HISTORY

OF THE

ANCIENT PEOPLES OF THE CLASSIC EAST

UNIVERSITY COLLEGE,
NOTTINGHAM.

Statue of Assur-nazir-pal
in the British Museum.

Printed by Wittmann in Paris (France)

THE
PASSING OF THE EMPIRES
850 B.C. TO 330 B.C.

BY

G. MASPERO

HON. D.C.L. AND FELLOW OF QUEEN'S COLLEGE, OXFORD
MEMBER OF THE INSTITUTE, AND PROFESSOR AT THE COLLEGE OF FRANCE

EDITED BY

A. H. SAYCE

PROFESSOR OF ASSYRIOLOGY, OXFORD

TRANSLATED BY M. L. McCLURE
MEMBER OF THE COMMITTEE OF THE EGYPT EXPLORATION FUND

WITH MAPS, THREE COLOURED PLATES, AND NUMEROUS ILLUSTRATIONS

LONDON
SOCIETY FOR PROMOTING CHRISTIAN KNOWLEDGE
NORTHUMBERLAND AVENUE, W.C.
1900

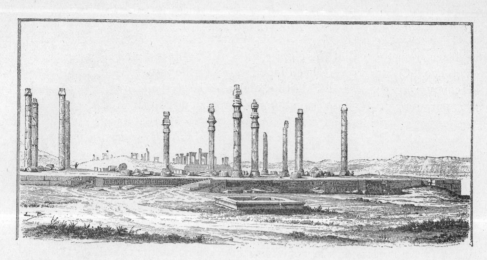

THE RUINS OF THE APADANA OF XERXES AT PERSEPOLIS.

EDITOR'S PREFACE.

WITH this third volume Professor Maspero concludes his monumental work on the history of the ancient East. The overthrow of the Persian empire by the Greek soldiers of Alexander marks the beginning of a new era. Europe at last enters upon the stage of history, and becomes the heir of the culture and civilisation of the Orient. The culture which had grown up and developed on the banks of the Euphrates and Nile passes to the West, and there assumes new features and is inspired with a new spirit. The East perishes of age and decrepitude; its strength is outworn, its power to initiate is past. The long ages through which it had toiled to build up the fabric of civilisation are at an end; fresh races are needed to carry on the work which it had achieved. Greece appears upon the scene, and behind Greece looms the colossal figure of the Roman empire.

Since the first volume of Professor Maspero's work was published, excavation has gone on apace in Egypt and Babylonia, and discoveries of a startling and unexpected nature have followed in the wake of excavation. Many pages of the volume will have to be rewritten in the light of them; such is always the fate of the historian of the past in this age of rapid and persistent research. Ages that seemed prehistoric step suddenly forth into the day-dawn of history; personages whom a sceptical criticism had consigned to the land of myth or fable are clothed once more with flesh and blood, and events which had been long forgotten demand to be recorded and described. In Babylonia, for example, the excavations at Niffer and Tello have shown that Sargon of Akkad, so far from being a creature of romance, was as much an historical monarch as Nebuchadrezzar himself; monuments of his reign have been discovered, and

b

we learn from them that the empire he is said to have founded had a very real existence. Contracts have been found dated in the years when he was occupied in conquering Syria and Palestine, and a cadastral survey that was made for the purposes of taxation mentions a Canaanite who had been appointed "governor of the land of the Amorites." Even a postal service had already been established along the high-roads which knit the several parts of the empire together, and some of the clay seals which franked the letters are now in the Museum of the Louvre.

At Susa, M. de Morgan, the late director of the Service of Antiquities in Egypt, has been excavating below the remains of the Achæmenian period, among the ruins of the ancient Elamite capital. Here he has found numberless historical inscriptions, besides a text in hieroglyphics which may cast light on the origin of the cuneiform characters. But the most interesting of his discoveries are two Babylonian monuments that were carried off by Elamite conquerors from the cities of Babylonia. One of them is a long inscription of about 1200 lines belonging to Manistusu, one of the early Babylonian kings, whose name has been met with at Niffer; the other is a monument of Naram-Sin, the son of Sargon of Akkad, which it seems was brought as booty to Susa by Simti-silkhak, the grandfather, perhaps, of Eriaku or Arioch.

In Armenia also equally important inscriptions have been found by Belck and Lehmann. More than two hundred new ones have been added to the list of Vannic texts. It has been discovered from them that the kingdom of Biainas or Van was founded by Ispuinis and Menuas, who rebuilt Van itself and the other cities which they had previously sacked and destroyed. The older name of the country was Kumussu, and it may be that the language spoken in it was allied to that of the Hittites, since a tablet in hieroglyphics of the Hittite type has been unearthed at Toprak Kaleh. One of the newly-found inscriptions of Sarduris III. shows that the name of the Assyrian god, hitherto read Ramman or Rimmon, was really pronounced Hadad. It describes a war of the Vannic king against Assur-nirari, son of Hadad-nirari (*A-da-di-ni-ra-ri*) of Assyria, thus revealing not only the true form of the Assyrian name, but also the parentage of the last king of the older Assyrian dynasty. From another inscription, belonging to Rusas II., the son of Argistis, we learn that campaigns were carried on against the Hittites and the Moschi in the latter years of Sennacherib's reign, and therefore only just before the irruption of the Kimmerians into the northern regions of Western Asia.

The two German explorers have also discovered the site and even the ruins of Muzazir, called Ardinis by the people of Van. They lie on the hill of Shkenna, near Topsanä, on the road between Kelishin and Sidek. In the immediate neighbourhood the travellers succeeded in deciphering a monument of Rusas I., partly in Vannic, partly in Assyrian, from which it appears that the Vannic king did not, after all, commit suicide when the news of the fall of Muzazir was brought to him, as is stated by Sargon, but that, on the contrary, he "marched against the mountains of Assyria" and restored the fallen city itself. Urzana, the King of Muzazir, had fled to him for shelter, and after the departure of the Assyrian army he was sent back by Rusas to his ancestral domains. The whole of the district in which Muzazir was situated was termed Lulu, and was regarded as the southern province of Ararat. In it was Mount Nizir, on whose summit the ark of the Chaldæan Noah rested, and which is therefore rightly described in the Book of Genesis as one of " the mountains of Ararat." It was probably the Rowandiz of to-day.

The discoveries made by Drs. Belck and Lehmann, however, have not been confined to Vannic texts. At the sources of the Tigris Dr. Lehmann has found two Assyrian inscriptions of the Assyrian king, Shalmaneser II., one dated in his fifteenth and the other in his thirty-first year, and relating to his campaigns against Aram of Ararat. He has further found that the two inscriptions previously known to exist at the same spot, and believed to belong to Tiglath-Ninip and Assur-nazir-pal, are really those of Shalmaneser II., and refer to the war of his seventh year.

But it is from Egypt that the most revolutionary revelations have come. At Abydos and Kom el-Ahmar, opposite El-Kab, monuments have been disinterred of the kings of the first and second dynasties, if not of even earlier princes; while at Negada, north of Thebes, M. de Morgan has found a tomb which seems to have been that of Menes himself. A new world of art has been opened out before us; even the hieroglyphic system of writing is as yet immature and strange. But the art is already advanced in many respects; hard stone was cut into vases and bowls, and even into statuary of considerable artistic excellence; glazed porcelain was already made, and bronze, or rather copper, was fashioned into weapons and tools. The writing material, as in Babylonia, was often clay, over which seal-cylinders of a Babylonian pattern were rolled. Equally Babylonian are the strange and composite animals engraved on some of the objects of this early age, as well as the structure of the tombs, which were built, not of stone, but of crude brick, with their external walls panelled and pilastered. Professor Hommel's theory, which brings Egyptian civilisation from Babylonia along with the ancestors of the historical Egyptians, has thus been largely verified.

But the historical Egyptians were not the first inhabitants of the valley of the Nile. Not only have palæolithic implements been found on the plateau of the desert; the relics of neolithic man have turned up in extraordinary abundance. When the historical Egyptians arrived with their copper weapons and their system of writing, the land was already occupied by a pastoral people, who had attained a high level of neolithic culture. Their implements of flint are the most beautiful and delicately finished that have ever been discovered; they were able to carve vases of great artistic excellence out of the hardest of stone, and their pottery was of no mean quality. Long after the country had come into the possession of the historical dynasties, and had even been united into a single monarchy, their settlements continued to exist on the outskirts of the desert, and the neolithic culture that distinguished them passed only gradually away. By degrees, however, they intermingled with their conquerors from Asia, and thus formed the Egyptian race of a later day. But they had already made Egypt what it has been throughout the historical period. Under the direction of the Asiatic immigrants and of the engineering science whose first home had been in the alluvial plain of Babylonia, they accomplished those great works of irrigation which confined the Nile to its present channel, which cleared away the jungle and the swamp that had formerly bordered the desert, and turned them into fertile fields. Theirs were the hands which carried out the plans of their more intelligent masters, and cultivated the valley when once it had been reclaimed. The Egypt of history was the creation of a twofold race: the Egyptians of the monuments supplied the controlling and directing power; the Egyptians of the neolithic graves bestowed upon it their labour and their skill.

The period treated of by Professor Maspero in his present volume is one for which there is an abundance of materials such as do not exist for the earlier portions of his history. The evidence of the monuments is supplemented by that of the Hebrew and classical writers. But on this very account it is in some respects more difficult to deal with, and the conclusions arrived at by the historian are more open to question and dispute. In some cases conflicting accounts are given of an event which seem to rest on equally good authority; in other cases, there is a sudden failure of materials just where the thread of the story becomes most complicated. Of this the decline and fall of the Assyrian empire is a prominent example; for our knowledge of it, we have still to depend chiefly on the untrustworthy legends of the Greeks. Our views must be coloured more or less by our estimate of Herodotos; those who, like myself, place little or no confidence in what he tells us about Oriental affairs will naturally form a very different idea of the death-struggle of Assyria from that formed by writers who still see in him the Father of Oriental History.

Even where the native monuments have come to our aid, they have not unfrequently introduced difficulties and doubts where none seemed to exist before, and have made the task of the critical historian harder than ever. Cyrus and his forefathers, for instance, turn out to have been kings of Anzan, and not of Persia, thus explaining why it is that the Neo-Susian language appears by the side of the Persian and the Babylonian as one of the three official languages of the Persian empire; but we still have to learn what was the relation of Anzan to Persia on the one hand, and to Susa on the other, and when it was that Cyrus of Anzan became also King of Persia. In the Annalistic Tablet, he is called "King of Persia" for the first time in the ninth year of Nabonidos.

Similar questions arise as to the position and nationality of Astyages. He is called in the inscriptions, not a Mede, but a Manda—a name which, as I showed many years ago, meant for the Babylonian a "barbarian" of Kurdistan. I have myself little doubt that the Manda over whom Astyages ruled were the Scythians of classical tradition, who, as may be gathered from a text published by Mr. Strong, had occupied the ancient kingdom of Ellipi. It is even possible that in the Madyes of Herodotos, we have a reminiscence of the

Manda of the cuneiform inscriptions. That the Greek writers should have confounded the Madâ or Medes with the Manda or Barbarians is not surprising ; we find even Berossos describing one of the early dynasties of Babylonia as " Median " where Manda, and not Madâ, must plainly be meant.

These and similar problems, however, will doubtless be cleared up by the progress of excavation and research. Perhaps M. de Morgan's excavations at Susa may throw some light on them, but it is to the work of the German expedition, which has just begun the systematic exploration of the site of Babylon, that we must chiefly look for help. The Babylon of Nabopolassar and Nebuchadrezzar rose on the ruins of Nineveh, and the story of the downfall of the Assyrian empire must still be lying buried under its mounds.

A. H. SAYCE.

TRANSLATOR'S PREFACE.

IN giving to the public the translation of the third and last volume of Professor Maspero's work, it is necessary to say a word on the want of uniformity, which will doubtless be remarked by the reader, in the orthography of the geographical and personal names which occur in these pages. Professor Maspero, to whom I have referred more than once on the subject, is apparently at greater pains to give to the student the various forms under which a town or province was known at different periods, than to preserve a uniform orthography of the name throughout his present work. He himself writes : " Souvent après avoir donné au début la forme authentique, j'ai employé dans la suite la forme usuelle." This lack of uniformity will be evident chiefly in the place-names in Palestine and Asia Minor, which of necessity varied, in the case of the former with the Egyptian, Assyrian, and Persian occupation, in that of the latter under its Assyrian, Lydian, Cimmerian, Phrygian, and Greek rulers. One of these many variants, and that often with an incorrect orthography, may be familiar to the English reader, and therefore must be mentioned in the translation, though the forms used in the French may be subsequently employed throughout the book without again identifying them with the popular one. I have, however, endeavoured to collect the various readings and place them in the index under one heading.

In rendering the passages from Holy Scripture cited by Professor Maspero in the course of his work, I have followed the Revised Version, but in the two or three instances where Professor Maspero's reading of the Hebrew original do not agree with that of the Revised Version, I have given a literal translation of his French, and have placed the Revised Version of the passage in a Translator's footnote. The forms of proper names occurring in Professor Maspero's quotations from the Bible, it may be well to note, are not in many cases those adopted by the Editors of our revised Text. No change, however slight, has been made without the Author's written permission, and such alterations as have been introduced are almost entirely confined to the correction of the errors of the French printers, and not one of them has any bearing on Biblical criticism.

The English title chosen by the Editor has met with Professor Maspero's entire approbation.

M. L. McClure.

November 20, 1899.

NOTE OF THE GENERAL LITERATURE
COMMITTEE OF THE S.P.C.K.

In bringing to a completion their undertaking to produce in English Professor Maspero's "History of the Ancient Peoples of the Classic East," the Committee wish it to be understood that they do not take upon themselves to pronounce on conclusions in the field of Biblical criticism deduced by the author from the events and documents discussed. While the great value of the materials embodied and their vivid presentment in Professor Maspero's books have seemed to the Committee to justify the publication of these volumes by the S.P.C.K., the author must be held responsible for the opinions which his study of these materials has led him to form.

ONE OF THE GATES OF THE TEMPLE OF ZEUS IN THE OASIS OF AMMON.

CONTENTS.

CHAPTER I.

THE ASSYRIAN REVIVAL AND THE STRUGGLE FOR SYRIA.

CHAPTER II.

TIGLATH-PILESER III. AND THE ORGANISATION OF THE ASSYRIAN EMPIRE FROM 745 TO 722 B.C.

CHAPTER III.

SARGON OF ASSYRIA AND SENNACHERIB (722–681 B.C.).

CHAPTER IV.

THE POWER OF ASSYRIA AT ITS ZENITH. ESARHADDON AND ASSUR-BANI-PAL.

CHAPTER V.

THE MEDES AND THE SECOND CHALDÆAN EMPIRE.

CHAPTER VI.

THE IRANIAN CONQUEST.

CHAPTER VII.

THE LAST DAYS OF THE OLD EASTERN WORLD.

THE ASSYRIAN REVIVAL

AND

THE STRUGGLE FOR SYRIA.

B

Shalmaneser III. (860–825 B.C.): the state of the empire at his accession—Urartu: its physical features, races, towns, temples, its deities—Shalmaneser's first campaign in Urartu: he penetrates as far as Lake Van (860 B.C.)—The conquest of Bît-Adini and of Naîri (859–855 B.C.).

The attack on Damascus: the battle of Qarqar (854 B.C.) and the war against Babylon (852–851 B.C.)—The alliance between Judah and Israel, the death of Ahab (853 B.C.); Damascus successfully resists the attacks of Assyria (849–846 B.C.)—Moab delivered from Israel, Mesha; the death of Ben-hadad (Adadidri) and the accession of Hazael; the fall of the house of Omri-Jehu (843 B.C.)—The defeat of Hazael and the homage of Jehu (842–839 B.C.).

Wars in Cilicia and in Namri (838–835 B.C.): the last battles of Shalmaneser III.; his building works, the revolt of Assur-dain-pal—Samsi-rammân IV. (825–812 B.C.), his first three expeditions, his campaigns against Babylon—Rammân-nirâri IV. (812–783 B.C.)—Jehu, Athaliah, Joash: the supremacy of Hazael over Israel and Judah—Victory of Rammân-nirâri over Mari, and the submission of all Syria to the Assyrians (803 B.C.).

The growth of Urartu: the conquests of Menuas and Argistis I., their victories over Assyria—Shalmaneser IV. (783–772 B.C.)—Assurdân III. (772–754 B.C.)—Assur-nirâri III. (754–745 B.C.)—The downfall of Assyria and the triumph of Urartu.

A MOUNTAIN RAID OF ASSYRIAN CAVALRY.[1]

CHAPTER I.

THE ASSYRIAN REVIVAL AND THE STRUGGLE FOR SYRIA.

Assur-nazir-pal (885–860) and Shalmaneser III. (860–825)—The kingdom of Urartu and its conquering princes: Menuas and Argistis.

ASSYRIA was the first to reappear on the scene of action. Less hampered by an ancient past than Egypt and Chaldæa, she was the sooner able to recover her strength after any disastrous crisis, and to assume again the offensive along the whole of her frontier line. During the years immediately following the ephemeral victories and reverses of Assurirba,[2] both the country and its rulers are plunged in the obscurity of oblivion. Two figures at length, though at what date is uncertain, emerge from the darkness—a certain Irbarammân and an Assur-nadinakhê II., whom we find engaged in building palaces and making a necropolis.[3] They were followed towards 950 by a Tiglath-pileser II., of whom nothing is known but his name.[4] He in his turn was succeeded about the year 935 by one Assurdân II., who appears to have concentrated his energies upon public works, for we hear of him digging a

---

[1] Drawn by Faucher-Gudin, from a bas-relief at Koyunjik of the time of Sennacherib; cf. LAYARD, *Monuments of Nineveh*, vol. ii. pl. 38. The initial cut, which is also by Faucher-Gudin, represents the broken obelisk of Assur-nazir-pal, the bas-reliefs of which are as yet unpublished; cf. HORMUZD RASSAM, *Asshur and the Land of Nimrod*, pp. 8, 9, and pl. iii.

[2] See what is said on this subject in MASPERO, *Struggle of the Nations*, pp. 664, 665.

[3] *Inscription on the Broken Obelisk*, col. ii. ll. 4–6; cf. PEISER, *Inschriften Aschur-nâsir-abal's*, in SCHRADER, *Keilinschriftliche Bibliothek*, vol. i. pp. 126, 127.

[4] Our only knowledge of Tiglath-pileser II. is from a brick, on which he is mentioned as being the grandfather of Rammân-nirâri II. (PINCHES, *A Guide to the Nimrod Central Saloon*, p. 9, No. 72; cf. WINCKLER, *Studien und Beiträge zu der Babylonisch-Assyrischen Geschichte*, in the *Zeitschrift für Assyriologie*, vol. ii. pp. 311, 312).

canal to supply his capital [1] with water, restoring the temples and fortifying towns.[2]   Rammân-nirâri III., who followed him in 912, stands out more distinctly from the mists which envelop the history of this period; he repaired the gate of the Tigris and the adjoining wall at Assur,[3] he enlarged its principal sanctuary,[4] reduced several rebellious provinces to obedience,[5] and waged a successful warfare against the neighbouring inhabitants of Karduniash.   Since the extinction of the race of Nebuchadrezzar I., Babylon had been a prey to civil discord and foreign invasion.[6]   The Aramæan tribes mingled with, or contiguous to the remnants of the Cossæans bordering on the Persian gulf, constituted possibly, even at this period, the powerful nation of the Kaldâ.[7]   It has been supposed, not without probability, that a certain Simashshikhu, Prince of the Country of the Sea, who immediately followed the last scion of the line of Pashê,[8] was one of their chiefs.   He endeavoured to establish order in the city, and rebuilt the temple of the Sun destroyed by the nomads at Sippar,[9] but at the end of eighteen years he was assassinated.   His son Eâmukinshumu remained at the head of affairs some three to six months; Kashshu-nadinakhê ruled three or six years, at the expiration of which a man of the house of Bâzi, Eulbar-shakinshumi by name, seized upon the crown.[10]   His dynasty consisted of three members, himself included, and it was overthrown after a duration of twenty years by an Elamite, who held authority for another seven.[11]   It was a period of calamity

[1] *Inscription on the Broken Obelisk*, col. ii. l. 20; cf. PEISER, *Inschriften Aschur-nâsir-abal's*, in SCHRADER, *Keilinschriftliche Bibliothek*, vol. i. pp. 128, 129.

[2] *Annals of Assur-nazir-pal*, col. i. ll. 30, 31; cf. *Keilinschriftliche Bibliothek*, vol. ii. pp. 56, 57.

[3] *Inscription on the Broken Obelisk*, col. ii. ll. 24–26.

[4] WINCKLER, *Studien und Beiträge*, in the *Zeitschrift für Assyriologie*, vol. ii. pp. 311, 312.

[5] *Annals of Assur-nazir-pal*, col. i. ll. 29, 30; cf. *Keilinschriftliche Bibliothek*, vol. ii. pp. 56, 57.

[6] For this subject, cf. MASPERO, *Struggle of the Nations*, p. 665.

[7] The names Chaldæa and Chaldæans being ordinarily used to designate the territory and people of Babylon, I shall employ the term Kaldu or Kaldâ in treating of the Aramæan tribes who constituted the actual Chaldæan nation.

[8] Cf. on this subject MASPERO, *Struggle of the Nations*, p. 669. The name of this prince has been read Simbarshiku by Peiser, a reading adopted by ROST, *Untersuchungen zur Altorientalischen Geschichte*, p. 26; Simbarshiku would have been shortened into Sibir, and we should have to identify it with that of the Sibir mentioned by Assur-nazir-pal in his *Annals*, col. ii. l. 84, as a king of Karduniash who lived before his (Assur-nazir-pal's) time (see p. 26 of the present volume).

[9] *Inscription of Nabubaliddin*, col. i. ll. 1–23, in RAWLINSON, *Cun. Ins. W. As.*, vol. v. pl. 60; cf. PINCHES, *Remarks upon the recent Discoveries of Mr. Rassam at Aboo-Habba*, in *Proceedings* of the Soc. of Biblical Arch., 1880–1881, vol. iii. pp. 110, 111, and the *Antiquities found by Mr. H. Rassam at Abu-Habbah* (Sippara), in *Transactions*, vol. viii. pp. 165–169; SCHEIL, *Inscrip. de Nabû-abil-iddin*, in the *Zeit. fur Assyr.*, vol. iv. pp. 325, 326; JEREMIAS, *Die Cultustafel von Sippar*, in the *Beit. zur Assyr.*, vol. i. pp. 269, 270; and PEISER, *Insch. des Nabû-abal-iddin*, in SCHRADER, *Keil. Bibl.*, vol. iii. pt. 1, pp. 174–183.

[10] The name of this king may be read Edubarshakîn-shumi (ROST, *Untersuchungen zur Altorientalischen Gesch.*, p. 27; cf. p. 19, note 3). The house of Bâzi takes its name from an ancestor who must have founded it at some unknown date, but who never reigned in Chaldæa. Winckler has with reason conjectured that the name subsequently lost its meaning to the Babylonians, and that they confused the Chaldæan house of Bâzi with the Arab country of Bâzu: this may explain why in his dynasties Berosos attributes an Arab origin to that one which comprises the short-lived line of Bît-Bâzi (WINCKLER, *Untersuch. zur Alt. Gesch.*, pp. 5, 6; cf. ROST, *Untersuch. zur Alt. Gesch.*, pp. 19, 20).

[11] Our knowledge of these events is derived solely from the texts of the Babylonian Canon

and distress, during which the Arabs or the Aramæans ravaged the country, and pillaged without compunction not only the property of the inhabitants, but also that of the gods. The Elamite usurper having died about the year 1030, a Babylonian of noble extraction expelled the intruders, and succeeded in bringing the larger part of the kingdom under his rule.[1] Five or six of his descendants had passed away, and a certain Shamash-mudammiq was feebly holding the reins of government, when the expeditions of Rammân-nirâri III. provoked war afresh between Assyria and Babylon. The two armies encountered each other once again on their former battle-field between the Lower Zab and the Turnat. Shamash-mudammiq, after being totally routed near the Yalmân mountains,[2] did not long survive, and Naboshumishkun, who succeeded him, showed neither more ability nor energy than his predecessor. The Assyrians wrested from him the fortresses of Bambala and Bagdad, dislodged him from the positions where he had entrenched himself, and at length took him prisoner while in flight, and condemned him to perpetual captivity.[3]

published and translated by G. Smith (*On Fragments of Inscriptions*, in the *Transactions* of the Soc. of Bibl. Arch., vol. iii. pp. 374-376), by Pinches (*The Babylonian Kings of the Second Period*, in the *Proceedings*, 1883–1884, vol. vi. pp. 196, 197), by Sayce (*The Dynastic Tablets*, in the *Records of the Past*, 2nd ser., vol. i. pp. 17, 21). The inscription of Nabubaliddin (col. i. ll. 24-30, col. ii. ll. 1-17) informs us that Kashu-nadînakhê and Eulbar-shâkinshumu continued the works begun by Simashshiku in the temple of the Sun at Sippar.

[1] The names of the first kings of this dynasty are destroyed in the copies of the Royal Canon which have come down to us. The three preceding dynasties are restored as follows :—

SIMASH-SHIKU	18 years 5 months	or according	17 years 3 months.
EÂMUKÎN-SHUMU	5 months	to another	3 months.
KASHU-NADÎNAKHÊ	3 years	computation	6 years.
Total for the dynasty of the Sea Country	21 years 5 months	,,	23 years 6 months.
EULBAR-SHÂKIN-SHUMU	17 years	,,	15 years.
NINIP-KUDURUSUR.	3 years	,,	2 years.
SHILANÎMSHUKAMUNA	3 months	,,	3 months.
Total for the dynasty of Bâzi	20 years 3 months.		

For the differences in the lengths of these reigns, cf. *Dawn of Civilization*, pp. 592–594 ; and further, FR. DELITZSCH, *Assyriologische Miscellen*, in the *Berichte* of the Academy of Sciences of Saxony, II., 1894, p. 189; and ROST, *Untersuchungen zur Altorientalischen Gesch.*, p. 26, note 2. A boundary stone, published by BELSER, *Bab. Kudurru Inschriften*, in the *Beiträge zur Ass.*, vol. ii. pp. 171-185, and translated by PEISER, *Texte juristischen und geschäftlichen Inhalts*, in the *Keilinschrift. Bibl.* vol. iv. pp. 82-93, bears the name of Ninip-kudurusur, dated in his third year, and also mentions a king Nabu-kînabal who appears to have reigned 24 years. According to Rost (*Untersuchungen zur Alt. Gesch.*, pp. 67, 68), this is the first king of the Babylonian dynasty which followed the dynasty of Bâzi ; a certain Irba-marduk, mentioned in an inscription of Merodach-baladan II. (PEISER and WINCKLER, *Inschriften Merodach-Baladan's* II., in SCHRADER, *Keil. Bibl.*, vol. iii. pp. 186, 187, col. ii. ll. 43, 44), ought to be placed among the five or six unknown princes who must have succeeded this Nabu-kînabal.

[2] For the variants of this name which occur in the inscriptions, cf. FR. DELITZSCH, *Wo lag das Paradies?* pp. 204, 205. As I have remarked elsewhere (*Struggle of the Nations*, p. 119, note 3), Winckler identifies the position of the countries around Yalmân with the present province of Holwân (*Gesch. Bab. und Ass.*, pp. 81, 82).

[3] Shamash-mudammiq appears to have died about 900. Naboshumishkun probably reigned only one or two years, from 900 to 899 or to 898. The name of his successor is destroyed in the *Synchronous History;* it might be Nabubaliddin, who seems to have had a long life, but it is wiser, until fresh light is thrown on the subject, to admit that it is some prince other than Nabubaliddin, whose name is as yet unknown to us (ROST, *Untersuchungen zur Alt. Gesch.*, p. 69).

His successor abandoned to the Assyrians most of the districts situated on the left bank of the Lower Zab between the Zagros mountains and the Tigris,[1] and peace, which was speedily secured by a double marriage, remained unbroken for nearly half a century.   Tukulti-ninip II. was fond of fighting; " he overthrew his adversaries and exposed their heads upon stakes," [2] but, unlike his predecessor, he directed his efforts against Naîri and the northern and western tribes.   We possess no details of his campaigns; we can only surmise that in six years, from 890 to 885,[3] he brought into subjection the valley of the Upper Tigris and the mountain provinces which separate it from the Assyrian plain.   Having reached the source of the river, he carved, beside the image of Tiglath-pileser I., the following inscription, which may still be read upon the rock.[4]   " With the help of Assur, Shamash, and Rammân, the gods of his religion, he reached this spot.   The lofty mountains he subjugated from the sun-rising to its down-setting; victorious, irresistible, he came hither, and like unto the lightning he crossed the raging rivers." [5]

He did not live long to enjoy his triumphs, but his death made no impression on the impulse given to the fortunes of his country.   The kingdom which he left to Assur-nazir-pal, the eldest of his sons, embraced scarcely any of the countries which had paid tribute to former sovereigns.[6]   Besides Assyria proper, it comprised merely those districts of Naîri which had been annexed within his own generation; the remainder had gradually regained their liberty : first the outlying dependencies—Cilicia, Melitene, Northern Syria, and then the provinces nearer the capital, the valleys of the Masios and the Zagros, the steppes of the Khabur, and even some districts such as Lubdi and Shupria, which had been allotted to Assyrian colonists at various times after successful campaigns.[7] Nearly the whole empire had to be reconquered under much the same

---

[1] *Synchronous Hist.*, col. iii. ll. 1–21 ; cf. SAYCE, *The Synchronous Hist. of Ass. and Babylonia,* in the *Records of the Past,* 2nd series, vol. iv. p. 32, and PEISER and WINCKLER, *Die sogenannte Synchron. Gesch.*, in SCHRADER, *Keilinschriftliche Bibliothek,* vol. i. pp. 200, 201.   For a restoration of this passage, see the *Synchronous History* in WINCKLER, *Altorientalische Forschungen,* vol. i. p. 246.

[2] *Annals of Assur-nazir-pal,* col. i. ll. 28, 29.

[3] The parts preserved of the Eponym canon (cf. *Struggle of the Nations,* pp. 620–621) begin their record in 893, about the end of the reign of Rammân-nirâri II.   The line which distinguishes the two reigns from one another is drawn between the name of the personage who corresponds to the year 890, and that of Tukulti-ninip who corresponds to the year 889 : Tukulti-ninip II., therefore, begins his reign in 890, and his death is six years later, in 885.   Cf. the list in SCHRADER, *Keilinschriftliche Bibliothek,* vol. i. p. 204.

[4] For the inscription of Tiglath-pileser I., cf. *Struggle of the Nations,* pp. 658, 659.

[5] SCHRADER, *Die Keilinschriften am Eingange der Quellgrotten des Sebeneh-Su,* pp. 14–19, 28.   This inscription and its accompanying bas-relief are mentioned in the *Annals of Assur-nazir-pal,* col. i. ll. 104, 105; cf. p. 19 of the present volume.

[6] For the details and extent of these first Assyrian conquests, cf. *Struggle of the Nations,* p. 604, et seq.

[7] An account of some of the secolonies is given in the *Struggle of the Nations,* pp. 608, 609, 640, 657, 665, 667, 668.   For Lubdi and Shupria, cf. WINCKLER, *Altorientalische Forschungen,* vol. ii. pp. 46–48.

conditions as in the first instance.   Assyria itself, it is true, had recovered the vitality and elasticity of its earlier days.   The people were a robust and energetic race, devoted to their rulers, and ready to follow them blindly and trustingly wherever they might lead.   The army, while composed chiefly of the same classes of troops as in the time of Tiglath-pileser I.,—spearmen, archers, sappers, and slingers,—now possessed a new element, whose appearance on the field of battle was to revolutionize the whole method of warfare; this was the

AN ASSYRIAN HORSEMAN ARMED WITH THE SWORD.[1]

cavalry, properly so called, introduced as an adjunct to the chariotry.   The number of horsemen forming this contingent was as yet small; like the infantry, they wore casques and cuirasses, but were clothed with a tight-fitting loin-cloth in place of the long kilt, the folds of which would have embarrassed their movements.   One-half of the men carried sword and lance, the other half sword and bow, the latter of a smaller kind than that used by the infantry. Their horses were bridled, and bore trappings on the forehead, but had no saddles; their riders rode bareback without stirrups; they sat far back with the chest thrown forward, their knees drawn up to grip the shoulder of the animal.   Each horseman was attended by a groom, who rode abreast of him, and held his reins during an action, so that he might be free to make use of his weapons.   This body of cavalry, having little confidence in its own powers,

[1] Drawn by Faucher-Gudin, from a bas-relief in bronze on the gate of Balawât.   The Assyrian artist has shown the head and legs of the second horse in profile behind the first, but he has forgotten to represent the rest of its body, and also the man riding it.

kept in close contact with the main body of the army, and was not used in independent manœuvres; it was associated with and formed an escort to the chariotry in expeditions where speed was essential, and where the ordinary foot soldier would have hampered the movements of the charioteers.[1]

A MOUNTED ASSYRIAN ARCHER WITH HIS ATTENDANT, CHARGING.[2]

The army thus reinforced was at all events more efficient, if not actually more powerful, than formerly; the discipline maintained was as severe, the military spirit as keen, the equipment as perfect, and the tactics as skilful as in former times.[3] A knowledge of engineering had improved upon the former methods of taking towns by sapping and scaling, and though the number of military engines was as yet limited, the besiegers were well able, when occasion demanded, to improvise and make use of machines capable of demolishing even the strongest walls.[4] The Assyrians were familiar with all the different kinds

---

[1] The history of the Assyrian cavalry has been briefly sketched by G. RAWLINSON, *The Five Great Monarchies*, 2nd edit., vol. i. p. 422, et seq. Isolated horsemen must no doubt have existed in the Assyrian just as in the Egyptian army (cf. on this point *Struggle of the Nations*, p. 218), but we never find any mention of a *body* of cavalry in inscriptions prior to the time of Assur-nazir-pal; the introduction of this new corps must consequently have taken place between the reigns of Tiglath-pileser and Assur-nazir-pal, probably nearer the time of the latter. Assur-nazir-pal himself seldom speaks of his cavalry (*Annals of Assur-nazir-pal*, col. ii. ll. 70–73, 103), but he constantly makes mention of the horsemen of the Aramæan and Syrian principalities, whom he incorporated into his own army (*Annals of Assur-nazir-pal*, col. iii. ll. 58, 60, 63, 69, 77).

[2] Drawn by Faucher-Gudin, from one of the bronze bas-reliefs of the gate of Balawât.

[3] For the organisation of the Assyrian armies and their military tactics previous to the use of cavalry, cf. *Struggle of the Nations*, pp. 626–642.

[4] For the Assyrian engines of war, see M. DIEULAFOY, *L'Acropole de Suse*, pp. 148–158, and JEREMIAS and BILLERBECK, *Der Untergang Nineveh's*, in the *Beiträge zur Assyriologie*, vol. iii. pp. 178–184 .

of battering-ram; the hand variety, which was merely a beam tipped with iron, worked by some score of men; the fixed ram, in which the beam was suspended from a scaffold and moved by means of ropes; and lastly, the movable ram, running on four or six wheels, which enabled it to be advanced or withdrawn at will. The military engineers of the day allowed full rein to their fancy in the

THE MOVABLE SOW MAKING A BREACH IN THE WALL OF A FORTRESS.[1]

many curious shapes they gave to this latter engine; for example, they gave to the mass of bronze at its point the form of the head of an animal, and the whole engine took at times the form of a sow ready to root up with its snout the foundations of the enemy's defences. The scaffolding of the machine was usually protected by a carapace of green leather or some coarse woollen material stretched over it, which broke the force of blows from projectiles; at times it had an additional arrangement in the shape of a cupola or turret in which archers were stationed to sweep the face of the wall opposite to the point of attack. The battering-rams were set up and placed in line at a short distance from the ramparts of the besieged town; the ground in front of them was then levelled and a regular causeway constructed, which was paved with

The battering-ram had already reached such a degree of perfection under Assur-nazir-pal, that it must have been invented some time before the execution of the first bas-reliefs on which we see it portrayed. Its points of resemblance to the Greek battering-ram furnished Hœfer with one of his main arguments for placing the monuments of Khorsabad and Koyunjik as late as the Persian or Parthian period (*Chaldée, Assyrie*, pp. 318, 319).

[1] Drawn by Faucher-Gudin, from one of the bronze bas-reliefs of the gate at Balawât.

bricks wherever the soil appeared to be lacking in firmness. These preliminaries accomplished, the engines were pushed forward by relays of troops till they reached the required range. The effort needed to set the ram in motion severely taxed the strength of those engaged in the work; for the size of the beam was enormous, and its iron point, or the square

THE TURRETED BATTERING-RAM ATTACKING THE WALLS OF A TOWN.[1]

mass of metal at the end, was of no light weight. The besieged did their best to cripple or, if possible, destroy the engine as it approached them. Torches, lighted tow, burning pitch, and stink-pots were hurled down upon its roofing; attempts were made to seize the head of the ram by means of chains or hooks, so as to prevent it from moving, or in order to drag it on to the battlements; in some cases the garrison succeeded in crushing the machinery with a mass of rock. The Assyrians, however, did not allow themselves to be discouraged by such trifling accidents; they would at once extinguish the fire, release, by sheer force of muscle, the beams which the enemy had secured, and if, notwithstanding all their efforts, one of the machines became injured, they had others ready to take its place, and the ram would be again at work after only a few minutes' delay. Walls, even when of burnt brick or faced with small stones, stood no chance against such an attack. The first blow of the ram sufficed to shake them, and an opening was rapidly made, so that in a few days, often in a few hours, they became a heap of ruins; the foot soldiers could then enter by the breach which the pioneers had effected.

[1] Drawn by Faucher-Gudin, from a bas-relief brought from Nimroud, now in the British Museum; cf. LAYARD, *Monuments of Nineveh*, vol. i. pl. 17.

It must, however, be remembered that the strength and discipline which the Assyrian troops possessed in such a high degree, were common to the military forces of all the great states—Elam, Damascus, Naîri, the Hittites, and Chaldæa. It was owing to this, and also to the fact that the armies of all these Powers were, as a rule, both in strength and numbers, much on a par, that no single state was able to inflict on any of the rest such a defeat as would end

THE BESIEGED ENDEAVOURING TO CRIPPLE OR DESTROY THE BATTERING-RAM.[1]

in its destruction. What decisive results had the terrible struggles produced, which stained almost periodically the valleys of the Tigris and the Zab with blood? After endless loss of life and property, they had nearly always issued in the establishment of the belligerents in their respective possessions, with possibly the cession of some few small towns or fortresses to the stronger party, most of which, however, were destined to come back to its former possessor in the very next campaign.[2] The fall of the capital itself was not decisive, for it left the vanquished foe chafing under his losses, while the victory cost his rival so dear that he was unable to maintain the ascendency for more than a few years. Twice at least in three centuries a king of Assyria had entered Babylon, and twice the Babylonians had expelled the intruder of the hour, and had forced him back with a blare of trumpets to the frontier. Although the Ninevite dynasties had persisted in their pretensions to

[1] Drawn by Faucher-Gudin, from a bas-relief from Nimroud, now in the British Museum; cf. LAYARD, *Monuments of Nineveh*, vol. i. pl. 19.

[2] For the little at present known of these wars between Assyria and Chaldæa, cf. *Struggle of the Nations*, pp. 592, 593, 595–597, 604–612, 662–664.

a suzerainty which they had generally been unable to enforce, the tradition of which, unsupported by any definite decree, had been handed on from one generation to another; yet in practice their kings had not succeeded in "taking the hands of Bel," * and in reigning personally in Babylon, nor in extorting from the native sovereign an official acknowledgment of his vassalage. Profiting doubtless by past experience, Assur-nazir-pal resolutely avoided those direct conflicts in which so many of his predecessors had wasted their lives. If he did not actually renounce his hereditary pretensions, he was content to let them lie dormant. He preferred to accommodate himself to the terms of the treaty signed a few years previously by Rammân-nirâri, even when Babylon neglected to observe them; he closed his eyes to the many ill-disguised acts of hostility to which he was exposed,[1] and devoted all his energies to dealing with less dangerous enemies. Even if his frontier touched Karduniash to the south, elsewhere he was separated from the few states strong enough to menace his kingdom by a strip of varying width, comprising several less important tribes and cities;—to the east and north-east by the barbarians of obscure race whose villages and strongholds were scattered along the upper affluents of the Tigris or on the lower terraces of the Iranian plateau; to the west and north-west by the principalities and nomad tribes, mostly of Aramæan extraction, who now for a century had peopled the mountains of the Tigris and the steppes of Mesopotamia. They were high-spirited, warlike, hardy populations, proud of their independence and quick to take up arms in its defence or for its recovery, but none of them possessed more than a restricted domain, or had more than a handful of soldiers at its disposal. At times, it is true, the nature of their locality befriended them, and the advantages of position helped to compensate for their paucity of numbers. Sometimes they were entrenched behind one of those rapid watercourses like the Radanu, the Zab, or the Turnat, which are winter torrents rather than streams, and are overhung by steep banks, precipitous as a wall above a moat; sometimes they took refuge upon some wooded height and awaited attack amid its rocks and pine woods. Assyria was superior to all of them, if not in the valour of its troops, at least numerically, and, towering in the midst of them, she could single out at will whichever tribe offered the easiest prey, and falling on it suddenly, would crush it by sheer force of weight. In such a case the surrounding tribes, usually only too well pleased to witness in safety the fall of a dangerous rival, would not attempt to interfere; but their turn was ere long sure to come, and the pity which they had declined to show to their neighbours was in like

* [For the meaning of this expression, see *Struggle of the Nations*, p. 24, note 1.—TR.]
[1] It will be seen later on (pp. 28-30 of the present volume) that he did not make the presence of Cossæan troops among the allies of the Sukhi a *casus belli*, even though they were commanded by a brother and by one of the principal officers of the King of Babylon.

manner refused to them. The Assyrians ravaged their country, held their chiefs to ransom, razed their strongholds, or, when they did not demolish them, garrisoned them with their own troops who held sway over the country. The revenues gleaned from these conquests would swell the treasury at Nineveh, the native soldiers would be incorporated into the Assyrian army, and when the smaller tribes had all in turn been subdued, their conqueror would, at length, find himself confronted with one of the great states from which he had

THE ESCARPMENTS OF THE ZAB.[1]

been separated by these buffer communities; then it was that the men and money he had appropriated in his conquests would embolden him to provoke or accept battle with some tolerable certainty of victory.

Immediately on his accession, Assur-nazir-pal turned his attention to the parts of his frontier where the population was most scattered, and therefore less able to offer any resistance to his projects.[2] He marched towards the north-

---

[1] Drawn by Boudier, from a photograph by M. Binder, sent by Father Scheil.

[2] The principal document for the history of Assur-nazir-pal is the "Monolith of Nimrud," discovered by Layard in the ruins of the temple of Ninip; it bears the same inscription on both its sides. It is a compilation of various documents, comprising, first, a consecutive account of the campaigns of the king's first six years, terminating in a summary of the results obtained during that period; secondly, the account of the campaign of his sixth year, followed by three campaigns not dated, the last of which was in Syria; and thirdly, the history of a last campaign, that of his eighteenth year, and a second summary. The inscription, of which several copies (mostly incomplete) are known, has been published by H. RAWLINSON, *Cun. Ins. W. As.*, vol. i. pls. 17–26; cf. pl. 27, and vol. iii. pl. 6. It has been translated *in extenso* into French by OPPERT, *Hist. des Empires de Chaldée et d'Assyrie*, pp. 72–102, and by MÉNANT, *Annales des rois d'Assyrie*, pp. 66–93; into English by RODWELL, *Annals of Assur-nasir-pal*, in the *Records of the Past*, 1st ser., vol. iii.

western point of his territory, suddenly invaded Nummi,[1] and in an incredibly short time took Gubbê, its capital, and some half-dozen lesser places, among them Surra, Abuku, Arura, and Arubi. The inhabitants assembled upon a mountain ridge which they believed to be inaccessible, its peak being likened to "the point of an iron dagger," and the steepness of its sides such that "no winged bird of the heavens dare venture on them." In the short space of three days Assur-nazir-pal succeeded in climbing its precipices and forcing the entrenchments which had been thrown up on its summit: two hundred of its defenders perished sword in hand, the remainder were taken prisoners. The Kirruri,[2] terrified by this example, submitted unreservedly to the conqueror, yielded him their horses, mules, oxen, sheep, wine, and brazen vessels, and accepted the Assyrian prefects appointed to collect the tribute. The neighbouring districts, Adaush, Gilzân, and Khubushkia, followed their example;[3] they

pp. 37–80, and by SAYCE, *The Standard Inscription of Assur-natsir-pal*, in the *Records of the Past*, 2nd ser., vol. ii. pp. 128–177; into German by PEISER, *Insch. Aschur-nâsir-abal's*, in SCHRADER, *Keil. Bibl.*, vol. i. pp. 50–119; a translation of the first column (ll. 1–99), with a specimen of a detailed commentary, was edited in 1885 by H. LHOTZKY, *Die Annalen Asurnazirpals* (884–860 B.C.), etc. A monolith found in the ruins of Kurkh, at some distance from Diarbekîr, and published by H. RAWLINSON, *Cun. Ins. W. As.*, vol. iii. pl. 6, contains some important additions to the account of the campaigns of the fifth year (ll. 42–52). The other numerous inscriptions of Assur-nazir-pal which have come down to us do not contain any information of importance which is not found in the text of the Annals; the dedication of the *plaques* (LAYARD, *Ins. in the Cun. Character*, pls. 1–11), fragments of which are dispersed in the various museums of Europe, has been translated into English by FOX TALBOT, *Standard Inscription of Ashur-akh-bal*, in the *Records of the Past*, 1st ser., vol. vii. p. 9, et seq., and into German by SCHRADER, *Insch. Assur-nasir-habal's*, etc., 1879. The inscription of the broken Obelisk, from which I have often quoted, contains in the second column some mention of the works undertaken by this king.

[1] Nummi or Nimmi, mentioned already in the Annals of Tiglath-pileser I. (col. iv. l. 71), has been placed by Hommel (*Gesch. Bab. und Ass.*, p. 554) in the mountain group which separates Lake Van from Lake Urumiah, but by Tiele in the regions situated to the south-east of Nineveh (*Bab. Ass. Gesch.*, p. 180); the observations of Delattre (*Encore un mot sur la Géographie Ass.*, pp. 6–12) show that we ought perhaps to look for it to the north of the Arzania, certainly in the valley of that river. It appears to me to answer to the cazas of Varto and Boulanîk in the sandjak of Mush. If the name of the capital, read Libiê-Libu by Oppert (*Hist. des Empires de Chald. et d'Ass.*, p. 76), ought to be read Gubbi-Gubbê, as Peiser believes (*Insch. Aschur-nâsir-abal's*, in SCHRADER, *Keil. Bibl.*, vol. i. pp. 60, 61, l. 46), it may be identified with the present Gop, chief town of the caza of Boulanîk (VITAL CUINET, *La Turquie d'Asie*, vol. ii. pp. 588, 589); in this case Abuku might be represented by the village of Biyonkh.

[2] The Kirruri must have had their habitat in the depression around Lake Urumiah, on the western side of the lake, if we are to believe Schrader (*Keil. und Gesch.*, pp. 163–169), whose identifications on this subject have been accepted with certain reservations by Hommel (*Gesch. Bab. und Ass.*, p. 554), by Tiele (*Bab.-ass. Gesch.*, pp. 168, 172, 180), by Delitzsch and Mürdter (*Gesch. Bab. und Ass.*, 2nd edit., p. 161), and by Winckler (*Gesch. Bab. und Ass.*, p. 215); Delattre has pointed out that it ought to be sought elsewhere, near the sources of the Tigris, not far from the Murad-su (*Encore un mot*, etc., p. 10, note 4). The connection in which it is here cited obliges us to place it in the immediate neighbourhood of Nummi, and its relative position to Adaush and Gilzân makes it probable that it is to be sought to the west and south-west of Lake Van, in the cazas of Mush and Sassun in the sandjak of Mush.

[3] For Adaush, cf. *Struggle of the Nations*, p. 646, note 2. Kirzâu, also transcribed Gilzân and Guzân, has been relegated by the older Assyriologists to Eastern Armenia, and the site further specified as being between the ancient Araxes and Lake Urumiah, in the Persian provinces of Khoî and Marand, by Schrader (*Keilinsch. und Geschichtsforschung*, pp. 167–169; cf. HOMMEL, *Gesch. Bab. und Ass*, p. 554; TIELE, *Bab. Ass. Gesch.*, pp. 168, 187; WINCKLER, *Gesch. Bab. und Ass.*, pp. 197, 200). The indications given in our text and the passages brought together by Schrader, which

sent the king considerable presents of gold, silver, lead, and copper, and their alacrity in buying off their conqueror saved them from the ruinous infliction of a garrison. The Assyrian army defiling through the pass of Khulun next fell upon

the Kirkhi, dislodged the troops stationed in the fortress of Nishtun, and pillaged the cities of Khatu, Khatara, Irbidi, Arzania, Tela, and Khalua;[1] Bubu, the Chief of Nishtun,[2] was sent to Arbela, flayed alive, and his skin nailed to the city wall. In a small town near one of the sources of the Tigris, Assur-nazir-

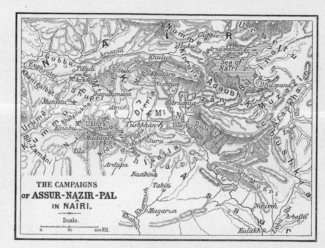

THE CAMPAIGNS of **ASSUR-NAZIR-PAL** IN NAÎRI.

pal founded a colony on which he imposed his name; he left there a statue of himself, with an inscription celebrating his exploits carved on its base, and having done this, he returned to Nineveh laden with booty.[3] A few weeks had sufficed for him to complete, on this side, the work bequeathed to him by his

place Gilzân in direct connection with Kirruri on one side and with Kurkhi on the other, oblige us to locate the country in the upper basin of the Tigris, and I should place it near Bitlis-tchaî, where different forms of the word occur many times on the map, such as Ghalzan in Ghalzan-dagh ; Kharzan, the name of a caza of the sandjak of Sert (CUINET, *La Turquie d'Asie*, vol. ii. pp. 612–614) ; Khizan, the name of a caza of the sandjak of Bitlis (IDEM., *ibid.*, vol. ii. pp. 566–568). Girzân-Kilzân would thus be the Roman province of Arzanene, Ardzn in Armenian, in which the initial *g* or *k* of the ancient name has been replaced in the process of time by a soft aspirate. Khubushkia or Khutushkia has been placed by Lenormant to the east of the Upper Zab, and south of Arapkha, and this identification has been approved by Schrader (*Keilinsch. und Gesch.*, pp. 163–167) and also by Delitzsch (*Die Sprache der Kossäer*, p. 33, et seq.) ; according to the passages that Schrader himself has cited, it must, however, have stretched northwards as far as Shatakh-su, meeting Gilzân at one point of the sandjaks of Van and Hakkiari.

[1] Assur-nazir-pal, in going from Kirruri to Kirkhi in the basin of the Tigris (cf., for Kirkhi or Kurkhi, *Struggle of the Nations*, p. 643, note 4), could go either by the pass of Bitlis or that of Sassun ; that of Bitlis is excluded by the fact that it lies in Kirruri, and Kirruri is not mentioned in what follows. But if the route chosen was by the pass of Sassun, Khulun necessarily must have occupied a position at the entrance of the defiles, perhaps that of the present town of Khorukh. The name Khatu recalls that of the Khoith tribe which the Armenian historians mention as in this locality (TOMASCHEK, *Sassoun und das Quellengebiet des Tigris*, pp. 6–8, etc.). Khaturu is perhaps Hatera in the caza of Lidjê, in the sandjak of Diarbekîr, and Arzania the ancient Arzan, Arzn, the ruins of which may be seen near Sheikh-Yunus. Tila-Tela is not the same town as the Tela in Mesopotamia, which we shall have occasion to speak of later, but is probably to be identified with Tîl or Tilleh, at the confluence of the Tigris and the Bohtan-tcha. Finally, it is possible that the name Khalua may be preserved in that of Halewi, which Layard gives as belonging to a village situated almost halfway between Rundvan and Tîl (*Nineveh and Babylon*, map 1).

[2] Nishtun was probably the most important spot in this region; from its position on the list, between Khulun and Khataru on one side and Arzania on the other, it is evident we must look for it somewhere in Sassun or in the direction of Mayafarrîkin.

[3] *Annals of Assur-nazir-pal*, col. i. ll. 43–69; cf. PEISER, *Inschriften Aschur-nâsir-abal's*, in SCHRADER, *Keil. Bibl.*, vol. i. pp. 58–63.

father, and to open up the neighbourhood of the north-east provinces; he was
not long in setting out afresh, this time to the north-west, in the direction of
the Taurus.[1]   He rapidly skirted the left bank of the Tigris, burned some score
of scattered hamlets at the foot of Nipur and Pazatu,[2] crossed to the right bank,
above Amidi, and, as he approached the Euphrates, received the voluntary
homage of Kummukh and the Mushku.[3]   But while he was complacently

THE SITE OF SHADIKANNI AT ARBÂN, ON THE KHABUR.[4]

engaged in recording the amount of vessels of bronze, oxen, sheep, and jars of wine
which represented their tribute, a messenger of bad tidings appeared before him.
Assyria was bounded on the east by a line of small states, comprising the Katna[5]

[1] The text of the "Annals" declares that these events took place "in this same limmu" (col. i.
l. 69), in what the king calls higher up in the column "the beginning of my royalty, the first year
of my reign" (col. i. ll. 43, 44).   We must therefore suppose that he ascended the throne almost at the
beginning of the year, since he was able to make two campaigns under the same eponym (TIELE,
Bab. Ass. Gesch., p. 179; HOMMEL, *Gesch. Bab. und Ass.*, pp. 552, 553).

[2] Nipur or Nibur is the Nibaros of Strabo (XI. xiv. § 2, p. 527), as Finzi recognized (*Ricerche
per lo Studio dell' Antichità Assira*, pp. 244–246; cf. DELATTRE, *The People and the Empire of the
Medes*, p. 71).   If we consider the general direction of the campaign, we are inclined to place Nipur
close to the bank of the Tigris, east of the regions traversed in the preceding campaign, and to
identify it, as also Pazatu, with the group of high hills called at the present day the Ashît-dagh,
between the Kharzan-su and the Batman-tchai (CUINET, *La Turquie d'Asie*, vol. ii. p. 551).

[3] Cf. what is said of Kummukh in the *Struggle of the Nations*, p. 590, note 6.   The Mushku
(Moschiano or Meshek) mentioned here do not represent the main body of the tribe, established in
Cappadocia (cf. on this subject, *ibid.*, pp. 591, 643); they are the descendants of such of the
Mushku as had crossed the Euphrates and contested the possession of the regions of Kashiari with
the Assyrians (HOMMEL, *Gesch. Bab. und Ass.*, p. 557).

[4] Drawn by Boudier, from a sketch taken by LAYARD, *Nineveh and Babylon*, p. 232.

[5] The name has been read sometimes Katna (OPPERT, *Hist. des Empires de Chald. et d'Ass.*, p. 91;
HOMMEL, *Gesch. Bab. und Ass.*, p. 557), sometimes Shuna (E. MEYER, *Gesch. des Alterthums*, vol. i.
p. 333; DELATTRE, *L'Asie Occidentale*, etc., pp. 8–11; WINCKLER, *Gesch. Bab. und Ass.*, pp. 183, 184;
PEISER, *Die Insch. Aschur-nâsir-abal's*, pp. 64, 65, 96, 97).   The country included the two towns of

ONE OF THE WINGED BULLS FOUND AT ARBÂN.[2]

and the Bît-Khalupi,[1] whose towns, placed alternately like sentries on each side the Khabur, protected her from the incursions of the Bedâwin. They were virtually Chaldæan cities, having been, like most of those which flourished in the Mesopotamian plains, thoroughly impregnated with Babylonian civilisation. Shadikanni, the most important of them, commanded the right bank of the Khabur, and also the ford where the road from Nineveh crossed the river on the route to Harrân and Carchemish. The palaces of its rulers were decorated with

winged bulls, lions, stelæ, and bas-reliefs carved in marble brought from the hills

Kamani and Dur-Katlimi (*Annals of Assur-nazir-pal*, col. iii. ll. 4–6), and on the south adjoined Bît-Khalupi; this identifies it with the districts of Margada and Sheddadîyeh, and, judging by the information with which Assur-nazir-pal himself furnishes us, it is not impossible that Dur-Katlimi may have been on the site of the present Magarda, and Kamani on that of Sheddadîyeh. Ancient ruins have been pointed out on both these spots (LAYARD, *Nineveh and Babylon*, pp. 254, 255; SACHAU, *Reise in Syrien und Mesopotamien*, p. 296).

[1] Peiser (*Die Inschriften Aschur-nâsir-abal's*, pp. 64, 65, 96, 97) and Winckler (*Gesch. Bab. und Ass.*, pp. 183–186) read as Bît-Khadippi the name that Oppert transcribed Bît-Khalupi (*Hist. des Emp. de Chald. et d'Assyrie*, pp. 78, 91, 92). Suru, the capital of Bît-Khalupi, was built upon the Khabur itself where it is navigable, for Assur-nazir-pal relates further on (*Annals*, col. iii. ll. 28, 29) that he had his royal barge built there at the time of the cruise which he undertook on the Euphrates in the VIth year of his reign. The itineraries of modern travellers mention a place called es-Sauar or es-Saur, eight hours' march from the mouth of the Khabur on the right bank of the river, situated at the foot of a hill some 220 feet high; the ruins of a fortified enclosure and of an ancient town are still visible (SACHAU, *Reise in Syrien und Mesopotamien*, p. 292). Following Tomkins (*Notes on the Geography from the Nile to the Euphrates*, in the *Bab. and Oriental Record*, vol. iii. p. 114), I should there place Suru, the chief town of Khalupi; Bît-Khalupi would be the territory in the neighbourhood of es-Saur.

[2] Drawn by Faucher-Gudin, from a sketch by LAYARD, *Nineveh and Babylon*, pp. 242; cf. pp. 235, 237.

[3] Drawn by Faucher-Gudin, from Layard's sketch, *ibid.*, p. 237.

STELE FROM ARBÂN.[3]

C

of Singar.[1] The people seem to have been of a capricious temperament, and, notwithstanding the supervision to which they were subjected, few reigns elapsed in which it was not necessary to put down a rebellion among them. Bît-Khalupi and its capital Suru had thrown off the Assyrian yoke after the death of Tukultininip; the populace, stirred up no doubt by Aramæan emissaries, had assassinated the Hamathite who governed them, and had sent for a certain Akhiababa, a man of base extraction from Bît-Adini,[2] whom they had proclaimed king. This defection, if not promptly dealt with, was likely to entail serious consequences, since it left an important point on the frontier exposed; and there now remained nothing to prevent the people of Adini or their allies from spreading over the country between the Khabur and the Tigris, and even pushing forward their marauding bands as far as the very walls of Singar and Assur. Without losing a moment, Assur-nazir-pal marched down the course of the Khabur, hastily collecting the tribute of the cities through which he passed. The defenders of Suru were disconcerted by his sudden appearance before their town, and their rulers came out and prostrated themselves at the king's feet: "Dost thou desire it? it is life for us;—dost thou desire it? it is death;—dost thou desire it? what thy heart chooseth, that do to us!" But the appeal to his clemency was in vain; the alarm had been so great and the danger so pressing, that Assur-nazir-pal was pitiless. The town was handed over to the soldiery, all the treasure it contained was confiscated, and the women and children of the best families were made slaves; some of the ringleaders paid the penalty of their revolt on the spot; the rest, with Akhiababa, were carried away and flayed alive, some at Nineveh, some elsewhere. An Assyrian garrison was installed in the citadel, and an ordinary governor, Azilu by name, replaced the dynasty of native princes. The report of this terrible retribution induced the Laqî[3] to tender their submission, and their example was followed by Khaian, king of Khindanu on the

---

[1] Shadikanni, which has been read Gardikanni (PEISER, *Insch. Aschur-nâzir-abal's*, in SCHRADER, *Keil. Bibl.*, vol. i. pp. 64, 65, 96, 97; WINCKLER, *Gesch. Bab. und Ass.*, pp. 183, 184), is certainly Arbân on the Khabur, as Rawlinson has already shown (*The Five Great Monarchies*, 2nd edit., vol. i. p. 205, and vol. ii. p. 84; cf. G. SMITH, *Hist. of Ass.*, p. 37; ED. MEYER, *Gesch. des Alterthums*, vol. i. pp. 333, 334; HOMMEL, *Gesch. Bab. und Ass.*, pp. 557, 558). For the ruins of Arbân, cf. LAYARD, *Nineveh and Babylon*, pp. 230–242; the possible identification of the prince whose name is met with on the sculptures of this locality, with a personage mentioned on a cylinder found at Sherif-Khan, has been pointed out by G. SMITH, *Hist. of Ass.*, p. 37, and admitted by ED. MEYER, *Gesch. des Alterthums*, vol. i. p. 334. Winckler attributes these monuments to the pre-Assyrian age of Mesopotamia, anterior to the time of the Aramæan invasion (*Gesch. Bab. und Ass.*, p. 150, and *Altorientalische Forschungen*, vol. i. p. 385, note 2). It is impossible to decide whether this is the case as long as we possess merely rough sketches which do not permit us to judge of the technique or the artistic merit of the objects in question.

[2] For the position of Bît-Adini on both banks in the bend of the Euphrates, cf. *Struggle of the Nations*, p. 590, note 9.

[3] The Laqî were situated on both banks of the Euphrates, principally on the right bank, between the Khabur and the Balikh (DELATTRE, *L'Asie Occidentale dans les Inscrip. Ass.*, pp. 12–16; HOMMEL, *Gesch. Bab. und Ass.*, p. 557), interspersed among the Sukhi, of whom they were perhaps merely a dissentient fraction.

Euphrates. He bought off the Assyrians with gold, silver, lead, precious stones, deep-hued purple, and dromedaries; he erected a statue of Assur-nazir-pal in the centre of his palace as a sign of his vassalage, and built into the wall near the gates of his town an inscription dedicated to the gods of the conqueror.[1] Six, or at the most eight, months had sufficed to achieve these rapid successes over various foes, in twenty different directions—the expeditions in Nummi and Kirruri, the occupation of Kummukh, the flying marches across the mountains and plains of Mesopotamia—during all of which the new sovereign had given ample proof of his genius. He had, in fine, shown himself to be a thorough soldier, a conqueror of the type of Tiglath-pileser, and Assyria by these victories had recovered her rightful rank among the nations of Western Asia.

The second year of his reign was no less fully occupied, nor did it prove less successful than the first. At its very beginning, and even before the return of the favourable season, the Sukhi on the Euphrates made a public act of submission, and their chief, Ilubâni, brought to Nineveh on their behalf a large sum of gold and silver. He had scarcely left the capital when the news of an untoward event effaced the good impression he had made. The descendants of the colonists, planted in bygone times by Shalmaneser I. on the western slope of the Masios, in the district of Khalzidipkha, had thrown off their allegiance, and their leader, Khulaî, was besieging the royal fortress of Damdamusa.[2] Assur-nazir-pal marched direct to the sources of the Tigris, and the mere fact of his presence sufficed to prevent any rising in that quarter. He took advantage of the occasion to set up a stele beside those of his father Tukulti-ninip and his ancestor Tiglath-pileser,[3] and then having halted to receive the tribute of Izalla,[4] he turned southwards, and took up a position on the slopes of the Kashiari. At

[1] *Annals of Assur-nazir-pal*, col. i. ll. 69–99; cf. PEISER, *Insch. Aschur-nâṣir-abal's*, pp. 62–69.

[2] The position of Khalzidipkha or Khalzilukha, as well as that of Kinabu, its stronghold, is shown approximately by what follows. Assur-nazir-pal, marching from the sources of the Supnat towards Tela, could pass either to the east or west of the Karajah-dagh; as the end of the campaign finds him at Tushkhân, to the south of the Tigris, and he returns to Naîri and Kirkhi by the eastern side of the Karajah-dagh, we are led to conclude that the outgoing march to Tela was by the western side, through the country situated between the Karajah-dagh and the Euphrates. [See p. 20, note 2.—TR.] On referring to a modern map, two rather important places will be found in this locality: the first, Arghana, commanding the road from Diarbekîr to Kharput; the other, Severek, on the route from Diarbekîr to Orfah. Arghana appears to me to correspond to the royal city of Damdamusa, which would thus have protected the approach to the plain on the north-west. Severek corresponds fairly well to the position which, according to the Assyrian text, Kinabu must have occupied; hence the country of Khalzidipkha (Khalzilukha) must be the district of Severek.

[3] Cf. the mention of these stelæ in the *Struggle of the Nations*, pp. 658, 659 [The Supnat is there written Subnat.—TR.], and p. 6 of the present volume.

[4] Izalla, written also Izala, Azala, paid its tribute in sheep and oxen, and also produced a wine for which it continued to be celebrated down to the time of Nebuchadrezzar II. (FR. LENORMANT, *Étude sur quelques parties des Syllab. cun.*, pp. 122, 123; DELATTRE, *L'Asie Occidentale*, pp. 24, 25. Lenormant and Finzi (*Ricerche per lo Studio dell' Antichità Assira*, pp. 111, 558) place this country near to Nisibis, where the Byzantine and Syrian writers mention a district and a mountain of the same name, and this conjecture is borne out by the passages of the *Annals of Assur-nazir-pal* (col. ii. ll. 21, 22, col. iii. ll. 57–60) which place it in the vicinity of Bît-Adini and Bît-Bakhiâni. It has also been adopted by most of the historians who have recently studied the question.

the first news of his approach, Khulai had raised the blockade of Damdamusa and had entrenched himself in Kinabu ; the Assyrians, however, carried the place by storm, and six hundred soldiers of the garrison were killed in the attack. The survivors, to the number of three thousand, together with many women and children, were thrown into the flames. The people of Mariru hastened to the rescue ; [1] the Assyrians took three hundred of them prisoners and burnt them alive ; fifty others were ripped up, but the victors did not stop to reduce their town. The district of Nirbu was next subjected to systematic ravaging, and half of its inhabitants fled into the Mesopotamian desert, while the remainder sought refuge in Tela at the foot of the Ukhira.[2] The latter place was a strong one, being surrounded by three enclosing walls, and it offered an obstinate resistance. Notwithstanding this, it at length fell, after having lost three thousand of its defenders :—some of its garrison were condemned to the stake, some had their hands, noses, or ears cut off, others were deprived of sight, flayed alive, or impaled amid the smoking ruins. This being deemed insufficient punishment, the conqueror degraded the place from its rank of chief town, transferring this, together with its other privileges, to a neighbouring city, Tushkhân, which had belonged to the Assyrians from the beginning of their conquests.[3] The king enlarged the place, added to it a strong enclosing wall, and installed within it the survivors of the older colonists who had been dispersed by the war, the majority of whom had taken refuge in Shupria.[4] He constructed a palace there, built storehouses for the reception of the grain of the province ; and, in

[1] The site of Mariru is unknown ; according to the text of the *Annals*, it ought to lie near Severek (Kinabu) to the south-east, since, after having mentioned it, Assur-nazir-pal speaks of the people of Nirbu whom he engaged in the desert before marching against Tela.

[2] Tîla or Tela is the Tela Antoninopolis of the writers of the Roman period and the present Veranshehr. The district of Nirbu, of which it was the capital, lay on the southern slope of the Karajah-dagh at the foot of Mount Ukhira, the central group of the range. The name Kashiari is applied to the whole mountain group which separates the basins of the Tigris and Euphrates to the south and south-west (HOMMEL, *Gesch Bab. und Ass.*, pp. 563–565.

[3] From this passage we learn that Tushkhân, also called Tushkha, was situated on the border of Nirbu, while from another passage in the campaign of the Vth year we find that it was on the right bank of the Tigris (*Annals*, col. ii. ll. 103–105). Following H. Rawlinson (*Assyrian Discovery*, in the *Athenæum*, 1863, vol. i. p. 228 ; cf. G. RAWLINSON, *The Five Great Monarchies*, vol. ii. p. 84, note 5), I place it at Kurkh, near the Tigris, to the east of Diarbekîr, where the monolith was found mentioned on p. 13, note 2, of this volume. The existence in that locality of an inscription of Assur-nazir-pal appears to prove the correctness of this identification ; we are aware, in fact, of the particular favour in which this prince held Tushkhân, for he speaks with pride of the buildings with which he embellished it (*Annals*, col. ii. l. 7). Hommel (*Gesch. Bab. und Ass.*, p. 572, note 5), however, identifies Kurkh with the town of Matiâtê, of which mention is made further on (see p. 26).

[4] Shupria or Shupri, a name which has been read Ruri, had been brought into submission from the time of Shalmaneser I. (cf. *The Struggle of the Nations*, p. 608). We gather from the passages in which it is mentioned that it was a hilly country, producimg wine, rich in flocks (*Annals*, col. ii. ll. 12–14), and lying at a short distance from Tushkhân ; perhaps Mariru, mentioned above, note 1, was one of its towns. I think we may safely place it on the north-western slopes of the Kashiari, in the modern caza of Tchernik, which possesses several vineyards held in high estimation (V. CUINET, *La Turquie d'Asie*, vol. ii. p. 493). Knudtzon, to whom we are indebted for the reading of this name, places the country rather further north, within the fork formed by the two upper branches of the Tigris (*Assyrische Gebete an den Sonnengott*, vol. ii. pp. 151, 152).

short, transformed the town into a stronghold of the first order, capable of serving as a base of operations for his armies. The surrounding princes, in the meanwhile, rallied round him, including Ammibaal of Bît-Zamani, and the rulers of Shupria, Naîri, and Urumi;[1] the chiefs of Eastern Nirbu alone held aloof, emboldened by the rugged nature of their mountains and the density of their forests. Assur-nazir-pal attacked them on his return journey, dislodged them from the fortress of Ishpilibria where they were entrenched, gained the pass of Buliani, and emerged into the valley of Luqia.[2] At Ardupa a brief halt was made to receive the ambassadors of one of the Hittite sovereigns and others from the kings of Khanigalbat, after which he returned to Nineveh, where he spent the winter.[3] As a matter of fact, these were but petty wars, and their immediate results appear at the first glance quite inadequate to account for the contemporary enthusiasm they excited. The sincerity of it can be better understood when we consider the miserable state of the country twenty years previously. Assyria then comprised two territories, one in the plains of the middle, the other in the districts of the upper, Tigris, both of considerable extent, but almost without regular intercommunication. Caravans or isolated messengers might pass with tolerable safety from Assur and Nineveh to Singar, or even to Nisibis; but beyond these places they had to brave the narrow defiles and steep paths in the forests of the Masios, through which it was rash to venture without keeping eye and ear ever on the alert. The mountaineers and their chiefs recognized the nominal suzerainty of Assyria, but refused to act upon this recognition unless constrained by a strong hand; if this control were relaxed they levied contributions on, or massacred, all who came within their reach, and the king himself never travelled from his own city of Nineveh to his own town of Amidi unless accompanied by an army. In less than the short space of three years, Assur-nazir-pal had remedied this evil. By the slaughter of some two hundred men in one place, three hundred in

---

[1] The position of Bît-Zamani on the banks of the Euphrates was determined by DELATTRE, *L'Asie Occidentale*, etc., pp. 39, 40. Urumi (see *The Struggle of the Nations*, p. 645) was situated on the right bank of the same river in the neighbourhoood of Sumeisat, and the name has survived in that of Urima, a town in the vicinity so called even as late as Roman times (PTOLEMY, v. 15, § 14). Nirdun, with Madara as its capital, occupied part of the eastern slopes of the Kashiari towards Ortaveran, as we gather from the *Annals of Assur-nazir-pal*, col. ii. ll. 98–101, compared with *Annals*, col. ii. l. 13

[2] Hommel identifies the Luqia with the northern affluent of the Euphrates called on the ancient monuments Lykos, and he places the scene of the war in Armenia (*Gesch. Bab. und Ass.*, pp. 562, 563). The context obliges us to look for this river to the south of the Tigris, to the north-east and to the east of the Kashiari. The king coming from Nirbu, the pass of Buliani, in which he finds the towns of Kirkhi, must be the valley of Khaneki, in which the road winds from Mardîn to Diarbekîr, and the Luqia is probably the most important stream in this region, the Sheikhân-Su, which waters Savur, chief town of the caza of Avineh (V. CUINET, *La Turquie d'Asie*, vol. ii. p. 518). Ardupa must have been situated near, or on the actual site of, the present Mardîn, whose Assyrian name is unknown to us; it was at all events a military station on the road to Nineveh, along which the king returned victorious with the spoil.

[3] *Annals of Assur-nazir-pal*, col. i. ll. 99–118, col. ii. ll. 1–13; cf. PEISER, *Inschriften Aschurnâsir-abal's*, in SCHRADER, *Keil. Bibl.*, vol. ii. pp. 68–75.

another, two or three thousand in a third, by dint of impaling and flaying refractory sheikhs, burning villages and dismantling strongholds, he forced the
marauders of Naîri and Kirkhi to respect his frontiers and desist from pillaging
his country. The two divisions of his kingdom, strengthened by the military
colonies in Nirbu, were united, and became welded together into a compact whole
from the banks of the Lower Zab to the sources of the Khabur and the Supnat.

During the following season the course of events diverted the king's efforts
into quite an opposite direction (B.C. 882). Under the name of Zamua there
existed a number of small states scattered along the western slope of the
Iranian Plateau north of the Cossæans.[1] Many of them—as, for instance, the
Lullumê—had been civilized by the Chaldæans almost from time immemorial ;
the most southern among them were perpetually oscillating between the
respective areas of influence of Babylon and Nineveh, according as one or
other of these cities was in the ascendant, but at this particular moment they
acknowledged Assyrian sway. Were they excited to rebellion against the latter
power by the emissaries of its rival, or did they merely think that Assur-nazir-pal
was too fully absorbed in the affairs of Naîri to be able to carry his arms effectively elsewhere ? At all events they coalesced under Nurrammân, the sheikh
of Dagara, blocked the pass of Babiti which led to their own territory, and there
massed their contingents behind the shelter of hastily erected ramparts.[2] Assur-
nazir-pal concentrated his army at Kakzi,[3] a little to the south of Arbela, and
promptly marched against them ; he swept all obstacles before him, killed
fourteen hundred and sixty men at the first onslaught, put Dagara to fire
and sword, and soon defeated Nurrammân, but without effecting his capture. As the campaign threatened to be prolonged, he formed an entrenched
camp in a favourable position, and stationed in it some of his troops to

[1] According to Hommel (*Gesch. Bab. und Ass.*, pp. 565, 599) and Tiele (*Bab. Ass. Gesch.*, p. 199),
Zamua would be the country extending from the sources of the Radanu to the southern shores of the
lake of Urumiah ; Schrader (*Die Namen der Meere*, p. 194) believes it to have occupied a smaller
area, and places it to the east and south-west of the lesser Zab. Delattre (*Encore un mot sur la
Géographie Ass.*, pp. 15–18) has shown that a distinction must be made between Zamua on Lake Van
and the well-known Zamua upon the Zab. Zamua, as described by Assur-nazir-pal, answers approximately to the present sandjak of Suleimaniyeh in the vilayet of Mossul.

[2] Hommel (*Gesch. Bab. und Ass.*, p. 567) believes that Assur-nazir-pal crossed the Zab near
Altin-keupru, and he is certainly correct ; but it appears to me from a passage in the *Annals* (col. ii.
ll. 51–55), of which a summary will be found below (see pp. 23, 24), that instead of taking the road
which leads to Bagdad by Kerkuk and Tuz-Khurmati, he marched along that which leads eastwards
in the direction of Suleimaniyeh. The pass of Babiti must have lain between Gawardis and Bibân,
facing the Kissê-tchai, which forms the western branch of the Radanu. Dagara would thus be
represented by the district to the east of Kerkuk at the foot of the Kara-dagh.

[3] Kakzi, sometimes read Kalzi, must have been situated, as Oppert has pointed out (*Expédition en
Mésopotamie*, vol. i. p. 318 ; cf. G. SMITH, *Hist. of Sennacherib*, pp. 165, 166 ; HOMMEL, *Gesch. Bab. und Ass.*,
p. 566, n. 5), at Shemamek or Shamamik, near Hazeh, to the south-west of Erbil, the ancient Arbela, at
the spot where Jones noticed important Assyrian ruins (*Topography of Nineveh*, in *Jour. of R. Asiatic
Soc.*, vol. xv. p. 374) excavated by Layard (*Nineveh and Bab.*, p. 189). Bricks from Kakzi are mentioned
in RAWLINSON, *Cun. Ins. W. As.*, vol. i. pls. vii. and viii., H ; cf. OPPERT, *Exp. en Mésop.*, vol. i. p. 226.

guard the booty, while he dispersed the rest to pillage the country on all sides. One expedition led him to the mountain group of Nizir, at the end of the chain known to the people of Lullumê as the Kinipa.[1] He there reduced to ruins seven towns whose inhabitants had barricaded themselves in urgent haste, collected the few herds of cattle he could find, and driving them back to the camp, set out afresh towards a part of Nizir as yet unsubdued by any conqueror. The strong hold of Larbusa fell before the battering-ram, to be followed shortly by the capture of Bara. Thereupon the chiefs of Zamua, convinced of their helplessness, purchased the king's departure by presents of horses, gold, silver, and corn.[2] Nurrammân alone

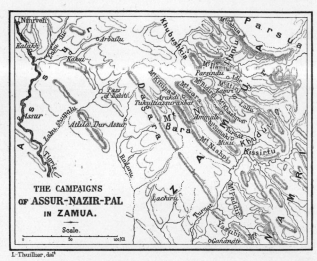

THE CAMPAIGNS OF ASSUR-NAZIR-PAL IN ZAMUA.

remained impregnable in his retreat at Nishpi, and an attempt to oust him resulted solely in the surrender of the fortress of Birutu.[3] The campaign, far from having been decisive, had to be continued during the winter in another direction where revolts had taken place,—in Khudun, in Kissirtu, and in the fief of Arashtua,[4] all three of which extended over the upper valleys of the lesser Zab, the Radanu, the Turnat, and their affluents. The king once more set out from Kakzi, crossed the Zab and the Radanu, through the gorges of Babiti, and halting on the ridges of Mount Simaki, peremptorily demanded tribute from Dagara.[5] This was, however, merely a ruse to deceive the enemy,

[1] See what is said of Nizir in the *Dawn of Civilization*, p. 570, note 1 : Mount Kinipa is a part of Nizir, the Khalkhalân-dagh, if we may judge from the direction of the Assyrian campaign.

[2] None of these places can be identified with certainty. The gist of the account leads us to gather that Bara was situated to the east of Dagara, and formed its frontier ; we shall not be far wrong in looking for all these districts in the fastnesses of the Kara-dagh, in the caza of Suleimaniyeh. Mount Nishpi is perhaps the Segirmê-dagh of the present day.

[3] *Annals of Assur-nazir-pal*, col. ii. ll. 23–49 ; cf. PEISER, *Inschriften Aschur-nâsir-abal's*, pp. 74–79. The Assyrian compiler appears to have made use of two slightly differing accounts of this campaign ; he has twice repeated the same facts without noticing his mistake.

[4] The fief of Arashtua, situated beyond the Turnat, is probably the district of Suleimaniyeh (HOMMEL, *Gesch. Bab. und Ass.*, pp. 566–568) ; it is, indeed, at this place only that the upper course of the Turnat is sufficiently near to that of the Radanu to make the marches of Assur-nazir-pal in the direction indicated by the Assyrian scribe possible. According to the account of the *Annals* (col. ii. ll. 54–59), it seems to me that we must seek for Khudun and Kissirtu to the south of the fief of Arashtua, in the modern cazas of Gulanbar or Shehrizôr.

[5] The *Annals of Assur-nazir-pal* go on to mention (col. ii. ll. 82, 83) that Mount Simaki extended as

for taking one evening the lightest of his chariots and the best of his horsemen, he galloped all night without drawing rein, crossed the Turnat at dawn, and pushing straight forward, arrived in the afternoon of the same day before the walls of Ammali, in the very heart of the fief of Arashtua.[1] The town vainly attempted a defence; the whole population was reduced to slavery or dispersed in the forests, the ramparts were demolished, and the houses reduced to ashes. Khudun with twenty, and Kissirtu with ten of its villages, Bara, Kirtiara, Dur-Lullumê, and Bunisa, offered no further resistance, and the invading host halted within sight of the defiles of Khashmar.[2] One kinglet, however, Amika of Zamru, showed no intention of capitulating. Entrenched behind a screen of forests and frowning mountain ridges, he fearlessly awaited the attack. The only access to the remote villages over which he ruled, was by a few rough roads hemmed in between steep cliffs and beds of torrents; difficult and dangerous at ordinary times, they were blocked in war by temporary barricades, and dominated at every turn by some fortress perched at a dizzy height above them. After his return to the camp, where his soldiers were allowed a short respite, Assur-nazir-pal set out against Zamru, though he was careful not to approach it directly and attack it at its most formidable points. Between two peaks of the Lara and Bidirgi ranges he discovered a path which had been deemed impracticable for horses, or even for heavily armed men. By this route, the king, unsuspected by the enemy, made his way through the mountains, and descended so unexpectedly upon Zamru, that Amika had barely time to make his escape, abandoning everything in his alarm—palace, treasures, harem, and even his chariot.[3] A body of Assyrians pursued him hotly beyond the fords of the Lallu, chasing him as far as Mount Itini; then, retracing their steps to headquarters, they at once set out on a fresh track, crossed the Idir, and proceeded to lay waste the plains of Ilaniu and Suâni.[4] Despairing of taking

far as the Turnat, and that it was close to Mount Azîra. This passage, when compared with that in which the opening of the campaign is described (col. ii. ll. 52, 53), obliges us to recognise in Mounts Simaki and Azîra two parts of the Shehrizôr chain, parallel to the Seguirmé-dagh. The fortress of Mizu, mentioned in the first of these two texts (l. 82), may perhaps be the present Gurân-kaleh.

[1] Hommel thinks that Ammali is perhaps the present Suleimaniyeh (*Gesch. Bab. und Ass.*, p. 568); it is, at all events, on this side that we must look for its site.

[2] I do not know whether we may trace the name of the ancient Mount Khashmar-Khashmir in the present Azmir-dagh; it is at its feet, probably in the valley of Suleimanabad, that we ought to place the passes of Khashmar. For the Cossæan origin of this name, cf. FR. DELITZSCH, *Die Sprache der Kossäer*, pp. 37, 38.

[3] This raid, which started from the same point as the preceding one, ran eastwards in an opposite direction and ended at Mount Itini. Leaving the fief of Arashtua in the neighbourhood of Suleimaniyeh, Assur-nazir-pal crossed the chain of the Azmir-dagh near Pir-Omar and Gudrun, where we must place Mounts Lara and Bidirgi, and emerged upon Zamru; the only places which appear to correspond to Zamru in that region are Kandishin and Suleimanabad. Hence the Lallu is the river which runs by Kandishîn and Suleimanabad, and Itini the mountain which separates this river from the Tchami-Kizildjîk.

[4] I think we may recognise the ancient name of Ilaniu in that of Alân, now borne by a district on

Amika prisoner, Assur-nazir-pal allowed him to lie hidden among the brushwood of Mount Sabua, while he himself called a halt at Parsindu,[1] and set to work to organise the fruits of his conquest. He placed garrisons in the principal towns—at Parsindu, Zamru, and at Arakdi in Lullumê, which one of his predecessors had re-named Tukulti-Ashshur-azbat,[2]—" I have taken the

THE ZAB BELOW THE PASSES OF ALÂN, THE ANCIENT ILANIU.[3]

help of Assur." He next imposed on the surrounding country an annual tribute of gold, silver, lead, copper, dyed stuffs, oxen, sheep, and wine. Envoys from neighbouring kings poured in—from Khudun, Khubushkia, and Gilzân, and the whole of Northern Zamua bowed " before the splendour of his arms ; " it now needed only a few raids resolutely directed against Mounts Azîra and Simaki, as far as the Turnat, to achieve the final pacification of the South.

the Turkish and Persian frontier, situated between Kunekdji-dagh and the town of Serdesht. The expedition, coming from the fief of Arashtua, must have marched northwards : the Idir in this case must be the Tchami-Kızıldjîk, and Mount Sabua the chain of mountains above Serdesht.

[1] Parsindu, mentioned between Mount Ilaniu and the town of Zamru, ought to lie somewhere in the valley of Tchami-Kizildjîk, near Murana.

[2] The approximate site of Arakdi is indicated in the itinerary of Assur-nazir-pal itself (*Annals*, col. ii. ll. 76–78) ; the king comes from Zamru in the neighbourhood of Suleimanabad, crosses Mount Lara, which is the northern part of the Azmir-dagh, and arrives at Arakdi, possibly somewhere in Surtash. In the course of the preceding campaign (*Annals*, col. ii. ll. 48, 49), after having laid waste Bara (cf. p. 23, note 2), he set out from this same town (Arakdi) to subdue Nishpi (see p. 23), all of which bears out the position I have indicated. The present town of Bazîân would answer fairly well for the site of a place destined to protect the Assyrian frontier on this side.

[3] Drawn by Boudier, from a photograph by M. de Morgan ; cf. J. DE MORGAN, *Mission en Perse*, vol. iv. pl. xxiv., and vol. ii. pl. iii., where the same view is given under the title of " Valley of the Lesser Zab at Bechast."

While in this neighbourhood, his attention was directed to the old town of Atlîla,[1] built by Sibir,[2] an ancient king of Karduniash, but which had been half ruined by the barbarians. He re-named it Dur-Assur, "the fortress of Assur," and built himself within it a palace and storehouses, in which he accumulated large quantities of corn, making the town the strongest bulwark of his power on the Cossæan border. The two campaigns of B.C. 882 and 881 had cost Assur-nazir-pal great efforts, and their results had been inadequate to the energy expended. His two principal adversaries, Nurrammân and Amika, had eluded him, and still preserved their independence at the eastern extremities of their former states. Most of the mountain tribes had acknowledged the king's supremacy merely provisionally, in order to rid themselves of his presence; they had been vanquished scores of times, but were in no sense subjugated, and the moment pressure was withdrawn, they again took up arms. The districts of Zamua alone, which bordered on the Assyrian plain, and had been occupied by a military force, formed a province, a kind of buffer state between the mountain tribes and the plains of the Zab, protecting the latter from incursions.

Assur-nazir-pal, feeling himself tolerably safe on that side, made no further demands, and withdrew his battalions to the westward part of his northern frontier. He hoped, no doubt, to complete the subjugation of the tribes who still contested the possession of various parts of the Kashiari, and then to push forward his main guard as far as the Euphrates and the Arzania, so as to form around the plain of Amidi a zone of vassals or tutelary subjects like those of Zamua. With this end in view, he crossed the Tigris near its source at the traditional fords, and made his way unmolested in the bend of the Euphrates from the palace of Tilluli, where the accustomed tribute of Kummukh was brought to him, to the fortress of Ishtarâti, and from thence to Kibaki. The town of Matiatê, having closed its gates against him, was at once sacked, and this example so stimulated the loyalty of the Kurkhi chiefs, that they hastened to welcome him at the neighbouring military station of Zazabukha. The king's progress continued thence as before, broken by frequent halts at the most favourable points for levying contributions on the inhabitants.[3] Assur-nazir-pal

[1] Given its position on the Chaldæan frontier, Atlîla is probably to be identified with the Kerkuk of the present day.

[2] Hommel is inclined to believe that Sibir was the immediate predecessor of Nabubaliddin, who reigned at Babylon at the same time as Assur-nazir-pal at Nineveh (Gesch. Bab. und Ass., p. 570), as we shall see further on (p. 28); consequently he would be a contemporary of Rammân-nirâri III. and of Tukulti-ninip II. Peiser and Rost have identified him, as we have seen, with Simmash-shikhu; see p. 4, note 8, of the present work.

[3] It is difficult to place any of these localities on the map: they ought all to be found between the ford of the Tigris, at Diarbekîr and the Euphrates, probably at the foot of the Mihrab-dagh and the Kirwântchemen-dagh. Matiatê may have been situated at Tchernîk (V. CUINET, La Turquie d'Asie, vol. ii. pp. 492, 493), and Tilluli near the environs of Lake Geuldîk. Rawlinson places Matiatê at Midiâd (The Five Great Monarchies, 2nd edit., vol. ii. p. 86), but this does not fall in with the facts given in the Assyrian text.

encountered no serious difficulty except on the northern slopes of the Kashiari, but there again fortune smiled on him ; all the contested positions were soon ceded to him, including even Madara, whose fourfold circuit of walls did not avail to save it from the conqueror.[1] After a brief respite at Tushkhân, he set out again one evening with his lightest chariots and the pick of his horsemen, crossed the Tigris on rafts, rode all night, and arrived unexpectedly the next morning before Pitura, the chief town of the Dirræans.[2] It was surrounded by a strong double enceinte, through which he broke after forty-eight hours of continuous assault : 800 of its men perished in the breach, and 700 others were impaled before the gates. Arbaki, at the extreme limits of Kirkhi, was the next to succumb, after which the Assyrians, having pillaged Dirra, carried the passes of Matni after a bloody combat, spread themselves over Naîri, burning 250 of its towns and villages, and returned with immense booty to Tushkhân. They had been there merely a few days when the news arrived that the people of Bît-Zamâni, always impatient of the yoke, had murdered their prince Ammibaal, and had proclaimed a certain Burramman in his place. Assur-nazir-pal marched upon Sinabu[3] and repressed the insurrection, reaping a rich harvest of spoil—chariots fully equipped, 600 draught-horses, 130 pounds of silver and as much of gold, 6600 pounds of lead and the same of copper, 19,800 pounds of iron, stuffs, furniture in gold and ivory, 2000 bulls, 500 sheep, the entire harem of Ammibaal, besides a number of maidens of noble family together with their dresses. Burramman was by the king's order flayed alive, and Arteanu his brother chosen as his successor. Sinabu and the surrounding towns formed part of that network of colonies which in times past Shalmaneser I. had organised as a protection from the incursions of the inhabitants of Naîri ; Assur-nazir-pal now used it as a rallying-place for the remaining Assyrian families, to whom he distributed lands and confided the guardianship of the neighbouring strongholds. The results of this measure were not long in making themselves felt : Shupria, Ulliba, and Nirbu, besides other districts,

---

[1] Madara belonged to a certain Lapturi, son of Tubusi, mentioned in the campaign of the king's second year (*Annals*, col. ii. 12, 13). In comparing the facts given in the two passages, we see it was situated on the eastern slope of the Kashiari, not far from Tushkhan on one side, and Ardupa—that is probably Mardîn (cf. p. 21, note 2)—on the other. The position of Ortaveran, or of one of the "tells" in its neighbourhood, answers fairly well to these conditions.

[2] According to the details given in the *Annals*, col. ii. ll. 103–110, we must place the town of Bitura (or Pitura) at about 19 miles from Kurkh, on the other side of the Tigris, in a northeasterly direction, and consequently the country of Dirrâ would be between the Hazu-tchaî and the Batman-tchaî. The Matni, with its passes leading in to Naîri, must in this case be the mountain group to the north of Mayafarrikîn, known as the Dordoseh-dagh or the Darkôsh-dagh.

[3] Hommel (*Gesch. Bab. und Ass.*, p. 575) thinks that Sinabu is very probably the same as the Kinabu mentioned above (p. 19, note 2) ; but it appears from Assur-nazir-pal's own account (*Annals*, col. i. ll. 102–110) that this Kinabu was in the province of Khalzidipkha (Khalzilukha) on the Kashiari, whereas Sinabu was in Bît-Zamâni (*Monolith of Kurkh*, l. 42, supplementing the *Annals*, col. ii. ll. 118–125).

paid their dues to the king, and Shura in Khamanu,[1] which had for some time held out against the general movement, was at length constrained to submit[2] (880 B.C.). However high we may rate the value of this campaign, it was eclipsed by the following one. The Aramæans on the Khabur and the middle Euphrates had not witnessed without anxiety the revival of Ninevite activity, and had begged for assistance against it from its rival. Two of their principal tribes, the Sukhi and the Laqi, had addressed themselves to the sovereign then reigning at Babylon. He was a restless, ambitious prince, named Nabu-baliddin, who asked nothing better than to excite a hostile feeling against his neighbour, provided he ran no risk by his interference of being drawn into open warfare. He accordingly despatched to the Prince of Sukhi the best of his Cossæan troops, commanded by his brother Zabdanu and one of the great officers of the crown, Bel-baliddin.[3] In the spring of 879 B.C., Assur-nazir-pal determined once for all to put an end to these intrigues. He began by inspecting the citadels flanking the line of the Kharmish[4] and the Khabur,—Tabiti,[5] Magarisi,[6] Shadikanni, Shuru in Bît-Khalupi, and Sirki.[7] Between the embouchures of the Khabur and the Balîkh, the Euphrates winds across a vast table-land, ridged with marly hills; the left bank is dry and sterile, shaded at rare intervals by sparse woods of poplars or groups of palms. The right bank, on the contrary, is seamed with fertile valleys, sufficiently well watered to permit the growth of cereals and the raising of cattle. The river-bed is almost everywhere wide, but strewn with dangerous rocks and sandbanks which render navigation perilous. On nearing the ruins of Halebiyeh, the river narrows as it enters the Arabian hills, and cuts for itself a regular defile of three or four hundred paces in length,

[1] Shura is mentioned on the return to Naîri (*Monolith of Kurkh*, l. 52), possibly on the road leading from Amidi and Tushkhân to Nineveh. Hommel believes that the country of Khamanu was the Amanos in Cilicia, and he admits, but unwillingly, that Assur-nazir-pal made a detour beyond the Euphrates (*Gesch. Bab. und Ass.*, pp. 575, 576). I should look for Shura, and consequently for Khamanu, in the Tur-Abdîn, and should identify them with Saur (SACHAU, *Reise in Syrien und Mesop.*, p. 421), in spite of the difference of the two initial articulations.

[2] *Annals of Assur-nazir-pal*, col. ii. ll. 86–125, supplemented by the text of the *Monolith of Kurkh*, ll. 42–54; cf. PEISER, *Insch. Aschur-nâsir-abal's*, in the *Keil. Bibliothek*, vol. i. pp. 84–95.

[3] *Annals*, etc., col. iii. ll. 17–20, in the *Keil. Bibl.*, vol. i. pp. 98, 99.

[4] The Kharmish has been identified with the Hirmâs, the river flowing by Nisibis, and now called the Nahr-Jaghjagha (G. RAWLINSON, *The Five Great Monarchies*, vol. ii. p. 87, note 2; SCHRADER, *Keilinschriften und Gesch.*, pp. 140–532). Nöldeke dismisses this identification by reminding his readers that Hirmâs is an abbreviation of Nahr-Mâs (*Z. d. D. M. G.*, vol. xxxiii. p. 328); Hommel justly remarks (*Gesch. Bab. und Ass.*, p. 577, note 2) that Nahr-Mâs is the popular interpretation of the old name Hirmâs, and he rightly maintains the identity of Hirmâs with Kharmish.

[5] Tabiti is, as Hommel has pointed out (*Gesch. Bab. und Ass.*, p. 577), the Thebeta (Thebet) of Roman itineraries and Syrian writers (NÖLDEKE, *Zwei Völker Vorderasiens*, in the *Z. d. D. M. G.*, vol. xxxiii. pp. 157, 158), situated, according to Peutinger's Table, 33 miles from Nisibis and 52 from Singara, on the Nahr-Hesawy or one of the neighbouring wadys.

[6] Magarisi ought to be found on the present Nahr-Jaghjagha, near its confluence with the Nahr-Jerrâhi and its tributaries; unfortunately, this part of Mesopotamia is still almost entirely unexplored, and no satisfactory map of it exists as yet.

[7] Sirki is Circesium at the mouth of the Khabur, as Fox Talbot was the first to point out (*Assyrian Texts*, p. 31).

which is approached by the pilots with caution.[1]   Assur-nazir-pal, on leaving
Sirki, made his way along the left bank, levying toll on Supri, Naqarabâni,
and several other villages in his course.   Here and there he called a halt
facing some town on the opposite bank, but the boats which could have put

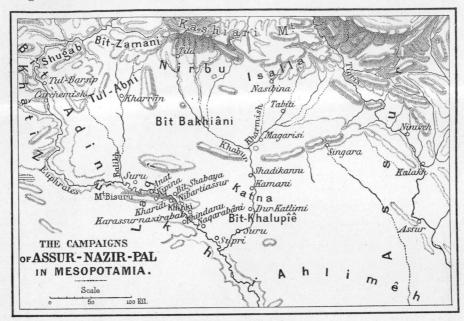

him across had been removed, and the fords were too well guarded to permit
of his hazarding an attack.   One town, however, Khindânu, made him a voluntary offering which he affected to regard as a tribute, but Kharidi and Anat
appeared not even to suspect his presence in their vicinity, and he continued
on his way without having obtained from them anything which could be
construed into a mark of vassalage.[2]   At length, on reaching Shuru, Shadadu,

[1] CHESNEY, *The Expedition of the Survey of the Rivers Euphrates and Tigris*, vol. i. pp. 48, 49, 417–
419 ; PETERS, *Nippur or Explorations and Adventures on the Euphrates*, vol. i. pp. 108–114.   It is at
this defile of El-Hammeh (HOMMEL, *Gesch. Bab. und Ass.*, p. 577), and not at that of Birejîk at the
end of the Taurus (DELITZSCH, *Wo lag das Paradies?* p. 173), that we must place the *Khinqi sha
Purati*—the narrows of the Euphrates—so often mentioned in the account of this campaign
(*Annals*, etc., col. iii. ll. 29, 30, 44).   The aspect presented by the country at this spot is shown in
the illustration on p. 25 of *The Struggle of the Nations*.

[2] The detailed narrative of the *Annals* (col. iii. ll. 13, 14) informs us that Assur-nazir-pal
encamped on a mountain between Khindânu and Bît-Shabaia, and this information enables us to
determine on the map with tolerable certainty the localities mentioned in this campaign.   The
mountain in question can be none other than El-Hammeh, the only one met with on this bank of
the Euphrates between the confluents of the Euphrates and the Khabur (HOMMEL, *Gesch. Bab. und
Ass.*, p. 577).   Khindânu is therefore identical with the ruins of Tabus, the Dabausa of Ptolemy
(SACHAU, *Reise in Syrien*, pp. 267–269 ; PETERS, *Nippur*, vol. i. p. 108) ; hence Supri and Naqabarâni
are situated between this point and Sirki, the former in the direction of Tayebeh, the latter towards
El-Hoseîniyeh.   On the other hand, the ruins of Kabr Abu-Atîsh (SACHAU, *Reise in Syrien*, pp. 255, 266 ;
PETERS, *Nippur*, vol. i. p. 108) would correspond very well to Bît-Shabaia : is the name of Abu-Sbé
borne by the Arabs of that neighbourhood a relic of that of Shabaia?   Kharidi ought in that case to be
looked for on the opposite bank, near Abu-Subân and Aksubi, where Chesney (*The Expedition of the
Survey*, vol. i., map) points out ancient remains.   A day's march beyond Kabr Abu-Atîsh brings us to

the Prince of Sukhi, trusting in his Cossæans, offered him battle; but he was defeated by Assur-nazir-pal, who captured the King of Babylon's brother, forced his way into the town after an assault lasting two days, and returned to Assyria laden with spoil.[1] This might almost be considered as a repulse; for no sooner had the king quitted the country than the Aramæans in their turn crossed the Euphrates and ravaged the plains of the Khabur.[2] Assur-nazir-pal resolved not to return until he was in a position to carry his arms into the heart of the enemy's country. He built a flotilla at Shuru in Bît-Khalupi on which he embarked his troops. Wherever the navigation of the Euphrates proved to be difficult, the boats were drawn up out of the water and dragged along the banks over rollers until they could again be safely launched; thus, partly afloat and partly on land, they passed through the gorge of Halebiyeh, landed at Kharidi, and inflicted a salutary punishment on the cities which had defied the king's wrath on his last expedition. Khindânu, Kharidi, and Kipina were reduced to ruins, and the Sukhi and the Laqi defeated, the Assyrians pursuing them for two days in the Bisuru mountains as far as the frontiers of Bît-Adini.[3] A complete submission was brought about, and its permanency secured by the erection of two strongholds, one of which, Kar-assur-nazir-pal, commanded the left, and the other, Nibarti-assur, the right bank of the Euphrates.[4]

This last expedition had brought the king into contact with the most important of the numerous Aramæan states congregated in the western region of Mesopotamia. This was Bît-Adini, which lay on both sides of the middle course of the Euphrates.[5] It included, on the right bank, to the north of

El-Khass, so that the town of Anat (Ilat in PEISER, *Inschriften Aschur*, etc., pp. 98, 99) would be in the Isle of Moglah, as Hommel supposes (*Gesch. Bab. und Ass.*, p. 57). Shuru must be somewhere near one of the two Tell-Menakhîrs on this side the Balikh.

[1] *Annals*, col. iii. ll. 1–16; cf. PEISER, *Inschriften Aschur.*, etc., pp. 96–99.

[2] The *Annals* do not give us either the *limmu* or the date of the year for this new expedition (col. iii. ll. 26–28). The facts taken altogether prove that it was a continuation of the preceding one, and it may therefore be placed in the year B.C. 878 (TIELE, *Bab. Ass. Gesch.*, pp. 174, 175; HOMMEL, *Gesch. Bab. und Ass.*, p. 578; DELITZSCH and MÜRDTER, *Gesch. Bab. und Ass.*, 2nd edit., p. 164; WINCKLER, *Gesch. Bab. und Ass.*, pp. 184, 185).

[3] The campaign of B.C. 878 had for its arena that part of the Euphrates which lies between the Khabur and the Balikh, and not, as Hommel thinks (*Gesch. Bab. und Ass.*, p. 578), the course of the Euphrates below the mouth of the Khabur; this time, however, the principal operations took place on the right bank. If Mount Bisuru is the Jebel-Bishri (HOMMEL, *Gesch. Bab. und Ass.*, p. 579), the town of Kipina, which is mentioned between it and Kharidi, ought to be located between Maidân and Sabkha.

[4] *Annals*, col. iii. ll. 26–50, where the account is confused, and contains perhaps some errors with regard to the facts, as Tiele has pointed out (*Bab. Ass. Gesch.*, pp. 184, 185). The site of the two towns is nowhere indicated, but a study of the map shows that the Assyrians could not become masters of the country without occupying the passes of the Euphrates; I am inclined to think that Kar-assur-nazir-pal is El-Halebiyeh, and Nibarti-assur, Zalebiyeh, the Zenobia of Roman times. For the ruins of these towns, cf. SACHAU, *Reise in Syrien und Mesop.*, pp. 256–259, and PETERS, *Nippur or Explorations and Adventures on the Euphrates*, vol. i. pp. 109–114.

[5] Cf. what I have already said in the *Struggle of the Nations*, p. 590, note 9. Bît-Adini appears to have occupied, on the right bank of the Euphrates, a part of the cazas of Aîn-Tab, Rum-kaleh, and Birejîk, that of Suruji, minus the nakhiyeh of Harrân, the larger part of the cazas of Membîj and of Rakkah, and part of the caza of Zôr, the cazas being those represented on the maps of VITAL CUINET, *La Turquie d'Asie*, vol. ii.

Carchemish, between the hills on the Sajur and Arabân-Su, a mountainous but fertile district, dotted over with towns and fortresses, the names of some of which have been preserved—Pakarrukhbuni, Sursunu, Paripa, Dabigu, and Shitamrat.[1] Tul-Barsip, the capital, was situated on the left bank, commanding the fords of the modern Birejîk,[2] and the whole of the territory between this latter and the Balîkh acknowledged the rule of its princes, whose authority also extended eastwards as far as the basaltic plateau of Tul-Abâ, in the Mesopotamian desert. To the south-east, Bît-Adini bordered upon the country of the Sukhi and the Laqi,[3] lying to the east of Assyria; other principalities, mainly of Aramæan origin, formed its boundary to the north and north-west—Shugab in the bend of the Euphrates, from Birejîk to Samosata,[4] Tul-Abnî around Edessa,[5] the district of Harrân,[6] Bît-Zamani, Izalla in the Tektek-dagh and on the Upper Khabur,[7] and Bît-Bakhiâni in the plain extending from the Khabur to the Kharmish.[8] Bît-Zamani had belonged to Assyria by right of conquest ever since the death of Ammibaal;[9] Izalla and Bît-Bakhiâni had fulfilled their duties as vassals whenever Assur-nazir-pal had appeared in their neighbourhood;[10] Bît-Adini alone had remained independent, though its strength was more apparent than real. .The districts which it included had never been able to form a basis for a powerful state.[11] If by chance some small kingdom arose within it, uniting under one authority the tribes scattered over the burning plain or along the river banks, the first conquering dynasty which sprang up in the

---

[1] FR. DELITZSCH, *Wo lag das Paradies?* p. 264. None of these localities can be identified with certainty, except perhaps Dabigu, a name we may trace in that of the modern village of Dehbek.

[2] The identification of Tul-Barsip with Birejîk, proposed by G. SMITH, *Assyrian Discoveries*, p. 34, has been adopted by SCHRADER, *Keilinschriften und Gesch.*, p. 219, note 2, by DELITZSCH, *Wo lag das Paradies?* p. 163, and by HOMMEL, *Gesch. Bab. und Ass.*, p. 607.

[3] In his previous campaign Assur-nazir-pal had taken two towns of Bît-Adini, situated on the right bank of the Euphrates, at the eastern extremity of Mount Bisuru (for this mountain cf. p. 30, note 3), near the frontier of the Lâqi (*Annals*, col. iii. ll. 41–44).

[4] The country of Shugab is mentioned between Birejîk (Tul-Barsip) and Bît-Zamani, in one of the campaigns of Shalmaneser III. (*Monolith*, col. ii. ll. 40, 41), which obliges us to place it in the caza of Rum-kaleh; the name has been read Sumu (WINCKLER, *Inschriften Salmanassar's II.*, in SCHRADER, *Keilinschriftliche Bibl.*, vol. i. pp. 164, 165).

[5] Tul-Abnî, which was at first sought for near the sources of the Tigris (IDEM., *ibid.*, p. 195, note 4), has been placed in the Mesopotamian plain by Hommel (*Gesch. Bab. und Ass.*, p. 579, note 3) and by Delattre (*L'Asie Occidentale*, pp. 18, 19). The position which it occupies among the other names (*Annals*, col. iii. ll. 55, 56, 63, 64) obliges us to put it near Bît-Adini and Bît-Zamani: the only possible site that I can find for it is at Orfah, the Edessa of classical times.

[6] The country of Harrân is nowhere mentioned as belonging either to Bît-Adini or to Tul-Abnî: we must hence conclude that at this period it formed a little principality independent of those two states.

[7] For Izalla, cf. p. 19, note 4.

[8] The situation of Bît-Bakhiâni is shown by the position which it occupies in the account of the campaign, and by the names associated with it in another passage of the *Annals*, col. ii. ll. 21–23 (SCHRADER, *Keilinschriftliche Bibl.*, vol. i. pp. 74, 75).

[9] See the mention made of this personage above on p. 21.

[10] *Annals*, col. i. l. 106, col. ii. ll. 21–23.

[11] This point has been elucidated by NÖLDEKE, *Harrân*, in the *Zeitschrift für Ass.*, vol. xi. pp. 107–109; cf., for a contrary opinion, WINCKLER, *Alt. Forschungen*, vol. i. p. 380, et seq.

neighbourhood would be sure to effect its downfall, and absorb it under its own leadership.   As Mitâni, saved by its remote position from bondage to Egypt, had not been able to escape from acknowledging the supremacy of the Khâti,[1] so Bît-Adini was destined to fall almost without a struggle under the yoke of the Assyrians.   It was protected from their advance by the volcanic groups of the Urâa and Tul-Abâ, which lay directly in the way of the main road from the marshes of the Khabur to the outskirts of Tul-Barsip.   Assur-nazir-pal, who might have worked round this line of natural defence to the north through Nirbu, or to the south through his recently acquired province of Lâqi, preferred to approach it in front ; he faced the desert, and, in spite of the drought, he invested the strongest citadel of Tul-Abâ in the month of June, 877 B.C.   The name of the place was Kaprabi, and its inhabitants believed it impregnable, clinging as it did to the mountain-side "like a cloud in the sky."[2]   The king, however, soon demolished its walls by sapping and by the use of the ram, killed 800 of its garrison, burned its houses, and carried off 2400 men with their families, whom he installed in one of the suburbs of Calah.   Akhuni, who was then reigning in Bît-Adini, had not anticipated that the invasion would reach his neighbourhood : he at once sent hostages and purchased peace by a tribute ; the Lord of Tul-Abnî followed his example, and the dominion of Assyria was carried at a blow to the very frontier of the Khâti.[3]   It was about two centuries before this that Assurirba had crossed these frontiers with his vanquished army, but the remembrance of his defeat had still remained fresh in the memory of the people,[4] as a warning to the sovereign who should attempt the old hazardous enterprise, and repeat the exploits of Sargon of Agadê or of Tiglath-pileser I.   Assur-nazir-pal made careful preparations for this campaign, so decisive a one for his own prestige and for the future of the empire.   He took with him not only all the Assyrian troops at his disposal, but requisitioned by the way the armies of his most recently acquired vassals, incorporating them with his own, not so much for the purpose of augmenting his power of action, as to leave no force in his rear when once he was engaged hand to hand with the Syrian legions.   He left Calah in the latter days of April, 876 B.C.,[5] receiving the customary taxes from Bît-Bakhiâni, Izalla,

---

[1] Cf. for these facts *Struggle of the Nations*, pp. 358, 590.

[2] The name is commonly interpreted " Great Rock," and divided thus—Kap-rabi (FR. DELITZSCH, *Wo lag das Paradies?* p. 264; HOMMEL, *Gesch. Bab. und Ass.*, p. 579).   It may also be considered, like Kapridargila (FR. DELITZSCH, *ibid.*, p. 164) or Kapranishâ (*Annals*, col. ii. l. 89), as being formed of *Kapru* and *abi*; this latter element appears to exist in the ancient name of Telaba, Thallaba, now Tul-Abâ.   Kapr-abi might be a fortress of the province of Tul-Abâ.

[3] *Annals*, col. iii. ll. 50–56; cf. PEISER, *Inschriften Aschur.*, etc., pp. 102–105.

[4] For Assurirba, cf. *Struggle of the Nations*, p. 665.   The fact of his defeat is known only from a passage on the *Monolith* of Shalmaneser III. (ll. 37, 38).

[5] On the 8th Iyyâr (*Annals*, col. iii. l. 56), but without any indication of *limmu*, or any number

and Bît-Adini, which comprised horses, silver, gold, copper, lead, precious stuffs, vessels of copper and furniture of ivory; having reached Tul-Barsip, he accepted the gifts offered by Tul-Abni, and crossing the Euphrates upon rafts of inflated skins, he marched his columns against Carchemish.[1]

The political organisation of Northern Syria had remained entirely un-altered since the days when Tiglath - pileser made his first victorious inroad into the country. The Cilician empire which succeeded to the Assyrian—if indeed it ever extended as far as some suppose—did not last long enough to disturb the balance of power among the various races occupying Syria: it had subjugated them for a time, but had not been able to break them up and reconstitute them.[2] At the downfall of the Cilician Empire the small states were still intact, and occupied, as of old, the territory comprising the ancient Naharaim of

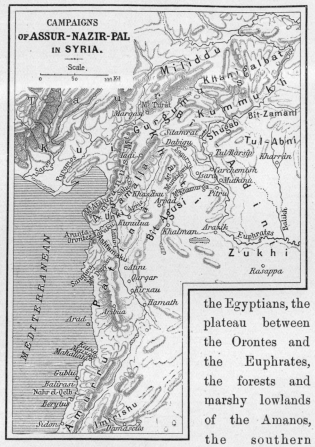

the Egyptians, the plateau between the Orontes and the Euphrates, the forests and marshy lowlands of the Amanos, the southern slopes of Taurus, and the plains of Cilicia. Of these states, the most famous, though not then the most redoubtable, was that with which the name of the Khâti is indissolubly connected, and which had Carchemish as its capital. This ancient city, seated on the banks of the Euphrates, still maintained its supre-macy there, but though its wealth and religious ascendency were undiminished, its territory had been curtailed. The people of Bît-Adini had intruded them-selves between this state and Kummukh, Arazik hemmed it in on the

---

of the year or of the campaign; the date 876 B.C. is admitted by the majority of historians (ED. MEYER, *Gesch. des Alterthums*, vol. i. p. 409; HOMMEL, *Geschichte Bab. und Ass.*, p. 580).

[1] *Annals of Assur-nazir-pal*, col. iii. ll. 56–64; cf. PEISER, *Die Inschriften Aschur-nâsir-abal's*, pp. 104, 105.

[2] For the state of Syria in the time of the wars of Tiglath-pileser I., cf. *Struggle of the Nations*, pp. 588–592, 656–658; on the subject of the Cilician empire, cf. pp. 667–669 of the same work.

south, Khazazu and Khalmân confined it on the west, so that its sway was only freely exercised in the basin of the Sajur.[1] On the north-west frontier of the Khâti lay Gurgum, whose princes resided at Marqasi and ruled over the central valley of the Pyramos together with the entire basin of the Ak-su. Mikhri,[2] Iaudi, and Samalla lay on the banks of the Saluara, and in the forests of the Amanos to the south of Gurgum. Kuî maintained its uneventful existence amid the pastures of Cilicia, near the marshes at the mouth of the Pyramos.[3] To the south of the Sajur, Bît-Agusi[4] barred the way to the Orontes; and from their lofty fastness of Arpad, its chiefs kept watch over the caravan road, and closed or opened it at their will. They held the key of Syria, and though their territory was small in extent, their position was so strong that for more

BAS-RELIEF FROM A BUILDING AT SINJÎRLI.[5]

than a century and a half the majority of the Assyrian generals preferred to avoid this stronghold by making a detour to the west, rather than pass beneath its walls. Scattered over the plateau on the borders of Agusi, or hidden in the valleys of Amanos, were several less important principalities, most of them owing allegiance to Lubarna, at that time king of the Patinâ and the most

[1] The territory of the Khâti has been determined with precision by SCHRADER, *Keilinschriften und Geschichtsforschung*, pp. 221–236; Assur-nazir-pal understands by this name merely the kingdom of Carchemish (FR. DELITZSCH, *Wo lag das Paradies?* pp. 269, 270).

[2] Mikhri or Ismikhri, *i.e.* "the country of larches," was the name of a part of the Amanos, possibly near the Pyramos (HOMMEL, *Geschichte Babyloniens und Assyriens*, pp. 530, 531; cf. DELATTRE, *L'Asie Occidentale dans les Inscriptions Assyr.*, p. 50).

[3] For the countries of Gurgum, Samalla, and Kuî, cf. *Struggle of the Nations*, p. 590; SACHAU, *Inschrift des Königs Panammû*, in the *Ausgrabungen in Sendschirli*, vol. i. p. 58; and WINCKLER, *Altorientalische Forschungen*, vol. i. p. 1, et seq.

[4] The real name of the country was Iakhânu (*Annals of Assur-nazir-pal*, col. iii. l. 77), but it was called Bît-Gusi or Bît-Agusi, like Bît-Adini, Bît-Bakhiâni, Bît-Omri, after the founder of the reigning dynasty (SCHRADER, *Keilinsch. und Gesch.*, p. 207, note). Delattre (*L'Asie Occid. dans les Inscr. Assyr.*, pp. 52, 53) places Iakhânu near the sources of the Kara-su and the Afrîn; we must rather place it to the south of Azaz, in the neighbourhood of Arpad, with this town as its capital (WINCKLER, *Alt. Forsch.*, vol. i. p. 8; MASPERO, *Notes au jour le jour*, § 32, in the *Proceedings of the Bibl. Arch. Soc.*, 1898, vol. xx. pp. 131–133).

[5] Drawn by Faucher-Gudin, from a sketch by PERROT and CHIPIEZ, *Histoire de l'art dans l'Antiquité*, vol. iv. p. 534; cf. LUSCHAN, *Ausgrab. in Sendschirli*, vol. i. p. 11.

powerful sovereign of the district. The Patinâ had apparently replaced the Alasia of Egyptian times, as Bît-Adini had superseded Mitâni; the fertile meadow-lands to the south of Samalla on the Afrîn and the Lower Orontes, together with the mountainous district between the Orontes and the sea as far as the neighbourhood of Eleutheros, also belonged to the Patinâ. On the southern frontier of the Patinâ lay the important Phœnician cities, Arvad,

JIBRÎN, A VILLAGE OF CONICAL HUTS, ON THE PLATEAU OF ALEPPO.[1]

Arka, and Sina; and on the south-east, the fortresses belonging to Hamath and Damascus.[2] The characteristics of the country remained unchanged.[3] Fortified towns abounded on all sides, as well as large walled villages of conical huts, like those whose strange outlines on the horizon are familiar to the traveller at the present day. The manners and civilisation of Chaldæa pervaded even more than formerly the petty courts, but the artists clung persistently to Asianic tradition, and the bas-reliefs which adorned the palaces and temples were similar in character to those we find scattered throughout Asia Minor;[4] there is the same inaccurate drawing, the same rough execution, the same tentative and awkward composition. The scribes from force of custom still employed the cuneiform syllabary in certain official religious or royal inscriptions, but, as it was difficult to manipulate and limited in application, the speech of the Aramæan immigrants and the Phœnician alphabet gradually superseded

[1] Drawn by Boudier, from a photograph reproduced in PETERS, *Nippur or Explorations and Adventures on the Euphrates,* vol. i. p. 81; cf. LAYARD, *Nineveh and Babylon,* p. 94.

[2] For the Patinâ, cf. *Struggle of the Nations,* p. 589. The limits of this country have been indicated by SCHRADER, *Keilinschr. und Gesch.,* pp. 214–221, by DELATTRE, *L'Asie Occid. dans les Inscr. Assyr.,* pp. 45–52, and by WINCKLER, *Altorient. Forsch.,* vol. i. p. 3, et seq.

[3] For the state of the country at the time of the first Assyrian conquest, cf. *Struggle of the Nations,* p. 588.

[4] Cf. what is said about this Asianic art in *Struggle of the Nations,* pp. 647–653.

the ancient language and mode of writing.[1] Thus these Northern Syrians became by degrees assimilated to the people of Babylon and Nineveh, much as the inhabitants of a remote province nowadays adapt their dress, their architecture, their implements of husbandry and handicraft, their military equipment and organisation, to the fashions of the capital.[2] Their armies were modelled on similar lines, and consisted of archers, pikemen, slingers, and those troops of horsemen which accompanied the chariotry on flying raids;[3] the chariots, moreover, closely followed the Assyrian type, even down to the padded bar with embroidered hangings which connected the body of the chariot with the end of the pole. The Syrian princes did not adopt the tiara, but they wore the long fringed robe, confined by a girdle at the waist, and their mode of life, with its ceremonies, duties,

THE WAR-CHARIOT OF THE KHÂTI OF THE NINTH CENTURY.[4]

and recreations, differed little from that prevailing in the palaces of Calah or Babylon. They hunted big game, including the lion, according to the laws of the chase recognised at Nineveh, priding themselves as much on their

[1] There is no monument bearing an inscription in this alphabet which can be referred with any certainty to the time of Assur-nazir-pal, but the inscriptions of the kings of Samalla date back to a period not more than a century and a half later than his reign (SACHAU, *Inschr. des Königs Panammû*, in *Ausgrab. in Sendschirli*, vol. i. pp. 81–84); we may therefore consider the Aramæan alphabet as being in current use in Northern Syria at the beginning of the ninth century, some forty years before the date of Mesha's inscription (*i.e.* the Moabite stone).

[2] One can judge of their social condition from the enumeration of the objects which formed their tribute (*Annals of Assur-nazir-pal*, col. iii. ll. 65–68, 71, 73–76, 78; *Monolith of Shalmaneser III.*, col. i. l. 41, col. ii. ll. 12, 13, 20–30, 82–86), or the spoil which the Assyrian kings carried off from their country.

[3] The composition of the Syrian armies is determined by various passages in the *Annals of Assur-nazir-pal*, col. iii. ll. 68, 69, 77.

[4] Drawn by Boudier, from a bas-relief not yet published, discovered by Fossey and Perdrizet.

exploits in hunting, as on their triumphs in war. Their religion was derived from the common source which underlay all Semitic religions, but a con-

THE ASSYRIAN WAR-CHARIOT OF THE NINTH CENTURY B.C.[1]

siderable number of Babylonian deities were also worshipped; these had been introduced in some cases without any modification, whilst in others they had

A KING OF THE KHÂTI HUNTING A LION IN HIS CHARIOT.[2]

been assimilated to more ancient gods bearing similar characteristics : at Nerab, among the Patinâ, Nusku and his female companion Nikal, both of Chaldæan origin, claimed the homage of the faithful, to the disparagement of Shahr

[1] Drawn by Faucher-Gudin, from a bronze bas-relief on the gates of Balawât.
[2] Drawn by Boudier, from a photograph by Hogarth, published in the *Recueil de Travaux*, vol. xvii. p. 25.

the moon and Shamash the sun.[1] Local cults often centred round obscure deities held in little account by the dominant races; thus Samalla reverenced Uru the light, Rekubêl the wind, the chariot of El, not to mention El

himself, Resheph, Hadad, and the Cabiri, the servants of Resheph.[2] These deities were mostly of the Assyrian type, and if one may draw any conclusion from the few representations of them already discovered, their rites must have been celebrated in a manner similar to that followed in the cities on the Lower Euphrates. Scarcely any signs of Egyptian influence survived, though here and there a trace of it might be seen in the figures of calf or bull, the vulture of Mut or the sparrow-hawk of Horus. Assur-nazir-pal, marching from the banks of the Khabur to Bît-Adini, and from Bît-Adini passing on to Northern Syria, might almost have imagined himself still in his own dominions, so gradual and imperceptible were the changes in language and civilisation in the country traversed between Nineveh and Assur, Tul-Barsip and Samalla.

His expedition was unattended by danger or blood-shed. Lubarna, the reigning prince of the Patinâ, was possibly at that juncture meditating the formation of a Syrian empire under his rule. Unki, in which lay his capital of Kunulua, was one of the richest countries of Asia,[4] being well watered by the Afrîn, Orontes, and

THE GOD HADAD.[3]

Saluara;[5] no fields produced such rich harvests as his, no meadows pastured such cattle or were better suited to the breeding of war-horses. His mountain

---

[1] CLERMONT-GANNEAU, Études d'Archéologie Orientale, vol. ii. pp. 182–223; HOFFMANN, Aramaïsche Inschriften aus Nérab bei Aleppo, in the Zeitschrift fur Assyriologie, vol. xi. pp. 258–272; JENSEN, Nik(k)al-Scharratu, in the Zeitschr. fur Assyr., vol. xi. pp. 293–301.

[2] For these gods, who are enumerated in the Aramæan inscriptions at Sinjirli, cf. HALÉVY, Les deux Inscriptions hétéennes de Zindjîrli, in the Revue Sémitique, vol. ii. pp. 25–31.

[3] Drawn by Faucher-Gudin, from the photograph in LUSCHAN, Ausgrab. in Sendschirli, vol. i. pl. vi.

[4] The Unki of the Assyrians, the Uniuqa of the Egyptians (MARIETTE, Karnak, pl. 20, No. 147), is the valley of Antioch, the Ἀμύκης πεδίον of Polybius (v. 59), the Amk of the present day (SAYCE, Monuments of the Hittites, in the Transactions of the Bibl. Arch. Soc., vol. vii. p. 292; FR. LENORMANT, Les Origines de l'Histoire, vol. iii. p. 324; TOMKINS, Notes on the Geography of Northern Syria, in the Babyl. and Orient. Record, vol. iii. p. 6; WINCKLER, Altorient. Forsch., vol. i. p. 9). Kunulua or Kinalia, the capital of the Patinâ, has been identified with the Gindaros of Greek times (SAYCE, Mon. of the Hittites, in the Transactions, vol. vii. p. 292); I prefer, with Tomkins (Notes on the Geography of Northern Syria, p. 6), to identify it with the existing Tell-Kunâna, written for Tell-Kunâla by the common substitution of n for l at the end of proper names.

[5] The Saluara of the Assyrian texts is the present Kara-su, which flows into the Ak-Denîz, the lake of Antioch (DELATTRE, L'Asie Occid. dans les Inscr. Assyr., p. 52; SACHAU, Zur historischen Geographie von Nordsyrien, pp. 17–24; cf. Struggle of the Nations, p. 7, note 3).

provinces yielded him wood and minerals, and provided a reserve of semi-savage woodcutters and herdsmen from which to recruit his numerous battalions. The neighbouring princes, filled with uneasiness or jealousy by his good fortune, saw in the Assyrian monarch a friend and a liberator rather than an enemy.   Carchemish opened its gates and laid at his feet the best of its treasures—twenty talents of silver, ingots, rings and daggers of gold, a hundred talents of copper, two hundred talents of iron, bronze bulls, cups decorated with scenes in relief or outline, ivory in the tusk or curiously wrought, purple and embroidered stuffs, and the state chariot of its King Shangara.   The Hittite troops, assembled in haste, joined forces with the Aramæan auxiliaries, and the united host advanced on Cœle - Syria.   The scribe commissioned to record the

RELIGIOUS SCENE DISPLAYING EGYPTIAN FEATURES.[1]

history of this expedition has taken a delight in inserting the most minute details.   Leaving Carchemish, the army followed the great caravan route, and, winding its way between the hills of Munzigâni and Khamurga, skirting Bît-Agusi, at length arrived under the walls of Khazazu among the Patinâ.[2] The town having purchased immunity by a present of gold and of finely woven stuffs, the army proceeded to cross the Apriê, on the bank of which an entrenched camp was formed for the storage of the spoil. Lubarna offered no resistance, but nevertheless refused to acknowledge his inferiority ; after some delay, it was decided to make a direct attack on his capital, Kunulua, whither he had retired.   The appearance of the Assyrian vanguard put a speedy end to his ideas of resistance : prostrating himself before his powerful adversary, he offered hostages, and emptied his palaces and stables to provide a ransom. This comprised twenty talents of silver, one talent of gold, a hundred talents of lead, a hundred talents of iron, a thousand bulls, ten thousand sheep,

---

[1] Drawn by Faucher-Gudin, from the impression taken from a Hittite cylinder.

[2] Khazazu being the present Azaz (SAYCE, *Mon. of the Hittites*, in the *Transactions*, vol. vii. p. 292 ; FR. DELITZSCH, *Wo lag das Paradies?* p. 294), the Assyrian army must have followed the route which still leads from Jerabîs to this town.   Mounts Munzigâni and Khamurga, mentioned between Carchemish and Akhânu or Iakhânu (cf. *supra*, p. 34, note 4), must lie between the Sajur and the Koweîk, near Shehab, at the only point on the route where the road passes between two ranges of lofty hills.

daughters of his nobles with befitting changes of garments, and all the para-
phernalia of vessels, jewels, and costly stuffs which formed the necessary
furniture of a princely household.   The effect of his submission on his own
vassals and the neighbouring tribes was shown in different ways.   Bît-Agusi at
once sent messengers to congratulate the conqueror, but the mountain provinces
awaited the invader's nearer approach before following its example.   Assur-
nazir-pal, seeing that they did not take the initiative, crossed the Orontes,
probably at the spot where the iron bridge now stands, and making his way
through the country between Iaraku and Iaturi,[1] reached the banks of the
Sangura[2] without encountering any difficulty.   After a brief halt there in
camp, he turned his back on the sea, and passing between Saratini and
Duppâni,[3] took by assault the fortress of Aribua.[4]   This stronghold commanded
all the surrounding country, and was the seat of a palace which Lubarna at
times used as a summer residence.   Here Assur-nazir-pal took up his quarters,
and deposited within its walls the corn and spoils of Lukhuti;[5] he established
here an Assyrian colony, and, besides being the scene of royal festivities, it became
henceforth the centre of operations against the mountain tribes.   The forts of
the latter were destroyed, their houses burned, and prisoners were impaled
outside the gates of their cities.   Having achieved this noble exploit, the king
crossed the intervening spurs of Lebanon and marched down to the shores of

[1] The spot where Assur-nazir-pal must have crossed the Orontes is determined by the respective
positions of Kunulua and Tell-Kunâna.   At the iron bridge, the modern traveller has the choice of
two roads : one, passing Antioch and Beît-el-Mâ, leads to Urdeh on the Nahr-el-Kebîr; the other
reaches the same point by a direct route over the Gebel Kosseir.   If, as I believe, Assur-nazir-pal
took the latter route, the country and Mount Iaraku must be the northern part of Gebel Kosseir
in the neighbourhood of Antioch, and Iaturi the southern part of the same mountain near Derkush ;
cf. DELATTRE, *L'Asie Occid. dans les Inscr. Assyriennes*, p. 49.   Iaraku is mentioned in the same position
by Shalmaneser III., who reached it after crossing the Orontes, on descending from the Amanos
(LAYARD, *Inscr. in the Cuneiform Character*, pl. 47, l. 23) *en route* for the country of Hamath.

[2] The Sangura or Sagura has been identified by Delattre (*L'Asie Occid. dans les Inscr. Assyr.*,
p. 50) with the Nahr-el-Kebîr, not that river which the Greeks called the Eleutheros, but that
which flows into the sea near Latakia ; cf. HOMMEL, *Gesch. Babyloniens und Assyr.*, p. 581 ;
WINCKLER, *Altorient. Forsch.*, vol. i. p. 5.   Before naming the Sangura, the *Annals* mention a
country, whose name, half effaced, ended in -*ku* (col. iii. l. 80) : I think we may safely restore this
name as [Ashtama]kou, mentioned by Shalmaneser III. in this region, after the name of Iaraku
(LAYARD, *Inscr. in the Cuneiform Character*, pl. 47, l. 23).   The country of Ashtamaku would thus
be the present canton of Urdeh, which is traversed before reaching the banks of the Nahr-el-Kebîr.

[3] The mountain cantons of Saratini and Duppâni (Kalpâni ? Adpâni ?), situated immediately to
the south of the Nahr-el-Kebîr, correspond to the southern part of Gebel-el-Akrad, but I cannot
discover any names on the modern map at all resembling them.

[4] Beyond Duppâni, Assur-nazir-pal encamped on the banks of a river whose name is unfortunately
effaced (*Annals*, col. iii. l. 81), and then reached Aribua ; this itinerary leads us to the eastern slope
of the Gebel Ansarieh in the latitude of Hamath.   The only site I can find in this direction fulfilling
the requirements of the text is that of Masiad, where there still exists a fort of the Assassins.   The
name Aribua is perhaps preserved in that of Rabaô, er-Rabahu, which is applied to a wady and
village in the neighbourhood of Masiad.

[5] Lukhuti must not be sought in the plains of the Orontes, where Assur-nazir-pal would have run
the risk of an encounter with the King of Hamath or his vassals ; it must represent the part of the
mountain of Ansarieh liyng between Kadmus, Masiad, and Tortosa.

the Mediterranean. Here he bathed his weapons in the waters, and offered the customary sacrifices to the gods of the sea, while the Phœnicians, with their wonted prudence, hastened to anticipate his demands—Tyre, Sidon, Byblos, Mahallat, Maîza, Kaîza,[1] the Amorites and Arvad,[2] all sending tribute. One point strikes us forcibly as we trace on the map the march of this victorious hero, namely, the care with which he confined himself to the left bank of the Orontes, and the restraint he exercised in leaving untouched the fertile fields of its valley, whose wealth was so calculated to excite his cupidity. This discretion would be inexplicable, did we not know that there existed in that region a formidable power which he may have thought it imprudent to provoke. It was Damascus which held sway over those territories whose frontiers he respected, and its kings, also suzerains of Hamath and masters of half Israel, were powerful enough to resist, if not conquer, any enemy who might present himself. The fear inspired by Damascus naturally explains the attitude adopted by the Hittite states towards the invader, and the precautions taken by the latter to restrict his operations within somewhat narrow limits. Having accepted the complimentary presents of the Phœnicians, the king again took his way northwards—making a slight detour in order to ascend the Amanos for the purpose of erecting there a stele commemorating his exploits, and of cutting pines, cedars, and larches for his buildings—and then returned to Nineveh amid the acclamations of his people.[3]

In reading the history of this campaign, its plan and the principal events which took place in it appear at times to be the echo of what had happened some centuries before. The recapitulation of the halting-places near the sources of the Tigris and on the banks of the Upper Euphrates, the marches through the valleys of the Zagros or on the slopes of Kashiari, the crushing one by one of the Mesopotamian races, ending in a triumphal progress through Northern Syria, is almost a repetition, both as to the names and order of the places mentioned, of the expedition made by Tiglath-pileser in the first

[1] For these three towns, cf. *Struggle of the Nations*, p. 172.

[2] The point where Assur-nazir-pal touched the sea-coast cannot be exactly determined : admitting that he set out from Masiad or its neighbourhood, he must have crossed the Lebanon by the gorge of the Eleutheros, and reached the sea-board somewhere near the mouth of this river. The assertion that he penetrated as far as the Nahr-el-Kelb rests on a false interpretation of the passage in the *Annals*, col. iii. l. 89, where he relates how he set up a stele recording his victories. Boscawen (*The Monuments and Inscriptions on the Rocks at the Nahr-el-Kelb*, in the *Transactions* of the Bibl. Arch. Soc., vol. vii. p. 339) has not noticed that this text refers to the Amanos, and, referring it to the Lebanon, he has conjectured that one of the stelæ now illegible on the Nahr-el-Kelb might be attributed to Assur-nazir-pal. Hommel followed him in this mistake (*Gesch. Babyl. und Assyr.*, p. 582). If Assur-nazir-pal had reached the Nahr-el-Kelb, he would have given us his detailed itinerary, noting the towns along the route, as he has done in that portion of his campaign which has to do with the Khâti and the Patinâ.

[3] *Annals of Assur-nazir-pal*, col. iii. ll. 64–92; cf. PEISER, *Die Inschriften Aschur-nâsir-abal's*, pp. 106–111.

five years of his reign.   The question may well arise in passing whether Assur-nazir-pal consciously modelled his campaign on that of his ancestor, as, in Egypt, Ramses III. imitated Ramses II.,[1] or whether, in similar circumstances, he instinctively and naturally followed the same line of march.   In either case, he certainly showed on all sides greater wisdom than his predecessor, and having attained the object of his ambition, avoided compromising his success by injudiciously attacking Damascus or Babylon, the two powers who alone could have offered effective resistance.   The victory he had gained, in 879, over the brother of Nabu-baliddin had immensely flattered his vanity.   His panegyrists vied with each other in depicting Karduniash bewildered by the terror of his majesty, and the Chaldæans overwhelmed by the fear of his arms; [2] but he did not allow himself to be carried away by their extravagant flatteries, and continued to the end of his reign to observe the treaties concluded between the two courts in the time of his grandfather Rammân-nirâri.[3]   He had, however, sufficiently enlarged his dominions, in less than ten years, to justify some display of pride.   He himself described his empire as extending, on the west of Assyria proper, from the banks of the Tigris near Nineveh to Lebanon and the Mediterranean; [4] besides which, Sukhi was subject to him, and this included the province of Rapiku on the frontiers of Babylonia.[5]   He had added to his older provinces of Amidi, Masios and Singar, the whole strip of Armenian territory at the foot of the Taurus range, from the sources of the Supnat to those of the Bitlis-tchaî, and he held the passes leading to the banks of the Arzania, in Kirruri and Gilzân, while the extensive country of Naîri had sworn him allegiance.   Towards the south-east the wavering tribes, which alternately gave their adherence to Assur or Babylon according to circumstances, had ranged themselves on his side, and formed a large frontier province beyond the borders of his hereditary kingdom, between the Lesser Zab and the Turnat.[6] But, despite repeated blows inflicted on them, he had not succeeded in welding these various factors into a compact and homogeneous whole; some small

[1] Cf. *Struggle of the Nations*, pp. 454, 455.

[2] *Annals of Assur-nazir-pal*, col. iii. ll. 23, 24; cf. PEISER, *Die Inschr. Aschur-nâsir-abal's*, in SCHRADER, *Keilinschr. Bibliothek*, vol. i. pp. 98, 99.

[3] His frontier on the Chaldæan side, between the Tigris and the mountains (*Annals*, col. ii. ll. 129, 130, col. iii. ll. 123, 124), was the boundary fixed by Rammân-nirâri (*Synchronous History*, col. iii. ll. 20, 21); cf. *supra*, pp. 5, 6.

[4] The expression employed in this description and in similar passages, *ishtu ibirtan nâru* (col. ii. ll. 127, 129, col. iii. ll. 121, 123), translated *from the ford over the river*, or better, *from the other side of the river*, must be understood as referring to Assyria proper: the territory subject to the king is measured in the direction indicated, starting from the rivers which formed the boundaries of his hereditary dominions.   *From the other bank of the Tigris* means from the bank of the Tigris opposite Nineveh or Calah, whence the king and his army set out on their campaigns.

[5] Rapiku is mentioned in several texts as marking the frontier between the Sukhi and Chaldæa (*Synchronous History*, col. ii. l. 24; *Annals of Assur-nazir-pal*, col. ii. l. 128, col. iii. l. 121).

[6] *Annals of Assur-nazir-pal*, col. ii. ll. 127–131, col. iii. ll. 118–126; the two descriptions contained in these passages differ in some points of detail.

proportion of them were assimilated to Assyria, and were governed directly by royal officials,[1] but the greater number were merely dependencies, more or less insecurely held by the obligations of vassalage or servitude. In some provinces the native chiefs were under the surveillance of Assyrian residents;[2] these districts paid an annual tribute proportionate to the resources and products of their country: thus Kirruri and the neighbouring states contributed horses, mules, bulls, sheep, wine, and copper vessels;[3] the Aramæans gold, silver, lead, copper, both wrought and in the ore, purple, and coloured or embroidered stuffs;[4] while Izalla, Nirbu, Nirdun, and Bît-Zamâni had to furnish horses, chariots, metals, and cattle.[5] The less civilised and more distant tribes were not, like these, subject to regular tribute, but each time the sovereign traversed their territory or approached within reasonable distance, their chiefs sent or brought to him valuable presents as fresh pledges of their loyalty. Royal outposts, built at regular intervals and carefully fortified, secured the fulfilment of these obligations, and served as depôts for storing the commodities collected by the royal officials; such outposts were, Damdamusa on the north-west of the Kashiari range,[6] Tushkhân on the Tigris,[7] Tilluli between the Supnat and the Euphrates,[8] Aribua among the Patinâ,[9] and others scattered irregularly between the Greater and Lesser Zab, on the Khabur, and also in Naîri.[10] These strongholds served as places of refuge for the residents and their guards in case of a revolt, and as food-depôts for the armies in the event of war bringing them into their neighbourhood.[11] In addition to these, Assur-nazir-pal also strengthened the defences of Assyria proper by building fortresses at the points most open to attack; he repaired or completed the defences of Kaksi, to command the plain between the Greater and

---

[1] There were royal governors in Suru in Bît-Khalupi (*Annals of Assur-nazir-pal*, col. i. ll. 75, 89), in Matiâte (col. ii. ll. 90, 91), in Madara (col. ii. l. 100), and in Naîri (H. RAWLINSON, *Cun. Ins. W. As.*, vol. iii. pl. 6, ll. 50, 51).

[2] There were Assyrian residents in Kirruri and the neighbouring countries (*Annals of Assur-nazir-pal*, col. i. l. 56), in Kirkhi (col. i. l. 67), and in Naîri (col. ii. l. 15).

[3] Tribute from Kirruri, Simisi, Simira, Adaush (*Annals*, col. i. ll. 54–56).

[4] Tribute from Shadikanni and Katna (*Annals*, col. i. ll. 78, 79, col. iii. l. 4), from the kings of Laqî (col. i. ll. 94, 95), from Khindanu (col. i. ll. 96, 97, col. iii. ll. 13, 47, 48), from the Aramæans round the Khabur and Euphrates (col. iii. ll. 6–7, 8–9, 9–10, 11), from Bît-Adini (col. iii. ll. 55, 56, 61, 62), from Bît-Bakhiâni (col. iii. ll. 55–58), from Tul-Abnî (col. iii. ll. 55, 56, 63, 64).

[5] Tribute from Izalla (*Annals*, col. i. l. 106, col. ii. ll. 22, 23, col. iii. ll. 59, 60, 94, 95), from Nirbu (col. ii. l. 11), from Nirdun (col. ii. ll. 101, 102), from Bît-Zamâni (col. ii. ll. 12–14).

[6] *Annals of Assur-nazir-pal*, col. i. l. 103; H. RAWLINSON, *Cun. Ins. W. As.*, vol. iii. pl. 6, ll. 47, 48.

[7] *Annals of Assur-nazir-pal*, col. ii. ll. 2–7, 101, 102, 117, 118, col. iii. ll. 104–109; H. RAWLINSON, *Cun. Ins. W. As.*, vol. iii. pl. 6, ll. 47, 48.

[8] *Annals of Assur-nazir-pal*, col. ii. l. 87; cf. *supra*, p. 26.

[9] *Annals of Assur-nazir-pal*, col. iii. ll. 81–83; cf. *supra*, p. 40.

[10] Atlîla or Dur-Assur, in the country of Zamua (*Annals*, col. ii. ll. 84–86); cf. *supra*, p. 26.

[11] Assur-nazir-pal halted at Tilluli (*Annals*, col. ii. l. 87), in Tushkhân (col. ii. ll. 101, 102), in Amidi (col. iii. ll. 107–109).

Lesser Zab and the Tigris; he rebuilt the castles or towers which guarded the river-fords and the entrances to the valleys of the Gebel Makhlub, and erected at Calah the fortified palace which his successors continued to inhabit for the ensuing five hundred years.

Assur-nazir-pal had resided at Nineveh from the time of his accession to the throne; from thence he had set out on four successive campaigns, and thither he had returned at the head of his triumphant troops; [1] there he had received the kings who came to pay him homage,[2] and the governors who implored his

THE MOUNDS OF CALAH.[3]

help against foreign attacks; [4] thither he had sent rebel chiefs, and there, after they had marched in ignominy through the streets, he had put them to torture and to death before the eyes of the crowd, and their skins were perchance still hanging nailed to the battlements when he decided to change the seat of his capital.[5] The ancient palace no longer suited his present state as a conqueror; the accommodation was too restricted, the decoration too poor, and probably the number of apartments was insufficient to house the troops of women and slaves brought back from his wars by its royal master. Built on the very bank of the Tebilti, one of the tributaries of the Khusur, and hemmed in by three

[1] Campaigns of the first year (*Annals of Assur-nazir-pal*, col. i. ll. 69, 70), and of second year (col. i. l. 104); there is no notice of the ensuing campaigns, but, in the account of that in the fourth year, it is stated that the kings of Zamua had representatives at Calah (col. ii. ll. 79, 80).

[2] Ilubâni, King of Sukhi, came in the second year to pay homage to the king in Nineveh, with his brothers and sons (*Annals*, col. i. ll. 99–101); cf. *supra*, p. 19.

[3] Drawn by Boudier from LAYARD, *Mon. of Nineveh*, vol. i. pl. 98. The pointed mound on the left near the centre of the picture represents the ziggurât of the great temple.

[4] *Annals of Assur-nazir-pal*, col. i. ll. 101–103, where the king at Nineveh receives tidings of the revolt of Khulaî (cf. *supra*, p. 19). While there, too, he hears of the insurrection of Dagara (col. ii. ll. 23–25), and of that of Amîka (col. ii. ll. 49, 50).

[5] Akhiababa was carried to Nineveh and flayed alive (*Annals*, col. i. l. 93), and his skin exposed on the wall; cf. *supra*, p. 18.

temples, there was no possibility of its enlargement—a difficulty which often occurs in ancient cities.[1] The necessary space for new buildings could only have been obtained by altering the course of the stream, and sacrificing a large part of the adjoining quarters of the city: Assur-nazir-pal therefore preferred to abandon the place and to select a new site where he would have ample space at his disposal. He found what he required close at hand in the half-ruined city of Calah, where many of his most illustrious predecessors had in times past sought refuge from the heat of Assur.[2] It was now merely an obscure and sleepy town about twelve miles south of Nineveh, on the right bank of the Tigris, and almost at the angle made by the junction of this river with the Greater Zab. The place contained a palace built by Shalmaneser I., which, owing to many years' neglect, had become uninhabitable. Assur-nazir-pal not only razed to the ground the palaces and temples, but also levelled the mound on which they had been built; he then cleared away the soil down to the water-level, and threw up an immense and almost rectangular terrace on which to lay out his new buildings. The king chose Ninip, the

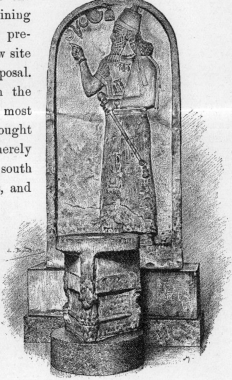

STELE OF ASSUR-NAZIR-PAL AT CALAH.[3]

god of war, as the patron of the city, and dedicated to him, at the north-west corner of the terrace, a ziggurât with its usual temple precincts. Here the god was represented as a bull with a man's head and bust, in gilded alabaster, and two yearly feasts were instituted in his honour, one in the month Sebat, the other in the month Ulul. The ziggurât was a little over two hundred feet high, and was probably built in seven stages, of which only one now remains intact:[4] around it are found several independent series of chambers

---

[1] These details are borrowed from the inscriptions of Sennacherib, the king who rebuilt Nineveh (MEISSNER and ROST, *Die Bauinschriften Sanheribs*, pp. 8, 9).

[2] The building of the palace and temples of Calah is mentioned several times in the *Annals of Assur-nazir-pal,* col. ii. ll. 131–135, col. iii. ll. 132–136, and in the inscription on the *Monolith* (RAWLINSON, *Cun. Ins. W. As.*, vol. i. pl. 27, No. 2, col. i. ll. 1–23). I have supplemented the information in these texts from the results of Layard's excavations, as described in his two chief works, *Nineveh and its Remains,* and *Nineveh and Babylon.*

[3] Drawn by Faucher-Gudin, from a photograph by Mansell; cf. LAYARD, *Mon. of Nin.,* vol. ii. pl. 4.

[4] Cf. LAYARD, *Nineveh and Babylon,* pp. 103–109, for the plan and elevation of the ruins as they existed in the middle of the nineteenth century A.D.

and passages, which may have been parts of other temples, but it is now impossible to say which belonged to the local Belît, which to Sin, to Gula, to Rammân, or to the ancient deity Eâ.   At the entrance to the largest chamber, on a rectangular pedestal, stood a stele with rounded top, after the Egyptian

THE WINGED BULLS OF ASSUR-NAZIR-PAL.[1]

fashion. On it is depicted a figure of the king, standing erect and facing to the left of the spectator; he holds his mace at his side, his right hand is raised in the attitude of adoration, and above him, on the left upper edge of the stele, are grouped the five signs of the planets; at the base of the stele stands an altar with a triangular pedestal and circular slab ready for the offerings to be presented to the royal founder[2] by priests or people.   The palace extended along the south side of the terrace facing the town, and with the river in its rear; it covered a space one hundred and thirty-one yards in length and a hundred and nine in breadth.[3] In the centre was a large court, surrounded by seven or eight spacious halls, appropriated to state functions; between these and the court were many rooms of different sizes, forming the offices and private apartments of the royal house.   The whole palace was built of brick faced with stone.   Three gateways, flanked by winged, human-headed bulls, afforded access to the largest apartment, the hall of audience, where the king received his subjects or the envoys of foreign powers.[4]   The doorways and walls of some of the rooms were decorated with glazed tiles, but the majority of them were covered with bands of coloured[5] bas-reliefs which portrayed various episodes in the life of the king—

---

[1] Drawn by Faucher-Gudin, from a sketch of Layard (*Nineveh and Babylon*, p. 300).

[2] LAYARD, *Nineveh and Babylon*, pp. 302, 303, where the vignette on p. 303 shows the situation of the monument to the right of the door. For a temple of the time of Assur-nazir-pal, discovered between the palace and the ziggurât, cf. the short notice by HORMUZD RASSAM, *Excav. and Discov. in Assyria*, in the *Transactions* of the Bibl. Arch. Soc., vol. viii. pp. 57, 58; and *Asshur and the Land of Nimrod*, pp. 225–227.

[3] LAYARD, *Nineveh and its Remains*, vol. i. pp. 62–71, 115, 116, 124–130, 144–146, 331–347, 381–390, the description of each room in turn with the sculptures discovered in it; vol. ii. pp. 4–14, 76–79; *Nineveh and Babylon*, pp. 149-170.

[4] At the east end of the hall Layard found a block of alabaster covered with inscriptions, forming a sort of platform on which the king's throne may have stood (*Nineveh and its Remains*, vol. i. pp. 133, 134, 383, No. 23).

[5] Layard points out the traces of colouring still visible when the excavations were made (*Nineveh*

his state-councils, his lion-hunts, the reception of tribute, marches over mountains and rivers, chariot-skirmishes, sieges, and the torture and carrying away of captives.[1] Incised in bands across these pictures are inscriptions extolling the omnipotence of Assur, while at intervals genii with eagles' beaks, or deities in human form, imperious and fierce, appear with hands full of offerings, or in the act of brandishing thunderbolts against evil spirits.[2] The architect who designed this imposing decoration, and the sculptors who executed it, closely followed the traditions of ancient Chaldæa in the drawing and composition of their designs, and in the use of colour or chisel; but the qualities

GLAZED TILE FROM PALACE OF CALAH.[3]

and defects peculiar to their own race gave a certain character of originality to this borrowed art. They exaggerated the stern and athletic aspect of their models, making the figures thick-set, the muscles extraordinarily enlarged, and the features ludicrously accentuated. Their pictures produce an impression of awkwardness, confusion and heaviness, but the detail is so minute and the animation so great that the attention of the spectator is forcibly arrested; these uncouth beings impress us with the sense of their self-reliance and their

and its Remains, vol. i. pp. 64, 126, and vol. ii. pp. 306–312; cf. G. RAWLINSON, *The Five Great Monarchies,* 2nd edit., vol. i. pp. 357–365, and PERROT and CHIPIEZ, *Histoire de l'Art dans l'Antiquité,* vol. ii. pp. 653–661).

[1] A certain number of these scenes have been already reproduced in *The Dawn of Civilization, The Struggle of the Nations,* and the present volume. For several episodes connected with the hunting of the lion or urus, see *The Dawn of Civilization,* pp. 558, 559, 769; *Struggle of the Nations,* pp. 621–623; for soldiers, see *ibid.,* pp. 559, 625; for chariots, *ibid.,* 626, 632; for the crossing of a river, *ibid.,* p. 628, and *supra,* p. 2; for a camp, a fortified town, and siege scenes, *Struggle of the Nations,* pp. 632–636, and *supra,* pp. 10, 11; for a convoy of prisoners, *Struggle of the Nations,* p. 640; for apes brought as tribute, *ibid.,* p. 662.

[2] Cf. the eagle-headed or human-headed genii given in *The Dawn of Civilization,* pp. 539, 557; a fish-god, *ibid.,* p. 547; the strife of Bel-Marduk with Tiamât, *ibid.,* p. 541.

[3] Drawn by Boudier, after LAYARD, *Mon. of Nin.,* vol. ii. pl. 55; cf. PERROT and CHIPIEZ, *Hist. de l'Art dans l'Antiq.,* vol. ii. pl. xiv., where the tile is reproduced in its original colouring, from the plate in Layard's work.

confidence in their master, as we watch them brandishing their weapons or hurrying to the attack, and see the shock of battle and the death-blows given and received.[1]   The human-headed bulls, standing on guard at the gates,

LION FROM ASSUR-NAZIR-PAL'S PALACE.[2]

exhibit the calm and pensive dignity befitting creatures conscious of their strength, while the lions passant who sometimes replace them, snarl and show their teeth with an almost alarming ferocity.   The statues of men and gods, as a rule, are lacking in originality.   The heavy robes which drape them from head to foot give them the appearance of cylinders tied in at the centre and slightly flattened towards the top.   The head surmounting this shapeless bundle is the only lifelike part, and even the lower half of this is rendered heavy by the hair and beard, whose tightly curled tresses lie in stiff rows one above the other.   The upper part of the face which alone is visible is correctly drawn; the expression is of rather a commonplace type of nobility—respectable but self-sufficient.   The features—eyes, forehead, nose, mouth—are all those of Assur-nazir-pal; the hair is arranged in the fashion he affected, and the robe is embroidered with his jewels; but amid all this we miss the keen intelligence always present in Egyptian sculpture, whether under the royal head-dress of Cheops or in the expectant eyes of the sitting scribe: the Assyrian sculptor could copy the general outline of his model fairly well, but could not infuse soul into the face of the conqueror, whose " countenance beamed above the destruction around him." [3]

The water of the Tigris being muddy, and unpleasant to the taste, and the wells at Calah so charged with lime and bitumen as to render them unwholesome, Assur-nazir-pal supplied the city with water from the neighbouring Zab.[4]   An abundant stream was diverted from this river at the spot now called

[1] G. RAWLINSON, The Five Great Monarchies, 2nd edit., vol. i. pp. 344-347; PERROT and CHIPIEZ, Hist. de l'Art dans l'Antiq., vol. ii. pp. 613-618.

[2] Drawn by Boudier, from a photograph of the sculpture in the British Museum; cf. LAYARD, Mon. of Nin., vol. ii. pl. 2.

[3] The commonplace character of Assyrian statuary has been noticed by all observers: G. RAWLINSON, The Five Great Monarchies, 2nd edit., vol. i. p. 344; PERROT and CHIPIEZ, Hist. de l'Art dans l'Antiq., vol. ii. pp. 536-540; BABELON, Manuel d'Archéologie Orientale, pp. 96-99.

[4] Annals of Assur-nazir-pal, col. iii. l. 135, and Inscription on Monolith, col. i. ll. 5-10; cf. PEISER,

Negub, and conveyed at first by a tunnel excavated in the rock, and thence by an open canal to the foot of the great terrace : at this point the flow of the water was regulated by dams, and the surplus was utilised for irrigation [1] purposes by means of openings cut in the banks. The aqueduct was named Bâbilat-khigal—the bringer of plenty [2]—and, to justify the epithet, date-palms,

A CORNER OF THE RUINED PALACE OF ASSUR-NAZIR-PAL AT CALAH.[3]

vines, and many kinds of fruit trees were planted along its course, so that both banks soon assumed the appearance of a shady orchard interspersed with small towns and villas. The population rapidly increased, partly through the spontaneous influx of Assyrians themselves, but still more through the repeated introduction of bands of foreign prisoners : [4] forts, established at the fords of

Inschriften Aschur-nâsir-abal's, in SCHRADER, Keilinschriftliche Bibliothek, vol. i. pp. 114, 115, 118, 119. The presence of bitumen in the waters of Calah is due to the hot springs which rise in the bed of the brook Shor-derreh (JONES, Topography of Nineveh, in the J. R. As. P., vol. xv. p. 342).

[1] The canal of Negub—Negub signifies hole in Arabic—was discovered by Layard, who describes it in Nineveh and its Remains, vol. i. pp. 80, 81, and Nineveh and Babylon, pp. 525–527; see also Jones (Topog. of Nineveh, in the J. R. As. Soc., vol. xv. pp. 310, 311, 342, 343). The Zab having changed its course to the south, and scooped out a deeper bed for itself, the double arch, which serves as an entrance to the canal, is actually above the ordinary level of the river, and the water flows through it only in flood-time.

[2] Monolith Inscription, col. i. pp. 6, 7; in the Annals of Assur-nazir-pal, col. iii. l. 135, the name is given in the form Pati-khigal.

[3] Drawn by Boudier, from a photograph by Rassam, contributed by Father Scheil; cf. HORMUZD RASSAM, Asshur and the Land of Nimrod, p. 222.

[4] For example, Assur-nazir-pal expressly says that he established at Calah a colony of 2000 Aramæan soldiers taken prisoners at Kaprabi, in Tul-Abâ (Annals, col. iii. ll. 53, 54); cf. supra p. 32.

E

the Zab, or commanding the roads which cross the Gebel Makhlub, kept the country in subjection and formed an inner line of defence at a short distance from the capital. Assur-nazir-pal kept up a palace, garden, and small temple, near the fort of Imgur-Bel, the modern Balawât : thither he repaired for intervals of repose from state affairs, to enjoy the pleasures of the chase and cool air in the hot season.[1] He did not entirely abandon his other capitals, Nineveh and Assur, visiting them occasionally, but Calah was his favourite seat, and on its adornment he spent the greater part of his wealth and most of his leisure hours. Only once again did he abandon his peaceful pursuits and take the field, about the year 897 B.C., during the eponymy of Shamashnurî. The tribes on the northern boundary of the empire had apparently forgotten the lessons they had learnt at the cost of so much bloodshed at the beginning of his reign : many had omitted to pay the tribute due, one chief had seized the royal cities of Amidi and Damdamusa, and the rebellion threatened to spread to Assyria itself. Assur-nazir-pal girded on his armour and led his troops to battle as vigorously as in the days of his youth. He hastily collected, as he passed through their lands, the tribute due from Kipâni, Izalla,[2] and Kummukh, gained the banks of the Euphrates, traversed Gubbu burning everything on his way, made a detour through Dirria and Kirkhi, and finally halted before the walls of Damdamusa. Six hundred soldiers of the garrison perished in the assault and four hundred were taken prisoners : these he carried to Amidi and impaled as an object-lesson round its walls ; but, the defenders of the town remaining undaunted, he raised the siege and plunged into the gorges of the Kashiari. Having there reduced to submission Udâ, the capital of Lapturi, son of Tubusi, he returned to Calah, taking with him six thousand prisoners whom he settled as colonists around his favourite residence.[3] This was his last exploit : he never subsequently quitted his hereditary domain, but there passed the remaining seven years of his life in peace, if not in idleness. He died in 860 B.C., after a reign of twenty-five years. His portraits represent him as a vigorous man, with a brawny neck and broad shoulders, capable of bearing the weight of his armour for many hours at

---

[1] Two copies of an inscription discovered by H. Rassam at Balawât (*Excav. and Discov. in Assyr.*, in the *Transactions* of the Bibl. Arch. Soc., vol. vii. pp. 53–55 ; *Asshur and the Land of Nimrod*, pp. 216, 217), translated by Budge (*On a recently discovered Text of Assur-natsir-pal*, in the *Transactions*, vol. vii. pp. 59–82), and by A. Strong (*A Votive Inscription of Assur-natsir-pal*, in the *Records of the Past*, 2nd ser., vol. iv. pp. 80–85).

[2] For Izalla, cf. *supra*, p. 19, note 4. Kipâni, according to Lehmann, corresponds to the Kephenes of Stephen of Byzantium and the Kephenia of Pliny (BELCK and LEHMANN, *Ein neuer Herrscher von Khaldia*, in the *Zeitschrift für Assyriologie*, vol. ix. p. 88, note), perhaps between Batman-tchaî and Bitlis-tchaî.

[3] *Annals of Assur-nazir-pal*, col. iii. ll. 92–113 ; cf. PEISER, *Inschr. Aschur-nâsir-abal's*, in SCHRADER, *Keilinschr. Bibliothek*, vol. i. pp. 110–113. The new localities mentioned in this passage cannot at present be satisfactorily identified with any modern site.

a time. He is short in the head, with a somewhat flattened skull and low forehead ; his eyes are large and deep-set beneath bushy eyebrows, his cheek-bones high, and his nose aquiline, with a fleshy tip and wide nostrils, while his mouth and chin are hidden by moustache and beard. The whole figure is instinct with real dignity, yet such dignity as is due rather to rank and the habitual exercise of power, than to the innate qualities of the man.[1] The character of Assur-nazir-pal, as gathered from the dry details of his Annals, seems to have been very complex. He was as ambitious, resolute, and active as any prince in the world ; yet he refrained from offensive warfare as soon as his victories had brought under his rule the majority of the countries formerly subject to Tiglath-pileser I. He knew the crucial moment for ending a campaign, arresting his progress where one more success might have brought him into collision with some formidable neighbour; and this wise prudence in his undertakings enabled him to retain the principal acquisitions won by his arms. As a worshipper of the gods he showed devotion and gratitude ; he was just to his subjects, but his conduct towards his

SHALMANESER III.[2]

enemies was so savage as to appear to us cruel even for that terribly pitiless age : no king ever employed such horrible punishments, or at least none has described with such satisfaction the tortures inflicted on his vanquished foes. Perhaps such measures were necessary, and the harshness with which he repressed insurrection prevented more frequent outbreaks and so averted greater sacrifice of life. But the horror of these scenes so appals the modern reader, that at first he can only regard Assur-nazir-pal as a royal butcher of the worst type.[3]

[1] MÉNANT, *Remarques sur les portraits des rois assyro-chaldéens*, pp. 9, 10. Perrot and Chipiez do not admit that the Assyrian sculptors intended to represent the features of their kings ; for this they rely chiefly on the remarkable likeness between all the figures in the same series of bas-reliefs (*Histoire de l'Art dans l'Antiquité*, vol. ii. pp. 550–552). My own belief is that in Assyria, as in Egypt, the sculptors took the portrait of the reigning sovereign as the model for all their figures.

[2] Drawn by Boudier from a photograph by Mansell, taken from the original stele in the British Museum.

[3] The cruelties of Assur-nazir-pal have been exaggerated by GUTSCHMID, *Neue Beiträge zur Geschichte des Alten Orients*, pp. 148–150, and palliated by HOMMEL, *Gesch. Babyl. und Assyr.*, p. 588. Tiele struck the right note on the subject (*Babylonisch-Assyrische Geschichte*, p. 177), and I adopt his conclusions.

Assur-nazir-pal left to his successor an overflowing treasury, a valiant army, a people proud of their progress and fully confident in their own resources, and a kingdom which had recovered, during several years of peace, from the strain of its previous conquests.　Shalmaneser III.* drew largely on the reserves of men and money which his father's foresight had prepared, and his busy reign of thirty-five years saw thirty-two campaigns, conducted almost without a break, on every side of the empire in succession.[1]　A double task awaited him, which he conscientiously and successfully fulfilled.　Assur-nazir-pal had thoroughly reorganised the empire and raised it to the rank of a great power: he had confirmed his provinces and vassal states in their allegiance, and had subsequently reduced to subjection, or, at any rate, penetrated at various points, the little buffer principalities between Assyria and the powerful kingdoms of Babylon, Damascus, and Urartu; but he had avoided engaging any one of these three great states in a struggle of which the issue seemed doubtful.　Shalmaneser could not maintain this policy of forbearance without loss of prestige in the eyes of the world: conduct which might seem prudent and cautious in a victorious monarch like Assur-nazir-pal would in him have argued timidity or weakness, and his rivals would soon have provoked a quarrel if they thought him lacking in the courage or the means to attack them.　Immediately after his accession, therefore, he assumed the offensive, and decided to measure his strength first against Urartu, which for some years past had been showing signs of restlessness.　Few countries

---

* [The Shalmaneser III. of the text is the Shalmaneser II. of the notes.—Tr.]

[1] A fortunate occurrence has preserved for us the summary of the chief events of thirty-one out of the thirty-five years of the reign of Shalmaneser III. recorded on the Black Obelisk of Nimroud, discovered by Layard (*Nineveh and its Remains*, vol. i. pp. 345–347; *Monuments of Nineveh*, vol. i. pls. 53–56; and *Inscr. in the Cuneif. Char.*, pls. 87–90; cf. ABEL and WINCKLER, *Keilschrifttexte*, pp. 7–12), and preserved in the British Museum: the inscription has been translated into French by OPPERT, *Expédition de Mésopotamie*, vol. i. pp. 342–347, and *Hist. des Empires de Chaldée et d'Assyrie*, pp. 108–117; and by MÉNANT, *Annales des Rois d'Assyrie*, pp. 97–104; into English by SAYCE, *The Black Obelisk Inscription of Shalmaneser II.*, in *Records of the Past*, 1st ser., vol. v. p. 27; and by SCHEIL, *Inscr. of Shalmaneser II.*, in *Records of the Past*, 2nd ser., vol. iv. pp. 38–52; into German by WINCKLER, *Annaleninschrift des Obelisks von Nimrûd*, in SCHRADER, *Keilins. Bibliothek*, vol. i. pp. 128–151. A detailed narration of the events which occurred in the first six years was inscribed on the monolith of Kurkh (H. RAWLINSON, *Cun. Ins. W. As.*, vol. iii. pls. 7, 8); this has been translated into French by MÉNANT, *Annales des rois d'Assyrie*, pp. 105–113; into English by SAYCE, *Kurkh Inscr. of Shalmaneser*, in *Records of the Past*, 1st ser., vol. iii. pp. 81–100; by CRAIG, *Monolith Inscr. of Salmaneser II.*, 1887, New Haven, extract from *Hebraica*, vol. iii. pp. 201–231; and by SCHEIL, *Monolith Inscr. of Shalmaneser II.*, in *Records of the Past*, 2nd ser., vol. iv. pp. 53–71; into German by PEISER, *Die Monolith-Inschrift*, in SCHRADER, *Keilins. Bibliothek*, vol. i. pp. 150–175. Some other inscriptions engraved on the two bulls from Nimroud (LAYARD, *Inscr. in the Cuneif. Char.*, pp. 12–16, 46–47) add further details to the history of several of the campaigns. The bronze gates of Balawât (PINCHES, *The Bronze Gates discovered by M. Rassam at Balawât*, in the *Proceedings* of the Bibl. Arch. Soc., vol. vii. pp. 89–111; and SCHEIL, *Inscr. of Shalmaneser II. on the Gates of Balawât*, in *Records of the Past*, 2nd ser., vol. iv. pp. 72–79) give, besides a written text, a series of reliefs in bronze (partly published by the Bibl. Arch. Soc.) illustrating the wars which occupied the early years of the reign. All these documents have been chronologically classified, transcribed, and translated into French by AMIAUD and SCHEIL, *Les Inscr. de Salmanasar II., roi d'Assyrie*, 860–824, Paris, 1890.

are more rugged or better adapted for defence than that in which his armies were about to take the field. The volcanoes to which it owed its configuration in geological times, had become extinct long before the appearance of man, but the surface of the ground still bears evidence of their former activity; layers of basaltic rock, beds of scoriæ and cinders, streams of half-disintegrated mud and lava, and more or less perfect cones, meet the eye at every turn. Subterranean disturbances have not entirely ceased even

THE TWO PEAKS OF MOUNT ARARAT.[1]

now, for certain craters—that of Tandurek, for example—sometimes exhale acid fumes; while hot springs exist in the neighbourhood, from which steaming waters escape in cascades to the valley, and earthquakes and strange subterranean noises are not unknown. The backbone of these Armenian mountains joins towards the south the line of the Gordyæan range; it runs in a succession of zigzags from south-east to north-west, meeting at length the mountains of Pontus and the last spurs of the Caucasus. Lofty snow-clad peaks, chiefly of volcanic origin, rise here and there among them, the most important being Akhta-dagh, Tandurek, Ararat, Bingœl, and Palandœken. The two unequal pyramids which form the summit of Ararat are covered with perpetual snow, the higher of them being 16,916 feet above the sea-level. The spurs which issue from the principal chain cross each other in all directions, and make a network of rocky basins where in former times water collected and formed lakes, nearly all of which are now dry in consequence of the breaking down of one or other of their enclosing sides. Two

[1] Drawn by Boudier, from a photograph by A. Tissandier.

only of these mountain lakes still remain, entirely devoid of outlet, Lake Van in the south, and Lake Urumiah[1] further to the south-east. The Assyrians called the former the Upper Sea of Naîri, and the latter the Lower Sea,[2] and both constituted a defence for Urartu against their attacks. To reach the centre of the kingdom of Urartu, the Assyrians had either to cross the mountainous strip of land between the two lakes, or by making a detour to the north-west, and descending the difficult slopes of the valley of the Arzania, to approach the mountains of Armenia lying to the north of Lake Van. The march was necessarily a slow and painful one for both horses and men, along narrow winding valleys down which rushed rapid streams, over raging torrents, through tangled forests where the path had to be cut as they advanced, and over barren wind-swept plateaux where rain and mist chilled and demoralized soldiers accustomed to the warm and sunny plains of the Euphrates. The majority of the armies which invaded this region never reached the goal of the expedition : they retired after a few engagements, and withdrew as quickly as possible to more genial climes. The main part of Urartu remained almost always unsubdued behind its barrier of woods, rocks, and lakes, which protected it from the attacks levelled against it, and no one can say how far the kingdom extended in the direction of the Caucasus. It certainly included the valley of the Araxes and possibly part of the valley of the Kur, and the steppes sloping towards the Caspian Sea. It was a region full of contrasts, at once favoured and ill-treated by nature in its elevation and aspect : rugged peaks, deep gorges, dense thickets, districts sterile from the heat of subterranean fires, and sandy wastes barren for lack of moisture, were interspersed with shady valleys, sunny vine-clad slopes, and wide stretches of fertile land covered with rich layers of deep alluvial soil, where thick-standing corn and meadow-lands, alternating with orchards, repaid the cultivator for the slightest attempt at irrigation.[3]

History does not record who were the former possessors of this land ; but towards the middle of the ninth century it was divided into several principalities, whose position and boundaries cannot be precisely determined. It is thought that Urartu lay on either side of Mount Ararat and on both banks

[1] For a detailed description of the mountain groups of Armenia and the region of the two lakes, cf. ÉLISÉE RECLUS, Nouvelle Géographie Universelle, vol. ix. pp. 180-185, 321, et seq.

[2] SCHRADER, Die Namen der Meere in den Assyrischen Inschriften, pp. 189–193, and Zur Geographie des Assyrischen Reichs, p. 7. Delattre, who strongly combated this identification (Esquisse de Géogr. Assyr., pp. 15–18), was afterwards converted to Schrader's opinion (Encore un mot sur la Géogr. Assyr., pp. 15–18).

[3] The renowned fertility of Urartu, specially of that part watered by the Araxes, is attested, among others, by S. Jerome : " Ararat autem regio in Armenia campestris est, per quam Araxes fluit, incredibilis ubertatis, ad radices Tauri montis qui usque illuc extenditur " (Comm. ad Jes., xxxvii. 36, et seq.).

of the Araxes, that Biainas lay around Lake Van,[1] and that the Mannai occupied the country to the north and east of Lake Urumiah;[2] the positions of the other tribes on the different tributaries of the Euphrates or the slopes of the Armenian mountains are as yet uncertain. The country was probably peopled by a very mixed race, for its mountains have always afforded a safe

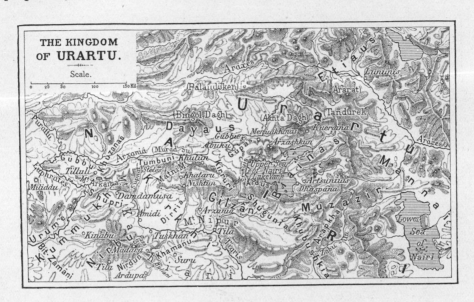

asylum for refugees, and at each migration, which altered the face of Western Asia, some fugitives from neighbouring nations drifted to the shelter of its fastnesses. The principal element, the Khaldi,[3] were akin to that great

---

[1] HYVERNAT, in MÜLLER(-SIMONIS), *Du Caucase au Golfe Persique*, pp. 523, 524. Urartu is the only name by which the Assyrians knew the kingdom of Van; it has been recognised from the very beginning of Assyriological studies, as well as its identity with the Ararat of the Bible and the Alarodians of Herodotus (H. RAWLINSON, *On the Alarodians of Herodotus*, in G. RAWLINSON, *Herodotus*, vol. iv. pp. 203–206). It was also generally recognised that the name Biainas in the Vannic inscriptions, which Hincks read Bieda, corresponded to the Urartu of the Assyrians, but in consequence of this mistaken reading, efforts have been made to connect it with Adiabene. Sayce was the first to show that Biainas was the name of the country of Van, and of the kingdom of which Van was the capital (*The Cuneiform Inscriptions of Van, deciphered and translated*, in the *J. R. As. Soc.*, new series, vol. xiv. pp. 388–396); the word Bitâni which Sayce connects with it is not a secondary form of the name of Van, but a present day term, and should be erased from the list of geographical names (SCHRADER, *Keilins. und Geschichtsf.*, p. 147, note, and *Zur Geographie des Assyrischen Reichs*, p. 14, note 1).

[2] The Mannai were at first identified with the people of Van (FR. LENORMANT, *Lettres assyriologiques*, vol. i. p. 22). Sayce first recognised that they should be located in the neighbourhood of Lake Urumiah (*The Cuneif. Inscript. of Van*, in the *J. R. As. Soc.*, new series, vol. xiv. pp. 388–400), to the north and east of that lake (BELCK, *Das Reich der Mannæer*, in the *Verhandlungen der Berliner anthropologischen Gesellschaft*, 1896, p. 480). They are the Minni of Jeremiah (li. 27), and it is in their country of Minyas that one tradition made the ark rest after the Deluge (NICHOLAS OF DAMASCUS, Fragm. 76, in MÜLLER-DIDOT, *Fragmenta Historicorum Græcorum*, vol. iii. p. 415; cf. JOSEPHUS, *Ant. Jud.*, I. iii. § 6).

[3] The application of the name Khaldi to the indigenous race, guessed at by Sayce (*The Ancient

family of tribes which extended across the range of the Taurus, from the shores of the Mediterranean to the Euxine, and included the Khalybes, the Mushku, the Tabal, and the Khâti. The little preserved of their language resembles what we know of the idioms in use among the people of Arzapi and Mitânni, and their religion seems to have been somewhat analogous to the ancient worship of the Hittites.[1]   The character of the ancient Armenians, as revealed to us by the monuments, resembles in its main features that of the Armenians of the present time. They appear as tall, strong, muscular, and determined, full of zest for work and fighting, and proud of their independence.[2] Some of them led a pastoral life, wandering about with their flocks during the greater part of the year, obliged to seek pasturage in valley, forest, or mountain height according to the season, while in winter they remained frost-bound in semi-subterranean dwellings similar to those in which their descendants immure themselves at the present day.[3]   Where the soil lent itself to

FRAGMENT OF A VOTIVE SHIELD OF URARTIAN WORK.[4]

agriculture, they proved excellent husbandmen, and obtained abundant crops. Their ingenuity in irrigation was remarkable, and enabled them to bring water by a system of trenches from distant springs to supply their fields and gardens;[5]

Empires of the East, Herodotus I.–III., p. 17, note 6) and by Hommel (Geschichte Babyl. und Assyr., p. 627, note 2), has been clearly shown by Lehmann (BELCK and LEHMANN, Ueber neuerlich aufgefundene armenische Keilinschriften, in the Zeitschrift für Ethnologie, 1892, pp. 131, 132; Ein neuer Herrscher von Chaldia, in the Zeitschrift für Assyriologie, vol. ix. pp. 83–90; Chaldische Forschungen, in the Verhandlungen der Berliner anthropologischen Gesellschaft, 1895, pp. 578–592). Jensen alone has up to now raised objections against this identification (Grundlagen für eine Entzifferung der Khatischen oder Cilicischen Inschriften, p. 124; cf. Z. d. D. Morgenl. Gesells., vol. xlviii. p. 434).

[1] JENSEN, Vorstudien zur Entzifferung des Mitanni, in the Zeitschrift für Assyriologie, vol. vi. pp. 59, 60, 65, et seq., and Grundlagen für eine Entzifferung, p. 128, et seq.; BELCK and LEHMANN, Ueber neuerlich aufgefundene Keilinschriften in russisch und türkisch Armenien, in the Zeitschrift für Ethnologie, 1892, pp. 129, 130. Fr. Lenormant tried to compare the inscriptions of Urartu with those of Georgia (Lettres assyriologiques, vol. i. pp. 124–133).

[2] Cf. Xenophon on the Khaldi of his time: Ἐλέγοντο δὲ οἱ Χαλδαῖοι ἐλεύθεροί τε καὶ ἄλκιμοι εἶναι (Anabasis, IV. iii. § 4; V. v. § 17), and the picture he gives of their warlike customs in the Cyropædia, III. ii. § 7.

[3] ELISÉE RECLUS, Nouvelle Géographie Universelle, vol. ix. p. 355. Xenophon describes one of these underground villages which lay between the Northern Euphrates and the country of the Chalybes (Anabasis, IV. v. §§ 25–27).

[4] Drawn by Faucher-Gudin, from a photograph by Hormuzd Rassam; cf. HORMUZD RASSAM, Asshur and the Land of Nimrod, p. 378.

[5] For the irrigation trenches, and the traces which remain of them, and for the use the people of

besides which, they knew how to terrace the steep hillsides so as to prevent the rapid draining away of moisture. Industries were but little developed among them, except perhaps the working of metals; for were they not akin to those Chalybes of the Pontus, whose mines and forges already furnished iron to the Grecian world? Fragments have been discovered in the ruined cities of Urartu of statuettes, cups, and votive shields, either

SITE OF AN URARTIAN TOWN AT TOPRAH-KALEH.[1]

embossed or engraved, and decorated with concentric bands of animals or men, treated in the Assyrian manner, but displaying great beauty of style and remarkable finish of execution. Their towns were generally fortified or perched on heights, rendering them easy of defence, as, for example, Van and Toprah-Kaleh. Even such towns as were royal residences were small, and not to be compared with the cities of Assyria or Aram; their ground-plan generally assumed the form of a rectangular oblong, not always traced with equal

Urartu made of them, cf. BELCK and LEHMANN, *Ueber neuerlich aufgefundene Keilinschriften*, in the *Zeitschrift für Ethnologie*, 1892, pp. 136–147; *Mittheilung über weitere Ergebnisse ihrer Studien*, in the *Verhandlungen der Berliner anthropologischen Gesellschaft*, 1892, pp. 477–483; and *Chaldische Forschungen*, in the same periodical, 1896, pp. 309–315. Armenian tradition, agreeing with classical tradition, attributes the construction of these canals to Semiramis, *Storia di Mose Corenese*, Venice, 1841, pp. 51–54.

[1] Drawn by Boudier, from a photograph by M. Binder, contributed by Father Scheil.

exactitude. The walls were built of blocks of roughly hewn stone, laid in regular courses, but without any kind of mortar or cement; they were surmounted by battlements, and flanked at intervals by square towers, at the foot of which were outworks to protect the points most open to attack. The entrance was approached by narrow and dangerous pathways, which sometimes ran on ledges across the precipitous face of the rock.[1] The dwelling-houses were of very simple construction, being merely square cabins of stone or brick, devoid of any external ornament, and pierced by one low doorway, but sometimes surmounted by an open colonnade supported by a row of small pillars; a flat

THE RUINS OF A PALACE OF URARTU AT TOPRAH-KALEH.[2]

roof with a parapet crowned the whole, though this was often replaced by a gabled top, which was better adapted to withstand the rains and snows of winter. The palaces of the chiefs differed from the private houses in the size of their apartments and the greater care bestowed upon their decoration. Their façades were sometimes adorned with columns, and ornamented with bucklers or carved discs of metal; slabs of stone covered with inscriptions lined the inner halls, but we do not know whether the kings added to

[1] BELCK and LEHMANN, *Chaldische Forschungen*, in the *Verhandlungen der Berliner anthropologischen Gesellschaft*, 1895, pp. 601–614.

[2] Drawn by Boudier, from a photograph by Hormuzd Rassam; cf. HORMUZD RASSAM, *Asshur and the Land of Nimrod*, p. 376.

TEMPLE OF KHALDIS, AT MUZAZÎR, PILLAGED BY THE ASSYRIANS.

Drawn by Faucher-Gudin, from Botta, *Le Monument de Ninive*, vol. ii. pl. 141.

their dedications to the gods and the recital of their victories, pictures of the battles they had fought and of the fortresses they had destroyed. The furniture resembled that in the houses of Nineveh, but was of simpler workmanship, and perhaps the most valuable articles were imported from Assyria or were of Aramæan manufacture. The temples seem to have differed little from the palaces, at least in external appearance. The masonry was more regular and more skilfully laid; the outer court was filled with brazen lavers and statues; the interior was furnished with altars, sacrificial stones, idols in human or animal shape, and bowls identical with those in the sanctuaries on the Euphrates, but the nature and details of the rites in which they were employed are unknown.[1]   One supreme deity, Khaldis, god of the sky, was, as far as we

ASSYRIAN SOLDIERS CARRYING OFF OR DESTROYING THE FURNITURE OF AN URARTIAN TEMPLE.[2]

can conjecture, the protector of the whole nation, and their name was derived from his, as that of the Assyrians was from Assur, the Cosseans from Kashshu, and the Khâti from Khâtu. This deity was assisted in the government of the universe by Teisbas, god of the air, and Ardinis the sun-god. Groups of secondary deities were ranged around this sovereign triad—Auis, the water; Ayas, the earth; Selardis, the moon; Kharu-bainis, Irmusinis, Adarutas, and Arzimelas: one single inscription enumerates forty-six, but some of these were worshipped in special localities only. It would appear as if no goddesses were included in the native Pantheon. Saris, the only goddess known to us at present, is probably merely a variant of the Ishtar of Nineveh or Arbela, borrowed from the Assyrians at a later date.[3]

The first Assyrian conquerors looked upon these northern regions as an

---

[1] Illustrations of these may be seen in pls. 140, 141 of *Monument de Ninive* by Botta; portions of them are reproduced in the vignettes on pp. 59 and 60 of the present work.

[2] Drawn by Faucher-Gudin, from BOTTA, *Monument de Ninive*, vol. ii. pl. 140. Scribes are weighing gold, and soldiers destroying the statue of a god with their axes.

[3] SAYCE, *Cuneiform Inscriptions of Van deciphered and translated*, in the *J. R. As. Soc.*, new series, vol. xiv. pp. 412–417.

integral part of Naîri, and included them under that name.[1]   They knew of no single state in the district whose power might successfully withstand their own, but were merely acquainted with a group of hostile provinces whose internecine conflicts left them ever at the mercy of a foreign foe.[2]   Two kingdoms had, however, risen to some importance about the beginning of the ninth century—that of the Mannai in the east, and that of Urartu in the centre of the country.   Urartu comprised the district of Ararat proper, the province of

SHALMANESER III. CROSSING THE MOUNTAINS IN HIS CHARIOT.[3]

Biaina, and the entire basin of the Arzania.   Arzashkun, one of its capitals, situated probably near the sources of this river, was hidden, and protected against attack, by an extent of dense forest almost impassable to a regular army.   The power of this kingdom, though as yet unorganised, had already begun to inspire the neighbouring states with uneasiness.   Assur-nazir-pal speaks of it incidentally as lying on the northern frontier of his empire,[4] but the care he took to avoid arousing its hostility shows the respect in which he held it.   He was, indeed, as much afraid of Urartu as of Damascus, and though he approached quite close to its boundary in his second campaign, he preferred to check his triumphant advance rather than risk attacking it.   It appears to

[1] See SCHRADER, *Keilins. und Geschichtsf.*, p. 579, for the enumeration of the countries included under the term Naîri.   We shall see further on how one of the most powerful kings of Urartu, Aramê, called himself King of Naîri ; cf. *infra*, p. 62.

[2] The single inscription of Tiglath-pileser I. contains a list of twenty-three kings of Naîri (*Annals*, col. iv. ll. 71–83), and mentions sixty chiefs of the same country (*ibid.*, ll. 96–98); cf. MASPERO, *Struggle of the Nations*, pp. 653, 654.

[3] Drawn by Faucher-Gudin, from one of the bas-reliefs on the bronze gates of Balawât.

[4] *Monolith of Shalmaneser III.*, col. ii. ll. 47–54.   Arzashku, Arzashkun, seems to be the Assyrian form of an Urartian name ending in -*ka* (SAYCE, *The Cuneiform Inscriptions of Van*, pp. 429, 430, 436), formed from a proper name Arzash, which recalls the name Arsene, Arsissa, applied by the ancients to part of Lake Van (STRABO, XI. xiv. § 8, p. 529).   Arzashkun might represent the Ardzîk of the Armenian historians, west of Malasgert.

have been at that time under the undisputed rule of a certain Sharduris, son of Lutipri,[1] and subsequently, about the middle of Assur-nazir-pal's reign, to have passed into the hands of Aramê, who styled himself King of Naîri, and whose ambition may have caused those revolts which forced Assur-nazir-pal to take up arms in the eighteenth year of his reign.   On this occasion the Assyrians again confined themselves to the chastisement of their own vassals, and checked

THE PEOPLE OF SHUGUNIA FIGHTING AGAINST THE ASSYRIANS.[3]

their advance as soon as they approached Urartu.[2] Their success was but temporary; hardly had they withdrawn from the neighbourhood, when the disturbances were renewed with even greater violence, very probably at the instigation of Aramê. Shalmaneser III. found matters in a very unsatisfactory state both on the west and south of Lake Van: some of the peoples who had been subject to his father — the Khubush-

kia, the pastoral tribes of the Gordyæan mountains, and the Aramæans of the Euphrates[4]—had transferred their allegiance elsewhere. He immediately took measures to recall them to a sense of their duty, and set out from Calah only a few days after succeeding to the crown. He marched at first in an easterly direction, and, crossing the pass of Simisi, burnt the city of Aridi, thus proving that he was fully prepared to treat rebels after the same fashion as his father.[5] The lesson had immediate effect.   All the neighbouring tribes, Khargæans,

[1] The position of Sharduris, who must be called for the present Sharduris I., has been indicated by BELCK, Das Reich der Mannäer (in the Verhandl. der Berliner anthropol. Gesellschaft, 1894, p. 486), and by LEHMANN, Schar Kischschati (in the Zeitschrift für Assyriologie, vol. xi. p. 201, 202).

[2] Cf. the story of this campaign, supra, p. 50.

[3] Drawn by Faucher-Gudin, from one of the bas-reliefs on the bronze gates of Balawât.

[4] Lehmann (Schar Kischschati, in the Zeitschrift für Assyriologie, pp. 201, 202) has with reason attributed this recoil of the Assyrian power to the extension of the kingdom of Urartu.

[5] A passage on the Black Obelisk, 1. 190, states that one could "descend to the borders of Khalman by the pass of Simisi," which decided Hommel (Geschichte Babyloniens und Assyriens, p. 593) to make this first expedition ascend to the table-land of Media by the passes near Holwân. The same names occur in the country traversed by Shalmaneser as were noted by Assur-nazir-pal in one of his campaigns, and consequently it must be sought in the east or north-east, though I cannot fix the exact position on the map of all the localities mentioned.

Kharmasæans, Simisæans, the people of Simira, Sirisha, and Ulmania, hastened to pay him homage even before he had struck his camp near Aridi. Hurrying across country by the shortest route, which entailed the making of roads to enable his chariots and cavalry to follow him, he fell upon Khubushkia, and reduced a hundred towns to ashes, pursuing the king Kakia into the depths of the forest,

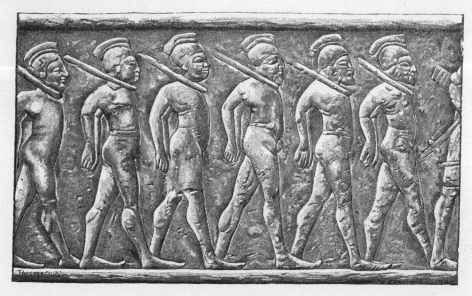

PRISONERS FROM SHUGUNIA, WITH THEIR ARMS TIED AND YOKES ON THEIR NECKS.[1]

and forcing him to an unconditional surrender. Ascending thence to Shugunia, a dependency of Aramê's, he laid the principality waste, in spite of the desperate resistance made on their mountain slopes by the inhabitants; then proceeding to Lake Van, he performed the ceremonial rites incumbent on an Assyrian king whenever he stood for the first time on the shores of a new sea. He washed his weapons in the waters, offered a sacrifice to the gods, casting some portions of the victim into the lake, and before leaving carved his own image on the surface of a commanding rock. On his homeward march he received tribute from Gilzân.[2] This expedition was but the prelude of further successes. After a few weeks' repose at Nineveh, he again set out to make his authority felt in the western portions of his dominions. Akhuni, chief of Bît-Adini, whose position was the first to be menaced, had formed a league with the chiefs of all the cities which had formerly bowed before Assur-nazir-pal's victorious arms, Gurgum, Samalla, Kuî, the Patinâ, Carchemish, and the Khâti.

---

[1] Drawn by Faucher-Gudin, from one of the bas-reliefs on the bronze gates of Balawât.
[2] The summary of this first campaign is found on the *Black Obelisk*, ll. 22–26; the detailed account on the *Monolith*, col. i. ll. 14–29. Cf. PEISER, *Die Monolith-Inschrift*, in SCHRADER, *Keilins. Bibliothek*, vol. i. pp. 152–157, and AMIAUD and SCHEIL, *Les Inscr. de Salmanasar II.*, pp. 8–13.

Shalmaneser seized Lalati[1] and Burmarana, two of Akhuni's towns, drove him across the Euphrates, and, following close on his heels, collected as he passed the tribute of Gurgum, and fell upon Samalla.   Under the walls of Lutibu[2] he overthrew the combined forces of Adini, Samalla, and the Patinâ, and raised a trophy to commemorate his victory at the sources of the Saluara;[3] then turning sharply to the south, he crossed the Orontes in pursuit of Shapalulmê, King of the Patinâ.   Not far from Alizir he encountered a fresh army raised by Akhuni and the King of Samalla, with contingents from Carchemish, Kuî, Cilicia, and Iasbuki:[4] having routed it, he burnt the fortresses of Shapalulmê, and after occupying himself by cutting down cedars and cypress trees on the Amanos in the province of Atalur, he left a triumphal stele engraved on the mountain-side.   Next turning eastwards, he received the homage offered with alacrity by the towns of Taia,[5] Khazazu, Nulia, and Butamu, and, with a final tribute from Agusi, he returned in triumph to Nineveh.[6] The motley train which accompanied him showed by its variety the immense extent of country he had traversed during this first campaign.   Among the prisoners were representatives of widely differing races;—Khâti with long robes and cumbrous head-dresses, following naked mountaineers from Shugunia, who marched with yokes on their necks, and wore those close-fitting helmets with short crests which have such a strangely modern look on the Assyrian bas-reliefs.   The actual results of the campaign were, perhaps, hardly commensurate with the energy expended.   This expedition from east to west had certainly inflicted considerable losses on the rebels against whom it had been directed; it had cost them dearly in men and cattle, and booty of all kinds, and had extorted from them a considerable amount of tribute, but they remained, notwithstanding, still unsubdued.   As soon as the Assyrian troops had quitted their neighbourhood, they flattered themselves they were

[1] Lalati is probably the Lulati of the Egyptians (*List of Thutmôsis III.*, No. 142) as recognised by Tomkins, *Notes on the Geography of N. Syria*, in the *Babylonian and Oriental Record*, vol. iii. p. 42.   The modern site is not known, nor is that of Burmarana.

[2] The name may also be read Tibtibu, Dibdibu; on the termination -*ib* of certain proper names in this district, cf. Sachau, *Inschrift des Königs Panammû*, in Luschan, *Ausgrabungen in Sendschirli*, vol. i. p. 9.   Perhaps Tibtibu, Dibdibu, may correspond with the modern village of Domdomu, Dumdum Huyuk.

[3] The Karasu, as was stated in Maspero, *Struggle of the Nations*, p. 7, note 3.

[4] The country of Iasbuki is represented by Ishbak, a son of Abraham and Keturah, mentioned in Genesis (xxv. 2) in connection with Shuah (Fr. Delitzsch, *Assyriologische Notizen zum Alten Testament*, in the *Zeitschrift für Keilforschung*, vol. ii. p. 92).

[5] Taia may be Kefer-Daya on Rey's map, a place situated some way south of Azaz and Tennîb; Tomkins (*Notes on the Geogr. of N. Syria*, in the *Babylonian and Oriental Record*, vol. iii. p. 6) prefers the Kefr-Taî of Sachau (*Reise in Syrien und Mesopotamien*, p. 459) to the west of Aleppo.

[6] *Black Obelisk*, ll. 26–31, and *Monolith*, col. i. ll. 29–54, col. ii. ll. 1–13; cf. Peiser, *Die Monolith-Inschrift*, in Schrader, *Keilins. Bibliothek*, vol. i. pp. 156–161, and Amiaud and Scheil, *Les Inscr. de Salmanasar II.*, pp. 12–19.

SACRIFICE OFFERED BY SHALMANESER III. TO THE GODS OF LAKE VAN AND ERECTION OF A TRIUMPHAL STELE.

Drawn by Faucher-Gudin, from one of the bas-reliefs on the bronze gates of Balawât.

F

safe from further attack. No doubt they thought that a show of submission would satisfy the new invader, as it had satisfied his father; but Shalmaneser was not disposed to rest content with this nominal dependence. He intended to exercise effective control over all the states won by his sword, and the proof of their subjection was to be the regular payment of tribute and fulfilment of other obligations to their suzerain. Year by year he unfailingly enforced his rights, till the subject states were obliged to acknowledge their master and resign themselves to servitude.

The narrative of his reiterated efforts is a monotonous one. The king advanced against Adini in the spring of 859 B.C., defeated Akhuni near Tul-barsip, transported his victorious regiments across the Euphrates on rafts of skins, seized Surunu, Paripa, and Dabigu,[1] besides six fortresses and two hundred villages, and then advanced into the territory of Carchemish, which he proceeded to treat with such severity that the other Hittite chiefs hastened to avert a similar fate by tendering their submission. The very enumeration of their offerings proves not only their wealth, but the terror inspired by the advancing Assyrian host : Shapalulmê of the Patinâ, for instance, yielded up three talents of gold, a hundred talents of silver, three hundred talents of copper, and three hundred of iron, and paid in addition to this an annual tribute of one talent of silver, two talents of purple, and two hundred great beams of cedar-wood. Samalla, Agusi, and Kummukh were each laid under tribute in proportion to their resources, but their surrender did not necessarily lead to that of Adini.[2] Akhuni realised that, situated as he was on the very borders of Assyrian territory, there was no longer a chance of his preserving his semi-independence, as was the case with his kinsfolk beyond the Euphrates ; proximity to the capital would involve a stricter servitude, which would soon reduce him from the condition of a vassal to that of a subject, and make him merely a governor where he had hitherto reigned as king. Abandoned by the Khâti, he sought allies further north, and entered into a league with the tribes of Naîri and Urartu. When, in 858 B.C., Shalmaneser III. forced an entrance into Tul-barsip, and drove back what was left of the garrison on the right bank of the Euphrates, a sudden movement of Aramê obliged him to let

---

[1] Fr. Lenormant (*Les Origines de l'Histoire*, vol. iii. p. 328) identified the Assyrian Paripa with the Fariua of the Egyptians (*List of Thutmôsis III.*, No. 247); the site of the modern El-Farâ, proposed for both by Tomkins (*Notes on the Geography of N. Syria*, in the *Babyl. and Orient. Record*, vol. iii. p. 42), is too far to the south. Shalmaneser crossed the Euphrates near Tul-barsip, which would lead him into the country between Birejîk, Rum-kaleh, and Aintab, and it is in that district that we must look for the towns subject to Akhuni. Dabigu, I consider, corresponds to Dehbek on Rey's map, a little to the north-east of Aintab (cf. *supra*, p. 31, note 1); the sites of Paripa and Surunu are unknown.

[2] *Obelisk*, ll. 32–35, and *Monolith*, col. ii. ll. 13–30; cf. PEISER, *Die Monolith-Inschrift*, in SCHRADER, *Keilins. Bibliothek*, vol. i. pp. 160–163, and AMIAUD and SCHEIL, *Les Inscriptions de Salmanasar II.*, pp. 18–23.

the prey escape from his grasp. Rapidly fortifying Tul-barsip, Nappigi,
Aligu, Pitru, and Mutkînu, and garrisoning them with loyal troops to command the fords of the river, as his ancestor Shalmaneser I. had done six
centuries before,[1] he then re-entered Naîri by way of Bît-Zamani, devastated
Inziti with fire and sword, forced a road through to the banks of the Arzania,
pillaged Sukhmi and Dayaîni, and appeared under the walls of Arzashkun.
Aramê withdrew to Mount Adduri and awaited his attack in an almost
impregnable position; he was nevertheless defeated: 3400 of his soldiers fell
on the field of battle; his camp, his treasures, his chariots, and all his baggage

SHUA, KING OF GILZÂN, BRINGING A WAR-HORSE FULLY CAPARISONED TO SHALMANESER.[2]

passed into the hands of the conqueror, and he himself barely escaped with
his life. Shalmaneser ravaged the country "as a savage bull ravages and
tramples under his feet the fertile fields;" he burnt the villages and the
crops, destroyed Arzashkun, and raised before its gates a pyramid of human
heads, surrounded by a circle of prisoners impaled on stakes. He climbed
the mountain chain of Iritia, and laid waste Aramali and Zanziuna at his
leisure, and descending for the second time to the shores of Lake Van,
renewed the rites he had performed there in the first year of his reign, and
engraved on a neighbouring rock an inscription recording his deeds of prowess.

---

[1] Cf. MASPERO, *Struggle of the Nations*, pp. 657, 665. Pitru, the Pethor of the Bible (*Numb.* xxii.
5), is situated near the confluence of the Sajur and the Euphrates (*Monolith of Shalmaneser*, col. ii.
l. 36), somewhere near the encampment called Oshériyéh by Sachau (*Reise in Syrien*, pp. 156–158).
Mutkînu was on the other bank, perhaps at Kharbet-Beddaî, nearly opposite Pitru. Nappigi was
on the left bank of the Euphrates, which excludes its identification with Mabog-Hierapolis, as
proposed by Hommel (*Gesch. Babyl. und Assyr.*, p. 607); Nabigath, mentioned by Tomkins (*Notes
on the Geography of N. Syria*, in the *Babyl. and Orient. Record*, vol. iii. p. 42), is too far east.
Nappigi and Aligu must both be sought in the district between the Euphrates and the town of Saruj.

[2] Drawn by Faucher-Gudin, from one of the bas-reliefs on the Black Obelisk; cf. LAYARD, *Mon.
of Nineveh*, vol. i. pl. 54.

He made his way back to Gilzân, where its king, Shua, brought him a war-horse fully caparisoned, as a token of homage. Shalmaneser graciously deigned to receive it, and further exacted from the king the accustomed contributions of chariot-horses, sheep, and wine, together with seven dromedaries, whose strange forms amused the gaping crowds of Nineveh. After quitting Gilzân, Shalmaneser encountered the people of Khubushkia, who ventured to bar his way; but its king, Kakia, lost his city of Shilaia, and three thousand soldiers, besides bulls, horses, and sheep innumerable. Having enforced submission in Khubushkia, Shalmaneser at length returned to Assur

DROMEDARIES FROM GILZÂN.[1]

through the defiles of Kirruri, and came to Calah to enjoy a well-earned rest after the fatigues of his campaign.[2] But Akhuni had not yet lost heart. Though driven back to the right bank of the Euphrates, he had taken advantage of the diversion created by Aramê in his favour, to assume a strong position among the hills of Shitamrat with the river in his rear.[3] Shalmaneser attacked his lines in front, and broke through them after three days' preliminary skirmishing; then finding the enemy drawn up in battle array before their last stronghold, the king charged without a moment's hesitation, drove them back and forced them to surrender. Akhuni's life was spared, but he was sent with the remainder of his army to colonise a village in the neighbourhood of Assur, and Adini became henceforth an integral part of Assyria. The war on the western frontier was hardly brought to a close when another broke out in the opposite direction. The king rapidly crossed the pass

---

[1] Drawn by Faucher-Gudin, from one of the bas-reliefs on the bronze gates of Balawât.

[2] *Obelisk,* ll. 35–44; *Inscription of Balawât,* col. ii. ll. 5, 6, col. iii. ll. 1–3; *Monolith,* col. ii. ll. 30–66: cf. PEISER, *Die Monolith-Inschrift,* in SCHRADER, *Keilins. Bibliothek,* vol. i. pp. 162–169, and AMIAUD and SCHEIL, *Les Inscr. de Salmanasar II.,* pp. 22–31.

[3] The position of Shitamrat may answer to the ruins of the fortress of Rum-kaleh, which protected a ford of the Euphrates in Byzantine times.

of Bunagishlu and fell upon Mazamua: the natives, disconcerted by his impetuous onslaught, nevertheless hoped to escape by putting out in their boats on the broad expanse of Lake Urumiah. Shalmaneser, however, constructed rafts of inflated skins, on which his men ventured in pursuit right out into the open. The natives were overpowered; the king "dyed the sea with their blood as if it had been wool," and did not withdraw until he had forced them to appeal for mercy.[1]

In five years Shalmaneser had destroyed Adini, laid low Urartu, and confirmed the tributary states of Syria in their allegiance; but Damascus and

TRIBUTE FROM GILZÂN.[2]

Babylon were as yet untouched, and the moment was at hand when he would have to choose between an arduous conflict with them, or such a repression of the warlike zeal of his opening years, that, like his father Assur-nazir-pal, he would have to repose on his laurels. Shalmaneser was too deeply imbued with the desire for conquest to choose a peaceful policy: he decided at once to assume the offensive against Damascus, being probably influenced by the news of Ahab's successes,[3] and deeming that if the King of Israel had gained the ascendency unaided, Assur, fully confident of its own superiority, need have no fear as to the result of a conflict. The forces, however, at the disposal of Benhadad II. (Adadidri) were sufficient to cause the Assyrians some uneasiness. The King of Damascus was not only lord of Cœle-Syria and the Haurân, but he exercised a suzerainty more or less defined over Hamath, Israel, Ammon,

---

[1] *Obelisk*, ll. 45–52; *Inscription of Balawâi*, col. iii. ll. 3–6; and *Monolith*, col. ii. ll. 66–78: cf. PEISER, *Die Monolith-Inschrift*, in SCHRADER, *Keilins. Bibliothek*, vol. i. pp. 168–171, and AMIAUD and SCHEIL, *Les Inscr. de Salmanasar II.*, pp. 30, 31.

[2] Drawn by Faucher-Gudin, from one of the bas-reliefs on the Black Obelisk; cf. LAYARD, *The Monuments of Nineveh*, vol. i. pl. 56.

[3] For the wars of Ahab with Ben-hadad (Adadidri), cf. MASPERO, *Struggle of the Nations*, p. 785, et seq.

the Arabian and Idumean tribes, Arvad and the principalities of Northern Phœnicia, Usanata, Shianu, and Irkanata;[1] in all, twelve peoples or twelve kings owned his sway, and their forces, if united to his, would provide at need an army of nearly 100,000 men: a few years might see these various elements merged in a united empire, capable of withstanding the onset of any foreign foe.[2] Shalmaneser set out from Nineveh on the 14th day of the month Iyyâr, 854 B.C., and chastised on his way the Aramæans of the Balikh, whose sheikh Giammu had shown some inclination to assert his independence. He crossed the Euphrates at Tul-barsip, and held a species of durbar at Pitru for his Syrian subjects: Sangar of Carchemish, Kundashpi of Kummukh, Aramê of Agusi, Lalli of Melitene, Khaiani of Samalla, Garparuda who had succeeded Shapalulmê among the Patinâ, and a second Garparuda of Gurgum,[3] rallied around him with their presents of welcome, and probably also with their troops. This ceremony concluded, he hastened to Khalmân and reduced it to submission, then plunged into the hill-country between Khalmân and the Orontes, and swept over the whole territory of Hamath. A few easy victories at the outset enabled him to exact ransom from, or burn to the ground, the cities of Adinnu, Mashgâ, Arganâ, and Qarqar, but just beyond Qarqar he encountered the advance-guard of the Syrian army.[4] Ben-hadad had called together, to give him a fitting

---

[1] Irkanata, the Egyptian Arqanatu (MAX MÜLLER, Asien und Europa, p. 246), perhaps the Irqata of the Tel-el-Amarna tablets (WINCKLER, Die Thontafeln von Tell-el-Amarna, pp. 170–173), is the Arka of Phœnicia. The other countries enumerated are likewise situated in the same locality. Shianu (for a long time read as Shizanu), the Sin of the Bible (Gen. x. 17), is mentioned by Tiglath-pileser III. under the name Sianu (cf. MASPERO, Struggle of the Nations, p. 172, note 5). Ushanat is called Uznu by Tiglath-pileser, and Delitzsch thought it represented the modern Kalaat-el-Hosn (Wo lag das Paradies? p. 282). With Arvad it forms the ancient Zahi of the Egyptians, which was then subject to Damascus.

[2] The suzerainty of Ben-hadad over these twelve peoples is proved by the way in which they are enumerated in the Assyrian documents: his name always stands at the head of the list (Obelisk, ll. 59–61, 88, 89, Bull No. 1, in LAYARD, Inscriptions, pl. 14, ll. 16, 17, 32, 33, 37, 38, 45, 46, and Monolith, col. ii. ll. 90–95.) The manner in which the Assyrian scribes introduce the names of these kings, mentioning sometimes one, sometimes two among them, without subtracting them from the total number 12, has been severely criticised, and Schrader excused it by saying that 12 is here used as a round number somewhat vaguely (Keilinschriften und Geschichtsforschung, p. 46). The detailed list on the Monolith, ll. 90–95, contains only 11 kings. When the scribe speaks of Ben-hadad, Irkhulini and the 12 kings of Syria, I think he intends to include the two he has named in the twelve. The proof of the correctness of this view is furnished by the various renderings of the same story: thus, where the Obelisk, ll. 91, 92, speaks of 12 kings, without naming any individually, the Bull No. 1, ll. 45, 46, mentions Ben-hadad (Adadidri), Irkhulini, with 12 kings; and where the Obelisk, ll. 59–61, gives Adadidri, Irkhulini, "with the kings of the Khâti," the Bull No. 1 mentions Adadidri, Irkhulini, "with 12 kings of the sea-coast," and the Monolith, ll. 90–95, enumerates 11 kings. Has one of the twelve been forgotten? It is quite certain that, in the phraseology of Shalmaneser, Ben-hadad, Irkhulini, with 12 kings really signifies Ben-hadad, Irkhulini, and others; in all, 12 kings of Syria and Phœnicia.

[3] Winckler (Gesch. Bab. und Ass., p. 193) considers that the Karparuda or Kalparuda of Gurgum is the same as the Karparuda of the Patinâ: the Patinâ and Gurgum would in this case be two provinces of a single kingdom, and the Assyrian scribes must have had two lists before them in drawing up this portion of the Annals, one calling Karparuda King of the Patinâ, the other entitling him King of Gurgum.

[4] The position of these towns is uncertain: the general plan of the campaign only proves that they must lie on the main route from Aleppo to Kalaat-Sejar, by Barâ or by Maarêt-en-Nômân and Kalaat-el-Mudîq. It is agreed that Qarqar must be sought not far from Hamath, whatever the exact site may be. An examination of the map shows us that Qarqar corresponds to the present Kalaat-el-

reception, the whole of the forces at his disposal: 1200 chariots, 1200 horse, 20,000 foot-soldiers from Damascus alone; 700 chariots, 700 horse and 10,000 foot from Hamath; 2000 chariots and 10,000 foot belonging to Ahab, 500 soldiers from Kuî, 1000 mountaineers from the Taurus,[1] 10 chariots and 10,000 foot from Irkanata, 200 from Arvad, 200 from Usanata, 30 chariots and 10,000 foot from Shianu, 1000 camels from Gindibu the Arab, and 1000 Ammonites.

TRIBUTE FROM GARPARUDA, KING OF THE PATINÂ.[2]

The battle was long and bloody, and the issue uncertain; Shalmaneser drove back one wing of the confederate army to the Orontes, and forcing the other wing and the centre to retire from Qarqar to Kirzau, claimed the victory, though the losses on both sides were equally great.[3] It would seem as if the battle were indecisive—the Assyrians, at any rate, gained nothing by it; they beat a retreat immediately after their pretended victory, and returned to their own land without prisoners and almost without booty.[4] On the whole, this first conflict had not been unfavourable to Damascus: it had demonstrated the power of that state in the eyes of the most incredulous, and proved how easy resistance would be, if only

Mudîq, the ancient Apamæa of Lebanon; the confederate army would command the ford which led to the plain of Hamath by Kalaat-Sejar.

[1] For Kuî, cf. MASPERO, *Struggle of the Nations*, p. 590, note 3. The people of the Muzri next enumerated have long been considered as Egyptians; the juxtaposition of their name with that of Kuî shows that it refers here to the Muzri of the Taurus; the use of the name is discussed in MASPERO, *Struggle of the Nations*, p. 608, note 3, and p. 655 (TIELE, *Babylonisch-Assyrische Geschichte*, p. 201, note 1; HOMMEL, *Gesch. Bab. und Ass.*, p. 609; WINCKLER, *Alttestament. Forsch.*, p. 172).

[2] Drawn by Faucher-Gudin, from one of the bas-reliefs on the Black Obelisk; cf. LAYARD, *Mon. of Nineveh*, vol. i. pl. 53.

[3] The number of the slain varies in different accounts of the battle: the *Obelisk*, ll. 65, 66, gives 20,500; the *Bull No. 1*, l. 18, 25,000; the *Monolith*, ll. 97, 98, only 14,000. On these divergencies, cf. SCHRADER, *Keilins. und Geschichtsforschung*, p. 47.

[4] *Obelisk*, ll. 54–66; *Monolith*, col. ii. ll. 78–102; *Bull No. 1*, ll. 12–19: cf. PEISER, *Die Monolith-Insch.*, in SCHRADER, *Keilins. Bibliothek*, vol. i. pp. 170–175, and AMIAUD and SCHEIL, *Les Inscr. de Salmanasar II.*, pp. 36–48. The detailed history on the *Monolith* ends in a very abrupt manner just after the battle of Qarqar.

the various princes of Syria would lay aside their differences and all unite under the command of a single chief. The effect of the battle in Northern Syria and among the recently annexed Aramæan tribes was very great; they began to doubt the omnipotence of Assyria, and their loyalty was shaken. Sangar of Carchemish and the Khâti refused to pay their tribute, and the Emirs of Tul-Abnî and Mount Kashiari broke out into open revolt. Shalmaneser spent a whole year in suppressing the insurrection;[1] complications, moreover, arose at Babylon which obliged him to concentrate his attention and energy on Chaldæan affairs. Nabu-baliddin had always maintained peaceful and friendly relations with Assyria, but he had been overthrown, or perhaps assassinated, and his son Marduk-nâdin-shumu had succeeded him on the throne,[2] to the dissatisfaction of a section of his subjects. Another son of Nabu-baliddin, Marduk-belusâtê, claimed the sovereign power, and soon won over so much of the country that Marduk-nâdin-shumu had fears for the safety of Babylon itself. He then probably remembered the pretensions to Karduniash,[3] which his Assyrian neighbours had for a long time maintained, and applied to Shalmaneser to support his tottering fortunes. The Assyrian monarch must have been disposed to lend a favourable ear to a request which allowed him to intervene as suzerain in the quarrels of the rival kingdom: he mobilised his forces, offered sacrifices in honour of Rammân at Zabân, and crossed the frontier in 853 B.C.[4]

The war dragged on during the next two years. The scene of hostilities was at the outset on the left bank of the Tigris, which for ten centuries had served as the battle-field for the warriors of both countries. Shalmaneser, who had invested Mê-Turnat at the fords of the Lower Dîyalah, at length captured that fortress, and after having thus isolated the rebels of Babylonia proper, turned his steps towards Gananatê.[5] Marduk-belusâtê, "a vacillating king, incapable of directing his own affairs," came out to meet him, but although repulsed and driven within the town, he defended his position with such spirit that Shalmaneser was at length obliged to draw off his troops after having cut down all the young corn, felled the fruit trees, disorganised the whole system of irrigation,—in short, after having effected all the damage

[1] *Obelisk*, ll. 67–72, and *Bull No. 1*, 20–23; cf. AMIAUD and SCHEIL, *Les Inscr. de Salmanasar II.*, ll. 42, 43.

[2] *Synchronous History*, col. iii. ll. 22–27; cf. PEISER and WINCKLER, *Die sogenannte Synchronistische Geschichte*, in SCHRADER, *Die Keilins. Bibliothek*, vol. i. pp. 200, 201.

[3] Cf. *supra*, pp. 11, 12.

[4] *Inscription of Balawât*, col. iv. ll. 1–3; cf. AMIAUD and SCHEIL, *Les Inscr. de Salmanasar II.*, pp. 46, 47. The town of Zabân is situated on the Lesser Zab, but it is impossible to fix the exact site.

[5] Mê-Turnat, Mê-Turni, "the water of the Turnat," stood upon the Dîyalah, probably near the site of Bakuba, where the most frequented route crosses the river; perhaps we may identify it with the Artemita of classical authors (ISIDOROS OF CHARAX, in the *Geographi Græci Minores*, ed. MULLER-DIDOT, vol. i. pp. 249, 250). Gananatê must be sought higher up near the mountains, as the context points out; I am inclined to place it near the site of Khanekîn, whose gardens are still celebrated, and the strategic importance of which is considerable (VITAL CUINET, *La Turquie d'Asie*, vol. iii. pp. 126, 127).

he could. He returned in the following spring by the most direct route; Lakhiru fell into his hands,[1] but Marduk-belusâtê, having no heart to contend with him for the possession of a district ravaged by the struggle of the preceding summer, fell back on the mountains of Yasubi and concentrated his forces round Armân.[2] Shalmaneser, having first wreaked his vengeance upon Gananatê, attacked his adversary in his self-chosen position; Armân fell after a desperate defence, and Marduk-belusâtê either perished or disappeared in a last attempt at retaliation. Marduk-nadîn-shumu, although rid of his rival, was not yet master of the entire kingdom. The Aramæans of the Marshes, or, as they called themselves, the Kaldâ, had refused him their allegiance, and were ravaging the regions of the Lower Euphrates by their repeated incursions.[3] They constituted not so much a compact state, as a confederation of little states, alternately involved in petty internecine quarrels, or temporarily reconciled under the precarious authority of a sole monarch. Each separate state bore the name of the head of the family—real or mythical—from whom all its members prided themselves on being descended,—Bît-Dakkuri, Bît-Adini, Bît-Amukkâni, Bît-Shalani, Bît-Shalli, and finally Bît-Yakîn, which in the end asserted its predominance over all the rest.[4] In demanding Shalmaneser's help, Marduk-nadîn-shumu had virtually thrown on him the responsibility of bringing these turbulent subjects to order, and the Assyrian monarch accepted the duties of his new position without demur. He marched to Babylon, entered the city and went direct to the temple of E-shaggîl: the people beheld him approach with reverence their deities Bel and Belît, and visit all the sanctuaries of the local gods, to whom he made endless propitiatory libations and pure offerings. He had worshipped Ninip in Kuta; he was careful not to forget Nabo of Borsippa, while on the other hand he officiated in the temple of Ezida, and consulted its ancient oracle, offering upon its altars the flesh of splendid oxen and fat lambs. The inhabitants had their part in the festival as well as

---

[1] Lakhiru comes before Gananatê on the direct road from Assyria, to the south of the Lower Zab, as we learn from the account of the campaign itself: we shall not do wrong in placing this town either at Kifri, or in its neighbourhood on the present caravan route.

[2] For the identity of Armân with Khalmân, and of both these with the present Holwân, cf. *Struggle of the Nations*, pp. 119, note 2, 615, 616. Mount Yasubi is the mountainous district which separates Khanekîn from Holwân.

[3] For the Kaldâ, cf. *Struggle of the Nations*, p. 669, and p. 4 of the present volume. The part played by the Kaldâ was first defined by DELATTRE, *Les Chaldéens jusqu'à la formation de l'empire de Nabuchodonosor* (extracted from the *Revue des Questions historiques*, 1877, and republished in 1889 with *Considérations sur un récent livre de M. Hugo Winckler*), then by WINCKLER, *Untersuchungen zur Altorient. Gesch.*, pp. 47–64; cf. WINCKLER, *Plagiat? Antwort auf die von A. J. Delattre S. J. gegen mich erhobenen Beschuldigungen*, 1889, and DELATTRE, *Réponse au Plaidoyer de M. H. Winckler*, 1889.

[4] FR. DELITZSCH, *Wo lag das Paradies?* pp. 201–203. As far as we can judge, Bît-Dakkuri and Bît-Adini were the most northerly, the latter lying on both sides of the Euphrates (*Inscrip. of Balawât*, col. vi. ll. 6, 7), the former on the west of the Euphrates, to the south of the Bahr-i-Nejîf; Bît-Yakîn was at the southern extremity near the mouths of the Euphrates, and on the western shore of the Persian Gulf. For Bît-Amukkâni the inscription of the *Bull No. 2*, l. 29, has the variant Bît-Ukâni, perhaps, as Hommel points out (*Gesch. Bab. und Ass.*, p. 596, note 2), through the intermediate form Aukâni.

the gods; Shalmaneser summoned them to a public banquet, at which he distributed to them embroidered garments, and plied them with meats and wine; then, after renewing his homage to the gods of Babylon, he recommenced his campaign, and set out in the direction of the sea. Baqâni, the first of the Chaldæan cities which lay on his route, belonged to Bît-Adini,[1] one of the tribes of Bît-Dakkuri; it appeared disposed to resist him, and was therefore promptly dismantled and burnt—an example which did not fail to cool the warlike inclinations which had begun to manifest themselves in other parts of Bît-Dakkuri. He next crossed the Euphrates, and pillaged Enzudî, the fate of which caused the remainder of Bît-Adini to lay down arms, and the submission of the latter brought about that of Bît-Yakîn and Bît-Amukkani. These were all rich provinces, and they bought off the conqueror liberally: gold, silver, tin, copper, iron, acacia-wood, ivory, elephants' skins, were all showered upon the invader to secure his mercy.[2] It must have been an intense satisfaction to the pride of the Assyrians to be able to boast that their king had deigned to offer sacrifices in the sacred cities of Accad, and that he had been borne by his war-horses to the shores of the Salt Sea; these facts, of little moment to us now, appeared to the people of those days of decisive importance. No king who was not actually master of the country would have been tolerated within the temple of the eponymous god, for the purpose of celebrating the rites which the sovereign alone was empowered to perform. Marduk-nadîn-shumu, in recognising Shalmaneser's right to act thus, thereby acknowledged that he himself was not only the king's ally, but his liegeman. This bond of supremacy doubtless did not weigh heavily upon him; as soon as his suzerain had evacuated the country, the two kingdoms remained much on the same footing as had been established by the treaties of the three previous generations. Alliances were made between private families belonging to both, peace existed between the two sovereigns, interchange of commerce and amenities took place between the two peoples, but with one point of difference which had not existed formerly: Assur protected Babel, and, by taking precedence of Marduk, he became the real head of the peoples of the Euphrates valley.[3] Assured of the subordination, or at least of the friendly neutrality of Babylon, Shalmaneser had now a free hand to undertake a campaign in the remoter regions of Syria,

---

[1] The site of Baqâni is unknown; it should be sought for between Lamlum and Warka, and Bît-Adini in Bît-Dakkuri should be placed between the Shatt-et-Kaher and the Arabian desert, if the name of Enzudî, the other royal town, situated to the west of the Euphrates, is found, as is possible, under a popular etymology, in that of Kalaat ain-Saîd or Kalaat ain-es-Saîd in the modern maps.

[2] *Obelisk*, ll. 73–84; *Bull No. 1*, ll. 23–29; *Balawât Inscrip.*, cols. iv.–vi.: cf. AMIAUD and SCHEIL, *Les Inscriptions de Salmanasar II.*, pp. 42-51. The account is very succinct, and the two campaigns are not distinguished in the *Synchronous History*, col. iii. ll. 22–35; cf. PEISER and WINCKLER, *Die sogenannte Synch. Gesch.*, in SCHRADER, *Keil. Bibl.*, vol. i. ll. 200, 201.

[3] For the nature of this suzerainty, cf. WINCKLER, *Untersuchungen*, etc., pp. 50, 51; for the consequent changes which this would produce in the Protocol of the Kings of Assyria, cf. WINCKLER, *Ein Beitrag zur Gesch. der Assyriologie in Deutschland*, pp. 20–23, 42, 43.

without being constantly haunted by the fear that his rival might suddenly swoop down upon him in the rear by the valleys of the Radanu or the Zabs. He now ran no risks in withdrawing his troops from the south-eastern frontier, and in marshalling his forces on the slopes of the Armenian Alps or on the banks of the Orontes, leaving merely a slender contingent in the heart of Assyria proper to act as the necessary guardians of order in the capital.

Since the indecisive battle of Qarqar, the western frontier of the empire had receded as far as the Euphrates, and Shalmaneser had been obliged to forego the collection of the annual Syrian tribute. It would have been an excellent opportunity for the Khâti, while they enjoyed this accidental respite, to come to an understanding with Damascus, for the purpose of acting conjointly against a common enemy; but they let the right moment slip, and their isolation made submission inevitable. The effort to subdue them cost Shalmaneser dear, both in time and men; in the spring of each year he appeared at the fords of Tul-barsip and ravaged the environs of Carchemish, then marched upon the Orontes to accomplish the systematic devastation of some fresh district, or to inflict a defeat on such of his adversaries as dared to encounter him in the open field. In 850 B.C. the first blow was struck at the Khâti; Agusi[2] was the next to suffer, and its king, Aramê, lost Arniê, his royal city, with some hundred more townships and strongholds.[2] In 849 B.C. it was the turn of Damascus. The league of which Ben-hadad had proclaimed himself the suzerain was still in existence, but it had recently narrowly escaped dissolution, and a revolt had almost deprived it of the adherence of Israel and the house of Omri—after Hamath, the most active of all its members. The losses suffered at Qarqar had doubtless been severe enough to shake Ahab's faith in the strength of his master and ally. Besides this, it would appear that the latter had not honourably fulfilled all the conditions of the treaty of peace he had signed three years

---

[1] Historians have up to the present admitted that this campaign of the year 850 took place in Armenia (TIELE, *Bab. Ass. Gesch.*, pp. 187, 201; WINCKLER, *Gesch. Bab. und Ass.*, p. 197). The context of the account itself shows us that, in his tenth year, Shalmaneser advanced against the towns of Aramê, immediately after having pillaged the country of the Khâti, which inclines me to think that these towns were situated in Northern Syria. I have no doubt that the Aramê in question is not the Armenian king of that name, but, as Fr. Lenormant (*Lettres assyriologiques*, vol. i. p. 138) thought, Aramê the sovereign of Bît-Agusi, who is named several times in the *Annals* of Shalmaneser (*Monolith*, col. ii. ll. 12, 83); cf. MASPERO, *Notes au jour le jour*, § 32, in the *Proceedings* of the Soc. of Bibl. Archæology, 1898, vol. xx. pp. 130–133.

[2] *Obelisk*, ll. 85, 86; *Bull No. 1*, ll. 29–82: cf. AMIAUD and SCHEIL, *Les Inscriptions de Salmanasar II.*, pp. 50–53. The text of *Bull No. 1* adds to the account of the war against Aramê, that of a war against the Damascene league (ll. 32–34), which merely repeats the account of Shalmaneser's eleventh year. It is generally admitted that the war against Aramê falls during his tenth year, and the war against Ben-hadad during his eleventh year. The scribes must have had at their disposal two different versions of one document, in which these two wars were described without distinction of year. The compiler of the inscription of the Bulls would have considered them as forming two distinct accounts, which he has placed one after the other (TIELE, *Bab. Ass. Gesch.*, pp. 201, 202; HOMMEL, *Gesch. Bab. und Ass.*, p. 111, note 4). For the interpretation which I have adopted in the text, cf. MASPERO, *Notes au jour le jour*, § 32, in *Proceedings* of the Soc. of Bibl. Arch., 1898, vol. xx. pp. 125–133.

previously;[1] he still held the important fortress of Ramoth-gilead, and he delayed handing it over to Ahab in spite of his oath to restore it. Finding that he could not regain possession of it by fair means, Ahab resolved to take it by force.[2] A great change in feeling and politics had taken place at Jerusalem. Jehoshaphat, who occupied the throne, was, like his father Asa, a devout worshipper of Jahveh, but his piety did not blind him to the secular needs of the moment. The experience of his predecessors had shown that the union of the twelve tribes under the rule of a scion of Judah was a thing of the past for ever; all attempts to restore it had ended in failure and bloodshed, and the house of David had again only lately been saved from ruin by the dearly bought intervention of Ben-hadad I. and his Syrians.[3] Jehoshaphat from the outset clearly saw the necessity of avoiding these errors of the past; he accepted the situation and sought the friendship of Israel. An alliance between two princes so unequal in power could only result in a disguised suzerainty for one of them and a state of vassalage for the other; what Ben-hadad's alliance was to Ahab, that of Ahab was to Jehoshaphat, and it served his purpose in spite of the opposition of the prophets.[4] The strained relations between the two countries were relaxed, and the severed tribes on both sides of the frontier set about repairing their losses; while Hiel the Bethelite at length set about rebuilding Jericho on behalf of Samaria,[5] Jehoshaphat was collecting around him a large army, and strengthening himself on the west against the Philistines and on the south against the Bedawîn of the desert.[6] The marriage of his eldest son Jehoram * with Athaliah subsequently bound the two courts together by still closer ties;[7] mutual visits were exchanged, and it

---

[1] Cf. what is said on the subject of this peace in *The Struggle of the Nations*, pp. 786, 787.

[2] 1 *Kings* xxii. 3, where the LXX. reads *Rama* of Gilead.

[3] Cf. *Struggle of the Nations*, pp. 778, 779.

[4] The subordinate position of Jehoshaphat is clearly indicated by the reply which he makes to Ahab when the latter asks him to accompany him on this expedition: "I am as thou art, my people as thy people, my horses as thy horses" (1 *Kings* xxii. 4). This dependence of Judah, suspected by Kittel (*Gesch. der Hebräer*, vol. ii. p. 39), has been fully demonstrated by Winckler (*Gesch. Israels*, vol. i. pp. 145, 146, 162–164, 165, 176).

[5] 1 *Kings* xvi. 34, where the writer has preserved the remembrance of a double human sacrifice, destined, according to the common custom in the whole of the East, to create guardian spirits for the new building: "he laid the foundation thereof with the loss of Abiram his firstborn, and set up the gates thereof with the loss of his youngest son Segub; according to the word of the Lord." [For the curse pronounced on whoever should rebuild Jericho, see *Josh.* vi. 26.—Tr.]

[6] 2 *Chron.* xvii. 10–19, where the narrative must have some basis of truth.

* [Following the distinction in spelling given in 2 *Kings* viii. 25, I have everywhere written Joram (of Israel) and Jehoram (of Judah), to avoid confusion.—Tr.]

[7] Athaliah is sometimes called the daughter of Ahab (2 *Kings* viii. 18), and sometimes the daughter of Omri (2 *Kings* viii. 26; cf. 2 *Chron.* xxii. 2), and several authors prefer the latter filiation (RENAN, *Histoire du Peuple d'Israel*, vol. ii. p. 310), while the majority see in it a mistake of the Hebrew scribe (STADE, *Gesch. des Volkes Israel*, vol. i. p. 524, note 2). It is possible that both attributions may be correct, for we see by the Assyrian inscriptions that a sovereign is called the son of the founder of his line even when he was several generations removed from him: thus, Merodach-baladan, the adversary of Sargon of Assyria, calls himself son of Iakîn, although the founder of the Bît-Iakîn had been dead many centuries before his accession. The document used in 2 *Kings* viii. 26 may have employed the term *daughter of Omri* in the same manner merely to indicate that the Queen of Jerusalem belonged to the house of Omri.

was on the occasion of a stay made by Jehoshaphat at Jezreel that the expedition against Ramoth was finally resolved on. It might well have appeared a more than foolhardy enterprise, and it was told in Israel that Micaiah, a prophet, the son of Imlah, had predicted its disastrous ending. " I saw," exclaimed the prophet, " the Lord sitting on His throne, and all the host of heaven standing on His right hand and on His left. And the Lord said, Who shall entice Ahab that he may go up and fall at Ramoth-gilead ? And one said on this manner, and another said on that manner. And there came forth a spirit, and stood before the Lord, and said, I will entice him. And the Lord said unto him, Wherewith ? And he said, I will go forth, and will be a lying spirit in the mouth of all his prophets. And He said, Thou shalt entice him, and shalt prevail also : go forth, and do so. Now therefore, behold, the Lord hath put a lying spirit in the mouth of all these thy prophets ; and the Lord hath spoken evil concerning thee." [1]

The two kings thereupon invested Ramoth, and Ben-hadad hastened to the defence of his fortress. Selecting thirty-two of his bravest charioteers, he commanded them to single out Ahab only for attack, and not fight with others until they had slain him. This injunction happened in some way to come to the king's ears, and he therefore disguised himself as a common soldier, while Jehoshaphat retained his ordinary dress. Attracted by the richness of the latter's armour, the Syrians fell upon him, but on his raising his war-cry they perceived their mistake, and turning from the King of Judah they renewed their quest of the Israelitish leader. While they were vainly seeking him, an archer drew a bow " at a venture," and pierced him in the joints of his cuirass. " Wherefore he said to his charioteer, Turn thine hand, and carry me out of the host ; for I am sore wounded." Perceiving, however, that the battle was going against him, he revoked the order, and remained on the field the whole day, supported by his armour-bearers. He expired at sunset, and the news of his death having spread panic through the ranks, a cry arose, " Every man to his city, and every man to his country !" The king's followers bore his body to Samaria,[2] and Israel again relapsed into the position of a vassal,

---

[1] 1 *Kings* xxii. 5–23, reproduced in 2 *Chron.* xviii. 4–22.

[2] 1 *Kings* xxii. 29–38 (cf. 2 *Chron.* xviii. 28–34), with interpolations in verses 35 and 38. It is impossible to establish the chronology of this period with any certainty, so entirely do the Hebrew accounts of it differ from the Assyrian. The latter mention Ahab as alive at the time of the battle of Qarqar in 854 B.C., and Jehu on the throne in 842 B.C. We must, therefore, place in the intervening twelve years, first, the end of Ahab's reign ; secondly, the two years of Ahaziah ; thirdly, the twelve years of Joram ; fourthly, the beginning of the reign of Jehu—in all, possibly fourteen years. The reign of Joram has been prolonged beyond reason by the Hebrew annalists, and it alone lends itself to be curtailed. Admitting, as I have done (*Struggle of the Nations*, p. 785, note 5), that the siege of Samaria preceded the battle of Qarqar, we may surmise that the three years which elapsed, according to the tradition (1 *Kings* xxii. 1), between the triumph of Ahab and his death, fall into two unequal periods, two previous to Qarqar, and one after it, in such a manner that the revolt of Israel would have been the result of the defeat of the Damascenes ; Ahab must have died in 853 B.C., as most modern historians agree (SCHRADER, *Keilinschriften und Geschichtsforschung*, pp. 356, 357 ; ED. MEYER, *Gesch. des Alterthums*, vol. i. p. 393 ; WINCKLER, *Gesch. Israels*, vol. i.

probably under the same conditions as before the revolt.   Ahaziah survived his father two years, and was succeeded by his brother Joram.[1]   When Shalmaneser, in 849 B.C., reappeared in the valley of the Orontes, Joram sent out against him his prescribed contingent, and the conquered Israelites once more fought for their conqueror.   The Assyrians had, as usual, maltreated the Khâti.   After having pillaged the towns of Carchemish and Agusi, they advanced on the Amanos, held to ransom the territory of the Patinâ enclosed within the bend of the Orontes, and descending upon Hamath by way of the districts of Iaraku and Ashtamaku, they came into conflict with the army of the twelve kings, though on this occasion the contest was so bloody that they were forced to withdraw immediately after their success.   They had to content themselves with sacking Apparazu, one of the citadels of Aramê, and with collecting the tribute of Garparuda of the Patinâ; which done, they skirted the Amanos and provided themselves with beams from its cedars.[2]   The two following years were spent in harrying the people of Paqarakhbuni, on the right bank of the Euphrates, in the dependencies of the ancient kingdom of Adini (848 B.C.), and in plundering the inhabitants of Ishtaratê in the country of Iaîti, near the sources of the Tigris (847 B.C.),[3] till in 846 they returned to try their fortune again in Syria.   They transported 120,000 men across the Euphrates, hoping perhaps, by the mere mass of such a force, to crush their enemy in a single battle; but Ben-hadad was supported by his vassals, and their combined army must have been as formidable numerically as that of the Assyrians.   As usual, after the engagement, Shalmaneser claimed the victory, but he did not succeed in intimidating the allies or in wresting from them a single rood of territory.[4]   Discouraged, doubtless, by so many fruitless attempts, he decided to suspend hostilities, at all events for the present.   In 845 B.C. he visited Naîri, and caused an " image of his royal Majesty " to be carved at the

pp. 164, 165).   On the other hand, it is scarcely probable that Jehu ascended the throne at the very moment that Shalmaneser was defeating Hazael in 842 B.C.; we can only carry back his accession to the preceding year, possibly 843.   The duration of two years for the reign of Ahaziah can only be reduced by a few months, if indeed as much as that, as it allows of a full year, and part of a second year (cf. 1 *Kings* xxii. 51, where it is said that Ahaziah ascended the throne in the 17th year of Jehoshaphat, and 2 *Kings* iii. 1, where it states that Joram of Israel succeeded Ahaziah in the 18th year of the same Jehoshaphat); in placing these two years between 853 and 851, there will remain for the reign of Joram the period comprised between 851 and 843, namely, eight years, instead of the twelve attributed to him by biblical tradition.

[1] The Hebrew documents merely make mention of Ahaziah's accession, length of reign, and death (1 *Kings* xxii. 40, 51-53, and 2 *Kings* i. 2-17).   The Assyrian texts do not mention his name, but they state that in 849 " the twelve kings " fought against Shalmaneser, and, as we have already seen (cf. *supra*, p. 70, note 1), one of the twelve was King of Israel, here, therefore necessarily Ahaziah, whose successor was Joram.

[2] *Obelisk*, ll. 88, 89; *Bull No. 1*, ll. 35-41: cf. AMIAUD and SCHEIL, *Les Inscr. de Salmanasar II.*, pp. 52-55.

[3] *Obelisk*, ll. 89-91; *Bull No. 1*, ll. 41-44: cf. AMIAUD and SCHEIL, *ibid.*, pp. 54-57.

[4] *Obelisk*, ll. 91, 92; *Bull No. 1*, ll. 44-47: cf. AMIAUD and SCHEIL, *ibid.*, pp. 56, 57.   The care which the king takes to specify that " with 120,000 men he crossed the Euphrates in flood-time " very probably shows that this number was for him in some respects an unusual one.

source of the Tigris close to the very spot where the stream first rises. Pushing forward through the defiles of Tunibuni, he next invaded Urartu, and devastated it as far as the sources of the Euphrates; on reaching these he purified his arms in the virgin spring, and offered a sacrifice to the gods. On his return to the frontier, the chief of Dayaini " embraced his feet," and presented him with some thoroughbred horses.[1] In 844 B.C. he crossed the Lower Zab and plunged into the heart of Namri; this country had long been under Babylonian influence, and its princes bore Semitic names. Marduk-mudammiq, who was then its ruler, betook himself to the mountains to preserve his life; but his treasures, idols, and troops were carried off to Assyria, and he was superseded on the throne by Ianzu, the son of Khambân, a noble of Cossæan origin.[2] As might be expected after such severe exertions, Shalmaneser apparently felt that he deserved a time of repose, for his chroniclers merely note the date of 843 B.C. as that of an inspection, terminating in a felling of cedars in the Amanos.[3] As a fact, there was nothing stirring on the frontier. Chaldæa itself looked upon him as a benefactor, almost as a suzerain, and by its position between Elam and Assyria, protected the latter from any quarrel with Susa. The nations on the east continued to pay their tribute without coercion, and Namri, which alone entertained pretensions to independence, had just received a severe lesson. Urartu had not acknowledged the supremacy of Assur, but it had suffered in the last invasion, and Aramê had shown no further sign of hostility. The tribes of the Upper Tigris—Kummukh and Adini—accepted their position as subjects, and any trouble arising in that quarter was treated as merely an ebullition of local dissatisfaction, and was promptly crushed. The Khâti were exhausted by the systematic destruction of their towns and their harvests. Lastly, of the principalities of the Amanos, Gurgum, Samalla, and the Patinâ, if some had occasionally taken part in the struggles for independence, the others had always remained faithful in the performance of their duties as vassals. Damascus alone held out, and the valour with which she had endured all the attacks made on her showed no signs of abatement; unless any internal disturbance arose to diminish her strength, she was likely to be able to resist the growing power of Assyria for a long time to come.

It was at the very time when her supremacy appeared to be thus firmly established that a revolution broke out, the effects of which soon undid the work of the preceding two or three generations. Ben-hadad, disembarrassed of Shalmaneser, desired to profit by the respite thus gained to make a final

[1] *Obelisk*, ll. 92, 93 ; *Bull No. 1*, ll. 47–50 : cf. AMIAUD and SCHEIL, *Les Inscr. de Salmanasar II.*, pp. 56–59.

[2] *Obelisk*, ll. 92, 93; *Bull No. 1*, ll. 47–50 : cf. AMIAUD and SCHEIL, *ibid.*, pp. 56–59. Ianzu, the name of the new Prince of Namri, appears to be a Cossæan term signifying *king*, applicable to all sovereigns, as that of Pharaoh in Egypt (FR. DELITZSCH, *Die Sprache der Kossäer*, pp. 25, 37–39) ; cf. *Struggle of the Nations*, p. 114.

[3] *Obelisk*, ll. 96, 97 ; cf. AMIAUD and SCHEIL, *Les Inscriptions de Salmanasar II.*, pp. 58, 59.

reckoning with the Israelites. It would appear that their fortune had been on the wane ever since the heroic death of Ahab. Immediately after the disaster at Ramoth, the Moabites had risen against Ahaziah,[1] and their king, Mesha, son of Kamoshgad, had seized the territory north of the Arnon which belonged to the tribe of Gad; he had either killed or carried away the Jewish population in order to colonise the district with Moabites, and he had then fortified most of the towns, beginning with Dhibon, his capital.[2] Owing to the shortness of his reign, Ahaziah had been unable to take measures to hinder him; but Joram, as soon as he was firmly seated on the throne, made every effort to regain possession of his province, and claimed the help of his ally or vassal Jehoshaphat.[3] The latter had done his best to repair the losses caused by the war with Syria. Being Lord of Edom, he had been tempted to follow the example of Solomon, and the deputy who commanded in his name had constructed a vessel * at Ezion-geber " to go to Ophir for gold; " but the vessel was wrecked before quitting the port, and the disaster was regarded by the king as a punishment from Jahveh, for when Ahaziah suggested that the enterprise should be renewed at their joint expense, he refused the offer.[4] But the sudden insurrection of Moab threatened him as much as it did Joram, and he gladly acceded to the latter's appeal for help. Apparently the simplest way of approaching the enemy would have been from the north, choosing Gilead as a base of operations; but the line of fortresses constructed by Mesha at this vulnerable point of his frontier was so formidable, that the allies resolved to attack from the south after passing the lower extremity of the Dead Sea. They marched for seven days in an arid desert, digging wells as they proceeded for the necessary supply of water. Mesha awaited them with his hastily

---

[1] 2 Kings iii. 5. The text does not name Ahaziah, and it might be concluded that the revolt took place under Joram (WINCKLER, Gesch. Israels, vol. i. pp. 206, 207); the expression employed by the Hebrew writer, however, " when Ahab was dead . . . the King of Moab rebelled against the King of Israel," does not permit of it being placed otherwise than at the opening of Ahaziah's reign.

[2] Inscription of Mesha, ll. 7–33; the name of the father of Mesha is uncertain, and the latter part of it has been read " malak: " Kamosh-malak would answer as well as Kamoshgad.

[3] 2 Kings iii. 6, 7, where Jehoshaphat replies to Joram in the same terms which he had used to Ahab (cf. supra, p. 76, note 4). The chronological difficulties induced ED. MEYER, Gesch. des Alterthums, vol. i. p. 395, to replace the name of Jehoshaphat in this passage by that of his son Jehoram. As Stade has remarked (Gesch. des Volkes Israel, vol. i. p. 536, note 1), the presence of two kings both bearing the name of Jehoram in the same campaign against Moab would have been one of those facts which strike the popular imagination, and would not have been forgotten; if the Hebrew author has connected the Moabite war with the name of Jehoshaphat, it is because his sources of information furnished him with that king's name.

* [Both in the Hebrew and the LXX. (MS. A.) the ships are in the plural number in 1 Kings xxii. 48, 49..—TR.]

[4] 1 Kings xxii. 48, 49, where the Hebrew writer calls the vessel constructed by Jehoshaphat a " ship of Tarshish; " that is, a vessel built to make long voyages. The author of the Chronicles thought that the Jewish expedition to Ezion-geber on the Red Sea was destined to go to Tarshish in Spain. He has, moreover, transformed the vessel into a fleet, and has associated Ahaziah in the enterprise, contrary to the testimony of the Book of Kings; finally, he has introduced into the account a prophet named Eliezer, who represents the disaster as a chastisement for the alliance with Ahaziah (2 Chron. xx. 35–37).

assembled troops on the confines of the cultivated land ; the allies routed him and blockaded him within his city of Kir-hareseth.[1] Closely beset, and despairing of any help from man, he had recourse to the last resource which religion provided for his salvation ; taking his firstborn son, he offered him to Chemosh, and burnt him on the city wall in sight of the besiegers. The Israelites knew what obligations this sacrifice entailed upon the Moabite god, and the succour which he would be constrained to give to his devotees in consequence. They therefore raised the siege and disbanded in all directions.[2] Mesha, delivered at the very moment that his cause seemed hopeless, dedicated a stele in the temple of Dhibôn, on which he recorded his victories and related what measures he had taken to protect his people.[3] He still feared a repetition of the invasion, but this misfortune was spared him ; Jehoshaphat was gathered to his fathers,[5] and his Edomite subjects revolted on receiving the news of his death. Jehoram,

THE MOABITE STONE OR STELE OF MESHA.[4]

his son and successor, at once took up arms to bring them to a sense of their duty ; but they surrounded his camp, and it was with difficulty that he cut his

[1] Kir-Hareseth or Kir-Moab is the present Kerak, the Krak of mediæval times.

[2] The account of the campaign (2 *Kings* iii. 8–27) belongs to the prophetic cycle of Elisha, and seems to give merely a popular version of the event. A king of Edom is mentioned (9–10, 12–13), while elsewhere, under Jehoshaphat, it is stated " there was no king in Edom " (1 *Kings* xxii. 47) ; the geography also of the route taken by the expedition is somewhat confused. Finally, the account of the siege of Kir-hareseth is mutilated, and the compiler has abridged the episode of the human sacrifice, as being too conducive to the honour of Chemosh and to the dishonour of Jahveh. The main facts of the account are correct, but the details are not clear, and do not all bear the stamp of veracity.

[3] This is the famous Moabite Stone or stele of Dhibôn, discovered by Clermont-Ganneau in 1868, and now preserved in the Louvre.

[4] From a photograph by Faucher-Gudin, retouched by Massias from the original in the Louvre. The fainter parts of the stele are the portions restored in the original.

[5] The date of the death of Jehoshaphat may be fixed as 849 or 848 B.C. The biblical documents give us for the period of the history of Judah following on the death of Ahab : First, eight years

way through their ranks and escaped during the night. The defection of the old Canaanite city of Libnah followed quickly on this reverse,[1] and Jehoram was powerless to avenge himself on it, the Philistines and the Bedâwin having threatened the western part of his territory and raided the country.[2] In the midst of these calamities Judah had no leisure to take further measures against Mesha, and Israel itself had suffered too severe a blow to attempt retaliation. The advanced age of Ben-hadad, and the unsatisfactory result of the campaigns against Shalmaneser, had furnished Joram with an occasion for a rupture with Damascus. War dragged on for some time apparently, till the tide of fortune turned against Joram, and, like his father Ahab in similar circumstances, he shut himself within Samaria, where the false alarm of an Egyptian or Hittite invasion produced a panic in the Syrian camp, and restored the fortunes of the Israelitish king.[3] Ben-hadad did not long survive the reverse he had experienced; he returned sick and at the point of death to Damascus, where he was assassinated by Hazael, one of his captains. Hebrew tradition points to the influence of the prophets in all these events. The aged Elijah had disappeared, so ran the story, caught up to heaven in a chariot of fire, but his mantle had fallen on Elisha, and his power still survived in his disciple.[4] From far and near Elisha's counsel was sought, alike by Gentiles as by the followers of the true God; whether the suppliant was the weeping Shunamite mourning for the loss of her only son,[5] or Naaman the captain of the Damascene chariotry,[6]

of Jehoshaphat, from the 17th year of his reign (1 *Kings* xxii. 51) to his 25th (and last) year (1 *Kings* xxii. 42); secondly, eight years of Jehoram, son of Jehoshaphat (2 *Kings* viii. 17); thirdly, one year of Ahaziah, son of Jehoram (2 *Kings* viii. 26)—in all 17 years, which must be reduced and condensed into the period between 853 B.C., the probable date of the battle of Ramoth, and 843, the equally probable date of the accession of Jehu. The reigns of the two Ahaziahs are too short to be further abridged; we must therefore place the campaign against Moab at the earliest in 850, during the months which followed the accession of Joram of Israel, and lengthen Jehoshaphat's reign from 850 to 849. There will then be room between 849 and 844 for five years (instead of eight) for the reign of Jehoram of Judah.

[1] 2 *Kings* viii. 20–22; cf. 2 *Chron.* xxi. 8–10.

[2] This war is mentioned only in 2 *Chron.* xxi. 16, 17, where it is represented as a chastisement from Jahveh; the Philistines and "the Arabs which are beside the Ethiopians" (Kush) seem to have taken Jerusalem, pillaged the palace, and carried away the wives and children of the king into captivity, "so that there was never a son left him, save Jehoahaz (Ahaziah), the youngest of his sons." The occurrence of the name of Kush, which had helped to discredit this passage, was first explained by Winckler (*Alttestamentliche Untersuchungen*, p. 635, etc.), who imagined it denoted the Cossæans; and subsequently by Hommel (*Inschriftliche Ergebnisse der vierten Reise Eduard Glaser's*, in the *Actes du Congrès de Genève*, 2nd sect., p. 112), who recognised in it the Kushites of Arabia, as did Glaser (*Skizze*, vol. ii. p. 339). Winckler (*Musri, Meluhha, Main*, i. pp. 1–3) has since adopted the opinion shared by Glaser and Hommel.

[3] Kuenen has proposed to take the whole account of the reign of Joram, son of Ahab, and transfer it to that of Jehoahaz, son of Jehu, and this theory has been approved by several recent critics and historians (KITTEL, *Geschichte der Hebræer*, vol. ii. pp. 186, 235, 249, 250; CORNILL, *Einleitung in das Alte Testament*, 2nd edit., p. 127). On the other hand, some have desired to connect it with the account of the siege of Samaria in Ahab's reign (WINCKLER, *Gesch. Israels*, vol. i. pp. 150, 151). I fail to see any reasonable argument which can be brought against the authenticity of the main fact, whatever opinion may be held with regard to the details of the biblical narrative.

[4] 2 *Kings* ii. 1–15.   [5] 2 *Kings* iv. 8–37.   [6] 2 *Kings* v.

he granted their petitions, and raised the child from its bed, and healed the soldier of his leprosy. During the siege of Samaria, he had several times frustrated the enemy's designs, and had predicted to Joram not only the fact but the hour of deliverance, and the circumstances which would accompany it.[1] Ben-hadad had sent Hazael to the prophet to ask him if he should recover, and Elisha had wept on seeing the envoy—"Because I know the evil that thou wilt do unto the children of Israel; their strongholds wilt thou set on fire, and their young men wilt thou slay with the sword, and wilt dash in pieces their little ones, and rip up their women with child. And Hazael said, But what is thy servant which is but a dog, that he should do this great thing? And Elisha answered, The Lord hath showed me that thou shalt be king over Syria." On returning to Damascus Hazael gave the results of his mission in a reassuring manner to Ben-hadad, but "on the morrow . . . he took the coverlet and dipped it in water, and spread it on his face, so that he died."[2]

The deed which deprived it of its king, seriously affected Damascus itself. It was to Ben-hadad that it owed most of its prosperity; he it was who had humiliated Hamath and the princes of the coast of Arvad, and the nomads of the Arabian desert. He had witnessed the rise of the most energetic of all the Israelite dynasties, and he had curbed its ambition; Omri had been forced to pay him tribute; Ahab, Ahaziah, and Joram had continued it; and Ben-hadad's suzerainty, recognised more or less by their vassals, had extended through Moab and Judah as far as the Red Sea. Not only had he skilfully built up this fabric of vassal states which made him lord of two-thirds of Syria, but he had been able to preserve it unshaken for a quarter of a century, in spite of rebellions in several of his fiefs and reiterated attacks from Assyria; Shalmaneser, indeed, had made an attack on his line, but without breaking through it, and had at length left him master of the field. This superiority, however, which no reverse could shake, lay in himself and in himself alone; no sooner had he passed away than it suddenly ceased, and Hazael found himself restricted from the very outset to the territory of Damascus proper.[3] Hamath, Arvad, and the northern peoples deserted the league, to return to it no more; Joram of Israel called on his nephew Ahaziah, who had just succeeded to Jehoram of Judah, and both together marched to besiege Ramoth. The Israelites were not successful in their methods of carrying on sieges; Joram, wounded in a skirmish, retired to his palace at Jezreel, where Ahaziah joined him a few days later, on the pretext of inquiring after his welfare.[4] The

---

[1] 2 *Kings* vi. 8–33; vii.   [2] 2 *Kings* viii. 7–15.

[3] From this point onward, the Assyrian texts which mentioned *the twelve kings of the Khâti*, Irkhulini of Hamath and Adadidri (Ben-hadad) of Damascus (cf. *supra*, p. 70, note 2), now only name *Khazailu of the country of Damascus* (*Obelisk*, ll. 97, 98, 103; cf. H. RAWLINSON, *Cun. Ins. W. As.*, vol. iii. pl. 5, No. 6, p. 41).   [4] 2 *Kings* viii. 28, 29.

prophets of both kingdoms and their followers had never forgiven the family of Ahab their half-foreign extraction, nor their eclecticism in the matter of religion. They had numerous partisans in both armies, and a conspiracy was set on foot against the absent sovereigns; Elisha, judging the occasion to be a propitious one, despatched one of his disciples to the camp with secret instructions. The generals were all present at a banquet, when the messenger arrived; he took one of them, Jehu, the son of Nimshi, on one side, anointed him, and then escaped. Jehu returned, and seated himself amongst his fellow-officers, who, unsuspicious of what had happened, questioned him as to the errand. "Is all well? Wherefore came this mad fellow to thee? And he said unto them, Ye know the man and what his talk was. And they said, It is false; tell us now. And he said, Thus and thus spake he to me, saying, Thus saith the Lord, I have anointed thee king over Israel. Then they hasted, and took every man his garment and put it under him on the top of the stairs, and blew the trumpet, saying, Jehu is king." He at once marched on Jezreel, and the two kings, surprised at this movement, went out to meet him with scarcely any escort. The two parties had hardly met when Joram asked, "Is it peace, Jehu?" to which Jehu replied, "What peace, so long as the whoredoms of thy mother Jezebel and her witchcrafts are so many?" Whereupon Joram turned rein, crying to his nephew, "There is treachery, O Ahaziah." But an arrow pierced him through the heart, and he fell forward in his chariot. Ahaziah, wounded near Ibleam, managed, however, to take refuge in Megiddo, where he died, his servants bringing the body back to Jerusalem.[1] When Jezebel heard the news, she guessed the fate which awaited her. She painted her eyes and tired her head, and posted herself in one of the upper windows of the palace. As Jehu entered the gates she reproached him with the words, "Is it peace, thou Zimri—thy master's murderer? And he lifted up his face to the window and said, Who is on my side—who? Two or three eunuchs rose up behind the queen, and he called to them, Throw her down. So they threw her down, and some of her blood was sprinkled on the wall and on the horses; and he trode her under foot. And when he was come in he did eat and drink; and he said, See now to this cursed woman and bury her; for she is a king's daughter." But nothing was found of her except her skull, hands, and feet, which they buried as best they could. Seventy princes, the entire family of Ahab, were slain, and their heads piled up on either side of the gate. The priests and worshippers of Baal remained to be dealt with. Jehu summoned them to

---

[1] According to the very curtailed account in 2 *Chron.* xxii. 9, Ahaziah appears to have hidden himself in Samaria, where he was discovered and taken to Jehu, who had him killed. This account may perhaps have belonged to the different version of which a fragment has been preserved in 2 *Kings* x. 12–17 (cf. *infra*, p. 85, note 2).

Samaria on the pretext of a sacrifice, and massacred them before the altars of their god.[1] According to a doubtful tradition, the brothers and relatives of Ahaziah, ignorant of what had happened, came to salute Joram, and perished in the confusion of the slaughter, and the line of David narrowly escaped extinction with the house of Omri.[2] Athaliah assumed the regency, broke the tie of vassalage which bound Judah to Israel, and by a singular irony of fate, Jerusalem offered an asylum to the last of the children of Ahab.[3] The treachery of Jehu, in addition to his inexpiable cruelty, terrified the faithful, even while it served their ends. Dynastic crimes were common in those days, but the tragedy of Jezreel eclipsed in horror all others that had preceded it; it was at length felt that such avenging of Jahveh was in His eyes too ruthless, and a century later the Prophet Hosea saw in the misery of his people the divine chastisement of the house of Jehu for the blood shed at his accession.[4]

The report of these events, reaching Calah, awoke the ambition of Shalmaneser. Would Damascus, mistrusting its usurper, deprived of its northern allies, and ill-treated by the Hebrews, prove itself as invulnerable as in the past? At all events, in 842 B.C., Shalmaneser once more crossed the Euphrates, marched along the Orontes, probably receiving the homage of Hamath and Arvad by the way. Restricted solely to the resources of Damascus, Hazael did not venture to advance into Cœle-Syria as Ben-hadad had always done; he barricaded the defiles of Anti-Lebanon, and, entrenched on Mount Shenir with the flower of his troops, prepared to await the attack. It proved the most bloody battle that the Assyrians had up to that period ever fought. Hazael lost 16,000 foot-soldiers, 470 horsemen, 1121 chariots, and yet succeeded in falling back on Damascus in good order. Shalmaneser, finding it impossible to force the city, devastated the surrounding country, burnt numberless villages and farms, and felled all the fruit trees in the Haurân up to the margin of the desert. This district had never, since the foundation of the kingdom by Rezon a century before, suffered at the hands of an enemy's army, and its population, enriched as much by peaceful labour as by the spoil of its successful wars, offered a prize of incalculable value. On his return march Shalmaneser raided the Bekaa, entered Phœnicia, and carved a

---

[1] 2 *Kings* ix.; x. 1–12, 18–27. For the date 843 B.C., which I should ascribe to these events, cf. *supra*, p. 77, note 2.

[2] 2 *Kings* x. 12–14. Stade (*Miscellen*, in the *Zeitschrift für Alttestamentliche Wissenschaft*, vol. v. p. 275, et seq.; cf. *Gesch. des Volkes Israel*, vol. i. pp. 544, 545) has shown that this account is in direct contradiction with its immediate context, and that it belonged to a version of the events differing in detail from the one which has come down to us. According to the latter, Jehu must at once have met Jehonadab the son of Rechab, and have entered Samaria in his company (vers. 15–17); this would have been a poor way of inspiring the priests of Baal with the confidence necessary for drawing them into the trap. According to 2 *Chron.* xxii. 8, the massacre of the princes of Judah preceded the murder of Ahaziah.

[3] 2 *Kings* xi. 1; cf. 2 *Chron.* xxii. 10.   [4] *Hosea* i. 4, 5.

triumphal stele on one of the rocks of Baalirasi.[1] The Kings of Tyre and
Sidon hastened to offer him numerous gifts, and Jehu, who owed to his
presence temporary immunity from a Syrian invasion, sent his envoys to greet
him, accompanied by offerings of gold and silver in bars, vessels of gold of
various forms, *situlæ*, salvers, cups, drinking-vessels, tin, sceptres, and wands
of precious woods. Shalmaneser's pride was flattered by this homage, and
he carved on one of his monuments the representation of this first official
connection of Assyria with Israel. The chief of the embassage is shown

JEHU, KING OF ISRAEL, SENDS PRESENTS TO SHALMANESER.[2]

prostrating himself and kissing the dust before the king, while the rest
advance in single file, some with vessels in their hands, some carrying sceptres,
or with metal bowls supported on their heads. The prestige of the house of
Omri was still a living influence, or else the Ninevite scribes were imperfectly
informed of the internal changes which had taken place in Israel, for the
inscription accompanying this bas-relief calls Jehu the son of Omri, and
grafts the regicide upon the genealogical tree of his victims.[3] Shalmaneser's
victory had been so dearly bought, that the following year the Assyrians
merely attempted an expedition for tree-felling in the Amanos (841 B.C.).
Their next move was to push forward into Kuî, in the direction of the Pyramos

---

[1] The site of Baalirasi is left undecided by Assyriologists. Fr. Delitzsch places it in the neighbourhood of Tyre or Sidon (*Wo lag das Paradies?* p. 104), and Schrader confines himself to translating the name (*Die Keilinschriften*, etc., 2nd ed., p. 211). The events which follow enable us to
affirm with tolerable certainty that the point on the coast where Shalmaneser received the tributes of
Tyre and Sidon is none other than the mouth of the Nahr-el-Kelb: the name Baalirasi, "the master
of the head," would then be applicable to the rocky point which rises to the south of the river, and
on which Egyptian kings had already sculptured their stelæ (cf. *Struggle of the Nations*, pp. 278, 427).

[2] Drawn by Faucher-Gudin, from one of the scenes represented on the Black Obelisk; cf. LAYARD,
The Monuments of Nineveh, vol. i. pl. 53. Cf. another bas-relief of the same monument, representing
the Jews, on the opposite page.

[3] *Obelisk*, ll. 97–99, where the defeat of Hazael is alone mentioned. The other events are known
to us from a fragment published in H. RAWLINSON, *Cun. Ins. W. As.*, vol. iii. pl. 5, No. 6, ll. 40–65;
cf. AMIAUD and SCHEIL, *Les Inscriptions de Salmanasar II.*, pp. 56–59.

and Saros (840 B.C.).[1] In the summer of 839 they once more ventured southwards, but this time Hazael changed his tactics: pitched battles and massed movements, in which the fate of a campaign was decided by one cast of the dice, were now avoided, and ambuscades, guerilla warfare, and long and tedious sieges became the order of the day.   By the time that four towns had been taken, Shalmaneser's patience was worn out; he drew off his troops and

PART OF ISRAEL'S TRIBUTE TO SHALMANESER.[2]

fell back on Phœnicia, laying Tyre, Sidon, and Byblos under tribute before returning into Mesopotamia.[3]   Hazael had shown himself possessed of no less energy than Ben-hadad; and Damascus, isolated, had proved as formidable a foe as Damascus surrounded by its vassals; Shalmaneser therefore preferred to leave matters as they were, and accept the situation.   Indeed, the results obtained were of sufficient importance to warrant his feeling some satisfaction. He had ruthlessly dispelled the dream of Syrian hegemony which had buoyed up Ben-hadad, he had forced Damascus to withdraw the suzerainty it had exercised in the south, and he had conquered Northern Syria and the lower basin of the Orontes.   Before running any further risks, he judged it prudent to strengthen his recently acquired authority over these latter countries, and to accustom the inhabitants to their new position as subjects of Nineveh.

He showed considerable wisdom by choosing the tribes of the Taurus and of the Cappadocian marches as the first objects of attack. In regions so difficult of access, war could only be carried on with considerable hardship and

---

[1] *Obelisk*, ll. 99–102; cf. AMIAUD and SCHEIL, *Les Inscriptions de Salmanasar II.*, pp. 60, 61.

[2] Drawn by Faucher-Gudin, from one of the bas-reliefs of the Black Obelisk; cf. LAYARD, *The Monuments of Nineveh*, vol. i. pl. 56.

[3] *Obelisk*, ll. 102–104; cf. AMIAUD and SCHEIL, *ibid.*, pp. 60–63.

severe loss. The country was seamed by torrents and densely covered with undergrowth, while the towns and villages, which clung to the steep sides of the valleys, had no need of walls to become effective fortresses, for the houses rose abruptly one above another, and formed so many redoubts which the enemy would be forced to attack and take one by one. Few pitched battles could be fought in a district of this description; the Assyrians wore themselves out in incessant skirmishes and endless petty sieges,

A MOUNTAIN VILLAGE.[1]

and were barely compensated by the meagre spoil which such warfare yielded. In 838 B.C. Shalmaneser swept over the country of Tabal and reduced twenty-four of its princes to a state of subjection; proceeding thence, he visited the mountains of Turat,[2] celebrated from this period downwards for their silver mines and quarries of valuable marbles. In 837 he seized the stronghold of Uêtash in Melitene, and laid Tabal under a fresh contribution; this constituted a sort of advance post for Assyria in the sight of those warlike and continually fluctuating races situated between the sources of the Halys and the desert border of Asia Minor.[3] Secure on this side, he was about to bring matters to

---

[1] Drawn by Boudier, from a photograph by Alfred Boissier.

[2] The position of the mountains of Turat is indicated by the nature of their products: "We know of *a silver mine* at Marash and an iron mine not worked, and *two fine quarries*, one of pink and the other of black marble" (VITAL CUINET, *La Turquie d'Asie*, vol. ii. p. 138; cf. p. 231). Turat, therefore, must be the Marash mountain, the Aghir-Dagh and its spurs; hence the two sorts of stone mentioned in the Assyrian text would be, the one the pink, the other the black marble (MASPERO, *Notes au jour le jour*, § 33, in the *Proceedings* of the Bibl. Arch. Soc., 1898, vol. xx. pp. 133, 134).

[3] *Obelisk*, ll. 104–110; cf. AMIAUD and SCHEIL, *Les Inscriptions de Salmanasar II.*, pp. 62, 63. A fragment of an anonymous list, discovered by Delitzsch, puts the expedition against the Tabal in 837 B.C. instead of in 838, and consequently makes the entire series of ensuing expeditions one year

a close in Cilicia, when the defection of Ianzu recalled him to the opposite
extremity of the empire. He penetrated into Namri by the defiles of
Khashmur,[1] made a hasty march through Sikhisatakh, Bît-Tamul, Bît-Shakki,

ELEPHANT AND MONKEYS BROUGHT AS A TRIBUTE TO NINEVEH BY THE PEOPLE OF MUZRI.[2]

and Bît-Shedi, surprised the rebels and drove them into the forests; he then
bore down on Parsua[3] and plundered twenty-seven petty kings consecutively;
skirting Misi, Amadai, Araziash,[4] and Kharkhar, and most of the districts

later, up to the revolt of Assur-dain-pal. This is evidently a mistake of the scribe who compiled
this edition of the Canon, and the chronology of a contemporary monument, such as the Black
Obelisk, ought to obtain until further light can be thrown on the subject.

[1] For the site of Khashmur or Khashmar, cf. *supra*, p. 24, note 2. The other localities cannot as
yet be identified with any modern site; we may conjecture that they were scattered about the basin
of the upper Dîyalah.

[2] Drawn by Faucher-Gudin, from one of the bas-reliefs of the Black Obelisk; cf. LAYARD, *The
Monuments of Nineveh*, vol. i. pl. 55.

[3] Parsua, or with the native termination Parsuash, has been identified first with Persia and then
with Parthia, and Rost still persists in its identification, if not with the Parthia of classical
geographers, at least with the Parthian people (*Untersuchungen zur altorientalischen Geschichte*,
p. 74, note 2). Schrader has shown that it ought to be sought between Namri on the south and the
Mannai on the north, in one of the valleys of the Gordyæan mountains (*Keilinschriften*, etc., pp. 169–
179), and his demonstration has been accepted with a few modifications of detail by most scholars
(DELATTRE, *Le Peuple et l'Empire des Mèdes*, pp. 68–72; HOMMEL, *Gesch. Bab. und Ass.*, pp. 593, 594;
WINCKLER, *Gesch. Bab. und Ass.*, p. 199). I believe it to be possible to determine its position with
still further precision. Parsua on one side lay on the border of Namri, which comprises the districts
to the east of the Dîyalah in the direction of Zohab (cf. *Struggle of the Nations* for Namar or Namri,
p. 606), and was contiguous to the Medes on the other side (*Obelisk*, ll. 119–121), and also to the
Mannai, who occupied the southern regions of Lake Urumiah (*Great Inscription of Samsi-rammân*,
col. ii. ll. 39, 40, *Slab Inscription of Rammân-nirâri*, l. 8, *Cylinder Inscription of Sargon*, l. 15); it
also lies close to Bît-Khamban, the principal of the Cossæan tribes (FR. DELITZSCH, *Die Sprache der
Kossäer*, pp. 35–37), as it would appear (*Cylinder Inscr. of Sargon*, l. 15). I can find only one position
on the map which would answer to all these requirements: this is in the main the basin of the
Gavê-rud and its small affluents, the Ardelân and the sources of the Kizil-Uzên, and I shall there
place Parsua until further information is forthcoming on the subject.

[4] Amadaî is a form of Madaî, with a prothetical *a*, like Agusi or Azala, by the side of Guzi and
Zala. The inscription of Shalmaneser III. thus gives us the first mention of the classical Medes, as
H. Rawlinson has from the first pointed out (*J. R. As. Soc.*, 1st ser., vol. xv. p. 242). This identifica-
tion has not been contested of latter years except by Delattre (*Le Peuple et l'Empire des Mèdes*, p. 74).
Araziash, placed too far to the east in Sagartenê by Fr. Lenormant (*Lettres Assyriologiques*, vol. i.

lying on the middle heights of the table-land of Iran, he at length came up with Ianzu, whom he seized and brought back prisoner to Assyria, together with his family and his idols.[1] It was at this juncture, perhaps, that he received from the people of Muzri the gift of an elephant and some large monkeys, representations of which he has left us on one of his bas-reliefs. Elephants were becoming rare, and it was not now possible to kill them by the hundred, as formerly, in Syria:[2] this particular animal, therefore, excited the wonder of the Ninevites, and the possession of it flattered the vanity of the conqueror. This was, however, an interlude of short duration, and the turbulent tribes of the Taurus recalled him to the west as soon as spring set in. He laid waste Kuî in 836 B.C., destroyed Timur, its capital, and on his return march revenged himself on Aramê of Agusi, whose spirit was still unbroken by his former misfortunes. Tanakun and Tarsus fell into his hands 835 B.C.; Shalmaneser replaced Kati, the King of Kuî, by his brother Kirri, and made of his dominions a kind of buffer state between his own territory and that of Pamphylia and Lycaonia.[3] He had now occupied the throne for a quarter of a century, not a year of which had elapsed without seeing the monarch gird on his armour and lead his soldiers in person towards one or other points of the horizon. He was at length weary of such perpetual warfare, and advancing age perchance prevented him from leading his troops with that dash and vigour which are necessary to success; however this might be, on his return from Cilicia he laid aside his armour once for all, and devoted himself to peaceful occupations.

But he did not on that account renounce all attempts at conquest. Conducting his campaigns by proxy, he delegated the command of his army to his Tartan Dayân-assur,[4] and the northern tribes were the first on whom this general gave proof of his prowess. Urartu had passed into the hands of another sovereign since its defeat in 845 B.C., and a second Sharduris[5] had

---

p. 25), has been located further westwards by Schrader (*Keilinschriften*, etc., p. 178), near the upper course of the Kerkhâ; but the documents of all periods which Schrader himself cites (*op. cit.*, p. 172, 173) show us that on one side it adjoined Kharkhar, that is the basin of the Gamas-âb, on the other side Media, that is the country of Hamadan. It must, therefore, be placed between the two, in the northern part of the ancient Cambadenê (ISIDOROS OF CHARAX, § 85, in MÜLLER-DIDOT, *Geographi Græci minores*, vol. i. p. 250), in the present Tchamabadân. Kharkhar in this case would be in the southern part of Cambadene, on the main road which leads from the gates of the Zagros to Hamadan, as Lenormant pointed out some time ago, while ascribing too large an area to it (*Lettres Assyriologiques*, vol. i. pp. 24, 43, 44); an examination of the general features of the country leads me to believe that the town of Kharkhar should occupy the site of Kirmânshahân, or rather of the ancient city which preceded that town (J. DE MORGAN, *Mission Scientifique en Perse*, etc., vol. ii. pp. 100–104).

[1] *Obelisk*, ll. 110–126; cf. AMIAUD and SCHEIL, *Les Inscriptions de Salmanasar II.*, pp. 62–65; ROST, *Untersuchungen zur alt. Gesch.*, pp. 74–76.

[2] See *Struggle of the Nations*, pp. 265, 284, 285.

[3] *Obelisk*, ll. 126–141; cf. AMIAUD and SCHIEL, *op. cit.*, pp. 64–67. The fragment of the eponym list, pointed out by Delitzsch (HOMMEL, *Ges. Bab. und Ass.*, p. 616, n.), inserts here, by mistake, a fresh expedition to Kuî, which obliges the scribe to antedate by a year all the ensuing expeditions (cf. *supra*, p. 88, n. 3).

[4] For the function of the Tartan, and the rank occupied by this officer at the Assyrian court, cf. *Struggle of the Nations*, pp. 620, 621.

[5] The name is written Siduri or Seduri in the text of the Obelisk (l. 144), probably in accordance

taken the place of the Aramê who had ruled at the beginning of Shalmaneser's reign. It would appear that the accession of this prince, who was probably young and active, was the signal for a disturbance among the people of the Upper Tigris and the Masios—a race always impatient of the yoke, and ready to make common cause with any fresh enemy of Assyria. An insurrection broke out in Bît-Zamani and the neighbouring districts. Dayân-assur quelled it offhand; then, quitting the basin of the Tigris by the defiles of Armash, he crossed the Arzania, and entered Urartu. Sharduris came out to meet him, and was defeated, if we may give credence to the official record of the campaign. Even if the account be an authentic one, the victory was of no advantage to the Assyrians, for they were obliged to retreat before they had subjugated the enemy,[1] and an insurrection among the Patinâ prevented them from returning to the attack in the following year. With obligations to their foreign master on one hand and to their own subjects on the other, the princes of the Syrian states had no easy life. If they failed to fulfil their duties as vassals, then an Assyrian invasion would pour in to their country, and sooner or later their ruin would be assured; they would have before them the prospect of death by impaling or under the knife of the flayer, or, if they escaped this, captivity and exile in a far-off land. Prudence therefore dictated a scrupulous fidelity to their suzerain. On the other hand, if they resigned themselves to their dependent condition, the people of their towns would chafe at the payment of tribute, or some ambitious relative would take advantage of the popular discontent to hatch a plot and foment a revolution, and the prince thus threatened would escape from an Assyrian reprisal only to lose his throne or fall by the blow of an assassin. In circumstances such as these the people of the Patinâ murdered their king, Lubarna II., and proclaimed in his room a certain Surri, who had no right to the crown, but who doubtless undertook to liberate them from the foreigner. Dayân-assur defeated the rebels and blockaded the remains of their army in Kinalua. They defended themselves at first energetically, but on the death of Surri from some illness, their courage failed them, and they offered to deliver over the sons of their chief if their own lives might be spared. Dayân-assur had the poor wretches impaled, laid the inhabitants under a heavy contribution, and appointed a certain Sâsi, son of Uzza,[2] to be their king. The remainder of Syria gave no further trouble—a fortunate circumstance, for the countries on the Armenian

---

with some popular pronunciation, in which the *r* was but slightly rolled and finally disappeared. The identity of Seduri and Sharduris, pointed out by Sayce (*The Cuneiform Inscriptions of Van*, in the *J. R. As. Soc.*, vol. xiv. p. 44), has been adopted by recent historians (TIELE, *Babylonisch-Assyrische Gesch.*, pp. 203, 215; HOMMEL, *Gesch. Bab. und Ass.*, pp. 600–602; WINCKLER, *Gesch. Bab. und Ass.*, pp. 197, 198). Belck and Lehmann have shown that this Seduri was not Sharduris, son of Lutipris, but a Sharduris II., probably the son of Aramê; cf. for this first Sharduris, p. 62 of the present work.

[1] *Black Obelisk*, ll. 141–146; cf. AMIAUD and SCHEIL, *Les Inscriptions de Salmanasar II.*, pp. 66, 67.
[2] *Black Obelisk*, ll. 146–156; cf. AMIAUD and SCHEIL, *ibid.*, pp. 66, 67.

border revolted in 832 B.C., and the whole year was occupied in establishing order among the herdsmen of Kirkhi.   In 831 B.C., Dayân-assur pushed forward into

Khubushkia, and traversed it from end to end without encountering any resistance.   He next attacked the Mannai.   Their prince, Ualki, quailed before his onslaught; he deserted his royal city Zirtu,[1] and took refuge in the mountains.   Dayân-assur pursued him thither in vain, but he was able to collect considerable booty, and turning in a south-easterly direction, he fought his way along the base of the Gordyæan mountains till he reached Parsua, which he laid under tribute.[2]   In 830 B.C. it was the turn of Muzazir, which hitherto had escaped invasion, to receive a visit from the Tartan.   Zapparia, the capital, and fifty-six other towns were given over to the flames.   From thence, Dayân-assur passed into Urartu proper; after having plundered it, he fell back on the southern provinces, collecting by the way the tribute of Guzân, of the Mannai, of Andiu,[3] and Parsua; he then pushed on into the heart of Namri, and having razed to the ground two hundred and fifty of its towns, returned with his troops to Assyria by the defiles of Shimishi and through Khalman.[5]   This was perhaps the last foreign campaign of Shalmaneser III.'s reign; it is at all events the last of which we possess any history.   The record of his exploits ends, as it had begun more than thirty years

BLACK OBELISK OF SHALMANESER III.[4] previously, with a victory in Namri.

The aged king had, indeed, well earned the right to end his allotted days in peace.   Devoted to Calah, like his predecessor, he had there accumulated

[1] The town is elsewhere called Izirtu (*Great Inscription of Sargon at Khorsabad*, l. 42), and appears to have been designated in the inscriptions of Van by the name of Sisiri-Khadiris (SAYCE, *The Cuneiform Inscriptions of Van*, in the *J. R. As. Soc.*, vol. xiv. p. 400).

[2] *Black Obelisk*, ll. 166–174; cf. AMIAUD and SCHEIL, *Les Inscriptions de Salmanasar II.*, pp. 66–69.

[3] Andia or Andiu is contiguous to Naîri (*Slab Inscr. of Rammân-nirâri IV.*, l. 19; cf. L. ABEL, *Inschriften Rammân-nirâri's III.*, in SCHRADER, *Keilinschriften Bibl.*, vol. i. pp. 188, 189), to Zikirtu and to Karalla, which latter borders on Manna (*Inscription on the Bulls of Sargon*, ll. 8, 9); it bordered on the country of Misa or Misi, into which it is merged under the name of Misianda in the time of Sargon (*Inscription des Fastes*, l. 37). Delattre (*Le Peuple et l'Empire des Mèdes*, pp. 82, 83) places Andiu in the country of the classical Matienæ, between the Matiænian mountains and Lake Urumiah. The position of Misu on the confines of Araziash and Media, somewhere in the neighbourhood of Talyantu-Dagh, obliges us to place Andiu lower down to the south-east, near the district of Kurdasir.

[4] Drawn by Faucher-Gudin, from the cast in the Louvre. [The original is in the Brit. Mus.—TR.]

[5] *Obelisk*, ll. 174–190; cf. AMIAUD and SCHEIL, *Les Inscriptions de Salmanasar II.*, pp. 70, 71. The fragment of the eponymous list pointed out by Delitzsch (cf. *supra*, p. 88, note 3) omits this last

the spoils of his campaigns, and had made it the wealthiest city of his empire. He continued to occupy the palace of Assur-nazir-pal, which he had enlarged. Wherever he turned within its walls, his eyes fell upon some trophy of his wars or panegyric of his virtues, whether recorded on mural tiles covered with inscriptions and bas-reliefs, or celebrated by statutes, altars, and triumphal stelæ. The most curious among all these is a square-based block terminating in three receding stages, one above the other, like the stump of an Egyptian obelisk surmounted by a stepped pyramid. Five rows of bas-reliefs on it represent scenes most flattering to Assyrian pride;—the reception of tribute

STAG AND LIONS OF THE COUNTRY OF SUKHI.[1]

from Gilzân, Muzri, the Patinâ, the Israelitish Jehu, and Marduk-abal-uzur, King of the land of Sukhi. The latter knew his suzerain's love of the chase, and he provided him with animals for his preserves, including lions, and rare species of deer. The inscription on the monument briefly relates the events which had occurred between the first and the thirty-first years of Shalmaneser's reign;—the defeat of Damascus, of Babylon and Urartu, the conquest of Northern Syria, of Cilicia, and of the countries bordering on the Zagros.[2] When the king left Calah for some country residence in its neighbourhood, similar records and carvings would meet his eye. At Imgur-Bel, one of the gates of the palace was covered with plates of bronze, on which the skilful artist has embossed and engraved with the chisel episodes from the campaigns

expedition, for which no available place could be found, after the insertion of the campaign against the Kuî, mentioned on p. 90, note 3, of the present work. For Khalman, see *Struggle of the Nations*, p. 615 ; as it corresponds, as Lenormant was the first to point out (*Lettres Assyriologiques*, vol. i. p. 41 ; cf. Fr. Delitzsch, *Die Sprache der Kossäer*, pp. 31, 34), to Khalonê (Diodorus Siculus, xvii. 110) or to Khala (Isidoros of Charax, § 53, in Müller-Didot, *Geographi Græci Minores*, vol. i. p. 250) of the classical period, the passes of Simishi necessarily coincide with the gates of the Zagros (Lenormant, *Lettres Assyriologiques*, vol. i. p. 41).

[1] Drawn by Faucher-Gudin, from one of the bas-reliefs of the Black Obelisk ; cf. Layard, *The Monuments of Nineveh*, vol. i. pl. 53.

[2] Most of the scenes on the Black Obelisk of Shalmaneser III. have been reproduced in the *Struggle of the Nations*, p. 661, and on pp. 86, 87, 89, and 93 of the present work.

on the Euphrates and the Tigris, the crossing of mountains and rivers, the assault and burning of cities, the long lines of captives, the *mêlée* with the enemy and the pursuit of the chariots.[1] All the cities of Assyria,— Nineveh,[2] Arbela, Assur, even to the more distant towns of Harrân[3] and Tushkhân,[4]—vied with each other in exhibiting proofs of his zeal for their gods and his affection for their inhabitants; but his predilection for Calah filled them with jealousy, and Assur particularly could ill brook the growing aversion with which the Assyrian kings regarded her. It was of no avail that she continued to be the administrative and religious capital of the empire, the storehouse of the spoil and annual tribute of other nations,[5] and was continually embellishing herself with fresh monuments:[6] a spirit of discontent was daily increasing, and merely awaited some favourable occasion to break out into open revolt. Shalmaneser enjoyed the dignity of *limmu* for the second time after thirty years, and had celebrated this jubilee of his inauguration by a solemn festival in honour of Assur and Rammân.[7] It is possible that he may have thought this a favourable moment for presenting to the people the son whom he had chosen from among his children to succeed him. At any rate, Assur-dain-pal, fearing that one of his brothers might be preferred before him, proclaimed himself king, and nearly the whole of Assyria gathered around his standard. Assur and twenty-six more of the most important cities revolted in his favour— Nineveh, Imgurbel, Sibaniba, Durbalat, Arbela, Zabân in the Chaldæan marches, Arrapkha in the valley of the Upper Zab, and most of the colonies,

[1] This monument, discovered by native diggers, was first brought into notice by G. Schlumberger, who bought small fragments of it, which were at once explained by Fr. Lenormant (*Bas-reliefs de bronze Assyriens*, in the *Gazette Archéologique*, 1878, pp. 119–129, and pls. xxii.–xxiv.). Nearly all the bas-reliefs were subsequently discovered and acquired for the authorities of the British Museum by Hormuzd Rassam, and published under the auspices of the Bibl. Arch. Soc. (BIRCH, *The Bronze Ornaments of the Palace Gate from Balawât*, Nos. 1–4; cf. HORMUZD RASSAM, *Asshur and the Land of Nimrod*, p. 200, et seq.). Numerous parts of them have been reproduced in the *Struggle of the Nations*, pp. 629, 630, 631, 638, 639, 641, 657, 658, 660, and also on pp. 7, 8, 9, 37, 61, 62, 63, 65, 68 of the present work.

[2] Nineveh is mentioned as the starting-place of nearly all the first campaigns in the inscription on the *Monolith*, col. i. No. 29, col. ii. ll. 14, 30, 67, 78; also in the Balawât inscription, col. iv. l. 5; on the other hand, towards the end of the reign, Calah is given as the residence of the king on the *Black Obelisk*, ll. 146, 147, 159, 160, 175, 176.

[3] Mention of the buildings of Shalmaneser III. at Harrân occurs in an inscription of Nabonidus (H. RAWLINSON, *Cun. Ins. W. As.*, vol. v. pl. 64, col. ii. l. 4; cf. LATRILLE, *Der Nabonid Cylinder V R 64*, in the *Zeitschrift für Keilforschung*, vol. ii. pp. 246, 247, 335).

[4] The Monolith discovered at Kurkh (RAWLINSON, *Cun. Ins. W. As.*, vol. iii. pls. 7, 8) is in itself a proof that Shalmaneser executed works in this town, the Tushkhân of the inscriptions (cf. for this town, *supra*, p. 20).

[5] Indications of booty and tribute brought in to the city of Assur, *Monolith*, col. i. ll. 27–29, col. ii. ll. 23, 24, 64, 65, 75–81; *Black Obelisk*, l. 140.

[6] These works are described in the inscription on the statue of Kalah-Shergât (LAYARD, *Inscriptions in the Cuneiform Character*, pls. 76, 77; cf. AMIAUD and SCHEIL, *Les Inscr. de Salmanasar II.*, pp. 74–77; J. A. CRAIG, *The Throne-Inscription of Salmanasar II.*, in *Hebraica*, vol. ii. pp. 140–146).

[7] *Obelisk*, ll. 174, 175; cf. AMIAUD and SCHEIL, *Les Inscr. de Salmanasar II.*, pp. 70, 71. Any connection established between this thirty-year jubilee and the thirty years' festival of Egypt (TIELE, *Bab. Ass. Gesch.*, p. 204) rests on facts which can be so little relied on, that it must be accepted with considerable reserve.

both of ancient and recent foundation—Amidi on the Tigris, Khindanu near the mouths of the Khabur and Tul-Abni on the southern slopes of the Masios. The aged king remained in possession only of Calah and its immediate environs—Nisibis, Harrân, Tushkhân, and the most recently subdued provinces on the banks of the Euphrates and the Orontes. It is probable, however, that the army remained faithful to him, and the support which these well-tried troops afforded him enabled the king to act with promptitude. The weight of years did not permit him to command in person; he therefore entrusted the conduct of operations to his son Samsi-rammân, but he did not live to see the end of the struggle. It embittered his last days, and was not terminated till 822 B.C., at which date Shalmaneser had been dead two years.[1] This prolonged crisis had shaken the kingdom to its foundations; the Syrians, the Medes, the Babylonians, and the peoples of the Armenian

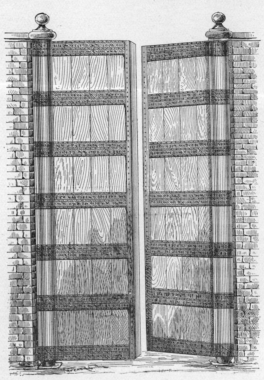

THE BRONZE-COVERED GATES OF BALAWÂT.[2]

and Aramæan marches were rent from it, and though Samsi-rammân IV. waged continuous warfare during the twelve years that he governed, he could only partially succeed in regaining the territory which had been thus lost.[3]

---

[1] *Eponym Canon* in DELITZSCH, art. *Sanherib*, in the *Bibel-Lexicon*, p. 392, where, from the thirty-third year of Shalmaneser (827 B.C.) to the third year of Samsi-rammân (822), we read, after the eponymous name, the word for "revolt;" the list of the rebel towns has been preserved at the beginning of the *Monolith Inscription of Samsi-rammân,* col. i. ll. 35–53; cf. AMIAUD and SCHEIL, *Les Inscriptions de Salmanasar II.,* pp. 84, 85, and SCHEIL, *Inscription Assyrienne archaïque de Shamshi-Rammân IV.,* pp. 6, 7. Tiele attributes the revolt of Assur-dain-pal to the jealousy which that prince entertained for the Tartan Dayân-assur (*Bab. Ass. Gesch.,* pp. 193, 194); Hommel believes that Assur-dain-pal had hoped to be called to the throne after the celebration of the thirtieth year, and that the disappointment he felt induced him to revolt (*Gesch. Bab. und Ass.,* pp. 615, 616).

[2] Drawn by Faucher-Gudin, from the sketch by PINCHES, in the *Transactions of the Bibl. Arch. Soc.,* vol. vii., plate between pp. 86 and 87.

[3] All that we know of the reign of Samsi-rammân IV. comes from the inscription in archaic characters, published in H. RAWLINSON, *Cun. Ins. W. As.,* vol. i. pls. 29, 34, translated into English by SAYCE, *Monolith Inscription of Samas-Rimmon,* in the *Records of the Past,* 1st ser., vol. i. pp. 9–22; into German by L. ABEL, *Inschrift Schamschi-Rammân's,* in SCHRADER, *Keilinschriftliche Bibliothek,* vol. i. pp. 174–187; into French by OPPERT, *Hist. des Empires de Chaldée et d'Assyrie,* pp. 122–128; by MÉNANT, *Annales des Rois d'Assyrie,* pp. 119–124; and by SCHEIL, *L'Inscription de Shamshi-Rammân IV. roi d'Assyrie* (824–811 B.C.), etc., 1889, in-4°. It contains the account of four campaigns, without giving the years of each reign or the *limmu,* and historians have classified them

His first three campaigns were directed against the north-eastern and eastern provinces. He began by attempting to collect the tribute from Naîri, the payment of which had been suspended since the outbreak of the revolution, and he re-established the dominion of Assyria from the district of Paddir to the township of Kar-Shulmânasharid, which his father had founded at the fords of the Euphrates opposite to Carchemish [1] (821 B.C.). In the following campaign he did not personally take part, but the Rabshakeh Mutarriz-assur pillaged the shores of Lake Urumiah, and then made his way towards Urartu, where he destroyed three hundred towns [2] (820). The third expedition was directed against Misi and Gizilbunda beyond the Upper Zab and Mount Zilar.[3] The inhabitants of Misi entrenched themselves on a wooded ridge commanded by three peaks, but were defeated in spite of the advantages which their position secured for them; [4] the people of Gizilbunda were not more fortunate than their neighbours, and six thousand of them perished at the assault of Urash, their capital.[5] Mutarriz-assur at once turned upon the

---

in different ways. Tiele believes that the last of them falls at the latest in 818 (*Bab.–Ass. Gesch.*, pp. 204, 205), and that none of the expeditions mentioned in it answer to those contained in the *Eponym Canon* (SCHRADER, *Keil. Bibl.*, vol. i. pp. 208, 209); to this opinion Winckler gives his adhesion (*Gesch. Bab. und Ass.*, pp. 202, 203). Hommel distributes them over the whole length of the reign, the three first from 822 to 818 (*Gesch. Bab. und Ass.*, p. 626), the fourth in 815 (*Id.*, p. 623).

[1] *Monolith Inscription of Samsi-rammân IV.*, col. i. l. 53, col. ii. ll. 1–16; cf. L. ABEL, *Inschrift Schamschi-Rammân's*, in SCHRADER, *Keil. Bibl.*, vol. i. pp. 178, 179, and SCHEIL, *Inscription assyrienne archaïque de Shamshi-Rammân IV.*, pp. 6–9.

[2] *Monolith Inscription of Samsi-rammân IV.*, col. ii. ll. 16–34; cf. L. ABEL, *Inschrift Schamschi-Rammân's*, pp. 178, 179, and SCHEIL, *Inscription ass. archaïque*, etc., pp. 8–11.

[3] Mount Zilar (Gullar in SCHEIL, *op. cit.*, pp. 10, 11) is beyond the Upper Zab, on one of the roads which lead to the basin of Lake Urumiah, probably in Khubushkia. There are two of these roads—that which passes over the neck of Kelishin, and the other which runs through the gorges of Alân; "with the exception of these two points the mountain chain is absolutely impassable" (J. DE MORGAN, *Mission scientifique en Perse, Études géographiques*, vol. ii. p. 46). According to the general direction of the campaign, it appears to me probable that the king crossed by the passes of Alân; Mount Zilâr would therefore be the group of chains which cover the district of Pîshder, and across which the Lesser Zab passes before descending to the plain.

[4] The country of Misi adjoined Gizilbunda (*Monolith Inscr.*, etc., col. ii. ll. 41–59), Media, Araziâsh (*Inscr. of Rammân-nirâri IV.*, ll. 6, 7), and Andiu (cf. *supra*, p. 92, note 3). All these circumstances incline us to place it in the south-eastern part of Kurdistan of Sihmeh, in the upper valley of Kisil-Uzên. The ridge, overlooked by three peaks, on which the inhabitants took refuge, cannot be looked for on the west, where there are few important heights: I should rather identify it with the part of the Gordyæan mountains which bounds the basin of the Kisil-Uzên on the west, and which contains three peaks of 12,000 feet—the Tchehel-tchechma, the Derbend, and the Nau-Kân (J. DE MORGAN, *Mission scientifique en Perse, Études géographiques*, vol. ii. p. 51).

[5] The name of the country has been read Giratbunda (OPPERT, *Hist. des Empires d'Assyrie et de Chaldée*, p. 125; MÉNANT, *Annales des rois d'Assyrie*, p. 121), Ginunbunda (SCHRADER, *Keil. und Geschichtsforschung*, p. 71, note 2), Girubbunda (SAYCE, *Monolith Inscription of Samas Rimmon*, in the *Records of the Past*, vol. i. p. 16); a variant, to which no objections can be made, has furnished Gizilbunda (HOMMEL, *Gesch. Bab. und Ass.*, p. 625, note 2; L. ABEL, *Inschrift Schamschi-Rammân's*, in SCHRADER, *Keil. Bibl.*, vol. i. p. 180). It was contiguous on one side to the Medes (*Monolith Inscr.*, etc., col. iii. ll. 7–27, *Inscription of Rammân-nirâri IV.*, l. 7), and on the other to the Mannai (*op. cit.*, ll. 7, 8), which obliges us to place it in Kurdistan of Gerrus, on the Kizil-Uzên. It may be asked if the word Kizil which occurs several times in the topographical nomenclature of these regions is not a relic of the name in question, and if Gizil-bunda is not a compound of the same class as Kizil-uzên, Kizil-gatchi, Kizil-alân, Kizil-lôk, whether it be that part of the population spoke a language analogous to the dialects now in use in these districts, or that the ancient word has been preserved by later conquerors and assimilated to some well-known word in their own language.

Medes, vanquished them, and drove them at the point of the sword into their remote valleys, returning to the district of Araziash, which he laid waste. A score of chiefs with barbarous names, alarmed by this example, hastened to prostrate themselves at his feet, and submitted to the tribute which he imposed on them. Assyria thus regained in these regions the ascendency which the victories of Shalmaneser III. in their time had won for her.[1]

Babylon, which had endured the suzerainty of its rival for a quarter of a century, seems to have taken advantage of the events occurring in Assyria to throw off the yoke, by espousing the cause of Assur-dain-pal. Samsi-rammân, therefore, as soon as he was free to turn his attention from Media (818), directed his forces against Babylonia. Meturnât, as usual, was the first city attacked ; it capitulated at once, and its inhabitants were exiled to Assyria. Karni to the south of the Turnat, and Dibina on Mount Yalmân, suffered the same fate, but Gananâtê held out for a time; its garrison, however, although reinforced by troops from the surrounding country, was utterly routed before its walls, and the survivors, who fled for refuge to the citadel in the centre of the town, were soon dislodged. The Babylonians, who had apparently been taken by surprise

MONOLITH OF SAMSI-RAMMÂN IV.[2]

at the first attack, at length made preparations to resist the invaders. The Prince of Dur-papsukal, who owned allegiance to Marduk-balatsu-ikbi, King of Babylon, had disposed his troops so as to guard the fords of the Tigris, in order to prevent the enemy from reaching his capital. But Samsi-rammân dispersed this advanced force, killing thirteen thousand, besides taking three thousand prisoners, and finally reduced Dur-papsukal to ashes. The respite thus obtained gave Marduk-balatsu-ikbi sufficient time to collect the main body of his troops: the army was recruited from Kaldâ and Elamites, soldiers from Namri, and Aramæan contingents, and the united force awaited the enemy behind the ruins of Dur-papsukal,

<hr />

[1] *Monolith Inscription of Samsi-rammân IV.*, col. ii. ll. 34–59; col. iii. ll. 1–70; cf. L. ABEL, *Inschrift Schamschi-Rammân's*, in SCHRADER, *Keilinschriftliche Bibliothek*, vol. i. pp. 178–183, and SCHEIL, *Inscr. assyrienne archaïque de Shamshi-Rammân IV.*, pp. 10–21.

[2] Drawn by Faucher-Gudin, from a photograph by Mansell. The original is in the British Museum.

H

along the banks of the Dabân canal. Five thousand footmen, two hundred horsemen, one hundred chariots, besides the king's tent and all his stores, fell into the hands of the Assyrians. The victory was complete; Babylon, Kuta, and Borsippa capitulated one after the other, and the invaders penetrated as far as the land of the Kaldâ, and actually reached the Persian Gulf. Samsi-rammân offered sacrifices to the gods, as his father had done before him, and concluded a treaty with Marduk-balatsu-ikbi, the terms of which included rectification of boundaries, payment of a subsidy, and the other clauses usual in such circumstances; the peace was probably ratified by a matrimonial alliance, concluded between the Babylonian princess Sammu-ramat and Rammân-nirâri, son of the conqueror.[1] In this manner the hegemony of Assyria over Karduniash was established even more firmly than before the insurrection; but all available resources had been utilised in the effort necessary to secure it. Samsi-rammân had no leisure to reconquer Syria or Asia Minor, and the Euphrates remained the western frontier of his kingdom, as it had been in the early days of Shalmaneser III.[2] The peace with Babylon, moreover, did not last long; Bau-akhiddîn, who had succeeded Marduk-balatsu-ikbi, refused to observe the terms of the treaty, and hostilities again broke out on the Turnat and the Tigris, as they had done six years previously. This war was prolonged from 813 to 812 B.C., and was still proceeding when Samsi-rammân died. His son Rammân-nirâri III. quickly brought it to a successful issue. He carried Bau-akhiddîn captive to Assyria, with his family and the nobles of his court, and placed on the vacant throne one of his own partisans, while he celebrated festivals in honour of his own supremacy at Babylon, Kuta, and Borsippa.[3] Karduniash made no attempt to rebel against Assyria during the next half-century. Rammân-nirâri proved himself an energetic and capable sovereign, and the thirty years

---

[1] *Monolith Inscription of Samsi-rammân IV.*, col. iii. ll. 70, 1–45; the history of the same expedition is recounted, but with several omissions, in the *Synchronous History* (PEISER and WINCKLER, *Die sogenannte Synchronistische Geschichte*, in SCHRADER, *Keilinschriftliche Bibliothek*, vol. i. pp. 200–203). The marriage of Sammu-ramat is not mentioned in any of the inscriptions referring to this war. For the possible identification of this princess with the legendary Semiramis, cf. OPPERT, *Hist. des Empires d'Assyrie et de Chaldée*, pp. 128–130; G. RAWLINSON, *The Five Great Monarchies*, vol. ii. pp. 119–121; HOMMEL, *Geschichte Babyloniens und Assyriens*, pp. 628–632. I agree with Tiele (*Babylonisch-assyrische Geschichte*, pp. 213, 214) that we must not attach much importance to this identification. It is not certain that Sammu-ramat was the wife of Rammân-nirâri; several historians think she was his mother (TIELE, *op. cit.*, pp. 212, 213; HOMMEL, *op. cit.*, p. 631).

[2] For the extent of the Assyrian Empire in the time of Samsi-rammân IV., cf. SCHRADER, *Keilins. und Geschichtsforschung*, p. 172, et seq.; and also DELATTRE, *Le Peuple et l'Empire des Mèdes*, pp. 72–74, and *Esquisse de Géographie assyrienne*, pp. 11–13.

[3] The notice of the wars of 813–812 against Chaldæa is taken from *The Eponym Canon* (SCHRADER, *Keilins. Bibliothek*, vol. i. pp. 208, 209); that of the wars of Rammân-nirâri from the *Synchronous History* (col. iv. ll. 1–21; cf. PEISER and WINCKLER, *Die sogenannte Synchronistische Geschichte*, in SCHRADER, *op. cit.*, vol. i. pp. 202, 203). I agree with Winckler (*Untersuchungen zur altorientalischen Geschichte*, p. 25; *Gesch. Babyl. und Assyr.*, pp. 117–120, 203; *Ein Beitrag zur Geschichte der Assyriologie in Deutschland*, pp. 24–27, 41, 42) that the fragment of the *Synchronous History*, col. iv. ll. 1–14, refers to Rammân-nirâri.

of his reign were by no means inglorious. We learn from the eponym lists what he accomplished during that time, and against which countries he waged war; but we have not yet recovered any inscription to enable us to fill in this outline, and put together a detailed account of his reign.[1] His first expeditions were directed against Media[2] (810), Gozân (809), and the Mannai (808–807); he then crossed the Euphrates, and in four successive years conducted as many vigorous campaigns against Arpad (806), Khazazu (805), the town of Baali (804), and the cities of the Phœnician sea-board (803). The plague interfering with his advance in the latter direction, he again turned his attention eastward and attacked Khubushkia in 802, 792, and 784; Media in 801–800, 794–793, and 790–787; Lushia in 799; Namri in 798; Diri in 796–795 and 785; Itua in 791, 783–782; Kishki in 785. This bare enumeration conjures up a vision of an enterprising and victorious monarch of the type of Assur-nazir-pal or Shalmaneser III., one who perhaps succeeded even where his redoubtable ancestors had failed. The panoramic survey of his empire, as unfolded to us in one of his inscriptions, includes the mountain ranges of Illipi as far as Mount Siluna, Kharkhar, Araziash, Misu, Media, the whole of Gizilbunda, Man, Parsua, Allabria, Abdadana,[3] the extensive territory of Naîri, far-off Andiu, and, westwards beyond the Euphrates, the Khâti, the entire country of the Amorites, Tyre, Sidon, Israel, Edom, and the Philistines. Never before had the Assyrian empire extended so far east in the direction of the centre of the Iranian tableland, nor so far to the south-west towards the frontiers of Egypt.[4]

In two only of these regions, namely, Syria and Armenia, do native documents add any information to the meagre summary contained in the Annals, and give us glimpses of contemporary rulers. The retreat of Shalmaneser, after his partial success in 839, had practically left the ancient

---

[1] *The Eponym Canon*, in Schrader, *Keilinschriftliche Bibliothek*, vol. i. pp. 202–205. The only inscription which contains any historical details has been published by H. Rawlinson, *Cun. Ins. W. As.*, vol. i. pl. 35, No. i., and translated into French by Oppert, *Histoire des Empires de Chaldée et d'Assyrie*, pp. 130, 131, and again by Ménant, *Annales des rois d'Assyrie*, pp. 126, 127, and into German by L. Abel, *Inschr. Rammân-nirâri's III.*, in Schrader, *op. cit.*, vol. i. pp. 190–193.

[2] The name is written in this place in the *Canon* (Schrader, *op. cit.*, vol. i. pp. 208, 209), *mat AA* (*mat-aî*), which G. Smith had already identified with *Madai, Matai*, the current name of Media, but Schrader (*zur Kritik der Inschriften Tiglath-Pileser's II.*, p. 26, note) had refused to accept this interpretation, and Delitzsch considered it a variant of the name Aîa, borne by a district of Kurdistan (*Wo lag das Paradies?* p. 247). Proofs that Smith's opinion is well founded are given by Hommel (*Gesch. Bab. und Assyr.*, p. 633, note 1), and in Rost (*Keilschrifttexte Tiglat-Pileser's III.*, vol. i. p. xxv.).

[3] On this survey, cf. especially Delattre, *Le Peuple et l'Empire des Mèdes*, pp. 75–84, and *Esquisse de Géogr. assyr.*, pp. 22–29.

[4] Allabria or Allabur is on the borders of Parsua (*Inscr. of Rammân-nirâri*, l. 8) and of Karalla (*Annals of Sargon*, ll. 48, 49), which allows us to locate it in the basins of the Kerkhorâh and the Saruk, tributaries of the Jagatu, which flow into Lake Urumiah. Abdadana, which borders on Allabria, and was, according to Rammân-nirâri, at the extreme end of Naîri (*Inscr. of Rammân-nirâri*, ll. 8, 9), was a little further to the east or north-east; if I am not mistaken, it corresponds pretty nearly to Uriâd, on the banks of the Kizil-Uzên.

allies of Ben-hadad II. at the mercy of Hazael,[1] the new King of Damascus, but he did not apparently attempt to assert his supremacy over the whole of Cœle-Syria, and before long several of its cities acquired considerable importance, first Mansuate, and then Hadrach,[2] both of which, casting Hamath into the shade, succeeded in holding their own against Hazael and his successors. He renewed hostilities, however, against the Hebrews, and did not relax his efforts till he had thoroughly brought them into subjection. Jehu suffered loss on all his frontiers, "from Jordan eastward, all the land of Gilead, the Gadites, the Reubenites, and the Manassites, from Aroer, which is by the valley of Arnon, even Gilead and Bashan."[3] Israel became thus once more entirely dependent on Damascus, but the sister kingdom of Judah still escaped its yoke through the energy of her rulers. Athaliah reigned seven years, not ingloriously; but she belonged to the house of Ahab, and the adherents of the prophets, whose party had planned Jehu's revolution, could no longer witness with equanimity one of the accursed race thus prospering and ostentatiously practising the rites of Baal-worship within sight of the great temple of Jahveh. On seizing the throne, Athaliah had sought out and put to death all the members of the house of David who had any claim to the succession; but Jehosheba, half-sister of Ahaziah, had with difficulty succeeded in rescuing Joash, one of the king's sons. Her husband was the high priest Jehoiada, and he secreted his nephew for six years in the precincts of the temple; at the end of that time, he won over the captains of the royal guard, bribed a section of the troops, and caused them to swear fealty to the child as their legitimate sovereign. Athaliah, hastening to discover the cause of the uproar, was assassinated. Mattan, chief priest of Baal, shared her fate; and Jehoiada at once restored to Jahveh the pre-eminence which the gods of the alien had for a time usurped [4] (837). At first his influence over his pupil was supreme, but

---

[1] Cf. the account of these events given *supra*, pp. 85–87.

[2] Mansuati successfully resisted Rammân-nirâri in 797 B.C. (*The Eponym Canon*, in SCHRADER, *Keilinschriftliche Bibliothek*, vol. i. pp. 208, 209), but he probably caused its ruin, for after this the Canon only mentions expeditions against Hadrach. Mansuati was in the basin of the Orontes (SCHRADER, *Keilinschriften und Geschichtsforschung*, pp. 121, 122), and the manner in which the Assyrian texts mention it in connection with Zimyra seems to show that it commanded the opening in the Lebanon range between Cœle-Syria and Phœnicia. The site of Khatarika, the Hadrach of Zech. ix. 1, is not yet precisely determined; but it must, as well as Mansuati, have been in the neighbourhood of Hamath (SCHRADER, *Keilins. und Geschichtsf.*, pp. 121, 122; FR. DELITZSCH, *Wo lag das Paradies?* p. 279), perhaps between Hamath and Damascus. It appears for the first time in 772 (*The Eponym Canon*, in SCHRADER, *Keilins. Bibliothek*, vol. i. pp. 210, 211).

[3] 2 *Kings* x. 32, 33. Even if verse 33 is a later addition (STADE, *Miscellen*, in the *Zeitschrift für das Alttestamentliche Wissenschaft*, vol. v. 1885, p. 179), it gives a correct idea of the situation, except as regards Bashan, which had been lost to Israel for some time already.

[4] 2 *Kings* xi.; cf. 2 *Chron.* xxii. 10–12, and xxiii. The author of 2 *Chron.* xxii. 11 alone states that Jehosheba was the wife of the high priest. For the value of the account as it stands, and the several sources which may be distinguished in the narrative, cf. STADE, in the *Zeitschrift für Alttestamentliche Wissenschaft*, 1885, vol. v. p. 279, et seq.

before long the memory of his services faded away, and the king sought only how to rid himself of a tutelage which had grown irksome. The temple had suffered during the late wars, and repairs were much needed. Joash ordained that for the future all moneys put into the sacred treasury—which of right belonged to the king—should be placed unreservedly at the disposal of the priests on condition that they should apply them to the maintenance of the services and fabric of the temple : the priests accepted the gift, but failed in the faithful observance of the conditions, so that in 814 B.C. the king was obliged to take stringent measures to compel them to repair the breaches in the sanctuary walls :[1] he therefore withdrew the privilege which they had abused, and henceforth undertook the administration of the Temple Fund in person. The beginning of the new order of things was not very successful. Jehu had died in 815, after a disastrous reign, and both he and his son Jehoahaz had been obliged to acknowledge the supremacy of Hazael : not only was he in the position of an inferior vassal, but, in order to preclude any idea of a revolt, he was forbidden to maintain a greater army than the small force necessary for purposes of defence, namely, ten thousand foot-soldiers, fifty horsemen, and ten chariots.[2] The power of Israel had so declined that Hazael was allowed to march through its territory unhindered on his way to wage war in the country of the Philistines ; which he did, doubtless, in order to get possession of the main route of Egyptian commerce. The Syrians destroyed Gath,[3] reduced Pentapolis to subjection, enforced tribute from Edom, and then marched against Jerusalem. Joash took from the treasury of Jahveh the reserve funds which his ancestors, Jehoshaphat, Joram, and Ahaziah, had accumulated, and sent them to the invader,[4] together with all the gold which was found in the king's house. From this time forward Judah became, like Israel, Edom, the Philistines and Ammonites, a mere vassal of Hazael ; with the possible exception of Moab, all the peoples of Southern Syria were now subject to Damascus, and formed a league as strong as that which had successfully resisted the power of Shalmaneser. Rammân-nirâri, therefore, did not

---

[1] 2 *Kings* xii. 4–16 ; cf. 2 *Chron.* xxiv. 1–14. The beginning of the narrative is lost, and the whole has probably been modified to make it agree with 2 *Kings* xxii. 3–7 ; cf. STADE, *Miscellen*, in the *Zeitschrift für Alttestamentliche Wissenschaft*, 1885, vol. v. p. 290.

[2] 2 *Kings* xiii. 1–7. It may be noticed that the number of foot-soldiers given in the Bible is identical with that which the Assyrian texts mention as Ahab's contingent at the battle of Qarqar, viz. 10,000 ; the number of the chariots is very different in the two cases (cf. *supra*, p. 71). Kuenen and other critics would like to assign to the reign of Jehoahaz the siege of Samaria by the Syrians, which the actual text of the Book of the Kings attributes to the reign of Joram (cf. *supra*, p. 82, note 5).

[3] The text of 2 *Kings* xii. 17 merely says that Hazael took Gath. Gath is not named by Amos among the cities of the Philistines (*Amos* i. 6–8), but it is one of the towns cited by that prophet as examples to Israel of the wrath of Jahveh (vi. 2). It is probable, therefore, that it was already destroyed in his time (STADE, *Geschichte des Volkes Israel*, vol. i. p. 566).

[4] 2 *Kings* xii. 17, 18 ; cf. 2 *Chron.* xxiv. 22–24, where the expedition of Hazael is represented as a punishment for the murder of Zechariah, son of Jehoiada.

venture to attack Syria during the lifetime of Hazael; but a change of sovereign is always a critical moment in the history of an Eastern empire, and he took advantage of the confusion caused by the death of the aged king to attack his successor Mari (803 B.C.). Mari essayed the tactics which his father had found so successful: he avoided a pitched battle, and shut himself up in

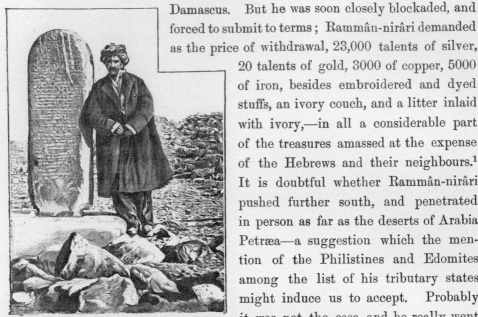

TRIUMPHAL STELE OF MENUAS AT KELISHIN.[2]

Damascus. But he was soon closely blockaded, and forced to submit to terms; Rammân-nirâri demanded as the price of withdrawal, 23,000 talents of silver, 20 talents of gold, 3000 of copper, 5000 of iron, besides embroidered and dyed stuffs, an ivory couch, and a litter inlaid with ivory,—in all a considerable part of the treasures amassed at the expense of the Hebrews and their neighbours.[1] It is doubtful whether Rammân-nirâri pushed further south, and penetrated in person as far as the deserts of Arabia Petræa—a suggestion which the mention of the Philistines and Edomites among the list of his tributary states might induce us to accept. Probably it was not the case, and he really went no further than Damascus. But the submission of that city included, in theory at least, the submission of all states subject to her sway, and these dependencies may have sent some presents to testify their desire to conciliate his favour; their names appear in the inscriptions in order to swell the number of direct or indirect vassals of the empire, since they were subject to a state which had been effectually conquered.[3]

Rammân-nirâri did not meet with such good fortune in the North; not only did he fail to obtain the brilliant successes which elsewhere attended his

[1] *Inscription of Rammân-nirâri*, ll. 15–21, in H. RAWLINSON, *Cun. Ins. W. As.*, vol. i. pl. 35, No. iii. The expedition mentioned here must be that of 803 B.C., "against the countries of the sea-coast" (*The Eponym Canon*, in SCHRADER, *Keilinschriftliche Bibliothek*, vol. i. pp. 208, 209). Mari is generally looked upon as a son of Hazael, and his name is interpreted "*my lord*" (TIELE, *Babylonisch-assyrische Geschichte*, pp. 211, 212), but Hommel places him after Ben-hadad III., and assigns the expedition of Rammân-nirâri to 797 (*Gesch. Bab. und Assyr.*, pp. 634, 635). Others identify Mari with the Biblical Ben-hadad III. (KITTEL, *Geschichte der Hebräer*, vol. ii. p. 250, note 5; WINCKLER, *Alttestamentliche Untersuchungen*, pp. 66, 67, and *Geschichte Israels*, vol. i. p. 154).

[2] Drawn by Faucher-Gudin, from a photograph by J. de Morgan; cf. J. DE MORGAN, *Mission Archéologique en Perse*, vol. iv. pl. xxv.

[3] H. RAWLINSON, *Cun. Ins. W. As.*, vol. i. pl. 35, No. iii. ll. 11–14.

arms, but he ended by sustaining considerable reverses. The Ninevite historians reckoned the two expeditions of 808 and 807 B.C. against the Mannai as victories, doubtless because the king returned with a train of prisoners and loaded with spoil; but the Vannic inscriptions reveal that Urartu, which had been rising into prominence during the reign of Shalmaneser, had now grown still more powerful, and had begun to reconquer those provinces on the Tigris and Euphrates of which the Assyrians thought themselves the undoubted lords. Sharduris II. had been succeeded, about 828, by his son Ishpuinis, who had perhaps measured his strength against Samsi-rammân IV.[1] Ishpuinis appears to have conquered and reduced to the condition of a province the neighbouring principality of Biainas, which up to that time had been governed by a semi-independent dynasty; at all events, he transferred thence his seat of government, and made Dhuspas his favourite residence.[2] Towards the end of his reign he associated with him on the throne his son Menuas,[3] and made him commander-in-chief of the army. Menuas proved a bold and successful general, and in a few years had doubled the extent of his dominions. He first delivered from the Assyrian yoke, and plundered on his father's account, the tribes on the borders of Lake Urumiah, Muzazir, Gilzân, and Kirruri; then, crossing the Gordyæan mountains, he burnt the towns in the valley of the Upper Zab, which bore the uncouth names of Teraîs, Ardis, Khanalis, Bikuras, Khatqanas, Inuas, and Nibur, laid waste the more fertile part of Khubushkia, and carved triumphal stelæ in the Assyrian and Vannic scripts upon the rocks in the pass of Rowandiz.[4] It was probably to recover this territory that Rammân-nirâri waged war three times in Khubushkia, in 802, 792, and 785, in a district which had formerly been ruled by a prefect from Nineveh, but had now fallen into the hands of the enemy.[5] Everywhere along the frontier, from

[1] Ishpuinis is probably the Ushpina mentioned by Samsi-rammân among the conquered kings of Naîri (*Monolith Inscr. of Samsi-rammân*, col. iv. ll. 16–30; cf. SCHEIL, *L'Inscription de Shamshi-Rammân IV.*, pp. 8–11; and L. ABEL, *Inschrift. Schamschi-Rammân's*, in SCHRADER, *Keilinschriftliche Bibliothek*, vol. i. pp. 178, 179). This is also the opinion of Belck and Lehmann (*Weitere Ergebnisse ihrer Studien an den neugefundenen armenischer Keilinschriften*, in the *Verhandlungen der Berliner anthropologischen Gesellschaft*, 1892, p. 483).

[2] BELCK and LEHMANN, *Chaldische Forschungen*, in the *Verhandlungen*, 1896, pp. 593–595.

[3] A certain number of Vannic inscriptions belong to the joint reign of Ishpuinis and Menuas, Nos. v., lvi., lviii., in Sayce (*The Cuneiform Inscriptions of Van*, in the *J. R. As. Soc.*, new series, vol. xiv. pp. 461–495, 663–673; and vol. xx. pp. 21–23) and No. 3 in Belck (*Ueber neuerlich aufgefundene Keilinschriften in rüssisch und türkisch Armenien*, in the *Zeitschrift für Ethnologie*, 1892, p. 124).

[4] Stelæ of Rowandiz, the most important of which, discovered by Schulz, has been transcribed and translated by Sayce (*op. cit.*, pp. 663–673, No. lvi.), and published more fully by Scheil and de Morgan (*La Stèle de Kel-i-chin*, in the *Recueil de Travaux*, vol. xiv. pp. 153–160). On the different stelæ of the same kind which exist in this region, and on the confusion to which they have given rise, cf. BELCK and LEHMANN, *Ueber die Kelishin-Stele*, in the *Verhandlungen*, 1893, pp. 389–400, and *Chaldische Forschungen*, 1896, p. 594.

[5] HOMMEL, *Geschichte Bab. und Assyr.*, p. 633, note 2. It is probable that the stele of Kelishin, belonging to the joint reign of Ishpuinis and Menuas, was intended to commemorate the events which led Rammân-nirâri to undertake his first expedition; the conquest by Menuas will fall then in 804

the Lower Zab to the Euphrates, Menuas overpowered and drove back the Assyrian outposts. He took from them Aîdus and Erinuis on the southern shores of Lake Van,[1] compelled Dayaîni to abandon its allegiance, and forced its king, Udhupursis, to surrender his treasure and his chariots; then gradually descending the valley of the Arzania, he crushed Seseti, Kulmê, and Ekarzu.[2] In one year he pillaged the Mannai in the east, and attacked the Khâti in the west, seizing their fortresses of Surisilis, Tarkhigamas, and Sarduras; in the province of Alzu he left 2113 soldiers dead on the field after one engagement;[3] Gupas yielded to his sway, followed by the towns of Khuzanas and Puteria, whereupon he even crossed the Euphrates and levied tribute from Melitene.[4] But the struggle against Assyria absorbed only a portion of his energy; we do not know what he accomplished in the east, in the plains sloping towards the Caspian Sea, but several monuments, discovered near Armavir and Erzerum, testify that he pushed his arms a considerable distance towards the north and north-west.[5] He obliged Etius to acknowledge his supremacy, sending a colony to its capital, Lununis, whose name he changed to Menua-lietzilinis.[6] Towards the end of his reign he partly subjugated the Mannai, planting colonies throughout their territory to strengthen his hold on the country.[7] By these campaigns he had formed a kingdom, which, stretching from the south side of the Araxes[8] to the upper reaches of the Zab and the

or 803 B.C. The inscription of Meher-Kapussi (SAYCE, *op. cit.,* vol. xiv. pp. 461–495) contains the names of the divinities belonging to several conquered towns, and may have been engraved on the return from this war (SAYCE, *op. cit.,* vol. xiv. p. 669).

[1] Inscriptions of Aghtamar, in SAYCE, *The Cuneiform Inscriptions of Van,* in the *J. R. As. Soc.,* vol. xiv. pp. 537–540, No. xxix. A–B. These inscriptions were removed to the mainland thirty years ago (BELCK and LEHMANN, *Weitere Ergebnisse ihrer Studien,* in the *Verhandlungen der Berliner anthropologische Gesellschaft,* 1892, p. 478, cf. 1893, p. 219).

[2] Inscriptions of Yazli-tash and Ismerd, in SAYCE, *op. cit.,* pp. 540–550, No. xxx., and pp. 468–570, No. xxxv. A.

[3] Inscriptions of Van, in SAYCE, *op. cit.,* pp. 555–558, No. xxxii., and vol. xx. p. 11.

[4] Inscription of Palu, first published in LAYARD, *Inscriptions in the Cuneiform Character,* pl. 64, translated and commented on in SAYCE, *op. cit.,* pp. 558–592, No. xxxiii.; Sayce recognises in Puteria the ancient name of the walled village of Palu, where the inscription was discovered, and in Khuzanas the name Khôzan, the district in which Palu is situated. Gupas is perhaps the district round the town Gubbi, pillaged by Assur-nazir-pal (see p. 14 of the present work).

[5] The inscription of Erzerum, discovered by F. de Saulcy and published by him (*Voyage autour de la Mer Morte,* pl. ii. 1), shows that Menuas was in possession of the district in which this town is situated, and that he rebuilt a palace there (SAYCE, *op. cit.,* p. 567, No. xxxv.).

[6] Inscriptions of Yazli-tash and Zolakert, in SAYCE, *op. cit.,* vol. xiv. pp. 562–577, No. xxxiv., and vol. xx. pp. 11–13. It follows from these texts that the country of Etius is the district of Armavir, and Lununis is the ancient name of this city. The new name by which Menuas replaced the name Lununis signifies *the abode of the people of Menuas;* like many names arising from special circumstances, it naturally passed away with the rule of the people who had imposed it.

[7] Inscription of Tash-tepê, rediscovered and interpreted by BELCK and LEHMANN, *Das Reich der Mannaër,* in the *Verhandlungen,* 1893, pp. 481, 482.

[8] Belck and Lehmann think that the conquests of Menuas did not extend beyond the Araxes (*Chaldische nova,* in the *Verhandlungen,* 1893, p. 221), and their opinion is confirmed by the position of the monuments at present discovered; but we must not forget that the country has been very little

Tigris, was quite equal to Assyria in size, and probably surpassed it in density of population, for it contained no barren steppes such as stretched across Mesopotamia, affording support merely to a few wretched Bedâwin. As their dominions increased, the sovereigns of Biainas began to consider themselves on an equality with the kings of Nineveh, and endeavoured still more to imitate them in the luxury and display of their domestic life, as well as in the energy of their actions and the continuity of their victories. They engraved everywhere on the rocks triumphal inscriptions, destined to show to posterity their own exploits and the splendour of their gods. Having made this concession to their vanity, they took effective measures to assure possession of their conquests. They selected in the various provinces sites difficult of access, commanding some defile in the mountains, or ford over a river, or at the junction of two roads, or the approach to a plain; on such spots they would build a fortress or a town, or, finding a citadel already existing, they would repair it and remodel its fortifications so as to render it impregnable.[1] At Kalajik,[2] Ashrut-Darga,[3] and the older Mukhrapert [4] may still be seen the ruins of ramparts built by Ishpuinis. Menuas finished the buildings his father had begun, erected others in all the districts where he sojourned, in time of peace or war, at Shushanz,[5] Sirka,[6] Anzaff,[7] Arzwapert,[8] Geuzak,[9] Zolakert,[10] Tashtepê, and

explored as yet, and that a methodical search might lead to discoveries which would oblige us to modify opinions formed on the basis of our present knowledge.

[1] On the system of construction adopted by the people of Urartu in their palaces and fortresses, cf. the short account on pp. 57–60 of the present work.

[2] Inscription of Kalajik, the Aralesk of the Armenians, in SAYCE, *The Cuneiform Inscriptions of Van*, in the *J. R. As. Soc.*, vol. xiv. pp. 453–460, No. iii; cf. BELCK and LEHMANN, *Archæologische Forschungen in Armenien*, in the *Verhandlungen der Berliner anthropologischen Gesellschaft*, 1893, p. 78.

[3] Information on this locality may be found in D. H. MÜLLER, *Die Keilinschrift von Ashrút-Darga;* cf. SAYCE, *op. cit.*, vol. xx. p. 21. The inscription of Ashrut-Darga belongs to the joint reign of Ishpuinis and Menuas.

[4] BELCK and LEHMANN, *Ueber neuerlich aufgefundene Keilinschriften in rüssisch und türkisch Armenien*, in the *Zeitschrift für Ethnologie*, 1892, p. 124; and *Archæologische Forschungen in Armenien*, in the *Verhandlungen*, 1893, p. 80; cf. SAYCE, *op. cit.*, vol. xxii. p. 5. The inscription of ancient Mukhrapert also belongs to the joint reign of Ishpunis and Menuas.

[5] SAYCE, *op. cit.*, vol. xiv. pp. 499, 500, Nos. viii., ix.; and pp. 505, 506, Nos. xii., xiii.; cf. BELCK and LEHMANN, *Chaldische Forschungen*, in the *Verhandlungen*, 1898, p. 613.

[6] SAYCE, *op. cit.*, vol. xiv. pp. 500–504, Nos. x., xi.; the name of the ancient place corresponding to the modern village of Sirka was probably Artsunis or Artsuyunis, according to the Vannic inscriptions.

[7] BELCK and LEHMANN, *Ueber neuerlich aufgefundene Keilinschriften*, in the *Zeitschrift für Ethnologie*, 1892, p. 125, and *Archæologische Forschungen*, in the *Verhandlungen*, 1893, p. 79.

[8] BELCK and LEHMANN, *Ueber neuerlich aufgefundene Keilinschriften*, in the *Zeitschrift für Ethnologie*, 1892, p. 125; and *Ueber weitere Ergebnisse ihrer Studien*, in the *Verhandlungen*, 1892, pp. 478, 479. The town appears to have been called Kueraînas, "belonging to the god Kueras;" cf. SAYCE, *op. cit.*, vol. xiv. p. 496, No. vi. A, l. 4.

[9] BELCK and LEHMANN, *Ueber neuerlich aufgefundene Keilinschriften*, in the *Zeitschrift für Ethnologie*, 1892, p. 125, and *Chaldische Forschungen*, in the *Verhandlungen*, 1895, p. 582.

[10] NIKOLSKY, *L'inscription cunéiforme de Kölany-Kirlany (Alutschalu) et autres inscriptions cunéiformes inédites de l'Arménie russe*, No. 3; cf. BELCK and LEHMANN, *Chaldische Forschungen*, in the *Verhandlungen*, 1895, p. 606.

in the country of the Mannai,[1] and it is possible that the fortified village of Melasgerd still bears his name.[2]   His wars furnished him with the men and materials necessary for the rapid completion of these works, while the statues, valuable articles of furniture, and costly fabrics, vessels of silver, gold, and copper carried off from Assyrian or Asiatic cities, provided him with surroundings as luxurious as those enjoyed by the kings of Nineveh.   His favourite residence was amid the valleys and hills of the south-western shore of Lake Van, the sea of the rising sun.   His father, Ishpuinis, had already done much to embellish the site of Dhuspas, or Khaldinas as it was called, from the god Khaldis; he had surrounded it with strong walls, and within them had laid the foundations of a magnificent palace.   Menuas carried on the work, brought water to the cisterns by subterranean aqueducts, planted gardens, and turned the whole place into an impregnable fortress, where a small but faithful garrison could defy a large army for several years.   Dhuspas, thus completed, formed the capital and defence of the kingdom during the succeeding century.

Menuas was gathered to his fathers shortly before the death of Rammân-nirâri, perhaps in 784 B.C.[3]   He was engaged up to the last in a quarrel with the princes who occupied the mountainous country to the north of the Araxes, and his son Argistis spent the first few years of his reign in completing his conquests in this region.[4]   He crushed with ease an attempted revolt in

---

[1] Inscription of Kelîshin, interpreted by BELCK, *Das Reich der Mannäer*, in the *Verhandlungen der Berliner anthropologischen Gesellschaft*, 1894, pp. 480–482.

[2] A more correct form than Melas-gerd is Manas-gert, *the city of Manas*, where Manas would represent Menuas: one of the inscriptions of Aghtamar (SAYCE, *The Cuneiform Inscriptions of Van*, in the *J. R. As. Soc.*, new ser., vol. xiv. p. 538, No. xxix. B.) speaks of a certain Menuakhinas, *city of Menuas*, which may be a primitive version of the same name (BELCK and LEHMANN, *Ueber weitere Ergebnisse ihrer Studien*, in the *Verhandlungen*, 1892, p. 478).

[3] This date seems to agree with the text of the *Annals of Argistis*, as far as we are at present acquainted with them (SAYCE, *op. cit.*, vol. xiv. pp. 571–628, Nos. xxxvii.–xliv.); Müller has shown, in fact, that they contain the account of fourteen campaigns, probably the first fourteen of the reign of Argistis (*Inschrift von Aschrût-Darga*, p. 27, et seq.), and he has recognised, in accordance with the observations of Stanislas Guyard, the formula which separates the campaigns one from another. There are two campaigns against the peoples of the Upper Euphrates mentioned before the campaigns against Assyria, and as these latter follow continuously after 781, it is probable that the former must be placed in 783–782, which would give 783 or 784 for the year of his accession.

[4] The *Annals of Argistis* are inscribed on the face of the rock which crowns the citadel of Van. They were copied by Schulz, and published after his death in the *Journal Asiatique*, 3rd ser., vol. ix., where they figured as Nos. ii.–viii.; the copies executed by Layard in 1850 have never been printed, but Sayce used them, as also those of Roberts (*Étude philologique sur les Inscriptions cunéiformes de l'Arménie*, 1876), to establish the text of the passages where the version of Schulz was incorrect.   The translation and commentary have been undertaken by Sayce (*op. cit.*, pp. 571–623); the results of this study have been criticised by Guyard (*Notes de Lexicographie Assyrienne*, pp. 113, 144), by Müller (*Die Keilinschrift von Aschrût-Darga*), and by Sayce himself (*op. cit.*, vol. xx. pp. 13–19), who gave a second English translation, *The Great Inscription of Argistis on the Rocks of Van*, in the *Records of the Past*, 2nd ser., vol. iv. pp. 114–133.   The inscription contains (as was stated above in note 3) the history of the first fourteen yearly campaigns of Argistis; I have followed in my arrangement the coincidences established between these wars and the data supplied by the Assyrian Eponym canon (SCHRADER, *Keilinschriftliche Bibliothek*, vol. i. pp. 210, 211), by D. H. Müller, and after him, by Hommel (*Geschichte Babyloniens und Assyriens*, pp. 630–642).

Dayaîni, and then invaded Etius, systematically devastating it, its king, Uduris, being powerless to prevent his ravages. All the principal towns succumbed one after another before the vigour of his assault, and, from the numbers killed and taken prisoners, we may surmise the importance of his victories in these barbarous districts, to which belonged the names of Seriazis, Silius, Zabakhas, Zirimutaras, Babanis, and Urmias,[1] though we cannot definitely locate the places indicated. On a single occasion, the assault on Ureyus, for instance,

THE GARDENS AND HILL OF DHUSPAS OR VAN.[2]

Argistis took prisoners 19,255 children, 10,140 men fit to bear arms, 23,280 women, and the survivors of a garrison which numbered 12,675 soldiers at the opening of the siege, besides 1104 horses, 35,016 cattle, and more than 10,000 sheep.[3] Two expeditions into the heart of the country, conducted between 784 and 782 B.C., had greatly advanced the work of conquest,[4] when the accession of a new sovereign in Assyria made Argistis decide to risk a change of front and to

[1] The site of these places is still undetermined. Seriazis and Silius (or Tarius) lay to the north-east of Dayaîni (SAYCE, *The Cuneiform Inscriptions of Van*, in the *J. R. As. Soc.*, vol. xiv. p. 579), and Urmias, Urmê, recalls the modern name of Lake Urumiah, but was probably situated on the left bank of the Araxes (SAYCE, *op. cit.*, p. 611).

[2] Drawn by Boudier, from a photograph by M. Binder, furnished by Father Scheil.

[3] *Annals of Argistis*, A, ll. 12–15; cf. SAYCE, *op. cit.*, p. 574.

[4] *Annals of Argistis*, A, ll. 1–43; B, ll. 1–3; cf. SAYCE, *op. cit.*, pp. 572–582. It is to these campaigns that the inscriptions of Surk Sahak seem to refer (SAYCE, *op. cit.*, pp. 623–631, Nos. xlv., xlvi.; and *Monolith Inscription of Argistis, King of Van*, in the *Records of the Past*, 2nd ser., vol. iv. pp. 134–146).

concentrate the main part of his forces on the southern boundary of his empire. Rammân-nirâri, after his last contest in Khubushkia in 784, had fought two consecutive campaigns against the Aramæan tribes of Itua, near the frontiers of Babylon, and he was still in conflict with them when he died in 782 B.C.[1] His son, Shalmaneser IV., may have wished to signalise the commencement of his reign by delivering from the power of Urartu the provinces which the kings of that country had wrested from his ancestors; or, perhaps, Argistis thought that a change of ruler offered him an excellent opportunity for renewing the struggle at the point where Menuas had left it, and for conquering yet more of the territory which still remained to his rival. Whatever the cause, the Assyrian annals show us the two adversaries ranged against each other, in a struggle which lasted from 781 to 778 B.C. Argistis had certainly the upper hand, and though his advance was not rapid, it was never completely checked. The first engagement took place at Nirbu, near the sources of the Supnat and the Tigris : Nirbu capitulated, and the enemy pitilessly ravaged the Hittite states, which were subject to Assyria, penetrating as far as the heart of Melitene (781).[2] The next year the armies encountered each other nearer to Nineveh, in the basin of the Bitlis-tchaî, at Khakhias ;[3] and, in 779, Argistis expressly thanks his gods, the Khaldises, for having graciously bestowed upon him as a gift the armies and cities of Assur.[4] The scene of the war had shifted, and the contest was now carried on in the countries bordering on Lake Urumiah, Bustus and Parsua.[5] The natives gained nothing by the change of invader, and were as hardly used by the King of Urartu as they had been by Shalmaneser III. or by Samsirammân : as was invariably the case, their towns were given over to the flames, their fields ravaged, their cattle and their families carried into captivity. Their resistance, however, was so determined that a second campaign was required to complete the conquest : and this time the Assyrians suffered a serious defeat at Surisidas (778),[6] and a year at least was needed for their recovery from the disaster.[7] During this respite, Argistis hastened to complete the

---

[1] *The Eponym Canon*, in SCHRADER, *Keilinschriftliche Bibliothek*, vol. i. pp. 210, 211.

[2] *Annals of Argistis*, B, ll. 4–24 ; cf. SAYCE, *The Cuneiform Inscriptions of Van*, in the *J. R. As. Soc.*, vol. xiv. pp. 582–685. For Nirbu, cf. p. 20, *supra.*

[3] *Annals of Argistis*, B, ll. 40–50 ; SAYCE, *op. cit.*, pp. 586, 587.

[4] *Annals of Argistis*, B, ll. 51–57, and C, ll. 1–22 ; cf. SAYCE, *op. cit.*, pp. 587, 588, 590–592. This passage concerns a certain Kharsitas, in whom Sayce thought he recognised the King of Assyria, Assurdân III., successor of Shalmaneser IV. (*op. cit.*, pp. 406, 407, 588–590). Tiele does not admit this identification, which is indeed somewhat far-fetched (*Babylonisch-assyriche Geschichte*, p. 216, note 1) ; Hommel suggests that the name Kharsitas represents the name of an Assyrian general, or perhaps of a chief in alliance with the Assyrians, and opposed to Argistis (*Geschichte Babyloniens und Assyriens*, p. 641), which seems a more reasonable theory.

[5] For Parsua, see *supra*, p. 88, note 3.

[6] *Annals of Argistis*, C, ll. 23–48 ; cf. SAYCE, *op. cit.*, pp. 593–596.

[7] The Eponym Canon notes in this year, 777, a campaign in the country of Itua (SCHRADER,

pacification of Bustus, Parsua, and the small portion of Man which had not been reduced to subjection by Menuas.[1]   When the Assyrians returned to the conflict, he defeated them again (776),[2] and while they withdrew to the Amanus, where a rebellion had broken out (775)[3], he reduced one by one the small states which

clustered round the eastern and southern shores of Lake Urumiah.[4] He was conducting a campaign in Namri, when Shalmaneser IV. made a last effort to check his advance; but he was again victorious (774),[5] and from henceforth these troubled regions, in which Nineveh had so persistently endeavoured for more than a century to establish her own supremacy, became part of the empire of Urartu. Argistis's hold of them proved, however, to be a precarious and uncertain one, and before long the same difficulties assailed him which had restricted the power of his rivals. He was forced to return again

URARTIAN STELE ON THE ROCKS OF AK-KEUPRU.[6]

and again to these districts, destroying fortresses and pursuing the inhabitants over plain and mountain: in 773 we find him in Urmes, the territory of

Keilinschriftliche Bibliothek, vol. i. pp. 210, 211); these expeditions against the Aramæan nomads were usually mere raids, which did not require a great effort.

[1] *Annals of Argistis*, C, ll. 48–71, D, ll. 1–20; cf. SAYCE, *The Cuneiform Inscriptions of Van*, in the *J. R. As. Soc.*, new ser., vol. xiv. pp. 596–598, 600, 601.

[2] *Annals of Argistis*, D, ll. 21–45; cf. SAYCE, *op. cit.*, pp. 602–604.

[3] *The Eponym Canon*, in SCHRADER, *Keilinschriftliche Bibliothek*, vol. i. pp. 210, 211, notes an expedition to the *Country of Cedars* for the year 775.

[4] *Annals of Argistis*, D, ll. 50–69; cf. SAYCE, *op. cit.*, pp. 604–606.

[5] *Annals of Argistis*, D, ll. 69–81; E, ll. 1–11; cf. SAYCE, *op. cit.*, pp. 606–609.   The *Eponym Canon* notes for this year an expedition to Urartu and Namri (SCHRADER, *op. cit.*, vol. i. pp. 210, 211), the last-mentioned in these regions for the reign of Shalmaneser IV.

[6] Drawn by Boudier, from a photograph by M. Ximénes, furnished by Father Scheil.

Bikhuras, and Bam, in the very heart of Namri;[1] in 772, in Dhuaras, and Gurqus, among the Mannai, and at the city of Uikhis, in Bustus.[2] Meanwhile, to the north of the Araxes, several chiefs had taken advantage of his being thus engaged in warfare in distant regions, to break the very feeble bond which held them vassals to Urartu. Etius was the fountain-head and main support of the rebellion ; the rugged mountain range in its rear provided its chiefs with secure retreats among its woods and lakes and valleys, through which flowed rapid torrents. Argistis inflicted a final defeat on the Mannai in 771, and then turned his forces against Etius. He took by storm the citadel of Ardinis which defended the entrance to the country, ravaged Ishqigulus,[3] and seized Amegu, the capital of Uidharus :[4] our knowledge of his wars comes to an end in the following year with an expedition into the land of Tarius.[5] The monuments do not tell us what he accomplished on the borders of Asia Minor : he certainly won some considerable advantages there, and the influence which Assyria had exercised over states scattered to the north of the Taurus, such as Melitene, and possibly Tabal and Kummukh, which had formed the original nucleus of the Hittite empire, must have now passed into his hands. The form of Argistis looms before us as that of a great conqueror, worthy to bear comparison with the most indefatigable and triumphant of the Pharaohs of Egypt or the lords of Chaldæa. The inscriptions which are constantly being discovered within the limits of his kingdom prove that, following the example of all Oriental sovereigns, he delighted as much in building as in battle : perhaps we shall some day recover a sufficient number of records to enable us to restore to their rightful place in history this great king, and the people whose power he developed more than any other sovereign.

Assyria had thus lost all her possessions in the northern and eastern parts of her empire ; turning to the west, how much still remained faithful to her ? After the expedition of 775 B.C. to the land of Cedars,[6] two consecutive campaigns are mentioned against Damascus (773) and Hadrach (772) ; it was during this latter expedition, or immediately after it, that Shalmaneser IV. died.[7] Northern Syria seems to have been disturbed by revolutions which seriously altered the balance of power within her borders. The ancient states, whose growth had been arrested by the deadly blows inflicted on them

[1] *Annals of Argistis*, E, ll. 12–20 ; F, G, ll. 1–14 ; cf. SAYCE, *The Cuneiform Inscriptions of Van,* in the *J. R. As. Soc.*, new ser., vol. xiv. pp. 609, 610, 612–614.

[2] *Annals of Argistis*, G, ll. 15–36 ; cf. SAYCE, *op. cit.*, pp. 614–616.

[3] Sayce (*op. cit.*, pp. 621, 631) shows that Ishqigulus was the district of Alexandropolis, to the east of Kars ; its capital, Irdanius, is very probably either the existing walled village of Kalinsha, or the neighbouring ruin of Ajuk-kaleh, on the Arpa-tchâî.

[4] *Annals of Argistis*, G, ll. 37–72 ; cf. SAYCE, *op. cit.*, pp. 616–619.

[5] *Annals of Argistis*, G, ll. 77–81 ; cf. SAYCE, *op. cit.*, pp. 619, 620.

[6] Cf. *supra*, p. 109, note 3.

[7] *The Eponym Canon*, in SCHRADER, *Keilinschriftliche Bibliothek*, vol. i. pp. 210, 211.

in the ninth century by Assur-nazir-pal and Shalmaneser III., had become reduced to the condition of second-rate powers, and their dominions had been split up. The Patinâ was divided into four small states—the Patinâ proper, Unki, Iaudi, and Samalla, the latter falling under the rule of an Aramæan family; [1] perhaps the accession of Qaral, the founder of this dynasty, had been accompanied by convulsions, which might explain the presence of Shalmaneser IV. in the Amanos in 775.[2] All these principalities, whether of ancient or recent standing, ranged themselves under one of two kingdoms— either Hadrach or Arpad, whose names henceforth during the following half-century appear in the front rank whenever a coalition is formed against Assyria. Carchemish, whose independence was still respected by the fortresses erected in its neighbourhood, could make no move without exposing itself to an immediate catastrophe : Arpad, occupying a prominent position a little in front of the Afrîn, on the main route leading to the Orontes, had assumed the *rôle* which Carchemish was no longer in a position to fill. Agusi became the principal centre of resistance; all battles were fought under the walls of its fortresses, and its fall involved the submission of all the country between the Euphrates and the sea, as in former times had been the case with Kinalua and Khazazu.[3] Similar to the ascendency of Arpad over the plateau of Aleppo was that of Hadrach in the valley of the Orontes. This city had taken the position formerly occupied by Hamath, which was now possibly one of its dependencies; it owed no allegiance to Damascus, and rallied around it all the tribes of Cœle-Syria, whose assistance Hadadezer, but a short while before, had claimed in his war with the foreigner.[4] Neither Arpad, Hadrach, nor Damascus ever neglected to send the customary presents to any sovereign who had the temerity to cross the Euphrates and advance into their neighbourhood, but the necessity for this act of homage became more and more infrequent. During his reign of eighteen years Assurdân III., son and successor of Shalmaneser IV., appeared only three times beneath their walls—at Hadrach in 766 and 755, at Arpad in 750, a few months only before his death.[5] Assyria was gradually becoming involved in difficulties, and the means necessary to

[1] The inscriptions of Tiglath-Pileser III. mention Unku, Iaudi, Samalla, and the Patinâ, in the districts where the texts of Assur-nazir-pal and Shalmaneser III. only know of the Patinâ (cf. for the Patinâ, *supra*, p. 35).

[2] For the founder of this dynasty, cf. SACHAU, *Inschrift des Königs Panammû*, in LUSCHÂN, *Die Ausgrabungen in Sendschirli*, vol. i. pp. 63-65.

[3] Hommel (*Geschichte Babyloniens und Assyriens*, p. 656) thinks that Arpad was in Unki. That Arpad was actually in Agusi (cf. for Agusi, *supra*, p. 34, note 4) is proved, among other places, by the inscriptions of Tiglath-pileser III., which show us from 743 to 741 the king at war with Matîlu of Agusi and his suzerain Sharduris III. of Urartu (*Annals of Tiglath-pileser III.*, ll. 59-73); the same events are noted in the *Eponym Canon* as taking place in the neighbourhood of Arpad (SCHRADER, *Keilinschriftliche Bibliothek*, vol. i. pp. 212, 213).

[4] For Hadrach, cf. *supra*, p. 100, note 2.

[5] *The Eponym Canon*, in SCHRADER, *op. cit.*, pp. 210-213.

the preservation of its empire were less available than formerly. Assurdân had frankly renounced all idea of attacking Urartu, but he had at least endeavoured to defend himself against his enemies on the southern and eastern frontiers; he had led his armies against Gananâtê (771, 767), against Itua (769), and against the Medes (766), before risking an attack on Hadrach (765), but more than this he had not attempted. On two occasions in eight years (768, 764) he had preferred to abstain from offensive action, and had remained inactive in his own country.[1] Assyria found herself in one of those crises of exhaustion which periodically laid her low after each outbreak of ambitious enterprise; she might well be compared to a man worn out by fatigue and loss of blood, who becomes breathless and needs repose as soon as he attempts the least exertion. Before long, too, the scourges of disease and civil strife combined with exhaustion in hastening her ruin. The plague had broken out in the very year of the last expedition against Hadrach (765), perhaps under the walls of that city.[2] An eclipse of the sun occurred in 763, in the month of Sivân, and this harbinger of woe was the signal for an outbreak of revolt in the city of Assur.[3] From Assur the movement spread to Arrapkha, and wrought havoc there from 761 to 760; it then passed on to Gozân, where it was not finally extinguished till 758. The last remains of Assyrian authority in Syria vanished during this period: Assurdân, after two years' respite, endeavoured to re-establish it, and attacked successively Hadrach (755) and Arpad (754). This was his last exploit. His son Assur-nirâri III. spent his short reign of eight years in helpless inaction; he lost Syria, he carried on hostilities in Namri from 749 to 748—whether against the Aramæans or Urartians is uncertain—then relapsed into inactivity, and a popular sedition drove him finally from Calah in 746. He died some months later, without having repressed the revolt; none of his sons succeeded him, and the dynasty, having fallen into disrepute through the misfortunes of its last kings, thus came to an end; for, on the 12th of Iyyâr, 745 B.C., a usurper, perhaps the leader of the revolt at Calah, proclaimed himself king under the name of Tiglath-pileser.[4]

---

[1] *The Eponym Canon*, in SCHRADER, *Keilinschriftliche Bibliothek*, vol. i. pp. 212, 213.

[2] According to the reasonable conjecture put forth by HOMMEL, *Geschichte Babyloniens und Assyriens*, p. 643, note 2.

[3] The text of *The Eponym Canon* does not mention it (SCHRADER, *op. cit.*, pp. 212, 213), but the ideas which Orientals held on the subject of comets renders the connection between the two events very likely, if not certain (HOMMEL, *op. cit.*, pp. 643, 644; TIELE, *Babylonisch-assyrische Geschichte*, p. 208).

[4] Many historians have thought that Tiglath-pileser III. was of Babylonian origin (HOMMEL, *op. cit.*, pp. 648, 649); most of them, however, rightly consider that he was an Assyrian (TIELE, *op. cit.*, pp. 226, 227; WINCKLER, *Geschichte Babyloniens und Assyriens*, pp. 221, 222; ROST, *Die Keilschrifttexte, Tiglat-pilesers III.*, vol. i. pp. 8, 9). The identity of Tiglath-pileser III. with Pulu, the Biblical Pul (2 *Kings* xv. 19), still contested by Oppert (*La non-identité de Phul et de Téglathphalazar prouvée par des textes cunéiformes*, in the *Revue d'Assyriologie*, vol. i. pp. 165–170), was first suggested by H. Rawlinson (*Athenæum*, 1862, No. 1869, p. 224), and by Lepsius (*Ueber die Assyrischen Epony-moslisten*, p. 56), and then demonstrated by Schrader (*Die Keilinschriften und das Alte Testament*,

The second Assyrian empire had lasted rather less than a century and a half, from Tukulti-ninip II. to Assur-nirâri III.[1]

In the manner in which it had accomplished its work, it resembled the Egyptian empire of eight hundred years before. The Egyptians, setting forth from the Nile valley, had overrun Syria and had at first brought it under their suzerainty, though without actually subduing it. They had invaded Amurru and Zahi, Naharaim and Mitanni, where they had pillaged, burnt, and massacred at will for years, without obtaining from these countries, which were too remote to fall naturally within their sphere of influence, more than a temporary and apparent submission; the regions in the neighbourhood of the isthmus alone had been regularly administered by the officers of Pharaoh, and when the country between Mount Seir and Lebanon seemed on the point of being organised into a real empire the invasion of the Peoples of the Sea had overthrown and brought to nought the work of three centuries. The Assyrians, under the leadership of ambitious kings, had in their turn carried their arms over the countries of the Euphrates and the Mediterranean, but, like those of the Egyptians before them, their expeditions resembled rather the destructive raids of a horde in search of booty than the gradual and orderly advance of a civilised people aiming at establishing a permanent empire. Their campaigns in Cœle-Syria and Palestine had enriched their own cities and spread the terror of their name throughout the Eastern world, but their supremacy had only taken firm root in the plains bordering on Mesopotamia, and just when they were preparing to extend their rule, a power had sprung up beside them, over which they had been unable to triumph: they had been obliged to withdraw behind the Euphrates, and they might reasonably have asked themselves whether, by weakening the peoples of Syria at the price of the best blood of their own

---

1st edit., pp. 120–134, and *Keilins. und Geschichtsforschung*, pp. 440–460), has been conclusively proved by the discovery of the *Babylonian Chronicle* (PINCHES, *The Babylonian Kings of the Second Period*, in the *Proceedings* of the Bibl. Arch. Soc., 1883–1884, vol. vi. pp. 198–202), where the Babylonian reigns of Tiglath-pileser III. and his son Shalmaneser V. are inserted where the dynastic lists give Pulu and Ululaî (SCHRADER, *Keilins. Bibliothek*, vol. ii. p. 287), the Poros and Eluloeos of Ptolemy.

[1] The list of the kings of Assyria down to Assur-irba is given in MASPERO, *Struggle of the Nations*, p. 665, note 3. Here is the concluding portion of the dynasty, from Irba-rammân to Assur-nirâri III.:—

IRBA-RAMMÂN	?	ASSUR-NAZIR-PAL III.	884–859
ASSUR-NADÎNAKHÊ II.	?	SHALMANU-SHARID [SHALMANESER III.]	859–824
TUKULTI-PAL-ESHARRA [TIGLATH-		SAMSI-RAMMÂN IV.	824–812
PILESER II.]	950–935?	RAMMÂN-NIRÂRI IV..	812–782
ASSUR-DÂN II.	935–911?	SHALMANESER IV.	782–772
RAMMÂN-NIRÂRI II.	911–890	ASSUR-DÂN III.	772–754
TUKULTI-NINIP II.	890–884	ASSUR-NIRÂRI	754–745

For the information we possess bearing on the first kings in this series, and the order in which they succeeded to the throne, cf. *supra*, pp. 4, 5.

I

nation, they had not merely laboured for the benefit of a rival power, and facilitated the rise of Urartu. Egypt, after her victory over the Peoples of the Sea, had seemed likely, for the moment, to make a fresh start on a career of conquest under the energetic influence of Ramses III., but her forces proved unequal to the task, and as soon as the master's hand ceased to urge her on, she shrank back, without a struggle, within her ancient limits, and ere long nothing remained to her of the Asiatic empire carved out by the warlike Pharaohs of the Theban dynasties. If Tiglath-pileser could show the same courage and capacity as Ramses III., he might well be equally successful, and raise his nation again to power; but time alone could prove whether Nineveh, on his death, would be able to maintain a continuous effort, or whether her new display of energy would prove merely ephemeral, and her empire be doomed to sink into irremediable weakness under the successors of her deliverer, as Egypt had done under the later Ramessides.

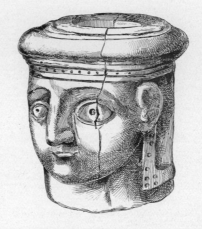

TIGLATH-PILESER III. AND THE ORGANI-SATION OF THE ASSYRIAN EMPIRE FROM 745 TO 722 B.C.

———•◆•———

FAILURE OF URARTU AND RE-CONQUEST OF SYRIA—EGYPT AGAIN UNITED UNDER ETHIOPIAN AUSPICES—PIÔNKHI—THE DOWNFALL OF DAMASCUS, OF BABYLON, AND OF ISRAEL.

Assyria and its neighbours at the accession of Tiglath-pileser III.: progress of the Aramœans in the basin of the Middle Tigris—Urartu and its expansion into the north of Syria—Damascus and Israel—Vengeance of Israel on Damascus—Jeroboam II.—Civilisation of the Hebrew kingdoms, their commerce, industries, private life, and political organisation—Dawn of Hebrew literature: the two historians of Israel—The priesthood and the prophets—The prophecy of Amos at Bethel; denunciation of Israel by Hosea.

Early campaigns of Tiglath-pileser III. in Karduniash and in Media—He determines to attack Urartu in Syria: defeat of Sharduris, campaign around Arpad, and capture of that city—Homage paid by the Syrian princes, by Menahem and Rezin II.—Second campaign against the Medes—Invasion of Urartu and end of its supremacy—Alliance of Pekah and Rezin against Ahaz: the war in Judœa and siege of Jerusalem.

Egypt under the kings of the XXIInd dynasty—The Theban principality, its priests, pallacides, and revolts; the XXIIIrd Tanite dynasty—Tafnakhti and the rise of the Saite family—The Egyptian kingdom of Ethiopia: theocratic nature of its dynasty, annexation of the Thebaid by the kingdom of Napata—Piônkhi-Mîamun; his generals in Middle Egypt; submission of Khmunu, of Memphis, and of Tafnakhti—Effect produced in Asia by the Ethiopian conquest.

The prophet Isaiah, his rise under Ahaz—Intervention of Tiglath-pileser III. in Hebrew affairs ; the campaign of 733 B.C. against Israel—Capture of Rezin, and the downfall of Damascus—Nabunazîr ; the Kaldâ and the close of the Babylonian dynasty ; usurpation of Ukînzîr—Campaign against Ukînzîr ; capture of Shapîa and of Babylon—Tiglath-pileser ascends the throne in the last-named city under the name of Pulu (729 B.C.)—Death of Tiglath-pileser III. (727 B.C.).

Reorganisation of the Assyrian empire ; provinces and feudatory states—Karduniash, Syria —Wholesale deportation of conquered races—Provincial administrators, their military and financial arrangements—Buildings erected by Tiglath-pileser at Calah—The Bît-Khilâni— Foundation of feudal lordships—Belharrân-beluzur—Shalmaneser V. and Egypt : rebellion of Hoshea, the siege of Samaria, and the prophecies of Isaiah—Sargon—Destruction of the kingdom of Israel.

COMBAT BEFORE THE WALLS OF A FORTRESS.[1]

CHAPTER II.

TIGLATH-PILESER III. AND THE ORGANISATION OF THE ASSYRIAN EMPIRE FROM 745 TO 722 B.C.

Failure of Urartu and re-conquest of Syria—Egypt again united under Ethiopian auspices—Piônkhi—The downfall of Damascus, of Babylon, and of Israel.

EVENTS proved that, in this period, at any rate, the decadence of Assyria was not due to any exhaustion of the race or impoverishment of the country, but was mainly owing to the incapacity of its kings and the lack of energy displayed by their generals. If Menuas and Argistis had again and again triumphed over the Assyrians during half a century, it was not because their bands of raw recruits were superior to the tried veterans of Rammân-nirâri in either discipline or courage. The Assyrian troops had lost none of their former valour, and their muster-roll showed no trace of diminution, but their leaders had lost the power of handling their men after the vigorous fashion of their predecessors, and showed less foresight and tenacity in conducting their campaigns. Although decimated and driven from fortress to fortress, and from province to province, hampered by the rebellions it was called upon to suppress, and distracted by civil discord, the Assyrian army still remained a strong and efficient force, ever ready to make its full power felt the

[1] Drawn by Boudier, from LAYARD, *Monuments of Nineveh*, vol. i. pl. 13. The initial, also by Boudier, represents a bronze statuette of Queen Karomama, now in the Louvre (PIERRET, *Catalogue de la Salle historique*, No. 23, p. 15; CHASSINAT, *Une Statuette en bronze de la reine Karomama*, in *Monuments Piot*, vol. iv. pp. 15–25, and pl. iii.).

moment it realised that it was being led by a sovereign capable of employing its good qualities to advantage. Tiglath-pileser had, doubtless, held a military command before ascending the throne, and had succeeded in winning the confidence of his men: as soon as he had assumed the leadership they regained their former prestige, and restored to their country that supremacy which its last three rulers had failed to maintain.[1]

The empire still included the original patrimony of Assur and its ancient colonies on the Upper Tigris, the districts of Mesopotamia won from the Aramæans at various epochs, the cities of Khabur, Khindanu, Laqî, and Tel-Abnî, and that portion of Bît-Adini which lay to the left of the Euphrates. It thus formed a compact mass capable of successfully resisting the fiercest attacks; but the buffer provinces which Assur-nazir-pal and Shalmaneser III. had grouped round their own immediate domains on the borders of Namri, of Naîri, of Melitene, and of Syria had either resumed their independence, or else had thrown in their lot with the states against which they had been intended to watch. The Aramæan tribes never let slip an opportunity of encroaching on the southern frontier. So far, the migratory instinct which had brought them from the Arabian desert to the swamps of the Persian Gulf had met with no

---

[1] The official documents dealing with the history of Tiglath-pileser III. have been seriously mutilated, and there is on several points some difference of opinion among historians as to the proper order in which the fragments ought to be placed, and, consequently, as to the true sequence of the various campaigns (G. SMITH, *The Annals of Tiglath-Pileser II.*, in the *Zeitschrift*, 1869, pp. 9–17; SCHRADER, *Keilinschriften und Geschichtsforschung*, pp. 224–236, *Zur Kritik der Inschriften Tiglath-Pileser's II., des Asarhaddon und des Aschurbanipal*, p. 1, et seq., and *Die Keilinschriften und das Alte Testament*, 1883, pp. 242–259; TIELE, *Babylonisch-Assyriche Geschichte*, pp. 224–236; HOMMEL, *Geschichte Babyloniens und Assyriens*, p. 649, et seq.; ROST, *Die Keilschrifttexte Tiglat-Pilesers III.*, vol. i. pp. i.–viii.). The principal documents are as follows: (1) The *Annals* in the Central Hall of the palace of Shalmaneser III. at Nimroud, partly defaced by Esarhaddon, and carried off to serve as materials for the south-western palace, whence they were rescued by Layard, and brought in fragments to the British Museum. Most of the legible portions have been published by LAYARD, *Inscriptions in the Cuneiform Character*, pls. 19, 24, 34 *a-b*, 45, 50 *a-b*, 65–68, 69 *I a-b*, *II a-b*, 71 *a-b*, 72, 73, and afterwards by ROST, *Die Keilschrifttexte Tiglat-Pilesers III.*, vol. ii. pls. i.–xxiv., who, after analysing them (*De Inscriptione Tiglat-Pileser III., regis Assyriæ, quæ vocatur Annalium*, 1892), transcribed and translated into German all that remains of them (*Die Keilschrifttexte Tiglat-Pilesers III.*, vol. i. pp. 2–41). (2) The *Tablets*, K. 3571 (H. RAWLINSON, *Cun. Ins. W. As.*, vol. ii. pl. 67, and ROST, *Die Keilschrifttexte Tiglat-Pilesers III.*, vol. ii., pls. xxxv., xxxvi.–xxxviii., and p. 15, et seq.), and *D. T. 3*, in the British Museum (SCHRADER, *Zur Kritik der Inschriften Tiglath-Pileser's II.*, p. 15, et seq.), translated into French by MÉNANT, *Annales des rois d'Assyrie*, pp. 140–144; by ENEBERG, *Inscription de Tiglat-Piléser II.*, in the *Journal Asiatique*, 1875, vol. vi. pp. 441–472; into English by G. SMITH, *Assyrian Discoveries*, pp. 256–266; and by STRONG, *The Nimrûd Inscription of Tiglath-Pileser III.*, in the *Records of the Past*, 2nd ser., vol. v. pp. 115–128; into German by SCHRADER, *Inschriften Tiglath-Pileser's III.*, in the *Keilinschriftliche Bibliothek*, vol. ii. pp. 8–25, afterwards by ROST, *Die Keilschrifttexte Tiglat-Pilesers III.*, pp. 54–77. (3) The *Slabs of Nimrud*, discovered by Layard and G. Smith, published by LAYARD, *Inscriptions in the Cuneiform Character*, pls. 17, 18, 19 *b*; afterwards by H. RAWLINSON, *Cun. Ins. W. As.*, vol. iii. pl. 10, Nos. 2, 3; partly translated into English by G. SMITH, *Assyrian Discoveries*, pp. 271, 272; into German by SCHRADER, *Inschriften Tiglath-Pileser's III.*, in the *Keilinschriftliche Bibliothek*, vol. ii. pp. 2–9; and by ROST, *Die Keilschrifttexte Tiglat-Pilesers III.*, vol. i. pp. 42–53. The *Eponym Canon* gives an outline of the reign with an official list of the campaigns (SCHRADER, *Keilinschriftliche Bibliothek*, vol. i. pp. 212–215), and PINCHES, *Babylonian Chronicle*, adds a few details, classified in chronological order, to what we had learnt from the other documents (col. i. ll. 1–26; cf. WINCKLER, *Babylonische Kronik B*, in SCHRADER'S *Keilinschriftliche Bibliothek*, vol. ii. pp. 274–277).

check.[1] Those who first reached its shores became the founders of that nation of the Kaldâ which had, perhaps, already furnished Babylon with one of its dynasties ; others had soon after followed in their footsteps, and passing beyond the Kaldâ settlement, had gradually made their way along the canals which connect the Euphrates with the Tigris till they had penetrated to the lowlands of the Uknu. Towards the middle of the eighth century B.C. they wedged themselves in between Elam and Karduniash, forming so many buffer states of varying size and influence. They extended from north to south along both banks of the Tigris, their different tribes being known as the Gambulu, the Puqudu, the Litau, the Damunu, the Ruuâ, the Khindaru, the Labdudu, the Harîlu, and the Rubuu ;[2] the Itua, who formed the vanguard, reached the valleys of the Turnat during the reign of Rammân-nirâri III.[3] They were defeated in 791 B.C., but obstinately renewed hostilities in 783, 782, 777, and 769 ; favoured by circumstances, they ended by forcing the cordon of Assyrian outposts, and by the time of Assur-nirâri had secured a footing on the Lower Zab.[4] Close by, to the east of them, lay Namri and Media, both at that time in a state of absolute anarchy. The invasions of Menuas and of Argistis had entirely laid waste the country, and Sharduris III., the king who succeeded Argistis, had done nothing towards permanently incorporating them with Urartu.[5] Sharduris, while still heir-apparent to the throne, had been appointed by his father governor of the recently annexed territory belonging to Etius and the Mannai :[6] he made Lununis his headquarters,[7] and set himself to subdue the barbarians who had settled between the Kur[8] and the Araxes. When he succeeded to the throne, about 760 B.C., the enjoyment of supreme power in no way lessened his activity. On the contrary,[9] he at once

---

[1] Cf. what has already been said on this point in the *Struggle of the Nations*, pp. 669, 670, and on pp. 4, 5 of the present work.

[2] The list of Aramæan tribes, and the positions occupied by them towards the middle of the eighth century, have been given us by Tiglath-pileser III. himself, *Slabs of Nimroud, No. 2*, ll. 4–11, and the *Nimroud Inscrip.*, Rev. ll. 5–10 ; cf. ROST, *Die Keilschrifttexte Tiglat-Pilesers III.*, vol. i. pp. 48, 49, 54–57. The list is given in its entirety in FR. DELITZSCH, *Wo lag das Paradies?* pp. 227–241.

[3] The position occupied by the Itua at the beginning of the reign of Tiglath-pileser is made sufficiently clear by a passage in the *Annals*, ll. 8–10, by *Slab No. 1*, ll. 6, 7, and by the *Inscriptions*, ll. 10, 11 (cf. ROST, *Die Keilschrifttexte Tiglat-Pilesers III.*, vol. i. pp. 2, 3, 42, 43, 56, 57), which connect them with Til-Khamri or Khumut, not far from the Lesser Zab (TIELE, *Babylonisch-assyrische Gesch.*, p. 227).

[4] As to what has been said about the campaigns against the Itua, cf. pp. 99, 112, *supra*.

[5] As will be apparent later on (cf. p. 142, *infra*), Tiglath-pileser did not encounter any Urartian forces in these regions, as would almost certainly have been the case had these countries remained subject to Urartu from the invasions of Menuas and Argistis onwards.

[6] Argistis tells us in the *Annals*, D, ll. 71–74, that he had made his son satrap over the provinces won from the Mannai and Etius (SAYCE, *The Cuneiform Inscriptions of Van*, vol. xiv. p. 606) : though his name is not mentioned, Sayce believes this son must have been Sharduris.

[7] As to the identity of the Lununis mentioned in the inscriptions of Van with the modern Armavir, cf. what has been said on p. 104, note 6, *supra*.

[8] BELCK and LEHMANN, *Ueber weitere Ergebnisse ihrer Studien*, in the *Verhandlungen der Berliner anthropologischen Gesellschaft*, 1892, p. 484.

[9] Sayce dates his accession about 750 (*The Cuneiform Inscriptions of Van*, vol. xiv. p. 405), and his

fixed upon the sort of wide isthmus which separates the Araxes from Lake Urumiah, as the goal of his incursions, and overran the territory of the Babilu;[1] there he carried by storm three royal castles, twenty-three cities, and sixty villages; he then fell back upon Etius, passing through Dakis, Edias, and Urmes on his way, and brought back with him 12,735 children, 46,600 women, 12,000 men capable of bearing arms, 23,335 oxen, 58,100 sheep, and 2,500 horses;[2] these figures give some idea of the importance of his victories and the wealth of the conquered territory. So far as we can learn, he does not seem to have attacked Khubushkia,[3] nor to have entered into open rivalry with Assyria; even under the rule of Assur-nirâri III. Assyria showed a bold enough front to deter any enemy from disturbing her except when forced to do so. Sharduris merely strove to recover those portions of his inheritance to which Assyria attached but little value, and his inscriptions tell us of more than one campaign waged by him with this object against the mountaineers of Melitene, about the year 758. He captured most of their citadels, one after another: Dhumeskis, Zapsas, fourteen royal castles, and a hundred towns, including Milid itself, where King Khitaruadas held his court.[4] At this point two courses lay open before him. He could either continue his march west-wards, and, penetrating into Asia Minor, fall upon the wealthy and industrious races who led a prosperous existence between the Halys and the Sangarios, such as the Tabal, the Chalybes, and the Phrygians, or he could turn southwards. Deterred, apparently, by the dreary and monotonous aspect of the Asianic steppes, he chose the latter course; he crossed Mount Taurus, descended into Northern Syria about 756, and forced the Khâti to swear allegiance to him. Their inveterate hatred of the Assyrians led the Bît-Agusi to accept without much reluctance the supremacy of the only power which had shown itself capable of withstanding their triumphant progress. Arpad became for several years an

view has been endorsed by most historians (TIELE, *Babylonisch-assyrische Geschichte*, pp. 215, 216; HOMMEL, *Geschichte Babyloniens und Assyriens*, p. 655).

[1] The name Babilus, wrongly read Babiluniè, was identified with that of Babylon by Hincks (*On the Inscriptions of Van*, in the *J. R. As. Soc.*, vol. ix. p. 398, and in LAYARD, *Nineveh and Babylon*, pp. 342, 343, 345). Fr. Lenormant (*Lettres Assyriologiques*, vol. i. pp. 156, 157) admitted the probable correctness of this identification; Sayce places the Babilu to the north of Lake Urumiah, in the Khoi district (*The Cuneiform Inscriptions of Van*, in the *J. R. As. Soc.*, vol. xiv. p. 400).

[2] *Inscriptions of Van*, in SAYCE, *The Cuneiform Inscriptions of Van*, vol. xiv. pp. 635–642; cf. vol. xx. pp. 18, 19. The totals of the number of prisoners and cattle given in the inscriptions do not correspond exactly with the figures quoted in the course of the campaign; at this distance of time it is impossible to determine on which side the error lies.

[3] It is evident from the account of the campaigns that Tiglath-pileser occupied Khubushkia from the very commencement of his reign; we must therefore assume that the invasions of Argistis had produced only transient effects. Cf. the narrative of the campaign given on p. 142, *infra*.

[4] *Inscription of Isoglu*, in SAYCE, *The Cuneiform Inscriptions of Van*, in the *J. R. As. Soc.*, vol. xiv. pp. 642–649; cf. vol. xx. p. 19. These campaigns must have preceded the descent into Syria, and I believe this latter to have been anterior to the expedition of Assur-nirâri against Arpad in 754 B.C. Assur-nirâri probably tried to reconquer the tribes who had just become subject to Sharduris. The descent of this latter into Syria probably took place about 756 or 755 B.C., and his wars against Melitene about 758 or 757 B.C.

unfailing support to Urartu and the basis on which its rule in Syria rested. Assur-nirâri had, as we know, at first sought to recover it, but his attempt to do so in 754 B.C. was unsuccessful, and merely served to demonstrate his own weakness: [1] ten years later, Carchemish, Gurgum, Kummukh, Samalla, Unki, Kuî—in a word, all the Aramæans and the Khâti between the Euphrates and the sea had followed in the steps of the Agusi, and had acknowledged the supremacy of Sharduris.[2] This prince must now have been sorely tempted to

A VISTA OF THE
ASIANIC STEPPE.[3]

adopt, on his own account, the policy of the Ninevite monarchs, and push on in the direction of Hamath, Damascus, and the Phœnician seaboard, towards those countries of Israel and Judah which were nearly coterminous with far-off Egypt. The rapidity of the victories which he had just succeeded in winning at the foot of Mount Taurus and Mount Amanus must have seemed a happy omen of what awaited his enterprise in the valleys of the Orontes and the Jordan. Although the races of southern and central Syria had suffered less than those of the north from the ambition of the Ninevite kings, they had, none the less, been sorely tried during the previous century; and it might be questioned whether they

[1] Cf. the account of this expedition on p. 112, *supra*.

[2] The *minimum* extent of the dominions of Sharduris in Syria may be deduced from the list of the allies assigned to him by Tiglath-pileser in 743 in the *Annals*, ll. 59–62 ; cf. *Inscriptions*, Obv., ll. 45, 46.

[3] Drawn by Boudier, from a photograph by Alfred Boissier.

had derived courage from the humiliation of Assyria, or still remained in so feeble a state as to present an easy prey to the first invader.

The defeat inflicted on Mari by Rammân-nirâri in 803[1] had done but little harm to the prestige of Damascus. The influence exercised by this state from the sources of the Litany to the brook of Egypt * was based on so solid a foundation that no temporary reverse had power to weaken it. Had the Assyrian monarch thrown himself more seriously into the enterprise, and reappeared before the ramparts of the capital in the following year, refusing to leave it till he had annihilated its armies and rased its walls to the ground, then, no doubt, Israel, Judah, the Philistines, Edom, and Ammon, seeing it fully occupied in its own defence, might have forgotten the ruthless severity of Hazael, and have plucked up sufficient courage to struggle against the Damascene yoke; as it was, Rammân-nirâri did not return, and the princes who had, perhaps, for the moment, regarded him as a possible deliverer, did not venture on any concerted action. Joash, King of Judah, and Jehoahaz, King of Israel, continued to pay tribute till both their deaths, within a year of each other, Jehoahaz in 797 B.C., and Joash in 796, the first in his bed, the second by the hand of an assassin.[2] Their children, Jehoash in Israel, Amaziah in Judah, were, at first, like their parents, merely the instruments of Damascus; but before long, the conditions being favourable, they shook off their apathy and initiated a more vigorous policy, each in his own kingdom. Mari had been succeeded by a certain Ben-hadad, also a son of Hazael,[3] and possibly this change of kings was accompanied by one of those revolutions which had done so much to weaken Damascus: Jehoash rebelled and defeated Ben-hadad near Aphek and in three subsequent engagements, but he failed to make his nation completely independent, and the territory beyond Jordan still remained in the hands of the Syrians.[4] We are told that before embarking on this venture he went to consult the aged Elisha, then on his deathbed. He wept to see him in this extremity, and bending over him, cried out, "My father, my father, the chariots of Israel and the horsemen thereof!" The prophet bade him take bow and arrows and shoot from the window toward the East. The king did

---

[1] Cf. what has been said on this subject on p. 102, *supra*.

* [Not the Nile, but the Wady el Arish, the frontier between Southern Syria and Egypt. Cf. *Josh.* xv. 47; 2 *Kings* xxiv. 7, called "river" of Egypt in the A.V.—TR.]

[2] 2 *Kings* xii. 20, 21, xiii. 9; cf. 2 *Chron.* xxiv. 22–26, where the death of Joash is mentioned as one of the consequences of the Syrian invasion (cf. p. 101, *supra*), and as a punishment for his crime in killing the sons of Jehoiada.

[3] 2 *Kings* xiii. 24, 25. Winckler is of opinion (cf. p. 102, note 1, *supra*) that Mari and Ben-hadad, son of Hazael, were one and the same person.

[4] 2 *Kings* xiii. 25. The term "saviour" in 2 *Kings* xiii. 5 is generally taken as referring to Joash: Winckler, however, prefers to apply it to the King of Assyria (*Geschichte Israels*, vol. i. p. 154). The biblical text does not expressly state that Joash failed to win back the districts of Gilead from the Syrians, but affirms that he took from them the cities which Hazael "had taken out of the hand of Jehoahaz, his father." Ramah of Gilead and the cities previously annexed by Jehoahaz must, therefore, have remained in the hands of Ben-hadad; cf. STADE, *Geschichte des Volkes Israel*, vol. i. p. 570.

so, and Elisha said, " The Lord's arrow of victory * over Syria; for thou shalt smite the Syrians in Aphek till thou have consumed them." Then he went on: " Take the arrows," and the king took them; then he said, " Smite upon the ground," and the king smote thrice and stayed. And the man of God was wroth with him, and said, " Thou shouldest have smitten five or six times; then hadst thou smitten Syria till thou hadst consumed it, whereas now thou shalt smite Syria but thrice." [1] Amaziah, on his side, had routed the Edomites in the Valley of Salt, one of David's former battle-fields, and had captured their capital, Sela.[2] Elated by his success, he believed himself strong enough to break the tie of vassalage which bound him to Israel, and sent a challenge to Jehoash in Samaria. The latter, surprised at his audacity, replied in a parable, " The thistle that was in Lebanon sent to the cedar that was in Lebanon, saying, Give thy daughter to my son to wife." But " there passed by a wild beast that was in Lebanon and trode down the thistle. Thou hast indeed smitten Edom, and thine heart hath lifted thee up: glory thereof and abide at home; for why shouldest thou meddle to thy hurt that thou shouldest fall, even thou, and Judah with thee?" They met near Beth-shemesh, on the border of the Philistine lowlands. Amaziah was worsted in the engagement, and fell into the power of his rival. Jehoash entered Jerusalem and dismantled its walls for a space of four hundred cubits, " from the gate of Ephraim unto the corner gate;" he pillaged the Temple, as though it had been the abode, not of Jahveh, but of some pagan deity, insisted on receiving hostages before he would release his prisoner, and returned to Samaria, where he soon after died (781 B.C.).[3] Jeroboam II. completed that rehabilitation of Israel, of which his father had but sketched the outline; he maintained his suzerainty, first over Amaziah, and when the latter was assassinated at Lachish (764),[4] over his son, the young Azariah.[5] After the defeat of Ben-hadad near Aphek, Damascus declined still further in power, and Hadrach, suddenly emerging from obscurity, completely barred the valley of the Orontes against it. An expedition under Shalmaneser IV. in 773 seems to have precipitated it to a lower depth than it had ever reached before:[6] Jeroboam was able to wrest from it, almost without a struggle, the cities which it had usurped in the days of Jehu, and Gilead was at last set free from a yoke which had oppressed it for more than a

---

* [Heb. " salvation;" A.V. "deliverance."—Tr.]

[1] 2 *Kings* xiii. 14–19.

[2] 2 *Kings* xiv. 7; cf. 2 *Chron.* xxv. 11, 12. Sela was rebuilt, and received the name of Joktheel from its Hebrew masters. The subjection of the country was complete, for, later on, the Hebrew chronicler tells of the conquest of Elath by King Azariah, son of Amaziah (2 *Kings* xiv. 22).

[3] 2 *Kings* xiv. 8–16; cf. 2 *Chron.* xxv. 17–24.

[4] 2 *Kings* xiv. 19, 20; cf. 2 *Chron.* xxv. 27, 28.

[5] The Hebrew texts make no mention of this subjection of Judah to Jeroboam II.; that it actually took place must, however, be admitted, at any rate in so far as the first half of the reign of Azariah is concerned, as a necessary outcome of the events of the preceding reigns.

[6] Cf. what has been said on this subject on pp. 110, 111, *supra*.

century.   Tradition goes so far as to affirm that Israel reconquered the Bekaa, Hamath, and Damascus, those northern territories once possessed by David, and it is quite possible that its rivals, menaced from afar by Assyria and hard pressed at their own doors by Hadrach, may have resorted to one of those propitiatory overtures which eastern monarchs are only too ready to recognise as acts of submission.   The lesser southern states, such as Ammon, the Bedâwin tribes of Hauran, and, at the opposite extremity of the kingdom, the Philistines,[1] who had bowed themselves before Hazael in the days of his prosperity, now transferred their homage to Israel.   Moab alone offered any serious resist-

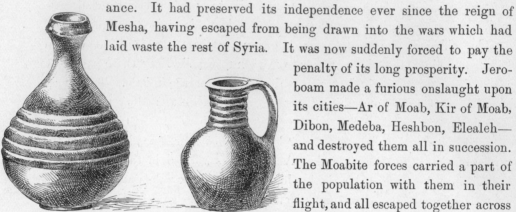

ance.   It had preserved its independence ever since the reign of Mesha, having escaped from being drawn into the wars which had laid waste the rest of Syria.   It was now suddenly forced to pay the penalty of its long prosperity.   Jeroboam made a furious onslaught upon its cities—Ar of Moab, Kir of Moab, Dibon, Medeba, Heshbon, Elealeh— and destroyed them all in succession. The Moabite forces carried a part of the population with them in their flight, and all escaped together across the deserts which enclose the southern basin of the Dead Sea.   On the

SPECIMENS OF HEBREW POTTERY.[2]

frontier of Edom they begged for sanctuary, but the King of Judah, to whom the Edomite valleys belonged, did not dare to shelter the vanquished enemies of his suzerain, and one of his prophets, forgetting his hatred of Israel in delight at being able to gratify his grudge against Moab, greeted them in their distress with a hymn of joy—" I will water thee with my tears, O Heshbon and Elealeh : for upon thy summer fruits and upon thy harvest the battle shout is fallen.   And gladness is taken away and joy out of the fruitful fields ; and in the vineyards there shall be no singing, neither joyful noise ; no treader shall tread out wine in the presses ; I have made the vintage shout to cease.   Wherefore my bowels sound like an harp for Moab, and mine inward parts for Kir-Heres.   And it shall come to pass, when Moab presenteth himself, when he wearieth himself upon the high place, and shall come to his sanctuary to pray, he shall not prevail ! "[3]

[1] The conquests of Jeroboam II. are indicated very briefly in 2 *Kings* xiv. 25-28 ; cf. *Amos* vi. 14, where the expressions employed by the prophet imply that at the time at which he wrote the whole of the ancient kingdom of David, Judah included, was in the possession of Israel.

[2] Drawn by Faucher-Gudin, from sketches by WARREN, *Plans, Elevations, Sections,* pl. xlv.

[3] *Isa.* xv. 1-9 ; xvi. 1-12.   This prophecy, which had been pronounced against Moab "in the old days," and which is appropriated by Isaiah (xvi. 13, 14), has been attributed by Hitzig (*Des Propheten Jona Orakel über Moab,* 1831) to Jonah, son of Amittaî, of Gath-Hepher, who actually lived

This revival, like the former greatness of David and Solomon, was due not so much to any inherent energy on the part of Israel, as to the weakness of the nations on its frontiers.   Egypt was not in the habit of intervening in the quarrels of Asia, and Assyria was suffering from a temporary eclipse.   Damascus had suddenly collapsed, and Hadrach or Mansuati,[1] the cities which sought to take its place, found themselves fully employed in repelling the intermittent attacks of the Assyrian ; the Hebrews, for a quarter of a century, therefore, had the stage to themselves, there being no other actors to dispute their possession

ISRAELITES OF THE HIGHER CLASS IN THE TIME OF SHALMANESER III.[2]

of it.   During the three hundred years of their existence as a monarchy they had adopted nearly all the laws and customs of the races over whom they held sway, and by whom they were completely surrounded.   The bulk of the people devoted themselves to the pasturing and rearing of cattle, and, during the better part of the year, preferred to live in tents, unless war rendered such a practice impossible.[3]   They had few industries save those of the potter[4] and the smith,[5] and their trade was almost entirely in the hands of foreigners.   We

in the time of Jeroboam II. (2 *Kings* xiv. 25).   It is now generally recognised as the production of an anonymous Judæan prophet, and the earliest authentic fragment of prophetic literature which has come down to us (CORNILL, *Einleitung in das Alte Testament*, 2nd edit., pp. 141, 142 ; DRIVER, *Introduction to the Literature of the Old Testament*, 5th edit., pp. 202, 203).

[1] Cf. what has been said on this subject on p. 100, note 2, and p. 111, *supra*.

[2] Drawn by Faucher-Gudin from one of the bas-reliefs of the Black Obelisk ; cf. LAYARD, *The Monuments of Nineveh*, vol. i. pl. 55.

[3] Cf. the passage in 2 *Kings* xiii. 5, "And the children of Israel dwelt in their tents as beforetime."   Although the word *ôhel* had by that time acquired the more general meaning of *habitation*, the context here seems to require us to translate it by its original meaning *tent*.

[4] Pottery is mentioned in 2 *Sam.* xvii. 28 ; numerous fragments dating from the monarchical period have been found at Jerusalem and at Lachish.

[5] The story of Tubal-Cain (*Gen.* iv. 22) shows the antiquity of the ironworker's art among the Israelites ; the smith is practically the only artisan to be found amongst nomadic tribes.

find, however, Hebrew merchants in Egypt,[1] at Tyre, and in Cœle-Syria, and they were so numerous at Damascus that they requested that a special bazaar might be allotted to them, similar to that occupied by the merchants of Damascus in Samaria from time immemorial.[2] The Hebrew monarchs had done their best to encourage this growing desire for trade. It was only the complicated state of Syrian politics that prevented them from following the example of Solomon, and opening communications by sea with the far-famed countries of Ophir, either in competition with the Phœnicians or under their guidance. Indeed, as we have seen, Jehoshaphat, encouraged by his alliance with the house of Omri, tried to establish a seagoing fleet, but found that peasants could not be turned into sailors at a day's notice, and the vessel built by him at Eziongeber was wrecked before it left the harbour.[3]

JUDÆAN PEASANTS.[4]

In appearance, the Hebrew towns closely resembled the ancient Canaanite cities. Egyptian influences still predominated in their architecture, as may be seen from what is still left of the walls of Lachish,[5] and they were fortified in such a way as to be able to defy the military engines of besiegers. This applies not only to capitals, like Jerusalem, Tirzah, and Samaria, but even to those towns which

[1] The accurate ideas on the subject of Egypt possessed by the earliest compilers of the traditions contained in Genesis and Exodus, prove that Hebrew merchants must have been in constant communication with that country about the time with which we are now concerned.

[2] 1 *Kings* xx. 34; cf. what has been said on this point in the *Struggle of the Nations*, pp. 781, 786.

[3] 1 *Kings* xxii. 49, 50; 2 *Chron.* xx. 35–37; cf. p. 80, *supra.*

[4] Drawn by Boudier, from LAYARD, *Monuments of Nineveh*, vol. i. pl. 23. These figures are taken from a bas-relief which represents Sennacherib receiving the submission of Judah before Lachish. The whole is given in Chapter III. of the present work.

[5] FLINDERS PETRIE, *Tell el Hesy*, pp. 23–27; cf. the vignette reproduced on p. 747 of the *Struggle of the Nations*. As to the appearance and defences of the Canaanite cities, cf. pp. 127–130, *ibid.*

commanded a road or mountain pass, the ford of a river, or the entrance to some fertile plain ; there were scores of these on the frontiers of the two kingdoms, and in those portions of their territory which lay exposed to the attacks of Damascus, Moab, Edom, or the Philistines.[1] The daily life of the inhabitants was, to all intents, the same as at Arpad, Sidon, or Gaza; and the dress, dwellings, and customs of the upper and middle classes cannot have differed in any marked degree from those of the corresponding grades of society in Syria. The men wore over their tunic a fringed kaftan, with short sleeves, open in front, a low-crowned hat, and sandals or shoes of pliant leather ;[2] they curled their beards and hair, painted their eyes and cheeks, and wore many jewels; while their wives adopted all the latest refinements in vogue in the harems of Damascus, Tyre, or Nineveh.[3] Descendants of ancient families paid for all this luxury out of the revenues of the wide domains they had inherited; others kept it up by less honourable means, by usury, corruption, and by the exercise of a ruthless violence towards neighbours who were unable to defend themselves. The king himself set them an evil example, and did not hesitate to

WOMEN AND CHILDREN OF JUDÆA.[4]

assassinate one of his subjects in order that he might seize a vineyard which he coveted ;[5] it was not to be wondered at, therefore, that the nobles of Ephraim "sold the righteous for silver, and the needy for a pair of

---

[1] 2 *Chron.* xi. 6–10, where we find a list of the towns fortified by Rehoboam : Bethlehem, Etam, Beth-zur, Soco, Adullam, Gath, Mareshah, Ziph, Adoraim, Lachish, Azekah, Zorah, Ajalon, Hebron.

[2] The kaftan met with in these parts seems to correspond to the *meîl* (R.V. " ephod ") of the biblical texts (1 *Sam.* ii. 19; xviii. 4, etc.).

[3] *Isa.* iii. 16-24 describes in detail the whole equipment of jewels, paint, and garments required by the fashionable women of Jerusalem during the last thirty years of the eighth century B.C.

[4] Drawn by Boudier, from the same source which furnished the illustration on p. 126.

[5] Cf. the well-known episode of Naboth and Ahab in 1 *Kings* xxi.

shoes;"[1] that they demanded gifts of wheat, and "turned the needy from their right" when they sat as a jury "at the gate."[2]   From top to bottom of the social ladder the stronger and wealthier oppressed those who were weaker or poorer than themselves, leaving them with no hope of redress except at the hands of the king.[3]   Unfortunately, the king, when he did not himself set the example of oppression, seldom possessed the resources necessary to make his decisions effective.   True, he was chief of the most influential family in either Judah or Israel, a chief by divine appointment, consecrated by the priests and prophets of Jahveh, a priest of the Lord,[4] and he was master in his own city of Jerusalem or Samaria, but his authority did not extend far beyond the walls.   It was not the old tribal organisation that embarrassed him, for the secondary tribes had almost entirely given up their claims to political independence.   The division of the country into provinces, a consequence of the establishment of financial districts by Solomon, had broken them up, and they gradually gave way before the two houses of Ephraim and Judah;[5] but the great landed proprietors, especially those who held royal fiefs, enjoyed almost unlimited power within their own domains.   They were, indeed, called on to render military service, to furnish forced labour, and to pay certain trifling dues into the royal treasury;[6] but, otherwise, they were absolute masters in their own domains, and the sovereign was obliged to employ force if he wished to extort any tax or act of homage which they were unwilling to render.   For this purpose he had a standing army distributed in strong detachments along the frontier, but the flower of his forces was concentrated round the royal residence to serve as a body-guard.   It included whole companies of foreign mercenaries, like those Cretan and Carian warriors who, since the time of David, had kept guard round the Kings of Judah;[7] these, in time of war,[8] were reinforced by militia, drawn entirely from among the landed proprietors, and the whole force, when commanded by an energetic leader, formed a host capable of meeting on equal terms the armies of Damascus,

---

[1] *Amos* ii. 6.   [2] *Amos* v. 11, 12.

[3] 2 *Kings* vi. 26–30; viii. 3–8, where, in both instances, it is a woman who appeals to the king. Cf. for the period of David and Solomon, 2 *Sam.* xiv. 1–20, and 1 *Kings* iii. 16–27.

[4] Cf. the anointing of Saul (1 *Sam.* ix. 16; x. 1; and xv. 1), of David (1 *Sam.* xvi. 1–3, 12, 13), of Solomon (1 *Kings* i. 34, 39, 45), of Jehu (2 *Kings* ix. 1–10), and compare it with the unction received by the priests on their admission to the priesthood (*Exod.* xxix. 7; xxx. 22, 23; cf. *Lev.* viii. 12, 30; x. 7).

[5] As to Solomon's districts, cf. *Struggle of the Nations*, pp. 738, 739.

[6] 1 *Kings* xv. 22 (cf. 2 *Chron.* xvi. 6), where "King Asa made a proclamation unto all Judah; none was exempted," the object in this case being the destruction of Ramah, the building of which had been begun by Baasha (cf. *Struggle of the Nations*, p. 779).

[7] The Carians or Cretans are again referred to in the history of Athaliah (2 *Kings* xi. 4).

[8] Taking the tribute paid by Menahem to Pul (2 *Kings* xv. 19, 20) as a basis, it has been estimated that the owners of landed estate in Israel, who were in that capacity liable to render military service, numbered 60,000 in the time of that king (ED. MEYER, *Gesch. des Alterthums*, vol. i. p. 449; cf. STADE, *Gesch. des Volkes Israel*, vol. i. p. 576, note 4); all others were exempt from military service.

Edom, or Moab, or even the veterans of Egypt and Assyria. The reigning prince was hereditary commander-in-chief, but the *shar zaba,* or captain of the troops, often took his place, as in the time of David, and thereby became the most important person in the kingdom. More than one of these officers had already turned against their sovereign the forces which he had entrusted to them, and these revolts, when crowned with success, had, on various occasions, in Israel at any rate, led to a change of dynasty: Omri had been *shar zaba* when he mutinied against Zimri, the assassin of Elah, and Jehu occupied the same position when Elisha deputed him to destroy the house of Omri.[1]

The political constitutions of Judah and Israel were, on the whole, very similar to those of the numerous states which shared the territory of Syria between them, and their domestic history gives us a fairly exact idea of the revolutions which agitated Damascus, Hamath, Carchemish, Arpad, and the principalities of Amanos and Lebanon about the same period. It would seem, however, that none of these other nations possessed a literary or religious life of any great intensity. They had their archives, it is true, in which were accumulated documents relating to their past history, their rituals of theology and religious worship, their collections of hymns and national songs; but none of these have survived, and the very few inscriptions that have come down to us merely show that they had nearly all of them adopted the alphabet invented by the Phœnicians.[2] The Israelites, initiated by them into the art of writing, lost no time in setting down, in their turn, all they could recall of the destinies of their race from the creation of the world down to the time in which they lived. From the beginning of the monarchical epoch onwards, their scribes collected together in the *Book of the Wars of the Lord,* the *Book of Jashar,* and in other works the titles of which have not survived, lyrics of different dates, in which nameless poets had sung the victories and glorious deeds of their national heroes, such as the Song of the Well, the Hymn of Moses, the triumphal Ode of Deborah, and the Blessing of Jacob.[3] They were able to

---

[1] Cf. what has been said about the rebellion of Omri in the *Struggle of the Nations,* p. 779, and about that of Jehu on pp. 84, 85, *supra.*

[2] Cf., in addition to the Mesha inscription quoted on p. 81, *supra,* the Aramæan inscriptions at Zinjirli (*Ausgrabungen in Sendschirli,* vol. i. pp. 55–84, and pls. vii., viii.) and at Nerab (CLERMONT-GANNEAU, *Études d'Archéologie Orientale,* vol. ii. pp. 182–223).

[3] The books of *Jashar* and of the *Wars of the Lord* appear to date from the IXth century B.C. (WILDEBOER, *Die Litteratur des Alten Testaments,* p. 73); as the latter is quoted in the Elohist narrative, it cannot have been compiled later than the beginning of the VIIIth century B.C. (CORNILL, *Einleitung in das Alte Testament,* 2nd edit., p. 69). The passage in *Numb.* xxi. 14b, 15, is the only one expressly attributed by the testimony of the ancients to the *Book of the Wars of the Lord,* but modern writers add to this the *Song of the Well* (*Numb.* xxi. 17b, 18), and the Song of Victory over Moab (*Numb.* xxi. 27b–30). The *Song of the Bow* (2 *Sam.* i. 19–27) admittedly formed part of the *Book of Jashar;* cf. *Struggle of the Nations,* pp. 720, 721. Joshua's Song of Victory over the Amorites (*Josh.* x. 13), and very probably the couplet recited by Solomon at the dedication of the Temple (1 *Kings* viii. 12, 13, placed by the LXX. after verse 53), also formed part of it, as also the *Song of Deborah* (cf. *Struggle of the Nations,* pp. 687, 688) and the Blessing of Jacob (*Gen.* xlix. 1–27).

K

draw upon traditions which preserved the memory of what had taken place in the time of the Judges ;[1] and when that patriarchal form of government was succeeded by a monarchy, they had narratives of the ark of the Lord and its wanderings, of Samuel, Saul, David, and Solomon,[2] not to mention the official records which, since then, had been continuously produced and accumulated by the court historians.[3]   It may be that more than one writer had already endeavoured to evolve from these materials an Epic of Jahveh and His faithful people, but in the second half of the IXth century B.C., perhaps in the time of Jehoshaphat, a member of the tribe of Judah undertook to put forth a fresh edition.[4]   He related how God, after creating the universe out of chaos, had chosen His own people, and had led them, after trials innumerable, to the conquest of the Promised Land.   He showed, as he went on, the origin of the tribes identified with the children of Israel, and the covenants made by Jahveh with Moses in the Arabian desert ; while accepting the stories connected with the ancient sanctuaries of the north and east at Shechem, Bethel, Peniel, Mahanaim, and Succoth, it was at Hebron in Judah that he placed the principal residence of Abraham and his descendants.   His style, while simple and direct, is at the same time singularly graceful and vivacious; the incidents he gives are carefully selected, apt and characteristic, while his narrative passes from scene to scene without trace of flagging, unburdened by useless details, and his dialogue, always natural and easy, rises without effort from the level of familiar conversation to heights of impassioned eloquence.   His aim was not merely to compile the history of his people : he desired at the same time to edify them, by showing how sin first came into the world through disobedience to the

[1] Wellhausen was the first to admit the existence of a Book of Judges prior to the epoch of Deuteronomy (BLEEK and WELLHAUSEN, *Einleitung in das Alte Testament*, 4th edit., § 92), and his opinion has been adopted by Kuenen (*Hist.-Kritik. Onderzoek*, vol. i. § 19, 11), by Driver (*An Introduction to the Literature of the Old Testament*, pp. 157, 158).   This book was probably drawn upon by the two historians of the IXth and VIIIth centuries B.C. of whom we are about to speak; some of the narratives, such as the story of Abimelech, and possibly that of Ehud, may have been taken from a document written at the end of the Xth or beginning of the IXth centuries B.C.

[2] The revolutions which occurred in the family of David (2 *Sam.* ix.–xx.; cf. *Struggle of the Nations*, pp. 734–736) bear so evident a stamp of authenticity that they have been attributed to a contemporary writer, perhaps Ahimaaz, son of Zadok (2 *Sam.* xv. 27), who took part in the events in question (KLOSTERMANN, *Die Bücher Samuelis und Könige*, p. xxxii., et seq.).   But apart from this, the existence is generally admitted of two or three books which were drawn up shortly after the separation of the tribes, containing a kind of epic of the history of the first two kings; the one dealing with Saul, for instance, was probably written in the time of Jeroboam I. (KITTEL, *Gesch. der Hebräer*, vol. ii. p. 32).

[3] The two lists in which the names of the principal personages at the court of David are handed down to us, mention a certain Jehoshaphat, son of Ahilud, who was *mazkir*, or recorder (2 *Sam.* viii. 16 and xx. 24); he retained his post under Solomon (1 *Kings* iv. 3).   As to the share attributable to these personages in the history of the two kingdoms that has come down to us, see the very lucid summary in CORNILL, *Einleitung in das Alte Testament*, 2nd edit., pp. 124, 125.

[4] The approximate date of the composition and source of this first *Jehovist* is still an open question.   Reuss (*Geschichte des Alten Testaments*, 2nd edit., p. 249, et seq.) and Kuenen (*H. C. Onderzoek*, vol. i. § 13, No. 9), not to mention others, believe the Jehovist writer to have been a native of the northern kingdom ; I have adopted the opposite view, which is supported by Dillmann, Stade, Wellhausen, Budde, and most modern critics.

commandments of the Most High, and how man, prosperous so long as he kept to the laws of the covenant, fell into difficulties as soon as he transgressed or failed to respect them. His concept of Jahveh is in the highest degree a concrete one: he regards Him as a Being superior to other beings, but made like unto them and moved by the same passions. He shows anger and is appeased, displays sorrow and repents Him of the evil.[1] When the descendants of Noah build a tower and a city, He draws nigh to examine what they have done, and having taken account of their work, confounds their language and thus prevents them from proceeding farther.[2] He desires, later on, to confer a favour on His servant Abraham: He appears to him in human form, and eats and drinks with him.[3] Sodom and Gomorrah had committed abominable iniquities, the cry against them was great and their sin very grievous; but before punishing them, He tells Abraham that He will "go down and see whether they have done according to the cry of it which is come unto Me; and if not, I will know."[4] Elsewhere He wrestles a whole night long with Jacob;[5] or falls upon Moses, seeking to kill him, until appeased by Zipporah, who casts the blood-stained foreskin of her child at her husband's feet.[6] This book, though it breathes the spirit of the prophets and was perhaps written in one of their schools, did not, however, include all the current narratives, and omitted many traditions that were passing from lip to lip; moreover, the excessive materialism of its treatment no longer harmonised with that more idealised concept of the Deity which had already begun to prevail. Consequently, within less than a century of its appearance, more than one version containing changes and interpolations in the narrative came to be circulated,[7] till a scribe of Ephraim, who flourished in the time of Jeroboam II., took up the subject and dealt with it in a different fashion.[8] Putting on one side the primitive accounts of the origin of the human

[1] *Exod.* iv. 14 and xxxii. 10, anger of Jahveh against Moses and against Israel; *Gen.* vi. 6, 7, where He repents and is sorry for having created man; and *Exod.* xxxii. 14, where He repents Him of the evil He had intended to do unto Israel. A collection of these and other similar expressions to be met with in the fragments of this first writer will be found in DILLMAN, *Die Genesis,* p. 46.

[2] *Gen.* xi. 5–8.   [3] *Gen.* xviii. (cf. the summary given on p. 68 of the *Struggle of the Nations*).

[4] *Gen.* xviii. and xix.   [5] *Gen.* xxxii. 24, 25 (cf. the summary on p. 69 of the *Struggle of the Nations*). [6] *Exod.* iv. 24–26.

[7] Schrader and Wellhausen have drawn attention to contradictions in the primitive history of humanity as presented by the Jehovist which forbid us to accept it as the work of a single writer. Nor can these inconsistencies be due to the influence of the Elohist, since the latter did not deal with this period in his book. Budde has maintained that the primitive work contained no account of the Deluge, and traced the descent of all the nations, Israel included, back to Cain, and he declares he can detect in the earlier chapters of Genesis traces of a first Jehovist, whom he calls J[1]. A second Jehovist, J[2], who flourished between 800 and 700 B.C., is supposed to have added to the contribution of the first, certain details borrowed from the Babylonian tradition, such as the Deluge, the story of Noah, of Nimrod, etc. Finally, a third Jehovist is said to have thrown the versions of his two predecessors into one, taking J[2] as the basis of his work. Cf. BUDDE, *Die Biblische Urgeschichte,* pp. 455–520, where a summary of the author's whole theory is given; in an *Appendix* (pp. 521–531) he gives a hypothetical text of J[1].

[8] The date and origin of the Elohist have given rise to no less controversy than those of the

race which his predecessors had taken pleasure in elaborating, he confined his attention solely to events since the birth of Abraham;[1] his origin is betrayed by the preference he displays for details calculated to flatter the self-esteem of the northern tribes. To his eyes, Joseph is the noblest of all the sons of Jacob, before whom all the rest must bow their heads, as to a king ; next to Joseph comes Reuben, to whom—rather than to Judah[2]—he gives the place as firstborn. He groups his characters round Bethel and Shechem, the sanctuaries of Israel ; even Abraham is represented as residing, not at Hebron in Judæa, but at Beersheba, a spot held in deep veneration by pilgrims belonging to the ten tribes.[3] It is in his concept of the Supreme Being, however, that he differs most widely from his predecessors. God is, according to him, widely removed from ordinary humanity. He no longer reveals Himself at all times and in all places, but works rather by night, and appears to men in their dreams, or, when circumstances require His active interference, is content to send His angels rather than come in His own person.[4] Indeed, such cases of active interference are of rare occurrence, and He prefers to accomplish His purpose through human agents, who act unconsciously, or even in direct contravention of their own clearly expressed intentions.[5] Moreover, it was only by degrees that He revealed His true nature and title ; the patriarchs, Abraham, Isaac, Jacob, and Joseph, had called Him Elohim, or " the gods," and it was not until the coming of Moses that He disclosed His real name of Jahveh to His worshippers.[6] In a word, this new historian shows us in every line that the theological instinct has superseded popular enthusiasm, and his work loses unmistakably in literary interest by the change. We feel that he is wanting in feeling and inspiration ; his characters no longer palpitate with life ; his narrative drags, its interest decreases, and his language is often deficient in force and colour.

But while writers, trained in the schools of the prophets, thus sought to bring home to the people the benefits which their God had showered on them, the people themselves showed signs of disaffection towards Him, or were, at any rate, inclined to associate with Him other gods borrowed from neighbouring states, and to overlay the worship they rendered Him with ceremonies and

Jehovist : the view most generally adopted is that he was a native of the northern kingdom, and flourished about 750 B.C. (STADE, *Geschichte des Volkes Israel*, vol. i. p. 59).

[1] Budde seems to have proved conclusively that the Elohist did not write any part of the primitive history of mankind (*Biblische Urgeschichte*, p. 493, et seq.).

[2] *Gen.* xxxvii. 21, 22, 29, 30 ; xlii. 22, 37 ; whereas in *Gen.* xliii. 3, 8–10, where the narrative is from the pen of the Jehovist, it is Judah that plays the principal part : it is possible that, in *Gen.* xxxvii. 21, Reuben has been substituted in the existing text for Judah.

[3] *Gen.* xxi. 31, 33 ; xxii. 19 ; the importance of Beersheba as a holy place resorted to by pilgrims from the northern kingdom is shown in 1 *Kings* xix. 3, and *Amos* v. 5 ; viii. 14.

[4] *Gen.* xx. 3–8 ; xxviii. 11–15 ; xxxi. 24 ; *Numb.* xxii. 8–12, 20.

[5] *Gen.* l. 20, end of the story of Joseph : " And as for you, ye meant evil against me ; but God meant it for good, to bring it to pass as it is this day, to save much people alive."

[6] *Exod.* iii. 13, 14 ; verse 15 is an interpolation of much later date.

ideas inconsistent with its original purity. The permanent division of the nation into two independent kingdoms had had its effect on their religion as well as on their political life, and had separated the worshippers into two hostile camps. The inhabitants of Judah still continued to build altars on their high places, as they had done in the time before David; there, the devout prostrated themselves before the sacred stones and before the Asherah, or went in unto the *kedeshôth* in honour of Astarte, and in Jahveh's own temple at Jerusalem they had set up the image of a brazen serpent to which they paid homage.[1] The feeling, however, that the patron deity of the chosen people could have but one recognised habitation—the temple built for Him by Solomon—and that the priests of this temple were alone qualified to officiate there in an effective manner, came to prevail more and more strongly in Judæa. The king, indeed, continued to offer sacrifices and prayer there,[2] but the common people could no longer intercede with their God except through the agency of the priests. The latter, in their turn, tended to develop into a close corporation of families consecrated for generations past to the priestly office; they came in time to form a tribe by themselves, which took rank among the other tribes of Israel, and claimed Levi, one of the twelve sons of Jacob, as its ancestor. Their head, chosen from among the descendants of Zadok, who had been the first high priest in the reign of Solomon, was by virtue of his office one of the chief ministers of the crown, and we know what an important part was played by Jehoiadah in the revolution which led to the deposition of Athaliah;[3] the high priest was, however, no less subordinate to the supreme power than his fellow-ministers, and the sanctity of his office did not avail to protect him from ill-treatment or death if he incurred the displeasure of his sovereign.[4] He had control over a treasury continually enriched by the offerings of the faithful, and did not always turn his trust to the best uses; in times of extreme distress the king used to borrow from him as a last resource, in order to bring about the withdrawal of an invader, or purchase the help of a powerful ally.[5] The

[1] Cf. what we are told of idolatrous practices in Judah under Rehoboam and Abijam (1 *Kings* xiv. 22–24; xv. 3), and of the tolerance of high places by Asa and Jehoshaphat (1 *Kings* xv. 14; xxii. 44); even at the period now under consideration neither Amaziah (2 *Kings* xiv. 4) nor Azariah (2 *Kings* xv. 4) showed any disposition to prohibit them. The brazen serpent was still in existence in the time of Hezekiah, at the close of the VIIIth century B.C. (2 *Kings* xviii. 4).

[2] 2 *Kings* xvi. 10–16, where Ahaz is described as offering sacrifice and giving instructions to the high priest Urijah as to the reconstruction and service of the altar; cf. 2 *Chron.* xxvi. 16–21, where similar conduct on the part of Uzziah is recorded, and where the leprosy by which he was attacked is, in accordance with the belief of later times, represented as a punishment of the sacrilege committed by him in attempting to perform the sacrifice in person.

[3] Cf. pp. 100, 101, *supra*.

[4] In order to form an idea of the relative positions occupied by the king and the high priest, we must read what is told of Jehoiadah and Joash (2 *Kings* xii. 6–16), or Urijah and Ahaz (2 *Kings* xvi. 10–16); the story runs that Zechariah was put to death by Joash (2 *Chron.* xxiv. 22).

[5] Asa did so in order to secure Ben-hadad's help against Baasha (1 *Kings* xv. 18, 19; cf. 2 *Chron.* xvi. 2, 3): as to the revenues by which the treasury of the temple was supported and the special dues appropriated to it, cf. 2 *Kings* xii. 4, 5, 7–16, and xxii. 4–7, 9.

capital of Israel was of too recent foundation to allow of its chapel royal becoming the official centre of national worship; the temple and priesthood of Samaria never succeeded in effacing the prestige enjoyed by the ancient oracles, though in the reign of both the first and second Jeroboam, Dan, Bethel, Gilgal, and Mizpah had each its band of chosen worshippers.[1] At these centres adoration was rendered to the animal presentment of Jahveh,[2] and even prophets like Elijah and Elisha did not condemn this as heretical; they had enough to do in hunting down the followers of Baal without entering into open conflict with the worshippers of the golden calf.[3] The priesthood of the northern kingdom was not confined to members of the family of Levi, but was recruited from all the tribes; it levied a tithe on the harvest, reserved to itself the pick

EGYPTIAN ALTAR AT DEIR-EL-BAHARI.[5]

of the offerings and victims, and jealously forbade a plurality of sanctuaries.[4] The *Book of the Covenant*[6] has handed down to us the regulations in force at one of these temples, perhaps that of Bethel, one of the wealthiest of them all. The directions in regard to ritual are extremely simple, and the moral code is based throughout on the inexorable *lex talionis*, "Life for life, eye for eye, tooth for tooth, hand for hand, foot for foot, burning for burning, wound for wound, stripe for stripe."[7] This brief code must have been almost universally applicable to every conjuncture of civil and religious life in Judah no less than in Israel. On one point only do we find a disagreement, and that is in connection with the one and only Holy of Holies to the possession of which the southern kingdom had begun to lay claim: in a passage full of significance Jahveh declares, "An altar of earth thou shalt make unto Me, and shalt sacrifice thereon thy burnt offerings and

---

[1] In regard to the foundations of Jeroboam I. at Bethel and Dan, cf. what is said in the *Struggle of the Nations*, pp. 754, 755. In the time of Jeroboam II., Bethel, Gilgal, and Dan are mentioned by Amos (iv. 4; v. 5, 6; viii. 14), by Hosea (iv. 15; ix. 15; xii. 12). Mizpah is mentioned by Hosea (v. 1), and so is Tabor. The altar of Jahveh on Mount Carmel was restored by Elijah (1 *Kings* xviii. 30).
[2] The golden calves at Dan and Bethel are referred to by Amos (viii. 14) and Hosea (x. 5), where Bethel is called Beth-aven; as to the golden calf at Samaria, cf. *Amos* viii. 14 and *Hos.* viii. 5, 6.
[3] KITTEL, *Geschichte der Hebräer*, vol. ii. p. 261.   [4] *Amos* iv. 4, 5; v. 21–23.
[5] Drawn by Faucher-Gudin, from a restoration by NAVILLE, *Deir-el-Bahari*, vol. i. pl. viii.
[6] This is the title given in *Exod.* xxiv. 7 to a writing in which Moses is said to have entered the covenant made between Jahveh and Israel; it is preserved, with certain interpolations and alterations, in *Exod.* xx. 23—xxiii. 33. It was inserted in its entirety in the Elohist narrative, there taking the place at present occupied by Deuteronomy in the Pentateuch, viz. that of the covenant made between Jahveh and Israel prior to the crossing of the Jordan (KUENEN, *H. C. Onderzoek*, i. § 13, No. 32). Reuss tries to make out that it was the code promulgated on the occasion of Jehoshaphat's legal reforms (*Geschichte der Heiligen Schriften*, 2nd edit., § 200, pp. 231–233), which is only referred to in 2 *Chron.* xvii. 7–9; cf. xix. 5. A more probable theory is that it was the "custom" of one of the great sanctuaries of the northern kingdom (probably that of Bethel, as suggested by OORT, *Oud-Israel's Rechtswezen*, pp. 19, 23), reduced to writing at the end of the Xth or during the IXth century B.C.   [7] *Exod.* xxi. 23–25.

thy peace offerings, thy sheep and thine oxen: in every place where I record My name I will come unto thee and I will bless thee. And if thou make Me an altar of stone, thou shalt not build it of hewn stones: for if thou lift up thy tool upon it, thou hast polluted it. Neither shalt thou go up by steps unto Mine altar, that thy nakedness be not discovered thereon."[1] The patriarchs and early ancestors of the race had performed their sacrifices in the open air, on rude and low altars, differing widely from lofty and elaborately ornamented erections like those at Jerusalem, which seem to have borne a resemblance to the altars of the Egyptians: the author of the *Book of the Covenant* advises the faithful to follow the example of those great men rather than that of the Levites of Judah. Nevertheless this multiplicity of high places was not without its dangers; it led the common people to confuse Jahveh with the idols of Canaan, and encouraged the spread of foreign superstitions. The misfortunes which had come thick and fast upon the Israelites ever since the division of the kingdom had made them only too ready to seek elsewhere that support and consolation which they could no longer find at home. The gods of Damascus and Assur who had caused the downfall of Gath, of Calneh, and of Hamath,[2] those of Tyre and Sidon who lavished upon the Phœnicians the wealth of the seas, or even the deities of Ammon, Moab, or Edom, might well appear more desirable than a Being Who, in spite of His former promises, seemed powerless to protect His own people. A number of the Israelites transferred their allegiance to these powerful deities, prostrated themselves before the celestial host, flocked round the resting-places of Kevan, the star of El, and carried the tabernacles of the King of heaven;[3] nor was Judah slow to follow their example. The prophets, however, did not view their persistent ill-fortune in the same light as the common people; far from accepting it as a proof of the power of other divinities, they recognised in it a mark of Jahveh's superiority. In their eyes Jahveh was the one God, compared with Whom the pagan deities were no gods at all, and could not even be said to exist. He might, had He so willed it, have bestowed His protection on any one of the numerous races whom He had planted on the earth; but as a special favour, which He was under no obligation to confer, He had chosen Israel to be His own people, and had promised them that they should occupy Canaan so long as they kept free from sin. But Israel had sinned, Israel had followed after idols; its misfortunes were, therefore, but the just penalty of its unfaithfulness. Thus conceived, Jahveh ceased to be merely the god of a nation—He became the God of the whole world; and it is in the guise of a universal Deity that some, at any rate, of the prophets begin to represent Him from the time of Jeroboam II. onwards.[4]

---

[1] *Exod.* xx. 24–26.

[2] *Amos* vi. 2; with regard to the destruction of Gath by Hazael, cf. p. 101, *supra.*   [3] *Amos* v. 26, 27.

[4] As to this change in the concept of the Being of God found in the prophets, cf. WELLHAUSEN,

This change of view in regard to the Being of Jahveh coincided with a no less marked alteration in the character of His prophets. At first they had taken an active part in public affairs; they had thrown themselves into the political movements of the time, and had often directed their course,[1] by persuasion when persuasion sufficed, by violence when violence was the only means that was left to them of enforcing the decrees of the Most High. Not long before this, we find Elisha secretly conspiring against the successors of Ahab, and taking a decisive part in the revolution which set the house of Jehu on the throne in place of that of Omri;[2] but during the half-century which had elapsed since his death, the revival in the fortunes of Israel and its growing prosperity under the rule of an energetic king had furnished the prophets with but few pretexts for interfering in the conduct of state affairs. They no longer occupied themselves in resisting the king, but addressed themselves to the people, pointed out the heinousness of their sins, and threatened them with the wrath of Jahveh if they persisted in their unfaithfulness: they came to be spiritual advisers rather than political partisans, and orators rather than men of action like their predecessors. Their discourses were carefully prepared beforehand, and were written down either by themselves or by some of their disciples for the benefit of posterity, in the hope that future generations would understand the dangers or witness the catastrophes which their contemporaries might not live to see. About 760 B.C., Amos of Tekôa,[3] a native of Judæa, suddenly made his appearance at Bethel, in the midst of the festivals which pilgrims had flocked to celebrate in the ancient temple erected to Jahveh in one of His animal forms. His opening words filled the listening crowd with wonder: "The high places of Isaac shall be desolate," he proclaimed, "and the

Abriss der Geschichte Israel's und Juda's, in *Skizzen und Vorarbeiten,* vol. i. p. 46, et seq.; and KUENEN, *Religion nationale et Religion universelle,* p. 86, et seq.

[1] Cf. the part taken by Nathan in the conspiracy which raised Solomon to the throne (1 *Kings* i. 8, et seq.), and previous to this in the story of David's amour with Bathsheba (2 *Sam.* xii. 1–25). Similarly, we find prophets such as Ahijah in the reign of Jeroboam I. (1 *Kings* xi. 29–39; cf. xiv. 1–18; xv. 29, 30), and Shemaîah in the reign of Rehoboam (1 *Kings* xii. 22–24), Jehu son of Hananiah under Baasha (1 *Kings* xvi. 1–4, 7, 12, 13), Micaiah son of Imla, and Zedekiah under Ahab (1 *Kings* xxii. 5–28), not to speak of those mentioned in the *Chronicles,* e.g. Azariah son of Oded (2 *Chron.* xv. 1–8), and Hanani under Asa (2 *Chron.* xvi. 7–10), Jahaziel (2 *Chron.* xx. 14–19), and Eliezer, son of Dodavahu (2 *Chron.* xx. 37), in the time of Jehoshaphat. No trace of any writings composed by these prophets is found until a very late date; but in *Chronicles,* in addition to a letter from Elijah to Jehoram of Juda (2 *Chron.* xxi. 12–15), we find a reference to the commentary of the prophet Iddo in the time of Abijah (2 *Chron.* xiii. 22), and to the "History of Jehu the son of Hanani, which is inserted in the book of the kings of Israel" (2 *Chron.* xx. 34), in the time of Jehoshaphat.

[2] Cf. what has been said on this subject on pp. 84, 85, *supra.*

[3] The title of the Book of Amos fixes the date as being "in the days of Uzziah king of Judah, and in the days of Jeroboam the son of Joash king of Israel" (i. 1), and the state of affairs described by him corresponds pretty closely with what we know of this period. Most critics fix the date somewhere between 760 and 750 B.C., but nearer 760 than 750 (CORNILL, *Einleitung in das Alte Testament,* 2nd edit., p. 177); the views of Zeydner (*Theologische Studien,* 1894, p. 94) and Valeton (*Amos en Hosea,* p. 10), who give the date as 744 or 745, *i.e.* at the accession of Tiglath-pileser III. and the beginning of the Assyrian revival, have up to the present time lacked general support.

sanctuaries of Israel shall be laid waste; and I will rise against the house of Jeroboam with the sword."[1] Yet Jeroboam had by this time gained all his victories, and never before had the King of Samaria appeared to be more firmly seated on the throne : what, then, did this intruder mean by introducing himself as a messenger of wrath in the name of Jahveh, at the very moment when Jahveh was furnishing His worshippers with abundant signs of His favour? Amaziah, the priest of Bethel, interrupted him as he went on to declare that "Jeroboam should die by the sword, and Israel should surely be led away captive out of his land." The king, informed of what was going on, ordered Amos into exile, and Amaziah undertook to communicate this sentence to him : "O thou seer, go, flee thee away into the land of Judah, and there eat bread, and prophesy there : but prophesy not again any more at Bethel : for it is the king's sanctuary, and it is a royal house." And Amos replied, "I was no prophet, neither was I a prophet's son; but I was a herdman, and a dresser of sycomore trees : and the Lord took me from following the flock, and the Lord said unto me, Go, prophesy unto My people Israel. Now therefore hear thou the word of the Lord : Thou sayest, Prophesy not against Israel, and drop not thy word against the house of Isaac : therefore thus saith the Lord : Thy wife shall be an harlot in the city, and thy sons and thy daughters shall fall by the sword, and thy land shall be divided by line; and thou thyself shalt die in a land that is unclean, and Israel shall surely be led away captive out of his land."[2] This prophecy, first expanded, and then written down with a purity of diction and loftiness of thought which prove Amos to have been a master of literary art,[3] was widely circulated, and gradually gained authority as portents indicative of the divine wrath began to accumulate, such as an earthquake which occurred two years after the incident at Bethel,[4] an eclipse of the sun, drought, famine, and pestilence.[5] It foretold, in the first place, the downfall of

---

[1] There has been much controversy as to whether the words spoken at Bethel are contained in the third or in the seventh chapter of the *Book of Amos* as we now have it. Cornill is of opinion that in the visions described in chaps. vii.–ix. we have the substance, if not the form, of this first prophecy (*Einleitung in das Alte Testament*, 2nd edit., pp. 176, 177). The verse quoted above (*Amos* vii. 9) gives, at any rate, its general tenor, and finds a pendant in the reply made by the prophet to Amaziah (*Amos* vii. 16) towards the end of the scene.

[2] *Amos* vii. 9–17.

[3] S. Jerome describes Amos as "rusticus" and "imperitus sermone," but modern writers are generally agreed that in putting forward this view he was influenced by the statement as to the peasant origin of the prophet. As to the characteristics of his style and method of composition, cf., amongst others, DRIVER, *An Introduction to the Literature of the Old Testament*, 5th edit., p. 29. The existing text has been modified in places, and some critics claim to have detected interpolations, especially in the verses referring to Judah (WELLHAUSEN, *Skizzen und Vorarbeiten*, vol. v. p. 69, et seq.); Cornill (*Einleitung*, pp. 177, 178) objects merely to the passages pointed out by Duhm (*Die Theologie der Propheten*, p. 119), *i.e.* the passages ii. 4, 5; iv. 13; v. 8, 9; ix. 5, 6, and perhaps a part of vi. 1.

[4] *Amos* i. 1; reference is made to it by the unknown prophet whose words are preserved in *Zech.* xiv. 5.

[5] The famine is mentioned in *Amos* iv. 6, the drought in *Amos* iv. 7, 8, the pestilence in *Amos* iv. 10; the pestilence was perhaps one of those mentioned in the *Eponym Canon* for 765 and

all the surrounding countries—Damascus, Gaza, Tyre, Edom, Ammon, Moab, and Judah ; then, denouncing Israel itself, condemned it to the same penalties for the same iniquities. In vain did the latter plead its privileges as the chosen people of Jahveh, and seek to atone for its guilt by endless sacrifices. " I hate, I despise your feasts," declared Jahveh, " and I will take no delight in your solemn assemblies. Yea, though ye offer Me your burnt offerings and meat offerings, I will not accept them : neither will I regard the peace offerings of your fat beasts. Take thou away from Me the noise of thy songs ; for I will not hear the melody of thy viols. But let judgment roll down as waters, and righteousness as a mighty stream." [1] The unfaithfulness of Israel, the corruption of its cities, the pride of its nobles, had sealed its doom ; even at that moment the avenger was at hand on its north-eastern border, the Assyrian appointed to carry out sentence upon it. [2] Then follow visions, each one of which tends to deepen the effect of the seer's words—a cloud of locusts, [3] a devouring fire, [4] a plumb-line in the hands of the Lord, [5] a basket laden with summer fruit [6]—till at last the whole people of Israel take refuge in their temple, vainly hoping that there they may escape from the vengeance of the Eternal. " There shall not one of them flee away, and there shall not one of them escape. Though they dig into hell, thence shall Mine hand take them ; and though they climb up to heaven, thence will I bring them down. And though they hide themselves in the top of Carmel, I will search and take them out thence ; and though they be hid from My sight in the bottom of the sea, thence will I command the serpent, and he shall bite them. And though they go into captivity before their enemies, thence will I command the sword, and it shall slay them ; and I will set Mine eyes upon them for evil and not for good." [7] For the first time in history a prophet foretold disaster and banishment for a whole people : love of country was already giving place in the heart of Amos to his conviction of the universal jurisdiction of God, and this conviction led him to regard as possible and probable a state of things in which Israel should have no part. Nevertheless, its decadence was to be merely temporary ; Jahveh, though prepared to chastise the posterity of Jacob severely, could not bring Himself to destroy it utterly. The kingdom of David was soon to flourish anew : " Behold, the days come, saith the Lord,

759 (SCHRADER, *Keilinschriftliche Bibliothek*, vol. i. pp. 210–213), which probably extended over the whole of Western Asia. So, too, the eclipse of the sun (*Amos* viii. 9) may perhaps be identical with that which occurred in 763, in the month of Sivan (SCHRADER, *Keilinschriftliche Bibliothek*, vol. i. pp. 210, 211). [1] *Amos* v. 21–24.

[2] Most commentators admit that the nation raised up by Jahveh to oppress Israel "from the entering in of Hamath unto the brook of the Arabah " (*Amos* vi. 14) was no other than Assyria. At the very period in which Amos flourished, Assurdân made two campaigns against Hadrach, in 765 and 755, which brought his armies right up to the Israelite frontier (SCHRADER, *Keilinschriftliche Bibliothek*, vol. i. pp. 210–213). [3] *Amos* vii. 1–3. [4] *Amos* vii. 4–6.

[5] *Amos* vii. 7–9. It is here that the speech delivered by the prophet at Bethel is supposed to occur (vii. 9 ; cf. pp. 136, 137, *supra*) ; the narrative of what afterwards happened follows immediately (*Amos* vii. 10–17). [6] *Amos* viii. 1–3. [7] *Amos* ix. 1–4.

that the plowman shall overtake the reaper, and the treader of grapes him that soweth seed; and the mountains shall drop sweet wine, and all the hills shall melt. And I will bring again the captivity of My people Israel, and they shall build the waste cities, and inhabit them; and they shall plant vineyards, and drink the wine thereof; they shall also make gardens, and eat the fruit of them. And I will plant them upon their land, and they shall no more be plucked up out of their land which I have given them, saith the Lord thy God." [1]

The voice of Amos was not the only one raised in warning. From the midst of Ephraim, another seer, this time a priest, Hosea, son of Beeri,[2] was never weary of reproaching the tribes with their ingratitude, and persisted in his foretelling of the desolation to come. The halo of grandeur and renown with which Jeroboam had surrounded the kingdom could not hide its wretched and paltry character from the prophet's eyes; "for yet a little while, and I will avenge the blood of Jezreel upon the house of Jehu, and will cause the kingdom of the house of Israel to cease. And it shall come to pass at that day that I will break the bow of Israel in the valley of Jezreel." [3] Like his predecessor, he, too, inveighed against the perversity and unfaithfulness of his people. The abandoned wickedness of Gomer, his wife, had brought him to despair. In the bitterness of his heart, he demands of Jahveh why He should have seen fit to visit such humiliation on His servant, and persuades himself that the faithlessness of which he is a victim is but a feeble type of that which Jahveh had suffered at the hands of His people. Israel had gone a-whoring after strange gods, and the day of retribution for its crimes was not far distant: "The children of Israel shall abide many days without king and without prince, and without sacrifice and without pillar, and without ephod or teraphim: afterward shall the children of Israel return, and seek the Lord their God, and David their king; and shall come with fear unto the Lord and to His goodness in the latter days." [4] Whether the decadence of the

---

[1] *Amos* ix. 13–15.

[2] Hoshea (or Hosea) was regarded by the rabbis as the oldest of the lesser prophets, and his writings were placed at the head of their collected works. The title of his book (*Hos.* i. 1), where he begins by stating that he preached "in the days of Jeroboam, the son of Joash (Jehoash), King of Israel," is a later interpolation; the additional mention of Uzziah, Jotham, Ahaz, and Hezekiah, kings of Judah, is due to an attempted analogy with the title of Isaiah (DRIVER, *An Introduction to the Literature of the Old Testament*, 5th edit., pp. 282, 283). Hosea was familiar with the prophecies of Amos, and his own predictions show that the events merely foreseen by his predecessor were now in course of fulfilment in his day. The first three chapters probably date from the end of the reign of Jeroboam, about 750 B.C.; the others were compiled under his successors, and before 734–733 B.C., since Gilead is there mentioned as still forming part of Israel (*Hos.* vi. 8; xii. 12), though it was in that year laid waste and conquered by Tiglath-pileser III. (cf. p. 187, *infra*). Duhm (*Die Theologie der Propheten*, p. 130) has suggested that Hosea must have been a priest from the tone of his writings, and this hypothesis is generally accepted by theologians (STADE, *Geschichte des Volkes Israel*, vol. i. pp. 577, 578; CORNILL, *Einleitung in das Alte Testament*, 2nd edit., p. 172).

[3] *Hos.* i. 4, 5; cf. p. 85, *supra*.

[4] *Hos.* i.–iii. Is the story of Hosea and his wife an allegory, or does it rest on a basis of actual

Hebrews was or was not due to the purely moral and religious causes indicated by the prophets, it was only too real, and even the least observant among their contemporaries must have suspected that the two kingdoms were quite unfitted, as to their numbers, their military organisation, and monetary reserves, to resist successfully any determined attack that might be made upon them by surrounding nations. An armed force entering Syria by way of the Euphrates could hardly fail to overcome any opposition that might be offered to it, if not at the first onset, at any rate after a very brief struggle; none of the minor states to be met upon its way, such as Damascus or Israel, much less those of Hamath or Hadrach, were any longer capable of barring its progress, as Ben-hadad and Hazael had arrested that of the Assyrians in the time of Shalmaneser III. The efforts then made by the Syrian kings to secure their independence had exhausted their resources and worn out the spirit of their peoples; civil war had prevented them from making good their losses during the breathing-space afforded by the decadence of Assyria, and now that Nature herself had afflicted them with the crowning misfortunes of famine and pestilence, they were reduced to a mere shadow of what they had been during the previous century. If, therefore, Sharduris, after making himself master of the countries of the Taurus and Amanos, had turned his steps towards the valley of the Orontes, he might have secured possession of it without much difficulty, and after that there would have been nothing to prevent his soldiers from pressing on, if need be, to the walls of Samaria or even of Jerusalem itself. Indeed, he seems to have at last made up his mind to embark on this venture, when the revival of Assyrian power put a stop to his ambitious schemes. Tiglath-pileser, hard pressed on every side by daring and restless foes, began by attacking those who were at once the most troublesome and most vulnerable—the Aramæan tribes on the banks of the Tigris. To give these incorrigible banditti, who boldly planted their outposts not a score of leagues from his capital, a free hand on his rear, and brave the fortune of war in Armenia or Syria, without first teaching them a lesson in respect, would have been simply to court serious disaster; an Aramæan raid occurring at a time when he was engaged elsewhere with the bulk of his army, might have made it necessary to break off a successful campaign and fall back in haste to the relief of Nineveh or Calah (Kalakh), just as he was on the eve of gaining some decisive advantage. Moreover, the suzerainty of Assyria over Karduniash entailed on him the duty of safe-guarding Babylon from that other horde of Aramæans which harassed it on

fact? Most critics now seem to incline to the view that the prophet has here set down an authentic episode from his own career, and uses it to point the moral of his work (BLEEK and WELLHAUSEN, *Einleitung*, 4th edit., pp. 406–408; ROBERTSON SMITH, *The Prophets*, p. 179, et seq.; CORNILL, *Einleitung in das Alte Testament*, 2nd edit., p. 172).

the east, while the Kaldâ were already threatening its southern frontier. It is not quite clear whether Nabunazîr who then occupied the throne implored his help:[1] at any rate, he took the field as soon as he felt that his own crown was secure, overthrew the Aramæans at the first encounter, and drove them back from the banks of the Lower Zab to those of the Uknu : all the countries which they had seized to the east of the Tigris at once fell again into the hands of the Assyrians. This first point gained, Tiglath-pileser crossed the river, and made a demonstration in force before the Babylonian fortresses. He visited, one after another, Sippar, Nipur, Babylon, Borsippa, Kuta, Kîshu, Dilbat, and Uruk, "cities without peer," and offered in all of them sacrifices to the gods,—to Bêl, to Zirbanît, to Nebo, to Tashmît, and to Nirgal. Karduniash bowed down before him, but he abstained from giving any provocation to the

CAMPAIGNS OF
TIGLATH-PILESER III
in **MEDIA**
Scale

Kaldâ, and satisfied with having convinced Nabunazîr that Assyria had lost none of her former vigour, he made his way back to his hereditary kingdom.[2] The lightly-won success of this expedition produced the looked-for result. Tiglath-pileser had set out a king *de facto ;* but now that the gods of the ancient sanctuaries had declared themselves satisfied with his homage,[3] and had granted him that religious consecration which had before been lacking, he returned a king *de jure* as well[4] (745 B.C.). His next campaign completed what the first had

[1] Nabunazîr is the Nabonassar who afterwards gave his name to the era employed by Ptolemy.

[2] Most historians believe that Tiglath-pileser entered Karduniash as an enemy ; that he captured several towns, and allowed the others to ransom themselves on payment of tribute (Ed. MEYER, *Geschichte des Alterthums,* vol. i. pp. 446, 447 ; TIELE, *Babylonisch-assyrische Geschichte,* pp. 217, 218 ; DELITZSCH and MÜRDTER, *Geschichte Babyloniens und Assyriens,* 2nd edit., pp. 180, 181 ; ROST, *Die Keilschrifttexte Tiglat-Pileser's III.,* vol. i. pp. 13, 14). The way in which the texts known to us refer to this expedition seems to me, however, to prove that he set out as an ally and protector of Nabonazir, and that his visit to the Babylonian sanctuaries was of a purely pacific nature—a view shared by HOMMEL, *Gesch. Bab. und Ass.,* pp. 651, 652 ; and WINCKLER, *Gesch. Bab. und Ass.,* pp. 121–123, 222, 223.

[3] *Nimroud Inscrip.,* Obv., ll. 11 and 12 ; cf. ROST, *Keilschrifttexte Tiglat-Pileser's III.,* pp. 56, 57.

[4] *Annals of Tiglath-pileser III.,* ll. 1–20 ; *Great Inscription of Khorsabad,* No. 1, ll. 1–7, 13–16, and No. 2, ll. 1–11 ; *Nimroud Inscrip.,* Obv., ll. 5–13 ; cf. ROST, *Keilschrifttexte Tiglat-Pileser's III.,* vol. i. pp. 2–5, 42–45, 48–51, 54–57. I follow Tiele (*Bab.-ass. Geschichte,* pp. 227, 228, 235, 236) in placing the submission of the Pukudu and Aramæan settlers on the shores of the Persian Gulf in the year 731 B.C.

begun. The subjugation of the plain would have been of little advantage if the
highlands had been left in the power of tribes as yet unconquered, and allowed
to pour down with impunity bands of rapacious freebooters on the newly liberated
provinces : security between the Zab and the Uknu could only be attained by
the pacification of Namri, and it was, therefore, to Namri that the seat of war
was transferred in 744 B.C.   All the Cossæan and Babylonian races intermingled
in the valleys on the frontier were put to ransom one after another.   These
included the Bît-Sangibuti, the Bît-Khambân, the Barrua, the Bît-Zualzash, the
Bît-Matti, the Umliash, the Parsua, the Bît-Zatti, the Bît-Zabdâdani, the Bît-
Ishtar, the city of Zakruti, the Ninâ, the Bustus, the Arakuttu, by which the conqueror gradually made his way into the heart of Media, reaching districts into
which none of his predecessors had ever penetrated.[1] Those least remote he
annexed to his own empire, converting them into a province under the rule of
an Assyrian governor; he then returned to Calah with a convoy of 60,500
prisoners, and countless herds of oxen, sheep, mules, and dromedaries.   Whilst
he was thus employed, Assur-dainâni, one of his generals to whom he had
entrusted the pick of his army, pressed on still further to the north-east,
across the almost waterless deserts of Media.   The mountainous district on
the shores of the Caspian had for centuries enjoyed a reputation for wealth and
fertility among the races settled on the banks of the Euphrates and Tigris.
It was from thence that they obtained their lapis-lazuli, and the hills from
which it was extracted were popularly supposed to consist almost entirely of
one compact mass of this precious mineral.   Their highest peak, now known
as the Demavend, was then called Bikni, a name which had come to be
applied to the whole district.   To the Assyrians it stood as the utmost
boundary mark of the known world, beyond which their imagination pictured
little more than a confused mist of almost fabulous regions and peoples.
Assur-dainâni caught a distant glimpse of the snow-capped pyramid of
Demavend, but approached no nearer than its lower slopes, whence he retraced
his steps after having levied tribute from their inhabitants.   The fame of
this exploit spread far and wide in a marvellously short space of time, and

[1] The presence of such names as Zikruti, Arakuttu, Ariarma, and Nissa in the list of conquered
nations led Norris (*Assyrian Dictionary*, s.v. *Namri, Zikruti, Ariarva, Arakuttu*) and Fr. Lenormant
(*Sur la campagne de Téglathphalazar II. dans l'Ariane*, in the *Zeitschrift*, 1870, pp. 48–56, 69–71) to
believe that Tiglath-pileser III. had made his way into Ariana and Arachosia, and as far as the
valley of the Indus.   This tempting hypothesis was overthrown by Patkanoff, whose paper, being
written in Russian, has remained inaccessible to most scholars; then by Delattre (*Esquisse de
Géographie assyrienne*, pp. 40–49, and *Le Peuple et la langue des Mèdes*, pp. 85–99).   More recently
Rost again called attention to the subject, and adopted on his own account several of the identifications formerly put forward by Fr. Lenormant(*Die Keilschrifttexte Tiglat-Pileser's III.*,vol. i. p. xvi. No. 2).

[2] The country of Bikni is probably Rhagian Media (DELATTRE, *Le Peuple et l'Empire des Mèdes*,
p. 101) and Mount Bikni, the modern Demavend (HOMMEL, *Gesch. Bab. und Ass.*, p. 653, note 5;
WINCKLER, *Gesch. Bab. und Ass.*, 270; ROST, *Die Keilschrifttexte Tiglat-Pileser's III.*, vol. i. p. xvii.).

chiefs who till then had vacillated in their decision now crowded the path of the victor, eager to pay him homage on his return: even the King of Illipi thought it wise to avoid the risk of invasion, and hastened of his own accord to meet the conqueror. Here, again, Tiglath-pileser had merely to show himself in order to re-establish the supremacy of Assyria: the races of the plain, for many years familiar with defeat, made no pretence of serious resistance, but bowed their necks beneath a fresh yoke almost without protest.[1]

Having thus secured his rear from attack for some years at any rate, Tiglath-pileser no longer hesitated to try conclusions with Urartu. The

PRINCIPAL PEAK OF MOUNT BIKNI
(DEMAVEND).[2]

struggle in which he now deliberately engaged could not fail to be a decisive one; for Urartu, buoyed up and borne on the wave of some fifty years of prosperity, had almost succeeded in reaching first rank among the Asiatic powers: one more victory over Nineveh, and it would become—for how long, none might say—undisputed mistress of the whole of Asia. Assyria, on the other hand, had reached a point where its whole future hung upon a single issue of defeat or victory. The prestige with which the brilliant campaigns of Assur-nazir-pal and Shalmaneser III. had invested its name, if somewhat diminished, had still survived its recent reverses, and the terror inspired by its arms was so great even among races who had witnessed them from a

---

[1] *Annals of Tiglath-pileser III.*, ll. 26–58; *Great Insc. of Khorsabad*, No. 1, ll. 17–20, and No. 2, ll. 18–29; *Nimroud Inscr.*, Obv., ll. 29–42; cf. SCHRADER, *Inschr. Tiglath-Pileser's III.*, in the *Keil. Bibl.*, vol. ii. pp. 6, 7, 16–19, and ROST, *Die Keilschr. Tiglat-Pileser's III.*, vol. i. pp. 6–11, 44, 45, 50, 51, 62–67.

[2] Drawn by Boudier, from a photograph by M. de Morgan; cf. J. DE MORGAN, *Mission Scientifique en Perse*, vol. i. pl. 1.

distance, that the image of Assyria rose involuntarily before the eyes of the Hebrew prophets as that of the avenger destined to punish Israel for its excesses.[1]   No doubt, during the last few reigns its prosperity had waned and its authority over distant provinces had gradually become relaxed; but now the old dynasty, worn out by its own activity, had given place to a new one, and with this change of rulers the tide of ill-fortune was, perhaps, at last about to turn.   At such a juncture, a successful campaign meant full compensation for all past disasters and the attainment of a firmer position than had ever yet been held; whereas another reverse, following on those from which the empire had already suffered, would render their effect tenfold more deadly, and, by letting loose the hatred of those whom fear alone still held in check, complete its overthrow.   It was essential, therefore, before entering on the struggle, to weigh well every chance of victory, and to take every precaution by which adverse contingencies might be, as far as possible, eliminated. The army, encouraged by its success in the two preceding campaigns, was in excellent fighting order, and ready to march in any direction without a moment's hesitation, confident in its ability to defeat the forces of Urartu as it had defeated those of the Medes and Aramæans; but the precise point of attack needed careful consideration.   Tiglath-pileser must have been sorely tempted to take the shortest route, challenge the enemy at his most vulnerable point on the shores of Lake Van, and by a well-aimed thrust deal him a blow from which he would never, or only by slow degrees, recover.   But this vital region of Urartu, as we have already pointed out,[2] presented the greatest difficulties of access.   The rampart of mountain and forest by which it was protected on the Assyrian side could only be traversed by means of a few byways, along which bands of guerrillas could slip down easily enough to the banks of the Tigris, but which were quite impassable to an army in full marching order, hampered by its horses, chariots, and baggage-train: compelled to thread its way, with columns unduly extended, through the woods and passes of an unknown country, which daily use had long made familiar to its adversaries, it would have run the risk of being cut to pieces man by man a dozen times before it could hope to range its disciplined masses on the field of battle.   Former Assyrian invasions had, as a general rule, taken an oblique course towards some of the spurs of this formidable chain, and had endeavoured to neutralise its defences by outflanking them, either by proceeding westwards along the basins of the Supnat and the Arzania, or

---

[1] Cf. the passage in Amos (vi. 4) referred to on pp. 137, 138, *supra*.

[2] As to the difficulties of an attack on Urartu by the most direct route, cf., in addition to what has been said on p. 54, *supra*, the remarks made by Belck in BELCK and LEHMANN, *Ein neuer Herrscher von Chaldia*, in the *Zeitschrift für Assyriologie*, vol. ix. p. 350, note 1.   Our knowledge of the country is as yet too scanty to allow us to regard the question as finally decided.

eastwards through the countries bordering on Lake Urumiah; but even this method presented too many difficulties and too little certainty of success to warrant Tiglath-pileser in staking the reviving fortunes of his empire on its adoption. He rightly argued that Sharduris would be most easily vulnerable in those provinces whose allegiance to him was of recent date, and he resolved to seek out his foe in the heart of Northern Syria. There, if anywhere, every chance was in his favour and against the Armenian. The scene of operations, while it had long been familiar to his own generals and soldiers, was, on the other hand, entirely new ground to those of the enemy; the latter, though

VIEW OF THE MOUNTAINS WHICH GUARD THE SOUTHERN BORDER OF URARTU.[1]

unsurpassed in mountain warfare, lost much of their superiority on the plains, and could not, with all their courage, make up for their lack of experience. Moreover, it must not be forgotten that a victory on the banks of the Afrîn or the Orontes would have more important results than a success gained in the neighbourhood of the lakes or of Urartu. Not only would it free the Assyrians from the only one of their enemies whom they had any cause to fear, but it would also bring back the Hittite kings to their allegiance, and restore the Assyrian supremacy over the wealthiest regions of Western Asia: they would thus disable Urartu and reconquer Syria at one and the same time. Tiglath-pileser, therefore, crossed the Euphrates in the spring of 743 B.C., neither Matîlu of Agusi, Kushtashpi of Kummukh, nor their allies daring to interfere with his progress. He thus advanced as far as Arpad,

[1] Drawn by Boudier, from a photograph by M. Binder, furnished by Father Scheil: it was taken at Julamerk, near the junction of the mountain tracks leading from the Zab valley to the south-eastern corner of the basin of Lake Van.

L

and, in the first moment of surprise, the town threw open its gates before him.[1] There, while he was making ready to claim the homage of the surrounding countries, he learnt that Sharduris was hastening up to the rescue. He at once struck his camp and marched out to meet his rival, coming up with him in the centre of Kummukh, not far from the Euphrates, between Kishtân and Khalpi. Sharduris was at the head of his Syrian contingents, including the forces of Agusi, Melitene, Kummukh, and Gurgum—a formidable army, probably superior in point of numbers to that of the Assyrians. The struggle lasted a whole day, and in the course of it the two kings, catching sight of one another on the field of battle, engaged in personal combat: at last, towards evening, the chariots and cavalry of Urartu gave way and the rout began. The victors made their way into the camp at the heels of their flying enemies. Sharduris abandoned his chariot, and could find nothing but a mare to aid him in his flight; he threw himself upon her back, careless of the ridicule at that time attached to the use of such a mount in Eastern countries,[2] fled at a gallop all through the night, hard pressed by a large body of cavalry, crossed the hills of Sibak, and with much difficulty reached the bridge over the Euphrates. His pursuers drew rein on the river-bank, and Sharduris re-entered his kingdom in safety. He had lost nearly 73,000 men, killed or taken prisoners, in addition to his chariots, and nearly the whole train of horses, asses, servants, and artisans attached to his army; he left his tent still standing, and those who were first to enter it laid hands on his furniture and effects, his royal ornaments, his bed and portable throne, with its cushions and bearing-poles, none of which had he found time to take with him. Tiglath-pileser burnt them all on the spot as a thank-offering to the gods who had so signally favoured him; the bed alone he retained, in order that he might dedicate it as a trophy to the goddess Ishtar of Nineveh.[3]

He had covered himself with glory, and might well be proud of his achievement, yet the victory was in no way a decisive one. The damage

---

[1] Different writers have given different versions of this campaign. Some think, with Hommel (*Gesch. Bab. und Ass.*, pp. 656, 657) and Rost (*Die Keilschrifttexte Tiglat-Pilesers III.*, vol. i. pp. xix.–xxi.), that Arpad resisted, and that Tiglath-pileser was laying siege to it, when the arrival of Sharduris compelled him to retire; others prefer to believe, with Tiele (*Babylonisch-assyrische Geschichte*, p. 219) and Belck and Lehmann (*Chaldische Forschungen*, in the *Verhandlungen der Berliner anthropologischen Gesellschaft*, 1896, pp. 324–325), that Arpad was still in the hands of the Assyrians, and that Tiglath-pileser used it as his base of operations. The formula *ina Arpadda* in the *Eponym Canon* (SCHRADER, *Keilinschriftliche Bibliothek*, vol. i. pp. 212, 213) proves that Tiglath-pileser was certainly *in Arpad :* since Arpad belonged to the Bît-Agusi and they were the allies or vassals of Sharduris, we must assume, as I have done here, that in the absence of the Urartians they did not dare to resist the Assyrians, and opened their gates to them.

[2] So, too, later on, in the time of Sargon (*Annals of Sargon*, ll. 108, 109), Rusas, when defeated, gets on the back of a mare and rides off; as to the impression of distress and almost ridicule suggested by an action of this kind, cf. the ingenious comment in BELCK and LEHMANN, *Chaldische Forschungen*, in the *Verhandlungen der Berliner anthropologischen Gesellschaft*, 1896, p. 325.

[3] *Annals of Tiglath-pileser III.*, ll. 59–73; *Great Inscription of Khorsabad*, No. 1, ll. 29–35; *Nimroud Inscrip.*, Obv., ll. 45–50; cf. ROST, *Die Keilschrifttexte Tiglat-Pilesers III.*, vol. i. pp. 12–15, 50–53, 66–69.

inflicted on the allies, considerable though it was, had cost him dear: the forces left to him were not sufficient to enable him to finish the campaign, and extort oaths of allegiance from the Syrian princes before they had recovered from the first shock of defeat. He returned to Nineveh, and spent the whole winter in reorganising his troops; while his enemies, on the other hand, made preparations to repel the attack energetically. Sharduris could not yet venture outside his mountain strongholds, but the hope of being reinforced by him, as soon as he had got together another army, encouraged the Syrian kings to remain faithful to him in spite of his reverses.[1] Matîlu of Agusi,

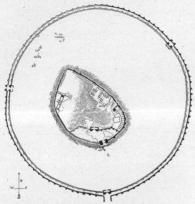

PLAN OF THE ANCIENT CITY OF ZINJIRLI.[2]

unable to carry the day against the Assyrians in the open field, distributed his men among his towns, and resisted all attacks with extraordinary persistence, confident that Sharduris would at length come to help him, and with this hope he held out for three years in his town of Arpad. This protracted resistance need no longer astonish us, now that we know, from observations made on the spot, the marvellous skill displayed in the fortification of these Asiatic towns. The ruins of

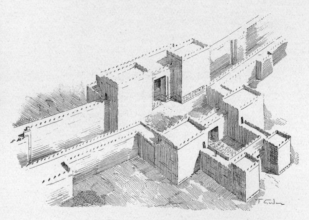

ONE OF THE GATES OF ZINJIRLI RESTORED.[3]

Arpad have yet to be explored, but those of Samalla have been excavated, and show us the methods adopted for the defence of a royal residence about the middle of the century with which we are now concerned.[4] The practice of building citadels on a square or rectangular plan, which prevailed so largely

[1] The part played by Sharduris in the events of the years which followed, passing mention of which was made by Winckler (*Gesch. Bab. und Ass.*, pp. 224, 225), have been fully dealt with by Belck and Lehmann (*Chaldische Forschungen*, in *Verhandl. der Berliner anthropol. Gesellschaft*, 1895, pp. 325–336.)

[2] A reproduction by Faucher-Gudin of the first plan published by LUSCHAN, *Ausgrabungen in Send-schirli*, vol. i. p. 10. A second and more complete plan is given in vol. ii. pl. xxix. of the same work.

[3] Reproduction by Faucher-Gudin of the sketch published by LUSCHAN, *Ausgrabungen in Send-schirli*, vol. ii. p. 112. This interesting restoration is the work of Robert Koldewey, the architect.

[4] The Tel of Zinjirli was excavated by a German expedition in 1892–1897, and the results were published, under the superintendence of Dr. von Luschan, in a fine work entitled *Ausgrabungen in Sendschirli*, two volumes of which appeared in 1896 and 1897.

under the Egyptian rule, had gradually gone out of fashion [1] as the knowledge of engineering advanced, and the use of mines and military engines had been more fully developed among the nations of Western Asia. It was found that the heavily fortified angles of the enclosing wall merely presented so many weak points, easy to attack but difficult to defend, no matter how carefully they might be protected by an accumulation of obstacles. In the case of fortresses built on a plain, where the plan was not modified by the nature of the site, the enclosing wall was generally round or oval in shape, and free from useless angles which might detract from its strength. The walls were surmounted by battlements, and flanked at short intervals by round or square towers, the tops of which rose but little, if indeed at all, above the level of the curtain. In front of this main wall was a second lower one, also furnished with towers and battlements, which followed the outline of the first all the way round at an interval of some yards, thus acting as a sort of continuous screen to it. The gates were little less than miniature citadels built into each line of ramparts; the gate of the outer wall was often surrounded by lower outworks, two square bastions and walls enclosing an outer quadrangle which had to be crossed before the real gate was reached. When a breach had been made in this double enclosure, though the town itself might be taken, the labours of the attacking force were not yet over. In the very centre of the place, on a sort of artificial mound or knoll, stood the royal castle, and resistance on the part of its garrison would make it necessary for the enemy to undertake a second siege no less deadly and protracted than the first. The keep of Zinjirli had only a single gate approached by a narrow causeway. Within, it was divided by walls into five compartments, each of which was independent of the rest, and had to be attacked separately. Matîlu knew he could hope for no mercy at the hands of the Assyrians; he therefore struggled on to the last, and when at length obliged to surrender, in the year 740 B.C., he paid for his obstinacy by the loss of his throne, and perhaps also of his life.[2] The inaction of Sharduris clearly showed that he was no longer in a position to protect his allies, and that the backbone of his kingdom was broken; the kings who had put faith in his help now gave him up, and ambassadors flocked in from all parts, even from those which were not as yet directly threatened. Kushtashpi of Kummukh, Tarkhulara of Gurgum, Pisiris of Carchemish, Uriaîk of Kuî, came to Arpad in person to throw themselves at the conqueror's feet, bringing with them offerings of gold and silver, of lead and iron, of ivory, carved and in the tusk, of purple, and of dyed or embroidered

[1] Cf. what has been said on this subject on pp. 127–130 of the *Struggle of the Nations.*

[2] Our knowledge of these events is imperfect, our only information being derived from the very scanty details given in the *Eponym Canon* (SCHRADER, *Keilinschriftliche Bibliothek*, vol. i. pp. 212, 213): up to the present we can do no more than trace the general course of events.

stuffs, and were confirmed in the possession of their respective territories; Hiram II. of Tyre, moreover, and Rezin of Damascus sent their greetings to him.[1] The Patinâ, who in days gone by had threatened the fortunes of Assur-nazir-pal, once again endeavoured to pose as the rivals of Assyria, and Tutammû, sovereign of Unki, the most daring of the minor states into which the Patinâ had been split up, declined to take part in the demonstrations made by his

BIRD'S-EYE VIEW OF THE ROYAL CASTLE OF ZINJIRLI AS RESTORED.[2]

neighbours. Tiglath-pileser marched on Kinalua, sacked it, built a fortress there, and left a governor and garrison behind him: Agusi and Unki henceforth sank to the level of mere provinces, administered by royal officers in the king's name, and permanently occupied by Assyrian troops.[3]

Northern Syria was thus again incorporated with the empire, but Urartu, although deprived of the resources with which Syria had supplied it, continued to give cause for apprehension; in 739 B.C., however, a large proportion of the districts of Naîri, to which it still clung, was wrested from it, and a fortress was built at Ulluba, with a view to providing a stable base of operations at this

---

[1] *Annals of Tiglath-pileser III.*, ll. 83–91 (cf. ROST, *Die Keilschrifttexte Tiglat-Pilesers III.*, vol. i. pp. 14–17), where the statement at the close indicates that Tiglath-pileser received the tributary kings of Syria "in Arpad," after he had captured that city.

[2] Drawn by Faucher-Gudin, from the plan published in LUSCHAN, *Ausgrabungen in Sendschirli*, vol. ii. pl. xxx. The restoration, as in the case of the preceding woodcut, is the work of Robert Koldewey, the architect.

[3] *Annals of Tiglath-pileser III.*, ll. 92–101; cf. ROST, *Keilschr. Tiglat-Pilesers III.*, vol. i. pp. 14–17.

point on the northern frontier.[1]   A rebellion, instigated, it may be, by his own agents, recalled Tiglath-pileser to the Amanus in the year 738.   The petty kings who shared with Assyria the possession of the mountains and plains of the Afrîn could not succeed in living at peace with one another, and every now and then their disputes broke out into open warfare.   Samalla was at that time subject to a family of which the first members known to history, Qaral and Panammu, shared Yaudi equally between them.   Barzur, son of Panammu I., had reigned there since about 765 B.C., and there can be little doubt that he must have passed through the same vicissitudes as his neighbours : faithful to Urartu as long as Sharduris kept the upper hand, and to Assyria as soon as Tiglath-pileser had humiliated Urartu, he had been killed in a skirmish by some rival.   His son, Panammu II., came to the throne merely as a nominee of his suzerain, and seems to have always rendered him faithful service ; [2] unfortunately, Yaudi was no longer subject to the house of Panammu, but obeyed the rule of a certain Azriyahu, who chafed at the presence of an alien power.[3]   Azriyahu took advantage of the events which kept Tiglath-pileser fully occupied in the east, to form a coalition in favour of himself among the states on the banks of the Orontes, including some seventeen provinces, dependencies of Hamath, and certain turbulent cities of Northern Phœnicia, such as Byblos, Arka, Zimyra, Usnû, Siannu, Cœle-Syria, and even Hadrach itself.[4]   It is not quite clear whether Damascus and the Hebrews took part in

[1] *Eponym Canon*, in SCHRADER, *Keil. Bib.*, vol. i. pp. 212, 213, and *Great Inscr. of Khorsabad*, No. 1, ll. 25–29 ; cf. ROST, *Die Keil. Tiglat-Pilesers III.*, vol. i. pp. 46, 47.   This campaign is regarded as having formed an episode in the wars against Urartu by Hommel (*Gesch. Bab. u. Ass.*, pp. 657–659), by Winckler (*Gesch. Bab. u. Ass.*, p. 225), and by Rost (*Die Keil. Tiglat-Pilesers III.*, vol. i. pp. xxii., xxiii.).

[2] Our knowledge of these events comes from the inscriptions on the statues at Zinjirli, published and translated by Sachau (*Die Ausgrabungen in Sendschirli*, vol. i. pls. vii., viii., and pp. 55–84), subsequently by Halévy (*Les Deux Inscriptions Hétéennes de Zindjirli*, in the *Revue Sémitique*, vol. i. pp. 138–167, 218–258, 319–336, and vol. ii. pp. 25–60).   Apart from differences in translation, the historical interpretations of the texts furnished by these two writers differ a good deal.   I have for the most part followed that given by Sachau.

[3] Azriyahu of Yaudi was identified with Azariah of Judah by G. Smith (*The Annals of Tiglath-Pileser II.*, in the *Zeitschrift*, 1869, pp. 12, 13, 16), and this identification, strenuously supported by Schrader (*Die Keilinschriften und das Alte Testament*, 1st edit., pp. 114–129, and 2nd edit., pp. 217–223), was for a long time accepted without question by most Assyriologists (TIELE, *Babylonisch-assyriche Geschichte*, pp. 530, 531 ; HOMMEL, *Gesch. Bab. und Ass.*, pp. 662, 663 ; WINCKLER, *Gesch. Bab. und Ass.*, pp. 225, 226 ; ROST, *Die Keilschrifttexte Tiglat-Pilesers III.*, vol. i. pp. xxii.–xxiv.).   Oppert rejected it from the first, and suggested that this Azriyahu was the son of Tabeel opposed by Pekah and Rezin to Ahaz, King of Judah (*La Chronologie Biblique fixée par les éclipses des Inscriptions cunéiformes*, 1869, pp. 30–35, and *Salomon et ses successeurs*, 1877, pp. 60–70) ; Wellhausen, without adopting Oppert's view, refused to be convinced by the arguments of Schrader (*Jahrbücher für die Deutsche Theologie*, vol. xx. pp. 632–699), cf. Schrader's reply (in the *Jahrbücher für protestantische Theologie*, 1876, pp. 373–384), and Gutschmidt made a violent attack on them (*Neue Beiträge zur Geschichte des Alten Orients*, pp. 55–65), which called forth a still more violent reply from Schrader (*Keilinschriften und Geschichtsforschung*, pp. 395–421).   Winckler has shown that the *Yaudi* of Tiglath-pileser III.'s inscriptions ought to be identified with the *Yadi* or *Yaudi* of the Zinjirli inscriptions (cf. p. 34, *supra*), and consequently that Azriyahu was not king of Judah, but a king of Northern Syria (*Altorientalische Forschungen*, vol. i. pp. 1–23).   His view has been accepted by Scheil (*Notes d'Épigr. et d'Arch. Assyriennes*, in the *Recueil de Travaux*, vol. xvi. p. 33), and appears to me to harmonise so well with what remains of the texts, and with our knowledge of the events, that I have had no hesitation in adopting it.

[4] The constitution of the league is furnished almost in its entirety by the list of towns and

this movement. Jeroboam had died in 740, after a prosperous reign of forty-one years, and on his death Israel seems to have fallen under a cloud: six months later, his son Zechariah was assassinated at Ibleam [1] by Shallum, son of Jabesh, and the prophecy of Amos, in which he declared that the house of Jeroboam should fall beneath the sword of Jahveh,[2] was fulfilled. Shallum himself reigned only one month: two other competitors had presented themselves immediately after his crime;[3] the ablest of these, Menahem, son of Gadi, had come from Tirzah to Samaria, and, after suppressing his rivals, laid hands on the crown.[4] He must have made himself master of the kingdom little by little, the success of his usurpation being entirely due to the ruthless energy invariably and everywhere displayed by him; as, for instance, when Tappuakh (Tiphsah) refused to open its gates at his summons, he broke into the town and slaughtered its inhabitants.[5] All the defects of organisation, all the sources of weakness, which for the last half-century had been obscured by the glories of Jeroboam II., now came to the surface, and defied all human efforts to avert their consequences. "Then," as Hosea complains, "is the iniquity of Ephraim discovered, and the wickedness of Samaria; for they commit falsehood: and the thief entereth in, and the troop of robbers spoileth without. And they consider not in their hearts that I (Jahveh) remember all their wickedness: now have their own doings beset them about; they are before My face. They make the king glad with their wickedness and the princes with their lies. They are all adulterers; they are as an oven heated by the baker. . . . They . . . devour their judges; all their kings are fallen; there is none among them that calleth unto Me." [6] In Judah, Azariah (Uzziah) had at first shown some signs of ability; he had completed the conquest of Idumæa [Edom], and had fortified Elath,[7] but he suddenly found himself stricken with leprosy, and was obliged to hand over the reins of government to Jotham.[8] His long life had been passed uneventfully, and

---

countries subdued after the defeat of Azriyahu (*Annals of Tiglath-pileser III.*, ll. 124–132; cf. ROST, *Die Keilschrifttexte Tiglat-Pilesers III.*, vol. i. pp. 20–23).

[1] The name Ibleam, corrupted in the received text (2 *Kings* xv. 10), has been restored by Stade (*Geschichte des Volkes Israel*, vol. i. p. 575, note 2).   [2] *Amos* vii. 9; cf. pp. 136, 137, *supra*.

[3] The nameless prophet, whose prediction is handed down to us in *Zech.* ix.–xi., speaks of three shepherds cut off by Jahveh in one month (xi. 8); two of these were Zechariah and Shallum; the third is not mentioned in the Book of Kings. Ewald tried to identify him with the mysterious *Kobolám* mentioned in 2 *Kings* xv. 10 (*Geschichte des Volkes Israel*, 3rd edit., vol. iii. p. 344); but Stade has shown that this is not the name of a man, but of the place where Zechariah was killed, viz. Ibleam. On the other hand, Niebuhr proposes to identify this anonymous king with the Lemuel referred to in *Prov.* xxxi. 1, 4 (*Die Chronologie der Geschichte Israels, Ægyptens, Babyloniens, und Assyriens*, pp. 25–28).   [4] 2 *Kings* xiv. 23–29; xv. 8–15.

[5] 2 *Kings* xv. 16. The Massoretic text gives the name of the town as Tipsah, but the LXX. has Taphôt, which led Thenius to suggest Tappuakh as an emendation of Tipsah: Stade (*Gesch. des Volkes Israel*, vol. i. p. 516) prefers the emendation Tirzah. Tappuakh was a town situated on the borders of Ephraim and Manasseh (*Josh.* xvi. 8; xvii. 7, 8).   [6] *Hos.* vii. 1–4, 7.

[7] 2 *Kings* xiv. 22; in 2 *Chron.* xxvi. 6–15 he is credited with the reorganisation of the army and of the Judæan fortresses, in addition to campaigns against the Philistines and Arabs.

[8] 2 *Kings* xv. 5; cf. 2 *Chron.* xxvi. 19–21. Azariah is also abbreviated into Uzziah.

without any disturbance, under the protection of Jeroboam; but the very same defects which had led to the ruin of Israel were at work also in Judah, and Menahem, in spite of his enfeebled condition, had nothing to fear in this direction.   The danger which menaced him came rather from the east and the north, where Damascus, aroused from its state of lethargy by Rezôn [Rezin] II., had again begun to strive after the hegemony of Syria.[1]   All these princes, when they found that the ambition of Tiglath-pileser threatened to interfere with their own intrigues, were naturally tempted to combine against him, and were willing

TIGLATH-PILESER III. IN HIS STATE CHARIOT.[2]

to postpone to a more convenient season the settlement of their own domestic quarrels.   But Tiglath-pileser did not give them time for this; he routed Azriyahu, and laid waste Kullani,[3] the chief centre of revolt, ravaged the valley of the Orontes, and carried off the inhabitants of several towns, replacing them with prisoners taken the year before during his campaign in Naîri.   After this feat the whole of Syria surrendered.   Rezin and Menahem were among the first to tender their homage,[4] and the latter paid a thousand talents of silver for the *firman* which definitely confirmed his tenure of the throne; the princes of Tyre, Byblos, Hamath, Carchemish, Milid, Tabal, and

[1] The name of this king, written Rezin in the Bible (2 *Kings* xv. 37; **xvi.** 5, 6, 9), is given as *Razunu* in the Assyrian texts (*Annals of Tiglath-pileser III.*, ll. 83, 150, 205, 236); he was therefore Rezôn II. (as to Rezôn I., cf. *Struggle of the Nations*, p. 778).   A passage in the *Annals*, l. 205, seems to indicate that Rezin's father was prince of a city dependent on Damascus, not king of Damascus itself; unfortunately the text is too much mutilated to warrant us in forming any definite conclusion on this point.

[2] Drawn by Faucher-Gudin, from a sketch published by LAYARD, *Nineveh and Babylon*, p. 527.

[3] Kullani is the Calno or Calneh mentioned by Isaiah (x. 9) and Amos (vi. 2), which lay somewhere between Arpad and Hamath; the precise spot is not yet known (TIELE, *Babylonisch-assyrische Geschichte*, p. 230; HOMMEL, *Gesch. Bab. und Ass.*, p. 660; WINCKLER, *Gesch. Bab. und Ass.*, p. 225).

[4] The name of Menahem was pointed out by Hincks in the *Athenæum*, 1852, vol. i., Jan. 3.

several others followed their example—even a certain Zabibi, queen of an Arab tribe, feeling compelled to send her gifts to the conqueror.[1]

A sudden rising among the Aramæan tribes on the borders of Elam obliged Tiglath-pileser to depart before he had time to take full advantage of his opportunity. The governors of Lullumi and Naîri promptly suppressed the outbreak, and, collecting the most prominent of the rebels together, sent them to the king in order that he might distribute them throughout the cities of Syria: a colony of 600 prisoners from the town of Amlati was established in

THE ROCK AND CITADEL OF VAN AT THE PRESENT DAY.[2]

the territory of Damaunu, 5400 from Dur were sent to the fortresses of Unki, Kunalia, Khuzarra, Taî, Tarmanazi, Kulmadara, Khatatirra, and Sagillu, while another 10,000 or so were scattered along the Phœnician seaboard and among the adjacent mountains.[3] The revolt had meanwhile spread to the nations of Media, where it was, perhaps, fomented by the agents of Urartu; and for the second time within seven years (737 B.C.) Tiglath-pileser trampled underfoot the countries over which he had ridden in triumph at the beginning of his career—the Bît-Kapsi, the Bît-Sangibuti, the Bît-Tazzakki, the Bît-Zualzash, the Bît-Matti, and Umliash. The people of Upash, among the Bît-Kapsi, entrenched themselves on the slopes of Mount Abirus; but he carried their entrenchments by storm. Ushuru of Taddiruta and Burdadda of Nirutakta were seized with alarm, and hid themselves in their mountain gorges; but he climbed up in pursuit of them, drove them out of their hiding-places, seized their possessions, and made them prisoners. Similar treatment was meted out to all those who proved refractory; some he despoiled, others he led captive, and "bursting upon the remainder like the downpour of

[1] Annals of Tiglath-pileser III., ll. 103–133, 150–157; cf. ROST, Die Keilschrifttexte Tiglat-Pilesers III., vol. i. pp. 18–23, 26, 27. In the Eponym Canon this is described as the campaign against Kullani (SCHRADER, Keilinschriftliche Bibliothek, vol. i. pp. 212, 213).

[2] Drawn by Boudier, from a photograph by M. Binder, furnished by Father Scheil.

[3] Annals, ll. 134–150; cf. ROST, Die Keilschrifttexte Tiglat-Pilesers III., vol. i. pp. 22–27.

Rammân," permitted none of them to escape.   He raised trophies all along his line of march : in Bau, a dependency of Bît-Ishtar, he set up a pointed javelin dedicated to Ninip, on which he had engraved a panegyric of the virtues of his master Assur; near Shilkhazi, a town founded, in bygone days, by the Babylonians, he erected a statue of himself, and a pillar consecrated to Marduk in Til-ashshur.[1]   In the following year he again attacked Urartu and occupied the mountain province of Nâl, which formed one of its out-lying defences (736).[2]   The year after he entered on the final struggle with Sharduris, and led the flower of his forces right under the walls of Dhuspas,[3] the enemy's capital.   Dhuspas really consisted of two towns joined together.   One of these, extending over the plain by the banks of the Alaîs and in the direction of the lake, was surrounded by fertile gardens and villas, in which the inhabitants spent the summer at their ease.   It was protected by an isolated mass of white and red nummulitic chalk, the steep sides of which are seamed with fissures and tunnelled with holes and caverns from top to bottom.   The plateau in which it terminates, and which rises to a height of 300 feet at its loftiest point, is divided into three main terraces, each completely isolated from the other two, and forming, should occasion arise, an independent fortress.   Ishpuinis, Menuas, Argistis, and Sharduris II. had laboured from generation to generation to make this stronghold impregnable, and they had succeeded in the attempt.[4]   The only access to it was from the western side, by a narrow bridle-path, which almost overhung the precipice as it gradually mounted to the summit.   This path had been partially levelled, and flanked with walls and towers which commanded the approach throughout its whole length; on the platforms at the summit a citadel had been constructed, together with a palace, temples, and storehouses, in which was accumulated a sufficient supply of arms and provisions to enable the garrison to tire out the patience of any ordinary foe;   treason or an unusually prolonged siege could alone get the better of such a position. Tiglath-pileser invested the citadel and ravaged its outskirts without pity, hoping, no doubt, that he would thus provoke the enemy into capitulating. Day after day, Sharduris, perched in his lofty eyrie, saw his leafy gardens laid bare under the hatchet, and his villages and the palaces of his nobles light

---

[1] *Annals of Tiglath-pileser III.*, ll. 157–176; cf. Rost, *Die Keilschrifttexte Tiglat-Pilesers III.*, vol. i. pp. 26–31.

[2] *Eponym Canon*, in Schrader, *Keilinschriftliche Bibliothek*, vol. i. pp. 212, 213.   Very probably the fragment of the *Annals of Tiglath-pileser III.*, ll. 176–190, refers to this campaign: cf. Tiele, *Bab.-ass. Gesch.*, pp. 231, 232; Rost, *Die Keilschr. Tiglat-Pilesers III.*, vol. i. pp. xxvi., xxvii.

[3] The name is written Turuspas in the inscriptions of Tiglath-pileser III. (Rost, *Die Keilschrift-texte Tiglat-Pilesers III.*, vol. i. pp. 46, 47, 52, 53).   There can be little or no doubt, however, that this is merely a variant of the name usually written as Tuspas, Tuspana, Dhuspana, the Thospia of classical times;   properly speaking, it was the capital of Biainas; for this country, cf. p. 55, note 1, *supra*.

[4] Cf. what has been said in regard to these buildings, p. 106, *supra*.

up the country round as far as the eye could reach : he did not flinch, however, and when all had been laid waste, the Assyrians set up a statue of their king before the principal gate of the fortress, broke up their camp, and leisurely retired. They put the country to fire and sword, destroyed its cities, led away every man and beast they could find into captivity, and then returned to Nineveh laden with plunder.[1] Urartu was still undaunted, and Sharduris remained king as before ; but he was utterly spent, and his power had sustained

ENTRANCE TO THE MODERN CITADEL OF VAN FROM THE WESTWARD.[2]

a blow from which it never recovered. He had played against Assur with the empire of the whole Asiatic world as the stake, and the dice had gone against him : compelled to renounce his great ambitions from henceforth, he sought merely to preserve his independence. Since then, Armenia has more than once challenged fortune, but always with the same result ; it fared no better under Tigranes in the Roman epoch, than under Sharduris in the time of the Assyrians ; it has been within an ace of attaining the goal of its ambitions, then at the last moment its strength has failed, and it has been forced to retire worsted from the struggle. Its position prevented it from exercising very wide influence ; hidden away in a corner of Asia at the meeting-point of three or four great mountain ranges, near the source of four rivers, all flowing in different directions, it has lacked that physical homogeneity without which no

[1] *Eponym Canon*, in SCHRADER, *Keilinschriftliche Bibliothek*, vol. i. pp. 212, 213. The only narrative of these events which has come down to us, that of *Slab No. 1*, ll. 23–25, and of *Slab No. 2*, ll. 35–40, introduces the siege of Turuspas after the defeat of Sharduris in Kummukh, thus making it appear as though the incidents of 735 followed in close succession after those of 743. The true order was re-established by Schrader, whose classification has been with good reason adopted by all recent historians (TIELE, *Bab.-ass. Gesch.*, pp. 231, 232 ; HOMMEL, *Gesch. Bab. und Ass.*, pp. 657–659 ; WINCKLER, *Gesch. Bab. und Ass.*, 227, 228 ; ROST, *Die Keilschrifttexte Tiglat-Pilesers III.*, vol. i. pp. 27, 28).

[2] Drawn by Boudier, from a photograph by M. Binder, furnished by Father Scheil.

people, however gifted, can hope to attain supremacy; nature has doomed it to remain, like Syria,[1] split up into compartments of unequal size and strength, which give shelter to half a score of independent principalities, each one of them perpetually jealous of the rest. From time to time it is invested with a semblance of unity, but for the most part it drags on an uneventful existence, dismembered into as many fragments as there happen to be powerful states around it, its only chance of complete reunion lying in the possibility of one or other of these attaining sufficient predominance to seize the share of the others and absorb it.

The subjection of Urartu freed Assyria from the only rival which could at this moment have disputed its supremacy on the banks of the Euphrates and the Tigris. The other nations on its northern and eastern frontiers as yet possessed no stability; they might, in the course of a passing outburst, cut an army to pieces or annex part of a province, but they lacked strength to follow up their advantage, and even their most successful raids were sure, in the long run, to lead to terrible reprisals, in which their gains were two or three times outweighed by their losses in men and treasure. For nearly a hundred years Nineveh found its hands free, and its rulers were able to concentrate all their energy on two main points of the frontier—to the south-west on Syria and Egypt, to the south-east on Chaldæa and Elam. Chaldæa gave little trouble, but the condition of Syria presented elements of danger. The loyalty of its princes was more apparent than real; they had bowed their necks after the fall of Unki, but afterwards, as the years rolled on without any seeming increase in the power of Assyria, they again took courage and began once more to quarrel among themselves. Menahem had died, soon after he had paid his tribute (737 B.C.); his son Pekahiah had been assassinated less than two years later (736),[2] and his murderer, Pekah, son of Remaliah, was none too firmly seated on the throne. Anarchy was triumphant throughout Israel; so much so that Judah seized the opportunity for throwing off the yoke it had borne for well-nigh a hundred years.[3] Pekah, conscious of his inability to suppress the rebellion, called in Rezin to help him.[4] The latter was already on the way when

---

[1] As to the natural divisions of Syria, cf. *Struggle of the Nations*, pp. 3, 4, 14.

[2] 2 *Kings* xv. 22–26. The chronology of the events which took place between the death of Menahem and the fall of Samaria, as presented by the biblical documents in the state in which they have been transmitted to us, is radically inaccurate: following the example of most recent historians, I have adhered exclusively to the data furnished by the Assyrian texts, merely indicating in the notes the reasons which have led me to adopt certain dates in preference to others.

[3] Winckler, in one place (*Gesch. Israels*, vol. i. p. 167), questions whether Judah was in a dependent position under Jeroboam II., and elsewhere (*Id.*, p. 179) admits that this was the case under Menahem; this latter view, in my opinion, alone explains the concatenation of events which followed. It is evident, from 2 *Kings* xv. 37, 38, that Jotham, not Ahaz, was the originator of the movement against Israel.

[4] Winckler declares that Pekah was merely a tool in the hands of Rezin, and in proof of this assertion points to the passage in 2 *Kings* xv. 25, where the author relates how the usurper killed Pekahiah with the help of fifty Gileadites: "he was helped by Gilead, which was itself under the

Jotham was laid with his fathers (736 B.C.), and it was Ahaz, the son of Jotham, who had to bear the brunt of the assault. He was barely twenty years old, a volatile, presumptuous, and daring youth, who was not much dismayed by his position.[1] Jotham had repaired the fortifications of Jerusalem, which had been left in a lamentable state ever since the damage done to them in the reign of Amaziah;[2] his successor now set to work to provide the city with the supply of water indispensable for its defence,[3] and, after repairing the ancient aqueducts, conceived the idea of constructing a fresh one in the spur of Mount Sion, which extends southwards. As time pressed, the work was begun simultaneously

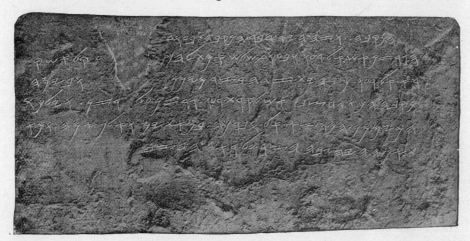

HEBREW INSCRIPTION ON THE SILOAM AQUEDUCT.[4]

at each end; the workmen had made a wide detour underground, probably in order to avoid the caves in which the kings of Judah had been laid to rest ever since the time of David,[5] and they were beginning to despair of ever uniting the two sections of the tunnel, when they suddenly heard one another through

rule of Damascus." But Gilead had been won back from Damascus; it belonged to Israel in the time of Jeroboam II. and of his successors, as Hosea himself tells us (vi. 8, where the prophet seems to refer to the assassination of Pekahiah, and xii. 2). Probably the rebellion of Judah was the sole cause which led Pekah to seek the aid of Rezin.

[1] 2 *Kings* xv. 38, xvi. 1, 2. Ahaz is called Iaukhazi, *i.e.* Jehoahaz, in the Assyrian texts (*Nimroud Inscrip.*, Rev., l. 11), and this would seem to have been the original form of the name (SCHRADER, *Die Keil. und das Alte Testament*, 2nd edit., pp. 263, 264; STADE, *Gesch. des Volkes Israel*, vol. i. p. 589, note 2).

[2] Cf. what has been said on p. 123, *supra.* The restoration of the walls of Jerusalem by Jotham is only mentioned in 2 *Chron.* xxvii. 3.

[3] We may deduce this from the words of Isaiah (vii. 3), where he represents Ahaz "at the end of the conduit of the upper pool, in the highway of the fuller's field." Ahaz had gone there to inspect the works intended for the defence of the aqueduct.

[4] A direct reproduction from a plaster cast now in Paris. The inscription discovered by Schick, in 1880, has since been mutilated, and only the fragments are preserved in the museum at Constantinople. Some writers think it was composed in the time of Hezekiah; cf., among the most recent, CLERMONT-GANNEAU, *Les Tombeaux de David et des rois de Juda*, pp. 396, 397. For my own part, I agree with Stade (*Geschichte des Volkes Israel*, vol. i. pp. 590–593) in assigning it to the period of Ahaz.

[5] This is the highly ingenious hypothesis put forward and defended with much learning by Clermont-Ganneau, in order to account for the large curve described by the tunnel (*Les Tombeaux de David et des rois de Juda et l'Aqueduc de Siloé*, in the *Comptes rendus de l'Académie des Inscriptions*, 1897, vol. xxv. pp. 383–427).

the wall of rock which divided them. A few blows with the pick-axe opened a passage between them, and an inscription on the wall adjoining the entrance on the east side, the earliest Hebrew inscription we possess, set forth the vicissitudes of the work for the benefit of future generations. It was scarcely completed when Rezin, who had joined forces with Pekah at Samaria, came up and laid regular siege to Jerusalem.[1] The allies did not propose to content themselves with exacting tribute from the young king; they meant to dethrone him, and to set up in his room a son of Tabeel, whom they had brought with them;[2] they were nevertheless obliged to retire without effecting a breach in his defences and leave the final assault till the following campaign. Rezin, however, had done as much injury as he could to Judah; he had laid waste both mountain and plain, had taken Elath by storm and restored it to the Edomites,[3] and had given a free hand to the Philistines (735).[4] The whole position seemed so hopeless, that a section of the people began to propose surrendering to the mercy of the Syrians.[5] Ahaz looked around him in search of some one on whom he might call for help. All his immediate neighbours were hostile; but behind them, in the background, were two great powers who might be inclined to listen to his appeal—Egypt and Assyria. Ever since the expedition of Sheshonq into Asia,[6] Egypt seemed to

BRONZE STATUETTE OF OSORKON I.[7]

have lost all interest in foreign politics. Osorkon had not inherited the warlike propensities of his father, and his son, Takelôti I., and his grandson, Osorkon II., followed his example.[8] These monarchs

---

[1] 2 *Kings* xvi. 5; cf. 2 *Chron.* xxviii. 5–8. It was on this occasion that Isaiah delivered the prophecies which, after subsequent revision, furnished the bulk of chaps. vi. 1—x. 4. Cf. what is said on this subject on pp. 184, 185, *infra.*

[2] *Isa.* vii. 4–9. The identity of this son of Tabeel has been, and still remains, the subject of conjecture. Oppert sought to identify him with the Azriyahu mentioned in the *Annals* of Tiglath-pileser III. (cf. p. 150, note 3, *supra*); some of the most recent writers have come back to the view that the son of Tabeel was Rezin himself (RENAN, *Histoire du Peuple d'Israel*, vol. ii. p. 508; WINCKLER, *Alttestamentliche Forschungen*, pp. 74–76, and *Geschichte Israels*, vol. i. p. 154).

[3] 2 *Kings* xvi. 6, where the Massoretic text states that the Syrians retained the town, while the LXX. maintain that he restored it to the Edomites. Winckler (*Geschichte Israels*, vol. i. p. 139, note 1, and p. 198) suppresses the reference to Rezin, and tries to make out that Elath had been won from Ahaz by a king of Edom.

[4] 2 *Chron.* xxviii. 18, where a list is given of the towns wrested from Judah by the Philistines. The delight felt by the Philistines at the sight of Judah's abasement seems to be referred to in the short prophecy of Isaiah (xiv. 29–32), wrongly ascribed to the year of Ahaz's death.

[5] This seems to be an obvious inference from the words of Isaiah (viii. 6): "Forasmuch as this people hath refused the waters of Shiloah that go softly, *and lose courage because of Rezin and Remaliah's son.*" [The R.V. reads "*rejoice in*" Rezin, etc.—TR.]

[6] As to the expedition of Sheshonq into Syria, cf. *Struggle of the Nations*, pp. 772–775.

[7] Drawn by Faucher-Gudin, from Lanzone's statuette; cf. LANZONE, *Descrizione di una Statuetta di bronzo*, in the *Atti* of the Turin Academy, 1875, vol. xi. p. 459, et seq., and MISS GONNINO, *Note on a Statuette of Osorkon I.*, in the *Proceedings* of the Soc. for Bibl. Arch., 1884–1885, vol. vi. pp. 205, 206.

[8] The chronology of this period is still very uncertain, and the stelæ of the Serapæum, which enable us to fix the order of the various reigns, yield no information as to their length. Sheshonq I. did

regarded themselves as traditionary suzerains of the country of Kharu, *i.e.* of Israel, Judah, Ammon, and Moab, and their authority may perhaps have been recognised by the Philistines in the main,[1] but they seldom stirred from their

THE GREAT TEMPLE OF BUBASTIS DURING NAVILLE'S EXCAVATIONS.[2]

own territory, and contented themselves with protecting their frontiers against the customary depredations of the Libyan and Asiatic nomads.[3]   Under their rule, Egypt enjoyed fifty years of profound peace, which was spent in works of public utility, especially in

not reign much longer than twenty-one years, which is his latest known date (CHAMPOLLION, *Monuments de l'Égypte et de la Nubie*, pl. cxxii. *bis;* LEPSIUS, *Denkm.* iii. 254 *c*), and we may take the reign of twenty-one years attributed to him by Manetho as being substantially correct.   The latest dates we possess are as follows : Osorkon I., twelfth year (LEGRAIN, *Textes gravés sur le quai de Karnak*, in the *Zeitschrift*, vol. xxxiv. p. 3, No. 2), and Takelôti I., sixth year (*Id.*, p. 3, No. 4) or seventh year (DARESSY, *Inscriptions inédites de la XXII*ᵉ *Dynastie*, in the *Recueil de Travaux*, vol. xviii. pp. 51, 52). Lastly, we have a twenty-ninth year in the case of Osorkon II. (*Id.*, p. 112, No. 14), with a reference in the case of the twenty-eighth year to the fifth year of a Takelôti whose first cartouche is missing (*Id.*, p. 112, No. 23), and who perhaps died before his father and co-regent.   In Manetho, Osorkon I. is credited with a reign of fifteen years, and his three next successors with a total of twenty-five years between them, which is manifestly incorrect, since the monuments give twenty-nine years, or twenty-three at the very least, if we take into account the double date in the case of the first two of these kings.   The wisest course seems to be to allow forty-five years to Osorkon and his two successors : if Sheshonq, as I believe, died in 924, the fifty years allotted to the next three Pharaohs would bring us down to 880, and it is in this year that I am, for the present, inclined to place the death of Osorkon II.

¹ Cf. *Struggle of the Nations*, p. 774.

² Drawn by Boudier, from a photograph by NAVILLE, *Bubastis*, pl. iii.

³ Repressive measures of this kind are evidently referred to in passages similar to those in which Osorkon II. boasts of having " overthrown beneath his feet the Upper and Lower Lotanu " (NAVILLE, *Bubastis*, p. 51, and *The Festival Hall of Osorkon II. in the Great Temple of Bubastis*, pl. vi., and p. 4), and speaks of the exploits of the sons of Queen Kalamâît against certain tribes whose name, though mutilated, seems to have been Libyan in character (DARESSY, *Inscriptions inédites de la XX*ᵉ *Dynastie*, in the *Recueil de Travaux*, vol. xviii. pp. 49–51).

the Delta, where, thanks to their efforts, Bubastis came to be one of the most splendid among the cities of secondary importance.[1]   Its temple, which had been rebuilt by Ramses II. and decorated by the Ramessides,[2] was in a sorry plight when the XXIInd dynasty came into power.   Sheshonq I. did little or nothing to it, but Osorkon I. entirely remodelled it,[3] and Osorkon II. added several new halls, including, amongst others, one in which he celebrated, in the twenty-second year of his reign, the festival of his deification.[4] A record of some of the ceremonies observed has come down to us in the mural paintings.   There we see the king, in a chapel, consecrating a statue of himself in accordance with the ritual in use since the time of Amenôthes III.,[5] and offering the figure devout and earnest worship; all the divinities of Egypt have assembled to witness the enthronement of this new member of their confraternity, and take part in the sacrifices accompanying his consecration. This gathering of the gods is balanced by a human festival, attended by Nubians and Kushites, as well as by the courtiers and populace.   The proceedings terminated, apparently, with certain funeral rites, the object being to make the identification of Osorkon with Osiris complete.   The Egyptian deities served in a double capacity, as gods of the dead as well as of the living, and no exception could be made in favour of the deified Osorkon; while yet living he became an Osiris, and his double was supposed to animate those prophetic statues in which he appeared as a mummy no less than those which represented him as still alive.   Another temple of small size, also dedicated to Bastît or Pasht, which had been built in the time of Ramses II., was enlarged by Osorkon I., and richly endowed with workshops, lands, cattle, slaves, and precious metals : Tumu-Khopri of Heliopolis, to mention but one of the deities worshipped there, received offerings of gold in value by weight £120,000, and silver ingots worth £12,000.[6]   A country which could afford to indulge in extravagances of this nature must have been in a flourishing condition, and everything goes to prove that Egypt prospered under the rule of the early Bubastite kings.

The very same causes, however, which had ruined the Ramessides and the Tanites were now openly compassing the downfall of the Bubastite dynasty.

[1] All our knowledge of the history of the temple of Bubastis dates from Naville's excavations, *Bubastis*, 1891, and *The Festival Hall of Osorkon II. in the Great Temple of Bubastis*, 1892.

[2] As to the origin of the temple of Bubastis, cf. what has been said in the *Dawn of Civilization*, pp. 364, 371, note 2, 422; and in regard to the successive restorations thereof prior to the XXIInd dynasty, cf. the *Dawn of Civilization*, pp. 503, 504, 530, and the *Struggle of the Nations*, pp. 59, 60, 423.

[3] NAVILLE, *Bubastis*, pp. 46–48.

[4] Naville has described this and explained the texts referring to it in a volume entitled *The Festival Hall of Osorkon II.*, etc.   The ceremony is that known as the *Sit-habu*, which Brugsch seeks to identify with the *Triakontæterides* of the Ptolemaic epoch, *i.e.* festivals which recurred every thirty years (cf. *Die Ægyptologie*, pp. 365, 366); my opinion of Brugsch's theory and of the nature of this festival has been briefly indicated in an article in the *Revue Critique*, 1892, vol. ii. pp. 386–398.

[5] As to the deification of Amenôthes III., cf. *Struggle of the Nations*, pp. 300–302.

[6] NAVILLE, *Bubastis*, pls. l.–lii., and pp. 60–62; this is the small temple afterwards described by Herodotus as being dedicated to Hermes (II. cxxxviii.; cf. WIEDEMANN, *Herodots Zweites Buch*, pp. 498, 499).

The military feudalism from which it had sprung, suppressed for a time by Sheshonq I., developed almost unchecked under his successors. They had thought to break it up and turn it to their own advantage, by transferring the more important religious functions and the principal fiefs to their own sons or nephews. They governed Memphis through the high priests of Phtah ;[1] a prince of the blood represented them at Khmunu,[2] another at Khninsu [3] (Heracleopolis), and others in various cities of the Delta,[4] each of them being at the head of several thousand Mashauasha, or Libyan soldiers on whose fidelity they could entirely rely.[5] Thebes alone had managed to exclude these representatives of the ruling dynasty, and its princes, guided in this particular by the popular prejudice, persistently re-

GATE OF THE FESTIVAL HALL AT BUBASTIS.[6]

fused to admit into their bodyguard any but the long-tried Mâzaîu.[7] Moreover, Thebes lost no opportunity of proving itself to be still the most turbulent of the

---

[1] Cf., on this point, STERN, *Die XXII Manethonische Dynastie*, in the *Zeitschrift*, 1883, pp. 18, 19, and DARESSY, *Inscriptions inédites de la XXIIᵉ dynastie*, in the *Recueil de Travaux*, vol. xviii. pp. 46–49.

[2] *E.g.* Namrôti, under Piônkhi-Mîamun, whose rights were such that he adopted the protocol of the Pharaohs (E. DE ROUGÉ, *La Stèle du roi éthiopien Piânkhi Meriamen*, pp. 1, 19, etc.).

[3] Stele 1959 of the Serapæum contains the names of five successive princes of this city, the first of whom was Namrôti, son of Osorkon II., and high priest of Thebes, who is dealt with later on (pp. 162–164, *infra*); a member of the same family, named Pefzââbastît, had taken cartouches under Osorkon III. of the XXIIIʳᵈ dynasty (E. DE ROUGÉ, *La Stèle du roi éthiopien Piânkhi Meriamen*, pp. 1, 35, etc.), as will be seen later on, pp. 167, 168, 176, *infra*. As to the principality of Khninsu, cf. STERN, *Die XXII Manethonische Dynastie*, in the *Zeitschrift*, 1883, p. 23.

[4] Cf. the list of princes of the Delta on the stele of Piônkhi-Mîamun (E. DE ROUGÉ, *La Stèle du roi éthiopien Piânkhi Meriamen*, pp. 67–70, 94).

[5] As to the Mashauasha and the prominent part played by them in the revolutions of Egypt from the latter part of the XXᵗʰ dynasty onwards, cf. *Struggle of the Nations*, pp. 765–768.

[6] Drawn by Faucher-Gudin, from a restoration by NAVILLE in *The Festival Hall of Osorkon II.*, a plate which serves as frontispiece to the volume.

[7] As to the absence of the Mashauasha from Thebes, cf. *Struggle of the Nations*, p. 767.

M

baronies. Its territory had suffered no diminution since the time of Hrihor, and half of Upper Egypt, from Elephantinê to Siut, acknowledged its sway.[1] Through all the changes of dynasty its political constitution had remained unaltered; Amon still ruled there supreme as ever, and nothing was done until he had been formally consulted in accordance with ancient usage.[2] Auputi, in spite of his being a son of Sheshonq, was compelled to adopt the title of high priest in order to rule in peace, and had married some daughter or niece of the last of the Paînotmu.[3] After his death, good care was taken to prevent the pontificate

SMALL BRONZE SPHINX OF SIAMUN.[4]

from passing to one of his children, as this would have re-established a Theban dynasty which might have soon proved hostile to that of Bubastis. To avoid this, Osorkon I. made over the office and fief to his own son Sheshonq. The latter, after a time, thought he was sufficiently powerful to follow the example of Paînotmu and adopt the royal cartouches; but, with all his ambition, he too failed to secure the succession to the male line of his descendants, for Osorkon II. appointed his own son Namrôti, already prince of Khninsu, to succeed him.[5] The amalgamation of these two posts invested the person on whom they were conferred with almost regal power; Khninsu was, indeed, as we know,[6] the natural rampart of Memphis and Lower Egypt against invasion from the south, and its possessor was in a position to control the fate of the empire almost as he pleased. Osorkon must have had weighty reasons for taking a step which placed him practically at the mercy of his son, and, indeed, events proved that but little reliance could be placed on the loyalty of the Thebans, and that energetic measures were imperative

---

[1] It is evident that this was so from the first steps taken by Piônkhi-Miamun's generals: they meet the army and fleet of Tafnakhti and the princes of the north right under the walls of Hermopolis, but say nothing of any feudal princes of the south (ll. 2–9). Their silence is explained if we assume that Thebes, being a dependency of Ethiopia, retained at that date, *i.e.* in the time of the XXIIIrd dynasty, the same or nearly the same boundaries which it had won for itself under the XXIst (cf. what has been said on this point in the *Struggle of the Nations*, pp. 564, 768, 769).

[2] As to the high priest Auputi, son of Sheshonq I., and the part played by him in Thebes at the beginning of the XXIInd dynasty, cf. what is said in the *Struggle of the Nations*, pp. 770, 771, 773.

[3] Cf., in regard to this marriage, the *Struggle of the Nations*, pp. 760, 761.

[4] Drawn by Faucher-Gudin, from the original now in the Louvre; cf. PIERRET, *Catalogue des Monuments de la Salle Historique*, No. 265, p. 56.

[5] MASPERO, *Les Momies royales de Deîr el-Baharî*, in *Mémoires de la Mission du Caire*, vol. i. pp. 734–738, where all the information we at present possess in regard to Namrôti is collected and discussed.

[6] As to the military and political influence of Khninsu (Heracleopolis), cf. what is said in the *Struggle of the Nations*, pp. 445–448.

to keep them in the path of duty or lead them back to it.   The decadence of
the ancient capital had sadly increased since the downfall of the descendants
of Hrihor.   The few public works which they had undertaken, and which
Sheshonq I. encouraged to the best of his ability, had been suspended owing
to want of money, and the craftsmen who had depended on them for support

RUINS OF THE TEMPLE AT KHNINSU AFTER NAVILLE'S EXCAVATIONS.[1]

were suffering from poverty : the makers of small articles of a religious or
funerary character, carvers of wood or stone, joiners, painters of mummy-cases,
and workers in bronze, alone managed to eke out a bare livelihood, thanks to
commissions still given to them by officials attached to the temples.   Theban
art, which in its best period had excelled in planning its works on a gigantic
scale, now gladly devoted itself to the production of mere knick-knacks, in
place of the colossal figures of earlier days.   We have statuettes some twelve or
fifteen inches high, crudely coloured, wooden stelæ, shapeless *ushabti* redeemed
from ugliness by a coating of superb blue enamel, and, above all, those miniature
sphinxes representing queens or kings, which present with two human arms
either a table of offerings or a salver decorated with cartouches.   The starving
populace, its interests and vanity alike mortified by the accession of a northern
dynasty, refused to accept the decay of its fortunes with resignation, and this
spirit of discontent was secretly fomented by the priests or by members of the
numerous families which boasted of their descent from the Ramessides.   Although
hereditary claims to the throne and the pontificate had died out or lost their

---

[1] Drawn by Boudier, from a photograph which serves as a frontispiece to NAVILLE, *Ahnas el-Medineh.*
The illustration shows what now remains of the portions of the temple rebuilt in the time of Ramses II.

force in the male line, they were still persistently urged by the women : consecrated from their birth to the service of Amon, and originally reserved to sing his praises or share his nuptial couch, those of them who married transmitted to their children, and more especially to their daughters, the divine germ which qualified them for the throne. They and their followers never ceased to look for the day when the national deity should shake off his apathy, and, becoming the champion of their cause against the Bubastite or Tanite usurpers, restore their city to the rank and splendour from which it had fallen. Namrôti married one of these Theban princesses, and thus contrived to ward off the danger of revolt during his lifetime ;[1] but on his death or disappearance an insurrection broke out. Sheshonq II. had succeeded Osorkon II., and he, in his turn, was followed by Takelôti II.[2] Takelôti chose Kalamâit, daughter of Namrôti, as his lawful wife, formally recognised her as queen, and set up numerous statues and votive monuments in her honour. But all in vain : this concession failed to conciliate the rebellious, and the whole Thebaid rose against him to a man. In the twelfth year of his reign he entrusted the task of putting down the revolt to his son Osorkon, at the same time conferring upon him the office of high priest. It took several years to repress the rising; defeated in the eleventh year, the rebels still held the field in the fifteenth year of the king, and it was not till some time after, between the fifteenth and twenty-second year of Takelôti II., that they finally laid down their arms.[3] At the end of this struggle the king's power was quite exhausted, while that of the feudal magnates had proportionately increased. Before long, Egypt was split up into a number of petty states, some of them containing but a few towns, while others, following the example of Thebes, boldly annexed several adjacent nomes. A last remnant of respect for the traditional monarchy kept them

---

[1] MASPERO, *Les Momies royales de Deîr el-Bahari*, pp. 738–740.

[2] The few references to these two Bubastite Pharaohs that have come down to us have been nearly all collected by WIEDEMANN, *Ægyptische Geschichte*, pp. 555–557, and *Supplement*, i. p. 64.

[3] The story of these events is told in several greatly mutilated inscriptions to be found at Karnak on the outer surface of the south wall of the Hall of Columns, and which have been published by LEPSIUS, *Denkm.*, iii. 256 *a*, 257 *a*; cf. CHAMPOLLION, *Monuments de l'Égypte et de la Nubie*, cclxxvii. 1, cclxxix. 1, and vol. ii. p. 22. One of them contains a phrase which Brugsch took to refer to an eclipse which occurred in the twenty-fourth day of Choiak in the fifteenth year of Takelôti II. (*Histoire d'Egypte*, p. 233), and which was made use of by Hincks to fix the date of the event as the 4th April, 945 B.C., assuming that it was an eclipse of the moon (*The Egyptian Dynasties of Manetho*, i. pp. 34–41), but afterwards, finding that an eclipse of the sun was meant, he altered the date to the 1st April, 927 (*Id.*, ii. p. 41). The accuracy of these deductions was disputed by Chabas, who maintained that the passage in question was purely mythological, and had no bearing on astronomy (*Mélanges Égyptologiques*, 2nd series, pp. 72–107). Thereupon a controversy ensued between Goodwin (*On an Inscription of Takelut II.*, in the *Zeitschrift*, 1868, pp. 25–29), Brugsch (*Eine Mondfinsterniss*, in the *Zeitschrift*, 1868, pp. 29–35), and Chabas (*Lettre à M. le Docteur Lepsius sur l'Inscription de Takellothis II.*, in the *Zeitschrift*, 1868, pp. 49–52), which ended in each of the disputants adhering to his own view while maintaining that he had refuted that of the others. Brugsch, who survived both Goodwin and Chabas by many years, persisted to the last in his opinion that the passage refers to an eclipse of the moon (*Geschichte Ægyptens*, p. 670).

from entirely repudiating the authority of Pharaoh.
They still kept up an outward show of submission
to his rule; they paid him military service when
called upon, and appealed to him as umpire in their
disputes, without, however, always accepting his
rulings, and when they actually came to blows
among themselves, were content to exercise their
right of private warfare under his direction.[1] The
royal domain gradually became narrowed down to
the Memphite nome and the private appanages of
the reigning house, and soon it no longer yielded
the sums necessary for the due performance of costly
religious ceremonies, such as the enthronement or
burial of an Apis. The pomp and luxury usually
displayed on such occasions grew less and less under
the successors of Takelôti II., Sheshonq III., Pimi,
and Sheshonq IV.[2] When the last of these passed
away after an inglorious reign of at least thirty-
seven years, the prestige of his race had so com-

KING PETUBASTIS AT PRAYER.[3]

pletely declined that the country would have no more of it; the sceptre passed
into the hands of another dynasty, this time of Tanite origin.[4] It was probably

[1] It is evident that this was so, from a romance discovered by KRALL, *Ein neuer Historischer
Roman in Demotischer Schrift*, p. 14, et seq.; cf. MASPERO, in the *Journal des Savants*, 1897, pp. 654–657.

[2] One need only go to the Louvre and compare the Apis stelæ erected during this period with
those engraved in the time of the XXVIth dynasty, in order to realise the low ebb to which the later
kings of the XXIInd dynasty had fallen: the fact that the chapel and monuments were built under
their direction shows that they were still masters of Memphis. We have no authentic date for
Sheshonq II., and the twenty-ninth year is the latest known in the case of Takelôti II. (CHAM-
POLLION, *Monuments de l'Égypte et de la Nubie*, vol. ii. pp. 22, 23; LEPSIUS, *Denkm.*, iii. 258 a), but we
know (MARIETTE, *Le Sérapéum de Memphis*, pl. 28; cf. MARIETTE, *Renseignements sur les soixante-
quatre Apis*, in the *Athénæum Français*, 1855, pp. 94–98, and BRUGSCH, *Geschichte Ægyptens*, p. 673)
that Sheshonq III. reigned fifty-two years, and, after two years of Pimi (MARIETTE, *Le Sérapéum*,
pl. 31, and *Renseignements*, etc., in the *Athénæum Français*, 1855, pp. 98–100), we find a reference to the
thirty-seventh year of Sheshonq IV. If we allow a round century for these last kings we are not likely
to be far out: this would place the close of the Bubastite dynasty somewhere about 780 B.C.

[3] Drawn by Faucher-Gudin, from a small door now in the Louvre; cf. PIERRET, *Catalogue de la
Salle Historique*, No. 649, p. 160.

[4] The following list gives the names of the Pharaohs of the XXIInd dynasty in so far as they
have been ascertained up to the present :—

    I. SHASHANQU I. MARIAMANU, UAZAKHPIRRÎ-SOTPUNIRÎ.
    II. UASARKANU I. MARIAMANU, SAKHMAKHPIRRÎ-SOTPUNIRÎ.
    III. TAKELÔTI I. SI-ISÎT MARIAMANU, USIRMÂRÎ-SOTPUNIAMANU.
    IV. UASARKANU II. SI-BASTÎT MARIAMANU, USIRMÂRÎ-SOTPUNIAMANU.
    V. SHASHANQU II. MARIAMANU, SAKHMAKHPIRRÎ-SOTPUNIAMANU.
    VI. TAKELÔTI II. SI-ISÎT MARIAMANU, UAZAKHPIRRÎ-SOTPUNIRÎ.
    VII. SHASHANQU III. SI-BASTÎT MARIAMANU, USIRMÂRÎ-SOTPUNIRÎ.
    VIII. PAIMÎ MARIAMANU, USIRMÂRÎ-SOTPUNIAMANU.
    IX. SHASHANQU IV. MARIAMANU, AKHPIRRÎ.

This list is identical with that drawn up by Lepsius (*Ueber die XXII ägyptischen Königs-dynastie*

a younger branch of the Bubastite family allied to the Ramessides and Theban Pallacides. Petubastis, the first of the line, secured recognition in Thebes,[1] and throughout the rest of Egypt as well, but his influence was little greater than that of his predecessors; as in the past, the real power was in the hands of the high priests. One of them, Auîti by name, even went so far, in the fourteenth or fifteenth year, as to declare himself king, and had his cartouches inscribed on official documents side by side with those of the Tanite monarch.[2] His kingship died with him, just as that of Paînotmu had done in similar circumstances, and two years later we find his successor, Harsiisît, a mere high priest without pretensions to royalty.[3] Doubtless his was not an isolated case; all the grandees who happened to be nearly related either to the dethroned or to the reigning houses acted in like manner, and for the first time for many years Egypt acknowledged the simultaneous sway of more than one legitimate Pharaoh. Matters became still worse under Osorkon III.; although he, too, introduced a daughter of Amon into his harem,[4] this alliance failed to give him any hold over Thebes, and even the Seven Nomes and the Delta were split up to such an extent that at one time they included something like a score of independent principalities, three of which, Hermopolis, Heracleopolis, and Tentramu, were administered by kings who boasted cartouches similar to those of Tanis and Bubastis.[5]

About 740 B.C. there appeared in the midst of these turbulent and extortionate nobles a man who, by sheer force of energy and talent, easily outstripped all competitors.[6] Tafnakhti was a chief of obscure origin, whose hereditary rights

nebst einigen Bemerkungen zu der XXVI und andern Dynastien des Neuen Reichs, pl. i., and *Königs-buch*, pls. xliv.–xlvi.), with one single exception. Stern had discovered that the prenomen attributed by Lepsius to Takelôti I. really belonged to Takelôti II. (*Die XXII Manethonische Dynastie*, in the *Zeitschrift*, 1882, pp. 16, 17); to Daressy, however, belongs the credit of indicating the protocol of Takelôti I. in his *Note additionnelle* addressed to BARSANTI, *Sur deux stèles d'Abydos au nom du Pharaon Takellothis Ier* (*Recueil de Travaux*, vol. xvi. pp. 174, 175), and in his *Inscriptions inédites de la XXIIe Dynastie* (*Recueil de Travaux*, vol. xviii. pp. 51, 52).

[1] This fact, disputed by Révillout (*Notice des Papyrus archaiques*, pp. 217, 233), has recently been placed beyond doubt by inscriptions found on the quay at Karnak near the water-marks of the Nile (LEGRAIN, *Textes gravés sur le quai de Karnak*, in the *Zeitschrift*, vol. xxxiv. p. 114, Nos. 26–29).

[2] No. 26 of Legrain's inscriptions (*Textes gravés*, etc., in the *Zeitschrift*, vol. xxxiv. p. 114) tells us the height of the Nile in the sixteenth year of Petubastît, which was also the second year of King Auîti (cf. LEGRAIN, *Les Crues du Nil*, in the *Zeitschrift*, vol. xxxiv. p. 121). Seeing that Auîti's name occurs in the place occupied by that of the high priest of Thebes in other inscriptions of the same king, I consider it probable that he was reigning in Thebes itself, and that he was a high priest who had become king in the same way as Paînotmu under the XXIst dynasty (cf. *Struggle of the Nations*, p. 760).

[3] Cf. Nos. 27, 28 of Legrain's inscriptions, in which the writer refers to a high priest of Amon, whose name is mutilated, but should be read Harsiisît (*Textes gravés sur le quai de Karnak*, in the *Zeitschrift*, vol. xxxiv. p. 114).

[4] LIEBLEIN, *Die Ægyptischen Denkmäler aus Saint-Petersburg, Helsingfors, Upsala und Kopenhagen*, pp. 6–11, and pl. 1, 2; cf. MASPERO, *Les Momies royales de Deîr el-Bahari*, pp. 741–754.

[5] E. DE ROUGÉ, *L'Inscription historique du roi Pianchi Mériamoun*, p. 18, et seq.; E. de Rougé was the first to identify the Osorkon, King of Bubastis, mentioned on an Ethiopian stele, with the Osorkon III. of the monuments, the second Pharaoh of the XXIIIrd Tanite dynasty.

[6] All our knowledge of this first Ethiopian campaign comes from a stele of King Piônkhi-Miamun, discovered at Gebel-Barkal in 1862, and transported to Bulaq (MARIETTE, *Lettre à M. le Vicomte de Rougé sur une stèle trouvée au Gebel-Barkal*, in the *Revue Archéologique*, 1863, vol. vii. pp. 413–422)

extended merely over the village of Nutirît and the outskirts of Sebennytos.[1] One or two victories gained over his nearest neighbours encouraged him to widen the sphere of his operations. He first of all laid hands on those nomes of the Delta which extended to the west of the principal arm of the Nile, the Saite, Athribite, Libyan, and Memphite nomes; these he administered through officers under his own immediate control; then, leaving untouched the eastern provinces, over which Osorkon III. exercised a make-shift, easy-going rule, he made his way up the river. Maitumu and the Fayum accepted him as their

VIEW OF A PART OF THE RUINS OF NAPATA.[2]

suzerain, but Khninsu and its king, Pefzââbastît, faithful to their allegiance,[3] offered strenuous resistance. He then crossed over to the right bank, and

and published by Mariette (*Monuments divers*, pls. 1–6, and *Texte*, pp. 1, 2), interpreted by E. de Rougé (*L'Inscription historique du roi Pianchi Meriamoun*, in the *Revue Archéologique*, 1863, vol. viii. p. 94, et seq., and *La stèle du roi éthiopien Piânkhi Meriamen*, in the *Chrestomathie Égyptienne*, vol. iv.), and, after him, translated into German by Lauth (*Die Pianchi-Stele*, in the *Sitzungsberichte* of the Munich Academy, 1869, pp. 13–49, and in the *Abhandlungen* of the same institution, 1870), then by Brugsch (*Die Siegesinschrift Königs Pianchi von Ethiopien*, in the *Nachrichten* of the Göttingen Institute of Sciences, 1876, No. 19, pp. 457–488, and *Geschichte Ægyptens*, pp. 676–707), into English by Cook (*Inscription of Pianchi Meramon, King of Egypt, in the Eighth Century B.C.*, 1873, reprinted with certain corrections in the *Records of the Past*, 1st series, vol. ii. pp. 79–104), and finally by Griffith (*Egyptian Literature*, in *Specimen Pages of a Library of the World's Best Literature*, pp. 5274–5295).

[1] E. DE ROUGÉ, *L'Inscription historique du roi Pianchi Mériamoun*, pp. 21, 22. The city of Nutirît was first of all identified by Brugsch (*Geographische Inschriften*, vol. i. pp. 289, 290) with Manuti, near Canopus; Brugsch has since then come to the conclusion that it is the Isæum of the Greco-Roman geographers, near Behbeît (BRUGSCH, *Dictionnaire Géographique*, pp. 366, 367). Tafnakhti is the Tnephakhtos, father of Bocchoris, mentioned by Diodorus Siculus (i. 45), whose name is incorrectly given as Tekhnatis (E. DE ROUGÉ, *L'Inscription historique du roi Pianchi Mériamoun*, pp. 22, 23) by the author of the treatise *De Iside* (§ 8, p. 13, PARTHEY's edit.).

[2] Reproduced by Faucher-Gudin, from a lithograph published in CAILLIAUD, *Voyage à Méroé*, *Atlas*, vol. i. pl. lxiii.

[3] Pefzââbastît, King of Heracleopolis, seems to be identical with the Pharaoh Pefzâbastît of the

received the homage of Heliopolis and Pnebtepahê ;[1] he put the inhabitants of Uabu to ransom, established a close blockade of Khninsu, and persuaded Namrôti, King of Khmunu, to take an oath of allegiance.[2] At length, those petty kings and princes of the Saîd and the Delta who still remained

GEBEL-BARKAL, THE SACRED MOUNTAIN OF NAPATA.[3]

unconquered called upon Ethiopia,[4] the only power capable of holding its ground against him, for help. The "vile Kaushu" (Cush) probably rose to be an independent state about the time when Sheshonq and the Bubastite kings came into power.[5] Peopled by Theban settlers, and governed by the civil and religious code of Thebes, the provinces which lay between the cataract of Hannek and the confluence of the two Niles soon became a second Thebaid, more barren and less wealthy than the first, but no less tied to the traditions of the past.[6] Napata, its capital, lay in the plain at the foot of a sandstone cliff, which rose perpendicularly to a height of nearly two hundred

Berlin sarcophagus (LEPSIUS, *Denkm.*, iii. 284 a), as pointed out by E. de Rougé (*Inscription du roi Pianchi Meriamoun*, pp. 18, 19) and Devéria (*Mémoires et Fragments*, vol. i. pp. 376, 377; cf. DARESSY, *Notes et Remarques*, § cxliii., in the *Recueil de Travaux*, vol. xix. pp. 20, 21).

[1] *Inscription of Piônkhi-Miamun*, ll. 2–4 ; cf. MARIETTE, *Monuments divers*, pl. i. ; E. DE ROUGÉ, *La Stèle du roi éthiopien Piânkhi Meriamen*, pp. 3–5.

[2] *Inscription of Piônkhi-Miamun*, ll. 4, 5 ; cf. MARIETTE, *Monuments divers*, pl. i. ; E. DE ROUGÉ, *La Stèle du roi éthiopien Piânkhi Meriamen*, p. 6.

[3] Reproduced by Faucher-Gudin, from a lithograph in CAILLIAUD, *Voyage à Méroé*, *Atlas*, vol. i. pl. l.

[4] *Inscription of Piônkhi-Miamun*, ll. 6–8 ; cf. MARIETTE, *Monuments divers*, pl. i. ; E. DE ROUGÉ, *La Stèle du roi éthiopien Piânkhi Meriamen*, pp. 7, 8.

[5] Cf. the *Struggle of the Nations*, p. 772.

[6] Cf. what is said in regard to Ethiopia in the *Struggle of the Nations*, pp. 299, 300.

feet, its summit, when viewed from the south-west, presenting an accidental resemblance to a human profile.[1] This was the *Du-uabu*, or Sacred Mount, in the heart of which the god was supposed to have his dwelling; the ruins of several temples can still be seen near the western extremity of the hill, the finest of them being dedicated to a local Amon-râ. This Amon was a replica of the Theban Amon on a smaller scale, and was associated with the same companions as his prototype, Maut, his consort, and Khonsu, his son. He owed his origin to the same religious concepts, and was the central figure of a similar myth, the only difference being that he was represented in composite shape, with a ram's head; perhaps a survival from some earlier indigenous deity, such as Didun, for instance,[3] who had been previously worshipped in those parts; his priests lived in accordance with the rules of the Theban hierarchy. We

RUINS OF THE TEMPLE OF AMON AT NAPATA.[2]

can readily believe that when Hrihor extorted the title of "Royal Son of Kaushu" from the weaklings who occupied the throne at the close of the Ramesside dynasty, he took care to install one of the members of his family as high priest at Napata, and from henceforward had the whole country at his bidding. Subsequently, when Païnotmu II. was succeeded by Auputi at

---

[1] CAILLIAUD, *Voyage à Méroé*, vol. iii. pp. 199, 200. The natives believe this profile to have been cut by human hands—an error which has been shared by more than one modern traveller.

[2] Reproduced by Faucher-Gudin, from a lithograph published by CAILLIAUD, *Voyage à Méroé*, *Atlas*, vol. i. pl. lix.

[3] As to Didun or Dudun, and the identification of this ancient Nubian deity with Amon and Khmunu, at the time of the Egyptian conquest, cf. *Struggle of the Nations*, p. 300. Lepsius believed that the introduction of the ram-headed Amon at Napata occurred at a comparatively recent date, and attributed it to the time of Taharqa (*Ueber die widderköpfigen Götter Ammon und Chnuphis, in Beziehung auf die Ammons-Oase*, in the *Zeitschrift*, 1876, pp. 14–16).

Thebes, it seems that the Ethiopian priests refused to ratify his election. Whether they conferred the supreme power on one of their own number, or whether some son of Paînotmu, flying from the Bubastite kings, arrived at the right moment to provide them with a master, is not quite clear. The kings of Ethiopia, priests from the first, never lost their sacerdotal character. They continued to be men of God, and as such it was necessary that they should be chosen by the god himself. On the death of a sovereign, Amon at once became regent in the person of his prophet, and continued to act until the funeral rites were celebrated. As soon as these ceremonies were completed, the army and the people collected at the foot of the Sacred Mount; the delegates of the various orders of the state were led into the sanctuary, and then, in their presence, all the males of the royal

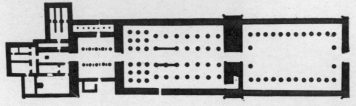

PLAN OF THE TEMPLE OF AMON AT NAPATA.[1]

family—"the king's brothers," as they were called—were paraded before the statue of the god; he on whom the god laid his hand as he passed was considered to be the chosen one of Amon, and consecrated king without delay.[2] As may be readily imagined, the new monarch thus appointed by divine dictation was completely under the control of the priests, and before long, if he failed to prove sufficiently tractable,[3] they claimed the right to dispense with him altogether; they sent him an order to commit suicide, and he obeyed. The boundaries of this theocratic state varied at different epochs; originally it was confined to the region between the First Cataract and the mouth of the Blue Nile. The bulk of the population consisted of settlers of Egyptian extraction and Egyptianised natives; but isolated, as they were, from Egypt proper by the rupture of the political ties which had bound them to the metropolis, they ceased to receive fresh reinforcements from the northern part of the valley as they had formerly done, and daily became more closely identified with the races of various origin which roamed through the deserts of Libya or Arabia. This constant infiltration of free or slavish Bedâwin blood and the large number of black women

---

[1] Reproduced by Faucher-Gudin, from the plan drawn up and published by CAILLAUD, *Voyage à Méroé, Atlas,* vol. i. pl. lxiv.; cf. LEPSIUS, *Denkm.,* i. 128.

[2] This is the ritual described in the *Stele of the Enthronement* (MARIETTE, *Monuments divers,* pl. 9; cf. MASPERO, *Mélanges de Mythologie et d'Archéologie Égyptiennes,* vol. iii. pp. 135–151, 229–233). Perhaps it was already in use at Thebes under the XXIst and XXIInd dynasties, at the election of the high priest, whether he happened to be a king or not; at any rate, a story of the Ptolemaic period told by Synesius in *The Egyptian* (MASPERO, *Mélanges de Mythologie,* vol. i. pp. 86–89) seems to point to this conclusion.

[3] DIODORUS SICULUS, iii. 6.

found in the harems of the rich, and even in the huts of the common people, quickly impaired the purity of the race, even among the upper classes of the nation, and the type came to resemble that of the negro tribes of Equatorial Africa.[1] The language fared no better in the face of this invasion, and the written character soon became as corrupt as the language; words foreign to the Egyptian vocabulary, incorrect expressions, and barbarous errors in syntax were multiplied without stint.[2] The taste for art decayed, and technical ability began to deteriorate, the moral and intellectual standard declined, and the mass of the people showed signs of relapsing into barbarism: the leaders of the aristocracy and the scribes alone preserved almost intact their inheri-

A NEARLY PURE ETHIOPIAN TYPE.[3]

tance from an older civilisation. Egypt still attracted them: they looked upon it as their rightful possession, torn from them by alien usurpers in defiance of all sense of right, and they never ceased to hope that some day, when the god saw fit, they would win back their heritage. Were not their kings of the posterity of Sibu, the true representatives of the Ramessides and the solar race, compared with whom the northern Pharaohs, even those whose mothers ranked as "worshippers" of Amon, were but mere mushroom kings? Thebes admitted the validity of their claims: it looked to them for help, and the revolts by which it had been torn ever since the reign of Osorkon II. were, perhaps, instigated by

MIXED NEGRO AND ETHIOPIAN TYPE.[4]

the partisans of Ethiopia.[5] In the time of Petubastis its high priests,

[1] Taharqa furnishes us with a striking example of this degeneration of the Egyptian type. His face shows the characteristic features of the black race, both on the Egyptian statue—the head of which is reproduced further on as a heading to the summary of Chapter IV. of this volume—as well as on the Assyrian stele of Sinjirli (LUSCHAN, *Die Ausgrabungen in Sendschirli*, vol. i. pl. i.).

[2] Cf. the phrases and grammatical forms in the Egyptian dialect of Ethiopia pointed out by MASPERO, *Mélanges de Mythologie et d'Archéologie Égyptiennes*, vol. iii. pp. 265-277, 279-284.

[3] Drawn by Faucher-Gudin, from LEPSIUS, *Denkm.*, iii. 303, No. 95. This is one of the kings who flourished about the Greco-Roman period.

[4] Drawn by Faucher-Gudin, from LEPSIUS, *Denkm.*, iii. 303, No. 96. Also a portrait of a king of the same period.

[5] Cf. what has been said on the subject of these revolts on pp. 161-165, *supra*.

Harsiisît and Takelôti, were still connected with the Tanites;[1] after that it placed itself under the immediate orders of Ethiopia, and the pontificate disappeared. The accession of a sovereign who was himself invested by hereditary right with the functions and title of high priest of Amon henceforth rendered the existence of such an office superfluous at Thebes: it would almost have meant an *imperium in imperio*. The administration of religious, and perhaps also of political, affairs was, therefore, handed over to the deputy prophet, and this change still further enhanced the importance of the "female worshippers of the god." In the absence of the king, who had his capital at Napata, they remained the sole representatives of legitimate authority in the Thebaid: the chief among them soon came to be regarded as a veritable *Lady of Thebes*, and, subject to the god, mistress of the city and its territory.[2]

It is not quite clear whether it was Piônkhi Miamun or one of his immediate predecessors who took possession of the city. The nomes dependent on Amon followed the example of the capital, and the whole Theban territory as far as Siut had been occupied by Ethiopian troops, when in the twenty-first year of the king's reign the princes of the Delta and Middle Egypt appealed to the court of Napata for help. Even had they not begged it to do so, it would have been compelled before long to intervene, for Tafnakhti was already on his way to attack it; Piônkhi charged Luâmarsakni and Puarama, the generals he had already stationed in the Thebaid, to hold Tafnakhti in check, till he was able to get together the remainder of his army and descend the Nile to support

---

[1] LEGRAIN, *Textes gravés sur le quai de Karnak*, in the *Zeitschrift*, vol. xxxiv. p. 114, Nos. 27–29; this disappearance of the office of high priest was first pointed out by MASPERO, *Les Momies Royales de Déir el-Bahari*, pp. 745–748.

[2] MASPERO, *Les Momies Royales de Déir el-Bahari*, p. 747, et seq.

them. Their instructions were to spare none of the rebellious towns, but to " capture their men and their beasts, and their ships on the river; to allow none of the fellaheen to go out into the fields, nor any labourer to his labour, but to attack Hermopolis and harass it daily." They followed out these orders, though, it would seem, without result, until the reinforcements from Nubia came up : their movements then became more actively offensive, and falling on Tafnakhti's ships, which were making for Thebes heavily laden with

men and stores, they sunk several of them. Anxious to profit by this first suc- cess, they made straight for Heracleopolis with a view to relieving it. Tafnakhti, ac- companied by the two kings Namrôti and Auputi, was directing the siege in person; he had under his command, in addition to contingents

RUINS OF OXYRRHYNCHOS AND THE MODERN TOWN OF BAHNESA.[1]

from Busiris, Mendès, Thoth, and Pharbæthos, all the vassals of Osorkon III., the successor of Petubastis and titular Pharaoh of the whole country. The Ethiopian fleet engaged the Egyptian ships at the end of the island of Heracleopolis, near the mouth of the canal leading from the Nile to the Bahr- Yusuf.[2] Tafnakhti was defeated, and the remnants of his squadron took refuge in Pipuga under cover of his land forces.[3] At dawn, the next day, the Ethiopians disembarked and gave battle. The struggle was long and fierce, but inde- cisive. Luâmarsakni and Puarama claimed the victory, but were obliged to effect a retreat on the day following their so-called success, and when they

[1] Drawn by Boudier, from an engraving in VIVANT DENON, Voyage dans le Haute Égypte, pl. 31, 2.

[2] The ancient geographers looked upon the nome of Heracleopolis as a large island (STRABO, XVII. i. § 35, p. 809 ; PTOLEMY, Geogr., vol. i. bk. iv. p. 120), its southern boundary being, probably, the canal of Harabshent (JOMART, Description de l'Heptanomide, in the Description de l'Égypte, vol. iii. pp. 400–402) : the end of the island, which the Egyptians called " the forepart of Khninsu " (Inscription of Piônkhi, l. 20), was probably Harabshent and its environs (MASPERO, Notes au jour le jour, § 31, in the Proceedings of the Soc. of Bibl. Arch., 1898, vol. xx. pp. 124, 125).

[3] Pi-puga, formerly identified by Lauth (Die Pianchi-Stele, 1870, p. 38) with Pushîn, the modern Bush, and by Brugsch (Dictionnaire Géographique, p. 228) with El-Beka, is probably El-Fokâ, on the Nile, to the north of Harabshent (MASPERO, Notes au jour le jour, § 31, in the Proceedings of the Soc. of Bibl. Arch., 1898, vol. xx. p. 125).

dropped anchor in the harbour of Hermopolis, they found that Namrôti had made his way back to the city by land and forestalled them. Powerless to hold the field without support, he collected all the men and cattle he could lay hands on, and awaited the progress of events behind his ramparts. The Ethiopians invested the town, and wrote to inform Piônkhi of what they had

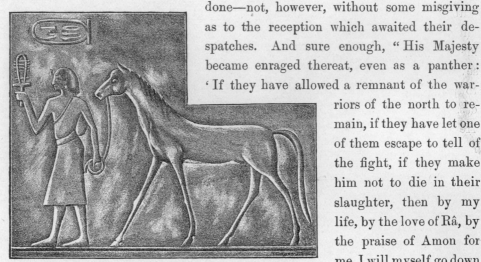

done—not, however, without some misgiving as to the reception which awaited their despatches. And sure enough, " His Majesty became enraged thereat, even as a panther: 'If they have allowed a remnant of the warriors of the north to remain, if they have let one of them escape to tell of the fight, if they make him not to die in their slaughter, then by my life, by the love of Râ, by the praise of Amon for me, I will myself go down and overthrow that which

KING NAMRÔTI LEADING A HORSE TO PIÔNKHI.[1]

Tafnakhti hath done,[2] I will compel him to give up war for ever! Therefore, after celebrating the festivals of the New Year, when I shall have sacrificed to Amon of [Napata], my father, in his excellent festival wherein he appears in his procession of the New Year, when he shall have sent me in peace to look upon the [Theban] Amon in his festivals at Thebes, and when I shall have carried his image in procession to Luxor, in the festival celebrated in his honour among the festivals of Thebes, on the night of the feast appointed in the Thebaid, established by Râ at the creation, when I have led him in the procession and brought him unto his throne, on the day for introducing the god, even the second of Athyr, then will I make the enemy taste the savour of my claws.' " The generals did their very utmost to appease their master's wrath before he appeared on the scene. They told off a force to keep watch over Hermopolis while they themselves marched against the nome of Uabu; they took Oxyrrhynchos by storm, with "the fury of a water-spout," and informed the king of this achievement; but "his heart was not softened thereby." They crossed over to the right bank; they crushed the people of the north

---

[1] Drawn by Faucher-Gudin, from an impression of the stele in the Gizeh Museum; cf. MARIETTE, *Monuments divers*, pl. 1.

[2] The king does not mention his adversary by name in the text; he is content to indicate him by a pronoun in the third person—"that which *he* hath done . . . then will I make him taste," etc.

under the walls of Tatehni,[1] they forced the walls of the town with the battering-ram, and killed many of the inhabitants, amongst others a son of Tafnakhti, whose body they sent to the king; but "his heart was not softened thereby." They then pushed on as far as Haît Bonu [2] and sacked it, but still failed to regain favour. On the 9th of Thoth, Piônkhi came down to Thebes, and after hasty

RUINS OF THE TEMPLE OF THOTH, AT HERMOPOLIS THE GREAT.[3]

attendance at the services to Amon, went to rejoin the vanguard of his army under the walls of Hermopolis. "No sooner had his Majesty quitted the cabin of his ship, than the horses were harnessed and the charioteers in their places; the fear of his Majesty spread even to the Nomads of Asia, and all hearts trembled before him." Piônkhi drove back the enemy behind their walls, pitched his tent to the south-west of the city, threw up earth-works, and built terraces so as to place his bowmen and slingers on a level with the battlements of its towers. At the end of three days, Namrôti, finding himself hard pressed on every side, resolved to surrender. He sent envoys to Piônkhi laden with rich presents, and despatched Queen Nsitentmahît after them to beg for mercy from the women who had accompanied the Ethiopian, his wives, concubines, daughters, or royal sisters. Their entreaties were graciously received, and Namrôti ventured to come in person, leading a horse with his right hand and shaking in his left a sistrum of gold and lapis-lazuli; he knelt down and presented with his salutations the long train of gifts which had gone before

[1] The modern Tehneh, on the right bank of the Nile, a little below Minieh (MASPERO, *Notes sur quelques points de Grammaire et d'Histoire*, in the *Mélanges d'Archéologie Égyptienne et Assyrienne*, vol. i. pp. 291, 292, and *Mélanges de Mythologie et d'Archéologie Egyptiennes*, vol. iii. pp. 278, 279; cf. BRUGSCH, *Dictionnaire Géographique*, p. 957, and DÜMICHEN, *Geschichte Ægyptens*, p. 196).

[2] Hâit-Bonu, or Hâbonu, is the Hipponon of the Greco-Roman geographers (J. DE ROUGÉ, *Textes Géographiques du temple d'Edfou*, in the *Revue Archéologique*, 1872, vol. xxiii. p. 72, note 3, and p. 76), which Dümichen places at el-Hibeh, almost opposite Feshn (*Geschichte Ægyptens*, pp. 196, 197. [Not to be confounded with Hibonu, opposite Minieh.—TR.]

[3] Drawn by Boudier, from an engraving in VIVANT DENON, *Voyage dans la Haute Égypte*, pl. 33, 1; cf. *Description de l'Égypte, Antiq.*, vol. iv. pl. 5. The portico was destroyed about 1820 by the engineers who constructed the sugar refinery at Rodah, and now only a few shapeless fragments of it remain.

him.   Piônkhi visited the temple of Thoth, and there, amidst the acclamations of soldiers and priests, offered up the customary sacrifices.   He then made his way to the palace and inspected its courts, chambers, treasury, and storehouses, and reviewed the whole household, including even Namrôti's own wives and daughters, though "he turned not his face towards any one of them."   He next went on to the stud-farms, and was indignant to find that the horses had suffered from hunger during the siege.   Thoroughbreds were probably somewhat scarce at Napata, and he had, no doubt, reckoned on obtaining new blood and a complete relay of chargers from the Egyptian stables; his chances of doing so seemed likely to vanish if brood mares and stallions had everywhere been debilitated by the hardships of war.   He reserved a part of the booty for himself, handed over the balance to the priests of Amon at Karnak, and also, before he left, received tribute from Heracleopolis.   Pefzââbastît brought him horses, the pick of his stables, slaves laden with gold and silver and precious stones; then burying his face in the dust, he offered worship to his liberator: "Hell had swallowed me up, I was plunged into darkness, and lo, now a light has been given me.   Since I have found no man to love me in the day of adversity, or to stand by me in the day of battle, save only thee, O victorious king, who hast torn away the night from above me, I will be thy servant, I and all my house, and Khninsu shall pay tribute into thy treasury.   For, as to thee, thou art Harmakhis, chief of the imperishable stars, thou art king, even as he is king, and even as he doth not destroy himself, neither shalt thou destroy thyself!"[1]

The downfall of Khmunu led all who might still have shown resistance in Middle Egypt to lay down their arms also.   The fortress of Pisakhmakhpirrî[2] dominated the gorges of Lahunît, and thus commanded the entrance to the Fayum; but the son of Tafnakhti agreed to surrender it, provided he were allowed to march out with the honours of war.   Shortly after, Maîtumu threw open its gates, and its example was followed by Titauî; at Maîtumu there was rioting among the Egyptians in the streets, one party wishing to hold out, the other to surrender, but in the end the latter had their way.[3]   Piônkhi discharged

[1] *Inscription of Piônkhi-Miamun*, ll. 8–76; MARIETTE, *Monuments divers*, pls. i.–iii.; E. DE ROUGÉ, *La Stèle du roi éthiopien Piânkhi Meriamen*, pp. 8–37.

[2] This fortress, which bears a name compounded with that of Osorkon I. (BRUGSCH, *Dictionnaire Géographique*, pp. 434, 435), must have been rebuilt by that monarch on the site of an earlier fort; the new name remained in use under the XXIInd and XXIIIrd dynasties, after which the old one reappears.   It is Illahun, where Petrie discovered the remains of a flourishing town of the Bubastite epoch (*Illahun, Kahun and Gurob*, p. 24, et seq.).

[3] Maritumu, or Maîtumu, is the modern Meîdum (LAUTH, *Die Pianchi-Stele*, p. 34; BRUGSCH, *Dictionnaire Géographique*, p. 82), associated in the inscription with the characteristic epithet, *Pisokari-Nibu-Suazu*, or "temple of Sokari, master of the transfiguration."   Titauî lay exactly on the frontier between Upper and Lower Egypt—hence its name, which signifies "commanding the two regions" (E. DE ROUGÉ, *La Stèle du roi éthiopien Piânkhi Meriamen*, p. 42, note 4); it was in the Memphite nome, and Brugsch identifies it with the Greek city of Acanthos, near Dahshur (*Diction-*

his priestly duties wherever he went, and received the local taxes, always being careful to reserve a tenth for the treasury of Amon-Râ; the fact that his army was kept under rigid control, and that he showed great clemency to the vanquished, helped largely to conciliate those who were not bound by close ties of interest to the cause of Tafnakhti. On reaching Memphis, Piônkhi at once had recourse to the persuasive methods which had hitherto served him so well, and entered into negotiations with the garrison. " Shut not yourselves up in forts, and fight not against the Upper Country,[1] for Shu the god of creation, when I enter, he entereth, and when I go out, he goeth out, and none may repel my attacks. I will present offerings to Phtah and to the divinities of the White Wall, I will honour Sokari in his mysterious coffer, I will contemplate Rîsânbuf,[2] then I will return from thence in peace. If ye will trust in me, Memphis shall be prosperous and healthy, even the children shall not cry therein. Behold the nomes of the South; not a soul has been massacred there, saving only the impious who blasphemed God, and these rebels have been executed." This eloquence, however, was of no avail. A detachment of archers, sailors, and engineers sent to make a reconnaissance of the harbour was taken by surprise and routed with loss, and on the following night Tafnakhti suddenly made his appearance on the spot. He had the 8000 men who were defending it paraded before him, and made them a speech, in which he pointed out the great natural strength of the position, the stoutness of the walls and the abundance of provisions; he then mounted his horse, and making his way a second time through the enemy's outposts, headed straight for the Delta in order to levy reinforcements there. The next day, Piônkhi went in person to examine the approaches of the city in which his ancestors had once been throned. There was a full Nile, and the river came right up to the walls. He sailed close in along the whole of the eastern front, and landed on the north, much vexed and discomfited at finding it so strongly fortified. Even the common soldiers were astonished, and began to discuss among themselves the difficulties of the undertaking with a certain feeling of discouragement. It would be necessary, they declared, to open a regular siege, " to make an inclined plane leading to the city, throw up earthworks against its walls, bind ladders, set up masts and erect spars all around it." Piônkhi burst into a rage when these remarks were repeated to him : a siege in set form

naire Géographique, pp. 983–985), but this position appears to me to be too close to Memphis and too far from the boundary of the nome; I should prefer to place Titauî at Kafr el-Ayat or thereabouts. Cf., as to this place, what is said in the *Struggle of the Nations*, vol. ii. p. 464, note 7.

[1] *I.e.* against Piônkhi, who was master of the Upper Country, that is, of Thebes and Ethiopia, and the forces from the whole of the valley to the south of Memphis who accompanied him.

[2] Lit., " He who is on the South of his Wall," a name given to one of the quarters of Memphis, and afterwards applied to the god Phtah, who was worshipped in that quarter (BRUGSCH, *Dictionnaire Géographique*, pp. 57, 58).

would have been a most serious enterprise, and would have allowed the allied princes time to get together fresh troops. He drove his ships full speed against the line of boats anchored in the harbour, and broke through it at the first onset; his sailors then scaled the bank and occupied the houses which overlooked it. Reinforcements concentrated on this point gradually penetrated into the heart of the city, and after two days' fighting the garrison threw down their arms. The victor at once occupied the temples to save them from pillage; he then purified Memphis with water and natron, ascended in triumph to the temple of Phtah, and celebrated there those rites which the king alone was entitled to perform. The other fortresses in the neighbourhood surrendered without further hesitation. King Auputi of Tentramu,[1] prince Akaneshu,[2] and prince Petisis tendered the homage of their subjects in person, and the other sovereigns of the Delta merely waited for a demonstration in force on the part of the Ethiopians before following their example. Piônkhi crossed the Nile and marched in state to Heliopolis, there to receive the royal investiture. He offered up prayers at the various holy places along the route, such as the sanctuary of Tumu at Khriâhu and the temple of the Ennead who dwelt in the cavern from which the Northern Nile was supposed to spring; he then crossed over Mount Ahu, bathed his face in the reputed source of the river, and at length penetrated into the dwelling-place of Râ. He ascended the steps leading to the great chapel in order that he might there "see Râ in Hâit-Banbonu even himself. All unattended, he drew the bolt, threw open the doors, contemplated his father Râ in Hâit-Banbonu, adjusted Râ's boat Mâdît and the Saktit of Shu,[3] then closed the doors again, affixed a seal of clay, and impressed it with the royal signet." He had thus submitted his conduct for the approval of the god in whom all attributes of royalty were vested, and the god had legitimatised his claims to universal rule: he was henceforth the master, not merely *de jure* but *de facto* as well, and the kings who had hitherto declined to recognise him were now obliged to bow reverently before his authority.[4]

[1] Probably the original of the statue discovered by Naville at Tel-el-Yahudîyeh (*The Mound of the Jews and the City of Onias*, pp. 10, 11, and pl. 1, and *Les Fouilles du Delta pendant l'hiver de 1887*, in the *Recueil de Travaux*, vol. x. p. 53). Tentramu and Taânu, the cities of Auputi, are, perhaps, as Brugsch suggests, identical with the biblical Elîm (*Exod.* xvi. 1) and the Daneon Portus of Pliny (*Hist. Nat.*, VI. xxxiii.) on the Red Sea (*Dict. Geogr.*, pp. 124, 125, 453–455), but Naville prefers to identify Daneon with the Tonu of the *Berlin Papyrus, No. 1* (*The Store-City of Pithom*, pp. 22, 23). I believe that we ought to look for the kingdom of Auputi in the neighbourhood of Menzaleh, near Tanis.

[2] Akaneshu ruled over Sebennytos and in the XVIIth nome (*Inscription of Piônkhi Miamun*, l. 115). Naville discovered at Samannud the statue of one of his descendants, a king of the same name, perhaps his grandson, who was prince of Sebennytos in the time of Psammetichus I. (*Les Fouilles du Delta pendant l'hiver de 1887*, in *Recueil de Travaux*, vol. x. p. 57, and *The Mound of the Jews*, pp. 24, 25, pl. v.).

[3] As to these two barques of the Sun, cf. what is said in the *Dawn of Civilization*, p. 90, notes 4, 5; *Mâdît* is a later form of *Mânzit* or *Mâzit*, a name frequently met with in the ancient texts.

[4] *Inscription of Piônkhi Miamun*, ll. 76–106; cf. MARIETTE, *Monuments divers*, pls. 3–5; E. DE ROUGÉ, *La Stèle du roi éthiopien Piânkhi Meriamen*, pp. 37–61.

Osorkon was the first to submit, and did so before the close of Piônkhi's stay at Heliopolis; when the latter pitched his camp near Kahani [1] in the Athribite nome, the nobles of the Eastern Delta, both small and great, came one after another with their followers; among them Patinifi of Pisapti, Paimau of Busiris, Pabîsa of Khriâhu and of Pihâpi,[2] besides a dozen others. He extended his favour to all alike, merely stipulating that they should give him the best of their horses, and undertake to keep careful watch over the prosperity of their stud farms. But Tafnakhti still held out, and seemed determined to defy him to the end; he had set fire to his palace and taken refuge in the islands on the river, and had provided a hiding-place for himself at Masudît among the marshes on the coast [3] in case of final defeat. A victory gained over him by the Ethiopian generals suddenly induced him to sue for peace. He offered to disband his men and pay tribute, provided he was guaranteed undisturbed possession of Sais and of the western districts of the Delta; he refused, however, to sue for pardon in person, and asked that an envoy should be sent to receive his oath of allegiance in the temple of Nît. Though deserted by his brother princes and allies, he still retained sufficient power to be a thorn in his conqueror's side; his ultimate overthrow was certain, but it would have entailed many a bloody struggle, while a defeat might easily have shaken the fidelity of the other feudatory kings, and endangered the stability of the new dynasty. Piônkhi, therefore, accepted the terms offered him without modification, and asked for no guarantee beyond the oath taken in the presence of the gods. News was brought him about this time that Cynopolis and Aphroditopolis had at last thrown open their gates, and accordingly he summoned his vassals for the last time to his camp near Athribis. With the exception of Tafnakhti, they all obeyed the call, including two minor kings of Upper and two of Lower Egypt, together with barons of lesser rank; but of these, Namrôti alone was admitted to the royal apartments, because he alone was circumcised and ate no fish; after this the camp was broken up, and the Ethiopians set out on their return journey southwards.[4] Piônkhi may well have been proud of the result of this

[1] Kahani is, perhaps, the modern Kaha, some distance to the north of Qaliub.

[2] Pisapti stood on the present site of Saft-el-Hineh (BRUGSCH, *Die Götter des Nomos Arabia*, in the *Zeitschrift*, 1881, pp. 16, 17, and NAVILLE, *Goshen and the Shrine of Saft-el-Henneh*, pp. 14, 15). Khriâhu, as we know, formed part of the Heliopolitan nome, and is, very possibly, to be identified with Babylon of Egypt, the Fostât of the Arabs (BRUGSCH, *Dict. Géogr.*, pp. 625–627); Pihâpi was a place not far from the supposed source of the Southern Nile (BRUGSCH, *Dict. Géogr.*, pp. 484, 485).

[3] The passage referring to these events, given in a mutilated form by Mariette (*Monuments divers*, pl. 6, ll. 120–123; E. DE ROUGÉ, *La Stèle du roi éthiopien Piânkhi-Meriamen*, pp. 70, 71), has been restored from the original by Brugsch (*Dictionnaire Géographique*, pp. 1135–1137), who proposes, with some hesitation, to identify Masudît with the Coptic Te-msiôti, the modern Pamsis.

[4] *Inscription of Piônkhi-Miamun*, ll. 106–159; cf. MARIETTE, *Monuments divers*, pls. 5, 6, and E. DE ROUGÉ, *La Stèle du roi éthiopien Piânkhi-Meriamen*, pp. 61–80.

campaign, both for himself and for his country. The empire of the Pharaohs, which had for the last hundred and fifty years been divided, was now re-established from the confluence of the Niles to the shores of the Mediterranean, but it was no longer Egypt that benefited by the change. It was now, after many years of slavery, the turn of Ethiopia to rule, and the seat of power was transferred from Thebes or Memphis to Napata. As a matter of fact, the fundamental constitution of the kingdom underwent no great modification; it had merely one king the more to rule over it—not a stranger, as we are often tempted to conclude, when we come to measure these old-world revolutions by our modern standards of patriotism, but a native of the south, who took the place of those natives of the north who had succeeded one another on the throne since the days of Smendes. In fact, this newly crowned son of Râ lived a very long way off; he had no troops of his own further north than Siut, and he had imposed his suzerainty on the rival claimants and reigning princes without thereby introducing any change in the constitution of the state. In tendering their submission to him, the heads of the different nomes had not the slightest intention of parting with their liberty; they still retained it, even though nominally dependent, and continued, as in the past, to abuse it without scruple. Namıôti was king at Khmunu, Pefzâābastît at Khninsu, Auputi at Tentramu, and Osorkon III. at Bubastis; the prestige investing the Tanite race persisted so effectively that the annalists give to the last-named precedence over the usurpers of the Ethiopian dynasty; the Tanites continued to be the incarnate representatives of legitimate power, and when Osorkon III. died, in 732, it was his son Psamutis who was regarded as the Lord of Egypt. Tafnakhti had, in his defeat, gained formal recognition of his royalty. He was no longer a mere successful adventurer, a hero of the hour, whose victories were his only title-deeds, whose rights rested solely on the argument of main force. Piônkhi, in granting him amnesty, had conferred official investiture on him and on his descendants. Henceforth his rule at Sais was every whit as legitimate as that of Osorkon at Bubastis, and he was not slow in furnishing material proof of this, for he granted himself cartouches, the uræus, and all the other insignia of royalty.[1] These changes must have been quickly noised abroad throughout Asia. Commercial intercourse between Syria and Egypt was maintained as actively as ever, and the merchant caravans and fleets

---

[1] Cf. the stele in the Museum at Athens, discovered and published by Mallet (*Quelques Monuments Égyptiens du Musée d'Athènes*, in the *Recueil de Travaux*, vol. xviii. pp. 1–6); cf. NAVILLE, *Additions et Corrections aux trois Inscriptions de la reine Hatasou, ibid.*, vol. xix. p. 214, where the reading of the cartouche prenomen is correctly given. The protocol of the sovereign is *Shopsisuri Tafnakhti*, and the date is in the eighth year of the reign. M. Révillout tries to make out that this usurpation was prior to the intervention of Piônkhi (*Notice des Papyrus démotiques archaiques*, p. 213, note a); I believe, with Mallet, that it took place after the invasion. If Tafnakhti had possessed royal titles, Piônkhi would have allowed him to retain them as he did in the case of the other local Pharaohs; one more king among his vassals would not have caused him additional trouble.

exported with regularity the news of events as well as the natural products of the soil or of industry. The tidings of an Ethiopian conquest and of the re-establishment of an undivided empire in the valley of the Nile, coming as they did at the very moment when the first effects of the Assyrian revival began to be so keenly felt, could not fail to attract the attention and arouse the hopes of Syrian statesmen. The Philistines, who had never entirely released themselves from the ties which bound them to the Pharaohs of the

KING TAFNAKHTI PRESENTS A FIELD TO TUMU AND TO BASTIT.[1]

Delta, felt no repugnance at asking for a renewal of their former protection. As for the Phœnicians, the Hebrews, Edom, Moab, Ammon, and Damascus, they began to consider whether they had not here, in Africa, among the members of a race favourably disposed towards them by the memories of the past and by its ambition, hereditary allies against Nineveh. The fact that Egypt was torn by domestic dissensions and divided into a score of rival principalities in no way diminished their traditional admiration for its wealth or their confidence in its power; Assyria itself was merely an agglomeration of turbulent provinces,

[1] Drawn by Boudier, from Mallet's photograph of the stele in the Museum at Athens.

vassal cities, and minor kingdoms, artificially grouped round the ancient domain of Assur, and yet the convulsions by which it was periodically shaken had not prevented it from developing into the most formidable engine of war that had ever threatened the peace of Asia. The African hosts, whether led by ordinary generals or by a king of secondary rank, formed none the less a compact army well fitted by numbers and organisation to hold its own against any forces which Tiglath-pileser might put into the field; and even should the supreme Pharaoh be unwilling to throw the full weight of his authority into the balance, yet an alliance with one of the lesser kings, such as the lord of Sais or of Bubastis, would be of inestimable assistance to any one fortunate enough to secure it. It is true that, in so far as the ultimate issue was concerned, there was little to be gained by thus pitting the two great powers together and persuading one to fight against the other; the victor must, in the long run, remain master alike of those who had appealed for help and of those who had fought against him, and if Egypt emerged triumphant, there would be nothing for it but to accept her supremacy. In either event, there could be no question of independence; it was a choice between the hegemony of Egypt or that of Assyria.

From the moment that Tiglath-pileser had made his appearance on the northern horizon, the nations of Southern Syria had instinctively looked to Pharaoh for aid. There seems to have been an Egyptian faction in Samaria, even during the disorders which broke out after the death of Jeroboam II., and perhaps it was a hope of overcoming it easily which led Menahem of his own accord to invoke the still remote suzerainty of Nineveh, after the fall of Unki in 738;[1] later on, when Pekah had assassinated Pekahiah and entered into alliance with Rezin, he adopted the view of those who saw no hope of safety save from the banks of the Nile, his only reason for doing so being, apparently, because the kings of the fallen dynasty had received support from the valley of the Tigris. Hosea continually reproached his countrymen with this vacillating policy, and pointed out the folly of it: " Ephraim is like a silly dove without understanding; they call unto Egypt, they go unto Assyria;

---

[1] As to the homage offered by Menahem, cf. p. 152, *supra.* The existence of an Egyptian faction at this period has been admitted by KITTEL, *Geschichte der Hebræer*, vol. ii. p. 282. Winckler, in a series of remarkable researches inserted in his *Alttestamentliche Untersuchungen*, pp. 168–174, and afterwards in his *Altorientalische Forschungen*, vol. i. pp. 24–41, 289, 290, 337, etc., which he completed by two articles on *Musri, Meluhha, Ma'in*, i., ii., in the *Mitt. der Vorderas. Ges.*, vols. i. and ii., has traced to the Arabian or Idumæan Muzri everything previously referred to Egypt. His arguments seem to me to be, in many cases, convincing, as I shall point out where necessary, but I think he carries his theory too far when he systematically excludes Egypt and puts Muzri in its place. Egypt, even in its decadent state, was a far more important power than the Arabian Muzri, and it seems unreasonable to credit it with such a limited share in the politics of the time. I cannot believe that any other power is intended in most of those passages in the Hebrew writings and Assyrian inscriptions in which the words Mizraîm and Muzri occur.

when they shall go I will spread My net upon them," said the Eternal.[1] They were to be given up to Assyria and dispersed, and while some were to go into Assur and eat unclean food, Ephraim was to return into Egypt; " for, lo, they are gone away from destruction, yet Egypt shall gather them up, Memphis shall bury them." [2] Nevertheless, they persisted in negotiating with Egypt, and though there was as yet no formal alliance between Samaria and Sais or Tanis, their relations were so close that no enemy of Israel could look for protection from Psamuti or his vassals. Ahaz had, therefore, nothing to hope from this quarter, and was compelled by the force of circumstances to throw himself into the arms of Assyria, if he decided to call in outside aid at all. His prophets, like those of Pekah, strenuously forbade him to do so, and among them was one who was beginning to exert a marvellous influence over all classes of society—Isaiah, the son of Amoz. He had begun his career in the year that Uzziah died,[3] and had continued to prophesy without interruption during the brief reign of Jotham.[4] When Jahveh first appeared to him, in the smoke of the altar, seated on a throne and surrounded by seraphim, a sense of his own unworthiness filled him with fear, but an angel purified his lips with a live coal, and he heard the voice of the Lord saying, " Whom shall I send, and who will go for us ? " and he replied, " Here am I ; send me," whereupon Jahveh gave him this message : " Hear ye indeed, but understand not ; and see ye indeed, but perceive not. Make the heart of this people fat, and make their ears heavy, and shut their eyes ; lest they see with their eyes and hear with their ears, and understand with their heart, and turn again and be healed." Then the prophet asked, " Lord, how long ? " And Jahveh answered, " Until cities be waste without inhabitant and houses without man, and the land become utterly waste, and Jahveh have removed men far away, and the forsaken places be many in the midst of the land. And if there be yet a tenth in it, it shall be eaten up ; as a terebinth, and as an oak, whose stock remaineth when they are felled, so the holy seed is the stock thereof." [5] Judah, though less powerful, was quite as corrupt as his brethren of Israel, and the divine wrath threatened him no less than them ; it rested with himself, however, to appease it by repentance, and to enter again into divine favour after suffering his punishment ; the Eternal would then gather together on Mount Sion those of His faithful people who had survived the crisis, and would assure them a long period of prosperity under His law. The prophet, convinced that men could

---

[1] *Hos.* vii. 11, 12.   [2] *Hos.* ix. 3-6.   [3] *Isa.* vi. 1.

[4] The fragments which can be assigned to this period now occur as follows : chap. ii. 2-5 (verses 2-4 are also found in *Micah* iv. 1-3, and were, perhaps, borrowed from some third prophet), ii. 6-22, iii., iv., v. 1-24 (the Parable of the Vineyard), and lastly, chap. vi., in so far as the substance is concerned ; it seems to have been put into its present form long after the events.

[5] *Isa.* vi. 9-13.

in no wise alter the decrees of the Highest, save by repentance alone, was astonished that the heads of the state should strive to impede the progress of events that were happening under their very eyes, by the elaborately useless combinations of their worldly diplomacy. To his mind, the invasion of Pekah and Rezin was a direct manifestation of the divine anger, and it filled him with indignation that the king should hope to escape from it by begging for an alliance against them with one of the great powers : when Jahveh should decide that the punishment was sufficient for the crime, He would know how to shatter His instruments without any earthly help. Indeed, Isaiah had already told his master, some days before the allied kings appeared, while the latter was busy superintending the works intended to supply Jerusalem with water, to "Take heed, and be quiet; fear not, neither let thy heart be faint, because of these two tails of smoking firebrands.[1] . . . Because Syria hath counselled evil against thee, Ephraim also, and the son of Remaliah, saying, Let us go up against Judah, hem it in, carry it by storm, and set up the son of Tabeel as king : [2] thus saith the Lord God, It shall not stand, neither shall it come to pass." [3] If, however, the course of the divine justice was to be disturbed by the intervention of a purely human agency, the city would doubtless be thereby saved, but the matter would not be allowed to rest there, and the people would suffer even more at the hands of their allies than they had formerly endured from their enemies. "Behold, a virgin shall conceive and bear a son, and shall call his name Immanuel—God with us. . . . For before the child shall know to refuse the evil and choose the good, the land whose two kings thou abhorrest shall be forsaken," and yet " Jahveh shall bring upon thee, and upon thy people, and upon thy father's house, days that have not come, from the day that Ephraim departed from Judah." [4] And then, employing one of those daring apologues, common enough in his time, the prophet took a large tablet and wrote upon it in large letters two symbolical names—*Spoil-speedeth, Prey-hasteth*—and set it up in a prominent place, and with the knowledge of credible witnesses went in unto the prophetess his wife. When the child was born in due course, Jahveh bade him call it *Spoil-speedeth, Prey-hasteth*, "for before he shall have knowledge to cry, My father, and, My mother, the riches of Damascus and the spoil of Samaria shall be carried away before the King of Assyria." But the Eternal added, "Forasmuch as this people hath refused the waters of Shiloah that go softly, and rejoice in Rezin and Remaliah's son ; now therefore, behold, the Lord bringeth up upon them

---

[1] An explanatory gloss, "the fierce anger of Rezin and Syria and of the son of Remaliah," which formed no part of the original prophecy, is here inserted in the text.

[2] As to the enigmatic personage thus designated by the prophet, cf. p. 158, note 2, *supra.*

[3] *Isa.* vii. 1–9.   [4] *Isa.* vii. 10–17.

the waters of the river [the Euphrates], strong and many:[1] and he shall come up over all his channels, and go over all his banks: and he shall sweep onward into Judah; he shall overflow and pass through; he shall reach even to the neck, and the stretching of his wings shall fill the breadth of thy land, O Immanuel [God-with-us]!"[2]

Finding that Egypt was in favour of his adversaries, Ahaz, in spite of the prophet's warnings, turned to Assyria.[3] At one time he had found himself so hard pressed that he invoked the aid of the Syrian gods, and made his eldest son pass through the fire in

[1] A marginal gloss has here been inserted in the text, indicating that it was "the King of Assyria and all his glory" that the prophet referred to.

[2] *Isa.* viii. 1–8.

[3] The following portions of Isaiah are accepted as belonging to the period of this Syrian war: in addition to chap. vii., chaps. viii.-ix. 6; xi. 1–9; xxii. 1–11; i. 4–9, 18–32; to these Kuenen adds chap. xxiii. 1–14.

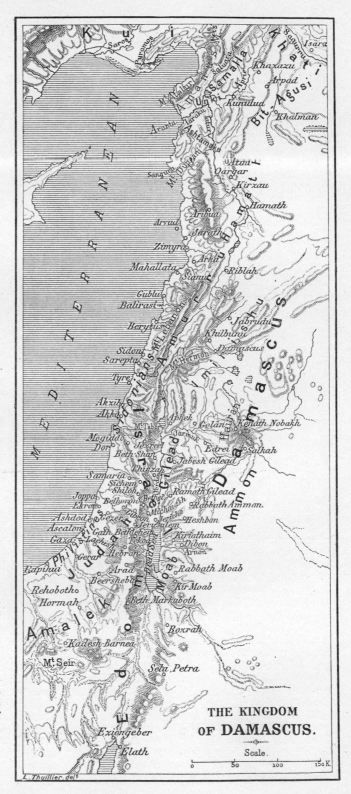

THE KINGDOM OF DAMASCUS.

Scale.

L. Thuillier del.

order to propitiate them ; [1] he collected together all the silver and gold he could find in his own treasury or in that of the temple and sent it to Tiglath-pileser, with this message : " I am thy servant and thy son : come up and save me out of the hand of the King of Syria, and out of the hand of the King of Israel, which rise up against me." [2] Tiglath-pileser came in haste, and Rezin and Pekah, at the mere tidings of his approach, desisted from their attack on Jerusalem, separated, and retired each to his own kingdom. The Assyrian king did not immediately follow them up. He took the road leading along the coast, after leaving the plains of the middle Orontes, and levied tribute from the Phœnician cities as he passed ; he then began by attacking the western frontier of Israel, and sent a body of troops against the Philistines, who were ceaselessly harassing Judah. Hannon, King of Gaza, did not await the attack, but fled to Egypt for safety, and Ahaz breathed freely, perhaps for the first time since his accession. [3] This, however, was only a beginning ; the real struggle took place in the following year, and was hotly contested. In spite of the sorry pass to which its former defeats and present discords had brought it, Damascus still possessed immense wealth, and its army, when reinforced by the Arabian and Israelite contingents, was capable of holding its own for a long time against the battalions of Assyria, even if it could not hope to conquer them. Unfortunately for its chances, Rezin had failed to inherit the military capacity of his great predecessors, Ben-hadad and Hazael ; he allowed Tiglath-pileser to crush the Hebrews without rendering them any effective assistance. Pekah fought his best, but he lost, one after another, the strongholds which guarded his northern frontier—Ijon, Abel-beth-maacah, Janoah, Kedesh, and Hazor ; he saw the whole of Naphtali and Gilead laid waste, and their inhabitants carried off into Assyria without his being able to prevent it ; he himself being obliged to evacuate Samaria and take refuge in the mountains almost unattended. [4] Judah followed, with mingled exultation

[1] 2 *Kings* xvi. 3 (cf. 2 *Chron.* xxviii. 3). There is nothing to indicate the date, but most historians place the event at the beginning of the Syrian war, a little before or during the siege (STADE, *Geschichte des Volkes Israel*, vol. i. p. 596; KITTEL, *Geschichte der Hebræer*, vol. ii. p. 291, note 2).

[2] 2 *Kings* xvi. 7, 8; cf. 2 *Chron.* xxviii. 16, 20, 21.

[3] *Slab Inscription*, published by H. RAWLINSON, *Cun. Ins. W. Ass.*, vol. iii. pl. 10, No. 3, ll. 1–11. The chronology of these events is still doubtful. The *Eponym Canon* (SCHRADER, *Keilinschrift-liche Bibliothek*, vol. i. pp. 212, 213) shows that the operations lasted three years, and it records one expedition against the Philistines (734), and two against Damascus (733–732). I have followed Rost (*Die Keilschrifttexte Tiglat-Pileser's III.*, pp. xxviii.–xxxii.) in my classification of the mutilated lines which precede the reference to Gaza in the campaign against the Philistines.

[4] 2 *Kings* xv. 29. Schrader (*Die Keilschriften und das Alte Testament*, 1883, pp. 254–259) thought himself justified in adding to the mutilated names in the inscription published by H. RAWLINSON, *Cun. Ins. W. Ass.*, vol. iii. pl. 10, those of Gilead and Abel-beth-maacah, to which Hommel added later on that of Naphtali the Great (*Ges. Bab. und Ass.*, p. 665, note 1). A careful collation of the mutilated texts has proved that in all probability the correct reading is Galza and Abilakka, which would preclude all possibility of identifying the biblical names with those which appear in the Assyrian text (ROST, *Die Keilschrifttexte Tiglat-Pileser's III.*, vol. i. pp. 78, 79). The campaign beyond the Jordan is mentioned in 1 *Chron.* v. 26, where the Hebrew writer has two distinct kings of Assyria, Pul and Tilgath-pilneser, in place of the one king known to modern historians.

and disquietude, the vicissitudes of the tragic drama which was thus enacted before its eyes, and Isaiah foretold the speedy ruin of the two peoples who had but yesterday threatened to enslave it. He could already see the following picture in his mind's eye: "Damascus is taken away from being a city, and it shall be a ruinous heap. The cities of Aroêr are forsaken: they shall be for flocks, which shall lie down, and none shall make them afraid.[1] The fortress also shall cease from Ephraim, and the kingdom from Damascus, and the

MOUNT HERMON.[2]

remnant of Syria: they shall be as the glory of the children of Israel, saith the Lord of hosts! And it shall come to pass in that day, that the glory of Jacob shall be made thin, and the fatness of his flesh shall wax lean. And it shall be as when the harvestman gathereth the standing corn, and his arm reapeth the ears; yea, it shall be as when one gleaneth ears in the valley of Rephaim. Yet there shall be left therein gleanings, as the shaking of an olive tree, two or three berries in the top of the uppermost bough, four or five in the outmost branches of a fruitful tree, saith Jahveh, the God of Israel! . . . In that day shall his strong cities be as the forsaken places in the wood, and on the mountain top, which were forsaken from before the children of Israel:[3] and it shall be as

---

[1] Both of these Aroêrs lay beyond Jordan—one in Reuben, afterwards Moab (*Judg.* xi. 26; *Jer.* xlviii. 19); the other in Ammon, afterwards Gad (*Josh.* xiii. 25; 2 *Sam.* xxiv. 5): here they stand for the countries beyond Jordan which Tiglath-pileser had just laid waste. The tradition preserved in 1 *Chron.* v. 26 stated that these inhabitants of Gad and Reuben were led into captivity by Pul, *i.e.* Tiglath-pileser.

[2] Drawn by Boudier, from a photograph brought back by Lortet; cf. LORTET, *La Syrie*, p. 563.

[3] This is probably an allusion to the warlike exploits performed during Rezin and Pekah's invasion of Judæa, a year or two previously; cf. p. 186, *supra*.

a desolation. For thou hast forgotten the God of thy salvation."[1] Samaria was doomed to helplessness for many a day to come, if not for ever, but it had taken a whole year to lay it low (733); Tiglath-pileser returned in 732, and devoted yet another year to the war against Damascus. Rezin had not been dismayed by the evil fortune of his friends, and had made good his losses by means of fresh alliances. He had persuaded first Mutton II. of Tyre, then Mitinti of Askalon, and with the latter a section of the Philistines, to throw in their lot with him; he had even won over Shamshieh, queen of the Arabs, and with her a number of the most warlike of the desert tribes; for himself, he had

AN ARAB.[2]

taken up a position on the further side of Anti-Lebanon, and kept strict watch from Mount Hermon on the roads leading from the valley of the Jordan to the plains of the Abana, in order to prevent the enemy from outflanking him and taking him in the rear. But all to no purpose; Tiglath-pileser bore directly down upon him, overwhelmed him in a pitched battle, obliged him to take refuge behind the walls of Damascus, and there besieged him. The city was well fortified, amply supplied with provisions, and strongly garrisoned; the siege was, therefore, a long one, and the Assyrians filled up the time by laying waste the fertile country at the foot of Anti-Lebanon. At last Rezin yielded, gave himself up unconditionally, and was forthwith executed: eight thousand of his followers were carried off to Kîr, on the confines of Elam,[3] his kingdom was abolished, and a Ninevite governor was installed in his palace, by whom the former domain of Damascus and the territory lately wrested from Israel were henceforth to be administered. The coalition he had formed did not long survive its leader.[4] Mutton hastily came

---

[1] *Isa.* xvii. 1–6, 9, 10.

[2] Drawn by Faucher-Gudin, from LAYARD, *Monuments of Nineveh,* vol. i. pl. 57.

[3] *2 Kings* xvi. 9. Kîr is generally located in Armenia, Media, or Babylonia (cf. SCHRADER, in RIEHM, *Handwörterbuch,* 2nd edit., vol. i. p. 845); a passage in Isaiah (xxii. 6), however, seems to point to its having been somewhere in the direction of Elam, and associated with the Aramæans on the banks of the Tigris (HALÉVY, *Recherches Bibliques,* pp. 57, 58; WINCKLER, *Alttestamentliche Untersuchungen,* pp. 177–179). The Assyrian monuments have not, as yet, yielded confirmation of the details given by the *Book of the Kings* in regard to the captivity of the inhabitants of Damascus. A fragmentary tablet, giving an account of the death of Rezin, was discovered by H. Rawlinson (*Assyrian Discovery,* in the *Athenæum,* 1862, vol. ii. p. 246), but it was left in Assyria (G. SMITH, *The Annals of Tiglath-Pileser II.,* in the *Zeitschrift,* 1869, p. 14), and no one knows what has since become of it.

[4] The following is a list of the kings of Damascus from the time of David, as far as is known up to the present time:—

REZIN I.	HAZAEL.
KHEZIÔN?	BEN-HADAD III.
TABRIMMÔN.	MARÎ.
BEN-HADAD I.	. . . .
ADADIDRI (BEN-HADAD II.).	REZIN II.

As to the possible omission of Kheziôn, cf. *Struggle of the Nations,* p. 778, note 3. As to the name Adadidri, called Ben-hadad [or Hadadezer] by the Hebrew writers, cf. p. 785, note 4, *ibid.*

to an understanding with the conqueror ; Mitinti, like Hannon, fled into Egypt, and his place was taken by Rukibtu, a partisan of Assyria. Hoshea, son of Elah, rebelled against Pekah, assassinated him, and purchased the right to reign over what was left of Israel for ten talents of gold.[1] Shamshieh alone held out. She imagined herself to be safe among the sands of the desert, and it never occurred to her that the heavy masses of the Assyrian army would dream of venturing into these solitudes. Detachments of light cavalry were sent in pursuit of her, and at first met with some difficulties; they were, however, eventually successful ; the Armenian and Cappadocian steeds of the Ninevite

horsemen easily rode down the queen's *meharis.* Their success made a great impression on the Arab tribes, and induced the Mashaî, Timaî Sabæans, Khaiapæans, Badanæans, and Khattiæans to bend the knee before Assyria. They all sent envoys bearing presents of gold and silver, camels, both male and

ARAB MEHARIS RIDDEN DOWN BY THE ASSYRIAN CAVALRY.[2]

female, and spices :[3] even the Muzri, whose territory lay to the south of the Dead Sea, followed their example, and a certain Idibiel was appointed as their chief.[4] While his lieutenants were settling outstanding issues in this fashion, Tiglath-pileser held open court at Damascus, where he received the visits and homage of the Syrians. They came to assure themselves by the evidence of their own eyes of the downfall of the power which had for more than one hundred years checked the progress of Assyria. Those who, like Uassarmi of Tabal, showed any sign of disaffection were removed, the remainder were confirmed in their dignities, subject to payment of the usual tribute, and Mutton of Tyre was obliged to give one hundred talents of gold to ransom his city. Ahaz came to salute his preserver, and to obtain a nearer view of the soldiers to whom he

---

[1] 2 *Kings* xv. 30. The inscription published by H. RAWLINSON, *Cun. Ins. W. Ass.*, vol. iii. pl. 10, No. 2, merely states that " they overthrew Pekah, their king, and I promoted Auzi [to the kingship] over them. I received [from him] X talents of gold and . . . talents of silver . . . (ll. 17–19; cf. ROST, *Die Keilschrifttexte Tiglat-Pileser's III.*, vol. i. pp. 80, 81). Cf. in WINCKLER, *Alttestamentliche Forschungen*, p. 24, an attempted restoration of the two earlier narratives on which the present Hebrew text is based.

[2] Drawn by Faucher-Gudin, from the bas-relief reproduced by LAYARD, *Mon. of Nineveh*, vol. i. pl. 57.

[3] Delitzsch (*Wo lag das Paradies?* pp. 301–304) has identified the names of several of these races with names mentioned in the Bible, such as the Temah, Massah, Ephah, Sheba ; cf. DELATTRE, *L'Asie Occidentale dans Inscriptions assyriennes*, pp. 140–146.

[4] The name Muzri, as Winckler has shown, here refers, not to Egypt, but to a canton near Edom, the Nabatæa of the Greco-Roman geographers (*Altorient. Forsch.*, vol. i. pp. 24–41, 289, 290, 337, 338).

owed continued possession of Jerusalem ;[1] the kings of Ammon, Moab, Edom, and Askalon, the Philistines and the nomads of the Arabian desert, carried away by the general example, followed the lead of Judah, until there was not a single prince or lord of a city from the Euphrates to the river of Egypt who had not acknowledged himself the humble vassal of Nineveh.[2]

With the downfall of Rezin, Syria's last hope of recovery had vanished ; the few states which still enjoyed some show of independence were obliged, if they wished to retain it, to make a parade of unalterable devotion to their Ninevite master, or—if they found his suzerainty intolerable—had to risk everything by appealing to Egypt for help.   Much as they may have wished from the very first to do so, it was too early to make the attempt so soon after the conference at Damascus ; Tiglath-pileser had, therefore, no cause to fear a rebellion among them, at any rate for some years to come, and it was just as well that this was so, for at the moment of his triumph on the shores of the Mediterranean his interests in Chaldæa were threatened by a serious danger. Nabonazîr, King of Karduniash, had never swerved from the fidelity which he had sworn to his mighty ally after the events of 745, but the tranquillity of his reign had been more than once disturbed by revolt.   Borsippa itself had risen on one occasion, and endeavoured to establish itself as an independent city side by side with Babylon.[3]   When Nabonazîr died, in 734, he was succeeded by his son Nabunâdinzîri, but at the end of a couple of years the latter was assassinated during a popular outbreak,[4] and Nabushumukîn, one of his sons, who had been implicated in the rising, usurped the crown (732).   He wore it for two months and twelve days, and then abdicated in favour of a certain Ukînzîr.[5]   The latter was

---

[1] 2 Kings xvi. 10–12.   The Nimroud Incrip., Rev., l. 11, merely mentions his tribute among that of the Syrian kings (Rost, Die Keilschrift. Tiglat-Pileser's III., vol. i. pp. 72, 73).

[2] Annals of Tiglath-pileser III., ll. 195–240 ; Nimroud Inscrip., Rev., ll. 2–16 ; Inscription published by H. Rawlinson, Cun. Ins. W. Ass., vol. iii. pl. 10, No. 2, ll. 12–28 ; cf. Rost, Die Keilschrifttexte Tiglat-Pileser's III., vol. i. pp. 34–41, 70–73, 80–83.   As to the various interpretations of the facts, cf. Tiele, Bab.-ass. Ges., pp. 220, 221, 232–235 ; Hommel, Ges. Bab. und Ass., pp. 664–670 ; Winckler, Ges. Bab. und Ass., pp. 228–231.

[3] Pinches' Babylonian Chronicle, col. i. ll. 6, 7 ; cf. Winckler, Babylonische Chronik B, in Schrader, Keilinschriftliche Bibliothek, vol. ii. pp. 274, 275.   This document was first discovered and analysed by Pinches, The Babylonian Kings of the Second Period, in the Proceedings of the Soc. for Bibl. Arch., 1883–1884, vol. vi. pp. 198–202, it was afterwards published and translated into English by him, in the J. R. As. Soc., 1887, vol. xix. p. 655 ; translated into Latin by Winckler, Chronicon Babylonicum editum et Commentario instructum, in the Zeitschrift für Assyriologie, vol. ii. pp. 148–168, 299–307, and into French by Oppert, Chronique babylonienne du Musée Britannique, in the Comptes rendus de l'Académie des Inscriptions, 1887, pp. 263–269.   The fragments of two duplicates were dis-covered by Bezold, On Two Duplicates of the Babylonian Chronicle, in the Proceedings, 1888–1889, vol. xi. pp. 131–138 ; the whole has been published in Abel and Winckler, Keilschrifttexte, pp. 47, 48, and translated into German by Winckler, Babylonische Chronik B, in Schrader, Keilinschrift-liche Bibliothek, vol. ii. pp. 274–285.

[4] Pinches' Babylonian Chronicle, col. i. ll. 11–15 ; cf. Winckler, Babylonische Chronik B, pp. 274–277, where the full name of the king, furnished by Pinches' Canon (Schrader, Die Grosse Babylonische Königsliste, in the Keilinschriftliche Bibliothek, vol. ii. p. 287), is abbreviated into Nadînu, and has passed thence into the Canon of Ptolemy under the form of Nadios.

[5] Pinches' Babylonian Chronicle, col. i. ll. 16–18 ; cf. Winckler, Die Babylonische Chronik B, pp.

chief of the Bît-Amukkâni, one of the most important among the Chaldæan communities;[1] the descendants of the Aramæan nomads were thus once more placed upon the throne, and their accession put an end to the relations which had existed for several centuries between Assyria and Karduniash. These marauders, who had always shown themselves impatient of any settled authority, and had never proffered more than a doubtful submission to even the most triumphant invader, were not likely to accept the subordinate position which members of the presiding dynasty had been, for the most part, content to occupy. It was more probable that they would, from the very first, endeavour to throw off the suzerainty of Nine-veh. Tiglath-pileser gave the new dynasty no time 'to settle itself firmly on the throne : the year after his return from Syria he got together an army and marched against it. He first cleared the right bank of the Tigris, where the Pukudu (Pekod) offered but a feeble resist-ance; he annexed their territory to the ancient province of Arrapkha, then crossed the river and attacked the Kaldi scattered among the plains and marshes of the Shatt el-

A KALDU.[2]

Haî. The Bît-Shilâni were the first to succumb ; their king Nabushabshi was impaled before one of the gates of his capital, Sarrabânu, the town itself was taken by storm, plundered and dismantled, and 55,000 of its inhabitants were led captive into Assyria. After the Bît-Shilâni, came the turn of the Bît-Shaalli. Dur-Illataî, their capital, was razed to the ground, and its population, numbering

276, 277, in which the name is shortened into Shumukîn. The chronicle states that Nabushumukîn was governor of a province, whereas the Royal Canon (SCHRADER, *Die Grosse Babylonische Königsliste*, in the *Keilinschriftliche Bibliothek*, vol. ii. p. 287) affirms that he was the son of his predecessor ; it is probable that both statements are correct. Winckler (*Ges. Bab. und Ass.*, p. 123, note 1) and Rost (*Die Keils. Tiglat-Pileser's III.*, vol. i. p. xxxvii., note 1) regard the entry in the Canon as a clerical error. The following is as complete a list as can at present be compiled of this Babylonian dynasty, the eighth of those registered in Pinches' *Canons* (cf. ROST, *Untersuch. zur altorient. Gesch.*, p. 27) :—

NABU-KÎNABAL ?	. . . .
. . . .	BAU-AKHIDDIN ?
. . . .	. . . .
SHAMASH-MUDAMMIQ.	. . . .
NABU-SHUMISHKUN I.	
. . . .	NABU-SHUMISHKUN II.
NABU-ABAL-IDDINA.	NABU-NÂZÎR (NABONASSAR).
MARDUK-NÂDIN-SHUMU.	NABU-NÂDIN-ZÎRI.
MARDUK-BALÂTSUIKBI.	NABU-SHUMUKÎN.

It included twenty-two kings, and lasted for about three hundred and fifty years.

[1] The chronicle is silent with regard to the origin of Ukînzir, but Tiglath-pileser, who declines to give him the title of " King of Babylon," says that he was *mar Amukkâni* = son of Amukkâni (*Nimroud Inscrip.*, Obv., l. 23 ; cf. ROST, *Die Keilschrifttexte Tiglat-Pileser's III.*, vol. i. pp. 60, 61). Pinches' *Canon* indicates that Ukînzir belonged to a dynasty the name of which may be read either Shashi or Shapi (SCHRADER, *Keilinschriftliche Bibliothek*, vol. ii. p. 287). The reading Shapi at once recalls the name of Shapîa, one of the chief cities of the Bît-Amukkâni (as to this town, cf. p. 192, *infra*) ; it would thus confirm the evidence of the Nimroud Inscription.

[2] Drawn by Faucher-Gudin, from a woodcut published by TOMKINS, *Abraham and his Times*, pl. iv.

50,400 men and women, was deported. Their chief, Lakiru, who had shown great bravery in the struggle, escaped impalement, but was sent into captivity with his people, a Ninevite governor being appointed in his place. Ukînzîr, who was, as we know, hereditary prince of the Bît-Amukkâni, came up in haste to defend his appanage, and threw himself into his fortress at Shapîa: Tiglath-pileser cut down the gardens and groves of palms which lent it beauty, burnt the surrounding farms and villages, and tried, without success, to make a breach in the walls; he still, however, maintained the siege, but when winter came on and the place still held out, he broke up his camp and retreated in good order, leaving the districts which he had laid waste occupied by an Assyrian force. Before his departure, he received homage and tribute from most of the Aramæan chiefs, including those of Balasu and the Bît-Dakkuri, of Nadînu, and even of the Bît-Yakîn and Merodach-baladan, whose ancestors had never before " kissed the foot " of an Assyrian conqueror.[1] In this campaign he had acquired nearly three-fourths of the whole Babylonian kingdom; but Babylon itself still refused to yield, and it was no easy task to compel it to do so. Tiglath-pileser spent the whole of the year 730 in preparing for another attack,[2] and in 729 he again appeared in front of Shapîa, this time with greater success; Ukînzîr fell into his hands, Babylon opened its gates, and he caused himself to be proclaimed King of Sumir and Akkad within its walls.[3] Many centuries had passed since the two empires had been united under the rule of a single master, or an Assyrian king had " taken the hands of Bel." [4] Tiglath-pileser accepted the condition attached to this solemn investiture, which obliged him to divide his time between Calah and Babylon, and to repeat at every festival of the New Year the mystic ceremony by which the god of the city confirmed him in his office.[5] His Babylonian subjects seem to have taken a liking to him, and perhaps in order to hide from themselves their dependent

---

[1] *Nimroud Slab*, No. 1, ll. 8–15, No. 2, ll. 11–17, and *Nimroud Inscrip.*, Obv., ll. 16–28; cf. ROST, *Die Keilschrifttexte Tiglat-Pileser's III.*, vol. i. pp. 42–45, 48–51, 56–63. In all these texts, the expedition of 731 is mentioned immediately after that of 745, and modern historians at first failed to separate the two. A comparison with the text of the *Annals*, however, enables us to assign to the campaign of 731 all the facts described after the defeat of the Pukudu (TIELE, *Bab.-ass. Gesch.*, pp. 235, 236; HOMMEL, *Gesch. Bab. und Ass.*, pp. 652, 653; WINCKLER, *Gesch. Bab. und Ass.*, pp. 123, 124, 231, 232; ROST, *Die Keilschrifttexte Tiglat-Pileser's III.*, vol. i. pp. xxxvii., xxxviii.). It is this expedition which the *Eponym Canon* refers to as having been directed against Shapîa (SCHRADER, *Keilinschriftliche Bibliothek*, vol. i. pp. 214, 215).

[2] The *Eponym Canon* refers to this year as having been spent "in the country" (SCHRADER, *Keilinschriftliche Bibliothek*, vol. i. pp. 214, 215).

[3] Contemporary documents do not furnish us with any information as to these events. The *Eponym Canon* tells us that "*the king took the hands of Bel*" (SCHRADER, *Keilinschriftliche Bibliothek*, vol. i. pp. 214, 215). Pinches' *Chronicle* adds that "in the third year of Ukînzîr, Tiglath-pileser marched against Akkad, laid waste the Bît-Amukkâni, and took Ukînzîr prisoner; Ukînzîr had reigned three years in Babylon. Tiglath-pileser followed him upon the throne of Babylon" (col. i. ll. 19–23).

[4] Not since Tukulti-ninip I.; cf. *Struggle of the Nations*, pp. 606–610.

[5] The *Eponym Canon* proves that in 728 B.C., the year of his death, he once more took the hands of Bel (SCHRADER, *Keilinschriftliche Bibliothek*, vol. i. pp. 214, 215).

condition, they shortened his purely Assyrian name of Tukulti-abal-esharra into the familiar sobriquet of Puru or Pulu, under which appellation the native chroniclers later on inscribed him in the official list of kings :[1] he did not long survive his triumph, but died in the month of Tebeth, 728 B.C., after having reigned eighteen years over Assyria, and less than two years over Babylon and Chaldæa.[2]

The formulæ employed by the scribes in recording historical events vary so little from one reign to another, that it is, in most cases, a difficult matter to make out, under the mask of uniformity by which they are all concealed, the true character and disposition of each successive sovereign. One thing, however, is certain—the monarch who now came upon the scene after half a century of reverses, and in a brief space restored to his armies the skill necessary to defeat such formidable foes as the Armenians or the Syrians of Damascus, must have been an able general and a born leader of men. Yet Nineveh had never suffered long from a lack of capable generals, and there would be little to distinguish Tiglath-pileser from any of his predecessors, if we could place nothing more than a few successful campaigns to his credit. His claim to a pre-eminent place amongst them rests on the fact that he combined the talents of the soldier with the higher qualities of the administrator, and organised his kingdom in a manner at once so simple and so effective, that most of the Oriental powers down to the time of the Grecian conquest were content to accept it as a model. As soon as the ambition of the Assyrian kings began to extend beyond the region confined between the Khabur and the Greater Zab, they found it necessary to parcel out their territory into provinces under the authority of prefects for the purpose of preserving order among the vanquished peoples, and at the same time of protecting them from the attacks of adjacent tribes ; these representatives of the central power were supported by garrisons, and were thus enabled to put down such minor insurrections as broke out from time to time. Some of these provinces were already in existence in the reigns of Shalmaneser or Tiglath-pileser I. ;[3] after the reverses in the time of Assurirba, their number decreased, but it grew rapidly again as Assur-nazir-pal and Shalmaneser III. gradually extended the field of their operations and of their victories. From this epoch onwards, the monuments mention over a score of them, in spite of the fact that the list thus furnished is not a complete one ; the provinces of which we know most are those whose rulers were successively

[1] Even the Royal Canon has the name Pulu (SCHRADER, *Keilinschriftliche Bibliothek*, vol. ii. p. 287), which appears under the form of Pôros in Ptolemy. Cf. what is said on this point on p. 112, note 4, *supra*.

[2] *Pinches' Chronicle*, col. 1, ll. 24–26; cf. WINCKLER, *Die Babylonische Kronik B*, in SCHRADER, *Keilinschriftliche Bibliothek*, vol. ii. pp. 276, 277.

[3] Cf. what is said as to this in the *Struggle of the Nations*, pp. 608, 657. Rawlinson (*Athenæum*, 1867, Nos. 2055, 2080) discovered the true character and rank of these personages, whom he had previously taken to be high priests (*Athenæum*, 1862, No. 1812, p. 724, et seq.).

appointed to act as *limmi*, each of them giving their name to a year of a reign.[1] Assyria proper contained at least four, viz. Assur (called *the country*, as distinguished from all others), Calah, Nineveh, and Arbela.   The basin of the Lesser Zab was divided into the provinces of Kakzi, Arrapkha, and Akhizukhîna;[2] that of the Upper Tigris into those of Amidi, Tushkhân, and Gôzan.   Kirruri was bounded by Mazamua, and Mazamua by Arrapkha and Lake Urumiah.[3]   We hear of the three spheres of Nazibina (Nisibis), Tela, and Razappa in Mesopotamia,[4] the two former on the southern watersheds of the Masios, on the highways leading into Syria; the latter to the south of the Euphrates, in the former kingdom of the Laqî.   Most of them included—in addition to the territory under the immediate control of the governor—a number of vassal states, kingdoms, cities, and tribes, which enjoyed a certain measure of independence, but were liable to pay tribute and render military service.   Each new country was annexed, as soon as conquered, to the nearest province, or, if necessary, was converted into a distinct province by itself; thus we find that Assur-nazir-pal, after laying hands on the upper valleys of the Radanu and the Turnat, rebuilt the ruined city of Atlîla, re-named it Dur-Assur, placed a commandant, cavalry, and eunuchs there, and established within it storehouses for the receipt of contributions from the neighbouring barbarians.[5]   He followed the same course on each occasion when the fortune of war brought him fresh subjects;[6] and his successors, Shalmaneser III., Samsi-rammân IV., and Rammân-nirâri did the same thing in Media, in Asia Minor, and in Northern Syria;[7] Tiglath-pileser III. had only to follow their example and extend the application of their system to the countries which he gradually forced to submit to his rule.[8]   In his case, however, certain elements came into play

[1] As to the functions of the *Limmi*, cf. *Struggle of the Nations*, pp. 620, 621.

[2] Akhizukhîna is probably identical with Arzukhîna = "the City of Zukhîna" (FR. DELITZSCH, *Wo lag das Paradies?* p. 187), which is referred to in the *Synch. Hist.* as being situated in the basin of the Lesser Zab (col. ii. B, ll. 14–16).   As to the position of Kakzi, cf. what has been said on p. 22, n. 3, *supra*.

[3] As to Gôzan and Tushkhân, cf. p. 14, note 3, and p. 20, note 3, *supra*; in regard to Kirruri and Mazamua, cf. p. 14, note 2, and p. 22, note 1, *supra*.

[4] Razappa is the biblical Rezeph (2 *Kings* xix. 12; *Isa.* xxxvii. 12) and the Resapha of Ptolemy (V. xv. 24), now Er-Rasafa, to the south of the Euphrates, on one of the routes leading to Palmyra.

[5] *Annals of Assur-nazir-pal*, col. ii. ll. 84–86; cf. pp. 25, 26, *supra*.

[6] We read of the appointment of a governor in Bît-Khalupi (*Annals of Assur-nazir-pal*, col. i. l. 89), at Tushkhân, in Naîri (col. ii. ll. 2–15), and in the country of the Patinâ (col. iii. ll. 81–83); cf. the summary of the reign (col. iii. ll. 125, 126, *ibid.*).

[7] The territory of the Bît-Adini was converted into a province by Shalmaneser III. (*Monolith*, col. ii. ll. 33–38; cf. p. 68, *supra*).

[8] We find the formation of an Aramæan province, with Kar-Assur as its capital, mentioned in the *Annals of Tiglath-pileser III.*, ll. 8–11; this took place after the events related on pp. 140, 141, *supra*. The prisoners taken were distributed over different provinces.   Provinces were also established in Media (ll. 36, 37, 49–51; cf. p. 112, *supra*), in Unki (col. 100, 101; cf. p. 149, *supra*), in the basin of the Orontes, and in Lebanon, from nineteen districts formerly belonging to Hamath (col. 125–130; cf. pp. 150, 152, *supra*), six maritime provinces in Northern Phœnicia and in Cœle-Syria (*Slab No. 3*, ll. 1–5), in Galilee (*Slab No. 3*, ll. 6–8), at Gaza (*Slab No. 3*, ll. 8–11; cf. p. 186, *supra*, for an account of the events which led to the establishment of this last province).

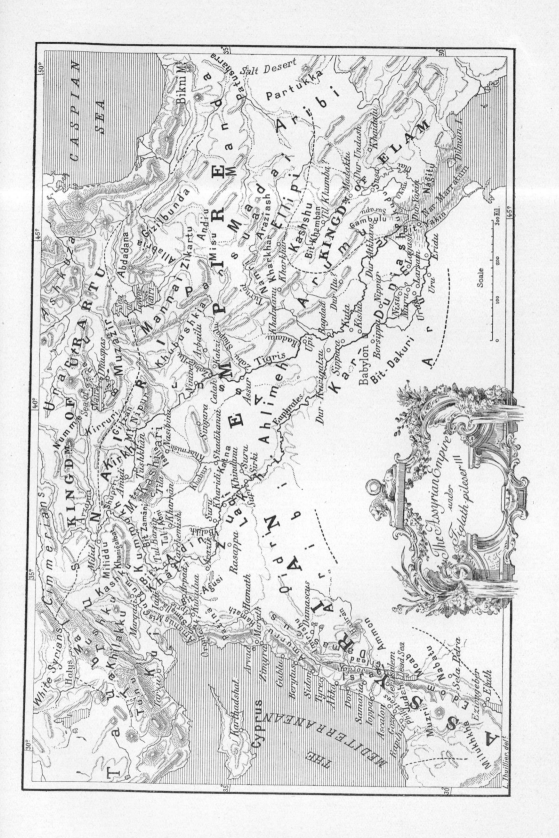

which forced him to modify several of their methods, and to have recourse to others which they had seldom or never employed. The majority of the countries hitherto incorporated had been near enough to the capital—whether it were Assur, Calah, or Nineveh—to permit of strict watch being kept for any sign of disaffection, and they could be promptly recalled to order if they attempted to throw off the yoke. These provinces were, moreover, of moderate area and sparsely populated: once drawn within the orbit of Assyria's attraction, they were unable to escape from its influence by their own unaided efforts; on the contrary, they gradually lost their individuality, and ended by becoming merged in the body of the nation. The Aramæan tribes of the Khabur and the Balikh, the Cossæans of the Turnat, the marauding shepherds of the Gordyæan hills and the slopes of the Masios, gradually became assimilated to their conquerors after a more or less protracted resistance, till at length—in spite of differences of origin, creed, and speech—they became the best of Assyrians, every whit as devoted to the person of their king and as jealous of his honour as the aboriginal Assyrians themselves. A similar result could not be looked for in the case of the cities recently subdued. It was not to be expected that Babylon and Damascus—to name but two of the most important—would allow themselves to be influenced and to become reconciled to their lot by artifices which had been successful enough with the Medes and in the country of Tul-Abnî.

To take the case of Babylon first. It was no mere conglomeration of tribes, nor a state of minor importance, but an actual empire, nearly as large as that of Assyria itself, and almost as solidly welded together. It extended from the Turnat and the mountains of Elam to the Arabian desert and the Nâr-Marratûm, and even though the Cossæans, Elamites, Kaldâ, Sumerians, Akkadians, and other remnants of ancient peoples who formed its somewhat motley population, had dwelt there for centuries in a state of chronic discord, they all agreed— in theory, at any rate—in recognising the common suzerainty of Babylon. Babylon was, moreover, by general acknowledgment, the ancient metropolis to which Assyria owed its whole civilisation; it was the holy city whose gods and whose laws had served as a prototype for the gods and laws of Assyria; from its temples and its archives the Assyrian scribes had drawn such knowledge as they had of the history of the ancient world, their religious doctrines and ceremonies, their methods of interpreting the omens and of forecasting the future—in short, their whole literature, both sacred and profane. The King of Nineveh might conquer Babylon, might even enter within its gates in the hour of triumph, and, when once he had it at his mercy, might throw down its walls, demolish its palaces, destroy its *ziggurât*, burn its houses, exterminate or carry off its inhabitants, and blot out its name from the list of nations; but, so long as he recoiled from the sacrilege involved in such irreparable destruction, he was not merely powerless to reduce it to the level of an ordinary leading provincial town, such as Tela or Tushkhân, but he could not even deprive it in any way of its rank as a capital, or hope to make it anything less than the second city of his empire. As long as it remained in existence, it necessarily took precedence of all others, thanks to its extensive area, the beauty and antiquity of its buildings, and the number of its inhabitants. The pride of its nobles and priests, subdued for a moment by defeat, would almost instantly have reasserted itself, had the victor sought to lower the dignity of their city; Babylon only consented to accept an alien master provided he bowed himself respectfully before its superiority, and was willing to forget that he was a stranger within its gates, and was ready to comply with its laws and masquerade as a Babylonian. Tiglath-pileser III. never dreamt, therefore, of treating the Babylonians as slaves, or of subordinating them to their Assyrian descendants, but left their liberties and territory alike unimpaired. He did not attempt to fuse into a single empire the two kingdoms which his ability had won for him; he kept them separate, and was content to be monarch of both on similar terms. He divided himself, as it were, into two persons, one of whom reigned in Calah, while the other reigned in Karduniash, and his Chaldæan subjects took care to invest this dual *rôle*—based on a fiction so soothing to their pride—with every appearance of reality; he received from them, together with all the titles of the Babylonian kings, that name of Pulu, which later on found its way into their chronicles, and which was so long a puzzle to historians, both ancient and modern.[1] Experience amply proved that this was the only means by which it was possible to yoke temporarily together the two great powers of the Euphrates and the Tigris. Among the successors of Tiglath-pileser, the only sovereigns to rule over Babylon without considerable difficulty were those who followed the precedent set by him and were satisfied to divide their functions and reign as dual kings over a dual kingdom.[2] This combination, while gratifying to the ambition of its rulers, was, perhaps, more a source of loss than of gain to Assyria itself. It is true that the power of Karduniash had decreased under the previous dynasty, but it had still been strong enough to hold back the Aramæans of the Persian Gulf on one side, and the Elamite hordes on the other. It lay like a broad barrier between these barbarians and the cities of the Middle Tigris; when an unusually vigorous attack compelled it to give way

---

[1] Cf. p. 112, note 4, *supra*.

[2] As we shall see later on, this was so in the case of Tiglath-pileser III.'s immediate successor, Shalmaneser V., of Esarhaddon, and of Assur-bani-pal; Shalmaneser was known at Babylon by the name of Ululaî (cf. p. 209, note 2), Assur-bani-pal by that of Kandalanu.

at some point, it appealed to Nineveh for help, and an Assyrian army, entering the country at the fords of the Zab, hastened to drive back the aggressors to the place from which they had set out. When, however, the kings of Assyria had become kings of Babylon as well, the situation was altered. Several branches of the Kaldâ had hitherto held possession of the city, and still possessed representatives and allies among the other tribes, especially among the Bît-Yakîn,[1] who believed themselves entitled to reassert their supremacy within it. The Elamite princes, on their part, accustomed to descend at will into the plains that lay between the Tigris and the Euphrates, and to enrich themselves by frequent raids,[2] could not make up their minds to change the habits of centuries, until they had at least crossed swords with the new despot, and put his mettle to the test. The Ninevite King of Babylon was thus in duty bound to protect his subjects against the same enemies that had ceaselessly harassed his native-born predecessors, and as the unaided resources of Karduniash no longer enabled him to do so effectively, he was, naturally, obliged to fall back on the forces at his disposal as King of Assyria. Henceforward it was no longer the Babylonian army that protected Nineveh, but rather that of Nineveh which had to protect Babylon, and to encounter, almost every year, foes whom in former days it had met only at rare intervals, and then merely when it chose to intervene in their affairs. Where the Assyrian sovereigns had gained a kingdom for themselves and their posterity, Assyria itself found little else but fresh battle-fields and formidable adversaries, in the effort to overcome whom its energies were all but exhausted.

In Syria and on the shores of the Mediterranean, Tiglath-pileser had nations of less stubborn vitality to deal with, nor was he bound by the traditions of a common past to show equal respect to their prejudices. Arpad, Unki, the Bekâa, Damascus, and Gilead were all consecutively swallowed up by Assyria, but, the work of absorption once completed, difficulties were encountered which now had to be met for the first time. The subordinate to whom he entrusted the task of governing these districts [3] had one or two Assyrian regiments assigned him as his body-guard,[4] and these exercised the

---

[1] As to the Bît-Yakîn and the territory occupied by them, cf. Fr. Delitzsch, *Wo lag das Paradies?* p. 203. I shall have occasion to refer to them more fully at the beginning of Chapter III. of the present volume.

[2] Cf. *Struggle of the Nations*, pp. 592, 596, 609, 610, 613–616, and the first few pages of Chapter III. of the present volume.

[3] The governor was called *Shaknu* = "he whom the king has established in his place," and *pekhu* = "the pilot," "the manager," whence *pikhatu* = "a district," and *bel-pikhati* = "the master of a district." It seems that the *shaknu* was of higher rank than the *bel-pikhati*, and often had the latter under his command. As to the duties and authority of those personages, cf. Tiele, *Bab.-ass. Gesch.*, pp. 497–499, and Winckler, *Gesch. Bab. und Ass.*, pp. 210, 211.

[4] Thus Assur-nazir-pal selected the horsemen and other soldiers who were to form the body-guard of the governor of Parzindu (*Annals*, col. ii. ll. 70, 71; cf. p. 25, *supra*).

same ascendency over the natives as the Egyptian archers had done in days gone by :[1] it was felt that they had the whole might of Assyria behind them, and the mere fact of their presence in the midst of the conquered country was, as a rule, sufficient to guarantee the safety of the Assyrian governor and ensure obedience to his commands. This body-guard was never a very numerous one, for the army would have melted away in the course of a campaign or two, had it been necessary, after each fresh conquest, to detach from it a sufficient force to guard against rebellion. It was strengthened, it is true, by auxiliaries enlisted on the spot, and the tributary chiefs included in the provincial district were expected to furnish a reasonable quota of men in case of need;[2] but the loyalty of all these people was, at the best, somewhat doubtful, and in the event of their proving untrustworthy at a critical moment, the little band of Assyrian horse and foot would be left to deal with the revolt unaided until such time as the king could come and relieve them. The distance between the banks of the Jordan or Abana and those of the Tigris was a long one, and in nearly every instance it would have been a question of months before help could arrive. Meanwhile, Egypt was at hand, jealous of her rival, who was thus encroaching on territory which had till lately been regarded as her exclusive sphere of influence, and vaguely apprehensive of the fate which might be in store for her if some Assyrian army, spurred by the lust of conquest, were to cross the desert and bear down upon the eastern frontiers of the Delta. Distrustful of her own powers, and unwilling to assume a directly offensive attitude, she did all she could to foment continual disturbances among the Hebrews and Phœnicians, as well as in Philistia and Aram ; she carried on secret intrigues with the independent princes, and held out tempting hopes of speedy intervention before the eyes of their peoples ; her influence could readily be traced in every seditious movement. The handful of men assigned to the governors of the earlier provinces close to the capital would have been of little avail against perils of this kind. Though Tiglath-pileser added colony to colony in the distant regions annexed by him, he organised them on a different plan from that which had prevailed before his time. His predecessors had usually sent Assyrians to these colonies, and filled the villages vacated by them with families taken from the conquered region :[3] a transfer of inhabitants was made, for instance, from Naîri

[1] Cf. what has been said in regard to these archers in the *Struggle of the Nations*, pp. 274, 275.

[2] In a despatch from Belibni to Assur-bani-pal (*K*, 10) we find Aramæans from the Persian Gulf submitting to the authority of an Assyrian officer, and fighting in Elam side by side with his troops (Obv., ll. 19–21 ; Rev., ll. 1–14; cf. C. JOHNSTON, *The Epistolary Literature of the Assyrians and Babylonians*, p. 143). Again, under Assur-bani-pal, an army sent to repress a revolt on the part of Kedar and the Nabatæans included contingents from Ammon, Moab, and Edom, together with the Assyrian garrisons of the Haurân and Zobah (G. SMITH, *History of Assurbanipal*, pp. 258, 259, 288, 289).

[3] Cf., in regard to these colonies and the exchange of populations to which they gave rise, *Struggle of the Nations*, pp. 608, 609, 666–668, 639, 640, 659, 665, and pp. 15, 18–21, 26, 27, 30, 40, etc., of the present volume.

or from Media into Assyria, and *vice versâ*. By following this system, Tiglath-pileser would soon have scattered his whole people over the dependencies of his empire, and have found his hereditary states peopled by a motley and incoherent collection of aliens ; he therefore left his Assyrians for the most part at home, and only effected exchanges between captives. In his earlier campaigns he brought back with him, on one occasion, 65,000 prisoners from the table-land of Iran, in order to distribute them over a province which he was organising on the banks of the Turnat and the Zab :[1] he levied contributions of this kind without mercy from all the states that he conquered from year to year, and dispersed the captives thus obtained over the length and breadth of his empire ; he transplanted the Aramæans of the Mesopotamian deserts, and the Kaldâ to the slopes of Mount Amanus or the banks of the Orontes,[2] the Patinians and Hamathæans to Ulluba,[3] the inhabitants of Damascus to Kîr or to the borders of Elam,[4] and the Israelites to some place in Assyria.[5] He allowed them to take with them their wives and their children, their herds, their chattels, their gods, and even their money. Drafted into the towns and country districts in batches sufficiently numerous to be self-supporting, but yet not large enough to allow of their at once re-establishing themselves as a distinct nation in their new home, they seem to have formed, even in the midst of the most turbulent provinces, settlements of colonists who lived unaffected by any native influence or resentment. The aborigines hated them because of their religion, their customs, their clothing, and their language ; in their eyes they were mere interlopers, who occupied the property of relations or fellow-countrymen who had fallen in battle or had been spirited away to the other end of the world. And even when, after many years, the native owners of the soil had become familiarised with them, this mutual antipathy had struck such deep root in their minds that any understanding between the natives and the descendants of the immigrants was quite out of the question : what had been formerly a vast kingdom, occupied by a single homogeneous race, actuated by a common patriotic spirit, became for many a year a region capriciously subdivided and torn by the dissensions of a number of paltry antagonistic communities. The colonists, exposed to the same hatreds as the original Assyrian conquerors, soon forgot to look upon the latter as the oppressors of all, and, allowing their present grudge to efface the memory of past injuries, did not hesitate to make common cause with them. In time of peace, the governor did his best to protect them against molestation on the part of the natives, and in return for this they rallied round

---

[1] *Nimroud Inscription*, Obv., l. 33 ; cf. p. 142, *supra*.

[2] *Annals of Tiglath-pileser III.*, ll. 135-148 ; cf. p. 142, *supra*.

[3] *Annals of Tiglath-pileser III.*, ll. 132, 133 ; *Nimroud Inscription*, Obv., ll. 15-21. As to the events which rendered this colonisation necessary, cf. pp. 149, 150, *supra*.

[4] 2 *Kings* xvi. 9 ; cf. p. 183, *supra*.   [5] 2 *Kings* xv. 29 ; cf. p. 186, *supra*.

him whenever the latter threatened to get out of hand, and helped him to stifle the revolt or hold it in check until the arrival of reinforcements. Thanks to their help, the empire was consolidated and maintained without too many violent outbreaks in regions far removed from the capital and beyond the immediate reach of the sovereign.[1]

We possess very few details with regard to the administration of these prefects.[2] The various functionaries, governors of towns, tax-collectors, heads of stations, and officers whose duty it was to patrol the roads and look after the safety of merchants, were, for the most part, selected from among natives who had thrown in their lot with Assyria, and probably few Assyrians were to be found outside the more turbulent cities and important fortresses. The kings and chiefs whose territory was attached to a given province, either took their instructions direct from Nineveh, or were sometimes placed under the control of a resident, or *kipu,* with some sort of escort at his back, who kept watch over their movements and reported them to the suzerain, and saw that the tribute was paid regularly, and that the military service provided for in the treaties was duly rendered.[3] Governors and residents alike kept up a constant correspondence with the court, and such of their letters as have chanced to come down to us show what a minute account of even the most trifling occurrences was required of them by the central authorities.[4] They were not only obliged to report any fluctuation in the temper or attitude of their subordinates,[5]

---

[1] This was the history of the only one of those colonies whose fate is known to us—that founded at Samaria by Sargon and his successors (*Annals of Sargon,* Winckler's edit., ll. 11–17, *Ezra* iv.; cf. WINCKLER, *Alttestamentliche Untersuchungen,* pp. 97–107).

[2] The texts contain a certain number of names of offices, the precise nature of which it is not easy to ascertain, *e.g.* the Khâzanu (FR. DELITZSCH, *Assyrische Studien,* p. 182; cf. *Assyrisches Handwörterbuch,* p. 272), the Labuttu (FR. DELITZSCH, *Ass. Handwört.,* p. 373), and others. One of them, read *Shu-ul-shak* by the Germans, seems as though it ought to be *Shuparshak,* and identical with one of the titles mentioned in Ezra (v. 6, vi. 6) as being in existence during the Persian epoch (WINCKLER, *Altorientalische Forschungen,* vol. i. p. 476, note 1). Cf., as to the provincial administration, TIELE, *Bab.-ass. Gesch.* pp. 497–499, where the title *shalat* discussed by the author is merely a variant of *shaknu,* and ought to be omitted from the nomenclature of offices.

[3] The part played by the *kipu* has been defined by WINCKLER, *Gesch. Bab. und Ass.,* p. 229, note 1, and *Altorient. Forsch.,* vol. i. p. 24. Idibiel was appointed *kipu* over the Arabian country of Muzri, on the borders of Egypt (*Slab No. 3,* ll. 29–33, *Annals of Tiglath-pileser III.,* l. 226); as to the events which led to his appointment, cf. p. 189, *supra.*

[4] G. Smith was the first to make use of these despatches in his *History of Assurbanipal,* pp. 181–190, 196–199, 201–204, 296–298, 323, 324; four of them were subsequently published and translated by Pinches (*Notes upon the Assyrian Report Tablets,* in the *Transactions* of Soc. of Bibl. Arch., vol. vi. pp. 209–243). No serious study was made of them till 1887, when it was undertaken by S. A. Smith (*Die Keilschrifttexte Asurbanipals,* vols. ii., iii., and *Assyrian Letters,* in the *Proceedings,* 1886–1887, vol. ix. pp. 240–256, and 1887–1888, vol. x. pp. 60–72, 155–177, 205–215), and by Fr. Delitzsch (*Zur assyrisch-babylonische Briefliteratur,* in the *Beiträge zur Assyriologie,* vol. i. pp. 185–248, 613–630; vol. ii. pp. 19–62); a very large part of those preserved in the British Museum have been reproduced by Harper (*Assyrian and Babylonian Letters of the Koyundjik Collection,* vols. i.–iv., 1892–1897). A translation and notes on several of them will be found in an article by C. JOHNSTON, *The Epistolary Literature of the Assyrians and Babylonians,* in the *Journal of the American Oriental Society,* vol. xviii. pp. 125–175, and vol. xix., 2nd pt., pp. 42–96.

[5] Cf. the report of Nabu-ushabshî, governor of Uruk, with regard to the intrigues of a certain

or any intrigues that were being entered into across the frontier;[1] they had also to record the transfer of troops,[2] the return of fugitives, the pursuit of deserters, any chance scuffle between soldiers and natives, as well as the punishment inflicted on the rebellious,[3] the appearance of a portent in the heavens, or omens noticed by the augurs.[4] There were plenty of envious or officious tongues among their followers to report to headquarters the slightest failure of duty, and to draw attention to their negligence. Moreover, it seems certain that the object of thus compelling them to refer to the king at every turn, was not merely in order to keep him informed of all that took place in his dependencies, but also to lay bare the daily life of his prefects before his eyes. The latter were entrusted with the command of seasoned troops; they had considerable sums of money passing through their hands, and were often obliged to take prompt decisions and enter into diplomatic or military transactions on their own responsibility; in short, those of them, at any rate, who were stationed at the furthest confines of the empire were really kings in all but title, insignia, and birth. There was always the danger lest some among them should be tempted to reassert, in their own interest, the independence of the countries under their rule, and seek to found a dynasty in their midst. The strict supervision maintained over these governors generally nipped any ambition of this kind in the bud; in some cases, however, it created the very danger it was intended to prevent. If a governor who had been recalled to Nineveh or Calah in order to explain his conduct failed to clear himself completely, he at once fell into disgrace; and disgrace in Assyria, as in other countries of the East, meant, nine times out of ten, confiscation of property, mutilation and lifelong imprisonment, or death in its most hideous form. He would, therefore, think twice before quitting his post, and if he had any reason to suppose himself suspected, or viewed with disfavour in high quarters, he

Piribel (PINCHES, Notes upon the Assyrian Report Tablets, in the Transactions of the Soc. of Bibl. Arch., vol. vi. pp. 217, 218, 233–239; and JOHNSTON, The Epistolary Literature, vol. xviii. pp. 146–148.

[1] Cf., in the time of Assur-bani-pal, Belibni's reports on what was going on on the Elamite frontier and in Elam, K 13 (G. SMITH, History of Assurbanipal, pp. 197–200; JOHNSTON, The Epistolary Literature, vol. xviii. pp. 138–142), K 524 (S. A. SMITH, Die Keilschrifttexte Asurbanipals, vol. ii. pp. 54–58, 77, 78, 87, 88; JOHNSTON, The Epistolary Literature, vol. xviii. pp. 134–138), K 577, 599 (G. SMITH, History of Assurbanipal, pp. 196, 197), K 1250 (WINCKLER, Sammlung von Keilschrifttexten, vol. ii. p. 59), K 1374 (WINCKLER, ibid., pp. 20, 21).

[2] Cf. a letter written by Nabu-ushabshî under Assur-bani-pal, in regard to an expedition against the Gambulu (PINCHES, Notes upon the Assyrian Record Tablets, in the Transactions of the Soc. of Bibl. Arch., vol. vi. pp. 217, 228–232; JOHNSTON, The Epistolary Literature, vol. xviii. pp. 144–146).

[3] Report of Sha-assurdubbu, governor of Tushkhân, in the time of Sargon (JOHNSTON, The Epistolary Literature, vol. xviii. pp. 151–153), and report of Assurdurpani, under Assur-bani-pal (S. A. SMITH, Die Keilschrifttexte Asurbanipals, vol. iii. pp. 30–36, 95, 96, and FR. DELITZSCH, Beiträge zur Erklärung der Babylonisch-assyrischen Briefliteratur, in the Beiträge zur Assyriologie, vol. ii. pp. 55–62).

[4] Cf., under Esarhaddon, the reports of Arad-eâ (HARPER, Assyrian and Babylonian Letters, Nos. 27–29) and of Balasi (Id., Nos. 74–79).

would be in no hurry to obey a summons to the capital. A revolt was almost certain to be crushed without fail, and offered merely a very precarious chance of escape, but the governor was seldom likely to hesitate between almost certain condemnation and the vague possibility of a successful rising; in such a case, therefore, he staked everything on a single throw.[1] The system was a defective one, in that it exposed to strong temptation the very functionaries whose loyalty

was most essential to the proper working of the administration, but its dangers were outweighed by such important advantages that we cannot but regard it as a very real improvement on the haphazard methods of the past. In the first place, it opened up a larger recruiting-ground for the army, and, in a measure, guaranteed it against that premature exhaustion which had already led more than once to an eclipse of the Assyrian power.[2] It may be

TIGLATH-PILESER III. BESIEGING A REBELLIOUS CITY.[3]

that the pick of these provincial troops were, preferably, told off for police duties, or for the defence of the districts in which they were levied, and that they seldom left it except to do battle in the adjacent territory;[4] but, even with these limitations they were none the less of inestimable value, since they relieved the main army of Assyria from garrison duties in a hundred scattered localities, and allowed the king to concentrate it almost in its entirety about his own person, and to direct it *en masse* upon those points where he wished to strike a decisive blow. On the other hand, the finances of the kingdom were put on a more stable and systematic basis. For nearly the whole of the two previous centuries, during which Assyria had resumed its victorious career, the treasury had been filled to some extent by taxes in kind or in money, and by various dues claimed from the hereditary kingdom and its few immediate dependencies,

---

[1] Winckler, *Geschichte Babyloniens und Assyriens*, pp. 210, 211.

[2] Cf., in regard to these stages of periodical exhaustion suffered by Assyria, the *Struggle of the Nations*, pp. 666, 667, and pp. 113, 114, 116–118, *supra*.

[3] Drawn by Boudier, from a photograph by Mansell.

[4] Thus, in the reign of Assur-bani-pal, we find the militia of the governor of Uruk marching to battle against the Gambulu (*Tablet K 528*; Johnston, *The Epistolary Literature*, vol. xviii. pp. 144–146).

but mainly by booty and by tribute levied after each campaign from the peoples who had been conquered or had voluntarily submitted to Assyrian rule. The result was a budget which fluctuated greatly, since all forays were not equally lucrative, and the new dependencies proved so refractory at the idea of perpetual tribute, that frequent expeditions were necessary in order to persuade them to pay their dues. We do not know how Tiglath-pileser III. organised the finances of his provinces, but certain facts recorded here and there in

A HERD OF HORSES BROUGHT IN AS TRIBUTE.[1]

the texts show that he must have drawn very considerable amounts from them.[2] We notice that twenty or thirty years after his time, Carchemish was assessed at a hundred talents, Arpad and Kuî at thirty each, Megiddo and Manzuatu at fifteen, though the purposes to which these sums were applied is not specified.[3] On the other hand, we know the precise object to which the contributions of several other cities were assigned ; as, for instance, so much for the maintenance of the throne in the palace, or for the divans of the ladies of the harem ; so much for linen garments, for dresses, and for veils ; twenty talents from Nineveh for the armaments of the fleet, and ten from the same city for firewood.[4] Certain provinces were expected to maintain the stud-farms, and their contributions of horses were specially valuable, now that cavalry played

---

[1] Drawn by Faucher-Gudin, from one of the bronze bas-reliefs on the gates of Balawat. The breed here represented seems to have been common in Urartu, as well as in Cappadocia and Northern Syria.

[2] Some fragments of tablets which contain documents referring to the collection or employment of taxes have been mentioned by H. RAWLINSON, *Assyrian Discovery*, in the *Athenæum*, 1863, vol. ii. p. 246, note 26, and published in his *Cun. Ins. W. As.*, vol. ii. pl. 53, Nos. 2–4. They have been translated by SAYCE, *The Assyrian Tribute-Lists*, in the *Records of the Past*, series 1, vol. xi. pp. 139–144, and in *Assyria, its Princes, Priests and People*, pp. 139–143.

[3] RAWLINSON, *Cun. Ins. W. As.*, vol. ii. pl. 53, No. 3, ll. 53–61.

[4] SAYCE, *The Assyrian Tribute-Lists*, in the *Records of the Past*, series 1, vol. xi. pp. 141, 142 ; cf. *Assyria, its Princes, Priests and People*, pp. 140, 145.

almost as important a part as infantry in military operations. The most highly prized animals came, perhaps, from Asia Minor; the nations of Mount Taurus, who had supplied chargers to Israel and Egypt five centuries earlier,[1] now furnished war-horses to the squadrons of Nineveh. The breed was small, but robust, inured to fatigue and hard usage, and in every way similar to that

TYPICAL CAPPADOCIAN HORSE.[2]

raised in these countries at the present day. In war, horses formed a very considerable proportion of the booty taken; in time of peace, they were used as part of the payment of the yearly tribute, and a brisk trade in them was carried on with Mesopotamia. After the king had deducted from his receipts enough to provide amply for the wants of his family and court, the salaries of the various functionaries and officials, the pay and equipment of his army, the maintenance and construction of palaces and fortresses, he had still sufficient left over to form an enormous reserve fund on which he and his successors might draw in the event of their ordinary sources of income being depleted by a series of repeated reverses.

Tiglath-pileser thus impressed upon Assyria the character by which it was known during the most splendid century of its history, and the organisation which he devised for it was so admirably adapted to the Oriental genius that it survived the fall of Nineveh, and served as a model for every empire-maker

---

[1] As to the horses obtained from Kuî and the Hittite country, and afterwards sold by Solomon in Egypt, cf. *Struggle of the Nations*, pp. 739, 740.

[2] Drawn by Boudier, from a photograph by M. Alfred Boissier.

down to the close of the Macedonian era and even beyond it. The wealth of the country grew rapidly, owing to the influx of capital and of foreign population;

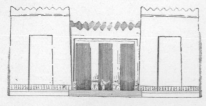

A SYRIAN BÎT-KHILÂNI.[1]

in the intervals between their campaigns its rulers set to work to remove all traces of the ruins which had been allowed to accumulate during the last forty years. The king had built himself a splendid palace at Calah, close to the monuments of Assur-nazir-pal and Shalmaneser III., and its terraces and walls overhung the waters of the Tigris. The main entrance consisted of a *Bît-khilâni,* one of those porticoes, flanked by towers and sup-

THE FOUNDATIONS OF A BÎT-
KHILÂNI AT ZINJIRLI.[2]

ported by columns or pillars, often found in Syrian towns, the fashion for which was now beginning to spread to Western Asia.[3] Those discovered at Zinjirli

---

[1] Reproduced by Faucher-Gudin, from the restoration published by LUSCHAN, *Ausgrabungen in Sendschirli,* vol. ii. No. 67, p. 168.

[2] Drawn by Boudier, from a sketch published by LUSCHAN, *Ausgrabungen in Sendschirli,* vol. i. p. 11.

[3] The precise nature of the edifices referred to in the inscriptions under the name of Bît-khilâni (ROST, *Die Keilschrifttexte Tiglat-Pilesers III.,* pp. 72, 73, 1. 18) is still a matter of controversy. Friedrich is of opinion that it was the name of the pillared hall, or audience-chamber, such as we find in Sargon's palace at Khorsabad (*Die Holztektonik Vorderasiens in Alterthum und der Hekal Mat Hatti,* pp. 10–16). Puchstein identifies it with edifices or portions of edifices which varied according to the period, but which were ornamented with columns (*Die Saüle in der Assyrischen Architektur,* in the *Jahrbuch des Deutschen Archæologischen Instituts,* 1892, vol. viii. pp. 1–24). It seems clear, however, from the passages quoted by Meissner and Rost (*Noch einmal das Bît-hillâni und die Assyriche Saüle,* 1891), that it was used of the whole series of chambers and buildings which formed the monumental gates of Assyrian palaces, something analogous to the *Migdol* of Ramses III. at Medinet-Habu (cf. *Struggle of the Nations,* pp. 128–130), and more especially to the gates at Zinjirli, as described and restored by Koldewey, in LUSCHAN, *Ausgrabungen in Sendschirli,* vol. ii. p. 136, et seq.

afford fine examples of the arrangements adopted in buildings of this kind; the lower part of the walls was covered with bas-reliefs, figures of gods and men, soldiers mounted or on foot, victims, and fantastic animal shapes; the columns, where there were any, rested on the back of a sphinx or on a pair of griffins of a type which shows a curious mixture of Egyptian and Semitic influences. The wood-work of the Ninevite *Bît-khilâni* was of cedar from Mount Amanus, the door-frames and fittings were of various rare woods, inlaid with ivory and metal. The entrance was guarded by the usual colossal figures, and the walls of the state reception-rooms were covered with slabs of alabaster; on these, in accordance with the usual custom,[1] were carved scenes from the royal wars, with explanatory inscriptions. The palace was subsequently dismantled, its pictures defaced and its inscriptions obliterated,[2] to mark the hatred felt by later generations towards the hero whom they were pleased to regard as a usurper; we can only

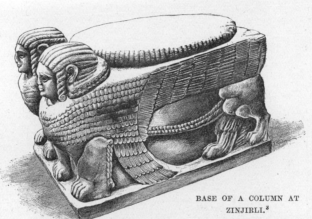

BASE OF A COLUMN AT ZINJIRLI.[3]

partially succeed in deciphering his annals by the help of the fragmentary sentences which have escaped the fury of the destroyer. The cities and fortresses which he raised throughout the length and breadth of Assyria proper and its more recently acquired provinces have similarly disappeared;[4] we can only conjecture that the nobles of his court, fired by his example, must have built and richly endowed more than one city on their hereditary estates, or in the territories under their rule. Bel-harrân-beluzur, the marshal of the palace, who twice gave his name to years of the king's reign, viz. in 741 and 727 B.C.,[5]

---

[1] The building of Tiglath-pileser's palace is described in the *Nimroud Inscription*, rev., ll. 17–36. It stood near the centre of the platform of Nimroud (LAYARD, *Nineveh and Babylon*, p. 526).

[2] The materials were utilised (LAYARD, *Nineveh and its Remains*, vol. i. pp. 34, 35, 39, et seq., etc.) by Esarhaddon, but it does not necessarily follow that the palace was dismantled by that monarch; this was probably done by Sargon or by Sennacherib.

[3] Drawn by Faucher-Gudin, from a photograph published by LUSCHAN, *Ausgrabungen in Sendschirli*, vol. ii. pl. xxxiii.

[4] Cf. the foundation of Kar-assur, between the Zab and the Radanu (*Annals of Tiglath-pileser III.*, ll. 8–11), and of Dur-Tiglath-pileser (*Annals*, ll. 21–24, where the name has been destroyed, but has been restored to all appearance correctly from a passage in the *Nimroud Inscrip.*, Obv., l. 40, where it is shown that this town was founded before the second campaign); cf. also the rebuilding of Nikur on the Median frontier (*Annals*, ll. 36, 37), of Kunulua in Unki (*Annals*, ll. 100, 101), and the foundation of Assur-ikîsha in Ulluba (*Slab No. 1*, ll. 28, 29, and *Slab No. 2*, ll. 43-45).

[5] *Eponym Canon*, in SCHRADER, *Keilinschriftliche Bibliothek*, vol. i. pp. 212–215.

possessed, it would seem, an important fief a little to the north of Assur, near the banks of the Tharthar, on the site of the present Tel-Abta.[1] The district was badly cultivated, and little better than a wilderness; by express order of the celestial deities—Marduk, Nabu, Shamash, Sin, and the two Ishtars—he dug

the foundations of a city which he called Dur-Bel-harrân-beluzur. The description he gives of it affords conclusive evidence of the power of the great nobles, and shows how nearly they approached, by their wealth and hereditary privileges, to the kingly rank. He erected, we are told, a *ziggurât* on a raised terrace, in which he placed his gods in true royal fashion; he assigned slaves, landed property, and a yearly income to their priests, in order that worship might be paid to them in perpetuity; he granted sanctuary to all freemen who settled within the walls or in the environs, exemption from forced labour, and the right to tap a water-course and construct a canal. A decree of foundation was set up in the temple in

STELE OF BEL-HARRÂN-BELUZUR.[2]

memory of Bel-harrân-beluzur, precisely as if he were a crowned king. It is a stele of common grey stone with a circular top. The dedicator stands erect against the background of the carving, bare-foot and bare-headed, his face clean-shaven, dressed in a long robe embroidered in a chess-board pattern, and with a tunic pleated in horizontal rows; his right elbow is supported by the left hand, while the right is raised to a level with his eyes, his fist is clenched, and the thumb inserted between the first and second fingers in the customary gesture of adoration. What the provost of the palace had done on his land, the

---

[1] SCHEIL, *Stèle de Bél-Harrân-bel-utsur*, in the *Recueil de Travaux*, vol. xvi. p. 176. All the details which follow have been taken from the monument published and commented on in that article.

[2] Drawn by Boudier, from the photograph published by Father Scheil, in his article in the *Recueil de Travaux*, vol. xvi.

other barons in all probability did on theirs; most of the departments which had fallen away and languished during the disturbances at the close of the previous dynasty, took a new lease of life under their protection. Private documents—which increase in number as the century draws to an end—contracts, official reports, and letters of scribes, all give us the impression of a wealthy and industrious country, stirred by the most intense activity, and in the enjoyment of unexampled prosperity. The excellent administration of Tiglath-pileser and his nobles had paved the way for this sudden improvement, and had helped to develop it, and when Shalmaneser V. succeeded his father on the throne it continued unchecked.[1] The new-comer made no changes in the system of government which had been so ably inaugurated. He still kept Assyria separate from Karduniash; his Babylonian subjects, faithful to ancient custom, soon devised a nickname for him, that of Ululai, as though seeking to persuade themselves that they had a king who belonged to them alone; and it is under this name that their annalists have inscribed him next to Pulu in the list of their dynasties.[2] His reign was, on the whole, a calm and peaceful one; the Kaldâ, the Medes, Urartu, and the races of Mount Taurus remained quiet, or, at any rate, such disorders as may have arisen among them were of too trifling a nature to be deemed worthy of notice in the records of the time. Syria alone was disturbed, and several of its independent states took advantage of the change of rulers to endeavour to shake off the authority of Assyria.

Egypt continued to give them secret encouragement in these tactics, though its own internal dissensions prevented it from offering any effective aid. The Tanite dynasty was in its death-throes. Psamuti, the last of its kings, exercised a dubious sovereignty over but a few of the nomes on the

---

[1] It was, for a long time, an open question with the earlier Assyriologists whether or not Shalmaneser and Sargon were different names for one and the same monarch. As for monuments, we possess only one attributed to Shalmaneser, a weight in the form of a lion, discovered by Layard at Nimroud (*Nineveh and its Remains*, vol. i. p. 128; cf. *Nineveh and Babylon*, pp. 510, 511), in the north-west palace (SCHRADER, *Inschrift Salmanassar's IV.*, in the *Keilinschriftliche Bibliothek*, vol. i. pp. 32, 33). The length of his reign, and the scanty details we possess concerning it, have been learnt from the *Eponym Canon* (SCHRADER, *Keilinschriftliche Bibliothek*, vol. i. pp. 205, 214, 215) and *Pinches' Babylonian Chronicle* (col. i. ll. 27–30; cf. WINCKLER, *Babylonische Chronik B*, in SCHRADER, *Keilinschriftliche Bibliothek*, vol. ii. pp. 276, 277), and also from the Hebrew texts (2 *Kings* xvii. 3–6; xviii. 9–12).

[2] The identity of Ululai and Shalmaneser V., though still questioned by Oppert (*La Non-identité de Phul et de Téglath-phalasar*, in the *Revue d'Assyriologie*, vol. i. pp. 166–168), has been proved by the comparison of Babylonian records, in some of which the names Pulu and Ululai occur in positions exactly corresponding with those occupied, in others, by Tiglath-pileser and Shalmaneser (PINCHES, *The Babylonian Kings of the Second Period*, in the *Proceedings* of the Soc. of. Bibl. Arch., 1883–4, vol. vi. pp. 197, 198; cf. SCHRADER, *Keilinschriftliche Bibliothek*, vol. ii. pp. 287, 290, 291). The name Ululai was given to the king because he was born in the month of Ulul (PINCHES, *The Babylonian Kings*, p. 197, note 6; OPPERT, *La Non-identité de Phul et de Téglath-phalasar*, p. 167); in Pinches' list we find a gloss, "Dynasty of Tinu," which probably indicates the Assyrian town in which Tiglath-pileser III. and his son were born.

P

Arabian frontier.[1] His neighbours the Saites were gradually gaining the upper hand in the Delta and in the fiefs of middle Egypt, at first under Tafnakhti, and then, after his death, under his son Bukunirînif, the Bocchoris of the Greek historians.[2] They held supremacy over several personages who, like themselves, claimed the title and rank of Pharaoh; amongst others, over a certain Rudamanu Mîamun, son of Osorkon:[3] their power did not, however, extend beyond Siut, near the former frontier of the Theban kingdom. The

CONE BEARING THE NAME OF KASHTA AND OF HIS DAUGHTER AMENERTAS.[5]

withdrawal of Piônkhi-Mîamun, and his subsequent death, had not disturbed the Ethiopian rule in the southern half of Egypt, though it somewhat altered its character. While an unknown Ethiopian king filled the place of the conqueror at Napata, another Ethiopian, named Kashta, made his way to the throne in Thebes.[4] It is possible that he was a son of Piônkhi, and may have been placed in supreme power by his father when the latter reinstated the city in its place as capital. With all their partiality for real or supposed descendants of the Ramesside dynasty, the Thebans were, before all things, proud of their former greatness, and eagerly hoped to regain it without delay. When, therefore, they accepted this Kushite king who, to their eyes, represented the only family possessed of a legitimate claim to the throne, it was mainly because they counted on him to restore them to their former place among the cities of Egypt. They must have been cruelly disappointed when he left them for the Sacred Mountain. His invasion, far from reviving their prosperity, merely served to ratify the suppression of that pontificate of Amon-Râ which was the last remaining evidence of their past splendour. All hope of re-estab-

[1] He is the Psammous mentioned by Manetho. The cartouches attributed to him by Lepsius (*Königsbuch*, pl. xlvi. No. 614) really belong to the Psammuthis of the XXIXth dynasty (WIEDEMANN, *Gesch. Ægypt. von Psammetich I. bis auf Alexander den Grossen*, p. 274, and *Ægypt. Gesch.*, pp. 577, 696–699; MASPERO, *Découverte d'un petit temple à Karnak*, in *Recueil de Travaux*, vol. vi. p. 20). It is possible that one of the marks found at Karnak indicating the level of the Nile (LEGRAIN, *Textes gravés sur le quai de Karnak*, in *Zeitschrift*, vol. xxxiv. p. 114, No. 24) belong to the reign of this monarch.

[2] As to Tafnakhti, King at Sais, cf. pp. 180, 181, *supra*.

[3] For the genealogy of this king, cf. DEVÉRIA, *Mémoires et fragments*, vol. i. pp. 376, 377, and DARESSY, *Notes et Remarques*, in the *Recueil de Travaux*, vol. xix. pp. 20, 21.

[4] As is frequently the case with the secondary kings of this period, no cartouche prenomen of Kashta has come down to us. His name, erroneously read at first as Katohet (WILKINSON, *Materia Hieroglyphica*, part ii. pl. iii.; ROSELLINI, *Mon. Storici*, vol. ii. p. 109, and pl. viii. 141 *e*; LEEMANS, *Lettre à M. Salvolini*, p. 132, and pl. xxvi. No. 259; E. DE ROUGÉ, *Notice de quelques textes hiéroglyphiques*, p. 48), then as Kashen (LEPSIUS, *Ueber die XXII ægyptische Königsdynastie*, pp. 300, 302, and pl. ii.), was supposed to be that of a son of Amenertas; his true relationship to this queen was divined by Prisse d'Avennes (*Notice sur le Musée du Caire*, pp. 13, 14), and the correct reading of his name was indicated by Lepsius, at first doubtfully (*Ueber die XXII ægyptische Königsdynastie*, p. 302), afterwards without hesitation (*Königsbuch*, pl. xlvi. Nos. 616, 617). This king has been identified by Lauth (*Die Pianchi-Stele*, pp. 59, 60, and *Aus Ægyptens Vorzeit*, pp. 393, 426, 427) with the Xêt or Zêt of Manetho.

Drawn by Faucher-Gudin, after PRISSE D'AVENNES, *Monuments égyptiens*, pl. xxvii.

lishing it had now to be abandoned, since the sovereign who had come to them from Napata was himself by birth and hereditary privilege the sole priest of Amon: in his absence the actual head of the Theban religion could lay claim only to an inferior office, and indeed, even then, the only reason for accepting a second prophet was that he might direct the worship of the temple at Karnak.   The force of circumstances compelled the Ethiopians to countenance in the Thebaid what their Tanite or Bubastite predecessors had been obliged to tolerate at Hermopolis, Heracleopolis, Sais, and in many another lesser city;[1] they turned it into a feudatory kingdom, and gave it a ruler who, like Auîti, half a century earlier, had the right to use the cartouches.[2]   Once installed, Kashta employed the usual methods to secure his seat on the throne, one of the first being a marriage alliance.   The disappearance of the high priests had naturally increased the importance of the princesses consecrated to the service of Amon.   From henceforward they were the sole visible intermediaries between the god and his people, the privileged guardians of his body and his double, and competent to perpetuate the line of the solar kings.   The Theban appanage constituted their dowry, and even if their sex prevented them from discharging all those civil, military, and religious duties required by their position, no one else had the right to do so on their behalf, unless he was expressly chosen by them for the purpose.   When once married they deputed their husbands to act for them; so long as they remained either single or widows, some exalted personage, the prophet of Amon or Montu, the ruler of Thebes, or the administrator of the Saîd, managed their houses and fiefs for them with such show of authority that strangers were at times deceived, and took him for the reigning monarch of the country.[3]   The Pharaohs had, therefore, a stronger incentive than ever to secure exclusive possession of these women, and if they could not get all of them safely housed in their harems, they endeavoured, at any rate, to reserve for themselves the chief among them, who by purity of descent or seniority in age had attained the grade of *Divine Worshipper*. Kashta married a certain Shapenuapît, daughter of Osorkon III. and a Theban pallacide;[4] it is uncertain whether he eventually became king over Ethiopia

---

[1] Cf. what has been said concerning the secondary Pharaohs on pp. 166–180, *supra*.

[2] LEGRAIN, *Textes gravés sur le quai de Karnak*, in the *Zeitschrift*, vol. xxxiv. p. 114, No. 26; also cf. what is said of this Pharaoh Auîti on p. 166, *supra*.

[3] Thus Harua, in the time of Amenertas, was prince and chief over the servants of the "Divine Worshipper" (EBERS, *Die Naophore Statue des Harual*, in the *Zeit. d. D. Morgenl. Ges.*, vol. xxvi. pp. 139, 140, 143 ; PIEHL, *Une Inscription de l'époque Saite*, pp. 3, 4, 9, 10, 13).   Mantumihâit, in the time of Taharqa and of Tanutamanu, was ruler of Thebes, and fourth prophet of Amon (E. DE ROUGÉ, *Étude sur quelques monuments du règne de Tahraka*, in the *Mélanges d'Archéologie*, vol. i. pp. 17–20), and it is he who is described in the Assyrian monuments as King of Thebes(*Annales d'Assurbanabal*, col. i. l. 109).

[4] LIEBLEIN, *Die Ægyptischen Denkmäler in St.-Petersburg, Helsingfors, Upsala und Copenhagen*, pp. 6–11; cf. MASPERO, *Les Momies royales de Deîr-el-Baharî*, in *Mém. de la Mission du Caire*, vol. i. pp. 752, 753.   It may be that, in accordance with a custom which obtained during the generations that followed, and which possibly originated about this period, this daughter of Osorkon III. was only the adoptive mother of Amenertas (ERMAN, *Zu den Legrain'schen Inschr.*, in the *Zeitschrift*, vol. xxxv. p. 29).

and the Sudan or not.   So far, we have no proof that he did, but it seems quite possible when we remember that one of his children, Shabaku (Sabaco), subsequently occupied the throne of Napata in addition to that of Thebes.[1] Kashta does not appear to have possessed sufficient energy to prevent the Delta and its nomes from repudiating the Ethiopian supremacy.   The Saites, under Tafnakhti or Bocchoris, soon got the upper hand, and it was to them that the Syrian vassals of Nineveh looked for aid, when death removed the conqueror who had trampled them so ruthlessly underfoot.   Ever since the fall of Arpad, Hadrach, and Damascus, Shabaraîn, a town situated somewhere in the valley of the Orontes or of the Upper Litany,[2] and hitherto but little known, had served as a rallying-point for the disaffected Aramæan tribes : on the accession of Shalmaneser V. it ventured to rebel, probably in 727 B.C., but was over-thrown and destroyed, its inhabitants being led away captive.   This achievement proved, beyond the possibility of doubt, that in spite of their change of rulers the vengeance of the Assyrians was as keen and sharp as ever.   Not one of the Syrian towns dared to stir, and the Phœnician seaports, though their loyalty had seemed, for a moment, doubtful, took care to avoid any action which might expose them to the terrors of a like severity.[3]   The Israelites and Philistines, alone of the western peoples, could not resign themselves to a prudent policy ; after a short period of hesitation they drew the sword from its scabbard, and in 725 war broke out.[4]

[1] The relationship between Kashta and Shabaku, first suggested by E. de Rougé (*Études sur quelques monuments du règne de Tahraka*, in the *Mélanges d'Archéologie*, vol. i. pp. 87, 88), was proved by the inscription on a statuette afterwards discovered and published by Lieblein (*Die Ægyptische Denkmäler in St.-Petersburg, Helsingfors, Upsala und Copenhagen*, pp. 6–11).

[2] Shabaraîn was originally confounded with Samaria by the early commentators on the Babylonian Chronicle. Halévy, very happily, referred it to the biblical Sepharvaîm, a place always mentioned in connection with Hamath and Arpad (2 *Kings* xvii. 24, 31 ; xviii. 34 ; xix. 13 ; cf. *Isa.* xxxvi. 19 ; xxxvii. 13), and to the Sibraîm of Ezekiel (xlvii. 16), called in the *Septuagint* Samarêim (*Mélanges de Critique et d'Histoire*, p. 162 ; *Notes Assyriologiques*, in the *Zeitschrift für Assyriologie*, vol. ii. pp. 401, 402 ; *Communications*, § i., in the *Journal Asiatique*, 1889, vol. xi. pp. 280–282). Its identification with Samaria has, since then, been generally rejected, and its connection with Sibraîm admitted (WINCKLER, *Nachtrag*, in the *Zeitschrift für Assyriologie*, vol. ii. pp. 350–352, and *Noch einmal Samaria, ibid.*, vol. iii. pp. 108–111 ; *Alttestamentliche Untersuchungen*, p. 101, note 1 ; SCHRADER, *Sepharvaim*, in RIEHM, *Handwörterbuch*, 2nd edit., vol. i. p. 480). Sibraîm (or Sepharvaîm, or Samarêim) has been located at Shomerîyeh, to the east of the Bahr-Kades, and south of Hamath.

[3] *Pinches' Babylonian Chronicle*, col. i. l. 28 ; cf. WINCKLER, *Babylonische Chronik B*, in SCHRADER, *Keilinschriftliche Bibliothek*, vol. ii. pp. 276, 277. The siege of Tyre, which the historian Menander, in a passage quoted by Josephus, places in the reign of Shalmaneser (for the different forms of this name which appear here, cf. SCHRADER, Σελάμψas = *Salmanassar*, in the *Zeitschrift für Assyriologie*, vol. i. pp. 126, 127), ought really to be referred to the reign of Sennacherib (G. SMITH, *History of Sennacherib*, pp. 69, 70 ; ED. MEYER, *Geschichte des Alterthums*, vol. i. pp. 435, 467 ; HOMMEL, *Gesch. Bab. und Ass.*, p. 676 ; STADE, *Geschichte des Volkes Israel*, vol. i. p. 599, note 2, 619 ; FR. JEREMIAS, *Tyrus bis zur Zeit Nebukadnezar's*, pp. 29–33), or the fragment of Menander must be divided into three parts dealing with three different Assyrian campaigns against Tyre, under Tiglath-pileser, Senna-cherib, and Esarhaddon respectively (LANDAU, *Beiträge zur Alterthumskunde des Orients*, pp. 5–16).

[4] The war cannot have begun earlier, for the *Eponym Canon*, in dealing with 726, has the words " in the country," thus proving that no expedition took place in that year ; in the case of the year 725, on the other hand, it refers to a campaign against some country whose name has dis-appeared (SCHRADER, *Keilinschriftliche Bibliothek*, vol. i. pp. 214, 215) ; it was probably Palestine (WINCKLER, *Alttestamentliche Untersuchungen*, p. 17). The passages in the *Books of Kings* (2 *Kings* xvii.

Hoshea, who had ascended the throne with the consent of Tiglath-pileser, was unable to keep them quiet. The whole of Galilee and Gilead was now an Assyrian province, subject to the governor of Damascus; Jerusalem, Moab, Ammon, and the Bedâwin had transferred their allegiance to Nineveh; and Israel, with merely the central tribes of Ephraim, Manasseh, and Benjamin left, was now barely equal in area and population to Judah. Their tribute weighed heavily on the Israelites; passing armies had laid waste their fields, and townsmen, merchants, and nobles alike, deprived of their customary resources, fretted with impatience under the burdens and humiliations imposed on them by their defeat; convinced of their helplessness, they again looked beyond their own borders for some nation or individual who should restore to them their lost prosperity. Amid the tottering fortunes of their neighbours, Egypt alone stood erect, and it was, therefore, to Egypt that they turned their eyes. Negotiations were opened, not with Pharaoh himself, but with Shabi, one of the petty kings on the eastern frontier of the Delta, whose position made him better qualified than any other to deal with Syrian affairs.[1] Hannon of Gaza had by this time returned from exile, and it was, doubtless, owing to Shabi's support that he had been able to drive out the Assyrian generals and recover his crown.[2] The Israelite aristocracy was led away by his example,

1–6, and xviii. 9–12) which deal with the close of the kingdom of Israel, have been interpreted in such a way as to give us two campaigns by Shalmaneser against Hoshea: (1) Hoshea having failed to pay the tribute imposed upon him by Tiglath-pileser, Shalmaneser made war upon him and compelled him to resume its payment (2 *Kings* xvii. 1–3); (2) Hoshea having intrigued with Egypt, and declined to pay tribute, Shalmaneser again took the field against him, made him prisoner, and besieged Samaria for three years (2 *Kings* xvii. 4–6; xviii. 9–12). The first expedition must, in this case, have taken place in 727, while the second must have lasted from 725–722 (TIELE, *Babylonisch-assyrische Geschichte*, pp. 237, 238). Most modern historians believe that the Hebrew writer has ascribed to Shalmaneser the subjection of Hoshea which was really the act of Tiglath-pileser, as well as the final war against Israel (STADE, *Geschichte des Volkes Israel*, vol. i. p. 600, note 1; HOMMEL, *Geschichte Babyloniens und Assyriens*, pp. 674–676; KITTEL, *Geschichte der Hebräer*, vol. ii. pp. 295, 296): according to Winckler, the two portions of the narrative must have been borrowed from two different versions of the final war, which the final editor inserted one after the other, heedless of the contradictions contained in them (*Alttestamentliche Untersuchungen*, pp. 15–25).

[1] This individual is called Sua, Seveh, and So in the Hebrew text (2 *Kings* xvii. 4), and the LXX. gives the transliteration Sebek side by side with Sêgôs. He is found again under the forms Shibahi, Shabi, Shabé, in Sargon's inscriptions (*Annals*, ll. 27, 29; *Great Inscription of Khorsabad*, ll. 26, 27, Winckler's edit., pp. 7, 101): Oppert was the first to identify him with Shabaku of the XXVth dynasty, and read the title which accompanies the name of Shabi in Assyrian as *shiltanu* = sultan (OPPERT, *Les Inscriptions assyriennes des Sargonides*, p. 22; *Grande Inscription du Palais de Khorsabad*, pp. 74, 75, and *Mémoire sur les rapports de l'Égypte et de l'Assyrie*, pp. 12–14), while Hincks followed Rawlinson in rendering it *turtanu*, the title applied to the commander-in-chief of the Assyrian armies, though he accepted Oppert's identification (*Assyrian Discovery*, in the *Athenæum*, 1863, vol. ii. p. 524). Rawlinson at first refused to recognise as a king of Egypt a person bearing the title *tartan*, and though obliged to admit the identification with Sabaco, he suggested that the reference in Sargon's text must have been made to Sabaco before he came to the throne, while he was still merely a general in the Egyptian army (*Assyrian Discovery*, in the *Athenæum*, 1863, vol. ii. p. 247, note 18); later on, Stade absolutely declined to admit any identity between Sabaco and Sua, maintaining that the latter was merely one of the petty kings of the Delta (*De Isaiæ Vaticiniis Æthiopicis*, pp. 39, 40, 54–56), but his opinion did not gain acceptance until Winckler took it up afresh and completed the evidence in its favour (*Untersuchungen zur Altorientalischen Geschichte*, pp. 92–94, 106–108).

[2] This seems to be the inference from Sargon's inscription, in which he is referred to as relying on the army of Shabi, the *tartan* of Egypt (*Annals of Sargon*, ll. 27–29; *Great Inscr. of Khorsabad*, ll. 26, 27).

but Shalmaneser hastened to the spot before the Egyptian bowmen had time to cross the isthmus.   Hoshea begged for mercy, and was deported into Assyria and condemned to lifelong imprisonment.[1]   Though deserted by her king, Samaria did not despair; she refused to open her gates, and, being strongly fortified, compelled the Assyrians to lay regular siege to the city.   It would seem that at one moment, at the beginning of operations, when it was rumoured on all sides that Pharaoh would speedily intervene, Ahaz began to fear for his own personal safety, and seriously considered whether it would not be wiser to join forces with Israel or with Egypt.[2]   The rapid sequence of events, however, backed by the counsel of Isaiah, speedily recalled him to a more reasonable view of the situation.   The prophet showed him Samaria spread out before him like one of those wreaths of flowers which the guests at a banquet bind round their brows, and which gradually fade as their wearers drink deeper and deeper.   " Woe to the crown of pride of the drunkards of Ephraim, and to the fading flower of his glorious beauty, which is on the head of the fat valley of them that are overcome with wine.   Behold, the Lord hath a mighty and strong one; as a tempest of hail, a destroying storm, as a tempest of mighty waters overflowing, shall he cast down to the earth with violence.   The crown of the pride of the drunkards of Ephraim shall be trodden underfoot, and the fading flower of his glorious beauty, which is on the head of the fat valley, shall be as the first ripe fig before the summer; which when he that looketh upon it seeth, while it is yet in his hand he eateth it up."   While the cruel fate of the perverse city was being thus accomplished, Jahveh Sabaoth was to be a crown of glory to those of His children who remained faithful to Him; but Judah, far from submitting itself to His laws, betrayed Him even as Israel had done. Its prophets and priests were likewise distraught with drunkenness; they staggered under the effects of their potations, and turned to scorn the true prophet sent to proclaim to them the will of Jehovah.   " Whom," they stammered between their hiccups—" whom will He teach knowledge? and whom will He make to understand the message? them that are weaned from the milk and drawn from the breasts?   For it is precept upon precept, precept

---

[1]   2 *Kings* xvii. 4.

[2]   The *Second Book of Kings* (xviii. 9, 10; cf. xvii. 6) place the beginning of the siege of Samaria in the seventh year of Hoshea (= fourth year of Hezekiah), and the capture of the town in the ninth year of Hoshea (= sixth year of Hezekiah); further on it adds that Sennacherib's campaign against Hezekiah took place in the fourteenth year of the latter's reign (2 *Kings* xviii. 13; cf. *Isa.* xxxvi. 1). Now, Sennacherib's campaign against Hezekiah took place (as will be shown later on, in Chapter III. of the present work) in 702 B.C., and Samaria was captured in 722 (cf. p. 216, *infra*). The synchronisms in the Hebrew narrative are therefore fictitious, and rest on no real historical basis—at any rate, in so far as the king who occupied the throne of Judah at the time of the fall of Samaria is concerned; Ahaz was still alive at that date, and continued to reign till 716 or 715 (ED. MEYER, *Geschichte des Alterthums*, vol. i. p. 433; STADE, *Geschichte des Volkes Israel*, vol. i. p. 605), or perhaps only till 720 (WINCKLER, *Alttestamentliche Untersuchungen*, pp. 78–80, 135–142, and *Geschichte Israels*, vol. i. pp. 180, 181; C. NIEBUHR, *Die Chronologie der Geschichte Israels*, pp. 22, 23).

upon precept, line upon line, line upon line, here a little and there a little!" And sure enough it was by the mouth of a stammering people, by the lips of the Assyrians, that Jahveh was to speak to them. In vain did the prophet implore them: "This is the rest, give ye rest to him that is weary;" they did not listen to him, and now Jahveh turns their own gibes against them: "Precept upon precept, precept upon precept, line upon line, line upon line, here a little and there a little,"—"that they may go and fall backward, and be broken and snared and taken." There was to be no hope of safety for Jerusalem unless it gave up all dependence on human counsels, and trusted solely to God for protection.[1] Samaria was doomed; this was the general belief, and men went about repeating it after Isaiah, each in his own words; every one feared lest the disaster should spread to Judah also, and that Jahveh, having once determined to have done with the northern kingdom, would turn His wrath against that of the south as well. Micah the Morashtite, a prophet born among the ranks of the middle class, went up and down the land proclaiming misery to be the common lot of the two sister nations sprung from the loins of Jacob, as a punishment for their common errors and weaknesses. "The Lord cometh forth out of His place, and will come and tread upon the high places of the earth. And the mountains shall be molten under Him, and the valleys shall be cleft, as wax before the fire, as waters that are poured down a steep place. For the transgression of Jacob is all this, and for the sins of the house of Israel. What is the transgression of Jacob? is it not Samaria? and what are the high places of Judah? are they not Jerusalem?" The doom pronounced against Samaria was already being carried out, and soon the hapless city was to be no more than "an heap of the field, and as the plantings of a vineyard; and I will pour down the stones thereof into the valley," saith the Lord, "and I will discover the foundations thereof. And all her graven images shall be beaten to pieces, and all her hires shall be burned with fire, and all her idols will I lay desolate: for of the hire of an harlot hath she gathered them, and unto the hire of an harlot shall they return." Yet, even while mourning over Samaria, the prophet cannot refrain from thinking of his own people, for the terrible blow which had fallen on Israel "is come even unto Judah; it reacheth unto the gate of my people, even to Jerusalem."[2] Doubtless the Assyrian generals kept a watchful eye upon Ahaz during the whole time of the siege, from 724 to 722, and when once the first heat of enthusiasm had cooled,

---

[1] *Isa.* xxviii. Giesebrecht has given it as his opinion that only verses 1-6, 23-29 of the prophecy were delivered at this epoch: the remainder he believes to have been written during Sennacherib's campaign against Judah, and suggests that the prophet added on his previous oracle to them, thus diverting it from its original application (*Beiträge zur Iesajakritik*, pp. 53-72). Others, such as Stade and Wellhausen, regard the opening verses as embodying a mere rhetorical figure. Jerusalem, they say, appeared to the prophet as though changed into Samaria, and it is this transformed city which he calls "the crown of pride of the drunkards of Ephraim."   [2] *Micah* i. 3-9.

the presence of so formidable an army within striking distance must have greatly helped the king to restrain the ill-advised tendencies of some of his subjects. Samaria still held out when Shalmaneser died at Babylon in the month of Tebeth, 722. Whether he had no son of fit age to succeed him, or whether a revolution, similar to that which had helped to place Tiglath-pileser on the throne, broke out as soon as he had drawn his last breath, is not quite clear. At any rate, Sargon, an officer who had served under him, was proclaimed king on the 22nd day of Tebeth, and his election was approved by the whole of Assyria. After some days of hesitation, Babylon declined to recognise him, and took the oath of allegiance to a Kaldu named Marduk-abalidinna,[1] or Merodach-baladan. While these events were taking place in the heart of the empire, Samaria succumbed; perhaps to famine, but more probably to force. It was sacked and dismantled, and the bulk of its population, amounting to 27,280 souls, were carried away into Mesopotamia and distributed along the Balîkh, the Khabur, the banks of the river of Gozân, and among the towns of the Median frontier.[2] Sargon made the whole territory into a province; an Assyrian governor was installed in the palace of the kings of Israel, and soon the altars of the strange gods smoked triumphantly by the side of the altars of Jahveh (722 B.C.).[3]

Thus fell Samaria, and with Samaria the kingdom of Israel, and with Israel the last of the states which had aspired, with some prospect of success, to rule over Syria. They had risen one after another during the four centuries

[1] *Pinches' Babylonian Chronicle*, col. i. ll. 29–33; WINCKLER, *Die Babylonische Chronik B*, in SCHRADER, *Keilinschriftliche Bibliothek*, vol. ii. pp. 276, 277.

[2] *Annals of Sargon*, ll. 10–17; *Great Inscription of Khorsabad*, ll. 23–25; WINCKLER's edit., pp. 4, 5, 100, 101. Sargon does not mention where he deported the Israelites to, but we learn this from the *Second Book of Kings* (xvii. 6; xviii. 11); as to the emendation *Balikh* for *Calah*, cf. WINCKLER, *Alttestamentliche Untersuchungen*, pp. 108–110. There has been much controversy as to whether Samaria was taken by Shalmaneser, as the Hebrew chronicler seems to believe (2 *Kings* xvii. 3–6; xviii. 9, 10), or by Sargon, as the Assyrian scribes assure us. At first, several scholars suggested a solution of the difficulty by arguing that Shalmaneser and Sargon were one and the same person (RAWLINSON, in the *J. R. As. Soc.*, vol. xii. p. 419; HAIGH, *Sardanapallus, his Place in History*, in the *Zeitschrift*, 1870, p. 88, note; SAYCE, *Ueber den Zerstörer Samaria's*, and *Der Belagerer Samaria's*, in *Studien und Kritiken*, 1871, pp. 318–322; 1872, pp. 722–734); afterwards the theory took shape that Samaria was really captured in the reign of Shalmaneser, but by Sargon, who was in command of the besieging army at the time, and who transferred this achievement, of which he was naturally proud, to the beginning of his own reign (VIGOUROUX, *La Bible et les Découvertes modernes*, 6th edit., pp. 555–558). The simplest course seems to be to accept for the present the testimony of contemporary documents, and place the fall of Samaria at the beginning of the reign of Sargon, being the time indicated by Sargon in his inscriptions.

[3] 2 *Kings* xvii. 24–41, a passage to which I shall have occasion to refer farther on in the present volume. The following is a list of the kings of Israel, after the division of the tribes:—

I. JEROBOAM I.	VI. OMRI.	XI. JEHOAHAZ.	XVI. MENAHEM.
II. *NADAB.*	VII. *AHAB.*	XII. JEHOASH.	XVII. *PEKAHIAH.*
III. BAASHA.	VIII. *AHAZIAH.*	XIII. JEROBOAM II.	XVIII. *PEKAH.*
IV. *ELAH.*	IX. *JORAM.*	XIV. *ZECHARIAH.*	XIX. HOSHEA.
V. *ZIMRI.*	X. JEHU.	XV. *SHALLUM.*	

[In this table father and son are shown by a perpendicular line. The king's name in italics signifies that he died a violent death.—TR.]

in which the absence of the stranger had left them masters of their own fate—
the Hittites in the North, the Hebrews and the Philistines in the South, and
the Aramæans and Damascus in the centre; each one of these races had
enjoyed its years of glory and ambition in the course of which it had seemed
to prevail over its rivals. Then those whose territory lay at the extremities
began to feel the disadvantages of their isolated position, and after one or two
victories gave up all hope of ever establishing a supremacy over the whole
country. The Hittite sphere of influence never at any time extended much
further southwards than the sources of the Orontes, while that of

the Hebrews in their palmiest
days cannot have gone beyond
the vicinity of Hamath. And
even progress thus far had cost
both Hebrews and Hittites a
struggle so exhausting that they
could not long maintain it. No
sooner did they relax their efforts,
than those portions of Cœle-
Syria which they had annexed
to their original territory, being
too remote from the seat of
power to feel its full attraction,
gradually detached themselves
and resumed their independence,
their temporary suzerains being
too much exhausted by the intensity of their own exertions to
retain hold over them. Damascus, which lay almost in the
centre, at an equal distance from

SARGON OF ASSYRIA AND HIS VIZIER.[1]

the Euphrates and the " river of Egypt," could have desired no better position for
grouping the rest of Syria round her. If any city had a chance of establishing a
single kingdom, it was Damascus, and Damascus alone. But lulled to blissful
slumbers in her shady gardens, she did not awake to political life and to the desire
of conquest until after all the rest, and at the very moment when Nineveh was beginning to recover from her early reverses. Both Ben-hadads had had a free hand
given them during the half-century which followed, and they had taken advantage
of this respite to reduce Cœle-Syria, the Lebanon, Arvadian Phœnicia, Hamath,
and the Hebrews—in fact, two-thirds of the whole country—to subjection, and

[1] Drawn by Faucher-Gudin, from a sketch by Flandin in BOTTA, *Le Monument de Ninive*, vol. i. pl. 12.

to organise that league of the twelve kings which reckoned Ahab of Israel among its leaders. This rudimentary kingdom had scarcely come into existence, and its members had not yet properly combined, when Shalmaneser III. arose and launched his bands of veterans against them; it however successfully withstood the shock, and its stubborn resistance at the beginning of the struggle shows us what it might have done, had its founders been allowed time in which to weld together the various elements at their disposal. As it was, it was doomed to succumb—not so much to the superiority of the enemy as to the insubordination of its vassals and its own internal discords. The league of the twelve kings did not survive Ben-hadad II.; Hazael and his successors wore themselves out in repelling the attacks of the Assyrians and in repressing the revolts of Israel; when Tiglath-pileser III. arrived on the scene, both princes and people, alike at Damascus and Samaria, were so spent that even their final alliance could not save them from defeat. Its lack of geographical unity and political combination had once more doomed Syria to the servitude of alien rule; the Assyrians, with methodical procedure, first conquered and then made vassals of all those states against which they might have hurled their battalions in vain, had not fortune kept them divided instead of uniting them in a compact mass under the sway of a single ruler. From Carchemish to Arpad, from Hamath to Damascus and Samaria, their irresistible advance had led the Assyrians on towards Egypt, the only other power which still rivalled their prestige in the eyes of the world; and now, at Gaza, on the frontier between Africa and Asia, as in days gone by on the banks of the Euphrates or the Balîkh, these two powers waited face to face, hand on hilt, each ready to stake the empire of the Asiatic world on a single throw of the dice.

SARGON OF ASSYRIA AND SENNACHERIB
(722-681 B.C.).

SARGON AS A WARRIOR AND AS A BUILDER—THE STRUGGLE OF SENNACHERIB WITH JUDÆA
AND EGYPT—DESTRUCTION OF BABYLON.

The origin of Sargon II.: the revolt of Babylon, Merodach-baladan and Elam—The kingdom of Elam from the time of the first Babylonian empire; the conquests of Shutruk-nakhunta I.; the princes of Malamîr—The first encounter of Assyria and Elam, the battle of Durîlu (721 B.C.)—Revolt of Syria, Iaubîdi of Hamath and Hannon of Gaza—Bocchoris and the XXIVth Egyptian dynasty; the first encounter of Assyria with Egypt, the battle of Raphia (720 B.C.).

Urartu and the coalition of the peoples of the north-east and north-west—Defeat of Zikartu (719 B.C.), of the Tabal (718), of the Khâti (717), of the Mannai, of the Medes and Ellipi (716), and of the Medes (715)—Commencement of XXVth Ethiopian dynasty: Sabaco (716)—The fall of Urzana and Rusas (714) and the formation of an Assyrian province in Cappadocia (713–710)—The revolt and fall of Ashdod.

The defeat of Merodach-baladan and of Shutruk-nakhunta II.: Sargon conquers Babylon (710–709 B.C.)—Success of the Assyrians at Mushki: homage of the Greeks of Cyprus (710)—The buildings of Sargon: Dur-sharrukîn—The gates and walls of Dur-sharrukîn; the city and its population—The royal palace, its courts, the ziggurât, the harem—Revolt of Kummukh (709 B.C.) and of Ellipi (708 B.C.)—Inauguration of Dur-sharrukîn (706 B.C.) —Murder of Sargon (705 B.C.): his character.

The upheaval of the entire Eastern world on the accession of Sennacherib—Revolt of Babylon : return of Merodach-baladan and his efforts to form a coalition against Assyria ; the battle of Kîsh (703 B.C.)—Belibni, King of Babylon (702–699 B.C.)—Sabaco, King of Egypt, Amenertas and Pionkhi, Shabî-toku—Tyre and its kings after Ethbaal II. : Phœnician colonisation in Libya and the foundation of Carthage—The kingdom of Tyre in the time of Tiglath-pileser III. and Sargon : Elulai—Judah and the reforms of Hezekiah : alliance of Judah and Tyre with Egypt, the downfall of the Tyrian kingdom (702 B.C.)—The battle of Altaku and the siege of Jerusalem : Sennacherib encamped before Lachish, his Egyptian expedition, the disaster at Pelusium.

Renewed revolt of Babylon and the Tabal (699 B.C.) : flight of the people of Bît-Yakîn into Elamite territory ; Sennacherib's fleet and descent on Nagîtu (697–696 B.C.)—Khalludush invades Karduniash (695 B.C.) ; Nirgal-ushezîb and Mushesîb-marduk at Babylon (693–689 B.C.)—Sennacherib invades Elam (693 B.C.) : battle of Khalulê (692 B.C.), siege and destruction of Babylon (689 B.C.)—Buildings of Sennacherib at Nineveh : his palace at Kouyunjik ; its decoration with battle, hunting, and building scenes.

THE MOUND OF KHORSABAD, BEFORE BOTTA'S EXCAVATIONS.[1]

CHAPTER III.

SARGON OF ASSYRIA AND SENNACHERIB (722-681 B.C.).

Sargon as a warrior and as a builder—The struggle of Sennacherib with Judæa and Egypt—
Destruction of Babylon.

WHETHER Sargon was even remotely connected with the royal line, is a question which for the present must remain unanswered. He mentions in one of his inscriptions the three hundred princes who had preceded him in the government of Assyria, and three lines further on he refers to the kings his ancestors, but he never mentions his own father by name, and this omission seems to prove that he was not a direct descendant of Shalmaneser V., nor of Tiglath-pileser III., nor indeed of any of their immediate predecessors.[2] It is, however, probable, if not certain, that he could claim some sort of kinship with them, though more or less remote. It was customary for the sovereigns of Nineveh to give their daughters in marriage to important officials or lords of their court, and owing to the constant contraction of such alliances through several centuries, there was hardly a noble family but had some royal blood in its veins; and that of Sargon was probably no exception to the rule. His genealogy was traced by the chroniclers, through

---

[1] Drawn by Boudier, after Flandin (BOTTA, Le Monument de Ninive, pl. 5). The vignette is copied by Faucher-Gudin, from a drawing in the same work, pl. 38.

[2] Cylinder Inscriptions, ll. 45–48, and Bull Inscription, ll. 43–49 (ed. LYON, pp. 34, 35, 42, 43). Oppert conjectured, at first, that Shar-kin meant actual king, established sovereign, true king, and that

several hundred generations of princes, to the semi-mythical heroes who had founded the city of Assur; but as Assur-nazir-pal and his descendants had claimed Bel-kapkapi and Sulili as the founders of their race, the Sargonids chose a different tradition, and drew their descent from Belbâni, son of Adasi.[1] The cause and incidents of the revolution which raised Sargon to the throne are unknown, but we may surmise that the policy adopted with regard to Karduniash was a factor in the case. Tiglath-pileser had hardly entered Babylon before the fascination of the city, the charm of its associations, and the sacred character of the legends which hallowed it, seized upon his imagination; he returned to it twice in the space of two years to "take the hands of Bel," and Shalmaneser V. much preferred it to Calah or Nineveh as a place of residence.[2] The Assyrians doubtless soon became jealous of the favour shown by their princes to their ancient enemy, and their discontent must have doubtless conduced to their decision to raise a new monarch to the throne.[3] The Babylonians, on the other hand, seem to have realised that the change in the dynasty presaged a disadvantageous alteration of government; for as soon as the news reached them a movement was set on foot and search made for a rival claimant to set up in opposition to Sargon.[4] Of all the nations who had

it was a surname of the usurper; he thought the original name of the king appeared in those of the eponym Bel-patis-assur, and of Enemessar mentioned in the Book of Tobit (*Les Inscriptions assyriennes des Sargonides et les Fastes de Ninive*, p. 89; *Grande Inscription du Palais de Khorsabad*, pp. 34–36). Sayce subsequently conjectured that Sargon was the Jareb, King of Assyria, twice mentioned in the Book of Hosea (v. 13 and x. 6), and that the primitive form of the name was either Yaribu or Eribu-Aribu (*Was Jareb the Original Name of Sargon?* in the *Babylonian and Oriental Record*, vol. ii. pp. 18–22; cf., in support of this hypothesis, NEUBAUER, *Sargon Yareb*, in the *Zeitschrift für Assyriologie*, vol. iii. p. 103, and against it, LYON, *The Meaning of Jareb in Hosea*, in the *Record*, vol. ii. pp. 127, 128), or, as Hommel prefers to read it, Irbâ, Iribâ (*Gesch. Bab. und Ass.*, p. 680). A simpler explanation still is to admit that Sargon is the name the usurper received in infancy, which he retained when he ascended the throne (TIELE, *Babylonisch-assyrische Geschichte*, pp. 255, 256); his subjects, both Babylonian and Assyrian, sometimes give him the epithet *arku*, the *later* Sargon (G. SMITH, *Assyrian History*, in the *Zeitschrift*, 1869, p. 93). The spelling varies in such a way as to allow of different readings; sometimes *Sharru-kinu*, the *legitimate king*, sometimes *Sharru-ukin*, the god *has instituted him king* (SCHRADER, *Die Assyrisch-babylonischen Keilinschriften*, pp. 157–163, *Die Sargonstele des Berliner Museums*, p. 28, et seq., and *Die Keilinschriften und das Alte Testament*, 1883, p. 392; cf. LYON, *Keilschrifttexte Sargons*, pp. ix., x., and WINCKLER, *Die Keilschrifttexte Sargons*, vol. i. pp. xiv., xv.).

[1] *Inscription of Negoub*, attributed to Sennacherib (ED. MEYER, *Geschichte des Alterthums*, vol. i. p. 220), but really belonging to Esarhaddon (G. SMITH, *Assyrian History*, in the *Zeitschrift*, 1869, pp. 93, 94), and published by LAYARD, *Inscriptions in the Cuneiform Character*, pl. 35; the truth of this theory is confirmed by the texts of Esarhaddon and Shamash-shumukîn brought together in WINCKLER, *Die Keilschrifttexte Sargons*, vol. i. p. 13, note 1. For Adasi and Bel-bâni or Bel-ibni, cf. *Struggle of the Nations*, p. 118, note 4.

[2] Cf. what is said on this subject, *supra*, pp. 192, 193, 209, 215.

[3] Sargon insists several times on the care he has taken to "make the rights of Assur prevail" (*Cylinder*, 1. 5, in LYON, *Keilschrifttexte Sargons*, pp. 1, 30, 31, 59), or to re-establish the liberties of *Assur and Harrân*, which had long fallen into abeyance (*Inscription des Fastes*, ll. 10, 11, in WINCKLER, *Die Keilschrifttexte Sargons*, vol. i. pp. 96–99).

[4] The succession of events, as indicated in *Pinches' Babylonian Chronicle*, col. i. ll. 29–31, seems indeed to imply that the Babylonians waited to ascertain the disposition of the new king before they decided what line to adopt. In fact, Shalmaneser died in the month Tebeth, and Sargon ascended

in turn occupied the plains of the Lower Euphrates and the marshes bordering on Arabia, the Kaldâ alone had retained their full vitality. They were constantly recruited by immigrants from their kinsfolk of the desert, and the continual infiltration of these semi-barbarous elements kept the race from becoming enervated by contact with the indigenous population, and more than compensated for the losses in their ranks occasioned by war. The invasion of Tiglath-pileser and the consequent deportations of prisoners had decimated

ASSYRIAN SOLDIERS PURSUING KALDÂ REFUGEES IN A BED OF REEDS.[1]

the tribes of Bît-Shilâni, Bît-Shaali, and Bît-Amukkâni, the principalities of the Kaldâ which lay nearest to Babylonian territory, and which had borne the brunt of attack in the preceding period; but their weakness brought into notice a power better equipped for warfare, whose situation in their rear had as a rule hitherto preserved it from contact with the Assyrians, namely, Bît-Yakîn.[2] The continual deposit of alluvial soil at the mouths of the rivers had greatly altered the coast-line from the earliest historic times downwards. The ancient estuary was partly filled up, especially on the western side, where the Euphrates enters the Persian Gulf: a narrow barrier of sand and silt extended

the throne at Assur in the same month, and it was only in the month Nisân that Merodach-baladan was proclaimed king. The three months intervening between the accession of Sargon and that of Merodach-baladan evidently represent a period of indecision, when it was not yet known if the king would follow the policy of his predecessors with regard to Babylon, or adopt a different attitude towards her.

[1] Drawn by Faucher-Gudin, from a bas-relief reproduced in LAYARD, *Monuments of Nineveh*, vol. i. pl. 25.

[2] For these wars of Tiglath-pileser III., cf. *supra*, pp. 190–192.

between the marshes of Arabia and Susiana, at the spot where the streams of fresh water met the tidal waters of the sea, and all that was left of the ancient gulf was a vast lagoon, or, as the dwellers on the banks called it, a kind of brackish river, *Nâr marratum.* Bît-Yakîn occupied the southern and western portions of this district, from the mouth of the Tigris to the edge

A REED-HUT OF THE BEDAWIN OF IRAK.[1]

of the desert. The aspect of the country was constantly changing, and presented no distinctive features; it was a region difficult to attack and easy to defend; it consisted first of a spongy plain, saturated with water, with scattered artificial mounds on which stood the clustered huts of the villages; between this plain and the shore stretched a labyrinth of fens and peat-bogs, irregularly divided by canals and channels freshly formed each year in flood-time, meres strewn with floating islets, immense reed-beds where the neighbouring peasants took refuge from attack, and into which no one would venture to penetrate without hiring some friendly native as a guide.[2] In this fenland dwelt the Kaldâ in their low, small conical huts of reeds, somewhat resembling giant beehives, and in all respects similar to those which the Bedawin of Irak inhabit at the present day. Dur-Yakîn, their capital, was probably situated on

[1] Drawn by Faucher-Gudin, from a photograph in PETERS, *Nippur*, vol. ii. p. 74.
[2] For Bît-Yakîn, cf. FR. DELITZSCH, *Wo lag das Paradies?* p. 203; for the description of the marshes the reader may refer to the illustration on p. 223 of this work, and to the illustrations in the *Dawn of Civilization*, pp. 552, 553.

the borders of the gulf, near the Euphrates, in such a position as to command the mouths of the river. Merodach-baladan, who was King of Bît-Yakîn at the time of Sargon's accession, had become subject to Assyria in 729 B.C., and had paid tribute to Tiglath-pileser, but he was nevertheless the most powerful chieftain who had borne rule over the Chaldæans since the death of Ukînzîr.[1] It was this prince whom the Babylonians chose to succeed Shalmaneser V. He presented himself before the city, was received with acclamation, and prepared without delay to repulse any hostilities on the part of the Assyrians.[2]

He found a well-disposed ally in Elam. From very ancient times the masters of Susa had aspired to the possession of Mesopotamia or the suzerainty over it, and fortune had several times favoured their ambitious designs. On one

[1] Dur-Yakîn was situated on the shores of the Persian gulf, as is proved by a passage in the *Bull Inscription*, ll. 33, 34 (cf. LYON, *Keilschrifttexte Sargons*, pp. 42, 43), where it is stated that Sargon threw into the sea the corpses of the soldiers killed during the siege; the neighbourhood of the Euphrates is implied in the text of the *Inscription des Fastes*, l. 128 (cf. WINCKLER, *Die Keilschrifttexte Sargons*, vol. i. p. 129, et seq.), and the *Annals*, ll. 324, 325 (*ibid.*, pp. 54–57), where the measures taken by Merodach-baladan to defend his capital are described. The name of Bît-Yakîn, and probably also that of Dur-Yakîn, have been preserved to us in the name of Aginis or Aginnê, the name of a city mentioned by Strabo (XV. iii. § 5, p. 729), and by the historians of Alexander (ANDREAS, *Aginis, Ampé, Alexandreia 13*, in PAULY-WISSOWA, *Real-Encyclopädie*, vol. i. pp. 810–816, 1390–1395, 1877–1880). Its site is uncertain, but can be located near the present town of Kornah (BILLERBECK, *Susa*, p. 81, note 1).

[2] The principal authority for the history of Sargon's reign is the text of his *Annals*, discovered at Khorsabad, and published by BOTTA, *Le Monument de Ninive*, pls. 63–92, 105–120, 155–160, and also by WINCKLER, *Die Keilschrifttexte Sargons*, vol. ii. pls. 1–29, in four versions, all much mutilated; the fragments of them have been translated into French by OPPERT, *Les Inscriptions de Dour-Sarkayan*, in PLACE, *Ninive et l'Assyrie*, vol. ii. pp. 309–319, and also by MÉNANT, *Annales des rois d'Assyrie*, pp. 158–179; into English by OPPERT, *The Annals of Sargon*, in the *Records of the Past*, 1st series, vol. viii. pp. 21–56; into German by WINCKLER, *Die Keilschrifttexte Sargons*, vol. i. pp. 2–79 for the three first versions, and pp. 80–95 for the fourth. The information furnished by the *Annals* is supplemented by that obtained from a considerable number of documents, for the most part discovered during the excavations at Khorsabad: (1) *Inscription des Fastes*, published by BOTTA, *op. cit.*, pls. 93–104, 121–154, 181, and by WINCKLER, *op. cit.*, vol. ii. pls. 30–36; translated into French by OPPERT and MÉNANT, *La Grande Inscription du Palais de Khorsabad*, in the *Journal Asiatique*, 1863, vol. i. pp. 5–26, vol. ii. pp. 475–517; 1864, vol. iii. pp. 5–62, 168–201, 209–265, 373–415; 1865, vol. vi. pp. 133–179, 289–330; and again by MÉNANT, *Annales des rois d'Assyrie*, pp. 180–192; into English by OPPERT, *The Great Inscription in the Palace of Khorsabad*, in the *Records of the Past*, 1st series, vol. iv. pp. 1–20; into German by WINCKLER, *op. cit.*, vol. i. pp. 96–135. (2) *The Inscription on the Pavement of the Gateway*, published by BOTTA, *op. cit.*, pp. 1–21; translated into French by MÉNANT, *op. cit.*, pp. 195, 196; into German by WINCKLER, *op. cit.*, vol. i. pp. 136–163. (3) *The Bull Inscription*, published by BOTTA, *op. cit.*, pp. 22–62, and by LYON, *op. cit.*, pls. 13–19; translated into French by OPPERT, *Les Inscr. de Dour-Sarkayan*, in PLACE, *Ninive et l'Assyrie*, vol. ii. pp. 283–291, and by MÉNANT, *op. cit.*, pp. 192–195; into English by OPPERT, *Bull Inscription of Khorsabad*, in the *Records*, 1st series, vol. xi. pp. 15–26; into German by LYON, *op. cit.*, pp. 40–47, 79–81. (4) *The Inscriptions on the back of the Slabs*, published by BOTTA, *op. cit.*, pl. 184, et seq.; translated into French by MÉNANT, *op. cit.*, p. 196, et seq.; into German by WINCKLER, *op. cit.*, vol. i. pp. 164–167. (5) *The Cylinder Inscription*, published by H. RAWLINSON, *Cun. Ins. W. As.*, vol. i. pl. 36; translated into French by OPPERT, *Les Inscr. de Dour-Sarkayan*, in PLACE, *op. cit.*, vol. ii. pp. 291–303, and by MÉNANT, *op. cit.*, pp. 199–204; translated into German by LYON, *op. cit.*, pp. 1–22, 30–39. (6) *Stele of Larnaka*, published by H. RAWLINSON, *op. cit.*, vol. iii. pl. 11; and again, with a German translation by SCHRADER, *Die Sargonsstele des Berliner Museums*, 1882. There are, besides, half a dozen more documents of less importance, which will be referred to as opportunity occurs. For the chronology of the reign of Sargon, cf. TIELE, *Babylonisch-assyrische Geschichte*, pp. 249–282, and WINCKLER, *op. cit.*, vol. i. pp. xiii., xiv.

Q

occasion they had pressed forward their victorious arms as far as the Mediterranean,[1] and from that time forward, though the theatre of their operations was more restricted, they had never renounced the right to interfere in Babylonian affairs, and indeed, not long previously, one of them had reigned for a period of seven years in Babylon in the interval between two dynasties.[2] Our information with regard to the order of succession and the history of these energetic and warlike monarchs is as yet very scanty; their names even are for the most part lost, and only approximate dates can be assigned to those of whom we catch glimpses from time to time.[3] Khumban-numena, the earliest of whom we have any record, exercised a doubtful authority, from Anshân to Susa, somewhere about the fourteenth century B.C., and built a temple to the god Kirisha in his capital, Liyan.[4] His son Undasgal carried on the works begun by his father,[5] but that is all the information the inscriptions afford concerning him, and the mist of oblivion which for a moment lifted and allowed us to discern dimly the outlines of this sovereign, closes in again and hides everything from our view for the succeeding forty or fifty years.

[1] For these earliest Elamite conquests in Babylonia, cf. MASPERO, Struggle of the Nations, pp. 29–40, 47, 49.

[2] For the conflicts between Elam and Karduniash, cf. ID., ibid., pp. 56, et seq., 596, 612–616; and for the Elamite who reigned at Babylon about the tenth century, cf. supra, pp. 4, 5.

[3] These names are in the majority of cases found written on stamped and baked bricks, which have been published by LOFTUS, Lithographic Fac-similes of Inscriptions in the Cuneiform Character, 1852, by FRANÇOIS LENORMANT, Choix de Textes Cunéiformes inédits ou incomplétement publiés, pp. 109–141; by DIEULAFOY, L'Acropole de Suse, pp. 308, 309, 311, 429 (No. 284); and by WEISSBACH, Anzanische Inschriften, pls. i.–v., and Neue Beiträge zur Kunde der Susichen Inschriften, pl. i. They were first compared with the names contained in the Annals of Sargon and his successors, and assimilated to those of the princes who were contemporary with Sennacherib and Assur-bani-pal (FR. LENORMANT, op. cit., pp. 111–113; OPPERT, Les Inscriptions en langue Susienne, in the Mémoires du Congrès International de Paris, 1873, vol. ii. pp. 180, 181; QUENTIN, Textes Susiens, in the Journal Asiatique, 1891, vol. xviii. pp. 152–155); then they were referred to the time of the great Elamite empire, and one of them was identified with that Kudur-Nakhunta who had pillaged Uruk (cf. Struggle of the Nations, p. 37) 1635 years before Assur-bani-pal (BILLERBECK, Susa, pp. 51–56). Finally, they were brought down again to an intermediate period (WINCKLER, Zu den Altsusischen Inschriften, in the Zeitschrift für Assyriologie, vol. vi. pp. 323–326), more precisely, to the fourteenth or thirteenth century B.C. (WEISSBACH, Neue Beiträge zur Kunde der Susischen Inschriften, pp. 733, 734). This last date appears to be justified, at least as the highest permissible, by the mention of Dur-kurigalzu (cf., for the foundation of this town, Struggle of the Nations, p. 596), in a text of Undasgal (OPPERT, op. cit., p. 193).

[4] Jensen was the first to recognise that Liyan was a place-name, and the inscriptions of Shilkhak-Inshusinak add that Liyan was the capital of the kingdom (WEISSBACH, Neue Beiträge zur Kunde der Susischen Inschriften, p. 735); perhaps it was the name of a part of Susa. Khumban-numena has left us no monuments of his own, but he is mentioned on those of his son (OPPERT, op. cit., pp. 191, 192, and Susian Texts, in Records of the Past, 1st ser., vol. vii. pp. 83, 84). Lenormant read the name as Khumban-igash (op. cit., pp. 111–113), and Oppert as Humbabbak-Masnagi, with the variant Hum-masmaki (Les Inscriptions en langue Susienne, p. 181), Winckler as Khum . . . khumashnagi, op. cit., pp. 321, 323); the reading Khumban-numena is Weissbach's (Anzanische Inschriften, p. 127).

[5] OPPERT, Les Inscriptions en langue Susienne, p. 192, where the name is rendered Undas-Arman (cf. ID., ibid., p. 181, and Susian Texts, in the Records of the Past, 1st ser., vol. vii. p. 83, note 2); Lenormant transcribed it Urtaki (Choix de Textes Cunéiformes, pp. 111, 113, 123–126). The reading Untasgal, Undasgal, of Weissbach (Anzanische Inschr., pp. 127, 142) is only provisional: it is not known what Susian god is denoted by the name written AN GAL, "the great god."

About the thirteenth century a gleam once more pierces the darkness, and a race of warlike and pious kings emerges into view—Khalludush-Inshushinak, his son Shutruk-nakhunta, the latter's two sons, Kutur-nakhunta and Shilkhak-Inshushinak,[1] and then perhaps a certain Kutir-khuban.[2] The inscriptions on their bricks boast of their power, their piety, and their inexhaustible wealth. One after another they repaired and enlarged the temple built by Khumban-numena at Liyan, erected sanctuaries and palaces at Susa, fortified their royal citadel, and ruled over Habardîp and the Cossæans as well as over Anshân and Elam.[3] They vigorously contested the possession of the countries on the right bank of the Tigris with the Babylonians, and Shutruk-nakhunta even succeeded in conquering Babylon itself. He deprived Zamâmâ-shu-middin, the last but one of the Cossæan kings, of his sceptre and his life, placed his own son Kutur-nakhunta

BRICK BEARING THE NAME OF THE SUSIAN KING SHILKHAK-INSHUSHINAK.[4]

on the throne, and when the vanquished Babylonians set up Bel-nadinshumu as a rival sovereign, he laid waste Karduniash with fire and sword. After the death of Bel-nadinshumu, the Pashê princes continued to offer resistance, but at first without success. Shutruk-nakhunta had taken away from the temple of Esagilla the famous statue of Bel-Merodach, whose hands had to be taken by each newly

[1] The order of succession of these princes is proved by the genealogies with which their bricks are covered (OPPERT, Les Inscriptions en langue Susienne, pp. 180, 181; WINCKLER, Zu den Altsusischen Inschriften, in the Zeitschrift für Assyriologie, vol. vi. pp. 320–323; WEISSBACH, Neue Beiträge zur Kunde der Susischen Inschr., pp. 732, 733). Jensen has shown that we ought to read Khalludush-Inshushinak and Shilkhak-Inshushinak (Elamitsche Eigennamen, p. 54), instead of the shorter forms Khalludush and Shilkhak read previously.

[2] The mutilated name found in a brick inscription published by Lenormant (Choix de textes Cunéiformes, p. 120, No. 34, 1. 1) has been plausibly restored by Weissbach as Kutir-khuban, and connected with the Kutir-khuban mentioned among the sons of Shilkhak-Inshushinak on a brick in Dieulafoy's collection, in the Louvre (WEISSBACH, Anzanische Inschriften, pp. 147, 148, D, ll. 5, 6, and Neue Beiträge, p. 735).

[3] OPPERT, Les Inscr. en langue Susienne, pp. 192, 193. On the identification of Habardip with the Amardians of classical times, cf. Struggle of the Nations, p. 35, note 1.

[4] Drawn by Faucher-Gudin, from a photograph by MARCEL DIEULAFOY, L'Acropole de Suse, p. 311, Fig. 194. The original was discovered in the excavations of Bender-Bushîr, and is now in the Louvre.

elected king of Babylon, and had carried it off in his waggons to Elam, together with much spoil from the cities on the Euphrates.[1] Nebuchadrezzar I. brought the statue back to Babylon after many vicissitudes, and at the same time recovered most of his lost provinces,[2] but he had to leave at Susa the bulk of the trophies which had been collected there in course of the successful wars. One of these represented the ancient hero Naram-sin standing, mace in hand, on the summit of a hill, while his soldiers forced their way up the slopes, driving before them the routed hosts of Susa. Shutruk-nakhunta left the figures and names untouched, but carved in one corner of the bas-relief a dedicatory inscription, transforming this ancient proof of Babylonian victories over Elam into a trophy of Elamite victories over Babylon. His descendants would assuredly have brought Mesopotamia into lasting subjection, had not the feudal organisation of their empire tolerated the existence of contemporary local dynasties, the members of which often disputed the supreme authority with the rightful king. The dynasty which ruled Habardîp[3] seems to have had its seat of government at Tarrisha in the valley of Malamîr.[4] Three hundred figures carved singly or in groups on the rocks of Kul-Firaun[6] portray its princes and their ministers in every posture of adoration, but most of them have no accompanying inscription. One large

BAS-RELIEF OF NARAM-SIN, TRANSPORTED TO SUSA BY SHUTRUK-NAKHUNTA.[5]

[1] For this episode in the Elamite wars, which was not known when the *Struggle of the Nations* was published, cf. the notice by WINCKLER, *Altorientalische Forschungen*, vol. i. pp. 534–543. The name of the king is destroyed on the Babylonian document, but the mention of Kutur-nakhunta as his son obliges us, till further information comes to light, to recognise in him the Shutruk-nakhunta of the bricks of Susa, who also had a son Kutur-nakhunta. This would confirm the restoration of Shutruk-nakhunta as the name of a sovereign who boasts, in a mutilated inscription, that he had pushed his victories as far as the Tigris, and even up to the Euphrates (FR. LENORMANT, *Choix de Textes Cunéiformes*, p. 128, No. 42; OPPERT, *Les Inscr. en langue Susienne*, pp. 192, 193).

[2] For the conquest of Namar, cf. *Struggle of the Nations*, pp. 612–616.

[3] The prince represented on the bas-reliefs gives himself the title Apirra, the man of Apîr, Apirti, or Habardîp (*Great Inscription of Malamîr*, l. 5).

[4] Tarrisha is, like Liyan (cf. *supra*, p. 226, note 4), the name of a town (WEISSBACH, *Neue Beiträge, zur Kunde der Susischen Inschriften*, p. 774), doubtless the capital of the fief of Malamîr; it is probably represented by the considerable ruins which Layard identified as the remains of the Sassanid city of Aidej (*A Description of the Province of Kúzistan*, in the *Journal of the R. Geog. Soc.*, 1846, vol. xvi. p. 74, et seq.).

[5] Drawn by Boudier, from a photograph by M. de Morgan, published in J. DE MORGAN, *Compte rendu sommaire des Travaux archéologiques exécutés du 3 novembre 1897 au 1er juin 1898*.

[6] The monuments of Malamîr were first described by Layard (*op. cit.*, pp. 74–80) and by Bode

bas-relief, however, forms an exception, and from its legend we learn the name
of Khanni, son of Takhkhi-khîkhutur.[1] This prince, even if possessed of no
royal protocol, was none the less a powerful and wealthy personage. His figure
dominates the picture, the central space of which it completely fills;[2] his

THE GREAT ROCK BAS-RELIEF OF MALAMÎR.[3]

expression is calm, but somewhat severe. His head is covered by a low cap,
from which long locks escape and flow over his shoulders; the hair on his

(*Notes on a Journey from Behbehán to Shúster*, in the *J. R. G. S.*, 1843, vol. xii. p. 86, et seq.). They
have been published by Layard (*Inscr. in the Cuneiform Character*, pls. 31, 32, 36, 37), by Flandin,
from the drawings of Baron de Bode (*Voyage en Perse*, vol. iv. pls. 226, 228), by Dieulafoy (*Note
relative à la découverte sur le tombeau de Darius de sept Inscriptions nouvelles*, in the *Revue Archéologique*, 1885, vol. vi. pl. xxiv., and *L'Acropole de Suse*, p. 33, Fig. 38). The inscriptions have been
studied by Oppert (*Les Inscr. en langue Susienne*, pp. 199–216), by Sayce (*The Inscr. of Mal-Amir and
the Language of the Second Column of the Akhæmenian Inscriptions*, in the *International Oriental Congress at Leyden*, vol. ii. pp. 637–756), and by Weissbach (*Neue Beiträge zur Kunde des Susischen
Inschriften*, pp. 742–777, and pls. ii.–iv.).

[1] The name of Khanni, already recognised by Oppert (*Les Inscr. en langue Susienne*, p. 215), has
been explained by Sayce as *the desirable*, and that of his father, Takhkhi-khîkhutur, as *help|this thy
servant* (*The Inscr. of Mal-Amir*, pp. 714, 715; cf. JENSEN, *Elamitische Eigennamen*, pp. 216, 225).

[2] Perrot and Chipiez (*Histoire de l'Art dans l'Antiquité*, vol. v. pp. 774, 775), misled by the analogy
of the Hittite bas-relief at Ibrîz (cf. the reproduction of this bas-relief in the *Struggle of the Nations*,
p. 653), took the largest figure for the image of a god. The inscription engraved on the robe, *U
Khanni shak Takkhi-khikutur*, "I am Khanni, son of Takhkhi-khîkhutur," leaves no doubt that the
figure represents the prince himself, and not a divinity.

[3] Drawn by Faucher-Gudin, from a photograph by Babin and Houssay, published by MARCEL
DIEULAFOY, in *Note relative*, etc. (quoted above), and in *L'Acropole de Suse*, p. 33, Fig. 28; cf.
FLANDIN, *Voyage en Perse*, vol. iv. pp. 226–228, and PERROT and CHIPIEZ, *op. cit.*, vol. iv. p. 775.

face is symmetrically curled above the level of his mouth, and terminates in a pointed beard. The figure is clothed from head to foot in a stiff robe and mantle adorned with tufted fringes, and borders of embroidered rosettes; a girdle at the waist completes the misleading resemblance to the gala-dress of a Ninevite monarch. The hands are crossed on the breast in an attitude of contemplation, while the prince gazes thoughtfully at a sacrifice which is being offered on his behalf. At the bottom of the picture stands a small altar, behind which a priest in a short tunic seems to be accomplishing some ceremonial rite, while two men are cutting the throat of a ram. Higher up the heads of three rams lie beside their headless trunks, which are resting on the ground, feet in the air, while a servant brandishes a short sword with which he is about to decapitate the fourth beast. Above these, again, three musicians march in procession, one playing on a harp, another on a five-stringed lyre, and the third on a tambourine. An attendant holding a bow, and the minister Shutsururazi, stand quietly waiting till the sacrifice is accomplished. The long text which runs across several of the figures is doubtless a prayer, and contains the names of peoples and princes mingled with those of deities. The memory of these provincial chiefs would be revived, and more of their monuments discovered, if the mountains and inaccessible valleys of ancient Elam could be thoroughly explored: it is evident, from the small portion of their history which has been brought to light, that they must have been great sources of trouble to the dynasties which reigned in Susa, and that their revolts must often have jeopardised the safety of the empire, in spite of the assistance afforded by the Aramæans from the tenth or eleventh centuries onwards. All the semi-nomadic tribes which densely peopled the banks of the Tigris, and whose advance towards the north had been temporarily favoured by the weakness of Assyria—the Gambulu, the Pukudu, the Rutu, and the Itua—had a natural tendency to join forces with Elam for the purpose of raiding the wealthy cities of Chaldæa, and this alliance, or subjection, as it might be more properly termed, always insured them against any reprisals on the part of their victims.[1] The unknown king who dwelt at Susa in 745 B.C. committed the error of allowing Tiglath-pileser to crush these allies.[2] Khumban-igash, who succeeded this misguided monarch in 742 B.C.,[3] did not take up arms to defend Bît-Amukkâni and the

---

[1] For the advance of these Aramæan tribes during the first half of the seventh century, cf. *supra*, pp. 118, 119.

[2] For this campaign of Tiglath-pileser against the Aramæan tribes bordering on the Tigris, cf. *supra*, pp. 140–142.

[3] The date of his accession is furnished by the passage in *Pinches' Babylonian Chronicle*, col. i. l. 9 (cf. WINCKLER, *Die Babylonische Chronik B*, in SCHRADER, *Keilinschriftliche Bibliothek*, vol. ii. pp. 274, 275), where it is stated that he ascended the throne of Elam in the fifth year of

other states of the Kaldâ from 731 to 729,[1] but experience must have taught him that he had made a mistake in remaining an unmoved spectator of their misfortunes ; for when Merodach-baladan, in quest of allies, applied to him, he unhesitatingly promised him his support.[2]

Assyria and Elam had hitherto seldom encountered one another on the field of battle. A wide barrier of semi-barbarous states had for a long time held them apart, and they would have had to cross the territory of the Babylonians or the Cossæans before coming into contact with each other. Tiglath-pileser I., however, had come into conflict with the northern districts of Elam towards the end of the twelfth century B.C.,[3] and more recently the campaigns of Assur-nazir-pal, Shalmaneser III., and Rammân-nirâri had frequently brought these sovereigns into contact with tribes under the influence of Susa; but the wildness and poverty of the country, and the difficulties it offered to the manœuvres of large armies, had always prevented the Assyrian generals from advancing far into its mountainous regions. The annexation of Aramæan territory beyond the Tigris, and the conquest of Babylon by Tiglath-pileser III., at length broke through the barrier and brought the two powers face to face at a point where they could come into conflict without being impeded by almost insurmountable natural obstacles, namely, in the plains of the Umliash and the united basins of the Lower Ulai and the Uknu. Ten years' experience had probably sufficed to convince Khumban-igash of the dangers to which the neighbourhood of the Assyrians exposed his subjects. The vigilant watch which the new-comers kept over their frontier rendered raiding less easy : and if one of the border chieftains were inclined to harry, as of old, an unlucky Babylonian or Cossæan village, he ran the risk of an encounter with a well-armed force, or of being plundered in turn by way of reprisal.[4] An irregular but abundant source of revenue was thus curtailed, without taking into consideration the wars to which such incidents must perforce lead sooner or later. Even unaided the Elamites considered themselves capable of repelling any attack ; allied with the Babylonians or the Kaldâ, they felt certain of victory in any circumstances. Sargon realised this fact almost as fully as did the Elamites themselves ; as soon, therefore, as his spies had forewarned him that an invasion

---

Nabonazir. The Assyrian and Babylonian scribes assimilated the Susian *b* to the *m*, and also suppressed the initial aspirate of the Elamite name, writing generally Umman-igash for Khumban-igash.

[1] For this second campaign, cf. *supra*, pp. 190–192.

[2] Sargon declares distinctly that Merodach-baladan had invoked the aid of Khumban-igash (*Fastes*, ll. 122, 123).

[3] For the campaign of Tiglath-pileser against the tribes settled in the northern districts of Elam, cf. *Struggle of the Nations*, pp. 662, 663.

[4] For frontier episodes of this kind in the reign of Assur-bani-pal, cf. the texts quoted by JOHNSTON, *The Epistolary Literature of the Assyrians and Babylonians*, pp. 134–146.

was imminent, he resolved to take the initiative and crush his enemies singly before they succeeded in uniting their forces. Khumban-igash had advanced as far as the walls of Durîlu, a stronghold which commanded the Umliash, and he there awaited the advent of his allies before laying siege to the town : it was, however, the Assyrian army which came to meet him and offered him battle. The conflict was a sanguinary one, as became an engagement between such valiant foes, and both sides claimed the victory. The Assyrians maintained their ground, forcing the Elamites to evacuate their positions, and tarried some weeks longer to chastise those of their Aramæan subjects who had made common cause with the enemy : they carried away the Tumuna, who had given up their sheikh into the hands of the emissaries of the Kaldâ, and transported the whole tribe, without Merodach-baladan making any attempt to save his allies, although his army had not as yet struck a single blow.[1] Having accomplished this act of vengeance, the Assyrians suspended operations and returned to Nineveh to repair their losses, probably intending to make a great effort to regain the whole of Babylonia in the ensuing year. Grave events which occurred elsewhere prevented them, however, from carrying this ambitious project into effect. The fame of their war against Elam had spread abroad in the Western provinces of the empire, and doubtless exaggerated accounts circulated with regard to the battle of Durîlu had roused the spirit of dissatisfaction in the west. Sargon had scarcely seated himself securely on a throne to which he was not the direct heir, when he was menaced by Elam and repudiated by Chaldæa, and it remained to be seen whether his resources would prove equal to maintaining the integrity of his empire, or whether the example set by Merodach-baladan would not speedily be imitated by all who groaned under the Assyrian yoke. Since the decline of Damascus and Arpad, Hamath had again taken a prominent place in Northern Syria : prompt submission had saved this city from destruction in the time of Tiglath-pileser III.,[2] and it had since prospered under the foreign rule; it was, therefore, on Hamath that all hopes of deliverance still cherished by rulers and people now centred. A low-

---

[1] The history of this first campaign against Merodach-baladan, which is found in a mutilated condition in the *Annals of Sargon*, ll. 18–23 (cf. WINCKLER, *Die Keilschrifttexte Sargons*, vol. i. pp. 4–7), exists nowhere else in a complete form, but the facts are very concisely referred to in the *Fastes*, ll. 23, 121–123, and in the *Cylinders*, l. 17 (cf. LYON, *Keilschrifttexte Sargon's*, pp. 32, 33). The general sequence of events is indicated by *Pinches' Babylonian Chronicle*, col. i. ll. 33–37, but the author places them in 720 B.C., the second year of Merodach-baladan, contrary to the testimony of the *Annals*, and attributes the victory to the Elamites in the battle of Durîlu, in deference to Babylonian patriotism. Tiele was the first to unravel the order of events (*Babylonisch-assyrische Geschichte*, pp. 239–258, 259, 614, 615), and his conclusions have been adopted in their entirety by Winckler (*op. cit.*, vol. i. pp. xvii., xviii.; *Geschichte Babyloniens und Assyriens*, pp. 125, 126, 237, 238). The course of events after the battle of Durîlu seems to prove clearly that the Assyrians remained masters of the field.

[2] For the revolt of Hamath, cf. *supra*, pp. 150–153.

born fellow, a smith named Iaubîdi,[1] rose in rebellion against the prince of Hamath for being mean-spirited enough to pay tribute, proclaimed himself king, and in the space of a few months revived under his own leadership the coalition which Hadadezer and Rezon II. had formed in days gone by. Arpad and Bît-Agusi, Zimyra and Northern Phœnicia, Damascus and its dependencies, all expelled their Assyrian garrisons, and Samaria, though still suffering from its overthrow, summoned up courage to rid itself of its governor.[2] Meanwhile, Hannon of Gaza, recently reinstated in his city by Egyptian support,[3] was carrying on negotiations with a view to persuading Egypt to interfere in the affairs of Syria. The last of the Tanite Pharaohs, Psamuti, was just dead, and Bocchoris, who had long been undisputed master of the Delta, had now ventured to assume the diadem openly (722 B.C.), a usurpation which the Ethiopians, fully engaged in the Thebaid and on the Upper Nile, seemed to regard with equanimity. As soon as the petty kings and feudal lords had recognised his suzerainty, Bocchoris listened favourably to the entreaties of Hannon, and promised to send an army to Gaza under the command of his general Shabê.[4] Sargon, threatened with the loss of the entire western half of his empire, desisted for a time from his designs on Babylon. Khumban-igash was wise enough to refrain from provoking an enemy who left him in peace, and Merodach-baladan did not dare to enter the lists without the support of his confederate : the victory of Durîlu, though it had not succeeded in gaining a province for Nineveh, had at least secured the south-eastern frontier from attack, at all events for so long as it should please Sargon to remain at a distance.

[1] This person is called Iaubîdi in the *Fastes*, l. 38, and in the *Nimroud Inscription*, l. 8, but Ilubîdi in the *Annals of Sargon*, l. 23, and the earliest Assyriologists were struck with the identity which these variants seemed to establish between the divine names Iahu and Ilu. The ideogram which follows his name is translated *smith* by OPPERT, *Great Inscription in the Palace of Khorsabad*, in the *Records of the Past*, 1st ser., vol. ix. p. 6, and *peasant, labourer*, by WINCKLER, *Altorientalische Forschungen*, vol. i. p. 548.

[2] *Annals of Sargon*, l. 25 ; cf. WINCKLER, *Die Keilschrifttexte Sargons*, vol. i. pp. 6, 7.

[3] For this restoration, cf. *supra*, p. 213.

[4] As long as the name Shibi, Shibahi, Shabê, in the Assyrian texts was identified with that of Shabaka (cf. *supra*, p. 213, note 1), it was necessary to recognise Sabaco in the king who supported Hannon and was conquered by Sargon. Since this hypothesis has been abandoned, the ascertained dates of Egyptian chronology force us to place these events in the reign of Bocchoris. By adding up the number of years assigned by the most trustworthy tradition to the reigns of the three Ethiopian kings, Sabaco twelve years, Shabîtoku twelve years, Taharqa (Tirhakah) twenty-six years, we arrive at 716 for the approximate date of the death of Bocchoris, and 722 for his accession. One tradition assigned him a reign of forty or forty-four years (MANETHO, in MÜLLER-DIDOT, *Fragmenta Historicum Græcorum*, vol. ii. p. 592), and M. Révillout consequently attributes to him a contract, preserved in the Louvre, which is dated " the sixteenth year," without giving the name of the king (*Notice des Papyrus démotiques archaïques*, pp. 212, 213); if this contract really belongs to the Ethiopian period, as it seems to do, it must belong to the reign of Taharqa. I agree with Lepsius (*Königsbuch*, pp. 86, 87, 91), Lauth (*Aus Ægyptens Vorzeit*, p. 428), and E. de Rougé (*Inscription historique du roi Piânchi-Mériamoun*, p. 26) in following the tradition which assigns a reign of only six years to Bocchoris, a tradition which agrees better with the known facts of contemporary history. The only authentic date of his reign is the sixth year, on the stelæ of the Serapeum (MARIETTE, *Notice des soixante-quatre Apis*, in the *Bulletin Archéologique de l'Athénæum Français*, 1856, pp. 58–62).

The league formed by Hamath had not much power of cohesion. Iaubîdi had assembled his forces and the contingents of his allies at the town of Qarqar as Hadadezer had done before: he was completely defeated, taken prisoner, and flayed alive. His kingdom was annexed to the Assyrian empire, Qarqar was burnt to the ground, the fortifications of Hamath were demolished, and the city obliged to furnish a force of two hundred charioteers and six hundred horsemen, probably recruited from among the families of the upper classes, to serve as hostages as well as auxiliaries. Arpad, Zimyra, Damascus, Samaria, all succumbed without serious opposition, and the citizens who had been most seriously compromised in the revolt paid for their disaffection with their lives.[1] This success confirmed the neighbouring states of Tyre, Sidon, Judah, Ammon, and Moab in their allegiance, which had shown signs of wavering since the commencement of hostilities;[2] but Gaza remained unsubdued, and caused the more uneasiness because it was perceived that behind her was arrayed all the majesty of the Pharaoh. The Egyptians, slow to bestir themselves, had not yet crossed the Isthmus when the Assyrians appeared beneath the walls of Gaza: Hannon, worsted in a preliminary skirmish, retreated on Raphia, where Shabê, the Egyptian general, had at length arrived, and the decisive battle took place before this town. It was the first time that the archers and charioteers of the Nile valley had measured forces with the pikemen and cavalry of that of the Tigris; the engagement was hotly contested, but the generals and soldiers of Bocchoris, fighting according to antiquated methods of warfare, gave way before the onset of the Assyrian ranks, who were better equipped and better led. Shabê fled " like a shepherd whose sheep have been stolen," Hannon was taken prisoner and loaded with chains, and Raphia fell into the hands of the conqueror; the inhabitants who survived the sack of their city were driven into captivity to the number of 9033 men, with their flocks and household goods.[2] The manifest superiority of Assyria was evident from the first encounter, but the contest had been so fierce and the result so doubtful that Sargon did not consider it prudent to press his advantage. He judged rightly that these troops, whom he had not dispersed without considerable effort, constituted merely an advanced guard. Egypt was not like the petty kingdoms of Syria or Asia Minor, which had but one army apiece, and could not risk more

---

[1] *Annals of Sargon*, ll. 23–25 (cf. OPPERT, *Annals of Sargon*, in *Records of the Past*, 1st series, vol. vii. p. 29; WINCKLER, *Die Keilschrifttexte Sargons*, vol. i. pp. 6, 7), where the account is much mutilated; *Inscription des Fastes*, ll. 33–36 (cf. OPPERT, *Great Inscr. in the Palace of Khorsabad*, in *Records of the Past*, 1st ser., vol. ix. p. 6; WINCKLER, *op. cit.*, vol. i. pp. 102–105); *Stele of Larnaka*, col. i. ll. 51–65 (cf. WINCKLER, *op. cit.*, vol. i. pp. 178, 179).

[2] *Annals*, ll. 27–31 (cf. OPPERT, *Annals of Sargon*, in *Records of the Past*, 1st ser., vol. vii. p. 29; WINCKLER, *op. cit.*, pp. 6, 7), *Inscription des Fastes*, ll. 25, 26 (cf. OPPERT, *Great Inscr. in the Palace of Khorsabad*, in *Records of the Past*, 1st ser., vol. ix. p. 5; WINCKLER, *op. cit.*, vol. i. pp. 100, 101, and *Untersuchungen zur Altorientalischen Geschichte*, pp. 92–94).

than one pitched battle. Though Shabê's force was routed, others would not fail to take its place and contend as fiercely for the possession of the country, and even if the Assyrians should succeed in dislodging them and curbing the power of Bocchoris, the fall of Sais or Memphis, far from putting an end to the war, would only raise fresh complications. Above Memphis stretched the

valley of the Nile, bristling with fortresses, Khininsu, Oxyrhynchus, Hermopolis, Siut, Thinis, and Thebes, the famous city of Amon, enthroned on the banks of the river, whose very name still evoked in the minds of the Asiatics a vivid remembrance of all its triumphal glories.[1] Thebes itself formed merely one stage in the journey towards Syene, Ethiopia, Napata, and the unknown regions of Africa which popular imagination filled with barbarous races or savage monsters,[2] and however far an alien army might penetrate in a

IAUBÎDI OF HAMATH BEING FLAYED ALIVE.[3]

southerly direction, it would still meet with the language, customs, and divinities of Egypt—an Egypt whose boundary seemed to recede as the invader advanced, and which was ever ready to oppose the enemy with fresh forces whenever its troops had suffered from his attacks. Sargon, having reached Raphia, halted on the very threshold of the unexplored realm whose portals stood ajar ready to admit him: the same vague disquietude which had checked the conquering career of the Pharaohs on the borders of Asia[4] now

---

[1] Thebes was at that time known among the Semites by its popular name of *the city of Amon—Nuît-Amonu*, Nuî-Amonu, or *the City* simply—Nuît, Nuî—which the Hebrew writers transcribed as Nô-Amon (*Nahum* iii. 8) or Nô alone (*Jer.* xlvi. 25; *Ezek.* xxx. 14, 15, 16), and the Assyrians by Ni (OPPERT, *Mémoire sur les rapports de l'Égypte et de l'Assyrie*, pp. 95–98).

[2] Cf. the description in *Isa.* xxx. 6 of the desert and the isthmus, "The land of trouble and anguish, from whence come the lioness and the lion, the viper and the fiery flying serpent."

[3] Drawn by Faucher-Gudin, from a sketch by Flandin in BOTTA, *Le Monument de Ninive*, vol. ii. pl. 120.

[4] For the hesitation of the Theban Pharaohs, cf. MASPERO, *Dawn of Civilization*, pp. 394, 469, et seq., and *Struggle of the Nations*, pp. 16, 17, 88, 100, 106, et seq.

stayed his advance, and bade him turn back as he was on the point of entering
Africa.   He had repulsed the threatened invasion, and as a result of his victory
the princes and towns which had invoked the aid of the foreigner lay at his
mercy ; he proceeded, therefore, to reorganise the provinces of Philistia and
Israel, and received the homage of Judah and her dependencies.   Ahaz, while
all the neighbouring states were in revolt, had not wavered in his allegiance ;
the pacific counsels of Isaiah had once more prevailed over the influence of the
party which looked for safety in an alliance with Egypt.[1]   The whole country
from the Orontes to the mountains of Seir and the river of Egypt[2] was again
reduced to obedience, and set itself by peaceful labours to repair the misfortunes which had befallen it during the previous quarter of a century.   Sargon
returned to his capital, but fate did not yet allow him to renew his projects
against Babylon.   Rarely did an insurrection break out in any part of the
country on the accession of a new king at Nineveh without awaking echoes in
the distant provinces of the empire.   The report of a revolt in Chaldæa roused
a slumbering dissatisfaction among the Syrians, and finally led them into
open rebellion : the episodes of the Syrian campaign, narrated in Armenia or
on the slopes of the Taurus with the thousand embellishments suggested by the
rancour of the narrators, excited the minds of the inhabitants and soon rendered
an outbreak inevitable.   The danger would have been serious if the suppressed
hatred of all had found vent at the same moment, and if insurrections in five or
six different parts of his empire had to be faced by the sovereign simultaneously ;
but as a rule these local wars broke out without any concentrated plan, and
in localities too remote from each other to permit of any possible co-operation
between the assailants ; each chief, before attempting to assert his independence, seemed to wait until the Assyrians had had ample time to crush the
rebel who first took the field, having done which they could turn the whole of
their forces against the latest foe.   Thus Iaubîdi did not risk a campaign till
the fall of Elam and Karduniash had been already decided on the field of

[1] Sargon probably alludes to homage received at this time, when he styles himself "the subduer
of far-off Judah " (Nimroud Inscr., l. 8; cf. WINCKLER, Die Keilschrifttexte Sargons, vol. i. pp. 108,
109).   It is not certain that Ahaz was still King of Judah ; it was for a long time admitted that
Hezekiah was already king when these events took place, in accordance with 2 Kings xviii. 9, 10,
where it is stated that Samaria was destroyed in the sixth year of Hezekiah (cf. supra, p. 216, note 2).
I consider, in agreement with several historians (ED. MEYER, Geschichte des Alterthums, vol. i. pp.
433, 567; STADE, Geschichte des Volkes Israel, vol. i. p. 606, note 2), that the date of Sennacherib's
invasion of Judah must have remained more firmly fixed in the minds of the Jewish historians than
that of the taking of Samaria, and as 2 Kings xviii. 13 places this invasion in the fourteenth year of
Hezekiah, which corresponds, as we shall see, to the third year of Sennacherib, or 702 B.C. (cf. infra,
p. 288), it seems better to place the accession of Hezekiah about 715, and prolong the reign of Ahaz
till after the campaign of Sargon against Hannon of Gaza.
[2] This is the boundary indicated by Sargon in the Cylinder Inscription, l. 13 (cf. OPPERT, Les
Inscriptions de Dour-Sarkayân, in PLACE, Ninive, vol. ii. p. 292 ; LYON, Keilschrifttexte Sargons,
pp. 30, 31).

Durîlu; in the same way, the nations of the North and East refrained from entering the lists till they had allowed Sargon time to destroy the league of Hamath and repel the attack of Pharaoh.

They were secretly incited to rebellion by a power which played nearly the same part with regard to them that Egypt had played in Southern Syria. Urartu had received a serious rebuff in 735 B.C., and the burning of Dhuspas had put an end to its ascendency,[1] but the victory had been effected at the cost of so much bloodshed that Tiglath-pileser was not inclined to risk losing the advantage already gained by pushing it too far: he withdrew, therefore, without concluding a treaty, and did not return, being convinced that no further hostilities would be attempted till the vanquished enemy had recovered from his defeat. He was justified in his anticipations, for Sharduris died about 730, without having again taken up arms, and his son Rusas I. had left Shalmaneser V. unmolested:[2] but the accession of Sargon and the revolts which harassed him had awakened in Rusas the warlike instincts of his race, and the moment appeared advantageous for abandoning his policy of inactivity. The remembrance of the successful exploits of Menuas and Argistis still lived in the minds of his people, and more than one of his generals had entered upon their military careers at a time when, from Arpad and Carchemish to the country of the Medes, quite a third of the territory now annexed to Assyria had been subject to the king of Urartu:[3] Rusas, therefore, doubtless placed before himself the possibility of reconquering the lost provinces, and even winning, by a stroke of fortune, more than had been by a stroke of fortune wrested from his father. He began by intriguing with such princes as were weary of the Assyrian rule, among the Mannai, in Zikartu,[4] among the Tabal, and even among the Khâti. Iranzu, who was at that time reigning over the Mannai, refused to listen to the suggestions of his neighbour, but two of his towns, Shuandakhul and Durdukka, deserted him in 719 B.C., and ranged themselves under Mitâtti, chief of the Zikartu, while about the same time the strongholds of Sukkia, Bala, and Abitikna, which were on the borders of Urartu, broke the ties which had long

---

[1] For this campaign in Urartu, cf. *supra*, pp. 154–156.

[2] The name of this king is usually written Ursa in the Assyrian inscriptions, but the *Annals of Sargon*, ll. 58, 75, give in each case the form Rusâ (WINCKLER, *Die Keilschrifttexte Sargons*, vol. i. pp. 12, 16), in accordance with which Sayce had already identified the Assyrian form Ursâ or Rusâ with the form Rusas found on some Urartian monuments (*The Cuneiform Inscriptions of Van*, p. 654). Belck and Lehmann have discovered several monuments of this Rusas I., son of Sharduris (*Ein neuer Herrscher von Chaldia*, in the *Zeitschrift für Assyriologie*, vol. ix. p. 348).

[3] Cf. *supra*, pp. 118–122, 140, 143–146.

[4] Zikruti, Zikirtu, Zikartu, may probably be identified with the Sagartians of Herodotus (I. cxxv.), as was first perceived by Norris, and this identification, on which Lenormant laid too much insistence (*Sur la campagne de Tiglathphalazar II. dans l'Ariane*, in the *Zeitschrift*, 1870, p. 52), has been adopted by Tiele (*Babylonisch-assyrische Geschichte*, pp. 261, 265), by Winckler (*Untersuchungen zur Altorientalischen Geschichte*, pp. 112, 113), and lastly by Hommel (*Gesch. Bab. und Ass.*, p. 712).

bound them to Assyria, and concluded a treaty of alliance with Rusas. Sargon was not deceived as to the meaning of these events, and at once realised that this movement was not one of those local agitations which broke out at intervals in one or other of his provinces. His officers and spies must have kept him informed of the machinations of Rusas and of the revolutions which the migrations of the last thirty years had provoked among the peoples of the Iranian table-land. A new race had arisen in their rear, that of the Cimmerians and Scythians, which, issuing in irresistible waves from the gorges of the Caucasus, threatened to overwhelm the whole ancient world of the East. The stream, after a moment's vacillation, took a westerly direction, and flooded Asia Minor from one end to the other.[1] Some tribes, however, which had detached themselves from the main movement sought an outlet towards the south-east, on to the rich plains of the Araxes and the country around Lake Urumiah. The native races, pressed in the rear by these barbarians, and hemmed in on either side and in front by Urartu and Assyria, were forced into closer proximity, and, conscious of their individual weakness, had begun to form themselves into three distinct groups, varying considerably in compactness,—the Medes in the south, Misianda in the north,[2] with Zikartu between them. Zikartu was at that time the best organised of these nascent states, and its king, Mitâtti, was not deficient either in military talent or political sagacity. The people over whom he ruled were, moreover, impregnated with the civilisation of Mesopotamia, and by constantly meeting the Assyrians in battle they had adopted the general principles of their equipment, organisation, and military tactics. The vigour of his soldiers and the warlike ardour which inspired them rendered his armies formidable even to leaders as experienced, and warriors as hardened, as the officers and soldiers of Nineveh. Mitâtti had strongly garrisoned the two rebel cities, and trusted that if the Assyrians were unable to recapture them without delay, other towns would not be long in following their example; Iranzu would, no doubt, be expelled, his place would be taken by a hostile chief, and the Mannai, joining hands with Urartu on the right and Zikartu on the left, would, with these two states, form a compact coalition, whose combined forces would menace the northern frontier of the empire from the Zagros to the Taurus. Sargon,

---

[1] I shall return later on, in Chapters IV. and V., to the little that is actually known of the Cimmerian invasion, and the grouping of tribes for which it was responsible. It had not sufficient influence on the policy of Assyria, at any rate at first, for the scope of this history to permit of me doing more than briefly mention it.

[2] I shall revert, in Chapters IV. and V. of this history, to the origin of the Median kingdom. The name of Misianda is formed by the union of two names, Andiu or Andia and Mîsu, which are found separately in the inscriptions of Shalmaneser III. (*Obelisk*, l. 182) and of Rammân-nirâri III. (*Slab Inscr. of Calah*, ll. 7, 9; cf. *supra*, p. 92, note 3, and p. 96, note 4). Andiu was the more important, for Sargon often mentions Andia or Andiu as synonymous with Misianda (WINCKLER, *Die Keilschrifttexte Sargons*, vol. i. pp. 82, 83, 148, 149, 176, 177).

putting all the available Assyrian forces into the field, hurled them against the rebels, and this display of power had the desired effect upon the neighbouring kingdoms: Rusas and Mitâtti did not dare to interfere, the two cities were taken by assault, burnt and razed to the ground, and the inhabitants of the surrounding districts of Sukkia, Bala, and Abitikna were driven into exile among the Khâti.[1] The next year, however, the war thus checked on the Iranian table-land broke out in the north-west, in the mountains of Cilicia. A Tabal chief, Kiakku of Shinukhta, refused to pay his tribute (718). Sargon

seized him and destroyed his city; his family and adherents, 7500 persons in all, were carried away captives to Assyria, and his principality was given to a rival chief, Mattî of Atuna, on a promise from the latter of an increased amount of tribute.[2] In 717 B.C. more serious dangers openly declared themselves. The Khâti had not forgotten that

TAKING OF A CASTLE IN ZIKÂRTU.[4]

they had once been the allies of Urartu, and that their king, Pisiris, together with Matîlu of Agusi,[3] had fought for Sharduris against Tiglath-pileser III. Pisiris conspired with Mitâ, chief of the Mushki, and proclaimed his independence; but vengeance swiftly and surely overtook him. He succumbed before his accomplice had time to come to his assistance, and was sent to join Kiakku and his adherents in prison, while the districts which he had ruled were incorporated into Assyrian territory, and Carchemish became

[1] Annals of Sargon, ll. 32–42: cf. OPPERT, The Annals of Sargon, in Records of the Past, 1st ser., vol. vii. pp. 29, 30; WINCKLER, Die Keilschrifttexte Sargons, vol. i. pp. 8, 9; Inscription des Fastes, l. 48; cf. OPPERT, Great Inscription in the Palace of Khorsabad, in Records of the Past, 1st ser., vol. ix. p. 7; WINCKLER, op. cit., vol. i. pp. 106, 107.

[2] Annals of Sargon, ll. 42–45; cf. OPPERT, The Annals of Sargon, in Records of the Past, 1st ser., vol. vii. p. 30; WINCKLER, op. cit., vol. i. pp. 8–11; Inscription des Fastes, ll. 28, 29; cf. OPPERT, Great Inscription in the Palace of Khorsabad, in Records of the Past, 1st ser., vol. ix. pp. 5, 6; WINCKLER, op. cit., vol. i. pp. 102, 103. The name of Atuna is a variant of the name Tuna, which is found in the inscriptions of Tiglath-pileser III. (Nimroud Inscr., obv., l. 59), and Tuna recalls the name of the old city of Tyana (LENORMANT, Les Origines de l'Histoire, vol. iii. pp. 212, 213, 238), or that of Tynna or Tunna, near Tyana, in the Taurus (RAMSAY, The Historical Geography of Asia Minor, pp. 68, 310, 311). Shinukhta, not far from Atuna, must be the capital of a district situated on the Karmalas or the Saros, on the borders of Cilicia or Cataonia; cf. DELATTRE, L'Asie Occid. dans les Inscr. Assyr., p. 68.

[3] Cf. supra, pp. 120, 121, 145–149.

[4] Drawn by Faucher-Gudin, from the facsimile by Flandin, published in BOTTA, Le Monument de Ninive, vol. ii. pl. 89.

the seat of an Assyrian prefect who ranked among the *limmi* from whom successive years took their names. The fall of Pisiris made no impression on his contemporaries. They had witnessed the collapse of so many great powers—Elam, Urartu, Egypt—that the misfortunes of so insignificant a personage awakened but little interest; and yet with him foundered one of the most glorious wrecks of the ancient world. For more than a century the Khâti had been the dominant power in North-western Asia, and had successfully withstood the power of Thebes; crushed by the Peoples of the Sea, hemmed in and encroached upon by the rising wave of Aramæan invasion, they had yet disputed their territory step by step with the Assyrian generals, and the area over which they spread can be traced by the monuments and inscriptions scattered over Cilicia, Lycaonia, Cappadocia, and Northern Syria as far as the basins of the Orontes and the Litany. So lasting had proved their influence on all around them, and so fresh was the memory of their greatness, that it would have seemed but natural that their vitality should survive this last blow, and that they should enjoy a prosperous future which should vie with their past. But events proved that their national life was dead, and that no recuperative power remained: as soon as Sargon had overthrown their last prince, their tribes became merged in the general body of Aramæans, and their very name ere long vanished from the pages of history.[1]

Up to this time Rusas had not directly interfered in these quarrels between the suzerain and his vassals : he may have incited the latter to revolt, but he had avoided compromising himself, and was waiting till the Mannai had decided to make common cause with him before showing his hand openly. Ever since the skirmish of the year 719, Mitâtti had actively striven to tempt the Mannai from their allegiance, but his intrigues had hitherto proved of no avail against the staunch fidelity first of Irânzu and then of Azâ, who had succeeded the latter about 718. At the beginning of the year 716 Mitâtti was more successful; the Mannai, seduced at length by his promises and those of Rusas, assembled on Mount Uaush, murdered their king, and leaving his corpse unburied, hastened to place themselves under the command of Bagadatti, regent of Umildîsh.[2] Sargon hurried to the spot, seized Bagadatti, and had him flayed alive on Mount Uaush, which had just witnessed the murder of Azâ, and exposed the mass of bleeding flesh before the gaze of the people to demonstrate the fate reserved for his enemies. But though he had acted speedily he was too late, and the fate of their chief, far from discouraging his subjects, confirmed

---

[1] *Annals of Sargon*, ll. 46–50 : cf. OPPERT, *The Annals of Sargon*, in *Records of the Past*, 1st ser., vol. vii. pp. 30, 31 ; WINCKLER, *Die Keilschrifttexte Sargons*, vol. i. pp. 10, 11.

[2] For Mildîsh or Umildîsh and the probable position of this country, cf. *Struggle of the Nations*, p. 645, note 1.

them in their rebellion. They had placed upon the throne Ullusunu, the brother of Azâ, and this prince had immediately concluded an alliance with Rusas, Mitâtti, and the people of Andia; his example was soon followed by other Eastern chiefs, Assurlî of Karallu and Itti of Allabria,[1] whereupon, as the spirit of revolt spread from one to another, most of the districts lately laid under tribute by Tiglath-pileser took up arms—Niksama, Bîtsagbati, Bîtkhir-mâmi, Kilambâti, Armangu, and even the parts around Kharkhar, and Ellipi,

TAKING OF THE CITY OF KISHÎSIM BY THE ASSYRIANS.[2]

with its reigning sovereign Dalta. The general insurrection dreaded by Sargon, and which Rusas had for five years been fomenting, had, despite all the efforts of the Assyrian government, at last broken out, and the whole frontier was ablaze from the borders of Elam to those of the Mushku. Sargon turned his attention to where danger was most urgent; he made a descent on the territory of the Mannai, and laid it waste " as a swarm of locusts might have done ; " he burnt their capital, Izirtu, demolished the fortifications of Zibia and Armaîd, and took Ullusunu captive, but, instead of condemning him to death, he restored to him his liberty and his crown on condition of his paying a regular tribute.

---

[1] For Allabria and its situation, cf. *supra*, p. 99, note 4.

[2] Drawn by Faucher-Gudin, from the facsimile by Flandin, published in Botta, *Le Monument de Ninive*, vol. i. pls. 68, 69. The figures resembling stags' horns, which crown three of the upper towers, are tongues of flame, as was indicated by the red colouring which still remained on them when the bas-relief was discovered.

R

This act of clemency, in contrast with the pitiless severity shown at the beginning of the insurrection, instantly produced the good effects he expected: the Mannai laid down their arms and swore allegiance to the conqueror, and their defection broke up the coalition. Sargon did not give the revolted provinces time to recover from the dismay into which his first victories had thrown them, but marched rapidly to the south, and crushed them severally; commencing with Andia, where he took 4200 prisoners with their cattle, he next attacked Zikartu, whose king, Mitâtti, took refuge in the mountains and thus escaped death at the hands of the executioner. Assurlî of Karalla had a similar fate to Bagadatti, and was flayed alive. Itti of Allabria, with half of his subjects, was carried away to Hamath. The towns of Niksama and Shurgadia were annexed to the province of Parsuash. The town of Kishîsim was reduced to ashes, and its king, Belsharuzur, together with the treasures of his palace, was carried away to Nineveh. Kharkhar succumbed after a short siege, received a new population, and was henceforward known as Kar-Sharrukîn; Dalta was restored to favour, and retained his dominion intact.[1] Never had so great a danger been so ably or so courageously averted. It was not without good reason that, after his victory over the Mannai, Sargon, instead of attacking Rusas, the most obstinate of his foes, turned against the Medes. Ellipi, Parsuash, and Kharkhar, comprising half the countries which had joined in the insurrection, were on the borders of Elam or had frequent relations with that state, and it is impossible to conjecture what turn affairs might have taken had Elam been induced to join their league, and had the Elamite armies, in conjunction with those of Merodach-baladan, unexpectedly fallen upon the Assyrian rear by the valleys of the Tigris or the Turnât. Had the Elamites, however, entertained a desire to mingle in the fray, the promptness with which Sargon had re-established order must have given them cause to reflect and induced them to maintain their neutrality. The year which had opened so inauspiciously thus ended in victory, though the situation was still fraught with danger. The agitation which had originated in the east and north-east in 716 reached the north-west in 715, and spread as far as the borders of Southern Syria. Rusas had employed the winter in secret negotiations with the Mannai, and had won over one of their principal chiefs, a certain Dayaukku, whose name seems to be identical with that which the Greeks transliterated as Deiokes.[2] As soon as spring had returned he

---

[1] *Annals of Sargon*, ll. 52-74: cf. OPPERT, *The Annals of Sargon*, in *Records of the Past*, 1st ser., vol. vii. pp. 31, 32; WINCKLER, *Die Keilschrifttexte Sargons*, vol. i. pp. 10–17. The events are confused with those of the following campaigns in the *Inscription des Fastes*, ll. 36–42, 44, 45, 49–56, 58–66 (cf. OPPERT, *The Great Inscription in the Palace of Khorsabad*, vol. ix. pp. 6–9; WINCKLER, *op. cit*, pp. 104–111), as well as in other contemporary documents.

[2] The identity of the name Dayaukku with that of Deiokes was at once recognised by G. SMITH, *Assyrian History* (in the *Zeitschrift*, 1869, p. 98); it has since been admitted by all historians. I shall have occasion to revert to this personage at the beginning of Chapter IV. of this work.

entered the territory of Ullusunu, and occupied twenty-two strongholds, which were probably betrayed into his hands by Dayaukku.[1] While this was taking place Mitâ of Mushki invaded Cilicia, and the Arab tribes of the Idumæan desert —the Thamudites, the Ibadites, the Marsimanu, and Khayapâ—were emboldened to carry their marauding expeditions into Assyrian territory.[2] The Assyrian monarch was thus called on to conduct three distinct wars simultaneously in three different directions; he was, moreover, surrounded by wavering subjects whom terror alone held to their allegiance, and whom the slightest imprudence or the least reverse might turn into open foes.

Sargon resolutely faced the enemy at all three points of attack. As in the previous year, he reserved for himself the position where danger was most threatening, directing the operations against the Mannai.[3] He captured one by one the twenty-two strongholds of Ullusunu which Rusas had seized, and laying hands on Dayaukku, sent him and his family into exile to Hamath. This display of energy determined Ianzu[4] of Naîri to receive the Assyrian monarch courteously within the royal residence of Khubushkia and to supply him with horses, cattle, sheep, and goats in token of homage. Proceeding from thence in an oblique direction, Sargon reached Andia and took prisoner its king Tilusînas. Having by this exploit reduced the province of Mannai to order, he restored the twenty-two towns to Ullusunu, and halting some days in Izirtu, erected there a statue of himself, according to his custom, as a visible witness of Assyrian supremacy, having done which, he retraced his steps to the south-east. The province of Kharkhar, which had been reduced to subjection only a few months previously, was already in open revolt, and the district of Kar-Sharrukîn alone remained faithful to its governor: Sargon had to reconquer it completely, town by town, imposing on the four citadels of Kishislu, Kindâu, Bît-Bagaiâ, and Zaria the new names of Kar-Nabu, Kar-Sin, Kar-Rammânu, and Kar-Ishtar, besides increasing the fortifications of Kar-Sharrukîn. The Medes once more acknowledged his suzerainty, and twenty-two of their chiefs came to tender the oath of allegiance at his feet;[5] two or three districts which remained insubordinate were given up to

---

[1] *Annals of Sargon*, ll. 75, 76 : cf. OPPERT, *The Annals of Sargon*, in *Records of the Past*, 1st ser., vol. vii. pp. 32, 33; WINCKLER, *Die Keilschrifttexte Sargons*, vol. i. pp. 14, 15.

[2] *Annals of Sargon*, ll. 92–95 : cf. OPPERT, *op. cit.*, p. 34; WINCKLER, *op. cit.*, pp. 20, 21.

[3] Tiele first remarked that these risings of the different peoples took place simultaneously on the eastern and western frontiers; Sargon could lead only the most important of his armies in person, viz. that which was directed against Rusas, the Mannai and the Medes (*Babylonisch-assyrische Geschichte*, p. 264). Winckler even suggests that the expeditions against Rusas and against the Medes were conducted simultaneously (*Die Keilschrifttexte Sargons*, vol. i. pp. xiv., xv.).

[4] Sargon's text seems to give this as the actual name of the king. Delitzsch has shown that it is the title of the kings in the local dialects (*Die Sprache der Kossäer*, pp. 25, 29–38; cf. *Struggle of the Nations*, p. 114).

[5] This is the number given in the *Annals*, l. 89; the *Fastes*, ll. 66, 67, give 34 instead of 22.

pillage as far as Bît-Khambân, and the inhabitants of Kimirra were sent into captivity.[1] The eastern campaign was thus brought to a most successful issue, fortune, meanwhile, having also favoured the Assyrian arms in the other menaced quarters. Mitâ, after pushing forward at one point as far as the Mediterranean, had been driven back into the mountains by the prefect of Kuî,

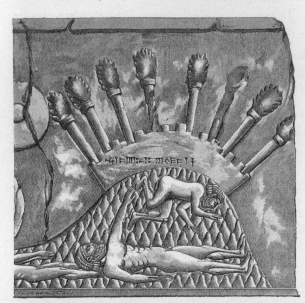

THE TOWN OF BÎT-BAGAÎA BURNT BY THE ASSYRIANS.[3]

and the Bedâwin of the south had sustained a serious reverse. These latter were mere barbarians, ignorant of the arts of reading and writing, and hitherto unconquered by any foreign power : their survivors were removed to Samaria, where captives from Hamath had already been established, and where they were soon joined by further exiles from Babylon.[2] This episode had greater effect than its importance warranted ; or perhaps the majority of the neighbouring states made it a convenient pretext for congratulating Sargon on his victories over more serious enemies. He received gifts from Shamshiê, the Arabian queen who had formerly fought against Tiglath-pileser,[4] from Itamar the Sabæan, and the sheîkhs of the desert, from the kings of the Mediterranean sea-board, and from the Pharaoh himself.[5] Bocchoris had died after a troublous reign of seven years.[6] His real character is unknown, but as he left a deep impression on the memories of his people, it is natural to conclude

[1] *Annals of Sargon*, ll. 76–90 : cf. OPPERT, *The Annals of Sargon*, in *Records of the Past*, 1st ser., vol. viii. pp. 33, 34 ; WINCKLER, *Die Keilschrifttexte Sargons*, vol. i. pp. 16–19. The text of the *Annals* is imperfect, but the sense can be restored by comparison with that of the *Fastes*, ll. 44, 45, 52–54, 63–67.

[2] *Annals of Sargon*, ll. 92–97, 99, 100 : cf. OPPERT, *op. cit.*, p. 34 ; WINCKLER, *op. cit.*, pp. 20, 21. For the colonisation of Samaria, cf. WINCKLER, *Alttestamentliche Untersuchungen*, pp. 97–107.

[3] Drawn by Faucher-Gudin, from the facsimile by Flandin, in BOTTA, *Le Monument de Ninive*, vol. i. p. 76. The tongues of flame which issue from the towers still bore traces of red and yellow colouring when the bas-relief was discovered.

[4] Cf. *supra*, pp. 188, 189.

[5] *Annals of Sargon*, ll. 97–99 : cf. OPPERT, *op. cit.*, p. 34 ; WINCKLER, *Die Keilschrifttexte Sargons*, vol. i. pp. 20, 21.

[6] For the duration of his reign, cf. *supra*, p. 233, note 4. The two dynasties of Tanis and Sais may be for the present reconstituted as follows :—

that he displayed, at times, both ability and energy. Many legends in which the miraculous element prevailed were soon in circulation concerning him. He was, according to these accounts, weak in body and insignificant in appearance,[1] but made up for these defects by mental ability and sound judgment. He was credited with having been simple in his mode of life,[2] and was renowned as one of the six great legislators produced by Egypt. A law concerning debt and the legal rates of interest,[3] was attributed to him; he was also famed for the upright-ness of his judgments, which were regarded as due to divine inspiration. Isis had bestowed on him a serpent, which, coiling itself round his head when he sat on the judgment-seat, covered him with its shadow, and admonished him not to

KING BOCCHORIS GIVING JUDGMENT BETWEEN TWO WOMEN, RIVAL CLAIMANTS
TO A CHILD.[4]

forget for a moment the inflexible principles of equity and truth.[5] A collec-tion of the decisions he was reputed to have delivered in famous cases existed in the Græco-Roman period, and one of them is quoted at length: he had very ingeniously condemned a courtesan to touch the shadow of a purse as payment for the shadowy favours she had bestowed in a dream on her lover.[6] An Alexandrian poet, Pancrates, versified the accounts of this juridical

XXIII. (Tanite) Dynasty.		XXIV. (Saite) Dynasty.	
I. Saharuri Patisibastît . .	Petubastis	I. Uahkarî Bukunirînif . . .	Bocchoris
II. Âkhpîrrî Sotpuniamonu			
Osorkon Mariamonu . .	Osorkon III.		
III. Psamuti	Psammuthis		

Neither Tafnakhti nor any of the local sovereigns mentioned on the stele of Piônkhi were comprised in the official computation; there is, therefore, no reason to add them to this list.

[1] Diodorus Siculus, i. 65, 94.

[2] Alexis, *Fragm.* 3, in Müller-Didot, *Fragmenta Historicorum Græcorum*, vol. iv. p. 299.

[3] Diodorus Siculus, i. 79, 94.

[4] Drawn by Faucher-Gudin, from a sketch published in the *Rendiconti della R. Accademia dei Lincei*, ser. v. vol. vi.

[5] Plutarch, *On false shame*, § 3; the serpent is nothing else than the uræus attached to the head-dress of the king, and which the Egyptians represented as alive.

[6] Clement of Alexandria, *Stromateis*, iv. 18. The existence of this collection was indicated by Lumbroso, in the *Atti dell' Accademia dei Lincei*, ser. iii., vol. xi. p. 203, et seq., and in the *Archivio per lo Studio delle tradizioni popolari*, vol. ii. p. 569, et seq.

collection,[1] and the artists of the Imperial epoch drew from it motives for mural decoration ; they portrayed the king pronouncing judgment between two mothers who disputed possession of an infant, between two beggars laying claim to the same cloak, and between three men asserting each of them his right to a wallet full of food.[2] A less favourable tradition represents the king as an avaricious and irreligious sovereign :[3] he is said one day to have conceived the sacrilegious desire to bring about a conflict between an ordinary bull and the Mnevis adored at Heliopolis.[4] The gods, doubtless angered by his crimes, are recorded to have called into being a lamb with eight feet, which, suddenly breaking into articulate speech, predicted that Upper and Lower Egypt would be disgraced by the rule of a stranger.[5] The monuments of his reign which have come down to us tell us nothing of his deeds ; we can only conjecture that after the defeat sustained by his generals at Raphia, the discords which had ruined the preceding dynasties again broke out with renewed violence. Indeed, if he succeeded in preserving his crown for several years longer, he owed the fact more to the feebleness of the Ethiopians than to his own vigour : no sooner did an enterprising prince appear at Barkal and demand that he should render an account of his usurpation, than his power came to an end. Kashto having died about 716,[7] his son Shabaku, the Sabaco of the Greeks, inherited the throne, and his daughter Amenertas the priesthood and principality of Thebes, in right of her mother Shapenuapît.[8] Sabaco was an able

SABACO.[6]

[1] Pancrates lived in the time of Hadrian (ATHENÆUS, *Deipnosophistæ*, p. 677 *e*), and Athenæus, who has preserved his memory for us, quotes the first book of his Bocchoreidion (p. 478 *a*).

[2] Considerable remains of this decorative cycle have been discovered at Pompeii and at Rome, in a series of frescoes, in which Lumbroso (*Atti dell' Accademia dei Lincei*, ser. iii. vol. xi. p. 303, et seq. ; cf. *Archivio per lo Studio delle tradizioni popolari*, vol. ii., 1883, p. 569, et seq.) and E. Lœwy (*Aneddoti Giudizari dipinti in un Fregio antico*, in the *Rendiconti della R. Accademia dei Lincei*, ser. v. vol. vi. pp. 27-45, pls. i., ii.) recognise the features of the legends of Bocchoris ; the dispute between the two mothers recalls the famous judgment of Solomon (1 *Kings* iii. 16-28).

[3] DIODORUS SICULUS, i. 65, 94.

[4] ÆLIAN, *Hist. Animal.*, xi. 11.

[5] This legend, preserved by Manetho and Ælian (*Hist. Animal.*, xii. 3) is also known from the fragments of a demotic papyrus at Vienna, discovered and published by Krall (*Vom König Bokchoris, nach einem demotischen Papyrus der Sammlung Erzherzog Rainer*, Innsbruck, 1898), which contains the prophecy of the lamb.

[6] Drawn by Faucher-Gudin, from LEPSIUS, *Denkmäler*, iii. 301, No. 79 ; cf. ROSELLINI, *Monumenti Storici*, pl. 12, No. 47.

[7] The date of the accession of Sabaco is here fixed at 716-715, because I follow the version of the lists of Manetho, which gives twelve years as the reign of that prince ; an inscription from Hammamât mentions his twelfth year (LEPSIUS, *Denkm.*, v. 1 *e*).

[8] For the genealogy of Sabaco, Kashto, and Amenertas suggested by E. DE ROUGÉ, *Étude sur quelques monuments du règne de Tahraka* (in the *Melanges d'Archéologie Égyptienne*, vol. i. pp. 87, 88), cf. MASPERO, *Les Momies royales de Deir-el-Bahari*, in the *Mémoires de la Mission Française*, vol. i. pp. 752, 753.

and energetic prince, who could by no means tolerate the presence of a rival Pharaoh in the provinces which Piônkhi had conquered. He declared war, and, being doubtless supported in his undertaking by all the petty kings and great feudal nobles whose jealousy was aroused by the unlooked-for prosperity of the Saite monarch, he defeated Bocchoris and took him prisoner. Tafnakhti had formerly recognised the Ethiopian supremacy, and Bocchoris, when he succeeded to his father's dominions, had himself probably sought investiture at the hands of the King of Napata. Sabaco treated him as a rebel, and either burnt or flayed him alive (715).[1] The struggle was hardly over, when the news of Sargon's victories reached Egypt. It was natural that the new king, not yet securely seated on his throne, should desire to conciliate the friendship of a neighbour who was so successful in war, and that he should seize the first available pretext to congratulate him. The Assyrian on his part received these advances with satisfaction and pride: he perceived in them a guarantee that Egyptian intrigues with Tyre and Jerusalem would cease, and that he could henceforth devote himself to his projects against Rusas without being distracted by the fear of an Ethiopian attack and the subversion of Syria in his rear.

Sargon took advantage of these circumstances to strike a final blow at Urartu. He began in the spring of 714 by collecting among the Mannai the tribute due from Ullusuna, Daltâ, and the Median chiefs; then pushing forward into the country of the Zikartu, he destroyed three forts and twenty-four villages, and burnt their capital, Parda. Mitatti escaped servitude, but it was at the price of his power: a proscribed fugitive, deserted by his followers, he took refuge in the woods, and never submitted to his conqueror; but he troubled him no further, and disappeared from the pages of history. Having achieved this result, Sargon turned towards the north-west, and coming at length into close conflict with Rusas, did not leave his enemy till he had crushed him. He drove him into the gorges of Uaush, slaughtered a large number of his troops, and swept away the whole of his body-guard— a body of cavalry of two hundred men, all of whom were connected by blood with the reigning family. Rusas quitted his chariot, and, like his father Sharduris on the night of the disaster at Kishtân, leaped upon a mare, and fled, overwhelmed with shame, into the mountains.[2] His towns, terror-stricken, opened their gates at the first summons to the victor; Sargon burnt those which he knew he could not retain, granted the district of Uaush to his

---

[1] According to Manetho, he was burnt alive (MÜLLER-DIDOT, *Fragm. Hist. Græc.*, vol. ii. p. 593; the tradition which mentions that he was flayed alive is found in John of Antioch (MÜLLER-DIDOT, *op. cit.*, vol. iv. p. 540).

[2] Cf., for this episode of the mare and the shame connected with it in the eyes of the ancients, *supra*, p. 146.

vassal Ullusunu as a recompense for his loyalty, and then marched up to rest awhile in Naîri, where he revictualled his troops at the expense of Ianzu of Khubushkia.[1] He had, no doubt, hoped that Urzana of Muzazîr, the last of the friends of Rusas to hold out against Assyria, would make good use of the respite thus, to all appearances unintentionally, afforded him, and would come to terms; but as the appeal to his clemency was delayed, Sargon

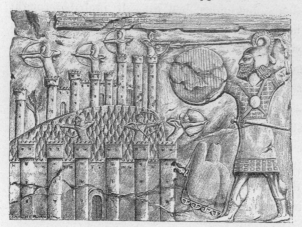

suddenly determined to assume the aggressive. Muzazîr, entrenched within its mountain ranges, was accessible only by one or two dangerous passes; Urzana had barricaded these, and believed himself in a position to defy every effort of the Assyrians. Sargon, equally convinced of the futility of a front attack, had recourse to a surprise. Taking with

TAKING OF A TOWN IN URARTU BY THE ASSYRIANS.[2]

him his chariots and one thousand picked horsemen, he left the beaten track, and crossing the four or five mountain chains—the Shiak, the Ardinshi, the Ulayau, and the Alluria—which lay between him and Muzazîr, he unexpectedly bore down upon the city. Urzana escaped after a desperate resistance, but the place was taken by assault and sacked, the palace destroyed, the temple overthrown, and the statues of the gods Khaldîa and Bagbartu dragged from their sanctuary.[3] The entire royal family were sent into slavery, and with them 20,170 of the inhabitants who had survived the siege, besides 690 mules, 920 oxen, 100,225 sheep, and incalculable spoils in gold, silver, bronze, iron, and precious stones and stuffs, the furniture of Urzana, and even his seal, being deposited in the treasury at Nineveh. The disaster at Muzazîr was the final blow to Urartu; it is impossible to say what took place where Rusas himself was, and whether the feudatories refused him any further allegiance, but in a short time he found himself almost forsaken, without friends, troops, or a place of refuge, and reduced to choose between death or the degradation of appealing to the mercy of the conqueror. He stabbed himself rather than yield; and Sargon,

---

[1] For Ianzu and the nature of the title he bore, cf. *Struggle of the Nations*, p. 114, and also p. 243, note 4, of the present work.

[2] Drawn by Faucher-Gudin, from the drawing by BOTTA, *Le Monument de Ninive*, vol. ii. pl. 90.

[3] Cf. *supra*, p. 59, for the pillaging of the temple of Muzazîr.

only too thankful to be rid of such a dangerous adversary, stopped the pursuit.[1]
Argistis II. succeeded to what was left of his father's kingdom,[2] and, being
anxious above all things to obtain peace for his subjects, suspended hostilities,
without however disarming his troops. As was the case under Tiglath-pileser III.,
Urartu neither submitted to Assyria, nor was there any kind of treaty between
the belligerents to prescribe the conditions of this temporary truce. Both sides
maintained their positions on their respective territories: Sargon kept the
frontier towns acquired by him in previous years, and which he had annexed to the border provinces, retain-
ing also his suzerainty over Muzazîr,
the Mannai, and the Median states implicated in the struggle; Argistis, on
his side, strengthened himself in the
regions around the sources of the
Euphrates and Lake Van—in Biaînas,
in Etius, and in the plains of the
Araxes. The material injuries which
he had received, however considerable

THE SEAL OF URZANA, KING OF MUZAZÎR.[3]

they may appear, were not irreparable, and, as a fact, the country quickly
recovered from them, but the people's confidence in their prince and his
chiefs was destroyed. The defeat of Sharduris, following as it did on a period
of advantageous victories, may have seemed to Argistis one of those unimportant occurrences which constantly take place in the career of the strongest
nations; the disaster of Rusas proved to him that, in attempting to wipe out his
first repulse, he had only made matters worse, and the conviction was borne
in upon his princes that they were not in a position to contest the possession
of Western Asia with the Assyrians. They therefore renounced, more from
instinct than as the result of deliberation, the project of enlarging their borders
to the south, and if they subsequently reappeared on the Mesopotamian plains,
it was in search of booty, and not to acquire territory. Any attempt to stop
their incursions, or to disturb them in their mountain fastnesses, found them
prepared to hold their own with the same obstinacy as of old, and they were

[1] *Annals of Sargon*, ll. 101–139: cf. OPPERT, *The Annals of Sargon*, in *Records of the Past*, 1st ser.,
vol. vii. pp. 34–37; WINCKLER, *Die Keilschrifttexte Sargons*, vol. i. pp. 20–27. The lacunæ in the
text of the *Annals* can be partly filled in by means of the *Fastes*, ll. 45–47, 72–78; for the sequence of
events, cf. TIELE, *Babylonisch-assyrische Geschichte*, pp. 265, 266.

[2] No text states positively that Argistis II. immediately succeeded his father; but he is found
mentioned as being King of Urartu from 708 onwards (*Fastes*, l. 113; cf. *infra*, pp. 257, 258), and
hence it has been concluded, not without some reason, that such was the fact. The Vannic inscriptions have not as yet given us this sovereign's name.

[3] Drawn by Faucher-Gudin, from an impression of the original seal which is preserved at the
Hague; cf. J. MÉNANT, *Catalogue des Cylindres Orientaux du Cabinet Royal des Médailles de La
Haye*, pl. vii. No. 32; LAJARD, *Introduction à l'Étude du Culte de Mithra*, pl. lxi. No. 9.

quite able to safeguard their independence against an intruder. Besides this, the Cimmerians and the Scythians were already pressing on their frontier, and were constantly harassing them. This fresh danger absorbed their entire attention, and from this time forward they ceased to play a part in general history; the century which had seen the rise and growth of their power was also a witness of their downfall under the attacks of Assyria.

THE ASSYRIANS TAKING A MEDIAN TOWN.[1]

During the last months of 714, the tribes which had formerly constituted the kingdom of Karalla mutinied against the tyranny of their governor, and invited Amitash-shi, the brother of their ancient lord Assurlî, to rule over them. Sargon attacked them in the spring of 713, dispersed their troops, held them to ransom, and after having once more exacted homage from Bît-Dayaukku,[2] Ellipi, and Allabria, made a raid extending as far as the confines of the Iranian desert, the barren steppes of Eastern Arabia,[3] and the district of Nagira belonging to the "powerful" Manda.[4] While he was thus preparing the way for peace in his Median domains, one of his generals crossed

[1] Drawn by Faucher-Gudin, from the facsimile by Flandin, published in BOTTA, *Le Monument de Ninive*, vol. ii. pl. 93. It seems that this town was called Amkaru, and its name appears, as far as I know, in none of the accounts which we possess of the campaigns. The town was apparently situated in Karalla or in Median territory.

[2] The Dayaukku who gave his name to this province was at first confounded with the personage who was entangled in the affairs of Ullusunu (cf. what is said of him, pp. 242, 243, *supra*), and was then banished by Sargon to Hamath (FR. LENORMANT, *Lettres Assyriologiques*, vol. i. p. 56, et seq.; TIELE, *Babylonisch-assyrische Geschichte*, p. 263, note 3; HOMMEL, *Geschichte Babyloniens und Assyriens*, p. 714; E. MEYER, *Geschichte des Alterthums*, vol. i. pp. 456, 555). The identity of the two persons was disputed by G. Rawlinson (*The Five Great Monarchies*, 2nd edit., vol. ii. p. 383, note 7) and by Sayce (E. BUNSEN, *Biblische Gleichzeitigkeiten*, p. 142, et seq.); a good number of historians now admit that they were different persons (DELATTRE, *Le Peuple et l'Empire des Mèdes*, p. 146, note 1; WINCKLER, *Untersuchungen zur Altorientalischen Geschichte*, pp. 117, 118). Bît-Dayaukku is evidently the district of Ecbatana, as Oppert (*Le Peuple et la Langue des Mèdes*, p. 20) was the first to point out; cf. WINCKLER, *Untersuchungen zur Altorientalischen Gesch.*, p. 118.

[3] The Eastern Arabs mentioned here were nomadic, and inhabited the confines of the Great Desert to the south-east of Media (DELATTRE, *Le Peuple et l'Empire des Mèdes*, p. 106), or the steppes of Northern Iran (WINCKLER, *op. cit.*, p. 112). They are those mentioned in a passage of Appian (*Syriaca*, § 55), together with Parthians, Bactrians, and Tapyræans, as having submitted to Seleucus.

[4] The "powerful" Manda, encamped in the mountain and desert (*Annals*, ll. 162, 163), and who were named after the Eastern Arabs, must be the peoples situated between the Caspian and the steppes of the Iranian plateau, and a branch of the Scythians who are soon to appear in Asiatic history.

the Euphrates to chastise the Tabal for their ill deeds. The latter had figured, about the year 740 B.C., among the peoples who had bowed before the supremacy of Urartu, and their chief, Uassarmi, had been the ally or vassal of Sharduris. Contemptuously spared at the taking of Arpad, he had not been able to resign himself to the Assyrian yoke, and had, in an ill-timed moment, thrown it off in 731; he had, however, been overcome and forced to surrender, and Tiglath-pileser had put in his place a man of obscure birth, named Khulli, whose fidelity had remained unshaken throughout the reign of Shalmaneser V. and the first years of Sargon.[1] Khulli's son, Ambaridis,[2] the husband of a Ninevite princess,[3] who had brought him as dowry a considerable part of Cilicia, had been unable to resist the flattering offers of Rusas; he had broken the ties which attached him to the new Assyrian dynasty, but had been left unmolested so long as Urartu and Muzazîr remained unshaken, since his position at the western extremity of the empire prevented him from influencing in the smallest degree the issue of the struggle, and it was well known that when the fall of Rusas took place, Ambaridis would be speedily brought to account. He was, in fact, seized, banished to the banks of the Tigris, and his hereditary fief of Bît-Burutash annexed to Cilicia under the rule of an Assyrian.[4] The following year was signalised by a similar execution at which Sargon himself deigned to preside in person. Tarkhunazi, the King of Miliddu, not only had taken advantage of the troubles consequent on the Armenian war to rebel against his master, but had attacked Gunzinânu, who held, and had ruthlessly pillaged, the neighbouring district of Kammanu.[5] Sargon overcame him in the open field, took from him his city of Miliddu, and stormed the town of Tulgarimmê in which he had taken refuge.[6] Here again the native kingdom disappeared, and was replaced by an Assyrian administration. Kammanu,

---

[1] Cf. what is said of this Uassarmi, p. 189, *supra*.

[2] This is the spelling of the *Annals*, 1. 168, but we find also Ambaris (*Annals*, 1. 175, *Inscription des Fastes*, 1. 29) and Amris (*Inscription des Fastes*, 1. 31).

[3] Winckler (*Altorientalische Forschungen*, vol. i. p. 365, note 3) is inclined to recognise in this princess the lady Akhatabîsha, whom Sennacherib, while still heir-apparent, mentions in a despatch addressed to Sargon (H. RAWLINSON, *Cun. Ins. W. As.*, vol. iv. pl. 26, No. 1, pp. 55–58).

[4] *Annals of Sargon*, ll. 168–178: cf. OPPERT, *The Annals of Sargon*, in *Records of the Past*, 1st ser., vol. vii. pp. 37, 38; WINCKLER, *Die Keilschrifttexte Sargons*, vol. i. pp. 28–31; *Inscription des Fastes*, ll. 29–32; cf. OPPERT, *Great Inscription in the Palace of Khorsabad*, in *Records of the Past*, 1st ser., vol. xi. p. 67; WINCKLER, *Die Keilschrifttexte Sargons*, vol. i. pp. 102, 103.

[5] Kammanu is probably not the Kammanênê of the Greek geographers (E. NORRIS, *Assyrian Dictionary*, v.s. *Kammanu*, p. 573; SCHRADER, *Keilinschriften und Geschichtsforschung*, p. 153), which is too far north relatively to Melitênê, but is probably Comana of Cappadocia and its district (DELATTRE, *L'Asie Antérieure*, p. 65, and *Encore un mot sur la Géographie Assyrienne*, pp. 31–33).

[6] Tulgarimmê has been connected with the Togarmah of the Bible (*Gen.* x. 3) by Halévy and Delitzsch (*Wo lag das Paradies?* p. 246), and their views on this subject have been adopted by most historians (FR. LENORMANT, *Les Origines de l'Histoire*, vol. ii. p. 410; WINCKLER, *Die Keilschrifttexte Sargons*, vol. i. p. xxix., note 5, and *Geschichte Babyloniens und Assyriens*, p. 246; HOMMEL, *Geschichte Babyloniens und Assyriens*, p. 715, note 1; TIELE, *Babylonisch-assyrische Geschichte*, p. 297; SCHRADER, *Die Keilinschriften und das Alte Testament*, 1883, p. 85).

wedged in between Urartu and Mushki, separated these two countries, sometimes rivals to each other, but always enemies to Nineveh. Its maintenance as an independent kingdom prevented them from combining their efforts, and obtaining that unity of action which alone could ensure for them, if not a definite triumph, at least preservation from complete extinction and an opportunity of maintaining their liberty; the importance of the position, however, rendered it particularly perilous to hold, and the Assyrians succeeded in so doing only by strongly fortifying it. Walls were built round ten cities, five on the Urartian frontier, three on that of Mushki, and two on the north, and the country which they protected was made into a new province, that of Tulgarimmê, the district of Miliddu being confided to the care of Mutallu, Prince of Kummukh (710).[1] An incident which took place in the following year furnished a pretext for completing the organisation and military defence of this western border province. Gurgum had been for thirty years or more in the possession of Tarkhulara; this prince, after having served Sharduris, had transferred his homage to Tiglath-pileser,[2] and he had thenceforward professed an unwavering loyalty to the Assyrian sovereigns. This accommodating personage was assassinated by his son Mutallu; and Sargon, fearing a revolt, hastened, at the head of a detachment of picked troops, to avenge him. The murderer threw down his arms almost without having struck a blow, and Gurgum was thenceforward placed under the direct rule of Nineveh.[3] The affair had not been brought to a close before an outbreak took place in Southern Syria, which might have entailed very serious consequences had it not been promptly dealt with. Egypt, united from end to end under the sceptre of Sabaco, jealously kept watch over the political complications in Asia, and though perhaps she was not sure enough of her own strength to interfere openly before the death of Rusas, she had renewed negotiations with the petty kingdoms of the Hebrews and Philistines. Ashdod had for some time past showed signs of discontent, and it had been found necessary to replace their king, Azuri, who had refused to pay tribute, by his brother

---

[1] *Annals of Sargon,* ll. 178–195: cf. OPPERT, *The Annals of Sargon,* in *Records of the Past,* 1st ser., vol. viii. pp. 38, 39; WINCKLER, *Die Keilschrifttexte Sargons,* vol. i. pp. 30–33; *Inscription des Fastes,* ll. 78–83; cf. OPPERT, *Great Inscription in the Palace of Khorsabad,* in *Records of the Past,* 1st ser., vol. ix. p. 10; WINCKLER, *Die Keilschrifttexte Sargons,* vol. i. pp. 112, 113. The scribe who drew up the inscriptions of Hall XIV. did not understand the sequence of events, and believed that Sargon had deprived Gunzinanû of his territory (ll. 9, 10; cf. WINCKLER, *Die Keilschrifttexte Sargons,* vol. i. pp. 82, 83); the scribe who had the inscriptions of the gateway floors cut fell into the same mistake (iv. ll. 23–27; cf. WINCKLER, *Die Keilschrifttexte Sargons,* vol. i. pp. 148, 149).

[2] Cf. what is said with regard to the government of Gurgum and its prince under Tiglath-pileser III., pp. 121, 148, 149, *supra.*

[3] *Annals of Sargon,* ll. 208–215: cf. OPPERT, *The Annals of Sargon,* in *Records of the Past,* 1st ser., vol. vii. pp. 39–50; WINCKLER, *Die Keilschrifttexte Sargons,* vol. i. pp. 32–35; *Inscription des Fastes,* ll. 83–89; cf. OPPERT, *Great Inscription of the Palace of Khorsabad,* in *Records of the Past,* 1st ser., vol. ix. pp. 12, 13; WINCKLER, *Die Keilschrifttexte Sargons,* vol. i. pp. 112–115.

Akhimiti; shortly after this, however, the people had risen in rebellion : they had massacred Akhimiti, whom they accused of being a mere thrall of Assyria, and had placed on the throne Yamani, a soldier of fortune, probably an adventurer of Hellenic extraction.[1] The other Philistine cities had immediately taken up arms ; Edom and Moab were influenced by the general movement,[2] and Isaiah was striving to avert any imprudent step on the part of Judah. Sargon despatched the Tartan,[3] and the rapidity with which that officer carried out the campaign prevented the movement from spreading beyond Philistia. He devastated Ashdod, and its vassal, Gath, carried off their gods and their inhabitants, and peopled the cities afresh with prisoners from Asia Minor, Urartu, and Media. Yamani attempted to escape into Egypt, but the chief of Milukhkha intercepted him on his way, and handed him over in chains to the conqueror.[4] The latter took care not to call either Moab, Edom, or Judah to account for the part they had taken in the movement, perhaps because they were not mentioned in his instructions, or because he preferred not to furnish them, by an untimely interference, with a pretext for calling in the help of Egypt.[5] The year was doubtless too far advanced to allow him to dream of marching against Pharaoh, and moreover that would have been one of those important steps which the king alone had the right to take. There was, however, no doubt that the encounter between the two empires was imminent, and Isaiah ventured to predict the precise date of its occurrence. He walked stripped and barefoot through the streets of Jerusalem—a strange

---

[1] This prince's name, usually written Yamani (*Annals of Hall XIV.*, l. 11 ; *Inscription des Fastes*, ll. 95, 101 ; *Fragment of the Campaign against Ashdod*, ll. 18, 40), is also written Yatnani in the *Annals*, l. 220, and this variation, which is found again in the name of the island of Cyprus and the Cypriotes, gives us grounds for believing that the Assyrian scribe took the race-name of the prince for a proper name : the new king of Ashdod would have been a Yamani, a Greek of Cyprus (WINCKLER, *Die Keilschr. Sargons*, vol. i. p. xxx., note 2 ; HOMMEL, *Gesch. Bab. und Ass.*, p. 703). Winckler would now be inclined to see in this man an Arab, a man of Yemen (*Musri, Meluhha, Ma'in*, i. p. 26, note 1).

[2] The *Annals* and the *Fastes* mention only the people of Ashdod, whom the scribe calls Khâti, probably from a reminiscence of the local tradition which placed some of the Hittites in Southern Syria (cf. *Struggle of the Nations*, p. 148); G. Smith's fragment expressly mentions along with them the Philistines, Judah, Moab, Edom, and Pharaoh, King of Egypt (ll. 29–36).

[3] The Assyrian narratives, as usual, give the honour of conducting the campaign to the king (*Annals*, l. 222, et seq. ; *Fastes*, l. 97, et seq.). Isaiah (xx. 1) distinctly says that Sargon sent the Tartan to quell the revolt of Ashdod.

[4] The *Annals*, ll. 225, 226, state that Yamani was made prisoner and taken to Assyria. The *Fastes*, ll. 101–103, more accurate on this point, state that he escaped to Muzri, and that he was given up by the King of Milukhkha. The Muzri mentioned in this passage would be, according to Winckler (*Altorientalische Forschungen*, vol. i. pp. 27, 28), the Arab district of that name ; but the mention of Pharaoh, King of Muzri, in Smith's fragment (ll. 33, 34), shows that Muzri very probably here means Egypt ; Winckler prefers to believe that Piru is not the transcript of Pharaoh, but the name of the Arab prince of Muzri (*Musri, Meluhha, Ma'in*, i. pp. 2–4, 14, 15).

[5] *Annals of Sargon*, ll. 215–228 : cf. OPPERT, *The Annals of Sargon*, in *Records of the Past*, 1st ser., vol. vii. p. 40 ; WINCKLER, *Die Keilschrifttexte Sargons*, vol. i. pp. 36–39 ; *Inscrip. des Fastes*, ll. 90–109 ; cf. OPPERT, *Great Inscription in the Palace of Khorsabad*, in *Records of the Past*, 1st ser., vol. ix. pp. 11, 12 ; WINCKLER, *Die Keilschrifttexte Sargons*, vol. i. pp. 114–117. A fragment of the *Annals*, discovered by G. Smith (*Assyrian History*, in the *Zeitschrift*, 1869, p. 107), published by Winckler (*op. cit.*, vol. i. pp. 186–189), gives a fully detailed account of the campaign ; unfortunately it is much mutilated.

procedure which he explained by the words which Jahveh had put into his lips: "Like as My servant Isaiah hath walked naked and barefoot three years for a sign and a wonder upon Egypt and upon Kush (Ethiopia); so shall the King of Assyria lead away the captives of Egypt and the exiles of Kush, young and old, naked and barefoot, and with buttocks uncovered, to the shame of Egypt. And they shall be dismayed and ashamed, because of Kush their expectation, and of Egypt their glory. And the inhabitants of this coastland shall say in that day, Behold, such is our expectation, whither we fled for help to be delivered from the King of Assyria: and we, how shall we escape?"[1]

The fulfilment of this prophecy did not take place as quickly as the prophet perhaps desired. Egypt appeared too strong to be openly attacked by a mere section of the battalions at the disposal of Assyria, and besides, it may have been deemed imprudent to involve the army to any serious extent on so distant a field as Africa, when Babylon was ready and waiting to fall upon the very heart of Assyria at the first news of a real or supposed reverse. Circumstances seemed, moreover, to favour a war against Merodach-baladan.[2] This sovereign, who had been received with acclamation by the Babylonians, had already lost the popularity he had enjoyed at his accession. The fickle character of the people, which made them nearly always welcome a fresh master with enthusiasm, soon led them from love and obedience to hatred, and finally to revolt. Merodach-baladan trusted to the Kaldâ[3] to help him to maintain his position, and their rude barbarity, even if it protected him against the fickleness of his more civilised subjects, increased the discontent at Kutha, Sippar, and Borsippa. He removed the statues of the gods from these towns, imprisoned the most turbulent citizens, confiscated their goods, and distributed them among his own followers;[4] the other cities took no part in the movement, but Sargon must have expected to find in them, if not effective support, at least sympathies which would facilitate his work of conquest. It is true that Elam, whose friendship for the Aramæan was still undiminished,

[1] Isa. xx.

[2] The early Assyriologists did not really understand the true nature of this war. They looked upon Merodach-baladan as the lawful King of Babylon, and Fr. Lenormant made him a Chaldæan patriot (*Les Premières Civilisations*, vol. ii. p. 202, et seq.), who was defending his fatherland against the invader. The real origin of Merodach-baladan, the part he played at Babylon, and the reasons for his impotence, were brought to light for the first time by DELATTRE, *Les Chaldéens jusqu'à la formation de l'Empire de Nabuchodonosor*, 2nd edit., pp. 9-12, and *Le Peuple et l'Empire des Mèdes*, pp. 109-190; then by TIELE, *Babylonisch-assyrische Geschichte*, pp. 277-279; and by WINCKLER, *Untersuchungen zur Altorientalischen Geschichte*, pp. 55, 56. For the question as to priority, cf. DELATTRE, *Un nouveau Livre sur l'Histoire Ancienne de l'Orient*, 1889, p. 12, and *Les Chaldéens jusqu'à la formation de l'Empire de Nabuchodonosor, précédé de considérations sur un récent livre de M. Hugo Winckler*, 1889, xii.-25 p.; WINCKLER, *Plagiat? Antwort auf die von A. J. Delattre S. J. gegen mich erhobenen Beschuldigungen*, 1889, 20 p.; and finally, DELATTRE, *Réponse au plaidoyer de M. Hugo Winckler*, 1889, p. 20.

[3] *Annals of Sargon*, ll. 235-238, 360, 361; *Inscription des Fastes*, ll. 121-125, 134-137.

[4] For these facts, cf. the passage in the *Annals*, 359-364, where the victorious Sargon relates how he undid the work of Merodach-baladan.

remained to be reckoned with, but Elam had lost much of its prestige in the last few years. The aged Khumban-igash had died in 717,[1] and his successor, Shutruk-nakhunta, had not apparently inherited all the energy of his father,[2] and it is possible that troubles had arisen among the vassals of his own kingdom which prevented him from interfering on behalf of his ally. Sargon took account of all these circumstances in arranging his plan of campaign. He divided his army into two forces, one of which, under his own command, was to be directed against Merodach-baladan, while the other was to attack the insurgent Aramæans on the left bank of the Tigris, and was to be manœuvred so as to drive Shutruk-nakhunta back on the marshes of the Uknu.[3] The eastern force was the first to be set in movement, and it pushed forward into the territory of the Gambulu. These latter had concentrated themselves round Dur-Atkharas, one of their citadels;[4] they had increased the height of the walls, and filled the ditches with water brought from the Shurappu by means of a canal, and having received a reinforcement of 600 horsemen and 4000 foot soldiers, they had drawn them up in front of the ramparts. A single morning sufficed to disperse them, and the Assyrians, entering the city with the fugitives, took possession of it on the same day. They made 16,490 prisoners, and seized horses, mules, asses, camels, and both sheep and oxen in large numbers. Eight of the chiefs of the neighbourhood, who ruled over the flat country between the Shurappu and the Uknu, begged for mercy as soon as they learned the result of the engagement. The name of Dur-Atkharas was changed to that of Dur-

---

[1] The date of the death of Khumban-igash is indirectly given in the passage of the *Babylonian Chronicle of Pinches*, col. ii. 32–34, where it is said that in the first year of Ashshur-nâdin-shumu, King of Babylon, Ishtar-khundu (= Shutruk-nakhunta) was dethroned by his brother, Khallushu, after having reigned over Elam eighteen years : these events actually took place, as we shall see below (cf. p. 299, *infra*), about the year 699 before our era.

[2] Shutruk-nakhunta is the Susian form of the name (cf. *supra*, pp. 127, 128); the Assyrian texts distort it into Shutur-nankhundi (*Annals of Sargon*, ll. 271, 286, 292, 406 ; *Inscription des Fastes*, l. 119), and the *Babylonian Chronicle of Pinches*, col. ii. ll. 32, 34, into Ishtar-khundu, owing to a faint resemblance in the sound of the name of the goddess Ishtar with the form *Shutur*, *Sthur*, itself derived from Shutruk, with which the name began.

[3] The earlier historians of Assyria, misled in the first place by the form in which the scribes have handed down the account in the *Annals* and the *Fastes*, assumed the existence of a single army, led by Sargon himself, and which would have marched on all the above-mentioned places of the country, one by one. Tiele was the first to recognise that Sargon must have left part of his forces to the command of one of his lieutenants (*Babylonisch-assyrische Geschichte*, p. 273), and Winckler, enlarging on this idea, showed that there were then two armies, engaged at different seats of war, but manœuvring as far as possible by mutual arrangement (*Die Keilschrifttexte Sargons*, vol. i. p. xxviii., note 1 ; cf. BILLERBECK, *Susa*, pp. 79–81, where one of the two armies, called by the author the army of the north, is said to have been itself divided into two corps).

[4] The site of Dur-Atkharas is unknown. Billerbeck places it hypothetically on the stream of Mendeli (*Susa*, p. 80), and his conjecture is in itself very plausible. I should incline, however, to place it more to the south, on account of the passage in which it is said that the Kaldâ, to complete the defences of the town, brought a canal from the Shurappu and fortified its banks. The Shurappu, according to Delitzsch, would be the Shatt Umm-el-Jemâl (*Wo lag das Paradies ?* p. 195); according to Delattre, the Kerkha (*Les Travaux hydrauliques en Babylonie*, p. 39, n. 4); the account of the campaign under consideration would lead me to recognise in it a watercourse like the Tîb, which runs into the Tigris near Amara, in which case the ruins of Kherîb would perhaps correspond with the site of Dur-Atkharas.

Nebo, the territory of the Gambulu was converted into a province, and its organisation having been completed, the army continued its march, sweeping before it the Ruâ, the Khindaru, the Puqudu, in short, all the tribes occupying the district of Yatbur.[1] The chiefs of these provinces sought refuge in the morasses of the lower Kerkha, but finding themselves surrounded and short of provisions, they were forced by famine to yield to the enemy, and came to terms with the Assyrians, who imposed a tribute on them and included them within the new province of Gambulu. The goal of this expedition was thus attained, and Elam separated from Karduniash, but the issue of the war remained undecided as long as Shutruk-nakhunta held the cities at the edge of the plain, from which he could emerge at will into the heart of the Assyrian position. The conqueror therefore turned in that direction, rapidly took from him the citadels of Shamuna and Babduri, then those of Lakhi-rimmu and Pillutu, and pitched his camp on the bank of the Naditi, from whence he despatched marauding bands to pillage the country. Dismay spread throughout the district of Rashi; the inhabitants, abandoning their cities— Tîl-Khumba, Durmishamash, Bubî, and Khamanu—migrated as far as Bît-Imbi; Shutruk-nakhunta, overcome with fear, took refuge, so it was said, in the distant mountains to preserve his life.[2] Sargon, meanwhile, had crossed the Euphrates with the other force, and had marched straight upon Bît-Dakkuri; having there noticed that the fortress of Dur-Ladînu was in ruins, he rebuilt it, and, firmly installed within the heart of the country, he patiently waited until the eastern force had accomplished its mission. Like his adversary, Merodach-baladan, he had no desire to be drawn into an engagement until he knew what chance there was of the latter being reinforced by the King of Elam. At the opening of hostilities Merodach-baladan claimed the help of the Elamite king, and lavished on him magnificent presents —a couch, a throne, a portable chair, a cup for the royal offerings, and his own pectoral chain; these all reached their destination in good condition, and were graciously accepted. But before long the Elamite prince, threatened

[1] For these peoples, cf. p. 119, *supra*.

[2] None of these places can be identified with certainty. So far as I can follow the account of this campaign on the map, it seems that the attacks upon Shutruk-nakhunta took place on the plain and in the mountains between the Ab-î-Gengir and the Tîb, so that the river Naditi would be the Aftâh or one of its tributaries. If this were so, Lakhirimmu and Pillutu would be situated somewhere near the Jughaî ben Ruan and the Têpê Ghulamen of de Morgan's map of Elam, Shamuna near Zirzir-têpî, Babdurî near Hosseiniyeh. But I wish it to be understood that I do not consider these comparisons as more than simple conjectures. Bît-Imbi was certainly out of the reach of the Assyrians, since it was used as a place of refuge by the inhabitants of Rashî; at the same time it must have been close to Rashî, since the people of this country fled thither. The site of Ghilân which de Morgan has adopted on his map seems to me to be too far north to comply with these conditions, and that of Tapa, approved by Billerbeck (*Susa*, p. 73), too southerly. If, as I believe, Rashî corresponds to the regions of Pushti-kuh which lie on both sides of the upper waters of the Mendeli stream, we ought to look for Bît-Imbi somewhere near the Desht-î-Ghoaur and the Zenjan, near a point where communication with the banks of the Ab-î-Kirind would be easy.

in his own domain, forgot everything except his own personal safety, and declared himself unable to render Merodach-baladan any assistance. The latter, on receiving this news, threw himself with his face in the dust, rent his clothes, and broke out into loud weeping; after which, conscious that his strength would not permit of his meeting the enemy in the open field, he withdrew his men from the other side of the Tigris, escaped secretly by night, and retired with his troops to the fortress of Ikbîbel. The inhabitants of Babylon and Borsippa did not allow themselves to be disconcerted; they brought the arks of Bel, Zarpanît, Nebo, and Tashmît out of their sanctuaries, and came forth with chanting and musical instruments to salute Sargon at Dûr-Ladînu. He entered the city in their company, and after he had celebrated the customary sacrifices, the people enthroned him in Merodach-baladan's palace. Tribute was offered to him, but he refused to accept any part of it for his personal use, and applied it to a work of public utility—the repairing of the ancient canal of Borsippa, which had become nearly filled up. This done, he detached a body of troops to occupy Sippara, and returned to Assyria, there to take up his winter quarters.[1]

Once again, therefore, the ancient metropolis of the Euphrates was ruled by an Assyrian, who united in one protocol the titles of the sovereigns of Assur and Karduniash. Babylon possessed for the kings of Nineveh the same kind of attraction as at a later date drew the German Cæsars to Rome. Scarcely had the Assyrian monarchs been crowned within their own domains, than they turned their eyes towards Babylon, and their ambition knew no rest till the day came for them to present themselves in pomp within the temple of its god and implore his solemn consecration. When at length they had received it, they scrupulously secured its renewal on every occasion which the law prescribed, and their chroniclers recorded among the important events of the year, the ceremony in which they "took the hand of Bel." Sargon therefore returned, in the month Nisan of the year 709, to preside over the procession of the god, and he devoutly accomplished the rites which constituted him the legitimate successor of the semi-fabulous heroes of the old empire, foremost among whom was his namesake Shargâni of Agadê.[2] He offered sacrifices to Bel, Nebo, and to the divinities of Sumir and Akkad, and he did not return to the camp until he had fulfilled all the duties incumbent on his new dignity.

[1] *Annals of Sargon*, ll. 228–316: cf. OPPERT, *The Annals of Sargon*, in the *Records of the Past*, 1st ser., vol. vii. pp. 40–46; WINCKLER, *Die Keilschrifttexte Sargons*, vol. i. pp. 38–55. The *Annals*, in spite of the mutilation they have suffered, are the only documents which furnish us with an almost complete picture of this campaign. In the *Fastes* the events are distributed under various headings, and the narrative is greatly abridged (ll. 18–21, 121–126, 140–144); the *Larnaka Stele* merely gives an account of the entry into Babylon (col. ii. ll. 1–22).

[2] As to Shargâni of Agadê (Sargon I.), cf. *Dawn of Civilization*, pp. 596–599.

He was involved that year in two important wars at opposite points of his empire. One was at the north-western extremity, against the Mushki and their king Mita, who, after having supported Rusas, was now intriguing with Argistis; the other in the south-east, against the Kaldâ, and probably also against Elam. He entrusted the conduct of the former to the governor of Kuî, but reserved to himself the final reckoning with Merodach-baladan. The Babylonian king had made good use of the respite given him during the winter months. Too prudent to meet his enemy in the open plain, he had transformed his hereditary principality into a formidable citadel. During the preceding campaign he had devastated the whole of the country lying between the marshes and the territory occupied by the Assyrians, and had withdrawn the inhabitants. Most of the towns—Ikbîbel, Uru, Uruk, Kishik, and Nimid-laguda—were also deserted, and no garrisons were left in them. He had added to the fortifications of Dur-Yakîn,[1] and enlarged the moat till it was two hundred cubits wide and eighteen deep, so as to reach the level of infiltration; he then turned into it the waters of the Euphrates, so that the town appeared to be floating on a lake, without either bridges or quays by means of which the besiegers might have brought their machines within range and their troops been able to approach for an assault. Merodach-baladan had been careful not to shut himself within the town, but had taken up a position in the marshes, and there awaited the arrival of the Assyrians. Sargon, having left Babylon in the month of Iyyâr, encountered him within sight of Dur-Yakîn. The Aramæan infantry were crushed by repeated charges from the Ninevite chariotry and cavalry, who pursued the fugitives to the outer side of the moat, and seized the camp with all its baggage and the royal train, including the king's tent, a canopy of solid silver which protected the throne, his sceptre, weapons, and stores of all kinds. The peasants, to the number of 90,580, crowded within the lines, also fell into their hands, together with their flocks and herds—2500 horses, 610 mules, and 854 camels, as well as sheep, oxen, and asses; the remainder of the fugitives rushed within the outworks for refuge " like a pack of wild boars," and finally were driven into the interior of the place, or scattered among the beds of reeds along the coast. Sargon cut down the groves of palm trees which adorned the suburbs, and piled up their trunks in the moat, thus quickly forming a causeway right up to the walls. Merodach-baladan had been wounded in the arm [2] during the engagement, but, nevertheless, fought stubbornly in defence of his city; when he saw that its

---

[1] As to the position occupied by Dur-Yakîn, near the modern town of Qornah, cf. p. 225, supra.

[2] The Inscription des Fastes, ll. 133, 134, states that he was made prisoner with all his family; the text of the Annals, l. 349, admits that he escaped. We shall find him reappearing again at the beginning of the reign of Sennnacherib; cf. pp. 274, 275, infra.

fall was inevitable, he fled to the other side of the gulf, and took refuge among the mud flats of the Lower Ulaî. Sargon set fire to Dur-Yakîn, levelled its towers and walls with the ground, and demolished its houses, temples, and palaces. It had been a sort of penal settlement, to which the Kaldâ rulers used to consign those of their subjects belonging to the old aboriginal race, who had rendered themselves obnoxious by their wealth or independence of character; the number of these prisoners was considerable, Babylon, Borsippa, Nipur, and Sippar, not to speak of Uru, Uruk, Eridu, Larsam, and Kishîk, having all of them furnished their share. Sargon released them all, and restored their gods to the temples; he expelled the nomads from the estates which, contrary to all justice, had been distributed among them in preceding years, and reinstated the former owners. Karduniash, which had been oppressed for twelve long years by a semi-barbarian despot, now breathed again, and hailed Sargon as its deliverer, while he on his part was actively engaged in organising his conquest. The voluntary submission of Upiri, King of Dilmun,[1] who lived isolated in the open sea, "as though in a bird's nest," secured to Sargon possession of the watercourses which flowed beyond the Chaldæan lake into the Persian Gulf: no sooner had he obtained it than he quitted the neighbourhood of Dur-Yakîn, crossed the Tigris, and reinforced the garrisons which lined his Elamite frontier on this side. He had just finished building a strongly fortified citadel on the site of Sagbat,[2] when ambassadors arrived from Mitâ.[3] The governor of Kuî had at length triumphed over the obstinacy of the Mushki, and after driving them from village to village, had compelled them to sue for terms: the tidings of the victories over the Kaldâ had doubtless hastened their decision, but they were still so powerful that it was thought wiser not to impose too rigorous conditions upon them. Mitâ agreed to pay tribute, and surrendered one or two districts, which were turned into an Aramæan settlement: the inhabitants were transferred to Bît-Yakîn, where they had to make the best they could of lands that had been devastated by war.[4] At this juncture the Greeks of Cyprus flattered the pride of the Assyrians in a most unexpected

[1] As to the site of Dilmun, cf. *Dawn of Civilization*, p. 562, note 7.

[2] This Sagbat, which must not be confused with the district of Bît-Sagbati mentioned in the reign of Tiglath-pileser III., seems to correspond with a post to the south of Durîlu, perhaps the ruins of Baksayeh, on the Tchengula.

[3] *Annals of Sargon*, ll. 317–371: cf. OPPERT, *The Annals of Sargon*, in the *Records of the Past*, 1st ser., vol. vii. pp. 46–49; WINCKLER, *Die Keilschrifttexte Sargons*, vol. i. pp. 54–63. An abridged narrative of the same events is found in the *Inscription des Fastes*, ll. 126–138, 144, 145; cf. OPPERT, *Great Inscription in the Palace of Khorsabad*, in the *Records of the Past*, 1st ser., vol. ix. pp. 14–17; WINCKLER, *Die Keilschrifttexte Sargons*, vol. i. pp. 120–125, 126, 127.

[4] *Annals of Sargon*, ll. 371–383: cf. OPPERT, *The Annals of Sargon*, in the *Records of the Past*, 1st ser., vol. vii. pp. 49, 50; WINCKLER; *Die Keilschrifttexte Sargons*, vol. i. pp. 62–65; *Inscription des Fastes*, ll. 149–153; cf. OPPERT, *Great Inscription in the Palace of Khorsabad*, in the *Records of the Past*, 1st ser., vol. ix. pp. 17, 18; WINCKLER, *Die Keilschrifttexte Sargons*, vol. i. pp. 126–129.

STELE AT LARNAKA.[4]

way : after the manner of their race they scoured the seas, and their fleets persistently devastated the coasts of Syria and Cilicia.[1] Seven of their kings were so far alarmed by the report of Sargon's achievements as to dread punishment for their misdeeds. They therefore sent him presents, and, for the moment, abandoned their piratical expeditions in Phœnician waters. The homage of these inveterate robbers raised Sargon in his own eyes and in those of his subjects.[2] Some years later, about 708 B.C., he presented them with a stele of black marble, on which he had engraved his own portrait, together with a long inscription setting forth his most glorious exploits. They set it up at Kition (Citium), where it has been preserved amongst the ruins, a priceless witness to the greatness of Assyria.[3]

While war thus raged around him, Sargon still found time for works of a peaceful character. He set himself to remodel and complete the system of irrigation in the Assyrian plain ; he repaired the dykes, and cleaned out and made good the beds of the canals which had been neglected during the troublous times of the last generation.[5] He erected buildings at Calah[6] and at Nineveh,[7] but in these cities everything seemed to recall too vividly the memory of the sovereigns who had gone before him : he wished for a capital which should belong to himself alone, where he would not be reminded of a past in which he had no part.[8] After meditating

---

[1] Their misdeeds are indicated in the *Cylinder Inscription* (l. 21; cf. LYON, *Keilschrifttexte Sargons*, pp. 32, 33), which was first accurately explained by Fr. Delitzsch (*Wo lag das Paradies?* p. 248), and in which Sargon boasts that he has "torn the Ionian from the midst of the seas and thus restored peace to the countries of Kuî and Tyre."

[2] *Annals of Sargon*, ll. 383–388 : cf. OPPERT, *The Annals of Sargon*, in *Records of the Past*, 1st ser., vol. vii. p. 51; WINCKLER, *Die Keilschrifttexte Sargons*, vol. i. pp. 64–66; *Inscrip. des Fastes*, ll. 145–149, where Winckler (*Keilschrifttexte Sargons*, vol. i. p. ix., note 6, and *Altorient. Forschungen*, vol. i. p. 367, note 1) regards the Assyrian expression *Ia-nagi* as a blundering transcription of the Greek 'Ιωνική.

[3] *Larnaka Stele*, col. ii. ll. 43–62; cf. WINCKLER, *Die Keilschrifttexte Sargons*, vol. i. pp. 182, 183. This stele was discovered at Larnaka, and is now in the Berlin Museum.

[4] Drawn by Faucher-Gudin, from the plaster cast in the Louvre.

[5] *Cylinder Inscription*, ll. 36, 37 : cf. OPPERT, *Les Inscriptions de Dour-Sarkayân*, in PLACE, *Ninive et l'Assyrie*, vol. ii. pp. 296, 297 ; LYON, *Keilschrifttexte Sargons*, pp. 34, 35. As to works of the same nature carried out in Babylon, cf. *Annals*, ll. 302–304.

[6] At Calah, he lived in an old palace of Assur-nazir-pal restored and adapted for his use, as shown by the inscription published by LAYARD, *Inscriptions in the Cuneiform Characters*, pl. xxxiii. ll. 13–22; cf. WINCKLER, *Die Keilschrifttexte Sargons*, vol. i. pp. 170–173.

[7] *Inscription on the Bricks at Kouyunjik* (in H. Rawlinson, *Cun. Ins. W. As.*, vol. i. pl. 6, No. 7 ; cf. WINCKLER, *Die Keilschrifttexte Sargons*, vol. i. p. 193), relating to the rebuilding of a temple of Nebo and Marduk.

[8] The account of the building of Dur-Sharrukîn is to be found in a more or less complete form at the end of all Sargon's historical inscriptions, *e.g.* in the *Annals*, ll. 414–460, in the *Inscription des Fastes*, ll. 153–194, in the *Annals of Room XIV.*, ll. 65–89, in the *Inscription on the Pavement of the*

day and night, his choice fell upon the
village of Maganubba, a
little to the north-east of
Nineveh, in a wide plain
which extends from the
banks of the Khuzur to the
hills of Muzri, and by a single
decree he expropriated all
its inhabitants. He then
built on the land which he
had purchased from them a
city of unrivalled magnificence, which he called by his
own name, Dur-Sharrukîn.[1]
The ground plan of it is of
rectangular shape, the sides
being about 1900 yards long
by 1800 yards wide, each
corner exactly facing one of
the four points of the compass.[3] Its walls rest on a

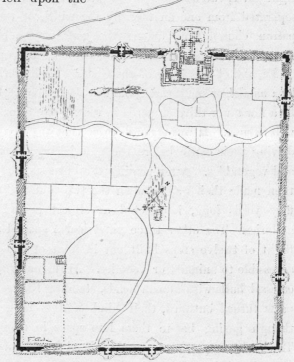

PLAN OF THE ROYAL CITY OF DUR-SHARRUKÎN.[2]

limestone sub-structure some three feet six inches high, and rise fifty-seven feet
above the ground; they are strengthened, every thirty yards or so, by battle-
mented towers which project thirteen feet from the face of the wall and stand
sixteen feet higher than the ramparts.[4] Access was gained to the interior by

Gates, ii. ll. 18–44, iii. ll. 23–45, iv. ll. 90–158, v. ll. 28–39, in the *Cylinder Inscription*, ll. 41–71, in
the *Inscription of the Bulls*, ll. 39–107; the *Inscription on the Reverse of the Slabs* is devoted to it, as
is also that of the *Foundation Tablets*.

[1] *Annals of Sargon*, ll. 414, 415. In most of the texts the village of Maganubba is not named; it
is mentioned in the *Cylinder Inscription*, l. 44, and this document is the only one which furnishes
details of the expropriation, etc. (ll. 44–52; cf. OPPERT, *Les Inscriptions de Dour-Sarkayân*, in PLACE,
Ninive et l'Assyrie, vol. ii. pp. 296, 297; LYON, *Keilschrifttexte Sargons*, pp. 34–37). The modern
name of the place is Khorsabad, *the city of Khosroes*, but the name of its founder was still associated
with its ruins, in the time of Yakut, who mentions him under the name of Sarghun. It was first
explored in 1843 by Botta, who published the result of his excavations in several works of very
varied range, in *Lettres sur les découvertes de Khorsabad*, and in *Le Monument de Ninive*, 1846-1850;
then by Place and Oppert, whose researches are embodied in the three volumes entitled *Ninive et
l'Assyrie*, 1866–1869. The antiquities collected there by Botta and Place constitute the bulk of the
Assyrian Museum in the Louvre; unfortunately, a part of the objects collected by Place went to the
bottom of the Tigris with the lighter which was carrying them.

[2] Reduction by Faucher-Gudin, from the plan published in PLACE, *Ninive et l'Assyrie*, pl. 2.

[3] PLACE, *Ninive et l'Assyrie*, vol. i. pp. 160, 161. Botta mistook the site for a "paradise" belonging to the palace; Place recognised it as the actual site of the city itself (*Ninive et l'Assyrie*, vol. i.
pp. 153–157).

[4] PLACE, *Ninive et l'Assyrie*, vol. i. pp. 161–167. Place reckoned the height of the wall at 75 feet,
a measurement adopted by Perrot and Chipiez (*Histoire de l'Art dans l'Antiquité*, vol. ii. p. 478);
Dieulafoy has shown that the height of the wall must be reduced to 47 feet, and that of the towers
about 65 feet (*L'Acropole de Suse*, p. 178).

eight gates, two on each side of the square, each of them marked by two towers separated from one another by the width of the bay. Every gate had its patron, chosen from among the gods of the city; there was the gate of Shamash, the gate of Rammân, those of Bel and Beltis, of Anu, of Ishtar, of Eâ, and of the Lady of the Gods.[1] Each of them was protected externally by a *migdol,* or small castle, built in the Syrian style,[2] and flanked at each corner by a low tower thirteen yards in width; five allowed of the passage of beasts as well as men. It was through these that the peasants came in every morning, driving their cattle before them, or jolting along in waggons laden with fruit and vegetables. After passing the outposts, they crossed a paved courtyard, then made their way between the two towers through a vaulted passage over fifty yards long, intersected at almost equal intervals by two transverse galleries. The other three gates had a special arrangement of their own; a flight of twelve steps built out in front of the courtyard rendered them inaccessible to animals or vehicles. At the entrance to the passage towered two colossal bulls with human heads, standing like sentinels—their faces and foreparts turned outward, their hind-quarters ranged along the inner walls—as though gazing before them into space in company with two winged genii. The arch supported by their mitred heads was ornamented by a course of enamelled bricks, on which other genii, facing one another in pairs, offered pinecones across a circular ornament of many colours. These were the mystic guardians of the city, who shielded it not only from the attacks of men, but also from invasions of evil spirits and pernicious diseases.[3] The rays of the sun made the forecourt warm in winter, while it was always cool under the archway in summer; the gates served as resorts for pleasure or business, where old men and idlers congregated to discuss their affairs and settle the destinies of the State, merchants bargained and disposed of their goods, and the judge and notables of the neighbouring quarter held their courts.[4] It was here that the king generally exposed to view the chieftains and kings whom he had taken captive; here they lay, chained like dogs in cages, dependent on the pity of

[1] The number of the gates and their names are given by Sargon himself, in an abbreviated form, in the *Inscription of the Bulls,* ll. 81–90, and in that of the *Cylinders,* ll. 66–70; they appear in a more complete form in the *Annals of Hall XIV.,* ll. 78–84.

[2] As already stated, this is what the inscriptions describe as a "*bit-khilâni* in the manner of the country of Khâti" (*Inscription on the Reverse of the Slabs,* ll. 20, 21; *Inscription on the Pavement of the Gates,* ll. 28–30; *Inscription des Fastes,* ll. 161, 162). Cf. the description and illustration of a *bit-khilâni,* on pp. 206, 207, *supra;* the parts described on the present page can be readily identified in the woodcut.

[3] For a description of the gates of the city, cf. PLACE, *Ninive et l'Assyrie,* vol. i. pp. 169–196. The part played by the sacred bulls as guardians has been briefly indicated in the *Dawn of Civilization,* p. 633.

[4] A vivid description of the uses of the gates is given by PLACE, *Ninive et l'Assyrie,* vol. i. pp. 183–188); cf. the same custom among the Hebrews (*Gen.* xix. 1; xxiii. 10, 16, 18; *Ruth* iv. 1, 2, 9–12; *Deut.* xxi. 18–21).

their guards or of passers-by for such miserable fare as might be flung to them, and, the first feeling of curiosity once passed, no longer provoking even the jeers of the crowd, until a day came when their victor took it into his head to remove them from their ignominious position, and either restored them to their thrones or sent them to the executioner.[1] The town itself, being built from plans drawn up by one mind, must have presented few of the irregularities of outline characteristic of ancient cities. The streets leading from the gates were of uniform breadth throughout, from one side of the enclosure to the other.

They were paved, had no sideways or footpaths, and crossed one another at right angles.[2] The houses on either side of them seem, for the most part, to have consisted of a single story. They were built of bricks, either baked or unbaked, the outer surfaces of which were covered with white or tinted rough-casting. The high and narrow doors were nearly

PART OF THE ENAMELLED COURSE OF A GATE.[3]

always hidden away in a corner of the front; the bare monotony of the walls was only relieved here and there at long intervals by tiny windows, but often instead of a flat roof the building was surmounted by a conical dome or by semi-cupolas, the concave sides of which were turned inwards.[4] The inhabitants varied greatly in race and language: Sargon had filled his city with prisoners collected from all the four quarters of his empire, from Elam, Chaldæa, and Media, from Urartu and Tabal, Syria and Palestine, and in order to keep these incongruous elements in check he added a number of Assyrians, of the mercantile, official, or priestly classes.[5] He could overlook the whole city from the palace which he had built on both sides the north-eastern wall of the town, half within and half without the ramparts. Like all palaces built on the Euphratean model, this royal castle stood on an artificial eminence of bricks formed of two rectangles joined

---

[1] To mention but a single instance, it was in this way that Assur-bani-pal treated the Arab kings captured by him (*Rassam Cylinder*, col. viii. ll. 8–14, 27, 28; col. ix. ll. 103–111).

[2] PLACE, *Ninive et l'Assyrie*, vol. i. pp. 198, 199; cf. PERROT and CHIPIEZ, *Histoire de l'Art dans l'Antiquité*, vol. ii. pp. 490–492.

[3] Drawn by Faucher-Gudin, from a drawing published in PLACE, *Ninive et l'Assyrie*, pl. 15.

[4] PLACE, *Ninive et l'Assyrie*, vol. i. pp. 208, 209; cf. PERROT and CHIPIEZ, *Histoire de l'Art dans l'Antiquité*, vol. ii. pp. 145, 146, 466–468.

[5] *Inscription of the Bulls*, ll. 92–97; *Cylinder Inscription*, ll. 72–74; *Annals of Hall XIV.*, ll. 87–89.

together in the shape of the letter T.[1] The only entrance to it was on the
city side, foot-passengers being admitted by a double flight of steps built out
in front of the ramparts, horsemen and chariots by means of an inclined plane
which rose in a gentle gradient along the right flank of the masonry work, and
terminated on its eastern front. Two main gates corresponded to these two
means of approach ; the one on the north-east led straight to the royal

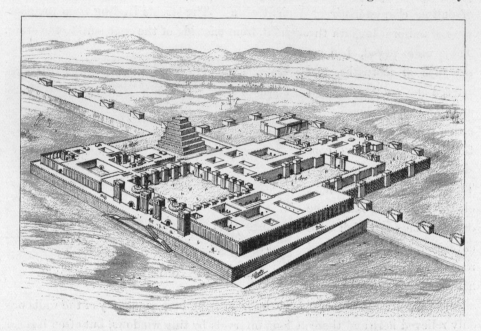

BIRD'S EYE VIEW OF SARGON'S PALACE AT DUR-SHARRUKÎN.[2]

apartments, the other faced the city and opened on to the double staircase. It
was readily distinguishable from a distance by its two flagstaffs bearing
the royal standard, and its two towers, at the base of which were winged
bulls and colossal figures of Gilgames crushing the lion.[3] Two bulls of
still more monstrous size stood sentry on either side of the gate, the arch
was outlined by a course of enamelled bricks, while higher up, immediately beneath the battlements, was an enamelled mosaic showing the king
in all his glory. This triumphal arch was reserved for his special use, the
common people being admitted by two side doors of smaller size less richly
decorated.

Sargon resided at Calah, where he had taken up his quarters in the

<hr />

[1] As to the construction of this mound, its dimensions and general arrangement, cf. PLACE,
Ninive et l'Assyrie, vol. i. pp. 23–40.

[2] Drawn by Boudier, from the restoration by Thomas in PLACE, *Ninive et l'Assyrie*, pl.
18 *bis*.

[3] One of these figures of Gilgames is reproduced in the *Dawn of Civilization*, p. 575.

former palace of Assur-nazir-pal,[1] while his new city was still in the hands of the builders. Every moment that he could spare from his military and administrative labours was devoted to hastening on the progress of the work, and whenever he gained a victory or pillaged a district, he invariably set aside a considerable part of the booty in order to meet the outlay which the building involved. Thus we find that on returning from his tenth campaign he brought with him an

ONE OF THE GATES OF THE PALACE AT DUR-SHARRUKÎN.[2]

immense convoy laden with timber, stone, and precious metals which he had collected in the neighbourhood of Mount Taurus or among the mountains of Assyria, including coloured marbles, lapis-lazuli, rock crystal, pine, cedar, and cypresswood, gold, silver, and bronze, all of which was destined for Dur-Sharrukîn ; the quantity of silver included among these materials was so great that its value fell to a level with that of copper.[3] The interior of the building, as in the case of the old Chaldæan palaces, was separated into two well-marked divisions.[4] The larger of these was used by the king in his public capacity, and to this the nobles and soldiers, and even the common people, were admitted under certain conditions and on certain days prescribed by custom.[5] The outer court was

[1] *Nimroud Inscription*, l. 13; cf. WINCKLER, *Die Keilschrifttexte Sargons*, vol. i. pp. 170, 171.

[2] Drawn by Faucher-Gudin, from the restoration by Thomas, in PLACE, *Ninive et l'Assyrie*, pl. 20.

[3] *Annals of Sargon*, ll. 196–208 : cf. OPPERT, *The Annals of Sargon*, in the *Records of the Past*, 1st ser., vol. vii. p. 39 ; WINCKLER, *Die Keilschrifttexte Sargons*, vol. i. pp. 34, 35.

[4] Cf. what has been said of the palace of Gudêa in the *Dawn of Civilization*, pp. 709–718.

[5] For a description of this part of the palace, cf. PLACE, *Ninive et l'Assyrie*, vol. i. pp. 47–105.

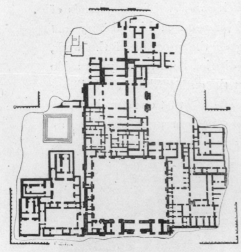

PLAN OF THE EXCAVATED PORTIONS OF THE
PALACE AT DUR-SHARRUKÎN.[5]

lined on three sides by warehouses and depôts, in which were stored the provisions, commodities, and implements required for the host of courtiers and slaves who depended on the sovereign for support.[1] Each room had, as may still be seen, its own special purpose There were cellars for wine and oil, with their rows of large oblong jars;[2] then there were store-rooms for implements of iron, which Place found full of rusty helmets, swords, pieces of armour, maces, and ploughshares; a little further on were rooms for the storage of copper weapons,[3] enamelled bricks,[4] and precious metals, and the king's private treasury, in which were hidden away the spoils of the vanquished or the regular taxes paid by his subjects; some fine bronze lions of marvellous workmanship and lifelike expression were found still shut up here.

ONE OF THE BRONZE LIONS FROM DUR-SHARRUKÎN.[7]

The kitchens adjoined the pantries, and the stables for horses and camels communicated direct with the coach-houses in which the state chariots were kept, while the privies were discreetly hidden in a secluded corner.[6] On the other side, among the buildings occupying the southern angle of the courtyard, the menials of the palace lived huddled together, each family quartered in small, dark rooms.[8] The royal apartments, properly so called, stood at the back of these domestic offices, facing the south-east, near the spot where the inclined plane debouched on to the city ramparts. The monumental entrance to these apartments was guarded, in accordance

---

[1] PLACE, *Ninive et l'Assyrie*, vol. i. pp. 80–82.

[2] PLACE, *Ninive et l'Assyrie*, vol. i. pp. 82, 83.

[3] PLACE, *Ninive et l'Assyrie*, vol. i. pp. 84–89; this is room 84 on Place's plan.

[4] PLACE, *Ninive et l'Assyrie*, vol. i. pp. 64–66, 89–90; the helmets were in rooms 16 and 17, the piles of arms in room 18, and the other implements in room 88.

[5] Drawn by Faucher-Gudin, from the plan by Thomas, in PLACE, *Ninive et l'Assyrie*, pl. 3.

[6] PLACE, *Ninive et l'Assyrie*, vol. i. p. 89.

[7] Drawn by Faucher-Gudin, from the original in the Louvre.

[8] PLACE, *Ninive et l'Assyrie*, vol. i. pp. 93–105.

with religious custom, by a company of winged bulls; behind this gate was a lawn, then a second gate, a corridor and a grand quadrangle in the very centre of the palace.[1] The king occupied a suite of some twenty rooms of a rather simple character; here he slept, ate, worked, and transacted the greater part of his daily business, guarded by his eunuchs and attended by his ministers and secretaries. The remaining rooms were apartments of state, all of the same pattern, in which the crowd of courtiers and employés assembled while waiting for a private audience or to intercept the king as he passed.[2] A subdued light made its way from above through narrow windows let into the massive arches.[3] The walls were lined

A HUNTING EXPEDITION IN THE WOODS NEAR DUR-SHARRUKÎN.[4]

to a height of over nine feet from the floor with endless bas-reliefs, in greyish alabaster, picked out in bright colours, and illustrating the principal occupations in which the sovereign spent his days, such as the audiences to ambassadors, hunting in the woods, sieges and battles. A few brief inscriptions interspersed above pictures of cities and persons indicated the names of the vanquished chiefs or the scenes of the various events portrayed; detailed descriptions were engraved on the back of the slabs facing the brick wall against which they rested. This was a precautionary measure, the necessity for which had been but too plainly proved by past experience. Every one—the king himself included —well knew that some day or other Dur-Sharrukîn would be forsaken just as

[1] For the gates of the palace, cf. the description given by PLACE, *Ninive et l'Assyrie,* vol. ii. pp. 21–28.

[2] These were the portions laid bare by Botta, illustrated and described by him, and afterwards studied afresh by PLACE, *Ninive et l'Assyrie,* vol. i. pp. 47–49.

[3] As to the lighting, cf. PLACE, *Ninive et l'Assyrie,* vol. i. pp. 307–315, and PERROT and CHIPIEZ, *Histoire de l'Art dans l'Antiquité,* vol. ii. pp. 186–196.

[4] Drawn by Faucher-Gudin, from a drawing by Flandin, in BOTTA, *Le Monument de Ninive,* vol. ii. pl. 108.

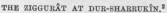

the palaces of previous dynasties had been, and it was hoped that inscriptions concealed in this manner would run a better chance of escaping the violence of man or the ravages of time; preserved in them, the memory of Sargon would rise triumphant from the ruins. The gods reigned supreme over the north-east angle of the platform, and a large irregular block of buildings was given up to their priests; their cells contained nothing of any particular interest, merely white walls and black plinths, adorned here and there with frescoes embellished by arabesques, and pictures of animals and symbolical genii.[1] The *ziggurât* rose to a height of some 141 feet

THE ZIGGURÂT AT DUR-SHARRUKÎN.[2]

above the esplanade. It had seven storeys dedicated to the gods of the seven planets, each storey being painted in the special colour of its god—the first white, the second black, the third purple, the fourth blue, the fifth a vermilion red; the sixth was coated with silver, and the seventh gilded. There was no chamber in the centre of the tower, but a small gilded chapel probably stood at its base, which was used for the worship of Assur or of Ishtar.[3] The harem, or *Bît-riduti*, was at the southern corner of the enclosure, almost in the shadow of the *ziggurât*.[4] Sargon had probably three queens when he founded his city, for the harem is divided into three separate apartments, of which the two larger look out on the same quadrangle. Two courses of enamelled bricks ran

SECTION OF A BEDROOM IN THE HAREM.[5]

along the base of the façade, while statues were placed at intervals

[1] PLACE, *Ninive et l'Assyrie*, vol. i. pp. 149–151.

[2] Drawn by Faucher-Gudin, from the restoration by Thomas, in PLACE, *Ninive et l'Assyrie*, pl. 37.

[3] PLACE, *Ninive et l'Assyrie*, vol. i. pp. 137–148; the four lower stories of the *ziggurât* are all that now remain. Cf. PERROT and CHIPIEZ, *Histoire de l'Art dans l'Antiquité*, vol. ii. pp. 403–406.

[4] PLACE, *Ninive et l'Assyrie*, vol. i. pp. 107–136.

[5] Drawn by Faucher-Gudin, from the restoration by Thomas, in PLACE, *Ninive et l'Assyrie*, pl. 25, 4.

against the wall, and the bay of the gateway was framed by two bronze
palm trees gilt: the palm being the emblem of fruitfulness and grace,
no more fitting decoration could have been chosen for this part of the
building.[1] The arrangement was the same in all three divisions: an ante-
chamber of greater width than length; an apartment, one half of which
was open to the sky, while the other was covered by a half-dome, and a

MAIN DOOR OF THE HAREM AT DUR-SHARRUKÎN.[2]

flight of twelve steps, leading to an alcove in which stood a high wooden
couch. The queens and princesses spent their lives in this prison-like *bît-
riduti*: their time was taken up with dress, embroidery, needlework, dancing
and singing, the monotony of this routine being relieved by endless quarrels,
feuds, and intrigues. The male children remained in the harem until the
age of puberty, when they left it in order to continue their education as
princes and soldiers under the guidance of their father.[3] This group of buildings was completed by a park, in which cedars of Lebanon, pines, cypresses,
gazelles, stags, wild asses and cattle, and even lions, were acclimatised, in
addition to a heterogeneous collection of other trees and animals. Here, the

[1] PLACE, *Ninive et l'Assyrie*, vol. i. pp. 116–127.
[2] Drawn by Faucher-Gudin, from the restoration by Thomas, in PLACE, *Ninive et l'Assyrie*,
pl. 24.
[3] An inscription of Assur-bani-pal, published by RAWLINSON, *Cun. Ins. W. As.*, vol. v.
pl. i. col. i. ll. 11–34, and afterwards translated by Jensen in the *Keilinschriftliche Bibliothek*,
vol. ii. pp. 154–157, gives a summary description of the life led in the harem by heirs to
the throne, and describes generally the kind of education received by them from their earliest
childhood.

king gave himself up to the pleasures of the chase, and sometimes invited one or other of his wives to come thither and banquet or drink with him.[1]

After Mitâ's surrender, Sargon had hoped to be allowed to finish building his city in peace; but an ill-advised movement in Kummukh obliged him to don his harness again (708 B.C.). King Mutallu had entered into an alliance with Argistis of Urartu, and took the field with his army; but when details of what had taken place in Chaldæa reached his ears, and he learnt the punishment that had been inflicted on the people of Bît-Yakin, his courage failed him. He fled without waiting for the Assyrians to appear, and so great was his haste that he had no time to take his family and treasure with him. Sargon annexed his kingdom, placed it under the government of the *tartan*, and incorporated into his own the whole army of Kummukh, including 150 chariots, 1500 horsemen, 20,000 archers, and 10,000 pikemen.[2] In the following year (707) his vassal Dalta died, leaving two sons, Nibi and Ishpabara, both of whom claimed possession of the fief of Ellipi; Nibi appealed to Elam for help, and Ishpabara at once turned for aid to Assyria. Sargon sent him a body of troops, commanded by seven of his generals, while Shutruk-nakhunta lent his *protégé* 4500 bowmen; Ishpabara won the day, took the city of Marubishti by storm, and compelled his brother to take refuge in Susian territory.[3] The affair was over so quickly that it caused practically no delay in the completion of the works at the capital. The consecration of a new city necessitated the observance of a host of complicated ceremonies, which extended over several months. First of all provision had to be made for its religious worship; the omens were consulted in order to determine which of the gods were to be invoked, and, when this was decided, there followed the installation of the various statues and arks which were to preside over the destinies of the city and the priests to whom they were intrusted; the solemn inauguration took place on the 22nd day of Tisri, in the year 707 B.C., and from that day forward Dur-Sharrukîn occupied the

---

[1] *Annals of Hall XIV.*, ll. 65, 66: cf. WINCKLER, *Die Keilschrifttexte Sargons*, vol. i. pp. 88–91; *Inscription of the Bulls*, ll. 41, 42; cf. LYON, *Die Keilschrifttexte Sargons*, pp. 42, 43. We shall see below the bas-relief showing Assur-bani-pal drinking with the queen in the palace garden.

[2] *Annals of Sargon*, ll. 388–401: cf. OPPERT, *The Annals of Sargon*, in *Records of the Past*, 1st ser., vol. vii. pp. 51, 52; WINCKLER, *Die Keils. Sargons*, vol. i. pp. 64–69; *Inscrip. des Fastes*, ll. 112–117; cf. OPPERT, *Great Inscrip. in Palace of Khorsabad*, in *Records*, etc., 1st ser., vol. ix. pp. 12, 13; WINCKLER, *Die Keils. Sargons*, vol. i. pp. 116–119. The date has been destroyed in the Annals, but the Eponym Canon places an expedition against Kummukh, which must be identical with that of the mutilated text, in the fifteenth year of the reign, in the eponymous year of office of Shamash-upakhkhir (SCHRADER, *Keil. Bibl.*, vol. i. pp. 209, 214, 215, vol. iii. 2nd pt., pp. 146, 147; cf. TIELE, *Bab.-ass. Gesch.*, pp. 179, 180).

[3] *Annals of Sargon*, ll. 402–414: cf. OPPERT, *The Annals of Sargon*, in *Records of the Part*, 1st ser., vol. vii. pp. 52–53; WINCKLER, *Die Keilschrifttexte Sargons*, vol. i. pp. 68–71; *Inscription des Fastes*, ll. 117–121; cf. OPPERT, *Great Inscription in the Palace of Khorsabad*, in *Records of the Past*, 1st ser., vol. xi. p. 13; WINCKLER, *Die Keilschrifttexte Sargons*, vol. i. pp. 118–121. The date is missing in the text of the Annals, and the campaign may have taken place in the same year as the campaign against Kummukh, that is to say, possibly in 708; it could not have been later than the year 707, for the *Inscription des Fastes* included, as the compiler himself asserted (l. 23), events which occurred from the beginning of the reign until the fifteenth year (TIELE, *Babylonisch-assyrische Geschichte*, p. 180).

rank officially assigned to it among the capitals of the empire. Sargon, however, did not formally take up his residence within it till six months later, on the 6th day of Iyyâr, 706.[1] He must, by this time, have been advancing in years, and even if we assume him to have been a young man when he ascended the throne, after the sixteen years of bodily fatigue and mental worry through which he had passed since coming into power, he must have needed repose. He handed over the government of the northern provinces to his eldest son Sin-akhê-irba, better known to us as Sennacherib, whom he regarded as his successor; to him he transferred the responsibility of keeping watch over the movements of the Mannai, of Urartu, and of the restless barbarians who dwelt beyond the zone of civilised states on the banks of the Halys, or at the foot of the distant Caucasus:[2] a revolt among the Tabal, in 706, was promptly suppressed by his young and energetic deputy.[3] As for Sargon himself, he was content to retain the direct control of the more pacific provinces, such as Babylon, the regions of the Middle Euphrates, and Syria, and he doubtless hoped to enjoy during his later years such tranquillity as was necessary to enable him to place his conquests on a stable basis. The envious fates, however, allowed him but little more than twelve short months: he perished early in 705 B.C., assassinated by some soldier of alien birth, if I interpret rightly the mutilated text which furnishes us with a brief mention of the disaster. Sennacherib was recalled in haste from the frontier, and proclaimed king immediately on his arrival, thus ascending unopposed to the throne on the 12th day of Ab.[4] His father's body had been left unburied, doubtless in order that he might verify with his own eyes the truth of what had been told him concerning his death, and thus have no ground for harbouring suspicions that would have boded ill for the safety of the late king's councillors and servants. He looked upon his father's miserable ending as a punishment for some unknown transgression, and consulted the gods to learn what it was that had aroused their anger, refusing to authorise the burial within the palace until the various expiatory rites suggested by the oracle had been duly performed.[5]

[1] The dates of the inauguration of Dur-Sharrukîn are supplied by a fragment of the *Eponym Canon*, of which the sense is still somewhat obscure (SCHRADER, *Keilinschriftliche Bibliothek*, vol. i. pp. 214, 215), and the first date is also indicated in the *Babylonian Chronicle of Pinches*, col. ii. l. 8.

[2] Winckler has discovered and published (*Sammlung von Keilschrifttexten : Texte von verschiedenen Inhalts*, pp. 8 and 11, Nos. 5464 and 1080) some of Sennacherib's despatches, in which he informs his father of the advances of the Cimmerians on Urartu; cf. WINCKLER, *Geschichte Israels*, vol. i. p. 185.

[3] *Bab. Chron. of Pinches*, col. ii. l. 9 (cf. WINCKLER, *Bab. Chronik B*, in SCHRADER, *Keil. Bibl.*, vol. ii. pp. 278, 279), where the conduct of the campaign is attributed, as is natural, to Sargon himself.

[4] *Eponym Canon*, in SCHRADER, *op. cit.*, vol. i. pp. 214, 215; cf. G. SMITH, *History of Sennacherib*, p. 10.

[5] This is my interpretation of the text published and translated by Winckler (*Sammlung von Keilschrifttexten : Texte von verschiedenen Inhalts*, p. 52, and *Altorientalische Forschungen*, vol. i. pp. 410–415). Winckler sees in it the account of a campaign during which Sargon was killed by mountaineers, as was Cyrus in later times by the Massagetæ; the king's body (according to him) remained unburied, and was recovered by Sennacherib only after considerable delay. In support of his version of this event Winckler cites the passage in *Isa.* xiv. 4–20a, which he takes as having been composed to exult over the death of Sargon, and then afterwards adapted to the death of a king of Babylon.

Thus mysteriously disappeared the founder of the mightiest dynasty that ever ruled in Assyria, perhaps even in the whole of Western Asia. At first sight, it would seem easy enough to determine what manner of man he was and to what qualities he owed his greatness, thanks to the abundance of documents which his contemporaries have bequeathed to us; but when we come to examine more closely, we soon find the task to be by no means a simple one. The inscriptions maintain so discreet a silence with regard to the antecedents of the kings before their accession, and concerning their education and private life, that at this distance of time we cannot succeed in forming any clear idea as to their individual temperament and character. The monuments record such achievements as they took pride in, in terms of uniform praise which conceal or obliterate the personality of the king in question; it is always the ideal Assyrian sovereign who is held up for our admiration under a score of different names, and if, here and there, we come upon some trait which indicates the special genius of this or that monarch, we may be sure that the scribe has allowed it to slip in by accident, quite unconscious of the fact that he is thus affording us a glimpse of his master's true character and disposition. A study of Sargon's campaigns as revealed in his annals will speedily convince us that he was something more than a fearless general, with a keen eye to plunder, who could see nothing in the most successful expedition but a means of enriching his people or adding to the splendours of his court. He was evidently convinced that certain nations, such as Urartu and Elam, would never really assimilate with his own subjects, and, in their case, he adhered strictly to the old system of warfare, and did all he could to bring about their ruin; other nations, on the contrary, he regarded as capable of amalgamation with the Assyrians, and these he did his best to protect from the worst consequences of their rebellion and resistance. He withdrew them from the influence of their native dynasties, and converted their territories into provinces under his own vigilant administration, and though he did not scruple to send the more turbulent elements among them into exile, and did his best to weaken them by founding alien colonies in their midst, yet he respected their religion, customs, and laws, and, in return for their obedience to his rule, guaranteed them an equitable and judicious government. Moreover, he took quite as much interest in their well-being as in his own military successes, and in the midst of his heroic struggles against Rusas and Merodach-baladan he contrived to find time for the consideration of such prosaic themes as the cultivation of the vine and of corn; he devoted his attention to the best methods of storing wine, and sought to prevent " oil, which is the life of man and healeth wounds, from rising in price, and the cost of sesame from exceeding that of wheat." [1] We seem to see

---

[1] *Cylinder Inscription*, ll. 39–42; LYON, *Die Keilschrifttexte Sargons*, pp. 34, 35.

in him, not only the stern and at times cruel conqueror, but also the gracious monarch, kind and considerate to his people, and merciful to the vanquished when policy permitted him to indulge his natural leaning to clemency.

Sennacherib either failed to inherit his father's good fortune, or lacked his ability.[1] He was not deficient in military genius, nor in the energy necessary to withstand the various enemies who rose against him at widely removed points of his frontier, but he had neither the adaptability of character nor the delicate tact required to manage successfully the heterogeneous elements combined under his sway. He lacked the wisdom to conciliate the vanquished, or opportunely to check his own repressive measures; he destroyed towns, massacred entire tribes, and laid whole tracts of country waste, and by failing to repeople these with captive exiles from other nations, or to import colonists in sufficient numbers, he found himself towards the end of his reign ruling over a sparsely inhabited desert where his father had bequeathed to him flourishing provinces and populous cities. His was the system of the first Assyrian conquerors, Shalmaneser III. and Assur-nazir-pal, substituted for that of Tiglath-pileser III. and Sargon. The assimilation of the conquered peoples to their conquerors was retarded, tribute was no longer paid regularly, and the loss of revenue under this head was not compensated by the uncertain increase in the spoils obtained by war; the recruiting of the army, rendered more difficult by the depopulation of revolted districts, weighed heavier still on those which remained faithful, and began, as in former times, to exhaust the

---

[1] The two principal documents for the reign of Sennacherib are engraved on cylinders: the *Taylor Cylinder* and the *Bellino Cylinder*, duplicates of which, more or less perfect, exist in the collections of the British Museum (cf. BEZOLD, *Inschriften Sanherib's*, in SCHRADER, *Keilins. Bibliothek*, vol. ii. p. 80, note 1). The *Taylor Cylinder* contains the history of the first eight years of the reign. It was found at Kouyunjik or Nebi-Yunus, and was published in H. RAWLINSON, *Cun. Ins. W. A.*, vol. i. pls. 37–42; it has been translated into French by OPPERT, *Les Inscr. Assyr. des Sargonides*, pp. 41–53, and by MÉNANT, *Annales des Rois d'Assyrie*, pp. 214–225; into English by FOX TALBOT, *Inscr. of Sennacherib, containing the Annals of the first eight years of his reign*, in *Records of the Past*, vol. i., 1st ser., pp. 33–53; into German by R. HÖRNING, *Das Sechsseitige Prisma des Sanherib in transcribirten Grundtexte und Uebersetzung*, 1878, in-8°, and by BEZOLD, *op. cit.*, pp. 80–113. The *Bellino Cylinder*, which is a sort of duplicate of the preceding, treats of the two first years of this reign. It has been published by GROTEFEND, *Bemerkungen zur Inschrift eines Thongefässes mit ninivitischer Keilschrift*, in the *Abhandlungen der Königl. Gesellschaft der Wissenschaften zu Göttingen*, 1850, and in LAYARD, *Inscr. in the Cuneiform Char.*, pls. 63, 64; it has been translated into French by OPPERT, *Expédition en Mesopotamie*, vol. i. p. 297, et seq., and by MÉNANT, *Annales des rois d'Assyrie*, pp. 225–230; into English by FOX TALBOT, *The Inscr. on the Bellino Cylinder*, comprising *the first two years of the reign of Sennacherib*, in *Records of the Past*, vol. i., 1st ser., pp. 23–32 (cf. the former translations by the same author in *J. R. As. Soc.*, 1860, vol. xviii. p. 76, et seq., and in the *Transactions of the R. Soc. of Literature*, vol. viii. p. 369, et seq.). The *Bavian Stele*, published from copies taken by Layard in H. RAWLINSON, *Cun. Ins. W. A.*, vol. iii. pl. 14, has been transcribed and commented on by POGNON, *L'Inscription de Bavian, Texte, traduction et commentaire philologique* in-8°, 1879–1880; cf. the former translations into French by MÉNANT, *Ninive et l'Assyrie*, pp. 234–237; into English by PINCHES, *The Bavian Inscr. of Sennacherib*, in *Records of the Past*, 1st ser., vol. ix. pp. 21–28. All these texts, and others which are less perfect or less important, were collected, transcribed, translated, and the paragraphs composing them classed in chronological order by G. Smith; this work, interrupted by the premature death of the author, when he had only sketched out the later portions, has been completed and edited by Sayce, under the title: *History of Sennacherib, translated from the Cuneiform Inscriptions*, 1878.

T

nation. The news of Sargon's murder, published throughout the Eastern world, had rekindled hope in the countries recently subjugated by Assyria, as well as in those hostile to her. Phœnicia, Egypt, Media, and Elam roused themselves from their lethargy and anxiously awaited the turn which events should take at Nineveh and Babylon. Sennacherib did not consider it to his interest to assume the crown of Chaldæa, and to treat on a footing of absolute equality a country which had been subdued by force of arms: he relegated it to the rank of a vassal state, and while reserving the suzerainty for himself, sent thither one of his brothers to rule as king.[1] The Babylonians were indignant at this slight. Accustomed to see their foreign ruler conform to their national customs, take the hands of Bel, and assume or receive from them a new throne-name, they could not resign themselves to descend to the level of mere tributaries: in less than two years they rebelled, assassinated the king who had been imposed upon them, and proclaimed in his stead Marduk-zâkir-shumu,[2] who was merely the son of a female slave (704 B.C.). This was the signal for a general insurrection in Chaldæa and the eastern part of the empire. Merodach-baladan, who had remained in hiding in the valleys on the Elamite frontier since his defeat in 709 B.C., suddenly issued forth with his adherents, and marched at once to Babylon; the very news of his approach caused a sedition, in the midst of which Marduk-zâkir-shumu perished, after having reigned for only one month.[3] Merodach-baladan re-entered his former

[1] The events which took place at Babylon at the beginning of Sennacherib's reign are known to us from the fragments of Berosus (MÜLLER-DIDOT, *Fragmenta Historicorum Græcorum*, vol. ii. p. 504; cf. SCHRADER, *Zur Kritik der Chronologischen Angaben des Alexander Polyhistor und des Abydenus*, 1880, pp. 1–15), compared with the Canon of Ptolemy and Pinches' Babylonian Canon (SCHRADER, *Keilinschriftliche Bibliothek*, pp. 290, 291). The first interregnum in the Canon of Ptolemy (704–702 B.C.) is filled in Pinches' Canon by three kings who are said to have reigned as follows: Sennacherib, two years; Marduk-zâkir-shumu, one month; Merodach-baladan, nine months. Berosus substitutes for Sennacherib one of his brothers, whose name apparently he did not know; and this is the version I have adopted, in agreement with most modern historians (ED. MEYER, *Geschichte des Alterthums*, vol. i. p. 464; TIELE, *Babylonisch-assyriche Geschichte*, pp. 285, 312; HOMMEL, *Gesch. Bab. und Ass.*, pp. 686, 731), as best tallying with the evident lack of affection for Babylon displayed by Sennacherib throughout his reign.

[2] The servile origin of this personage is indicated in Pinches' Babylonian Canon (*The Babylonian Kings of the Second Period*, in the *Proceedings* of the Bibl. Arch. Soc., 1883–1884, vol. vi. col. iv. l. 13); he might, however, be connected through his father with a princely, or even a royal, family, and thereby be in a position to win popular support. Among modern Assyriologists, some suppose that the name Akises in Berosus is a corruption of [Marduk-]zâkir[shumu], as Schrader (*Die Keilinschriftliche Babylonische Königsliste*, in the *Sitzungsberichte* of the Academy of Sciences in Berlin, 1887, p. 948, et seq.); others consider Akises-Akishu as being the personal name of the king, and Marduk-zâkir-shumu his throne-name (TIELE, *Babyl.-assyr. Geschichte*, p. 313, note 1; HOMMEL, *Gesch. Bab. und Ass.*, p. 686, note 3).

[3] Many authorities have thought the Merodach-baladan of Sennacherib's reign a different person from the king who bore that name under Sargon. Schrader, who at first defended this hypothesis (*Die Keilins. und das Alte Testament*, 1st edit., pp. 213–217; cf. ED. MEYER, *Gesch. des Alterthums*, vol. i. p. 464), has since renounced it (*Die Keilins. und das Alte Testament*, 2nd edit., pp. 341–343), and has returned to the opinion of the first interpreters (G. RAWLINSON, *The Five Great Monarchies*, 2nd edit., vol. ii. pp. 156, 157; FR. LENORMANT, *Les Premières Civilisations*, vol. ii. p. 263; MÉNANT,

capital, and as soon as he was once more seated on the throne, he endeavoured to form alliances with all the princes, both small and great, who might create a diversion in his favour. His envoys obtained promises of help from Elam ; other emissaries hastened to Syria to solicit the alliance of Hezekiah, and might have even proceeded to Egypt if their sovereign's good fortune had lasted long enough.[1] But Sennacherib did not waste his opportunities in lengthy preparations. The magnificent army left by Sargon was at his disposal, and summoning it at once into the field, he advanced on the town of Kîsh, where the Kaldâ monarch was entrenched with his Aramæan forces and the Elamite auxiliaries furnished by Shutruk-nakhunta. The battle issued in the complete rout of the confederate forces. Merodach-baladan fled almost unattended, first to Guzummanu, and then to the marshes of the Tigris, where he found a temporary refuge ; the troops who were despatched in pursuit followed him for five days, and then, having failed to secure the fugitive, gave up the search.[2] His camp fell into the possession of the victor, with all its contents—chariots, horses, mules, camels, and herds of cattle belonging to the commissariat department of the army : Babylon threw open its gates without resistance, hoping, no doubt, that Sennacherib would at length resolve to imitate the precedent set by his father and retain the royal dignity for himself. He did, indeed, consent to remit the punishment for this first insurrection, and contented himself with pillaging the royal treasury and palace, but he did not deign to assume the crown, conferring it on Belibni, a Babylonian of noble birth, who had been taken, when quite a child, to Nineveh and educated there under the eyes of Sargon.[3] While he was thus reorganising the government, his generals were bringing the campaign to a close: they

---

Babylone et la Chaldée, p. 158), adopted now by nearly all historians (DELATTRE, *Les Chaldéens jusqu'à la formation de l'Empire de Nabuchodonosor*, 2nd edit., pp. 12, 13 ; WINCKLER, *Untersuchungen zur Altorientalischen Geschichte*, p. 50, and *Gesch. Bab. und Ass.*, pp. 129, 259 ; HOMMEL, *Gesch. Bab. und Ass.*, p. 731) ; TIELE, *Babyl.-assyr. Geschichte*, p. 285, and p. 313, note 1, still hesitates which view to adopt.

[1] 2 *Kings* xx. 12–19 ; *Isa.* xxxix. The embassy to Hezekiah has been assigned to the first reign of Merodach-baladan, under Sargon (FR. LENORMANT, *Les Premières Civilisations*, vol. ii. pp. 231–241 ; TIELE, *Babyl.-assyr. Gesch.*, p. 319 ; HOMMEL, *Gesch. Bab. und Ass.*, p. 704 ; WINCKLER, *Die Keilschrifttexte Sargons*, vol. i. p. xxxi., note 2 ; *Alttestamentliche Untersuchungen*, pp. 155, 156 ; *Geschichte Israels*, vol. i. pp. 181, 182). In accordance with the information obtained from the Assyrian monuments, it seems to me that it could only have taken place during his second reign, in 703 B.C. ; cf. SCHRADER, *Die Keilins. und das Alte Testament*, 1883, pp. 343, 344 ; DELATTRE, *Les Chaldéens*, 2nd edit., p. 12 ; ED. MEYER, *Geschichte des Alterthums*, vol. i. p. 466 ; MÜRDTER and DELITZSCH, *Gesch. Bab. und Ass.*, 2nd edit., p. 197 ; STADE, *Gesch. des Volkes Israel*, vol. i. p. 614.

[2] The detail is furnished by the *Bellino Cylinder*, l. 10 ; cf. G. SMITH, *History of Sennacherib*, p. 26. Berosus affirmed that Merodach-baladan was put to death by Belibni (MÜLLER-DIDOT, *Frag. Hist. Græc.*, vol. ii. p. 504).

[3] The name is transcribed Belibos in Greek, and it seems as if the Assyrian variants justify the pronunciation Belibush (SCHRADER, *Zur Kritik des Chronologischen Angaben des Alexander Polyhistor und des Abydenus*, p. 9, note 1, and *Die Keilins. und das Alte Testament*, 1883, p. 349). *Pinches' Babylonian Chronicle*, col. ii. ll. 23, 24, 26, 28, gives the spelling Bel-ib-ni.

sacked, one after another, eighty-nine strongholds and eight hundred and twenty villages of the Kaldâ; they drove out the Arabian and Aramæan garrisons which Merodach-baladan had placed in the cities of Karduniash, in Uruk, Nipur, Kuta, and Kharshag-kalamma, and they re-established Assyrian supremacy over all the tribes on the east of the Tigris up to the frontiers of Elam, the Tumuna, the Ubudu, the Gambulu, and the Khindaru, as also over the Nabatæans and Hagarenes, who wandered over the deserts of Arabia to the west of the mouths of the Euphrates. The booty was enormous: 208,000 prisoners, both male and female, 7200 horses, 11,073 asses, 5230 camels, 80,100 oxen, 800,500 sheep, made their way like a gigantic horde of emigrants to Assyria under the escort of the victorious army. Meanwhile the Khirimmu remained defiant, and showed not the slightest intention to submit: their strongholds had to be attacked and the inhabitants annihilated before order could in any way be restored in the country. The second reign of Merodach-baladan had lasted barely nine months.[1]

The blow which ruined Merodach-baladan broke up the coalition which he had tried to form against Assyria. Babylon was the only rallying-point where states so remote, and such entire strangers to each other as Judah and Elam, could enter into friendly relations and arrange a plan of combined action. Having lost Babylon as a centre, they were once more hopelessly isolated, and had no means of concerting measures against the common foe: they renounced all offensive action, and waited under arms to see how the conqueror would deal with each severally. The most threatening storm, however, was not that which was gathering over Palestine, even were Egypt to be drawn into open war; for a revolt of the western provinces, however serious, was never likely to lead to disastrous complications, and the distance from Pelusium to the Tigris was too great for a victory of the Pharaoh to compromise effectually the safety of the empire. On the other hand, should intervention on the part of Elam in the affairs of Babylon or Media be crowned with success, the most disastrous consequences might ensue: it would mean the loss of Karduniash, or of the frontier districts won with such difficulty by Tiglath-pileser III. and Sargon; it would entail permanent hostilities on the Tigris and the Zab, and perhaps the appearance of barbarian troops under the walls of Calah or of Nineveh. Elam had assisted Merodach-baladan, and its soldiers had fought on the plains of Kîsh. Months had elapsed since that battle, yet Shutruk-nakhunta showed no disposition to take the initiative: he accepted his defeat at all events for the time, but though he put off the day of reckoning till a

---

[1] *Taylor Cylinder*, col. i. ll. 19–62 (BEZOLD, *Inschriften Sanherib's*, in SCHRADER, *Keilins Bibliothek*, vol. ii. pp. 82–87); cf. SMITH-SAYCE, *History of Sennacherib*, pp. 24–42.

more favourable opportunity, it argued neither weakness nor discouragement, and he was ready to give a fierce reception to any Assyrian monarch who should venture within his domain. Sennacherib, knowing both the character and resources of the Elamite king, did not attempt to meet him in the open field, but wreaked his resentment on the frontier tribes who had rebelled at the instigation of the Elamites, on the Cossæans, on Ellipi, and its king Ishpabara.[1] He pursued the inhabitants into the narrow valleys and forests of the Khoatras, where his chariots were unable to follow : proceeding with his troops, sometimes on horseback, at other times on foot, he reduced Bît-kilamzak, Khardishpi, and Bît-kubatti to ashes, and annexed the territories of the Cossæans and the Yasubigallâ to the prefecture of Arrapkha. Thence he entered Ellipi, where Ishpabara did not venture to come to close quarters with him in the open field, but led him on from town to town. He destroyed the two royal seats of Marubishti and Akkuddu, and thirty-four of their dependent strongholds; he took possession of Zizirtu, Kummalu, the district of Bitbarru, and the city of Elinzash, to which he gave the name Kar-Senna-cherib,—the fortress of Sennacherib,—and annexed them to the government of Kharkhar. The distant Medes, disquieted at his advance, sent him presents, and renewed the assurances of devotion they had given to Sargon, but Sennacherib did not push forward into their territory as his predecessors had done : he was content to have maintained his authority as far as his outlying posts, and to have strengthened the Assyrian empire by acquiring some well-situated positions near the main routes which led from the Iranian table-land to the plains of Mesopotamia.[2] Having accomplished this, he at once turned his attention towards the west, where the spirit of rebellion was still active in the countries bordering on the African frontier. Sabaco, now undisputed master of Egypt,[3] was not content, like Piônkhi, to bring Egypt proper into a position of dependence, and govern it at a distance, by means of his generals. He took up his residence within it, at least during part of every year, and played the *rôle* of Pharaoh so well that his Egyptian subjects, both at Thebes and in the Delta, were obliged to acknowledge his sovereignty and recognise him as the founder of a new dynasty. He kept a close watch over the vassal princes, placing garrisons in Memphis and the other principal citadels, and throughout the country he took in hand public works which had been almost completely

---

[1] For this individual, and the manner in which he had been raised to the throne by Sargon some years previously, cf. *supra*, p. 270.

[2] *Taylor Cylinder*, col. i. ll. 63–82, col. ii. ll. 1–33 (BEZOLD, *Inschriften Sanherib's*, in SCHRADER, *Keilins. Bibliothek*, vol. ii. pp. 88–91; cf. SMITH-SAYCE, *History of Sennacherib*, pp. 43–52). Delattre (*Le Peuple et l'Empire des Mèdes*, pp. 118–120) considerably reduces the successes of Sennacherib in these regions.

[3] For the accession of Sabaco, cf. *supra*, pp. 246, 247.

interrupted for more than a century owing to the civil wars : the highways were repaired, the canals cleaned out and enlarged, and the foundations of the towns raised above the level of the inundation.[1] Bubastis especially profited under his rule, and regained the ascendency it had lost ever since the accession of the second Tanite dynasty ; but this partiality was not to the detriment of other cities.[2] Several of the temples at Memphis were restored, and the inscriptions effaced by time were re-engraved.[3] Thebes, happy under the government of Amenertas and her husband Piônkhi, profited largely by the liberality of its Ethiopian rulers. At Luxor Sabaco restored the decoration of the principal gateway between the two pylons,[4] and repaired several portions of the temple

CLAY SEAL WITH CARTOUCHE OF SABACO.[7]

of Amon at Karnak.[5] History subsequently related that, in order to obtain sufficient workmen, he substituted forced labour for the penalty of death : a policy which, beside being profitable, would win for him a reputation for clemency.[6] Egypt, at length reduced to peace and order, began once more to flourish, and to display that inherent vitality of which she had so often given proof, and her reviving prosperity attracted as of old the attention of foreign powers. At the beginning of his reign, Sabaco had attempted to meddle in the intrigues of Syria, but the ease with which Sargon had quelled the revolt of Ashdod had inspired the Egyptian monarch with salutary distrust in his own power ; he had sent presents to the conqueror and received gifts in exchange, which furnished him with a pretext for enrolling the Asiatic peoples among the tributary nations whose names he inscribed on his triumphal lists.[8] Since then he had had some diplomatic correspondence with his powerful neigh-

---

[1] HERODOTUS, II. cxxxvii.; DIODORUS SICULUS, i. 65; cf. WIEDEMANN, *Herodot's Zweites Buch*, pp. 495, 496.

[2] HERODOTUS, II. cxxxviii. The excavations of Naville have not discovered any monument which bears signs of the restorations undertaken by Sabaco in the city of Bubastis.

[3] Cf. the fragments of statues bearing his name noted by MARIETTE, *Monuments Divers*, pl. 29 *d*. A demotic contract of the Ptolemaic era still mentions, at Memphis, the *street of Sabaco* (REVILLOUT, *Hypothèque légale de la femme*, in the *Revue Égyptologique*, vol. i. p. 126, note, and p. 148, note 1).

[4] CHAMPOLLION, *Monuments de l'Égypte et de la Nubie*, pl. cccxxxvii.; ROSELLINI, *Monumenti Storici*, pl. cli. 2, 3, and vol. iv. pp. 175, 176; cf. DARESSY, *Notice explicative des ruines du Temple de Louxor*, p. 27.

[5] CHAMPOLLION, *op. cit.*, vol. ii. p. 129, et seq.; ROSELLINI, *op. cit.*, vol. iv. pp. 176, 177; LEPSIUS, *Denkm.*, iii. 69 *d*, v. 1 *a*, *b*; BRUGSCH, *Reiseberichte aus Ægypten*, p. 170; MARIETTE, *Karnak*, pl. 45 *c*, and pp. 9, 10, 28, 69.

[6] HERODOTUS, II. cxxxvii.; DIODORUS, i. 65; cf. WIEDEMANN, *Herodot's Zweites Buch*, pp. 495, 496.

[7] Drawn by Faucher-Gudin, from a sketch by LAYARD, *Nineveh and Babylon*, p. 132.

[8] For these gifts, cf. *supra*, pp. 244, 247. It was probably with reference to this exchange of presents that Sabaco caused the bas-relief at Karnak to be engraved, in which he represents himself as victorious over both Asiatics and Africans (LEPSIUS, *Denkm.*, v. 1 *c*).

bour, and a document bearing his name was laid up in the archives at Calah, where the clay seal once attached to it has been discovered.[1] Peace had lasted for a dozen years, when he died about 703 B.C., and his son Shabîtoku ascended the throne.[2] The temporary embarrassments in which the Babylonian revolution had plunged Sennacherib must have offered a tempting opportunity for interference to this inexperienced king.

Tyre and Judah alone of all the Syrian states retained a sufficiently independent spirit to cherish any hope of deliverance from the foreign yoke. Tyre still maintained her supremacy over Southern Phœnicia, and her rulers were also kings of Sidon.[3] The long reign of Ethbaal and his alliance with the kings of Israel had gradually repaired the losses occasioned by civil discord, and had restored Tyre to the high degree of prosperity which it had enjoyed under Hiram. Few actual facts are known which can enlighten us as to the activity which prevailed under Eth-baal: we know, however, that he rebuilt the small town of Botrys, which had been destroyed in the course of some civil war, and that he founded the city of Auza in Libyan territory, at the foot of the mountains of Aures, in one of the richest mineral districts of modern Algeria.[4] In 876 B.C. Assur-nazir-pal had crossed the Lebanon and skirted the shores of the Mediterranean: Eth-baal, naturally compliant, had loaded him with gifts, and by this opportune submission had preserved his cities and country from the horrors of invasion.[5] Twenty years later Shalmaneser III. had returned to Syria, and had come into conflict with Damascus. The northern Phœnicians formed a league with Ben-hadad (Adadidri) to withstand him, and drew upon themselves the penalty of their rashness; the Tyrians, faithful to their usual policy, preferred to submit

---

[1] LAYARD, *Nineveh and Babylon*, pp. 132–134, with Birch's note on King Sabaco.

[2] One version of Manetho assigns twelve years to the reign of Sabaco (MÜLLER-DIDOT, *Fragmenta Historicorum Græcorum*, vol. ii. p. 593), and this duration is confirmed by an inscription in Hammamât, dated in his twelfth year (LEPSIUS, *Denkm.*, v. 1 *e*). Sabaco having succeeded to the throne in 716–715 B.C. (cf. *supra*, p. 233, note 4, and p. 246, note 7), his reign brings us down to 704 or 703 B.C., which obliges us to place the accession of Shabî-toku in the year following the death of Sargon.

[3] Eth-baal II., who, according to the testimony of the native historians (MENANDER, *Fragm.* 1, in MÜLLER-DIDOT, *op. cit.*, vol. iv. p. 446), belonged to the royal family of Tyre, is called King of the Sidonians in the Bible (1 *Kings* xvi. 31), and the Assyrian texts similarly call Elulai King of the Sidonians (*Taylor Cylinder*, col. ii. 1. 35), while Menander mentions him as King of Tyre (JOSEPHUS, *Ant. Jud.*, ix. 14, § 2). It is probable that the King of Sidon, mentioned in the Annals of Shalmaneser III. side by side with the King of Tyre, was a vassal of the Tyrian monarch.

[4] The two facts are preserved in a passage of Menander (*Fragm.* 4, in MÜLLER-DIDOT, *op. cit.*, vol. iv. p. 447). I admit the identity of the Auza mentioned in this fragment with the Auzea of Tacitus (*Annals*, iv. 25), and with the *Colonia Septimia Aur. Auziensium* of the Roman inscriptions (*Corpus Ins. Lat.*, vol. viii. No. 9062) the present Aumale. Gutschmid preferred to recognise in it the Uzita of Strabo (XVII. iii. § 12, p. 831) and of Ptolemy (iv. 3, 37), not far from Leptis the Less (*Kleine Schriften*, vol. ii. p. 59).

[5] Cf. *supra*, p. 41. The King of Tyre who sent gifts to Assur-nazir-pal is not named in the Assyrian documents: our knowledge of Tyrian chronology permits us with all probability to identify him with Eth-baal.

voluntarily and purchase peace. Their conduct showed the greater wisdom in that, after the death of Eth-baal, internal troubles again broke out with renewed fierceness and with even more disastrous results. His immediate successor was Balezor (854–846 B.C.), followed by Mutton I. (845–821 B.C.),[1] who flung himself at the feet of Shalmaneser III., in 842 B.C., in the camp at Baalirasi, and renewed his homage three years later, in 839 B.C.[2] The legends concerning the foundation of Carthage blend with our slight knowledge of his history. They attribute to Mutton I. a daughter named Elissa, who was married to her uncle Sicharbal, high priest of Melkarth, and a young son named Pygmalion (820–774 B.C.). Sicharbal had been nominated by Mutton as regent during the minority of Pygmalion, but he was overthrown by the people, and some years later murdered by his ward. From that time forward Elissa's one aim was to avenge the murder of her husband. She formed a conspiracy which was joined by all the nobles, but being betrayed and threatened with death, she seized a fleet which lay ready to sail in the harbour, and embarking with all her adherents set sail for Africa, landing in the district of Zeugitanê, where the Sidonians had already built Kambê. There she purchased a tract of land from Iarbas, chief of the Liby-phœnicians, and built on the ruins of the ancient factory a new town, Qart-hadshat, which the Greeks called Carchedo and the Romans Carthage.[3] The genius of Virgil has rendered the name of Dido illustrious: but history fails to recognise in the narratives which form the basis of his tale anything beyond a legendary account fabricated after the actual origin (814–813 B.C.) of the great Punic city had been forgotten. Thus weakened, Tyre could less than ever think of opposing the ambitious designs of Assyria: Pygmalion took no part in the rebellions of the petty Syrian kings against Samsî-rammân, and in 803 B.C. he received his suzerain Rammân-nirâri with the accustomed gifts, when that king passed through Phœnicia before attacking Damascus.[4] Pygmalion died about 774 B.C., and the names of his immediate successors are not known;[5] it may be

[1] MENANDER, *Fragm.* 1, in MÜLLER-DIDOT, *Fragm. Hist. Græc.*, vol. iv. p. 446; cf. G. RAWLINSON, *History of Phœnicia*, pp. 435, 436; PIETSCHMANN, *Geschichte der Phönizier*, pp. 298, 299. Mutton, transcribed Mitenna by the Assyrians, is the Phœnician form of the name Mattan, which occurs in the story of Athaliah (cf. *supra*, p. 100).

[2] Cf. *supra*, pp. 86, 87. Here again the Assyrian documents fail to supply the name of the king who paid the tribute.

[3] The narratives concerning the foundation of Carthage have been criticised by OTTO MELTZER, *Geschichte der Karthager*, vol. i. pp. 90–101; for the objections urged by Gutschmid (*Kleine Schriften*, vol. ii. pp. 89–94), cf. the reply of OTTO MELTZER, *op. cit.*, vol. ii. pp. 457, 458.

[4] For this campaign, cf. *supra*, pp. 99, 101, 102.

[5] The fragment of Menander which has preserved for us the list of Tyrian kings from Abî-baal to Pygmalion (*Fragm.* 1, in MÜLLER-DIDOT, *op. cit.*, vol. iv. pp. 445, 446), was only quoted by Josephus (*Contra Apionem*, 1, § 18), because, the seventh year of Pygmalion's reign corresponding to the date of the foundation of Carthage,—814–813 B.C. according to the chronological system of Timæus,—the Hebrew historian found in it a fixed date which seemed to permit of his establishing the chronology

supposed, however, that when the power of Nineveh temporarily declined, the ties which held Tyre to Assyria became naturally relaxed, and the city released herself from the burden of a tribute which had in the past been very irregularly paid. The yoke was reassumed half a century later, at the mere echo of the first victories of Tiglath-pileser III.; and Hiram II., who then reigned in Tyre, hastened to carry to the camp at Arpad assurances of his fidelity (742 B.C.). He gave pledges of his allegiance once more in 738 B.C.;[1] then he disappears, and Mutton II. takes his place about 736 B.C. This king cast off, unhappily for himself, his hereditary apathy, and as soon as a pretext offered itself, abandoned the policy of neutrality to which his ancestors had adhered so firmly. He entered into an alliance in 734 B.C. with Damascus, Israel and Philistia, secretly supported and probably instigated by Egypt; then, when Israel was conquered and Damascus overthrown, he delayed repairing his error till an Assyrian army appeared before Tyre: he had then to pay the price of his temerity by 120 talents of gold and many loads of merchandise (728 B.C.). The punishment was light and the loss inconsiderable in comparison with the accumulated wealth of the city, which its maritime trade was daily increasing:[*] Mutton thought the episode was closed,[2] but the peaceful policy of his house, having been twice interrupted, could not be resumed. Southern Phœnicia, having once launched on the stream of Asiatic politics, followed its fluctuations, and was compelled henceforth to employ in her own defence the forces which had hitherto been utilised in promoting her colonial enterprises.

But it was not due to the foolish caprice of ignorant or rash sovereigns that Tyre renounced her former neutral policy: she was constrained to do so, almost perforce, by the changes which had taken place in Europe.[3] The progress of the Greeks, and their triumph in the waters of the Ægean and Ionian Seas, and the rapid expansion of the Etruscan navy after the end of the ninth century, had gradually restricted the Phœnician merchantmen to the coasts of the Western Mediterranean and the Atlantic: they industriously exploited the mineral wealth of Africa and Spain, and traffic with the barbarous tribes of Morocco and Lusitania, as well as the discovery and working of the British tin mines,

of the kings of Israel and Judah on a trustworthy basis between the reign of Pygmalion and Hiram I., the contemporary of David and Solomon.

[1] Cf. *supra*, pp. 149, 152, 153, on the homage paid twice by Hiram II. to Tiglath-pileser.

[*] [For a description of the trade carried on by Tyre, cf. *Ezek.* xxvi., xxvii., and xxviii.—Tʀ.]

[2] For all these facts, cf. *supra*, pp. 188, 189. Pygmalion having died about 774 B.C., and Hiram II. not appearing till 742 B.C., it is probable that we should intercalate between these two kings at least one sovereign whose name is still unknown.

[3] The same reasons which compelled me to forego treating in my previous works, *The Dawn of Civilization* and *The Struggle of the Nations*, several matters which were comprised in my original scheme, compel me here to avoid any discussion on Tyrian colonisation and the Greek colonisation in Cyprus; I can only indicate briefly the facts necessary to the comprehension of the history of the Phœnicians of the continent as well as of that of the Assyrians.

had largely compensated for the losses occasioned by the closing of the Greek and Italian markets. Their ships, obliged now to coast along the inhospitable cliffs of Northern Africa and to face the open sea, were more strongly and scientifically built than any vessels hitherto constructed. The Egyptian undecked galleys, with stem and stern curving inwards, were discarded as a build ill adapted to resist the attacks of wind or wave. The new Phœnician galley had a long, low, narrow, well-balanced hull, the stern raised and curving inwards above the

A PHŒNICIAN GALLEY WITH TWO BANKS OF OARS.[1]

steersman, as heretofore, but the bows pointed and furnished with a sharp ram projecting from the keel, equally serviceable to cleave the waves or to stave in the side of an enemy's ship. Motive power was supplied by two banks of oars, the upper ones resting in row-locks on the gunwale, the lower ones in row-locks pierced in the timbers of the vessel's side. An upper deck, supported by stout posts, ran from stem to stern, above the heads of the rowers, and was reserved for the soldiers and the rest of the crew : on a light railing surrounding it were hung the circular shields of the former, forming as it were a rampart on either side. The mast, passing through both decks, was firmly fixed in the keel, and was supported by two stays made fast to stem and stern. The rectangular sail was attached to a yard which could be hoisted or lowered at will. The wealth which accrued to the Tyrians from their naval expeditions had rendered the superiority of Tyre over the neighbouring cities so manifest that they had nearly all become her vassals. Arvad and Northern Phœnicia were still independent, as also the sacred city of Byblos, but the entire coast from the Nahr-el-Kelb to the headland formed by Mount Carmel was directly subject to Tyre,[2] comprising the two Sidons, Bît-zîti, and Sarepta, the country from Mahalliba to the fords of the Litany, Ushu and its hinterland as far as Kana, Akzîb, Akko, and Dora; and this compact territory, partly protected by the

---

[1] Drawn by Faucher-Gudin, from LAYARD, *Mon. of Nineveh*, vol. i. pl. 71; for the rest of the bas-relief, cf. *infra*, p. 301. Sennacherib affirms that vessels of this type had been constructed by Syrian shipwrights, and were manned by Tyrian, Sidonian, and Ionian sailors (G. SMITH, *History of Sennacherib*, pp. 90, 91).

[2] The kings of Arvad and Byblos are still found mentioned at the beginning of Sennacherib's reign (*Taylor Cylinder*, col. ii. pp. 49, 50).

range of Lebanon, and secured by the habitual prudence of its rulers from the invasions which had desolated Syria, formed the most flourishing, and perhaps also the most populous, kingdom which still existed between the Euphrates and the Egyptian desert.[1] Besides these, some parts of Cyprus were dependent on Tyre, though the Achæan colonies, continually reinforced by fresh immigrants, had absorbed most of the native population and driven the rest into the mountains. A hybrid civilisation had developed among these early Greek settlers, amalgamating the customs, religions, and arts of the ancient eastern world of Egypt, Syria, and Chaldæa in variable proportions: their script was probably derived from one of the Asianic systems whose monuments are still but partly known, and it consisted of a syllabary awkwardly adapted to a language for which it had not been designed. A dozen petty kings, of whom the majority were Greeks, disputed possession of the northern and eastern parts of the island, at Idalion, Khytros, Paphos, Soli, Kourion, Tamassos, and Ledron. The Phœnicians had given way at first before the in-

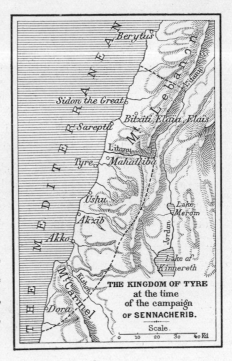

vaders, and had grouped themselves in the eastern plain round Kition; they had, however, subsequently assumed the offensive, and endeavoured to regain the territory they had lost. Kition, which had been destroyed in one of their wars, had been rebuilt, and thus obtained the name of Qart-hadshat, "the new city."[2]

---

[1] The extent of the kingdom of Tyre is indicated by the passage in which Sennacherib enumerated the cities which he had taken from Elulai (*Taylor Cylinder*, col. ii. ll. 38–44). For the situation of Little Sidon, Bît-zîti, Mahalliba, and Ushu, cf. MASPERO, *De quelques Localités voisines de Sidon*, in the *Recueil de Travaux*, vol. xvii. pp. 101–103. To these must be added Dor, to the south of Carmel, which was always regarded as belonging to the Tyrians, and whose isolated position between the headland, the sea, and the forest might cause the Assyrians to leave it unmolested.

[2] The name of this city, at first read as Amtikhadashti, and identified with Ammokhostos or with Amathous,—*Amti-Khadashti* would in this case be equivalent to *New Amathous* (SCHRADER, *Keilins. und Geschichtsf.*, p. 244, note 2),—is really Karti-Khadashti, as is proved by the variant reading discovered by Schrader (*Zur Kritik der Inschriften Tiglath-Pileser's*, p. 33), and this is identical with the native name of Carthage in Africa. For the identity of this Cyprian Carthage with Kition, cf. SIX, *Du Classement des Séries Cypriotes*, in the *Revue Numismatique*, 3rd ser., vol. i. p. 253, and more particularly SCHRADER, *Zur Geographie des Assyrischen Reichs*, pp. 17–24. This new city must have been of some antiquity by the time of Elulai, for it is mentioned on a fragment of a bronze vase found in Cyprus itself, and published in the *Corpus Inscriptionum Semiticarum*, vol. i. pl. iv.: this fragment belonged to a King Hiram, who according to some authorities would be Hiram II., according to others, Hiram I. (cf. *Struggle of the Nations*, p. 574).

Mutton's successor, Elulai,[1] continued, as we know, the work of defence and conquest: perhaps it was with a view to checking his advance that seven kings of Cyprus sent an embassy, in 709 B.C., to his suzerain, Sargon, and placed themselves under the protection of Assyria.[2] If this was actually the case, and Elulai was compelled to suspend hostilities against these hereditary foes, one can understand that this grievance, added to the reasons for uneasiness inspired by the situation of his continental dominions, may have given him the desire to rid himself of the yoke of Assyria, and contributed to his resolution to ally himself with the powers which were taking up arms against her. The constant intercourse of his subjects with the Delta, and his natural anxiety to avoid anything which might close one of the richest markets of the world to the Tyrian trade, inclined him to receive favourably the overtures of the Pharaoh: the emissaries of Shabîtoku found him as much disposed as Hezekiah himself to begin the struggle. The latter monarch, who had ascended the throne while still very young, had at first shown no ambition beyond the carrying out of religious reforms.[3] His father Ahaz had been far from orthodox, in spite of the influence exerted over him by Isaiah. During his visit to Tiglath-pileser at Damascus (729 B.C.) he had noticed an altar whose design pleased him. He sent a description of it to the high priest Urijah, with orders to have a similar one constructed, and erected in the court of the temple at Jerusalem: this altar he appropriated to his personal use, and caused the priests to minister at it, instead of at the old altar, which he relegated to an inferior position. He also effected changes in the temple furniture, which doubtless appeared to him old-fashioned in comparison with the splendours of the Assyrian worship which he had witnessed, and he made some alterations in the approaches to the temple, wishing, as far as we can judge, that the King of Judah should henceforth, like his brother of Nineveh, have a private means of access to his national god.[4] This was but the least of his offences: for had he not offered his own son as a holocaust at the moment he felt himself most menaced by the league of Israel and Damascus?[5] Among the people themselves there were many faint-hearted and faithless, who, doubting the power of the God of their forefathers, turned aside to the gods of the neighbouring nations, and besought from them the succour they despaired of receiving from any other source; the

---

[1] MENANDER, in JOSEPHUS, *Ant. Jud.*, viii. 5, § 3, where the reading of Gutschmid (*Kleine Schriften*, vol. ii. pp. 88, 89), according to which the fragment would refer to the people of Utica, does not seem to me preferable to the ancient reading, which makes it refer to the people of Kition (cf. LANDAU, *Beiträge zur Alterthumskunde des Orients*, pp. 18, 19).

[2] For the submission of the Cypriots, cf. *supra*, pp. 259, 260.

[3] For the date of Hezekiah's accession, cf. *supra*, p. 236, note 1.

[4] 2 *Kings* xvi. 10–18.

[5] Cf. *supra*, pp. 185, 186.

worship of Jahveh was confounded with that of Moloch in the valley of the children of Hinnom, where there was a sanctuary or Tophet, at which the people celebrated the most horrible rites: a large and fierce pyre was kept continually burning there, to consume the children whose fathers brought them to offer in sacrifice.[1]   Isaiah complains bitterly of these unbelievers who profaned the land with their idols, "worshipping the work of their own hands, that which their own fingers have made."[2]   The new king, obedient to the divine command, renounced the errors of his father; he removed the fetishes with which the superstition of his predecessors had cumbered the temple, and which they had connected with the worship of Jahveh, and in his zeal even destroyed the ancient brazen serpent, the Nehushtan, the origin of which was attributed to Moses.[3]   On the occasion of the revolt of Yamani, Isaiah counselled Hezekiah to remain neutral, and this prudence enabled him to look on in security at the ruin of the Philistines, the hereditary foes of his race.[4]   Under his wise administration the kingdom of Judah, secured against annoyance from envious neighbours by the protection which Assur freely afforded to its obedient vassals, and revived by thirty years of peace, rose rapidly from the rank of secondary importance which it had formerly been content to occupy.   "Their land was full of silver and gold, neither was there any end of their treasures; their land also was full of horses, neither was there any end of their chariots."[5] Now that the kingdom of Israel had been reduced to the condition of an Assyrian province, it was on Judah and its capital that the hopes of the whole Hebrew nation were centred.

Tyre and Jerusalem had hitherto formed the extreme outwork of the Syrian states; they were the only remaining barrier which separated the empires of Egypt and Assyria, and it was to the interest of the Pharaoh to purchase their alliance and increase their strength by every means in his power.   Negotiations must have been going on for some time between the three powers, but up to the time of the death of Sargon and the return of Merodach-baladan to Babylon their results had been unimportant, and it was possible that the disasters which had befallen the Kaldâ would tend to cool the ardour of the allies.   An unforeseen circumstance opportunely rekindled their zeal, and determined them to try their fortune.   The inhabitants of Ekron, dissatisfied with Padî, the chief whom the Assyrians had set over them, seized his person and sent

---

[1] *Isa.* xxx. 33, where the prophet describes the Tophet Jahveh's anger is preparing for Assyria.

[2] *Isa.* ii. 8.

[3] 2 *Kings* xviii. 4.   I leave the account of this religious reformation in the place assigned to it in the Bible; other historians relegate it to a time posterior to the invasion of Sennacherib (STADE, *Geschichte des Volkes Israel*, vol. i. pp. 607, 608).

[4] For the revolt of Yamani, cf. *supra*, pp. 252, 253.

[5] *Isa.* ii. 7, where the description applies better to the later years of Ahaz or the reign of Hezekiah than to the years preceding the war against Pekah and Rezin.

him in chains to Hezekiah.[1] To accept the present was equivalent to open rebellion, and a declaration of war against the power of the suzerain. Isaiah, as usual, wished Judah to rely on Jahveh alone, and preached against alliance with the Babylonians, for he foresaw that success would merely result in substituting the Kaldâ for the Ninevite monarch, and in aggravating the condition of Judah. "All that is in thine house," he said to Hezekiah, "and that which thy fathers have laid up in store unto this day, shall be carried to

THE CAMPAIGN OF SENNACHERIB in Judea.

Babylon; nothing shall be left, saith the Lord. And of thy sons that shall issue from thee, which thou shalt beget, shall they take away; and they shall be eunuchs in the palace of the King of Babylon." Hezekiah did not pay much heed to the prediction, for, he reflected, "peace and truth shall be in my days," and the future troubled him little.[2] When the overthrow of Merodach-baladan had taken place, the prophet still more earnestly urged the people not to incur the vengeance of Assyria without other help than that of Tyre or Ethiopia, and Eliakim, son of Hilkiah, spoke in the same strain; but Shebna, the prefect of the palace, declaimed against this advice, and the latter's counsel prevailed with his master.[3] Hezekiah agreed to accept the sovereignty over Ekron which its inhabitants offered to him, but a remnant of prudence kept him from putting Padî to death, and he contented himself with casting him into prison.[4] Isaiah, though temporarily out of favour with the king, ceased

[1] The name of the city, written Amgarruna (SMITH-SAYCE, *History of Sennacherib*, p. 57), and identified with Migron of Benjamin (*Isa.* x. 28) by Oppert (*Expédition en Mésopotamie*, vol. i. p. 370) and by Ménant (*Annales des rois d'Assyrie*, p. 218), is really Akkaron-Ekron, as Hincks (LAYARD, *Nineveh and Babylon*, p. 121) and Rawlinson (*Assyrian History*, in the *Athenæum*, Aug. 23, 1851) have recognised (cf. FINZI, *Ricerche per lo Studio dell' Antichità Assira*, pp. 385, 386; FR. LENORMANT, *Les Premières Civilisations*, vol. ii. pp. 273–275; FR. DELITZSCH, *Wo lag das Paradies?* p. 287; DELATTRE, *L'Asie Antérieure dans les Inscriptions Assyriennes*, p. 90).

[2] 2 *Kings* xx. 16–19.

[3] This follows from the terms in which the prophet compares the two men (*Isa.* xxii. 15–25).

[4] *Taylor Cylinder*, col. ii. ll. 69–72; cf. SMITH-SAYCE, *History of Sennacherib*, pp. 57, 58.

not to proclaim aloud in all quarters the will of the Almighty. "Woe to the rebellious children, saith the Lord, that take counsel, but not of Me; and that cover with a covering (form alliances), but not of My spirit, that they may add sin to sin: that walk to go down into Egypt, and have not asked at My mouth, to strengthen themselves in the strength of Pharaoh, and to trust in the shadow of Egypt! Therefore shall the strength of Pharaoh be your shame, and the trust in the shadow of Egypt your confusion. When your princes shall be at Tanis, and your messengers shall come to Heracleopolis,* you shall all be ashamed of a people that cannot profit you. . . . For Egypt helpeth in vain, and to no purpose: therefore have I called her Rahab that sitteth still."[1] He returned, unwearied and with varying imagery, to his theme, contrasting the uncertainty and frailty of the expedients of worldly wisdom urged by the military party, with the steadfast will of Jahveh and the irresistible authority with which He invests His faithful servants. "The Egyptians are men, and not God; and their horses flesh, and not spirit: and when the Lord shall stretch out His hand, both he that helpeth shall stumble, and he that is holpen shall fall, and they shall all fail together. For thus saith the Lord unto me, Like as when the lion growleth, and the young lion over his prey, if a multitude of shepherds be called forth against him, he will not be dismayed at their voice, nor abase himself for the noise of them: so shall the Lord of hosts come down to fight upon Mount Zion, and upon the hill thereof. As birds flying, so will the Lord of hosts protect Jerusalem: He will protect and deliver it. Turn ye unto Him from whom ye have deeply revolted, O children of Israel."[2] No one, however, gave heed to his warnings, either king or people; but the example of Phœnicia soon proved that he was right. When Sennacherib bestirred himself, in the spring of 702 B.C., either the Ethiopians were not ready, or they dared not advance to encounter him in Cœle-Syria, and they left Elulai to get out of his difficulties as best he might. He had no army to risk in a pitched battle; but fondly imagined that his cities, long since fortified, and protected on the east by the range of Lebanon, would offer a resistance sufficiently stubborn to wear out the patience of his assailant. The Assyrians, however, disconcerted his plans. Instead of advancing against him by the pass of Nahr-el-Kebir, according to their usual custom, they attacked him in flank, descending into the very midst of his positions by the *col* of Legnia or one of the neighbouring passes.[3] They captured in succession the two Sidons, Bît-zîti, Sarepta,

---

* [Heb. Hanes.—Tr.]

[1] *Isa.* xxx. 1–5, 7. In verses 4, 5, the original text employs the third person; I have restored the second person, to avoid confusion.

[2] *Isa.* xxxi. 3–6.

[3] This follows from the very order in which the cities were taken in the course of this campaign.

Mahalliba, Ushu, Akzîb, and Acco: Elulai, reduced to the possession of the island of Tyre alone, retreated to one of his colonies in Cyprus, where he died some years later, without having set foot again on the continent. All his former possessions on the mainland were given to a certain Eth-baal, who chose Sidon for his seat of government, and Tyre lost by this one skirmish the rank of metropolis which she had enjoyed for centuries.[1]

This summary punishment decided all the Syrian princes who were not compromised beyond hope of pardon to humble themselves before the suzerain. Menahem of Samsi-muruna,[2] Abdiliti of Arvad, Uru-malîk of Byblos, Pudu-îlu of Ammon, Chemosh-nadab of Moab, Malîk-rammu of Edom, Mitinti of Ashdod, all brought their tribute in person to the Assyrian camp before Ushu:[3] Zedekiah of Ashkelon and Hezekiah of Judah alone persisted in their hostility. Egypt had at length been moved by the misfortunes of her allies, and the Ethiopian troops had advanced to the seat of war, but they did not arrive in time to save Zedekiah: Sennacherib razed to the ground all his strongholds one after another, Beth-dagon, Joppa, Bene-berak, and Hazor,[4] took him prisoner at Ascalon, and sent him with his family to Assyria, setting up Sharludarî, son of Rukibti, in his stead. Sennacherib then turned against Ekron, and was about to begin the siege of the city, when the long-expected Egyptians at length made their appearance. Shabîtoku did not command them in person, but he had sent his best troops—the contingents furnished by the petty kings of the Delta, and the sheikhs of the Sinaitic peninsula, who were vassals of Egypt. The encounter took place near Altaku,[5] and on this occasion again, as at Raphia,

[1] *Taylor Cylinder*, col. ii. ll. 34–46: cf. SMITH-SAYCE, *Hist. of Sennacherib*, pp. 53–55, 67, 68; BEZOLD, *Inschriften Sanherib's*, in SCHRADER, *Keilins. Bibliothek*, vol. ii. pp. 90, 91. The Assyrian text gives for the name of the King of Sidon a shortened form Tu-baal instead of Eth-baal, paralleled by Lulia for Elulai.

[2] Several of the early Assyriologists read Usi-muruna, and identified the city bearing this name with Samaria (FOX TALBOT, in the *J. R. As. Soc.*, vol. xix. p. 144; NORRIS, *Assyrian Dictionary*, p. 292; FINZI, *Ricerche per lo Studio dell' Antichità Assira*, p. 379; SCHRADER, *Die Keilinschriften und das Alte Testament*, 1st edit., p. 93; SMITH-SAYCE, *Hist. of Sennacherib*, pp. 55–72), which was not approved of by H. Rawlinson nor by Fr. Lenormant (*Les Premières Civilisations*, vol. ii. p. 272, note 2). The discovery of the reading Samsi-muruna on a fragment of the time of Assur-bani-pal (cf. SCHRADER, *Zur Kritik der Inschriften Tiglatpilesers II.*, pp. 33, 34) no longer permits of this identification, and obliges us to look for the city in Phœnicia. Some time ago Fr. Lenormant (*ibid.*) ventured to suggest Orthosia: Halévy is content to explain the name as *Shamash is our lord* (*Mélanges de Critique et d'Histoire relatifs aux peuples sémitiques*, p. 35); Delitzsch recognises in it a Phœnician city (*Wo lag das Paradies?* pp. 286, 287), and other Assyriologists give its name without trying to locate it on the map.

[3] The last detail is found in *Bull Inscr. No. 4* (SMITH-SAYCE, *Hist. of Sennacherib*, p. 65; cf. BEZOLD, *Inschriften Sanherib's*, in SCHRADER, *Keilins. Bibliothek*, vol. ii. p. 91, note 42).

[4] These are the cities attributed to the tribes of Dan and Judah in *Josh.* xv. 25, 41; xix. 45. Beth-dagon is now Bêt-Dejân; Azuru is Yazûr, to the south-east of Joppa; Beni-barak is Ibn-Abrak, to the north-east of the same town.

[5] Altaku is certainly Eltekeh of Dan (*Josh.* xix. 44), as was seen from the outset; the site, however, of Eltekeh cannot be fixed with any certainty. It has been located at Bêt-Lukkieh, in the mountainous country north-west of Jerusalem, but this position in no way corresponds to the requirements of the Assyrian text, according to which the battle took place on a plain large enough for the evolutions of the Egyptian chariots, and situated between the group of towns formed by Beth-dagon,

the scientific tactics of the Assyrians prevailed over the stereotyped organisation of Pharaoh's army: the Ethiopian generals left some of their chariots in the hands of the conqueror, and retreated with the remnants of their force beyond the Isthmus. Altaku capitulated, an example followed by the neighbouring fortress of Timnath, and subsequently by Ekron itself, all three being made to feel Sennacherib's vengeance. "The nobles and chiefs who had offended, I slew," he remarks, "and set up their corpses on stakes in a circle round the city; those of the inhabitants who had offended and committed crimes, I took them prisoners, and for the rest who had neither offended nor transgressed, I pardoned them."[1] We may here pause to inquire how Hezekiah was occupied while his fate was being decided on the field of Altaku. He was fortifying Jerusalem, and storing within it munitions of war, and enrolling Jewish soldiers and mercenary troops from the Arab tribes of the desert.[3] He had suddenly become aware that large portions of the wall of the city of David had crumbled away, and he set about demolishing the neighbouring houses to obtain materials for repairing these breaches: he hastily strengthened the weak points in his fortifications, stopped up the springs which flowed into the Gihon, and cut off the brook itself, constructing a reservoir between the inner and outer city walls to store up the waters of

THE PASS OF LEGNIA, IN LEBANON.[2]

Joppa, Beni-barak, and Hazor, which Sennacherib had just captured, and the cities of Ekron, Timnath, and Eltekeh, which he took directly after his victory: a suitable locality must be looked for in the vicinity of Ramleh or Zernuka.

[1] Taylor Cylinder, col. iii. ll. 47–83, col. iv. ll. 1–7; cf. BEZOLD, Inschriften Sanherib's, in SCHRADER, Keilins. Bibliothek, vol. ii. pp. 90–95; SMITH-SAYCE, Hist. of Sennacherib, pp. 55–60.

[2] Drawn by Boudier, from a photograph given in LORTET, La Syrie d'aujourd'hui, p. 632.

[3] Taylor Cylinder, col. iv. ll. 31–33; cf. SMITH-SAYCE, Hist. of Sennacherib, p. 63. The Urbi mentioned in this passage are the Arabs of the North Arabian desert, connected with the Kaldâ and Eastern Aramæans (FR. DELITZSCH, Wo lag das Paradies? pp. 305, 306).

U

the ancient pool. These alterations [1] rendered the city, which from its natural position was well defended, so impregnable that Sennacherib decided not to attack it until the rest of the kingdom had been subjugated: with this object in view he pitched his camp before Lachish, whence he could keep a watch over the main routes from Egypt where they crossed the frontier, and then scattered his forces over the land of Judah, delivering it up to pillage in a systematic manner. He took forty-six walled towns, and numberless strongholds and villages, demolishing the walls and leading into captivity 200,150 persons of all ages and conditions, together with their household goods, their horses, asses, mules, camels, oxen, and sheep ; [2] it was a war as disastrous in its effects as that which terminated in the fall of Samaria, or which led to the final captivity in Babylon.[3] The work of destruction accomplished, the Rabshakeh brought up all his forces and threw up a complete circle of earthworks round Jerusalem: Hezekiah found himself shut up in his capital "like a bird in a cage." [4] The inhabitants soon became accustomed to this isolated life, but Isaiah was indignant at seeing them indifferent to their calamities, and inveighed against them with angry eloquence : "What aileth thee now, that thou art wholly gone up to the housetops ? O thou that art full of shoutings, a tumultuous city, a joyous town ; thy slain are not slain with the sword, neither are they dead in battle. All thy rulers fled away together, they are made prisoners without drawing the bow ; they are come hither from afar for safety, and all that meet together here shall be taken together." * The danger was urgent ; the Assyrians were massed in their entrenchments with their auxiliaries ranged behind them to support them : "Elam bare the quiver with chariots of men and horsemen, and Kir uncovered the shield (for the assault). And it came to pass that thy choicest valleys were full of chariots, and the horsemen set themselves in array at thy gate, and he took away the covering of Judah." In those days, therefore, Jahveh, without pity for His people, called them to "weeping, and to mourning, and to baldness, and to girding with sackcloth: and behold, joy and gladness, slaying oxen and killing sheep, eating flesh and drinking wine : let us eat and drink, for to-morrow we shall die. And the Lord of hosts revealed Himself in mine ears, Surely this iniquity shall not be purged from you till ye die, saith the Lord, the Lord of Hosts." [5] The prophet threw the blame on the courtiers,

---

[1] *Isa.* xxii. 8–11.

[2] *Taylor Cylinder*, col. iv. ll. 11–20 ; cf. SMITH-SAYCE, *Hist. of Sennacherib*, pp. 61, 62, 66, 69. An allusion to the sojourn of Sennacherib near Lachish is found in 2 *Kings* xviii. 14–17 ; xix. 8, and in *Isa.* xxxvi. 2 ; xxxvii. 8.

[3] It seems that the Jewish historian Demetrios considered the captivities under Nebuchadrezzar and Sennacherib to be on the same footing (MÜLLER-DIDOT, *Fragmenta Hist. Græc.*, vol. iii. p. 208).

[4] *Taylor Cylinder*, col. iv. l. 20 ; cf. SMITH-SAYCE, *op. cit.*, p. 62.	[5] *Isa.* xxii. 1–14.

* [The R.V. gives this passage as follows : "They were bound by the archers: all that were found of thee were bound together, they fled afar off."—TR.]

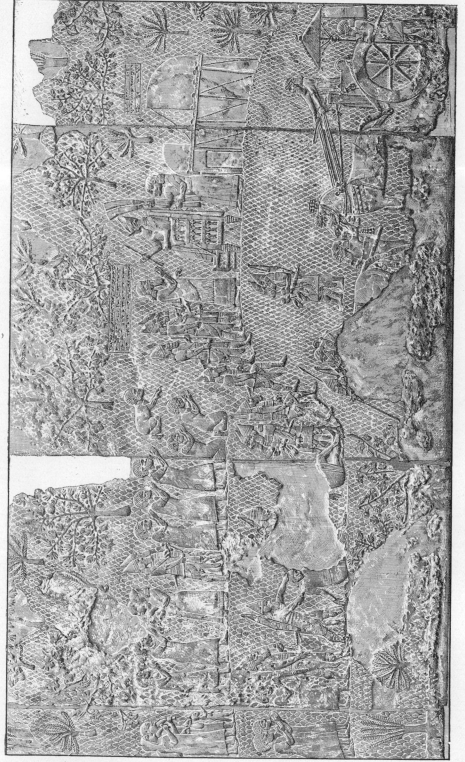

SENNACHERIB RECEIVING THE SUBMISSION OF THE JEWS IN HIS CAMP BEFORE LACHISH.

Drawn by Boudier, from LAYARD, *Monuments of Nineveh*, vol. ii. pl. 22.

especially Shebna, who still hoped for succour from the Egyptians, and kept up the king's illusions on this point. He threatened him with the divine anger; he depicted him as seized by Jahveh, rolled and kneaded into a lump, "and tossed like a ball into a large country : there shalt thou die, and there shall be the chariots of thy glory, thou shame of thy lord's house. And I will thrust thee from thy office, and from thy station he shall pull thee down!"[1] Meanwhile, day after day elapsed, and Pharaoh did not hasten to the rescue. Hezekiah's eyes were opened; he dismissed Shebna, and degraded him to the position of scribe, and set Eliakim in his place in the Council of State.[2] Isaiah's influence revived, and he persuaded the king to sue for peace while yet there was time.

Sennacherib was encamped at Lachish; but the Tartan and his two lieutenants received the overtures of peace, and proposed a parley near the conduit of the upper pool, in the highway of the fuller's field. Hezekiah did not venture to go in person to the meeting-place; he sent Eliakim, the new prefect of the palace, Shebna, and the chancellor Joah, the chief cupbearer, and tradition relates that the Assyrian addressed them in severe terms in his master's name: "Now on whom dost thou trust, that thou rebellest against me? Behold, thou trustest upon the staff of this bruised reed, even upon Egypt; whereon if a man lean, it will go into his hand and pierce it: so is Pharaoh, King of Egypt, to all that trust on him." Then, as he continued to declaim in a loud voice, so that the crowds gathered on the wall could hear him, the delegates besought him to speak in Aramaic, which they understood, but "speak not to us in the Jews' language, in the ears of the people that are on the wall!" Instead, however, of granting their request, the Assyrian general advanced towards the spectators and addressed them in Hebrew: "Hear ye the words of the great king, the King of Assyria. Let not Hezekiah deceive you; for he shall not be able to deliver you: neither let Hezekiah make you trust in the Lord, saying, The Lord will surely deliver ns: this city shall not be given into the hand of the King of Assyria. Hearken not to Hezekiah: for thus saith the King of Assyria, Make your peace with me, and come out to me; and eat ye every one of his vine, and every one of his fig tree, and drink ye every one the waters of his own cistern; until I come and take you away to a land like your own land, a land of corn and wine, a land of bread and vineyards. Beware lest Hezekiah persuade you, saying, The Lord will deliver us!" The specified conditions were less hard than might have been feared.[3] The Jewish king was to give up his wives and daughters as

---

[1] *Isa.* xxii. 15–19.

[2] In the duplicate narrative of these negotiations with the Assyrian generals, Shebna is in fact considered as a mere scribe, while Eliakim is the prefect of the king's house (2 *Kings* xviii. 18, 37; xix. 2; *Isa.* xxxvi. 3, 22; xxxvii. 2).

[3] The Hebrew version of these events is recorded in 2 *Kings* xviii. 13–37; xix., and in *Isa.* xxxvi.;

hostages, to pledge himself to pay a regular tribute, and disburse immediately a ransom of thirty talents of gold, and eight hundred talents of silver : he could only make up this large sum by emptying the royal and sacred treasuries, and taking down the plates of gold with which merely a short while before he had adorned the doors and lintels of the temple. Padî was released from his long captivity, reseated on his throne, and received several Jewish towns as an indemnity ; other portions of territory were bestowed upon Mitinti of Ashdod and Zillibel of Gaza as a reward for their loyalty.[1] Hezekiah issued from the struggle with his territory curtailed and his kingdom devastated ; the last obstacle which stood in the way of the Assyrians' victorious advance fell with him, and Sennacherib could now push forward with perfect safety towards the Nile. He had, indeed, already planned an attack on Egypt, and had reached the isthmus, when a mysterious accident arrested his further progress. The conflict on the plains of Altaku had been severe ; and the army, already seriously diminished by its victory, had been still further weakened during the campaign in Judæa, and possibly the excesses indulged in by the soldiery had developed in them the germs of one of those terrible epidemics which had devastated Western Asia several times in the course of the century : whatever may have been the cause, half the army was destroyed by pestilence before it reached the frontier of the Delta, and Sennacherib led back the shattered remnants of his force to Nineveh.[2] The Hebrews did not hesitate to ascribe the

xxxvii., with only one important divergence, namely, the absence from Isaiah of verses 14–16 of 2 *Kings* xviii. This particular passage, in which the name of the king has a peculiar form, is a detached fragment of an older document, perhaps the official annals of the kingdom, whose contents agreed with the facts recorded in the Assyrian text. The rest is borrowed from the cycle of prophetic narratives, and contains two different versions of the same events. The first comprises 2 *Kings* xviii. 13, 17–37 ; xix. 1–9a, 36b–37, where Sennacherib is represented as despatching a verbal message to Hezekiah by the Tartan and his captains. The second consists merely of 2 *Kings* xix. 9b–36a, and in this has been inserted a long prophecy of Isaiah's (xix. 21–31) which has but a vague connection with the rest of the narrative. In this Sennacherib defied Hezekiah in a letter, which the Jewish king spread before the Lord, and shortly afterwards received a reply through the prophet. The two versions were combined towards the end of the seventh or beginning of the sixth century, by the compiler of the *Book of Kings*, and passed thence into the collection of the prophecies attributed to Isaiah.

[1] *Taylor Cylinder*, col. iv. ll. 8–11, 20–41 ; cf. SMITH-SAYCE, *Hist. of Sennacherib*, pp. 60–64. The sequence of events is not very well observed in the Assyrian text, and the liberation of Padî is inserted in ll. 8–11, before the account of the war with Hezekiah. It seems very unlikely that the King of Judah would have released his prisoner before his treaty with Sennacherib ; the Assyrian scribe, wishing to bring together all the facts relating to Ekron, anticipated this event. Hebrew tradition fixed the ransom at the lowest figure, 300 talents of silver instead of the 800 given in the Assyrian document (2 *Kings* xviii. 14), and authorities have tried to reconcile this divergence by speculating on the different values represented by a talent in different countries and epochs (BRANDIS, *Münz-, Mass-, und Gewichtswesen in Vorderasien*, p. 98).

[2] The Assyrian texts are silent about this catastrophe, and the sacred books of the Hebrews seem to refer it to the camp at Libnah in Palestine (2 *Kings* xix. 8–35) ; the Egyptian legend related by Herodotus (II. cxli. ; cf. *infra*, p. 294) seems to prove that it took place near the Egyptian frontier. Josephus (*Ant. Jud.*, x. 1, § 4) takes the king as far as Pelusium, and describes the destruction of the Assyrian army as taking place in the camp before this town. He may have been misled by the meaning "mud," which attaches to the name of Libnah as well as to that of Pelusium. Oppert

event to the vengeance of Jahveh, and to make it a subject of thankfulness. They related that before their brutal conqueror quitted the country he had sent a parting message to Hezekiah: "Let not thy God in whom thou trustest deceive thee, saying, Jerusalem shall not be given into the hand of the King of Assyria. Behold, thou hast heard what the kings of Assyria have done to all lands, by destroying them utterly; and shalt thou be delivered? Have the gods of the nations delivered them which my fathers have destroyed, Gozan and Haran and Rezeph, and the children of Eden which were in Telassar? Where is the King of Hamath, and the King of Arpad, and the King of the city of Sepharvaim, of Hena, and Ivvah?" Hezekiah, having received this letter of defiance, laid it in the temple before Jahveh, and prostrated himself in prayer: the response came to him through the mouth of Isaiah. "Thus saith the Lord concerning the King of Assyria, He shall not come unto this city, nor shoot an arrow there, neither shall he come before it with a shield, nor cast a mount against it. By the way that he came, by the same shall he return, and he shall not come unto this city, saith the Lord. For I will defend this city to save it, for Mine own sake and for My servant David's sake. And it came to pass that night, that the angel of the Lord went forth, and smote in the camp of the Assyrians an hundred fourscore and five thousand: and when men arose early in the morning, behold, they were all dead corpses."[1] The Egyptians considered the event no less miraculous than did the Hebrews, and one of their popular tales ascribed the prodigy to Phtah, the god of Memphis. Sethon, the high priest of Phtah, lived in a time of national distress, and the warrior class, whom he had deprived of some of its privileges, refused to take up arms in his behalf. He repaired, therefore, to the temple to implore divine assistance, and, falling asleep, was visited by a dream. The god appeared to him, and promised to send him some auxiliaries who should ensure him success. He enlisted such of the Egyptians as were willing to follow him, shopkeepers, fullers, and sutlers, and led them to Pelusium to resist the threatened invasion. In the night a legion of field-mice came forth, whence no one knew, and, noiselessly spreading throughout the camp of the Assyrians, gnawed the quivers, the bowstrings, and the straps of the bucklers in such a way that, on the morrow, the enemy, finding themselves disarmed, fled after a mere pretence at resistance, and suffered severe losses. A statue was long shown in the temple at

---

upheld his opinion, and identified the Libnah of the biblical narrative with the Pelusium of Herodotus (*Mémoire sur les Rapports de l'Égypte et de l'Assyrie*, pp. 34–36). It is probable that each of the two nations referred the scene of the miracle to a different locality.

[1] 2 *Kings* xix. 8–35; *Isa.* xxxvii. 8–36; this is the second tradition of which mention has been made (cf. *supra*, p. 292, note 3), but already amalgamated with the first to form the narrative as it now stands.

Memphis portraying this Sethon: he was represented holding a mouse in his hand, and the inscription bade men reverence the god who had wrought this miracle.[1]

The disaster was a terrible one: Sennacherib's triumphant advance was suddenly checked, and he was forced to return to Asia when the goal of his ambition was almost reached. The loss of a single army, however much to be deplored, was not irreparable, since Assyria could furnish her sovereign with a second force as numerous as that which lay buried in the desert on the road to Egypt, but it was uncertain what effect the news of the calamity and the sight of the survivors might have on the minds of his subjects and rivals. The latter took no immediate action, and the secret joy which they must have experienced did not blind them to the real facts of the case; for though the power of Assyria was shaken, she was still stronger than any one of them severally, or even than all of them together, and to attack her or rebel against her now, was to court defeat with as much certainty as in past days. The Pharaoh kept himself behind his rivers; the military science and skill which had baffled his generals on the field of Altaku did not inspire him with any desire to reappear on the plains of Palestine. Hezekiah, King of Judah, had emptied his treasury to furnish his ransom, his strongholds had capitulated one by one, and his territory, diminished by the loss of some of the towns of the Shephelah,[2] was little better than a waste of smoking ruins. He thought himself fortunate to have preserved his power under the suzerainty of Assyria, and his sole aim for many years was to refill his treasury, reconstitute his army, and re-establish his kingdom. The Philistine and Nabatæan princes, and the chiefs of Moab, Ammon, and Idumæa, had nothing to gain by war, being too feeble to have any chance of success without the help of Judah, Tyre, and Egypt. The Syrians maintained a peaceful attitude, which was certainly their wisest policy; and during the following quarter of a century they loyally obeyed their governors, and gave Sennacherib no cause to revisit them. It was fortunate for him that they did so, for the peoples of the North and East, the Kaldâ, and, above all, the Elamites, were the cause of much trouble, and exclusively occupied his attention during several years. The inhabitants of Bît-Yakîn, urged on either by their natural restlessness or by the news of

---

[1] HERODOTUS, II. cxli.; cf. WIEDEMANN, *Herodot's Zweites Buch*, pp. 501–505. The statue with which this legend had been connected, must have represented a king offering the image of a mouse crouching on a basket, like the cynocephalus on the hieroglyphic sign which denotes centuries, or the frog of the goddess Hiqît. Historians have desired to recognise in Sethon a King Zêt of the XXIIIrd dynasty (LEPSIUS, *Königsbuch*, pp. 46, 47), or even Shabîtoku of the XXVth dynasty (LAUTH, *Aus Ægypten's Vorzeit*, pp. 439, 440); Krall identified him with Satni in the demotic story of *Satni-Khâmoîs* (*Ein neuer historischer Roman in Demotischer Schrift*, p. 1, note 3).

[2] Cf. *supra*, p. 293, for the portions of territory which Hezekiah had to cede to Padî of Ekron, Mitinti of Ashdod, and Zillibel of Gaza.

the misfortune which had befallen their enemy, determined once more to try the fortunes of war. Incited by Marduk-ushezîb,[1] one of their princes, and by Merodach-baladan, these people of the marshes intrigued with the courts of Babylon and Susa, and were emboldened to turn against the Assyrian garrisons stationed in their midst to preserve order. Sennacherib's vengeance fell first on Marduk-ushezîb, who fled from his stronghold of Bîttutu after sustaining a short siege. Merodach-baladan, deserted by his accomplice, put the statues of his gods and his royal treasures on board his fleet, and embarking with his followers crossed the lagoon, and effected a landing in the district of Nagîtu, in Susian territory, beyond the mouth of the Ulaî.[2] Sennacherib entered Bît-Yakîn without striking a blow, and completed the destruction of the half-deserted town ; he next proceeded to demolish the other cities one after the other, carrying off into captivity all the men and cattle who fell in his way. The Elamites, disconcerted by the rapidity of his action, allowed him to crush their allies unopposed ; and as they had not openly intervened, the conqueror refrained from calling them to account for their intrigues. Babylon paid the penalty for all: its sovereign, Belibni, who had failed to make the sacred authority of the suzerain respected in the city, and who, perhaps, had taken some part in the conspiracy, was with his family deported to Nineveh, and his vacant throne was given to Assur-nadin-shumu, a younger son of Sargon (699 B.C.).[3] Order was once more restored in Karduniash, but Sennacherib felt that its submission would be neither sincere nor permanent, so long as Merodach-baladan was hovering on its frontier possessed of an army, a fleet, and a supply of treasure, and prepared to enter the lists as soon as circumstances seemed favourable to his cause. Sennacherib resolved, therefore, to cross the head of the Persian Gulf and deal him such a blow as would once for all end the contest ; but troubles which broke out on the Urartian frontier as soon as he

---

[1] Three kings of Babylon at this period bore very similar names—Marduk-ushezîb, Nergal-ushezîb, and Mushezîb-marduk. Nergal-ushezîb is the elder of the two whom the texts call Shuzub, and whom Assyriologists at first confused one with another. Tiele was the first to distinguish them (*Schuzub de Babyloniër en Schuzub de Chaldæër Köningen van Babel*, in the *Études Archéologiques, Historiques et Linguistiques dédiées à M. Leemans*, pp. 109, 110, and *Babylonisch-assyrische-Geschichte*, pp. 321–323), and his view has been since accepted by all Assyriologists (SCHRADER, *Die Keilinschriftliche Baby-lonische Königsliste*, p. 12, note 1, and p. 25 ; HOMMEL, *Gesch. Bab. und Ass.*, p. 33, note 1 ; DELITZSCH and MÜRDTER, *Gesch. Bab. und Ass.*, pp. 178–201 ; WINCKLER, *Gesch. Bab und Ass.*, pp. 130–132, 306). The second of the two Shuzubs, Mushezîb-marduk, is the Mesesi-mordakos of the Royal Canon of Ptolemy.

[2] Nagîtu was bounded by the Nar-Marratum and the Ulaî (FR. DELITZSCH, *Wo lag das Paradies ?* pp. 323, 324), which allows us to identify it with the territory south of Edrisieh (BILLERBECK, *Susa*, p. 86).

[3] *Taylor Cylinder*, col. iii. pp. 42–65 : cf. SMITH-SAYCE, *Hist. of Sennacherib*, pp. 73–78 ; BEZOLD, *Inschriften Sanherib's*, in SCHRADER, *Keilins. Bibliothek*, vol. ii. pp. 96–99. Berosus, misled by the deposition of Belibni, thought that the expedition was directed against Babylon itself (MÜLLER-DIDOT, *Fragm. Historicorum Græcorum*, vol. ii. p. 504) ; he has likewise confounded Assur-nâdin-shumu with Esar-haddon, and he has given this latter, whom he calls Asordanes, as the immediate successor of Belibni. The date 699 B.C. for these events is indicated in *Pinches' Babylonian Chronicle*, col. ii. ll. 26–30, which places them in the third year of Belibni.

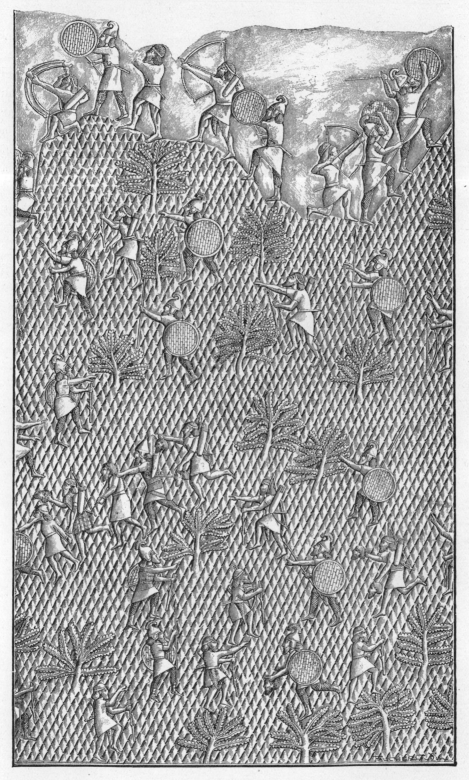

A RAID AMONG THE WOODS AND MOUNTAINS.

Drawn by Faucher-Gudin, from LAYARD, *Monuments of Nineveh*, vol. i. pl. 70.

returned forced him to put off his project. The tribes of Tumurru, who had placed their strongholds like eyries among the peaks of Nipur, had been making frequent descents on the plains of the Tigris, which they had ravaged unchecked by any fear of Assyrian power. Sennacherib formed an entrenched camp at the foot of their mountain retreat, and there left the greater part of his army, while he set out on an adventurous expedition with a picked body of infantry and cavalry. Over ravines and torrents, up rough and difficult slopes, they made their way, the king himself being conveyed in a litter, as there were no roads practicable for his royal chariot ; he even deigned to walk when the hillsides were too steep for his bearers to carry him ; he climbed like a goat, slept on the bare rocks, drank putrid water from a leathern bottle, and after many hardships at length came up with the enemy. He burnt their villages, and carried off herds of cattle and troops of captives ; but this exploit was more a satisfaction of his vanity than a distinct advantage gained, for the pillaging of the plains of the Tigris probably recommenced as soon as the king had quitted the country. The same year he pushed as far as Dayaîni, where similar tactics were employed. Constructing a camp in the neighbourhood of Mount Anara and Mount Uppa, he forced his way to the capital, Ukki, traversing a complicated network of gorges and forests which had hitherto been considered impenetrable. The king, Maniya, fled ; Ukki was taken by assault and pillaged, the spoil obtained from it slightly exceeding that from Tumurru (699 B.C.). Shortly afterwards the province of Tulgarimmê revolted in concert with the Tabal : Sennacherib overcame the allied forces, and led his victorious regiments through the defiles of the Taurus.[1] Greek pirates or colonists having ventured from time to time to ravage the seaboard, he destroyed one of their fleets near the mouth of the Saros, and took advantage of his sojourn in this region to fortify the two cities of Tarsus and Ankhialê, to defend his Cilician frontier against the peoples of Asia Minor.[2]

This was a necessary precaution, for the whole of Asia Minor was just then stirred by the inrush of new nations which were devastating the country,[3] and the effect of these convulsions was beginning to be felt in the country

[1] Taylor Cylinder, col. iii. ll. 66–82, col. iv. ll. 1–19 : cf. SMITH-SAYCE, Hist. of Sennacherib, pp. 79–87 ; BEZOLD, Inschriften Sanherib's, in SCHRADER, Keilins. Bibliothek, vol. ii. pp. 98–101. The dates of and connection between these two wars are not determined with any certainty. Some authorities assign them both to the same year, somewhere between 699 and 696 B.C. (TIELE, Babyl.-assyr. Gesch., pp. 297, 298, 320), while others assign them to two different years, the first to 699 or 696 B.C., the second to 698 or 695 B.C. (SMITH-SAYCE, op. cit., p. 87 ; HOMMEL, Gesch. Babyl. und Assyr., p. 718).

[2] The encounter of the Assyrians with the Greeks is only known to us from a fragment of Berosus (MÜLLER-DIDOT, Fragm. Hist. Græc., vol. ii. p. 504). The foundation of Tarsus is definitely attributed to Sennacherib in the same passage ; that of Ankhialê is referred to the fabulous Sardanapalus (STRABO, XIV. v. § 9, p. 672, quoting Aristobulus), but most historians with much probability attribute the foundation to Sennacherib (ED. MEYER, Gesch. des Alterthums, vol. i. pp. 471–473, vol. ii. p. 454 ; TIELE, Babyl.-assyr. Gesch., p. 298 ; HOMMEL, Gesch. Babyl. und. Assyr., p. 719, note 1).

[3] Cf. the summary account of these events, supra, p. 238.

to the south of the central plain, at the foot of the Taurus, and on the frontiers of the Assyrian empire. Barbarian hordes, attracted by the fame of the ancient Hittite sanctuaries in the upper basin of the Euphrates and the Araxes, had descended now and again to measure their strength against the advanced posts of Assyria or Urartu, but had subsequently withdrawn and disappeared beyond the Halys. Their movements may at this time have been so aggressive as to arouse serious anxiety in the minds of the Ninevite rulers; it is certain that Sennacherib, though apparently hindered by no revolt, delayed the execution of the projects he had formed against Merodach-baladan for three years; and it is possible his inaction may be attributed to the fear of some complication arising on his north-western frontier. He did not carry out his scheme till 695 B.C., when all danger in that quarter had passed away. The enterprise was a difficult one, for Nagîtu and the neighbouring districts were dependencies of Susa, and could not be reached by land without a violation of Elamite neutrality, which would almost inevitably lead to a conflict. Shutruk-nakhunta was no longer alive. In the very year in which his rival had set up Assur-nâdin-shumu as King of Karduniash, a revolution had broken out in Elam, which was in all probability connected with the events then taking place in Babylon. His subjects were angry with him for having failed to send timely succour to his allies the Kaldâ, and for having allowed Bît-Yakîn to be destroyed: his own brother Khalludush sided with the malcontents, threw Shutruk-nakhunta into prison, and proclaimed himself king.[1] This time the Ninevites, thinking that Elam was certain to intervene, sought how they might finally overpower Merodach-baladan before this interference could prove effectual. The feudal constitution of the Elamite monarchy rendered, as we know, the mobilisation of the army at the opening of a war a long and difficult task: weeks might easily elapse before the first and second grades of feudatory nobility could join the royal troops and form a combined army capable of striking an important blow.[2] This was a cause of dangerous inferiority in a conflict with the Assyrians, the chief part of whose forces, bivouacking close to the capital during the winter months, could leave their quarters and set out on a campaign at little more than a day's notice; the kings of Elam minimised the danger by keeping sufficient troops under arms on their northern and western frontiers to meet any emergency, but an attack by sea seemed to them so unlikely that they had not, for a long time past, thought of protecting their coast-line. The ancient Chaldæan cities, Uru, Lagash, Uruk, and Eridu had possessed fleets on the Persian Gulf; but the times were long past when they

---

[1] *Pinches' Babylonian Chronicle*, col. ii. ll. 32-35, where the new king is called Khallushu, instead of Khalludush, the form given in the inscriptions of Sennacherib.

[2] For all the difficulties which the feudal constitution of their empire caused the kings of Susa, cf. *supra*, pp. 228-230.

used to send to procure stone and wood from the countries of Magan and Melukhkha, and the seas which they had ruled were now traversed only by merchant vessels or fishing-boats. Besides this, the condition of the estuary seemed to prohibit all attack from that side. The space between Bît-Yakîn and the long line of dunes or mud-banks which blocked the entrance to it was not so much a gulf as a lagoon of uncertain and shifting extent; the water flowed only in the middle, being stagnant near the shores; the whole expanse was irregularly dotted over with mud-banks, and its surface was constantly altered by the alluvial soil brought down by the Tigris, the Euphrates, the Ulaî, and the Uknu. The navigation of this lagoon was dangerous, for the relative positions of the channels and shallows were

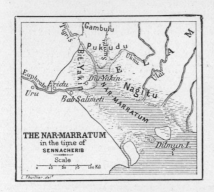

THE NAR-MARRATUM
in the time of
SENNACHERIB

constantly shifting, and vessels of deep draught often ran aground in passing from one end of it to the other.[1] Sennacherib decided to march his force to the mouth of the Euphrates, and, embarking it there, to bring it to bear suddenly on the portion of Elamite territory nearest to Nagîtu: if all went well, he would thus have time to crush the rising power of Merodach-baladan and regain his own port of departure before Khalludush could muster a sufficient army to render efficient succour to his vassal.

More than a year was consumed in preparations. The united cities of Chaldæa being unable to furnish the transports required to convey such a large host across the Nar-Marratum, it was necessary to construct a fleet, and to do so in such a way that the enemy should have no suspicion of danger. Sennacherib accordingly set up his dockyards at Tul-barsîp on the Euphrates and at Nineveh on the Tigris, and Syrian shipwrights built him a fleet of vessels after two distinct types. Some were galleys identical in build and equipment with those which the Mediterranean natives used for their traffic with distant lands.[2] The others followed the old Babylonian model, with stem and

---

[1] For the earliest configuration of these districts, cf. MASPERO, *Dawn of Civilization*, pp. 548, 549, 552, 553. The condition I describe here is very similar to what Alexander's admirals found 350 years later. Arrian has preserved for us the account of Nearchus' navigation in these waters (*Historia Indica*, §§ xli., xlii., in MÜLLER-DIDOT, *Geographi Græci Minores*, vol. i. pp. 365–368), and his description shows such a well-defined condition of the estuary that its main outline must have remained unchanged for a considerable time; the only subsequent alterations which had taken place must have been in the internal configuration, where the deposit of alluvium must have necessarily reduced the area of the lake since the time of Sennacherib. The little map inserted in the text has no pretension to scientific exactitude; its only object is to show roughly what the estuary of the Euphrates was like, and to illustrate approximately the course of the Assyrian expedition.

[2] Cf the vignette reproduced *supra*, p. 282.

stern both raised, the bows being sometimes distinguished by the carving of a horse's head, which justified the name of *sea-horse* given to a vessel of this kind. They had no masts, but propelling power was provided by two banks of oars one above the other, as in the galleys. The two divisions of the fleet were ready at the beginning of 694 B.C., and it was arranged that they should meet at Bît-Dakkuri, to the south of Babylon. The fleet from Tul-barsîp had merely to descend the Euphrates to reach the meeting-place,[1] but that from

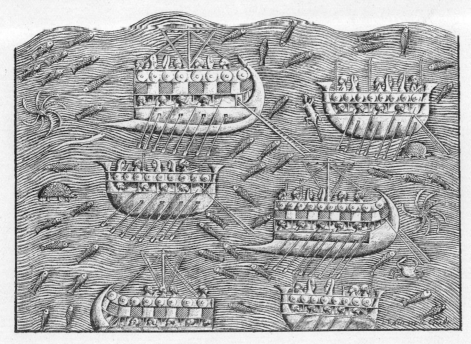

THE FLEET OF SENNACHERIB ON THE NAR-MARRATUM.[2]

Nineveh had to make a more complicated journey. By following the course of the Tigris to its mouth it would have had to skirt the coast of Elam for a considerable distance, and would inevitably have aroused the suspicions of Khalludush; the passage of such a strong squadron must have revealed to him the importance of the enterprise, and put him on his guard. The vessels therefore stayed their course at Upi, where they were drawn ashore and transported on rollers across the narrow isthmus which separates the Tigris from the

[1] The story of the preparations, as it has been transmitted to us in Sennacherib's inscriptions (SMITH-SAYCE, *Hist. of Sennacherib*, pp. 90–92, 102, 103), is curiously similar to the accounts given by the Greek historians of the vessels Alexander had built at Babylon and Thapsacus by Phœnician workmen, which descended the Euphrates to join the fleet in the Persian Gulf (ARRIAN, *Anabasis*, VII. xx. §§ 3–6; cf. PLUTARCH, *Life of Alexander*, § 68). This fleet consisted of quinqueremes, according to Aristobulus, who was present at their construction: Quintus-Curtius (x. 1, § 19) makes them all vessels with seven banks of oars, but he evidently confuses the galleys built at Thapsacus with those which came in sections from Phœnicia and which Alexander had put together at Babylon.
[2] Drawn by Faucher-Gudin, from LAYARD, *Monuments of Nineveh*, vol. i. pl. 71.

Arakhtu canal, on which they were then relaunched. Either the canal had not been well kept, or else it never had the necessary depth at certain places; but the crews managed to overcome all obstacles and rejoined their comrades in due time.[1] Sennacherib was ready waiting for them with all his troops—foot-soldiers, charioteers, and horsemen—and with supplies of food for the men, and of barley and oats for the horses; as soon as the last contingent had arrived, he gave the signal for departure, and all advanced together, the army marching along the southern bank, the fleet descending the current, to the little port of Bab-Salimeti, some twelve miles below the mouth of the river.[2] There they halted in order to proceed to the final embarcation, but at the last moment their inexperience of the sea nearly compromised the success of the expedition. Even if they were not absolutely ignorant of the ebb and flow of the tide, they certainly did not know how dangerous the spring tide could prove at the equinox under the influence of a south wind. The rising tide then comes into conflict with the volume of water brought down by the stream, and in the encounter the banks are broken down, and sometimes large districts are inundated: this is what happened that year, to the terror of the Assyrians. Their camp was invaded and completely flooded by the waves; the king and his soldiers took refuge in haste on the galleys, where they were kept prisoners for five days "as in a huge cage." As soon as the waters abated, they completed their preparations and started on their voyage. At the point where the Euphrates enters the lagoon, Sennacherib pushed forward to the front of the line, and, standing in the bows of his flag-ship, offered a sacrifice to Eâ, the god of the Ocean. Having made a solemn libation, he threw into the water a gold model of a ship, a golden fish, and an image of the god himself, likewise in gold; this ceremony performed, he returned to the port of Bab-Salimeti with his guard, while the bulk of his forces continued their voyage eastward. The passage took place without mishap, but they could not disembark on the shore of the gulf itself, which was unapproachable by reason of the deposits of semi-liquid mud which girdled it; they therefore put into the mouth of the Ulaî, and ascended the river till they reached a spot where the slimy reed-beds gave place to firm ground, which permitted them to draw their ships to land.[3] The inhabitants assembled hastily at sight of the enemy,

---

[1] Fr. Delitzsch, *Wo lag das Paradies?* p. 74, where the right sense of the passage, misunderstood by Smith, has been indicated for the first time.

[2] The mouth of the Euphrates being at that time not far from the site of Kornah, Bab-Salimeti, which was about twelve miles distant, must have been somewhere near the present village of Abu-Hatira, on the south bank of the river; cf. Billerbeck, *Geographische Untersuchungen*, p. 47. Fr. Delitzsch placed this town north of the Euphrates nearer to Kornah, on the map which accompanied his work entitled *Wo lag das Paradies?*

[3] Billerbeck recognises in the narrative of Sennacherib the indication of two attempts at debarcation, of which the second only can have been successful (*op. cit.*, pp. 47, 48); I can distinguish only one crossing.

and the news, spreading through the neighbouring tribes, brought together for their defence a confused crowd of archers, chariots, and horsemen. The Assyrians, leaping into the stream and climbing up the bank, easily overpowered these undisciplined troops. They captured at the first onset Nagîtu, Nagîtu-Dibîna, Khilmu, Pillatu, and Khupapânu; and raiding the Kaldâ, forced them on board the fleet with their gods, their families, their flocks, and household possessions, and beat a hurried retreat with their booty.

Merodach-baladan himself and his children once more escaped their clutches, but the State he had tried to create was annihilated, and his power utterly crushed. Sennacherib received his generals with great demonstrations of joy at Bab-Salimeti, and carried the spoil in triumph to Nineveh.[1] Khalludush, exasperated by the affront put upon him, instantly retaliated by invading Karduniash, where he pushed forward as far as Sippara, pillaging and destroying the inhabitants without opposition. The Babylonians who had accompanied Merodach-baladan into exile, returned in

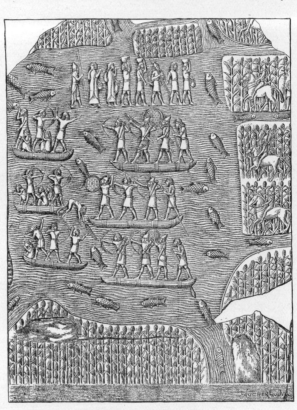

A SKIRMISH IN THE MARSHES.[2]

the train of the Elamites, and, secretly stealing back to their homes, stirred up a general revolt: Assur-nâdin-shumu, taken prisoner by his own subjects, was put in chains and despatched to Susa, his throne being bestowed on a Babylonian named Nergal-ushezîb,[3] who at once took the field (694 B.C.). His preliminary

[1] SMITH-SAYCE, *Hist. of Sennacherib*, pp. 88–100, 102, 103; cf. BEZOLD, *Inschriften Sanherib's*, in SCHRADER, *Keilins. Bibliothek*, vol. ii. pp. 100, 101. *Pinches' Babylonian Chronicle*, col. ii. ll. 36–39, places the taking of Nagîtu in the sixth year of Assur-nâdin-shumu, which supplies the date 694–693 B.C. for the expedition. For the appreciation of these events, see the observations of BILLERBECK, *Susa*, pp. 84–86, and *Geographische Untersuchungen*, pp. 46–48.

[2] Drawn by Faucher-Gudin, from LAYARD, *Monuments of Nineveh*, vol. ii. p. 27.

[3] This is the prince whom the Assyrian documents name Shuzub, and whom we might call Shuzub the Babylonian, in contradistinction to Mushezîb-marduk, who is Shuzub the Kaldu; cf. *supra*, p. 296, note 1.

efforts were successful : he ravaged the frontier along the Turnât with the help of the Elamites, and took by assault the city of Nipur, which refused to desert the cause of Sennacherib (693 B.C.). Meanwhile the Assyrian generals had captured Uruk (Erech) on the 1st of Tisri, after the retreat of Khalludush; and having sacked the city, were retreating northwards with their spoil when they were defeated on the 7th near Nipur by Nergal-ushezîb. He had already rescued the statues of the gods and the treasure, when his horse fell in the midst of the fray, and he could not disengage himself. His vanquished foes led him captive to Nineveh, where Sennacherib exposed him in chains at the principal gateway of his palace: the Babylonians, who owed to him their latest success, summoned a Kaldu prince, Mushezîb-marduk, son of Gahul, to take command. He hastened to comply, and with the assistance of Elamite troops offered such a determined resistance to all attack, that he was finally left in undisturbed possession of his kingdom (692 B.C.): the actual result to Assyria, therefore, of the ephemeral victory gained by the fleet had been the loss of Babylon.[1]

A revolution in Elam speedily afforded Assyria an opportunity for revenge. When Nergal-ushezîb was taken prisoner, the people of Susa, dissatisfied with the want of activity displayed by Khalludush, conspired to depose him: on hearing, therefore, the news of the revolutions in Chaldæa, they rose in revolt on the 26th of Tisri, and, besieging him in his palace, put him to death, and elected a certain Kutur-nakhunta as his successor.[2] Sennacherib, without a moment's hesitation, crossed the frontier at Durîlu, before order was re-established at Susa, and recovered, after very slight resistance, Raza and Bît-khaîri which Shutruk-nakhunta had taken from Sargon. This preliminary success laid the lower plain of Susiana at his mercy, and he ravaged it pitilessly from Raza to Bît-bunaki. " Thirty-four strongholds and the townships depending on them, whose number is unequalled, I besieged and took by assault, their inhabitants I led into captivity, I demolished them and reduced them to ashes : I caused the smoke of their burning to rise into the wide heaven, like the smoke of one great sacrifice." Kutur-nakhunta, still insecurely seated on the throne of Susa, retreated with his army towards Khaîdalu, in the almost unexplored regions which bordered the Iranian plateau,[3] and entrenched himself strongly in the heart of the mountains. The season was already well

[1] The order of events is given by *Pinches' Babylonian Chronicle*, col. ii. ll. 39–48, col. iii. ll. 1–9; the Assyrian texts add a certain number of contradictory details to the information it conveys (SMITH-SAYCE, *Hist. of Sennacherib*, pp. 100, 101, 103–105; cf. BEZOLD, *Inschriften Sanherib's*, in SCHRADER, *Keilins. Bibliothek*, vol. ii. pp. 100–103).

[2] *Pinches' Babylonian Chronicle*, col. iii. ll. 6–9, where the new king is called by the abbreviated name of Kudur; the full form Kudur-nankhundi is given by the Assyrian texts (*Taylor Cylinder*, col. iv. l. 70), the Susian original of which is Kutur-nakhunta.

[3] Khaîdalu is very probably the present Dîs Malkân (BILLERBECK, *Susa*, p. 72).

advanced when the Assyrians set out on this expedition, and November set in while they were ravaging the plain : but the weather was still so fine that Sennacherib determined to take advantage of it to march upon Madaktu. Hardly had he scaled the heights when winter fell upon him with its accompaniment of cold and squally weather. "Violent storms broke out, it rained and snowed incessantly, the torrents and streams overflowed their banks," so that hostilities had to be suspended and the troops ordered back to Nineveh.[1] The effect produced, however, by these bold measures was in no way diminished : though Kutur-nakhunta had not had the necessary time to

prepare for the contest, he was nevertheless discredited among his subjects for failing to bring them out of it with glory, and three months after the retreat of the Assyrians he was assassinated in a riot on the 20th of Ab, 692 B.C.[2] His younger brother, Ummân - minânu, assumed the crown, and though his enemies disdain- fully refused to credit him

THE HORSE OF NERGAL-USHEZÎB FALLING IN THE BATTLE.[3]

with either prudence or judgment, he soon restored his kingdom to such a formidable degree of power that Mushezîb-marduk thought the opportunity a favourable one for striking a blow at Assyria, from which she could never recover. Elam had plenty of troops, but was deficient in the resources necessary to pay the men and their chiefs, and to induce the tribes of the table-land to furnish their contingents. Mushezîb-marduk, there- fore, emptied the sacred treasury of Ê-sagilla, and sent the gold and silver of Bel and Zarpanit to Ummân-minânu with a message which ran thus: "Assemble thine army, and prepare thy camp, come to Babylon and strengthen our hands, for thou art our help." The Elamite asked nothing better than to avenge the provinces so cruelly harassed, and the cities consumed in the course of the last campaign : he summoned all his nobles, from the least

[1] *Taylor Cylinder*, col. iv. ll. 43–79 : cf. SMITH-SAYCE, *Hist. of Sennacherib*, pp. 106–110 ; BEZOLD, *Inschriften Sanherib's*, in SCHRADER, *Keilins. Bibliothek*, vol. ii. pp. 102–105.

[2] The Assyrian documents merely mention the death of Kutur-nakhunta less than three months after the return of Sennacherib to Nineveh (*Taylor Cylinder*, col. iv. ll. 79–90, col. v. ll. 1–4). *Pinches' Babylonian Chronicle*, col. iii. ll. 14–16, only mentions the revolution in which he perished, and informs us that he had reigned ten months. It contracts Ummân-minânu, the name of the Elamite king, to Minânu.

[3] Drawn by Faucher-Gudin, from LAYARD, *Monuments of Nineveh*, vol. i. pl. 64.

to the greatest, and enlisted the help of the troops of Parsuas, Ellipi, and Anzân, the Aramæan Puqudu and Gambulu of the Tigris, as well as the Aramæans of the Euphrates, and the peoples of Bît-Adini and Bît-Amukkâni, who had rallied round Samuna, son of Merodach-baladan, and joined forces with the soldiers of Mushezîb-marduk in Babylon. "Like an invasion of countless locusts swooping down upon the land, they assembled, resolved to give me battle, and the dust of their feet rose before me, like a thick cloud which darkens the copper-coloured dome of the sky." The conflict took place near the township of Khalulê, on the banks of the Tigris, not far from the confluence of this river with the Turnât.[1] At this point the Turnât, flowing through the plain, divides into several branches, which ramify again and again, and form a kind of delta extending from the ruins of Nayân to those of Reshadeh. During the whole of the day the engagement between the two hosts raged on this unstable soil, and their leaders themselves sold their lives dearly in the struggle. Sennacherib invoked the help of Assur, Sin, Shamash, Nebo, Bel, Nergal, Ishtar of Nineveh, and Ishtar of Arbela, and the gods heard his prayers. "Like a lion I raged, I donned my harness, I covered my head with my casque, the badge of war; my powerful battle-chariot, which mows down the rebels, I ascended it in haste in the rage of my heart; the strong bow which Assur entrusted to me, I seized it, and the javelin, destroyer of life, I grasped it: the whole host of obdurate rebels I charged, shining like silver or like the day, and I roared as Rammân roareth." Khumba-undash, the Elamite general, was killed in one of the first encounters, and many of his officers perished around him, "of those who wore golden daggers at their belts, and bracelets of gold on their wrists." They fell one after the other, "like fat bulls chained" for the sacrifice, or like sheep, and their blood flowed on the broad plain as the water after a violent storm: the horses plunged in it up to their knees, and the body of the royal chariot was reddened with it. A son of Merodach-baladan, Nabu-shumishkun, was taken prisoner, but Ummân-minânu and Mushezîb-marduk escaped unhurt from the fatal field. It seems as if fortune had at last decided in favour of the Assyrians, and they proclaimed the fact loudly, but their success was not so evident as to preclude their adversaries also claiming the victory with some show of truth. In any case,

---

[1] Fr. Delitzsch placed Khalulê near Bagdad, but was uncertain whether it lay on the right or left bank of the river (*Wo lag das Paradies?* p. 207). Billerbeck places the site on the left bank in the delta of the Dîyala (*Geographische Untersuchungen*, p. 11, note 1), perhaps on the site of the town of Hebheb in the present canton of Khalis (*Susa*, p. 90). Haupt (*The Battle of Halulê*, in the *Andover Review*, 1887, p. 542, et seq.) attributes to the name the signification *holes, bogs*, and this interpretation agrees well enough with the state of the country round the mouths of the Dîyala, in the low-lying district which separates that river from the Tigris; he compares it with the name Haulâyeh, quoted by Arab geographers in this neighbourhood, and with that of the canton of Hâleh, mentioned in Syrian texts as belonging to the district of Râdhân, between the Adhem and the Dîyala.

the losses on both sides were so considerable as to force the two belligerents to suspend operations; they returned each to his capital, and matters remained much as they had been before the battle took place.[1]

Years might have elapsed before Sennacherib could have ventured to recommence hostilities: he was not deluded by the exaggerated estimate of his victory in the accounts given by his court historians, and he recognised the fact that the issue of the struggle must be uncertain as long as the alliance subsisted between Elam and Chaldæa. But fortune came to his aid sooner than he had expected. Ummân-minânu was not absolute in his dominions any more than his predecessors had been, and the losses he had sustained at Khalulê, without obtaining any compensating advantages in the form of prisoners or spoil, had lowered him in the estimation of his vassals; Mushezîb-marduk, on the other hand, had emptied his treasuries, and though Karduniash was wealthy, it was hardly able, after such a short interval, to provide further subsidies to purchase the assistance of the mountain tribes. Sennacherib's emissaries kept him well informed of all that occurred in the enemy's court, and he accordingly took the field again at the beginning of 689 B.C., and on this occasion circumstances seemed likely to combine to give him an easy victory.[2] Mushezîb-marduk shut himself up in Babylon, not doubting that the Elamites would hasten to his succour as soon as they should hear of his distress; but his expectation was not fulfilled. Ummân-minânu was struck down by apoplexy, on the 15th of Nisân, and though his illness did not at once terminate fatally, he was left paralysed with distorted mouth, and loss of speech, incapable of action, and almost unfit to govern.[3] His seizure put a stop to his warlike preparations: and his ministers, preoccupied with the urgent question of the succession to the throne, had no desire to provoke a conflict with Assyria, the issue of which could not be foretold; they therefore

[1] *Taylor Cylinder*, col. v. ll. 5–85, col. vii. ll. 1–24: cf. SMITH-SAYCE, *Hist. of Sennacherib*, pp. 114–132; BEZOLD, *Inschriften Sanherib's*, in SCHRADER, *Keilins. Bibliothek*, vol. ii. pp. 104–111. An animated description of the battle has been given by Haupt (*The Battle of Halulé*, 691 B.C., in the *Andover Review*, 1886, p. 512, et seq.). *Pinches' Babylonian Chronicle*, col. iii. ll. 16–18, attributes the victory to the Elamites, and says that the year in which the battle was fought was unknown. The testimony of this chronicle is so often marred by partiality, that to prefer it always to that of the Ninevite inscriptions shows deficiency of critical ability: the course of events seems to me to prove that the advantage remained with the Assyrians, though the victory was not decisive. The date, which necessarily falls between 692 and 689 B.C., has been decided by general considerations as 691 B.C., the very year in which the *Taylor Cylinder* was written.

[2] The Assyrian documents insert the account of the capture of Babylon directly after the battle of Khalulê (*Bavian Inscription*, l. 43, et seq.), and modern historians therefore concluded that the two events took place within a few months of each other (ED. MEYER, *Geschichte des Alterthums*, vol. i. p. 470). The information afforded by *Pinches' Babylonian Chronicle*, col. iii. ll. 22–26, has enabled us to correct this mistake, and to bring down the date of the taking of Babylon to 689 B.C. (TIELE, *Bab.-ass. Gesch.*, pp. 305, 324; HOMMEL, *Gesch. Bab. und Ass.*, pp. 733, 734; MÜRDTER and DELITZSCH, *Gesch. Bab. und Ass.*, 2nd edit., pp. 201, 202; WINCKLER, *Gesch. Bab. und Ass.*, p. 132).

[3] *Pinches' Babylonian Chronicle*, col. iii. ll. 19–21.

left their ally to defend his own interests as best he might. Babylon, reduced to rely entirely on its own resources, does not seem to have held out long, and perhaps the remembrance of the treatment it had received on former occasions may account for the very slight resistance it now offered. The Assyrian kings who had from time to time conquered Babylon, had always treated it with great consideration. They had looked upon it as a sacred city, whose caprices and outbreaks must always be pardoned; it was only with infinite precautions that they had imposed their commands upon it, and even when they had felt that severity was desirable, they had restrained themselves in using it, and humoured the idiosyncrasies of the inhabitants. Tiglath-pileser III., Shalmaneser V., and Sargon had all preferred to be legally crowned as sovereigns of Babylon instead of remaining merely its masters by right of conquest, and though Sennacherib had refused compliance with the traditions by which his predecessors had submitted to be bound, he had behaved with unwonted lenity after quelling the two previous revolts. He now recognised that his clemency had been shown in vain, and his small stock of patience was completely exhausted just when fate threw the rebellious city into his power. If the inhabitants had expected to be once more let off easily, their illusions were speedily dissipated: they were slain by the sword as if they had been ordinary foes, such as Jews, Tibarenians, or Kaldâ of Bît-Yakîn, and they were spared none of the horrors which custom then permitted the stronger to inflict upon the weaker. For several days the pitiless massacre lasted. Young and old, all who fell into the hands of the soldiery, perished by the sword; piles of corpses filled the streets and the approaches to the temples, especially the avenue of winged bulls which led to Ê-sagilla,[1] and, even after the first fury of carnage had been appeased, it was only to be succeeded by more organised pillage. Mushezîb-marduk was sent into exile with his family, and immense convoys of prisoners and spoil followed him. The treasures carried off from the royal palace, the temples, and the houses of the rich nobles were divided among the conquerors; they comprised gold, silver, precious stones, costly stuffs, and provisions of all sorts. The sacred edifices were sacked, the images hacked to pieces or carried off to Nineveh: Bel-Marduk, introduced into the sanctuary of Assur, became subordinate to the rival deity amid a crowd of strange gods. In the inmost recess of a chapel were discovered some ancient statues of Rammân and Shala of Ê-kallati, which Marduk-nâdin-akhê had carried off in the time of Tiglath-pileser I., and these were brought back in triumph to their own land, after an absence of four hundred and eighteen years.[2] The buildings

[1] Cylinder of Assur-bani-pal, col. iv. ll. 70-73; cf. S. ALDEN-SMITH, Die Keilschrifttexte Asur-banipals, vol. i. pp. 34, 35.

[2] For this date, cf. Struggle of the Nations, p. 663.

themselves suffered a like fate to that of their owners and their gods. "The city and its houses, from foundation to roof, I destroyed them, I demolished them, I burnt them with fire; walls, gateways, sacred chapels, and the towers of earth and tiles, I laid them all low and cast them into the Arakhtu."[1] The incessant revolts of the people justified this wholesale destruction. Babylon, as we have said before,[2] was too powerful to be reduced for long to the second rank in a Mesopotamian empire : as soon as fate established the seat of empire in the districts bordering on the Euphrates and the middle course of the Tigris, its well-chosen situation, its size, its riches, the extent of its population, the number of its temples, and the beauty of its palaces, all conspired to make it the capital of the country. In vain Assur, Calah, or Nineveh thrust themselves into the foremost rank, and by a strenuous effort made their princes rulers of Babylon; in a short time Babylon replenished her treasury, found allies, soldiers, and leaders, and in spite of reverses of fortune soon regained the upper hand. The only treatment which could effectually destroy her ascendency was that of leaving in her not one brick upon another, thus preventing her from being re-peopled for several generations, since a new city could not at once spring up from the ashes of the old; until she had been utterly destroyed her conquerors had still reason to fear her. This fact Sennacherib, or his councillors, knew well. If he merits any reproach, it is not for having seized the opportunity of destroying the city which Babylon offered him, but rather for not having persevered in his design to the end, and reduced her to a mere name.

In the midst of these costly and absorbing wars, we may well wonder how Sennacherib found time and means to build villas or temples; yet he is neverthe-less, among the kings of Assyria, the monarch who has left us the largest number of monuments.[2] He restored a shrine of Nergal in the small town of Tarbizi;[3] he fortified the village of Alshi;[4] and in 704 B.C. he founded a royal residence[5]

[1] *Bavian Inscription*, ll. 43–54: cf. SMITH-SAYCE, *Hist. of Sennacherib*, pp. 132–135; POGNON, *L'Inscription de Bavian*, pp. 17–21, 85–95, 125; BEZOLD, *Inschriften Sanherib's*, in SCHRADER, *Keilins. Bibliothek*, vol. ii. pp. 116–119. *Pinches' Babylonian Chronicle*, col. iii. l. 24, attributes to the reign of Mushezîb-marduk a period of four years, which enables us to fix the date of the taking of the city as 689 B.C. (TIELE, *Babylonisch-assyrische Geschichte*, p. 324; HOMMEL, *Gesch. Bab. und Ass.*, pp. 733, 734; DELITZSCH and MÜRDTER, *Gesch. Bab. und Ass.*, 2nd edit., pp. 201, 202; WINCKLER, *Gesch. Bab. und Ass.*, p. 132).

[2] Cf. *supra*, pp. 196, 197.

[3] All the texts relating to the buildings of Sennacherib have been collected, translated, and commented on, for the first time, by MEISSNER and ROST, *Die Bauinschriften Sanheribs*, 1893.

[4] The erection of the temple at Tarbizi is known from inscriptions on bricks and stone (H. RAWLINSON, *Cun. Ins. W. As.*, vol. i. pl. 7, Nos. viii. and c.; cf. OPPERT, *Expédition en Mésopotamie*, vol. i. p. 348), and on clay tablets (H. RAWLINSON, *op. cit.*, vol. iii. pl. 3, No. 13), which come from Sherîf-Khan, that is to say, from the site where Tarbizi itself stood, as well as from a fragment discovered at Kouyunjik (MEISSNER and ROST, *op. cit.*, pp. 89, 92, 93).

[5] A brick from the Kalaa, or citadel of Shemamek (LAYARD, *Nineveh and Babylon*, pp. 190, 191),

in the fortress of Kakzi, which defended the approach to Calah from the south-east.[1]   He did not reside much at Dur-Sharrukîn, neither did he complete the decoration of his father's palace there : his pride as a victorious warrior suffered when his surroundings reminded him of a more successful conqueror than himself, and Calah itself was too full of memories of Tiglath-pileser III. and the sovereigns of the eighth century for him to desire to establish his court there.   He preferred to reside at Nineveh, which had been much neglected by his predecessors, and where the crumbling edifices merely recalled the memory of long-vanished splendours.   He selected this city as his residence at the very beginning of his reign, perhaps while he was still only crown prince, and began by repairing its ancient fortifications ; later on, when the success of his earlier

THE MOUNDS OF NINEVEH SEEN FROM THE TERRACE OF A HOUSE IN MOSUL.[2]

campaigns had furnished him with a sufficient supply of prisoners, he undertook the restoration of the whole city, with its avenues, streets, canals, quays, gardens, and aqueducts : the labour of all the captives brought together from different quarters of his empire was pressed into the execution of his plans—the Kaldâ, the Aramæans, the Mannai, the people of Kuî, the Cilicians, the Philistines, and the Tyrians ; the provinces vied with each other in furnishing him with materials without stint,—precious woods were procured from Syria, marbles from Kapri-dargîla, alabaster from Balad, while Bît-Yakîn provided the rushes to be laid between the courses of brickwork.   The river Tebilti, after causing the downfall of the royal mausolea and " displaying to the light of day the coffins which they concealed," had sapped the foundations of the palace of Assur-nazir-pal, and caused it to fall in :[3] a muddy pool now occupied the north-western quarter, between the court of Ishtar and the lofty ziggurât of Assur. This pool Sennacherib filled up, and regulated the course of the stream,

---

and preserved in the British Museum (H. RAWLINSON, *Cun. Ins. W. As.*, vol. i. pl. 7, No. viii. H) ; Kalaa is the site of the city of Alshi, which must not be confounded with the neighbouring fortress of Kalzi or Kakzi (MEISSNER and ROST, *Die Bauinschriften Sanheribs*, pp. 89, 90, 92, 93).

[1] Fragment of the Eponym Canon, published by H. RAWLINSON, *op. cit.*, vol. ii. pl. 69 ; cf. SCHRADER, *Keilinschriftliche Bibliothek*, vol. i. pp. 214, 215.

[2] Drawn by Boudier, from a lithograph in LAYARD, *Monuments of Nineveh*, vol. ii. pl. 70.

[3] For the palace of Assur-nazir-pal, cf. *supra*, pp. 44, 45.

providing against the recurrence of such accidents in future by building a
substructure of masonry, 454 cubits long by 289 wide, formed of large blocks of
stone cemented together by bitumen. On this he erected a magnificent palace,
a Bît-Khilâni in the Syrian style,[1] with woodwork of fragrant cedar and cypress
overlaid with gold and silver, panellings of sculptured marble and alabaster,
and friezes and cornices in glazed tiles of brilliant colouring: inspired by the

KING SENNACHERIB WATCHING THE TRANSPORT OF
A COLOSSAL STATUE.[2]

goddess Nin-kurra, he caused winged bulls of white alabaster and limestone
statues of the gods to be hewn in the quarries of Balad near Nineveh. He
presided in person at all these operations—at the raising of the soil, the making
of the substructures of the terrace, the transport of the colossal statues or blocks
and their subsequent erection; indeed, he was to be seen at every turn, standing
in his ebony and ivory chariot, drawn by a team of men. When the building
was finished, he was so delighted with its beauty that he named it "the
incomparable palace,"[3] and his admiration was shared by his contemporaries;
they were never wearied of extolling in glowing terms the twelve bronze lions,
the twelve winged bulls, and the twenty-four statues of goddesses which kept
watch over the entrance, and for the construction of which a new method of

[1] For the Bît-Khilâni in the Syrian style, and the aspect they presented, cf. *supra*, pp. 205-207.
[2] Drawn by Faucher-Gudin, from LAYARD, *Monuments of Nineveh*, vol. ii. pl. 12.
[3] For this "*incomparable palace*"—*Ekallu sha shanina la ishu*—and for the texts which describe
its erection, cf. MEISSNER and ROST, *Die Bauinschriften Sanheribs*, pp. 1-46.

rapid casting had been invented. Formerly the erection of such edifices cost much in suffering to the artificers employed on them, but Sennacherib brought his great enterprise to a prompt completion without extravagant outlay or unnecessary hardship inflicted on his workmen. He proceeded to annex the neighbouring quarters of the city, relegating the inhabitants to the suburbs

ASSYRIAN BAS-RELIEFS AT BAVIAN.[1]

while he laid out a great park on the land thus cleared; this park was well planted with trees, like the heights of Amanus, and in it flourished side by side all the forest growths indigenous to the Cilician mountains and the plains of Chaldæa. A lake, fed by a canal leading from the Khuzur, supplied it with water, which was conducted in streams and rills through the thickets, keeping them always fresh and green. Vines trained on trellises afforded a grateful shade during the sultry hours of the day; birds sang in the branches, herds of wild boar and deer roamed through the coverts, in order that the prince might enjoy the pleasures of the chase without quitting his own private grounds. The main part of these constructions was finished about 700 B.C., but many details were left incomplete, and the work was still proceeding after the court

[1] Drawn by Faucher-Gudin, from a sketch in LAYARD, *Nineveh and Babylon*, p. 182.

had long been in residence on the spot.   Meanwhile a smaller palace, as well as

GREAT ASSYRIAN STELE AT BAVIAN.[1]

barracks and a depôt for arms and provisions, sprang up elsewhere.[2]   Eighteen
aqueducts, carried across the country, brought the water from the Muzri to the

[1] Drawn by Boudier, from LAYARD, *Monuments of Nineveh*, vol. ii. pl. 51.
[2] The inscriptions referring to the arsenal—*bît-kutalli*—have been translated and commented on
in the special collection of MEISSNER and ROST, *Die Bauinschriften Sanheribs*, pp. 47–61.

Khuzur, and secured an adequate supply to the city; the Ninevites, who had hitherto relied upon rain-water for the replenishing of their cisterns, awoke one day to find themselves released from all anxiety on this score. An ancient and semi-subterranean canal, which Assur-nazir-pal had constructed nearly two centuries before, but which, owing to the neglect of his successors, had become choked up, was cleaned out, enlarged, and repaired, and made capable of bringing water to their doors from the springs of Mount Tas, in the same year as that in which the battle of Khalulê took place.[1] At a later date, magnificent bas-reliefs, carved on the rock by order of Esar-haddon, representing winged bulls, figures of the gods and of the king, with explanatory inscriptions, marked the site of the springs, and formed a kind of monumental façade to the ravine in which they took their rise.[2]

It would be hard to account for the rapidity with which these great works were completed, did one not remember that Sargon had previously carried out extensive architectural schemes, in which he must have employed all the available artists in his empire. The revolutions which had shattered the realm under the last descendants of Assur-nazir-pal, and the consequent impoverishment of the kingdom, had not been without a disastrous effect on the schools of Assyrian sculpture. Since the royal treasury alone was able to bear the expense of those vast compositions in which the artistic skill of the period could have free play, the closing of the royal workshops, owing to the misfortunes of the time, had the immediate effect of emptying the sculptors' studios. Even though the period of depression lasted for the space of two or three generations only, it became difficult to obtain artistic workmen; and those who were not discouraged from the pursuit of art by the uncertainty of employment, no longer possessed the high degree of skill attained by their predecessors, owing to lack of opportunity to cultivate it. Sculpture was at a very low ebb when Tiglath-pileser III. desired to emulate the royal builders of days gone by, and the awkwardness of composition noticeable in some of his bas-reliefs, and the almost barbaric style of the stelæ erected by persons of even so high a rank as Belharrân-beluzur, prove the lamentable deficiency of good artists at that epoch, and show that the king had no choice but to employ all the surviving members of the ancient guilds, whether good, bad, or indifferent workmen. The increased demand, however, soon produced an adequate supply

---

[1] Mount Tas is the group of hills enclosing the ravine of Bavian. These works were described in the Bavian inscription, of which they occupy the whole of the first part: cf. POGNON, *L'Inscription de Bavian*, pp. 6–15, 35–72; MEISSNER and ROST, *Die Bauinschriften Sanheribs*, pp. 66, 72–77.

[2] The Bavian text speaks of six inscriptions and statues which the king had engraved on the Mount of Tas, at the source of the stream (POGNON, *op. cit.*, pp. 20, 21); these are the monuments described and in some instances sketched in LAYARD, *Nineveh and Babylon*, pp. 176–183.

of workers, and when Sargon ascended the throne, the royal guild of sculptors had been thoroughly reconstituted; the inefficient workmen on whom Tiglath-pileser and Shalmaneser had been obliged to rely had been eliminated in course of time, and many of the sculptures which adorned the palace at Khorsabad display a purity of design and boldness of execution comparable to that of the best Egyptian art. The composition still shows traces of Chaldæan

AN ASSYRIAN CAVALRY RAID THROUGH THE WOODS.[1]

stiffness, and the exaggerated drawing of the muscles produces an occasionally unpleasing heaviness of outline, but none the less the work as a whole constitutes one of the richest and most ingenious schemes of decoration ever devised, which, while its colouring was still perfect, must have equalled in splendour the great triumphal battle-scenes at Ibsambul or Medinet-Habu. Sennacherib found ready to his hand a body of well-trained artists, whose number had considerably increased during the reign of Sargon, and he profited by the experience which they had acquired and the talent that many of them had developed.[2] What immediately strikes the spectator in the series of pictures produced under his auspices, is the great skill with which his artists covered the whole surface at their disposal without overcrowding it. They no longer

[1] Drawn by Faucher-Gudin, from LAYARD, Monuments of Nineveh, vol. i. pl. 81.
[2] The features of Assyrian sculpture, under Sennacherib, were first noted by RAWLINSON, The Five Great Monarchies, vol. ii. pp. 181–183 ; cf. PERROT and CHIPIEZ, Histoire de l'Art dans l'Antiquité, vol. ii. pp. 630–647.

treated their subject, whether it were a warlike expedition, a hunting excursion, a sacrificial scene, or an episode of domestic life, as a simple juxtaposition of groups of almost equal importance ranged at the same elevation along the walls, the subject of each bas-relief being complete in itself and without any necessary connection with its neighbour. They now selected two or three principal incidents from the subjects proposed to them for representation, and round these they grouped such of the less important episodes as lent themselves best to picturesque treatment, and scattered sparingly over the rest of the field the minor accessories which seemed suitable to indicate more precisely the scene of the action. Under the auspices of this later school, Assyrian foot-soldiers are no longer depicted attacking the barbarians of Media or Elam on backgrounds of smooth stone, where no line marks the various levels, and where the remoter figures appear to be walking in the air without anything to support them. If the battle represented took place on a wooded slope crowned by a stronghold on the summit of the hill, the artist, in order to give an impression of the surroundings, covered his background with guilloche patterns by which to represent the rugged surface of the mountains; [1] he placed here and there groups of various kinds of trees, especially the straight cypresses and firs which grew upon the slopes of the Iranian table-land: or he represented a body of lancers galloping in single file along the narrow woodland paths, and hastening to surprise a distant enemy, or again foot-soldiers chasing their foes through the forest or engaging them in single combat; while in the corners of the picture the wounded are being stabbed or otherwise despatched, fugitives are trying to escape through the under-growth, and shepherds are pleading with the victors for their lives. It is the actual scene the sculptor sets himself to depict, and one is sometimes inclined to ask, while noting the precision with which the details of the battle are rendered, whether the picture was not drawn on the spot, and whether the conqueror did not carry artists in his train to make sketches for the decorators of the main features of the country traversed and of the victories won. The masses of infantry seem actually in motion, a troop of horsemen rush blindly over uneven ground, and the episodes of their raid are unfolded in all their confusion with unfailing animation. For the first time a spectator can realise Assyrian warfare with its striking contrasts of bravery and unbridled cruelty; he is no longer reduced to spell out laboriously a monotonous narrative of a battle, for the battle takes place actually before his eyes. And after the return from the scene of action, when it is desired to show how the victor employed his prisoners for the greater honour of his gods and his own glory,

---

[1] See, among others, the illustration on p. 297 of this work.

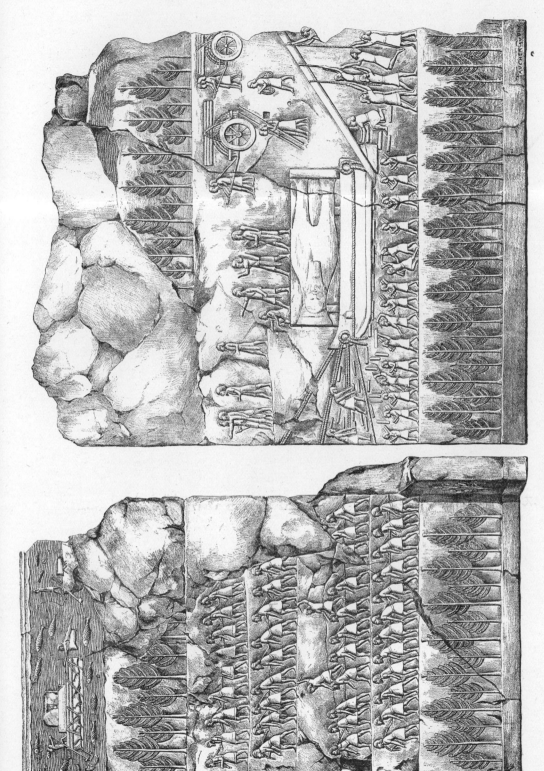

TRANSPORT OF A WINGED BULL ON A SLEDGE.

Drawn by Faucher-Gudin, from LAYARD, *Monuments of Nineveh*, vol. ii. pl. 13.

the picture is no less detailed and realistic. There we see them, the noble and the great of all the conquered nations, Chaldæans and Elamites, inhabitants of Cilicia, Phœnicia, and Judæa, harnessed to ropes and goaded by the whips of the overseers, dragging the colossal bull which is destined to mount guard at the gates of the palace : with bodies bent, pendant arms, and faces contorted with pain, they, who had been the chief men in their cities, now take the place of beasts of burden, while Sennacherib, erect on his state chariot, with steady glance and lips compressed, watches them as they pass slowly before him in their ignominy and misery.

After the destruction of Babylon there is a pause in the history of the conqueror, and with him in that of Assyria itself. It seems as if Nineveh had been exhausted by the greatness of her effort, and was stopping to take breath before setting out on a fresh career of conquest : the other nations also, as if overwhelmed by the magnitude of the catastrophe, appear to have henceforth despaired of their own security, and sought only how to avoid whatever might rouse against them the enmity of the master of the hour. His empire formed a compact and solid block in their midst, on which no human force seemed capable of making any impression. They had attacked it each in turn, or all at once, Elam in the east, Urartu in the north, Egypt in the south-west, and their efforts had not only miserably failed, but had for the most part drawn down upon them disastrous reprisals. The people of Urartu remained in gloomy inaction amidst their mountains, the Elamites had lost their supremacy over half the Aramæan tribes, and if Egypt was as yet inaccessible beyond the intervening deserts, she owed it less to the strength of her armies than to the mysterious fatality at Libnah. In one half-century the Assyrians had effectually and permanently disabled the first of these kingdoms, and inflicted on the others such serious injuries that they were slow in recovering from them. The fate of these proud nations had intimidated the inferior states—Arabs, Medes, tribes of Asia Minor, barbarous Cimmerians or Scythians, —all alike were careful to repress their natural inclinations to rapine and plunder. If occasionally their love of booty overpowered their prudence, and they hazarded a raid on some defenceless village in the neighbouring border territory, troops were hastily despatched from the nearest Assyrian garrison, who speedily drove them back across the frontier, and pursuing them into their own country, inflicted on them so severe a punishment that they remained for some considerable time paralysed by awe and terror. Assyria was the foremost kingdom of the East, and indeed of the whole world, and the hegemony which she exercised over all the countries within her reach cannot be accounted for solely by her military superiority. Not only did she excel in the art of conquest, as many before her had done—Babylonians, Elamites, Hittites, and Egyptians—but she did what none of them had been able to accomplish; she exacted lasting obedience from the conquered nations, ruling them with a firm hand, and accustoming them to live on good terms with one another in spite of diversity of race, and this with a light rein, with unfailing tact, and apparently with but little effort. The system of deportation so resolutely carried out by Tiglath-pileser III. and Sargon began to produce effect, and up to this time the most happy results only were discernible. The colonies which had been planted throughout the empire from Palestine to Media, some of them two generations previously, others within recent years, were becoming more and more acclimatised to their new surroundings, on which they were pro- ducing the effect desired by their conquerors; they were meant to hold in check the populations in whose midst they had been set down, to act as a curb upon them, and also to break up their national unity and thus gradually prepare them for absorption into a wider fatherland, in which they would cease to be exclusively Damascenes, Samaritans, Hittites, or Aramæans, since they would become Assyrians and fellow-citizens of a mighty empire.

SENNACHERIB.[1]

The provinces, brought at length under a regular system of government, protected against external dangers and internal discord by a well-disciplined soldiery, and enjoying a peace and security they had rarely known in the days of their independence, gradually became accustomed to live in concord under the rule of a common sovereign, and to feel themselves portions of a single empire. The speech of Assyria was their official language, the gods of Assyria were associated with their national gods in the prayers they offered up for the welfare of the sovereign, and foreign nations with whom they were brought into communication no longer distinguished between them and their conquerors, calling their country Assyria, and regarding its inhabitants as Assyrians. As is invariably the case, domestic peace and good administra- tion had caused a sudden development of wealth and commercial activity. Although Nineveh and Calah never became such centres of trade and industry as Babylon had been, yet the presence of the court and the sovereign attracted thither merchants from all parts of the world. The Medes, reaching the capital by way of the passes of Rowândîz and Suleimaniyeh, brought in the lapis-lazuli, precious stones, metals, and woollen stuffs of Central

---

[1] Drawn by Faucher-Gudin, from LAYARD, *Monuments of Nineveh*, vol. i. pl. 5.

Asia and the farthest East, while the Phœnicians and even Greeks, who were already following in their footsteps, came thither to sell in the bazaars of Assyria the most precious of the wares brought back by their merchant vessels from the shores of the Mediterranean, the Atlantic, and the farthest West. The great cities of the triangle of Assyria were gradually supplanting all the capitals of the ancient world, not excepting Memphis, and becoming the centres of universal trade ; unexcelled for centuries in the arts of war, Assyria was in a fair way to become mistress also in the arts of peace. A Jewish prophet thus described the empire at a later date : " The Assyrian was a cedar in Lebanon with fair branches, and with a shadowing shroud, and of an high stature ; and his top was among the thick clouds. The waters nourished him, the deep made him grow : therefore his stature was exalted above all the trees of the field, and his boughs were multiplied, and his branches became long by reason of many waters, when he shot them forth. All the fowls of the heaven made their nests in his boughs, and under his branches did all the beasts of the field bring forth their young, and under his shadow dwelt all great nations. Thus was he fair in his greatness, in the length of his branches : for his root was by many waters. The cedars in the garden of God could not hide him : the fir trees were not like his boughs, and the plane trees were not as his branches ; nor was any tree like unto him in beauty : so that all the trees of Eden, that were in the garden of God, envied him " (*Ezek.* xxxi. 3–9).

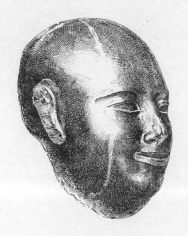

THE POWER OF ASSYRIA AT ITS ZENITH.
ESARHADDON AND ASSUR-BANI-PAL.

Y

Tanuatamanu reasserts the authority of Ethiopia in Egypt (664 B.C.), and Tammaritu of Elam invades Karduniash ; reconquest of the Said and sack of Thebes—Psammetichus I. and the rise of the XXVIth dynasty—Disturbances among the Medes and Mannai—War against Teummân and the victory of Tulliz (660 B.C.) : Elam yields to the Assyrians for the first time—Shamash-shumukîn at Babylon ; is at first on good terms with his brother, then becomes dissatisfied, and forms a coalition against the Ninevite supremacy.

The Uruk incident and outbreak of the war between Karduniash, Elam, and Assyria ; Elam disabled by domestic discords—Siege and capture of Babylon ; Assur-bani-pal ascends the throne under the name of Kandalanu (648–646 B.C.)—Revolt of Egypt : defeat and death of Gyges (642 B.C.) : Ardys drives out the Cimmerians and Dugdamis is killed in Cilicia—Submission of Arabia.

Revolutions in Elam—Attack on Indabigash—Tammaritu restored to power—Pillage and destruction of Susa—Campaign against the Arabs of Kedar and the Nabatœans : suppression of the Tyrian rebellion—Dying struggles of Elam—Capture of Madaktu and surrender of Khumbân-khaldash— The power of Assyria reaches its zenith.

ONE OF THE EGYPTIAN IVORIES FOUND IN ASSYRIA.[1]

CHAPTER IV.

THE POWER OF ASSYRIA AT ITS ZENITH.
ESARHADDON AND ASSUR-BANI-PAL.

The Medes and Cimmerians: Lydia—The conquest of Egypt, of Arabia, and of Elam.

AS we have already seen, Sennacherib reigned for eight years after his triumph; eight years of tranquillity at home, and of peace with all his neighbours abroad. If we examine the contemporary monuments or the documents of a later period, and attempt to glean from them some details concerning the close of his career, we find that there is a complete absence of any record of national movement on the part of either Elam, Urartu, or Egypt. The only event of which any definite mention is made is a raid across the north of Arabia, in the course of which Hazael, King of Adumu, and chief among the princes of Kedar, was despoiled of the images of his gods.[2] The older states of the Oriental world had, as we have pointed out, grown weary

---

[1] Drawn by Faucher-Gudin, after LAYARD, *Monuments of Nineveh*, vol. i. pl. 89, 11. The initial, also by Faucher-Gudin, represents Taharqa in a kneeling attitude, and is taken from a bronze statuette in the Macgregor collection, published by SCHÆFER, *Eine Bronzefigur des Taharka*, in the *Zeitschrift*, vol. xxxiii. pl. vi. 1.

[2] *Prism Inscription*, col. ii. ll. 55–58, col. iii. l. 1; cf. BUDGE, *The History of Esarhaddon*, pp. 52,

of warfare which brought them nothing but loss of men and treasure; but behind these states, on the distant horizon to the east and north-west, were rising up new nations whose growth and erratic movements assumed an importance that became daily more and more alarming. On the east, the Medes, till lately undistinguishable from the other tribes occupying the western corner of the Iranian table-land, had recently broken away from the main body, and, rallying round a single leader, already gave promise of establishing an empire formidable alike by the energy of its people and the extent of its domain. A tradition afterwards accepted by them attributed their earlier successes to a certain Deïokes, son of Phraortes, a man wiser than his fellows, who first set himself to deal out justice in his own household. The men of his village, observing his merits, chose him to be the arbiter of all their disputes, and, being secretly ambitious of sovereign power, he did his best to settle their differences on lines of the strictest equity and justice. "By these means he gained such credit with his fellow-citizens as to attract the attention of those who lived in the neighbouring villages, who had suffered from unjust judgments, so that when they heard of the singular uprightness of Deïokes and of the equity of his decisions they joyfully had recourse to him until at last they came to put confidence in no one else. The number of complaints brought before him continually increasing as people learnt more and more the justice of his judgments, Deïokes, finding himself now all-important, announced that he did not intend any longer to hear causes, and appeared no more in the seat in which he had been accustomed to sit and administer justice. 'It was not to his advantage,' he said, 'to spend the whole day in regulating other men's affairs to the neglect of his own.' Hereupon robbery and lawlessness broke out afresh and prevailed throughout the country even more than heretofore; wherefore the Medes assembled from all quarters and held a consultation on the state of affairs. The speakers, as I

54, 55. Winckler follows G. Smith (*History of Sennacherib*, pp. 137-139) in supposing that Sennacherib undertook, in his latter years, a second campaign against Palestine and Egypt, in the course of which Jerusalem was besieged a second time (*Alttestamentliche Untersuchungen*, pp. 36-38; *Gesch. Bab. und Ass.*, pp. 254, 255, 257, 258, 334; *Altorientalische Forschungen*, vol. i. p. 69). Adumu has by several Assyriologists been identified with the country of Edom (Norris, *Assyrian Dictionary*, p. 19; Tiele, *Bab.-ass. Gesch.*, p. 348; Hommel, *Gesch. Bab. und Ass.*, p. 708, where the city of Adumu is tentatively identified with Petra); Halévy has connected the name with that of the town of Udumeh, which lies near Yabrud, to the north-east of Damascus (*Essai sur les Inscriptions du Safa*, p. 121), and Winckler places it in Djauf (*Gesch. Bab. und Ass.*, p. 267), where Finzi had already (*Ricerche per lo Studio dell' Antichità Assira*, pp. 393, 394) sought to locate the biblical Dumah (*Gen.* xxv. 14; *Isa.* xxi. 11), the Dumaitha of Ptolemy (v. 19, § 7, cf. viii. 22, § 3), and Domata of Pliny (*H. Nat.*, vi. 32). It ought really to be looked for further north, in the country of Kedar, properly so called. It is, indeed, evident from a comparison of the texts that the Assyrians called the desert tribes to the north and south of Palmyra, Aribi or Qidri indifferently (Delitzsch, *Wo lag das Paradies?* p. 299; Delattre, *L'Asie Occidentale*, pp. 102-104, 120-122).

think, were chiefly friends of Deïokes. 'We cannot possibly,' they said, 'go on living in this country if things continue as they now are; let us, therefore, set a king over us, so that the land may be well governed, and we ourselves may be able to attend to our own affairs, and not be forced to quit our country on account of anarchy.' After speaking thus, they persuaded themselves that they desired a king, and forthwith debated whom they should choose. Deïokes was proposed and warmly praised by all, so they agreed to elect him." [1] Whereupon Deïokes had a great palace built, and enrolled a bodyguard to attend upon him. He next called upon his subjects to leave their villages, and " the Medes, obedient to his orders, built the city now called Agbatana,[2] the walls of which are of great size and strength, rising in circles one within the other. The walls are concentric, and so arranged that they rise one above the other by the height of their battlements. The nature of the ground, which is a gentle hill, favoured this arangement. The number of the circles is seven, the royal palace and the treasuries standing within the last. The circuit of the outer wall is very nearly the same as that of Athens. Of this wall the battlements are white, of the next black, of the third scarlet, of the fourth blue, of the fifth orange. The two last have their battlements coated respectively with silver and gold. All these fortifications Deïokes caused to be raised for himself and his own palace; the people he required to dwell outside the citadel. When the town was finished, he established a rule that no one should have direct access to the king, but that all communications should pass through the hands of messengers. It was declared to be unseemly for any one to see the king face to face, or to laugh or spit in his presence. This ceremonial Deïokes established for his own security, fearing lest his compeers who had been brought up with him, and were of as good family and parts as he, should be vexed at the sight of him and conspire against him: he thought that by rendering himself invisible to his vassals they would in time come to regard him as quite a different sort of being from themselves." [3]

Two or three facts stand out from this legendary background. It is probable that Deïokes was an actual person; that the empire of the Medes first took shape under his auspices; that he formed an important kingdom at the foot of Mount Elvend, and founded Ecbatana the Great, or, at any rate, helped to

---

[1] HERODOTUS, I. xcvi.–xcviii.

[2] Agbatana (ÆSCHYLUS, *Persæ*, 16; HERODOTUS, I. xcviii.; ARISTOPHANES, *Acharnians*, 64) or Ecbatana is the Greek form of the old Iranian name Hañgmatâna, Hagmatâna, borne by the city in the great inscription of Behistun (col. ii. l. 76; cf. WEISSBACH and BANG, *Die Altpersische Keilinschriften*, pp. 20, 21). Modern writers, inspired by Herodotus' legend, explain this name as "the meeting-place" of the tribes (G. RAWLINSON, *The Five Great Monarchies*, 2nd edit., vol. ii. p. 363; SPIEGEL, *Erânische Alterthumskunde*, vol. i. p. 103, note 1). It is now called Hamadân.

[3] HERODOTUS, I. xcviii., xcix.

raise it to the rank of a capital.[1] Its site was happily chosen, in a rich and fertile valley, close to where the roads emerge which cross the Zagros chain of mountains and connect Irân with the valleys of the Tigris and Euphrates, almost on the border of the salt desert which forms and renders sterile the central regions of the plateau. Mount Elvend shelters it, and feeds with its snows the streams that irrigate it, whose waters transform the whole country round into one vast orchard. The modern town has, as it were, swallowed up all traces of its predecessor; a stone lion, overthrown and mutilated, marks the site of the royal palace. The chronological reckoning of the native annalists,

STONE LION AT HAMADÂN.[3]

as handed down to us by Herodotus, credits Deïokes with a reign of fifty-three years, which occupied almost the whole of the first half of the seventh century, *i.e.* from 709 to 656, or from 700 to 647 B.C.[2] The records of Nineveh mention a certain Dayaukku who was governor of the Mannai, and an ally of the Assyrians in the days of Sargon, and was afterwards deported with his family to Hamath in 715;[4] two years later reference is made to an expedition across the territory of Bît-Dayaukku, which is described as lying between Ellipi and Karalla, thus corresponding to the modern province of Hamadân.[5] It is quite within the bounds of possibility that the Dayaukku who gave his name to this district

[1] The existence of Deïokes has been called in question by Grote (*History of Greece*, vol. iii. p. 307, et seq.) and by the Rawlinsons (*Herodotus*, vol. i. p. 321, and *The Five Great Monarchies*, 2nd edit., vol. ii. pp. 380–383). Most recent historians, however, accept the story of this personage as true in its main facts (FR. LENORMANT, *Lettres Assyriologiques*, 1st ser., vol. i. pp. 55–62; SPIEGEL, *Erânische Alterthumskunde*, vol. ii. pp. 248–252; DELATTRE, *Le Peuple et l'Empire des Mèdes*, pp. 129–146; NÖLDEKE, *Aufsätze zur Persischen Geschichte*, pp. 4–6; JUSTI, *Geschichte des Alten Persiens*, pp. 5–7); some believe him to have been merely the ancestor of the royal house which later on founded the united kingdom of the Medes (ED. MEYER, *Geschichte des Alterthums*, vol. i. p. 555; PRASHEK, *Medien und das Haus Kyaxares*, p. 40, and *Beiträge zur Medischen Geschichte*, in *Recueil de Travaux*, vol. xix. p. 202; WINCKLER, *Untersuchungen zur Altorientalischen Geschichte*, p. 118).

[2] Herodotus (I. cii.) expressly attributes a reign of fifty-three years to his Deïokes, and the total of a hundred and fifty years which we obtain by adding together the number of years assigned by him to the four Median kings (53 + 22 + 40 + 35) brings us back to 709–708, if we admit, as he does, that the year of the proclamation by Cyrus as King of Persia (559–558) was that in which Astyages was overthrown (I. cxxx.); we get 700–699 as the date of Deïokes' accession, if we separate the two facts, as the monuments compel us to do, and reckon the hundred and fifty years of the Median empire from the fall of Astyages in 550–549.

[3] Drawn by Faucher-Gudin, from FLANDIN and COSTE, *Voyage en Perse*, pl. 25, and p. 17.

[4] *Annals of Sargon*, ll. 75–77, and *Inscription des Fastes*, l. 49; cf. p. 243, *infra*.

[5] *Annals of Sargon*, l. 140; cf. p. 250, *infra*. As to the probable position of Ellipi and Karalla, cf. the map on p. 141, *infra*. The name Bît-Dayaukku is probably only the Assyrian equivalent of the native appellation.

was identical with the Deïokes of later writers.[1] He was the official ancestor of a royal house, a fact proved by the way in which his conqueror uses the name to distinguish the country over which he had ruled; moreover, the epoch assigned to him by contemporary chroniclers coincides closely enough with that indicated by tradition in the case of Deïokes. He was never the august sovereign that posterity afterwards made him out to be, and his territory included barely half of what constituted the province of Media in classical times; he contrived, however—and it was this that gained him

VIEW OF HAMADÂN AND MOUNT ELVEND IN WINTER.[2]

universal renown in later days—to create a central rallying-point for the Median tribes around which they henceforth grouped themselves. The work of concentration was merely in its initial stage during the lifetime of Sennacherib, and little or nothing was felt of its effects outside its immediate area of influence, but the pacific character ascribed to the worthy Deïokes by popular legends, is to a certain extent confirmed by the testimony of the monuments: they record only one expedition, in 702, against Ellipi and the neighbouring tribes, in the course of which some portions of the newly acquired territory were annéxed

---

[1] The form Deïokes, in place of Daïokes, is due to the Ionic dialect employed by Herodotus (cf. NÖLDEKE, *Aufsätze zur Persischen Geschichte*, pp. 6, 147). Justi (*Iranisches Namenbuch*, p. 76) regards the name as an abbreviated form of the ancient Persian *Dahyaupati* = "the master of a province," with the suffix -*ka*.

[2] Drawn by Boudier, from a photograph by M. de Morgan; cf. J. DE MORGAN, *Mission Scientifique en Perse*, vol. ii. pl. lvi.

to the province of Kharkhar,[1] and after mentioning this the annals have nothing further to relate during the rest of the reign. Sennacherib was too much taken up with his retaliatory measures against Babylon, or his disputes with Elam, to think of venturing on expeditions such as those which had brought Tiglath-pileser III. or Sargon within sight of Mount Bikni; while the Medes, on their part, had suffered so many reverses under these two monarchs that they probably thought twice before attacking any of the outposts scattered along the Assyrian frontier: nothing occurred to disturb their tranquillity during the early years of the seventh century, and this peaceful interval probably enabled Deïokes to consolidate, if not to extend, his growing authority. But if matters were quiet, at all events on the surface, in this direction, the nations on the north and north-west had for some time past begun to adopt a more threatening attitude. That migration of races between Europe and Asia, which had been in such active progress about the middle of the second millennium before our era, had increased twofold in intensity after the rise of the XXth Egyptian dynasty,[2] and from thenceforward a wave of new races had gradually spread over the whole of Asia Minor, and had either driven the older peoples into the less fertile or more inaccessible districts, or else had overrun and absorbed them. Many of the nations that had fought against Ramses II. and Ramses III., such as the Uashasha, the Shagalasha, the Zakkali, the Danauna, and the Tursha, had disappeared, but the Thracians, whose appearance on the scene caused such consternation in days gone by, had taken root in the very heart of the peninsula, and had, in the course of three or four generations, succeeded in establishing a thriving state.[3] The legend which traced the descent of the royal line[4] back to the fabulous hero Ascanius proves that at the outset the haughty tribe of the Ascanians must have taken precedence over their fellows;[5] it soon degenerated, however, and before long the

---

[1] Cf. what has been said on this subject on p. 277, *supra*.

[2] Cf., for the movements of these races, *The Struggle of the Nations*, pp. 362, 363, 461–470. Here, again, the limitations to which the original plan of my work has been subjected have obliged me to suppress nearly everything connected with what we know of the nations of Asia Minor; I have merely retained such few details of Phrygian and Lydian history as are necessary to enable the reader to understand the politics of the ancient empires of the East.

[3] Cf. what has been said on this subject in *The Struggle of the Nations*, pp. 586, 587. I may mention that several scholars, such as Ramsay, for instance (*A Study of Phrygian Art*, in *Jour. of Hellenic Studies*, 1888), place the arrival of the Phrygians in Asia Minor as late as the ninth century B.C.

[4] This Ascanius is mentioned in the *Iliad* (Bk. II. 862, 863: Φόρκυς αὖ Φρύγας ἦγε, καὶ 'Ασκάνιος θεοειδής,—τῆλ' ἐξ 'Ασκανίης; cf. STRABO, XII. iv. § 5, p. 564).

[5] The name of this tribe was retained by a district afterwards included in the province of Bithynia, viz. Ascania, on the shores of the Ascanian lake: the distribution of place and personal names over the face of the country makes it seem extremely probable that Ascania and the early Ascanians occupied the whole of the region bounded on the north by the Propontis; in other words, the very country in which, according to Xanthus of Lydia (MÜLLER-DIDOT, *Fragm. Hist. Græc.*, vol. i. p. 37), the Phrygians first established themselves after their arrival in Asia (STRABO, XII. viii. § 3, p. 572). As to the application of the name Ashkenaz (*Gen.* x. 3) by Rabbinical commentators, and its identification with Ascania and Phrygia, cf. FR. LENORMANT, *Les Orig. de l'Hist.*, vol. ii. pp. 388–395.

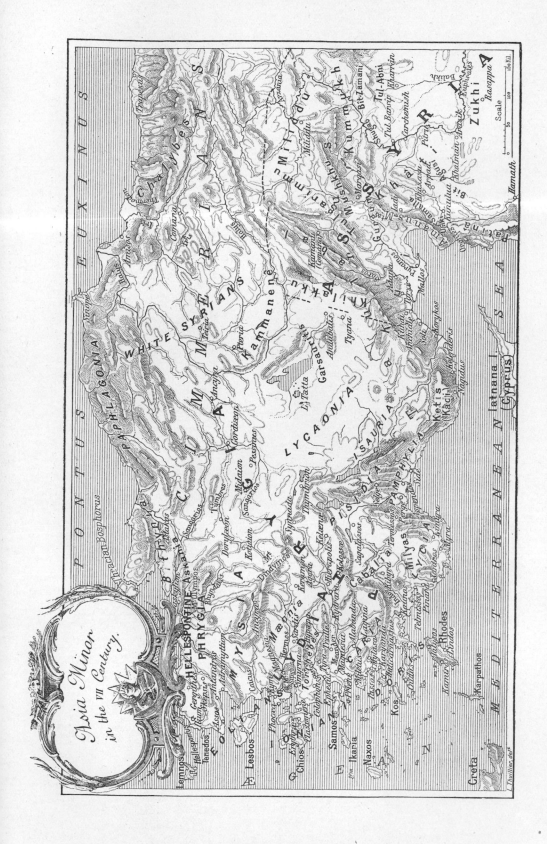

Asia Minor in the VII Century.

Scale
0   50   100   150 Kil.

I. Thuillier, del.^t

Phrygian tribe gained the upper hand and gave its name to the whole nation.[1]
Phrygia proper, the country first colonised by them, lay between Mount
Dindymus and the river Halys, in the valley of the Upper Sangarios and its
affluents : it was there that the towns and strongholds of their most venerated
leaders, such as Midaion, Dorylaion, Gordiaion, Tataion, and many others
stood close together, perpetuating the memory of Midas, Dorylas, Gordios, and
Tatas.[2] Its climate was severe and liable to great extremes of temperature,
being bitterly cold in winter and almost tropical during the summer months;
forests of oak and pine, however, and fields of corn flourished, while the mountain slopes favoured the growth of the vine ; it was, in short, an excellent and
fertile country, well fitted for the development of a nation of vine-dressers and
tillers of the soil. The slaying of an ox or the destruction of an agricultural
implement was punishable by death,[3] and legend relates that Gordios, the first
Phrygian king, was a peasant by birth. His sole patrimony consisted of a
single pair of oxen, and the waggon used by him in bringing home his sheaves
after the harvest was afterwards placed as an offering in the temple of Cybele
at Ancyra by his son Midas; there was a local tradition according to which
the welfare of all Asia depended on the knot which bound the yoke to the pole
being preserved intact.[4] Midas did not imitate his father's simple habits,
and the poets, after crediting him with fabulous wealth, tried also to make
out that he was a conqueror. The kingdom expanded in all directions, and
soon included the upper valley of the Mæander, with its primeval sanctuaries,
Kydrara, Colossæ, and Kylænæ, founded wherever exhalations of steam and
boiling springs betrayed the presence of some supernatural power. The southern
shores of the Hellespont, which formed part of the Troad, and was the former territory of Ascania, belonged to it, as did also the majority of the peoples scattered
along the coast of the Euxine between the mouth of the Sangarios and that of
the Halys; those portions of the central steppe which border on Lake Tatta
were also for a time subject to it,[5] Lydia was under its influence,[6] and it is no
exaggeration to say that in the tenth and eleventh centuries before our era

[1] As to the early form of their name, Bryges (HERODOTUS, VII. lxvii.; STRABO, VII. iii. § 2, p. 295,
and Fragm. 24, ed. MÜLLER-DIDOT, p. 278), cf. TOMASCHEK, Die Alten Thraker, and KRETSCHMER,
Einleitung in die Geschichte der Griechischen Sprache, p. 229.

[2] As to the derivation of the names of Phrygian towns and castles, cf. RAMSAY, The Historical
Geography of Asia Minor, pp. 144, 439.

[3] NICOLAUS OF DAMASCUS, Fragm. 128, in MÜLLER-DIDOT, Fragm. Hist. Græc., vol. iii. p. 461, who
probably took his facts from Xanthus of Lydia.

[4] ARRIAN, Anabasis, II. iii. §§ 2–4; QUINTUS CURTIUS, iii. 1; ÆLIAN, De Natura Animalium,
xiii. 1; cf. GUTSCHMID, Kleine Schriften, vol. iii. pp. 457–465.

[5] Salambria in Garsauria bears a name of Thracian and, consequently, Phrygian origin; cf.
KRETSCHMER, Einleitung in die Geschichte der Griechischen Sprache, p. 206.

[6] Cf. the traditions in regard to the Phrygian Sipylus, and in regard to the Phrygian origin of
Tantalus, Pelops, and Niobe (STRABO, XII. viii. § 2, p. 571; HERODOTUS, VII. ii.).

there was a regular Phrygian empire which held sway, almost without a rival, over the western half of Asia Minor.[1]

It has left behind it so few relics of its existence, that we can only guess at what it must have been in the days of its prosperity. Three or four ruined fortresses, a few votive stelæ, and a dozen bas-reliefs cut on the faces of cliffs in a style which at first recalls the Hittite and Asianic carvings of the preceding age, and afterwards, as we come down to later times, betrays the influence

MONUMENT COMMEMORATIVE OF MIDAS.[2]

of early Greek art.[3] In the midst of one of their cemeteries we come upon a monument resembling the façade of a house or temple cut out of the virgin rock; it consists of a low triangular pediment, surmounted by a double scroll, then a rectangle of greater length than height, framed between two pilasters and a horizontal string-course, the centre being decorated with a geometrical design of crosses in a way which suggests the pattern of a carpet; a recess is hollowed out on a level with the ground, and filled by

---

[1] As to the conclusions to be drawn from a study of geographical names with regard to the extension of the Phrygian empire, cf. KRETSCHMER, *Einleitung in die Geschichte der Griechischen Sprache*, pp. 203–208.

[2] Drawn by Faucher-Gudin, from a plate in PERROT and CHIPIEZ, *Histoire de l'Art dans l'Antiquité*, vol. v. p. 83.

[3] For a survey of the art of the Phrygian monuments, cf. RAMSAY, *A Study of Phrygian Art*, in the *Journal of Hellenic Studies*, vol. ix. pp. 350–382, and vol. x. pp. 147–189; also PERROT and CHIPIEZ, *Histoire de l'Art dans l'Antiquité*, vol. v. pp. 1–235, 899–902.

a blind door with rebated doorposts. Is it a tomb? The inscription carefully engraved above one side of the pediment contains the name of Midas, and seems to show that we have before us a commemorative monument, piously dedicated by a certain Ates in honour of the Phrygian hero.[1] Elsewhere we come upon the outlines of a draped female form, sometimes alone, sometimes

A PHRYGIAN GOD.[4]

accompanied by two lions, or of a man clothed in a short tunic, holding a sort of straight sceptre in his hand, and we fancy that we have the image of a god before our eyes, though we cannot say which of the deities handed down by tradition it may represent.[2] The religion of the Phrygians is shrouded in the same mystery as their civilisation and their art, and presents a curious mixture of European and Asianic elements. The old aboriginal races had worshipped from time immemorial a certain mother-goddess, Mâ, or Amma, the black earth, which brings forth without ceasing, and nourishes all living things.[3] Her central place of worship seems, originally, to have been in the region of the Anti-taurus, and it was there that her sacred cities— Tyana, Venasa, and the Cappadocian Comana—were to be found as late as Roman times; in these towns her priests were regarded as kings, and thousands of her priestesses spent lives of prostitution in her service; but her sanctuaries, with their special rites and regulations, were scattered over the whole peninsula.[5] She was sometimes worshipped under the form of a meteoric stone, or betyle

---

[1] This is the view taken by PERROT and CHIPIEZ, *Histoire de l'Art dans l'Antiquité*, vol. v. p. 102; other authorities take it to be the real tomb of some deceased Midas, and not a commemorative chapel in honour of the original Midas (cf. again RAMSAY, *A Study of Phrygian Art*, in the *Journal of Hellenic Studies*, vol. x. pp. 156–161).

[2] PERROT and CHIPIEZ, *Histoire de l'Art dans l'Antiquité*, vol. v. p. 146, et seq.

[3] *Etymologicon Magnum*, s.v. Ἀμμά, with its secondary forms Ἀμμάς and Ἀμμαία, Ἀμμία; among the Lydians Mâ was identified with the Greek Rhea (STEPHEN OF BYZANTIUM, s.v. Μάσταυρα).

[4] Drawn by Faucher-Gudin, from a sketch by RAMSAY, *Studies in Asia Minor*, in the *Journal of Hellenic Studies*, pl. xxi. B ; cf. PERROT and CHIPIEZ, *Histoire de l'Art dans l'Antiquité*, vol. iv. pp. 721, 722, and vol. v. p. 147, where the figure is described as that of a priest, not of a god.

[5] As to the constitution of Comana in Cappadocia, cf. STRABO, XII. ii. § 3, p. 535; a list of some of the towns in which it obtained is given by RAMSAY, *Pre-Hellenic Monuments of Cappadocia*, in the *Recueil de Travaux*, vol. xiv. p. 77, et seq.

similar to those found in Canaan ;[1] more frequently she was represented in female shape, with attendant lions, or placed erect on a lion in the attitude of walking.[2] A moon-god, Mên, shared divine honours with her,[3] and with a goddess Nana whose son Atys had been the only love of Mâ and the victim of her passion. We are told that she compelled him to emasculate himself in a fit of mad delirium, and then transformed him into a pine tree : thenceforward her priests made the sacrifice of their virility with their own hands at the moment of dedicating themselves to the service of the goddess.[4] The gods introduced from Thrace by the Phrygians showed a close affinity with those of the purely Asianic peoples. Precedence was universally given to a celestial divinity named Bagaios, Lord of the Oak, perhaps because he was worshipped under a gigantic

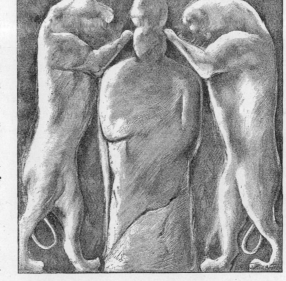

THE MOTHER-GODDESS BETWEEN LIONS.[5]

[1] *E.g.* at Mount Dindymus and at Pessinus, which latter place was supposed to possess the oldest sanctuary of Cybele (APPIAN, *De Bello Annibalico,* § lvi. ; HERODIAN, i. 11 ; AMMIANUS MARCELLINUS, XXII. ix. §§ 5–7). The Pessinus stone, which was carried off to Rome in 204 B.C., was small, irregular in shape, and of a dark colour. Another stone represented Cybele on Mount Ida (CLAUDIAN, *De Raptu Proserpinæ,* ll. 202–209).

[2] She is shown between two lions as in the illustration on this page; elsewhere she appears erect on the back of a lion, in one of the monuments reproduced by PERROT and CHIPIEZ, *Histoire de l'Art dans l'Antiquité,* vol. iv. pp. 650, 651.

[3] As to Mên and his associates, cf. WADDINGTON and LEBAS, *Voyage Archéologique, Explication des Inscriptions,* iii., Nos. 667, 668. Ramsay believes the god to be the Phrygian Manes, transformed into Mên by popular etymology during the Greek epoch, and then identified with a moon-god (*Cities and Bishoprics of Phrygia,* vol. i. pp. 169, 294); Kretschmer is inclined to accept this hypothesis (*Einleitung in die Geschichte der Griechischen Sprache,* p. 197, note 4). Seeing how little we know of the early attributes of this god, I am somewhat inclined to reverse Ramsay's theory : a native god, Mên, may have been changed to Manes by popular etymology, and afterwards identified with Manes, a purely Phrygian deity.

[4] Nana was made out to be the daughter of the river Sangarios. She is said to have conceived Atys by placing in her bosom the fruit of an almond tree which sprang from the hermaphrodite Agdistis (cf. the legends borrowed from Timotheus by ARNOBIUS, *Adversus Nationes,* v. 5–7, and those preserved by PAUSANIAS, VII. xviii. § 5). This was the form—extremely ancient in its main features —in which the legend was preserved at Pessinus. For other versions, cf. OVID, *Fasti,* iv. 221–224 ; JULIAN, *Serm. V., De Mater Deorum,* p. 165 B ; SALLUST PHIL., *De Diis et Mundo,* iv. ; DIODORUS SICULUS, iii. 58, 59 ; FIRMICUS MATERNUS, *De Erroribus prof. religion.,* 27, 1, ed. Halm. As to the Syrian origin of Atys or Attes and his supposed identity with Atê, cf. ED. MEYER, *Gesch. des Alterthums,* vol. i. pp. 307, 308, who declares unhesitatingly that it is nothing more than a plausible conjecture : the myth of Atys and that of Adonis subsequently became merged into one another during the Alexandrine period.

[5] Drawn by Faucher-Gudin, from a sketch by Ramsay, in the *Journal of Hellenic Studies,* 1884, vol. v. p. 285 ; cf. PERROT and CHIPIEZ, *Histoire de l'Art dans l'Antiquité,* vol. v. pp. 156, 157.

sacred oak ; [1] he was king of gods and men,[2] their father,[3] lord of the thunder and the lightning,[4] the warrior who charges in his chariot.[5] He, doubtless, allowed a queen-regent of the earth to share his throne,[6] but Sauazios,[7] another and, at first, less venerable deity had thrown this august pair into the shade.[8] The Greeks, finding this Sauazios at the head of the Phrygian Pantheon, identified him with their Zeus,[9] or, less frequently, with the Sun ; [10] he was really a variant of their Dionysos.[11] He became torpid in the autumn, and slept a death-

THE MOTHER-GODDESS AND ATYS.[12]

[1] The name Bagaios (HESYCHIUS, *s.v.l.*) was for a long time identified with the Sanscrit *bhága-*, the Old-Persian *baga* and the Old-Slavonic *bogu* = "god." Torp (*Indogermanische Forschungen*, v. p. 193) has recently sought to derive it from a Phrygian word *bāga*, which he connects with the O.H.G. *buohha* and Latin *fagus*, thus making the god the presiding genius of the oak, φηγοναῖος. This etymology has been adopted and defended by KRETSCHMER, *Einleitung in die Geschichte der Griechischen Sprache*, pp. 198, 199.

[2] In the inscriptions he is called βασιλεύς, "king," and τύραννος, "tyrant."

[3] In this capacity he bore the surname Papas. Cf. the fragment from ARRIAN, *Bythin.*, quoted by Eustathius, ἀνιόντες εἰς τὰ ἄκρα τῶν ὀρῶν Βίθυνοι ἐκάλουν Πάπαν τὸν Δία καὶ Ἄττιν τὸν αὐτόν, and the inscription at Prusa, dedicated to Ζεύς παππῷος (*Mittheilungen aus Œsterr.*, vol. vii. p. 174, et seq.).

[4] Βροντῶν. He is called Βροντῶν καὶ Ἀστράπτων in an inscription at Laodicea (*Athen. Mittheilungen*, vol. xiii. p. 235, No. 1).

[5] Βέννιος or Βεννεύς, from the Thracian *Benna*, "chariot" (RAMSAY, *A Study of Phrygian Art*, in the *Journal of Hellenic Studies*, 1887, p. 512).

[6] The existence of such a goddess may be deduced from the passage in which Dionysius of Halicarnassus (*Ant. Rom.*, i. 27) states that Manes, first king of the Phrygians, was the son of Zeus and Demeter.

[7] As to the various forms of this name, Sabazios or Sauazios, cf. KRETSCHMER, *Einleitung in die Geschichte der Griechischen Sprache*, pp. 195, 196; its original meaning is not known.

[8] This is proved by dedications to the Διὶ Σαβαζίῳ in Greek inscriptions in Phrygia; as to Sabazios-Sauazios, cf. RAMSAY, *The Cities and Bishoprics of Phrygia*, vol. i. pp. 294, 295.

[9] He is represented on votive bas-reliefs with a radiated crown on his head; cf. an inscription at Nicopolis quoted in the *Mitt. aus Œsterr.*, vol. x. p. 241, No. 6, Διὶ Ἡλίῳ Μεγάλῳ κυρίῳ Σαβαζίῳ ἁγίῳ.

[10] NYMPHIS, in MÜLLER-DIDOT, *Fragm. Hist. Græc.*, vol. iii. p. 14: Διονύσιος καὶ Σαβάζιος εἷς ἐστι θεός; cf. DIODORUS SICULUS, iv. 4.

[11] As to the nature of the god, cf. especially the *De Iside et Osiride*, PARTHEY's ed., § 69, pp. 121, 122, where his name Sauazios does not appear, but he is simply described as ὁ θεός; as to the meaning and possible derivation of the word Sauades, cf. KRETSCHMER, *op. cit.*, p. 196, note 2.

[12] Drawn by Faucher-Gudin, from a photograph by Chantre. It is one of the bas-reliefs at Iasili-kiaia (cf. PERROT and CHIPIEZ, *Histoire de l'Art dans l'Antiquité*, vol. iv. pp. 645, 646), to which we shall have occasion to refer later on in Chapter V. of the present volume.

like sleep all through the winter; but no sooner did he feel the warmth of the first breath of spring, than he again awoke, glowing with youth, and revelled during his summer in the heart of the forest or on the mountain-side, leading a life of riot and intoxication, guarded by a band of Sauades, spirits of the springs and streams, the Sileni of Greek mythology. The resemblances detected by the new-comers between the orgies of Thrace and those of Asia

THE GOD MÊN ASSOCIATED WITH THE SUN AND OTHER DEITIES.[1]

quickly led to confusion between the different dogmas and divinities. The Phrygians adopted Mâ, and made her their queen, the Cybele who dwells in the hills,[2] and takes her title from the mountain-tops which she inhabits— Dindymêne on Mount Dindymus, Sipylêne on Mount Sipylus. She is always the earth, but the earth untilled, and is seated in the midst of lions, or borne through her domain in a car drawn by lions, accompanied by a troop of Corybantes with dishevelled locks. Sauazios, identified with the Asianic Atys, became her lover and her priest, and Mên, transformed by popular etymology into Manes, the good and beautiful, was looked upon as the giver of good luck,

[1] Drawn by Faucher-Gudin, from a photograph by Perdrizet, in the *Bulletin de Correspondance Hellénique*, 1896, pl. vi. The last figure on the left is the god Mên; the Sun overlooks all the rest, and a god bearing an axe occupies the extreme right of the picture. The shapes of these ancient aboriginal deities have been modified by the influence of Graeco-Roman syncretism, and I merely give these figures, as I do many others, for lack of better representations.

[2] According to Hesychius, *kybela* is the Phrygian word for "mountain," "cave:" Κύβελα, ὄρη Φρυγίας καὶ ἄντρα καὶ θάλαμοι. As to this goddess, cf. Decharme's article in SAGLIO, *Dictionnaire des Antiquités*, vol. ii. p. 1679, et seq.

who protects men after death as well as in life. This religion, evolved from so many diverse elements, possessed a character of sombre poetry and sensual fanaticism which appealed strongly to the Greek imagination : they quickly adopted even its most barbarous mysteries, those celebrated in honour of the goddess and Atys, or of Sauazios. They tell us but little of the inner significance of the symbols and doctrines taught by its votaries, but have frequently described its outward manifestations. These consisted of aimless wanderings through the forests, in which the priest, incarnate representative of his god, led after him the ministers of the temple, who were identified with the Sauades and nymphs of the heavenly host. Men heard them passing in the night, heralded by the piercing notes of the flute provoking to frenzy, and by the clash of brazen cymbals, acompanied by the din of uproarious ecstasy : these sounds were broken

MIDAS OF PHRYGIA.[2]

at intervals by the bellowing of bulls and the roll of drums, like the rumbling of subterranean thunder.[1]

A Midas followed a Gordios, and a Gordios a Midas, in alternate succession, and under their rule the Phrygian empire enjoyed a period of prosperous obscurity. Lydia led an uneventful existence beside them, under dynasties which have received merely passing notice at the hands of the Greek chroniclers. They credit it at the outset with the almost fabulous royal line of the Atyadæ, in one of whose reigns the Tyrseni are said to have migrated into Italy.[3] Towards the twelfth century the Atyadæ were supplanted by a family of Heraclidæ, who traced their descent to a certain Agrôn, whose personality is only a degree less mythical than his ancestry; he was descended from Heracles through Alcæus, Belus, and Ninus. Whether these last two names point to intercourse with one or other of the courts on the banks of the Euphrates, it is difficult to say.[4] Twenty-one Heraclidæ, each one the son of his predecessor, are said to have followed Agrôn on the throne, their combined reigns giving a

    [1] Æschylus, *Hedon.*, Fragments 1–3, in Ahrens-Didot's edition, p. 178.

    [2] Drawn by Faucher-Gudin, from a specimen in the *Cabinet des Médailles.* It is a bronze coin from Prymnessos in Phrygia, belonging to the imperial epoch. The cast reproduced above was kindly lent to me by M. Babelon.

    [3] Cf. what has been said as to this migration of the Tyrseni, in *The Struggle of the Nations,* p. 587.

    [4] Herodotus, I. vii.; as to the Assyrian origin of these personages, cf. Fr. Lenormant, *Les Antiquités de la Troade,* pt. 1, pp. 68, 69, whence the theory has passed on to D'Arbois de Jubainville, *Les Premiers Habitants de l'Europe,* 2nd edit., vol. i. pp. 120, 121, 274–277; to Perrot and Chipiez, *Histoire de l'Art dans l'Antiquité,* vol. v. p. 245; to Schubert, *Geschichte der Könige von Lydien,* pp. 7, 8; and to Radet, *La Lydie et le Monde Grec au temps des Mermnades,* pp. 66, 67; while Sayce (*The Ancient Empires of the East,* vol. i. p. 427) is rather inclined to look on them as a survival of the Hittite dominion in Asia Minor. We have here probably merely a genealogy which was fabricated bit by bit at a period when a vague memory of the relations kept up by Gyges and Ardys with Assur-bani-pal and the court of Assyria still existed.

total of five hundred years.[1] Most of these princes, whether Atyadæ or Heraclidæ, have for us not even a shadowy existence, and what we know of the remainder is of a purely fabulous nature. For instance, Kambles is reported to have possessed such a monstrous appetite, that he devoured his own wife one night, while asleep.[2] The concubine of Meles, again, is said to have brought forth a lion, and the oracle of Telmessos predicted that the town of Sardes

THE STEEP BANKS OF THE HALYS FAILED TO ARREST THEM.[3]

would be rendered impregnable if the animal were led round the city walls; this was done, except on the side of the citadel facing Mount Tmolus, which was considered unapproachable, but it was by that very path that the Persians subsequently entered the town.[4] Alkimos, we are told, accumulated immense

---

[1] HERODOTUS, I. vii. The number is a purely conventional one, and Gutschmid has shown how it originated. The computation at first comprised the complete series of 22 Heraclidæ and 5 Mermnadæ, estimated reasonably at 4 kings to a century, *i.e.* $27 \times 25 = 675$ years, from the taking of Sardes to the supposed accession of Agrôn. As it was known from other sources that the 5 Mermnadæ had reigned 170 years, these were subtracted from the 675, to obtain the duration of the Heraclidæ alone, and by this means were obtained the 505 years mentioned by Herodotus (SCHUBERT, *Gesch. der Könige von Lydien*, p. 8; GUTSCHMID, *Kleine Schriften*, vol. ii. pp. 474, 475).

[2] XANTHUS OF LYDIA, *Fragm.* 14, in MÜLLER-DIDOT, *Fragmenta Hist. Græc.*, vol. i. pp. 38, 39. Another version, related by Nicolas of Damascus, refers the story to the time of Iardanos, a contemporary of Hercules (HEROD., I. vii.); it shows that the Lydian chronographers considered Kambles or Kamblitas as being one of the last of the Atyad kings (*Fragm.* 28, in MÜLLER-DIDOT, *Fragm. Hist. Græc.*, vol. iii. p. 372, note 4; SCHUBERT, *Gesch. der Könige von Lydien*, p. 5).

[3] Drawn by Faucher-Gudin, from a photograph by A. BOISSIER, *En Cappadoce*, pp. 16, 17. The road leading from Angora to Yuzgat crosses the river not far from the site shown here, near the spot where the ancient road crossed.

[4] HERODOTUS, I. lxxxiv.

Z

treasures, and under his rule his subjects enjoyed unequalled prosperity for fourteen years.[1] It is possible that the story of the expedition despatched into Palestine by a certain Akiamos, which ended in the foundation of Ascalon, is merely a feeble echo of the raids in Syrian and Egyptian waters made by the Tyrseni and Sardinians in the thirteenth century B.C.[2] The spread of the Phrygians, and the subsequent progress of Greek colonisation, must have curtailed the possessions of the Heraclidæ from the eleventh to the ninth centuries, but the material condition of the people does not appear to have suffered by this diminution of territory. When they had once firmly planted themselves in the ports along the Asianic littoral—at Kymê, at Phocæa, at Smyrna, at Clazomenæ, at Colophon, at Ephesus, at Magnesia, at Miletus—the Æolians and the Ionians lost no time in reaping the advantages which this position, at the western extremities of the great high-road through Asia Minor, secured to them. They overran all the Lydian settlements in Phrygia—Sardes, Leontocephalos, Pessinus, Gordiæon, and Ancyra. The steep banks and the tortuous course of the Halys failed to arrest them; and they pushed forward beyond the mysterious regions peopled by the White Syrians, where the ancient civilisation of Asia Minor still held its sway. The search for precious metals mainly drew them on— the gold and silver, the copper, bronze, and above all iron, which the Chalybes found in their mountains, and which were conveyed by caravans from the regions of the Caucasus to the sacred towns of Teiria and Pteria.[3] The friendly relations into which they entered with the natives on these journeys resulted before long in barter and intermarriage, though their influence made itself felt in different ways, according to the character of the people on whom it was brought to bear.[4] They gave as a legacy to Phrygia one of their alphabets, that of Kymê, which soon banished the old Hittite syllabary from the monuments,[5] and they borrowed in exchange Phrygian customs,

[1] XANTHUS OF LYDIA, Fragm. 10, in MÜLLER-DIDOT, Fragm. Hist. Græc., vol. i. p. 38; cf. NICOLAS OF DAMASCUS, Fragm. 49, in MÜLLER-DIDOT, op. cit., vol. iii. p. 382.

[2] XANTHUS OF LYDIA, Fragm. 23, in MÜLLER-DIDOT, op. cit., vol. i. p. 43; cf. NICOLAS OF DAMASCUS, Fragm. 26, in MÜLLER-DIDOT, op. cit., vol. iii. p. 372. The correction of Akiamos into Alkimos and their identification one with another is unjustifiable, as has been lately pointed out by SCHUBERT, Gesch. der Könige von Lydien, p. 3. Fragment 25 of Nicolas of Damascus (MÜLLER-DIDOT, op. cit., vol. iii. p. 372), which mentions the town of Nêrabos, the Nirabu of the Egyptian texts (cf. Struggle of the Nations, p. 142, note 6), belonged to the account of this campaign, and it may serve to indicate the pretended itinerary of the Lydian expedition.

[3] The site of Pteria has been fixed at Boghaz-keui by Texier, an identification which has been generally adopted; cf. PERROT and CHIPIEZ, Hist. de l'Art dans l'Antiquité, vol. iv. p. 596, et seq. Euyuk is very probably, as Radet conjectures (La Lydie et le Monde Grec au temps des Mermnades, p. 27, note 3), Teiria, a town of the Leucosyrians, mentioned by Hecatæus of Miletus in his work (Fragm. 194, in MÜLLER-DIDOT, op. cit., vol. i. p. 13).

[4] For all these facts, which want of space obliges me to curtail, I must refer the reader to the valuable work of RADET, La Lydie et le Monde Grec, etc., pp. 63–111.

[5] This is Ramsay's hypothesis in the Athenæum, 1884, pp. 864, 865, and A Study of Phrygian Art in the Journal of Hellenic Studies, vol. x. pp. 186–189.

musical instruments, traditions, and religious orgies. A Midas sought in marriage Hermodikê, the daughter of Agamemnon the Kymæan,[1] while another Midas, who had consulted the oracle of Delphi, presented to the god the chryselephantine throne on which he was wont to sit when he dispensed justice.[2] This interchange of amenities and these alliances, however, had a merely superficial effect, and in no way modified the temperament and life of

VIEW OVER THE PLAIN OF SARDES.[3]

the people in inner Asia Minor. They remained a robust, hardworking race, attached to their fields and woods, loutish and slow of understanding, unskilled in war, and not apt in defending themselves in spite of their natural bravery. The Lydians, on the contrary, submitted readily to foreign influence, and the Greek leaven introduced among them became the germ of a new civilisation, which occupied an intermediate place between that of the Greek and that of the Oriental world.[4] About the first half of the eighth century B.C. the Lydians had become organised into a confederation of several tribes, governed by hereditary chiefs, who were again in their turn subject to the Heraclidæ occupying Sardes.[5]

[1] HERACLIDES OF PONTUS, *Constitutions*, xi. § 3, in MÜLLER-DIDOT, *Frag. Hist. Græc.*, vol. ii. p. 216; cf. POLLUX, *Onomasticon*, ix. 83, where the wife is called Demodikê. The striking of the earliest Kymæan coins is attributed to her, which would oblige us to put her at the end of the eighth or the beginning of the seventh century. Her husband must be one of the last sovereigns bearing the name Midas.

[2] HERODOTUS, I. xiv.   [3] Drawn by Boudier from a photograph.

[4] PERROT and CHIPIEZ, *Hist. de l'Art dans l'Antiquité*, vol. v. p. 253, et seq., and particularly RADET, *La Lydie et le Monde Grec.*, etc., pp. 86–111, 260, et seq.

[5] Gelzer was the first, to my knowledge, to state that Lydia was a feudal state, and he defined its constitution (*Das Zeitalter des Gyges*, in the *Rheinisches Museum*, 1880, vol. xxxv. pp. 520–524); Radet (*op. cit.*, pp. 90, 91) refuses to recognise it as feudal in the true sense of the term, and he prefers to see in it a confederation of states under the authority of a single prince.

This town rose in terraces on the lower slopes of a detached spur of the Tmolus running in the direction of the Hermos, and was crowned by the citadel, within which were included the royal palace, the treasury, and the arsenals. It was surrounded by an immense plain, bounded on the south by a curve of the Tmolus, and on the west by the distant mountains of Phrygia Katakekaumenê. The Mæonians still claimed primacy over the entire race, and the reigning family was chosen from among their nobles.[1] The king, who was supposed to be descended from the gods, bore, as the insignia of his rank, a double-headed axe, the emblem of his divine ancestors. The Greeks of later times said that the axe was that of their Heracles, which was wrested by him

from the Amazon Hippolyta, and given to Omphalê.[2] The king was the supreme head of the priesthood, as also of the vassal chiefs and of the army, but he had as a subordinate a "companion" who could replace him when occasion demanded,[3] and he was assisted in the exercise of his functions by the counsel of "Friends," and further still in extraordinary circumstances by the citizens of the capital assembled in the public square.

THE AXE BORNE BY ZEUS LABRAUNDOS.[4]

This intervention of the voice of the populace was a thing unknown in the East, and had probably been introduced in imitation of customs observed among the Greeks of Æolia or Ionia; it was an important political factor, and might possibly lead to an outbreak or a revolution. Outside the pale of Sardes and the province of Mæonia, the bulk of Lydian territory was distributed among a very numerous body of landowners, who were particularly proud of their noble descent. Many of these country magnates held extensive fiefs, and had in their pay small armies, which rendered them almost independent, and the only way for the sovereign to succeed in ruling them was to conciliate them at all hazards, and to keep them in perpetual enmity with their fellows. Two of these rival families vied with each other in their efforts to secure the royal favour; that of the Tylonidæ and that of the Mermnadæ, the principal domain of which latter lay at Teira, in the valley of the Cayster, though they had also other possessions at Dascylion, in Hellespontine Phrygia.[5] The head sometimes of one and sometimes of the other

---

[1] Cf. RADET, *La Lydie et le Monde Grec au temps des Mermnades*, pp. 57–60.

[2] PLUTARCH, *Quæst. Gr.*, § 45, Didot's ed., *Moralia*, vol. i. p. 371. Gelzer sees in the legend about the axe related by Plutarch, a reminiscence of a primitive gynocracy (*Das Zeitalter des Gyges*, in the *Rheinisches Museum*, 1880, vol. xxxv. pp. 517, 518). The axe is the emblem of the god of war, and, as such, belongs to the king: the coins of Mylasa exhibit it held by Zeus Labraundos (BARCLAY HEAD, *Historia Nummorum*, pp. 528, 529).

[3] GELZER, *op. cit.*, in *Rheinisches Museum*, 1880, vol. xxxv. pp. 526, 527, and RADET, *op. cit.*, pp. 88, 89.

[4] Drawn by Faucher-Gudin, from a coin in the Cabinet des médailles.

[5] GELZER, *op. cit.*, in the *Rheinisches Museum*, 1880, vol. xxxv. pp. 523, 524; the name of the Lydian appanage, written "Teira" on the coins, is spelt Tyrrha or Tyrrhos in literary sources (RADET, *La Lydie et le Monde Grec*, etc., p. 16, note 1).

family would fill that post of "companion" which placed all the resources of the kingdom at the disposal of the occupant.

The first of the Mermnadæ of whom we get a glimpse is Daskylos, son of Gyges, who about the year 740 was "companion" during the declining years of Ardys, over whom he exercised such influence that Adyattes, the heir to the throne, took umbrage at it, and caused him to be secretly assassinated, where-upon his widow, fearing for her own safety, hastily fled into Phrygia, of which district she was a native. On hearing of the crime, Ardys, trembling with anger, convoked the Assembly, and as his advanced age rendered walking difficult, he caused himself to be carried to the public square in a litter. Having reached the place, he laid the assassins under a curse, and gave permission to any who could find them to kill them; he then returned to his palace, where he died a few years later, about 730 B.C. Adyattes took the name of Meles on ascending the throne,[1] and at first reigned happily, but his father's curse weighed upon him, and before long began to take effect. Lydia having been laid waste by a famine, the oracle declared that, before appeasing the gods, the king must expiate the murder of the Mermnad noble, by making every atonement in his power, if need be by an exile of three years' duration. Meles submitted to the divine decree. He sought out the widow of his victim, and learning that during her flight she had given birth to a son, called, like his father, Daskylos, he sent to entreat the young man to repair immediately to Sardes, that he might make amends for the murder; the youth, however, alleged that he was as yet unborn at the hour of his father's death, and therefore not entitled to be a party to an arrangement which did not personally affect him, and refused to return to his own country. Having failed in this attempt, Meles entrusted the regency of his kingdom to Sadyattes, son of Kadys, one of the Tylonidæ, who probably had already filled the post of companion to the king for some time past, and set out for Babylon. When the three years had elapsed, Sadyattes faithfully handed over to him the reins of government and resumed the second place.[2] Myrsos succeeded Meles about 716,[3] and his accession immediately became the cause of uneasiness to the younger Daskylos, who felt that he was no longer safe from the intrigues of the Heraclidæ; he therefore quitted Phrygia

[1] GELZER, *Das Zeitalter des Gyges*, in the *Rheinisches Museum*, 1880, vol. xxxv. pp. 524, 525, and after him SCHUBERT, *Gesch. der Könige von Lydien*, pp. 22, 23, still distinguish this Adyattes or Alyattes from Meles; Radet seems to have shown clearly that Adyattes or Alyattes and Meles are two names of one and the same person, the first being the sacred and the second the family name (*La Lydie et le Monde Grec*, pp. 77, 78).

[2] NICOLAS OF DAMASCUS, *Fragm.* 49, in MÜLLER-DIDOT, *Fragm. Hist. Græc.*, vol. iii. pp. 382, 383, after Xanthus of Lydia.

[3] The lists of Eusebius give 36 years to Ardys, 14 years to Meles or Adyattes, 12 years to Myrsos, and 17 years to Candaules (*Chronicorum Libri duo*, ed. SCHŒNE, vol. i. cols. 67–69, and vol. ii. pp. 76–82); that is to say, if we place the accession of Gyges in 687, the dates of the reign of Candaules are 704–687, of that of Myrsos 716–704, of that of Meles 730–716, of that of Ardys I. 766–730. GELZER, *op. cit.*, in the *Rheinisches Museum*, 1880, vol. xxxv. pp. 524, 525, thinks that the double names each represent a different king; RADET, *op. cit.*, p. 79, adheres to the four generations of Eusebius.

and settled beyond the Halys among the White Syrians, one of whom he took in marriage, and had by her a son, whom he called Gyges, after his ancestor.[1] The Lydian chronicles which have come down to us make no mention of him, after the birth of this child, for nearly a quarter of a century. We know, however, from other sources, that the country in which he took refuge had for some time past been ravaged by enemies coming from the Caucasus, known to us as the Cimmerians.[2] Previous to this period these had been an almost mythical race in the eyes of the civilised races of the Oriental world. They imagined them as living in a perpetual mist on the confines of the universe: " Never does bright Helios look upon them with his rays, neither when he rises towards

A CONFLICT WITH TWO GRIFFINS.[4]

the starry heaven, nor when he turns back from heaven towards the earth, but a baleful night spreads itself over these miserable mortals."[3] Fabulous animals, such as griffins with lions' bodies, having the neck and ears of a fox, and the wings and beak of an eagle, wandered over their plains, and sometimes attacked them; the inhabitants were forced to defend themselves with axes, and did not always emerge victorious from these terrible conflicts. The few merchants who had ventured to penetrate into their country had returned from their travels with less fanciful notions concerning the nature of the regions frequented by them, but little continued to be known of them, until an unforeseen occurrence obliged them to quit their remote steppes. The Scythians, driven from the plains of the Iaxartes by an influx of the Massagetæ, were urged forwards in a westerly direction beyond the Volga and the Don, and so

[1] NICOLAS OF DAMASCUS, *Fragm.* 49, in MÜLLER-DIDOT, *Fragm. Hist. Græc.*, vol. iii. p. 383.

[2] I would gladly have treated at length the subject of the Cimmerians with its accompanying developments, but lack of space prevents me from doing more than summing up here the position I have taken. Most modern critics have rejected that part of the tradition preserved by Herodotus which refers to the itinerary of the Cimmerians, and have confused the Cimmerian invasion with that of the Thracian tribes. I think that there is reason to give weight to Herodotus' statement, and to distinguish carefully between two series of events: (1) a movement of peoples coming from Europe into Asia, by the routes that Herodotus indicates, about the latter half of the eighth century B.C., who would be more especially the Cimmerians; (2) a movement of peoples coming from Europe into Asia by the Thracian Bosphorus, and among whom there was perhaps, side by side with the Treres, a remnant of Cimmerian tribes who had been ousted by the Scythians. The two streams would have had their confluence in the heart of Asia Minor, in the first half of the seventh century.

[3] *Odyssey*, xi. 14–19. It is this passage which Ephorus applies to the Cimmerians of his own time who were established in the Crimea, and which accounts for his saying that they were a race of miners, living perpetually underground (EPHORUS, *Frag.* 45, in MÜLLER-DIDOT, *Frag. Hist. Græc.*, vol. i. p. 245).

[4] Drawn by Faucher-Gudin, from one of the reliefs on the crown of the Great Blinitza; cf. the *Comptes rendus de la Commission Impériale Archéologique*, 1865, pl. i. 3.

great was the terror inspired by the mere report of their approach, that the Cimmerians decided to quit their own territory. A tradition current in Asia three centuries later, told how their kings had counselled them to make a stand against the invaders; the people, however, having refused to listen to their advice, their rulers and those who were loyal to them fell by each other's hands, and their burial-place was still shown near the banks of the Tyras. Some of their tribes took refuge in the Chersonesus Taurica, but the greater number pushed forward beyond the Mæotic marshes; a body of Scythians followed in their track, and the united horde pressed onwards till they entered Asia Minor, keeping to the shores of the Black Sea.[1] This heterogeneous mass of people came into conflict first with Urartu; then turning obliquely in a south-easterly direction, their advance-guard fell upon the Mannai. But they were repulsed by Sargon's generals; the check thus administered

SCYTHIANS ARMED FOR WAR.[2]

forced them to fall back speedily upon other countries less vigorously defended. The Scythians, therefore, settled themselves in the eastern basin of the Araxes, on the frontiers of Urartu and the Mannai, where they formed themselves into a kind of marauding community, perpetually quarrelling with their neighbours.[3] The Cimmerians took their way westwards, and established themselves upon the upper waters of the Araxes, the Euphrates, the Halys, and the Thermodon,[4] greatly to the vexation of the rulers of Urartu.

---

[1] HERODOTUS, IV. xi., xii. The version of Aristæas of Proconnesus, as given by Herodotus (IV. xiii.) and by Damastes of Sigæa (MÜLLER-DIDOT, *Fragm. Hist. Græc.*, vol. ii. p. 65), attributes a more complex origin to this migration, *i.e.* that the Arimaspes had driven the Issedonians before them, and that the latter had in turn driven the Scythians back on the Cimmerians.

[2] Drawn by Faucher-Gudin, from the reliefs on the silver vase of Kul-Oba.

[3] Winckler (*Altorientalische Forschungen*, vol. i. pp. 187, 188) was the first to show that the Scythians of the tradition preserved by Herodotus must have been the Ashguzai or Ishkuzai of the cuneiform documents. The original name must have been Skuza, Shkuza, with a sound in the second syllable that the Greeks have rendered by *th*, Σκυθαί, and the Assyrians by *z*: the initial vowel has been added, according to a well-known rule, to facilitate the pronunciation of the combination SK, SHK. An oracle of the time of Esarhaddon shows that they occupied one of the districts really belonging to the Mannai (KNUDTZON, *Assyrische Gebete an den Sonnengott*, p. 130): and it is probably they who are mentioned in a passage of *Jer.* li. 27, where the traditional reading *Ashchenaz* should be replaced by that of Ashkuz (SAYCE, *The Cuneiform Inscriptions of Van*, in *J. R. As. Soc.*, vol. xiv. pp. 394, 678: cf. FR. LENORMANT, *Les Orig. de l'Hist.*, vol. iii. p. 229, note 6; FR. DELITZSCH, in *Libri Daniel, Ezra, Nehemiah*, ed. BÆR, 1882, p. ix.; KNUDTZON, *op. cit.*, p. 131; WINCKLER, *op. cit.*, vol. i. pp. 292, 491, note 2).

[4] It is doubtless to these events that the tradition preserved by Pompeius Trogus, which is known to us through his abbreviator Justin (ii. 4, § 1), or through the compilers of a later period (QROSIUS, i. 15; ÆTHICUS ISTER, v. 68), refers, concerning the two Scythian princes Ylinus and Scolopitus: they seem to have settled along the coast, on the banks of the Thermodon and in the district of Themiscyra.

They subsequently felt their way along the valleys of the Anti-Taurus, but finding them held by Assyrian troops, they turned their steps towards the country of the White Syrians, seized Sinôpê, where the Greeks had recently founded a colony,[1] and bore down upon Phrygia. It would appear that they were joined in these regions by other hordes from Thrace which had crossed the Bosphorus a few years earlier, and among whom the ancient historians particularly make mention of the Treres;[2] the results of the Scythian invasion had probably been felt by all the tribes on the banks of the Dnieper, and had been the means of forcing them in the direction of the Danube and the Balkans, whence they drove before them, as they went, the inhabitants of the Thracian peninsula across into Asia Minor. It was about the year 750 B.C. that the Cimmerians had been forced to quit their first home, and towards 720 that they came into contact with the empires of the East; the Treres had crossed the Bosphorus about 710, and the meeting of the two streams of immigration may be placed in the opening years of the seventh century.[3] The combined hordes did not at once attack Phrygia itself, but spread themselves along the coast, from the mouths of the Rhyndakos to those of Halys, constituting a sort of maritime confederation of which Heraclea and Sinôpê were the chief towns.[4] This confederation must not be regarded as a regularly constituted state, but rather as a vast encampment in which the warriors could leave their families and their spoil in safety; they issued from it nearly every year to spread themselves over the neighbouring provinces, sometimes in one direction, sometimes in another.[5] The ancient sanctuaries of Pteria and the treasures they contained excited their cupidity, but they were not well enough equipped to undertake the siege of a strongly fortified place, and for want of anything better were content to hold it to ransom. The bulk of the indigenous population lived even then in those subterranean dwellings so difficult of access, which are still used as habitations by the tribes on the banks of the Halys, and it is possible that they helped

[1] HERODOTUS, IV. xii.; SCYMNUS OF CHIOS, Orbis Descriptio, 941-952, in MÜLLER-DIDOT, Geographi Græci Minores, vol. i. p. 236.

[2] Strabo says decisively that the Treres were both Cimmerians (Τρήρων . . . Κιμμερικοῦ ἔθνους, XIV. i. § 40, p. 617) and Thracians (Τρῆρες, καὶ οὗτοι Θρᾷκες, XIII. i. § 8, p. 386); elsewhere he makes the Treres synonymous with the Cimmerians (Κιμμέριοι, οὓς καὶ Τρῆρας ὀνομάζουσι, I. iii. § 22, p. 61). The Treres were probably the predominating tribe among the people which had come into Asia on that side.

[3] Gelzer (Das Zeitalter des Gyges, in the Rheinisches Museum, 1875, vol. xxx. pp. 256-264) thinks that the invasion by the Bosphorus took place about 705, and Radet (La Lydie et le Monde Grec au temps des Mermnades, pp. 125, 145, 175) about 708; and their reckoning seems to me to be so likely to be correct, that I do not hesitate to place the arrival of the Treres in Asia about the time they have both indicated—roughly speaking, about 710 B.C.

[4] For Sinôpê, cf. what is said above, p. 344, note 1; Arrian, in a passage of his Bithynica, speaks of their dwelling beyond the Sangarios, in the country of the Mariandynians, where several of their bands had been poisoned by eating hemlock (Fragm. 47, in MÜLLER-DIDOT, Fragm. Hist. Græc., vol. iii. p. 595).

[5] The nature of their empire was defined very exactly by FRÉRET, Mémoire sur les Cimmériens, in the Mémoires de l'Académie des Inscriptions, 1745, vol. xix. p. 609; cf. FR. LENORMANT, Les Origines de l'Histoire, vol. ii. pp. 355, 356; RADET, La Lydie et le Monde Grec au temps des Mermnades, pp. 175, 176.

to swell the marauding troops of the new-comers. In the declining years of Sennacherib, it would appear that the Ninevite provinces possessed an irresistible attraction for these various peoples. The fame of the wealth accumulated in the regions beyond the Taurus and the Euphrates, in Syria and Mesopotamia, provoked their cupidity beyond all bounds, and the time was at hand when the fear alone of the Assyrian armies would no longer avail to hold them in check.

The last years of Sennacherib had been embittered by the intrigues which

INHABITED CAVES ON THE BANKS OF THE HALYS.[1]

usually gathered around a monarch enfeebled by age and incapable of bearing the cares of government with his former vigour. A fierce rivalry existed between those of his sons who aspired to the throne, each of whom possessed his following of partisans, both at court and among the people, who were ready to support him, if need be even with the sword. One of these princes, probably the eldest of the king's remaining sons,[2] named Assur-akhê-iddin, called by us Esarhaddon, had already been nominated his successor, and had received the official investiture of the Babylonian kingdom under the name of Assur-etilmu-kîn-pal.[3] The catastrophe of 689 had not resulted in bringing about the

---

[1] Drawn by Boudier, from a photograph courteously sent by ALFRED BOISSIER.

[2] The eldest was perhaps that Assur-nadin-shumu who reigned in Babylon, and who was taken prisoner to Elam by King Khalludush; cf. what is said of this prince in pp. 296, 303 of this volume.

[3] The idea of an enthronisation at Babylon in the lifetime of Sennacherib, put forward by the earlier Assyriologists, Ménant (*Annales des rois d'Assyrie*, p. 238), Budge (*The History of Esarhaddon*, p. 2), Pinches (*On Babylonian Art as illustrated by M. H. Rassam's Discoveries*, in the *Proceedings* of the Society of Biblical Archæology, 1883–1884, vol. vi. pp. 14, 15, and in the *Transactions*, vol. viii. pp. 353, 354), based on an inscription on a lion's head discovered at Babylon (cf. the drawing of this object at the heading of chap. vi., p. 535, *Dawn of Civilization*), has been adopted and confirmed by Winckler (*Studien und Beiträge zur Bab.-ass. Gesch.*, in *Zeit. für Assyriologie*,

ruin of Babylon, as Sennacherib and his ministers had hoped. The temples, it is true, had been desecrated and demolished, the palaces and public buildings razed to the ground, and the ramparts thrown down, but, in spite of the fact that the city had been set on fire by the conquerors, the quarters inhabited by the lower classes still remained standing, and those of the inhabitants who had escaped being carried away captive, together with such as had taken refuge in the surrounding country or had hidden themselves in neighbouring cities, had gradually returned to their desolated homes. They cleared the streets, repaired the damage inflicted during the siege, and before long the city, which was believed to be hopelessly destroyed, rose once more with the vigour, if not with the wealth, which it had enjoyed before its downfall. The mother of Esarhaddon was a Babylonian, by name Naki'a;[1] and as soon as her son came into possession of his inheritance, an impulse of filial piety moved him to restore to his mother's city its former rank of capital. Animated by the strong religious feeling which formed the groundwork of his character, Esarhaddon had begun his reign by restoring the sanctuaries which had been the cradle of the Assyrian religion, and his intentions, thus revealed at the very outset, had won for him the sympathy of the Babylonians;[2] this, indeed, was excited sooner than he expected, and perhaps helped to secure to him his throne. During his absence from Nineveh, a widespread plot had been formed in that city, and on the 20th day of Tebeth, 681, at the hour when Sennacherib was praying before the image of his god, two of his sons, Sharezer and Adarmalik (Adrammelech), assassinated their father at the foot of the altar.[3] One half of the army proclaimed Sharezer

---

vol. ii. pp. 306–308; *Untersuchungen zur Altorient. Gesch.*, p. 11, n. 1; *Gesch. Bab. und Ass.*, p. 133; *Altorient. Forschungen*, vol. i. p. 418, vol. ii. pp. 56, 57). It was doubtless on this occasion that Esarhaddon received as a present from his father the objects mentioned in the document which Sayce (*Will of Sennacherib King of Assyria*, in *Records of the Past*, 1st ser., vol. i. p. 136) and Budge (*History of Esarhaddon*, pp. 14, 15) have called, without sufficient reason, the *Will of Sennacherib* (WINCKLER, *Altorient. Forschungen*, vol. ii. pp. 55–57).

[1] WINCKLER, *Altorientalische Forschungen*, vol. ii. p. 189.

[2] Fragment S 1079, in the British Museum, quoted by Winckler (*op. cit.*, vol. ii. pp. 56, 57), seems to show clearly that the restoration of the temples was begun even in the lifetime of Sennacherib.

[3] We possess three different accounts of the murder of Sennacherib: 1. In the *Babylonian Chronicle of Pinches* (col. iii. ll. 34–36; cf. WINCKLER, *Babylonische Chronik B*, in SCHRADER, *Keilinschriftliche Bibliothek*, vol. ii. pp. 280–283). 2. In the Bible (2 *Kings* xix. 36, 37; cf. *Isa.* xxxvii. 37, 38; 2 *Chron.* xxxii. 21). 3. In Berosus (*Fragm.* 12, in MÜLLER-DIDOT, *Fragm. Hist. Græc.*, vol. ii. p. 504). The biblical account alone mentions both murderers; the *Chronicle* and Berosus speak of only one, and their testimony seems to prevail with several historians (HOMMEL, *Geschichte Babyloniens und Assyriens*, pp. 688, 689; WINCKLER, *Studien und Beiträge zur Babylonisch-assyrischen Geschichte*, in the *Zeitschrift für Assyriologie*, vol. ii. pp. 392–396, and *Altorientalische Forschungen*, vol. ii. p. 59). I believe that the silence of the *Chronicle* and of Berosus is explained by the fact that Sharezer was chief in the conspiracy, and the one among the sons who aspired to the kingdom: the second murderer merely acted for his brother, and consequently had no more right to be mentioned by name than those accomplices not of the blood-royal who shared in the murder. The name Sharezer is usually considered as an abbreviation of the Assyrian name Nergal-sharuzur (TIELE, *Babylonisch-assyrische Geschichte*, p. 325), or Assur-sharuzur (HOMMEL, *Gesch. Bab. und Ass.*, p. 688). Winckler now thinks that he sees in it a corruption of Sharitir, abbreviated from Sharitir-assur, which he finds as a royal name on a fragment in the British Museum; he proposes to recognise in this Sharitir-assur, Sharezer enthroned after his father's death (*Altorientalische Forschungen*, vol. ii. pp. 58, 59; cf. pp. 6–8).

king; the northern provinces espoused his cause; and Esarhaddon must for the moment have lost all hope of the succession. His father's tragic fate overwhelmed him with fear and grief; he rent his clothes, groaned and lamented like a lion roaring, and could be comforted only by the oracles pronounced by the priests of Babylon. An assurance that the gods favoured his cause reached him even from Assyria, and Nineveh, after a few weeks of vacillation, acknowledged him as its sovereign, the rebellion being mercilessly crushed on the 2nd of Adar.[1] Although this was a considerable advantage to Esarhaddon's cause, it could not be considered as decisive, since the provinces of the Euphrates still declared for Sharezer; the gods, therefore, once more intervened. Ishtar of Arbela had long been considered as the recognised patroness and oracle of the dynasty. Whether it were a question of a foreign expedition or a rebellion at home, of a threatened plague or invasion, of a marriage or an alliance with some powerful neighbour, the ruling sovereign would invariably have recourse to her, always with the same formula, to demand counsel of her for the conduct of affairs in hand, and the replies which she vouchsafed in various ways were taken into consideration; her will, as expressed by the mouth of her ministers, would hasten, suspend, or modify the decisions of the king. Esarhaddon did not neglect to consult the goddess, as well as Assur and Sin, Shamash, Bel, Nebo, and Nergal; and their words, transcribed upon a tablet of clay, induced him to act without further delay: "Go, do not hesitate, for we march with thee and we will cast down thine enemies!" Thus encouraged, he made straight for the scene of danger without passing through Nineveh, so as to prevent Sharezer and his party having time to recover. His biographers depict Esarhaddon hurrying forward, often a day or more in advance of his battalions, without once turning to see who followed him, and without waiting to allow the horses of his baggage-waggons to be unharnessed or permitting his servants to pitch his tent; he rested merely for a few moments on the bare ground, indifferent to the cold and nocturnal frosts of the month of Sebat. It would appear as if Sharezer had placed his hopes on the Cimmerians, and had expected their chiefs to come to the rescue. This hypothesis seems borne out by the fact that the decisive battle took place beyond the Euphrates and the Taurus, in the country of Khanigalbat. Esar-

---

[1] The broken Cylinder of Esarhaddon, col. i. ll. 1–26: cf. BUDGE, *The History of Esarhaddon*, pp. 20–23; WINCKLER, *Die Inschrift des (zerbrochenen) Prismas B*, in SCHRADER, *Keilinschriftliche Bibliothek*, vol. ii. pp. 140–143. The Bible alone tells us that Sharezer retired to Urartu (2 *Kings* xix. 37). To explain the plan of this campaign, it is usually supposed that at the time of his father's death Esarhaddon was either beyond Mount Taurus or else on the Armenian frontier (TIELE, *Babylonisch-assyrische Geschichte*, pp. 309, 324, 325, 344, 345; HOMMEL, *Geschichte Babyloniens und Assyriens*, p. 689); the sequence of the dates in the *Babylonian Chronicle of Pinches*, col. iii. ll. 34–38, compels me to revert to the opinion, as Winckler has already done (*Untersuchungen zur Altorientalischen Geschichte*, p. 10, note 1; *Geschichte Babyloniens und Assyriens*, pp. 258, 259), that Esarhaddon marched from Babylon against the rebels, and pursued them as far as Mount Taurus, and beyond it to Khanigalbat (BUDGE, *The History of Esarhaddon*, p. 3).

haddon attributed his success to Ishtar, the goddess of bravery and of combat; she alone had broken the weapons of the rebels, she alone had brought confusion into their lines, and had inclined the hearts of the survivors to submit. They cried aloud, "This is our king!" and Sharezer thereupon fled into Armenia.[1] The war had been brought to a close with such rapidity that even the most unsettled of the Assyrian subjects and vassals had not had time to take advantage of it for their own purposes; the Kaldâ on the Persian Gulf, and the Sidonians on the Mediterranean, were the only two peoples who had openly revolted, and were preparing to enter on a struggle to preserve their independence thus once more regained. Yet the events of the preceding months had shaken the power of Nineveh more seriously than we should at first suppose. For the first time since the accession of Tiglath-pileser III. the almost inevitable troubles which accompany the change of a sovereign had led to an open war. The vast army of Sargon and Sennacherib had been split up, and the two factions into which it was divided, commanded as they were by able generals and composed of troops accustomed to conquer, must have suffered more keenly in an engagement with each other than in the course of an ordinary campaign against a common enemy. One part at least of the military staff had become disorganised; regiments had been decimated, and considerable contingents were required to fill the vacancies in the ranks. The male population of Assyria, suddenly called on to furnish the necessary effective force, could not supply the demand without drawing too great a proportion of men from the country; and one of those crises of exhaustion was imminent which come upon a nation after an undue strain, often causing its downfall in the midst of its success, and yielding it an easy prey to the wiles of its adversaries.[2]

[1] *Babylonian Chronicle of Pinches*, col. iii. l. 38; cf. SCHRADER, *Keilinschriftliche Bibliothek*, vol. ii. pp. 282, 283, and KNUDTZON, *Assyrische Gebete an den Sonnengott*, p. 69, note 2, where the correction of the 18th (?) of Adar for the 18th of Sivan is pointed out for the passage in the *Chronicle of Pinches*. The date of the accession of Esarhaddon was fixed in various ways by the Assyrians: some, reckoning the reign from the death of Sennacherib, made it begin under the *eponymous* year of Nabu-akh-ishshish (*Canon I., col. V.*, in SCHRADER, *Keilinschriftliche Bibliothek*, vol. i. p. 207), that is in 681; others, dating it from the day of the coronation, made it commence in the *eponymous* year of Dananu (*Tablet K 76*, in the *British Museum*, in G. SMITH, *The Assyrian Eponym Canon*, p. 92).

[2] The information we possess concerning Esarhaddon is gathered from: 1. *The Inscription of Cylinders A, B, C*, the second of the three better known as the *Broken Cylinder*. They have been published by LAYARD, *Inscriptions in the Cuneiform Character*, pls. 20–29, 54–58; by H. RAWLINSON, *Cun. Ins. W. As.*, vol. i. pls. 45–47, and vol. iii. pls. 15, 16; by ABEL and WINCKLER, *Keilschrifttexte*, pls. 25, 26; then translated into French by OPPERT, *Les Inscriptions des Sargonides*, pp. 53–60, and by MÉNANT, *Annales des Rois d'Assyrie*, pp. 240–247; into English at various times by FOX TALBOT, *Inscription of Esarhaddon* and *The Second Inscription*, in *Records of the Past*, 1st ser., vol. iii. pp. 102–124; then by R. F. HARPER, *Cylinder A of the Esarhaddon Inscriptions, transliterated and translated, with Textual Notes, from the Original Copy in the British Museum;* into German, Cylinders A–C by L. ABEL, *Die Inschrift der Prismen A und C*, and by WINCKLER, *Die Inschrift des (zerbrochenen) Prismas B*, in SCHRADER, *Keilinschriftliche Bibliothek*, vol. ii. pp. 124–151. These texts contain a summary of the king's wars, in which the subject-matter is arranged geographically, not chronologically: they cease with the *eponymy* of Akhazilu, *i.e.* the year 673. 2. Some mutilated fragments of the *Annals*, published and translated for the first time by BOSCAWEN, *Historical Inscription of Esarhaddon*, in the *Transactions* of the Society of Biblical Archæology, vol. iv. pp. 84–97. 3. *The Black Stone of Aberdeen*, on which

Esarhaddon was personally inclined for peace, and as soon as he was established on the throne he gave orders that the building works, which had been suspended during the late troubles, should be resumed and actively pushed forward;[1] but the unfortunate disturbances of the times did not permit of his pursuing his favourite occupation without interruption, and, like those of his warlike predecessors, his life was passed almost entirely on the field of battle. Babylon, grateful for what he had done for her, tendered him an unbroken fidelity throughout the stormy episodes of his reign, and showed her devotion to him by an unwavering obedience. The Kaldâ received no support from that quarter, and were obliged to bear the whole burden of the war which they had provoked. Their chief, Nabu-zîru-kînish-lîshir, who had been placed over them by Sennacherib, now harassed the cities of Karduniash, and Ningal-shumiddin, the prefect of Uru, demanded immediate help from Assyria. Esarhaddon at once despatched such a considerable force that the Kaldu chief did not venture to meet it in the open field, and after a few unimportant skirmishes he gave up the struggle, and took refuge in Elam. Khumbân-khaldash had died there in 680, a few months before the murder of Sennacherib, and his son, a second Khumbân-khaldash, had succeeded him;[2] this prince appears either to have shared the peaceful tastes of his brother-king of Assyria, or more probably did not feel himself sufficiently secure of his throne to risk the chance of coming into collision with his neighbour. He caused Nabu-zîru-kînish-lîshir to be slain, and Nâîd-marduk, the other son of Merodach-baladan, who had shared his brother's flight, was so terrified at his

the account of the rebuilding of Babylon is given, and which was published by H. RAWLINSON, *Cun. Ins. W. As.*, vol. i. pls. 49, 50, and translated into French by OPPERT, *Expédition de Mésopotamie*, vol. i. p. 180, et seq., and again by MÉNANT, *Annales des Rois d'Assyrie*, p. 248, and *Babylone et la Chaldée*, pp. 167, 168; into German by WINCKLER, *Inschrift des sogenannten schwarzen Steins*, in SCHRADER, *Keilinschriftliche Bibliothek*, vol. ii. pp. 120–125. 4. *The Stele of Zindjirli*, published by VON LUSCHAN, *Ausgrabungen in Sendschirli*, vol. i. pp. 11–29, and pls. i.–iv., translated into German with a commentary by SCHRADER, *Inschrift Asarhaddon's*, in the same work, pp. 29–43. 5. The consultations of the god Shamash by Esarhaddon in different circumstances of his reign, collected by J. A. KNUDTZON, *Assyrische Gebete an den Sonnengott für Staat und Königliches Haus aus der Zeit Asarhaddons und Assurbanipals*, vol. ii. pp. 72–264. 6. A considerable number of small inscriptions, some of which are enumerated and described in BEZOLD, *Kurzgefasster Ueberblick über die Babylonisch-assyrische Litteratur*, pp. 106, 107, and some tablets published in various places which I will mention if necessary when I have occasion to use them. The classification of the events of this reign presents serious difficulties, which have been partly overcome by passages in the *Babylonian Chronicle of Pinches* (col. iii. ll. 28–48, col. iv. ll. 1–32); cf. TIELE, *Babylonisch-assyrische Geschichte*, pp. 341–351, in which most of the proposed (chronological) arrangements have been permanently accepted. The principal monuments of the reign have been classified, transcribed, translated, and commented on by BUDGE, *The History of Esarhaddon, son of Sennacherib, King of Assyria, B.C. 681–668*, 1880; this work, though antiquated by reason of new discoveries, is still useful for reference. The texts relating to the buildings have been collected and translated, with comments by MEISSNER and ROST, *Die Bauinschriften Asarhaddons*, in the *Beiträge zur Assyriologie*, vol. iii. pp. 189–362.

[1] For the date of the decree for the rebuilding of Babylon, cf. MEISSNER and ROST, *Die Bauinschriften Asarhaddons*, in the *Beiträge zur Assyriologie*, vol. iii. pp. 277, 278.

[2] *Babylonian Chronicle of Pinches*, col. iii. ll. 30–33; cf. WINCKLER, *Babylonische Chronik B*, in SCHRADER, *Keilinschriftliche Bibliothek*, vol. ii. pp. 280, 281.

murder that he at once sought refuge in Nineveh; he was reinstated in his paternal domain on condition of paying a tribute, and, faithful to his oath of allegiance, he thenceforward came yearly in person to bring his dues and pay homage to his sovereign (679).[1] The Kaldâ rising had, in short, been little more than a skirmish, and the chastisement of the Sidonians would have involved neither time nor trouble, had not the desultory movements of the barbarians obliged the Assyrians to concentrate their troops on several points which were threatened on their northern frontier. The Cimmerians and the Scythians had not suffered themselves to be disconcerted by the rapidity with which the fate of Sharezer had been decided, and after a moment's hesitation they had again set out in various directions on their work of conquest, believing, no doubt, that they would meet with a less vigorous resistance after so serious an upheaval at Nineveh. The Cimmerians appear to have been the first to have provoked hostilities; [2] their king Tiushpa,[3] who ruled over their territory on the Black Sea, ejected the Assyrian garrisons placed on the Cappadocian frontier, and his presence in that quarter aroused all the insubordinate elements still remaining in the Cilician valleys. Esarhaddon brought him to a stand on the confines of the plain of Saros, defeated him in Khubushna,[4] and drove the remains of the horde back across the Halys.[5] Having thus averted the Cimmerian

[1] The date and the plan of the campaign are given by the *Babylonian Chronicle of Pinches*, col. iii. ll. 39–42; the details are taken from the *Broken Cylinder*, col. ii. ll. 1–26 (WINCKLER, *Die Inschrift des zerbrochenen Prismas B*, in SCHRADER, *Keilinschriftliche Bibliothek*, vol. ii. pp. 142–145, completed by the document published in WINCKLER, *Altorientalische Forschungen*, vol. i. pp. 522, 523), and from *Cylinders A–C*, col. ii. ll. 32–41; cf. BUDGE, *The History of Esarhaddon*, pp. 26–31.

[2] The campaign against the Cimmerians is usually placed in 679–678 (HOMMEL, *Geschichte Babyloniens und Assyriens*, p. 721; WINCKLER, *Untersuchungen zur Altorientalischen Geschichte*, p. 120; ROST, *Untersuchungen zur Altorientalischen Geschichte*, p. 87), in accordance with the mutilated passage in the *Babylonian Chronicle of Pinches*, col. iii. l. 58, col. iv. ll. 1–2, where Winckler has restored the reading Gimirri (*Studien und Beiträge*, in *Zeit. für Assyr.*, vol. ii. p. 305); Knudtzon alone has cast doubts on the legitimacy of this rendering (*Assyrische Gebete an den Sonnengott*, p. 69).

[3] The name Teushpa, Tiushpa, has all along been compared with that of Teispes, in Old Persian Chaîshpis; cf. JUSTI, *Iranisches Namenbuch*, p. 152.

[4] Several Assyriologists have thought that Khubushna might be an error for Khubushkhia, and have sought the seat of war on the eastern frontier of Assyria (TIELE, *Babylonisch-assyrische Geschichte*, p. 334, note 4; HOMMEL, *Geschichte Babyloniens und Assyriens*, p. 721): in reality the context shows that the place under discussion is a district in Asia Minor, identified with Kamisene by Gelzer (*Kappadokien und seine Bewohner*, in the *Zeitschrift*, 1875, p. 17, note 2), but left unidentified by most authorities (SCHRADER, *Keilinschriften und Geschichtsforschung*, p. 520; FR. LENORMANT, *Les Origines de l'Histoire*, vol. ii. p. 341; HALÉVY, *Recherches Bibliques*, pp. 329, 330; ED. MEYER, *Geschichte des Alterthums*, vol. i. p. 546; WINCKLER, *Geschichte Babyloniens und Assyriens*, p. 268). Jensen has shown that the name is met with as early as the inscriptions of Tiglath-pileser III. (*Annals*, l. 154), where we should read Khubishna, and he places the country in Northern Syria, or perhaps further north in the western part of Taurus (*Hittiter und Armenier*, pp. 115, 116). The determinative proves that there was a town of this name as well as a district, and this consideration encourages me to recognise in Khubushna or Khubishna the town of Kabissos-Kabessos, the Sis of the kingdom of Lesser Armenia (RAMSAY, *The Historical Geography of Asia Minor*, pp. 386, 451).

[5] *Cylinders A, C*, col. ii. ll. 6–9, and the *Broken Cylinder*, col. iii. ll. 1–2; cf. SCHRADER, *Keilinschriftliche Bibliothek*, vol. ii. pp. 128, 129, 144, 145, and WINCKLER, *Altorient. Forschungen*, vol. i. p. 523. Rost (*Untersuchungen zur Altorientalischen Geschichte*, p. 90) puts the campaign against Tiushpa after the Scythian attack, which will be treated on pp. 353, 354 of the present work.

danger, he was able, without much difficulty, to bring the rebels of the western provinces into subjection.[1] His troops thrust back the Cilicians and Duha into the rugged fastnesses of the Taurus, and razed to the ground one and twenty of their strongholds, besides burning numberless villages and carrying the inhabitants away captive.[2] The people of Parnaki, in the bend of the Euphrates between Tel-Assur and the sources of the Balîkh, had taken up arms on hearing of the brief successes of Tiushpa, but were pitilessly crushed by Esarhaddon.[3] The sheikh of Arzani, in the extreme south of Syria, close to the brook of Egypt, had made depredations on the Assyrian frontier, but he was seized by the nearest governor and sent in chains to Nineveh. A cage was built for him at the gate of the city, and he was exposed in it to the jeers of the populace, in company with the bears, dogs, and boars which the Ninevites were in the habit of keeping confined there.[4] It would appear that Esarhaddon set himself to come to a final reckoning with Sidon and Phœnicia, the revolt of which had irritated him all the more, in that it showed an inexcusable ingratitude towards his family. For it was Sennacherib who, in order to break the power of Elulai, had not only rescued Sidon from the dominion of Tyre, but had enriched it with the spoils taken from its former rulers, and had raised it to the first rank among the Phœnician cities.[5] Ethbaal in his lifetime had never been wanting in gratitude, but his successor, Abdimilkôt, forgetful of recent services, had chafed at the burden of a foreign yoke, and had recklessly thrown it off as soon as an occasion presented itself. He had thought to strengthen himself by securing the help of a certain Sanduarri, who possessed the two fortresses of Kundu and Sîzu, in the Cilician mountains;[6] but neither this alliance nor the insular position of his capital

---

[1] These expeditions are not dated in any of the documents that deal with them: the fact that they are mentioned along with the war against Tiushpa and Sidon makes me inclined to consider them as being a result of the Cimmerian invasion. They were, strictly speaking, the quelling of revolts caused by the presence of the Cimmerians in that part of the empire.

[2] *Cylinders A, C*, col. ii. ll. 10–21, and *Inscription of the Broken Cylinder*, col. iii. ll. 3–12; cf. SCHRADER, *Keilinschriftliche Bibliothek*, vol. ii. pp. 128, 129, 144, 145, and BUDGE, *The History of Esarhaddon*, pp. 42–45. The Duua or Duha of this campaign, who are designated as neighbours of the Tabal, lived in the Anti-taurus: the name of the town, Tyana, *Tuana*, is possibly composed of their name and of the suffix -*na*, which is met with in Asianic languages (KRETSCHMER, *Einleitung in die Geschichte der Griechischen Sprache*, p. 319).

[3] *Cylinders A, C*, col. ii. ll. 22–25, and *Inscription of the Broken Cylinder*, col. iii. ll. 13–15; cf. SCHRADER, *Keilinschriftliche Bibliothek*, vol. ii. pp. 128, 129, 144, 145, and BUDGE, *The History of Esarhaddon*, pp. 44, 45. On the probable situation of Barnaki or Parnaki,—Lenormant at first read *Masnaki* and identified it with the Mossynœkæ (*Lettres Assyriologiques*, vol. i. p. 77),—cf. WINCKLER, *Bericht über die Thontafeln von Tell-el-Amarna*, pp. 15, 16, and *Gesch. Bab. und Ass.*, pp. 269, 334–336.

[4] *Cylinders A, C*, col. i. ll. 55, 56, col. ii. ll. 1–5; cf. BUDGE, *The History of Esarhaddon*, pp. 40–43, and SCHRADER, *Keil. Bibl.*, vol. ii. pp. 126–129. For the site of Arzani and the river of Musri, cf. WINCKLER, *Altorientalische Forschungen*, vol. i. pp. 35, 338, 527, 528, and *Musri, Meluhha, Main*, i. p. 11.

[5] On this subject cf. above, pp. 287, 288 of the present volume.

[6] Some Assyriologists have proposed to locate these two towns in Cilicia (DELATTRE, *L'Asie Occidentale dans les inscriptions assyriennes*, pp. 80, 81; WINCKLER, *Geschichte Babyloniens und Assyriens*, p. 67); others place them in the Lebanon, Kundi being identified with the modern village of Ain-Kundiya (FR. DELITZSCH, *Wo lag das Paradies?* p. 283; TIELE, *Babylonisch-assyrische Geschichte*,

was able to safeguard him, when once the necessity for stemming the tide of the Cimmerian influx was over, and the whole of the Assyrian force was free to be brought against him. Abdimilkôt attempted to escape by sea before the last attack, but he was certainly taken prisoner, though the circumstances are unrecorded, and Sanduarri fell into the enemy's hands a short time after. The suppression of the rebellion was as vindictive as the ingratitude which prompted it was heinous. Sidon was given up to the soldiery and then burnt, while opposite to the ruins of the island city the Assyrians built a fortress on the mainland, which they called Kar-Esarhaddon.[1] The other princes of Phœnicia and Syria were hastily convoked, and were witnesses of the vengeance wreaked on the city, as well as of the installation of the governor to whom the new province was entrusted. They could thus see what fate awaited them in the event of their showing any disposition to rebel, and the majority of them were not slow to profit by the lesson. The spoil was carried back in triumph to Nineveh, and comprised, besides the two kings and their families, the remains of their court and people, and the countless riches which the commerce of the world had brought into the great ports of the Mediterranean—ebony, ivory, gold and silver, purple, precious woods, household furniture, and objects of value from all parts in such quantities that it was long before the treasury at Nineveh needed any replenishing.[2]

The reverses of the Cimmerians did not serve as a warning to the Scythians. Settled on the borders of Manna, partly, no doubt, on the territory formerly dependent on that state,[3] they secretly incited the inhabitants to revolt, and to join in the raids which they made on the valley of the Upper Zab, and they would even have urged their horses up to the very walls of Nineveh had the occasion presented itself. Esarhaddon, warned of their intrigues by the spies which he sent among them, could not bring himself either to anticipate their attack or to assume the offensive, but anxiously consulted the gods with

---

pp. 345, 346, with certain reservations). The name of Kundu so nearly recalls that of Kuinda, the ancient fort mentioned by Strabo (XIV. v. § 10, p. 671), to the north of Anchialê, between Tarsus and Anazarbus, that I do not hesitate to identify them, and to place Kundu in Cilicia.

[1] On the site of Kar-Esarhaddon, cf. the researches of WINCKLER, *Alttestamentalische Forschungen*, pp. 111–113, and *Altorientalische Forschungen*, vol. i. pp. 440, 441, 551–553. The town is mentioned in tablet *K 2711* in the British Museum, published by MEISSNER and ROST, *Die Bauinschriften Asarhaddons*, in the *Beiträge zur Assyriologie*, vol. iii. pp. 264, 265, l. 20.

[2] *Cylinders A, C*, col. i. ll. 10–54, and *Inscription of the Broken Cylinder*, col. i. ll. 27–30: cf. BUDGE, *The History of Esarhaddon*, pp. 32–41; SCHRADER, *Keilinschriftliche Bibliothek*, vol. ii. pp. 124–127, 144, 145. The importance of the event and the amount of the spoil captured are apparent, if we notice that Esarhaddon does not usually record the booty taken after each campaign; he does so only when the number of objects and of prisoners taken from the enemy is extraordinary. The *Babylonian Chronicle of Pinches*, col. iv. ll. 1–8, places the capture of Sidon in the second, and the death of Abdimilkôt in the fifth year of his reign. Hence Winckler has concluded that Abdimilkôt held out for fully two years after the loss of Sidon. The general tenor of the account, as given by the inscriptions, seems to me to be that the capture of the king followed closely on the fall of the town: Abdimilkôt and Sanduarri probably spent the years between 679 and 676 in prison.

[3] One of the oracles of Shamash speaks of the captives as dwelling in a canton of the Mannai (KNUDTZON, *Assyrische Gebete an den Sonnengott*, p. 130).

regard to them : "O Shamash," he wrote to the Sun-god, "great lord, thou whom I question, answer me in sincerity ! From this day forth, the 22nd day of this month of Simanu, until the 21st day of the month of Duzu of this year, during these thirty days and thirty nights, a time has been foreordained favourable to the work of prophecy. In this time thus foreordained, the hordes of the Scythians who inhabit a district of the Mannai, and who have crossed the Mannian frontier,—will they succeed in their undertaking ? Will they emerge from the passes of Khubushkia at the towns of Kharrânia and Anîsuskia ; will they ravage the borders of Assyria and steal great booty, immense spoil ? that doth thy high divinity know. Is it a decree, and in the mouth of thy high divinity, O Shamash, great lord, ordained and promulgated ? He who sees, shall he see it ; he who hears, shall he hear it ? "[1] The god comforted his faithful servant, but there was a brief delay before his answer threw light on the future, and the king's questions were constantly renewed as fresh couriers brought in further information. In 678 B.C. the Scythians determined to try their fortune, and their king, Ishpakai,[2] took the field, followed by the Mannai. He was defeated and driven back to the north of Lake Urumiah, the Mannai were reduced to subjection, and Assyria once more breathed freely.[3] The victory, however, was not a final one, and affairs soon assumed as threatening an aspect as before. The Scythian tribes came on the scene, one after another, and allied themselves to the various peoples subject either directly or indirectly to Nineveh.[4] On one occasion it was Kashtariti, the regent of Karkashshi,[5] who wrote to Mamitiarshu, one of the Median princes, to induce him to make common cause with himself

---

[1] KNUDTZON, *Assyrische Gebete an den Sonnengott*, pp. 129–132. The town of Anîsuskia is not mentioned elsewhere, but Kharrânia is met with in the account of the thirty-first campaign of Shalmaneser III. (*Obelisk*, l. 181) with Kharrâna as its variant.

[2] This king's name seems to be of Iranian origin. Justi (*Iranisches Namenbuch*, pp. 46, 143) has connected it with the name Aspakos, which is read in a Greek inscription of the Cimmerian Bosphorus (LATYSCHEF, *Inscriptiones antiquæ oris septentrionalis Ponti Euxini*, vol. ii. p. 264); both forms have been connected with the Sanskrit *Açvaka*. I question whether we should not rather see in it a derivative of the Median Σπάκα, *dog*, as in the female name Spakô (HERODOTUS, I. cx.).

[3] *Cylinders A, C*, col. ii. ll. 27–31, and *Inscription du Prisme brisé*, col. iii. ll. 16–18, in SCHRADER, *Keilinschriftliche Bibliothek*, vol. ii. pp. 128, 129, 146, 147; for the explanation of these events, see WINCKLER, *Altorientalische Forschungen*, vol. i. pp. 486, 487.

[4] This subdivision of the horde into several bodies seems to be indicated, as Winckler has observed (*Altorientalische Forschungen*, vol. i. p. 487), by the number of different royal names among the Scythians which are mentioned in the Assyrian documents.

[5] Karkashshi had been identified with Karkathiokertha or Karkasiokertha in Armenia, by Halévy (*Journal Asiatique*, vol. xv. 1880, pp. 530, 531), who later on withdrew this interpretation (*Recherches Bibliques*, pp. 324, 325): the site is unknown, but the list of Median princes subdued by Sargon (WINCKLER, *Die Keilschrifttextte Sargons*, vol. ii. pl. 44 B) shows that it was situated in Media. Kishshashshu is very probably the same as Kishisim or Kishisu, the town which Sargon subdued, and which he called Kar-nergal or Kar-ninib (*Inscription des Fastes*, ll. 59, 60, *Inscription of the Pavement of the Gates*, iv. l. 16; *Stele of Larnaka*, col. i. l. 30; cf. WINCKLER, *Die Keilschrifttexte Sargons*, vol. i. pp. 108, 109, 146, 147, 176, 177), and which is mentioned in the neighbourhood of Parsuash, Karalla, Kharkhar, Media, and Ellipi (cf. the illustration above, p. 241 of the present work). I think that it would be in the basin of the Gavê—Rud ; Billerbeck places it at the ruins of Siama, in the upper valley of the Lesser Zab (*Das Sandschak Suleimania*, pp. 97, 98).

in attacking the fortress of Kishshashshu on the eastern border of the empire.[1] At another time we find the same chief plotting with the Mannai and the Saparda to raid the town of Kilmân, and Esarhaddon implores the god to show him how the place may be saved from their machinations.[2] He opens negotiations in order to gain time, but the barbarity of his adversary is such that he fears for his envoy's safety, and speculates whether he may not have been put to death.[3] The situation would indeed have become critical if Kashtariti had succeeded in bringing against Assyria a combined force of Medes, Scythians, Mannai, and Cimmerians, together with Urartu and its king, Rusas III.; but, fortunately, petty hatreds made the combination of these various elements an impossibility, and they were unable to arrive at even a temporary understanding. The Scythians themselves were not united as to the best course to be pursued, and while some endeavoured to show their hostility by every imaginable outrage and annoyance, others, on the contrary, desired to enter into friendly relations with Assyria. Esarhaddon received on one occasion an embassy from Bar-tatua,[4] one of their kings, who humbly begged the hand of a lady of the blood-royal, swearing to make a lasting friendship with him if Esarhaddon would consent to the marriage. It was hard for a child brought up in the harem, amid the luxury and comfort of a civilised court, to be handed over to a semi-barbarous spouse; but state policy even in those days was exacting, and more than one princess of the line of Sargon had thus sacrificed herself by an alliance which was to the interest of her own people.[5] What troubled Esarhaddon was

---

[1] *Prayers Nos. 1, 2*, in KNUDTZON, *Assyrische Gebete an den Sonnengott*, pp. 72–82. These tablets, the first of the series to be made known, were attributed by Sayce (*Babylonian Literature*, pp. 20, 79, et seq.) and by Boscawen (*Babylonian dated Tablets and the Canon of Ptolemy*, in the *Transactions* of the Society of Biblical Archæology, vol. vi. pp. 21, 22, 107, 108) to a second Esarhaddon, who would have reigned after Assur-bani-pal: Kashtariti would have been none other than Cyaxares, the destroyer of the Assyrian empire. This opinion was adopted and for a long while maintained by many Assyriologists and historians (SCHRADER, *Keilinschriften und Geschichtsforschung*, pp. 518–521; FR. LENORMANT, *Les Origines de l'Histoire*, vol. ii. pp. 350–355; HALÉVY, *Recherches Bibliques*, pp. 319–325, 334, 343), but was rejected by many others (FR. DELITZSCH, *Wo lag das Paradies?* p. 245; ED. MEYER, *Geschichte des Alterthums*, vol. i. pp. 463, 464; TIELE, *Babylonisch-assyrische Geschichte*, pp. 334, 335; HOMMEL, *Geschichte Babyloniens und Assyriens*, pp. 721–724), and is now finally set aside, and the latest authors agree in seeing in the Esarhaddon of these tablets Esarhaddon, son of Sennacherib (KNUDTZON, *Assyrische Gebete an den Sonnengott*, pp. 67–71; WINCKLER, *Untersuchungen zur Altorientalischen Geschichte*, p. 120, and *Altorientalische Forschungen*, vol. i. p. 486, et seq.; ROST, *Untersuchungen zur Altorientalischen Geschichte*, p. 87, et seq.).

[2] *Prayer No. 11*, in KNUDTZON, *Assyrische Gebete an den Sonnengott*, pp. 92–96. The people of Saparda, called by the Persians Sparda, have been with good reason identified by Fr. Lenormant (*Lettres Assyriologiques*, vol. i. pp. 46, 47; *Les Origines de l'Histoire*, vol. ii. pp. 352, 353), and after him by Schrader (*Keilinschriften und Geschichtsforschung*, pp. 116–119; *Die Keilinschriften und das Alte Testament*, 1883, pp. 445–447), with the Sepharad of the prophet Obadiah (ver. 20): the Assyrian texts show that this country should be placed in the neighbourhood of the Mannai and of the Medes.

[3] *Prayers Nos. 9, 10*, in KNUDTZON, *Assyrische Gebete an den Sonnengott*, pp. 90–92.

[4] Bartatua is, according to Winckler's ingenious observation, the Protothyes of Herodotus (I. ciii.), the father of Madyes, with whom we shall deal below, pp. 472, 480 of this volume. [The name should more probably be read Masta-tua.—ED.]

[5] Sargon had in like manner given one of his daughters in marriage to Ambaris, King of Tabal, in order to attach him to the Assyrian cause (*Annals*, l. 172; *Fastes*, l. 30; cf. WINCKLER, *Die Keilschrifttexte Sargons*, vol. i. pp. 30, 31, 102, 103), but without permanent success; cf. *supra*, p. 251.

not the thought of sacrificing a sister or a daughter, but a misgiving that the sacrifice would not produce the desired result, and in his difficulty he once more had recourse to Shamash. " If Esarhaddon, King of Assyria, grants a daughter of the blood (royal) to Bartatua, the King of the Iskuza, who has sent an embassy to him to ask a wife, will Bartatua, King of the Iskuza, act loyally towards Esarhaddon, King of Assyria? will he honestly and faithfully enter into friendly engagements with Esarhaddon, King of Assyria? will he observe the conditions (made by) Esarhaddon, King of Assyria? will he fulfil them punctually? that thy high divinity knoweth. His promises, in a decree and in the mouth of thy high divinity, O Shamash, great lord, are they decreed, promulgated?"[1] It is not recorded what came of these negotiations, nor whether the god granted the hand of the princess to her barbarian suitor. All we know is, that the incursions and intrigues of the Scythians continued to be a perpetual source of trouble to the Medes, and roused them either to rebel against Assyria or to claim the protection of its sovereign. Esarhaddon, in the course of his reign, was more than once compelled to interfere in order to ensure peace and quietness to the provinces on the table-land of Iran, which Sargon had conquered and which Sennacherib had retained.[2] He had first to carry his arms to the extreme edge of the desert, into the rugged country of Patusharra, lying at the foot of Demavend, rich in lapis-lazuli, and as yet untrodden by any king of Assyria.[3] Having reached his destination, he captured two petty kings, Eparna and Shîtirparna,[4] and exiled them to Assyria, together with their people, their thoroughbred horses, and their two-humped camels,—in fine, all the possessions of their subjects.[5] Shortly after this, three other Median chiefs, hitherto intractable—

---

[1] *Prayer No. 29*, in KNUDTZON, *Assyrische Gebete an den Sonnengott*, pp. 119–122.

[2] Several recent historians (DELATTRE, *Le Peuple et l'Empire des Mèdes*, pp. 116–125, and WINCKLER, *Untersuchungen zur Altorientalischen Geschichte*, p. 87) allege that Sennacherib did not keep the territories that Sargon had conquered, and that the Assyrian frontier became contracted on that side; whereas the general testimony of the known texts seems to me to prove the contrary, namely, that he preserved nearly all the territory annexed by his father, and that Esarhaddon was far from diminishing this inheritance. If these two kings mention only insignificant deeds of arms in the western region, it is because the population, exhausted by the wars of the two preceding reigns, easily recognised the Ninevite supremacy, and paid tribute to the Assyrian governors with sufficient regularity to prevent any important military expedition against them.

[3] The country of Patusharra has been identified by Lenormant (*Lettres Assyriologiques*, vol. i. pp. 66, 69) with that of the Patischorians—Πατεισχορεῖς—mentioned by Strabo (XV. iii. § 1, p. 727) in Persia proper, who would have lived further north, not far from Demavend; cf. HOMMEL, *Geschichte Babyloniens und Assyriens*, p. 724; TIELE, *Babylonisch-assyrische Geschichte*, p. 348. Sachau (*Glossen zu der historischen Inschriften Assyrischer Könige*, in the *Zeitschrift für Assyriologie*, vol. xi. pp. 54–57) calls attention to the existence of a mountain chain Patashwar-gar or Padishwar-gir, in front of Choarêne, and he places the country of Patusharra between Demavend and the desert.

[4] Lenormant (*Lettres Assyriologiques*, vol. i. pp. 66, 67) sees in Eparna and Shîtirparna a transcript of the Iranian names Vifarna and Chithrafarna (cf. JUSTI, *Iranisches Namenbuch*, pp. 141, 164); as against the first of these identifications, cf. ROST, *Untersuchungen zur Altorientalischen Geschichte*, p. 111, n. 2.

[5] *Cylinders A, C*, col. iv. ll. 8–18, and *Inscription of the Broken Cylinder*, col. iv. ll. 3–9, in SCHRADER, *Keilinschriftliche Bibliothek*, vol. ii. pp. 132, 133, 146, 147; cf. BUDGE, *History of Esarhaddon*, pp. 66–69, and ROST, *Untersuchungen zur Altorientalischen Geschichte*, pp. 87, 88.

Uppis of Partakka, Zanasana of Partukka,[1] Ramatea of Urakazabarna—came to Nineveh to present the king with horses and lapis-lazuli, the best of everything they possessed, and piteously entreated him to forgive their misdeeds. They represented that the whole of Media was torn asunder by countless strifes, prince against prince, city against city, and an iron will was needed to bring the more turbulent elements to order. Esarhaddon lent a favourable ear to their prayers; he undertook to protect them on condition of their paying an annual tribute, and he put them under the protection of the Assyrian governors who were nearest to their territory.[2] Kharkhar, securely entrenched behind its triple ramparts, assumed the position of capital to these Iranian marches. It is difficult to determine the precise dates of these various events; we learn merely that they took place before 673, and we surmise that they must have occurred between the second and sixteenth year of the king's reign.[3] The outcome of them was a distinct gain to Assyria, in the acquisition of several new vassals. The recently founded kingdom of Ecbatana lacked as yet the prestige which would have enabled it to hold its own against Nineveh; besides which, Deïokes, the contemporary ruler assigned to it by tradition, was of too complaisant a nature to seek occasions of quarrel.[4] The Scythians, after having declared their warlike intentions, seem to have come to a more peaceable frame of mind, and to have curried favour with Nineveh; but the rulers of the capital kept a strict watch upon them, since their numbers, their intrepid character, and

[1] Partakka and Partukka seem to be two different adaptations of the name Paraituka (FR. LENORMANT, *Lettres Assyriologiques*, vol. i. p. 67), the Parætakênê of the Greek geographers; Tiele (*Babylonisch-assyrische Geschichte*, p. 348) thinks of Parthyênê. I think that these two names designate the northern districts of Parætakênê, the present Ashnakhor or the country near to it.

[2] *Cylinders A, C*, col. iv. ll. 19–37, in SCHRADER, *Keilinschriftliche Bibliothek*, vol. ii. pp. 132–135; cf. BUDGE, *The History of Esarhaddon*, pp. 68–73, and ROST, *Untersuchungen zur Altorientalischen Geschichte*, pp. 88, 89.

[3] The facts relating to the submission of Patusharra and of Partukka are contained in Cylinder A, dated from the eponymous year of Akhazilu, in 673. Moreover, the version which this document contains seems to have been made up of two pieces placed one at the end of the other: the first an account of events which occurred during an earlier period of the reign, and in which the exploits are classified in geographical order, from Sidon in the west (col. i. l. 10, et seq.) to the Arabs bordering on Chaldæa in the east (col. ii. l. 55, et seq.); and the second consisting of additional campaigns carried out after the completion of the former—which is proved by the place which these exploits occupy, out of their normal position in the geographical series—and making mention of Patusharra and Partukka (col. iv. ll. 8–37), as well as of Belikisha (col. iii. ll. 52–60, col. iv. ll. 1–7). The editor of the *Broken Cylinder* has tried to combine these latter elements with the former in the order adopted by the original narrator. As far as can be seen in what is left of the columns, he has placed, after the Chaldæan events (col. iii. ll. 19–28), the facts concerning Partukka (col. iv., where lines 1, 2 in the present state of the cylinder contain fragments which fit in to the end of the account preserved in *A–C*, col. iv. ll. 19–39), then those concerning Patusharra (col. iv. ll. 3–9), and finally the campaign against Bazu (col. iv. ll. 10–26), the extreme limit of Esarhaddon's activity in the south. Knowing that the campaign in the desert and the death of Abdimilkôt took place in 676 (*Babylonian Chronicle of Pinches*, col. iv. ll. 5–8), and that we find them already alluded to in the first part of the narrative, as well as the events of 675 relating to the revolt of Dakkuri, we may conclude that the submission of Patusharra and that of Partukka occurred in 674, or at latest in the beginning of 673.

[4] Cf. what is said on this subject, *supra*, pp. 324–328.

instinct for rapine made them formidable enemies—the most dangerous, indeed, that the empire had encountered on its north-eastern frontier for nearly a century.

This policy of armed *surveillance*, which proved so successful in these regions, was also carefully maintained by Esarhaddon on his south-eastern border against Assyria's traditional enemy, the King of Susa. Babylon, far from exhibiting any restlessness at her present position, showed her gratitude for the favours which her suzerain had showered upon her by resigning herself to become the ally of Assyria. She regarded her late disaster as the punishment inflicted by Marduk

THE TOWN OF KHARKHAR WITH ITS TRIPLE RAMPART.[1]

for her revolts against Sargon and Sennacherib. The god had let loose the powers of evil against her, and the Arakhtu, overflowing among the ruins, had swept them utterly away; indeed, for the space of ten years, destruction and desolation seemed to have taken the place of her former wealth of temples and palaces. In the eleventh year, the divine wrath was suddenly appeased. No sooner had Esarhaddon mounted the throne, than he entreated Shamash, Rammân, and even Marduk himself, to reveal to him their will with regard to the city; whereupon the omens, interpreted by the seers, commanded him to rebuild Babylon and to raise again the temple of Ê-sagilla. For this purpose he brought together all the captives taken in war that he had at his disposal, and employed them in digging out clay and in brick-making; he then prepared the foundations, upon which he poured libations of oil, honey, palm-wine, and other wines of various kinds; he himself took the mason's hod, and with tools of ebony, cypress wood, and oak, moulded a brick for the new sanctuary. The work was, indeed, a gigantic undertaking, and demanded years of uninterrupted

<hr />

[1] Drawn by Faucher-Gudin, from Flandin, in BOTTA, *Le Monument de Ninive*, pl. 55.

labour, but Esarhaddon pushed it forward, sparing neither gold, silver, costly stone, rare woods, or plates of enamel in its embellishment. He began to rebuild at the same time all the other temples and the two city walls—Imgurbel and Nimittibel; to clear and make good the canals which supplied the place with water, and to replant the sacred groves and the gardens of the palace. The inhabitants were encouraged to come back to their homes, and those who had been dispersed among distant provinces were supplied with clothes and food for their return journey, besides having their patrimony restored to them.[1] This rebuilding of the ancient city certainly displeased and no doubt alarmed her two former rivals, the Kaldâ and Elam, who had hoped one day to wrest her heritage from Assyria. Elam concealed its ill-feeling, but the Kaldâ of Bît-Dakkuri had invaded the almost deserted territory, and appropriated the lands which had belonged to the noble families of Babylon, Borsippa, and Sippara. When the latter, therefore, returned from exile, and, having been reinstituted in their rights, attempted to resume possession of their property, the usurpers peremptorily refused to relinquish it. Esarhaddon was obliged to interfere to ensure its restoration, and as their king, Shamash-ibni, was not inclined to comply with the order, Esarhaddon removed him from the throne, and substituted in his place a certain Nabushallim, son of Belesys, who showed more deference to the suzerain's wishes.[2] It is possible that about this time the Kaldâ may have received some support from the Aramæans of the desert and the Arab tribes encamped between the banks of the Euphrates and Syria, or, on the other hand, the latter may have roused the wrath of Assyria by inroads of a more than usually audacious character. However this may be, in 676 Esarhaddon resolved to invade their desert territory, and to inflict such reprisals as would force them thenceforward to respect the neighbouring border provinces. His first relations with them had been of a courteous and friendly nature. Hazael of Adumu, one of the sheikhs of Kedar, defeated by Sennacherib towards the end of his reign,[3] had taken the opportunity of the annual tribute to come to Nineveh with considerable presents, and to implore the restoration of the statues of his gods. Esarhaddon had caused these battered idols to be cleaned and repaired, had engraved upon them an inscription in praise of Assur, and had further married the suppliant sheikh to a woman of the royal harem, named Tabua. In consideration of this, he had imposed upon the Arab a supplementary tribute of sixty-five camels, and had restored

---

[1] The whole of this account is taken from inscriptions published and translated by MEISSNER and ROST, *Die Bauinschriften Asarhaddons*, in the *Beiträge zur Assyriologie*, vol. iii. pp. 218–269.

[2] *Cylinders A, C*, col. ii. ll. 42–54, and *Inscription of the Broken Cylinder*, col. iii. ll. 19–28, in SCHRADER, *Keilinschriftliche Bibliothek*, vol. ii. pp. 128–131, 146, 147; cf. BUDGE, *The History of Esarhaddon*, pp. 48–51.

[3] Cf. what is said of this prince on p. 323, *supra*.

to him his idols. All this took place, no doubt, soon after the king's accession. A few years later, on the death of Hazael, his son Yauta [1] solicited investiture, but a competitor for the chieftaincy, a man of unknown origin, named Uahab, treacherously incited the Arabs to rebel, and threatened to overthrow him. Esarhaddon caused Uahab to be seized, and exposed him in chains at the gate of Nineveh; but, in consideration of this service to the Arabs, he augmented the tribute which already weighed upon the people by a further demand for ten gold *minas*, one thousand precious stones, fifty camels, and a thousand measures of spicery.[2] The repression of these Arabs of Kedar thus confirmed Esarhaddon's supremacy over the extreme northern region of Arabia, between Damascus and Sippara or Babylon; but in a more southerly direction, in the wadys which unite Lower Chaldæa to the districts of the Jordan and the Dead Sea, there still remained several rich and warlike states—among others, Bazu,[3] whose rulers had never done homage to the sovereigns of either Assyria or Karduniash. To carry hostilities into the heart of their country was a bold and even hazardous undertaking; it could be reached only by traversing miles of arid and rocky plains, exposed to the rays of a burning sun, vast extents of swamps and boggy pasture land, desolate wastes infested with serpents and scorpions, and a mountain range of blackish lava known as Khâzu. It would have been folly to risk a march with the heavy Assyrian infantry in the face of such obstacles. Esarhaddon probably selected for the purpose a force composed of cavalry, chariots, and lightly equipped foot-soldiers, and despatched them with orders to reach the Jauf by forced marches through the Wady Haurân. The Arabs, who were totally unprepared for such a movement, had not time to

---

[1] The name of Hazael's son is written Yalu in Cylinder A, and Yata in Winckler's fragment (*Altorientalische Forschungen*, vol. i. pp. 527, l. 6), and we may conclude from these two variants that the original form was Yataïlu, which would give us a name often found in Himyaritic inscriptions; this Yauta has been confounded with the individual whom we shall find called Uaîtê and Yauta in the reign of Assur-bani-pal, and of whom we shall treat below, on pp. 417 and 430, 431.

[2] *Cylinders A, C,* col. ii. ll. 55–58, col. iii. ll. 1–24, in SCHRADER, *Keilinschriftliche Bibliothek*, vol. ii. pp. 130, 131; cf. BUDGE, *The History of Esarhaddon*, pp. 54–59. The account of these facts is no longer found in the *Broken Cylinder;* it was probably chronicled on one of the ends—now destroyed—of the columns. For a mutilated version in which the story of Uahab is told, cf. WINCKLER, *Altorientalische Forschungen*, vol. i. pp. 527–529, 532–534.

[3] The Bazu of this text is certainly the Buz which the Hebrew books name among the children of Nahor (*Gen.* xxii. 21; *Jer.* xxv. 23). The early Assyriologists identified Khazu with Uz, the son of Nahor (H. RAWLINSON, in the *Journ. R. As. Soc.*, 1864, vol. i. pp. 238, 239; NORRIS, *Assyrian Dictionary*, p. 412; FINZI, *Ricerche per lo Studio dell' Antichità Assira*, pp. 396, 397); Delitzsch (*Wo lag das Paradies?* p. 307) compares the name with that of Hazo (Huz), the fifth son of Nahor (*Gen.* xxii. 22), and his opinion is admitted by most scholars (SCHRADER, *Die Keilinschriften und das Alte Testament*, 1883, p. 141; TIELE, *Babylonisch-assyrische Geschichte*, p. 349). For the site of these countries I have followed the ideas of Delattre, who identifies them with the oases of Jauf and Meskakeh, in the centre of Northern Arabia (*L'Asie Occidentale dans les inscriptions assyriennes*, pp. 137, 138). The Assyrians must have set out by the Wady Haurân or by one of the wadys near to Babylon, and have returned by a more southern wady. Glaser makes them pass through the southern Nejed (*Skizze der Geschichte und der Geographie Arabiens*, vol. ii. pp. 5, 265), and Winckler adopts his conclusions (*Geschichte Babyloniens und Assyriens*, p 266).

collect their forces; eight of their chiefs were taken by surprise and killed one after another—among them Kisu of Khaldili, Agbaru of Ilpiati, Mansaku of Magalani,—and also some reigning queens. Lâ, the King of Yadi, at first took refuge in the mountains, but afterwards gave himself up to the enemy, and journeyed as far as Nineveh to prostrate himself at Esarhaddon's feet, who restored to him his gods and his crown, on the usual condition of paying tribute.[1] A vassal occupying a country so remote and so difficult of access could not be

SHABÎTOKU, KING OF EGYPT.[2]

supposed to preserve an unbroken fidelity towards his suzerain, but he no longer ventured to plunder the caravans which passed through his territory, and that in reality was all that was expected of him.

Esarhaddon thus pursued a prudent and unadventurous policy in the northern and eastern portions of his empire, maintaining a watchful attitude towards the Cimmerians and Scythians in the north, carrying on short defensive campaigns among the Medes in the east, preserving peace with Elam, and making occasional flying raids in the south, rather from the necessity for repressing troublesome border tribes than with any idea of permanent conquest. This policy must have been due to a presentiment of danger from the side of Egypt, or to the inception of a great scheme for attacking the reigning Pharaoh. After the defeat of his generals at Altaku,[3] Shabîtoku had made no further attempt to take the offensive; his authority over the feudal nobility of Egypt was so widely acknowledged that it causes us no surprise to meet with his cartouches on more than one ruin between Thebes and Memphis,[4] but his closing years were marred by misfortune. There was then living at Napata a certain Taharqa, one of those scions of the solar race who enjoyed the title of "Royal brothers," and from among whom Amon of the Holy Mountain was wont to choose his representative to reign over the land of

---

[1] *Cylinders A, C,* col. iii. ll. 25–52, and *Broken Cylinder,* col. iv. ll. 10–26, in SCHRADER, *Keilins. Bibliothek,* vol. ii. pp. 130–133, 146–149.

[2] Drawn by Faucher-Gudin, from LEPSIUS, *Denkmäler,* iii. 301, No. 81; cf. ROSELLINI, *Monumenti Storici,* pl. 12, No. 48.

[3] Cf. *supra,* pp. 288, 289.

[4] His name or monuments of his erection have been discovered at Karnak (CHAMPOLLION, *Monuments de l'Égypte et de la Nubie,* vol. ii. p. 265, et seq.; ROSELLINI, *op. cit.,* pl. cli. No. 5; LEPSIUS, *Denkmäler,* v. 3, 4), at Luxor (DARESSY, *Notice explicative des ruines du temple de Louxor,* p. 55), in the temple of Phtah at Memphis (MARIETTE, *Monuments Divers,* pl. 29 e, 1–3) in the Serapeum (MARIETTE, *Notice sur les soixante-quatre Apis,* in the *Bulletin archéologique de l'Athénæum Français,* 1856, p. 52; cf. the *Sérapéum de Memphis,* vol. i. p. 27).

Ethiopia whenever the throne became vacant.[1] It does not appear that the father of Taharqa ever held the highest rank; it was from his mother, Âkaluka, that he inherited his pretensions to the crown, and through her probably that he traced his descent from the family of the high priests.[2] Tradition asserts that he did not gain the regal power without a struggle;

TAHARQA AND HIS QUEEN DIKAHÎTAMANU.[3]

having been proclaimed king in Ethiopia at the age of twenty, as the result of some revolution, he is said to have marched against Shabîtoku, and, coming up with him in the Delta, to have defeated him, taken him prisoner, and put him to death.[4] These events took place about 693 B.C.,[5] and Taharqa employed the opening years of his reign in consolidating his authority over the double

---

[1] For Ethiopian "Royal brothers," see *supra*, p. 170.

[2] E. DE ROUGÉ, *Étude sur quelques monuments du règne de Tahraka*, in the *Mélanges d'Archéologie Égyptienne et Assyrienne*, vol. i. p. 12. The name of the queen, somewhat mutilated on the monuments, appears to have been Âkaluka.

[3] Drawn by Faucher-Gudin, from the coloured plate in LEPSIUS, *Denkmäler*, v. 5.

[4] Eusebius, who cites the fact, had his information from a trustworthy Greek source (UNGER, *Manetho*, p. 251), perhaps from Manetho himself (MÜLLER-DIDOT, *Fragm. Historicorum Græcorum*, vol. ii. p. 593). The inscription of Tanis seems to say that Taharqa was twenty years old at the time of his revolt (E. DE ROUGÉ, *op. cit.*, pp. 16–22, BIRCH; *On Some Monuments of the Reign of Tirhakah*, in the *Transactions* of the Bibl. Arch. Soc., vol. vii. pp. 194, 198, and *Inscription of Tirhakah*, in the *Zeitschrift*, 1880, p. 23).

[5] Most of the lists of kings taken from Manetho assign twelve years to the reign of Sébikhos; one alone, that of Africanus, assigns him fourteen years (MANETHO, in MÜLLER-DIDOT, *Fragm. Hist. Græc.*, vol. ii. p. 593).

kingdom. He married the widow of Sabaco, Queen Dikahîtamanu, and thus assumed the guardianship of Tanuatamanu, her son by her first husband, and this marriage secured him supreme authority in Ethiopia.[1] That he regarded Egypt as a conquered country can no longer be doubted, seeing that he inserted its name on his monuments among those of the nations which he had vanquished.[2] He nevertheless felt obliged to treat it with consideration; he respected the rights of the feudal princes, and behaved himself in every way like a Pharaoh of the old royal line. He summoned his mother from Napata, where he had left her, and after proclaiming her regent of the South and the North, he associated her with himself in the rejoicings at his coronation. This ceremony, celebrated at Tanis with the usages customary in the Delta,[3] was repeated at Karnak in accordance with the Theban ritual, and a chapel erected shortly afterwards on the northern quay of the great sacred lake has preserved to us the memory of it.[4] Âkaluka, installed with the rank and prerogatives of the " Divine Spouse " of Amon, presented her son to the deity, who bestowed upon him through his priests dominion over the whole world. She bent the bow, and let fly the arrows towards the four cardinal points, which she thereby symbolically delivered to him as wounded prisoners; the king, on his part, hurled against them bullets of stone, and by this attack figuratively accomplished their defeat.[5] His wars in Africa were crowned with a certain meed of success,[6] and his achievements in this quarter won for him in after-

---

[1] The text of *Cylinder A* of Assur-bani-pal (col. ii. l. 53), and that of several other documents (*K 228* and *K 2675*, cf. G. SMITH, *History of Assurbanipal*, pp. 29, 47), only mentioned that Tanuata-manu was the " son of his wife," which Oppert interpreted to mean son of Taharqa himself (*Mémoire sur les rapports de l'Égypte et de l'Assyrie dans l'Antiquité*, p. 104), while others see in him a son of Kashto, a brother of Amenertas (HINCKS, *The Assyrian Sacking of Thebes*, in the *Zeitschrift*, 1866, p. 2), or a son of Shabîtoku (G. SMITH, *Egyptian Campaigns of Esarhaddon and Assurbanipal*, in the *Zeitschrift*, 1868, p. 96). Rassam's Cylinder, No. 1 (col. ii. l. 22) gives the variant, Tandamanê, son of Sabaco, as was observed for the first time by G. SMITH, *Assyrian Discoveries*, pp. 318, 327.

[2] BRUGSCH, *Reiseberichte aus Ægypten*, p. 300; the parallel scene, where the name of Egypt was found, has been usurped by Nectanebo.

[3] The stele of Tanis, whose fragments were discovered by Mariette and Petrie, seems to refer to these coronation festivities at Tanis; cf. the translations of it given by E. de Rougé (*Étude sur quelques monuments du règne de Tahraka*, in the *Mélanges d'Archéologie Égyptienne*, vol. i. pp. 21–23), Birch (*On Some Monuments of the Reign of Tirhakah*, in the *Transactions* of the Bibl. Arch. Soc., vol. vii. pp. 194–199), and Griffith (PETRIE, *Tanis*, vol. ii. pp. 29, 30, pl. ix. No. 162).

[4] The scenes and inscriptions in this chapel, published by PRISSE D'AVENNES, *Monuments Égyptiens*, pls. xxxi.–xxxiii., have been carefully worked out by E. DE ROUGÉ only, *op. cit.*, pp. 14–16.

[5] PRISSE D'AVENNES, *op. cit.*, pl. xxxiii.; cf. E. DE ROUGÉ, *op. cit.*, p. 15.

[6] The list inscribed on the base of the statue discovered and published by Mariette (*Karnak*, pl. xlv. *a* 2) contains a large number of names belonging to Africa. They are the same as those met with in the time of the XVIIIth dynasty, and were probably copied from some monument of Ramses II., who had himself perhaps borrowed them from a document of the time of Thûtmosis III. (MARIETTE, *Karnak*, pp. 66, 67; cf. WIEDEMANN, *Ægyptische Geschichte*, p. 594). A bas-relief at Medinet-Habu shows him to us in the act of smiting a group of tribes, among which figure the Tepa, Doshrît, and "the humbled Kush" (CHAMPOLLION, *Monuments de l'Égypte et de la Nubie*, vol. i. pp. 319–321; ROSELLINI, *Monumenti Storici*, pl. cl. vol. iv. p. 182; LEPSIUS, *Denkmäler*, v. pl. i. *c*); this bas-relief was appropriated later on by Nectanebo.

time so much popularity among the Egyptians, that they extolled him to the Greeks as one of their most illustrious conquering Pharaohs; they related

THE COLUMN OF TAHARQA, AT KARNAK.[1]

that he had penetrated as far as the Pillars of Hercules in the west, and that he had invaded Europe in imitation of Sesostris.[2] What we know to be a fact is, that he secured to the valley of the Nile nearly twenty years of prosperity,

[1] Drawn by Faucher-Gudin, from a photograph by Beato, taken in 1886.
[2] STRABO, I. iii. § 21, p. 61; XV. i. § 6, p. 687: the latter passage is taken from Megasthenes (*Fragm.* 20, in MÜLLER-DIDOT, *Fragm. Hist. Græc.*, vol. ii. p. 416).

and recalled the glories of the great reigns of former days, if not by his
victories, at least by the excellence of his administration and his activity.   He
planned the erection at Karnak [1] of a hypostyle hall in front of the pylons of
Ramses II., which should equal, if not surpass, that of Seti I.[2]   The columns
of the central aisle were disposed in two lines of six pillars each, but only one of

THE HEMISFEOS OF HÂTHOR AND BÎSÛ, AT GEBEL-BARKAL.[3]

these now remains standing in its original place; its height, which is the same
as that of Seti's columns, is nearly sixty-nine feet.   The columns of the side
aisles, like those which should have flanked the immense colonnade at Luxor,
were never even begun, and the hall of Taharqa, like that of Seti I., remains

[1] Information as to the principal portions of his work at Karnak may be found in MARIETTE,
Karnak, pp. 10, 20, note 2, and in WIEDEMANN, *Ægyptische Geschichte*, pp. 595, 596.

[2] These columns have been looked upon as triumphal pillars, designed to support statues or
divine emblems (JOLLOIS and DE VILLIERS, *Description du palais de Karnak*, in the *Description de
l'Égypte*, vol. ii. pp. 422–425; E. DE ROUGÉ, *Étude des Monuments du Massif de Karnak*, in the
Mélanges d'Archéologie Égyptienne, vol. i. p. 67; STEINDORFF and BAEDEKER, *Egypten*, pp. 245, 246).
Mariette thinks that they supported "an edifice in the architectural style of the kiosk at Philæ and
the small hypæthral temple on the roof of Denderah" (*Karnak*, p. 19). I am of opinion that the architect
intended to make a hypostyle hall, but that when the columns were erected, he perceived that the
great width of the aisle they formed would render the strength of the roof very doubtful, and so
renounced the execution of his first design.

[3] Drawn by Faucher-Gudin, from a lithograph in CAILLAUD, *Voyage à Méroé*, vol. i. pl. lviii.

unfinished to this day.[1] He bestowed his favour on Nubia and Ethiopia, as well as on Egypt proper; even Napata owed to his munificence the most beautiful portions of its temples. The temple of Amon, and subsequently that of Mût, were enlarged by him;[2] and he decorated their ancient halls with bas-reliefs, representing himself, accompanied by his mother and his wife, in attitudes of adoration before the deity. The style of the carving is very good, and the hieroglyphics would not disgrace the walls of the Theban

ENTRANCE TO THE HEMISPEOS OF BÎSÛ (BES), AT GEBEL-BARKAL.[3]

temples. The Ethiopian sculptors and painters scrupulously followed the traditions of the mother-country, and only a few insignificant details of ethnic type or costume enable us to detect a slight difference between their works and those of pure Egyptian art. At the other extremity of Napata, on the western side of the Holy Mountain, Taharqa excavated in the cliff a rock-hewn shrine, which he dedicated to Hâthor and Bîsû (Bes), the patron of jollity and happiness, and the god of music and of war. Bîsû, who was at first relegated to the lowest rank among the crowd of genii adored by the people, had gradually risen to the highest place in the hierarchy of the gods, and his images predominated in chapels destined to represent the cradle of the infant gods, and

---

[1] For this colonnade at Luxor, cf. *Struggle of the Nations*, p. 379.

[2] CAILLAUD, *Voyage à Méroé*, vol. i. pls. lxiv.–lxvi., and vol. iii. pp. 218–225; LEPSIUS, *Denkmäler*, v. 5–13. The cartouches of Taharqa were recognised in this edifice from the outset by Champollion (Note in *Bulletin des Annonces*, 1824), and led him to attribute the erection of the building to this prince.

[3] Drawn by Faucher-Gudin, from a lithograph in CAILLAUD, *Voyage à Méroé*, vol. i. pl. lxxiv.; drawings of these pillars are reproduced in LEPSIUS, *Denkmäler*, v. 6 *a–b*.

the sacred spots where goddesses gave birth to their divine offspring. The portico erected in front of the pylon had a central avenue of pillars, against which stood monstrous and grinning statues of Bîsû, his hands on his hips, and his head crowned with a large bunch of lotus-flowers and plumes. Two rows of columns with Hathor-headed capitals flanked the central aisle, which led to a hall supported by massive columns, also with Hathor capitals, and beyond it again lay the actual shrine similarly excavated in the rocky hill; two statues of Bîsû, standing erect against their supporting columns, kept guard over the entrance, and their fantastic forms, dimly discernible in the gloom, must have

TAHARQA.[2]

appeared in ancient times to have prohibited the vulgar throng from approaching the innermost sanctuary. Half of the roof has fallen in since the building was deserted, and a broad beam of light falling through the aperture thus made reveals the hideous grotesqueness of the statues to all comers.[1]

The portraits of Taharqa represent him with a strong, square-shaped head, with full cheeks, vigorous mouth, and determined chin, such as belong to a man well suited to deal with that troubled epoch, and the knowledge we as yet possess of his conflict with Assyria fully confirms the character exhibited by his portrait statues. We may surmise that, when once absolute master of Egypt, he must have cast his eyes beyond the isthmus, and considered how he might turn to his own advantage the secret grudge borne by the Syrians against their suzerain at Nineveh, but up to the present time we possess no indications as to the policy he pursued in Palestine. We may safely assume, however, that it gave umbrage to the Assyrians, and that Esarhaddon resolved to put an end once for all to the uneasiness it caused him. More than half a century had elapsed since the day when the kings of Syria, alarmed at the earliest victories of Tiglath-pileser III., had conceived the idea of pitting their former conquerors against those of the day, and had solicited help from the Pharaohs against Assyria.[3] None of the sovereigns to whom they turned had refused to listen to their appeals, or failed to promise subsidies and reinforcements; but these engagements, however definite, had for the most part been left unfulfilled, and when an occasion for their execution had occurred, the Egyptian armies had merely

---

[1] CAILLAUD, *Voyage à Méroé*, vol. ii. pp. 212–215. The plan is given in CAILLAUD, *op. cit.*, vol. i. pl. lxviii.

[2] Drawn by Faucher-Gudin, from a cast of the fragment preserved at Gizeh; cf. MASPERO, *Guide du Visiteur au Musée de Boulaq*, p. 63, No. 101.

[3] Cf. *supra*, pp. 180–182.

appeared on the fields of battle to beat a hasty retreat : they had not prevented
the subjugation of Damascus, Israel, Tyre, the Philistines, nor, indeed, of any of
the princes or people who trusted to their renown ; yet, notwithstanding these
numerous disappointments, the prestige of the Egyptians was still so great
that insubordinate or rebel states invariably looked to them for support and
entreated their help. The Assyrian generals had learnt by experience to meet
them unmoved, being well aware that the Egyptian army was inferior to their
own in organisation, and used antiquated weapons and methods of warfare ;
they were also well aware that the Egyptian and even the Ethiopian soldiery
had never been able successfully to withstand a determined attack by the
Assyrian battalions, and that when once the desert which protected Egypt had
been crossed, she would, like Babylon, fall an easy prey to their arms. It would
merely be necessary to guard against the possible danger of opposition being
offered to the passage of the invading host by the Idumæan and Arab tribes
sparsely scattered over the country between the Nile and the Gulf of Akabah,
as their hostility would be a cause of serious uneasiness. An expedition,
sent against Milukhkha[1] in 675 B.C., had taught the inhabitants to respect
the power of Assyria ; but the campaign had not been brought to a satisfactory conclusion, for the King of Elam, Khumbân-khaldash II., seeing his
rival occupied at the opposite extremity of his empire, fell unexpectedly upon
Babylon, and pushing forward as far as Sippara, laid waste the surrounding
country ; and his hateful presence even prevented the god Shamash from
making his annual progress outside the walls of the city. The people of Bît-
Dakkuri seem to have plucked up courage at his approach, and invaded the
neighbouring territory, probably that of Borsippa. Esarhaddon was absent on
a distant expedition, and the garrisons scattered over the province were not
sufficiently strong in numbers to risk a pitched battle : Khumbân-khaldash,
therefore, marched back with his booty to Susa entirely unmolested. He died
suddenly in his palace a few days after his return, and was succeeded by his
brother, Urtaku, who was too intent upon seating himself securely on the throne
to send his troops on a second raid in the following year.[2] Esarhaddon deferred
his revenge to a more convenient season, and utilised the respite fate had
accorded him on the Elamite border to hasten his attack on Egypt (673 B.C.).[3]

---

[1] The name of Milukhkha, first applied to the countries in the neighbourhood of the Persian Gulf
(cf. *Dawn of Civilization*, p. 564, note 3, and p. 600), had been transferred to the western coasts of
Arabia, as well as that of Magan.

[2] *Pinches' Babylonian Chronicle*, col. iv. ll. 9–15; cf. WINCKLER, *Babylonische Chronik B*, in
SCHRADER, *Keilins. Bibl.*, vol. ii. pp. 282–288. This is the only document recording these events,
and it gives them in great confusion ; I have endeavoured to point out the bond which unites them.

[3] *Pinches' Babylonian Chronicle*, col. iv. l. 16 ; cf. WINCKLER, *op. cit.*, pp. 284, 285. Knudtzon (*Assyrische Gebete an den Sonnengott*, vol. i. p. 59) has established the reading " the Assyrians *were defeated*,"
—*diku*,—instead of " the Assyrians *came*,"—*illiku*,—as read by the first editors of this passage.

The expedition was a failure, and Taharqa was greatly elated at having issued with honour from this trial of strength. As most of the countries over which his enemy exercised his supremacy were those which had been ruled by his Theban ancestors in days gone by, Taharqa engraved on the base of his statue a list of nations and towns copied from one of the monuments of Ramses II. The Khâti, Carchemish, Mitanni, Arvad—in short, a dozen peoples already extinct or in their decline, and whose names were merely perpetuated in the stereotyped official lists,—were enumerated in the list of his vanquished foes side by side with Assyria.[1] It was a mere piece of bravado, for never, even when victorious, did he set foot on Syrian soil; but all the same the victory had caused the invading host to retire, and the fame of this exploit, spreading throughout Asia, was not without its effect on the minds of the inhabitants. The island of Tyre had never officially recognised the Assyrian suzerainty. The Tyrians had lived in peace since the defeat of Elulai, and had maintained constant commercial relations with the continent without interfering in active politics: they had, perhaps, even been permitted to establish some settlements on the coast of the mainland. Their king, Bâal, now deemed the moment a propitious one for coming forward and recovering his lost territory, and since the Greek princes of Cyprus had ranged themselves under the hegemony of Assyria, he thought he could best counterbalance their influence by seeking support from Egypt, whose ancient greatness was apparently reviving. He therefore concluded an alliance with Taharqa,[2] and it would be no cause for astonishment if we should one day discover that Judah had followed his example. Hezekiah had devoted his declining years to religious reformation, and the organisation of his kingdom under the guidance of Isaiah or the group of prophets of which Isaiah was the leader. Judah had increased in population, and had quickly recovered its prosperity; when Hezekiah died, about 686 B.C.,[3] it had entirely regained its former vigour, but the memory of the disasters of 701 was still sufficiently fresh in the minds of the people to prevent the change of sovereign being followed by a change of policy. Manasseh, who succeeded his father, though he did not walk, as Hezekiah had done, in the ways of the Lord,[4] at least remained loyal to his Assyrian masters. It is, however, asserted that he afterwards rebelled, though his reason for doing so is not explained, and that he was carried captive to Babylon as a punishment for this crime: he

---

[1] Mariette, *Karnak*, pl. 45 *a*, and pp. 66, 67.

[2] The alliance of Bâal with Taharqa is mentioned in the fragment of the *Annals*, reproduced by Budge (*The History of Esarhaddon*, pp. 116, 117, l. 12), under the date of year X., and the name Bâal is still decipherable amid the defaced lines which contained the account of events which took place before that year (pp. 114, 115, l. 2). I think we may reasonably assign the first understanding between the two sovereigns, either to the actual year of the first campaign or to the following year, and this is the present opinion of Winckler (*Altorientalische Forschungen*, vol. i. pp. 525, 526).

[3] For the dates of Hezekiah's reign, cf. *supra*, pp. 236, 284.

[4] 2 *Kings* xxi. 1, 2; cf. 2 *Chron.* xxxiii. 1, 2.

succeeded, nevertheless, in regaining favour, and was reinstated at Jerusalem on condition of not repeating his offence. If this statement is true, as I believe it to be, it was probably after the Egyptian campaign of 673 B.C.[1] that his conspiracy with Bâal took place. The Assyrian governors of the neighbouring provinces easily crushed these attempts at independence, but, the islands of Tyre being secure from attack, they were obliged to be content with establishing a series of redoubts along the coast, and with prohibiting the Tyrians from having access to the mainland.[2]

The promptitude of their action quenched the hopes of the Egyptian party and prevented the spread of the revolt. Esarhaddon was, nevertheless, obliged to put off the fulfilment of his schemes longer than he desired : complications arose on his northern frontiers, near the sources of the Tigris, which distracted his attention from the intrigues taking place on the banks of the Nile. Urartu, hard pressed by the Cimmerians and Scythians, had lived for a quarter of a century in a condition of sullen peace with Assyria, and its kings avoided anything which could bring them into conflict with their hereditary rival. Argistis II. had been succeeded by one of his sons, Rusas II., and both of them had been more intent upon strengthening their kingdom than on extending its area ; they had rebuilt their capital, Dhuspas, on a magnificent scale, and from the security of their rocky home they watched the course of events without taking any part in it, unless forced to do so by circumstances.[3] Andaria, chief of Lubdi, one of the remote mountain districts, so difficult of access that it always retained its independence in spite of frequent attacks, had seized Shupria, a province which had been from very early times subject to the sovereigns of Nineveh, and was the first to be colonised by them.[4] The inhabitants, forgetful

[1] The fact of Manasseh's captivity is only known to us from the testimony of 2 *Chron.* xxxiii. 10–13, and most modern critics consider it apocryphal (STADE, *Geschichte des Volkes Israel*, vol. i. pp. 639, 640). The moral development which accompanies the narrative, and the conversion which follows it, are certainly later additions, but I think, with Halévy (*Mélanges de Critique et d'Histoire relatifs aux peuples Sémitiques*, pp. 36, 37), that the story may have some foundation in fact ; we shall see later on (*infra*, p. 386) that Necho I., King of Sais, was taken prisoner, led into captivity, and received again into favour in the same way as Manasseh is said to have been. The exile to Babylon, which at one time appeared to demonstrate the unauthenticity of the passage, would be rather in favour of its authenticity, as G. Smith had already remarked (*The Assyrian Eponym Canon*, pp. 165, 166). Esarhaddon was King of Babylon during the whole of his reign, and the great works which he executed in that city obliged him, we know, to transport thither a large proportion of the prisoners whom he brought back from his wars.

[2] WINCKLER, *Altorientalische Forschungen*, vol. i. pp. 525, 526, assigns the opening of the blockade to this date ; I had independently arrived at the same conclusion, when Winckler himself pushed back the date for the commencement of operations to 675 B.C. (*Gesch. Bab. und Assyr.*, p. 335), and Landau brought it down to 670 B.C. (*Beiträge zur Altertumskunde des Orients*, pp. 11, 12).

[3] For the order and succession of the kings of Urartu at this epoch, I have followed the ideas set forth by BELCK and LEHMANN, *Ein neuer Herrscher von Chaldia*, in the *Zeitschrift für Assyriologie*, vol. ix. pp. 82–99, 339–360.

[4] For these colonies, cf. *Struggle of the Nations*, p. 608, note 2. The name is there given under the form Ruri, the inaccuracy of which was shown at the very time that work began to appear ; cf. *supra*, p. 20, note 4.

2 B

of their origin, had yielded voluntarily to Andaria; but this prince, after receiving their homage, was seized with alarm at his own audacity. He endeavoured to strengthen his position by an alliance with the Cimmerians,[1] and the spirit of insubordination which he aroused spread beyond the Euphrates; Mugallu of Milid, a king of the Tabal, resorted to such violent measures that Esarhaddon was alarmed lest the wild mountaineers of the Taurus should pour down upon the plain of Kuî and lay it waste.[2] The danger would indeed have been serious had all these tribes risen simultaneously; but the Cimmerians were detained in Asia Minor by their own concerns,[3] and Mugallu, when he saw the Assyrian troops being concentrated to bring him to reason, remained quiet.[4] The extension of Lubdi was not likely to meet with favour in the eyes of Rusas; he did not respond to the advances made to him,[5] and Esarhaddon opened his campaign against the rebels without having to dread the intervention of Urartu. Andaria, besieged in his capital of Ubbumi,[6] laid aside his royal robes, and, assuming the ragged garments of a slave, appeared upon the ramparts and pleaded for mercy in a voice choked with tears: "Shupria, the country which has sinned against thee, will yield to thee of her own accord; place thy officers over her, she will vow obedience to thee; impose on her a ransom and an annual tribute for ever. I am a robber, and for the crime I have committed I will make amends fifty-fold." Esarhaddon would listen to no terms before a breach had been effected in the city walls. This done, he pardoned the prince who had taken refuge in the citadel, but resumed possession of Shupria: its inhabitants were mercilessly punished, being condemned to slavery, and their lands and goods divided among new colonists. Many Urartians were numbered among the captives: these Esarhaddon separated from the rest, and sent back to Rusas as a reward for his having remained neutral. All this had barely occupied the space of one month, the month of Tebet. The firstfruits of the spoil reserved

---

[1] This seems, indeed, to be proved by a tablet in which Esarhaddon, addressing the god Shamash, asks him if the Cimmerians or Urartians will unite with a certain prince who can be no other than the King of Shupria (KNUDTZON, *Assyrische Gebete an den Sonnengott*, pp. 149–153; cf. WINCKLER, *Altorient. Forsch.*, vol. ii. pp. 50, 51).

[2] I should like to refer to this date the oracular "consultations," Nos. 55, 56, 57, 58, which belong to the reign of Esarhaddon, as Knudtzon (*op. cit.*, pp. 158–165) has pointed out; cf. WINCKLER, *op. cit.*, vol. ii. p. 125, et seq.

[3] It was about this time they were dealing the death-blow to the kingdom of Phrygia; cf. *infra*, pp. 391, 392.

[4] This concentration of Assyrian troops is the subject of oracular "consultation," No. 56 (KNUDTZON, *op. cit.*, pp. 160–163). Mugallu shut himself up in one of his strongholds as soon as he heard of it, and it seems as if the affair went no further, for we find him still King of Tabal some years later, under Assur-bani-pal; cf. *infra*, p. 387.

[5] That Esarhaddon dreaded the formation of an alliance between Rusas and the chiefs of Lubdi and Shupria, follows from oracle No. 48 in KNUDTZON, *op. cit.*, p. 150, rev., l. 6, et seq., where the name Rusas must be restored, as the editor has clearly seen (*op. cit.*, p. 152); cf. WINCKLER, *Altorient. Forsch.*, vol. ii. p. 52, where he raises some objections to this restoration.

[6] The town is named Bumu in KNUDTZON, *op. cit.*, No. 48, obv., l. 9, p. 150.

for Uruk had already reached that town by the month Kislev,[1] and the year was not so far advanced as to render further undertakings impossible, when the death of the queen, on the 5th Adar, suspended all warlike enterprises.[2] The last months of the year were given up to mourning, and the whole of 671 B.C. passed without further action. The Ethiopian king was emboldened by this inactivity on the part of his foe to renew his intrigues with Syria with redoubled energy; at one moment, indeed, the Philistines of Ashkelon, secretly instigated, seemed on the point of revolt.[3] They held themselves, however, in check, and Esarhaddon, reassured as to their attitude, entered into negotiations with the sheikhs of the Arab tribes, and purchased their assistance to cross the desert of Sinai. He bade them assemble at Raphia, at the western extremity of Palestine, each chief bringing all the camels he could command, and as many skins of water as their beasts could carry: this precaution, a wise one at any time, might secure the safety of the army in case Taharqa should have filled up the wells which marked the stages in the caravan route.[4] When all was ready, Esarhaddon consulted the oracle of Shamash, and, on receiving a favorable reply from the god, left Nineveh in the beginning of the month Nisân, 670 B.C., to join the invading army in Syria.[5] He made a detour in order to inspect the lines of forts which his generals had established along the coast opposite Tyre, and strengthened their garrisons to prevent Bâal from creating a diversion in the rear of his base of operations; he then proceeded southwards to the

[1] *Pinches' Bab. Chron.*, col. iv. l. 22; cf. WINCKLER, *Die Bab. Chron. B*, in SCHRADER, *Keil. Bibl.*, vol. ii. pp. 284, 285. Winckler thinks that in l. 21 of this document the name of Nineveh should be substituted for that of Uruk (*Alt. Forsch.*, vol. ii. p. 46, note 1), but I do not see the necessity for this. The Babylonian chronicler naturally reported the events connected with the towns of his own land, and the arrival of a portion of the booty, the offering of the king to the temple in Uruk, touched him more nearly than the arrival of the whole amount of the spoil at Nineveh would have done.

[2] All these facts are revealed to us by the great tablet in the British Museum, the fragments of which were first published and translated by WINCKLER, *Altorient. Forsch.*, vol. ii. pp. 27–52; cf. vol. i. pp. 529–532. The date is fixed by a passage in *Pinches' Babylonian Chronicle* (col. iv. ll. 19–21; cf. WINCKLER, *Die Babylonische Chronik B*, in SCHRADER, *Keilins. Bibliothek*, vol. ii. pp. 284, 285), where it is stated that in *the eighth year*, in the month of Tebet, the king conquered the land of *Shupriza*: Shupriza is certainly an error of the Babylonian scribe for Shupria (KNUDTZON, *Assyrische Gebete an den Sonnengott*, p. 152; WINCKLER, *Alt. Forsch.*, vol. ii. p. 46). In the fragment of the *Annals* there occurs, immediately before the second expedition into Egypt, a much mutilated account which seems to be that of the campaign against Shupria; cf. BUDGE, *Hist. of Esarhaddon*, pp. 114, 115.

[3] Ashkelon is mentioned in two of the prayers (Nos. 70, 71) in which Esarhaddon consults Shamash on the subject of his intended campaign in Egypt (KNUDTZON, *op. cit.*, pp. 178–181); he seems to fear lest that city and the Bedâwin of the Idumæan desert should espouse the cause of the King of Ethiopia.

[4] This information is furnished by the fragment of the *Annals*, rev., ll. 1, 2; cf. BUDGE, *op. cit.*, pp. 118, 119; WINCKLER, *Untersuchungen zur Altorient. Gesch.*, p. 98, and *Musri, Meluhha, Main*, i. p. 6. The Assyrian text introduces this into the narrative in such a manner that it would appear as if these negotiations were carried on at the very commencement of the campaign; it is, however, more probable that they were concluded beforehand, as occurred later on, in the time of Cambyses, when the Persians invaded Egypt (HERODOTUS, III. iv.–ix.).

[5] KNUDTZON, *op. cit.*, pp. 174–181, where it is shown that the published texts refer to the second Egyptian campaign of Esarhaddon. The reply of the god is not easy to interpret, but it was certainly favourable, since the expedition took place.

neighbourhood of Aphek, in the territory of the tribe of Simeon.[1] The news which there met him must doubtless have informed him that the Bedâwin had been won over in the interval by the emissaries of Taharqa, and that he would run great risk by proceeding with his campaign before bringing them back to a sense of their duty. On leaving Aphek [2] he consequently turned southwards, and plunged into the heart of the desert, as if he had renounced all designs upon Egypt for that season, and was bent only on restoring order in Milukhkha and Magân before advancing further. For six weeks he marched in short stages, without other water than the supply borne, in accordance with his commands, by the Arab camels, passing through tracts of desert infested by strange birds and double-headed serpents; [3] when he had at length dispersed the bands which had endeavoured to oppose his advance, he suddenly turned in a north-westerly direction, and, following the dry bed of the torrent of Muzur, at length reached Raphia.[4] From thence he did not select the usual route, which follows the coast-line and leads to Pelusium, a place which he may have feared was too well defended, but he again pressed forward across the sands of the desert, and in the first days of Tammuz reached the cultivated land of the Delta by way of the Wady Tumilât. The frontier garrisons, defeated on the 3rd of Tammuz near Ishkhupri,[5] retreated in good order. Taharqa, hastening to their succour, disputed the ground inch by inch, and engaged the invaders in several conflicts, two at least of which, fought on the 16th and 18th of Tammuz, were regular pitched battles, but in every case the Assyrian tactics triumphed in spite of the dashing onslaught of the Egyptians;

[1] *Annals*, obv., l. 10; cf. BUDGE, *The History of Esarhaddon*, pp. 116, 117, and WINCKLER, *Musri, Meluhha, Maîn*, i. p. 6.

[2] The defaced name of the country in which this Aphek was situated was read as Samirina and translated "Samaria" by the first editor (BOSCAWEN, *Historical Inscription of Esarhaddon*, in the *Transactions* of the Bibl. Arch. Soc., vol. iv. pp. 85, 87, 93). This interpretation has been adopted by most historians (TIELE, *Babylonisch-assyrische Geschichte*, pp. 338, 350, note 1; DELITZSCH, *Wo lag das Paradies?* pp. 178, 179, 286, 287; DELATTRE, *L'Asie Occid. dans les Inscrip. Assyr.*, pp. 90, 91), who have seen in Aphek the town of this name belonging to the western portion of Manasseh. Budge read it Samina (*Hist. of Esarhaddon*, pp. 118, 119, l. 16), and this reading, verified by Craig, gave Winckler the idea of identifying Samina or Simina with the tribe of Simeon, and Aphek with the Aphekah (*Josh.* xv. 53) in the mountains of Judah (*Musri, Meluhha, Maîn*, i. pp. 8, 9).

[3] Cf. the winged serpents from Arabia whose bones were shown to Herodotus in Heliopolis (II. lxxv.; cf. WIEDEMANN, *Herodots Zweites Buch*, pp. 318, 319).

[4] Winckler (*op. cit.*, i. p. 8, et seq.) has fully explained the general plan of the campaign. I do not clearly understand, from his explanation, if he has noticed that the enumeration of days spent on the march and of districts traversed falls naturally into two divisions: a first itinerary of 30 *kashbu-kakkar* (obv., ll. 16–18, and rev., ll. 1–11), which apparently gives the stages of the journey from Aphek to Raphia; a second itinerary of 40 *kashbu-kakkar*, probably from Raphia to Ishkhupri. All this narrative must remain obscure until a well-preserved copy of this part of the *Annals* is discovered.

[5] The text on the stele at Zinjirli (SCHRADER, *Inschrift Asarhaddon's*, in LUSCHAN, *Ausgrabungen in Sendschirli*, vol. i. pp. 40, 41) gives a total of fifteen days' march from Ishkhupri to Memphis, while *Pinches' Babyl. Chron.*, col. iv. pp. 24–26, indicates three battles as having been fought on the 3rd, 16th, and 18th of Tammuz, and the taking of Memphis as occurring on the 22nd of the same month. If fifteen days is precisely accurate for the length of march, Esarhaddon would have reached Ishkhupri about the 27th of Sivan.

Memphis succumbed on the 22nd, after an assault lasting merely a few hours, and was mercilessly sacked. The Ethiopian king, with his army decimated and exhausted, gave up the struggle, and beat a hasty retreat southwards. The attack had been made with such rapidity that he had had no time to remove his court from the "palace of the White Wall" to the Saîd ; the queen, therefore, together with other women of less exalted rank, fell into the hands of the conqueror, besides the crown-prince, Ushana-horu, several younger sons and daughters, and such of the children of Sabaco and Shabîtoku as

SOUTHERN PROMONTORY AT THE MOUTH OF THE NAHR-EL-KELB.[1]

resided at court. But the victory had cost the Assyrians dearly, and the enemy still appeared to them so formidable that Esarhaddon prudently abstained from pursuing him up the Nile valley. He favourably received those feudal lords and petty kings who presented themselves to pay him homage, and confirmed them in possession of their fiefs, but he placed over them Assyrian governors and imposed new official names on their cities ; thus Athribis was officially called Limir-pateshî-assur, and other cities received the names Assur-makan-tishkul, Bît-marduk-sha-assur-taru, Shaîmuk-assur. He further imposed on them a heavy annual tribute of more than six talents of gold and six hundred talents of silver, besides robes and woven stuffs, wine, skins, horses, sheep, and asses ; and having accomplished this, he retraced his steps towards the north-east with immense booty and innumerable convoys of prisoners.[2] The complete defeat of the Ethiopian power filled not only

[1] Drawn by Boudier, from a photograph recently brought back by Lortet.
[2] The chronology of this campaign is furnished by *Pinches' Bab. Chron.*, col. iv. ll. 23–28 (cf. WINCKLER, *Die Babylonische Chronik B*, in SCHRADER, *Keilins. Bibliothek*, vol. ii. pp. 284, 285); the

Esarhaddon himself but all Asia with astonishment. His return to Nineveh was a triumphal progress; travelling through Syria by short stages, he paraded his captives and trophies before the peoples and princes who had so long relied on the invincible power of the Pharaoh. Esarhaddon's predecessors

STELE OF ESARHADDON AT THE NAHR-EL-KELB.[2]

had more than once inscribed the record of their campaigns on the rocks of the Nahr-el-Kelb, beside the bas-relief engraved there by Ramses II.,[1] and it had been no small gratification to their pride thus to place themselves on a footing of equality with one of the most illustrious heroes of the ancient Egyptian empire. The footpath which skirts the southern bank of the river, and turning to the south is continued along the seashore, was bordered by the great stelæ in which, one after another, they had thought to immortalise their glory; following their example, Esarhaddon was in like manner pleased to celebrate his prowess, and exhibit the ancient lords of the world subjugated to his will.[3] He erected numerous triumphal monuments along his route, and the stele which was discovered at one of the gates of Zinjirli is, doubtless, but an example of those which he

details are given in the fragment of the *Annals* first translated by G. Smith (*The Assyrian Eponym Canon*, pp. 141–143: cf. BUDGE, *Hist. of Esarhaddon*, pp. 114–123; WINCKLER, *Untersuchungen zur Altorient. Gesch.*, pp. 97–99, and *Musri, Meluhha, Main*, i. p. 5, et seq.), as well as in the inscription of Zinjirli (SCHRADER, *Inschrift Asarhaddon's Königs von Assyrien*, in LUSCHAN, *Ausgrab. in Sendschirli*, vol. i. pp. 30–43; cf. WINCKLER, *Untersuch. zur Altor. Gesch.*, pp. 99, 100), and in the fragments of a cylinder of Esarhaddon, which have been published by WINCKLER, *Altorient. Forsch.*, vol. ii. pp. 21–23.

[1] For the stelæ of Ramses II., cf. *Struggle of the Nations*, pp. 278, note 1, 389, 427; for the stelæ of Assyrian kings, cf. *ibid.*, p. 367, and *supra*, p. 41, note 2.

[2] Drawn by Faucher-Gudin, from a photograph brought back by Lortet.

[3] A translation of this inscription from the cast in the British Museum is to be found in G. SMITH, *The Assyrian Eponym Canon*, pp. 167–169; cf. BOSCAWEN, *The Monuments and Inscriptions on the Rocks at the Nahr-el-Kelb*, in the *Transactions* of the Bibl. Arch. Soc., vol. vii. pp. 345–349.

erected in other important cities. He is represented on the Zinjirli stele standing erect, while at his feet are two kneeling prisoners, whom he is holding by a bridle of cord fastened to metal rings passed through their lips ; these figures represent Bâal of Tyre and Taharqa of Napata, the latter with the uræus on his

forehead.[1] As a matter of fact, these kings were safe beyond his reach, one surrounded by the sea, the other above the cataracts, and the people were well aware that they did not form part of the band of prisoners which defiled before their eyes ; but they were accustomed to the vain and extravagant boastings of their conquerors, and these very exaggerations enabled them to understand more fully the extent of the victory. Esarhaddon thenceforward styled himself King of Egypt, King of the Kings of Egypt, of the Saîd and of Kush,[2] so great was his pride at having trampled underfoot the land of the Delta. And, in fact, Egypt had, for a century, been the only one of the ancient Eastern states which had always eluded the grasp of Assyria. The Elamites had endured disastrous defeats, which had cost them some of their provinces ; the Urartians had been driven back into their mountains, and no longer attempted to emerge from them ; Babylon had nearly been annihilated in her struggles for independence ; while the

STELE OF ZINJIRLI.[3]

Khâti, the Phœnicians, Damascus, and Israel had been absorbed one after another in the gradual extension of Ninevite supremacy. Egypt, although she had had a hand in all their wars and revolutions, had never herself paid the penalty of

[1] Inscription on one of the tiles of the palace of Esarhaddon at Nimroud, published in LAYARD, *Inscr. in the Cuneiform Character*, pl. 19 *a* ; cf. OPPERT, *Expédition de Mésopotamie*, vol. i. p. 334 ; MÉNANT, *Annales des rois d'Assyrie*, p. 240 ; SCHRADER, *Keilins. Bibliothek*, vol. ii. pp. 150–153. Contrary to the generally admitted opinion, Winckler considers that, by Muzur, Esarhaddon designates in this inscription Arabia, not Egypt (*Musri, Meluhha, Maîn*, i. pp. 13, 14).

[2] H. RAWLINSON, *Cun. Ins. W. As.*, vol. i. pl. 48, No. 5 ; cf. OPPERT, *Mémoire sur les rapports de l'Égypte et de l'Assyrie dans l'Antiquité*, pp. 40–43, where the name Paturîsi of the Assyrian text is for the first time compared with the biblical Pathros (*Isa.* xi. 11 ; *Jer.* xliv. 1, 15 ; *Ezek.* xxx. 14), and interpreted, after E. de Rougé, by the Egyptian Pa-to-rîsi, the land of the South, the Thebaid, the present Saîd.

[3] Drawn by Faucher-Gudin, from a photograph of the original, which is preserved in the Berlin Museum ; cf. LUSCHAN, *Ausgrabungen in Sendschirli*, vol. i. pl. i.

her intrigues, and even when she had sometimes risked her troops on the battle-fields of Palestine, her disasters had not cost her more than the loss of a certain number of men: having once retired to the banks of the Nile, no one had dared to follow, and the idea had gained credence among her enemies as well as among her friends that Egypt was effectually protected by the desert from every attack. The victory of Esarhaddon proved that she was no more invulnerable than the other kingdoms of the world, and that before a bold advance the obstacles, placed by nature in the path of an invader, disappeared; the protecting desert had been crossed, the archers and chariots of Egypt had fled before the Assyrian cavalry and pikemen, her cities had endured the ignominy and misery of being taken by storm, and the wives and daughters of her Pharaohs had been carried off into servitude in common with the numerous princesses of Elam and Syria of that day. Esarhaddon filled his palaces with furniture and woven stuffs, with vases of precious metal and sculptured ivories, with glass ornaments and statuettes looted from Memphis: his workers in marble took inspiration from the sphinxes of Egypt to modify the winged, human-headed lions upon which the columns of their palaces rested, and the plans of his architects became more comprehensive at the mere announcement of such a vast amount of spoil. The palace they had begun to build at Nineveh, on the ruins of an ancient edifice, already surpassed all previous architectural efforts. The alabaster quarries of the Assyrian mountains and the forests of Phœnicia had alike been put under contribution to face the walls of its state apartments; twenty-two chiefs of the country of the Khâti, of Phœnicia, and of the Mediterranean littoral—among them the Greek kings of Cyprus—had vied with one another in supplying Esarhaddon with great beams of pine, cedar, and cypress for its construction.[1] The ceilings were of cedar supported by pillars of cypress-wood encircled by silver and iron; stone lions and bulls stood on either side of the gates, and the doors were made of cedar and cypress, incrusted or overlaid with iron, silver, and ivory.[2] The treasures of Egypt enabled Esarhaddon to complete this palace and begin a new one at Calah, where the buildings erected somewhat hurriedly by Tiglath-pileser III. had already fallen into ruin. Some of the slabs on which the latter conqueror had engraved his Annals, and recounted the principal episodes of his campaigns, were removed and transferred to the site selected by Esarhaddon, and one of the surfaces of each was pared down in order to receive

[1] *Inscriptions on Cylinders A, C*, col. v. ll. 11–26; cf. ABEL, *Die Inschrift der Prismen A und C*, in SCHRADER, *Keilins. Bibliothek*, vol. ii. pp. 136–187. The list of names of these kings is found in the *Inscription on the Broken Cylinder*, col. v. ll. 13–26; cf. BUDGE, *The History of Esarhaddon*, pp. 100–103.

[2] For the inscriptions relating to works executed in the palace of Nineveh, cf. MEISSNER and ROST, *Die Bauinschriften Asarhaddons*, in the *Beiträge sur Assyriologie*, vol. iii. pp. 196–205, 210–215.

new pictures and fresh inscriptions. They had, however, hardly been placed in the stonemason's hands when the work was interrupted.[1] It may have been that Esarhaddon had to suspend all his operations while putting down some conspiracy. At any rate, we know that in 669 B.C. many high personages of his court were seized and executed.[2] The question of the succession to the throne was still undecided; Sinidinabal, the son whom Esarhaddon had previously designated as his heir presumptive, was dead,[3] and the people feared lest he should choose from among his other sons some prince who had not their interests at heart. The king's affection for Babylon had certainly aroused jealousy and anxiety among his Assyrian subjects, and perhaps some further tokens of preference made them uneasy lest he should select Shamash-shumukîn,[5] one of his children who manifested the same tendencies, and who was, moreover, the son of a Babylonian wife.[6] Most of the nobles who had been led to join the conspiracy paid

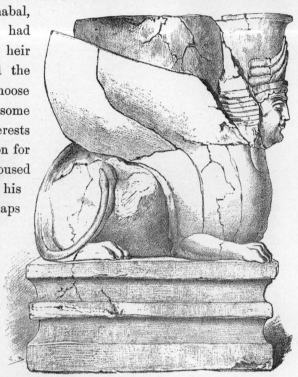

ASSYRIAN SPHINX IN EGYPTIAN STYLE SUPPORTING THE BASE OF A COLUMN.[4]

for their indiscretion with their heads, but their opposition gave the sovereign

---

[1] The date of the building of the palace at Calah is furnished by the inscriptions, in which Esarhaddon assumes the title of King of Egypt; cf. MEISSNER and ROST, *Die Bauinschriften Asarhaddons,* in the *Beiträge zur Assyriologie,* vol. iii. pp. 191–194, 206, 207.

[2] *Pinches' Babylonian Chronicle,* col. iv. l. 29; cf. WINCKLER, *Babylonische Chronik B,* in SCHRADER, *Keil. Bibl.,* vol. ii. pp. 284, 285.

[3] This personage was at first identified with Assur-bani-pal by G. Smith (*Hist. of Assurbanipal,* p. 324), and the identification was accepted by many Assyriologists, but Knudtzon (*Assyr. Gebete an den Sonnengott,* No. 107, pp. 218–221), in publishing the oracle relating to him, has shown that Sinidinabal was probably a son of Esarhaddon, who died before his father.

[4] Drawn by Boudier, from the alabaster sculpture reproduced by LAYARD, *The Monuments of Nineveh,* vol. i. pl. 95, 1.

[5] The name of this prince, which has been read very differently at different times, was for the first time accurately deciphered by Fr. Delitzsch (cf. SCHRADER, *Zur Kritik der historischen Angaben des Alexander Polyhistor und Abydenus,* in the *Berichte* of the Academy of Saxony, 1880, p. 2, note 3); it was transcribed Σαοσδούχινος and Sammughes by the chronologists of the Hellenistic period. The history of the decipherment, and of the interpretation given to these diverse forms, is very clearly set forth in LEHMANN, *Schamaschschumukin,* pp. 6–16.

[6] Shamash-shumukîn speaks of Babylon as " the place where his mother was born." Lehmann

cause for reflection, and decided him to modify his schemes. Convinced that it was impossible to unite Babylon and Nineveh permanently under the same ruler, he reluctantly decided to divide his kingdom into two parts—Assyria, the strongest portion, falling naturally to his eldest son, Assur-bani-pal, while Babylonia was assigned to Shamash-shumukîn, on condition of his paying homage to his brother as suzerain.[1] The best method to ensure his wishes being carried into effect was to prepare the way for their fulfilment while he was still alive; and rebellions which broke out about this time beyond the isthmus afforded a good opportunity for so doing.

Egypt was at this period divided into twenty states of various dimensions, very nearly the same as had existed a century before, when Piônkhi had, for the first time, brought the whole country under Ethiopian rule.[2] In the south, the extensive Theban province occupied both sides of the river from Assuan to Thinis and Khemmis. It was nominally governed by Amenertas or her daughter, Shapenuapît, but the administration was, as usual, entrusted to a member of the priestly college, at that time to Montumihâît, Count of Thebes, and fourth prophet of Amon.[3] The four principalities of Thinis, Siut, Hermopolis, and Heracleopolis separated it from the small kingdom of Memphis and Sais, and each of the regions of the Delta was divided into one or two fiefs, according to the number and importance of the towns it contained. In the south, Thebes was too directly under the influence of Ethiopia to be able to exercise an independent policy with regard to the rest of the country. In the north, two families contested the supremacy more or less openly. One of them, whose hereditary domains included the Arabian, and parts of the

(*Schamaschschumukin*, part 2, pp. 6, 7, 33, 34) translates this "the place where my mother gave me birth" (cf. JENSEN, *Inschriften Schamaschschumukin's*, in SCHRADER, *Keil. Bibl.*, vol. iii. pp. 198, 199); I have adopted the interpretation given by WINCKLER, *Altorient. Forsch.*, vol. i. p. 417. Lehmann had, however, proved convincingly that Shamash-shumukîn had a Babylonian mother, viz. the queen whose death is noticed in *Pinches' Babylonian Chronicle* (cf. *supra*, p. 371), and that he was born in Babylon (*Schamaschschumukin*, part 1, pp. 30–32).

[1] Winckler considers that Assur-bani-pal was the leader of the conspiracy, and that he obliged his father to recognise him as heir to the crown of Assyria (*Altorient. Forsch.*, vol. i. pp. 415–418), and to associate him on the throne.

[2] Cf. *supra*, pp. 160–166. The list of the principalities in the time of Esarhaddon and Assur-bani-pal is found on the cylinders of Assur-bani-pal (G. SMITH, *Hist. of Assurbanipal*, pp. 20–22), and was first commented on by Oppert (*Mémoire sur les rapports de l'Égypte et de l'Assyrie*, pp. 89–114), in accordance with the views of E. de Rougé. It has been studied several times since then by Haigh (*To the Editor*, in the *Zeitschrift*, 1868, pp. 82, 83; *Assyro-Ægyptiaca*, in the *Zeitschrift*, 1871, pp. 112–117), by Brugsch (*Bemerkungen zu den Assyro-Ægyptiaca*, in the *Zeitschrift*, 1872, pp. 29, 30; *Gesch. Ægyptens*, pp. 720–722), by Wiedemann (*Ægyptische Gesch.*, pp. 591, 592), and by Steindorff (*Die Keilschriftliche Wiedergabe ägyptischer Eigennamen*, in the *Beiträge zur Assyriologie*, vol. i. pp. 344–361, 593–612).

[3] The Assyrian name of this personage, spelt first Mantimiankhi by Oppert (*op. cit.*, p. 111), has been more accurately transcribed Mantimikhi by Steindorff (*op. cit.*, vol. i. pp. 354–356). The identification with the Montumihâît of the Theban documents, proposed by E. de Rougé (*Étude sur quelques monuments du règne de Tahraka*, in the *Mélanges d'Archéol. Égypt. et Assyr.*, vol. i. p. 20), is now generally adopted.

surrounding nomes, was then represented by a certain Pakruru.[1]   He had united under his banner the numerous petty chiefs of the eastern side of the Delta, the heirs of the ancient dynasties of Tanis and Bubastis, and his energy or ability must have made a good impression on the minds of his contemporaries, for they handed down his memory to their successors, who soon metamorphosed him into a popular legendary hero, famed both for his valour and wisdom.   The nobles of the western nomes acknowledged as their overlords the regents of Sais, the descendants of that Bocchoris who had for a short while brought the whole valley of the Nile under his sway.   Sabaco, having put his rival to death, had installed in his hereditary domains an Ethiopian named Ammeris, but this Ammeris had disappeared from the scene about the same time as his patron, in 704 B.C., and after him three princes at least had succeeded to the throne, namely, Stephinates, Nekhepsos, and Necho.[2]   Stephinates had died about 680 B.C., without accomplishing anything which was worth recording.   Nekhepsos had had no greater opportunities of distinguishing himself than had fallen to the lot of his father, and yet legends grew up round his name as round that of Pakruru: he was reputed to have been a great soothsayer, astrologist, and magician, and medical treatises were ascribed to him, and almanacs much esteemed by the superstitious in the Roman period.[3]   Necho had already occupied the throne for three or four years when the invasion of 670 B.C. delivered him from the Ethiopian supremacy.   He is represented as being brave, energetic, and enterprising, ready to hazard everything in order to attain the object towards which the ambition of his ancestors had been tending for a century past, namely, to restore unity to the ancient kingdom under the rule

---

[1] Pakruru plays the principal part in the "Adventure of a Breastplate" discovered and published by Krall (*Ein neuer Historischer Roman in Demotischer Schrift*, in the *Mittheilungen aus der Sammlungen der Papyrus Erzherzog Rainer*, vol. iii. pp. 19–80); for the interpretation to be given to the incidents of the romance, and the date to be assigned to its action, cf. MASPERO, *Un Nouveau Conte Égyptien*, in the *Journal des Savants*, 1897, pp. 649–659, 717–731.

[2] The lists of Eusebius give the series Ammeres, Stephinates, Nekhepsos, Necho I. (MANETHO, in MÜLLER-DIDOT, *Fragmenta Historicorum Græcorum*, vol. ii. pp. 593, 594), but Lepsius displaced Ammeres and identified him with the queen Amenertas (*Königsbuch*, p. 88 ; cf. WIEDEMANN, *Ægyptische Gesch.*, p. 590); others have thought to recognise in him Miamun Piônkhi, or Tanuatamanu, the successor of Taharqa (LAUTH, *Die Pianchi-Stele*, in the *Sitzungsberichte* of the Academy of Sciences at Munich, 1869, vol. i. pp. 29–32, and *Academy of Sciences* of Bavaria, vol. i. p. 307, et seq. ; *Aus Ægypten's Vorzeit*, pp. 442, 443; ED. MEYER, *Gesch. des Alterthums*, vol. i. p. 478).   He must, however, be left in this place in the list (WINCKLER, *Untersuch. zur Altorient. Gesch.*, p. 107, note 1), and we may perhaps consider him as the founder of the XXVIth dynasty (SCHÆFER, *Ein Porträt Psammetichs I.*, in the *Zeitschrift*, vol. xxxiii. pp. 117, 118).   If the number of *seven* years for the reign of Stephinates is adopted, we must suppose either that Manetho passed over the name of a prince at the beginning of the XXVIth dynasty, or that Ammeris was only enthroned at Memphis after the death of Sabaco; but the lists of the Syncellus and of Sothis assign 27 years to the reign of Stephinates.

[3] The astrological works of Nekhepsos are cited, among others, by PLINY, *H. Nat.*, II. xxi., VIII. xlix., l., and it is probably he whom a Greek papyrus of the Salt Collection mentions under the name of Nekheus.   Wiedemann objected to the identification of the astrologer with the King Nekhepsos (*Gesch. Ægyptens von Psammitich I. bis auf Alexander den Grossen*, pp. 156, 157, and *Ægyptische Gesch.*, pp. 600, 601), which Lauth vigorously insisted on (*König Nechepsos, Petosiris und die Triacontaëteris*, in the *Sitzungsberichte* of the Academy of Sciences at Munich, 1875, vol. ii.).

of the house of Sais.   The extent of his realm, and, above all, the possession
of Memphis, gave him a real superiority, and Esarhaddon did not hesitate
to esteem him above his competitors; the Ninevite scribes placed him in the
first rank, and he heads the list of the Egyptian vassals.   He soon had an
opportunity of proving his devotion to his foreign suzerain.   Taharqa did
not quietly accept his defeat, and Egypt looked to him to be revenged on
the Assyrian as soon as he should have reorganised his army.   He once more,
accordingly, took the field in the middle of 669 B.C.; the barons of the Saîd
rallied to his standard without hesitation, and he soon re-entered the " White
Wall," but there his advance was arrested.   Necho and the neighbouring chiefs
of the Delta, held in check by the presence of Semitic garrisons, did not venture
to proclaim themselves on his side, and awaited under arms the arrival of
Assyrian reinforcements.[1]   Esarhaddon, in spite of failing health, assumed
command of the troops, and before leaving home carried out the project to
which the conspiracy of the preceding year had given rise; he assigned the
government of Babylon to Shamash-shumukîn, and solemnly designated
Assur-bani-pal as the heir to Assyria proper, and to the suzerainty over the
whole empire.[2]   On the 12th of Iyyar, 668 B.C., on the day of the feast of Gula,
he presented their new lord to all the inhabitants of Assyria, both small and
great, who had assembled to be present at the ceremony, which ended in the
installation of the prince in the palace of Bîtriduti,[3] reserved for the heirs-
apparent.   A few weeks later Esarhaddon set out for Egypt, but his malady
became more serious on the journey, and he died on the 10th of Arakhsamna, in
the twelfth year of his reign.[4]   When we endeavour to conjure up his image

[1] *Annals of Assur-bani-pal*, col. i. ll. 52–63; cf. G. SMITH, *Hist. of Assurbanipal*, pp. 5–17, 36, 37;
JENSEN, *Inschriften Aschurbanipal's*, in SCHRADER, *Keil. Bibl.*, vol. ii. pp. 158, 159.   The first Egyptian
campaign of Assur-bani-pal is also the last campaign of Esarhaddon, and Assur-bani-pal appropriated
all the earlier incidents of it, some of which belong to the sole reign of his father, and some to the
few weeks in which he shared the throne with him; for this, cf. WINCKLER, *Altorient. Forsch.*, vol. i.
pp. 477–481.

[2] The association of Assur-bani-pal with his father on the throne was pointed out by G. Smith,
(*Egyptian Campaigns of Esarhaddon and Assur-bani-pal*, in the *Zeitschrift*, 1868, pp. 94, 95;
Hist. of Assurbanipal, p. 14; *Assyrian Discoveries*, pp. 416, 417), who thought he could fix the date
about 673 B.C., three or four years before the death of Esarhaddon (*Assyrian Eponym Canon*
pp. 163–165).   Tiele showed that Assur-bani-pal was then only made viceroy, and assigned his
association in the sovereignty to the year 671 or 670 B.C., about the time of the second Egyptian
campaign (*Bab.-assyr. Gesch.*, pp. 351, 369–371), while Hommel brought it down to 669 (*Gesch. Bab.
und Ass.*, p. 694).   Winckler has, with much reason, placed the date in 668 B.C. (*Gesch. Babyloniens
und Ægyptens*, p. 272, and *Altorient. Forsch.*, vol. i. pp. 415–418).   The Assyrian documents do not
mention the coronation of Shamash-shumukîn, for Assur-bani-pal afterwards affected to consider his
brother a mere viceroy, appointed by himself after the death of his father Esarhaddon; but an
examination of all the circumstances has shown that the enthronement of Shamash-shumukîn at
Babylon was on a par with that of Assur-bani-pal at Nineveh, and that both owed their elevation to
their father (E. MEYER, *Gesch. Alterthums*, vol. i. p. 477; LEHMANN, *Schamaschschumukin*, p. 33,
et seq.; WINCKLER, *Gesch. Bab. und Ass.*, pp. 133, 134, 272).

[3] *Annals of Assur-bani-pal*, col. i. ll. 11–24.

[4] *Pinches' Babylonian Chronicle*, col. iv. 30, 31; cf. WINCKLER, *Babylonische Chronik B*, in

before us, we fancy we are right in surmising that he was not cast in the ordinary mould of Assyrian monarchs. The history of his campaigns shows that he was as active and resolute as Assur-nazir-pal and Shalmaneser III., but he did not add to these good qualities their inflexible harshness towards their subjects, nor their brutal treatment of conquered foes. Circumstances in which they would have shown themselves merciless, he seized upon as occasions for clemency, and if massacres and executions are recorded among the events of his reign, at least he does not class them among the most important: the records of his wars do not continually speak of rebels flayed alive, kings impaled before the gates of their cities, and whole populations decimated by fire and sword. Of all the Assyrian conquerors, he is almost the only one for whom the historian can feel any regard, or from the study of whose reign he passes on with regret to pursue that of others in due course.

As soon as Esarhaddon had passed away, the separation of the two parts of the empire which he had planned was effected almost automatically: Assur-bani-pal proclaimed himself King of Assyria, and Shamash-shumukîn, in like manner, King of Babylon. One fact, which seems insignificant enough to us when we read it in the Annals, but was decisive in the eyes of their contemporaries, sanctioned the transformation thus accomplished: Bel and the gods of Accad quitted Assur in the month of Iyyâr and returned to their resting-place in Babylon. The restoration of the images to their own country became necessary as soon as it was decided to have a king in Karduniash, even though he were an Assyrian. To enable him to exercise legitimate authority, he must have celebrated the rites and "taken the hands of Bel," but it was a question whether this obligation could be fulfilled if Bel remained a prisoner in the neighbouring capital. Assur-bani-pal believed for a moment that this difficulty could be obviated, and consulted Shamash on this delicate question: "Shamash-shumukîn, the son of Esarhaddon, the King of Assyria, can he in this year take the hands of Bel, the mighty lord Marduk, in this very city, and then go to Babylon with the favour of Bel! If that would be pleasing to thy great divinity and to the mighty lord Marduk, thy great divinity must know it."[1] The reply was not favourable, and Shamash gave it as his opinion that Bel could not act as a sovereign lord while still languishing in prison in a city which was not his own. Assur-bani-pal had to resign himself to the release of his captive, and he did it

SCHRADER, *Keil. Bibl.*, vol. ii. pp. 284, 285. Arakhsamna corresponds to the Jewish Marcheswân, and to our month of May.

[1] KNUDTZON, *Assyrische Gebete an den Sonnengott*, pp. 267–269. Knudtzon has shown that *the city* mentioned in the text was Assur; the consultation of the oracle must, therefore, be interpreted in the fashion I have indicated, and the obedience accorded by Assur-bani-pal to Shamash, in spite of his instinctive objection to this impolitic proceeding, shows how powerful the oracles were at this epoch.

with a good grace.[1] He proceeded in pomp to the temple of Assur, where Marduk was shut up, and humbly entreated the exiled deity to vouchsafe to return to his own country. "Think on Babylon, which thou didst bring to nought in the rage of thy heart, and turn thy face towards the temple of Ê-sagilla, the lofty seat of thy divinity! Revisit thy city which thou hast forsaken to inhabit a place which is not worthy of thee, and do thou thyself, O Marduk,

lord of the gods, give the command to return to Babylon."[2] The statue set out on its journey, and was escorted by a solemn procession headed by the two kings.[3] The gods, by one accord, came forth from their cities and saluted the traveller as he passed by—Beltis of Agadê, Nebo of Borsippa, Shamash of Sippara, and Nirgal. At length he reached his beloved city, and entered Ê-sagilla in the midst of an immense throng of people. The kings headed the cortège, and the delighted multitude joined their two names with that of the god in their acclamations: it was a day never to be forgotten. Assur-bani-pal, in his capacity of suzerain, opened the sacred edifice, and then presented his brother, who thereupon "took the hands of Bel." A quarter of a century had not passed since the victorious Sennacherib had, as he thought, inflicted a mortal blow on the one power which stood in the way of Assyria's supremacy in Western Asia; already, in spite of his efforts, the city had sprung up from its ruins as vigorous as ever, and his son and grandsons had felt themselves irresistibly drawn to resuscitate that which their ancestors had desired to

ASSUR-BANI-PAL AS A BEARER OF OFFERINGS.[4]

[1] Pinches' Babylonian Chron., col. iv. 34–36; cf. WINCKLER, Babyl. Chronik B, in SCHRADER, Keil. Bibl., vol. ii. pp. 284, 285. For the significance of the ceremony in which the king took the hands of Bel, cf. Dawn of Civilization, p. 705; for the return of the gods and the date of the event, cf. LEHMANN, Schamaschschumukin, i. p. 43 i., 38, et seq.

[2] Tablet K 2050–K 2694 of the British Museum, col. ii. ll. 26–33, in LEHMANN, op. cit., pl. xxxvii., and ii. pp. 24–27.

[3] The substance of this account is taken from Tablet K 3050–K 2694, whose value has been first shown by LEHMANN, op. cit., i. pp. 43–56, where all the questions touching the accession of Shamash-shumukîn have been discussed at length. For the relative position of the two sovereigns, cf., lastly, WINCKLER, Altorient. Forsch., vol. i. pp. 415–418.

[4] Drawn by Boudier, from a photograph in LEHMANN, Schamaschschumukin, i., Frontispiece.

annihilate irrevocably. Babylon had rebuilt her palaces, her walls, and her temples; she had received back her gods without a war, and almost without any agitation, by the mere force of the prestige she exercised over all around her, and even over her conquerors. As a matter of fact, she had not regained her former position, and was still depressed and enfeebled by the blow which had laid her low; in addition to this, her king was an Assyrian, and a vassal of Assyria,[1] but nevertheless he was her own king, and hers alone. Her independence was already half regained. Shamash-shumukîn established his court at Babylon, and applied himself from the outset to restore, as far as he was able, the material and moral forces of his kingdom. Assur-bani-pal, on his side, met with no opposition from his subjects, but prudence cautioned him not to estrange them; the troubles of the preceding year were perhaps not so completely suppressed as to prevent the chiefs who had escaped punishment from being encouraged by the change of sovereign to renew their intrigues. The king, therefore, remained in Nineveh to inaugurate his rule, and confided to his generals the charge of conducting the expeditions which had been undertaken during his father's lifetime.[3] One of these undertakings was unimportant. Tandaî of Kirbît, a petty chief, was continually engaged in harassing the inhabitants of Yamutbal; he

SHAMASH-SHUMUKÎN AS A BEARER OF OFFERINGS.[2]

bore down upon them every year, and, after dealing a blow, retreated to his hiding-place in the mountains. He was attacked in his stronghold, and carried

---

[1] *Pinches' Babylonian Chron.*, col. iv. l. 38; cf. WINCKLER, *Bab. Chron. B*, in SCHRADER, *Keilinschriftliche Bibliothek*, ii. pp. 284, 285.

[2] Drawn by Boudier, from a photograph in LEHMANN, *Schamaschschumukin*, i., Frontispiece.

[3] The documents relating to the reign of Assur-bani-pal are so numerous that I cannot here give the bibliography of even the chief ones. I shall confine myself to indicating the two collections in which the most important of those which relate to the actual history are brought together and partially classified: G. SMITH, *History of Assurbanipal*, in 8vo, 1871, and SAMUEL ALDEN SMITH, *Die Keilschrifttexte Asurbanipals, Königs von Assyrien (678–626 v. Chr.) nach dem selbst in London copierten Grundtext mit Transcription, Uebersetzung, Kommentar und vollständigem Glossar*, in 8vo, Leipzig, 1887–1889, besides the selected texts transcribed and translated by JENSEN, *Inschriften Aschurbanipal's*, in SCHRADER, *Keil. Bibl.*, vol. ii. pp. 152–269. In these documents the facts are arranged in geographical order, not by the dates of the successive expeditions, and the chronological order of the campaigns is all the more difficult to determine accurately, as *Pinches' Babylonian Chronicle* fails us after the beginning of this reign, immediately after the mention of the above-mentioned war with Kirbît. Even the *Eponym Canon* is only accurate down to 666 B.C.; in that year

away captive with all his people into Egypt, at the furthest extremity of the empire, to serve in Assyrian garrisons in the midst of the fellahîn.[1]

Meanwhile, the army which Esarhaddon had been leading against Taharqa pursued its course under command of the Tartan.[2] Syria received it submissively, and the twenty-two kings who still possessed a shadow of autonomy in the country sent assurances of their devotion to the new monarch: even Yakînlu, King of Arvad, who had aroused suspicion by frequent acts of insubordination,[3] thought twice before rebelling against his terrible suzerain, and joined the rest in paying both homage and tribute. Cyprus and also Phœnicia remained faithful to their allegiance, and, what was of still more consequence, the states which lay nearest to Egypt—Philistia, Judah, Moab, and Ammon; the Assyrians were thus able to push forward to the Delta without losing time in repressing rebellions along their route. The Ethiopians had entrenched themselves at Karbanîti;[4] they were, however, once more defeated, and left

there is a break, and although we possess for the succeeding period more than forty names of eponyms, their classification is not at present absolutely certain (G. SMITH, *History of Assurbanipal*, pp. 320, 321, and the *Assyrian Eponym Canon*, pp. 67–71). The first to succeed in disentangling the chaos of dates and criticise the documents was TIELE, *Bab.-assyr. Gesch.*, pp. 366–376, 386–389, 399, 400, and his views are those which I have generally adopted; a certain number of new combinations have been suggested and sometimes demonstrated by WINCKLER, *Altorient. Forsch.*, i., ii., to which I shall duly refer as occasion offers. The inscriptions relating to the reign of Shamash-shumukîn have been collected, translated, and commented on with much care by LEHMANN, *Schamaschschumukin, König von Babylonien, 668–643 v. Chr., Inschriftliches Material über den Beginn seiner Regierung, grossentheils zum ersten Male herausgegeben, übersetzt und erläutert*, in 4to, 1892; cf. JENSEN, *Inschr. Schamaschschumukin's*, in SCHRADER, *Keil. Bibl.*, vol. iii. part 1, pp. 194–207. For the editions, translations, and commentaries published before 1866, see BEZOLD, *Kurzgefasster Ueberblick über die Babylonisch-assyrische Literatur*, pp. 108–121.

[1] *Pinches' Babylonian Chronicle*, col. iv. 1. 37; WINCKLER, *Bab. Chron. B*, in SCHRADER, *Keil. Bibl.*, vol. ii. pp. 284, 285. The expedition against Kirbît is omitted in certain documents, such as *Cylinder A of the Brit. Mus.*; it is inserted in the others in the fourth place, between the wars in Asia Minor and the campaign against the Mannai (G. SMITH, *Hist. of Assurbanipal*, pp. 79–88). The place assigned to it in the *Bab. Chron.*, quite in the beginning of the reign, is confirmed by a fragment of a tablet quoted by WINCKLER, *Altorient. Forsch.*, vol. i. pp. 474–477. Perhaps it was carried out by a Babylonian army; though Assur-bani-pal claimed the glory of it, by reason of his suzerainty over Karduniash.

[2] The text of *Tablet K 2675–K 228 of the Brit. Mus.*, obv., ll. 11–13 (G. SMITH, *Hist. of Assurbanipal*, p. 38), states distinctly that the Tartan commanded the first army. For the identity of this expedition with the last of those conducted by Esarhaddon, cf. *supra*, p. 380, note 1.

[3] Assur-bani-pal, acting in the name of his father, Esarhaddon, King of Assyria, had consulted Shamash on the desirability of sending troops against Arvad: the prince of this city is called Ikkalu (KNUDTZON, *Assyrische Gebete an den Sonnengott*, pp. 170–172), which is a variant of Yakînlu. Winckler concluded that the campaign against Arvad, which will be mentioned later on (*infra*, p. 387), took place before 668 B.C., in the reign of Esarhaddon (*Altorient. Forsch.*, vol. i. pp. 477, 478). It seems to me more natural to place it on the return from Egypt, when the people of Arvad were demoralised by the defeat of the Pharaoh whose alliance they had hoped for.

[4] I had compared Karbanîti with the Qarbîna mentioned in the *Great Harris Papyrus* (cf. *Struggle of the Nations*, p. 456), and this identification was accepted by Brugsch (*Geschichte Ægyptens*, pp. 188, 189, 717, 718), and subsequently by most Egyptologists, even after Brugsch himself recognised in Qarbîna the name of Canopus or a town near Canopus (*Dictionnaire Géographique*, pp. 654, 655). It has been contested by Steindorff (*Die Keilschriftliche Wiedergabe Ægyptischer Eigennamen*, in the *Beiträge zur Assyriologie*, vol. i. pp. 595, 596), and, in fact, Karbanîti could not be identified with Canopus, any more than the Qarbîna of the Harris Papyrus; its site must be looked for in the eastern or central part of the Delta.

so many of their soldiers dead upon the field, that Taharqa had not sufficient troops left to defend Memphis. He retreated upon Thebes, where he strongly fortified himself; but the Tartan had not suffered less than his adversary, and he would have been unable to pursue him, had not reinforcements promptly reached him. The Rabshakeh, who had been despatched from Nineveh with some Assyrian troops, had summoned to his aid the principal Syrian feudal chiefs, who, stimulated by the news of the victories achieved on the banks of the Nile, placed themselves unreservedly at his disposal. He ordered their vessels to proceed along the coast as far as the Delta, where he purposed to collect a fleet to ascend the river, while their troops augmented the force already under his command.[1] The two Assyrian generals, the Tartan and the Rabshakeh, quitted Memphis, probably in the early part of 667 B.C., and, cautiously advancing southwards, covered the distance separating the two Egyptian capitals in a steady march of forty days. When the Assyrians had advanced well up the valley, the princes of the Delta thought the opportunity had arrived to cut them off by a single bold stroke. They therefore opened cautious negotiations with the Ethiopian king, and proposed an arrangement which should secure their independence: "We will divide the country between us, and neither of us shall exercise authority over the other." However secretly these negotiations were conducted, they were certain to come to the knowledge of the Assyrian generals: the couriers were intercepted; and discovering from the despatches the extent of the danger, the Assyrians seized as many of the leaders of the league as they could. As a warning they sacked Sais, Mendes, and Tanis, demolishing the fortifications, and flaying or impaling the principal citizens before their city gates; they then sent two of the intriguing chiefs, Necho and Sharludari of Pelusium, bound hand and foot with chains, to Nineveh. Pakruru, of the Arabian nome, managed, however, to escape them. Taharqa, thus bereft of his allies, was no longer in a condition to repel the invader: he fled to Ethiopia, abandoning Thebes to its fate. The city was ransomed by despoiling the temple of Amon of half its treasures: Montumihâît transferred his allegiance unhesitatingly to Assur-bani-pal, and the whole of Egypt from the Mediterranean to the first cataract once more became Assyrian territory.[2] The victory was so complete that Assur-bani-pal thought

---

[1] The despatch of reinforcements under command of the Rabshakeh is expressly mentioned in *K 2675–K 218*, obv., ll. 25–99; cf. G. SMITH, *History of Assurbanipal*, pp. 40, 41.

[2] Tiele has shown (*Bab.-assyr. Gesch.*, p. 372) that the only account of an authentic character which we possess of the first Egyptian war of Assur-bani-pal, is that which is written on tablets *K 2675–K 228* of the British Museum. The official version on the Cylinders has confused the order of events, and has sometimes attributed to the king himself the actions of his generals. Winckler has completed Tiele's work on certain points, and has better indicated the chronological sequence of events (*Untersuchungen zur Altorient. Gesch.*, pp. 101–106, and *Altorient. Forsch.*, vol. i. pp. 478–483), but his scepticism has perhaps led him rather too far: I have, as a rule, kept closer to the Assyrian

2 C

he might without risk show clemency to his prisoners. He summoned them to his presence, and there, instead of putting out their eyes or subjecting them to some horrible form of torture, he received them back into favour, and confirmed Necho in the possession of all the honours which Esarhaddon had conceded to him. He clothed him in a mantle of honour, and bestowed on him a straight-bladed sword with an iron scabbard ornamented with gold, engraved with

MONTUMIHÂÎT, PRINCE OF THEBES.[1]

his names and titles, besides rings, gold bracelets, chariots, horses, and mules; in short, all the appurtenances of royalty. Not content with restoring to him the cities of Sais and Memphis, he granted him the fief of Athrîbis for his eldest son, Psammetichus. Moreover, he neglected no measure likely to show his supremacy. Athrîbis received the new name of Limir-patesi-assur, *may the high priest of Assur be glorious*, and Sais that of Kar-bel-matâti, *the fortress of the lord of the countries*. Psammetichus was called Nebo-shezib-anni, *Nebo, deliver me*, and residents were installed at his court and that of his father, who

texts than he has done. For the whole number of monuments referring to this campaign, see G. SMITH, *Hist. of Assurbanipal*, pp. 15–23, 30–44; S. ALDEN SMITH, *Die Keilschrifttexte Asurbanipals*, vol. i. pp. 4–11; and JENSEN, *Inschriften Aschurbanipal's*, in SCHRADER, *Keil. Bibl.*, vol. ii. pp. 158–167, 236, 237.

    [1] Drawn by Boudier, from the photograph by Miss Benson, published in the *Recueil de Travaux*, vol. xx.; cf. BENSON and GOURLAY, *The Temple of Mut in Asher*, pl. xxiv. It is not quite certain that this statue represents Montumihâit, as the inscription is wanting: the circumstances of the discovery, however, render it very probable (ID., *ibid.*, pp. 261, 262).

were entrusted with the *surveillance* of their conduct, and the task of keeping them to the path of duty : Necho, thus well guarded, thenceforward never faltered in his allegiance.[1]

The subjection of Egypt reacted on Syria and Asia Minor. Of the only two states still existing along the Phœnician seaboard, one, namely Tyre, had been in revolt for many years, and the other, Arvad, showed symptoms of disaffection. Esarhaddon, from lack of a sufficient fleet, had never been able to subdue the former, but he had interrupted the communications of the island with the mainland, and the blockade, which was constantly increasing in strictness, had already lasted for four years.[2] On receipt of the news from Egypt, Bâal realised that further resistance was hopeless; he therefore delivered up to the victor his heir-apparent, Yahî-melek, and one of his daughters, together with other hostages, besides silver, gold, and wood, and intreated for pardon. Assur-bani-pal left him in possession of his kingdom on condition of paying the regular tribute,[3] but Yakînlu, the King of Arvad, met with harsher treatment. In vain did he give up his sons, his daughters, and all his treasures; his intractability had worn out the patience of his suzerain :

PSAMMETICHUS I.[4]

he was carried away captive to Nineveh, and replaced by Azîbaal, his eldest son.[5] Two chiefs of the Taurus—Mugallu of Tabal, who had given trouble to Esarhaddon in the last years of his life,[6] and Sanda-sarmê of Cilicia—purchased immunity from the punishment due for various acts of brigandage, by gifts of horses, and by handing over each of them a daughter, richly

[1] *K 2675–K 228*, obv., ll. 51–65; cf. G. SMITH, *Hist. of Assurbanipal*, pp. 44–47. For later versions of the same events, see ID., *ibid.*, pp. 27–29; S. ALDEN SMITH, *Die Keilschrifttexte Asurbanipals*, vol. i. pp. 12, 13; JENSEN, *Inschriften Aschurbanipal's*, in SCHRADER, *Keil. Bibl.*, vol. ii. pp. 166, 167.

[2] Cf. *supra*, p. 369. Assur-bani-pal recounts the events at the beginning of his reign, as if they had been ordered and carried out directly by himself or his generals (*Cylinders A–B*, col. ii. ll. 84–88; cf. G. SMITH, *op. cit.*, pp. 58, 59); the constructions necessary for the blockade were begun some years previously by his father, Esarhaddon (WINCKLER, *Altorient. Forsch.*, vol. i. pp. 524–526; vol. ii. pp. 69, 70).

[3] G. SMITH, *op. cit.*, pp. 58–60, 68, 69; S. ALDEN SMITH, *op. cit.*, pp. 14–17; JENSEN, *op. cit.*, in SCHRADER, *op. cit.*, pp. 168–171.

[4] Drawn by Faucher-Gudin, from a bas-relief in the British Museum.

[5] G. SMITH, *op. cit.*, pp. 60, 61, 69–71; S. ALDEN SMITH, *op. cit.*, pp. 16–19; JENSEN, *op. cit.*, in SCHRADER, *op. cit.*, pp. 170–173.

[6] Cf. *supra*, p. 370.

dowered, to the harem of the king at Nineveh.[1] But these were incidents of slight moment, and their very insignificance proves how completely resigned to foreign domination the nations of the Mediterranean coast had now become. Vassal kings, princes, cities, peasants of the plain or shepherds of the mountains, all who were subject directly or indirectly to Assyria, had almost ceased to imagine that a change of sovereign afforded them any chance of regaining their independence. They no longer considered themselves the subjects of a conqueror whose death might free them from allegiance; they realised that they were the subjects of an empire whose power did not depend on the genius or incapacity of one man, but was maintained from age to age in virtue of the prestige it had attained, whatever might be the qualities of the reigning sovereign. The other independent states had at length come to the same conclusion, and the news of the accession of a fresh Assyrian king no longer awakened among them hopes of conquest or, at all events, of booty; such an occasion was regarded as a suitable opportunity for strengthening the bonds of neighbourly feeling or conciliatory friendship which united them to Assyria, by sending an embassy to congratulate the new sovereign. One of these embassies, which arrived about 667 B.C., caused much excitement at the court of Nineveh, and greatly flattered the vanity of the king. Reports brought back by sailors or the chiefs of caravans had revealed the existence of a kingdom of Lydia in the extreme west of Asia Minor, at the place of embarcation for crossing the sea.[2] It was known to be celebrated for its gold and its horses, but no direct relations between the two courts had ever been established, and the Lydian kings had hitherto affected to ignore the existence of Assyria. A revolution had broken out in this province a quarter of a century previously, which had placed on the throne of the Heraclidæ that family of the Mermnadæ whose previous history had been so tragic.[3] Dascylus, who had made his home for a long time among the White Syrians, had no intention of abandoning his adopted country, when one day, about the year 698 B.C., a messenger arrived bidding him repair to Sardes without delay.[4] His uncle Ardys, prince of Tyrrha, having no children, had applied to Sadyattes, beseeching him to revoke the sentence of banishment passed on his nephew. "My house is desolate," said he, "and all my kinsfolk are dead; and furthermore, Dascylus and his house have

[1] G. SMITH, Hist. of Assurbanipal, pp. 61, 62, 69, 70, 75; S. ALDEN SMITH, Die Keilschrifttexte Asurbanipals, pp. 16, 17; JENSEN, Inschriften Aschurbanipal's, in SCHRADER, Keil. Bibl., vol. ii. pp. 170–173. The oracular consultation, No. 55, attributed by Knudtzon to the time of Esarhaddon (Assyr. Gebete an den Sonnengott, pp. 15157–8), more probably refers to the period of Assur-bani-pal (WINCKLER, Altorient. Forsch., vol. ii. p. 127).

[2] It is called nagu sha nibirti tâmtim (Rassam Cylinder, col. ii. l. 95), "the country of the crossing of the sea," or more concisely, "the country this side the sea." Cf. for the explanation of this text, GELZER, Das Zeitalter des Gyges, in the Rheinisches Museum, 1875, vol. xxx. p. 221, note 4.

[3] Cf. supra, pp. 341, 342.

RADET, La Lydie et le Monde Grec, etc., pp. 143–145, has shown this date to be very probable.

already been pardoned by thine ancestors." Sadyattes consented, but Dascylus, preferring not to return, sent his son Gyges, then about eighteen years of age, in his stead. Gyges was a tall and very beautiful youth, and showed unusual skill as a charioteer and in the use of weapons, so that his renown soon spread throughout the country. Sadyattes desired to see him, and being captivated by his bold demeanour, enrolled him in his bodyguard, loaded him with presents, and took him into his entire confidence. Gyges was clever enough to utilise the king's favour in order to enlarge his domains and increase his riches, and thus win partisans among the people and the body of " Friends." Carian mercenaries at that time formed one of the most vigorous and best disciplined contingents in the armies of the period.[1] The Carians were, above all, a military race, and are said to have brought the shield and helmet to their highest perfection ;[2] at Sardes they formed the garrison of the citadel, and their captains were in high favour with the king. Gyges formed a fast friendship with Arselis of Mylasa, one of the chief of these officers, and thus made sure of the support of the garrison, and of the possibility of recruiting a corps among the Carian clans who remained in their own country.[3] He thus incurred the bitter jealousy of the Tylonidæ, whose chief, Lixos, was ready to adopt any measures which might damage his rival, even going so far as to simulate madness and run through the streets of Sardes crying out that Gyges, the son of Dascylus, was about to assassinate the king; but this stratagem did not succeed any better than his other treacherous devices. Meanwhile Sadyattes had sought the hand of Toudô,[4] daughter of Arnossos of Mysia, and sent his favourite to receive his affianced bride at the hand of her father. Gyges fell in love with her on the journey, and tried in vain to win her favour. She repulsed his advances with indignation, and on the very night of her marriage complained to her husband of the insult which had been offered her. Sadyattes swore that he would avenge her on the morrow; but Gyges, warned by a servant, slew the king before daybreak. Immediately after thus assassinating his sovereign, Gyges called together the " Friends," and ridding himself of those who were hostile to him, induced the others by bribes to further his designs; then descending to the place of public assembly, he summoned the people to a conclave. After a long and stormy debate, it was decided to consult the oracle at Delphi, which,

---

[1] Archilochus of Paros, a contemporary of Gyges, mentions the Carian mercenaries, Καὶ δὴ ἐπίκουρος ὥστε Κὰρ κεκλήσομαι (BERGK, *Poetæ Lyrici Græci*, vol. i. p. 690, *Fragm.* 24), and later on Ephorus said of them, that they had been the first to sell their services to strangers (*Fragm.* 23, in MÜLLER-DIDOT, *Fragm. Hist. Græc.*, vol. i. p. 239).

[2] For the weapons of the Carian mercenaries, cf. HERODOTUS, I. ccxxi., II. clii., and POLYÆNUS, *Stratagems*, vii. 3.

[3] The connection between Arselis and Gyges is mentioned by PLUTARCH, *Quæstiones Græcæ*, § 45, in the *Moralia*, ed. DIDOT, vol. i. pp. 371, 372.

[4] It is not certain whether the name is Toudô or Trydô ; I have followed the spelling of MÜLLER-DIDOT, *Fragm. Hist. Græc.*, vol. iii. p. 384, note 54.

corrupted by the gold from the Pactolus, enjoined on the Lydians to recognise Gyges as their king. He married Toudô, and by thus espousing the widow of the Heraclid sovereign, obtained some show of right to the crown; but the decision of the oracle was not universally acceptable, and war broke out, in which Gyges was victorious, thanks to the bravery of his Carian mercenaries.[1]

His career soon served as the fabric on which the popular imagination was continually working fresh embroideries. He was reported at the outset to have been of base extraction, a mere soldier of fortune, who had raised himself by degrees to the highest posts and had finally supplanted his patron. Herodotus, following the poet Archilochus of Paros, relates how the last of the Heraclidæ, whom he calls by his private name of Kandaules, and not his official name of Sadyattes,[2] forcibly insisted on exposing to the admiration of Gyges the naked beauty of his wife; the queen, thus outraged, called upon the favourite to avenge the insult to her modesty by the blood of her husband, and then bestowed on him her hand, together with the crown.[3] Plato made this story the groundwork of a most fantastic tale. Gyges, according to him, was originally a shepherd, who, after a terrible storm, noticed a fissure in the ground, into which he crept; there he discovered an enormous bronze horse, half broken, and in its side the corpse of a giant with a gold ring on his finger. Chance revealed to him that this ring rendered its wearer invisible: he set out for the court in quest of adventures, seduced the queen, murdered the king and seized his crown, accomplishing all this by virtue of his talisman.[4] According to a third legend, his crime and exaltation had been presaged by a wondrous prodigy. Two eagles of supernatural size had alighted on the roof of Toudô's room while she was still dwelling in her father's house, and the soothsayers who were consulted prognosticated that the princess would be the wife of two kings in a single night; and, in fact, Gyges, having stabbed Sadyattes when

[1] NICOLAS OF DAMASCUS, Fragm. 49, in MÜLLER-DIDOT, Fragm. Hist. Græc., vol. iii. pp. 383–385, who slavishly copies Xanthus the Lydian; cf. SCHUBERT, Geschichte der Könige von Lydien, pp. 24–35, and RADET, La Lydie et le Monde Grec, etc., pp. 124–139. The date of this revolution has been fixed at 587 B.C. by GELZER, Das Zeitalter des Gyges, in the Rheinisches Museum, 1875, vol. xxx. pp. 230–256.

[2] For the connection of the two names applied to the same person, cf. RADET, op. cit., pp. 76, 77, 124. Schubert (op. cit., pp. 31–34) considers that the names Sadyattes and Kandaules belong to two distinct persons. Kandaules, according to him, was probably a second son of Myrsos, who, after the murder of Sadyattes, disputed the possession of the crown with Gyges; in this case he was killed in battle by the Carian commander, Arselis, as related by Plutarch (Quæst. Græc., § 45), and Gyges was not really king till after the death of Kandaules.

[3] HERODOTUS, I. viii.–xiv. The improbability of the account given by Herodotus was demonstrated in the last century by FRÉRET, Recherches sur la Chronologie de l'Histoire de Lydie, in the Mémoires de l'Académie des Inscriptions, 1725, vol. v. p. 282; cf. GELZER, Das Zeitalter des Gyges, in the Rheinisches Museum, 1880, vol. xxxv. pp. 515, 518, et seq., where are collected examples of similar legends attached to the names of several historical characters—Sargon of Agadê (cf. Dawn of Civilization, pp. 597, 598), Cyrus, Arsaces the Parthian, and others.

[4] PLATO, Republic, Bk. II. iii., ed. DIDOT, vol. ii. pp. 23, 24; cf. CICERO, De Officiis, iii. 9. This version is curious, because it has preserved for us one of the earliest examples of a ring which renders its wearer invisible; it is well known how frequently such a talisman appears in Oriental tales of a later period.

his marriage was but just consummated, forced Toudô to become his wife on the spot without waiting for the morrow.[1]   Other stories were current, in which the events were related with less of the miraculous element, and which attributed the success of Gyges to the unbounded fidelity shown him by the Carian Arselis.[2]   In whatever manner it was brought about, his accession marked the opening of a new era for Lydia.   The country had always been noted for its valiant and warlike inhabitants, but the Heraclidæ had not expended its abundant resources on foreign conquest, and none of the surrounding peoples suspected that it could again become the seat of a brilliant empire as in fabulous times.[3]   Gyges endeavoured to awaken the military instincts of his subjects.   If he were not actually the first to organise that admirable cavalry corps which for nearly a century proved itself invincible on the field of battle, at least he enlarged and disciplined it, giving it cohesion

LYDIAN HORSEMEN.[4]

and daring; and it was well he did so, for a formidable danger already menaced his newly acquired kingdom.   The Cimmerians and Treres, so long as they did not act in concert, had been unable to overcome the resistance offered by the Phrygians; their raids, annually renewed, had never resulted in more than the destruction of a city or the pillaging of an ill-defended district.   But from 690 to 680 B.C. the Cimmerians, held in check by the bold front displayed by Sennacherib and Esarhaddon, had at last broken away from the seductions of the east, and poured down in force on the centre of the peninsula.   King Midas, after an heroic defence, at length gave way before their overwhelming numbers, and, rather than fall alive into the hands of the barbarians, poisoned himself by drinking the blood of a bull (676 B.C.).[5]   The flower of his nobility perished with him, and the

[1] XANTHUS OF LYDIA, according to NICOLAS OF DAMASCUS, *Fragm*. 49, in MÜLLER-DIDOT, *Fragm. Hist. Græc.*, vol. iii. pp. 384, 385.

[2] PLUTARCH, *Quæst. Græc.*, § 45.   For the authenticity of this narrative, cf. GELZER, *Das Zeitalter Gyges*, in the *Rheinisches Museum*, 1880, vol. xxxv. p. 528; SCHUBERT, *Gesch. der Könige von Lydien*, pp. 31–34; RADET, *La Lydie et le Monde Grec au temps des Mermnades*, pp. 133, 134.

[3] For this first Lydian empire, cf. *Struggle of the Nations*, pp. 364, 587, and *supra*, pp. 336–338.

[4] Drawn by Faucher-Gudin, from a Lydian bas-relief found in one of the tombs at Bin-Tepê, and now preserved in the British Museum.

[5] STRABO, I. iii. § 21, p. 61.   The date of 676 B.C. has been borrowed from Julius Africanus

people of lower rank who survived were so terrified by the invasion, that they
seemed in one day to lose entirely the brave and energetic character which had
hitherto been their safeguard.   The Cimmerians seized town after town; [1] they
descended from the basin of the Sangarios into that of the Rhyndakos; they
laid waste the Troad, and, about 670 B.C., they established themselves securely
in the stronghold of Antandros, opposite the magnificent Æolian island of
Lesbos, and ere long their advanced posts were face to face on all sides with
the outposts of Lydia. [2]   Gyges resolutely held his own, and successfully
repulsed them; but the struggle was too unequal between their vast hordes,
recruited incessantly from their reserves in Thrace or the Caucasus, and his
scanty battalions of Lydians, Carians, and Greeks.   Unaided, he had no chance
of reopening the great royal highway, which the fall of the Phrygian monarchy
had laid at the mercy of the barbarians along the whole of its middle course,
and yet he was aware that a cessation of the traffic which passed between the
Euphrates and the Hermos was likely to lead in a short time to the decay of
his kingdom.   If the numerous merchants who were wont to follow this ancient
traditional route were once allowed to desert it and turn aside to one of the coast-
roads which might replace it—either that of the Pontus in the north or of the
Mediterranean in the south—they might not be willing to return to it even
when again opened to traffic, and Lydia would lose for ever one of her richest
sources of revenue. [3]   We may well conceive that Gyges, whose fortune and very
existence was thus in jeopardy, would seek assistance against these barbarians from
the sovereign whose interests appeared identical with his own.   The renown of
the Assyrian empire had penetrated far into the west; the Achæans of Cyprus
who were its subjects, the Greek colonists of Cilicia, and the sailors whom the
exigencies of the coast-trade brought to Syrian ports, must all have testified to
its splendour; and the fame of its conquests over the Tabal and the peoples on
the Halys had spread abroad more than once during the previous century, and

by the Christian chronologists of the Byzantine period ; these latter made the fall of the Phrygian
kingdom coincide with the reign of Amon in Judæa, and this date is accepted by most modern
historians (GELZER, *Das Zeitalter des Gyges*, in the *Rheinisches Museum*, 1875, vol. xxx. pp. 252, 253,
257, 261–263 ; ED. MEYER, *Gesch. des Alterthums*, vol. i. pp. 545, 546, vol. ii. pp. 455, 456 ; RADET, *La
Lydie et le Monde Grec au temps des Mermnades*, p. 176).

[1] One fact alone, probably taken from the *Lydiaca* of Xanthus, is known to us concerning their
operations in Phrygia, namely, the taking of Syassos and the capture of enormous stores of corn which
were laid up in the silos in that city ; cf. STEPHEN OF BYZANTIUM, *s.v.* Σύασσος.

[2] ARISTOTLE, *Constitutions, Fragm.* 190, in MÜLLER-DIDOT, *Fragmenta Historicorum Græcorum*,
vol. ii. p. 162, ταύτην ὠνομάσθαι καὶ Κιμμερίδα Κιμμερίων ἐνοικούντων ἑκατὸν ἔτη; cf. PLINY, *H. Nat.*,
v. 32, § 2.

[3] Radet deserves credit for being the first to point out the economic reasons which necessarily led
Gyges to make his attempt at forming an alliance with Assur-bani-pal (*op. cit.*, p. 177).   He has thus
definitely dismissed the objections which some recent critics, especially Gutschmid, had raised against
the authenticity of this episode in order to defend classic tradition and diminish the authority of the
Assyrian texts (*Neue Beiträge zur Geschichte des Alten Orients*, pp. x., xi.).

had reached as far as the western extremity of the peninsula of Asia Minor, by means of the merchants of Sardes or Ionia. The Cimmerians had harassed Assyria, and still continued to be a source of anxiety to her rulers; Gyges judged that participation in a common hatred or danger would predispose the king in his favour, and a dream furnished him with a pretext for notifying to the court of Nineveh his desire to enter into friendly relations with it. He dreamed that a god, undoubtedly Assur, had appeared to him in the night, and commanded him to prostrate himself at the feet of Assur-bani-pal : " In his name thou shalt overcome thine enemies." The next morning he despatched horsemen to the great king, but when the leader of the embassy reached the frontier and met the Assyrians for the first time, they asked him, " Who, then, art thou, brother, thou from whose land no courier has as yet visited our country ? " The language he spoke was unknown to them; they only gathered that he desired to be conducted into the presence of the king, and consequently sent him on to Nineveh under good escort. There the same obstacle presented itself, for none of the official interpreters at the court knew the Lydian tongue ; however, an interpreter was at length discovered, who translated the story of the dream as best he could.[1] Assur-bani-pal joyfully accepted the homage offered to him from such a far-off land, and from thenceforward some sort of alliance existed between Assyria and Lydia—an alliance of a very Platonic order, from which Gyges at least derived no sensible advantage. Some troops sent into the country of the White Syrians may have disquieted the Cimmerians, and, by causing a diversion in their rear, procured a respite for Lydia ; but the caravan route across Asia Minor was only of secondary importance to the prosperity of Nineveh and the Syrian provinces, since the Phœnician navy provided sufficient outlets for their trade in the west. Assur-bani-pal lavished friendly speeches on the Lydians, but left them to bear the brunt of the attack alone, and devoutly thanked Assur for the security which their determined courage procured for the western frontier of his empire.[2]

The Cimmerian peril being, for the present at least, averted, there no longer remained any foe to trouble the peace of the empire on the northern or eastern

---

[1] The detailed account of the events concerning the arrival of the ambassador is known to us only from *Cylinder E of the British Museum*, ll. 1–11, published by G. SMITH, *History of Assurbanipal*, pp. 76, 77 ; cf. JENSEN, *Inschriften Aschurbanipal's*, in SCHRADER, *Keilinschriftliche Bibliothek*, vol. ii. pp. 172, 173.

[2] The embassy sent by Gyges is mentioned in *K 2675*, rev., ll. 13–21 (G. SMITH, *op. cit.*, pp. 73–75), and with some variations in *Cylinder B*, col. ii. ll. 86–93 (ID., *ibid.*, pp. 71, 72) : the other documents in which it is mentioned, mostly connect with it the story of the death of Gyges and the victory of Ardys over the Cimmerians (ID., *ibid.*, pp. 64–68 ; S. ALDEN SMITH, *Die Keilschrifttexte Asurbanipals*, vol. i. pp. 18–21 ; JENSEN, *Inschriften Aschurbanipal's*, in SCHRADER, *Keilinschriftliche Bibliothek*, vol. ii. pp. 172–177), that is to say, with events much posterior to these first communications between Lydia and Assyria.

frontier, Urartu, the Mannai, and the Medes having now ceased to be formidable.   Urartu, incessantly exposed to the ravages of the barbarians, had drawn
closer and closer to Assyria; and though not actually descending to the point of
owning its rival's superiority in order to obtain succour against these terrible
foes, it yet carefully avoided all pretexts for war, and persistently maintained
friendly relations with its powerful neighbour.   Its kings, Rusas II. and his
successor Erimenas, no longer meditated feats of arms and successful raids, but
devoted themselves to building their city walls, erecting palaces and temples,
and planning pleasant retreats in the mountain fastnesses, where they lived
surrounded by gardens planted at great cost, watered by streams brought
thither from distant springs.[1]   The Mannai submitted without a murmur to
their Assyrian governors, and the Medes, kept in check by the garrisons of Parsua
and Kharkhar, seemed to have laid aside much of their fierce and turbulent
disposition.   Esarhaddon had endeavoured to conciliate the good will of Elam
by a signal service.   He had supplied its inhabitants with corn, wine, and
provisions of all sorts during a famine which had afflicted the country about
670 B.C.;   nor had his good will ended there.   He refused to bring into servitude those Elamite subjects who had taken refuge with their families on Assyrian
territory to escape the scourge, although the rights of nations authorised him
so to do, but having nourished them as long as the dearth lasted, he then sent
them back to their fellow-citizens.   Urtaku of Elam had thenceforward maintained a kind of sullen neutrality, entering only into secret conspiracies against
the Babylonian prefects on the Tigris.   The Aramæans in the valleys of the Ulaî,
indeed, were restless, and several of their chiefs, Bel-ikîsha of the Gambulâ, and
Nabo-shumirîsh, plotted in secret with Marduk-shumibni, the Elamite general
in command on the frontier.[2]   But no hint of this had yet transpired, and peace
apparently reigned there as elsewhere.   Never had the empire been so respected;
never had it united so many diverse nations under one sceptre—Egyptians,
Syrians, tribes of the Taurus, and the mountain districts round the Tigris and
Euphrates, Mannai, Medes, Babylonians, and Arabs; never, moreover, had it
possessed greater resources wherewith to compel obedience from the provinces
or defend them against foreign attack.   Doubtless the population of Assyria
proper, and the ancient districts whose contingents formed the nucleus of the

[1] For the succession of the kings of Urartu at this epoch, see BELCK and LEHMANN, *Ein neuer
Herrscher von Khaldia*, in the *Zeitschrift für Assyriologie*, 1894, vol. ix. pp. 82–99, 339–360. For the
foundation or restoration of the city and gardens of Toprak-Kaleh by Rusas II. and III., cf., besides the
memoir mentioned above, BELCK and LEHMANN, *Ueber neuer aufgefundenen Armenischen Keilinschriften*,
in the *Zeitschrift für Ethnologie*, 1892, pp. 144–147; *Weitere Ergebnisse*, in the *Verhandlungen der Berliner
anthropologischer Gesellschaft*, 1892, p. 486; *Chaldische Nova*, in the *Verhandlungen*, 1893, pp. 223, 224,
and *Chaldische Forschungen*, in the *Verhandlungen*, 1895, pp. 595–601.
[2] G. SMITH, *History of Assurbanipal*, pp. 100–102, 108, 109.

army, were still suffering from the results of the civil war which had broken out more than fifteen years before, after the assassination of Sennacherib;[1] but under the easy rule of Esarhaddon the natural increase of population, unchecked by any extraordinary call for recruits, must have almost repaired their losses. The Egyptian campaigns, partially carried out by Syrian auxiliaries, had not sensibly retarded this progress, and, provided that peace were maintained for some years longer, the time seemed at hand when the king, having repaired his losses, could call upon the nation to make fresh efforts in offensive or defensive warfare, without the risk of seeing his people melt and disappear before his eyes. It seems, indeed, as if Assur-bani-pal, either by policy or natural disposition,

was inclined for peace. But this did not preclude, when occasion demanded, his directing his forces and fighting in person like any other Assyrian monarch; he, however, preferred repose, and when circumstances forced war upon him, he willingly delegated the conduct of the army to his generals. He would probably have renounced possession of Egypt if he could have done so with safety and such a course would not have been without wisdom, the retention of this newly acquired province being difficult and costly. Not to speak of differences in language, religion, and manners, which would prevent it from ever becoming assimilated to Assyria

ASSUR-BANI-PAL.[2]

as Damascus, Hamath, and Samaria, and most of the Asiatic states had been, it was merely connected with the rest of the empire by the thin chain of rocks, desert, and marshes stretching between the Red Sea and the Mediterranean. A revolt of the cities of the Philistines, or of one of the Idumæan sheikhs, would have sufficed to isolate it, and, communications once interrupted, the safety of the numerous Assyrian officers and garrisons would be seriously jeopardised, all of whom must be maintained there if the country was to be permanently retained. The inclination to meddle in the affairs of Syria always displayed by the Pharaohs, and their obsolete claims to rule the whole country as far as the Euphrates, did not allow of their autonomy being restored to them at the risk of the immediate renewal of their intrigues with Tyre or Judah, and the fomenting of serious rebellions among the vassal princes of Palestine. On the other hand, Egypt was by its natural position so detached

---

[1] Cf. *supra*, p. 348.

[2] Drawn by Faucher-Gudin, from one of the bas-reliefs from Kouyunjik preserved in the British Museum.

from the rest of the empire that it was certain to escape from the influence of Nineveh as soon as the pressure of circumstances obliged the suzerain to relax his efforts to keep it in subjection. Besides this, Ethiopia lay behind Egypt, almost inaccessible in the fabled realms of the south, always ready to provoke conspiracies or renew hostilities when the occasion offered. Montumihâît had already returned to Thebes on the retreat of the Assyrian battalions, and though Taharqa, rendered inactive, as it was said, by a dream which bade him remain at Napata,[1] had not reappeared north of the cataract, he had sent Tanuatamanu, the son of his wife by Sabaco, to administer the province in his name.[2] Taharqa died shortly after (666 B.C.), and his stepson was preparing to leave Thebes in order to be solemnly crowned at Gebel Barkal, when he saw one night in a dream two serpents, one on his right hand, the other on his left. The sooth-sayers whom he consulted on the matter prognosticated for him a successful career: "Thou holdest the south countries; seize thou those of the north, and let the crowns of the two regions gleam upon thy brow!" He proceeded at once to present himself before his divine father Amon of Napata, and, encountering no opposition from the Ethiopian priests or nobles, he was able to fulfil the prediction almost immediately after his coronation.[3] The Saîd hailed his return with joy, and the inhabitants, massed upon either bank of the river, acclaimed him as he glided past them on his boat: "Go in peace! mayest thou have peace! Restore life to Egypt! Rebuild the ruined temples, set up once more the statues and emblems of the deities! Re-establish the endowments raised to the gods and goddesses, even the offerings to the dead! Restore the priest to his place, that he may minister at all the rites!"

The Assyrian officials and the princes of the north, with Necho at their head, were drawn up beneath the walls of Memphis to defy him. He overcame them, however, captured the city, and pushed on into the Delta in pursuit of the retreating foe. Necho either fell in a skirmish, or was taken prisoner and

---

[1] The legend quoted by Herodotus (II. clii., cf. WIEDEMANN, *Herodots Zweites Buch*, pp. 543, 544) relates that Sabaco, having slain Necho I., the father of Psammetichus, evacuated Egypt which he had conquered, and retired to Ethiopia in obedience to a dream. The name of Sabaco was very probably substituted for that of Taharqa in the tradition preserved in Sais and Memphis, echoes of which reached the Greek historian in the middle of the fifth century B.C.

[2] It appears, from the *Stele of the Dream*, ll. 3–7, that Tanuatamanu was in the Thebaid at the time of his accession to the throne (MASPERO, *Mélanges de Mythologie et d'Archéologie Égyptiennes*, vol. iii. p. 9; SCHÆFER, *Zur Erklärung der Traumstele*, in the *Zeitschrift*, vol. xxxv. p. 69).

[3] Steindorff (*Keilschriftliche Wiedergabe ägyptischer Eigennamen*, in the *Beiträge für Assyriologie*, vol. i. pp. 358, 359) thinks that Tanuatamanu had been officially associated with himself on the throne by Taharqa, and Schæfer (*op. cit.*, pp. 67, 68) supposes that the dream dates from the first year of their joint reign. The presence of Tanuatamanu beside Taharqa, in the small Theban temple, the bas-reliefs of which were published by MARIETTE, *Monuments Divers*, pls. 79–85, does not necessarily prove that the two kings reigned conjointly: it may equally well indicate that the one accomplished the work commenced by the other.

put to death : his son Psammetichus escaped to Syria,[1] but the remaining princes shut themselves up, each in his own stronghold, to await reinforcements from Asia, and a series of tedious and interminable sieges began. Impatient at this dilatory method of warfare, Tanuatamanu at length fell back on Memphis,

KING TANUATAMANU IN ADORATION BEFORE THE GODS OF THEBES.[2]

and there opened negotiations in the hope of securing at least a nominal submission, which might enable him to withdraw from the affair with honour. The princes of the east received his overtures favourably, and consented to prostrate themselves before him at the White Wall under the auspices of Pakruru. "Grant us the breath of life, for he who acknowledges thee not cannot live, and we will be thy vassals, as thou didst declare at the beginning,

---

[1] HERODOTUS, II. clii., who appears to have been well informed on this point : it is certain that the name of Necho I. disappears from the Assyrian records directly after the accession of Tanuatamanu.

[2] Drawn by Boudier, after a photograph by Legrain, taken in the small temple at Thebes ; cf. MARIETTE, *Monuments Divers*, pl. 86.

on the day in which thou becamest king!" The heart of his Majesty was filled with joy when he heard this discourse: he bestowed upon them in abundance bread, beer, and all manner of good things. After sojourning some days at the court of Pharaoh their lord, they said to him, "Why stay we here, O prince our master?" His Majesty replied, "Wherefore?" They answered then, "Graciously permit us to return to our own cities, that we may give commands to our subjects, and may bring thee our tribute offerings!" They returned ere long, bringing the promised gifts, and the king withdrew to Napata loaded with spoil.[1] The Delta proper at once ceased to obey him, but Memphis, as well as Thebes, still acknowledged his sway for some two or three years longer.[2] It was neither indolence nor fear which had kept Assur-bani-pal from marching to the succour of his subjects as soon as the movement under Tanuatamanu became manifest, but serious complications had arisen in the south-east which had for the moment obliged him to leave Egypt to itself. Elam had at last laid aside the mask, and Urtaku, yielding to the entreaties of the Aramæan sheikhs, who were urged on by Marduk-shumibni,[3] had crossed the Tigris. Shamash-shumukîn, thus taken unawares, could only shut himself up in Babylon, and in all haste send information of his plight to his brother and suzerain. Assur-bani-pal, preoccupied with the events taking place on the Nile, was for a moment in doubt whether this incursion was merely a passing raid or the opening of a serious war, but the reports of his scouts soon left no doubt as to the gravity of the danger: "The Elamite, like a swarm of grasshoppers, covers the fields, he covers Accad; against Babylon he has pitched his camp and drawn out his lines." The city was too strong to be taken by storm. The Assyrians hastened to relieve it, and threatened to cut off the retreat of the aggressors: the latter, therefore, gave up the siege, and returned to their own country, but their demeanour was still so undaunted that Assur-bani-pal did not cross the frontier in pursuit of them (665 B.C.). He doubtless fully expected that they would

---

[1] MARIETTE, *Monuments Divers*, pls. 7, 8, and p. 2 : cf. MASPERO, *Mélanges de Mythologie et d'Archéologie Égyptiennes*, vol. iii. pp. 5–18, 217–223; BRUGSCH, *Geschichte Ægyptens*, pp. 707–715; and SCHÆFER, *Zur Erklärung der Traumstele*, in the *Zeitschrift*, vol. xxxv. pp. 67–70. Tanuatamanu was at first identified by Haigh (*To the Editor*, in the *Zeitschrift*, 1868, pp. 80–83) with the person whose name Assyriologists read as Urdamani, but the impossibility of recognising the name *Tanuatamanu* in *Urdamani* decided E. de Rougé (*Étude sur quelques monuments du règne du Tahraka*, in the *Mélanges*, vol. i. pp. 89–91), and subsequently others (MASPERO, *Histoire des peuples de l'Orient*, 4th edit., pp. 459, 526–528), to admit an Urdamani different from Tanuatamanu. The discovery of the right reading of the name *Tandamanu* by Steindorff (*Die Keilschriftliche Wiedergabe ägyptischer Eigennamen*, in the *Beiträge zur Assyriologie*, vol. i. pp. 356–359) has banished all doubts, and it is now universally admitted that the person mentioned in the Assyrian documents is identical with the king who erected the *Stele of the Dream* at Gebel Barkal.

[2] A monument still exists which was dedicated at Thebes in the third year of Tanuatamanu: it was first brought to notice by Champollion (*Monuments de l'Égypte et de la Nubie*, pl. ccclix.), and is now preserved in the Berlin Museum (ERMAN, *Ausführliches Verzeichniss*, pp. 169, 170, No. 2096), with another undated document of the same king (ID., *ibid.*, p. 170, No. 2097).

[3] For these sheikhs, cf. *supra*, pp. 358, 367.

soon return in larger numbers, and perhaps his fear would not have proved unfounded had not fate suddenly deprived them of all their leaders. Bel-ikîsha was killed in hunting by a wild boar, Nabu-shumirîsh was struck down by dropsy, and Marduk-shumibni perished in a mysterious manner. Finally Urtaku succumbed to an attack of apoplexy, and the year which had been so fatal to his allies proved not less so to himself (664 B.C.).[1] It now seemed as if Assur-bani-pal might breathe freely, and inflict his long-deferred vengeance on Tanuatamanu, but the death of Urtaku did not remove all causes of uneasiness. Peace was not yet concluded, and it depended on the new King of Elam whether hostilities would be renewed. Fortunately for the Assyrians, the transmission of power had rarely taken place at Susa for a century past without a disturbance, and Urtaku himself had gained the throne by usurpation, possibly accompanied by murder. As he had treated his elder brother Khumbân-khaldash and the children of the latter, so did his younger brother Tammaritu now treat his sons. Tammaritu was "a devil" incarnate, whose whole thoughts were of murder and rapine; at least, this was the idea formed of him by his Assyrian contemporaries, who declared that he desired to put to death the sons of his two predecessors out of sheer cruelty. But we do not need a very vivid imagination to believe that these princes were anxious to dethrone him, and that in endeavouring to rid himself of them he was merely forestalling their secret plots. They escaped his murderous designs, however, and fled to Assyria,—Khumbân-igash, Khumbân-appa, and Tammaritu, sons of Urtaku, and Kuduru and Parru, sons of Khumbân-khaldash, followed by sixty other princes of royal blood, together with archers and servants—forming, in fact, a small army of Elamites. Assur-bani-pal received them with honour, for their defection furnished him with a powerful weapon against the usurper : by succouring them he could rouse half Elam and involve it in civil war, in which the pretenders would soon exhaust their resources. It was now a favourable moment to renew hostilities in Egypt, while Tammaritu, still insecure on his throne, would not venture to provoke a conflict.[2] As a matter of fact, Tanuatamanu did not risk the defence of Memphis, but concentrated his forces at Thebes. Once more the Assyrian generals ascended the Nile, and, after a

---

[1] G. Smith, *History of Assurbanipal*, pp. 100–109; Jensen, *Inschriften Aschurbanipal's*, in Schrader, *Keilinschriftliche Bibliothek*, vol. ii. pp. 244–247.

[2] The time of the war against Urtaku and the expedition against Tanuatamanu is indicated by a passage in a cylinder as yet unedited (*Rassam 281 of the British Museum*), quoted by Winckler, *Altorient. Forschungen*, vol. i. p. 478, note 2. There we read that the invasion of Urtaku took place at the moment when Tanuatamanu ascended the throne. These preliminary difficulties with Elam would thus have coincided with the two years which elapsed between the accession of Tanuatamanu and his conquest of Memphis, up to the third year mentioned in the Berlin inscription (for this inscription, cf. *supra*, p. 398, note 2); the testimony of the Egyptian monuments would thus be in almost complete accord with the Assyrian documents on this point.

voyage lasting six weeks, at length reached the suburbs of the great city. Tanuatamanu had fled towards Kipkip, leaving Thebes at the mercy of the invaders. It was given up to pillage, its population was carried off into slavery, and its temples and palaces were despoiled of their treasures—gold, silver, metals, and precious stones, broidered and richly dyed stuffs, and horses of the royal stud. Two of the obelisks which adorned the temple of Amon were taken down from their pedestals and placed on rafts to be transported to Nineveh, and we shall perhaps unearth them some day from its ruins. This work of reprisal accomplished, the conquerors made their way northwards, and the bulk of the army recrossed the isthmus: Ethiopian rule had ceased

ASSYRIAN HELMET FOUND
AT THEBES.[2]

north of the cataract, and Egypt settled down once more under the Assyrian yoke (663–662 B.C.).[1]

Impoverished and decayed as Thebes had now long since become, the nations whom she had afflicted so sorely in the days of her glory had retained for her feelings of respect and almost of awe: the rumour of her fall, spread through the Eastern world, filled them with astonishment and pity. The Hebrews saw in it the chastisement inflicted by their God on the tyrant who had oppressed their ancestors, and their prophets used it to impress upon the minds of their contemporaries the vanity of human prosperity. Half a century later, when Nineveh, menaced in her turn, was desperately arming herself to repel the barbarians, Nahum the Elkoshite demanded of her, amid his fierce denunciations, whether she vaunted herself to be better than " No-amon (city of Amon), that was situate among the rivers, that had the waters round about her; whose rampart was the sea, and her wall was of the sea? Ethiopia and Egypt were her strength, and it was infinite. Put and Lubim (Libya and the Nubians) came to her succour. Yet was she carried away, she went into captivity: her young children also were dashed in pieces at the top of all the streets: and they cast lots for her honourable men, and all her great men were bound in chains." [3] Assur-bani-pal, lord of Egypt and conqueror of Ethiopia,

[1] The account of the campaign against Tanuatamanu is found on *Tablet K 2675*, obv., ll. 70–74, rev., ll. 1–5, in G. SMITH, *History of Assurbanipal*, pp. 55–57 ; for variant renderings, cf. G. SMITH, *op. cit.*, pp. 52–55 ; S. ALDEN SMITH, *Die Keilschrifttexte Asurbanipals*, vol. i. pp. 12–16 ; JENSEN, *Inschriften Aschurbanipal's*, in SCHRADER, *Keil. Bibl.*, vol. ii. pp. 166–169. The dates which I have adopted follow from the date of 666 B.C. given for the death of Taharqa and the accession of Psammetichus I. The expedition against Thebes must have taken place at the end of the third or beginning of the fourth year of the reign of Tanuatamanu, shortly after the inscription of the third year, and was engraved (for this inscription, cf. *supra*, p. 398, note 2) either in 663 or 662 B.C. at the latest.

[2] Drawn by Faucher-Gudin, from the photograph by PETRIE, *Six Temples at Thebes*, pl. xxi.

[3] *Nahum* iii. 8–10.

might reasonably consider himself invincible ; it would have been well for the princes who trembled at the name of Assur-bani-pal, if they had taken this lesson to heart, and had learned from the downfall of Tanuatamanu what fate awaited them in the event of their daring to arouse the wrath of Assyria by any kind of intrigue. Unfortunately, many of them either failed to see the warning or refused to profit by it. The Mannai had quickly recovered from the defeat inflicted on them by Esarhaddon,[1] and their king, Akhsheri, in

spite of his advancing years, believed that his own energy and resources were sufficient to warrant him in anticipating a speedy revenge. Perhaps a further insight into the real character of Assur-bani-pal may have induced him to venture on hostilities. For the king's contemporaries had begun to realise that, beneath his apparent bravery and ostentation, he was by nature indolent, im-

A LION ISSUING FROM ITS CAGE.[2]

patient of restraint, and fond of ease and luxury. When not absorbed in the routine of the court and the pleasures of the harem, he spent his leisure in hunting on the Mesopotamian plains, or in the extensive parks which had been laid out by himself or his predecessors in the vicinity of their summer palaces. Urus-stalking had become merely a memory of the past : these animals had been so persistently hunted for centuries that the species had almost become extinct ; solitary specimens only were occasionally met with in remote parts of the forest or in out-of-the-way marshes. The wild ass was still to be found in large numbers, as well as the goat, the ostrich, and small game,[3] but the lion was now rarely met with, and the beaters were no longer sure of finding him in his ancient haunts. Specimens had to be sought by the royal gamekeepers in the provinces, and when successfully trapped were forthwith despatched to one or other of the king's country seats.

---

[1] For the defeat of the Mannai in the reign of Esarhaddon, cf. *supra*, pp. 352–354.

[2] Drawn by Faucher-Gudin, from a photograph taken from the original in the British Museum ; cf. PLACE, *Ninive et l'Assyrie*, vol. iii. pl. 50.

[3] The representation of a wild-ass hunt, reproduced in *The Dawn of Civilization*, p. 559, belongs to the reign of Assur-bani-pal.

The beast was often kept for several days in a cage while preparations were made for a fête, at which he was destined to form one of the chief attractions, and when the time came he was taken to the appointed place and let loose; the sovereign pursued him either in a chariot or on horseback, and did not desist from the chase till he had pierced his quarry with arrows or lance. Frequently the beast would be turned loose in the park, and left there till accustomed to his surroundings, so that later on he might be run down under conditions somewhat resembling his native freedom. Assur-bani-pal did not shun a personal encounter with an infuriated lion; he displayed in this hazardous sport a bravery and skill which rivalled that of his ancestors, and he never relegated to another the task of leading the attack or dealing the final death-blow. This, however, was not the case when it was a question of starting on some warlike expedition; he would then leave to his Tartans, or to the Rabshakeh, or to some other chosen officer, the entire conduct of all operations.[1] This did not preclude the king from taking an interest in what was passing beyond the frontier, nor did he fail in his performance of the various religious duties which custom imposed on an Assyrian sovereign: he consulted the oracles of Shamash or Ishtar, he offered sacrifices, he fasted and humbled himself in the temples to obtain the success of his troops, and when they returned laden with spoil from the campaign, he attributed their victories no less to his prayers than to their courage or to the skill of their leaders. His generals, thoroughly equipped for their task, and well supported by their troops, had no need of the royal presence to ensure their triumph over any foe they might encounter; indeed, in the absence of the king they experienced a liberty of action and boldness in pressing their victories to the uttermost which they would not have enjoyed had he been in command. Foreigners, accustomed to see the sovereigns of Nineveh conduct their armies in person, as long as they were not incapacitated by age, thought that the indolence of Assur-bani-pal was the unconscious expression of weariness or of his feeble control of the empire, and Akhsheri determined to be one of the first to take advantage of it. Events proved that he was mistaken in his calculations. No sooner had his intentions become known, than a division of Assyrian troops appeared on his frontier, and prepared to attack him. Resolving to take the initiative, he fell one night unexpectedly upon the Assyrian camp, but fortune declared against him: he was driven back, and his broken ranks were closely pursued for a distance of twenty-three miles. Eight of his strongholds fell one after the other, and he was at length forced to abandon his capital of Izirtu, and flee precipitately to his fortress of

---

[1] We have seen, for example, that after the death of Esarhaddon, the Egyptian campaign was conducted by one of the Tartans and the Rabshakeh (cf. *supra*, pp. 384, 385); for the campaign against Tiummân, and the reasons which hindered the king from conducting it in person, see *infra*, p. 405.

Adrana in the heart of the mountains. Even there he did not find the security he desired, for the conqueror pursued him thither, methodically devastating by the way the districts through which he passed : he carried off everything—men, slaves, and herds of cattle—and he never retired from a city or village without previously setting it on fire. Paddir, Arsiyanîsh, and Eristiana were thus laid waste, after which the Assyrians returned to their camp, having re-established the authority of their master over several districts which had been lost to them for some generations previously. Akhsheri had shown no sign of yielding, but his people, weary of a hopeless resistance, put him to death, and hurling his corpse over the wall of Adrana, proclaimed his son Ualli as king. The new sovereign hastened to conclude a treaty with the Assyrians on reasonable terms : he gave up his eldest son, Erisinni, and one of his daughters as hostages, and promised to pay the former tribute augmented by an annual present of thirty horses ;[1] peace was not again disturbed on this side except by some unimportant skirmishes. In one of these, a Median chieftain, named Biriz-khadri, made an alliance with two princes of the people of the Sakhi, Sarâti, and Parikhia, sons of Gâgu,[2] to ravage the marches of the Greater Zab ; but their territory was raided in return, and they themselves taken prisoners.[3] A little later, Andaria, prince of Lubdi, forgetful of his oath of allegiance to the aged Esarhaddon,[4] made a night attack on the towns of Kullimir and Ubbumî : the inhabitants armed in haste, and he was not only defeated, but was taken captive, and his head cut off to be sent to Nineveh.[5] The garrisons and military colonies along

[1] G. Smith, *Hist. of Assurbanipal*, pp. 84–99; S. Alden Smith, *Die Keilschrifttexte Asurbanipals*, vol. i. pp. 20–23 ; Jensen, *Inschriften Aschurbanipal's*, in Schrader, *Keil. Bibl.*, vol. ii. pp. 176–179, 240–243. As Tiele has shown (*Bab.-assyr. Gesch.*, p. 374), the narrative of *Cylinder B*, col. iii. ll. 16–102 (G. Smith, *op. cit.*, pp. 89–97), is the most authentic account of this campaign extant. The others are abridged, and the castle in which Akhsheri took refuge is called in them Ishtattu instead of Adrana. The exact date of the expedition is still unknown.

[2] The name of Biriz-khadri has an Iranian appearance. The first element *Biriz* recalls the Zend *bereza, berez*, "tall, large;" the second, which appears in the names Bisi-khadir and Khali-khadri (*Annals of Tiglath-pileser III.*, ll. 33, 43, ed. Rost, pp. 8–11), is of uncertain derivation, and has been connected with *atar*, "fire" (Tiele, *Bab.-assyr. Gesch.*, p. 361, note 4), or with *khwathra*, "brilliance" (Rost, *Untersuchungen zur Altorient. Gesch.*, p. 90, note 2). Gâgu, which is found as the name of a people (Gagâti) in the Tel-el-Amarna tablets (Bezold and Budge, *The Tell el Amarna Tablets in the Brit. Mus.*, No. i. l. 38), has been identified from the first with the name of Gog, prince of Rosh, Meshech, and Tubal (*Ezek.* xxxviii. 2, 3 ; xxxix. 1: cf. Fr. Lenormant, *Les Origines de l'Histoire*, vol. ii. pp. 461–466; G. Smith, *op. cit.*, p. 99 ; Schrader, *Keil. und Geschichtsforschung*, p. 159, note ; Delitzsch, *Wo lag das Paradies?* p. 247 ; Tiele, *Bab.-assyr. Gesch.*, p. 361, note 41 ; Hommel, *Gesch. Bab. und Ass.*, p. 727 ; Rost, *op. cit.*, p. 91, note 1). The name of the country of Sakhi, which has not been met with elsewhere, has been compared with that of the Sacæ, which seems to have existed not only in the name of the province of Sakasenê mentioned by the classical geographers (Strabo, XI. viii. § 4, pp. 509, 511), but in that of Shakê known to the old Armenian geographers (Justi, *Iranisches Namenbuch*, p. 243); the country itself, however, as it seems to me, cannot be sought in the direction of Sakasenê, and consequently the proposed identification cannot hold good. ;

[3] G. Smith, *op. cit.*, pp. 97, 98 ; Jensen, *op. cit.*, in Schrader, *Keil. Bibl.*, vol. ii. pp. 178–181; this campaign is not mentioned in the *Rassam Cylinder*, nor is the skirmish of Andaria.

[4] Cf. *supra*, pp. 369, 370.

[5] G. Smith, *op. cit.*, pp. 97–99 ; Jensen, *op. cit.*, in Schrader, *op. cit.*, vol. ii. pp. 180, 181.

the north-east frontier were constantly required to be on the alert; but they usually had sufficient available resources to meet any emergency, and the enemies who molested them were rarely dangerous enough to necessitate the mobilisation of a regular army.

This was not the case, however, in the south-west, where Tiummân, counting on the military strength of Elam, made continual hostile demonstrations. He was scarcely settled on his throne before he hastened to form alliances with those Aramæan states which had so often invoked the aid of his predecessors against the ancestors of Assur-bani-pal.[1] The Kaldâ rejected his proposals, as did most of the tribes of the littoral; but the Gambulâ yielded to his solicitations, and their king, Dunânu, son of Bel-ikîsha, entered into an offensive and defensive alliance with Elam. Their defection left the eastern frontier of Karduniash unprotected, and, by opening to the Elamite the fords of the Tigris, permitted him to advance on Babylon unhindered by any serious obstacle. As soon as the compact was sealed, Tiummân massed his battalions on the middle course of the Uknu, and, before crossing the frontier, sent two of his generals, the Susian Khumba-darâ and the Chaldæan Nabu-damîq, as the bearers of an insolent ultimatum to the court of Nineveh: he offered the king the choice between immediate hostilities, or the extradition of the sons of Urtaku and Khumbân-khaldash, as well as of their partisans who had taken refuge in Assyria.[2] To surrender the exiles would have been an open confession of inferiority, and such a humiliating acknowledgment of weakness promptly reported throughout the Eastern world might shortly have excited a general revolt: hence Assur-bani-pal disdainfully rejected the proposal of the Elamite sovereign, which had been made rather as a matter of form than with any hope of its acceptance, but the issue of a serious war with Susa was so uncertain that his refusal was accompanied with serious misgivings. It needed many favourable omens from the gods to encourage him to believe in his future success. The moon-god Sin was the first to utter his prediction: he suffered eclipse in the month of Tammuz, and for three successive days, at nightfall, showed himself in the sky surrounded by strange appearances which heralded the death of a king in Elam, and foretold calamity to that country. Then Assur and Ishtar struck Tiummân with violent convulsions; they caused his lips and eyes to be horribly distorted, but he despised their warning, and as soon as his seizure had passed, set out to assume command of his army. The news of his action reached Nineveh in the month of Ab, on the morning of the solemn festival of Ishtar.

---

[1] For the contests waged by the united forces of Elamites and Aramæans against Sargon, Sennacherib, and Esarhaddon, cf. *supra*, pp. 222–225, 230–232, 254–257, 274–276, 295, 296, 299–307, 349, 350, 358.

[2] Cf. *supra*, p. 399.

Assur-bani-pal was at Arbela, celebrating the rites in honour of the goddess, when the messenger appeared before him and repeated, together with the terms of the declaration of war, the scornful words which Tiummân had uttered against him and his patroness: "This prince whose wits have been crazed by Ishtar— I will let him escape no more, when once I have gone forth and measured my strength against him!" This blasphemy filled the Assyrian king with horror. That very evening he betook himself to the sanctuary, and there, prostrate before the image of the goddess, he poured forth prayers mingled with tears: "Lady of Arbela, I am Assur-bani-pal, King of Assyria, the creature of thy hands, the offspring of a father whom thou didst create! Behold now, this Tiummân, the King of Elam, who despises the gods of Assyria, hath sent forth his host and prepared himself for the conflict; he hath called for his arms to rush to attack Assyria. Do thou, O archer of the gods, like a bolt falling in the midst of the battle, overthrow him, and let loose upon him a tempest, and an evil wind!"[1] Ishtar heard his prayer, and her voice sounded through the gloom: "Fear not," said she, comforting him: "since thou hast raised thy hands to me in supplication, and thine eyes are bedewed with tears, I grant thee a boon!" Towards the end of that night, a seer slept in the temple and was visited by a dream. Ishtar of Arbela appeared to him, with a quiver on either side, a bow in one hand and a drawn sword in the other. She advanced towards the king, and spoke to him as if she had been his mother: "Make war boldly! whichever way thou turnest thy countenance, there will I go!" And the king replied to her, "Where thou goest, will I go with thee, sovereign lady!" But she answered, "Stay thou here. Dwell in this home of Nebo, eat thy food and drink thy wine, listen to joyful songs and honour my divinity, until I have gone and accomplished this work. Let not thy countenance grow pale, nor thy feet fail under thee, and expose not thyself to the danger of battle." "And then, O king," added the seer, "she hid thee in her bosom as a mother, and protected thy image. A flame shall spring forth before her, and shall spread abroad to destroy thine enemies: against Tiummân, King of Elam, who has angered her, has she set her face!" Like Mînephtah of old, in the days of the Libyan invasions of Egypt,[2] Assur-bani-pal allowed himself to be readily convinced by the decision of the gods; he did not quit Arbela, but gave orders to his troops to proceed to the front. His generals opened the campaign in the month of Elul, and directed the main body of their forces against the

---

[1] The discourse is somewhat mutilated on *Cylinder B*, col. v. ll. 30–46, which alone has preserved this text (G. SMITH, *Hist. of Assurbanipal*, pp. 119–123; JENSEN, *Inschr. Aschurbanipal's*, in SCHRADER, *Keil. Bibl.*, vol. ii. pp. 250, 251; cf. S. ALDEN SMITH, *Die Keilschr. Asurbanipals*, vol. iii. pp. 11–17). I have given the general sense of the passage rather than an actual translation.

[2] For the dream of Mînephtah and the order he received not to be present at the battle against the Libyans, cf. *Struggle of the Nations*, p. 434.

fortress of Durîlu, at the point on the frontier nearest to Susa. Tiummân was not expecting such a prompt and direct attack: he had reckoned doubtless on uniting his forces with those of Dunânu with a view to invading Karduniash, and suddenly realised that his adversary had forestalled him and was advancing on the heart of his empire. He slowly withdrew his advanced guard, and con-

ITUNI BREAKS HIS BOW WITH A BLOW OF HIS SWORD, AND GIVES HIMSELF UP TO THE EXECUTIONER.[1]

centrated his forces round the town of Tullîz, a few leagues on this side of Susa, and there awaited the enemy's attack.[2]

His position was a strong one, flanked on the right by a wood and on the left by the Ulaî, while the flower of the Elamite nobility was ranged around him. The equipment of his soldiers was simpler than that of the enemy: consisting of a low helmet, devoid of any crest, but furnished with a large pendant tress of horsehair to shade the neck; a shield of moderate dimensions; a small bow, which, however, was quite as deadly a weapon as that of the Assyrians, when wielded by skilful hands; a lance, a mace, and a dagger. He had only a small body of cavalry, but the chariotry formed an important force, and presented

[1] Drawn by Boudier, from a photograph taken from the original in the British Museum; cf. LAYARD, *The Monuments of Nineveh*, vol. ii. pls. 45, 46. The translation of the inscription is given in G. SMITH, *History of Assurbanipal*, pp. 143, 144.

[2] The site of Tullîz is unknown. Billerbeck considers, and with reason, I think, that the battle took place to the south of Susa, on the river Shavur, which would correspond to the Ulaî, on the lowest spurs of the ridge of hills bordering the alluvial plain of Susiana (*Susa*, p. 174, note 17).

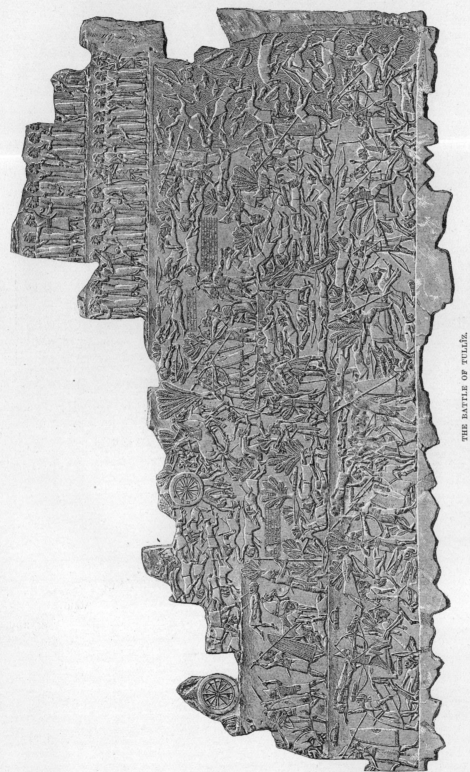

THE BATTLE OF TULLÎZ.

Drawn by Boudier, from a photograph of the original in the British Museum.

several original features.   The chariot did not follow the classic model, rounded in front and open at the back; it was a kind of light car, consisting of a square footboard placed flat on the axle of the wheels, and furnished with triangular side-pieces on two sides only, the vehicle being drawn by a pair of horses.   Such chariots were easier to manage, better adapted for rapid motion, and must have been more convenient for a reconnaissance or for skirmishes with infantry; but when thrown in a mass against the heavy chariotry of the peoples of the Euphrates, they were far too slightly built to overthrow the latter, and at close quarters were of necessity crushed by the superior weight of the

URTAKU, COUSIN OF TIUMMÂN, SURRENDERING TO AN ASSYRIAN.[1]

adversary.   Tiummân had not succeeded in collecting all his forces before the first columns of the Assyrian army advanced to engage his front line, but as he was expecting reinforcements, he endeavoured to gain time by despatching Ituni, one of his generals, with orders to negotiate a truce.   The Assyrian commander, suspecting a ruse, would not listen to any proposals, but ordered the envoy to be decapitated on the spot: Ituni broke his bow with a blow of his sword, and stoically yielded his neck to the executioner.[2]   The issue of the battle was for a long time undecided, but the victory finally remained with the heavy regiments of Assyria. The left wing of the Susians, driven into the Ulaî, perished by drowning, and the river was choked with the corpses of men and horses, and the *débris* of arms and broken chariots.   The right wing took to flight under cover of a wood, and the survivors tried to reach the mountains.   Urtaku, the cousin of Tiummân,

<hr />

[1] Drawn by Boudier, from a photograph of the original in the British Museum; cf. LAYARD, *Mon. of Nineveh*, vol. ii. pl. 45.   The translation of the inscription is given in G. SMITH, *Hist. of Assurbanipal*, pp. 144, 145.

[2] *Tablet K 2674 of the British Museum*, obv., ll. 31–33, in S. ALDEN SMITH, *Die Keilschrifttexte Asurbanipals*, vol. iii. pp. 2, 5; inscription from one of the bas-reliefs of the battle, in G. SMITH, *op. cit.*, pp. 145, 146.

was wounded by an arrow; perceiving an Assyrian soldier coming up to him, he told him who he was, and recommended him to carry his head to the general: "He will pay you handsomely for it," he added.[1] Tiummân had led in person several charges of his body-guard; and on being wounded, his son Tammaritu had succeeded in rescuing him from the thick of the fight: both seated together in a chariot, were in full flight, when one of the wheels caught against a tree and was shattered, the shock flinging the occupants to the ground.[2] A large body of Assyrians were in close pursuit, led by one

THE LAST ARROW OF TIUMMÂN AND HIS SON.[3]

of the exiled Susian princes, a second Tammaritu, son of Urtaku. At the first discharge an arrow wounded Tiummân in the right side, and brought him to his knee. He felt that all was over, and desiring at all events to be revenged, he pointed out the deserter prince to his companion, crying indignantly, "Let fly at him." The arrow missed its mark, and a flight of hostile darts stretched the young man on the ground: the traitor Tammaritu dealt the son his death-blow with his mace, while an Assyrian decapitated the father.[4] The corpses were left on the field, but the head of the king, after being taken to the general in command, was carried through the camp on one of the chariots captured during the action, and was eventually sent to the palace

---

[1] *Tablet K 2674*, obv., ll. 27–30, in S. ALDEN SMITH, *Die Keilschrifttexte Asurbanipals*, vol. iii. pp. 2–5; inscription from one of the bas-reliefs of the battle, in G. SMITH, *History of Assurbanipal*, pp. 144, 145.

[2] *Tablet K 2674*, obv., ll. 14–26; cf. G. SMITH, *op. cit.*, pp. 142, 143; S. ALDEN SMITH, *op. cit.*, pp. 1, 4, 5.

[3] Drawn by Boudier, from a photograph taken in the British Museum; cf. LAYARD, *Mon. of Nineveh*, vol. ii. pl. 46. The translation of the inscription is given in G. SMITH, *op. cit.*, p. 143.

[4] Inscriptions from one of the bas-reliefs of the battle, in G. SMITH, *op. cit.*, pp. 143, 144.

of Arbela by the hand of a well-mounted courier.[1]   The day concluded with the making of an inventory of the spoil, and by an enumeration of the heads of the slain : prisoners from the rank and file were beaten to death according to custom, and several of the principal officers had their tongues torn out or were flayed alive.   The news of the disaster was brought to Susa towards evening by the fugitives, and produced a revolution in the city.   The partisans of the exiled princes, seizing the adherents of Tiummân, put them in chains, and delivered

DEATH OF TIUMMÂN AND HIS SON.[2]

them up to the conqueror.   The shattered remnants of the army rallied round them, and a throng of men and women in festal garb issued forth along the banks of the Ulaî to meet the Assyrians.   The priests and sacred singers marched to the sound of music, marking the rhythm with their feet, and filling the air with the noise of their harps and double flutes, while behind them came a choir of children, chanting a hymn under the direction of the consecrated eunuchs. The Tartan met them, and, acting in accordance with the orders of Assur-bani-pal, presented to the multitude Khumbân-igash, the eldest son of Urtaku, as their king.[3]   The people joyfully hailed the new sovereign, and the

[1] Inscription on one of the bas-reliefs of the battle, in G. Smith, *Hist. of Assurbanipal*, p. 144.
[2] Drawn by Boudier, from a photograph taken in the British Museum; cf. Layard, *Monuments of Nineveh*, vol. ii. pl. 46. The translation of the inscription is given in G. Smith, *op. cit.*, pp. 143, 144.
[3] Inscription on one of the bas-reliefs of the battle, in G. Smith, *Hist. of Assurbanipal*, p. 146.

KHUMBÂN-IGASH ACCLAIMED AS KING AFTER THE BATTLE OF TULLÎZ.

Drawn by Boudier, from a photograph of the original in the British Museum.

Assyrians, after exacting tribute from him and conferring the fief of Khaîdalu on his brother Tammaritu, withdrew, leaving to the new princes the task of establishing their authority outside the walls of Susa and Madaktu. As they returned, they attacked the Gambulâ, speedily reducing them to submission. Dunânu, besieged in his stronghold of Shapîbel, surrendered at discretion, and was carried away captive with all his family. Thus Assur-bani-pal had scrupulously obeyed the orders of Ishtar. While his generals were winning his victories

THE HEAD OF TIUMMÂN SENT TO NINEVEH.[1]

he had been eating and drinking, hunting, dallying with his wives, and living in the open air. He was taking his pleasure with the queen in the palace garden when the head of Tiummân was brought to him : he caused it to be suspended from the branch of a pine tree in full view of the whole court, and continued his banquet to the sound of harps and singing. Rusas III., King of Urartu, died about this time, and his successor, Sharduris III., thought it incumbent on him to announce his accession at Nineveh. Assur-bani-pal received the embassy at Arbela, with the graciousness befitting a suzerain whom a faithful vassal honours by his dutiful homage, and in order to impress

---

[1] Drawn by Boudier, from a photograph taken in the British Museum; cf. LAYARD, *Monuments of Nineveh*, vol. ii. pl. 45. The chariot speeding along at a gallop in the topmost series of pictures carries a soldier bearing the head of Tiummân in his hand; behind him, under a tent, scribes are registering the heads which are brought in. In the two lower bas-reliefs are displayed the closing scenes of the battle. The translation of the inscription is given in G. SMITH, *History of Assurbanipal*, p. 144.

the Urartians still further with an idea of his power, he showed them the two Elamite delegates, Khumba-darâ and Nabu-damîq, in chains at his feet.[1]   These wretched men had a more cruel ordeal yet in store for them : when the Assyrian army re-entered Nineveh, Assur-bani-pal placed them on the route along which the cortège had to pass, and made them realise to the full the humiliation of their country.   Dunânu walked at the head of the band of captive chiefs, with the head of Tiummân, taken from its tree, suspended round his neck.   When the delegates perceived it, they gave way to despair : Khumba-darâ tore out his beard by handfuls, and Nabu-damîq, unsheathing the dagger which hung from his belt, plunged it into his own breast.   The triumphal entry was followed by the usual tortures.   The head of Tiummân was fixed over the gate of

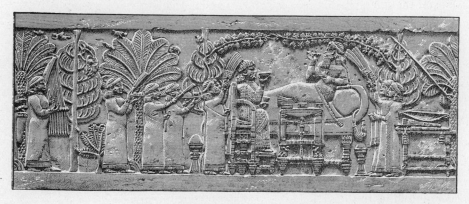

ASSUR-BANI-PAL BANQUETING WITH HIS QUEEN.[2]

Nineveh, to rot before the eyes of the multitude.   Dunânu was slowly flayed alive, and then bled like a lamb ; his brother Shamgunu had his throat cut, and his body was divided into pieces, which were distributed over the country as a warning.   Even the dead were not spared : the bones of Nabu-shumirîsh were disinterred and transported to Assyria, where his sons were forced to bray them in a mortar.[3]   We may estimate the extent of the alarm which had been felt at

---

[1] G. Smith, *Hist. of Assurbanipal*, pp. 115, 116, 146, 147.   Belck and Lehmann (*Ein neuer Herrscher von Chaldia*, in the *Zeitschrift für Assyriologie*, vol. ix. pp. 342–345) have very ingeniously connected the embassy, mentioned in the Assyrian documents, with the fact of the accession of the king who sent it.

[2] Drawn by Boudier, from a photograph of the original in the British Museum.   The head of Tiummân hangs on the second tree on the left-hand side.

[3] The fullest text of all those which narrate the campaign against Tiummân and Dunânu is that on *Cylinder B of the British Museum*, col. iv. ll. 82–95, col. v. ll. 1–104, col. vi. ll. 2–92, published and translated by G. Smith, *op. cit.*, pp. 116–138 ; cf. Jensen, *Inschr. Aschurbanipal's*, in Schrader, *Keil. Bibl.*, vol. ii. pp. 246–259.   It pretends, as usual, that the king led the army in person, but the words which the seer places in the mouth of Ishtar (col. v. ll. 63–70, cf. *supra*, p. 405) prove that the king remained at Arbela by divine command, and the inscription on one of the bas-reliefs (G. Smith, *op. cit.*, p. 146, cf. *supra*, p. 413), as well as *Tablet K 2674* (G. Smith, *op. cit.*, p. 140 ; S. Alden Smith, *Die Keilschr. Asurbanipals*, vol. iii. pp. 2, 5), mentions, without giving his name, the general who was sent against Susa.   The other documents relating to this expedition have been collected in

Nineveh by the outburst of brutal joy with which the victory was hailed. The experience of the past showed what a terrible enemy Assyria had in Elam, and how slight was the chance of a successful issue in a war against her. Her kings had often invaded Chaldæa, and had more than once brought it directly under their sway ; they had ravaged its cities and pillaged its temples, and the sanctuaries of Susa were filled with statues of the gods or with bas-reliefs which they had dedicated after their campaigns on the Euphrates. Although they had not been successful against Assyria to the same extent, they had at least always victoriously repelled her attacks : they had held their own against Sargon, given much trouble to Sennacherib, and defied the power of Esarhaddon with impunity. Never till now had an Assyrian army gained such an important victory over Elam, and though it was by no means decisive, we can easily believe that Assurbani-pal was filled with pride and delight, since it was the first time that a king of Nineveh had imposed on Elam a sovereign of his own choice.

Since homage was voluntarily rendered him by the rulers of foreign nations, Assur-bani-pal doubtless believed that he might exact it without hesitation from the vassal princes dependent on the empire; and not from the weaker only like those who were still to be found in Syria, but also from the more powerful, not excepting the lord of Karduniash. Shamash-shumukîn had fully risen to his position as King of Babylon, and the unbroken peace which he had enjoyed since the death of Urtaku [1] had enabled him almost to complete the restoration of the kingdom begun under Esarhaddon. He had finished the rebuilding of the walls of Babylon, and had fortified the approaches to the city, thus rendering it capable of withstanding a long siege ; [2] he had repaired the temple of Sippara, which had never recovered from the Elamite invasion; [3] and while unstintingly lavishing his treasures in honour of the gods and for the safety of his capital, he watched with jealous care over the interests of his subjects. He obtained for them the privilege of being treated on the same footing as the Assyrians throughout his father's ancestral domains ; they consequently enjoyed the right of trading without restriction throughout the empire, and met with the same degree of protection from the officials of Nineveh as from the magistrates of their own country.

G. SMITH, Hist. of Assurbanipal, pp. 110–114, 139–146, and in S. ALDEN SMITH, Die Keilschrifttexte Asurbanipals, vol. i. pp. 22–27; cf. JENSEN, Inschriften Aschurbanipal's, in SCHRADER, Keil. Bibl., vol. ii. pp. 180–183. The exact date of this war is unknown; it may be approximately given as 655 B.C.

[1] See supra, pp. 398, 399, for a short account of the expedition of Urtaku against Babylon.

[2] Cylindre de la Bibliothèque Nationale à Paris, published by LEHMANN, Schamaschschumukin, pl. xxx., and vol. i. pp. 27, 54, ii. p. 62. Assur-bani-pal, from whom this cylinder emanates, claims the merit of these works himself.

[3] Bilingual Inscription, ll. 23–29 ; London Cylinder, ll. 16–18; cf. LEHMANN, Schamaschschumukin, vol. ii. pp. 8, 9, 18, 19.

Assur-bani-pal had at the outset furthered the wishes of his brother to the utmost of his power : he had granted the privileges demanded, and whenever a Chaldæan of noble birth arrived at his court, he received him with special marks of favour.[1] The two states enjoyed a nearly absolute equality during the opening years of his reign, and though the will of Esarhaddon had made Babylon dependent on Assyria, the yoke of vassalage was far from heavy. The suzerain reserved to himself the honour of dedicating the mighty works begun by his father, the restoration of the temple of Bel-Marduk and of the double wall of fortification;[2] he claimed, in his inscriptions, the whole merit of the work, but he none the less respected his brother's rights, and in no way interfered in the affairs of the city

TWO ELAMITE CHIEFS FLAYED ALIVE AFTER THE BATTLE OF TULLÎZ.[3]

except in state ceremonies in which the assertion of his superior rank was indispensable. But with success his moderation gradually gave place to arrogance. In proportion as his military renown increased, he accentuated his supremacy, and accustomed himself to treat Babylon more and more as a vassal state.[4] After the conquest of Elam his infatuated pride knew no bounds, and the little consideration he still retained for Shamash-shumukîn vanished completely. He thenceforward refused to regard him as being more than a prefect bearing a somewhat higher title than his fellows, a viceroy owing his crown, not to

---

[1] *Cylinder A*, col. iv. ll. 22–27 ; cf. G. SMITH, *Hist. of Assurbanipal*, pp. 153, 154 ; *Rassam Annals*, col. iii. ll. 87–95 ; cf. S. ALDEN SMITH, *Die Keils. Asurbanipals*, vol. i. pp. 26, 27 ; JENSEN, *Inschr. Aschurbanipal's*, in SCHRADER, *Keil. Bibl.*, vol. ii. pp. 184, 185.

[2] For the commencement of the restoration of the temple of Marduk, cf. *supra*, pp. 382, 383.

[3] Drawn by Boudier, from a photograph taken in the British Museum; cf. LAYARD, *Monuments of Nineveh*, vol. ii. pl. 47. The translation of the two inscriptions is given in G. SMITH, *Hist. of Assurbanipal*, p. 148. The names of the two persons under torture were left blank on the original monument.

[4] Thus, in *Tablet K 891 of the British Museum*, obv., ll. 11–13, he affects to enumerate on an equal footing his three brothers, Shamash-shumukîn, Assur-mukîn-palîya, and Assur-etil-shamê-uirziti-balasu, as all alike invested by himself with important charges; the first with the kingdom of Karduniash, the other two with important offices in the priesthood (LEHMANN, *Schamaschschumukin*, vol. ii. pp. 20, 21 ; cf. for other analogous facts, ID., *ibid.*, vol. ii. pp. 16–19).

the will of their common father, but to the friendship of his brother, and liable to be deprived of it at any moment through the caprice of the sovereign. He affected to consider all that took place at Babylon as his own doing, and his brother as being merely his docile instrument, not deserving mention any more than the ordinary agents who carried out his designs ; and if, indeed, he condescended to mention him, it was with an assumption of disdainful superiority. It is a question whether Shamash-shumukîn at this juncture believed that his brother was meditating a design to snatch the reins of government from his hand, or whether he merely yielded to the impulse of wounded vanity in resolving to shake off a yoke which had become intolerable. Knowing that his power was not equal to that of Assur-bani-pal, he sought to enter into relations with foreign allies who shared the same fears, or nursed a similar feeling of bitterness. The nobles and priests of the ancient Sumerian and Accadian cities were already on his side, but the Aramæans had shown themselves hostile at his accession, and had brought down on him the forces of Elam. He found means, however, to conciliate them, together with the tribes which dwelt on the Tigris and the Uknu, as well as those of the lower Euphrates and the Arabian desert. He won over to his projects Nabu-bêlzikri, the chief of the Kaldâ— grandson of that Merodach-baladan who had cherished invincible hatred against Sargon and Sennacherib—besides the lords of the Bît-Dakkuri and Bît-Amukkâni, and the sheikh of the Pukudu.[1] Khumbân-igash ought to have remained loyal to the friend to whom he owed his kingdom, but he chafed at the patronage of Assyria, and Assur-bani-pal had just formulated a demand to which he, not unreasonably, hesitated to accede. The archaic statue of Nanâ, stolen from Uruk by Kutur-nakhunta sixteen centuries before,[2] and placed by that prince in one of the temples of Susa, had become so naturalised in its new abode that the kings of Elam, not content with rendering it an official cult, were wont to send presents to Babylonia, to the image which had replaced it in its original sanctuary.[3] Assur-bani-pal now required Khumbân-igash to give back the original statue,[4] but the Elamite could not obey this mandate without imperilling both his throne and his person : he would thereby have risked incurring the displeasure both of the nobles, whose pride would have suffered at the loss of so precious a trophy, and of the common people, who would have thus been deprived of one of their most venerable objects of devotion. The messengers

---

[1] The part taken by the Aramæans in the rebellion is known to us from a certain number of despatches from Assyrian governors, which were first deciphered and utilised by G. Smith, *Hist. of Assurbanipal*, pp. 201, 202.

[2] For this statue, cf. *Struggle of the Nations*, p. 37.

[3] PINCHES, *Assyrian Report Tablets*, in *The Records of the Past*, 1st ser., vol. xi. p. 76, despatch of Nabu-ibashshi.

[4] *Tablet K 2644 of the British Museum*, quoted first by G. SMITH, *op. cit.*, pp. 200, 201.

of Shamash-shumukîn, arriving at the moment when this question was agitating the court of Susa, found the way already prepared for a mutual understanding. Besides, they held in their hands an irresistible argument, the treasures of Bel-Marduk of Babylon, of Nebo of Borsippa, and of Nergal of Kuta, which had been confided to them by the priests with a view to purchasing, if necessary, the support of Elam. Khumbân-igash thereupon promised to send a detachment of troops to Karduniash, and to invade the provinces of Assyria the moment war should be declared. The tribes of Guti were easily won over, and were followed by the kings of Phœnicia and the Bedâwin of Melukhkha, and perhaps Egypt itself was implicated in the plot.[1] The Prince of Kedar, Amuladdin, undertook to effect a diversion on the frontiers of Syria, and Uatê, son of Layali, one of the Arab kings who had paid homage to Esarhaddon, was not behindhand in furnishing his contingent of horsemen and wild native infantry.[2] The coalition already extended from the shores of the Mediterranean and the Red Sea to the Persian Gulf before Assur-bani-pal became aware of its existence.

An unforeseen occurrence suddenly broke in upon his peace and revealed the extent of the peril which threatened him.[3] Kudur, the Assyrian prefect of Uruk, learnt from Sin-tabnî-uzur, the governor of Uru, that certain emissaries of Shamash-shumukîn had surreptitiously entered that city and were secretly fomenting rebellion among the people. Sin-tabnî-uzur himself had been solicited to join the movement, but had absolutely refused to do so, and considering himself powerless to repress the disaffection with the few soldiers at his disposal, he had demanded reinforcements. Kudur first furnished him with five hundred men of his own troops, and subsequently sent some battalions which were under the command of the governors of Arrapkha and Amidi, but which were, for some unknown reason, encamped in the neighbourhood. It would appear that Shamash-shumukîn, finding his projects interfered with by this premature exposure, tried to counteract its effects by protestations of friendship : a special embassy was despatched to his brother to renew the assurances of his devotion,

---

[1] *Cylinder B*, col. vi. ll. 93–97, col. vii. l. 1 ; cf. G. SMITH, *Hist. of Assurbanipal*, pp. 170, 171. For the preliminaries of this war, see the texts collected by G. SMITH, *op. cit.*, pp. 151–156, 158, 169, 170, 171, 174, 175, 186–188, and by S. ALDEN SMITH, *Die Keilschrifttexte Asurbanipals*, vol. i. pp. 26–29 ; cf. JENSEN, *Inschriften Aschurbanipal's*, in SCHRADER, *Keil. Bibl.*, vol. ii. pp. 182–187, 262–265.

[2] *Cylinder A*, col. vii. ll. 97–116 ; cf. G. SMITH, *op. cit.*, pp. 256–258.

[3] The chronology of this war has been determined by G. Smith from the dates attached to the documents in the British Museum, which give the names of three *limmi*, Assur-duruzur, Zagabbu, and Bel-kharrân-shadua : these he assigned respectively to the years 650, 649, and 648 B.C. (*op. cit.*, pp. 321, 322, and *The Assyrian Eponym Canon*, pp. 95, 96). Tiele (*Bab.-assyr. Gesch.*, pp. 388, 389) has shown that these three *limmi* must be assigned to the years 652–650 B.C., and his opinion has been adopted by LEHMANN, *Schamaschschumukin*, p. 6 ; though these dates seem in the highest degree probable, we must wait before we can consider them as absolutely certain till chance restores to us the missing parts of the Canon.

2 E

and he thus gained the time necessary to complete his armaments.[1] As soon as he felt himself fully prepared, he gave up further dissimulation, and, throwing away the mask, proclaimed himself independent of Assyria, while at the same moment Khumbân-igash despatched his army to the frontier and declared war on his former protector. Assur-bani-pal was touched to the quick by what he truly considered the ingratitude of the Babylonians. "As for the children of Babylon, I had set them upon seats of honour, I had clothed them in robes of many colours, I had placed rings of gold upon their fingers; the children of Babylon had been established in Assyria, and were admitted into my presence. But Shamash-shumukîn, the false brother, he has not observed my ordinances, but has raised against me the peoples of Akkad, the Kaldâ, the Aramæans, the peoples of the country of the sea, from Akabah to Bab-salimêti!" Nineveh was at first in a state of trepidation at this unexpected blow; the sacred oracles gave obscure replies, and presaged evil four times out of five. At last, one day, a seer slept and dreamed a dream, in which he saw this sentence written on the ground in the temple of Sin: "All those who are meditating evil against Assur-bani-pal, King of Assyria, and who are preparing themselves to fight with him, I will inflict on them a terrible death: by the swift sword, by flinging them into fire, by famine and by pestilence, will I destroy their lives!"[2] The courage of the people being revived by this prophecy, Assur-bani-pal issued a proclamation to the Babylonians, in which he denounced his brother's treason, and commanded them to remain quiet as they valued their lives,[3] and, having done this, he boldly assumed the offensive (652 B.C.).[4] The only real danger came from the side of Elam; this state alone was in a condition to oppose him with as numerous and determined an army as that which he himself could put into the field; if Elam were disabled, it would be impossible for Babylon to be victorious, and its fall would be a mere question of time. The opening of the campaign was a difficult matter. Khumbân-igash, having sold his support dearly, had at all events spared no pains to satisfy his employer, and had furnished him with the flower of his

[1] *Tablet K 5457 of the British Museum*, utilised by G. SMITH, *Hist. of Assurbanipal*, p. 201; *Cylinder A*, col. iv. ll. 16–19, and *Rassam Cylinder*, col. iii. ll. 85, 86: cf. G. SMITH, *op. cit.*, pp. 152–154; S. ALDEN SMITH, *Die Keilschr. Asurbanipals*, vol. i. pp. 26, 27; JENSEN, *Inschr. Aschurbanipal's*, in SCHRADER, *Keil. Bibl.*, vol. ii. pp. 184, 185.

[2] *Tablet K 4 of the British Museum*, in G. SMITH, *op. cit.*, pp. 186, 187; *Cylinder A of the Brit. Mus.*, col. iv. 48, 49, and *Rassam Cylinder*, col. iii. ll. 118–127: cf. G. SMITH, *op. cit.*, pp. 157–159; S. ALDEN SMITH, *op. cit.*, vol. i. pp. 28, 29; JENSEN, *op. cit.*, in SCHRADER, *op. cit.*, vol. ii. pp. 186, 187.

[3] *Tablet K 84 of the British Museum*, containing the proclamation of Assur-bani-pal to the Babylonians, discovered and utilised by G. SMITH, *op. cit.*, p. 181, published in H. RAWLINSON, *Cun. Ins. W. As.*, vol. iv. pl. 52, No. 1.

[4] The proclamation is dated in the eponymous year of Assur-duruzur, corresponding to 652 B.C. (TIELE, *Bab.-assyr. Gesch.*, p. 309); the events which immediately preceded the proclamation ought, very probably, to be assigned to the same year.

nobility, comprising Undashi, one of the sons of Tiummân; Zazaz, prefect of Billatê; Parru, chief of Khilmu; Attamîtu, commanding the archers; and Nesu, commander-in chief of his forces. In order to induce Undashi to serve under him, he had not hesitated to recall to his memory the sad fate of Tiummân: "Go, and avenge upon Assyria the murder of the father who begat thee!" [1] The two opposing forces continued to watch one another's movements without any serious engagement taking place during the greater part of the year 651 B.C.; though the Assyrians won some slight advantages, killing Attamîtu in a skirmish [2] and sending his head to Nineveh, some serious reverses soon counterbalanced these preliminary successes. Nabo-bel-shumi had arrived on the scene with his Aramæan forces, and had compelled the troops engaged in the defence of Uruk and Uru to lay down their arms: their leaders, including Sin-tabnî-uzur himself, had been forced to renounce the supremacy of Assyria, and had been enrolled in the rebel ranks. [3] Operations seemed likely to be indefinitely prolonged, and Assur-bani-pal, anxious as to the issue, importunately besought the gods to intervene on his behalf, when discords breaking out in the royal family of Elam caused the scales of fortune once more to turn in his favour. The energy with which Khumbân-igash had entered on the present struggle had not succeeded in effacing the disagreeable impression left on the minds of the majority of his subjects, by the fact that he had returned to his country in the chariots of the stranger and had been enthroned by the decree of an Assyrian general. Tammaritu, of Khaîdalu, who had then fought at his side in the ranks of the invaders, was now one of those who reproached him most bitterly for his conduct. He frankly confessed that his hand had cut off the head of Tiummân, but denied that he did so in obedience to the hereditary enemies of his country: he had but avenged his personal injuries, whereas Khumbân-igash, following the promptings of ambition, had kissed the ground at the feet of a slave of Assur-bani-pal and had received the crown as a recompense for his

---

[1] *Cylinder B of the British Museum*, col. vi. ll. 93–97, and col. vii. ll. 1–22; cf. G. SMITH, *Hist. of Assurbanipal*, pp. 170–173, and JENSEN, *Inschr. Aschurbanipal's*, in SCHRADER, *Keil. Bibl.*, vol. ii. pp. 262–265.

[2] *Cylinder B of the British Museum*, col. vii. ll. 23–29; cf. G. SMITH, *op. cit.*, p. 173.

[3] The official accounts say nothing of the intervention of Nabo-bel-shumi at this juncture, but the information furnished by *Tablet K 159* in the British Museum (G. SMITH, *op. cit.*, pp. 183, 184) makes up for their silence. The objection raised by Tiele (*Bab.-assyr. Gesch.*, p. 389) to the interpretation given by G. Smith (*Hist. of Assurbanipal*, p. 188) that this passage cannot refer to Assyrian deserters, falls to the ground if one admits that the Assyrian troops led into Elam at a subsequent period by Nabo-bel-shumi (*Cylinder C of the British Museum*, ll. 88–94; cf. G. SMITH, *op. cit.*, pp. 178, 179), and which will be referred to later on (*infra*, p. 422), were none other than the garrisons of the Lower Euphrates which were obliged to side with the insurgents in 651 B.C. The two despatches, *K 4696* and *K 28* in the British Museum, which refer to the defection of Sin-tabnî-uzur, are dated the 8th and 11th Abu in the eponymous year of Zagabbu (G. SMITH, *op. cit.*, pp. 184, 185), corresponding to the year 651 B.C., as indicated by Tiele with very good reason, in my opinion (*Bab.-assyr. Gesch.*, pp. 388, 389).

baseness.[1]   Putting his rival to death, Tammaritu seized the throne, and in order
to prove that he was neither consciously nor unconsciously an instrument of
Ninevite policy, he at once sent reinforcements to the help of Babylon without
exacting in return any fresh subsidy.   The Assyrians, taking advantage of the
isolated position of Shamash-shumukîn, had pressed forward one of their divisions
as far as the districts on the sea coast, which they had recovered from the power
of Nabo-bel-shumi, and had placed under the administration of Belibni, a person
of high rank.[2]   The arrival of the Elamite force was on the point of further
compromising the situation, and rekindling the flames of war more fiercely than
ever, when a second revolution broke out, which shattered for ever the hopes
of Shamash-shumukîn.   Assur-bani-pal naturally looked upon this event as
the result of his supplications and sacrifices : Assur and Ishtar, in answer to
his entreaties, raised up Indabigash, one of the most powerful feudal lords of
the kingdom of Susa, and incited him to revolt.   Tammaritu fled to the
marshes which bordered the Nâr-marratum, and seizing a vessel, put out
to sea with his brothers, his cousins, seventeen princes of royal blood,
and eighty-four faithful followers : the ship, driven by the wind on to the
Assyrian shore, foundered, and the dethroned monarch, demoralised by sea-
sickness, would have perished in the confusion had not one of his followers
taken him on his back and carried him safely to land across the mud.[3]   Belibni
sent him prisoner to Nineveh with all his suite,[4] and Assur-bani-pal, after allowing him to humble himself before him, raised him from the ground, embraced
him, and assigned to him apartments in the palace and a train of attendants
befitting the dignity which he had enjoyed for a short time at Susa.   Indabigash
was too fully occupied with his own affairs to interfere again in the quarrel
between the two brothers : his country, disorganised by the successive shocks it
had sustained, had need of repose, for some years at least, before re-entering the
lists, except at a disadvantage.   He concluded no direct treaty with the Assyrian
king, but he at once withdrew the troops which had entered Karduniash, and
abstained from all hostile demonstrations against the garrisons of the border provinces : [5] for the moment, indeed, this was all that was required of him (650 B.C.).

¹ *Cylinder A of the British Museum*, col. iv. ll. 74–80 : cf. G. SMITH, *History of Assurbanipal*,
pp. 159, 160 ; JENSEN, *Inschr. Aschurbanipal's*, in SCHRADER, *Keil. Bibl.*, vol. ii. pp. 188, 189.
² *Tablet K 312 of the British Museum*, utilised for the first time by G. SMITH, *op. cit.*, pp. 189,
190, and dated in the eponymous year of Bel-kharrân-shadua, corresponding to the year 650 B.C.
(TIELE, *Bab.-assyr. Gesch.*, pp. 381, 389).
³ All the details of the war of Tammaritu against Khumbân-igash, his defeat by Indabigash, his
flight, his voyage, his arrival on the Assyrian coast, were illustrated by a number of bas-reliefs, the
inscriptions of which have been preserved for us on *Tablet K 4457 of Brit. Mus.*; cf. G. SMITH, *op. cit.*,
pp. 191–194.
⁴ *Tablet K 599 of the British Museum* contains the despatch in which Belibni announces the
arrival of Tammaritu and his departure for Nineveh ; cf. G. SMITH, *op. cit.*, pp. 196, 197.
⁵ For the texts relating to the revolutions in Elam, cf. G. SMITH, *op. cit.*, pp. 158–162, 170–176 ;
S. ALDEN SMITH, *Die Keilschrifttexte Asurbanipals*, vol. i. pp. 30–33 ; JENSEN, *op. cit.*, in SCHRADER,
op. cit., vol. ii. pp. 186–191.

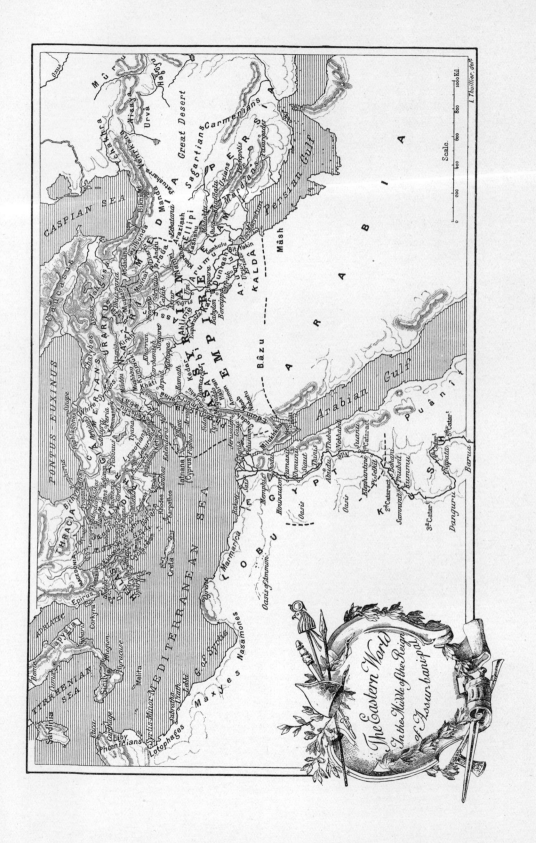

The Eastern World
In the Middle of the Reign
of Assur-bani-pal

Deprived of the support of Elam, Babylon was doomed to fall. The Aramæans deserted her cause, and Nabu-bel-shumi, grandson of Merodach-baladan, despairing of ever recovering the heritage of his family, withdrew to his haunts among the reed beds of the Uknu, taking back with him as hostages the Assyrians whom he had forced to join his army at the beginning of the campaign.[1] Shamash-shumukîn, however, was not disconcerted: he probably hoped that his distant allies might yet effect a diversion in his favour, and thus oblige his brother to withdraw half of the forces employed against him. Indeed, after the blockade had already begun, a band of Arabs under the two sheikhs Abiyatê and Aamu forced a way through the besieging lines and entered the city.[2] This was the last succour which reached Babylon from without: for many long months all communication between her citizens and the outer world was completely cut off. The Assyrians laid waste the surrounding country with ruthless and systematic cruelty, burning the villages, razing to the ground isolated houses, destroying the trees, breaking down the dykes, and filling up the canals. The year 649 B.C. was spent in useless skirmishes; the city offered an energetic and obstinate resistance, and as the walls were thick and the garrison determined, it would not have succumbed had not the supply of provisions finally failed. Famine raged in the city, and the inhabitants devoured even their own children, while pestilence spreading among them mowed them down by thousands. The Arab auxiliaries at this juncture deserted the cause of the defenders, and their sheikhs surrendered to Assur-bani-pal, who received and pardoned them;[3] but the Babylonians themselves, knowing that they could expect no mercy, held out some time longer: at length, their courage and their strength exhausted, they rose against their chiefs, whose ambition or patriotic pride had brought them to such a pass, and determined to capitulate on any terms. Shamash-shumukîn, not wishing to fall alive into the hands of his brother, shut himself up in his palace, and there immolated himself on a funeral pyre with his wives, his children, his slaves, and his treasures at the moment when his conquerors were breaking down the gates and penetrating into the palace precincts.[4] The city presented a terrible spectacle, and shocked even

[1] *Cylinder B of the British Museum*, col. vii. ll. 76–81, and *Cylinder C*, ll. 88–93; cf. G. SMITH, *History of Assurbanipal*, pp. 176–179.

[2] *Cylinder A of the British Museum*, col. viii. ll. 30–36; cf. G. SMITH, *op. cit.*, pp. 262, 263.

[3] *Cylinder A of the British Museum*, col. viii. ll. 37–41; cf. G. SMITH, *op. cit.*, 263, 264. For the private texts which prove the growing misery in the city, and the portents of ill omen which affrighted the inhabitants, cf. OPPERT, *Une Éclipse lunaire du règne de Saosduchin, roi de Babylone*, in the *Comptes rendus de l'Académie des Inscriptions et Belles-Lettres*, 1896, vol. xxv. pp. 423–438, 602, 603.

[4] G. Smith thought that the Babylonians, rendered furious by their sufferings, had seized Shamash-shumukîn and burnt him to death (*Hist. of Assurbanipal*, pp. 163, 203; cf. TIELE, *Bab.-assyr. Gesch.*, p. 382). It is, however, certain that Shamash-shumukîn killed himself, according to the Eastern custom, to escape the tortures which awaited him if he fell alive into the hands of his enemies. The memory of this event, transferred by the popular imagination to Assur-bani-pal, appears in the concluding portion of the legendary history of Sardanapalus.

the Assyrians, accustomed as they were to horrors of this sort. Most of
the numerous victims to pestilence or famine lay about the streets or in the
public squares, a prey to the dogs and swine; such of the inhabitants and of
the soldiery as were comparatively strong had endeavoured to escape into
the country, and only those remained who had not sufficient strength left
to drag themselves beyond the walls. Assur-bani-pal pursued the fugitives,
and, having captured nearly all of them, vented on them the full fury of his
vengeance. He caused the tongues of the soldiers to be torn out, and then had
them clubbed to death. He massacred the common folk in front of the great
winged bulls which had already witnessed a similar butchery half a century
before, under his grandfather Sennacherib; [1] the corpses of his victims remained
long unburied, a prey to all unclean beasts and birds. When the executioners
and the king himself were weary of the slaughter, the survivors were pardoned;
the remains of the victims were collected and piled up in specified places, the
streets were cleansed, and the temples, purified by solemn lustrations, were
reopened for worship.[2] Assur-bani-pal proclaimed himself king in his brother's
room: he took the hands of Bel, and, according to custom, his Babylonian
subjects gave him a new name, that of Kandalanu, by which he was henceforth known among them.[3] Had he been wise, he would have completed the
work begun by famine, pestilence, and the sword, and, far from creating a new
Babylon, he would have completed the destruction of the ancient city. The
same religious veneration which had disarmed so many of his predecessors

---

[1] Cf. *supra*, p. 308.

[2] For the siege of Babylon, cf. the texts collected by G. SMITH, *Hist. of Assurbanipal*, pp. 162–
170; S. ALDEN SMITH, *Die Keilschr. Asurbanipals*, vol. i. pp. 32–37; JENSEN, *Inschr. Aschurbanipal's*, in SCHRADER, *Keil. Bibl.*, vol. ii. pp. 190–195. The date of 648–647 B.C. for the taking of
Babylon and the death of Shamash-shumukîn is corroborated by the Canon of Ptolemy and the
fragments of Berosus, both of which attribute twenty or twenty-one years to the reign of Saosdukhîn
(Sammughes). Lehmann points out a document dated in the XXth year of Shamash-shumukîn,
which confirms the exactitude of the information furnished by the Greek chronologists (*Schamasch-
shumukîn*, i. p. 6).

[3] The Canon of Ptolemy gives as the successor of Saosdukhîn a certain Kinêladan, who corresponds to Kandalanu, whose date has been fixed by contemporary documents (PINCHES, *Some Recent
Discoveries*, in the *Proceedings* of the Bibl. Arch. Soc., 1882–1883, vol. v. p. 6). The identity of
Kinêladan with Assur-bani-pal was known from the Greek chronologists, for whereas Ptolemy puts
Kinêladan after Saosdukhîn, the fragments of Berosus state that the successor of Sammughes was
his *brother;* that is to say, Sardanapalus or Assur-bani-pal. This identification had been proposed
by G. Smith, who tried to find the origin of the form Kinêladan in the name of Sinidinabal,
which seems to be borne by Assur-bani-pal in *Tablet K 195 of the British Museum* (*Hist. of Assurbanipal*, pp. 323, 324), and which is really the name of his elder brother (cf. *supra*, p. 377, note 2);
it found numerous supporters as soon as Pinches had discovered the tablets dated in the reign of
Kandalanu, and Schrader endeavoured to demonstrate its truth in a special memoir, *Kineladan und
Asurbanipal* (*Zeitschrift für Keilforschung*, vol. i. pp. 222–232). Oppert combatted the arguments
of Schrader (*La Vraie Personnalité et les dates du roi Chinaladan* in the *Revue d'Assyriologie*, vol. i.
pp. 1–11), and he has affirmed the existence of two distinct kings whenever an occasion has offered,
but the majority of Assyriologists and historians hold that Kandalanu and Assur-bani-pal are one
and the same person (TIELE, *Bab.-assyr. Gesch.*, pp. 368, 369, 412–414; DELITZSCH and MÜRDTER,
Gesch. Bab. und Ass., 2nd edit., p. 230; WINCKLER, *Gesch. Bab. und Ass.*, pp. 135, 282, 289).

probably withheld him from giving free rein to his resentment, and not daring to follow the example of Sennacherib, he fell back on the expedient adopted by Tiglath-pileser III. and Sargon, adhering to their idea of two capitals for two distinct states, but endeavouring to unite in his own person the two irreconcilable sovereignties of Marduk and Assur.   He delegated the administration of Babylonian affairs to Shamash-danâni, one of his high officers of State,[1] and re-entered Nineveh with an amount of spoil almost equalling that taken from Egypt after the sack of Thebes.   Kuta, Sippara, and Borsippa, the vassal states of Babylon, which had shared the misfortune of their mistress, were, like her, cleared of their ruins, rebuilt and repeopled, and were placed under the authority of Shamash-danâni : such was their inherent vitality that in the short space of ten or a dozen years they had repaired their losses and reattained their wonted prosperity.   Soon no effect of their disaster remained except an additional incentive for hating Nineveh, and a determination more relentless than ever not to spare her when the day of her overthrow should come and they should have her in their power.

It was impossible for so violent and so prolonged a crisis to take place without in some degree injuring the prestige of the empire.   Subjects and allies of long standing remained loyal, but those only recently subjugated by conquest, as well as the neighbouring independent kingdoms, without hesitation threw off the yoke of suzerainty or of obligatory friendship under which they had chafed.   Egypt freed herself from foreign domination as soon as the possibilities of war with Elam had shown themselves, and it was Psammetichus of Sais,[2] son of Necho, one of the princes most favoured by the court of Nineveh, who set on foot this campaign against his former patron.   He expelled the Assyrian garrisons, reduced the petty native princes to submission, and once more set up the kingdom of the Pharaohs from Elephantinê to the Syrian desert, without Assur-bani-pal having been able to spare a single soldier to prevent him, or to bring him back to a sense of his duty.   The details of his proceedings are unknown to us: we learn only that he owed his success to mercenaries imported from Asia Minor, and the Assyrian chroniclers, unaccustomed to discriminate between the different peoples dwelling on the shores of the Ægean, believed that these auxiliaries were supplied to the Pharaoh by the only sovereign with whom they had had any dealings, namely, Gyges, King of Lydia.[3]   That Gyges had had negotiations with Psammetichus and procured

---

[1] This Shamash-danâni, who was *limmu* in 644 B.C. (G. SMITH, *The Assyrian Eponym Canon*, p. 97 ; TIELE, *Bab.-assyr. Gesch.*, pp. 368, 369), was called at that date prefect of Akkad, that is to say, of Babylon (*Cylinder A of the British Museum*, in G. SMITH, *Hist. of Assurbanipal*, p. 316).   He probably entered on this office immediately after the taking of the city.

[2] Cf. what is said of Psammetichus, *supra*, p. 386.

[3] For what we know of the auxiliaries of Psammetichus, cf. *infra*, pp. 487–498.   The Assyrian

assistance for him has not yet been proved, but to assert that he was incapable of conceiving and executing such a design is quite a different matter. On the contrary, all the information we possess concerning his reign shows that he was daring in his political undertakings, and anxious to court alliances with the most distant countries. The man who tried to draw Assur-bani-

PSAMMETICHUS I.[2]

pal into a joint enterprise against the Cimmerians would not have hesitated to ally himself with Psammetichus if he hoped to gain the least profit from so doing. Constant intercourse by sea took place between Ionia or Caria and Egypt, and no event of any importance could occur in the Delta without being promptly reported in Ephesus or Miletus.[1] Before this time the Heraclid rulers of Sardes had lived on excellent terms with most of the Æolian or Ionian colonies: during the anxious years which followed his accession Gyges went still further, and entered into direct relations with the nations of Greece itself. It was no longer to the gods of Asia, to Zeus of Telmissos, that he addressed himself in order to legitimatise his new sovereignty, but, like Midas of Phrygia, he applied to the prophetic god of Hellas, to the Delphian Apollo and his priests.[3] He recompensed them lavishly for pronouncing judgment in his favour: beside the silver offerings with which he endowed the temple at Delphi, he presented to it a number of golden vases, and, among others, six *craters* weighing thirty talents each, which, placed by the side of the throne of Midas, were still objects of admiration in the treasury

texts relating to the intervention of Gyges in the affairs of Egypt have been collected by G. SMITH, *History of Assurbanipal*, pp. 66, 67; S. ALDEN SMITH, *Die Keilschrifttexte Asurbanipals*, vol. i. pp. 18–21; JENSEN, *Inschriften Aschurbanipal's*, in SCHRADER, *Keilinschriftliche Bibliothek*, vol. ii. pp. 174–177. The various spellings of the name identified by Smith with that of Psammetichus, Pishamilki, and Tushamilki, at first called forth objections from Oppert (*Journal Asiatique*, 1872, vol. xix. p. 112): all doubts, however, seem to have been now dissipated (STEINDORFF, *Die Keilschriftliche Wiedergabe ägyptischer Eigennamen*, in the *Beiträge zur Assyriologie*, vol. i. pp. 360, 361).

[1] For the communications between Asia Minor and the shores of the Delta, cf. *infra*, pp. 496, 497.

[2] Drawn by Boudier, from a photograph.

[3] Cf. what is stated on this subject, *supra*, p. 339.

of the Corinthians in the time of Herodotus.[1]   To these he added at various times such valuable gifts that the Pythian priestess, who had hitherto been poor, was in later times accounted to have owed to him her wealth.[2]   Having made sure of the good will of the immortals, Gyges endeavoured to extend his influence among the Greek colonies along the coast, and if he did not in every case gain a footing amongst them, his failure seems to have been due, not to his incapacity, but to the force of circumstances or to the ambiguous position which he happened to occupy with regard to these colonies.   Ambition naturally incited him to annex them and make them into Lydian cities, but the bold disposition of their inhabitants and their impatience of constraint never allowed any foreign rule to be established over them : conquest, to be permanent, would have to be preceded by a long period of alliance on equal terms, and of discreet patronage which might insensibly accustom them to recognise in their former friend, first a protector, and then a suzerain imbued with respect for their laws and constitution.   Gyges endeavoured to conciliate them severally, and to attach them to himself by treaties favourable to their interests or flattering to their vanity, and by timely and generous assistance in their internecine quarrels ; and thus, secretly fostering their mutual jealousies, he was able to reduce some by force of arms without causing too much offence to the rest.[3]   He took Colophon,[4] and also, after several fruitless campaigns, the Magnesia which lay near Sardes, Magnesia of Sipylos, tradition subsequently adorning this fortunate episode in his history with various amusing anecdotes.   According to one account he had a favourite in a youth of marvellous beauty called Magnes, whom the Magnesians, as an act of defiance to Gyges, had mutilated till he was past recognition ; and it was related that the king appealed to the fortune of war to avenge the affront.[5] By a bold stroke he seized the lower quarters of Smyrna, but was unable to take the citadel,[6] and while engaged in the struggle with this city, he entered into a friendly understanding with Ephesus and Miletus.   Ephesus, situated at the mouth of the river Cayster, was the natural port of Sardes, the market in

[1] HERODOTUS, I. xiv.

[2] PHANIAS OF ERESOS, *Fragm.* 14, in MÜLLER-DIDOT, *Fragm. Hist. Græc.*, vol. ii. p. 297.

[3] The policy of Gyges and his successors with regard to the Greek colonies has been described with much sagacity and, I think, with much judgment by RADET, *La Lydie et le Monde Grec au temps des Mermnades*, pp. 169–174.

[4] HERODOTUS, I. xv.   Grote (*Hist. of Greece*, vol. iv. p. 298) thought that he captured the lower town of Colophon, τὸ ἄστυ, not the citadel, and his opinion has been adopted by Max Duncker (*Gesch. des Alterthums*, 5th edit., vol. ii. p. 583, note 2).   Schubert (*Gesch. der Könige von Lydien*, p. 36) thinks that he took both town and citadel.

[5] NICOLAS OF DAMASCUS, *Fragm.* 62, in MÜLLER-DIDOT, *op. cit.*, vol. iii. p. 396, where the town is called simply Magnesia ; it was evidently the Magnesia near Sardes, Magnesia ad Sipylum (SCHUBERT, *op. cit.*, p. 37 ; RADET, *op. cit.*, p. 171).

[6] HERODOTUS, I. xiv., mentions this war without entering into any details.   We know from Pausanias (iv. 21, § 3) that the people of Smyrna defended themselves bravely, and that the poet Mimnermus composed an elegy on this episode in their history (ix. 19, § 4).

which the gold of Lydia, and the commodities imported from the East by the
caravans which traversed the royal route, might be exchanged for the products
of Hellas and of the countries of the West visited by the Greek mariners. The
city was at this time under the control of a family of rich shipowners, of whom the
head was called Melas: Gyges gave him his daughter in marriage, and by this
union gained free access to the seaboard for himself and his successors.[1] The
reason for his not pushing his advantages further in this direction is not hard
to discover: since the fall of the kingdom of Phrygia had left his eastern
frontier unprotected,[2] the attacks of the Cimmerians had obliged him to
concentrate his forces in the interior, and though he had always successfully
repulsed them, the obstinacy with which these inroads were renewed year after
year prevented him from further occupying himself with the Greek cities. He
had carefully fortified his vast domains in the basin of the Rhyndakos, he had
reconquered the Troad, and though he had been unable to expel the barbarians
from Adramyttium, he prevented them from having any inland communications. Miletus rendered vigorous assistance in this work of consolidating his
power, for she was interested in maintaining a buffer state between herself and
the marauders who had already robbed her of Sinope; and it was for this reason
that Gyges, after mercilessly harassing her at the beginning of his reign,[3] now
preferred to enter into an alliance with her. He had given the Milesians permission to establish colonies along the Hellespont and the Propontid at the
principal points where communication took place between Europe and Asia;
Abydos, Lampsacus, Parium, and Cyzicus, founded successively by Milesian
admirals, prevented the tribes which remained in Thrace from crossing over to
reinforce their kinsfolk who were devastating Phrygia.[4]

Gyges had hoped that his act of deference would have obtained for him the
active support of Assur-bani-pal, and during the following years he perse-
veringly continued at intervals to send envoys to Nineveh: on one occasion
he despatched with the embassy two Cimmerian chiefs taken in battle, and
whom he offered in token of homage to the gods of Assyria.[5] Experience,
however, soon convinced him that his expectations were vain; the Assyrians, far
from creating a diversion in his favour, were careful to avoid every undertaking which might draw the attention of the barbarians on themselves. As
soon as Gyges fully understood their policy, he broke off all connection with

---

[1] ÆLIAN, *Variæ Historiæ*, iii. 26; on the importance of Ephesus for the kings of Lydia, cf. the
observations of RADET, *La Lydie et le Monde Grec au temps des Mermnades*, pp. 31, 108, 172.

[2] For the fall of the kingdom of Phrygia, cf. *supra*, pp. 391, 392.

[3] HERODOTUS, I. xiv.

[4] For the policy followed by Gyges towards the Milesian colonies on the Hellespont and the
Propontis, cf. RADET, *op. cit.*, pp. 172–175.

[5] G. SMITH, *Hist. of Assurbanipal*, pp. 65, 66; S. ALDEN SMITH, *Die Keilschr. Asurbanipals*,
vol. i. pp. 18, 19.

them, and thenceforth relied on himself alone for the protection of his interests. The disappointment he thus experienced probably stirred up his anger against Assyria, and if he actually came to the aid of Psammetichus, the desire of giving expression to a secret feeling of rancour no doubt contributed to his decision. Assur-bani-pal deeply resented this conduct, but Lydia was too far off for him to wreak his vengeance on it in a direct manner, and he could only beseech the gods to revenge what he was pleased to consider as base ingratitude: he therefore prayed Assur and Ishtar that "his corpse might lie outstretched before his enemies, and his bones be scattered far and wide."[1] A certain Tugdami was at that time reigning over the Cimmerians, and seems to have given to their hitherto undisciplined hordes some degree of cohesion and guidance.[2] He gathered under his standard not only the Trêres, the Thracian kinsfolk of the Cimmerians, but some of the Asianic tribes, such as the Lycians,[3] who were beginning to feel uneasy at the growing prosperity of Gyges, and let them loose upon their Lydian quarry. Their heavy cavalry, with metal helmets and long steel swords, overran the peninsula from end to end, treading down everything under their horses' hoofs. Gyges did his best to stand up against the storm, but his lancers quailed beneath the shock and fled in confusion: he himself perished in the flight, and his corpse remained in the enemy's hands (652 B.C.).[4] The whole of Lydia was mercilessly ravaged, and the lower town of Sardes was taken by storm.[5] Ardys, who had succeeded his

---

[1] *Cylinder A of the Brit. Mus.*, col. iii. ll. 30–32, in G. SMITH, *Hist. of Assurbanipal*, pp. 66, 67: cf. S. ALDEN SMITH, *Die Keilschr. Asurbanipals*, vol. i. pp. 18–21; JENSEN, *Inschr. Aschurbanipal's*, in SCHRADER, *Keil. Bibl.*, vol. ii. pp. 176, 177.

[2] The name Tugdami, mentioned in the hymn published by STRONG, *Un Texte inédit d' Asurbanipal*, in the *Journal Asiatique*, 1893, vol. i. pp. 368, 375, 378, has been identified by Sayce, in the *Academy*, 1893, p. 277, with the Cimmerian chief mentioned by Strabo (I. iii. § 21, p. 61) under the name of Lygdamis: the received reading of this name (Λύγδαμις) must be corrected into Δύγδαμις. The opinion of Sayce has been adopted by other Assyriologists (MESSERSCHMIDT, *Die Inschrift der Stele Nabuna'id's*, p. 61; WINCKLER, *Altorientalische Forschungen*, vol. i. p. 485, note 3). The inscription makes Tugdami a king of the Manda, and thus overthrows the hypothesis that Lygdamis or Dygdamis was a Lycian chief who managed to discipline the barbarian hordes (RADET, *La Lydie et le Monde Grec au temps des Mermnades*, pp. 180, 181).

[3] The alliance of the Lycians with the Cimmerians and Trêres is known from the evidence of Callisthenes preserved for us by Strabo (XIII. iv. § 8, p. 627); it is probable that many of the marauding tribes of the Taurus—Isaurians, Lycaonians, and Pamphylians—similarly joined the Cimmerians.

[4] *Cylinder A of the Brit. Mus.*, col. iii. ll. 32–36, in G. SMITH, *op. cit.*, p. 67: cf. S. ALDEN SMITH, *op. cit.*, vol. i. pp. 20, 21; JENSEN, *op. cit.*, in SCHRADER, *op. cit.*, vol. ii. pp. 176, 177. The date 652 B.C. given for the death of Gyges is gathered from the facts collected and discussed by GELZER, *Das Zeitalter des Gyges*, in the *Rheinisches Museum*, 1875, vol. xxx. pp. 256–264. Winckler has attempted to return to the date 657 B.C. (*Altorient. Forsch.*, vol. i. pp. 495, 496), relying on the epoch assumed for the compilation of the different Cylinder-inscriptions of Assur-bani-pal; it does not seem to me at present that his calculations outweigh those of Gelzer.

[5] HERODOTUS, I. xv.: Σάρδεις πλὴν τῆς ἀκροπόλιος εἷλον; and Strabo states definitely that it was Lygdamis who took the city (I. iii. § 21, p. 61). The account given by the same author of a double destruction of Sardes in 652 and 682 B.C. is due to an unfortunate borrowing from the work of Callisthenes (STRABO, XIII. iv. § 8, p. 627, XIV. i. § 40, p. 647; cf. MÜLLER-DIDOT, *Scriptores rerum Alexandri Magni*, p. 18).

father on the throne, was able, however, to save the citadel: he rallied around him the remnants of his army and once more took the field. The cities of Ionia made common cause with him; their hoplites issued victorious from more than one engagement, and their dogs, trained to harry fearlessly the horses of the enemy, often took an active part in the battle.[1] City after city was attacked by the barbarians, and the suburbs plundered. Ephesus, on account of the wealth it contained, formed their chief attraction, but their forces dashed themselves fruitlessly against its walls; they avenged themselves for their failure by setting on fire the temple of Artemis which stood in the outskirts. This

BATTLE OF THE CIMMERIANS AGAINST THE GREEKS ACCOMPANIED BY THEIR DOGS.[2]

act of sacrilege profoundly stirred the whole Hellenic world, and when the first fury of pillage was exhausted, the barbarians themselves seemed to have been struck with superstitious horror at their crime: deadly fevers contracted in the marshes near the city thinned their ranks, and in the scourge which struck down their forces they recognised the chastisement of the goddess.[3] The survivors abandoned the siege and withdrew in disorder towards the mountains of the interior. On their way they surprised Magnesia on the

---

[1] On the employment of dogs in warfare at this period among both Hellenic and barbarian peoples in Asia Minor, cf. the passages from ancient authors recently collected by SALOMON REINACH, *Un nouveau sarcophage peint de Clazomènes*, in the *Revue des Études Grecques*, 1895, vol. viii. pp. 175–179, and by A. S. MURRAY, *Sarcophage de Clazomènes appartenant au Musée Britannique*, in the *Mémoires Piot*, vol. iv. pp. 27–52. Many of these dogs are represented in the woodcut reproduced in the text on this page; they are depicted harrying the horses of the Cimmerians and biting their haunches.

[2] Drawn by Faucher-Gudin, from the sarcophagus of Clazomenæ reproduced in the *Mémoires Piot*, vol. iv. pl. v.

[3] The invasion of Ionia by the Cimmerians is indicated in general terms by HERODOTUS, I. vi.; the details of the attack on Ephesus and the destruction of the temple of Artemis are preserved in a passage of Callimachus (*Hymns*, iii. 251–258), and in the fragments quoted by HESYCHIUS, *s.v.* Λύγδαμις and Σκύθων ἐρημία. Cf., for the details of these events and the different questions to which they give rise, GELZER, *Das Zeitalter des Gyges*, in the *Rheinisches Museum*, 1875, vol. xxx. p. 258; SCHUBERT, *Geschichte der Könige von Lydien*, pp. 40–42; RADET, *La Lydie et le Monde Grec au temps des Mermnades*, pp. 187–189.

Mæander and entirely destroyed it, but this constituted their sole military success : elsewhere, they contented themselves with devastating the fields without venturing to attack the fortified towns.[1]   Scarcely had Ardys freed himself from their unwelcome presence, than, like his father before him, he tried to win the support of Assyria.   He sent an envoy to Nineveh with a letter couched in very humble terms : " The king whom the gods acknowledge, art thou; for as soon as thou hadst pronounced imprecations against my father, misfortune overtook him.   I am thy trembling servant; receive my homage graciously, and I will bear thy yoke ! "   Assur-bani-pal did not harden his heart to this suppliant who confessed his fault so piteously, and circumstances shortly constrained him to give a more efficacious proof of his favour to Ardys than he had done in the case of Gyges.[2]   On quitting Lydia, Tugdami, with his hordes, had turned eastwards, bent upon renewing in the provinces of the Taurus and the Euphrates the same destructive raids which he had made among the peoples of the Ægean seaboard ; but in the gorges of Cilicia he came into contact with forces much superior to his own, and fell fighting against them about the year 645 B.C.   His son Sanda-khshatru led the survivors of this disaster back towards the centre of the peninsula, but the conflict had been so sanguinary that the Cimmerian power never fully recovered from it.   Assur-bani-pal celebrated the victory won by his generals with a solemn thanks-giving to Marduk, accompanied by substantial offerings of gold and objects of great value.[3]   The tranquillity of the north-west frontier was thus for a time secured, and this success most opportunely afforded the king leisure to turn his attention to those of his vassals who, having thrown off their allegiance during the war against Shamash-shumukîn, had not yet returned to their obedience. Among these were the Arabs and the petty princes of Egypt.   The contingents furnished by Yauta, son of Hazael, had behaved valiantly during the siege of Babylon, and when they thought the end was approaching, their leaders, Abiyatê and Aamu, had tried to cut a way through the Assyrian lines : being repulsed, they had laid down their arms on condition of their lives being spared.[4]

---

[1] STRABO, XIV. i. § 40, p. 647, and HESYCHIUS, s.v. Σκύθων ἐρημία ; Callinus and Archilochus had sung of the destruction of Magnesia (ATHENÆUS, xii. 29).

[2] Cylinder A of the Brit. Mus., col. iii. ll. 36–42, in G. SMITH, Hist. of Assurbanipal, pp. 67, 68. The name of the Lydian king is mutilated, but the final . . . su permits of the restoration Ardusu, which is confirmed by the expression ablu-su, " his son," after the mutilated name.

[3] Strabo (I. iii. § 21, p. 61) was aware, perhaps from Xanthus of Lydia, that Lygdamis had fallen in battle in Cilicia. The hymn to Marduk, published by Strong (Un texte inédit d'Assourbani-pal, in the Journal Asiatique, 1893, vol. i. pp. 368, 375, 378 ; MESSERSCHMIDT, Die Inschrift der Stele Nabuna'id's, pp. 63–67 ; cf. WINCKLER, Altorient. Forsch., vol. i. pp. 492, 493), informs us that the Cimmerian chief fell upon the Assyrians, and that his son Sanda-khshatru carried on hostilities some time longer. Sanda-khshatru is an Iranian name of the same type as that of the Median king Uva-khshatra or Cyaxares.

[4] Cf. supra, p. 422.

There now remained the bulk of the Arab tribes to be reduced to submission, and the recent experiences of Esarhaddon had shown the difficulties attending this task. Assur-bani-pal entrusted its accomplishment to his subjects in Edom, Moab, Ammon, the Haurân, and Damascus, since, dwelling on the very borders of the desert, they were familiar with the routes and the methods of warfare best suited to the country. They proved victorious all along the line. Yauta, betrayed by his own subjects, took refuge with the Nabatæans; but their king, Nadanu, although he did not actually deliver him up to the Assyrians, refused to grant him an asylum, and the unhappy man was finally obliged to surrender to his pursuers. His cousin Uatê, son of Birdadda, was made chief in his place by the Assyrians, and Yauta was sent to Nineveh, where he was exposed at one of the city gates, chained in a niche beside the watch-dogs. Amuladdin, the leading prince of Kedar, met with no better fate: he was overcome, in spite of the assistance rendered him by Adîya, the queen of a neighbouring tribe, and was also carried away into captivity. His defeat completed the discouragement of the tribes who still remained unsubdued. They implored mercy, which Assur-bani-pal granted to them, although he deposed most of their sheikhs, and appointed as their ruler that Abiyatê who had dwelt at his court since the capitulation of Babylon. Abiyatê took the oath of fidelity, and was sent back to Kedar, where he was proclaimed king of all the Arab tribes under the suzerainty of Assyria.[1]

Of all the countries which had thrown off their allegiance during the late troubles, Egypt alone remained unpunished, and it now seemed as if its turn had come to suffer chastisement for its rebellion. It was, indeed, not to be tolerated that so rich and so recently acquired a province should slip from the grasp of the very sovereign who had completed its conquest, without his making an effort on the first opportunity to reduce it once more to submission. Such inaction on his part would be a confession of impotence, of which the other vassals of the empire would quickly take advantage: Tyre, Judah, Moab, the petty kings of the Taurus, and the chiefs of Media, would follow the example of Pharaoh, and the whole work of the last three centuries would have to be done over again. There can be no doubt that Assur-bani-pal cherished the secret hope of recovering Egypt in a short campaign, and that he hoped to attach it to the empire by more permanent bonds than before, but as a

---

[1] The texts relating to this part of the wars against the Arabs have been collected by G. SMITH, *Hist. of Assurbanipal*, pp. 256–265, 283–293, 295, 296, and in S. ALDEN SMITH, *Die Keilschrifttexte Asurbanipals*, vol. i. pp. 58–63; cf. JENSEN, *Inschr. Aschurbanipal's*, in SCHRADER, *Keil. Bibl.*, vol. ii. pp. 214–221. The *Cylinder B of the Brit. Mus.*, col. vii. ll. 87–92 (cf. G. SMITH, *op. cit.*, pp. 283, 284), attributes to the reign of Assur-bani-pal a whole series of events, comprising the first submission of Yauta and the restitution of the statues of Atarsamaîn, which had taken place under Esarhaddon (cf. *supra*, pp. 358–360). The Assyrian annalists do not seem to have always clearly distinguished between Yauta, son of Hazael, and Uatê, son of Birdadda.

preliminary to executing this purpose it was necessary to close and settle if possible the account still open against Elam. Recent events had left the two rival powers in such a position that neither peace nor even a truce of long duration could possibly exist between them. Elam, injured, humiliated, and banished from the plains of the Lower Euphrates, over which she had claimed at all times an almost exclusive right of pillage, was yet not sufficiently enfeebled by her disasters to be convinced of her decided inferiority to Assyria. Only one portion of her forces, and that perhaps the smallest, had taken the field and sustained serious reverses : she had still at her disposal, besides the peoples of the plain and the marshes who had suffered the most, those almost inexhaustible reserves of warlike and hardy mountaineers, whose tribes were ranged on the heights which bounded the horizon, occupying the elevated valleys of the Uknu, the Ulaî, and their nameless affluents, on the western or southern slopes or in the enclosed basins of the Iranian table-land. Here Elam had at her command at least as many men as her adversaries could muster against her, and though these barbarian contingents lacked discipline and systematic training, their bravery compensated for the imperfection of their military education. Elam not only refused to admit herself conquered, but she believed herself sure of final victory, and, as a matter of fact, it is not at all certain that Assur-bani-pal's generals would ever have completely triumphed over her, if internal discords and treason had not too often paralysed her powers. The partisans of Khumbân-igash were largely responsible for bringing about the catastrophe in which Tiummân had perished, and those who sided with Tammaritu had not feared to provoke a revolt at the moment when Khumbân-igash was occupied in Chaldæa; Indabigash in his turn had risen in rebellion in the rear of Tammaritu, and his intervention had enabled the Assyrians to deal their final blow at Shamash-shumukîn. The one idea of the non-reigning members of the royal house was to depose the reigning sovereign, and they considered all means to this end as justifiable, whether assassination, revolt, desertion to the enemy, or defection on the very field of battle. As soon as one of them had dethroned another, hatred of the foreigner again reigned supreme in his breast, and he donned his armour with a firm determination to bring the struggle to an end, but the course he had pursued towards his predecessor was now adopted by one of his relatives towards himself; the enemy meanwhile was still under arms, and each of these revolutions brought him a step nearer to the goal of his endeavours, the complete overthrow of the Elamite kingdom and its annexation to the empire of Nineveh. Even before the struggle with Babylon was concluded, Assur-bani-pal had demanded of Indabigash the release of the Assyrians whom Nabo-bel-shumu had carried off in his train, besides the extradition of that personage himself. Indabigash had no desire for war at this juncture, but hesitated to surrender the Kaldâ, who had always served him faithfully : he entered into negotiations which were interminably prolonged, neither of the two parties being anxious to bring them to a close. After the fall of Babylon, Assur-bani-pal, who was tenacious in his hatred, summoned the Elamite ambassadors, and sent them back to their master with a message conceived in the following menacing terms : " If thou dost not surrender those men, I will go and destroy thy cities, and lead into captivity the inhabitants of Susa, Madaktu, and Khaîdalu. I will hurl thee from thy throne, and will set up another thereon : as aforetime I destroyed Tiummân, so will I destroy thee." A detachment of troops was sent to enforce the message of defiance, but when the messengers had reached the frontier town of Dêri, Indabigash was no longer there : his nobles had assassinated him, and had elected Khumbân-khaldash, the son of Attamêtush, king in his stead.[1] The opportunity was a favourable one to sow the seeds of division in the Elamite camp, before the usurper should have time to consolidate his power : Assur-bani-pal therefore threw himself into the cause of Tammaritu, supporting him with an army to which many malcontents speedily rallied. The Aramæans and the cities of the marsh-lands on the littoral, Khilmu, Billatê, Dummuku, Sulâa, Lakhiru, and Dibirîna, submitted without a struggle, and the invaders met with no resistance till they reached Bît-Imbi. This town had formerly been conquered by Sennacherib, but it had afterwards returned to the rule of its ancient masters, who had strongly fortified it. It now offered a determined resistance, but without success : its population was decimated, and the survivors mutilated and sent as captives into Assyria—among them the commander of the garrison, Imbappi, son-in-law of Khumbân-khaldash, together with the harem of Tiummân, with his sons and daughters, and all the members of his family whom his successors had left under guard in the citadel. The siege had been pushed forward so rapidly that the king had not been able to make any attempt to relieve the defenders : besides this, a pretender had risen up against him, one Umbakhabua, who had been accepted as king by the important district of Bubîlu. The fall of Bît-Imbi filled the two competitors with fear : they abandoned their homes and fled, the one to the mountains, the other to the lowlands on the shores of the Nar-Marratum. Tammaritu entered Susa in triumph and was enthroned afresh ; but the insolence and rapacity of his auxiliaries was so ruthlessly manifested, that at the end of some days he resolved to rid himself of them by the sword. A

---

[1] G. SMITH, *History of Assurbanipal*, pp. 177–181. Tablet K 13 of the British Museum, first utilised by G. Smith (pp. 197–199), refers to these events, and contains some details of the death of Indabigash. Cf. JENSEN, *Inschr. Aschurbanipal's*, in SCHRADER, *Keilinschriftliche Bibliothek*, vol. ii. pp. 266–269.

2 F

traitor having revealed the design, Tammaritu was seized, stripped of his royal apparel, and cast into prison. The generals of Assur-bani-pal had no one whom they could proclaim king in his stead, and furthermore, the season being well advanced, the Elamites, who had recovered from their first alarm, were returning in a body, and threatened to cut off the Assyrian retreat : they therefore evacuated Susa, and regained Assyria with their booty. They burnt all the towns along the route whose walls were insufficient to protect them against a sudden escalade or an attack of a few hours' duration, and the country between the capital and the frontier soon contained nothing but heaps of smoking ruins (647 B.C.)[1]

The campaign, which had been so successful at the outset, had not produced all the results expected from it. The Assyrians had hoped henceforth to maintain control of Elam through Tammaritu, but in a short time they had been obliged to throw aside the instrument with which they counted on effecting the complete humiliation of the nation : Khumbân-khaldash had reoccupied Susa, following on the heels of the last Assyrian detachment, and he reigned as king once more without surrendering Nabo-bel-shumi, or restoring the statue of Nana, or fulfilling any of the conditions which had been the price of a title to the throne. Assur-bani-pal was not inclined to bear patiently this partial reverse ; as soon as spring returned he again demanded the surrender of the Chaldæan and the goddess, under pain of immediate invasion. Khumbân-khaldash offered to expel Nabo-bel-shumi from Lakhiru where he had entrenched himself, and to thrust him towards the Assyrian frontier, where the king's troops would be able to capture him. His offer was not accepted, and a second embassy, headed by Tammaritu, who was once more in favour, arrived to propose more trenchant terms. The Elamite might have gone so far as to grant the extradition of Nabo-bel-shumi, but if he had yielded the point concerning Nana, a rebellion would have broken out in the streets of Susa : he preferred war, and prepared in desperation to carry it on to the bitter end. The conflict was long and sanguinary, and the result disastrous for Elam. Bît-Imbi opened its gates, the district of Rashi surrendered at discretion, followed by the city of Khamanu and its environs, and the Assyrians approached Madaktu : Khumbân-khaldash evacuated the place before they reached it, and withdrew beneath the walls of Dur-Undasi, on the western bank of the Ididi. His enemies pursued him thither, but the stream was swift and

---

[1] G. SMITH, *History of Assurbanipal*, pp. 205–217 ; S. ALDEN SMITH, *Die Keilschr. Asurbanipals*, vol. i. pp. 36–43 ; cf. JENSEN, *Inschr. Aschurbanipal's*, in SCHRADER, *Keil. Bibl.*, vol. ii. pp. 195–199. The difficulty we experience in locating on the map most of the names of Elamite towns is the reason why we cannot determine with any certainty the whole itinerary followed by the Assyrian army.

swollen by rain, so that for two days they encamped on its bank without daring to cross, and were perhaps growing discouraged, when Ishtar of Arbela once more came to the rescue. Appearing in a dream to one of her seers, she said, " I myself go before Assur-bani-pal, the king whom my hands have created; " the army, emboldened by this revelation, overcame the obstacle by a vigorous effort, and dashed impetuously over regions as yet unvisited by any conqueror. The Assyrians burnt down fourteen royal cities, numberless small towns, and destroyed the cornfields, the vines, and the orchards ; Khumbân-khaldash, utterly exhausted, fled to the mountains " like a young dog." Banunu and the districts of Tasarra, twenty cities in the country of Khumir, Khaîdalu, and Bashimu, succumbed one after another, and when the invaders at length decided to retrace their steps to the frontier, Susa, deserted by her soldiers and deprived of her leaders, lay before them an easy prey. It was not the first time in the last quarter of a century that the Assyrians had had the city at their mercy. They had made

STATUES OF THE GODS CARRIED OFF BY ASSYRIAN SOLDIERY.[1]

some stay in it after the battle of Tullîz, and also after the taking of Bît-Imbi in the preceding year; but on those occasions they had visited it as allies, to enthrone a king owing allegiance to their own sovereign, and political exigencies had obliged them to repress their pillaging instincts and their long-standing hatred. Now that they had come as enemies, they were restrained by no considerations of diplomacy : the city was systematically pillaged, and the booty found in it was so immense that the sack lasted an entire month. The royal treasury was emptied of its gold and silver, its metals and the valuable objects which had been brought to it from Sumir, Accad, and Karduniash at successive periods from the most remote ages down to that day, in the course of the successful invasions conducted by the princes of Susa beyond the Tigris ; among them, the riches of the Babylonian temples, which Shamash-shumukîn had lavished on Tiummân to purchase his support, being easily

[1] Drawn by Faucher-Gudin, from LAYARD, *The Monuments of Nineveh*, vol. ii. pl. 30. Cf. the plates (vol. i. pl. 65, and vol. ii. pl. 50) of the same work, and the vignette reproduced in *Struggle of the Nations*, p. 36.

distinguishable. The furniture of the palace was sent to Nineveh in a long procession; it comprised beds and chairs of ivory, and chariots encrusted with enamel and precious stones, the horses of which were caparisoned with gold. The soldiers made their way into the ziggurât, tore down the plates of ruddy copper, violated the sanctuary, and desecrated the prophetic statues of the gods who dwelt within it, shrouded in the sacred gloom, and whose names were only uttered by their devotees with trembling lips. Shumudu, Lagamar, Partikira, Ammankasibar, Udurân, Sapak, Aîpaksina, Bilala, Panintimri, and Kindakarpu, were now brought forth to the light, and made ready to be carried into exile together with their belongings and their priests. Thirty-two statues of the kings, both ancient and modern, in silver, gold, bronze, and marble, escorted the gods on their exodus, among their number being those of Khumbânigash, son of Umbadarâ, Shutruk-nakhunta, and Tammaritu II., the sovereigns who had treated Assyria with the greatest indignity. The effigy of Khalludush was subjected to humiliating outrage: "his mouth, with its menacing smile, was mutilated; his lips, which breathed forth defiance, were slit; his hands, which had brandished the bow against Assur, were cut off," to avenge, though tardily, the ill success of Sennacherib.[1] The sacred groves shared the fate of the temples, and all the riches collected in them by generations of victors were carried off in cartloads. They contained, amongst other edifices, the tombs of the ancient heroes of Elam, who had feared neither Assur nor Ishtar, and who had often brought trouble on the ancestors of Assur-bani-pal. Their sepulchres were violated, their coffins broken open, their bones collected and despatched to Nineveh, to crumble finally into dust in the land of exile: their souls, chained to their mortal bodies, shared their captivity, and if they were provided with the necessary sustenance and libations to keep them from annihilation, it was not from any motives of compassion or pity, but from a refinement of vengeance, in order that they might the longer taste the humiliation of captivity. The image of Nana was found among those of the native gods: it was now separated from them, and after having been cleansed from pollution by the prescribed ceremonies, it was conducted to Uruk, which it entered in triumph on the 1st of the month Kislev. It was reinstated in the temple it had inhabited of old: sixteen hundred and thirty-five years had passed since it had been carried off, in the reign of Kutur-nakhunta, to dwell as a prisoner in Susa.[2]

Assur-bani-pal had no intention of preserving the city of Susa from destruction, or of making it the capital of a province which should comprise

---

[1] See what is stated on this subject, *supra*, pp. 303, 304.

[2] G. SMITH, *Hist. of Assurbanipal*, pp. 218–237, 243–251; S. ALDEN SMITH, *Die Keilschr. Asurbanipals*, vol. i. pp. 42–51: cf. JENSEN, *Inschr. Aschurbanipal's*, in SCHRADER, *Keil. Bibl.*, vol. ii. pp. 198–211, and, for the whole history of this war, BILLERBECK, *Susa*, pp. 112–118. On the value of the chronological data respecting Nana, cf. *Struggle of the Nations*, p. 37, note 2.

THE GREAT TUMULUS OF SUSA.

Drawn by Boudier, from a photographic panorama by Dieulafoy.

the plain of Elam. Possibly it appeared to him too difficult to defend as long as the mountain tribes remained unsubdued, or perhaps the Elamites themselves were not so completely demoralised as he was pleased to describe them in his inscriptions, and the attacks of their irregular troops would have rendered the prolonged sojourn of the Assyrian garrison difficult, if not impossible. Whatever the reason, as soon as the work of pillage was fully accomplished, the army continued its march towards the frontier, carrying with it the customary spoil of the captured towns, and their whole population, or all, at least, who had not fled at the approach of the enemy. The king reserved for himself the archers and pikemen, whom he incorporated into his own bodyguard, as well as the artisans, smelters, sculptors, and stonemasons, whose talents he turned to account in the construction and decoration of his palaces; the remainder of the inhabitants he apportioned, like so many sheep, to the cities and the temples, governors of provinces, officers of state, military chiefs, and private soldiers. Khumbân-khaldash reoccupied Susa after the Assyrians had quitted it, but the misery there was so great that he could not endure it: he therefore transferred his court to Madaktu, one of the royal cities which had suffered least from the invasion, and he there tried to establish a regular government. Rival claimants to the throne had sprung up, but he overcame them without much difficulty: one of them, named Paê, took refuge in Assyria, joining Tammaritu and that little band of dethroned kings or pretenders to the throne of Susa, of whom Assur-bani-pal had so adroitly made use to divide the forces of his adversary. Khumbân-khaldash might well believe that the transportation of the statue of Nana and the sack of Susa had satisfied the vengeance of the Assyrians, at least for a time, and that they would afford him a respite, however short; but he had reckoned without taking into consideration the hatred which had pursued Nabo-bel-shumi during so many years: an envoy followed him as far as Madaktu, and offered Khumbân-khaldash once more the choice between the extradition of the Chaldæan or the immediate reopening of hostilities. He seems to have had a moment's hesitation, but when Nabo-bel-shumi was informed of the terms offered by the envoy, "life had no more value in his eyes: he desired death." He ordered his shield-bearer to slay him, and when the man refused to do so, declaring that he could not live without his master, they stabbed each other simultaneously, and perished, as they had lived, together. Khumbân-khaldash, delivered by this suicide from his embarrassments, had the corpse of the master and the head of the faithful shield-bearer duly embalmed, and sent them to Nineveh. Assur-bani-pal mutilated the wretched body in order to render the conditions of life in the other world harder for the soul: he cut off its head, and forbade the burial of the remains, or the rendering to the dead of the most simple offerings.[1] About this time the inhabitants of Bît-Imbi, of Til-Khumba, and a dozen other small towns, who had fled for refuge to the woods of Mount Saladri, came forth from their hiding-places and cast themselves on the mercy of the conqueror: he deigned to receive them graciously, and enrolled them in his guard, together with the prisoners taken in the last campaign. He was contented to leave Elam to itself for the moment, as he was disquieted at the turn affairs were taking in Arabia.[2] Abiyatê, scarcely seated on the throne, had refused to pay tribute, and had persuaded Uatê and Nadanu to join him in his contumacy; several cities along the Phœnician seaboard, led away by his example, shut their gates and declared themselves independent. Assur-bani-pal had borne all this patiently, while the mass of his troops were engaged against Khumbân-khaldash; but after the destruction of Susa, he determined to revenge himself. His forces left Nineveh in the spring of 642 B.C., crossed the Euphrates, and the line of wooded hills which bordered the course of the river towards the west, provisioned themselves with water at the halting-place of Laribda, and plunged into the desert in search of the rebels. The Assyrians overran the country of Mash, from the town of Iarki to Azalla, where "there dwell no beasts of the field, where no bird of the sky builds its nest," and then, after filling their water-skins at the cisterns of Azalla, they advanced boldly into the thirsty lands which extend towards Qurazite; they next crossed the territory of Kedar, cutting down the trees, filling up the wells, burning the tents, and reached Damascus from the north-east side, bringing in their train innumerable flocks of asses, sheep, camels, and slaves. The Bedâwin of the north had remained passive, but the Nabatheans, encouraged by the remoteness of their country and the difficulty of access to it, persisted in their rebellion. The Assyrian generals did not waste much time in celebrating their victory in the Syrian capital: on the 3rd of Ab, forty days after leaving the Chaldæan frontier, they started from Damascus towards the south, and seized the stronghold of Khalkhuliti, at the foot of the basaltic plateau overlooked by the mountains of the Haurân; they then destroyed all the fortresses of the country one after another, driving the inhabitants to take shelter in the rugged range of volcanic rocks, where they were blockaded, and finally reduced by famine: Abiyatê capitulated, Nadanu ransomed himself by a promise of tribute, and the whole desert between Syria and the Euphrates fell once more into the condition of an Assyrian province. Before returning to Nineveh, Assur-bani-pal's generals

[1] For the belief presupposed by this, cf. what is stated concerning the kings of Susa, *supra*, p. 436.

[2] G. SMITH, *History of Assurbanipal*, pp. 237–243; S. ALDEN SMITH, *Die Keilschrifttexte Asur-banipals*, vol. i. pp. 52–57: cf. JENSEN, *Inschr. Aschurbanipal's*, in SCHRADER, *Keilinschriftliche Bibliothek*, vol. ii. pp. 210–215.

inflicted chastisement on Akko and Ushu, the two chief Tyrian cities which had revolted, and this vigorous action confirmed the fidelity of the Assyrian vassals in Palestine. Uatê's life was spared, but his lip and cheek were pierced by the hand of the king himself, and he was led by a cord passed through the wounds, as if he had been a wild beast intended for domestication; a dog's collar was riveted round his neck, and he was exposed in a cage at one of the gates of Nineveh. Aamu, the brother of Abiyatê, was less fortunate, for he was flayed alive before the eyes of the mob. Assyria was glutted with the spoil: the king, as was customary, reserved for his own service the able-bodied men for the purpose of recruiting his battalions, distributing the remainder among his officers and soldiers. The camels captured were so numerous that their market-value was for a long time much reduced; they were offered in the open market, like sheep, for a half-shekel of silver apiece, and the vendor thought himself fortunate to find a purchaser even at this price.[1]

The final ruin of Elam followed swiftly on the subjugation of Arabia. While one division of the army was scouring the desert, the remainder were searching the upland valleys of the Ulaî and the Uknu, and relentlessly pursuing Khumbân-khaldash. The wretched monarch was now in command of merely a few bands of tattered followers, and could no longer take the field; the approach of the enemy obliged him to flee from Madaktu, and entrench himself on the heights. Famine, misery, and probably also the treachery of his last adherents, soon drove him from his position, and, despairing of his cause, he surrendered himself to the officers who were in pursuit of him. He was the third king of Elam whom fate had cast alive into the hands of the conqueror: his arrival at Nineveh afforded the haughty Assur-bani-pal an occasion for celebrating one of those triumphal processions in which his proud soul delighted, and of going in solemn state to thank the gods for the overthrow of his most formidable enemy. On the day when he went to prostrate himself before Assur and Ishtar, he sent for Tammaritu, Paê, and Khumbân-khaldash, and adding to them Uatê, who was taken out of his cage for the occasion, he harnessed all four to his chariot of state, and caused himself to be drawn through Nineveh by this team of fallen sovereigns to the gate of the temple of Ê-mashmash.[2] And, indeed, at that moment, he might reasonably consider himself as having reached the zenith of his power. Egypt, it is true, still remained unpunished,

[1] G. SMITH, *Hist. of Assurbanipal*, pp. 263–283, 294–296; S. ALDEN SMITH, *Die Keilschr. Asurbani-pals*, vol. i. pp. 64–75: cf. JENSEN, *Inschr. Aschurbanipal's*, in SCHRADER, *Keil. Bibl.*, vol. ii. pp. 218–229. For the general direction of the marches executed by the Assyrian army across the desert, from the banks of the Euphrates to Damascus and the Haurân, I have followed the indications of DELATTRE, *L'Asie Occid. dans les Inscr. Assyr.*, pp. 108–120.

[2] G. SMITH, *op. cit.*, pp. 300–306; S. ALDEN SMITH, *op. cit.*, vol. i. pp. 74–77: cf. JENSEN, *op. cit.*, in SCHRADER, *op. cit.*, vol. ii. pp. 228–231.

and its renewed vitality under the influence of the Saïte Pharaohs allowed no hope of its being speedily brought back into subjection, but its intrigues no longer exerted any influence over Syria, and Tyre itself appeared to be resigned to the loss of its possessions on the mainland. Lydia under the rule of Ardys continued to maintain intermittent intercourse with its distant protector. The provinces of the Taurus, delivered from the terror inspired by the Cimmerians, desired peace above all things, and the Mannai had remained quiet since the defeat of Akhsheri. Babylon was rapidly recovering from the ills she had endured. She consoled herself for her actual servitude by her habitual simulation of independence; she called Assur-bani-pal Kandalanu, and this new name allowed her to fancy she had a separate king, distinct from the King of Assyria. Elam no longer existed. Its plains and marsh lands were doubtless occupied by Assyrian garrisons, and formed an ill-defined annexation to Nineveh; the mountain tribes retained their autonomy, and although still a source of annoyance to their neighbours by their raids or sudden incursions, they no longer constituted a real danger to the state : if there still remained some independent Elamite states, Elam itself, the most ancient, except Babylon, of all the Asiatic kingdoms, was erased from the map of the world. The memories of her actual history were soon effaced, or were relegated to the region of legend, where the fabulous Memnon supplanted in the memory of men those lines of hardy conquerors who had levied tribute from Syria in the days when Nineveh was still an obscure provincial town. Assyria alone remained, enthroned on the ruins of the past, and her dominion seemed established for all time ; yet, on closer investigation, indications were not wanting of the cruel sufferings that she also had endured. Once again, as after the wars of Tiglath-pileser I. and those of Assur-nazir-pal and Shalmaneser III., her chiefs had overtaxed her powers by a long series of unremitting wars against vigorous foes. Doubtless the countries comprised within her wide empire furnished her with a more ample revenue and less restricted resources than had been at the command of the little province of ancient days, which had been bounded by the Khabur and the Zab, and lay on the two banks of the middle course of the Tigris ; but, on the other hand, the adversaries against whom she had measured her forces, and whom she had overthrown, were more important and of far greater strength than her former rivals. She had paid dearly for humiliating Egypt and laying Babylon in the dust. As soon as Babylon was overthrown, she had, without pausing to take breath, joined issue with Elam, and had only succeeded in triumphing over it by drawing upon her resources to the utmost during many years : when the struggle was over, she realised to what an extent she had been weakened by so lavish an outpouring of the blood of her citizens. The

Babylonian and Elamite recruits whom she incorporated into her army after each of her military expeditions, more or less compensated for the void which victory itself had caused in her population and her troops ; but the fidelity of these vanquished foes of yesterday, still smarting from their defeat, could not be relied on, and the entire assimilation of their children to their conquerors was the work of at least one or two generations. Assyria, therefore, was on the eve of one of those periods of exhaustion which had so often enfeebled her national vitality and imperilled her very existence. On each previous occasion she had, it is true, recovered after a more or less protracted crisis, and the brilliancy of her prospects, though obscured for a moment, appeared to be increased by their temporary eclipse. There was, therefore, good reason to hope that she would recover from her latest phase of depression ; and the only danger to be apprehended was that some foreign power, profiting by her momentary weakness, might rise up and force her, while still suffering from the effects of her heroic labours, to take the field once more.

THE MEDES AND THE SECOND
CHALDÆAN EMPIRE.

———◆———

THE FALL OF NINEVEH AND THE RISE OF THE CHALDÆAN AND MEDIAN EMPIRES— THE XXVIth
EGYPTIAN DYNASTY: CYAXARES, ALYATTES, AND NEBUCHADREZZAR.

*The legendary history of the kings of Media and the first contact of the Medes with the
Assyrians: the alleged Iranian migrations of the Avesta—Media proper, its fauna and flora;
Phraortes and the beginning of the Median empire—Persia proper and the Persians: conquest of
Persia by the Medes—The last monuments of Assur-bani-pal: the library of Kouyunjik—
Phraortes defeated and slain by the Assyrians.*

*Cyaxares and his first attack on Nineveh—The Assyrian triangle and the defence of Nineveh:
Assur-bani-pal summons the Scythians to his aid—The Scythian invasion—Judah under
Manasseh and Amon: development in the conceptions of the prophets—The Scythians in Syria
and on the borders of Egypt: they are defeated and driven back by Cyaxares—The last kings
of Nineveh and Nabopolassar—Taking and destruction of Nineveh: division of the Assyrian
empire between the Chaldæans and the Medes (608 B.C.).*

*The XXVIth Egyptian dynasty—Psammetichus I. and the Ionian and Carian mercenaries;
final retreat of the Ethiopians and the annexation of the Theban principality; the end of Egypt
as a great power—First Greek settlements in the Delta; flight of the Mashauasha and the
reorganisation of the army—Resumption of important works and the renaissance of art in Egypt
—The occupation of Ashdod, and the Syrian policy of Psammetichus I.*

Josiah, King of Judah : the discovery and public reading of the Book of the Covenant ; the religious reform—Necho II. invades Syria : Josiah slain at Megiddo, the battle of Carchemish— Nebuchadrezzar II. : his policy with regard to Media—The conquests of Cyaxares and the struggles of the Mermnadæ against the Greek colonies—The war between Alyattes and Cyaxares : the battle of the Halys and the peace of 585 B.C.—Necho reorganises his army and his fleet : the circumnavigation of Africa—Jeremiah and the Egyptian party in Jerusalem : the revolt of Jehoiakim and the captivity of Jehoiachin.

Psammetichus I. and Zedekiah—Apries and the revolt of Tyre and of Judah : the siege and destruction of Jerusalem—The last convulsions of Judah and the submission of Tyre ; the successes of Apries in Phœnicia—The Greeks in Libya and the founding of Cyrene : the defeat of Irasa and the fall of Apries—Amasis and the campaign of Nebuchadrezzar against Egypt— Relations between Nebuchadrezzar and Astyages—The fortifications of Babylon and the rebuilding of the Great Ziggurât—The successors of Nebuchadrezzar : Nabonidus.

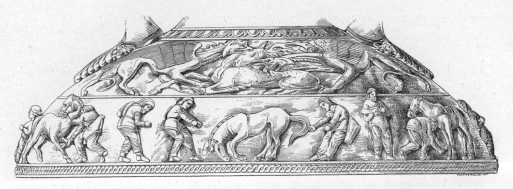

SCYTHIANS LASSOING HORSES.[1]

CHAPTER V.

THE MEDES AND THE SECOND CHALDÆAN EMPIRE.

The fall of Nineveh and the rise of the Chaldæan and Median empires—The XXVIth Egyptian dynasty: Cyaxares, Alyattes, and Nebuchadrezzar.

THE East was ever a land of kaleidoscopic changes and startling dramatic incidents. An Oriental empire, even when built up by strong hands and watched over with constant vigilance, scarcely ever falls to pieces in the slow and gradual process of decay arising from the ties that bind it together becoming relaxed or its constituent elements growing antiquated. It perishes, as a rule, in a cataclysm; its ruin comes like a bolt from the blue, and is consummated before the commencement of it is realised. One day it stands proud and stately in the splendour of its glory; there is no report abroad but that which tells of its riches, its industry, its valour, the good government of its princes and the irresistible might of its gods, and the world, filled with envy or with fear, deeming its good fortune immutable, never once applies to it, even in thought, the usual commonplaces on the instability of human things. Suddenly an ill wind, blowing up from the distant horizon, bursts upon it in destructive squalls, and it is overthrown in the twinkling of an eye, amid the glare of lightning, the resounding crash of thunder, whirlwinds of dust and rain: when the storm has passed away as quickly as it came, its mutterings heralding the desolation which it bears to other climes, the brightening sky

[1] Drawn by Faucher-Gudin, from the silver vase of Tchertomlitsk, now in the museum of the Hermitage. The initial is also drawn by Faucher-Gudin, and represents an Egyptian torso in the Turin museum; the cartouche which is seen upon the arm is that of Psammetichus I.

no longer reveals the old contours and familiar outlines, but the sun of history rises on a new empire, emerging, as if by the touch of a magic wand, from the ruins which the tempest has wrought. There is nothing apparently lacking of all that, in the eyes of the many, invested its predecessor with glory; it seems in no wise inferior in national vigour, in the number of its soldiers, in the military renown of its chiefs, in the proud prosperity of its people, or in the majesty of its gods; the present fabric is as spacious and magnificent, it would seem, as that which has but just vanished into the limbo of the past. No kingdom ever shone with brighter splendour, or gave a greater impression of prosperity, than the kingdom of Assyria in the days succeeding its triumphs over Elam and Arabia : precisely at this point the monuments and other witnesses of its activity fail us, just as if one of the acts of the piece in which it had played a chief part having come to an end, the drop-curtain must be lowered, amid a flourish of trumpets and the illuminations of an apotheosis, to allow the actors a little breathing-space. Half a century rolls by, during which we have a dim perception of the subdued crash of falling empires, and of the trampling of armies in fierce fight; then the curtain rises on an utterly different drama, of which the plot has been woven behind the scenes, and the exciting *motif* has just come into play. We no longer hear of Assyria and its kings; their palaces are in ruins; their last faithful warriors sleep in unhonoured graves beneath the ashes of their cities, their prowess is credited to the account of half a dozen fabulous heroes such as Ninus, Sardanapalus, and Semiramis—heroes whose names call up in the memory of succeeding generations only vague but terrible images, such as the phantasies of a dream, which, although but dimly remembered in the morning, makes the hair to stand on end with terror. The nations which erewhile disputed the supremacy with Assyria have either suffered a like eclipse—such as the Khâti, Urartu, the Cossæans, and Elam—or have fallen like Egypt and Southern Syria into the rank of second-rate powers. It is Chaldæa which is now in the van of the nations, in company with Lydia and with Media, whose advent to imperial power no one would have ventured to predict forty or fifty years before.

The principality founded by Deïokes about the beginning of the seventh century B.C., seemed at first destined to play but a modest part;[1] it shared the fortune of the semi-barbarous states with which the Ninevite conquerors came in contact on the western boundary of the Iranian plateau, and from which the governors of Arrapkha or of Kharkhar had extorted tribute to the utmost as often as occasion offered. According to one tradition, it had only three kings in an entire century : Deïokes up till 655 B.C., Phraortes from 655 to 633, and

---

[1] Cf. on this subject, *supra*, pp. 324-328.

after the latter year Cyaxares, the hero of his race.[1] Another tradition claimed an earlier foundation for the monarchy, and doubled both the number of the kings and the age of the kingdom.[2] This tradition ignored the monarchs who had rendered the second Assyrian empire illustrious, and substituted for them a line of inactive sovereigns, reputed to be the descendants of Ninus and Semiramis. The last of them, Sardanapalus, had, according to this account, lived a life of self-indulgence in his harem, surrounded by women, dressing himself in their garb, and adopting feminine occupations and amusements. The satrap of Media, Arbakes, saw him at his toilet, and his heart turned against yielding obedience to such a painted doll: he rebelled in concert with Belesys the Babylonian. The imminence of the danger thus occasioned roused Sardanapalus from his torpor, and revived in him the warlike qualities of his ancestors; he placed himself at the head of his troops, overcame the rebels, and was about to exterminate them, when his hand was stayed by the defection of some Bactrian auxiliaries. He shut himself up in Nineveh, and for two whole years heroically repulsed all assaults; in the third year, the Tigris, swollen by

[1] This is the tradition gleaned by Herodotus (I. xcv.–ciii.), probably at Sardes, from the mouths of Persians (I. xcv.) residing in that city.

[2] This is the tradition derived from the court of Artaxerxes by Ctesias of Cnidus (*Fragm.* 25, in MÜLLER-DIDOT, *Ctesiæ Cnidii Fragmenta*, pp. 41–53). Volney (*Recherches sur l'Histoire Ancienne*, vol. i. p. 144, et seq.) discovered the principle upon which the chronology of his Median dynasty was based by Ctesias. If we place his list side by side with that of Herodotus—

HERODOTUS.		CTESIAS.	
Interregnum	*x*	Arbakes	28
Deïokes	53	Mandaukas	50
		Sosarmos	30
		Artykas	50
Phraortes	22	Arbianes	22
		Artaios	40
		Artynes	22
Cyaxares	40	Astibaras	40

we see that, while rejecting the names given by Herodotus, Ctesias repeats twice over the number of years assigned by the latter to the reigns of his kings, at least for the four last generations—

Phraortes . . . 22 $\begin{cases} \text{Arbianes . . . 22} \\ \text{Artynes . . . 22} \end{cases}$ $\begin{cases} \text{Artaios . . . 40} \\ \text{Astibaras . . . 40} \end{cases}$ Cyaxares . . . 40

At the beginning Herodotus gives before Deïokes an interregnum of uncertain duration. Ctesias substituted the round number of fifty years for the fifty-three assigned to Deïokes, and replaced the interregnum by a reign which he estimated at the mean duration of a human generation, thirty years; he then applied to this new pair of numbers the process of doubling he had employed for the couple mentioned above—

Deïokes . . . 53 $\begin{cases} \text{Mandaukas . . 50} \\ \text{Artykas . . . 50} \end{cases}$ $\begin{cases} \text{Arbakes . . . 28} \\ \text{Sosarmos . . . 30} \end{cases}$ *Interregnum* . . *x*

The number twenty-eight has been attributed to the reign of Arbakes, instead of the number thirty, to give an air of truthfulness to the whole catalogue. For the end of the list of Ctesias and the numbers which must be inserted in it, cf. MARQUART, *Die Assyriaka des Ktesias*, in the *Philologus*, Supplement, vol. v. pp. 562, 563.

the rains, overflowed its banks and broke down the city walls for a distance of twenty stadia. The king thereupon called to mind an oracle which had promised him victory until the day when the river should betray him. Judging that the prediction was about to be accomplished, he resolved not to yield himself alive to the besieger, and setting fire to his palace, perished therein, together with his children and his treasures, about 788 B.C.[1] Arbakes, thus rendered an independent sovereign, handed down the monarchy to his son Mandaukas, and he in his turn was followed successively by Sosarmos, Artykas, Arbianes, Artaios, Artynes, and Astibaras.[2] These names are not the work of pure invention; they are met with in more than one Assyrian text: among the petty kings who paid tribute to Sargon are enumerated some which bear such names as Mashdaku,[3] Ashpanda,[4] Arbaku, and Khartukka,[5] and many others, of whom traces ought to be found some day among the archives of princely families of later times.[6] There were in these archives, at the disposal of scribes and strangers inclined to reconstruct the history of Asia, a supply of materials of varying value—authentic documents inscribed on brick tablets, legends of fabulous exploits, epic poems and records of real victories and conquests, exaggerated in accordance with the vanity or the interest of the composer: from these elements it was easy to compile lists of Median kings which had no real connection with each other as far as their names, order of succession, or duration of reign were concerned.[7] The Assyrian chronicles have handed down to us, in place of these dynasties which were alleged to have exercised authority over the whole territory, a considerable number of noble houses scattered over the country, each of them autonomous, and a rival of its neighbour, and only brought into agreement with one another at rare intervals by their common hatred of the invader. Some of them were representatives of ancient races akin to the Susians, and perhaps to the first inhabitants of Chaldæa;[8] others belonged to tribes of a fresh stock, that of the Aryans, and more particularly to the Iranian

---

[1] For the legend of Sardanapalus and Arbakes, see the narratives of CTESIAS, *Fragm.* 20–22, in MÜLLER-DIDOT, *Ctesiæ Cnidii Fragmenta*, pp. 36–41; cf. DIODORUS SICULUS, ii. 23–28.

[2] Oppert thought that the names given by Herodotus represented "Aryanised forms of Turanian names, of which Ctesias has given the Persian translation" (*Le Peuple et la langue des Mèdes*, p. 17, et seq.).

[3] Mashdaku is identified by Rost (*Untersuchungen zur Altorient. Gesch.*, p. 115) with the Mandaukas or Maydaukas of Ctesias, which would then be a copyist's error for Masdaukas. The identification with Vashd[t]aku, Vashtak, the name of a fabulous king of Armenia, proposed by Justi (*Iranisches Namenbuch*, p. 359), is rejected by Rost (*op. cit.*, p. 111, note 3); Mashdaku would be the Iranian Mazdaka, preserved in the Mazakes of Arrian (*Anabasis*, III. i. § 2).

[4] Ashpanda is the Aspandas or Aspadas which Ctesias gives instead of the Astyages of Herodotus (*Fragm.* 25, in MÜLLER-DIDOT, *op. cit.*, p. 43); cf. JUSTI, *op. cit.*, p. 45).

[5] The name of Artykas is also found in the secondary form Kardikeas, which is nearer the Khartukka of the Assyrian texts (ROST, *op. cit.*, p. 115).

[6] These names are taken from the list discovered by G. Smith (*Assyrian Discoveries*, pp. 288, 289), and interpreted by Rost (*op. cit.*, pp. 111–115).

[7] ROST, *Untersuchungen zur Altorientalischen Geschichte*, pp. 110, 111, 115, 116.

[8] On this point, cf. *Struggle of the Nations*, pp. 32–36, 113, 114.

branch of the Aryan family. We catch glimpses of them in the reign of Shalmaneser III., who calls them the Amadaî ;[1] then, after this first brush with Assyria, intercourse and conflict between the two nations became more and more frequent every year, until the "distant Medes" soon began to figure among the regular adversaries of the Ninevite armies, and even the haughtiest monarchs refer with pride to victories gained over them. Rammân-nirâri waged ceaseless war against them,[2] Tiglath-pileser III. twice drove them before him from the south-west to the north-east as far as the foot of Demavend,[3] while Sargon, Sennacherib, and Esarhaddon, during their respective reigns, kept anxious watch upon them, and endeavoured to maintain some sort of authority over the tribes which lay nearest to them.[4] Both in the personal names and names of objects which have come down to us in the records of these campaigns, we detect Iranian characteristics, in spite of the Semitic garb with which the inscriptions have invested them: among the names of countries we find Partukka, Diristânu, Patusharra, Nishaîa, Urivzân, Abîruz, and Ariarma, while the men bear such names as Ishpabarra, Eparna, Shîtirparna, Uarzân, and Dayaukku.[5] As we read through the lists, faint resemblances in sound awaken dormant classical memories, and the ear detects familiar echoes in the names of those Persians whose destinies were for a time linked with those of Athens and Sparta in the days of Darius and of Xerxes: it is like the first breath of Greek influence, faint and almost imperceptible as yet, wafted to us across the denser atmosphere of the East.

The Iranians had a vague remembrance of a bygone epoch, during which they had wandered, in company with other nations of the same origin as themselves, in that cradle of the Aryan peoples, Aryanem-Vaêjô.[6] Modern historians at first placed their mythical birthplace in the wilder regions of Central Asia, near the Oxus and the Jaxartes, and not far from the so-called table-land of Pamir, which they regarded as the original point of departure of

---

[1] For the identity of Amadaî or the Madaî—or in other words, the Medes—cf. p. 89, n. 4, *supra.*

[2] For Rammân-nirâri IV. and his wars against the Medes, cf. p. 99, *supra.*

[3] The campaigns of Tiglath-pileser III. against the Medes have been described on pp. 142, 143, 153, 154, *supra.*

[4] The little we know of the relations of the Medes with the Sargonide kings has already been dealt with in the present volume, on pp. 240–244, 247–259 in the case of Sargon, and on pp. 276, 277 and pp. 252–256 in the case of Sennacherib and Esarhaddon respectively; it would seem that at least one-half of the plateau must at that time have been either directly or indirectly under the rule of Assyria.

[5] The Iranian equivalents of these names have already been given in the present volume—in the case of Partukka on p. 356, note 1, of Patusharra on p. 355, note 3, of Eparna and Shîtirparna on p. 355, note 4. Urivzân has been connected with the Avestic Urvâ (Fr. Lenormant, *Lettres Assyriologiques*, vol. i. p. 31), and if so, would correspond to Urva-Zâna (Rost, *Die Keilschrifttexte Tiglat-Pileser's III.*, vol. i. p. xvii., and *Untersuchungen zur Altorientalischen Geschichte*, p. 78, note 5). Abîruz seems to me to contain the element *bereza,* "high," which is found in the name Elburz. Uarzân is, perhaps, Varzan or Varezâna, which the Greeks transliterated into Barzanes (Justi, *Iranisches Namenbuch*, p. 65, and Rost, *Untersuchungen zur Altorientalischen Geschichte*, p. 113, note 1).

[6] J. Darmesteter, *The Zend-Avesta*, vol. ii. p. 5, note 4.

2 G

the Indo-European races. They believed that a large body of these primitive Aryans must have descended southwards into the basin of the Indus and its affluents, and that other detachments had installed themselves in the oases of Margiana and Khorasmia, while the Iranians would have made their way up to the plateau which separates the Caspian Sea from the Persian Gulf, where they sought to win for themselves a territory sufficient for their wants.[1] The compilers of the sacred books of the Iranians claimed to be able to trace each stage of their peregrinations, and to describe the various accidents which befell them during this heroic period of their history. According to these records, it was no mere chance or love of adventure which had led them to wander for years from clime to clime, but rather a divine decree. While Ahurômazdaô, the beneficent deity whom they worshipped, had provided them with agreeable resting-places, a perverse spirit, named Angrômaînyus, had on every occasion rendered their sojourn there impossible, by the plagues which he inflicted on them. Bitter cold, for instance, had compelled them to forsake Aryanem-Vaêjô and seek shelter in Sughdhâ and Mûru.[2] Locusts had driven them from Sughdhâ; the incursions of the nomad tribes, coupled with their immorality, had forced them to retire from Mûru to Bâkhdhî, "the country of lofty banners,"[3] and subsequently to Nisaya, which lies to the south-east, between Mûru and Bâkhdhî. From thence they made their way into the narrow valleys of the Harôyu, and overran Vaêkereta, the land of noxious shadows.[4] From this point forwards,

---

[1] The theory that the first chapter of the Vendidâd throws valuable light on the early history of the Aryan races and Iranian migrations dates from the beginning of this century. Heeren (*Ideen zur Alten Geschichte*, vol. i. p. 498) and, later on, Rohde (*Die Heilige Sage des Zendvolks*, p. 61) first advanced the view that it describes the state of Iran as it was in the time of Zoroaster; Rohde even went so far as to assert that the order in which the provinces are enumerated corresponds with the successive stages of the Iranian conquest. Lassen, starting from this hypothesis, suggested that Aryanem-Vaêjô, which occupies the first place in the list, was the cradle of the race (*Indische Alterthumskunde*, 1st edit., vol. i. p. 526), and soon afterwards Haug proposed to regard the whole chapter as a sort of diary composed during the course of the migration (*Das Erste Kapitel des Vendidads*, in BUNSEN, *Ægypten's Stellung in der Weltgeschichte*, vol. v. pt. 2, pp. 104–127). These views held the field until they were refuted by Kiepert in the *Monatsberichte* of the Berlin Academy of Sciences, 1856, p. 621, et seq., and until Bréal proved in his paper *De la Géographie de l'Avesta*, published in the *Journal Asiatique* for 1862, and reproduced in *Mélanges de Mythologie et de Linguistique*, p. 187, et seq., that "the geography of the Avesta is fabulous from beginning to end." This is the view now generally accepted (J. DARMESTETER, *The Zend-Avesta*, vol. ii. pp. 1–4).

[2] Sughdhâ is Sogdiana; Mûru, in ancient Persian Margush (*Inscription of Behistun*, col. iii. l. 11), is the modern Merv, the Margiana of classical geographers.

[3] Bâkhdhî is identical with Bactriana, but, as Spiegel points out, this Avestic form, when compared with the Bakhtrish of the Achæmenian inscriptions (*Inscription of Persepolis E, epoch of Darius*, l. 16, and *Inscription of Naksh-i-Rustem*, l. 23) and the Greek Βάκτρα, is comparatively recent, and readily suggests the modern Balkh, in which the consonants have become weakened.

[4] The Avesta places Nisaya between Mûru and Bâkhdhî (J. DARMESTETER, *The Zend-Avesta*, vol. ii. p. 9), to distinguish it from other districts of the same name to be found in this part of Asia: Eugène Burnouf is probably correct in identifying it with the Nêsæa of Strabo (XI. vii. § 3, p. 509) and of Ptolemy (vi. 10, 4), which lay to the south of Margiana, at the junction of the roads leading to Hyrcania in one direction and Bactriana in the other. Harôyu or Haraêva is the Greek Aria, the modern province of Herat. The Pehlevi commentators identify Vaêkereta with Kabulistan, and also volunteer the following interpretation of the title which accompanies the name: "The shadow of the trees there is injurious to the body, or as some say, the shadow of the mountains," and it produces

the countries mentioned by their chroniclers are divided into two groups, lying in opposite directions: Arahvaiti, Haêtumant, and Haptahindu [1] on the east; and on the west, Urvâ,[2] Khnenta-Vehrkâna,[3] Rhagâ,[4] and Chakhra,[5] as far as the districts of Varena [6] and the basin of the Upper Tigris.[7] This legend was

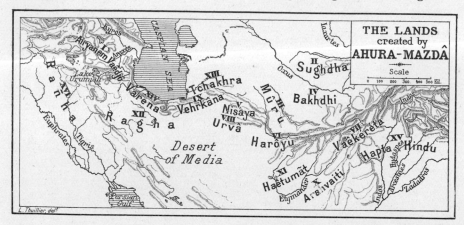

composed long after the event, in order to explain in the first place the relationship between the two great families into which the Oriental Aryans were divided,

fever there. Arguing from passages of similar construction, Lassen was led to recognise in the epithet *duzhako-shayanem* a place-name, "inhabitant of Duzhakô," which he identified with a ruined city in this neighbourhood called Dushak; Haug (*Das erste Kapitel des Vendidads*, in BUNSEN, *Ægypten's Stellung*, vol. v. p. 132) believed he had found a confirmation of this hypothesis in the fact that the Pairika Khnâthaiti created there by Angrô-maînyus recalls in sound, at any rate, the name of the people Parikani mentioned by classical writers (HEROD., III. xciv.; PLINY, *Hist. Nat.*, vi. 16) as inhabiting these regions.

[1] Arahvaiti, the Harauvatish of the Achæmenian inscriptions (*Inscription E of Persepolis*, l. 17), is the Greek Arachosia, and Haêtumant the basin of their Etymander, the modern Helmend; in other words, the present province of Seîstan. Hapta-Hindu is the western part of the Indian continent, *i.e.* the Punjaub.

[2] The Pehlevi commentators identify Urvâ with Mesênê, mentioned by classical writers, at the confluence of the Tigris and Euphrates (J. DARMESTETER, *The Zend-Avesta*, vol. ii. p. 11, note 24), or perhaps the plain around Ispahan which bore the name of Masân in the Sassanid period (J. DARMESTETER, *The Zend-Avesta*, vol. i. p. 2). Fr. Lenormant (*Lettres Assyriol.*, vol. i. p. 31) had connected it with the name Urivzân (cf. p. 449, note 5, *supra*), which is applied in the Assyrian inscriptions to a district of Media in the time of Tiglath-pileser III. (*Tablet K 3571*, obv., l. 30, ed. ROST, vol. i. pp. 62, 63).

[3] The name Khnenta seems to have been Hellenised into that of Kharindas, borne by a river which formed the frontier between Hyrcania and Media (AMMIANUS MARCELLINUS, XXIII. ii. § 20); according to the Pehlevi version it was really a river of Hyrcania, the Djordjân (J. DARMESTETER, *The Zend-Avesta*, vol. ii. p. 12, note 23). The epithet Vehrkâna, which qualifies the name Khnenta, has been identified by Burnouf (*Commentaire sur le Yaçna*, p. lxi.) with the Hyrcania of classical geographers.

[4] Raghâ is identified with Azerbaijân in the Pehlevi version of the Vendidâd (J. DARMESTETER, *The Zend-Avesta*, vol. ii. p. 13, note 33), but is, more probably, the Rhagæ of classical geographers (STRABO, XI. xiii. § 6, p. 524; ARRIANUS, *Anabasis*, iii. 20), the capital of Eastern Media.

[5] Chakhra seems to be identical with the country of Karkh, at the north-western extremity of Khorassan, as suggested by Haug (cf. J. DARMESTETER, *The Zend-Avesta*, vol. i. p. 9, note 1, and *The Zend-Avesta*, vol. ii. p. 13, note 36).

[6] Varena is identified by the Pehlevi commentators with Patishkhvargâr (J. DARMESTETER, *The Zend-Avesta*, vol. ii. p. 14, note 38), *i.e.* probably the Patusharra of the Assyrian inscriptions (cf. p. 355, note 3, *supra*).

[7] Haug proposed to identify this last station with the regions situated on the shores of the Caspian, near the south-western corner of that sea. But, as Garrez points out, the Pehlevi commentators prove that it must be the countries on the Upper Tigris (*Journal Asiatique*, 1869, vol. ii. p. 186; cf. J. DARMESTETER, *The Zend-Avesta*, vol. ii. p. 15, note 44).

viz. the Indian and Iranian, and in the second to account for the peopling by the Iranians of a certain number of provinces between the Indus and the Euphrates. As a matter of fact, it is more likely that the Iranians came originally from Europe, and that they migrated from the steppes of Southern Russia into the plains of the Kur and the Araxes by way of Mount Caucasus.[1] It is possible that some of their hordes may have endeavoured to wedge themselves in between the Halys and the Euphrates as far as the centre of Asia Minor. Their presence in this quarter would explain why we encounter Iranian personal names in the Sargonide epoch on the two spurs of Mount Taurus, such as that of the Kushtashpi, King of Kummukh, in the time of Tiglath-pileser III., and of the Kundashpi mentioned in the *Annals* of Shalmaneser III. in the ninth century B.C.[2] The main body, finding its expansion southwards checked by Urartu, diverged in a south-easterly direction, and sweeping before it all the non-Aryan or Turanian tribes who were too weak to stem its progress, gradually occupied the western edge of the great plateau, where it soon became mainly represented by the two compact groups, the Persians to the south on the farthest confines of Elam, and the Medes between the Greater Zab, the Turnât, and the Caspian. It is probable that the kingdom founded by Deïokes originally included what was afterwards termed *Media Magna* by the Græco-Roman geographers.[3] This sovereignty was formed by the amalgamation under a single monarch of six important tribes—the Buzæ, Parætakeni, Struchatæ, Arizanti, Budii, and Magi.[4] It extended north-westwards as far as the Kizil-uzên, which formed the frontier between the Persians and the Mannai on this side. Northwards, it reached as far as Demavend; the salt desert that rendered Central Iran a barren region, furnished a natural boundary on the east; on both the south and west, the Assyrian border-lands of Ellipi, Kharkhar, and Arrapkha prevented it from extending to the chief ranges of the Zagros and Gordiæan mountains. The soil, though less fertile than that of Chaldæa or of

[1] Spiegel has argued that Aryanem-Vaêjô is probably Arrân, the modern Kazabadagh, the mountainous district between the Kur and the Aras (*Eranische Alterthumskunde*, vol. i. pp. 194, 211, 212), and his opinion, adopted by Darmesteter (*The Zend-Avesta*, vol. i. p. 3, *The Zend-Avesta*, vol. ii. p. 5, note 4), is now gaining acceptance. The settlement of the Iranians in Russia, and their entrance into Asia by way of the Caucasus, have been admitted by Rost (*Untersuch. zur Altorient. Gesch.*, pp. 78–80). Classical writers reversed this order of things, and derived the Sauromatæ and other Scythian tribes from Media (DIODORUS SICULUS, ii. 43; PLINY, *Hist. Nat.*, vi. 19; AMMIANUS MARCELLINUS, XXXI. ii. 17).

[2] Cf. persons mentioned on pp. 70, 148, *supra*. The name Kushtashpi has been compared with that of Vistâspa or Gushtâsp by Fr. Lenormant (*Lettres Assyriologiques*, vol. i. p. 144), the name Kundashpi with that of Vindâspa by Gutschmid (*Neue Beiträge zur Geschichte des Alten Orients*, pp. 95, 96), and, later on, Ball has added to these a long list of names in Egyptian and Assyrian inscriptions which he looks upon as Iranian (*Iranian Names amongst the Hetta-Hatte*, in *Proc.* of Bibl. Arch. Soc., 1887–1888, vol. x. pp. 424–436). Kundashpi recalls at first sight Gundobunas, a name of the Sassanid epoch, if this latter form be authentic (JUSTI, *Iranisches Namenbuch*, p. 120). Tiele adopts the identification of Kushtashpi with Vistâspa (*Bab.-ass. Gesch.*, p. 229, note 1), and Justi has nothing to say against it, nor against the identification of Kundashpi with Vindâspa (*Iran. Namenbuch*, p. 378).

[3] Cf. p. 325, et seq., *supra*.   [4] HERODOTUS, I. lvi.

Egypt, was by no means deficient in resources. The mountains contained copper, iron, lead, some gold and silver,[1] several kinds of white or coloured marble,[2] and precious stones, such as topaz, garnets, emeralds, sapphires, cornelian, and lapis-lazuli, the latter being a substance held in the highest esteem by Eastern jewellers from time immemorial; Mount Bikni was specially celebrated for the fine specimens of this stone which were obtained there.[3] Its mountains were in those days clothed with dense forests, in which the pine, the oak, and the poplar grew side by side with the eastern plane tree, the cedar, lime, elm, ash, hazel, and terebinth.[4] The intermediate valleys were veritable orchards, in which the vegetation of the temperate zones mingled with tropical growths. The ancients believed that the lemon tree came originally from Persia.[5] To this day the peach, pear, apple, quince, cherry, apricot, almond, filbert, chestnut, fig, pistachio-nut, and pomegranate[6] still flourish there: the olive is easily acclimatised,[7] and the vine produces grapes equally suitable for the table or the winepress.[8] The plateau presents a poorer and less promising appearance —not that the soil is less genial, but the rivers become lost further inland, and the barrenness of the country increases as they come to an end one after another. Where artificial irrigation has been introduced, the fertility of the country is quite as great as in the neighbourhood of the mountains;[9] outside this irrigated region no trees are to be seen, except a few on the banks of rivers

[1] Rawlinson, in the *Journal of the Geographical Society*, vol. x. p. 55, has collected traditions in reference to gold and silver mining among the mountains in the neighbourhood of Takht-i-Suleimân; one of these is still called *Zerreh-Sharân*, the mount of the *gold-washers*.

[2] The best known was the so-called Tauris marble quarried from the hills in the neighbourhood of Lake Urumiyah.

[3] The list of precious stones which Pliny tells us (*Hist. Nat.*, xxxvii. 5, 8, 10, 11) were found in Media, contains several kinds which we are unable to identify, *e.g.* the Zathênê, the gassinades and narcissitis (cf. DIONYSIUS PERIEGETES, v. 1030, 1031). Pliny calls lapis-lazuli *sapphirus*, and declares that the bright specks of pyrites it contained rendered it unsuitable for engraving (xxxvii. 8). In the Assyrian inscriptions Mount Bikni, the modern Demavend (cf. p. 142, note 2, *supra*), is described as a mountain of Uknu, or lapis-lazuli.

[4] G. RAWLINSON, *The Five Great Monarchies*, 2nd edit., vol. ii. pp. 289, 290, where references are given to the authors who mention the existence in their time of each of the species enumerated in the text. A large part of the mountains and plains is now treeless, but it is manifest, both from the evidence of the inscriptions and from the observations of travellers, that the whole of Media was formerly well wooded; cf. OLIVIER, *Voyage dans l'Empire Othoman*, vol. iii. pp. 119–121, and J. DE MORGAN, *Mission Archéologique en Perse*, vol. ii. pp. 16, 17, 52, 88–91.

[5] The apple obtained from Media was known as the *Medicum malum*, and was credited with the property of being a powerful antidote to poison (VIRGIL, *Georgics*, ii. 126–135): it was supposed that it would not grow anywhere outside Media (PLINY, *Hist. Nat.*, xii. 3).

[6] G. RAWLINSON, *The Five Great Monarchies*, 2nd edit., vol. ii. p. 290.

[7] M. de Morgan (*Mission Archéologique en Perse*, vol. iv. p. 239, note 1) denies that the olive can exist in Media, but H. Rawlinson asserts that it is found in various parts of the country (*Journal of the Geographical Society*, vol. x. p. 3).

[8] In some places, as, for instance, at Kirmânshahân (OLIVIER, *Voyage dans l'Empire Othoman*, vol. iii. p. 14), the vine-stocks have to be buried during the winter to protect them from the frost. As to the making of wine, cf. OLIVIER, *Voyage dans l'Empire Othoman*, vol. iii. pp. 157–159.

[9] Irrigation was effected formerly, as now, by means of subterranean canals with openings at intervals, known as *kanât*; they have been described by Olivier (*op.cit.*, vol. iii. pp. 172–174), and more recently, with explanatory drawings and sectional plans, by J. de Morgan (*op. cit.*, vol. i. pp. 300–303).

or ponds, but wheat, barley, rye, oats, and an abundance of excellent vegetables grow readily in places where water is present. The fauna include, besides wild beasts of the more formidable kinds, such as lions, tigers, leopards, and bears,[1] many domestic animals, or animals capable of being turned to domestic use, such as the ass, buffalo, sheep, goat, dog, and dromedary, and the camel with

NISÆAN HORSES HARNESSED TO A ROYAL CHARIOT.[4]

two humps, whose gait caused so much merriment among the Ninevite idlers when they beheld it in the triumphal processions of their kings;[2] there were, moreover, several breeds of horses, amongst which the Nisæan steed was greatly prized on account of its size, strength, and agility.[3] In short, Media was large enough and rich enough to maintain a numerous population, and offered a stable foundation to a monarch ambitious of building up a new empire.[5]

The first person to conceive the idea of establishing one was, perhaps, a certain Fravartish, the Phraortes of the Greeks, whom Herodotus declares to

---

[1] G. Rawlinson has collected the evidence of modern writers in regard to the actual existence of these animals in Persia in his *Five Great Monarchies*, 2nd edit., vol. ii. pp. 294, 295.

[2] Cf. the two-humped camels reproduced on p. 68, *supra*, from one of the bronze bas-reliefs on the gates of Balawât.

[3] HERODOTUS, VII. xl. In the time of the Seleucides, Media supplied nearly the whole of Asia with these animals (POLYBIUS, x. 27, § 2), and the grazing-lands of Bagistana, the modern Behistun, are said to have supported 160,000 of them (DIODORUS SICULUS, xvii. 110). Under the Parthian kings Media paid a yearly tribute of 3000 horses (STRABO, XI. xiii. § 8, p. 525), and the Nisæan breed was still celebrated at the beginning of the Byzantine era (AMMIANUS MARCELLINUS, xxiii. 6, § 30). Horses are mentioned among the tribute paid by the Medic chiefs to the kings of Assyria (*Annals of Tiglath-pileser III.*, ll. 30, 46, 170, 182, ROST's edit., vol. i. pp. 6, 7, 10, 11, 30–33 ; *Annals of Sargon*, ll. 166, 167, WINCKLER's edit., vol. i. pp. 28, 29).

[4] Drawn by Boudier, from a bas-relief from Persepolis, reproduced from a photograph of the original now in the British Museum.

[5] The history of the Medes remains shrouded in greater obscurity than that of any other Asiatic race. We possess no original documents which owe their existence to this nation, and the whole of our information concerning its history is borrowed from Assyrian and Babylonian inscriptions, and from the various legends collected by the Greeks, especially by Herodotus and Ctesias, from Persian magnates in Asia Minor or at the court of the Achæmenian kings, or from fragments of vanished works such as the writings of Berosus. And yet modern archæologists and philologists have, during the last thirty years, allowed their critical faculties, and often their imagination as well, to run riot when dealing with this very period. After carefully examining, one after another, most of the theories put forward, I have adopted those hypotheses which, while most nearly approximating to the classical legends, harmonise best with the chronological framework—far too imperfect as yet— furnished by the inscriptions dealing with the closing years of Nineveh ; I do not consider them all to be equally probable, but though they may be mere stop-gap solutions, they have at least the merit of reproducing in many cases the ideas current among those races of antiquity who had been in direct communication with the Medes and with the last of their sovereigns.

have been the son and successor of Deïokes.[1] He came to the throne about
655 B.C., at a time when the star of Assur-bani-pal was still in the ascendant,
and at first does not seem to have thought of trying to shake off the incubus
of Assyrian rule. He began very wisely by annexing such of the petty
neighbouring states as had
hitherto remained inde-
pendent, and then set himself to attack the one other
nation of Iranian blood
which, by virtue of the
number and warlike quali-
ties of its clans, was in a
position to enter into rivalry
with his own people.[2] The
Persians, originally concentrated in the interior,
among the steep valleys
which divide the plateau
on the south, had probably
taken advantage of the misfortunes of Elam to extend
their own influence at its

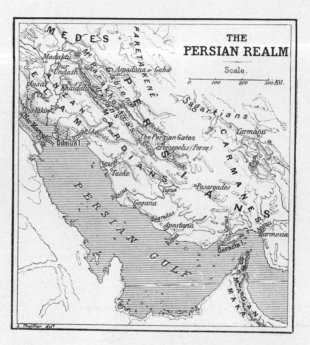

expense. Their kings were chosen from among the descendants of a certain
Akhâmanish, the Achæmenes of the Greeks, who at the time of the Iranian
invasion had been chief of the Pasargadæ, one of the Persian clans. Achæmenes
is a mythical hero rather than a real person; he was, we are told, fed during
infancy by an eagle—that mighty eagle whose shadow, according to a Persian
belief in mediæval times, assured the sovereignty to him on whom it chanced

---

[1] HERODOTUS, I. cii. The ancient form of the name, Fravartish or Frawarti, has been handed
down to us by a passage in the great inscription of Behistun (col. ii. l. 14) ; it means the man who
proclaims faith in Ahura-mazda, the believer (JUSTI, *Iranisches Namenbuch*, p. 105). The
existence of Phraortes was called in question by the Rawlinsons (*Herodotus*, vol. i. pp. 330, 331 ;
The Five Great Monarchies, 2nd edit., vol. ii. p. 883, note 10), and Winckler has brought forward
fresh arguments in support of their view in his *Untersuchungen zur Altorientalischen Geschichte*,
pp. 123, 124 (cf. *Altorientalische Forschungen*, vol. i. p. 490). Büdinger had endeavoured to prove, at
some length, that Phraortes is merely the Fravartish of the Behistun inscription, transported bodily
into the past (*Ausgang des Medischen Reiches*, pp. 22–24) ; Winckler, without going so far as this,
admits that the Phraortes of the legends owes his existence to the Oriental habit of giving grandchildren the names of their paternal grandfathers, and believes that Phraortes, father of Cyaxares,
grew out of the fact that the Fravartish who flourished in the time of Darius called himself
the son of Cyaxares. Floigl (*Kyrus und Herodot*, pp. 95–113), and after him Unger (*Kyaxares
und Astyages*, pp. 39–41) and Prashek (*Medien und das Haus des Kyaxares*, pp. 51–63), admit that
Phraortes really existed, but seek to identify him with the Astyages who, according to the Babylonian tradition, married one of his daughters to Nebuchadrezzar (cf. p. 484, *supra*).

[2] HERODOTUS, I. cii., where the author follows the tradition of the Harpagides, which he had picked
up in Asia Minor.

to fall.[1] Achæmenes would seem to have been followed by a certain Chaispi —or Teispes—a less fabulous personage, described in the legends as his son. It was, doubtless, during his reign that Assur-bani-pal, in hot pursuit of Tiummân and Khumbân-khaldash, completed the downfall of Susa; Chaispi claimed the eastern half of Elam as his share of the spoil, and on the strength of his victory styled himself King of Anshân—a title on which his descendants still prided themselves a hundred years after his death.[2] Persia, as then constituted, extended from the mouths of the Oroatis—the modern Tab—as far as the entrance to the Straits of Ormuzd.[3] The coast-line, which has in several places been greatly modified since ancient times by the formation of alluvial deposits, consists of banks of clay and sand, which lie parallel with the shore, and extend a considerable distance inland; in some places the country is marshy, in others parched and rocky, and almost everywhere barren and unhealthy. The central region is intersected throughout its whole length by several chains of hills, which rise terrace-like, one behind the other, from the sea to the plateau; some regions are sterile, more especially in the north and east, but for the most part the country is well wooded, and produces excellent crops of cereals. Only a few rivers, such as the Oroatis, which forms the boundary between Persia and Susiana,[4] the Araxes, and the Bagradas succeed in breaking through the barriers that beset their course, and reach the Persian Gulf;[5]

---

[1] ÆLIAN, Variæ Hist., xii. 21; cf., for the connection between this legend and that of Humaî, NÖL-DEKE, Aufsätze zur Persischen Gesch., p. 16, n. 1, and Das Iranische Nationalepos, in Grundriss der Iran. Philol., vol. ii. p. 133; Spiegel (Eranische Alterthums, vol. ii. p. 262) prefers to see in it the Simurgh.

[2] HERODOTUS, I. cxxv. The fact that Teispes was the immediate successor of Achæmenes, indicated by Herodotus (VII. xi.), is affirmed by Darius himself in the Behistun inscription (col. i. ll. 5, 6). Oppert, in drawing up |the pedigree of these kings, assumed that Achæmenes was a contemporary of Phraortes, and that the Iranian invasion of Persia must have taken place several reigns earlier, about the middle of the eighth century B.C. (Expédition de Mésopotamie, vol. ii. p. 201, et seq.; cf. FR. LENORMANT, Lettres Assyriologiques, vol. i. pp. 68–71), and that, consequently, there must have been a gap of greater or less duration in the chronological series between Achæmenes and Teispes; other writers, carrying this theory a step further, have intercalated three kings into this interval (BÜDINGER, Neuentdeckten Inschriften über Cyrus, pp. 6, 7). The Babylonian monuments of Cyrus, which credit this king and his three predecessors with the title "King of Anshân" (Cylinder, ll. 20, 21, in HAGEN; Keilschrifturkunden zur Geschichte des Königs Cyrus, pp. 6, 7, in the Beiträge zur Assyriologie, vol. ii. pp. 20, 21), have induced Rawlinson, and a good many other modern writers after him, to regard Teispes as the Persian king who conquered that part of Elam known as Anshân (H. RAWLINSON, Notes on a Newly-discovered Clay-Cylinder of Cyrus the Great, in the J. R. As. Soc., 1880, vol. xii. p. 75, et seq.; KEIPER, Die neuentdeckten Inschriften über Cyrus, pp. 18, 19; ED. MEYER, Geschichte des Alterthums, vol. i. pp. 559, 560); so far as I am aware, Floigl (Kyrus und Herodot, pp. 8–14) was the first and only writer to place this conquest in the reign of Achæmenes, father of Teispes, but he has since attributed it to Teispes himself (Geschichte des Semitischen Alterthums, Tabelle VI.). According to Billerbeck (Susa, p. 127), the Anzân (Anshân) of the early Achæmenides was merely a very small part of the ancient Anzân (Anshân), viz. the district on the east and south-east of Kuh-i-Dena, which includes the modern towns of Yezdeshast, Abadeh, Yeklîd, and Kushkiserd.

[3] Herodotus (I. cxxv.) imagined Carmania and Persia Proper to be one and the same province; from the Alexandrine period onwards historians and geographers drew a distinction between the two (STRABO, XV. iii. § 1, p. 727; PLINY, Hist. Nat., vi. 26; ARRIAN, vi. 28).

[4] The form of the name varies in different writers. Strabo calls it the Oroatis (XV. iii. §§ 1, 5, pp. 727, 729), Nearchus the Arosis (ARRIAN, Historia Indica, xxxix. 8); in Pliny it appears as Oratis and Zarotis (Hist. Nat., vi. 26, 28), and in Ammianus Marcellinus as Oroates (XXIII. vi. § 26).

[5] The Araxes (STRABO, XV. iii. § 6, p. 729) is the modern Bendamîr. The Kyros, which flowed

SCENE IN THE MOUNTAINS OF PERSIA.

Drawn by Boudier, from Coste and Flandin, *Voyage en Perse*, vol. i. pl. xcvi.

most of the others find no outlet, and their waters accumulate at the bottom of the valleys, in lakes whose areas vary at the different seasons. The mountainous district is furrowed in all directions by deep ravines, with almost vertical sides, at the bottom of which streams and torrents follow a headlong course. The landscape wears a certain air of savage grandeur; giant peaks rise in needle-like points perpendicularly to the sky; mountain paths wind upward, cut into the sides of the steep precipices; the chasms are spanned by single-arched bridges, so frail and narrow that they seem likely to be swept away in the first gale that blows. No country could present greater difficulties to the movements of a regular army or lend itself more readily to a system of guerrilla warfare. It was unequally divided between some ten or twelve tribes:[1] chief among these were the Pasargadæ, from which the royal family took its origin; after them came the Maraphii and Maspii. The chiefs of these two tribes were elected from

HEAD OF A PERSIAN ARCHER.[2]

among the members of seven families, who, at first taking equal rank with that of the Pasargadæ, had afterwards been reduced to subjection by the Achæmenides, forming a privileged class at the court of the latter, the members of which shared the royal prerogatives and took a part in the work of government.[3] Of the remaining tribes, the Panthialæi, Derusiæi, and Carmenians lived a sedentary life, while the Dai, Mardians, Dropici, and Sagartians[4] were nomadic in their habits. Each one of these tribes occupied its own allotted territory, the limits of which were not always accurately defined; we know that Sagartia, Parætakênê, and Mardia lay towards the north, on the confines of Media and the salt desert,[5] Taokênê extended along the seaboard, and Carmania lay to the east. The tribes had constructed large villages, such as Armuza, Sisidôna, Apostana, Gogana, and Taôkê, on the

past Persepolis, is now the Pulwar, an affluent of the Bendamîr. The Bagradas of Ptolemy, called the Hyperis by Juba (PLINY, Hist. Nat., vi. 26, § 99), is the modern Nabend.

[1] Herodotus only mentions ten Persian tribes (I. cxxv.); Xenophon (Cyropædeia, I. ii.) speaks of twelve.

[2] Drawn by Boudier, from a photograph of the Naksh-i-Rustem bas-relief taken by Dieulafoy.

[3] As to these seven royal families, cf. HERODOTUS, III. cxxvi.; JOSEPHUS, Ant. Jud., xi. 2.

[4] On all these points, cf. ELISÉE RECLUS, Géographie universelle, vol. ix. pp. 168–171, 177, 180, 185–187.

[5] Parætakênê, which has already been identified with the Partukkanu (or Partakkanu) of the Assyrian inscriptions (cf. p. 356, supra), is placed by Ptolemy in Persia (vi. 4); Mardia corresponds to the mountainous district of Bebahan and Kazrun.

sea-coast (the last named possessing a palace which was one of the three chief residences of the Achæmenian kings),[1] and Carmana, Persepolis, Pasargadæ, and Gabæ in the interior.[2] The Persians were a keen-witted and observant race, inured to all kinds of hardships in their occupation as mountain shepherds, and they were born warriors. The type preserved on the monuments differs but little from that which still exists at the present day in the more remote districts. It was marked by a tall and slender figure, with sturdy shoulders and loins, a small head, with a thick shock of hair and curling beard, a straight nose, a determined mouth, and an eye steady and alert. Yet, in spite of their valour, Phraortes overpowered them, and was henceforward able to reckon the princes of Anshân among his vassals; strengthened by the addition of their forces to his own, he directed his efforts to the subjection of the other races of the plateau. If we may believe the tradition of the Hellenic epoch, he reduced them to submission, and, intoxicated by his success, ventured at last to take up arms against the Assyrians, who for centuries past had held rule over Upper Asia.[3]

This was about 635 B.C., or less than ten years after the downfall of Elam, and it does not seem likely that the vital forces of Assyria can have suffered any serious diminution within so short a space of time.[5] Assur-bani-pal, weary of fighting, even

A PERSIAN.[4]

---

[1] The position of most of these towns is still somewhat doubtful. Armuza is probably Ormuz (or Hormuz) on the mainland, the forerunner of the insular Hormuz of the Portuguese, as the French scholar d'Anville has pointed out (*Recherches géog. sur le golfe Persique*, in the *Mémoires de l'Acad. des Insc.*, vol. xxx. p. 141); Sisidôna (NEARCHUS in ARRIAN, *Historia Indica*, xxxvii. 8) has been identified with the modern village of Mogu, near Ras-Jerd, Apostana (NEARCHUS, xxxvii. 5) with the town of Shewâr, the name seeming to be perpetuated in that of the Jebel Asban which rises not far from there (VINCENT, *Periplus*, p. 381). Gogana (NEARCHUS, xxxvii. 7) is probably Bender Kongûn, and Taokê, at the mouth of the Granis (NEARCHUS, xxxix. 3), is either Khor Gasseîr or Rohilla at the mouth of the Bishawer. The palace, which was one of the three principal residences of the Achæmenian kings, is probably mentioned by Strabo (XV. iii. § 3, p. 728, where we must read τὴν Ταόκην in place of τὴν Ὤκην), and possibly in Dionysius Periegetes (1069, where the Τασκοί of the MSS. is doubtless equivalent to Τωκοί).

[2] Carmana (PTOLEMY, vi. 8) is the modern Kermân; the exact position of Gabæ, which also possessed a palace (PTOLEMY, vi. 4; STRABO, XV. iii. § 3, p. 728; DIONYSIUS PERIEGETES, 1069, where we ought to read Τάβαι instead of Σαβαί), is not known. As to the name and position of Pasargadæ and Persepolis, cf. SPIEGEL, *Eranische Alterthumskunde*, vol. ii. pp. 617–621; NÖLDEKE, *Aufszätze zur Persischen Geschichte*, pp. 135–146.   [3] HERODOTUS, I. cii.

[4] Drawn by Boudier, from a photograph of one of the bas-reliefs at Persepolis, in DIEULAFOY, *L'Acropole de Suse*, p. 289.

[5] The date is indicated by the figures given by Herodotus in regard to the Medic kings, based on the calculations of himself or his authorities. Phraortes died in 634 B.C., after a reign of twenty-two years

though he no longer directed operations in person, had apparently determined to remain entirely on the defensive, and not to take the field, unless absolutely compelled to do so by rebellion at home or an attack from outside. In view of the growing need of rest for the Assyrian nation, he could not have arrived at a wiser decision, provided always that circumstances allowed of its being carried into effect, and that the tributary races and frontier nations were willing to fall in with his intentions. They did so at first, for the fate of Elam had filled even the most unruly among them with consternation, and peace reigned supreme from the Persian Gulf to the Mediterranean. Assur-bani-pal took advantage of this unexpected lull to push forward the construction of public works in the valleys of the Tigris and Euphrates. The palace of Sennacherib, though it had been built scarcely fifty years before, was already beginning to totter on its foundations; Assur-bani-pal entirely remodelled and restored it—a proceeding which gave universal satisfaction. The common people had, as usual, to make the bricks with their own hands and convey them to the spot, but as the chariots employed for this purpose formed part of the booty recently brought back from Elam, the privilege of using these trophies did something to lighten the burden of the tasks imposed on them. Moreover, they had the satisfaction of seeing at work among the squads of labourers several real kings, the Arabian chiefs who had been pursued and captured in the heart of the desert by Assur-bani-pal's generals; they plodded along under their heavy baskets, stimulated by the crack of the whip, amid insults and jeers.[1] This palace was one of the largest and most ornate ever built by the rulers of Assyria. True, the decoration does not reveal any novel process or theme; we find therein merely the usual scenes of battle or of the chase, but they are designed and executed with a skill to which the sculptor of Nineveh had never before attained. The animals, in particular, are portrayed with a light and delicate touch—the wild asses pursued by hounds, or checked while galloping at full speed by a cast of the lasso; the herds of goats and gazelles hurrying across the desert; the wounded lioness, which raises herself with a last dying effort to roar at the beaters.[2] We are conscious of Egyptian influence underlying the Asiatic work, and the skilful arrangement of the scenes from the Elamite campaigns also reminds us of Egypt. The picture of the battle of Tullîz recalls, in the variety of its episodes and the arrangement of the

(HERODOTUS, I. cii.), and as the last year of his reign coincides with the war against Assyria, the preparations for it cannot have been much earlier than 635 or 636 B.C., a year or two before the catastrophe.

[1] G. SMITH, *Hist. of Assurbanipal*, pp. 308–319; S. ALDEN SMITH, *Die Keilschrifttexte Asurbanipals*, vol. i. pp. 76–83; cf. JENSEN, *Inschr. Aschurbanipal's*, in SCHRADER, *Keil. Bibl.*, vol. ii. pp. 230–237.

[2] For specimens of these bas-reliefs, dealing with battle-scenes, cf. *Struggle of the Nations*, p. 635, and pp. 406–412, 415, *supra*; and for scenes of the chase, *Dawn of Civilization*, p. 559, *Struggle of the Nations*, pp. 622, 624, and pp. 401, 461, *supra*. The banqueting scene which appears on p. 413, *supra*, also comes from the same place.

perspective, the famous engagement at Qodshu, of which Ramses II. has left such numerous presentments on the Theban pylons. The Assyrians, led by the vicissitudes of invasion to Luxor and the Ramesseum, had, doubtless, seen these masterpieces of Egyptian art in a less mutilated state than that in which we now possess them, and profited by the remembrance when called upon to depict the private life of their king and the victories gained by his armies. It was in this magnificent residence that Assur-bani-pal led an existence of indolent splendour, such as the chroniclers of a later age were wont to ascribe to all the Assyrian monarchs from the time of Semiramis onwards.[1] We would gladly

A HERD OF WILD GOATS—A BAS-RELIEF OF THE TIME OF ASSUR-BANI-PAL.[2]

believe that he varied the monotony of his hunting expeditions, his banquets, and entertainments in the gardens in company with the women of the harem, by pleasures of a more refined nature, and that he took an unusual interest in the history and literature of the races who had become subject to his rule. As a matter of fact, there have been discovered in several of the ruined chambers of his palaces the remains of a regular library, which must originally have contained thousands of clay tablets, all methodically arranged and catalogued for his use.[3] A portion of them furnish us at first-hand with the records of his reign, and include letters exchanged with provincial governors,[4] augural

---

[1] Stories of the effeminacy of Sardanapalus had been collected by Ctesias of Cnidus (*Ctesiæ Cnidii Fragmenta*, in MÜLLER-DIDOT, pp. 35–39); they soon grew under the hands of historians in the time of Alexander, and were passed on by them to writers of the Roman and Byzantine epochs.

[2] Drawn by Faucher-Gudin, from the sketch by PLACE, *Ninive et l'Assyrie*, vol. iii. pl. 56.

[3] For a general description of the discovery and arrangement of this library, cf. the little book by J. MÉNANT, *La Bibliothèque du Palais de Ninive*, which gives all the necessary information.

[4] As to this part of the collection, cf. the papers by PINCHES, *Notes upon the Assyrian Report*

predictions, consultation of oracles,[1] observations made by the royal astrologers, standing orders, accounts of income and expenditure, even the reports of physicians in regard to the health of members of the royal family or of the royal household :[2] these documents reveal to us the whole machinery of government in actual operation, and we almost seem to witness the secret mechanism by which the kingdom was maintained in activity.   Other tablets contain authentic copies of works which were looked upon as classics in the sanctuaries of the Euphrates. Probably, when Babylon was sacked, Sennacherib had ordered the books which lay piled up in Ê-Sagilla and the other buildings of the city to be collected and carried away to Nineveh along with the statues and property of the gods.   They had been placed in the treasury, and there they remained until Esarhaddon re-established the kingdom of Karduniash, and Assur-bani-pal was forced to deliver up the statue of Marduk and restore to the sanctuaries, now rebuilt, all the wealth of which his grandfather had robbed them : but before sending back the tablets, he ordered copies to be made of them, and his secretaries set to work to transcribe for his use such of these works as they considered worthy of reproduction.   The majority of them were treatises compiled by the most celebrated adepts in the sciences for which Chaldæa had been famous from time immemorial ; they included collections of omens, celestial and terrestrial, in which the mystical meaning of each phenomenon and its influence on the destinies of the world was explained by examples borrowed from the Annals of world-renowned conquerors, such as Naramsin and Sargon of Agadê ;[3] then there were formulæ for exorcising evil spirits from the bodies of the possessed, and against phantoms, vampires, and ghosts, the recognised causes of all disease ; prayers and psalms, which had to be repeated before the gods in order to obtain pardon for sin ; and histories of divinities and kings from the time of the creation down to the latest date.[4]   Among these latter were several versions

Tablets, in the *Transactions* of the Biblical Archæological Society, vol. vi. pp. 209–243; *Assyrian Report Tablets*, in the *Records of the Past*, 1st series, vol. xi. pp. 75–78, and *Specimens of Assyrian Correspondence*, *ibid.*, 2nd series, vol. iii. pp. 178–189, by S. ALDEN SMITH, *Keilschrifttexte Asur-banipals*, vol. ii., and *Assyrian Letters* (reprinted from the *Proceedings* of the Biblical Archæological Society, vol. ix. pp. 240–256, 1886–1887, and vol. x., 1887–1888, pp. 60–72, 155–177, 305–315), by FR. DELITZSCH, *Beiträge zur Erklärung der Babylonisch-assyrischen Briefliteratur*, in the *Beiträge zur Assyriologie*, vol. i. pp. 184–248, 613–663, vol. ii. pp. 19–62, and by CHRISTOPHER JOHNSTON, *The Epistolary Literature of the Assyrians and Babylonians*, in the *Journal of the American Oriental Society*, vol. xviii. pp. 125–175, vol. xix. pp. 42–96, where a complete Bibliography of the whole subject is given, pp. 94–96.

    [1] On this subject, cf. the frequently quoted work of KNUDTZON, *Assyrische Gebete an den Sonnengott*, and the article by A. STRONG, *On some Oracles to Esarhaddon and Assur-bani-pal*, in the *Beiträge zur Assyriologie*, vol. ii. pp. 627–636.

    [2] Cf. the letter *K 515* in regard to the recovery of Nabu-nâdin-shumu (FR. DELITZSCH, *Beiträge zur Erklärung der Babylonisch-assyrischen Briefliteratur*, in the *Beiträge zur Assyriologie*, vol. i. pp. 196–198), and the letter *K 81* in regard to the cure of Kudurru, ID., *ibid.*, pp. 298–302.

    [3] Cf. *Dawn of Civilization*, pp. 599–773.

    [4] In regard to most of these works, cf. *Dawn of Civilization*, pp. 750–782.

of the epic of Gilgames, the story of Etana, of Adapa, and many others ; [1] and we may hope to possess all that the Assyrians knew of the old Chaldæan literature in the seventh century B.C., as soon as the excavators have unearthed from the mound at Kouyunjik all the tablets, complete or fragmentary, which still lie hidden there. Even from the shreds of information which they have already yielded to us, we are able to piece together so varied a picture that we can

REMAINS OF ASSUR-BANI-PAL'S WALL AT NIPPUR.[2]

readily imagine Assur-bani-pal to have been a learned and studious monarch, a patron of literature and antiquarian knowledge. Very possibly he either read himself, or had read to him, many of the authors whose works found a place in his library: the kings of Nineveh, like the Pharaohs, desired now and then to be amused by tales of the marvellous, and they were doubtless keenly alive to the delightful rhythm and beautiful language employed by the poets of the past in singing the praises of their divine or heroic ancestors. But the mere fact that his palace contained the most important literary collection which the ancient East has so far bequeathed to us, in no way proves that Assur-bani-pal displayed a more pronounced taste for literature than his predecessors; it

---

[1] The epic of Gilgames has been analysed fully in the *Dawn of Civilization*, pp. 566–572, 574–589 ; as to the poems of Etana and Adapa, cf. pp. 573, 659–661, 698–700, *ibid*.

[2] Drawn by Faucher-Gudin, from the photograph published by PETERS, *Nippur, or Explorations and Adventures on the Euphrates*, vol. ii. p. 164.

indicates merely the zeal and activity of his librarians, their intelligence, and their respect and admiration for the great works of the past.   Once he had issued his edict ordering new editions of the old masters to be prepared, Assurbani-pal may have dismissed the matter from his mind, and the work would go on automatically without need for any further interference on his part.   The scribes enriched his library for him, in much the same way as the generals won his battles, or the architects built his monuments : they were nothing more than nameless agents, whose individuality was eclipsed by that of their master, their skill and talent being all placed to his credit.   Babylonia shared equally with Assyria in the benefits of his government.   He associated himself with his brother Shamash-shumukîn in the task of completing the temple of Ê-Sagilla ; [1] afterwards, when sole monarch, he continued the work of restoration, not only in Babylon, but in the lesser cities as well, especially those which had suffered most during the war, such as Uru, Uruk, Borsippa, and Cutha. [2]   He remodelled the temple of Bel at Nippur, the walls built there by him being even now distinguishable from the rest by the size of the bricks and the careful dressing of the masonry. [3]   From the shores of the Persian Gulf to the mountains of Armenia, Assyria and Karduniash were covered with building-yards just as they had been in the most peaceful days of the monarchy.

It was at this unique juncture of apparent grandeur and prosperity that Phraortes resolved to attack Assur-bani-pal.   There is nothing to indicate that his action took place simultaneously with some movement on the part of other peoples, or with a serious insurrection in any of the Assyrian provinces.   For my part, I prefer to set it down to one of those sudden impulses, those irresistible outbursts of self-confidence, which from time to time actuated the princes tributary to Nineveh or the kings on its frontier.   The period of inactivity to which some previous defeat inflicted on them or on their predecessors had condemned them, allowed them to regain their strength, and one or two victories over less powerful neighbours served to obliterate the memory of former humiliation and disaster ; they flew to arms full of hope in the result, and once more drew down defeat upon their heads, being lucky indeed if their abortive rising led to nothing worse than the slaughter of their armies, the execution of their generals, and an increase in the amount of their former tribute.   This was the fate that overtook Phraortes ; the conqueror of the Persians, when confronted by the veteran troops of Assyria, failed before their superior discipline, and was

---

[1] Cf. pp. 382, 383, *supra*.

[2] He refers to the works at Borsippa and Kuta towards the end of the account of his campaign against Shamash-shumukîn (G. SMITH, *History of Assurbanipal*, pp. 167, 168), and to those at Uruk in describing the war against Khumbân-khaldash (G. SMITH, *History of Assurbanipal*, p. 236).

[3] A description of the parts built by Assur-bani-pal will be found in PETERS, *Nippur*, vol. ii. pp. 162–164, 261.

left dead upon the field of battle with the greater part of his army.[1] So far the affair presented no unusual features; it was merely one more commonplace repetition of a score of similar episodes which had already taken place in the same region, under Tiglath-pileser III. or the early Sargonides; but Huvakshatara, the son of Phraortes, known to the Greeks as Cyaxares,[2] instead of pleading for mercy, continued to offer a stubborn resistance. Cyaxares belongs to history, and there can be no doubt that he exercised a decisive influence over the destinies of the Oriental world, but precise details of his exploits are wanting, and his personality is involved in such obscuring mists that we can scarcely seize it; the little we have so far been able to glean concerning him shows us, not so much the man himself, as a vague shadow of him seen dimly through the haze. His achievements prove him to have been one of those perfect rulers of men, such as Asia produces every now and then, who knew how to govern as well as how to win battles—a born general and lawgiver, who could carry his people with him, and shone no less in peace than in war.[3] The armies at the disposal of his predecessors had been little more than heterogeneous assemblies of feudal militia; each clan furnished its own contingent of cavalry, archers, and pikemen, but instead of all these being combined into a common whole, with kindred elements contributed by the other tribes, each one acted separately, thus forming a number of small independent armies within the larger one. Cyaxares saw that defeat was certain so long as he had nothing but these ill-assorted masses to match against the regular forces of Assyria: he therefore broke up the tribal contingents and rearranged the units of which they were composed according to their natural affinities, grouping horsemen with horsemen, archers with archers, and pikemen with pikemen, taking the Assyrian cavalry and infantry as his models.[4] The foot-soldiers

[1] HERODOTUS, I. cii.

[2] The original form of the name is furnished by passages in the Behistun inscription (col. ii. ll. 15, 81, and iv. 19, 22), where Chitrantakhma of Sagartia and Fravartish of Media, two of the claimants for the throne who rose against Darius, are represented as tracing their descent from Huvakshatara (Cyaxares); cf. JUSTI, *Eranisches Namenbuch*, p. 140.

[3] G. Rawlinson (*The Five Great Monarchies*, 2nd edit., vol. ii. pp. 414, 415) takes a somewhat different view of Cyaxares' character; he admits that Cyaxares knew how to win victories, but refuses to credit him with the capacity for organisation required in order to reap the full benefits of conquest, giving as his reason for this view the brief duration of the Medic empire. The test applied by him does not seem to me a conclusive one, for the existence of the second Chaldæan empire was almost as short, and yet it would be decidedly unfair to draw similar inferences touching the character of Nabopolassar or Nebuchadrezzar from this fact.

[4] HERODOTUS, I. ciii., where we are told that Cyaxares was "the first to divide the Asiatics into different regiments, separating the pikemen from the archers and horsemen; before his time, these troops were all mixed up haphazard together." I have interpreted his evidence in the sense which seems most in harmony with what we know of Assyrian military tactics. It seems incredible that the Medic armies can have fought pell-mell, as Herodotus declares, seeing that for two hundred years past the Medes had been frequently engaged against such well-drilled troops as those of Assyria; if the statement be authentic, it merely means that Cyaxares converted all the small feudal armies which had

wore a high felt cap known as a tiara; they had long tunics with wide sleeves, tied in at the waist by a belt, and sometimes reinforced by iron plates or scales, as well as gaiters, buskins of soft leather, and large wickerwork shields covered with ox-hide, which they bore in front of them like a movable bulwark; their weapons consisted of a short sword, which depended from the belt and lay along the thigh, one or two light javelins, a bow with a strongly pronounced curve, and a quiver full of arrows made from reeds.[1]   Their horsemen, like those of other

warlike nations of the East, used neither saddle nor stirrups, and though they could make skilful use of lance and sword, their favourite weapon was the bow.[2]   Accustomed from their earliest childhood to all kinds of equestrian exercises, they seemed to sit their horses as though they actually formed part of the animal.[3]   They seldom fought in line, but, from the very beginning of an action, hung like a

MEDIC AND PERSIAN FOOT-SOLDIERS.[4]

dense cloud on the front and flanks of the enemy, and riddled them with missiles, without, however, coming to close quarters.   Like the Parthians of a later epoch, they waited until they had bewildered and reduced the foe by their ceaseless evolutions before giving the final charge which was to rout them completely.   No greater danger could threaten the Assyrians than the establishment of a systematically organised military power within the borders of Media.   An invader starting from Egypt or Asia Minor, even if he succeeded in overthrowing the forces sent out to meet him, had still a long way to go before he could penetrate to the heart of the empire.   Even if Cilicia and Syria

hitherto fought side by side on behalf of the king into a single royal army in which the different kinds of troops were kept separate.

[1] HERODOTUS, VII. lxi., where the historian describes the equipment of the Persians in much the same terms as I have used above, and then adds in the following chapter that "the Medes had the same equipment, for it is the equipment of the Medes and not that of the Persians."

[2] HERODOTUS, VII. lxxxvi., where he says that the Medic horsemen were armed in the same manner as the infantry.

[3] As to the education they received, cf. XENOPHON, *Cyropædia*, I. iv. § 4.

[4] Drawn by Faucher-Gudin, after COSTE and FLANDIN, *La Perse Ancienne*, pl. ci.   The first and third figures are Medes, the second and fourth Persians.

should be conquered, nothing was easier than to oppose a further advance at the barrier of the Euphrates; and should the Euphrates be crossed, the Khabur still remained, and behind it the desert of Singar, which offered the last obstacle between Nineveh and the invaders. The distances were less considerable in the case of an army setting out from Urartu and proceeding along the basin of the Tigris or its affluents; but here, too, the difficulties of transit were so serious that the invader ran a great risk of gradually losing the best part of his forces on the road. On the north-east and east, however, the ancient heritage of Assur lay open to direct and swift attack. An enemy who succeeded in destroying or driving back the garrisons stationed as outposts on the rim of the plateau, from Kharkhar to Parsua,[1] if he ventured to pursue his advantage and descended into the plain of the Tigris, had no less than three routes to choose from —the Kirind road on the south, the Baneh road on the north, and the Sulei-

A MEDIC HORSEMAN.[2]

manyeh road between the two. The last was the easiest of all, and led almost straight to the fords of Altun-Keupri and the banks of the Lesser Zab, on the confines of Assyria proper, close under the walls of Arbela, the holy city of Ishtar. He needed but to win two victories, one upon leaving the mountains, the other at the passage of the Zab, and two or three weeks' steady marching would bring him from Hamadân right up to the ramparts of Nineveh.[3]

Cyaxares won a victory over Assur-bani-pal's generals, and for the first time in over a hundred years Assyria proper suffered the ignominy of foreign invasion.[4] The various works constructed by twenty generations of kings had gradually transformed the triangle enclosed between the Upper Zab, the Tigris, and the Jebel-Makhlub into a regular fortified camp. The southern point of this triangle was defended by Calah from the attacks of Chaldæa or from foes coming down from Media by Holwân and Suleimanyeh, while Nineveh guarded it on the north-east, and several lines of walled cities—among which Dur-

[1] As to these garrisons, cf. pp. 243, 356, *supra*.

[2] Drawn by Faucher-Gudin, from a cast of the Medic intaglio in the Cabinet des Médailles; cf. LAJARD, *Le Culte de Mithra*, pl. xxv., No. 7, and MÉNANT, *La Glyptique Orientale*, vol. ii. p. 153.

[3] Cf. the noteworthy paper by Billerbeck, in BILLERBECK and JEREMIAS, *Der Untergang Nineveh's und die Weissagungsschrift des Nahum*, in the *Beiträge zur Assyriologie*, vol. iii. pp. 131–144.

[4] HERODOTUS, I. ciii.

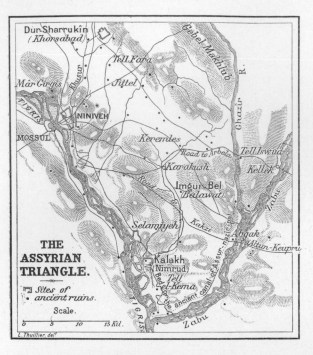

THE
ASSYRIAN
TRIANGLE.

Sites of
ancient ruins.

Scale.

Sharrukîn and Imgur-Bel can still be identified— protected it on the north and east, extending from the Tigris as far as the Ghazîr and Zab.[1] It was necessary for an enemy to break through this complex defensive zone, and even after this had been successfully accomplished and the walls of the capital had been reached, the sight which would meet the eye was well calculated to dismay even the most resolute invader. Viewed as a whole, Nineveh appeared as an irregular quadrilateral figure, no two sides of which were parallel, lying on the left bank of the Tigris. The river came right up to the walls on the west, and the two mounds of Kouyunjik and Nebi-Yunus, on which stood the palaces of the Sargonides, were so skilfully fortified that a single wall connecting the two sufficed to ward off all danger of attack on this side. The south wall, which was the shortest of the four, being only about 870 yards in length, was rendered inaccessible by a muddy stream, while the north wall, some 2150 yards long, was protected by a wide moat which could be

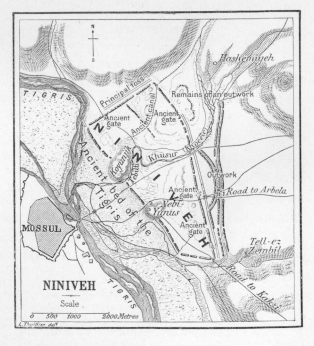

NINIVEH

Scale

---

[1] BILLERBECK and JEREMIAS, *Der Untergang Nineveh's und die Weissagungsschrift des Nahum von Elkosch*, in the *Beiträge zur Assyriologie*, vol. iii. pp. 127–131.

filled from the waters of the Khuzur. The eastern front had for a long
time depended for its safety on a single wall reinforced by a moat, but
Sennacherib, deeming it insufficiently protected against a sudden attack, had
piled up obstacles [1] in front of it, so that it now presented a truly formidable appearance. It was skirted throughout its whole length by a main
rampart, 5400 yards long, which described a gentle curve from north to south,
and rose to a height of about 50 feet,[2] being protected by two small forts
placed closed to the main gates. The fosse did not run along the foot of the
wall, but at a distance of about fifty yards in front of it, and was at least some

PART OF THE FOSSE AT NINEVEH.[3]

20 feet deep and over 150 feet in width. It was divided into two unequal
segments by the Khuzur: three large sluice-gates built on a level with the
wall and the two escarpments allowed the river to be dammed back, so that its
waters could be diverted into the fosse and thus keep it full in case of siege.
In front of each segment was a kind of demi-lune, and—as though this was not
precaution enough—two walls, each over 4300 yards long, were built in front of
the demi-lunes, the ditch which separated them being connected at one end
with the Khuzur, and allowed to empty itself into a stream on the south.[4] The

[1] As to the fortifications undertaken by Sennacherib, cf. MEISSNER and ROST, *Die Bauinschriften
Sanherib's*, pp. 68–72, etc.; also cf. p. 310, *supra*.

[2] This was still the approximate height of the ruins, when Jones drew up a plan of them about
the middle of the present century (*Topography of Nineveh*, in the *J. R. As. Soc.*, 1855, vol. xv. p. 322,
where the height is estimated at forty-six English feet).

[3] Drawn by Boudier, from a sketch in LAYARD, *Nineveh and Babylon*, p. 563.

[4] The remains of the fortifications at Nineveh have been surveyed by Jones (*Topography of
Nineveh*, in the *J. R. As. Soc.*, 1855, vol. xv. pp. 297–335), whose data furnished material for G.
Rawlinson (*The Five Great Monarchies*, 2nd edit., pp. 252–261), and, with some modifications, for
Billerbeck and Jeremias as well (*Der Untergang Nineveh's*, in the *Beiträge zur Assyriologie*, vol. iii.
pp. 118–127).

number of inhabitants sheltered behind these defences was perhaps 300,000 souls;[1] each separate quarter of the city was enclosed by ramparts, thus forming, as it were, a small independent town, which had to be besieged and captured after a passage had been cut through the outer lines of defence. Cyaxares might well have lost heart in the face of so many difficulties, but his cupidity, inflamed by reports of the almost fabulous wealth of the city, impelled him to attack it with extraordinary determination : the spoils of Susa, Babylon, and Thebes, in fact, of the whole of Western Asia and Ethiopia, were, he felt, almost within his reach, and would inevitably fall into his hands provided his courage and perseverance did not fail him.   After shutting up the remnant of the Assyrian army inside Nineveh he laid patient siege to the city, and the fame of his victories being noised abroad on all sides, it awoke among the subject races that longing for revenge which at one time appeared to have been sent to sleep for ever.   It almost seemed as though the moment was approaching when the city of blood should bleed in its turn, when its kings should at length undergo the fate which they had so long imposed on other monarchs.   Nahum the Elkoshite,[2] a Hebrew born in the Assyrian province of Samaria, but at that time an exile in Judah, lifted up his voice, and the echo of his words still resounds in our ears, telling us of the joy and hope felt by Judah, and with Judah, by the whole of Asia, at the prospect.   Speaking as the prophet of Jahveh, it was to Jahveh that he attributed the impending downfall of the oppressor : " Jahveh is a jealous God and avengeth ; Jahveh avengeth and is full of wrath ; Jahveh taketh vengeance on His adversaries, and He reserveth wrath for His enemies.   Jahveh is slow to anger and great in power, and will by no means clear the guilty ; Jahveh hath His way in the whirlwind and in the storm, and the clouds are the dust of His feet.   He rebuketh the sea and maketh it dry, and drieth up all the rivers : Bashan languisheth, and Carmel, and the flower of Lebanon languisheth." [3]   And, " Behold upon the mountains the feet of him that bringeth good tidings." [4]   Then he goes on to unfold

---

[1] This is the estimate given by BILLERBECK and JEREMIAS, *Untergang Nineveh's*, in the *Beiträge zur Assyriologie*, vol. iii. pp. 119, 120 ; Jones (*Topography of Nineveh*, in the *J. R. As. Soc.*, 1855, vol. xv. p. 324) and G. Rawlinson credit Nineveh with a population of not more than 175,000 (*The Five Great Monarchies*, 2nd edit., vol. i. p. 256).

[2] Elkosh is identified by Eusebius (*Onomasticon*, PARTHEY'S, edit., pp. 182, 183) with Elkese, which St. Jerome (*Proleg. Comm. Nahum*) declares to have been in Galilee, the modern el-Kauzeh, two and a half hours' walk south of Tibnîn.   The prophecy of Nahum has been taken by some as referring to the campaign of Phraortes against Assyria (EWALD, *Propheten des Alten Bundes*, 2nd edit., vol. ii. p. 3, et seq.), but more frequently to the destruction of Nineveh by the Medes and Chaldæans (ED. MEYER, *Geschichte des Alterthums*, vol. i. pp. 574, 575 ; TIELE, *Babylonisch-assyrische Geschichte*, p. 412 ; WELLHAUSEN, *Skizzen und Vorarbeiten*, vol. v. pp. 155, 156).   It undoubtedly refers to the siege interrupted by the Scythian invasion, as is admitted by Kuenen (*K. H. Onderzoek*, vol. ii. § 75, et seq.), Cornill (*Einleitung in das Alte Testament*, 2nd edit., p. 188), Kittel (*Geschichte der Hebräer*, vol. ii. p. 322), and many others.

[3] *Nahum* i. 2–4.

[4] *Nahum* i. 15.

before the eyes of his hearers a picture of Nineveh, humiliated and in the last extremity. There she lies, behind her bastions of brick, anxiously listening for the approach of the victorious Medes. " The noise of the whip, and the noise of the rattling of wheels ; and prancing horses and jumping chariots ; the horsemen mounting, and the flashing sword, and the glittering spear; and a multitude of slain and a great heap of carcases : and there is no end of the corpses ; they stumble upon their corpses : because of the multitude of the whoredoms of the well-favoured harlot, the mistress of witchcrafts, that selleth nations through her whoredoms, and families through her witchcrafts. Behold, I am against thee, saith Jahveh of hosts, and I will discover thy skirts upon thy face ; and I will show the nations thy nakedness, and the kingdoms thy shame. And I will cast abominable filth upon thee, and make thee vile, and will set thee as a gazing-stock. And it shall come to pass that all they that look upon thee shall flee from thee, and say, Nineveh is laid waste : who will bemoan her? Whence shall I seek comforters for thee ? " [1] Thebes, the city of Amon, did not escape captivity ; why then should Nineveh prove more fortunate ? " All thy fortresses shall be like fig trees with the firstripe figs : if they be shaken they fall into the mouth of the eater. Behold, thy people in the midst of thee are women ; the gates of thy land are set wide open unto thine enemies : the fire hath devoured thy bars. Draw thee water for the siege, strengthen thy fortresses : go into the clay and tread the mortar, make strong the brick-kiln. There shall the fire devour thee ; the sword shall cut thee off, . . . make thyself many as the cankerworm, make thyself many as the locusts. Thou hast multiplied thy merchants as the stars of heaven : the cankerworm spoileth and flieth away. Thy crowned are as the locusts and thy marshals as the swarms of grasshoppers, which camp in the hedges in the cold day, but when the sun ariseth they flee away, and their place is not known where they are. Thy shepherds slumber, O King of Assyria : thy worthies are at rest : thy people are scattered upon the mountains, and there is none to gather them. There is no assuaging of thy hurt ; thy wound is grievous : all that hear the bruit of thee clap the hands over thee ; for upon whom hath not thy wickedness passed continually ? " [2]

On this occasion Nineveh escaped the fate with which the prophet had threatened it, but its safety was dearly bought. According to the tradition accepted in Asia Minor two hundred years later, a horde of Scythians under King Madyes, son of Protothyes, setting out from the Russian steppes in pursuit of the Cimmerians, made their appearance on the scene in the nick of time. We are told that they flung themselves through the Caspian Gates

---

[1] *Nahum* iii. 2–7.   [2] *Nahum* iii. 12–19.

into the basin of the Kur, and came into contact with the Medes at the foot
of Mount Caucasus.   The defeat of the Medes here would necessarily
compel them to raise the siege of Nineveh.[1]   This crisis in the history of
Asia was certainly not determined by chance.   For eighty years Assyria
had been in contact with the Scythians, and the Assyrian kings had
never ceased to keep an eye upon their movements, or lose sight of the
advantage to which their bellicose temper might be turned in circumstances
like the present.   They had pitted them against the Cimmerians, then
against the Medes, and probably against the kings of Urartu as well, and
the intimacy between the two peoples came to be so close that the Scythian
king Bartatua did not hesitate to demand one of the daughters of Esarhaddon
in marriage.[2]   From the very beginning of his reign [3] Assur-bani-pal had
shown them the utmost consideration, and when King Madyes, son of his ally
Bartatua, intervened thus opportunely in the struggle, he did so, not by mere
chance, as tradition would have us believe, but at the urgent request of
Assyria.[4]   He attacked Media in the rear, and Cyaxares, compelled to raise the
siege of Nineveh, hastened to join battle with him.   The engagement probably
took place on the banks of the Lower Araxes or to the north of Lake Urumiah,
in the region formerly inhabited by the Mannai; but after defeating his foe
and dictating to him the terms of submission, Madyes, carried away by the lust
of conquest, did not hesitate to turn his arms against his ally.   Exhausted by
her recent struggle, Assyria lay at his mercy, her fortresses alone being able to
offer any serious resistance : he overran the country from end to end, and
though the walled cities withstood the fury of his attack, the rural districts
were plundered right and left, and laid desolate for many a year to come.
The Scythians of this epoch probably resembled those whom we find represented on the monuments of Greek art two centuries later.   Tall, fierce-looking
men, with unkempt beards, their long and straggling locks surmounted by
the *kyrbasis*,[5] or pointed national cap of felt; they wore breeches and a blouse
of embroidered leather, and were armed with lances, bows, and battle-axes.
They rode bareback on untrained horses, herds of which followed their tribes

---

[1] HERODOTUS, I. ciii., civ.; cf. the details borrowed by Justin (ii. 3) and Jordanes (*De Origine
Getarum*, 6) from Trogus Pompeius, who was probably indebted for his facts to Dinon.

[2] As to the Scythians in the time of Esarhaddon, cf. pp. 352–355, *supra*.

[3] Cf. pp. 354, 355, *supra*.

[4] This is the view taken by FLOIGL, *Cyrus und Herodot*, pp. 157, 158 (where the author pushes his
ingenious hypothesis too far when he tries to make out that every one of the Scythian expeditions
was undertaken by the order or at the request of Assur-bani-pal), by PRASHEK, *Medien und das Haus
des Kyaxares*, p. 69, and above all by WINCKLER, *Altorientalische Forschungen*, vol. i. pp. 489, 490, who
rightly looks upon the Scythian invasion as a natural outcome of the policy previously followed by
the Assyrian kings in dealing with the northern barbarians.   Madyes is the form given by Herodotus
(I. ciii.); Strabo gives the name as Madys (I. iii. § 21, p. 61).

[5] HERODOTUS, VII. lxiv., where he refers to the Sakæ or Sacæ of the Iaxartes.   For an explanation
of this passage, cf. KONDAKOFF and REINACH, *Les Antiquités du Bosphore Cimmérien*, pp. 136, 137.

about on their wanderings; each man caught the animal he required with the help of a lasso, put bit and bridle on him, and vaulting on to his back at a single bound, reduced him to a state of semi-obedience. No troops could stand their ground before the frantic charge of these wild horsemen; like the Huns of Roman times, the Scythians made a clean sweep of everything they found in their path. They ruined the crops, carried off or slaughtered the herds, and set fire to the villages from sheer love of destruction, or in order to inspire terror; every one who failed to fly to the mountains or take refuge in some fortress, was either massacred on the spot or led away into slavery. Too ignorant of the arts of war to undertake a siege in the regular way, they usually contented themselves with levying ransoms on fortified towns; occasionally, however, when the wealth accumulated behind the walls held out a prospect of ample booty, they blockaded the place until famine compelled it to surrender. More than one ancient city which, thanks to the good government of its rulers and the industry of its citizens, had amassed treasure of inestimable value, was put to fire

SCYTHIANS TENDING THEIR WOUNDED.[1]

and sword, and more than one fertile and populous region left untilled and deserted.[2] Most of the states which for the last three centuries had fought so stubbornly against the Assyrians for independence, went down before the storm, including the kingdoms of Urartu, of the Mushku, and of the Tabal,[3] their miserable end furnishing the Hebrew prophets full fifty years later with a theme of sombre rejoicing. "There is Meshech, Tubal, and all her multitude; her graves are round about her: all of them uncircumcised, slain by the sword; for they caused their terror in the land of the living. And they shall not lie with the mighty that are fallen of the uncircumcised, which are gone down to hell with their weapons of war, and have laid their swords under their heads,[4] and their iniquities are upon their

[1] Drawn by Faucher-Gudin, from the reliefs on a silver vase from Kul-Oba. As to the capture of horses by means of the lasso, cf. the illustration at the beginning of the present chapter, p. 445, *supra*.

[2] This may be deduced from the passage in Herodotus (I. cvi.), where he says that "the Scythians were masters of Asia for twenty-eight years, and overturned everything by their brutality and stupidity: for, in addition to tribute, they exacted from every one whatever they chose, and, moreover, they prowled here and there, plundering as they thought good."

[3] STRABO, XI. viii. § 4, p. 511, refers in general terms to the presence of Scythians (or, as he calls them, *Sacæ*) in Armenia, Cappadocia, and on the shores of the Black Sea.

[4] This, doubtless, means that the Mushku and Tabal had been so utterly defeated that they could not procure honourable burial for their dead, *i.e.* with their swords beneath their heads and their weapons on their bodies.

bones; for they were the terror of the mighty in the land of the living."[1]   The Cimmerians, who, since their reverses in Lydia and on Mount Taurus,[2] had concentrated practically the whole of their tribes in Cappadocia and in the regions watered by the Halys and Thermodon, shared the good fortune of their former adversaries.   At that time they lived under the rule of a certain Kôbos, who seems to have left a terrible reputation behind him; tradition gives him a place beside Sesostris among the conquerors of the heroic age, and no doubt, like his predecessor Dugdamis, he owed this distinction to some expedition or other against the peoples who dwelt on the shores of the Ægean Sea, but our knowledge of his career is confined to the final catastrophe which overtook him.   After some partial successes, such as that near Zela, for instance,[3] he was defeated and made prisoner by Madyes.[4]   His subjects, as vassals of the Scythians, joined them in their acts of brigandage,[5] and together they marched from province to province, plundering as they went; they overran the western regions of the Assyrian kingdom from Melitene and Mesopotamia to Northern Syria, from Northern Syria to Phœnicia, Damascus, and Palestine,[6] and at length made their appearance on the Judæan frontier.   Since the day when Sennacherib had been compelled to return to Assyria without having succeeded in destroying Jerusalem,[7] or even carrying it by storm, Judah had taken little or no part in external politics.   Divided at first by a conflict between the party of prudence, who advised submission to Nineveh, and the more warlike spirits who advocated an alliance with Egypt, it had ended by accepting its secondary position, and had on the whole remained fairly loyal to the dynasty of Sargon.   On the death of Hezekiah, his successor, Manasseh, had, as we know,[8] been tempted to intervene in the revolutions of the hour, but the prompt punishment which followed his first attempt put an end for ever to his desire for independence.   His successor, Amon, during his brief reign of two years,[9] had no time to desert the ways of his father, and Josiah,[10] who came to the throne in 638 B.C., at the age of eight, had so far manifested no hostility towards Assyria.   Thus, for more than fifty years, Judah enjoyed

---

[1] *Ezek.* xxxii. 26, 27.   [2] Cf. p. 430, *supra.*

[3] STRABO, XI. viii. § 4, p. 511, where the defeat of the Scythians is wrongly attributed to Persia.

[4] STRABO, I. iii. § 21, p. 61.

[5] It seems probable that this was so, when we consider the confusion between the Scythians or Sakæ, and the Cimmerians in the Babylonian and Persian inscriptions of the Achæmenian epoch (SCHRADER, *Keilinschriften und Geschichtsforschung*, p. 150; FR. LENORMANT, *Les Origines de l'Histoire*, vol. ii. pp. 347–350).

[6] Their migration from Media into Syria and Palestine is expressly mentioned by HERODOTUS, I. cv.

[7] Cf. pp. 288–295, *supra.*

[8] As to Manasseh's rebellion, cf. pp. 368, 369, *supra.*

[9] 2 *Kings* xxi. 18–26; cf. 2 *Chron.* xxxiii. 20–25. The reign of fifty-five years attributed to Manasseh by the Jewish annalists cannot be fitted into the chronology of the period; we must either take off ten years, thus reducing the duration of the reign to forty-five years, or else we must assume the first ten of Manasseh to be synchronous with the last ten of Hezekiah.

[10] 2 *Kings* xxii. 1; cf. 2 *Chron.* xxxiv. 1.

almost unbroken peace, and led as happy and prosperous an existence as the barrenness of its soil and the unruly spirit of its inhabitants would permit.

But though its political activity had been almost nothing during this interval, its spiritual life had seldom been developed with a greater intensity. The reverse sustained by Sennacherib had undoubtedly been a triumph for Isaiah, and for the religious party of which we are accustomed to regard him as the sole representative. It had served to demonstrate the power of Jahveh, and His aversion for all idolatrous worship and for all foreign alliances. In vain did the partisans of Egypt talk loudly of Pharaoh and of all those principalities of this world which were drawn round in Pharaoh's orbit; Egypt had shown herself incapable of safeguarding her friends, and things had gone steadily from bad to worse so long as these latter held the reins of government; their removal from office had been, as it were, the signal

IRANIAN SOLDIERS FIGHTING AGAINST THE SCYTHIANS.[1]

for a welcome change in the fortunes of the Jews. Jahveh had delivered His city the moment when, ceasing to rely upon itself, it had surrendered its guidance into His hands, and the means of avoiding disaster in the future was clearly pointed out to it. Judah must be content to follow the counsels which Isaiah had urged upon it in the name of the Most High, and submissively obey the voice of its prophets. "Thine eyes shall see thy teachers: and thine ears shall hear a word behind thee, saying, This is the way, walk ye in it, when ye turn to the right hand, and when ye turn to the left. And ye shall defile the overlaying of thy graven images of silver, and the plating of thy molten images of gold: thou shalt cast them away as an unclean thing; thou shalt say unto it, Get thee hence."[2] Isaiah seems to disappear after his triumph, and none of his later prophecies have come down to us: yet the influence of his teaching lasted throughout the reign of Hezekiah, and the court, supported by the more religious section of the people, not only abjured the worship of false gods, but forsook the high places and discontinued the practices which he had so strenuously denounced. The great bulk of the nation, however, soon returned to their idolatrous practices, if, indeed, they had ever given them up,

---

[1] Drawn by Faucher-Gudin, from the cast of a cylinder given by CUNNINGHAM, *Relics from Ancient Persia*, in the *Journal of the R. Asiatic Society of Bengal*, vol. i. The cylinder is usually described as Persian, but the dress is that of the Medes as well as of the Persians (cf. what has been said on this subject on p. 466, note 1, *supra*.   [2] *Isa.* xxx. 20-22.

and many of the royal advisers grew weary of the rigid observances which it was sought to impose upon them; rites abhorrent to Jahveh found favour even among members of the king's own family, and on Hezekiah's death, about 686 B.C., a reaction promptly set in against both his religious views and the material reforms he had introduced.[1] Manasseh was only thirteen years old when he came to the throne, and his youth naturally inclined him towards the less austere forms of divine worship: from the very first he tolerated much that his father had forbidden, and the spirit of eclecticism which prevailed among his associates rendered him, later on, an object of special detestation to the orthodox historians of Jerusalem. Worshippers again began openly to frequent the high places; they set up again the prostrate idols, replanted the sacred groves, and even "built altars for all the host of heaven in the two courts of the house of Jahveh." The chariots and horses of the sun reappeared within the precincts of the temple, together with the sacred courtesans. Baal and the Phœnician Astarte were worshipped on Mount Sion. The valley of Hinnom, where Ahaz had already burnt one of his children during a desperate crisis in the Syrian wars,[2] was again lighted up by the flames of the sacred pyre. We are told that Manasseh himself set the example by passing his son through the flames; he also had recourse to astrologers, soothsayers, fortune-tellers, and sorcerers of the lowest type. The example of Assyria in matters of this kind exercised a preponderant influence on Jewish customs, and certainly it would have been a miracle if Jerusalem had succeeded in escaping it; did not Nineveh owe the lofty place it occupied to these occult sciences and to the mysterious powers of its gods? In thus imitating its conqueror, Judah was merely borrowing the weapons which had helped him to subdue the world. The partisans of the ancient religions who were responsible for these innovations must have regarded them as perfectly legitimate reforms, and their action was received with favour in the provinces: before long the latter contained as many sanctuaries as there were towns,[3] and by thus multiplying the centres of worship, they hoped that, in accordance with ancient belief, the ties which existed between Jahveh and His chosen people would also be increased. The fact that the provinces had been ravaged from end to end in the days of Sennacherib, while Jerusalem had been spared, was attributed to the circumstance that Hezekiah had destroyed the provincial sanctuaries, leaving the temple on Mount Sion alone standing. Wherever Jahveh possessed altars, He kept guard over His people, but His protection was not extended to those places where sacrifices were no longer offered

[1] 2 *Kings* xxi. 2–7 (cf. 2 *Chron.* xxxiii. 2–7), where, in spite of manifest recensions of the text, the facts themselves seem to have been correctly set forth.

[2] Cf. pp. 185, 186, 284, *supra*.

[3] *Jer.* ii. 26–30. For the quotation see also *Jer.* xi. 13: "For according to the number of thy cities are thy gods, O Judah; and according to the number of the streets of Jerusalem have ye set up altars to the shameful thing, even altars to burn incense unto Baal."

to Him. The reaction was not allowed to take place without opposition on the part of the prophets and their followers. We are told that Manasseh "shed innocent blood very much till he had filled Jerusalem from one end to another;" there is even a Rabbinic tradition to the effect that, weary of the admonitions of the aged Isaiah, he put him to death by shutting him up in the hollow trunk of a tree, and causing him to be sawn in two.[1] For a long time after this no instance can be found of a prophet administering public affairs or directing the actions of the king himself; the priests and reformers, finding no outlet for their energy in this direction, fell back on private preaching and literary propaganda. And, above all, they applied themselves to the task of rewriting the history of Israel, which, as told by the chroniclers of the previous century, presented the national Deity in too material a light, and one which failed to harmonise with the ideals then obtaining. So long as there were two separate Hebrew kingdoms, the existence of the two parallel versions of the Elohist and Jahvist gave rise to but little difficulty: each version had its own supporters and readers, whose consciences were readily satisfied by the interpolation of a few new facts into the text as occasion arose. But now that Samaria had fallen, and the whole political and religious life of the Hebrew race was centred in Judah alone, the necessity for a double and often contradictory narrative had ceased to exist, and the idea occurred of combining the two in a single work. This task, which was begun in the reign of Hezekiah and continued under Manasseh, resulted in the production of a literature of which fragments have been incorporated into the historical books of our Bible.[2]

The reign of Amon witnessed no alteration in the policy initiated by his predecessor Manasseh; but when, after less than two years' rule, he was suddenly struck down by the knife of an assassin, the party of reform carried the day, and the views of Hezekiah and Isaiah regained their ascendency. Josiah had been king, in name at any rate, for twelve years,[3] and was learning to act on his own responsibility, when the Scythian danger appeared on the horizon. This

---

[1] 2 *Kings* xxi. 16. The tradition in regard to the fate of Isaiah took its foundation in this text, and it is perhaps indirectly referred to in *Heb.* xi. 37.

[2] The scheme of the present work prevents me from doing more than allude in passing to these preliminary stages in the composition of the Priestly Code. I shall have occasion to return briefly to the subject at the close of the present volume.

[3] The date is supplied by the opening passage of the prophecy of Jeremiah, "to whom the word of Jahveh came in the days of Josiah, the son of Amon, King of Judah, in the thirteenth year of his reign" (i. 2). Volney recognised that chaps. i., iv., v., and vi. of Jeremiah refer to the Scythian invasion, and since his time it has been admitted that, with the exception of certain interpolations in chaps. i. and iii., the whole of the first six chapters date from this period (STADE, *Geschichte des Volkes Israel*, vol. i. p. 646, et seq.; WILDEBOER, *Die Literatur des Alten Testaments*, p. 205), but that they underwent slight modifications in the recension which was made in the fourth year of Jehoiachin in order to make them applicable to the threatened Chaldæan invasion. The date is important, since by using it as a basis we can approximately restore the chronology of the whole period. If we assume the thirteenth year of Josiah to have been 627–626 B.C., we are compelled to place all the early Medic wars in the reign of Assur-bani-pal, as I have done.

barbarian invasion, which burst upon the peace of Assyria like a thunderbolt from a cloudless sky, restored to the faithful that confidence in the omnipotence of their God which had seemed about to fail them; when they beheld the downfall of states, the sack of provinces innumerable, whole provinces in flames and whole peoples irresistibly swept away to death or slavery, they began to ask themselves whether these were not signs of the divine wrath, indicating that the day of Jahveh was at hand. Prophets arose to announce the approaching judgment, among the rest a certain Zephaniah, a great-grandson of Hezekiah:[1] " I will utterly consume all things from off the face of the ground, saith Jahveh. I will consume man and beast; I will consume the fowls of the heaven, and the fishes of the sea, and the stumbling-blocks with the wicked; and I will cut off man from the face of the earth, saith Jahveh. And I will stretch out My hand upon Judah, and upon all the inhabitants of Jerusalem; and I will cut off the remnant of Baal from this place, and the name of the Chemarim with the priests; and them that worship the host of heaven upon the housetops; and them that worship, which swear to Jahveh and swear by Malcham; and them that are turned back from following Jahveh; and those that have not sought Jahveh nor inquired after Him. Hold thy peace at the presence of the Lord Jahveh; for the day of Jahveh is at hand; for Jahveh hath prepared a sacrifice, He hath sanctified His guests."[2] " That day is a day of wrath, a day of trouble and distress, a day of wasteness and desolation, a day of darkness and gloominess, a day of clouds and thick darkness, a day of the trumpet and alarm, against the fenced cities, and against the high battlements. And I will bring distress upon men, that they shall walk like blind men, because they have sinned against Jahveh: and their blood shall be poured out as dust, and their flesh as dung. Neither their silver nor their gold shall be able to deliver them in the day of Jahveh's wrath; but the whole land shall be devoured by the fire of His jealousy; for He shall make an end, yea, a terrible end, of all them that dwell in the land."[3] During this same period of stress and terror, there came forward another prophet, one of the greatest among the prophets of Israel—Jeremiah, son of Hilkiah. He was born in the village of Anathoth, near Jerusalem, being descended from one of those priestly families in which the faith had been handed down from generation to generation in all its original purity.[4] When Jahveh called him, he cried out in amazement,

---

[1] Zephaniah gives his own genealogy at the beginning of his prophecy (i. 1), though, it is true, he does not add the title " King of Judah " after the name of his ancestor Hezekiah.

[2] *Zeph.* i. 2–7.   [3] *Zeph.* i. 15–18.

[4] The descent and birthplace of Jeremiah are given at the beginning of his prophecies (i. 1). He must have been quite young in the thirteenth year of Josiah, as is evident from the statement in i. 6. We are told in chap. xxxvi. that in the fourth year of Jehoiakim he dictated a summary of all the prophecies delivered by him from the thirteenth year of Josiah up to the date indicated to his servant Baruch, and that later on he added a number of others of the same kind. As to the contents of this first collection and the form in which it now appears, cf. CORNILL, *Einleitung in das Alte Testament*,

"Ah, Lord God! behold, I cannot speak: for I am a child." But Jahveh reassured him, and touching his lips, said unto him, "Behold, I have put My words in thy mouth: see, I have this day set thee over the nations and over the kingdoms, to pluck up and to break down, and to destroy and to over-throw, to build and to plant." Then the prophet perceived a seething cauldron, the face of which appeared from the north, for the Eternal declared to him that "Out of the north evil shall break out upon all the inhabitants of the land."[1] Already the enemy is hastening: "Behold, he shall come up as clouds, and his chariots shall be as the whirlwind: his horses are swifter than eagles. Woe unto us! for we are spoiled. O Jerusalem, wash thine heart from wickedness, that thou mayest be saved. How long shall thine evil thoughts lodge within thee? For a voice declareth from Dan, and publisheth evil from the hills of Ephraim: make ye mention to the nations; behold, publish against Jerusalem!" The Scythians had hardly been mentioned before they were already beneath the walls, and the prophet almost swoons with horror at the sound of their approach. "My bowels, my bowels! I am pained at my very heart: my heart is disquieted in me; I cannot hold my peace; because thou hast heard, O my soul, the sound of the trumpet, the alarm of war. Destruction upon destruction is cried; for the whole land is spoiled, and my curtains in a moment. How long shall I see the standard and hear the sound of the trumpet?"[2] It would seem that the torrent of invasion turned aside from the mountains of Judah; it flowed over Galilee, Samaria, and the Philistine Shephelah, its last eddies dying away on the frontiers of Egypt. Psammetichus is said to have bribed the barbarians to retire. As they fell back they plundered the temple of Derketô, near Ashkelon: we are told that in order to punish them for this act of sacrilege, the goddess visited them with a disease which caused serious ravages amongst them, and which the survivors carried back with them to their own country.[3] There was, however, no need to introduce a supernatural agency in order to account for their rapid disappearance. The main body of invaders had never quitted Media or the northern part of the Assyrian empire, and only the southern regions of Syria were in all probability exposed to the attacks of isolated bands. These stragglers, who year after year embarked in one desperate adventure after another, must have found great difficulty in filling up the gaps

2nd edit., pp. 157, 158; DRIVER, *An Introduction to the Literature of the Old Testament*, 5th edit., pp. 254, 255; WILDEBOER, *Die Literatur des Alten Testaments*, pp. 204–206.

[1] *Jer.* i. 4–14.   [2] *Jer.* iv. 13–16, 19–21.

[3] HERODOTUS, I. cv., where the author calls the goddess Aphroditê Urania, by which we must understand Derketô or Atargatis (cf. *Struggle of the Nations*, vol. ii. p. 698), who is mentioned by several other classical authors, *e.g.* Xanthus of Lydia (*Fragm.* 11, in MÜLLER-DIDOT'S *Fragm. Hist. Græc.*, vol. i. p. 38), Diodorus Siculus (ii. 4), Strabo (XVI. iv. § 17, p. 785), Pliny (*Hist. Nat.*, v. 23). According to Justin (ii. 3), the Scythians were stopped only by the marshes of the Delta. The disease by which the Scythians were attacked is described by Hippocrates (*De aere, aquâ et locis*, vi. § 108); but in spite of what he tells us about it, its precise nature has not yet been determined.

which even victories made in their ranks; enervated by the relaxing nature of the climate, they could offer little resistance to disease, and excess completed what the climate had begun, the result being that most of them died on the way, and only a few survived to rejoin the main body with their booty. For several months the tide of invasion continued to rise, then it ebbed as quickly as it had risen, till soon nothing was left to mark where it had passed save a pathway of ruins, not easily made good, and a feeling of terror which it took many a year to efface. It was long before Judah forgot the "mighty nation, the ancient nation, the nation whose language thou knowest not, neither understandest thou what they say." [1] Men could still picture in imagination their squadrons marauding over the plains, robbing the fellah of his crops, his bread, his daughters, his sheep and oxen, his vines and fig trees, for "they lay hold on bow and spear; they are cruel and have no mercy; their voice roareth like the sea, and they ride upon horses; every one set in array as a man to the battle,[2] against thee, O daughter of Sion. We have heard the fame thereof; our hands wax feeble; anguish hath taken hold of us, and pangs as of a woman in travail." [3]

The supremacy of the Scythians was of short duration. It was said in after-times that they had kept the whole of Asia in a state of terror for twenty-eight years, dating from their defeat of Cyaxares; but the length of this period is exaggerated.[4] The Medes soon recovered from their disaster, but before engaging their foes in open conflict, they desired to rid themselves of the prince who had conquered them, and on whom the fortunes of the whole Scythian nation depended. Cyaxares, therefore, invited Madyes and his officers to a banquet, and after plying them to excess with meat and drink, he caused them all to be slain.[5] The barbarians made a brave resistance, in spite

---

[1] *Jer.* v. 15; it seems curious that the Hebrew prophet should use the epithet "ancient," when we remember that the Scythians claimed to be the oldest nation in the world, older than even the Egyptians themselves (JUSTIN, ii. 1; cf. *Struggle of the Nations*, p. 56).

[2] An obvious allusion to the regular formation adopted by the Scythian squadrons.

[3] *Jer.* v. 17; vi. 23, 24.

[4] HERODOTUS, I. cvi. The authenticity of the number of years given in Herodotus has been energetically defended by some modern historians (cf. FLOIGL, *Cyrus und Herodot*, pp. 156, 157), and not less forcibly denied by others, who reduce it, for example, in accordance with a doubtful passage of Justin (ii. 5, 1), to eight years (F. DE SAULCY, *Chronologie des Empires de Ninive, de Babylone et d'Ebcatane*, p. 69; cf. G. RAWLINSON, *The Five Great Monarchies*, 2nd edit., vol. ii. pp. 226, 227, 391–393; FR. LENORMANT, *Lettres assyriologiques*, vol. i. pp. 74–83, and *Les Origines de l'Histoire*, vol. ii. p. 444). By assigning all the events relating to the Scythian invaders to the mean period of twenty years, we should obtain the length of time which best corresponds to what is actually known of the general history of this epoch.

[5] HERODOTUS, I. cv. This episode is regarded as legendary by many modern historians (ED. MEYER, *Gesch. des Alterthums*, vol. i. p. 558; PRASHEK, *Medien und das Haus des Kyaxares*, p. 75; WINCKLER, *Untersuch. zur Altorient. Gesch.*, p. 125; *Einige Bemerkungen zur Nabunid-Stele*, in MESSERSCHMIDT, *Die Insch. der Stele Nabuna'id's*, pp. 71, 72, and *Altorient. Forsch.*, vol. i. p. 491). Winckler even goes so far as to deny the defeat of the Scythians: according to his view, they held possession of Media till their chief, Astyages, was overthrown by Cyrus. This theory was accepted first by Tiele (*Zeitschrift für Assyriologie*, vol. iv. pp. 425, 426), then by Lehmann (*Zu Nabonid's Bericht über die Besiegung des Astyages durch Kyros*, in the *Zeitschrift*, vol. v. p. 84), by Billerbeck and Jeremias (*Der Untergang Nineveh's*, in the *Beiträge zur Assyriologie*, vol. iii. p. 96, note 1); Rost has gone even further (*Untersuch.*

of the treason which had deprived them of their leaders: they yielded only after a long and bloody campaign, the details of which are unknown to us. Iranian legends wove into the theme of their expulsion all kinds of fantastic or romantic incidents. They related, for instance, how, in combination with the Parthians, the Scythians, under the leadership of their queen Zarinæa, several times defeated the Medes: she consented at last to conclude a treaty on equal terms, and peace having been signed, she retired to her capital of Roxanakê, there to end her days.[1] One body of the survivors re-entered Europe through the Caspian Gates,[2] another wandered for some time between the Araxes and the Halys, seeking a country adapted to their native instincts and customs.[3] Cyaxares, relieved from the pressure put upon him by the Scythians, immediately resumed his efforts against Assyria, and was henceforward able to carry his plans to completion without encountering any serious obstacle. It would be incorrect to say that the Scythian invasion had overthrown the empire of the Sargonids: it had swept over it like a whirlwind, but had not torn from it one province, nor, indeed, even a single city. The nations, already exhausted by their struggles for independence, were incapable of displaying any energy when the barbarians had withdrawn, and continued to bow beneath the Ninevite yoke as much from familiarity with habitual servitude as from inability to shake themselves free. Assur-bani-pal had died about the year 625 B.C., after a reign of forty-two years, and his son Assur-etililâni had assumed the double crown of Assyria and Babylon without opposition.[4] Nineveh had been saved from pillage by the strength of her ramparts, but

---

zur Altorient. Gesch., p. 93, et seq.), deeming even Cyaxares himself to have been a Scythian. For my part, I see no reason to reject the tradition of the fatal banquet. Without referring to more ancient illustrations, Nöldeke recalls the fact that in a period of only ten years, from 1030 to 1040 A.D., the princes reigning over the Iranian lands rid themselves by similar methods of the Turcoman bands which harassed them (*Aufsätze zur Persischen Geschichte*, p. 8, note 2). Such a proceeding has never been repugnant to Oriental morality, and it is of a kind to fix itself in the popular mind: far from wishing to suppress it, I should be inclined to see in it the nucleus of the whole tradition.

[1] The legend is recounted in a slightly different manner by the authors who have drawn upon Ctesias of Cnidus (*Fragm.* 26, 27, in MÜLLER-DIDOT, *Ctesiæ Cnidii Fragmenta*, pp. 4-45), such as Diodorus Siculus (ii. 34), Nicolas of Damascus (*Fragm.* 12, in MÜLLER-DIDOT, *Fragm. Hist. Græc.*, vol. iii. pp. 364, 365), and the anonymous author of the treatise *De Claris mulieribus*, § 2.

[2] HERODOTUS, IV. i.–iv.

[3] HERODOTUS, I. lxxiii., lxxiv., speaks of these Scythians as having lived at first on good terms with Cyaxares (cf. *infra*, p. 525).

[4] The date of Assur-bani-pal's death is not furnished by any Assyrian monument, but is inferred from the Canon of Ptolemy, where Saosduchîn or Shamash-shumukîn and Chinaladan or Assur-bani-pal each reigns forty-two years, from 668 or 667 to 626 or 625 B.C. The order of succession of the last Assyrian kings was for a long time doubtful, and Sin-shar-ishkun was placed before Assur-etililâni (TIELE, *Bab.-ass. Gesch.*, pp. 405, 406; HOMMEL, *Gesch. Bab. und Ass.*, pp. 742, 743); the inverse order (DELITZSCH and MÜRDTER, *Gesch. Bab. und Ass.*, 2nd edit., p. 233; WINCKLER, *Untersuch. zur Alt. Gesch.*, pp. 60-63, and *Gesch. Bab. und Ass.*, pp. 290, 291; HOMMEL, *Gesch. des Alten Morgenlandes*, pp. 150, 151; MESSERSCHMIDT, *Die Inschrift der Stele Nabuna'id's*, p. 12, note 1) seems to be now conclusively proved. The documents which seemed at one time to prove the existence of a last king of Assyria named Esarhaddon, identical with the Saracos of classical writers, really belong to Esarhaddon, the father of Assur-bani-pal (cf. *supra*, p. 354, note 1). [Another king, Sin-sum-lisir, is mentioned in a contract dated at Nippur in his accession year. He may have been the immediate predecessor of Sarakos.—ED.]

the other fortresses, Assur, Calah, and Dur-Sharrukîn, had been destroyed during the late troubles; the enemy, whether Medes or Scythians, had taken them by storm or reduced them by famine, and they were now mere heaps of ruin, deserted save for a few wretched remnants of their population.[1] Assur-etililâni made some feeble attempts to restore to them a semblance of their ancient splendour. He erected at Calah, on the site of the palaces which had been destroyed by fire, a kind of castle rudely built, and still more rudely decorated, the rooms of which were small and low, and the walls of sun-dried brick were panelled only to the height of about a yard with slabs of limestone roughly squared, and without sculpture or inscription: the upper part of the walls was covered with a coating of uneven plaster.[2] We do not know how long the inglorious reign of Assur-etililâni lasted, nor whether he was assassinated or died a natural death. His brother, Sin-shar-ishkun,[3] who succeeded him about 620 B.C.,[4] at first exercised authority, as he had done, over Babylon as well as Nineveh,[5] and laboured, like his predecessor,

[1] Layard has ascertained that the palace of Esarhaddon at Calah was destroyed by fire, and that of Assur-etililâni built on a higher level (Nineveh and Babylon, p. 558). Both Rawlinsons (The Five Great Monarchies, 2nd edit., vol. ii. p. 228) attribute its destruction to the Scythians, and this hypothesis has been pretty commonly accepted since their time; nothing, however, proves that the destruction may not be referred to the first invasion of Cyaxares, a theory of which G. Rawlinson himself admits the possibility in his Herodotus, 2nd edit., vol. i. p. 398.

[2] This palace is at present only known to us from the researches and descriptions of LAYARD, Nineveh and its Remains, vol. ii. pp. 38, 39; Nineveh and Babylon, p. 558.

[3] The name of this king was discovered by G. Smith on the fragments of a cylinder brought from Kouyunjik (Assyrian Discoveries, pp. 103, 382–384), where he read it as Bel-zakir-iskun. As the first characters were doubtful, so that Schrader thought it prudent to transcribe the name as X-shum-ishkun (Zur Kritik der Chronologischen Angaben des Alexander Polyhistor und des Abydenus, pp. 28–30, 33–41; Die Keilins. und das Alte Testament, 2nd edit., p. 360), which was reduced to X-?-iskun by Winckler (Einige neuer Inschriftenfragmente des letzten Assyrischen Königs, in the Revue d'Assyriologie, vol. ii. pp. 66, 67), while Tiele (Bab.-assyr. Gesch., pp. 405, 406, 412–488) kept the form Bel-zakir-ishkun, and Hommel (Gesch. Bab. und Assyr., p. 742) proposed Belshumishkun in default of anything better. The real reading is Sin-shar-ishkun, and the similarity of this name with that of Saracos, the last king of Assyria according to Greek tradition, strikes one immediately. The relationship of this king to Assur-etililâni was pointed out by Father Scheil (Sin-shar-ishkun, fils d'Ashshurbanipal, in the Zeitschrift für Assyriologie, vol. xi. pp. 47–49) from the fragment of a tablet on which Sin-shar-ishkun is declared to be the son of Assur-bani-pal, king of Assyria.

[4] A contract discovered at Nipur by Hilprecht (Keilinschriftliche Fund in Niffer, in the Zeitschrift, vol. iv. pp. 166–169) is dated in the fourth year of Assur-etililâni. On the other hand, a contract from Uruk published by King (Sinsharishkun and his Rule in Babylonia, in the Zeitschrift für Assyriologie, vol. ix. pp. 396–400) is dated in the seventh year of Sin-shar-ishkun. We have, therefore, eleven years attributed with certainty, out of the seventeen or eighteen which separate the death of Assur-banipal in 626 or 625 B.C. from the fall of Nineveh in 608. Since, on the other hand, it is unlikely that a contract of Uruk should have been dated in the reign of a king of Assyria after the revolt of Nabopolassar, which occurred in 611 or 610 at the latest, we cannot push the accession of Sin-shar-ishkun further back than 620 or 619 B.C.

[5] This may be deduced from a passage of Abydenus (Fragm. 7, in MÜLLER-DIDOT, Fragm. Hist. Græc., vol. iv. p. 282), where Saracos or Sin-shar-ishkun sends Bussalossoros (that is, Nabopolassar) to defend Chaldæa against the invasion of the peoples of the sea; so according to Abydenus, or rather Berosus, from whom Abydenus indirectly obtained his information, Saracos was King of Babylon as well as of Nineveh at the beginning of his reign. The contract dated in the year VII., quoted in the preceding note, brings material proof of this fact, since it comes from Uruk, and its testimony is confirmed by that of two other tablets, dated in the king's second year, which come from Sippara, one of which is preserved in the British Museum (EVETTS, Inscriptions of the Reigns of Evil-Merodach, Neriglissar, and Laborosoarchod, pp. 90, 91), and the other in the museum at Berlin.

to repair the edifices which had suffered by the invasion, making war on his neighbours, perhaps even on the Medes, without incurring serious losses.[1] The Chaldæans, however, merely yielded him obedience from force of habit, and the moment was not far distant when they would endeavour to throw off his yoke. Babylon was at that time under the rule of a certain Nabu-bal-uzur, known to us as Nabopolassar, a Kaldu of ancient lineage, raised possibly by Assur-bani-pal to the dignity of governor, but who, in any case, had assumed the title of king on the accession of Assur-etililâni.[2] His was but a local sovereignty, restricted probably to the city and its environs; and for twelve or thirteen years he had rested content with this secondary position, when an unforeseen incident presented him with the opportunity of rising to the first rank.[3] Tradition asserted that an immense army suddenly landed at the mouths of the Euphrates and the Tigris; probably under this story is concealed the memory of one of those revolts of the Bît-Yakîn and the tribes dwelling on the shores of the Nar-Marratum, such as had often produced consternation in the minds of the Sargonid kings.[4] Sin-shar-ishkun, distracted doubtless by other anxieties, acted as his ancestors had done in similar circumstances, and enjoined on his vassal to march against the aggressors and drive them into the sea; but Nabopolassar, instead of obeying his suzerain, joined forces with the rebels, and declared his independence. Assur-etililâni and his younger brother had possibly neglected to take the hands of Bel, and were therefore looked upon as illegitimate sovereigns. The annalists of later times erased their names from the Royal Canon, and placed Nabopolassar immediately after Assur-bani-pal, whom they called Kandalanu. But however feeble Assyria had become, the cities on the Lower Euphrates feared her still,

---

[1] This seems to follow from the fragments published by Winckler (*Einige neuer Inschriftenfragmente des letzen Assyrischen Königs*, in the *Revue d'Assyriologie*, vol. ii. p. 67).

[2] The Canon of Ptolemy makes Nabopolassar the direct successor of Chinaladan, and his testimony is justified by the series of Babylonian contracts which exist in fairly regular succession from the second to the twenty-first years of Nabopolassar. The account given by Berosus makes him a general of Saracos, but the contradiction which this offers to the testimony of the Canon can be explained if he is considered as a vassal-king; the kings of Egypt and of Media were likewise only satraps, according to Babylonian tradition (BEROSUS, *Fragm.* 12, 14, in MÜLLER-DIDOT, *Fragm. Hist. Græc.*, vol. ii. pp. 505, 506).

[3] Fixing the date of the fall of Nineveh in 608 or 607, and keeping in view the fact, that the contract dated in the year VII., mentioned *supra*, p. 482, notes 4, 5, comes from Uruk, it appears difficult to place the invasion of the barbarians more than three or four years before the final catastrophe, viz. in 612 or 611 B.C.

[4] See the account of the revolts and wars occasioned by these invasions, *supra*, pp. 222–225, 231, 232, 254–257, 274–276, 295, 296, 299–304, 349, 350, 358, 394, 398, 404, 412, 416, 434, 438, 439. Formerly these barbarians were identified with the remains of the Scythian hordes (BRANDIS, *Rerum Assyriacarum Tempora Emendata*, p. 31), and this hypothesis has been recently revived by Prashek (*Medien und das Haus des Kyaxares*, p. 645). G. Rawlinson long ago recognised that the reference must be to the Chaldæans, who were perhaps joined by the Susians (*Herodotus*, 2nd edit., vol. i. pp. 399–415, and the *Four Great Monarchies*, 2nd edit., vol. iii. p. 44), and this opinion has been rightly accepted by Unger (*Kyaxares und Astyages*, p. 39, note 2), by Tiele (*Bab.-assyr. Gesch.*, p. 421), and by Rost (*Untersuch. zur Altorient. Gesch.*, p. 94), while Hommel (*Gesch. Bab. und Assyr.*, p. 743) thinks an invasion of Elamites alone is meant.

and refused to ally themselves with the pretender.   Nabopolassar might perhaps have succumbed, as so many before him had done, had he been forced to rely entirely on his own resources, and he might have shared the sad fate of Merodach-baladan or of Shamash-shumukîn; but Marduk, who never failed to show favour to his faithful devotees, "raised up help for him and secured him an ally."[1]   The eyes of all who were oppressed by the cruel yoke of Nineveh were now turned on Cyaxares, and from the time that he had dispersed the Scythian hordes it was to him that they looked for salvation.   Nabopolassar besought his assistance, which the Median king graciously promised;[2] it is even affirmed that a marriage concluded between one of his daughters, Amytis, and Nebuchadrezzar, the heir to the throne of Babylon, cemented the alliance.[3]   The western provinces of the empire did not permit themselves to

[1] *Cylinder of Nabonidos*, col. ii. ll. 1-12.   This cylinder, the only original document in which allusion is made to the destruction of Nineveh, was discovered, published, and translated into French by FATHER SCHEIL, *Inscr. de Nabonide*, in the *Recueil de Travaux*, vol. xviii. pp. 15-29, and pls. i.-iii.; it was at once republished and retranslated into German by L. MESSERSCHMIDT, *Die Inschrift der Stele Nabuna'id's, Königs von Babylon*, in the *Mitteilungen der Vorderasiatischen Gesellschaft*, 1896, No. 1. Father Scheil first read as Iriba-tuktê the characters at the end of line 13, col. ii., and saw in them the name of the king of the Manda who conducted the war (*op. cit.*, pp. 16, 24), while Oppert thought that the passage relating to Nineveh referred, not to the final destruction of that city, but to the abortive attempt of Phraortes (*Sur l'inscr. de Nabonide*, in the *Comptes rendus de l'Académie des Inscriptions*, 1896, vol. xxiv. pp. 129, 130); he thought also that the words Iriba-tuktê represented the name of the Median king who attacked Nineveh, but explained it as Arbatyktes or Phraortes. Winckler first showed that these words did not represent a proper name (*Berlin Phil. Wochenschrift*, 1895, No. 1435), and his opinion is now generally adopted; cf., however, with slight divergences, LEHMANN, *Iribatukte*, in the *Zeitschrift für Assyriologie*, vol. xi. pp. 339-344.

[2] The text of Nabonidos speaks here of the Ummân-Manda and their king, whom it does not name (col. ii. ll. 3, 4, 14), and it has been agreed to recognise Cyaxares in this sovereign (MESSER-SCHMIDT, *op. cit.*, pp. 2-14; ROST, *Untersuch. zur Altorient. Gesch.*, pp. 96, 97).   On the other hand, the name of Ummân-Manda certainly designates in the Assyrian texts the wandering Iranian tribes to whom the Greeks gave the name of Sakæ or Scythians (DELATTRE, *Le Peuple et l'Empire des Medes*, p. 190; WINCKLER, *Untersuch. zur Altorient. Gesch.*, pp. 112, 124, 125); the result, in the opinions of several Assyriologists of the present day, is that neither Astyages nor Cyaxares were Medes in the sense in which we have hitherto accepted them as such on the evidence of Herodotus, but that they were Scythians, the Scythians of the great invasion.   This conclusion does not seem to me at present justified.   The Babylonians, who up till then had not had any direct intercourse either with the Madai or the Ummân-Manda, did as the Egyptians had done whether in Saite or Ptolemaic times, continuing to designate as Kharî, Kafîti, Lotanu, and Khâti the nations subject to the Persians or Macedonians; they applied a traditional name of olden days to present circumstances, and I see, at present, no decisive reason to change, on the mere authority of this one word, all that the classical writers have handed down concerning the history of the epoch according to the tradition current in their days.

[3] The name of the princess is written Amuhia (EUSEBIUS, *Armenian Translation*, ed. MAI, p. 19), Amyitis (SYNCELLUS, p. 396, note 1, probably from an extract from Berosus; cf. MÜLLER-DIDOT, *Fragm. Hist. Græc.*, vol. ii. p. 505).   The classical sources, the only ones which mention her, make her the daughter of Astyages, and this has given rise to various hypotheses.   According to some, the notice of this princess has no historical value (WINCKLER, *op. cit.*, pp. 62, 63, and *Altor. Forsch.*, vol. i. pp. 178, 179; BILLERBECK and JEREMIAS, *Der Untergang Nineveh's*, in the *Beiträge zur Assyrio-logie*, vol. iii. p. 113, note 2; MESSERSCHMIDT, *op. cit.*, p. 11; ROST, *Untersuch. zur Alt. Gesch.*, p. 100). According to others, the Astyages mentioned as her father is not Cyaxares the Mede, but a Scythian prince who came to the succour of Nabopolassar (ROST, *op. cit.*, pp. 99, 100), perhaps a predecessor of Cyaxares on the Median throne, and in this case Phraortes himself under another name (UNGER, *Kyaxares und Astyages*, pp. 39-41; PRASHEK, *Medien und das Haus des Kyaxares*, pp. 53-58).   The most prudent course is still to admit, as Nöldeke has done (*Aufsätze zur Persischen Geschichte*, p. 9), that Abydenus, or one of the compilers of extracts to whom we owe the information, has substituted

be drawn into the movement, and Judah, for example, remained faithful to its suzerain till the last moment,[1] but Sin-shar-ishkun received no help from them, and was obliged to fight his last battles single-handed. He shut himself up in Nineveh, and held out as long as he could; but when all his resources were exhausted—ammunitions of war, men and food supplies—he met his fate as a king, and burnt himself alive in his palace with his children and his wives, rather than fall alive into the hands of his conquerors (608 B.C.).[2] The Babylonians would take no part in pillaging the temples, out of respect for the gods, who were practically identical with their own, but the Medes felt no such scruples. "Their king, the intrepid one, entirely destroyed the sanctuaries of the gods of Assur, and the cities of Accad which had shown themselves hostile to the lord of Accad, and had not rendered him assistance. He destroyed their holy places, and left not one remaining; he devastated their cities, and laid them waste as it were with a hurricane."[3] Nineveh laid low, Assyria no longer existed. After the lapse of a few years, she was named only among the legends of mythical days: two centuries later, her very site was forgotten, and a Greek army passed almost under the shadow of her dismantled towers, without a suspicion that there lay before it all that remained of the city where Semiramis had reigned in her glory.[4] It is true that Egypt, Chaldæa, and the other military nations of the East, had never, in their hours of prosperity, shown the slightest consideration for their vanquished foes; the

the name of the last king of Media for that of his predecessor, either by mistake, or by reason of some chronological combinations. Amyitis, transported into the harem of the Chaldæan monarch, served, like all princesses married out of their own countries, as a pledge for the faithful observance by her relatives of the treaty which had been concluded.

[1] It was to oppose the march of Necho *against the King of Assyria* that Josiah fought the battle of Megiddo (2 *Kings* xxiii. 29, 30; cf. 2 *Chron.* xxxv. 20–24, where the mention of the King of Assyria is suppressed).

[2] Cf. what is said about the death of Shamash-shumukîn, *supra*, pp. 422, 423; we shall see later on that Crœsus ended his reign in like fashion. I have followed the account of Abydenus (*Fragm.* 7, in MÜLLER-DIDOT, *Fragm. Hist. Græc.*, vol. iv. pp. 282, 283); for the criticisms passed upon it I confine myself to referring to the works of Winckler and Rost cited in the course of the preceding notes, the principal ideas of which I shall have occasion to point out in subsequent pages.

[3] *Cylinder of Nabonidos*, col. ii. ll. 2–41; cf. SCHEIL, *Inscr. de Nabonide*, in the *Recueil de Travaux*, vol. xviii. p. 24, and MESSERSCHMIDT; *Die Inschrift der Stele Nabuna'id's*, pp. 25, 26. Winckler had reopened the old controversy as to the part which must be assigned to each of the allied powers in the ruin of Nineveh, and concluded, from an analysis of the texts known before Father Scheil's discovery, that the Medes alone took Nineveh without the help of the Babylonians (*Untersuch. zur Altorient. Gesch.*, pp. 63–68, and *Altor. Forsch.*, vol. i. pp. 170–182); since then his view has been confirmed (*Altor. Forsch.*, vol. i. pp. 490, 491), and is shared by Lehmann (*Schamaschschumukin*, vol. ii. p. 185), by Billerbeck and Jeremias (*Der Untergang Nineveh's*, in the *Beiträge zur Assyriologie*, vol. iii. pp. 112, 113), by Rost (*Untersuch. zur Alt. Gesch.*, pp. 92–100). Messerschmidt has given, I believe, the true solution of the problem when he says that the Babylonians and Medes together destroyed the empire, but the Medes alone destroyed the city of Nineveh (*Die Inschrift der Stele Nabuna'id's*, p. 14).

[4] This is what the *Ten Thousand* did when they passed before Larissa and Mespila (XENOPHON, *Anabasis*, III. iv. § 1). The name remained famous, and later on the town which bore it attained a relative importance, as is shown by the texts brought together by Lincke, in his two memoirs, *Continuance of the Names of Assyria and Nineveh after 607–606 B.C.* (*Memoirs of the IX. Oriental Congress at London in 1891*), and *Assyria und Nineveh in Geschichte und Sage der Mittelmeervölker* (*nach 607–606*), 1894.

Theban Pharaohs had mercilessly crushed Africa and Asia beneath their feet, and had led into slavery the entire population of the countries they had subdued. But the Egyptians and Chaldæans had, at least, accomplished a work of civilisation whose splendour redeemed the brutalities of their acts of reprisal. It was from Egypt and Chaldæa that the knowledge and the arts of antiquity—astronomy, medicine, geometry, physical and natural sciences— spread to the ancestors of the classic races; and though Chaldæa yields up to us unwillingly, with niggard hand, the monuments of her most ancient kings, the temples and tombs of Egypt still exist to prove what signal advances the earliest civilised races made in the arts of the sculptor and the architect. But on turning to Assyria, if, after patiently studying the successive centuries during which she held supreme sway over the Eastern world, we look for other results besides her conquests, we shall find she possessed nothing that was not borrowed from extraneous sources. She received all her inspirations from Chaldæa—her civilisation, her manners, the implements of her industries and of agriculture, besides her scientific and religious literature: one thing alone is of native growth, the military tactics of her generals and the excellence of her soldiery. From the day when Assyria first realised her own strength, she lived only for war and rapine; and as soon as the exhaustion of her population rendered success on the field of battle an impossibility, the reason for her very existence vanished, and she passed away.

Two great kingdoms rose simultaneously from her ruins. Cyaxares claimed Assyria proper and its dependencies on the Upper Tigris, but he specially reserved for himself the yet unconquered lands on the northern and eastern frontiers, whose inhabitants had only recently taken part in the political life of the times. Nabopolassar retained the suzerainty over the lowlands of Elam, the districts of Mesopotamia lying along the Euphrates, Syria, Palestine, and most of the countries which had hitherto played a part in history;[1] he claimed to exert his supremacy beyond the Isthmus, and the Chaldæan government looked upon the Egyptian kings as its feudatories because for some few years they had owned the suzerainty of Nineveh.[2] The Pharaoh, however, did not long tolerate this pretension, and far from looking forward to bend the knee

[1] There was no actual division of the empire, as has been often asserted, but each of the allies kept the portion which fell into his power at the moment of their joint effort. The two new states gradually increased in power by successive conquests, each annexing by degrees the ancient provinces of Assyria nearest to its own frontier.

[2] This seems to be implied by the terms in which Berosus speaks of Necho: he considers him as a rebel satrap over the provinces of Egypt, Cœle-Syria, and Phœnicia, and enumerates Egypt in conjunction with Syria, Phœnicia, and Arabia among the dependencies of Nabopolassar and Nebuchad- rezzar (Fragm. 14, in MÜLLER-DIDOT, Fragm. Hist. Græc., vol. ii. p. 506). Just as the Egyptian state documents never mentioned the Lotanu or the Kharu without entitling them Children of Rebellion, so the Chaldæan government, the heir of Assyria, could only look upon the kings of Syria, Arabia, and Egypt as rebellious vassals.

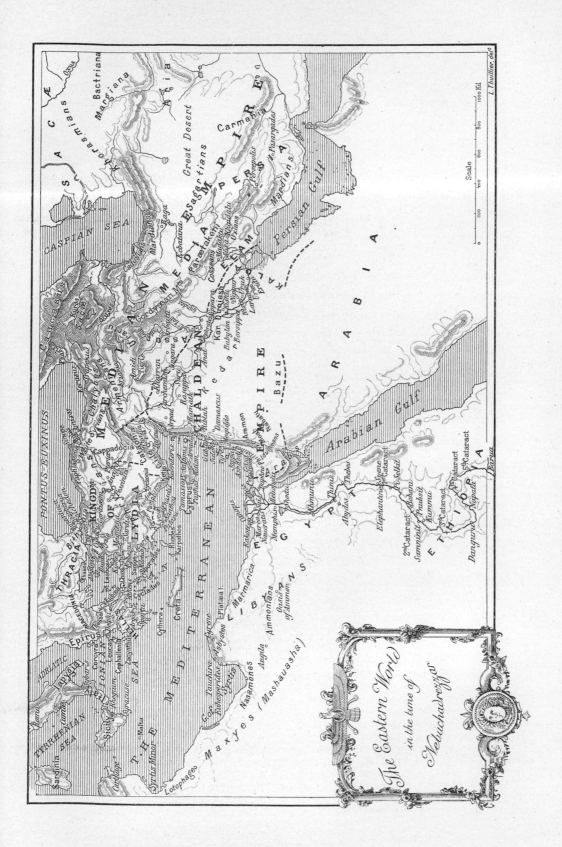

The Eastern World in the time of Nebuchadrezzar

L. Thuillier, del.

before a Chaldæan monarch, he believed himself strong enough to reassert his ancestral claims to the possession of Asia.   Egypt had experienced many changes since the day when Tanuatamanu, returning to Ethiopia, had abandoned her to the ambition of the petty dynasties of the Delta.[1]   One of the romances current among the people of Sais in the fifth century B.C. related that at that time the whole land was divided between twelve princes.   They lived peaceably side by side in friendly relations with each other, until an oracle predicted that the whole valley would finally belong to that prince among them who should pour a libation to Phtah into a brazen cup, and thenceforward they jealously watched each other each time they assembled to officiate in the temple at Memphis.   One day, when they had met together in state, and the high priest presented to them the golden cups they were wont to use, he found he had mistaken their number, and had only prepared eleven. Psammetichus was therefore left without one, and in order not to disarrange the ceremonial he took off his brazen helmet and used it to make his libation; when the rest perceived this, the words of the oracle came to their remembrance, and they exiled the imprudent prince to the marshes along the sea-coast, and forbade him ever to quit them.   He secretly consulted the oracle of Isis of Buto to know what he might expect from the gods, and she replied that the means of revenge would reach him from the sea, on the day when brazen soldiers should issue from its waters.   He thought at first that the priests were mocking him, but shortly afterwards Ionian and Carian pirates, clad in their coats of mail, landed not far from his abode.   The messenger who brought tidings of their advent had never before seen a soldier fully armed, and reported that brazen men had issued from the waves and were pillaging the country.   Psammetichus, realising at once that the prediction was being fulfilled, ran to meet the strangers, enrolled them in his service, and with their aid overthrew successively his eleven rivals.[2]   A brazen helmet and an oracle had dethroned him; another oracle and brazen men had replaced him on his

---

[1] Cf. what is stated on this subject, *supra*, pp. 399, 400.

[2] HERODOTUS, II. cxlvii.–clii.   The account given by Diodorus of these events (i. 66) is in general derived from that of Herodotus, with additional details borrowed directly or indirectly from some historian of the same epoch, perhaps Hellanicus of Mitylene : the reason of the persecution endured by Psammetichus is, according to him, not the fear of seeing the prediction fulfilled, but jealousy of the wealth the Saite prince had acquired by his commerce with the Greeks.   I have separated the narrative of Herodotus from his account of the Labyrinth which did not originally belong to it, but was connected with a different cycle of legends.   The original romance was part of the cycle which grew up around the oracle of Buto, so celebrated in Egypt at the Persian epoch, several other fragments of which are preserved in Herodotus (II. cxi., *Story of Pheron* ; II. cxxxiii., *Story of Mycerinus* ; III. lxiv., *Story of Cambyses*) ; it had been mixed up with one of the versions of the stories relating to the Labyrinth, probably by some dragoman of the Fayyûm.   The number twelve does not correspond with the information furnished by the Assyrian texts, which enumerate more than twenty Egyptian princes (cf. *supra*, pp. 378, 379) ; it is perhaps of Greek origin, like the *twelve* great gods which the informants of Herodotus tried to make out in Egypt (II. xliii.), and was introduced into the Egyptian version by a Greek interpreter (MALLET, *Les Premiers établissements des Grecs en Egypte*, p. 37, note 2).

throne. A shorter version of these events made no mention of the twelve kings, but related instead that a certain Pharaoh named Tementhes had been warned by the oracle of Amon to beware of cocks. Now Psammetichus had as a companion in exile a Carian named Pigres, and in conversing with him one day, he learned by chance that the Carians had been the first people to wear crested helmets; he recalled at once the words of the oracle, and hired from Asia a number of these "cocks," with whose assistance he revolted and over- threw his suzerain in battle under the walls of Memphis, close to the temple of Isis.[1] Such is the legendary account of the Saite renaissance; its true history is not yet clearly and precisely known. Egypt was in a state of com- plete disintegration when Psammetichus at length revived the ambitious projects of his family, but the dissolution of the various component parts had not everywhere taken place in the same manner. In the north, the Delta and the Nile

THREE HOPLITES IN ACTION.[2]

valley, as far as Siut, were in the power of a military aristocracy, supported by irregular native troops and bands of mercenaries, for the most part of Libyan extraction, who were always designated by the generic name of Mashauasha. Most of these nobles were in possession of not more than two or three cities apiece: they had barely a sufficient number of supporters to main- tain their precarious existence in their restricted domains, and would soon have succumbed to the attacks of their stronger neighbours, had they not found a powerful protector to assist them. They had finally separated themselves into two groups, divided roughly by the central arm of the Nile. One group comprised the districts that might be designated as the Asiatic zone of the country—Heliopolis, Bubastis, Mendes, Tanis, Busiris, and Sebennytos—and it recognised as chief the lord of one or other of those wealthy cities, now the ruler of Bubastis, now of Tanis, and lastly Pakruru of Pisaptit. The second

---

[1] POLYÆNUS, *Stratagemata*, vii. 3; very probably from the lost work of Aristagoras of Miletus. Gutschmid, who pointed out the origin of the story (*Kleine Schriften*, vol. i. pp. 135–138, 177), maintained that the narrative given by Aristagoras represented a Theban version of the romance of the "twelve kings," relying on the name of Amon attributed to the god who delivered the oracle. Considering the period we have reached, I should prefer to see in it a variant in which the oracle of the Libyan Amon—Amon of the Oasis—received all the honour of the prediction which others claimed for the rival oracle of Butô.

[2] Drawn by Faucher-Gudin, from an archaic vase-painting in the collection of SALZMANN, *La Nécropole de Camiros*, pl. 53, No. 1.

group centred in the lords of Sais, to whom the possession of Memphis had secured a proponderating voice in the counsels of the state for more than a century.[1] The fiefs and kingdoms of Middle Egypt wavered between the two groups, playing, however, a merely passive part in affairs : abandoning themselves to the stream of events rather than attempting to direct it, they owed allegiance to Sais and Tanis alternately as each prevailed over its rival. On passing thence into the Thebaid a different world appeared to be entered. There Amon reigned, ever increasingly supreme, and the steady advance of his influence had transformed his whole domain into a regular theocracy, where the women occupied the highest position and could alone transmit authority. At first, as we have seen, it was passed on to their husbands and their children,[2] but latterly the rapidity with which the valley had changed masters had modified this law of succession in a remarkable way. Each time the principality shifted its allegiance from one king to another, the new sovereign naturally hastened to install beside the *divine female worshipper* a man devoted to his interests, who should administer the fief to the best advantage of the suzerain. It is impossible to say whether he actually imposed this minister on her as a husband, or whether the time came when she was obliged to submit to as many espousals as there occurred revolutions in the destinies of Egypt.[3] However this may be, we know that from the first half of the seventh century B.C. the custom arose of placing beside " the divine worshipper" a princess of the dominant family, whom she adopted, and who thus became her heiress-designate.   Taharqa had in this way associated one of his sisters, Shapenuapît II., with the queen Amenertas when the latter had lost her husband, Piônkhi ; and Shapenuapît, succeeding her adopted mother, had reigned over Thebes in the Ethiopian interest during many years.[4] There is nothing to show that she was married, and perhaps she was compensated for her official celibacy by being authorised to live the free life of an ordinary Pallacide ;[5] her

---

[1] This grouping, which might already have been suspected from the manner in which the Assyrian and Egyptian monuments of the period show us the feudal princes rallying round Necho I. and Pakruru (cf. the passages relating to these personages, *supra*, pp. 378, 379), is indicated by the details in the demotic romance published by Krall (*Ein neuer Historischer Roman in Demotischer Schrift*, 1897), where the foundation of the story is the state of Egypt in the time of the "twelve kings" (Maspero, *Un Nouveau Conte égyptien*, in the *Journal des Savants*, 1897, pp. 652–654).

[2] Cf. what is stated on this subject, *supra*, p. 164, et seq.

[3] They would have been, in fact, in the same condition as the Hova queens of our century, who married the ministers who reigned in their names.

[4] Cf. Erman (*Zu den Legrain'schen Inschriften*, in the *Zeitschrift*, vol. xxxv. pp. 28, 29), after an inscription given in Legrain (*Deux Stèles trouvées à Karnak*, in the *Zeitschrift*, vol. xxxv. pp. 16–19). Cf., for Shapenuapît I. and Amenertas, *supra*, pp. 246, 247.

[5] It is perhaps these last female descendants of the high priests that are intended in a passage where Strabo (XVII. i. § 46, p. 817) speaks of the Pallacides who were chosen from among the most noble families of the city. Diodorus mentions their tombs, quoting from Hecatæus of Abdera (i. 47), but he does not appear to know the nature of their life ; but the name of Pallacides which he applies to them proves that their manner of life was really that which Strabo describes.

minister Montumihâît directed her affairs for her so completely that the
Assyrian conquerors looked upon him as petty king of Thebes.[1] Tanuatamanu
confirmed him in his office when the Assyrians evacuated the Said, and the
few years which had elapsed since that event had in no way modified the *régime*
established immediately on their departure.

It is uncertain how long Assur-bani-pal in the north, and Tanuatamanu in
the south, respectively maintained a precarious sovereignty over the portions of Egypt nearest to their own
capitals. The opening of the reign of Psammetichus
seems to have been fraught with difficulties, and the
tradition which represents him as proscribed by his
peers, and confined to the marshes of the sea-coast, has
probably a certain basis of truth.   Pakruru, who had
brought all the western part of the Delta under his
own influence, and who, incessantly oscillating between
Assyria and Ethiopia, had yet been able to preserve his
power and his life, had certainly not of his own free
will renounced the hope of some day wearing the
double crown. It was against him or his successor that
Psammetichus must have undertaken his first wars,
and it was perhaps with the help of Assyrian governors that the federal coalition drove him back to the
coast. He extricated himself from this untoward situation by the help of Greek and Asiatic mercenaries,
his Ionians and Carians. Some historians stated that
the decisive battle was fought near Memphis, in sight
of the temple of Isis;[2] others affirmed that it took
place at Momemphis, that several of the princes

STATUE OF A THEBAN QUEEN.[3]

perished in the conflict, and that the rest escaped into Libya, whence
they never returned;[4] others, again, spoke of an encounter on the Nile,

[1] Cf. what is stated concerning this personage, *supra*, pp. 378, 385, 386, 396.

[2] POLYÆNUS, *Strat.*, vii. 3 : probably after Aristagoras of Miletus, as was stated *supra*, p. 489,
note 2.

[3] Drawn by Boudier, from a photograph by M. de Bissing. The statue, whose feet are missing,
represents either Amenertas I. or Mutertas; it was never completely finished, and several of the parts
have never received their final polish.

[4] DIODORUS SICULUS, I. 66. It is possible that this version is only a transposition of the events,
which happened a century later, on the fall of Apries, which were narrated by Herodotus (II. clxiii.),
but it is useless to suppose with Wiedemann (*Geschichte Ægyptens von Psammetich I. bis auf Alexander*,
p. 124) that Momemphis should be corrected to Memphis. Diodorus, or rather the historian whom
he followed in this matter, having located the site of the battle between Apries and Amasis (i. 68), at
Marea, was free to place at Momemphis the battle between Psammetichus and the eleven kings, the
locality of which was not known to Herodotus.

when the fleet of the Saite king dispersed that of his rivals.[1] It is, in fact, probable that a single campaign sufficed for Psammetichus, as formerly for the Ethiopian pretenders, to get the upper hand, and that the Egyptian feudal lords submitted after one or two defeats at most,[2] hoping that, as in days gone by, when the first dash made by the new Pharaoh was over, his authority would decline, and their own would regain the ascendency. Events showed that they were deceived. Psammetichus, better served by his Hellenes than Tafnakhti or Bocchoris had been by their Libyans, or Piônkhi and Tanuatamanu by their Ethiopians, soon consolidated his rule over the country he had conquered. From 660 or 659 B.C. he so effectively governed Egypt that foreigners, and even the Assyrians themselves, commonly accorded him the title of king. The fall of the Ninevite rule had been involved in that of the feudal lords, but it was generally believed that Assur-bani-pal would leave no means untried to recall the countries of the Nile to their obedience : Psammetichus knew this, and knew also that, as soon as they were no longer detained by wars or rebellions elsewhere, the Assyrian armies would reappear in Egypt. He therefore entered into an alliance with Gyges,[3] and subsequently, perhaps, with Shamash-shumukîn also ; then, while his former suzerain was waging war in Elam and Chaldæa, he turned southwards, in 658 B.C., and took possession of the Thebaid without encountering any opposition from the Ethiopians, as his ancestor Tafnakhti had from Piônkhi-Miamun. Montumihâît negotiated this capitulation of Thebes, as he had already negotiated so many others ; in recompense for this service, he was confirmed in his office, and his queen retained her high rank.[4] A century or two earlier Psammetichus would have married one of the princesses of sacerdotal lineage, and this union would have sufficed to legalise his position ;[5] perhaps he actually associated Shapenuapît with himself by a show of marriage, but in any case he provided her with an adopted

---

[1] STRABO, XVII. i. § 18, p. 801, where this event is connected with the founding of Naucratis ; the name of Inaros, which is mixed up with this legend, is evidently a reminiscence of the Egyptian wars of Artaxerxes I. (MALLET, *Les Premiers Établissements des Grecs en Égypte*, pp. 46, 47).

[2] This is what happened in the times of Piônkhi Mariamonu, Sabaco, and Tanuatamanu ; cf. *supra*, pp. 166–181, 244–247, 396–400).

[3] For the relations between Gyges and Psammetichus, cf. what was stated *supra*, pp. 424, 425, 428. Legrain's inscription (*Deux Stèles trouvées à Karnak en février 1897*, in the *Zeitschrift*, vol. xxxv. pp. 16–19) proves that the annexation of the Thebaid and the consequent pacification of Egypt was an accomplished fact in the year IX. of Psammetichus I. The analogy of similar documents, *e.g.* the stele of the high priest Menkhopirrî (cf. *Struggle of the Nations*, p. 762), shows that the ceremony of adoption which consecrated the reunion of Upper and Lower Egypt cannot have been separated by a long interval from the completion of the reunion itself : in placing this at the end of the year VIII., we should have for the two events the respective dates of 658–657 and 657–656 B.C.

[4] The part played by Montumihâît in this affair is easily deduced : (1) from our knowledge of his conduct some years previously under Taharqa and Tanuatamanu (cf. *supra*, pp. 378, 385, 396) ; (2) from the position he occupied at Thebes, in the year IX., with regard to Shapenuapît, according to the stele of Legrain.

[5] Cf. what is stated on this subject, *supra*, pp. 164, 166.

daughter according to the custom instituted by the Ethiopian Pharaohs. She already had one daughter by adoption, whom she had received at the hands of Taharqa, and who, in changing her family, had assumed the name of Amenertas in honour of the queen who had preceded Shapenuapît: Psammetichus forced her to replace the Ethiopian princess by one of his own daughters, who was henceforth called Shapenuapît, after her new mother. A deputation of the nobles and priests of Thebes came to escort the princess from Memphis, in the month of Tybi, in the ninth year of the reign: Psammetichus formally presented her to them, and the ambassadors, having listened to his address, expatiated in the customary eulogies on his splendour and generosity. "They shall endure as long as the world lasteth; all that thou ordainest shall endure. How beautiful is that which God hath done for thee, how glorious that which thy divine father hath done for thee! He is pleased that thy double should be commemorated, he rejoices in the pronouncing of thy name, for our lord Psammetichus has made a gift to his father Amon, he has given him his eldest daughter, his beloved Nitauqrît Shapenuapît, to be his divine spouse, that she may shake the sistrum before him!" On the 28th of Tybi the princess left the harem, clothed in fine linen and adorned with ornaments of malachite, and descended to the quay, accompanied by an immense throng, to set out for her new home. Relays stationed along the river at intervals made the voyage so expeditious that at the end of sixteen days the princess came in sight of Thebes. She disembarked on the 14th of Khoiak, amid the acclamations of the people: "She comes, the daughter of the King of the South, Nitauqrît, to the dwelling of Amon, that he may possess her and unite her to himself; she comes, the daughter of the King of the North, Shapenuapît, to the temple of Karnak, that the gods may there chant her praises." As soon as the aged Shapenuapît had seen her coadjutor, "she loved her more than all things," and assigned her a dowry, the same as that which she had received from her own parents, and which she had granted to her first adopted daughter Amenertas. The magnates of Thebes—the aged Montumihâît, his son Nsiphtah, and the prophets of Amon—vied with each other in their gifts of welcome: Psammetichus, on his side, had acted most generously, and the temples of Egypt assigned to the princess an annual income out of their revenues, or bestowed upon her grants of houses and lands, in all constituting a considerable inheritance, which some-what consoled the Thebans for their subjection to a dynasty emanating from the cities of the north.[1] The rest of the principality imitated the example of

---

[1] All the facts relating to the enthronement of the princess are made known to us by the stele discovered and published by Legrain, which was first closely examined by Erman (LEGRAIN, *Deux Stèles trouvées à Karnak en février 1897*, in the *Zeitschrift*, vol. xxxv. pp. 16–19, and ERMAN, *Zu den Legrain'schen Inschriften*, in the *Zeitschrift*, vol. xxxv. pp. 24–29).

Thebes, and the whole of Egypt, from the shores of the Mediterranean to the rocks of the first cataract, once more found itself reunited under the sceptre of an Egyptian king. A small part of Nubia, the portion nearest to Elephantinê, followed this movement, but the greater part refused to cut itself off from the Ethiopians. These latter were henceforth confined to the regions along the middle course of the Nile, isolated from the rest of the world by the deserts, the Red Sea, and Egypt. It is probable that they did not give up without a struggle the hope of regaining the ground they had lost, and that their armies made more than one expedition in a northerly direction. The inhabitants of the Thebaid could hardly fail to remain faithful to them at heart, and to recognise in them the legitimate representatives of the posterity of Amon; it is possible that now and again they succeeded in penetrating as far as the ancient capital, but if so, their success was always ephemeral, and their sojourn left no permanent traces. The same causes, however, which had broken up the constituent elements, and destroyed the unity of Greater Egypt at the end of the Theban period, were still at work in Saite times to prevent the building up again of the empire. The preservation of the balance of power in this long and narrow strip of country depended on the centre of attraction and on the seat of government being nearly equidistant from the two extremities. This condition had been fulfilled as long as the court resided at Thebes; but as the removal of the seat of government to the Delta caused the loss and separation of the southern provinces, so its sudden return to the extreme south, with a temporary sojourn at Napata, necessarily produced a similar effect, and led to the speedy secession of the northern provinces. In either case, the dynasty placed at one extremity of the empire was unable to sustain for any length of time the weight depending on it at the other; when once the balance became even slightly disturbed, it could not regain its equilibrium, and there was consequently a sudden dislocation of the machinery of government.

The triumph of the Saite dynasty accomplished the final ruin of the work begun under the Papis, and brought to completion by the Amenemhâîts and the Usirtasens. Greater Egypt ceased to exist, after more than twenty centuries of glorious life, and was replaced by the Little Egypt of the first ages of history. The defeat of the military chiefs of the north, the annexation of the principality of Amon, and the final expulsion of the Ethiopians and the Asiatics had occupied scarcely nine years, but these feats constituted only the smaller part of the work Psammetichus had to accomplish: his subsequent task lay in restoring prosperity to his kingdom, or, at all events, in raising it from the state of misery into which two centuries of civil wars and invasions had plunged it. The important cities had suffered grievously: Memphis had been besieged and taken by assault by both Piônkhi and Esarhaddon, Thebes had been twice sacked by the veterans of Assur-bani-pal, and from Syenê to Pelusium there was not a township but had suffered at the hands of foreigners or of the Egyptians themselves. The country had enjoyed a moment's breathing-space under Sabaco, but the little good which this prince had been able to accomplish was effaced immediately after his death : the canals and dykes had been neglected, the supervision of the police relaxed, and the population, periodically decimated or driven to take refuge in the strongholds, had often allowed the lands to lie waste, so that famine had been superadded to the other evils under which the land already groaned. Psammetichus, having forced the feudal lords to submit to his supremacy, deprived them of the royal titles they had unduly assumed ; he no longer tolerated their habits of private warfare, but restricted them to the functions of hereditary governors, which their ancestors had exercised under the conquering dynasties of former times,[1] and this enforced peace soon allowed the rural population to devote themselves joyfully to their regular occupations. With so fertile a soil, two or three years of security, during which the fellahîn were able to sow and reap their crops free from the fear of marauding bands, sufficed to restore abundance, if not wealth, to the country, and Psammetichus succeeded in securing both these and other benefits to Egypt, thanks to the vigilant severity of his administration. He would have been unable to accomplish these reforms had he relied only on the forces which had been at the disposal of his ancestors—the native troops demoralised by poverty, and the undisciplined bands of Libyan mercenaries, which constituted the sole normal force of the Tanite and Bubastite Pharaohs and the barons of the Delta and Middle Egypt. His experience of these two classes of soldiery had decided him to look elsewhere for a less precarious support, and ever since chance had brought him in contact with the Ionians and Carians, he had surrounded himself with a regular army of Hellenic and Asiatic mercenaries. It is impossible to exaggerate the terror that the apparition of these men produced in the minds of the African peoples, or the revolution they effected, alike in peace or war, in Oriental states :[2] the charge of the Spanish soldiery among the lightly clad foot-soldiers of Mexico and Peru could not have caused more dismay than did that of the hoplites from beyond the sea among the half-naked archers and pikemen of Egypt and Libya. With their

---

[1] During the last few years records of a certain number of persons have been discovered whose names and condition prove that they were the descendants of semi-independent princes of the Ethiopian and Bubastite periods : *e.g.* a certain Akaneshu, who was prince of Sebennytos under Psammetichus I. (NAVILLE, *The Mound of the Jews and the City of Onias*, pp. 24, 25, pl. v.), and who very probably was the grandson of Akaneshu, prince of the same town under Piônkhi (cf. *supra*, p. 178, note 2) ; and a Sheshonq of Busiris, who was perhaps a descendant of Sheshonq, prince of Busiris under Piônkhi (NAVILLE, *op. cit.*, p. 28, pl. vii. *c*).

[2] For the impression caused by the hoplites, cf. MALLET, *Les Premiers Établissements des Grecs en Égypte*, pp. 38–45.

bulging corselets, the two plates of which protected back and chest, their greaves made of a single piece of bronze reaching from the ankle to the knee, their square or oval bucklers covered with metal, their heavy rounded helmets fitting closely to the head and neck, and surmounted by crests of waving plumes, they were, in truth, men of brass, invulnerable to any Oriental weapon. Drawn up in close array beneath their " tortoise," they received almost unhurt the hail of arrows and stones hurled against them by the lightly armed infantry, and then, when their own trumpet sounded the signal for attack, and they let themselves fall with their whole weight upon the masses of the enemy, brandishing their

THE SAITE FORTRESS OF DAPHNÆ.[1]

spears above the upper edge of their bucklers, there was no force of native troops or company of Mashauasha that did not waver beneath the shock, and finally give way before their attack. The Egyptians felt themselves incapable of overcoming them except by superior numbers or by stratagem, and it was the knowledge of their own hopeless inferiority which prevented the feudal lords from attempting to revenge themselves on Psammetichus. To make themselves his equals, they would have been obliged either to take a sufficient number of similar warriors into their own pay—and this they were not able to afford—or they must have won over those already in the employ of their suzerain; but the liberality with which Psammetichus treated his mercenaries gave them good cause to be faithful, even if military honour had not sufficed to keep them loyal to their employer. Psammetichus granted to them and their compatriots, who were attracted by the fame of Egypt, a concession of the fertile lands of the Delta stretching along the Pelusiac branch of the Nile, and he was careful to separate the Ionians from the Carians by the whole breadth of the river: this was a wise precaution, for their union beneath a common flag had not extinguished their inherited hatred of one another, and the authority of the general did not always suffice to prevent fatal quarrels breaking out between contingents of different nationalities.[2] They occupied, moreover, regularly entrenched camps, enclosed within massive walls, containing a collection of mud huts or houses of brick, the whole enclosure commanded by a fortress which formed the headquarters of the general

---

[1] Drawn by Faucher-Gudin, from a restoration by FL. PETRIE, Ten Years' Digging in Egypt, p. 52.
[2] HERODOTUS, II. cliv. This observation was made by KENRICK, Ancient Egypt under the Pharaohs, vol. ii. p. 223.

and staff of officers.[1] Some merchants from Miletus, emboldened by the presence of their fellow-countrymen, sailed with thirty vessels into the mouth of the Bolbitine branch of the Nile, and there founded a settlement which they named the Fort of the Milesians,[2] and, following in their wake, successive relays of emigrants arrived to reinforce the infant colony. The king entrusted a certain number of Egyptian children to the care of these Greek settlers, to be instructed in their language,[3] and the inter- preters thus educated in their schools increased in proportion as the bonds of commercial and friendly intercourse between Greece and Egypt became strengthened, so that ere long, in the towns of the Delta, they constituted a regular

EGYPTIAN GREEK.[4]

class, whose function was to act as intermediaries between the two races. By thus bringing his subjects in contact with an active, industrious, and enterprising nation, full of youthful vigour, Psammetichus no doubt hoped to inspire them with some of the qualities which he discerned in the colonists, but Egypt during the last two centuries had suffered too much at the hands of foreigners of all kinds to be favourably disposed to these new-comers. It would have been different had they presented themselves in humble guise like the Asiatics and Africans to whom Egypt had opened her doors so freely after the XVIIIth dynasty, and if they had adopted the obsequious manners of the Phœnician and Hebrew merchants; but they landed from their ships fully equipped for war, and, proud of their own courage and ability, they vied with the natives of the ancient race, whether of plebeian or noble birth, for

EGYPTIAN GREEK.[5]

the favour of the sovereign. Their language, their rude military customs,

---

[1] Such as that at Daphnæ, whose ruins at Tel-Defenneh have been excavated and described by W. FLINDERS PETRIE, *Nebesheh (Am) and Defenneh (Tahpanhes)*, pp. 47–67.

[2] STRABO, XVII. i. § 18, p. 801, where the account of the founding of the *Fort of the Milesians*, Μιλησίων τεῖχος, is mixed up with that of the foundation of Naucratis. Mallet is inclined to believe this event prior to the Saite epoch (*Les Premiers Établ. des Grecs en Égypte*, pp. 28–34, 37, 38, etc.).

[3] HERODOTUS, II. cliv. Diodorus, or rather the historian whom he follows, assures us that Psammetichus went still further, and gave his own children a Greek education (i. 66); what is possible and even probable, is, that he had them taught Greek. A bronze Apis in the Gizeh Museum was dedicated by an interpreter who inscribed on it a bilingual inscription in hieroglyphics and Carian (MARIETTE, *Monuments divers*, pl. 106 a, and p. 30; cf. MASPERO, *Guide du Visiteur*, p. 180, No. 1576, and SAYCE, *The Karian Language and Inscriptions*, in *Trans.* of Bibl. Arch. Soc., vol. ix. pp. 126, 146).

[4] Drawn by Faucher-Gudin, from FL. PETRIE, *Naukratis*, vol. i. pl. i. 2, and p. 36. The original statuette in alabaster is now in the Gizeh Museum; the Cyprian style of the figure is easily recognised.

[5] Drawn by Faucher-Gudin, from FL. PETRIE, *Naukratis*, vol. i. pl. ii. 1. The original limestone statuette is in the Gizeh Museum.

2 K

their cunning devices in trade, even the astonishment they manifested at the civilisation of the country, rendered them objects of disdain, as well as of jealous hatred to the Egyptian. The food of which they partook made them unclean in native estimation, and the horrified fellah shunned contact with them from fear of defiling himself, refusing to eat with them, or to use the same knife or cooking-vessel:[1] the scribes and members of the higher classes, astonished at their ignorance, treated them like children with no past history, whose ancestors a few generations back had been mere savages.

Although unexpressed at first, this hostility towards the Hellenes was not long in manifesting itself openly. The Saite tradition attributed it to a movement of wounded vanity. Psammetichus, to recompense the prowess of his Ionian and Carian soldiers, had attached them to his own person, and assigned to them the post of honour on the right wing when the army was drawn up for review or in battle array.[2] They reaped thus the double advantage of the glory, which they greatly prized, and of the higher pay attached to the title of body-guard,[3] but the troops who had hitherto enjoyed these advantages were naturally indignant at losing them, and began to murmur. One particularly galling circumstance at last caused their discontent to break out. The eastern and southern frontiers of Egypt were conterminous with those of two conquering empires, Assyria and Ethiopia, and on the west the Libyan tribes along the shores of the Mediterranean were powerful enough to demand constant vigilance on the part of the border garrisons. Psammetichus, among other reforms, had reorganised the ancient system of defence. While placing outposts at the entrance to the passes leading from the desert into the Nile valley,[4] he had concentrated considerable masses of troops at the three most vulnerable points—the outlets of the road to Syria, the country surrounding Lake Mareotis, and the first cataract; he had fortified Daphnæ, near the old town of Zalu, as a defence against the Assyrians, Marea against the Libyan Bedâwin, and Elephantinê against the Ethiopians. These advanced posts had been garrisoned with native troops who were quartered there for a year at a time. To be condemned to such an exile for so long a period raised in them a sense of profound indignation, but when the king apparently forgot them and left them there three years without sending other troops to relieve them, their anger knew no bounds. They resolved to put an end to such treatment, and as the hope of a successful

---

[1] HERODOTUS, II. xli.; cf. WIEDEMANN, *Herodots Zweites Buch*, pp. 187–193.

[2] DIODORUS SICULUS, i. 67, where it is stated that it was during the Syrian war that the king thus honoured his mercenary troops. Wiedemann thinks this is an erroneous inference drawn from the passage of Herodotus (II. xxx.), in which he explains the meaning of the word Asmakh (*Herodots Zweites Buch*, pp. 128, 129).

[3] HERODOTUS, II. clxviii., where the details of this high pay are given at length; cf. *infra*, p. 500.

[4] For these posts established at the entrances to the valley, cf. *Dawn of Civilization*, pp. 293, 294.

rebellion seemed but small, they decided to leave the country.   Two hundred and forty thousand of them assembled on a given day with their arms and baggage, and marched in good order towards Ethiopia.   Psammetichus, warned of their intentions when it was too late, hastened after them with a handful of followers, and coming up with them, besought them not to desert their national gods, their wives, and their children.   He had nearly prevailed on them to return, when one soldier, with a significant gesture, intimated that while manhood lasted they had power to create new families wherever they might chance to dwell.[1]   The details of this story betray the popular legend, but nevertheless have a basis of truth.   The inscriptions from the time of Psammetichus onwards never mention the Mashauasha, while their name and their exploits constantly recur in the history of the preceding dynasties : henceforth they and their chiefs vanish from sight, and discord and brigandage simultaneously cease in the Egyptian nomes.   It was very probably the most turbulent among these auxiliaries who left the country in the circumstances above narrated : since they could not contest the superiority of their Greek rivals, they concluded that their own part was played out, and rather than be relegated to the second rank, they preferred to quit the land in a body.[2]   Psammetichus, thus deprived of their support at the moment when Egypt had more than ever need of all her forces to regain her rightful position in the world, reorganised the military system as best he could.   He does not seem to have relied much upon the contingents from Upper Egypt, to whom was doubtless entrusted the defence of the Nubian frontier, and who could not be withdrawn from their posts without danger of invasion or revolt.   But the source of imminent peril did not lie in this direction, where Ethiopia, exhausted by the wars of Taharqa and Tanuatamanu, perhaps needed repose even more than Egypt itself, but rather on the Asiatic side, where Assur-bani-pal, in spite of the complications constantly arising in Karduniash and Elam, had by no means renounced his claims to the suzerainty of Egypt.   The Pharaoh divided the feudatory militia of the Delta into two classes, which resided apart in different sets of nomes.   The first group, who were popularly called Hermotybies, were stationed at Busiris, Sais, and Khemmis, in the island of Prosopitis, and in one half of Natho—in fact, in the district which for the last century had formed the centre of the principality of the Saite dynasty : perhaps they were mostly of Libyan origin,

---

[1] HERODOTUS, II. xxx.

[2] The classical references to this emigration were collected a century ago by HEEREN, *Commentatio de Militum Ægyptiorum in Æthiopiam Migratione*, in the *Mémoires de l'Académie de Göttingen, Phil. Hist. Classe*, vol. xii. p. 48.   Their authenticity has been controverted several times by Wiedemann (*Die Griechische Inschrift von Abusimbel*, in the *Rheinisches Museum*, 1880, pp. 365, 366; *Geschichte Ægyptens*, pp. 134–138, *Herodots Zweites Buch*, pp. 128–133 ; *Ægypt. Gesch.*, pp. 617, 618); I have elsewhere given my reasons for the conclusions I have adopted in the text (*Études de Myth. et d'Arch. Égyptiennes*, vol. iii. pp. 398–402 ; cf. MALLET, *Les Premiers Établissements des Grecs en Égypte*, pp. 77–82).

and represented the bands of Mashauasha who, from father to son, had served under Tafnakhti and his descendants. Popular report numbered them at 160,000 men, all told, and the total number of the other class, known as the Calasiries, at 250,000; these latter belonged, in my opinion, to the pure Egyptian race, and were met with at Thebes, while the troops of the north, who were more generally called out, were scattered over the territory which formerly supported the Tanite and Bubastite kings, and latterly Pakruru, and which comprised the towns of Bubastis, Aphthis, Tanis, Mendes, Sebennytos, Athribis, Pharbæthos, Thmuis, Onuphis, Anysis, and Myecphoris. Each year one thousand Hermotybies and one thousand Calasiries were chosen to form the royal body-guard, and these received daily five minæ of bread apiece, two minæ of beef, and four bowls of wine; the jealousy which had been excited by the Greek troops was thus lessened, as well as the discontent provoked by the emigration.[1] The King of Napata gladly welcomed the timely reinforcements which arrived to fill up the vacancies in his army and among his people, weakened by a century of rapid changes, and generously gave them permission to conquer for themselves some territory in the possession of his enemies! Having driven out the barbarians, they established themselves in the peninsula formed by the White and Blue Niles, and their numbers increased so greatly that in course of time they became a considerable nation. They called themselves Asmakh, the men who stand on the king's left hand, in memory of the affront put upon them, and which they had avenged by their self-exile: Greek travellers and geographers called them sometimes Automoli, sometimes Sembrites, names which clung to them till almost the beginning of our present era.[2]

This departure of the Mashauasha was as the last blast of wind after a storm: the swell subsided by degrees, and peace reigned in the interior.

[1] HERODOTUS, II. clxiv.–clxviii.; cf. WIEDEMANN, Herodots Zweites Buch, pp. 573–580. Calasiris is, as Birch saw fifty years ago (Lettre à M. Letronne sur le mot Calasiris, in the Revue Archéologique, 1847, vol. iv. p. 195, et seq.), the exact transcription of Khala-shiri, Khala-shere, signifying young man. The meaning and original of the word transcribed Hermotybies by Herodotus, and Hermotymbies according to a variant given by Stephen of Byzantium, is as yet unknown, but it seems to me to conceal a title analogous to that of Hir-mazaiu, and to designate what remained of Libyan soldiers in Egypt. This organisation of the army is described by Herodotus as existing in his own days, and there were Calasiries and Hermotybies in the Egyptian contingent which accompanied the army of Mardonius to Greece (HERODOTUS, II. xxxii.); it is nowhere stated that it was the work of Psammetichus, but everything points to the conclusion that it was so, at all events in the form in which it was known to the Greeks.

[2] HERODOTUS, II. xxx.; cf. MALLET, Les Premiers Établissements des Grecs en Égypte, pp. 95, 96. The name Asmakh is sometimes given as Askham in the manuscripts, which has led Wiedemann (op. cit., pp. 128, 129) to reject the etymology proposed by M. de Horrack (Lettre à propos d'un mot égyptien significant la gauche, récemment signalé par M. F. Chabas, in the Revue Archéologique, 1862, vol. ii. pp. 368, 369), according to which Asmakh would be the exact transcription of Smahi, the left. It is certain that the Egyptians, whatever may have been the real signification of the name, had in their minds the word indicated by M. de Horrack, and the very expression used by Herodotus, οἱ ἐξ ἀριστερῆς χειρός, proves it: it was doubtless this popular etymology which suggested to the romance-writers the original cause they assigned to the quarrel.

Thebes accommodated itself as best it could to the new order of things under the nominal administration of the Divine Spouses, the two Shapenuapîts. Building works were recommenced at all points where it appeared necessary, and the need of restoration was indeed pressing after the disorders occasioned by the Assyrian invasion and the Ethiopian suzerainty. At Karnak, and in the great temples on both banks of the Nile, Psammetichus, respecting the fiction which assigned the chief authority to the Pallacides, effaced himself in favour of them, allowing them to claim all the merit of the work; in the cities they erected small chapels, in which they are portrayed as queens fulfilling their sacerdotal functions, humbly escorted by the viceroy who in other respects exercised the real power.[1] The king's zeal for restoration is manifest all along the Nile, at Coptos,[2] Abydos,[3] and in the plains of the Delta, which are crowded with memorials of him. His two favourite capitals were Memphis and Sais, on both of which he impartially lavished his favours. At Memphis he built the propylons on the south side of the temple of Phtah, and the court in which the living Apis took his exercise and was fed: this court was surrounded by a colonnade, against the pillars of which were erected statues twelve cubits high, probably representing Osiris as in the Ramesseum and at Medinet-Habu.[4] Apis even when dead also received his share of attention. Since the days when Ramses II. had excavated the subterranean Serapeum as a burial-place of the sacred bulls, no subsequent Pharaoh who had reigned at Memphis had failed to embellish their common tomb, and to celebrate with magnificence their rites of sepulture. The body of the Apis, carefully embalmed, was sealed up in a coffin or sarcophagus of hard stone, the mouth of the vault was then walled up, and against the fresh masonry, at the foot of the neighbouring rocks, on the very floor of the passage, or wherever there was a clear space available, the high dignitaries, the workmen or the priests who had taken any part in the ceremonial, set up a votive stele calling down upon themselves and their families divine benedictions. The gallery was transformed by degrees into a kind of record-office, where each dynasty in turn recorded its name, whenever a fresh apotheosis afforded them the opportunity: these records were discovered in our own time by Mariette, almost perfect in spite of the destroying hand of men, and comprised inscriptions by the Bubastites, by Bocchoris, and even by the Ethiopians. Taharqa, when menaced by the Assyrians, had stayed at Memphis, only a year before his death, in the interval between two

---

[1] PETRIE, *Koptos*, pl. xxxvi. 1, and p. 17; the fragment seems to me to belong to Psammetichus I.

[2] MARIETTE, *Abydos*, vol. i. pl. ii. *b*, where Psammetichus is accompanied by Nitauqrît.

[3] The first Egyptologists attributed the prenominal cartouche of Psammetichus I. to Psammetichus II., and *vice versâ*: this error must always be kept in mind in referring to their works.

[4] HERODOTUS, II. cliii.; cf. DIODORUS, i. 67, where the propylons attributed to Psammetichus I. are those on the east. Strabo (XVII. i. § 31, p. 807) also describes the court.

campaigns, in order to bury an Apis, and Psammetichus likewise took care not to neglect this part of his regal duties.   He at first was content to imitate his predecessors, but a subsidence having occurred in that part of the Serapeum where the Apis who had died in the twentieth year of his reign reposed, he ordered his engineers to bore another gallery in a harder vein of limestone, and he performed the opening ceremony in his fifty-second year.   It was the commencement of a thorough restoration. The vaults in which the sacred bulls were entombed were severally inspected, the wrappings were repaired together with the mummy cases, the masonry of the chapel was strength- ened, and the building endowed with woods, stuffs, perfumes, and the necessary oils.[1]   No less activity apparently was displayed at Sais, the native home and favourite residence of the Pharaoh ; but all the monuments which adorned the place,

CHAMBER AND SARCOPHAGUS OF AN APIS.[2]

including the temple of Nît, and the royal palace, have been entirely destroyed ; the enclosing wall of unbaked bricks alone remains, and here and there, amid the *debris* of the houses, may be seen some heaps of shattered stone where the public buildings once stood.   On several blocks the name and titles of Psam- metichus may yet be deciphered, and there are few cities in the Delta which cannot make a similar show.[3]   From one end of the Nile valley to the other the quarries were reopened, and the arts, stimulated by the orders which flowed in,

[1] MARIETTE, *Renseignements sur les soixante-quatre Apis trouvés dans les souterrains du Sérapéum*, in the *Bulletin Archéologique de l'Athénæum Français*, 1855, pp. 47, 48, and vol. ii. p. 78; cf. *Le Séra- péum de Memphis*, 2nd edit., vol. i. pp. 118–121.

[2] Drawn by Faucher-Gudin, from an engraving published in MARIETTE, *Choix de Monuments du Sérapeum*, pl. vi.

[3] For the ruins of Sais, see the descriptions of CHAMPOLLION, *Lettres écrites d'Égypte*, 3rd edit., pp. 50–53, and pls. i., ii., and of WILKINSON, *Topography of Thebes and General Views of Egypt*, p. 296, as well as the plan of G. FOUCART, *Notes prises dans le Delta*, in the *Recueil de Travaux*, vol. xx. p. 169.

soon flourished anew. The engraving of hieroglyphics and the art of painting both attained a remarkable degree of elegance; fine statues and bas-reliefs were executed in large numbers, and a widely spread school of art was developed. The local artists had scrupulously observed and handed down the traditions which obtained in the time of the Pyramids, and more especially those of the

THE GREAT GALLERY OF THE SERAPEUM.[1]

first Theban period; even the few fragments that have come down to us of the works of these artists in the age of the Ramessides recall rather the style of the VIth and XIIth dynasties than that of their Theban contemporaries. Their style, brought to perfection by evident imitation of the old Memphite masters, pleases us by its somewhat severe elegance, the taste shown in the choice of detail, and the extraordinary skill displayed in the working of the stone. The Memphites had by preference used limestone for their sculpture, the Thebans red and grey granite or sandstone; but the artists of the age of Psammetichus unhesitatingly attacked basalt, breccia, or serpentine, and obtained marvellous effects from these finely grained materials of regular and even texture. The artistic renaissance which they brought to its height had been already inaugurated under the Ethiopians, and many of the statues we possess of the reign of Taharqa are examples of excellent workmanship. That of Amenertas was over-praised at the time of its discovery; the face, half buried

---

[1] Drawn by Faucher-Gudin, from an engraving of Devéria, published in MARIETTE, *Choix de Monuments du Sérapéum*, pl. v.

by the wig which we usually associate with the statues of the goddesses, has a dull and vacant expression in spite of its set smile, and the modelling of the figure is rather weak, but nevertheless there is something easy and refined in the gracefulness of the statue as a whole. A statuette of another "Divine Spouse," though mutilated and unfinished, is pleasing from its greater breadth of style,[1] although such breadth is rarely found in the works of this school, which toned down, elongated, and attenuated the figure till it often lost in vigour what it gained in distinction. The one point in which the Saite artists made a real advance, was in the treatment of the heads of their models. The expression is often refined and idealised as in the case of older works, but occasionally the portraiture is exact even to coarseness. It was not the idealised likeness of

MEMPHITE BAS-RELIEF OF THE SAITE EPOCH.[2]

Montumihâît which the artist wished to portray, but Montumihâît himself, with his low forehead, his small close-set eyes, his thin cheeks, and the deep lines about his nose and mouth.[3] And besides this, the wrinkles, the crows' feet, the cranial projections, the shape of ear and neck, are brought out with minute fidelity. A statue was no longer, as in earlier days, merely a piece of sacred stone, the support of the divine or human double, in which artistic value was an accessory of no importance and was esteemed only as a guarantee of resemblance: without losing aught of its religious significance, a statue henceforward became a work of art, admired and prized for the manner in which the sculptor faithfully represented his model, as well as for its mystic utility.

The reign of Psammetichus lasted till nearly the end of the century, and was marked by peace both at home and abroad. No doubt skirmishes of some kind took place in Lydia and Nubia, but we know nothing of them, nor have we any account of engagements with the Asiatics which from time to time must have taken place during this reign. Psammetichus followed with a vigilant eye the

---

[1] See this statue reproduced, *supra*, p. 491.

[2] Drawn by Boudier, from a heliogravure in MARIETTE, *Monuments Divers*, pl. 35 b. The bas-relief was worked into the masonry of a house in Memphis in the Byzantine period, and it was in order to fit it to the course below that the masons bevelled the lower part of it.

[3] See the portrait in question, *supra*, p. 386.

Queen Amenertas

Gizeh Museum

Printed by Wittmann in Paris (France)

revolutionary changes beyond the isthmus, actuated at first by the fear of an
offensive movement on the part of Syria, and when that ceased to be a danger,
by the hope of one day recovering, in Southern Syria, at all events, that
leading position which his predecessors had held so long. Tradition asserts

THE RUINS OF SAIS.[1]

that he wisely confined his ambition to the conquest of the Philistine
Pentapolis; it is even reported that he besieged Ashdod for twenty-nine
years before gaining possession of it. If we disregard the cipher, which
is evidently borrowed from some popular romance, the fact in itself is in
no way improbable. Ashdod was a particularly active community, and had
played a far more important part in earlier campaigns than any other
member of the Pentapolis. It possessed outside the town proper, which
was situated some little distance from the coast, a seaport similar to that
of Gaza, and of sufficient size to shelter a whole fleet. Whoever held
this harbour could exercise effective control over the main routes leading
from Syria into Egypt. Psammetichus probably undertook this expedition
towards the end of his life, when the victories gained by the Medes had
demonstrated the incapacity of Assyria to maintain the defence of her distant

[1] Drawn by Boudier, from a photograph by Golénischeff, taken in 1888.

provinces.[1] The attack of the Scythians, which might have proved dangerous to Egypt, had it been pushed far enough, had left her unharmed, and was in the end even advantageous to her.[2] It was subsequent to the retreat of the barbarians, no doubt, that Psammetichus sent his troops into Philistia and succeeded in annexing the whole or part of it. After this success he was content to wait and watch the course of events. The surprising revival of Egypt must have had the effect of infusing fresh life into the Egyptian factions existing in all the autonomous states, and in the prefectures of Syria. The appearance of the Pharaoh's troops, and the toleration of their presence within the territory of the Assyrian empire, aroused on all sides the hope of deliverance, and incited the malcontents to take some immediate action.

We do not know what may have happened at Tyre and Sidon, or among the peoples of Edom and Arabia, but Judah, at any rate, under the rule of Josiah, carefully abstained from any action inconsistent with the pledge of fidelity which it had given to Assyria. Indeed, the whole kingdom was completely absorbed in questions of a theological nature, and the agitations which affected the religious life of the nation reacted on its political life as well. Josiah, as he grew older, began to identify himself more and more with the doctrines taught by the prophets, and, thanks to his support, the party which sought to complete the reforms outlined by Hezekiah gained fresh recruits every day. The opposition which they had formerly aroused among the priests of the temple had gradually died out, partly as the result of genuine conviction, and partly because the priests had come to realise that the establishment of a single exclusive sanctuary would work for their own interest and advantage. The high priest Hilkiah took up the line followed by Jeremiah, and was supported by a number of influential personages such as Shaphan the scribe, son of Azaliah, Ahikam, Achbor son of Micaiah, and a prophetess named Huldah, who had married the keeper of the royal wardrobe. The terrors of the Scythian invasion had oppressed the hearts and quickened the zeal of the orthodox. Judah, they declared, had no refuge save Jahveh alone; all hope was lost if it persisted in the doctrines which had aroused against the faithless the implacable wrath of Jahveh; it must renounce at once those idols and superstitious rites with which His worship had been disfigured, and overthrow the altars which were to be found in every part of

---

[1] HERODOTUS, II. clvii.; DIODORUS SICULUS, i. 67. At one time I was inclined to explain this period of twenty-nine years by assuming that the fall of Ashdod took place in the twenty-ninth year of the king's reign, and that Herodotus had mistaken the date of its surrender for the duration of the siege: such an hypothesis is, however, unnecessary, since it is very probable that we have here one of those exaggerated estimates of time so dear to the hearts of popular historians. If we are to believe the account given by Diodorus, it was in Syria that Psammetichus granted the honour of a place in the right wing of his army to the Greek mercenaries: the capture of Ashdod must, in this case, have occurred before the emigration of the native troops. In *Jer.* xxv. 20, reference is made to "the remnant of Ashdod," in the fourth year of Jehoiakim, *i.e.* about 603 B.C., and the decadence of the city is generally attributed to the war with Egypt; it might with equal probability be ascribed to the Scythian invasion.

[2] Cf. what has been said in regard to the Scythian invasion on p. 479, *supra*.

the country in order to concentrate all its devotion on the temple of Solomon. In a word, Judah must return to an observance of the strict letter of the law, as it had been followed by their forefathers. But as this venerable code was not to be found either in the "Book of the Covenant" or in any of the other writings held sacred by Israel, the question naturally arose as to where it was now hidden. In the eighteenth year of his reign, Josiah sent Shaphan the scribe to the temple in order to audit the accounts of the sums collected at the gates for the maintenance of the building. After the accounts had been checked, Hilkiah suddenly declared that he had "found the Book of the Law" in the temple, and thereupon handed the document to Shaphan, who perused it forthwith. On his return to the palace, the scribe made his report: "Thy servants have emptied out the money that was found in the house, and have delivered it into the hand of the workmen;" then he added, "Hilkiah the priest hath delivered me a book," and proceeded to read it to the king. When the latter had heard the words contained in this Book of the Law, he was seized with anguish, and rent his garments; then, unable to arrive at any decision by himself, he sent Hilkiah, Shaphan, Ahikam, Achbor, and Asaiah to inquire of Jahveh for him and for his people, "for great is the wrath of the Lord that is kindled against us, because our fathers have not hearkened unto the words of this book, to do according unto all that which is written concerning us." The envoys betook themselves not to the official oracle or the recognised prophets, but to a woman, the prophetess Huldah, who was attached to the court in virtue of her husband's office; and she bade them, in the name of the Most High, to summon a meeting of the faithful, and, after reading the new code to them, to call upon all present to promise that they would henceforth observe its ordinances: thus Jahveh would be appeased, and since the king had "rent his garments and wept before Me, I also have heard thee, saith Jahveh. Therefore, behold, I will gather thee to thy fathers, and thou shalt be gathered to thy grave in peace." Josiah thereupon having summoned the elders of Judah and Jerusalem, went up into the temple, and there, standing on the platform, he read the Book of the Law in the presence of the whole people.[1]

It dealt with questions which had been frequent subjects of debate in prophetic circles since the days of Hezekiah, and the anonymous writer who had compiled it was so strongly imbued with the ideas of Jeremiah, and had so closely followed his style, that some have been inclined to ascribe the work to Jeremiah himself.[2] It has always been a custom among Orientals to affirm

---

[1] 2 *Kings* xxii. 3–20; xxiii. 1, 2. The narrative has undergone slight interpolation in places, *e.g.* verses 4*b*, 5*a*, 6, and 7, where the compiler has made it harmonise with events previously recorded in connection with the reign of Joash (2 *Kings* xii. 6–16; cf. p. 101, *supra*). The beginning of Huldah's prophecy was suppressed, when the capture of Jerusalem proved that the reform of divine worship had not succeeded in averting the wrath of Jahveh. It probably contained directions to read the *Book of the Covenant* to the people, and to persuade them to adopt its precepts, followed by a promise to save Judah provided it remained faithful to its engagements.

[2] RENAN, *Histoire du Peuple d'Israel*, vol. iii. pp. 233–236.

that any work for which they profess particular esteem was discovered in the temple of a god; the Egyptian priests, for instance, invented an origin of this nature for the more important chapters of their Book of the Dead, and for the leading treatises in the scientific literature of Egypt.[1] The author of the Book of the Law had ransacked the distant past for the name of the leader who had delivered Israel from captivity in Egypt. He told how Moses, when he began to feel the hand of death upon him, determined to declare in Gilead the decrees which Jahveh had delivered to him for the guidance of His people.[2] In these ordinances the indivisible nature of God, and His jealousy of any participation of other deities in the worship of His people, are strongly emphasised. " Ye shall surely destroy all the places wherein the nations which ye shall possess served their gods, upon the high mountains and upon the hills, and under every green tree : and ye shall break down their altars, and dash in pieces their pillars, and burn their Asherim with fire ; and ye shall hew down the graven images of their gods; and ye shall destroy their name out of that place." [3] Even were a prophet or dreamer of dreams to arise in the midst of the faithful and direct them by a sign or a miracle to turn aside after those accursed gods, they must not follow the teaching of these false guides, not even if the sign or miracle actually came to pass, but must seize and slay them. Even " if thy brother, the son of thy mother, or thy son, or thy daughter, or the wife of thy bosom, or thy friend which is as thine own soul, entice thee secretly, saying, Let us go and serve other gods, . . . thou shalt not consent unto him nor hearken unto him : neither shall thine eye pity him, neither shalt thou spare, neither shalt thou conceal him : but thou shalt surely kill him; thine hand shall be first upon him to put him to death, and afterwards the hand of all the people. And thou shalt stone him with stones that he die ; because he hath sought to draw thee away from Jahveh! " [4] And this Jahveh was not the Jahveh of any special place. He was not the Jahveh of Bethel, or of Dan, or of Mizpah, or of Geba, or of

---

[1] Cf. the instances which I have mentioned on pp. 224, 225, *supra*.

[2] Even St. Jerome (*Contra Jovinianum*, i. 5) and St. John Chrysostom (*Homilia de Matth.*, 9, p. 135*b*) admitted that Deuteronomy was the book discovered by Hilkiah in the temple during the reign of Josiah, and this view is accepted at present, though it is applied, not to the book of Deuteronomy as it appears in the Pentateuch, but rather to the nucleus of this book, and especially chaps. xii.–xxvi. For an accurate statement of the whole question, and an indication of the issues raised by it which are still undecided, I cannot do better than refer the reader to one of the numerous text-books on the subject, such as Cornill's *Einleitung in das Alte Testament*, 2nd edit., pp. 29–45, or Driver's *Introduction to the Literature of the Old Testament*, 5th edit., pp. 65–96. The numerous editions of these works present an almost annual record of the existing state of critical knowledge. I may here repeat that I am not writing the individual history of the Hebrews, but a general history of the nations of the East. I confine myself to using such results of modern criticism as seem to me calculated to explain the march of political events, without laying stress on questions which belong more exclusively to the history of religious ideas.

[3] *Deut.* xii. 2, 3.   [4] *Deut.* xiii. 1–10.

Beersheba; He is simply Jahveh.[1] Yet the seat of His worship was not a matter of indifference to Him. " Unto the place which Jahveh shall choose out of all your tribes to put His name there, even unto His habitation shall ye seek, and thither shalt thou come : and thither shall ye bring your . . . sacrifices and your tithes." [2] Jerusalem is not mentioned by name, but the reference to it was clear, since every one knew that the suppression of the provincial sanctuaries must necessarily benefit it. One part of the new code dealt with the relations between different members of the community. The king was to approximate as closely as possible to the ideal priest; he was not to lift up his heart above his brethren, nor set his mind on the possession of many chariots, horses, or wives, but must continually read the law of God and ponder over His ordinances, and observe them word for word all the days of his life.[3] Even in time of war he was not to put his trust in his soldiers or in his own personal valour; here again he must allow himself to be guided by Jahveh, and must undertake nothing without first consulting Him through the medium of His priests. The poor,[4] the widow, and the orphan,[5] the bondservant,[6] and even the stranger within the gates—in remembrance of the bondage in Egypt [7] —were all specially placed under the divine protection; every Jew who had become enslaved to a fellow-countryman was to be set at liberty at the end of six years, and was to receive a small allowance from his master which would ensure him for a time against starvation.[8] The regulations in regard to divine worship had not as yet been drawn up in that spirit of hair-splitting minuteness which, later on, became a characteristic of Hebrew legislation. Only three great festivals are mentioned in the Book of the Law. The Passover was celebrated in the month of Abîb, when the grain is in the ear, and had already come to be regarded as commemorative of the Exodus; but the other two, the Feast of Weeks and the Feast of Tabernacles, were merely associated with the agricultural seasons, and took place, the former seven weeks after the beginning of the harvest, the latter after the last of the crops had been housed.[9] The

---

[1] *Deut.* vi. 4. The expression found in *Zech.* xiv. 9 was borrowed from the second of the introductions added to *Deuteronomy* at a later date ; the phrase harmonises so closely with the main purpose of the book itself, that there can be no objection to employing it here.

[2] *Deut.* xii. 5, 6.

[3] *Deut.* xvii. 14–20 ; cf. xx. 1–9 for the regulations in regard to the levying of troops.

[4] As to the poor, and the charitable obligations towards them imposed by their common religion, cf. *Deut.* xv. 7–11 ; as to the rights of the hired servant, cf. xxiv. 14, 15.

[5] *Deut.* xxiv. 17–22 forbids the taking of a widow's clothing in pledge, and lays down regulations in regard to gleaning permitted to widows and orphans (cf. *Lev.* xix. 9, 10); reference is also made to their share in triennial tithe (*Deut.* xiv. 28, 29; xxvi. 12, 13) and in the solemn festivals (*Deut.* xvi. 11–14).

[6] Slaves were allowed to share in the rejoicings during the great festivals (*Deut.* xvi. 11, 14), and certain rights were accorded to women taken prisoners in war who had become their captors' concubines (*Deut.* xxi. 10–14).

[7] Participation of the stranger in the triennial tithe (*Deut.* xiv. 28, 29 ; xxvi. 12, 13).

[8] *Deut.* xv. 12–18.   [9] *Deut.* xvi. 1–17.

claim of the priest to a share in the victim and in the offerings made on various occasions is maintained, and the lawgiver allows him to draw a similar benefit from the annual and triennial tithes which he imposes on corn and wine and on the firstborn of cattle, the produce of this tithe being devoted to a sort of family festival celebrated in the Holy Place.[1]   The priest was thus placed on the same footing as the poor, the widow, the orphan, and the stranger, and his influence was but little greater than it had been in the early days of the monarchy.   It was to the prophet and not to the priest that the duty belonged of directing the public conscience in all those cases for which the law had made no provision.   "I will put My words into his mouth (said Jahveh), and he shall speak unto them all that I shall command him.   And it shall come to pass that whosoever will not hearken unto My words which he shall speak in My name, I will require it of him.   But the prophet which shall speak a word presumptuously in My name, which I have not commanded him to speak, or that shall speak in the name of other gods, that same prophet shall die.   And if thou say in thine heart, How shall we know the word which the Lord hath not spoken?—when a prophet speaketh in the name of Jahveh, if the thing follow not, nor come to pass, that is the thing which Jahveh hath not spoken: the prophet hath spoken it presumptuously; thou shalt not be afraid of him."[2]

When the reading of the law had ended, Josiah implored the people to make a covenant with Jahveh; that is to say, "to walk after Jahveh, and to keep His commandments, and His testimonies, and His statutes, with all their hearts and all their souls, to confirm the words of this covenant that were written in this book."   The final words, which lingered in every ear, contained imprecations of even more terrible and gloomy import than those with which the prophets had been wont to threaten Judah.   "If thou wilt not hearken unto the voice of Jahveh thy God, to observe to do all His commandments and His statutes which I command thee this day; then all these curses shall come upon thee, and overtake thee.   Cursed shalt thou be in the city, and cursed shalt thou be in the field.   Cursed shall be thy basket and thy kneading-trough.   Cursed shall be the fruit of thy body, and the fruit of thy ground, the increase of thy kine, and the young of thy flock. . . .   Thou shalt betroth a wife, and another man shall lie with her: thou shalt build an house, and shalt not dwell therein: thou shalt plant a vineyard, and shalt not use the fruit thereof.   Thine ox shall be slain before thine eyes, and thou shalt not eat thereof. . . . Thy sons and thy daughters shall be given unto another people; and thine eyes shall look, and fail with longing for them all the day:

---

[1] *Deut.* xviii. 1–8; as to the share in the triennial tithe, cf. *Deut.* xiv. 28, 29; xxvi. 12, 13.
[2] *Deut.* xviii. 9-22.

and there shall be naught in the power of thine hand. . . . Jahveh shall bring a nation against thee from far, from the end of the earth, as the eagle flieth ; a nation whose tongue thou shalt not understand ; a nation of fierce countenance, which shall not regard the person of the old, nor show favour to the young." This enemy was to burn and destroy everything : " and he shall besiege thee in all thy gates, throughout all thy land, which Jahveh thy God hath given thee. And thou shalt eat the fruit of thine own body, the flesh of thy sons and of thy daughters . . . in the straitness wherewith thine enemies shall straiten thee." Those who escape must depart into captivity, and there endure for many a long year the tortures of direst slavery ; " thy life shall hang in doubt before thee ; and thou shalt fear night and day, and shalt have none assurance of thy life : in the morning thou shalt say, Would God it were even ! and at even thou shalt say, Would God it were morning ! for the fear of thine heart which thou shalt fear, and for the sight of thine eyes which thou shalt see." [1] The assembly took the oath required of them, and the king at once displayed the utmost zeal in exacting literal performance of the ordinances contained in the Book of the Law. His first step was to purify the temple : Hilkiah and his priests overthrew all the idols contained in it, and all the objects that had been fashioned in honour of strange gods—the Baals, the Asherim, and all the Host of Heaven—and, carrying them out of Jerusalem into the valley of the Kidron, cast them into the flames, and scattered the ashes upon the place where all the filth of the city was cast out. The altars and the houses of the Sodomites which defiled the temple courts were demolished, the chariots of the sun broken in pieces, and the horses of the god sent to the stables of the king's chamberlain ; * the sanctuaries and high places which had been set up at the gates of the city, in the public places, and along the walls were razed to the ground, and the Tophet, where the people made their children pass through the fire, was transformed into a common sewer. The provincial sanctuaries shared the fate of those of the capital ; in a short time, from Geba to Beersheba, there remained not one of those " high places," at which the ancestors of the nation and their rulers had offered prayers for generations past. The wave of reform passed even across the frontier and was borne into the Assyrian province of Samaria ; the temple and image which Jeroboam had set up at Bethel were reduced to ashes, and human bones were burnt upon the altar to desecrate it beyond possibility of purification.[2] The governor offered

---

[1] *Deut.* xxviii. The two sets of imprecations (xxvii., xxviii.) which terminate the actual work are both of later redaction, but the original MS. undoubtedly ended with some analogous formula. I have quoted above the most characteristic parts of the twenty-eighth chapter.

* [The Hebrew text admits of this meaning, which is, however, not clear in the English A.V.—TR.]

[2] 2 *Kings* xxiii. 3–20, 24–27, where several glosses and interpolations are easily recognisable, such as the episode at Bethel (v. 15–20), the authenticity of which is otherwise incontestable (STADE, in the *Zeitschrift für Alttestamentliche Wissenschaft*, 1885, p. 292, et seq.). The account in 2 *Chron.*

no objection to these acts ; he regarded them, in the first place, as the private affairs of the subjects of the empire, with which he had no need to interfere, so long as the outburst of religious feeling did not tend towards a revolt : we know, moreover, that Josiah, guided on this point by the prophets, would have believed that he was opposing the divine will had he sought to free himself from the Assyrian yoke by ordinary political methods ; besides this, in 621, under Assur-etililâni, five years after the Scythian invasion, the prefect of Samaria had possibly not sufficient troops at his disposal to oppose the encroachments of the vassal princes.   It was an affair of merely a few months.   In the following year, when the work of destruction was over, Josiah commanded that the Passover should be kept in the manner prescribed in the new book ; crowds flocked into Jerusalem, from Israel as well as from Judah, and the festival made a deep impression on the minds of the people.   Centuries afterwards the Passover of King Josiah was still remembered : "There was not kept such a Passover from the days of the Judges . . . nor in all the days of the Kings of Israel, nor of the Kings of Judah." [1]   The first outburst of zeal having spent itself, a reaction was ere long bound to set in both among the ruling classes and among the people, and the spectacle that Asia at that time presented to their view was truly of a nature to incite doubts in the minds of the faithful. Assyria—that Assyria of which the prophets had spoken as the irresistible emissary of the Most High—had not only failed to recover from the injuries she had received at the hands, first of the Medes, and then of the Scythians, but had with each advancing year seen more severe wounds inflicted upon her, and hastening her irretrievably to her ruin.   And besides this, Egypt and Chaldæa, the ancient kingdoms which had for a short time bent beneath her yoke, had now once more arisen, and were astonishing the world by their renewed vigour.   Psammetichus, it is true, after having stretched his arm across the desert and laid hands upon the citadel which secured to him an outlet into Syria for his armies, had proceeded no further, and thus showed that he was not inclined to reassert the ancient rights of Egypt over the countries of the Jordan and the Orontes ; but he had died in 611, and his son, Necho II., who

xxxiv. is a defaced reproduction of that of 2 *Kings*, and it places the reform, in part at least, before the discovery of the new law.

[1] 2 *Kings* xxiii. 21–23; cf. 2 *Chron.* xxxv. 1–19.   The text of the LXX. appears to imply that it was the first Passover celebrated in Jerusalem.   It also gives in chap. xxii. 3, after the mention of the eighteenth year, a date of the seventh or eighth month, which is not usually accepted, as it is in contradiction with what is affirmed in chap. xxiii. 21–23, viz. that the Passover celebrated at Jerusalem was in the same year as the reform, in the eighteenth year.   It is to do away with the contradiction between these two passages that the Hebrew text has suppressed the mention of the month.   I think, however, it ought to be considered authentic and be retained, if we are allowed to place the celebration of the Passover in what would be one year after.   To do this it would not be needful to correct the regnal date in the text: admitting that the reform took place in 621, the Passover of 620 would still quite well have taken place in the eighteenth year of Josiah, that being dependent on the time of year at which the king had ascended the throne.

succeeded him, did not manifest the same peaceful intentions.[1]   If he decided
to try his fortune in Syria, supported by his Greek and Egyptian battalions,
what would be the attitude that Judah would assume between moribund Assyria
and the kingdom of the Pharaohs in its renewed vigour?

It was in the spring of 608 that the crisis occurred.   Nineveh, besieged by
the Medes, was on the point of capitulating, and it was easy to foresee that the
question as to who should rule there would shortly be an open one : [2] should
Egypt hesitate longer in seizing what she believed to be her rightful heritage,
she would run the risk of finding the question settled and another in possession.   Necho quitted Memphis and made his way towards the Asiatic frontier
with the army which his father had left to him.[3]   It was no longer composed
of the ill-organised bands of the Ethiopian kings or the princes of the Delta,
temporarily united under the rule of a single leader, but all the while divided
by reciprocal hatreds and suspicions which doomed it to failure.   All the troops
which constituted it—Egyptians, Libyans, and Greeks alike—were thoroughly
under the control of their chief, and advanced in a compact and irresistible
mass " like the Nile : like a river its volume rolls onward.   It said : I arise, I
inundate the earth, I will drown cities and people !   Charge, horses !   Chariots,
fly forward at a gallop !   Let the warriors march, the Ethiopian and the Libyan
under the shelter of his buckler, the fellah bending the bow !" [4]   As soon as
Josiah heard the news, he called together his troops and prepared to resist the
attack.   Necho affected not to take his demonstrations seriously, and sent a
disdainful message recommending him to remain neutral : " What have I to do
with thee, thou King of Judah ?   I come not against thee this day, but against
the house wherewith I have war ; and God hath commanded me to make
haste : forbear thee from meddling with God who is with me, that He destroy
thee not !" [5]   Having despatched the message, probably at the moment of
entering the Shephelah, he continued in a northerly direction, nothing doubting
that his warning had met a friendly reception ; but however low Nineveh
had fallen, Josiah could not feel that he was loosed from the oaths which
bound him to her, and, trusting in the help of Jahveh, he threw himself

[1] The last dated stele of Psammetichus I. is the official epitaph of the Apis which died in his
fifty-second year (MARIETTE, *Renseignements sur les soixante-quatre Apis,* in the *Bulletin Archéologique
de l'Athénæum Français,* 1856, pp. 78–80).   On the other hand, an Apis, born in the fifty-third year of
Psammetichus, died in the sixteenth year of Necho, after having lived 16 years, 7 months, 17 days.
A very simple calculation shows that Psammetichus I. reigned fifty-four years, as stated by Herodotus
(II. clvii.) and Manetho, according to Julius Africanus (MÜLLER-DIDOT, *Fragm. Hist. Græc.,* vol. ii. pp.
593–595).   Cf. on this subject LEPSIUS, *Einige von Herrn Mariette brieflich übersendete Apis-Daten,* in
Transactions of Acad. of Sciences at Berlin, 1854, where the calculation was made for the first time.

[2] Cf. *supra,* pp. 484, 485.

[3] HERODOTUS, II. clix., where it is distinctly said that Necho took the land route.

[4] *Jer.* xlvi. 7–9, where the prophet describes, not the army which marched against Josiah, but that
which was beaten at Carchemish.   With a difference of date of only three or four years, the constituent
elements of the army were certainly the same, so that the description of one would apply to the other.

[5] The message of Necho to Josiah is known to us from 2 *Chron.* xxxv. 20–22.

resolutely into the struggle. The Egyptian generals were well acquainted with the route as far as the further borders of Philistia, having passed along it a few years previously, at the time of the campaign of Psammetichus; but they had no experience of the country beyond Ashdod, and were solely dependent for guidance on the information of merchants or the triumphant records of the old Theban Pharaohs. These monuments followed the traditional road which had led their ancestors from Gaza to Megiddo, from Megiddo to Qodshu, from Qodshu to Carchemish, and they were reckoning on passing through the valley of the Jordan, and then that of the Orontes, without encountering any resistance, when, at the entrance to the gorges of Carmel, they were met by the advance guard of the Judæan army. Josiah, not having been warned in time to meet them as they left the desert, had followed a road parallel to their line of march, and had taken up his position in advance of them on the plain of Megiddo, on the very spot where Thutmosis III. had vanquished the Syrian confederates nearly ten centuries before. The King of Judah was defeated and killed in the confusion of the battle, and the conqueror pushed on northwards without, at that moment, giving the fate of the scattered Jews a further thought.[1] He rapidly crossed the plain of the Orontes by the ancient caravan track, and having reached the Euphrates, he halted under the walls of Carchemish. Perhaps he may have heard there of the fall of Nineveh, and the fear of drawing down upon himself the Medes or the Babylonians prevented him from crossing the river and raiding the country of the Balikh, which, from the force of custom, the royal scribes still persisted in designating by the disused name of Mitanni.[2] He returned southwards, after having collected the usual tributes and posted a few garrisons at strategic points; at Riblah he held a kind of *Durbar* to receive the homage of the independent Phœnicians[3] and of the old vassals of Assyria, who, owing to the rapidity of his movements, had not been able to tender their offerings on his outward march. The Jews had rescued the body of their king and had brought it back in his chariot to

---

[1] 2 *Kings* xxiii. 29; cf. 2 *Chron.* xxxv. 22, 23. It is probably to this battle that Herodotus alludes (II. clix.) when he says that Necho overcame the Syrians at Magdôlos. The identity of Magdôlos and Megiddo, accepted by almost all historians, was disputed by Gutschmid (*Kleine Schriften*, vol. iv. pp. 496, 497), who sees in the Magdôlos of Herodotus the Migdol of the Syro-Egyptian frontier, and in the engagement itself, an engagement of Necho with the Assyrians and their Philistine allies; also by Th. Reinach (*La Bataille de Mageddo et la chute de Ninive*, pp. 4, 5), who prefers to identify Magdôlos with one of the Migdols near Ascalon, and considers this combat as fought against the Assyrian army of occupation. If the information in Herodotus were indeed borrowed from Hecatæus of Miletus (WIEDEMANN, *Herodot's Zweites Buch*, pp. 567, 568), and by the latter from the inscription placed by Necho in the temple of Branchidæ (TH. REINACH, *La Bataille de Mageddo*, p. 4), it appears to me impossible to admit that Magdôlos does not here represent Megiddo.

[2] The text of 2 *Kings* xxiii. 29 says positively that Necho was marching towards the Euphrates. The name Mitanni is found even in Ptolemaic times.

[3] The submission of the Phœnicians to Necho is gathered from a passage in Berosus (*Fragm.* 14, in MÜLLER-DIDOT, *Fragm. Hist. Græc.*, vol. ii. p. 506), where he says that the Egyptian army beaten at Carchemish comprised *Phœnicians*, besides Syrians and Arabs. For the similar gathering held by Tiglath-pileser III. at Damascus, cf. pp. 189, 190 of the present volume.

Jerusalem; they proclaimed in his stead, not his eldest son Eliakim, but the youngest, Shallum, who adopted the name of Jehoahaz on ascending the throne. He was a young man, twenty-three years of age, light and presumptuous of disposition, opposed to the reform movement, and had doubtless been unwise enough to display his hostile feelings towards the conqueror. Necho summoned him to Riblah, deposed him after a reign of three months, condemned him to prison, and replaced him by Eliakim, who changed his name to that of Jehoiakim—" he whom Jahveh exalts; " and after laying Judah under a tribute of one hundred talents of silver and one of gold, the Egyptian monarch returned to his own country.[1] Certain indications lead us to believe that he was obliged to undertake other punitive expeditions. The Philistines, pro-bably deceived by false rumours of his defeat, revolted against him about the time that he was engaged in hostilities in Northern Syria, and on receiving news not only of his safety, but of the victory he had gained, their alarm was at once aroused. Judah forgot her own sorrows on seeing the peril in which they stood, and Jeremiah pronounced against them a prophecy full of menace.

VICTORIOUS NECHO.[2]

" Behold," he cried, " waters rise up out of the north, and shall become an overflowing stream, and shall overflow the land and all that is therein, the city and them that dwell therein : and the men shall cry, and all the inhabitants of the land shall howl . . . for the Lord will spoil the Philistines, the remnant of the Isle of Caphtor. Baldness is come upon Gaza ; Ascalon is dumb with terror, and you, all that are left of the giants, how long will ye tear your faces in your mourning ? " * Ascalon was sacked and then Gaza,[3] and Necho at length was able to re-enter his domains, doubtless by the bridge of Zalu, following in this his models, his heroic ancestors of the great Theban dynasties. He wished thereupon to perpetuate the memory of the Greeks who had served him so bravely, and as soon as the division of the spoil had been made, he sent as an offering to the temple of Apollo at Miletus, the cuirass which he had worn throughout the campaign.[4]

---

[1] 2 *Kings* xxiii. 30–55; cf. 2 *Chron.* xxxvi. 1–4, and for the name of Shallum, *Jer.* xxii. 11.

[2] Drawn by Faucher-Gudin, from a photograph published in MARIETTE, *Album photographique du Musée de Boulaq*, pl. 36. This scarab, now in the Gizeh Museum (MARIETTE, *Notice des prin. Mon.*, 1876, p. 207, and *Mon. Divers*, pl. 48 c), is the only Egyptian monument which alludes to the victories of Necho. Above, the king stands between Nît and Isis ; below, the vanquished are stretched on the ground.

* [R.V., "Ashkelon is brought to nought, the remnant of their valley: how long wilt thou cut thyself ? "—TR.]

[3] *Jer.* xlvii., which is usually attributed to a period subsequent to the defeat at Carchemish or even later ; the title, which alone mentions the Egyptians, is wanting in the LXX. If we admit that the enemy coming from the north is the Egyptian and not the Chaldæan, as do most writers, the only time that danger could have threatened Philistia from the Egyptians coming from the north, was when Necho, victorious, was returning from his first campaign. In this case, the Kadytis of Herodotus (II. clix.), which has caused so much trouble to commentators, would certainly be Gaza, and there would be no difficulty in explaining how the tradition preserved by the Greek historian placed the taking of this town after the battle of Megiddo.

[4] HERODOTUS, II. clix., probably following Hecatæus of Miletus; cf. WIEDEMANN, *Herodot's Zweites Buch*, pp. 567, 568.

We can picture the reception which his subjects gave him, and how the deputations of priests and nobles in white robes flocked out to meet him with garlands of flowers in their hands, and with acclamations similar to those which of old had heralded the return of Seti I. or Ramses II.[1] National pride, no doubt, was flattered by this revival of military glory, but other motives than those of vanity lay at the root of the delight exhibited by the whole country at the news of the success of the expedition. The history of the century which was drawing to its close, had demonstrated more than once how disadvantageous it was to Egypt to be separated from a great power merely by the breadth of the isthmus. If Taharqa, instead of awaiting the attack on the banks of the Nile, had met the Assyrians at the foot of Carmel, or even before Gaza, it would have been impossible for Esarhaddon to turn the glorious king-dom of the Pharaohs into an Assyrian province after merely a few weeks of fighting. The dictates of prudence, more than those of ambition, rendered, therefore, the conquest of Syria a necessity, and Necho showed his wisdom in undertaking it at the moment when the downfall of Nineveh reduced all risk of opposition to a minimum; it remained to be seen whether the conquerors of Sin-shar-ishkun would tolerate for long the interference of a third robber, and would consent to share the spoil with these Africans, who, having had none of the trouble, had hastened to secure the profit. All the Mediterranean dependencies of Assyria, such as Mesopotamia, Syria, and Judæa, fell natur-ally within the sphere of Babylon rather than that of Media, and, indeed, Cyaxares never troubled himself about them; and Nabopolassar, who con-sidered them his own by right, had for the moment too much in hand to permit of his reclaiming them. The Aramæans of the Khabur and the Balikh, the nomads of the Mesopotamian plain, had not done homage to him, and the country districts were infested with numerous bands of Cimmerians and Scythians, who had quite recently pillaged the sacred city of Harrân and violated the temple of the god Sin.[2] Nabopolassar, who was too old to command his troops in person, probably entrusted the conduct of them to Nebuchadrezzar, who was the son he had appointed to succeed him, and who had also married the Median princess. Three years sufficed this prince to carry the frontier of the new Chaldæan empire as far as the Syrian fords of the Euphrates, within sight of Thapsacus and Carchemish. Harrân remained

---

[1] Cf. the picture given of the reception of Seti I. at Zalu on his return from his first Syrian campaign (*Struggle of the Nations*, pp. 123, 371, 372).

[2] *Inscrip. of the Cylinder of Nabonidus*, col. x. ll. 12–21, where the pillage of Harrân is mentioned as having taken place fifty-four years before the date of its restoration by Nabonidus. This was begun, as we know, in the third year of that king (*Cylinder of Nabonidus*, col. i. ll. 8–38; cf. PEISER, *In-schriften Nabonid's*, in SCHRADER, *Keilinschrift. Bibl.*, vol. iii., 2nd part, pp. 96–99), possibly in 554–3. The date of the destruction is, therefore, 608–7, that is to say, a few months before the destruction of Nineveh.

in the hands of the barbarians,[1] probably on condition of their paying a tribute, but the district of the Subaru was laid waste, its cities reduced to ashes,[2] and the Babylonian suzerainty established on the southern slopes of the Masios. Having brought these preliminary operations to a successful issue, Nabopolassar, considering himself protected on the north and north-east by his friendship with Cyaxares, no longer hesitated to make an effort to recover the regions dominated by Egyptian influence, and, if the occasion presented itself, to reduce to submission the Pharaoh who was in his eyes merely a rebellious satrap.[3] Nebuchadrezzar again placed himself at the head of his troops ; Necho, warned of his projects, hastened to meet him with all the forces at his disposal, and, owing probably to the resistance offered by the garrisons which he possessed in the Hittite fortresses, he had time to continue his march as far as the Euphrates. The two armies encountered each other at Carchemish ; the Egyptians were completely defeated in spite of their bravery and the skilful tactics of their Greek auxiliaries, and the Asiatic nations, who had once more begun to rely on Egypt, were obliged to acknowledge that they were as unequal to the task of overcoming Chaldæa as they had been of sustaining a struggle with Assyria.[4] The religious party in Judah, whose hopes had been disappointed by the victory of Pharaoh at Megiddo, now rejoiced at his defeat, and when the remains of his legions made their way back across the Philistine plain, closely pressed by the enemy, Jeremiah hailed them as they passed with cutting irony. Two or three brief, vivid sentences depicting the spirit that had fired them a few months before, and then the picture of their disorderly flight : " Order ye the buckler and shield, and draw near to battle. Harness the horses ; and get up, ye horsemen, and stand forth with your helmets ; furbish the spears, put on the coats of mail. Wherefore have I seen it ? They are dismayed and turn backward ; and their mighty ones are beaten down, and are fled apace, and look not back ; terror is on every side, saith the Lord. Let not the swift flee

---

[1] The passage in the *Cylinder of Nabonidus*, cited on note 2 of p. 516, shows that the barbarians remained in possession of the town.

[2] *Cylinder of Nabopolassar*, col. ii. ll. 1–4, where the text, incomplete when published by Winckler (*Einige neuveröffentlichte Texte Hammurabis, Nabopolassars und Nebukadnezars*, in the *Zeitschrift für Assyriologie*, vol. ii. pp. 145, 146 ; cf. STRASSMAYER, *Inschriften Nabopolassars und Smerdis*, in the *Zeitschrift für Ass.*, vol. iv. 108), has been corrected from the copy discovered by Hilprecht (*The Babylonian Expedition of the University of Pennsylvania*, vol. i. p. 33, col. i. ll. 27–29). Messerschmidt has pointed out its value, but he would see in it a preliminary attack of the Chaldæans against Nineveh prior to its fall (*Die Inschrift der Stele Nabunaid's*, pp. 7, 8) : it appears to me more reasonable, until further light shall be cast on the question, to recognise in this war, as a natural result of the fall of Nineveh, the submission of the peoples of the Masios, shortly before the campaign against Necho. For the Subaru, cf. *Struggle of the Nations*, pp. 597, note 1, 605, 607.

[3] Cf. *supra*, p. 486, note 2.

[4] *Jer.* xlvi. 2 ; cf. 2 *Kings* xxiv. 7, where the editor, without mentioning the battle of Carchemish, recalls in passing that " the King of Babylon had taken, from the brook of Egypt unto the river Euphrates, all that pertained to the King of Egypt."

away, nor the mighty man escape ; in the north by the river Euphrates have they stumbled and fallen. . . . Go up into Gilead, and take balm, O virgin daughter of Egypt ; in vain dost thou use many medicines ; there is no healing for thee. The nations have heard of thy shame, and the earth is full of thy cry : for the mighty man hath stumbled against the mighty, they are fallen both of them together." [1] Nebuchadrezzar received by the way the submission of Jehoiakim and of the princes of Ammon, Moab, and the Philistines ; [2] he was nearing Pelusium on his way into Egypt, when a messenger brought him the news of his father's death. He feared lest a competitor should dispute his throne—perhaps his younger brother, that Nabu-shum-lishir who had figured at his side at the dedication of a temple to Marduk.[3] He therefore concluded an armistice with Necho, by the terms of which he remained master of the whole of Syria between the Euphrates and the Wady el-Arish, and then hastily turned homewards. But his impatience could not brook the delay occasioned by the slow march of a large force, nor the ordinary circuitous route by Carchemish and through Mesopotamia. He hurried across the Arabian desert, accompanied by a small escort of light troops, and presented himself unexpectedly at the gates of Babylon. He found all in order. His Chaldæan ministers had assumed the direction of affairs, and had reserved the throne for the rightful heir ; he had only to appear to be acclaimed and obeyed (B.C. 605).[4]

His reign was long, prosperous, and on the whole peaceful. The recent changes in Asiatic politics had shut out the Chaldæans from the majority of the battle-fields on which the Assyrians had been wont to wage warfare with the tribes on their eastern and northern frontiers. We no longer see stirring on the border-land those confused masses of tribes and communities of whose tumultuous life the Ninevite annals make such frequent record : Elam as an independent state no longer existed, neither did Ellipi and Namri, nor the Cossæans, nor Parsua, nor the Medes with their perpetual divisions, nor the Urartians and the Mannai in a constant state of ferment within their mountain territory ; all that remained of that turbulent world now constituted a single empire, united under the hegemony of the Medes, and the rule of a

<hr/>

[1] *Jer.* xlv. 3–6, 11, 12.

[2] The submission of all these peoples is implied by the passage already cited in 2 *Kings* xxiv. 7; Berosus speaks of the Phœnician, Jewish, and Syrian prisoners whom Nebuchadrezzar left to his generals, when he resolved to return to Babylon by the shortest route (*Fragment* 14, in MÜLLER-DIDOT, *Fragmenta Historicorum Græcorum*, vol. ii. p. 506; cf. JOSEPHUS, *Ant. Jud.*, bk. x.

[3] *Cylinder of Nabopolassar*, col. iii. ll. 6–25 ; cf. WINCKLER, *Inschrift. Nabopolassar's*, in SCHRADER, *Keil. Bibl.*, vol. iii., 2nd part, pp. 6, 7.

[4] BEROSUS, *Fragm.* 14, in MÜLLER-DIDOT, *Fragm. Hist. Græc.*, vol. ii. pp. 506, 507; cf. for the details, JOSEPHUS, *Ant. Jud.*, bk. x.

successful conqueror. The greater part of Elam was already subject to those Achæmenides who called themselves sovereigns of Anshân as well as of Persia, and whose fief was dependent on the kingdom of Ecbatana :[1] it is probable that Chaldæa received as her share of the ancient Susian territory the low countries of the Uknu and the Ulai, occupied by the Aramæan tribes of the Puqudu, the Rutu, and the Gambulu ;[2] but Susa fell outside her portion, and was soon transformed into a flourishing Iranian town. The plains bordering the right bank of the Tigris, from the Uknu to the Turnat or the Radanu, which had belonged to Babylon from the very earliest times, were no doubt still retained by her ;[3] but the mountain district which commanded them certainly remained in the hands of Cyaxares, as well as the greater part of Assyria proper, and there is every reason to believe that from the Radanu northwards the Tigris formed the boundary between the two allies, as far as the confluence of the Zab. The entire basin of the Upper Tigris and its Assyrian colonies, Amidi and Tushkân, were now comprised in the sphere of Medic influence, and the settlement of the Scythians at Harrân, around one of the most venerated of the Semitic sanctuaries, shows to what restrictions the new authority of Chaldæa was subjected, even in the districts of Mesopotamia, which were formerly among the most faithful possessions of Nineveh. If these barbarians had been isolated, they would not long have defied the King of Babylon, but being akin to the peoples who were subject to Cyaxares, they probably claimed his protection, and regarded themselves as his liege men ; it was necessary to treat them with consideration, and tolerate the arrogance of their presence upon the only convenient road which connected the eastern with the western provinces of the kingdom.[4] It is therefore evident that there was no opening

[1] Cf. *supra*, pp. 456, 459. "The king and the princes of Elam " mentioned in *Jer.* xxv. 25, xlix. 35–39, and in *Ezek.* xxxii. 24, 25, in the time of Nebuchadrezzar, are probably the Persian kings of Anshân and their Elamite vassals—not only, as is usually believed, the kings and native princes conquered by Assur-bani-pal ; the same probably holds good of the Elam which an anonymous prophet associates with the Medes under Nabonidus, in the destruction of Babylon (*Isa.* xxi. 2). The princes of Malamîr, whom Billerbeck places about this time (*Susa*, pp. 122–125), appear to me to belong to an anterior epoch, as I have said above (cf. *supra*, pp. 228, 230).

[2] The enumeration given in *Ezek.* xxiii. 23, "the Babylonians and all the Chaldæans, *Pekôd*, and Shoa, and Koa," shows us probably that the Aramæans of the Lower Tigris represented by Pekôd, as those of the Lower Euphrates are by the Chaldæans, belonged to the Babylonian empire in the time of the prophet. They are also considered as belonging to Babylon in the passage of an anonymous prophet (*Jer.* l. 21), who wrote in the last days of the Chaldæan empire: " Go up against the land of Merathaim, even against it and the inhabitants of Pekod." Translators and commentators have until quite recently mistaken the import of the name Pekôd.

[3] This is what appears to me to follow from the account of the conquest of Babylon by Cyrus, as related by Herodotus (I. clxxvii., clxxxviii., clxxxix.).

[4] This is the opinion of G. Rawlinson (*The Five Great Monarchies*, 2nd edit., vol. ii. p. 440), adopted by most modern historians (ED. MEYER, *Gesch. des Alterthums*, vol. i. pp. 577, 578 ; TIELE, *Babylonisch-assyrische Gesch.*, p. 422 ; HOMMEL, *Geschichte Babyloniens und Assyriens*, pp. 745, 746 ; WINCKLER, *Geschichte Babyloniens und Assyriens*, pp. 291, 292). For the presence of the Scythians at Harrân, cf. *supra*, p. 516.

on this side for those ever-recurring struggles in which Assyria had exhausted her best powers; one war was alone possible, that with Media, but it was fraught with such danger that the dictates of prudence demanded that it should be avoided at all costs, even should the alliance between the two courts cease to be cemented by a royal marriage. However great the confidence which he justly placed in the valour of his Chaldæans, Nebuchadrezzar could not hide from himself the fact that for two centuries they had always been beaten by the Assyrians, and that therefore he would run too great a risk in provoking hostilities with an army which had got the better of the conquerors of his people. Besides this, Cyaxares was fully engaged in subjecting the region which he had allotted to himself, and had no special desire to break with his ally. Nothing is known of his history during the years which followed the downfall of Nineveh, but it is not difficult to guess what were the obstacles he had to surmount, and the result of the efforts which he made to overcome them. The country which extends between the Caspian and the Black Sea—the mountain block of Armenia, the basins of the Araxes and the Kur, the valleys of the Halys, the Iris, and the Thermodon, and the forests of the Anti-Taurus and the Taurus itself—had been thrown into utter confusion by the Cimmerians and the Scythians. Nothing remained of the previous order of things which had so long prevailed there, and the barbarians who for a century and a half had destroyed everything in the country seemed incapable of organising anything in its place. Urartu had shrunk within its ancient limits around Ararat, and it is not known who ruled her; the civilisation of Argistis and Menuas had almost disappeared with the dynasty which had opposed the power of Assyria, and the people, who had never been much impregnated by it, soon fell back into their native rude habits of life. Confused masses of European barbarians were stirring in Etiaus and the regions of the Araxes, seeking a country in which to settle themselves, and did not succeed in establishing themselves firmly till a much later period in the district of Saka-sênê, to which was attached the name of one of their tribes.[1] Such of the Mushku and the Tabal as had not perished had taken refuge in the north, among the mountains bordering the Black Sea, where they were ere long known to the Greeks as the Moschi and the Tibarenians.[2] The remains of the Cimmerian hordes had taken their place in Cappadocia, and the Phrygian population which had followed in their wake had spread themselves over the basin of the Upper Halys and over the ancient Milidu, which before long took

[1] Strabo (XI. viii. § 4, p. 511) states that Armenia and the maritime regions of Cappadocia suffered greatly from the invasion of the Scythians. For the identity of the diminished Urartu with the country of the Alarodians of Herodotus (III. xciv., VII. lxxix.), cf. H. RAWLINSON, On the Alarodians of Herodotus, in G. RAWLINSON, Herodotus, vol. iv. pp. 203–206.

[2] FR. LENORMANT, Les Origines de l'Histoire, vol. iii. pp. 243-246.

from them the name of Armenia.[1] All these elements constituted a seething, struggling, restless mass of people, actuated by no plan or method, and subject merely to the caprice of its chiefs; it was, indeed, the "seething cauldron" of which the Hebrew prophets had had a vision, which at times overflowed over the neighbouring nations, and at others was consumed within and wasted itself in fruitless ebullition.[2]

It took Cyaxares years to achieve his conquests; he finally succeeded, however, in reducing the various elements to subjection—Urartians, Scythians, Cimmerians, Chaldæi, and the industrious tribes of the Chalybes and the White Syrians—and, always victorious, appeared at last on the right bank of the Halys;[3] but having reached it, he found himself face to face with foes of quite a different calibre from those with whom he had hitherto to deal. Lydia had increased both in wealth and in vigour since the days when her king Ardys informed his ally Assur-bani-pal that he had avenged the death of his father and driven the Cimmerians from the valley of the Mæander.[4] He had by so doing averted all immediate danger; but as long as the principal horde remained unexterminated, another invasion was always to be feared; besides which, the barbarian inroad, although of short duration, had wrought such havoc in the country that no native power in Asia Minor appeared, nor in reality was, able to make the effort needful to destroy them. Their king Dugdamis, it will be remembered, met his death in Cilicia at the hands of the Assyrians about the year 640, and Kôbos, his successor, was defeated and killed by the Scythians under Madyes about 633.[5] The repeated repulses they had suffered had the effect of quickly relieving Lydia, Phrygia, and the remaining states of the Ægean and the Black Sea from their inroads; the Milesians wrested Sinope from them about 630,[6] and the few bands left behind when the main body set out for the countries of the Euphrates were so harried and decimated by the people over whom they had terrorised for nearly a century, that they had soon no refuge except round the fortress of Antandros, in the mountains of the Troad.[7] Most of the kingdoms whose downfall they had caused never

---

[1] The Phrygian origin of the Armenians is pointed out by Herodotus (VII. lxxiii.) and by Eudoxius (EUSTATHIUS, *Ad Dionysium Periegeten*, v. 694, in MÜLLER-DIDOT, *Geographi Græci Minores*, vol. ii. p. 341); cf., lastly, KRETSCHMER, *Einleitung in die Geschichte der Griechischen Sprache*, pp. 208–210.

[2] *Jer.* i. 13; for the Cimmerians, cf. *supra*, pp. 478–480.

[3] HERODOTUS, I. ciii., knows none of the details of the conquests of Cyaxares: he merely describes this prince as τὴν Ἅλυος ποταμοῦ ἄνω Ἀσίην πᾶσαν συστήσας ἑωυτῷ, and he seems to understand by the expression ἄνω Ἀσίην πᾶσαν all the countries included in the XIIIth, XVIIIth, and XIXth satrapies of Darius, and in the eastern half of the IIIrd satrapy.

[4] For this, cf. *supra*, pp. 429, 430.

[5] For these events, cf. *supra*, pp. 430, 474.

[6] EUSEBIUS, *Chronicon*, ed. SCHŒNE, vol. ii. p. 89, after St. Jerome: cf. GELZER, *Das Zeitalter des Gyges*, in the *Rheinisches Museum*, vol. xxx., 1875, p. 257.

[7] For this settlement at Antandros, cf. *supra*, p. 392. According to Aristotle, the Cimmerians must have held the town for a hundred years (STEPHEN OF BYZANTIUM, *s.v.* Ἄντανδρος), which would be until about 580.

recovered from their reverses; but Lydia, which had not laid down its arms since the death of Gyges, became possessed by degrees of the whole of their territory; Phrygia proper came back to her in the general redistribution, and with it most of the countries which had been under the rule of the dynasty of Midas, from the mountains of Lycia to the shores of the Black Sea. The transfer was effected, apparently, with very slight opposition and with little loss

A VIEW IN THE MOUNTAINS OF THE MESSOGIS.[1]

of time, since in the four or five years which followed the death of Kôbos, Ardys had risen in the estimation of the Greeks to the position enjoyed by Gyges; and when, in 628, Aristomenes, the hero of the Messenian wars, arrived at Rhodes, it is said that he contemplated proceeding from thence, first to Sardes and then to Ecbatana, for the purpose of gaining the adherence of Lydia and Media to his cause. Death put an end to his projects, but he would not for a moment have entertained them had not Ardys been at that time at the head of a renowned and flourishing kingdom.[2] The renewal of international commerce followed closely on the re-establishment of peace, and even if the long period of Scythian invasion, followed by the destruction of Nineveh, rendered the overland route less available for regular traffic than before, at all events relations between the inhabitants of the Euphrates valley and those of

---

[1] Drawn by Boudier, from the heliogravure of RAYET and THOMAS, *Milet et le golfe Latmique*, pl. 3.

[2] PAUSANIAS, iv. 24, §§ 2, 3; cf. RADET, *La Lydie et le Monde Grec au temps des Mermnades*, p. 192.

the Ægean littoral were resumed to such good purpose that before long several fresh marts were opened in Lydia. Kymê and Ephesus put the region of the Messogis and the Tmolus into communication with the sea, but the lower valleys of the Hermos and the Mæander were closed by the existence of Greek colonies at Smyrna, Clazomenæ, Colophon, Priênê, and Miletus—all hostile to

THE SITE OF PRIENE.[1]

the Mermnadæ—which it would be necessary to overcome if these countries were to enjoy the prosperity shared by other parts of the kingdom; hence the principal effort made by the Lydians was either directly to annex these towns, or to impose such treaties on them as would make them their dependencies.[2] Ardys seized Priênê towards 620, and after having thus established himself on the northern shore of the Latmic Gulf,[3] he proceeded to besiege Miletus in 616, at the very close of his career. Hostilities were wearily prolonged all through the reign of Sadyattes (615–610), and down to the sixth year of Alyattes.[4] The position of Miletus was too strong to permit

[1] Drawn by Boudier, from the heliogravure of RAYET and THOMAS, *Milet et le golfe Latmique*, pl. 5.

[2] For the policy of the Lydian kings towards the Greek colonies, cf. the remarks of RADET, *La Lydie et le Monde Grec au temps des Mermnades*, p. 192, et seq.

[3] HERODOTUS, I. xv. The well-known story that Priênê was saved under Alyattes by a stratagem of the philosopher Bias (DIOGENES LAERTES, i. 83) is merely a fable, of which several other examples are found (HERODOTUS, I. xxi., xxii.; POLYÆNUS, *Stratagemata*, vii. 36). It would not be possible to conclude from it, as Grote did (*History of Greece*, vol. iii. p. 301), that Ardys' rule over the town was but ephemeral.

[4] The periods of duration assigned here to the reigns of these princes are those of Eusebius—that is to say, 15 years for Crœsus, 37 for Alyattes, 5 for Sadyattes, 37 for Ardys (*Chronicle*, ed. SCHŒNE, vol. i. p. 69); Julius Africanus gives 15 for Sadyattes and 38 for Ardys (SCHŒNE, vol. i., App. VI., p. 220),

of its being carried by a *coup de main;* besides which, the Lydians were
unwilling to destroy at one blow a town whose colonies, skilfully planted
at the seaports from the coasts of the Black Sea to those of Egypt, would
one day furnish them with so many outlets for their industrial products.
Their method of attacking it resolved itself into a series of exhausting
raids. "Every year, as soon as the fruit crops and the harvests began to
ripen, Alyattes set out at the head of his troops, whom he caused to march and
encamp to the sound of instruments. Having arrived in the Milesian territory,
he completely destroyed the crops and the orchards, and then again withdrew." [1]
In these expeditions he was careful to avoid any excesses which would have
made the injury inflicted appear irretrievable; his troops were forbidden to
destroy dwelling-houses or buildings dedicated to the gods; indeed, on one
occasion, when the conflagration which consumed the lands accidentally spread
to the temple of Athena near Assêsos, he rebuilt two temples for the goddess
at his own expense.[2] The Milesians sustained the struggle courageously, until
two reverses at Limeneion and in the plain of the Mæander at length induced
them to make terms. Their tyrant, Thrasybulus, acting on the advice of the
Delphic Apollo and by the mediation of Periander of Corinth, concluded a
treaty with Alyattes in which the two princes, declaring themselves the guest
and the ally one of the other, very probably conceded extensive commercial
privileges to one another both by land and sea (604).[3] Alyattes rewarded
the oracle by the gift of a magnificent bowl, the work of Glaucus of Chios,
which continued to be shown to travellers of the Roman period as one of the
most remarkable curiosities of Delphi.[4] Alyattes continued his expeditions
against the other Greek colonies, but directed them prudently and leisurely, so
as not to alarm his European friends, and provoke the formation against
himself of a coalition of the Hellenic communities scattered over the isles
or along the littoral of the Ægean. We know that towards the end of
his reign he recovered Colophon, which had been previously acquired by
Gyges, but had regained its independence during the Cimmerian crisis;[5] he

---

while Herodotus suggests 14 for Crœsus (I. lxxxvi.), 57 for Alyattes (I. xxv.), 12 for Sadyattes (I.
xvi.), and 59 for Ardys (I. xvi.).

[1] HERODOTUS, I. xvii.   [2] HERODOTUS, I. xix., xxii.

[3] HERODOTUS, I. xv.–xxv.; Thrasybulus' stratagem is said to have taken place at Priênê by Diogenes
Laertes (i. 83) and by Polyænus (vii. 36). For the Milesian wars I have followed the arrangement
adopted by Radet (*La Lydie et le Monde Grec au temps des Mermnades,* pp. 193–196). The war begins
under Ardys (HERODOTUS, I. xv.), lasts for five years under Sadyattes, instead of the six years which
Herodotus attributes to it (I. xviii.), and five years under Alyattes (HERODOTUS, I. xviii.).

[4] HERODOTUS, I. xxv.; PAUSANIAS, X. xvi. § 1.

[5] POLYÆNUS, *Stratagem.,* vii. 2, 2, tells the story of the trick by which Alyattes, after he had
treated with the people of Colophon, destroyed their cavalry and seized on their town. The fact that
a treaty was made seems to be confirmed by a fragment of Phylarchus (*Fragm.* 62, in MÜLLER-DIDOT,
Fragm. Hist. Græc., vol. i. p. 353), and the surrender of the town to the Lydians by a fragment of

razed Smyrna to the ground, and forced its inhabitants to occupy unfortified towns, where his suzerainty could not be disputed;[1] he half devastated Clazomenæ, whose citizens saved it by a despairing effort,[2] and he renewed the ancient alliances with Ephesus, Kymê, and the cities of the region of the Caicus and the Hellespont,[3] though it is impossible to attribute an accurate date to each of these particular events. Most of them had already taken place or were still proceeding when the irruption of the Medes across the Halys obliged him to concentrate all his energies on the eastern portion of his kingdom.

The current tradition in Lydia of a century later attributed the conflict of the two peoples to a romantic cause. It related that Cyaxares had bestowed his favour on the bands of Scythians who had become his mercenaries on the death of Madyes, and that he had entrusted to them the children of some of the noblest Medic families, that they might train them to hunt and also teach them the use of the bow. One day, on their returning from the chase without any game, Cyaxares reproached them for their want of skill in such angry and insulting terms, that they resolved on immediate revenge. They cut one of the children in pieces, which they dressed after the same manner as that in which they were accustomed to prepare the game they had killed, and served up the dish to the king; then, while he was feasting upon it with his courtiers, they fled in haste and took refuge with Alyattes. The latter welcomed them, and refused to send them back to Cyaxares; hence the outbreak of hostilities.[4] It is, of course, possible that the emigration of a nomad horde may have been the cause of the war,[5] but graver reasons than this had set the two nations at variance. The hardworking inhabitants of the valleys of the Iris and the

Xenophanes, quoted in Athenæus (xii. 31)). Schubert (*Geschichte der Könige von Lydien*, pp. 49, 50) does not seem to believe that the town was taken by Alyattes; I have adopted the opinion of Radet on this point (*La Lydie et le Monde Grec au temps des Mermnades*, pp. 197, 198).

[1] HERODOTUS, I. xvi., and NICOLAS OF DAMASCUS, *Fragm.* 64 (in MÜLLER-DIDOT, *Fragm. Hist. Græc.*, vol. iii. p. 397), confine themselves to relating the capture of the city; STRABO, XIV. i. § 37, p. 646, adds that the Lydians compelled the inhabitants to dwell in unfortified towns. Schubert (*Geschichte der Könige von Lydien*, pp. 48, 49) thinks that the passage in Strabo refers, not to the time of Alyattes, but to a subsequent event in the fifth century; he relies for this opinion on a fragment of Pindar (*Fragment* 204, in BERGK, vol. i., 4th edit., p. 449), which represents Smyrna as still flourishing in his time. But, as Busolt has pointed out, the intention of the text of Pindar is to represent the state of the city at about the time of Homer's birth, and not in the fifth century (*Griechische Geschichte*, vol. i. p. 582, note 3).

[2] HERODOTUS, I. xvi.

[3] The peace between Ephesus and Lydia must have been troubled for a little while in the reign of Sadyattes (NICOLAS OF DAMASCUS, *Fragm.* 63, in MÜLLER-DIDOT, *Fragm. Hist. Græc.*, vol. iii. p. 396), but it was confirmed under Alyattes by the marriage of Melas II. with one of the king's daughters (ÆLIAN, *Hist. Var.*, iii. 26).

[4] HERODOTUS, I. lxxiii., lxxiv.

[5] Grote (*History of Greece*, vol. iii. p. 310, note 1) has collected a certain number of examples in later times to show that the journeying of a nomad horde from one state to another may provoke wars, and he concludes therefrom that at least the basis of Herodotus' account may be considered as true; his opinion, which is questioned by G. Rawlinson (*Herodotus*, vol. i. pp. 302, 303), is, on the other hand, admitted by Schubert (*Geschichte der Könige von Lydien*, p. 51).

Halys were still possessed of considerable riches, in spite of the losses they had suffered from the avaricious Cimmerians, and their chief towns, Comana, Pteria and Teiria, continued to enjoy prosperity under the rule of their priest-kings. Pteria particularly had developed in the course of the century, thanks to her favourable situation, which had enabled her to offer a secure refuge to the neighbouring population during the late disasters. The town itself was crowded into a confined plain, on the left bank of a torrent which flowed into the Halys, and the city walls may still be clearly traced upon the soil; the outline of the houses, the silos, cisterns, and rock-cut staircases are still visible

THE RUINS OF PTERIA.[1]

in places, besides the remains of a palace built of enormous blocks of almost rough-hewn limestone. The town was defended by wide ramparts, and also by two fortresses perched upon enormous masses of rock, while a few thousand yards to the east of the city, on the right bank of the torrent, three converging ravines concealed the sanctuary of one of those mysterious oracles whose fame attracted worshippers from far and wide during the annual fairs. The bas-reliefs which decorate them belong to that semi-barbarous art which we have already met with in the monuments attributed to the Khâti, near the Orontes and Euphrates, on both slopes of the Amanus, in Cilicia, and in the ravines of the Taurus. Long processions of priests and votaries defile before figures of the gods and goddesses standing erect upon their sacred animals; in one scene, a tall goddess, a Cybele or an Anaitis, leans affectionately upon her chosen lover,[2] and seems to draw

[1] Drawn by Boudier, from CHARLES TEXIER, *Description de la Chersonèse d'Asia*, pl. vi.
[2] See the reproduction of this scene in the illustration on p. 334 of the present volume.

him with her towards an image with a lion's body and the head of a youth.[1]
Pteria and its surrounding hills formed a kind of natural fortress which over-

THE ENTRANCE TO THE SANCTUARY OF PTERIA.[2]

looked the whole bend of the Halys; it constituted, in the hands of the Lydians,

[1] On these ruins and the monuments which they contain, cf. PERROT and CHIPIEZ, *Histoire de l'Art dans l'Antiquité*, vol. iv. pp. 603–656. Without entering into an examination of the contradictory hypotheses of different authors suggested by the study of these bas-reliefs, I will confine myself to saying that they seem to me to have been executed at about the time with which we are dealing, or perhaps a few years later—in any case, before the Persian conquest.

[2] Drawn by Boudier, from a photograph by Chantre.

an outpost which effectually protected their possessions in Phrygia and Paphlagonia against an attack from the East; in the hands of the Medes it would be a dominant position which would counteract the defensive features of the Halys, and from it they might penetrate into the heart of Asia Minor without encountering any serious obstacles. The struggle between the two sovereigns was not so unequal as might at first appear. No doubt the army of Alyattes was inferior in numbers, but the bravery of its

ONE OF THE PROCESSIONS IN THE RAVINE OF PTERIA.[1]

component forces and the ability of its leaders compensated for its numerical inferiority, and Cyaxares had no troop to be compared with the Carian lancers, with the hoplites of Ionia, or with the heavy Mæonian cavalry. During six years the two armies met again and again—fate sometimes favouring one and sometimes the other—and were about to try their fortune once more, after several indecisive engagements, when an eclipse of the sun suspended operations (585). The Iranian peoples would fight only in full daylight, and their adversaries, although warned, so it is said, by the Milesian philosopher Thales of the phenomenon about to take place in the heavens, were perhaps not completely reassured as to its significance, and the two hosts accordingly separated without coming to blows.[2]

---

[1] Drawn by Faucher-Gudin, from a photograph by Chantre.

[2] This eclipse was identified at one time with that of Sept. 30, 610 (GROTE, *History of Greece*, vol. iii. p. 312, note; MAX DUNCKER, *Geschichte des Alterthums*, vol. ii. pp. 476, 589), at another with that of May 28, 585 (AIRY, *On the Eclipses of Agathocles, Thales, and Xerxes*, in the *Transactions of the R. Soc. of Astronomers*, 1853, p. 193). The latter of these two dates appears to me to be the correct one, and this opinion is shared by Gelzer (*Das Zeitalter des Gyges*, in the *Rheinisches Museum*, 1875, vol. xxx. pp. 264–268), by Unger (*Kyaxares und Astyages*, pp. 33–37), by Radet (*La Lydie et le Monde*

Nebuchadrezzar had followed, not without some misgivings, the vicissitudes of the campaign, and his anxiety was shared by the independent princes of Asia Minor, who were allies of the Lydians; he and they alike awaited with dread a decisive action, which, by crushing one of the belligerents beyond hope of recovery, would leave the onlookers at the mercy of the victor in the full flush of his success. Tradition relates that Syennesis of Cilicia and the Babylonian Nabonidus had taken advantage of the alarm produced by the eclipse to negotiate an armistice, and that they were soon successful in bringing the rival powers to an agreement.[1] The Halys remained the recognised frontier of the two kingdoms, but the Lydians probably obtained advantages for their commerce, which they regarded as compensatory for the abandonment of their claim to the district of Pteria. To strengthen the alliance, it was agreed that Alyattes should give his daughter Aryenis in marriage to Ishtuvigu, or, as the Greeks called him, Astyages, the son of Cyaxares.[2] According to the custom of the times, the two contracting parties, after taking the vow of fidelity, sealed the compact by pricking each other's arms and sucking the few drops of blood which oozed from the puncture.[3] Cyaxares died in the following year (584), full of days and renown, and was at once succeeded by Astyages. Few princes could boast of having had such a successful career as his, even in that century of unprecedented fortunes and boundless ambitions. Inheriting a disorganised army, proclaimed king in the midst of mourning, on the morrow of a defeat in which the fate of his kingdom had hung in the balance, he succeeded within a quarter of a century in overthrowing his enemies and substituting his supremacy for theirs throughout the whole of Western Asia. At his accession Media had occupied only

Grec au temps des Mermnades, p. 203, note 2), and by Schubert (*Gesch. der Könige von Lydien*, pp. 52–55), and is the only one which agrees with what we know of the general history of the sixth century.

[1] The name Labynetos given by Herodotus (I. lxxiv.) is a transcript of Nabonidus, but cannot here designate the Babylonian king of that name, for the latter reigned more than thirty years after the peace was concluded between the Lydians and the Medes. If Herodotus has not made the mistake of putting Labynetos for Nebuchadrezzar, we may admit, with G. Rawlinson (*Herodotus*, vol. i. p. 169, note 4), that this Labynetos was a prince of the royal family, or simply a general who was commanding the Chaldæan auxiliaries of Cyaxares.

[2] The form Ishtuvigu is given us by the Chaldæan documents (*Chronicle of Nabonidus*, obv., col. ii. l. 2; *Cylinder of Abu-Habbah*, col. i. l. 32). Its exact transcript was Astuigas, Astyigas, according to Ctesias (*Fragment 29*, in MÜLLER-DIDOT, *Ctesiæ Cnidii Fragmenta*, p. 45); in fact, this coincides so remarkably with the Babylonian mode of spelling, that we may believe that it faithfully reproduces the original pronunciation.

[3] HERODOTUS, I. lxxiii., lxxiv. Many ancient authors have spoken of this war, or at least of the eclipse which brought it to an end. Several of them place the conclusion of peace not in the reign of Cyaxares, but in that of Astyages—Cicero (*De Divinatione*, i. 49, 112), Solinus (ed. MOMMSEN, p. 95), and the Armenian Eusebius—and their view has been adopted by some modern historians (GELZER, *Das Zeitalter des Gyges*, in the *Rheinisches Museum*, 1875, vol. xxx. pp. 266, 267; CURTIUS, *History of Greece*, vol. ii. pp. 136, 137). The two versions of the account can be reconciled by saying, as Radet does (*La Lydie et le Monde Grec*, etc., p. 204, note 3), that Astyages was commanding the Median army instead of his father, who was too old to do so, but such an explanation is unnecessary, and Cyaxares, though over seventy, might still have had sufficient vigour to wage war. The substitution of Astyages for Cyaxares by the authors of Roman times was probably effected with the object of making the date of the eclipse agree with a different system of chronology from that followed by Herodotus.

a small portion of the Iranian table-land; at his death, the Median empire
extended to the banks of the Halys. It is now not difficult to understand why
Nebuchadrezzar abstained from all expeditions in the regions of the Taurus, as
well as in those of the Upper Tigris. He would inevitably have come into contact
with the allies of the Lydians, perchance with the Lydians themselves, or with
the Medes, as the case might be; and he would have been drawn on to take an
active part in their dangerous quarrels, from which, after all, he could not hope
to reap any personal advantage. In reality, there was one field of action only
open to him, and that was Southern Syria, with Egypt in her rear. He found
himself, at this extreme limit of his dominions, in a political situation almost
identical with that of his Assyrian predecessors, and consequently more or less

under the obligation of repeating their
policy. The Saites, like the Ethiopians
before them, could enjoy no assured sense of
security in the Delta, when they knew that
they had a great military state as their
nearest neighbour on the other side of the
isthmus: they felt with reason that the
thirty leagues of desert which separated

AN EGYPTIAN VESSEL OF THE SAITE PERIOD.[1]

Pelusium from Gaza was an insufficient protection from invasion, and they
desired to have between themselves and their adversary a tract of country
sufficiently extensive to ward off the first blows in the case of hostilities.
If such a buffer territory could be composed of feudal provinces or tributary
states, Egyptian pride would be flattered, while at the same time the security
of the kingdom would be increased, and indeed the victorious progress of Necho
had for the moment changed their most ambitious dreams into realities. Driven
back into the Nile valley after the battle of Carchemish, their pretensions had
immediately shrunk within more modest limits; their aspirations were now
confined to gaining the confidence of the few surviving states which had preserved some sort of independence in spite of the Assyrian conquest, to detaching them from Chaldæan interests and making them into a protecting zone
against the ambition of a new Esarhaddon. To this work Necho applied himself as soon as Nebuchadrezzar had left him in order to hasten back to Babylon.
The Egyptian monarch belonged to a persevering race, who were never cast
down by reverses, and had not once allowed themselves to be discouraged during
the whole of the century in which they had laboured to secure the crown for
themselves; his defeat had not lessened his tenacity, nor, it would seem, his
certainty of final success. Besides organising his Egyptian and Libyan troops,

[1] Drawn by Faucher-Gudin, from a photograph kindly sent to me by G. Bénédite; the original is
in the Egyptian Museum at the Louvre.

he enrolled a still larger number of Hellenic mercenaries, correctly anticipating that the restless spirits of the Phœnicians and Jews would soon furnish him with an opportunity of distinguishing himself upon the scene of action.

It was perhaps at this juncture that he decided to strengthen his position by the co-operation of a fleet. The superiority of the Chaldæan battalions had been so clearly manifested, that he could scarcely hope for a decisive victory if he persisted in seeking it on land; but if he could succeed in securing the command of the sea, his galleys, by continually cruising along the Syrian coast, and conveying troops, provisions, arms, and money to the Phœnician towns, would so successfully foster and maintain a spirit of rebellion, that the

THE ANCIENT HEAD OF THE RED SEA, NOW THE NORTHERN EXTREMITY OF THE BITTER LAKES.[1]

Chaldæans would not dare to venture into Egypt until they had dealt with this source of danger in their rear. He therefore set to work to increase the number of his war-vessels on the Red Sea, but more especially on the Mediterranean, and as he had drawn upon Greece for his troops, he now applied to her for ship-builders.[2] The trireme, which had been invented by either the Samian or Corinthian naval constructors, had as yet been little used, and possibly Herodotus is attributing an event of his own time to this earlier period when he affirms that Necho filled a dockyard with a whole fleet of these vessels; he possessed, at any rate, a considerable number of them, and along with them

[1] Drawn by Boudier, from a photograph taken from the railway between Ismaïlia and Suez, on the eastern shore of the lake.

[2] HERODOTUS, II. clix.; cf. WIEDEMANN, *Herodots Zweites Buch*, pp. 564, 565. Herodotus tells us that in his time the ruins of the docks which Necho had made for the building of his triremes could still be seen on the shore of the Red Sea as well as on that of the Mediterranean. He seems also to say that the building of the fleet was anterior to the first Syrian expedition.

other vessels of various build, in which the blunt stem and curved poop of the Greeks were combined with the square-cabined barque of the Egyptians.[1] At the same time, in order to transport the squadron from one sea to another when occasion demanded, he endeavoured to reopen the ancient canal of Seti I., which had been silted up ever since the last years of the XXth dynasty. He improved its course and widened it so as to permit of two triremes sailing abreast or easily clearing each other in passing. The canal started from the Pelusiac branch of the Nile, not far from Patumos, and skirted the foot of the Arabian hills from west to east ; it then plunged into the Wady Tumilat, and finally entered the head of the bay which now forms the Lake of Ismaïlia. The narrow channel by which this sheet of water was anciently connected with the Gulf of Suez was probably obstructed in places, and required clearing out at several points, if not along its entire extent. A later tradition states that after having lost 100,000 men in attempting this task, the king abandoned the project on the advice of an oracle, a god having been supposed to have predicted to him that he was working for the barbarians.[2] Another of Necho's enterprises excited the admiration of his contemporaries, and remained for ever in the memory of the people. The Carthaginians had discovered on the ocean coast of Libya, a country rich in gold, ivory, precious woods, pepper, and spices, but their political jealousy prevented other nations from following in their wake in the interests of trade. The Egyptians possibly may have undertaken to dispute their monopoly, or the Phœnicians may have desired to reach their colony by a less frequented highway than the Mediterranean. The merchants of the Said and the Delta had never entirely lost touch with the people dwelling on the shores of the Red Sea, and though the royal fleets no longer pursued their course down it on their way to Punt as in the days of Hâtshopsîtu and Ramses III., private individuals ventured from time to time to open trade communications with the ancient "Ladders of Incense." Necho despatched the Phœnician captains of his fleet in search of new lands, and they started from the neighbourhood of Suez, probably accompanied by native pilots accustomed to navigate in those waters. The undertaking, fraught with difficulty even in the last century, was, indeed, a formidable one for the small vessels of the Saite period. They sailed south for months with the east to the left of them, and on their right the continent which seemed to extend indefinitely before them. Towards the

---

[1] Cf. the illustration on p. 530. This is one of the two Egyptian ornaments acquired by the Louvre some years ago ; for further information on Necho's triremes, cf. MALLET, Les Premiers Établissements des Grecs en Égypte, pp. 99–105.

[2] HERODOTUS, II. clviii. ; cf. WIEDEMANN, Herodots Zweites Buch, pp. 560–564. The figures, 100,000 men, are evidently exaggerated, for in a similar undertaking, the digging of the Mahmudiyeh canal, Mehemet-Ali lost only 10,000 men, though the work was greater. For the canal itself, see EBERS, Durch Gosen zum Sinai, p. 471, et seq., and MALLET, Les Premiers Établissements des Grecs en Égypte, pp. 105–108.

autumn they disembarked on some convenient shore, sowed the wheat with which they were provided, and waited till the crop was ripe; having reaped the harvest, they again took to the sea. Any accurate remembrance of what they saw was soon effaced; they could merely recollect that, having reached a certain point, they observed with astonishment that the sun appeared to have reversed its course, and now rose on their right hand. This meant that they had turned the southern extremity of Africa and were unconsciously sailing northwards. In the third year they passed through the pillars of Hercules and reached Egypt in safety. The very limited knowledge of navigation possessed by the mariners of that day rendered this voyage fruitless; the dangerous route thus opened up to commerce remained unused, and its discovery was remembered only as a curious feat devoid of any practical use.[1] In order to obtain any practical results from the arduous voyage, it would have been necessary for Egypt to devote a considerable part of its resources to the making of such expeditions, whereas the country preferred to concentrate all its energies on its Tyrian policy. Necho certainly possessed the sympathies of the Tyrians, who had transferred their traditional hatred of the Assyrians to the Chaldæans. He could also count with equal certainty on the support of a considerable party in Moab, Ammon, and Edom, as well as among the Nabatæans and the Arabs of Kedar; but the key of the whole position lay with Judah—that ally without whom none of Necho's other partisans would venture to declare openly against their master. The death of Josiah had dealt a fatal blow to the hopes of the prophets, and even long after the event they could not recall it without lamenting the fate of this king after their own heart. "And like unto him," exclaims their chronicler, "was there no king before him, that turned to the Lord with all his heart and with all his soul and with all his might, according to all the law of Moses; neither after him arose there any like him."[2] The events which followed his violent death— the deposition of Jehoahaz, the establishment and fall of the Egyptian supremacy, the proclamation of the Chaldæan suzerainty, the degradation of the king and the misery of the people brought about by the tribute exacted from them by their foreign masters,—all these revolutions which had succeeded each other

---

[1] HERODOTUS, IV. xlii.; the Greek writers after Herodotus denied the possibility of such a voyage (EPHORUS, *Fragment* 96 *a*, in MÜLLER-DIDOT, *Fragm. Hist. Græc.*, vol. i. p. 261), and they thought that it could not be decided whether Africa was entirely surrounded by water (POLYBIUS, iii. 38), and that certainly no traveller had ever journeyed above 5000 stadia beyond the entrance to the Red Sea (STRABO, XVI. iii. § 10). Modern writers are divided on the point, some denying and others maintaining the authenticity of the account; the latest geographer and historian, H. BERGER, *Geschichte der Wissenschaftlichen Erdkunde der Griechen*, vol. i. pp. 37–40, has pronounced against it. The observation made by the navigators of the apparent change in the course of the sun, which Herodotus has recorded, and which neither he nor his authorities understood, seems to me to be so weighty an argument for its authenticity, that it is impossible to reject the tradition until we have more decided grounds for so doing.

[2] 2 *Kings* xxiii. 25.

without break or respite had all but ruined the belief in the efficacy of the reform due to Hilkiah's discovery, and preached by Jeremiah and his followers. The people saw in these calamities the vengeance of Jahveh against the presumptuous faction which had overthrown His various sanctuaries and had attempted to confine His worship to a single temple; they therefore restored the banished attractions, and set themselves to sacrifice to strange gods with greater zest than ever.

A like crisis occurred and like party divisions had broken out around Jehoiakim similar to those at the court of Ahaz and Hezekiah a century earlier. The populace, the soldiery, and most of the court officials, in short, all who adhered to the old popular form of religion or were attracted to strange devotions, hoped to rid themselves of the Chaldæans by earthly means, and since Necho declared himself an implacable enemy of their foe, their principal aim was to come to terms with Egypt. Jeremiah, on the contrary, and those who remained faithful to the teaching of the prophets, saw in all that was passing around them cogent reasons for rejecting worldly wisdom and advice, and for yielding themselves unreservedly to the Divine will in bowing before the Chaldæan of whom Jahveh made use, as of the Assyrian of old, to chastise the sins of Judah. The struggle between the two factions constantly disturbed the public peace, and it needed little to cause the preaching of the prophets to degenerate into an incitement to revolt. On a feast-day which occurred in the early months of Jehoiakim's reign, Jeremiah took up his station on the pavement of the temple and loudly apostrophised the crowd of worshippers. "Thus saith the Lord: If ye will not hearken unto Me, to walk in My law, which I have set before you, to hearken to the words of My servants the prophets, whom I send unto you, even rising up early and sending them, but ye have not hearkened; then will I make this house like Shiloh, and will make this city a curse to all the nations of the earth." Such a speech, boldly addressed to an audience the majority of whom were already moved by hostile feelings, brought their animosity to a climax; the officiating priests, the prophets, and the pilgrims gathered round Jeremiah, crying, "Thou shalt surely die." The people thronged into the temple, the princes of Judah went up to the king's house and to the house of the Lord, and sat in council in the entry of the new gate. They decreed that Jeremiah, having spoken in the name of the Lord, did not merit death, and some of their number, recalling the precedent of Micaiah the Morasthite, who in his time had predicted the ruin of Jerusalem, added, "Did Hezekiah King of Judah and all Judah put him at all to death?" Ahikam, the son of Shaphan, one of those who had helped in restoring the law, took the prophet under his protection and prevented the crowd from injuring him, but some others were not able to escape the popular fury. The prophet

Uriah of Kirjath-jearim, who unweariedly prophesied against the city and country after the manner of Jeremiah, fled to Egypt, but in vain; Jehoiakim despatched Elnathan, the son of Achbor, "and certain men with him," who brought him back to Judah, "slew him with the sword, and cast his dead body into the graves of the common people." [1] If popular feeling had reached such a pitch before the battle of Carchemish, to what height must it have risen when the news of Nebuchadrezzar's victory had given the death-blow to the hopes of the Egyptian faction! Jeremiah believed the moment ripe for forcibly arresting the popular imagination while it was swayed by the panic of anticipated invasion. He dictated to his disciple Baruch the prophecies he had pronounced since the appearance of the Scythians under Josiah, and on the day of the solemn fast proclaimed throughout Judah during the winter of the fifth year of the reign, a few months after the defeat of the Egyptians, he caused the writing to be read to the assembled people at the entry of the new gate.[2] Micaiah, the son of Gemariah, was among those who listened, and noting that the audience were moved by the denunciations which revived the memory of their recent misfortunes, he hastened to inform the ministers sitting in council within the palace of what was passing. They at once sent for Baruch, and begged him to repeat to them what he had read. They were so much alarmed at its recital, that they advised him to hide himself in company with Jeremiah, while they informed the king of the matter. Jehoiakim was sitting in a chamber with a brazier burning before him on account of the severe cold: scarcely had they read three or four pages before him when his anger broke forth; he seized the roll, slashed it with the scribe's penknife, and threw the fragments into the fire. Jeremiah recomposed the text from memory, and inserted in it a malediction against the king. "Thus saith the Lord concerning Jehoiakim, King of Judah: He shall have none to sit upon the throne of David; and his dead body shall be cast out in the day to the heat, and in the night to the frost. And I will punish him and his seed and his servants for their iniquity: and I will bring upon them, and upon the inhabitants of Jerusalem, and upon the men of Judah, all the evil that I have pronounced against them; but they hearkened not." [3] The Egyptian tendencies evinced at court, at

---

[1] *Jer.* xxvi., where the scene takes place at the beginning of Jehoiakim's reign, *i.e.* under the Egyptian domination.

[2] The date given in *Jer.* xxxvi. 9 makes the year begin in spring, since the ninth month occurs in winter; this date belongs, therefore, to the later recensions of the text (STADE, *Geschichte des Volkes Israel*, vol. i. p. 677, note 1). It is nevertheless probably authentic, representing the exact equivalent of the original date according to the old calendar.

[3] *Jer.* xxxvi. Attempts have been made to reconstruct the contents of Jeremiah's roll, and most of the authors who have dealt with this subject think that the roll contained the greater part of the fragments which, in the book of the prophet, occupy chaps. i. 4–19, ii., iii. 1–5, 19–25, iv.–vi., vii., viii., ix. 1–21, x. 17–25, xi., xii. 1–6, xvii. 19–27, xviii., xix. 1–13, which it must be admitted have not in every case been preserved in their original form, but have been abridged or rearranged

first discreetly veiled, were now accentuated to such a degree that Nebu-chadrezzar became alarmed, and came in person to Jerusalem in the year 601. His presence frustrated the intrigues of Pharaoh. Jehoiakim was reduced to order for a time, but three years later he revolted afresh at the instigation of Necho, and this time the Chaldæan satraps opened hostilities in earnest. They assembled their troops, which were reinforced by Syrian, Moabite, and Ammonite contingents, and laid siege to Jerusalem.[1] Jehoiakim, left to himself, resisted with such determination that Nebuchadrezzar was obliged to bring up his Chaldæan forces to assist in the attack. Judah trembled with fear at the mere description which her prophet Habakkuk gave of this fierce and sturdy people, " which march through the breadth of the earth to possess dwelling-places which are not theirs. They are terrible and dreadful: their judgment and their dignity proceed from themselves. Their horses also are swifter than leopards, and are more fierce than the evening wolves; and their horsemen spread themselves; yea, their horsemen come from far; they fly as an eagle that hasteneth to devour. They come all of them for violence; their faces are set eagerly as the east wind, and they gather captives as the sand. Yea, he scoffeth at kings, and princes are a derision unto him: he derideth every stronghold: for he heapeth up dust and taketh it. Then shall he sweep by as a wind, and shall pass over the guilty, even he whose might is his god." [2] Nebuchadrezzar's army must have presented a spectacle as strange as did that of Necho. It contained, besides its nucleus of Chaldæan and Babylonian infantry, squadrons of Scythian and Median cavalry, whose cruelty it was, no doubt, that had alarmed the prophet, and certainly bands of Greek hoplites, for the poet Alcæus had had a brother, Antimenidas by name, in the Chaldæan monarch's service.[3] Jehoiakim died before the enemy appeared beneath the walls of Jerusalem, and was at once succeeded by his son Jeconiah,* a youth of eighteen years, who assumed the name of Jehoiachin.[4] The new king continued

---

after the exile. Other chapters evidently belong to the years previous to the fifth year of Jehoiakim, as well as part of the prophecies against the barbarians, but they could not have been included in the original roll, as the latter would then have been too long to have been read three times in one day.

[1] 2 *Kings* xxiv. 1–4. The passage is not easy to be understood as it stands, and it has been differently interpreted by historians. Some have supposed that it refers to events immediately following the battle of Carchemish, and that Jehoiakim defended Jerusalem against Nebuchadrezzar in 605 (WINCKLER, *Alttestamentliche Untersuchungen*, pp. 81–87). Others think that, after the battle of Carchemish, Jehoiakim took advantage of Nebuchadrezzar's being obliged to return at once to Babylon, and would not recognise the authority of the Chaldæans; that Nebuchadrezzar returned later, towards 601, and took Jerusalem, and that it is to this second war that allusion is made in the *Book of Kings* (TIELE, *Babylonisch-assyrische Geschichte*, pp. 425–427; STADE, *Gesch. des Volkes Israel*, vol. i. p. 678; KITTEL, *Gesch. der Hebræer*, vol. ii. p. 318). It is more simple to consider that which occurred about 600 as a first attempt at rebellion which was punished lightly by the Chaldæans.

[2] *Hab.* i. 6–11. [3] STRABO, XIII. ii. § 3, p. 617.

* [Jehoiachin is called Coniah in *Jer.* xxii. 24 and xxiv. 1, and Jeconiah in 1 *Chron.* iii. 16.—TR.]

[4] 2 *Kings* xxiv. 5–10; cf. 2 *Chron.* xxxvi. 6–9, where the writer says that Nebuchadrezzar bound Jehoiakim "in fetters, to carry him to Babylon."

the struggle at first courageously, but the advent of Nebuchadrezzar so clearly convinced him of the futility of the defence, that he suddenly decided to lay down his arms. He came forth from the city with his mother Nehushta, the officers of his house, his ministers, and his eunuchs, and prostrated himself at the feet of his suzerain. The Chaldæan monarch was not inclined to proceed to extremities; he therefore exiled to Babylon Jehoiachin and the whole of his seditious court who had so ill-advised the young king, the best of his officers, and the most skilful artisans, in all 3023 persons, but the priests and the bulk of the people remained at Jerusalem. The conqueror appointed Mattaniah, the youngest son of Josiah, to be their ruler, who, on succeeding to the crown, changed his name, after the example of his predecessors, adopting that of Zedekiah. Jehoiachin had reigned exactly three months over his besieged city (596).[1]

The Egyptians made no attempt to save their ally, but if they felt themselves not in a condition to defy the Chaldæans on Syrian territory, the Chaldæans on their side feared to carry hostilities into the heart of the Delta. Necho died two years after the disaster at Jerusalem, without having been called to account by, or having found an opportunity of further annoying, his rival, and his son Psammetichus II. succeeded peacefully to the throne.[2] He was a youth at this time,[3] and his father's ministers conducted the affairs of State on his behalf, and it was they who directed one of his early campaigns, if not the very first, against Ethiopia.[4] They organised a small army for him

---

[1] 2 *Kings* xxiv. 11–17; cf. 2 *Chron.* xxxvi. 10.

[2] The length of Necho's reign is fixed at sixteen years by Herodotus (II. clix.), and at six or at nine years by the various abbreviators of Manetho (MÜLLER-DIDOT, *Fragm. Hist. Græc.*, vol. ii. pp. 593, 594). The contemporaneous monuments have confirmed the testimony of Herodotus on this point as against that of Manetho, and the stelæ of the Florentine Museum (ROSELLINI, *Monumenti Storici*, vol. ii. pp. 150, 151, where the author gives only six years to Necho), of the Leyden Museum (LEEMANS, *Lettre à M. François Salvolini*, pp. 125–132, where Rosellini's error is maintained), and of the Louvre (S. 2243, 2244; cf. E. DE ROUGÉ, *Notice sommaire des Mon. Égyptiens*, 1855, p. 47) have furnished certain proof that Necho died in the sixteenth year, after fifteen and a half years' reign (WIEDEMANN, *Gesch. Ægypt.* pp. 116–119).

[3] His sarcophagus, discovered in 1883, and now preserved in the Gizeh Museum, is of such small dimensions that it can have been used only for a youth (MASPERO, *Notes sur quelques points de Grammaire et d'Histoire*, in the *Zeitschrift*, 1884, pp. 78–80, and *Guide du Visiteur*, pp. 25, 26).

[4] HERODOTUS, II. clxi. The graffiti of Abu-Simbel have been most frequently attributed to Psammetichus I., and until recently I had thought it possible to maintain this opinion (cf. MALLET, *Les Premiers Établissements des Grecs en Égypte*, pp. 82–95). A. von Gutschmid was the first, in his German translation of Sharpe's *History of Egypt* (p. 82, note), to restore them to Psammetichus II., and his opinion has gained ground since Wiedemann's vigorous defence of it in his works (*Die Griechische Inschrift von Abu-Simbel*, in the *Rheinisches Museum*, vol. xxxv. pp. 364–372; *Geschichte Ægyptens*, pp. 157, 158; *Ægyptische Geschichte*, pp. 631, 632). The Ialysian mercenary's graffito, ὅκα βασιλεὺς ἤλασε τὸν στρατὸν τὸ πρᾶτον [ἔνθαδε ἅ]μα Ψαμειτίχ[ῳ..], contains the Greek translation of the current Egyptian phrase "when his Majesty came on his first military expedition into this country" (cf., *e.g.*, LEPSIUS, *Denkm.*, iii. 81–91, l. 5), which seems to point to no very early date in a reign for a first campaign. Moreover, one of the generals in command of the expedition is a Psammetichus, son of Theocles, that is, a Greek with an Egyptian name (cf. Psammetichus, nephew of Periander, ARISTOTLE, *Politics*, v. 9, 22, and NICOLAS OF DAMASCUS, *Fragment* 68, in MÜLLER-DIDOT, *Fragm. Hist. Græc.*, vol. iii. p. 394). A considerable lapse of time must have taken place since Psammetichus' first dealings with the Greeks, for otherwise the person named after the king would not have been of sufficiently mature age to be put at the head of a body of troops.

composed of Egyptians, Greeks, and Asiatic mercenaries, which, while the king was taking up his residence at Elephantinê, was borne up the Nile in a fleet of large vessels.[1]   It probably went as far south as the northern point of the second cataract, and not having encountered any Ethiopian force,[2] it retraced its course and came to anchor at Abu-Simbel.   The officers in command, after having admired the rock-cut chapel of Ramses II., left in it a memento of their visit in a fine inscription cut on the right leg of one of the colossi.   This inscription informs us that " King Psammatikhos having come to Elephantinê, the people who were with Psammatikhos, son of Theocles, wrote this.   They ascended above Kerkis, to where the river ceases ; Potasimto[3] commanded the foreigners, Amasis the Egyptians.   At the same time also wrote Arkhôn, son of Amoibikhos, and Peleqos, son of Ulamos." Following the example of their officers, the soldiers also wrote their names here and there, each in his own language—Ionians, Rhodians, Carians, Phœnicians, and perhaps even Jews ; e.g. Elesibios of Teos, Pabis of Colophon, Telephos of Ialysos, Abdsakon son of Petiehvê, Gerhekal son of Hallum.[4] The whole of this part of the country, brought to ruin in the gradual dismemberment of Greater Egypt, could not have differed much from the Nubia of to-day ; there were the same narrow strips of cultivation along the river banks, gigantic temples half buried by their own ruins, scattered towns and villages, and everywhere the yellow sand creeping insensibly down towards the Nile. The northern part of this province remained in the hands of the Saite Pharaohs, and the districts situated further south just beyond Abu-Simbel formed at that period a sort of neutral ground

[1] The chief *graffito* at Abu-Simbel says, in fact, that the king came to Elephantinê, and that only the troops accompanying the General Psammetichus, the son of Theocles, went beyond Kerkis.   It was probably during his stay at Elephantinê, while awaiting the return of the expedition, that Psammetichus II. had the inscriptions containing his cartouches engraved upon the rocks of Bigga, Abaton, Philæ, and Konosso (CHAMPOLLION, *Monuments de l'Égypte et de la Nubie*, vol. i. pp. 163, 616, 631 ; ROSELLINI, *Monumenti Storici*, pl. cxlii. *a*, and vol. ii. pp. 129, 130 ; LEPSIUS, *Denkm.*, iii. 274 *e* ; J. DE MORGAN, *De la Frontière de Nubie à Kom-Ombos*, p. 69, No. 14), or among the ruins of Elephantinê and of Philæ (CHAMPOLLION, *Monuments de l'Égypte et de la Nubie*, vol. i. p. 225 ; LEPSIUS, *Denkm.*, iii. 274 *d* ; J. DE MORGAN, *De la Frontière de Nubie à Kom-Ombos*, p. 114).

[2] The Greek inscription says *above Kerkis*. Wiedemann (*Die Griechische Inschrift von Abu-Simbel*, in the *Rheinisches Museum*, vol. xxxv. p. 372 ; cf. KRALL, *Potasimto*, in *Wiener Studien*, 1882, p. 165) has corrected *Kerkis* into *Kortis*, the Korte of the first cataract, but the reading Kerkis is too well established (PŒHL, *Inscriptiones Græciæ antiquissimæ*, No. 482) for there to be any reason for change. The simplest explanation is to acknowledge, with Ebers (*Ægypten und die Bücher Moses*, pp. 162–164), that the inscription refers to a place situated a few miles above Abu-Simbel, towards Wady-Halfa. Mallet has reminded us of names of similar form found in Nubia (*Les Premiers Établissements des Grecs en Égypte*, p. 83, note 2).

[3] On the identity of the name Potasimto in the inscription with the Egyptian name Potasimtoui, cf. KRALL, note *Potasimto*, in *Wiener Studien*, 1882, pp. 164–166, slightly amended by MALLET, *Les Premiers Établissements des Grecs en Égypte*, p. 85, note 4. The name signifies *the gift of the god Simtoui*, the god who unites the two lands, Horus.

[4] The Greek, Carian, and Semitic graffiti have been collected for the first time in almost complete fashion by LEPSIUS, *Denkm.*, vi. 98, et seq. ; cf. *Corpus Inscriptionum Semiticarum*, vol. i. pp. 128–137. For the rare Carian graffiti, see SAYCE, *The Karian Language and Inscriptions*, in the *Transactions* of the Bibl. Arch. Soc., 1887, vol. ix. pp. 144, 145.

between their domain and that of the Pharaohs of Napata. While all this was going on, Syria continued to plot in secret, and the faction which sought security in a foreign alliance was endeavouring to shake off the depression caused by the reverses of Jehoiakim and his son; and the tide of popular feeling setting in the direction of Egypt became so strong, that even Zedekiah, the creature of Nebuchadrezzar, was unable to stem it. The prophets who were inimical to religious reform, persisted in their belief that the humiliation of the country was merely temporary. Those of them who still remained in Jerusalem repeated at every turn, "Ye shall not serve the King of Babylon . . . the vessels of the Lord's house shall now shortly be brought again from Babylon."[1] Jeremiah endeavoured to counteract the effect

THE FAÇADE OF
THE GREAT TEMPLE
OF ABU-SIMBEL.[2]

of their words, but in vain; the people, instead of listening to the prophet, waxed wroth with him, and gave themselves more and more recklessly up to their former sins. Incense was burnt every morning on the roofs of the houses and at the corners of the streets in honour of Baal, lamentations for Tammuz again rent the air at the season of his festival;[3] the temple was invaded by uncircumcised priests and their idols,[4] and the king permitted the priests of Moloch to raise their pyres in the valley of Hinnom.[5] The exiled Jews, surrounded on all sides by heathen peoples, presented a no less grievous

---

[1] *Jer.* xxvii. 9, 16.

[2] Drawn by Boudier, from a photograph by Daniel Héron, taken in 1881. Cf. the general view of the mountain of Abu-Simbel in *Struggle of the Nations*, p. 413.

[3] *Ezek.* viii. 14, 15. [Cf. *Struggle of the Nations*, p. 178.—Tr.]

[4] *Jer.* xxxii. 34; *Ezek.* viii. 7–13, 16.   [5] *Jer.* xxxii. 35; *Ezek.* xvi. 21, xxiii. 37.

spectacle than their brethren at Jerusalem ; some openly renounced the God of their fathers,[1] others worshipped their chosen idols in secret,[2] while those who did not actually become traitors to their faith, would only listen to such prophets as promised them a speedy revenge—Ahab, Zedekiah, son of Maaseiah, and Shemaiah.   There was one man, however, who appeared in their midst, a priest, brought up from his youth in the temple and imbued with the ideas of reform—Ezekiel, son of Buzi, whose words might have brought them to a more just appreciation of their position, had they not drowned his voice by their clamour ; alarmed at their threats, he refrained from speech in public, but gathered round him a few faithful adherents at his house in Tel-Abîb, where the spirit of the Lord first came upon him in their presence about the year 592.[3]   This little band of exiles was in constant communication with the mother-country, and the echo of the religious quarrels and of the controversies provoked between the various factions by the events of the political world, was promptly borne to them by merchants, travelling scribes, or the king's legates who were sent regularly to Babylon with the tribute.[4]   They learnt, about the year 590, that grave events were at hand, and that the moment had come when Judah, recovering at length from her trials, should once more occupy, in the sight of the sun, that place for which Jahveh had destined her. The kings of Moab, Ammon, Edom, Tyre, and Sidon had sent envoys to Jerusalem, and there, probably at the dictation of Egypt, they had agreed on what measures to take to stir up a general insurrection against Chaldæa.[5]   The report of their resolutions had revived the courage of the national party, and of its prophets ; Hananiah, son of Azzur, had gone through the city announcing the good news to all.[6]   " Thus speaketh the Lord of hosts, the God of Israel, saying, I have broken the yoke of the King of Babylon.   Within two full years will I bring again into this place all the vessels of the Lord's house . . . and Jeconiah the son of Jehoiakim, King of Judah, with all the captives of Judah that went to Babylon ! "   But Jeremiah had made wooden yokes and had sent them to the confederate princes, threatening them with divine punishment if they did not bow their necks to Nebuchadrezzar ; the prophet himself bore one on his own neck, and showed himself in the streets on all occasions thus accoutred, as a living emblem of the slavery in which Jahveh permitted His people to remain for their spiritual good.   Hananiah, meeting the prophet by

[1] Jer. xxix. 21–32.   [2] Ezek. xiv. 1–8.
[3] Ezek. i. 1, 2.   We see him receiving the elders in his house in chaps. viii. 1, xiv. 1, xx. 1, et seq.
[4] Jer. xxix. 3 gives the names of two of these transmitters of the tribute—Elasah the son of Shaphan, and Gemariah the son of Hilkiah, to whom Jeremiah had entrusted a message for those of the captivity.
[5] Jer. xxvii. 1–3.   The statement at the beginning of this chapter: In the beginning of the reign of Jehoiakim, contains a copyist's error ; the reading should be : In the beginning of the reign of Zedekiah (see ver. 12).   [6] Jer. xxvii., xxviii.

chance, wrested the yoke from him and broke it, exclaiming, "Thus saith the Lord : Even so will I break the yoke of Nebuchadrezzar, King of Babylon, within two full years from off the neck of all the nations." The mirth of the bystanders was roused, but on the morrow Jeremiah appeared with a yoke of iron, which Jahveh had put "upon the neck of all the nations, that they may serve Nebuchadrezzar, King of Babylon." Moreover, to destroy in the minds of the exiled Jews any hope of speedy deliverance, he wrote to them : " Let not your prophets that be in the midst of you, and your diviners, deceive you, neither hearken ye to your dreams which ye cause to be dreamed. For they prophesy falsely unto you in My name : I have not sent them, saith the Lord." [1] The prophet exhorted them to resign themselves to their fate, at all events for the time, that the unity of their nation might be preserved until the time when it might indeed please Jahveh to restore it : " Build ye houses and dwell in them, and plant gardens and eat the fruit of them : take ye wives and beget sons and daughters, and take wives for your sons, and give your daughters to husbands, that they may bear sons and daughters ; and multiply ye there and be not diminished. And seek the peace of the city whither I have caused you to be carried away captive, and pray unto the Lord for it : for in the peace thereof shall ye have peace." [2]

Psammetichus II. died in 589,[3] and his reign, though short, was distinguished by the activity shown in rebuilding and embellishing the temples. His name is met with everywhere on the banks of the Nile—at Karnak, where he completed the decoration of the great columns of Taharqa,[4] at Abydos,[5] at Heliopolis, and on the monuments that have come from that town, such as the obelisk set up in the Campus Martius at Rome.[6] The personal influence of the young sovereign did not count for much in the zeal thus displayed ; but the impulse that had been growing during three or four generations, since the time of the expulsion of the Assyrians, now began to have its full effect. Egypt, well armed, well governed by able ministers, and more and more closely bound to Greece by

---

[1] *Jer.* xxix. 8, 9. [2] *Jer.* xxix. 5–7.

[3] Herodotus reckoned the length of the reign of Psammetichus II. at six years (II. clxi.), in which he agrees with the Syncellus, while the abbreviators of Manetho fix it at seventeen years (MÜLLER-DIDOT, *Fragm. Hist. Græc.*, vol. ii. pp. 593, 594). The results given by the reading of the stele of the Louvre S. 2210 enable us to settle that the figure 6 is to be preferred to the other, and to reckon the length of the reign at five years and a half; cf. WIEDEMANN, *Geschichte Ægyptens*, pp. 117, 118, 172, 173.

[4] CHAMPOLLION, *Monuments de l'Égypte et de la Nubie*, p. 8, et seq.; ROSELLINI, *Monumenti Storici*, pl. ii. pp. 129, 130 ; MARIETTE, *Karnak, Texte*, pp. 9, 20 ; cf. what is said of these columns above, pp. 364, 365. I would mention once more (cf. above, p. 501, note 3) that the monuments recorded by the early Egyptologists as belonging to Psammetichus II. belong really to Psammetichus I., and *vice versâ*.

[5] MARIETTE, *Abydos*, vol. i. pl. 2 *b*.

[6] UNGARELLI, *Interpretatio obeliscorum*, pl. 2, and p. 125. [Two obelisks were set up originally before the Temple of Serapis and Isis in the Campus Martius ; that in the text now stands before the Pantheon, and though cut by Rameses II., was appropriated by Psammetichus II. See p. 550, *infra.*—TR.]

both mercantile and friendly ties, had risen to a very high position in the estimation of its contemporaries; the inhabitants of Elis had deferred to her decision
in the question whether they should take part in the Olympic games in which
they were the judges, and following the advice she had given on the matter, they
had excluded their own citizens from the sports so as to avoid the least suspicion
of partiality in the distribution of the prizes.[1] The new king, probably the brother
of the late Pharaoh, had his prenomen of Uahibri from his grandfather Psammetichus I., and it was this sovereign that the Greeks called indifferently Uaphres
and Apries.[2] He was young, ambitious, greedy of fame and military glory, and

APRIES, FROM A SPHINX IN THE LOUVRE.[4]

longed to use the weapon that
his predecessors had for some
fifteen years past been carefully whetting; his emissaries,
arriving at Jerusalem at the
moment when the popular
excitement was at its height,
had little difficulty in overcoming Zedekiah's scruples.
Edom, Moab, and the Philis-
tines, who had all taken their share in the conferences of the rebel party,[3] hesitated at the last moment, and refused to sever their relations with Babylon. Tyre
and the Ammonites alone persisted in their determination, and allied themselves
with Egypt on the same terms as Judah. Nebuchadrezzar, thus defied by three
enemies, was at a loss to decide upon which to make his first attack. Ezekiel,
whose place of exile put him in a favourable position for learning what was
passing, shows him to us as he "stood at the parting of the way, at the head of
the two ways, to use divination: he shook the arrows to and fro, he consulted
the teraphim, he looked in the liver."[5] Judah formed as it were the bridge
by which the Egyptians could safely enter Syria, and if Nebuchadrezzar could
succeed in occupying it before their arrival, he could at once break up the
coalition into three separate parts incapable of rejoining one another—Ammon
in the desert to the east, Tyre and Sidon on the seaboard, and Pharaoh beyond

---

[1] HERODOTUS, II. clx.; cf. WIEDEMANN, *Herodots Zweites Buch*, pp. 568, 569. DIODORUS SICULUS,
i. 95, has transferred the anecdote to Amasis, and the decision given is elsewhere attributed to one
of the seven sages. The story is a popular romance, of which Herodotus gives the version current
among the Greeks in Egypt.

[2] MALLET, *Les Premiers Établissements des Grecs en Égypte*, p. 116, note 2. According to Herodotus
(II. clxi.), Apries was the son of Psammis. The size of the sarcophagus of Psammetichus II., suitable
only for a youth, makes this filiation improbable. Psammetichus, who came to the throne when he
was hardly more than a child, could have left behind him only children of tender age, and Apries
appears from the outset as a prince of full mental and physical development.

[3] Cf. above, p. 540 of the present volume.

[4] Drawn by Boudier, from the bronze statuette in the Louvre Museum; cf. PIERRET, *Catalogue de
la Salle historique*, No. 267, p. 57.   [5] *Ezek*. xxi. 21.

his isthmus to the south-west. He therefore established himself in a central position at Riblah on the Orontes, from whence he could observe the progress

of the operations, and hasten with his reserve force to a threatened point in the case of unforeseen difficulties ; having done this, he despatched the two divisions of his army against his two principal adversaries. One of these divisions crossed the Lebanon, seized its fortresses, and, leaving a record of its victories on the rocks of the Wady Brissa, made its way southwards along the coast to blockade Tyre.[1] The other force bore down upon Zedekiah, and made war

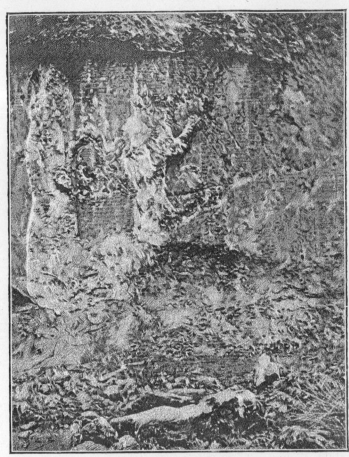

STELE OF NEBUCHADREZZAR.[2]

upon him ruthlessly. It burnt the villages and unwalled towns, gave the rural

---

[1] The account of this Phœnician campaign is contained in one of the inscriptions discovered and commented on by POGNON, *Les Inscriptions Babyloniennes du Wadi Brissa*, pp. 20-22, 120-126. Winckler, the only one to my knowledge who has tried to give a precise chronological position to the events recorded in the inscription, places them at the very beginning of the reign, after the victory of Carchemish, about the time when Nebuchadrezzar heard that his father had just died (*Altorientalische Forschungen*, vol. i. pp. 504-506). I think that this date is not justified by the study of the inscription, for the king speaks therein of the great works that he had accomplished, the restoration of the temples, the rebuilding of the walls of Babylon, and the digging of canals, all of which take us to the middle or the end of his reign. We are therefore left to choose between one of two dates, namely, that of 590-587, during the Jewish war, and that from the King's thirty-seventh year to 568 B.C., during the war against Amasis which will be treated below. I have chosen the first, because of Nebuchadrezzar's long sojourn at Riblah, which gave him sufficient time for the engraving of the stelæ on Lebanon : the bas-reliefs of Wady Brissa could have been cut before the taking of Jerusalem, for no allusion to the war against the Jews is found in them. The enemy mentioned in the opening lines is perhaps Apries, whose fleet was scouring the Phœnician coasts.

[2] Drawn by Boudier, from a photograph by POGNON, *Les Inscriptions Babyloniennes du Wady Brissa*, pl. ii. The figures have been carefully defaced with the hammer, but the outline of the king can still be discerned on the left ; he seizes the rampant lion by the right paw, and while it raises its left paw against him, he plunges his dagger into the body of the beast.

districts over as a prey to the Philistines and the Edomites, surrounded the two fortresses of Lachish and Azekah, and only after completely exhausting the provinces, appeared before the walls of the capital. Jerusalem was closely beset when the news reached the Chaldæans that Apries was approaching Gaza; Zedekiah, in his distress, appealed to him for help, and the promised succour at length came upon the scene.[1] The Chaldæans at once raised the siege with the object of arresting the advancing enemy, and the popular party, reckoning already on a Chaldæan defeat, gave way to insolent rejoicing over the prophets of evil. Jeremiah, however, had no hope of final success. "Deceive not yourselves, saying, The Chaldæans shall surely depart from us; for they shall not depart. For though ye had smitten the whole army of the Chaldæans that fight against you, and there remained but wounded men among them, yet should they rise up every man in his tent, and burn this city with fire."[2] What actually took place is not known; according to one account, Apries accepted battle and was defeated;[3] according to another, he refused to be drawn into an engagement, and returned haughtily to Egypt.[4] His fleet probably made some effective raiding on the Phœnician coast. It is easy to believe that the sight of the Chaldæan camp inspired him with prudence, and that he thought twice before compromising the effects of his naval campaign and risking the loss of his fine army—the only one which Egypt possessed—in a conflict in which his own safety was not directly concerned. Nebuchadrezzar, on his side, was not anxious to pursue so strongly equipped an adversary too hotly, and deeming himself fortunate in having escaped the ordeal of a trial of strength with him, he returned to his position before the walls of Jerusalem.

The city receiving no further succour, its fall was merely a question of time, and resistance served merely to irritate the besiegers. The Jews nevertheless continued to defend it with the heroic obstinacy and, at the same time, with the frenzied discord of which they have so often shown themselves capable. During the respite which the diversion caused by Apries afforded them, Jeremiah had attempted to flee from Jerusalem and seek refuge in Benjamin, to which tribe he belonged. Arrested at the city gate on the pretext of treason, he was unmercifully beaten, thrown into prison, and the king, who had begun to believe in him, did not venture to deliver him. He was confined in the court of the palace, which served as a gaol, and allowed a ration of a loaf of bread for his daily food.[5] The courtyard was a public place, to which all

---

[1] *Ezek.* xvii. 15.   [2] *Jer.* xxxvii. 5–10.

[3] JOSEPHUS, *Jewish Antiquities*, x. 7, § 3, where the Hebrew historian probably thought that the language used by Jeremiah (xxxvii. 7) implied a defeat of the Egyptians.

[4] That, at least, is what Jeremiah seems to say (xxxvii. 7): "Behold, Pharaoh's army, which is come forth to help you, shall return to Egypt into their own land." There is no hint here of defeat or even of a battle.

[5] *Jer.* xxxvii. 11–21.

comers had access who desired to speak to the prisoners, and even here the prophet did not cease to preach and exhort the people to repentance : " He that abideth in this city shall die by the sword, by the famine, and by the pestilence ; but he that goeth forth to the Chaldæans shall live, and his life shall be unto him for a prey, and he shall live. Thus saith the Lord, This city shall surely be given into the hand of the army of the King of Babylon, and he shall take it." The princes and officers of the king, however, complained to Zedekiah of him : " Let this man, we pray thee, be put to death ; forasmuch as he weakeneth the hands of the men of war, and the hands of all the people

PRISONERS UNDER TORTURE HAVING THEIR TONGUES TORN OUT.[1]

in speaking such words." Given up to his accusers and plunged in a muddy cistern, he escaped by the connivance of a eunuch of the royal household, only to renew his denunciations with greater force than ever. The king sent for him secretly and asked his advice, but could draw from him nothing but threats : " If thou wilt go forth unto the King of Babylon's princes, then thy soul shall live, and this city shall not be burned with fire, and thou shalt live and thine house : but if thou wilt not go forth to the King of Babylon's princes, then shall this city be given into the hand of the Chaldæans, and they shall burn it with fire, and thou shalt not escape out of their hand." [2] Zedekiah would have asked no better than to follow his advice, but he had gone too far to draw back now. To the miseries of war and sickness the horrors of famine were added, but the determination of the besieged was unshaken ; bread was failing, and yet they would not hear of surrender.[3] At length, after a year and a half of sufferings heroically borne, in the eleventh year of Zedekiah, the eleventh month, and the fourth day of the month, a portion of the city wall fell before the attacks of the battering-rams, and the Chaldæan army entered by the breach. Zedekiah

---

[1] Drawn by Boudier, from a photograph of the original in the British Museum ; cf. LÀYARD, *The Monuments of Nineveh*, vol. ii. pl. 47.

[2] *Jer.* xxxviii.   [3] *Jer.* xxxviii. 2, 9, 24–27, and 2 *Kings* xxv. 3.

assembled his remaining soldiers, and took counsel as to the possibility of cutting his way through the enemy to beyond the Jordan; escaping by night through the gateway opposite the Pool of Siloam, he was taken prisoner near Jericho, and carried off to Riblah, where Nebuchadrezzar was awaiting with impatience the result of the operations. The Chaldæans were accustomed to torture their prisoners in the fashion we frequently see represented on the monuments of Nineveh, and whenever an unexpected stroke of good fortune brings to light any decorative bas-relief from their palaces, we shall see represented on it the impaling stake, rebels being flayed alive, and chiefs having their tongues torn out. Nebuchadrezzar, whose patience was exhausted, caused the sons of Zedekiah to be slain in the presence of their father, together with all the prisoners of noble birth, and then, having put out his eyes, sent the king to Babylon loaded with chains. As for the city which had so long defied his wrath, he gave it over to Nebuzaradan, one of the great officers of the crown, with orders to demolish it and give it up systematically to the flames.

A KING PUTTING OUT THE EYES OF A PRISONER.[1]

The temple was despoiled of its precious wall-coverings, the pillars and brazen ornaments of the time of Solomon which still remained were broken up, and the pieces carried off to Chaldæa in sacks, the masonry was overthrown and the blocks of stone rolled down the hill into the ravine of the Kedron. The survivors among the garrison, the priests, scribes, and members of the upper classes, were sent off into exile, but the mortality during the siege had been so great that the convoy barely numbered eight hundred and thirty-two persons. Some of the poorer population were allowed to remain in the environs, and the fields and vineyards of the exiles were divided among them.[2] Having accomplished the work of destruction, the Chaldæans retired, leaving the government in the

---

[1] Drawn by Faucher-Gudin, from several engravings in BOTTA, *Le Monument de Ninive*. The mutilated remains of several bas-reliefs have been combined so as to form a tolerably correct scene; the prisoners have a ring passed through their lips, and the king holds them by a cord attached to it.

[2] 2 *Kings* xxv. 4–21, in *Jer.* lii. 6–27, 29; cf. *Jer.* xxxix. 2–10, and 2 *Chron.* xxxvi. 17–20.

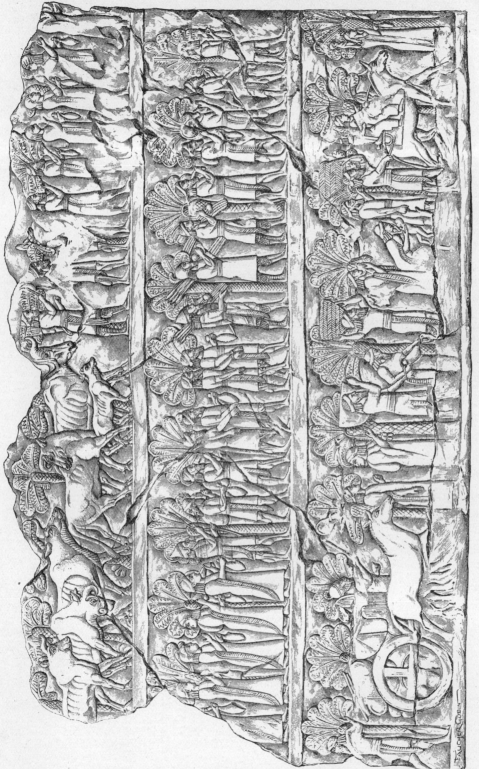

A PEOPLE CARRIED AWAY INTO CAPTIVITY WITH THEIR HOUSEHOLD GOODS AND CATTLE.

Drawn by Faucher-Gudin, from LAYARD, *The Monuments of Nineveh,* vol. ii. pl. 35.

hands of Gedaliah, son of Ahikam,[1] a friend of Jeremiah. Gedaliah established himself at Mizpah, where he endeavoured to gather around him the
remnant of the nation, and fugitives poured in from Moab, Ammon, and Edom.
It seemed that a Jewish principality was about to rise again from the ruins of
the kingdom. Jeremiah was its accredited counsellor, but his influence could
not establish harmony among these turbulent spirits, still smarting from their
recent misfortunes.[2] The captains of the bands which had been roaming over
the country after the fall of Jerusalem refused, moreover, to act in concert with
Gedaliah, and one of them, Ishmael by name, who was of the royal blood,
assassinated him, but, being attacked in Gibeon by Johanan, the son of Kareah,
was forced to escape almost alone and take refuge with the Ammonites.[3] These
acts of violence aroused the vigilance of the Chaldæans; Johanan feared
reprisals, and retired into Egypt, taking with him Jeremiah, Baruch, and the
bulk of the people.[4] Apries gave the refugees a welcome, and assigned them
certain villages near to his military colony at Daphnæ, whence they soon spread
into the neighbouring nomes as far as Migdol, Memphis, and even as far as the
Thebaid.[5] Even after all these catastrophes Judah's woes were not yet at an
end. In 581, the few remaining Jews in Palestine allied themselves with the
Moabites and made a last wild effort for independence; a final defeat, followed
by a final exile, brought them to irretrievable ruin.[6] The earlier captives had
entertained no hope of advantage from these despairing efforts, and Ezekiel
from afar condemned them without pity : "They that inhabit those waste
places in the land of Israel speak, saying, Abraham was one, and he inherited
the land : but we are many ; the land is given us for inheritance. . . . Ye
lift up your eyes unto your idols and shed blood : and shall ye possess the
land ? Ye stand upon your sword, ye work abomination, and ye defile every

The following is the table of the kings of Judah from the death of Solomon to the destruction of
Jerusalem :—

I. REHOBOAM.	VI. AHAZIAH.	XI. JOTHAM.	XVI. JOSIAH.
II. ABIJAH.	VII. ATHALIAH.	XII. AHAZ.	XVII. JEHOAHAZ.
III. ASA.	VIII. JOASH.	XIII. HEZEKIAH.	XVIII. JEHOIAKIM.
IV. JEHOSHAPHAT.	IX. AMAZIAH.	XIV. MANASSEH.	XIX. JEHOIACHIN.
V. JEHORAM.	X. UZZIAH (AZARIAH).	XV. AMON.	XX. ZEDEKIAH.

[1] 2 *Kings* xxv. 22 ; *Jer.* xl. 5–7.

[2] For the manner in which Jeremiah was separated from the rest of the captives, set at liberty
and sent back to Gedaliah, see *Jer.* xxxix. 11–18, xl. 1–6.

[3] 2 *Kings* xxv. 23–25, and *Jer.* xl. 7–16, xli. 1–15, where these events are recorded at length.

[4] 2 *Kings* xxv. 26 ; *Jer.* xli. 16–18, xlii., xliii. 1–7.

[5] *Jer.* xliv. 1, where the word of the Lord is spoken to "all the Jews . . . which dwelt at Migdol,
and at Tahpanhes (Daphnæ), and at Noph (corr. *Moph*, Memphis), and in the country of Pathros."

[6] JOSEPHUS, *Ant. Jud.*, x. 9, § 7; 11, § 1, following Berosus, speaks of a war against the Moabites
and the Ammonites, followed by the conquest of Egypt in the twenty-third year of Nebuchadrezzar.
To this must be added a Jewish revolt if we are to connect with these events the mention of the third
captivity, carried out in the twenty-third year of Nebuchadrezzar by Nebuzaradan (*Jer.* lii. 30).

one his neighbour's wife: and shall ye possess the land? . . . Thus saith the Lord God : As I live, surely they that are in the waste places shall fall by the sword, and him that is in the open field will I give to the beasts to be devoured, and they that be in the strongholds and in the caves shall die of the pestilence."[1] The first act of the revolution foreseen by the prophets was over; the day of the Lord, so persistently announced by them, had at length come, and it had seen not only the sack of Jerusalem, but the destruction of the earthly kingdom of Judah. Many of the survivors, refusing still to acknowledge the justice of the chastisement, persisted in throwing the blame of the disaster on the reformers of the old worship, and saw no hope of salvation except in their idolatrous practices. " As for the word that thou hast spoken unto us in the name of the Lord, we will not hearken unto thee. But we will certainly perform every word that is gone forth out of our mouth, to burn incense unto the queen of heaven, and to pour out drink offerings unto her, as we have done, we and our fathers, our kings and our princes, in the cities of Judah and in the streets of Jerusalem : for then had we plenty of victuals, and were well and saw no evil. But since we left off to burn incense to the queen of heaven and to pour out drink offerings unto her, we have wanted all things, and have been consumed by the sword and by the famine."[2]

There still remained to these misguided Jews one consolation which they shared in common with the prophets—the certainty of seeing the hereditary foes of Israel involved in the common overthrow: Ammon had been already severely chastised; Tyre, cut off from the neighbouring mainland, seemed on the point of succumbing, and the turn of Egypt must surely soon arrive in which she would have to expiate in bitter sufferings the wrongs her evil counsels had brought upon Jerusalem. Their anticipated joy, however, of witnessing such chastisements was not realised. Tyre defied for thirteen years the blockade of Nebuchadrezzar, and when the city at length decided to capitulate, it was on condition that its king, Ethbaal III., should continue to reign under the almost nominal suzerainty of the Chaldæans (574 B.C.).[3] Egypt continued not only to preserve her independence, but seemed to increase in prosperity in proportion to the intensity of the hatred which she had stirred up against her. Apries set about repairing the monuments and embellishing the temples: he erected throughout the country stelæ, tables of offerings, statues and obelisks, some of which, though of small size, like that which

---

[1] *Ezek.* xxxiii. 23–27. [2] *Jer.* xliv. 16–18.

[3] MENANDER, *Fragm.* 2, in MÜLLER-DIDOT, *Fragm. Hist. Græc.*, vol. iv. p. 447. The majority of Christian writers have imagined, contrary to the testimony of the Phœnician annals, that the island of Tyre was taken by Nebuchadrezzar; they say that the Chaldæans united the island to the mainland by a causeway similar to that constructed subsequently by Alexander. It is worthy of notice that a local tradition, still existing in the eleventh century of our era, asserted that the besiegers were not successful in their enterprise (WILLIAM OF TYRE, *Historia*, xiii. 4).

adorns the Piazza della Minerva at Rome,* erected so incongruously on the back of a modern elephant, are unequalled for purity of form and delicacy of cutting. The high pitch of artistic excellence to which the schools of the reign of Psammetichus II. had attained was maintained at the same exalted level. If the granite sphinxes[1] and bronze lions of this period lack somewhat in grace of form, it must be acknowledged that they display greater refinement and elegance in the technique of carving or moulding than had yet

BRONZE LION OF BOHBAÎT.[2]

been attained. While engaged in these works at home, Apries was not unobservant of the revolutions occurring in Asia, upon which he maintained a constant watch, and in the years which followed the capitulation of Tyre, he found the opportunity, so long looked for, of entering once more upon the scene. The Phœnician navy had suffered much during the lengthy blockade of their country, and had become inferior to the Egyptian, now well organised by the Ionians: Apries therefore took the offensive by sea, and made a direct descent on the Phœnician coasts. Nebuchadrezzar opposed him with the forces of the recently subjugated Tyrians, and the latter, having cooled in their attachment to Egypt owing to the special favour shown by the Pharaoh to their rivals the Hellenes, summoned their Cypriote vassals to assist them in repelling the attack. The Egyptians dispersed the combined fleets, and taking possession of Sidon, gave it up to pillage. The other maritime cities surrendered of their own accord,[3] including Gebal, which received an Egyptian garrison, and where the officers of Pharaoh founded a temple to the goddess whom they identified with the Egyptian Hâthor.[4]

* [One of the two obelisks of the Campus Martius, on which site the Church of S. Maria Sopra Minerva was built.—Tr.]

[1] Above the summary of the contents of the present chapter, will be found one of these sphinxes which was discovered in Rome.

[2] Drawn by Faucher-Gudin, from an engraving in MARIETTE, Monuments divers, pl. 41; cf. MASPERO, Guide du Visiteur au Musée de Boulaq, pp. 51, 52, No. 465.

[3] HERODOTUS, II. clxi., and DIODORUS SICULUS, i. 68, where is inserted information gathered from another author, perhaps Ephorus or Theopompus. The war of Apries against the Phœnicians cannot have taken place before the capitulation of Tyre in 574 B.C., because the Tyrians took part in it by order of Nebuchadrezzar, and on the other hand it cannot be put later than 569 B.C., the date of the revolt of Amasis; it must therefore be assigned to about 571 B.C. For the reasons which determined the Phœnicians to make common cause with the Chaldæans, cf. MALLET, Les Premiers Établissements des Grecs en Égypte, pp. 118, 119.

[4] RENAN, Mission de Phénicie, pp. 26, et seq., 179, and the memoir published concerning the Egyptian remains at Byblos, by E. DE ROUGÉ, Lettres à M. Renan, in the Revue Archéologique, 1864, vol. vii. pp. 194–198. Wiedemann (Gesch. Ægyptens, p. 131; Ægyptische Gesch., p. 614) prefers to attribute these buildings to the time of Psammetichus I.

The object at which Necho and Psammetichus II. had aimed for fifteen years was thus attained by Apries at one fortunate blow, and he could legitimately entitle himself "more fortunate than all the kings his predecessors," and imagine, in his pride, that "the gods themselves were unable to injure him."[1] The gods, however, did not allow him long to enjoy the fruits of his victory.

Greeks had often visited Libya since the time when Egypt had been thrown open to the trade of the Ægean. Their sailors had discovered that the most convenient course thither was to sail straight to Crete, and then to traverse the sea between this island and the headlands of the Libyan plateau; here they fell in with a strong current setting towards the east, which carried them quickly and easily as far as Rakotis and Canopus, along the Marmarican shore. In these voyages they learned to appreciate the value of the country; and about 631 B.C. some Dorians of Thera, who had set out to seek for a new home at the bidding of the Delphic oracle, landed in the small desert island of Platæa, where they built a strongly fortified settlement. Their leader, Battos,[2] soon crossed over to the main-

THE SMALL OBELISK IN THE PIAZZA DELLA MINERVA AT ROME.[3]

land, where, having reached the high plateau, he built the city of Cyrene on the borders of an extremely fertile region, watered by abundant springs. The tribes of the Labu, who had fought so valiantly against the Pharaohs of old, still formed a kind of loose confederation, and their territory stretched across the

---

[1] HERODOTUS, IV. clxix.

[2] Herodotus seems to have been ignorant of the real name of the founder of Cyrene, which has been preserved for us by Pindar (*Pythians*, v. 87), by Callimachus (*Hymn to Apollo*, 75), by the spurious Heraclides of Pontus (MÜLLER-DIDOT, *Fragm. Hist. Græc.*, vol. ii. p. 212), and by the chronologists of the Christian epoch. Herodotus says that *Battos* signifies *king* in the language of Libya (IV. clv.); on the resemblance which has been discerned between this name and that of a Libyan chieftain in the time of Mînephtah, cf. *Struggle of the Nations*, p. 431, note 5.

[3] Drawn by Boudier, from a photograph taken at Rome, about 1889.

deserts from the Egyptian frontier to the shores of the Syrtes. The chief of this confederation assumed the title of king, as in the days of Mînephtah or of Ramses III.[1] The most civilised of these tribes were those which now dwelt nearest to the coast: first the Adyrmakhides, who were settled beyond Marea, and had been semi-Egyptianised[2] by constant intercourse with the inhabitants of the Delta; then the Giligammes,[3] who dwelt between the port of Plynus and the island of Aphrodisias; and beyond these, again, the Asbystes, famed for their skill in chariot-driving, the Cabales, and the Auschises.[4] The oases of the hinterland were in the hands of the Nasamones[5] and of the Mashauasha, whom the Greeks called Maxyes.[6] One of the revolutions so

THE OASIS OF AMON AND THE SPRING OF THE SUN.[7]

frequent among the desert tribes had compelled the latter to remove from their home near the Nile valley, to a district far to the west, on the banks of the river Triton. There they had settled down in a permanent fashion, dwelling in houses of stone, and giving themselves up to the cultivation of the soil. They continued, however, to preserve in their new life some of their ancient customs, such as that of painting their bodies with vermilion, and of shaving off the hair from their heads, with the exception of one lock which hung over the right ear. The Theban Pharaohs had formerly placed garrisons in the most important oases, and had consecrated temples there to their god Amon. One of these sanctuaries, built close to an intermittent spring, which gave forth alternately hot and cold water, had risen to great eminence, and the oracle of these Ammonians was a centre of pilgrimage from far and near.[8] The first

[1] For what is known of these kings, cf. *Struggle of the Nations*, pp. 430–437, 456–461, 470–474. The description given by Herodotus of these Libyan tribes (IV. clxvii.–cxcviii.) agrees with the slight amount of information furnished by the Egyptian monuments for the thirteenth century B.C.

[2] HERODOTUS, IV. clxviii.   [3] HERODOTUS, IV. clxix.,clxx.

[4] HERODOTUS, IV. clxx., clxxi.   [5] HERODOTUS, IV. clxxii.–cxc.

[6] HERODOTUS, IV. cxci. For the identity of the Mashauasha with the Maxyes, cf. *Struggle of the Nations*, p. 430, note 4.

[7] Drawn by Boudier, from MINUTOLI, *Caravanenzug durch die Libysche Wüste*, pl. v. No. 1.

[8] HERODOTUS, IV. clxxxi. For the temples of the Theban Amon erected in these oases, cf. the article of LEPSIUS, *Ueber de widderköpfigen Götter Ammon und Chnumis, in Beziehung auf die Ammons-Oase und die gehörnten Köpfe auf griechischen Münzen*, in the *Zeitschrift*, 1877, pp. 8–22.

A PORTION OF THE RUINS OF CYRENE, THE NECROPOLIS.

Drawn by Boudier, from Pacho, *Voyage dans la Marmarique.*

Libyans who came into contact with the Greeks, the Asbystes and the Giligammes, received the new-comers kindly, giving them their daughters in marriage; from the fusion of the two races thus brought about sprang, first under Battos and then under his son Arkesilas I., an industrious and valiant race. The main part of their revenues was derived from commerce in silphium and woollen goods, and even the kings themselves did not deem it beneath their

LIBYA
in the VIᵗʰ Cent. B.C.

dignity to preside in person at the weighing of the crop, and the storing of the trusses in their magazines. The rapid increase in the wealth of the city having shortly brought about a breach in the friendly relations hitherto maintained between it and its neighbours, Battos the Fortunate, the son of Arkesilas I., sent for colonists from Greece: numbers answered to his call, on the faith of a second oracular prediction, and in order to provide them with the necessary land, Battos did not hesitate to dispossess his native allies. The latter appealed to Adikrân, king of the confederacy, and this prince, persuaded that his irregular militia would not be able to withstand the charge of the hoplites, thereupon applied in his turn to Apries for assistance.[1]

There was much tempting spoil to be had in Cyrene, and Apries was fully aware of the fact, from the accounts of the Libyans and the Greeks. His covetousness must have been aroused at the prospect of such rich booty, and perhaps he would have thought of appropriating it sooner, had he not been deterred from the attempt by his knowledge of the superiority of the Greek fleets, and of the dangers attendant on a long and painful march over an almost desert country through disaffected tribes. Now that he could rely on the support of the Libyans, he hesitated no longer to run these risks. Deeming it imprudent, with good reason, to employ his mercenary troops against their own compatriots, Apries mobilised for his encounter with Battos an army

THE SILPHIUM PLANT.[2]

exclusively recruited from among his native reserves. The troops set out full of confidence in themselves and of disdain for the enemy, delighted moreover at an opportunity for at length convincing their kings of their error in preferring barbarian to native forces. But the engagement brought to nought all their boastings. The Egyptians were defeated in the first encounter near Irasa, hard by the fountain of Thestê, near the spot where the high plateaus of

[1] HERODOTUS, IV. cl.–clix. For the questions relating to the primitive history of Cyrene, I refer to BUSOLT, *Griechische Geschichte*, vol. i. pp. 342–349, where the bibliography of this subject is given.

[2] Drawn by Faucher-Gudin, from the cast of a coin of Cyrene, kindly furnished by M. Babelon.

Cyrene proper terminate in the low cliffs of Marmarica : and the troops suffered so severely during the subsequent retreat that only a small remnant of the army regained in safety the frontier of the Delta.[1]   This unexpected reverse was the occasion of the outbreak of a revolution which had been in preparation for years.   The emigration to Ethiopia of some contingents of the military class had temporarily weakened the factions hostile to foreign influence ; these

WEIGHING SILPHIUM IN PRESENCE OF KING ARKESILAS.[2]

factions had felt themselves powerless under the rule of Psammetichus I., and had bowed to his will, prepared all the while to reassert themselves when they felt strong enough to do so successfully.   The reorganisation of the native army furnished them at once with the means of insurrection, of which they had temporarily been deprived.   Although Pharaoh had lavished privileges on the Hermotybies and Calasiries, he had not removed the causes for discontent which had little by little alienated the good will of the Mashauasha : to do so would have rendered necessary the disbanding of the Ionian guard, the

[1] HERODOTUS, IV. clix., from whom DIODORUS SICULUS, i. 68, borrowed the story of this expedition. The interpretation I have given to the sentiments of the Egyptian army follows clearly enough from the observation of Herodotus, that "the Egyptians, having never experienced themselves the power of the Greeks, had felt for them nothing but contempt."   The sito of Irasa and the fountain of Thestê has been fixed with much probability in the fertile district watered still by the fountain of Ersen, Erazem, or Erasân (PACHO, *Voyage dans la Marmarique*, pp. 84, 85).

[2] Drawn by Faucher-Gudin, from a photograph taken of the original in the Coin Room in the Bibliothèque Nationale at Paris.   The king here represented is Arkesilas II. the Bad.

object of their jealousy, and to take this step neither he nor his successors could submit themselves. The hatred of these mercenaries, and the irritation against the sovereigns who employed them, grew fiercer from reign to reign, and now wanted nothing but a pretext to break forth openly : such a pretext was furnished by the defeat at Irasa. When the fugitives arrived at the entrenched camp of Marea, exasperated by their defeat, and alleging doubtless that it was due to treachery, they found others who affected to share their belief that Pharaoh had despatched his Egyptian troops against Cyrene with the view of consigning to certain death those whose loyalty to him was suspected, and it was not difficult to stir up the disaffected soldiers to open revolt.[1] It was not the first time that a military tumult had threatened the sovereignty of Apries. Some time previous to this, in an opposite quarter of the Nile valley, the troops stationed at Elephantinê, composed partly of Egyptians, partly of Asiatic and Greek mercenaries—possibly the same who had fought in the Ethiopian campaign under Psammetichus II.—had risen in rebellion owing to some neglect in the payment of their wages : having devastated the Thebaid, they had marched straight across the desert to the port of Shashirît, in the hope of there seizing ships to enable them to reach the havens of Idumæa or Nabatæa. The governor of Elephantinê, Nsihor, had at first held them back with specious promises; but on learning that Apries was approaching with reinforcements, he attacked them boldly, and driving them before him, hemmed them in between his own force and that of the king and massacred them all.[2] Apries thought that the revolt at Marea would have a similar issue, and that he might succeed in baffling the rebels by fair words; he sent to them as his representative Amasis, one of his generals, distantly connected probably with the royal house.[3] What took place in the camp is not clearly known, for the actual events have been transformed in the course of popular transmission into romantic legends. The story soon took shape that Amasis was born of humble parentage in the village of Siuph, not far from Sais;[4] he was fond, it was narrated, of wine, the pleasures of the table, and women, and replenished his empty purse by stealing what he could lay his hands on from his neighbours

[1] HERODOTUS, IV. clxi.

[2] Statue A 90 in the Louvre, published by PIERRET, Recueil d'inscriptions, vol. i. pp. 21–29, interpreted by MASPERO, Notes sur quelques points de Gram. et d'Hist., in the Zeitschrift, 1884, pp. 87–90, and by BRUGSCH, Beiträge, in the Zeitschrift, 1884, pp. 93–97 ; cf. ED. MEYER, Gesch. Ægyptens, p. 365. This is the inscription in which Wiedemann thought he discerned an allusion to the conquest of Egypt by Nebuchadrezzar (Der Zug Nebucadnezar's gegen Ægypten, in the Zeitschrift, 1878, pp. 2–6, 87–90).

[3] MM. Piehl (Petites Études Egyptolog., pp. 29–36) and Révillout (La Femme et la Mère d'Amasis, in the Revue Egyptologique, vol. ii. pp. 96–98) thought they had found the wife and the mother of Amasis on two monuments in the Museums of Stockholm and the Louvre ; M. Piehl subsequently abandoned this view, which he had only brought forward as a hypothesis (Doit-on accepter l'hypothèse d'un règne simultané d'Apriès et d'Amasis ? in Zeitschrift, vol. xxviii. p. 9, et seq.). In fact, nothing certain is known of the relationship between Amasis and Apries, and it is merely a conjecture that the former is connected with the royal line. Diodorus, however, asserts that he was of good family (i. 68).

[4] HERODOTUS, II. clxxii. ; Plato (Timæus, ed. DIDOT, vol. ii. p. 169) makes him a native of Sais. Siuph is the present es-Seffeh.

or comrades—a gay boon-companion all the while, with an easy disposition and sarcastic tongue. According to some accounts, he conciliated the favour of Apries by his invariable affability and good humour;[1] according to others, he won the king's confidence by presenting him with a crown of flowers on his birthday.[2] The story goes on to say that while he was haranguing the rebels, one of them, slipping behind him, suddenly placed on his head the rounded helmet of the Pharaohs: the bystanders immediately proclaimed him king, and after a slight show of resistance he accepted the dignity. As soon as the rumour of these events had reached Sais, Apries despatched Patarbemis, one of his chief officers, with orders to bring back the rebel chief alive. The latter was seated on his horse, on the point of breaking up his camp and marching against his former patron, when the envoy arrived. On learning the nature of his mission, Amasis charged him to carry back a reply to the effect that he had already been making preparation to submit, and besought the sovereign to grant him patiently a few days longer, so that he might bring with him the Egyptian subjects of Pharaoh. Tradition adds that, on receiving this insolent defiance, Apries fell into a violent passion, and without listening to remonstrance, ordered the nose and ears of Patarbemis to be cut off, whereupon the indignant people, it is alleged, deserted his cause and ranged themselves on the side of Amasis. The mercenaries, however, did not betray the confidence reposed in them by their Egyptian lords. Although only thirty thousand against a whole people, they unflinchingly awaited the attack at Momemphis (569 B.C.); but, being overwhelmed by the numbers of their assailants, disbanded and fled, after a conflict lasting one day.[3] Apries, taken prisoner in the rout, was at first well treated by the conqueror, and seems even to have retained for a time the external pomp of royalty; but the populace of Sais demanding his execution with vehemence, Amasis was at length constrained to deliver him up to their vengeance, and Apries was strangled by the mob.[4] He was honourably interred between the royal palace and the temple of Nît, not far

[1] HERODOTUS, II. clxxiv.

[2] HELLANICUS OF LESBOS, *Fragm.* 151, in MÜLLER-DIDOT, *Fragm. Hist. Græc.*, vol. i. p. 66. The king to whom Amasis made this offering is called Patarmis, and the similarity of this name with the Patarbemis of Herodotus seems to indicate a variant of the legend, in which Patarmis or Patarbemis took the place of Apries.

[3] HERODOTUS, II. clxii., clxiii., clxix.; cf. WIEDEMANN, *Herodots Zweites Buch*, pp. 571, 572, 580–583. DIODORUS SICULUS, i. 68, places the scene of the engagement near Marea itself.

[4] HERODOTUS, II. clxix. Dr. Wiedemann thought he had discovered some monuments of this joint reign, one on a bas-relief in Cairo (CHAMPOLLION, *Monuments de l' Égypte et de la Nubie*, pl. ccccxliii. 1), the other on a seal of fine clay (WIEDEMANN, *Der Zug Nebucadnezar's gegen Ægypten*, in the *Zeitschrift*, 1878, pp. 5, 6, and *Notes et Remarques*, in the *Recueil de Travaux*, vol. xx. pp. 103, 134). M. Piehl has shown reason to believe that the former monument contains an ancient usurpation or an error in the reading of the cartouche (*Doit-on accepter*, etc., in the *Zeitschrift*, vol. xxviii. pp. 9–15), and the testimony of the other monument does not appear to be decisive. The account given by Herodotus does not render less likely the hypothesis that there was a kind of fictitious joint reign, during which, the two kings having existed side by side, it was possible to place the name of the conquered monarch beside that of his conqueror.

from the spot where his predecessors reposed in their glory,[1] and the usurper made himself sole master of the country. It was equivalent to a change of dynasty, and Amasis had recourse to the methods usual in such cases to consolidate his power. He entered into a marriage alliance with princesses of the Saïte line, and thus legitimatised his usurpation as far as the north was concerned.[2] In the south, the "divine worshippers" had continued to administer the extensive heritage of Amon, and Nitocris, heiress of Shapenuapît, had adopted in her old age a daughter of her great-nephew, Psammetichus II., named Ankhnasnofiribrî: this princess was at this time in possession of Thebes, and Amasis appears to have entered into a fictitious marriage with her in order to assume to himself her rights to the crown.[3] He had hardly succeeded in establishing his authority on a firm basis when he was called upon to repel the Chaldæan invasion. The Hebrew prophets had been threatening Egypt with this invasion for a long time, and Ezekiel, discounting the future, had already described the entrance of Pharaoh into Hades, to dwell among the chiefs of the nations—Assur, Elam, Meshech, Tubal, Edom, and Philistia—who, having incurred the vengeance of Jahveh, had descended into the grave one after the other: "Pharaoh and all his army shall be slain by the sword, saith the Lord God! For I have put this terror in the land of the living: and he shall be laid in the midst of the uncircumcised, with them that are slain by the sword, even Pharaoh and all his multitude, saith the Lord God!"[4] Nebuchadrezzar had some hesitation in hazarding his fortune in a campaign on the banks of the Nile: he realised tolerably clearly that Babylon was not in command of such resources as had been at the disposal of Nineveh under Esarhaddon or Assur-bani-pal, and that Egypt in the hands of a Saïte dynasty was a more formidable foe than when ruled by the Ethiopians. The report of the revolution of which Apries had become a victim at length determined him to act; the annihilation of the Hellenic troops, and the dismay which the defeat at Irasa had occasioned in the hearts of the Egyptians, seemed to offer an opportunity too favourable to be neglected. The campaign was opened by Nebuchadrezzar about 568, in the thirty-seventh year of his reign,[5] but we

---

[1] HERODOTUS, II. clxix., clxx. It was probably from this necropolis that the coffin of Psammetichus II. came, referred to *supra*, p. 537, note 4.

[2] The wife of Amasis, who was mother of Psammetichus III., the queen Tintkhîti, daughter of Petenît, prophet of Phtah, was probably connected with the royal family of Saïs (*S 4034 in the Louvre*, cf. E. DE ROUGÉ, *Notice de quelques Textes Hiéroglyphiques*, pp. 56, 57).

[3] For the adoption of the queen Ankhnasnofiribrî by Nitocris, and for the filiation of this princess, cf. ERMAN, in SCHWEINFURTH, *Alte Baureste*, p. 22, and *Zu den Legrain'schen Inschriften*, in the *Zeitschrift*, vol. xxxv. pp. 24–29; MASPERO, *Les Momies royales de Deir-el-Bahari*, pp. 758, 759; DARESSY, *Notes et Remarques*, in the *Recueil de Travaux*, vol. xx. p. 84.

[4] *Ezek.* xxxii. 31, 32.

[5] A fragment of his *Annals*, discovered by Pinches, mentions in the thirty-seventh year of his reign a campaign against [Ah]masu, King of Egypt; and Wiedemann, from the evidence of this document combined with the information derived from one of the monuments in the Louvre (*A 90*, PIERRET, *Recueil d'Inscriptions hiéroglyphiques inédites*, pp. 21–26), thought that the fact of a conquest o Egypt as far as Syenê might be admitted; at that point the Egyptian general Nsihor would have

have no certain information as to the issue of his enterprise. According to Chaldæan tradition, Nebuchadrezzar actually invaded the valley of the Nile and converted Egypt into a Babylonian province, with Amasis as its satrap.[1] We may well believe that Amasis lost the conquests won by his predecessor in Phœnicia, if, indeed, they still belonged to Egypt at his accession : but there is nothing to indicate that the Chaldæans ever entered Egypt itself and repeated the Assyrian exploit of a century before.

This was Nebuchadrezzar's last war, the last at least of which history makes any mention. As a fact, the kings of the second Babylonian empire do not seem to have been the impetuous conquerors which we have fancied them to be. We see them as they are depicted to us in the visions of the Hebrew prophets, who, regarding them and their nation as a scourge in the hands of God, had no colours vivid enough or images sufficiently terrible to portray them. They had blotted out Nineveh from the list of cities, humiliated Pharaoh, and subjugated Syria, and they had done all this almost at their first appearance in the field—such a feat as Assyria and Egypt in the plenitude of their strength had been unable to accomplish : they had, moreover, destroyed Jerusalem and carried Judah into captivity. There is nothing astonishing in the fact that this Nebuchadrezzar, whose history is known to us almost entirely from Jewish sources, should appear as a fated force let loose upon the world. " O thou sword of the Lord, how long will it be ere thou be quiet? put up thyself into the scabbard ; rest and be still ! How canst thou be quiet, seeing the Lord hath given thee a charge ? "[2] But his campaigns in Syria and Africa, of which the echoes transmitted to us still seem so formidable, were not nearly so terrible in reality as those in which Elam had perished a century previously; they were, moreover, the only conflicts which troubled the peace of his reign. The Arabian chroniclers affirm, indeed, that the fabulous wealth of Yemen had incited him to invade that region. Nebuchadrezzar, they relate, routed, not far from the town of Dhât-îrk, the Joctanides of Jorhom, who had barred his road to the Kaabah, and after seizing Mecca, reached the borders of the children of Himyâr : the exhausted condition of his soldiers having prevented him from

---

defeated the Chaldæans and repelled the invasion, and this event would have taken place during the joint reign of Apries and Amasis (*Der Zug Nebucadnezar's gegen Ægypten*, and *Nebucadnezar und Ægypten*, in the *Zeitschrift*, 1878, pp. 2–6, 87–89). A more attentive examination of the Egyptian monument shows that it refers not to a Chaldæan war, but to a rebellion of the garrisons in the south of Egypt, including the Greek and Semitic auxiliaries (MASPERO, *Notes sur quelques points de Gram. et d'Hist.*, in the *Zeitschrift*, 1884, pp. 87–90, and BRUGSCH, *Beiträge*, in the *Zeitschrift*, 1884, pp. 93–97); M. Wiedemann has, nevertheless, held to his own interpretation (*Ægypt. Gesch., Supplement*, p. 70), which has been adopted by many historians who are not Egyptologists (TIELE, *Bab.-ass. Gesch.*, pp. 433–438 ; WINCKLER, *Gesch. Bab. und Ass.*, pp. 312, 313). Winckler (*Alt. Forsch.*, vol. i. pp. 511–515) thought he recognised in the Chaldæan fragment the mention of Pittacus of Lesbos as the ally of Amasis.

[1] JOSEPHUS, *Ant. Jud.*, x. 9, § 7; 11, § 1, following Berosus. These events would have taken place in the twenty-third year of Nebuchadrezzar; the reigning king (Apries) being killed and his place taken by one of his generals (Amasis), who remained a satrap of the Babylonian empire.

[2] *Jer.* xlvii. 6, 7.

pressing further forward in his career of conquest, he retraced his steps and returned to Babylon with a great number of prisoners, including two entire tribes, those of Hadhurâ and Uabar, whom he established as colonists in Chaldæa.[1] He never passed in this direction beyond the limits reached by Assur-bani-pal, and his exploits were restricted to some successful raids against the tribes of Kedar and Nabatæa.[2] The same reasons which at the commencement of his reign had restrained his ambition to extend his dominions towards the east and north, were operative up to the end of his life. Astyages had not inherited the martial spirit of his father Cyaxares, and only one warlike expedition, that against the Cadusians, is ascribed to him.[3] Naturally indolent, lacking in decision, superstitious and cruel, he passed a life of idleness amid the luxury of a corrupt court, surrounded by pages, women, and eunuchs, with no more serious pastime than the chase, pursued within the limits of his own parks or on the confines of the desert. But if the king was weak, his empire was vigorous, and Nebuchadrezzar, brought up from his youth to dread the armies of Media, retained his respect for them up to the end of his life, even when there was no longer any occasion to do so. Nebuchadrezzar was, after all, not so much a warrior as a man of peace, whether so constituted by nature or rendered so by political necessity in its proper sense, and he took advantage of the long intervals of quiet between his campaigns to complete the extensive works which more than anything else have won for him his renown. During the century which had preceded the fall of Nineveh, Babylonia had had several bitter experiences; it had suffered almost entire destruction at the hands of Sennacherib; it had been given up to pillage by Assur-bani-pal, not to mention the sieges and ravages it had sustained in the course of continual revolts.[4] The other cities of Babylonia, Sippara, Borsippa, Kutha, Nipur, Uruk, and Uru, had been subjected to capture and recapture, while the surrounding districts, abandoned in turn to Elamites, Assyrians, and the Kaldâ, had lain uncultivated for many years. The canals at the same time had become choked with mud, the banks had fallen in, and the waters, no longer kept under control, had over-flowed the land, and the plains long since reclaimed for cultivation had returned to their original condition of morasses and reed-beds; at Babylon itself the Arakhtu, still encumbered with the *débris* cast into it by Sennacherib, was no longer navigable, and was productive of more injury than profit to the city:[5]

---

[1] CAUSSIN DE PERCEVAL, *Histoire des Arabes*, vol. i. pp. 81–99. Most of the Arabic legends relating to these conquests of Nebuchadrezzar are indirectly derived from the biblical story; but it is possible that the history of the expeditions against Central Arabia are founded on fact.

[2] This seems to follow from Jeremiah's imprecations upon Kedar (*Jer*. xlix. 28–33).

[3] NICOLAS OF DAMASCUS, *Fragm*. 61, in MÜLLER-DIDOT, *Fragm. Hist. Græc.*, vol. iii. p. 399. Moses of Chorene (i. 23–29) attributes to him long wars against an Armenian king named Tigranes; but this is a fiction of a later age.

[4] For the destruction by Sennacherib and the sack by Assur-bani-pal, cf. *supra*, pp. 307–309, and 422, 423.   [5] Cf. what is stated on this subject, *supra*, p. 357.

in some parts the aspect of the country must have been desolate and neglected as at the present day, and the work accomplished by twenty generations had to be begun entirely afresh. Nabopolassar had already applied himself to the task in spite of the anxieties of his Assyrian campaigns, and had raised many earthworks in both the capital and the provinces.[1] But a great deal more still remained to be done, and Nebuchadrezzar pushed forward the work planned by his father, and carried it to completion undeterred and undismayed by any difficulties.[2] The combined system of irrigation and navigation introduced by the kings of the first Babylonian empire twenty centuries previously, was ingeniously repaired; the beds of the principal canals, the Royal river and the Arakhtu, were straightened and deepened; the drainage of the country between the Tigris and the Euphrates was regulated by means of subsidiary canals and a network of dykes; the canals surrounding Babylon or intersecting in the middle of the city were cleaned out, and a waterway was secured for navigation from one river to the other, and from the plateau of Mesopotamia to the Nar-Marratum.[3] We may well believe that all Nebuchadrezzar's undertakings were

---

[1] The works undertaken by Nabopolassar are known to us from the evidence of several contemporary documents: (1) a cylinder published and translated into German by STRASSMAIER, *Inschriften von Nabopolassar und Smerdis,* in the *Zeitschrift für Assyriologie,* vol. iv. pp. 106–113, 129–136, and by WINCKLER, *Inschriften Nabopolassar's,* in SCHRADER, *Keil. Bibl.,* vol. iii., 2nd part, pp. 2–7; (2) a cylinder published by STRASSMAIER and WINCKLER, *Ein Text Nabopolassar's,* in the *Zeitschrift,* vol. ii. pp. 69–75, 144, 145, which deals with the restoration of the canal at Sippara; (3) a cylinder published by STRASSMAIER and WINCKLER, *Nachtrag zu "Ein Text Nabopolassar's,"* in the *Zeitschrift,* vol. ii. pp. 144–147, 172, 173, which concerns the rebuilding of the temple of Belît at Sippara. These last two texts are reproduced by WINCKLER, *Inschriften Nabopolassar's,* in SCHRADER, *Keil. Bibl.,* vol. iii., 2nd part, pp. 6–9.

[2] The only long inscriptions of Nebuchadrezzar which we possess, are those commemorating the great works he designed and executed: (1) the long *Inscription of the East India Company* (and its duplicate the *Broken Cylinder of Ker Porter*), published in 1803 by the care of HARFORD JONES BRIDGES, *An Inscription of the Size of the Original, copied from a Stone lately found among the Ruins of Babylon,* reproduced in archaic characters, and transcribed in H. RAWLINSON, *Cun. Ins. W. As.,* vol. i. pls. 53–64; transl. into French by OPPERT, *L'Inscr. de Nabuchodonosor sur les merveilles de Babylone,* 1866 (read at the *Imperial Academy of Reims,* 1865), and by MÉNANT, *Babylone et la Chaldée,* pp. 200–208; into English by RODWELL, *Inscription of Nebuchadnezzar,* in the *Records of the Past,* 1st ser., pp. 111–135, and by BALL, *Inscriptions of Nebukadrezzar,* in the *Proceedings* of the Bibl. Arch. Soc., 1887–1888, vol. x. pp. 87–129; into German by FLEMMING, *Die Grosse Steinplatteninschrift Nebukadnezzar's II. in transcribierten Babylonischen Grundtext, nebst Uebersetzung und Commentar,* 1883, and by WINCKLER, *Inschr. Nebukadnezar's,* in SCHRADER, *Keil. Bibl.,* vol. iii., 2nd part, pp. 10–31; (2) the *Cylinder of Philipps,* published by GROTEFEND, *Bemerkungen zur Inschrift eines Thongefasses mit Babylonischer Keilschrift,* 1848 (extract from the *Memoirs of the Academy of Sciences at Göttingen,* vol. iv.), and in H. RAWLINSON, *Cun. Ins. W. As.,* vol. i. pp. 65, 66; transl. into French by OPPERT, *Expédition en Mésopotamie,* vol. i. p. 230, et seq., and by MÉNANT, *op. cit.,* pp. 208–212; into English by BALL, *op. cit.,* pp. 215–230; into German by WINCKLER, *op. cit.,* pp. 32–39; (3) the *Inscriptions of Wady Brissa,* discovered, publ. and transl. into French by POGNON, *Les Inscr. Babyloniennes du Ouady Brissa,* 1887; (4) *Ball's Cylinder,* publ. and transl. into English by BALL, *op. cit.,* pp. 358–368; transl. into German by WINCKLER, *op. cit.,* pp. 46–53. To these must be added a series of lesser inscriptions enumerated in BEZOLD, *Kurzgefasster Ueberblick über die babylonish-assyrische Literatur,* pp. 126–135, the bibliography of which I shall indicate as I shall have occasion to refer to them.

[3] The irrigation works of Nebuchadrezzar are described at length, and perhaps exaggerated, by ABYDENUS, *Fragm.* 9, in MÜLLER-DIDOT, *Fragm. Hist. Græc.,* vol. iv. p. 284, who merely quotes Berosus more or less inaccurately. The completion of the quays along the Arakhtu, begun by Nabopolassar, is noticed in the *East India Company's Inscription,* col. v. ll. 2–33. A special inscription, publ. by

carried out in accordance with a carefully prepared scheme for perfecting the defences of the kingdom while completing the system of internal communication. The riches of Karduniash, now restored to vigour by continued peace, and become the centre of a considerable empire, could not fail to excite the jealousy of its neighbours, and particularly that of the most powerful among them, the Medes of Ecbatana. It is true that the relations between Nebuchadrezzar and Astyages continued to be cordial, and as yet there were no indications of a rupture; but it was always possible that under their successors the good under-

CITY DEFENDED BY A TRIPLE WALL.[1]

standing between the two courts might come to an end, and it was needful to provide against the possibility of the barbarous tribes of Iran being let loose upon Babylon, and attempting to inflict on her the fate they had brought upon Nineveh. Nebuchadrezzar, therefore, was anxious to interpose, between himself

and these possible foes, such a series of fortifications that the most persevering enemy would be worn out by the prolonged task of forcing them one after another, provided that they were efficiently garrisoned. He erected across the northern side of the isthmus between the two rivers a great embankment, faced with bricks cemented together with bitumen, called the *wall of Media*; this wall, starting from Sippara, stretched from the confluence of the Saklauiyeh with the Euphrates to the site of the modern village of Jibbara on the Tigris; on both sides of it four or five deep trenches were excavated, which were passable on raised causeways or by bridges of boats, so arranged as to be easily broken up in case of invasion.[2] The eastern frontier was furnished with a

H. RAWLINSON, *Cun. Ins. W. As.*, vol. i. pl. 52, note 4, and transl. into French by OPPERT, *Expédition de Mésopotamie*, vol. ii. p. 285, et seq. (cf. MÉNANT, *Babylone et la Chaldée*, pp. 213, 214), into German by WINCKLER, *Inschr. Nebukadnezar's*, in SCHRADER, *Keil. Bibl.*, vol. iii. pp. 60, 61, gives an account of the repairing of the canal Libil-khigallu, which crossed Babylon; cf. for these operations, and the possible plan of some of the canals, DELATTRE, *Les Travaux hydrauliques en Babylonie*, pp. 43, 44.

[1] Drawn by Faucher-Gudin, from a bas-relief of the time of Sargon, in the Museum of the Louvre; cf. M. DIEULAFOY, *L'Acropole de Suse*, p. 195.

[2] The building of this wall of Media is referred to in *L'Inscription en caractères cursifs de l'Ouady Brissa*, col. vi. ll. 15–31; edit. POGNON, pp. 16, 17; cf. LAYARD, *Nineveh and Babylon*, who has partially restored the plan from the ruins of the wall, and also, for the interpretation of these texts, WINCKLER, *Altorient. Forsch.*, vol. i. pp. 507–510, and above all, BILLERBECK, *Geographische Unter-suchungen*, pp. 1–6. The wall of Media is shortly described in XENOPHON, *Anabasis*, II. iv. § 12.

rampart protected by a wide moat, following, between Jibbara and Nipur, the contours of a low-lying district which could be readily flooded.[1]   The western boundary was already protected by the Pallakottas, and the lakes or marshes of Bahr-î-Nejîf: Nebuchadrezzar multiplied the number of the dikes, and so arranged them that the whole country between the suburbs of Borsippa and Babylon could be inundated at will.[2]   Babylon itself formed as it were the citadel in the midst of these enormous outlying fortifications, and the engineers both of Nabopolassar[3] and of his son expended all the resources of their art on rendering it impregnable.   A triple rampart surrounded it and united it to Borsippa, built on the model of those whose outline is so frequently found on the lowest tier of an Assyrian bas-relief.   A moat of great width, with banks of

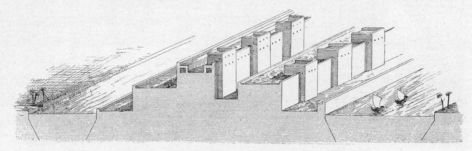

PROBABLE SECTION OF THE TRIPLE WALL OF BABYLON.[4]

masonry, communicating with the Euphrates, washed the foot of the outer wall, which retained the traditional name of Imgur-bel; behind this wall rose Nimitti-bel, the true city wall, to a height of more than ninety feet above the level of the plain, appearing from a distance, with its battlements and towers, more like a mountain chain than a rampart built by the hand of man; finally, behind Nimitti-bel ran a platform on the same level as the curtain of Imgur-bel, forming a last barrier behind which the garrison could rally before finally owning itself defeated and surrendering the city.   Large square towers rose at intervals along the face of the walls, to the height of some eighteen feet above the battlements; a hundred gates fitted with bronze-plated doors, which could be securely shut at need, gave access to the city.[5]

---

[1] The works on the east front are described by Nebuchadrezzar himself in the *East India Company's Inscription*, col. iv. ll. 39–52; cf., for the probable plan of the lines of fortification, the observations of BILLERBECK, *Geographische Untersuchungen*, pp. 6–8.

[2] For the utilisation of the canals on this side of Babylon, cf. DELATTRE, *Les Travaux hydrauliques en Babylonie*, pp. 24–28.

[3] The restoration of Imgur-bel and Nimitti-bel had been begun by Nabopolassar, as is testified by Nebuchadrezzar himself, *East India Company's Inscription*, col. iv. ll. 66–73, col. v. ll. 1–4.

[4] Reproduced by Faucher-Gudin from the restoration by DIEULAFOY, *L'Acropole de Suse*, p. 193.

[5] The description of the fortifications of the city is furnished by HERODOTUS, I. clxxviii., clxxix., who himself saw them still partially standing; the account of their construction has been given by Nebuchadrezzar himself, in the *East India Company's Inscription*, col. iv. ll. 66–73, col. v. ll. 1–65,

The space within the walls was by no means completely covered by houses, but contained gardens, farms, fields, and, here and there, the ruins of deserted buildings.   As in older Babylon, the city proper clustered round the temple of Merodach, with its narrow winding streets, its crowded bazaars, its noisy and dirty squares, its hostelries and warehouses of foreign merchandise.   The pyramid of Esarhaddon and Assur-bani-pal, too hastily built, had fallen into

FRAGMENT OF A BABY-
LONIAN BAS-RELIEF.[4]

ruins : Nebuchadrezzar reconstructed its seven stages, and erected on the topmost platform a shrine furnished with a table of massive gold, and a couch on which the priestess chosen to be the spouse of the god might sleep at night.[1]   Other smaller temples were erected here and there on both banks of the river,[2] and the royal palace, built in the marvellously short space of fifteen days, was celebrated for its hanging gardens, where the ladies of the harem might walk unveiled, secure from vulgar observation.[3]   No trace of all these extensive works remains at the present day.   Some scattered fragments of crumbling walls alone betray the site of the great ziggurât, a few bas-reliefs are strewn over the surface of the ground, and a lion of timeworn stone, lying on its back in a depression of the soil, is perhaps the last survivor of those which kept watch,

col. vi. ll. 1–55 ; cf. the *Inscriptions of Ouady Brissa*, ed. POGNON, pp. 15–19.   One special inscription on terra-cotta cylinders has been published in H. RAWLINSON, *Cun. Ins. W. As.*, vol. i. pl. 52, note 3, and translated into French by OPPERT, *Expéd. en Mésopotamie*, vol. i. p. 232, et seq., and by MÉNANT, *Babylone et la Chaldée*, pp. 212, 213 ; into English by BALL, *Inscr. of Nebuchadrezzar II.*, in the *Proceedings* of the Bibl. Arch. Soc., 1887–1888, vol. x. pp. 292, 293 ; into German by WINCKLER, *Inschr. Nebukadnezar's*, in SCHRADER, *Keil. Bibl.*, vol. iii., 2nd part, pp. 54–59.   For the height of the walls and the distribution of the means of defence, I refer the reader to MARCEL DIEULAFOY, *L'Acropole de Suse*, pp. 183–198, whose conclusions I have adopted.

[1] For the reconstruction of the temple of Merodach by Esarhaddon and Assur-bani-pal, see *supra*, pp. 357, 358, 382, 383, 415.   The restoration by Nebuchadrezzar is mentioned in the *East India Company's Inscription*, col. ii. ll. 40–65, col. iii. ll. 1–10, and more or less at length in the other known inscriptions of this king.   We only know the object of the uppermost platform from the testimony of HERODOTUS, I. clxxxi.

[2] For these other temples, cf. the *East India Company's Inscr.*, col. iii. ll. 13–72, col. iv. ll. 1–64.

[3] The building of the royal palace is referred to in *ibid.*, col. vii. ll. 34–63, col. viii., col. ix. ll. 1–42 ; the account given by Berosus (*Fragm.* 14, in MÜLLER-DIDOT, *Fragm. Hist. Græc*, vol. ii. p. 507) also stated that the palace was erected in fifteen days.   The hanging gardens are only known to us from the testimony of the classical writers, Berosus (*Fragm.* 14, in MÜLLER-DIDOT, *Fragm. Hist. Græc.*, vol. ii. p. 507), Diodorus Siculus (ii. 10), and Strabo (XVI. i. § 5, p. 738).

[4] Drawn by Faucher-Gudin, from a sketch in LAYARD, *Nineveh and Babylon*, p. 433.

according to custom, at the gates of the palace. But the whole of this vast work of reconstruction and ornamentation must not be attributed to Nebuchadrezzar alone. The plans had been designed by Nabopolassar under the influence of one of his wives, who by a strange chance bears in classic tradition the very Egyptian name of Nitocris;[1] but his work was insignificant compared with that accomplished by his son, and the name of Nebuchadrezzar was justly connected with the marvels of Babylon by all ancient writers. But even his reign of fifty-five years did not suffice for the completion of all his undertakings, and many details still remained imperfect at his death in the beginning of 562 B.C.

RUINS OF THE ZIGGURÂT OF THE TEMPLE OF BEL.[2]

Though of Kaldu origin, and consequently exposed to the suspicions and secret enmity of the native Babylonians, as all of his race, even Merodach-Baladan himself, had been before him,[3] he had yet succeeded throughout the whole of his reign in making himself respected by the turbulent inhabitants of his capital, and in curbing the ambitious pretensions of the priests of Merodach. As soon as his master-hand was withdrawn, the passions so long repressed broke forth, and proved utterly beyond the control of his less able or less fortunate successors.[4] As far as we are able to judge by the documents which

---

[1] HERODOTUS, I. clxxxv.–clxxxviii.

[2] Drawn by Faucher-Gudin, from a sketch in LAYARD, *Nineveh and Babylon*, p. 415.

[3] Cf. what is stated on this subject, *supra*, p. 254, et seq.

[4] The sequel of this history is known from the narrative of BEROSUS, *Fragm.* 14, in MÜLLER-DIDOT, *Fragm. Hist. Græc.*, vol. ii. pp. 507, 508. Its authenticity is proved by passages on the *Cylinder*

have come down to us, two factions had arisen in the city since the fall of Nineveh, both of which aspired to power and strove to gain a controlling influence with the sovereign. The one comprised the descendants of the Kaldâ who had delivered the city from the Assyrian yoke, together with those of the ancient military nobility. The other was composed of the great priestly families and their adherents, who claimed for the gods or their representatives the right to control the affairs of the state, and to impose the will of heaven on the rulers of the kingdom. The latter faction seems to have prevailed at first at the court of Amil-marduk, the sole surviving son and successor of Nebuchadrezzar. This prince on his accession embraced a policy contrary to that pursued by his father: and one of his first acts was to release Jehoiachin, King of Judah, who had been languishing in chains for twenty-seven years, and to ameliorate the condition of the other expatriated Jews.[1] The official history of a later date represented him as having been an unjust sovereign, but we have no information as to his misdeeds, and know only that after two years a conspiracy broke out against him, led by his own brother-in-law, Nergal-sharuzur, who assassinated him and seized the vacant throne (560 B.C.).[2] Nergal-sharuzur endeavoured to revive the policy of Nebuchadrezzar, and was probably supported by the military party, but his reign was a short one; he died in 556 B.C., leaving as sole heir a youth of dissipated character named Labashi-marduk, whose name is stigmatised by the chroniclers as that of a prince who knew not how to rule.[3] He was murdered at the end of nine months, and his place taken by a native Babylonian, a certain Nabonâîd (Nabonidus), son of Nabo-balatsu-ikbi, who was not connected by birth with his immediate predecessors on the throne (556–555 B.C.).[4]

of Nabonidus, col. iv. ll. 1–42, col. v. ll. 1–34, with which it has been compared by Messerschmidt (Die Inschrift der Stele Nabuna'ids, pp. 17–22). Messerschmidt considers that Amil-marduk and Labashi-marduk were overthrown by the priestly faction, but a passage on the Cylinder (col. v. ll. 14–18), which he does not seem to have noticed, in which Nabonidus represents himself as inheriting the political views of Nebuchadrezzar and Nergal-sharuzur, leads me to take the opposite view. We know what hatred Nabonidus roused in the minds of the priests of Merodach (cf. what is stated infra, in Chap. VI.) because his principles of government were opposed to theirs: the severe judgment he passed on the rule of Amil-marduk and Labashi-marduk seems to prove that he considered them as belonging to the rival party in the state, that is, to the priestly faction. The forms of the names and the lengths of the several reigns have been confirmed by contemporary monuments, especially by the numerous contract tablets. The principal inscriptions belonging to the reign of Nergal-sharuzur (BEZOLD, Inschriften Neriglissar's, in SCHRADER, Keil. Bibl., vol. iii., 2nd part, pp. 70–79) deal only with public works and the restoration of monuments.

[1] 2 Kings xxv. 27–30; cf. Jer. lii. 31–34.

[2] BEROSUS, Fragm. 14, in MÜLLER-DIDOT, Fragm. Hist. Græc., vol. ii. p. 507, where the expression προστὰς τῶν πραγμάτων ἀνόμως καὶ ἀσελγῶς seems almost a translation of a passage on the Cylinder of Nabonidus, col. iv. ll. 25–34, as Messerschmidt has observed (Die Inschr. der Stele Nabuna'ids, p. 18); Berosus, although belonging to the priestly caste, had as his sole sources of information documents proceeding from the opposite party, which was unfavourable to Labashi-marduk.

[3] BEROSUS, Fragm. 14, in MÜLLER-DIDOT, Fragm. Hist. Græc., vol. ii. p. 507; cf. the Cylinder of Nabonidus, col. v. ll. 34–42.

[4] BEROSUS, Fragm. 14, in MÜLLER-DIDOT, Fragm. Hist. Græc., vol. ii. p. 508.

No Oriental empire could escape from the effects of frequent and abrupt changes in its rulers: like so many previous dynasties, that of Nabopolassar became enfeebled as if from exhaustion immediately after the death of its most illustrious scion, and foundered in imbecility and decrepitude. Popular imagination, awe-struck by such a sudden downfall from exalted prosperity, recognised the hand of God in the events which brought about the catastrophe. A Chaldæan legend, current not long after, related how Nebuchadrezzar, being seized towards the end of his life with the spirit of prophecy, mounted to the roof of his palace, and was constrained, as a punishment for his pride, to predict to his people, with his own lips, the approaching ruin of their city; thereupon the glory of its monarch suffered an eclipse from which there was no emerging.[1] The Jews, nourishing undying hatred for the conqueror who had overthrown Jerusalem and destroyed the Temple of Solomon, were not satisfied with a punishment so inadequate.

THE STONE LION OF BABYLON.[2]

According to them, Nebuchadrezzar, after his victorious career, was so intoxicated with his own glory that he proclaimed himself the equal of God. "Is not this great Babylon," he cried, "which I have built for the royal dwelling-place, by the might of my power, and for the glory of my majesty!" and while he thus spake, there came a voice from heaven, decreeing his metamorphosis into the form of a beast. "He was driven from men, and did eat grass as oxen, and his body was wet with the dew of heaven, till his hair was grown like eagles' feathers, and his nails like birds' claws." For seven years the king remained in this state, to resume his former shape at the end of this period, and recover his kingdom after having magnified the God of Israel.[3] The founder of the dynasty which replaced that of Nebuchadrezzar, Nabonidus, was certainly ill fitted to brave the storms already threatening to break over his kingdom. It has not been ascertained whether he had any natural right to the throne, or by what means he attained supreme

[1] ABYDENUS, *Fragm.* 8, quoted from Berosus, in EUSEBIUS, *Præparatio evangelica*, ix. 41; cf. MÜLLER-DIDOT, *Fragm. Hist. Græc.*, vol. iv. p. 283.

[2] Drawn by Faucher-Gudin, from a photograph kindly furnished by Father Scheil.

[3] *Dan.* iv.

power, but the way in which he dwells on the names of Nebuchadrezzar and Ner-gal-sharuzur renders it probable that he was raised to the throne by the military faction.   He did not prove, as events turned out, a good general, nor even a soldier of moderate ability, and it is even possible that he also lacked that fierce courage of which none of his predecessors was ever destitute.   He allowed his army to dwindle away and his fortresses to fall into ruins ; the foreign alliances existing at his accession, together with those which he himself had concluded, were not turned to the best advantage ; his provinces were badly administered, and his subjects rendered discontented : his most salient characteristic was an insatiable curiosity concerning historical and religious antiquities, which stimulated him to undertake excavations in all the temples, in order to bring to light monuments of ages long gone by.   He was a monarch of peaceful disposition, who might have reigned with some measure of success in a century of unbroken peace, or one troubled only by petty wars with surrounding inferior states ; but, unfortunately, the times were ill suited to such mild sovereignty. The ancient Eastern world, worn out by an existence reckoned by thousands of years, as well as by its incessant conflicts, would have desired, indeed, no better fate than to enjoy some years of repose in the condition in which recent events had left it ; but other nations, the Greeks and the Persians, by no means anxious for tranquillity, were entering the lists.   For the moment the efforts of the Greeks were concentrated on Egypt, where Pharaoh manifested for them inexhaustible good will, and on Cyprus, two-thirds of which belonged to them : the danger for Chaldæa lay in the Persians, kinsfolk and vassals of the Medes, whose semi-barbarous chieftains had issued from their mountain homes some eighty years previously to occupy the eastern districts of Elam.

THE IRANIAN CONQUEST.

———◆———

Egypt under Amasis: building works, support given to the Greeks; Naukratis, its temples, its constitution, and its prosperity—Preparations for defence and the unpopularity of Amasis with the native Egyptians—The death of Cyrus and legends relating to it: his palace at Pasargadæ and his tomb—Cambyses and Smerdis—The legendary causes of the war with Egypt —Psammetichus III., the battle of Pelusium; Egypt reduced to a Persian province.

Cambyses' plans for conquest: the abortive expeditions to the Oasis of Ammon and Carthage— The kingdom of Ethiopia, its kings, its customs: the Persians fail to reach Napata, the madness of Cambyses—The fraud of Gaumâta, the death of Cambyses and the reign of the pseudo-Smerdis, the accession of Darius—The revolution in Susiana, Chaldæa, and Media: Nebuchad-rezzar III. and the fall of Babylon, the death of Orœtes, the defeat of Khshatrita, restoration of peace throughout Asia, Egyptian affairs and the re-establishment of the royal power.

The organisation of the country and its division into satrapies: the satrap, the military commander, the royal secretary; couriers, main roads, the Eyes and Ears of the king—The financial system and the provincial taxes: the daric—Advantages and drawbacks of the system of division into satrapies; the royal guard and the military organisation of the empire—The conquest of the Hapta-Hindu and the prospect of war with Greece.

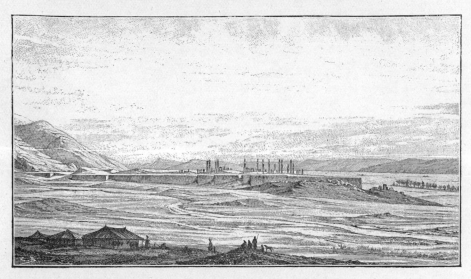

THE RUINS OF PERSEPOLIS, AS SEEN FROM THE NORTH.[1]

CHAPTER VI.

THE IRANIAN CONQUEST.

The Iranian religions—Cyrus in Lydia and at Babylon ; Cambyses in Egypt—Darius and the organisation of the empire.

THE Median empire is the least known of all those which held sway for a time over the destinies of a portion of Western Asia. The reason of this is not to be ascribed to the shortness of its duration: the Chaldæan empire of Nebuchadrezzar lasted for a period quite as brief, and yet the main outlines of its history can be established with some certainty in spite of large blanks and much obscurity. Whereas at Babylon, moreover, original documents abound, enabling us to put together, feature by feature, the picture of its ancient civilisation and of the chronology of its kings, we possess no contemporary monuments of Ecbatana to furnish direct information as to its history. To form any idea of the Median kings or their people, we are reduced to haphazard notices gleaned from the chroniclers of other lands, retailing a few isolated facts, anecdotes, legends, and conjectures, and, as these materials reach

---

[1] Drawn by Boudier, from the engraving in COSTE and FLANDIN, *La Perse Antique,* pl. 67. The initial, drawn by Faucher-Gudin, was designed from a statuette in terra-cotta, found in Southern Russia, representing a young Scythian; cf. KONDAKOF and REINACH, *Les Antiquités de la Russie Méridionale,* p. 204.

us through the medium of the Babylonians or the Greeks of the fifth or sixth century B.C., the picture which we endeavour to compose from them is always imperfect or out of perspective. We seemingly catch glimpses of ostentatious luxury, of a political and military organisation, and a method of government analogous to that which prevailed at later periods among the Persians, but more imperfect, ruder, and nearer to barbarism—a Persia, in fact, in the rudimentary stage, with its ruling spirit and essential characteristics as yet undeveloped.[1] The machinery of state had doubtless been adopted almost in its entirety from the political organisations which obtained in the kingdoms of Assyria, Elam, and Chaldæa, with which sovereignties the founders of the Median empire had held in turns relations as vassals, enemies, and allies;[2] but once we penetrate this veneer of Mesopotamian civilisation and reach the inner life of the people, we find in the religion they profess—mingled with some borrowed traits—a world of unfamiliar myths and dogmas of native origin.

The main outlines of this religion were already fixed when the Medes rose in rebellion against Assur-bani-pal; and the very name of *Confessor*—Fravartîsh —applied to the chief of that day, proves that it was the faith of the royal family.[3] It was a religion common to all the Iranians, the Persians as well as the Medes, and legend honoured as its first lawgiver and expounder an ancient prophet named Zarathustra, known to us as Zoroaster.[4] Most classical writers relegated Zoroaster to some remote age of antiquity—thus he is variously said to have lived six thousand years before the death of Plato,[5] five thousand before the Trojan war,[6] one thousand before Moses,[7] and six hundred before Xerxes' campaign against Athens;[8] while some few only affirmed that he had lived at

---

[1] NÖLDEKE, *Aufsätze zur Persische Geschichte*, pp. 11, 12, where the ruder aspect of the Median civilisation is left a little too much in the background.

[2] G. RAWLINSON, *The Five Great Monarchies*, 2nd edit., vol. ii. pp. 310–312.

[3] For the meaning of the name, cf. *supra*, p. 455, note 1.

[4] The name Zarathustra has been interpreted in a score of different ways. The Greeks sometimes attributed to it the meaning of ἀστροθύτης, worshipper of the stars, probably by reason of the similarity in sound of the termination -αστρης of Zoroaster with the word ἄστρον (DINON, *Fragm.* 5, in MÜLLER-DIDOT, *Fragm. Hist. Græc.*, vol. ii. p. 90). Among modern writers, H. Rawlinson derived it from the Assyrian Zîru-Ishtar, *the Seed of Ishtar* (*Notes on the Early History of Babylonia*, in the *J. R. As. Soc.*, 1855, vol. xv. p. 245, note 2), but the etymology now most generally accepted is that of Burnouf, according to which it would signify "the man with gold-coloured camels," the "possessor of tawny camels;" cf. JAMES DARMESTETER, *Le Zend-Avesta*, vol. iii. p. lxxvi., note 1, who, after proposing the meaning *red, gold-colour* (*Ormuzd et Ahriman*, p. 194), fell back on the explanation of Burnouf. The ordinary Greek form Zoroaster seems to be derived from some name quite distinct from Zarathustra (JUSTI, *Iranisches Namenbuch*, p. 381).

[5] This was, as Pliny records (*Hist. Nat.*, xxx. 1, § 2), the opinion of Eudoxus; not Eudoxus of Cnidus, pupil of Plato, as is usually stated, but a more obscure personage, Eudoxus of Rhodes.

[6] This was the statement of Hermodorus (DIOGENES LAERTIUS, *Procemium*, 2) and Hermippus (MÜLLER-DIDOT, *Fragm. Hist. Græc.*, vol. iii. pp. 53, 54; cf. *De Iside et Osiride*, § 46, ed. PARTHEY, p. 81).

[7] PLINY, *H. Nat.*, xxx. 1, § 2.

[8] XANTHUS OF LYDIA, *Fragm.* 29, in MÜLLER-DIDOT, *Fragm. Hist. Græc.*, vol. i. p. 44, where the alteration of 600 into 6000 is supported, in accordance with the testimony of two manuscripts of Diogenes Laertius; but this reading seems to have been interpolated in the text from a desire to make the testimony of the ancient historian agree with that of the followers of Plato, and Rapp justly

a comparatively recent period, and made him out a disciple of the philosopher Pythagoras, who flourished about the middle of the fifth century B.C.[1] According to the most ancient national traditions, he was born in the Aryanem-vaêjô, or, in other words, in the region between the Araxes and the Kur, to the west of the Caspian Sea.[2] Later tradition asserted that his conception was attended by supernatural circumstances, and the miracles which accompanied his birth announced the advent of a saint destined to regenerate the world by the revelation of the True Law. In the belief of an Iranian, every man, every living creature now existing or henceforth to exist, not excluding the gods themselves, possesses a Frôhar, or guardian spirit, who is assigned to him at his entrance into the world, and who is thenceforth devoted entirely to watching over his material and moral well-being.[3] About the time appointed for the appearance of the prophet, his Frôhar was, by divine grace, imprisoned in the heart of a Haoma,[4] and was absorbed, along with the juice of the plant, by the priest Purushâspa,[5] during a sacrifice, a ray of heavenly glory descending at the same time into the bosom of a maiden of noble race, named Dughdôva, whom Purushâspa shortly afterwards espoused. Zoroaster was engendered from the mingling of the Frôhar with the celestial ray.[6] The evil spirit, whose supremacy he threatened, endeavoured to destroy him as soon as he saw the light, and despatched one of his agents, named Bôuiti, from the country of the far north to oppose him; but the infant prophet immediately pronounced the formula with which the psalm for the offering of the waters opens: "The will of the Lord is the rule of good!" and proceeded to pour libations in honour

prefers the lower figure of the ordinary manuscripts (*Die Religion und Sitte der Perser und übrigen Iranier nach den griechischen und römischen Quellen*, in the *Z. d. D. Morgenl. Gesells.*, vol. xix. pp. 25, 26). The authenticity of the testimony of Xanthus has been most recently contested by J. MARQUART, *Die Assyriaka des Ktesias*, in the *Philologus, Supplément*, vol. vi. pp. 530, 531.

[1] PORPHYRY, *Life of Pythagoras*, ed. NAUCK, p. 12, which is supposed by a passage in the Byzantine historian Agathias (ii. 24), according to whom "the Persians of the present day assert that Zoroaster lived in the reign of Hystaspes, without making it clear whether they refer to the father of Darius or to another Hystaspes." This legend rests on the confusion of the well-known Hystaspes, father of Darius, with Vîshtâspa or Hystaspes, who is said to have been King of Bactria in the days of the prophet.

[2] WINDISCHMANN, *Zoroastrische Studien*, p. 47, et seq., has collected and commented upon all the passages of the Avesta and the Bundehesh which locate the birthplace and earliest home of Zoroaster in the Aryanem-Vaêjô (for the position of this country, cf. *supra*, p. 452, note 1). Most Western historians of the classical period adopted the legend which locates the birthplace of Zoroaster to the east of the Caspian Sea, in Bactriana (RAPP, *op. cit.*, pp. 29, 30).

[3] The Fravashi (for *fravarti*, from *fra-var*, "to support, nourish"), or the *frôhar* (*feruer*), is, properly speaking, the nurse, the genius who nurtures (OPPERT, *Inscriptions des Achéménides*, p. 105); on his *rôle* and history, cf. J. DARMESTETER, *Le Zend-Avesta*, vol. ii. pp. 500–505, and the *Yast* 13, which is entirely occupied with the glorification of the Fravashis. Many of the practices relating to the conception and cult of the Fravashis seem to me to go back to the primitive period of the Iranian religions.

[4] The haoma is an *Asclepias Sarcostema Viminalis*.

[5] The name signifies "He who has many horses;" cf. JUSTI, *Iranisches Namenbuch*, pp. 254, 255.

[6] J. DARMESTETER, *Le Zend-Avesta*, vol. iii. p. lxxviii., where the contents of the seventh book of the Dinkart are summed up in a few lines.

of the river Darêja,[1] on the banks of which he had been born a moment before, reciting at the same time the profession of faith which puts evil spirits to flight. Bôuiti fled aghast, but his master set to work upon some fresh device. Zoroaster allowed him, however, no time to complete his plans; he rose up, and undismayed by the malicious riddles propounded to him by his adversary, advanced against him with his hands full of stones—stones as large as a house—with which the good deity supplied him. The mere sight of him dispersed the demons, and they regained the gates of their hell in headlong flight, shrieking out, " How shall we succeed in destroying him ? For he is the weapon which strikes down evil beings; he is the scourge of evil beings." [2] His infancy and youth were spent in constant disputation with evil spirits : ever assailed, he ever came out victorious, and issued more perfect from each attack. When he was thirty years old, one of the good spirits, Vôhumanô, appeared to him, and conducted him into the presence of Ahura-mazdâ, the Supreme Being. When invited to question the deity, Zoroaster asked, " Which is the best of the creatures which are upon the earth ? " The answer was, that the man whose heart is pure, he excels among his fellows. He next desired to know the names and functions of the angels, and the nature and attributes of evil. His instruction ended, he crossed a mountain of flames, and underwent a terrible ordeal of purification, during which his breast was pierced with a sword, and melted lead poured into his entrails without his suffering any pain : only after this ordeal did he receive from the hands of Ahura-mazdâ the Book of the Law, the Avesta, and he was then sent back to his native land bearing his precious burden.[3] At that time, Vîshtâspa, son of Aurvatâspa, was reigning over Bactria. For ten years Zoroaster had only one disciple, his cousin Maidhyoi-Mâonha, but after that he succeeded in converting, one after the other, the two sons of Hvôgva, the grand vizir Jâmâspa, who afterwards married the prophet's daughter, and Frashaoshtra, whose daughter Hvôgvi he himself espoused ; the queen, Hutaosa, was the next convert, and afterwards, through her persuasions, the king Vîshtâspa himself became a disciple. The triumph of the good cause was hastened by the result of a formal disputation between the prophet and the wise men of the court : for three days they essayed to bewilder him with their captious objections and their magic arts, thirty standing on his right hand and thirty on his left, but he baffled their wiles, aided by grace from above, and having forced them to avow themselves at the end of their resources, he

---

[1] *Bundehesh*, xxiv. 15; cf. *Vendidad, Fargard,* 19, § 4 (J. DARMESTETER, *Le Zend-Avesta,* vol. ii. p. 260).

[2] *Vendidad, Fargard,* 19, which is devoted entirely to this episode; cf. J. DARMESTETER, *op. cit.,* vol. ii. pp. 256–275. The context shows that the attack was directed against the prophet at the very moment after his birth. Cf., for the legends relating to the birth of Zoroaster and the miracles which preceded, accompanied, or followed that event, the documents brought together by SPIEGEL, *Erânische Alterthumskunde,* vol. i. pp. 688–692.

[3] SPIEGEL, *Erânische Alterthumskunde,* vol. i. pp. 693–697.

completed his victory by reciting the Avesta before them.[1] The legend adds, that after rallying the majority of the people round him, he lived to a good old age, honoured of all men for his saintly life. According to some accounts, he was stricken dead by lightning,[2] while others say he was killed by a Turanian soldier, Brâtrôk-rêsh, in a war against the Hyaonas.[3]

The question has often been asked whether Zoroaster belongs to the domain of legend or of history. The only certain thing we know concerning him is his name; all the rest is mythical, poetic, or religious fiction.[4] Classical writers attributed to him the composition or editing of all the writings comprised in Persian literature: the whole consisted, they said, of two hundred thousand verses which had been expounded and analysed by Hermippus in his commentaries on the secret doctrines of the Magi.[5] The Iranians themselves averred that he had given the world twenty-one volumes—the twenty-one *Nasks* of the Avesta,[6] which the Supreme Deity had created from the twenty-one words of the Magian profession of faith, the *Ahuna Vairya.* King Vîshtâspa is said to have caused two authentic copies of the Avesta—which contained in all ten or twelve hundred chapters[7]—to be made, one of which was consigned to the archives of the empire, the other laid up in the treasury of a fortress, either Shapîgân, Shîzîgân, Samarcand, or Persepolis.[8] Alexander

---

[1] SPIEGEL, *Erânische Alterthumskunde*, vol. i. pp. 697–703.

[2] This is, under very diverse forms, the version preferred by Western historians of the post-classical period (RAPP, *Die Religion und Sitte der Perser und übrigen Iranier*, in the *Z. d. D. Morgenl. Gesell.*, vol. xxx. pp. 34–45).

[3] J. DARMESTETER, *Le Zend-Avesta*, vol. ii. p. 19, and vol. iii. pp. lxxviii., lxxix.; cf. SPIEGEL, *Erânische Alterthumskunde*, vol. i. p. 706.

[4] The mythical conception of Zoroaster has been defended more especially by Dutch critics, by Kern (*Over het woord Zarathustra en den mythischen Persoon van dien Naam*, in the *Memoirs* of the Academy of Sciences at Amsterdam, 1867), by Tiele (*Is Zarathustra een mythisch Persoon*, in the same *Memoirs*, immediately following the preceding), and accepted in other countries, among others, by Justi (*Göttinger gelehrte Anzeigen*, 1867, note 51) and by Darmesteter. Spiegel, on the contrary, admits the possibility of his having been a real person (*Erânische Alterthumskunde*, vol. i. pp. 707–710); cf. ED. MEYER, *Gesch. des Alterthums*, vol. i. p. 540.

[5] PLINY, *H. Nat.*, xxx. 2; cf., for the other testimonies in classical writers, RAPP, *op. cit.*, pp. 35, 36.

[6] The word *Avesta*, in Pehlevi *Apastâk*, whence come the Persian forms *âvasta*, *ôstâ*, is derived from the Achæmenian word *Abasta*, which signifies *law* in the inscriptions of Darius (OPPERT, *Note sur les mots Avesta et Zend*, in the *Journal Asiatique*, 1872, vol. xix. pp. 293–297; cf. J. DE HARLEZ, *Note sur le sens des mots Avesta-Zend*, in the *Journal Asiatique*, 1876, vol. viii. p. 487, et seq. The term Zend-Avesta, commonly used to designate the sacred book of the Persians, is incorrectly derived from the expression *Apastâk u Zend*, which in Pehlevi designates first the law itself, and then the translation and commentary in more modern language which conduces to a *knowledge* (*Zend*) of the law. The customary application, therefore, of the name Zend to the language of the Avesta is incorrect (J. DARMESTETER, *Le Zend-Avesta*, vol. i. pp. xxxix.-xli.).

[7] The Dinkart (viii. 1, § 20) fixes the number of chapters at 1000, and the Shâh-Nâmak at 1200, written on plates of gold (BLOCHET, *Liste Géographique des villes de l'Irân*, in the *Recueil de Travaux*, vol. xvii. pp. 165, 171). According to Masudi (*Les Prairies d'or*, ed. BARBIER DE MEYNARD, vol. ii. p. 125), the book itself and the two commentaries formed 12,000 volumes, written in letters of gold, the twenty-one Nasks each contained 200 pages, and the whole of these writings had been inscribed on 12,000 cow-hides.

[8] The site of Shapîgân or Shaspîgân (WEST, *Dinkart*, p. 413, note 4) is unknown. J. Darmesteter suggests that it ought to be read as *Shizîgân*, which would permit the identification of the place with Shîz, one of the ancient religious centres of Iran, whose temple was visited by the Sassanids on their accession to the throne (*Le Zend-Avesta*, vol. iii. p. xxi., n. 2). According to the Ardâ-Vîrâf the

is said to have burnt the former copy: the latter, stolen by the Greeks, is reported to have been translated into their language and to have furnished them with all their scientific knowledge. One of the Arsacids, Vologesus I., caused a search to be made for all the fragments which existed either in writing or in the memory of the faithful,[1] and this collection, added to in the reign of the Sassanid king, Ardashîr Bâbagan, by the high priest Tansar,[2] and fixed in its present form under Sapor I., was recognised as the religious code of the empire in the time of Sapor II., about the fourth century of the Christian era.[3] The text is composed, as may be seen, of three distinct strata, which are by no means equally ancient;[4] one can, nevertheless, make out from it with sufficient certainty the principal features of the religion and cult of Iran, such as they were under the Achæmenids, and perhaps even under the hegemony of the Medes. It is a complicated system of religion, and presupposes a long period of development. The doctrines are subtle; the ceremonial order of worship, loaded with strict observances, is interrupted at every moment by laws prescribing minute details of ritual,[5] which were only put in practice by priests and strict devotees, and were unknown to the mass of the faithful. The primitive base of this religion is difficult to discern clearly: but we may recognise in it most of those beings or personifications of natural phenomena which were the chief objects of worship among all the ancient nations of Western Asia—the stars, Sirius, the moon, the sun, water and fire, plants, animals beneficial to mankind, such as the cow and the dog, good and evil spirits everywhere present, and beneficent or malevolent souls of mortal men, but all systematised, graduated, and reduced to sacerdotal principles, according to the prescriptions of a powerful priesthood.[6] Families consecrated to the

law was preserved at Istakhr, or Persepolis, according to the Shâh-Nâmak at Samarcand in the temple of the Fire-god (BLOCHET, *Liste Géogr. des villes de l'Irân*, in *Recueil de Travaux*, vol. xvii. p. 165).

[1] Tradition speaks simply of a King Valkash, without specifying which of the four kings named Vologesus is intended. James Darmesteter has given good reasons for believing that this Valkash is Vologesus I. (50–75 A.D.), the contemporary of Nero (*The Zend-Avesta*, vol. i. pp. xxxiii.–xxxv., *Le Zend-Avesta*, vol. iii. pp. xxii.–xxiv.).

[2] For the high priest Tansar, cf. the notice which J. DARMESTETER, *Lettre au roi de Tabaristan* (in the *Journal Asiatique*, 1894, vol. iii. pp. 185-188), has placed at the commencement of his edition of a writing of this high priest.

[3] This is the tradition reproduced in two versions of the Dinkart (WEST, *Dinkart*, pp. xxx., xxxi., 412-415); it has been contested by SPIEGEL, *Erânische Alterthumskunde*, vol. iii. p. 782, note 1, defended and authenticated by J. DARMESTETER, *The Zend-Avesta*, vol. i. pp. xxxii.–xxxviii., and *Le Zend-Avesta*, vol. iii. pp. xx.–xxxvi.

[4] Darmesteter (*Le Zend-Avesta*, vol. iii. pp. lxx.–lxxiv.) declares that ancient Zoroastrianism is, in its main lines, the religion of the Median Magi, even though he assigns the latest possible date to the composition of the Avesta as now existing, and thinks he can discern in it Greek, Jewish, and Christian elements (*Le Zend-Avesta*, vol. iii. pp. xlii.–lxxii.).

[5] Renan defined the Avesta as " the Code of a very small religious sect; it is a Talmud, a book of casuistry and strict observance. I have difficulty in believing that the great Persian empire, which, at least in religious matters, professed a certain breadth of ideas, could have had a law so strict. I think, that had the Persians possessed a sacred book of this description, the Greeks must have mentioned it" (*Rapport sur les Travaux de la Société Asiatique*, 1880, vol. vii. p. 29).

[6] To distinguish the ideas which formed the basis of the ancient religions of Iran other than

service of the altar had ended, as among the Hebrews, by separating themselves from the rest of the nation and forming a special tribe, that of the Magi, which was the last to enter into the composition of the nation in historic times.[1] All the Magi were not necessarily devoted to the service of religion, but all who did so devote themselves sprang from the Magian tribe; the Avesta, in its

THE AHURA-MAZDÂ OF THE BAS-RELIEFS OF PERSEPOLIS.[2]

oldest form, was the sacred book of the Magi, as well as that of the priests who handed down their religious tradition under the various dynasties, native or foreign, who bore rule over Iran.

The Creator was described as "the whole circle of the heavens,"[3] "the most steadfast among the gods," for "he clothes himself with the solid vault of the firmament as his raiment,"[4] the most beautiful, the most intelligent, he whose members are most harmoniously proportioned; his body was the light and the sovereign glory,[5] the sun and the moon were his eyes."[6] The theologians had gradually spiritualised the conception of this deity without absolutely disconnecting him from the material universe. He remained under ordinary circumstances invisible to mortal eyes, and he could conceal his identity even

Zoroastrianism, cf. the *résumé* of M. Ed. Lehmann, in CHANTEPIE DE LA SAUSSAYE, *Lehrbuch der Religions-geschichte*, vol. ii. pp. 164–172.

[1] For the Median tribes, cf. *supra*, p. 452.

[2] Drawn by Faucher-Gudin, from FLANDIN and COSTE, *La Perse Ancienne*, pl. clvi.; cf. pl. clxiv.

[3] HERODOTUS, I. cxxxi.: τὸν κύκλον πάντα τοῦ οὐρανοῦ Δία καλέοντες, where Ahura-mazdâ is identified with Zeus, as in the bilingual inscription, in Greek and Pehlevi, on the bas-relief at Nakhsh-î-Rustem, which represents Ardashîr receiving the investiture from the Supreme Deity (DIEULAFOY, *L'Art Antique de la Perse*, vol. v. p. 114, and pl. xiv.); cf. the illustration on p. 579, *supra*.

[4] *Yasna* 30, § 5, in DARMESTETER, *Le Zend-Avesta*, vol. i. pp. 221, 222.

[5] *Yasna* 1, § 1, in ID., *ibid.*, pp. 7, 8; cf. the passage of PORPHYRY, *Life of Pythagoras*, ed. NAUCK, p. 41, Ὡρομάζου ἐοικέναι τὸ μὲν σῶμα φωτί.

[6] *Yasna* 68, § 22, in DARMESTETER, *Le Zend-Avesta*, vol. i. p. 423, where mention is made of the "prayer addressed to the two eyes of Ahura-mazdâ:" the pair formed by the moon and the sun, as shown by the title assumed by the Sassanids, *brother of the Sun and the Moon* (AMMIANUS MARCELLINUS, xvii. 5, § 3, xxiii. 6, § 5).

2 P

from the highest gods, but he occasionally manifested himself in human form.[1] He borrowed in such case from Assyria the symbol of Assur, and the sculptors depict him with the upper part of his body rising above that winged disk which is carved in a hovering attitude on the pediments of Assyrian monuments or stelæ.[2] In later days he was portrayed under the form of a king of imposing stature and majestic mien, who revealed himself from time to time to the princes of Iran.[3] He was named Ahurô-mazdâo or Ahura-mazdâ, the omniscient lord,[4] *Spentô-mainyus*, the spirit of good, *Mainyus-spenishtô*,[5] the most beneficent of spirits. Himself uncreate, he is the creator of all things, but he is assisted in the administration of the universe by legions of beings, who are all subject to him.[7] The most powerful among his ministers were

AN IRANIAN GENIUS IN FORM OF A WINGED BULL.[6]

---

[1] For the nature of the body of Ahura-mazdâ and his manifestations, cf. DARMESTETER, *Le Zend-Avesta*, vol. i. pp. 7, 8, note 4.

[2] SPIEGEL, *Erânische Alterthumskunde*, vol. ii. pp. 24, 25.

[3] In a passage of Philo of Byblos the god is described as having the head of a falcon or an eagle (*Fragm.* 9, in MÜLLER-DIDOT, *Fragm. Hist. Græc.*, vol. iii. pp. 572, 573), perhaps by confusion with one of the genii represented on the walls of the palaces.

[4] *Ahura* is derived from *Ahu* = Lord: *Mazdâo* can be analysed into the component parts, *maz* = great, and *dâo* = he who knows (J. DARMESTETER, *Le Zend-Avesta*, vol. i. p. 21, notes 1, 2). At first the two terms were interchangeable, and even in the Gâthas the form Mazdâ Ahura is employed much more often than the form Ahura Mazdâ (TIELE, *Zur Frage nach dem Alter des Avesta*, in the *Archiv für Religionswissenchaft*, vol. i. pp. 355–357). In the Achæmenian inscriptions, Auramazdâ is only found as a single word, except in an inscription of Xerxes, where the two terms are in one passage separated and declined *Aurahya mazdâha* (WEISSBACH and BANG, *Die Altpersischen Keilinschriften*, pp. 42, 43). The Greeks transliterated it as Αὐρομάσδης, Ὀρομάζης, Ὁρμίσδας (JUSTI, *Iranisches Namenbuch*, p. 7); the form Ormuzd, Ormazd, usually employed by Europeans, is that assumed by the name in modern Persian.

[5] These two names are given to him more especially in connection with his antagonism to Angrô-mainyus. The interpretation of this name and of its superlative form are but approximative (J. DARMESTETER, *Le Zend-Avesta*, vol. i. p. 21); the real sense would be "the spirit of increase" (SPIEGEL, *Erânische Alterthumskunde*, vol. ii. p. 22).

[6] Drawn by Boudier, from a photograph.

[7] Darius styles Ahura-mazdâ, *mathishta bagânâm*, the greatest of the gods (WEISSBACH and BANG, *op. cit.*, pp. 34, 35), and Xerxes invokes the protection of Ahura-mazdâ along with that of the gods, *Auramazdâ . . . hadâ bagaibish* (ID., *ibid.*, pp. 40–45). The classical writers also mention gods alongside of Ahura-mazdâ, as recognised not only among the Achæmenian Persians, but also among the Parthians, and a list of the principal passages which mention them has been made up by RAPP, *Die Religion und Sitte der Perser und übrigen Iranier nach den Griechischen und Römischen Quellen*, in the *Z. d. D. Morgenl. Gesells.*, vol. xxx. pp. 45–47. Darmesteter considers that the earliest

originally nature-gods, such as the sun, the moon, the earth, the winds, and the waters.[1] The sunny plains of Persia and Media afforded abundant witnesses of their power, as did the snow-clad peaks, the deep gorges through which rushed roaring torrents, and the mountain ranges of Ararat or Taurus, where the force of the subterranean fires was manifested by so many startling exhibitions of spontaneous conflagration.[2] The same spiritualising tendency which had already

AHURA-MAZDÂ BESTOWING THE TOKENS OF ROYALTY ON AN IRANIAN KING.[3]

considerably modified the essential concept of Ahura-mazdâ, affected also that of the inferior deities, and tended to tone down in them the grosser traits of their character. It had already placed at their head six genii of a superior order, six ever-active energies, who, after assisting their master at the creation of the universe, now presided under his guidance over the kingdoms and forces of nature.[4]

Achæmenids worshipped Ahura-mazdâ alone, "placing the other gods together in a subordinate and anonymous group: May Ahura-mazdâ and the other gods protect me," *hadâ vithaibish bagabish* (*Le Zend-Avesta*, vol. ii. pp. 364, 365); Tiele has established the real sense of the passage (*Zur Frage nach dem Alter des Avesta*, in the *Archiv für Religionswissenchaft*, vol. i. p. 338, note 1).

[1] HERODOTUS, I. cxxxi.: θύουσι δὲ ἡλίῳ τε καὶ σελήνῃ καὶ γέᾳ καὶ πυρὶ καὶ ὕδαι καὶ ἀνέμοισι.

[2] All these inferior deities, heroes, and genii who presided over Persia, the royal family, and the different parts of the empire, are often mentioned in the most ancient classical authors that have come down to us—Herodotus (III. lxv., V. cvi., VII. liii.: θεοὶ, οἵ Περσίδα γέαν λελόγχασι), Xenophon (*Cyropædia*, II. i. § 1, III. iii. § 22), and the later writers whose evidence has been collected by RAPP, *Die Religion und Sitte der Perser und übrigen Iranier*, in the *Z. d. D. Morgenl. Gesells.*, vol. xxx. pp. 66–68.

[3] Drawn by Boudier, from a photograph by DIEULAFOY, *L'Art Antique de la Perse*, vol. iv. pl. xiv., and *L'Acropole de Suse*, p. 408.

[4] The six Amesha-spentas, with their several characteristics, are enumerated in a passage of the *De Iside* (§ 47, ed. PARTHEY, p. 82): καὶ ὁ μὲν ἓξ θεοὺς ἐποίησε, τὸν μὲν πρῶτον εὐνοίας, τὸν δὲ δεύτερον

These benevolent and immortal beings—*Amesha-spentas*[1]—were, in the order of precedence, Vohu-manô (good thought), Asha-vahista (perfect holiness), Khshathra-vairya (good government), Spenta-armaiti (meek piety), Haurvatât (health), Ameretât (immortality). Each of them had a special domain assigned to him in which to display his energy untrammelled : Vohu-manô had charge of cattle, Asha-vahista of fire, Khshathra-vairya of metals, Spenta-armaiti of the earth, Haurvatât and Ameretât of vegetation and of water.[2] They were

MÂO, THE MOON-GOD.[5]

represented in human form, either masculine as Vohu-manô and Asha-vahista,[3] or feminine[4] as Spenta-armaiti, the daughter and spouse of Ahura-mazdâ, who became the mother of the first man, Gâyomaretan, and, through Gâyomaretan, ancestress of the whole human race.[7] Sometimes

VÂTO, GOD OF THE WIND.[6]

Ahura-mazdâ is himself included among the Amesha-spentas, thus bringing their number up to seven;[8] sometimes his place is taken by a certain Sraôsha (obedience to the law), the first who offered sacrifice and recited the prayers of the ritual.[9] Subordinate to these great spirits were the Yazatas, scattered by

ἀληθείας, τὸν δὲ τρίτον εὐνομίας, τῶν δὲ λοιπῶν τὸν μὲν σοφίας, τὸν δὲ πλούτου, τὸν δὲ τῶν ἐπὶ τοῖς καλοῖς ἡδέων δημιουργόν. This exposition of Persian doctrine is usually attributed to Theopompus, from which we may deduce the existence of a belief in the Amesha-spentas in the Achæmenian period. J. Darmesteter (*Le Zend-Avesta*, vol. iii. p. lxv., note 3) affirms, on the contrary, that "the author describes the Zoroastrianism of his own times (the second century A.D.), and quotes Theopompus for a special doctrine, that of the periods of the world's life." Although this last point is correct, the first part of Darmesteter's theory does not seem to me justified by investigation. The whole passage of Plutarch is a well-arranged composition of uniform style, which may be regarded as an exposition of the system described by Theopompus, probably in the eighth of his *Philippics*; cf. TIELE, *Zur Frage nach dem Alter des Avesta*, in the *Archiv für Religionswissenschaft*, vol. i. pp. 341–344.

[1] The translation of this word is only approximate. Anquetil-Duperron and Eugène Burnouf (*Commentaire sur le Yaçna*, p. 172) proposed *the beneficent Immortals*; a more literal translation would be *the Immortals who give increase*, with the sense of *Spenta* as indicated above, *supra*, p. 578, note 6. The current French term to designate them, *Amschaspand*, is borrowed from modern Persian.

[2] For the order, the functions and attributes of the Amesha-spentas, cf. SPIEGEL, *Erânische Alterthumskunde*, vol. ii. pp. 28–40 ; also J. DARMESTETER, *Le Zend-Avesta*, vol. i. pp. 23–25, and especially vol. ii. pp. 307–322, where is given the translation of Siroza, in which these beings are defined.

[3] The image of Asha-vahista is known to us from coins of the Indo-Scythian kings of Bactriana (AUREL STEIN, *Zoroastrian Deities on Indo-Scythian Coins*, in the *Babylonian and Oriental Record*, vol. i. pp. 165, 166). Vohu-manô is described as a young man.

[4] For the differentiation of the Amesha-spentas into male and female, cf. *Yasna* 21, in J. DARMESTETER, *Le Zend-Avesta*, vol. i. pp. 175–177. Haurvatât and Ameretât are feminine by the form of their names, and are classed among the female Amesha-spentas.

[5] Drawn by Faucher-Gudin, from a coin of King Kanishka, published by PERCY GARDNER, *The Coins of the Greek and Scythian Kings of Bactria and India*, pl. xxvi. No. 9.

[6] *Ibid.*, pl. xxvii. No. 6.

[7] On the Khêtûk-das or incestuous marriage of Spenta-armaiti with her father Ahura-mazdâ, and then with her own son Gâyomaretan, cf. J. DARMESTETER, *Le Zend-Avesta*, vol. i. pp. 128, 129.

[8] SPIEGEL, *Erânische Alterthumskunde*, vol. ii. pp. 27–29.

[9] For Sraosha, cf. SPIEGEL, *op. cit.*, vol. ii. pp. 87–91, and J. DARMESTETER, *op. cit.*, vol. i. pp. 357–372, and vol. ii. pp. 481–489, where is given a translation with commentary of the two *Yashts* relating to this goddess.

thousands over creation, presiding over the machinery of nature and maintaining it in working order.[1]   Most of them received no special names, but many exercised wide authority, and several were accredited by the people with an influence not less than that of the greater deities themselves.   Such were the regent of the stars—Tishtrya, the bull with golden horns, Sirius, the

sparkling one;[2] Mâo, the moon-god;[3] the wind, Vâto; the atmosphere, Vayu, the strongest of the strong, the warrior with

golden armour, who gathers the storm and hurls it against the demon;[5] Âtar, fire under its principal forms, divine fire, sacred fire and earthly fire;[7] Vere-

AURVATASPA.[6]

thraghna, the author of war and giver of victory;[8] Aurvataspa, the son of the waters, the lightning born among the clouds; and lastly, the spirit of the dawn, the watchful Mithra, "who, first of the celestial Yazatas, soars above Mount Hara,[9] before the immortal sun with his swift steeds, who, first in golden splendour,

MITHRA.[10]

passes over the beautiful mountains and casts his glance benign on the dwellings of the Aryans."[11]   Mithra was a charming youth of beautiful countenance,

---

[1] For the Yazatas, cf. SPIEGEL, *Erânische Alterthumskunde*, vol. ii. p. 41, et seq., and J. DARMESTETER, *Le Zend-Avesta*, vol. i. pp. 5–19, and vol. ii. pp. 296–322, where we have the translation with commentary of the texts which supply the list of the most important of these divinities. *Yazata,* in modern Persian *izat, ized, yazd,* signifies literally *he who should receive the sacrifice.*

[2] SPIEGEL, *Erânische Alterthumskunde,* vol. ii. pp. 70–76.

[3] ID., *ibid.,* p. 70; for the representation of Mâo on coins of the Indo-Scythian kings of Bactriana, cf. AUREL STEIN, *Zoroastrian Deities on Indo-Scythian Coins,* in the *Babylonian and Oriental Record,* vol. i. p. 157, and the illustration on p. 580, *supra.*

[4] Drawn by Faucher-Gudin, from a coin of King Kanishka, published by PERCY GARDNER, *The Coins of the Greek and Scythian Kings,* pl. xxvi. No. 4.

[5] SPIEGEL, *op. cit.,* vol. ii. pp. 101–104; and for the representation of the god, AUREL STEIN, *op. cit.,* p. 158.

[6] Drawn by Faucher-Gudin, from coin published by PERCY GARDNER, *op. cit.,* pl. xxvi. No. 7.

[7] SPIEGEL, *op. cit.,* vol. ii. pp. 41–51; J. DARMESTETER, *op. cit.,* vol. i. pp. 149–157; and for the representation of the god, AUREL STEIN, *op. cit.,* pp. 158, 159; cf. the illustration given above.

[8] SPIEGEL, *op. cit.,* pp. 98–101, where Aurvataspa is studied under the form Apañm-napât; for the representation of the god, cf. AUREL STEIN, *op. cit.,* pp. 157, 158, and the objections urged by J. DARMESTETER, *op. cit.,* vol. ii. p. 432.

[9] Hara is Haroberezaïti, or Elburz, the mountain over which the sun rises, "around which many a star revolves, where there is neither night nor darkness, no wind of cold or heat, no sickness leading to a thousand kinds of death, nor infection caused by the Daêvas, and whose summit is never reached by the clouds" (*Yasht* 12, § 23, in J. DARMESTETER, *op. cit.,* vol. ii. p. 496).

[10] Drawn by Faucher-Gudin, from a coin of King Huvishka, published by PERCY GARDNER, *op. cit.,* pl. xxviii. No. 5.

[11] This is the Mithra whose religion became so powerful in Alexandrian and Roman times.   His sphere of action is defined in the Bundehesh (J DARMESTETER, *Le Zend-Avesta,* vol. ii. pp. 314, 315); cf., for information about this deity borrowed from Iranian documents, SPIEGEL, *Erânische Alterthumskunde,* vol. ii. pp. 77–87, and, from classical authors, RAPP, *Die Religion und Sitte der Perser,* in the *Z. d. D. Morgenl. Gesells.,* vol. xxx. pp. 53–60.

his head surrounded with a radiant halo. The nymph Anâhita was adored under the form of one of the incarnations of the Babylonian goddess Mylitta, a youthful and slender female, with well-developed breasts and broad hips,

sometimes represented clothed in furs and sometimes nude.[1] Like the foreign goddess to whom she was assimilated, she was the dispenser of fertility and of love; the heroes of antiquity, and even Ahura-mazdâ himself, had vied with one another in their worship of her, and she had lavished her favours freely on all.[2] The less important Yazatas were hardly to be distinguished from the innumerable multitude of Fravashis. The Fravashis are the divine types of all intelligent beings.[3] They were originally brought into being by Ahura-mazdâ as a distinct species from the human, but they had allowed themselves to be

MYLITTA-ANÂHITA.[4]

entangled in matter, and to be fettered in the bodies of men, in order to hasten the final destruction of the demons and the advent of the reign of good.[5]

Once incarnate, a Fravashis devotes himself to the well-being of the mortal with whom he is associated;[6] and when once more released from the flesh, he continues the struggle against evil with an energy whose efficacy is proportionate to the virtue and purity displayed in life by the mortal to whom he has been temporarily joined. The last six days of the year are dedicated to the Fravashis. They leave their heavenly abodes at this time to visit the spots which were their earthly dwelling-places, and they wander through the villages inquiring, " Who wishes to hire us ? Who will offer us a sacrifice ? Who will make us their own, welcome us, and receive us with plenteous offerings of food and raiment, with a prayer which bestows sanctity on him who offers

NANA-ANÂHITA.[7]

[1] WEISSBACH and BANG, *Die Altpersischen Keilinschriften*, pp. 44–47; the popularity of these two deities was already well established at the period we are dealing with, for Herodotus mentions Mithra and confuses him with Anâhita (I. cxxxi.). He is represented as described in the text on the coins of the Indo-Scythian kings; cf. AUREL STEIN, *Zoroastrian Deities on Indo-Scythian Coins*, in the *Babylonian and Oriental Record*, vol. i. pp. 156, 157.

[2] *Yasht* 5, in J. DARMESTETER, *Le Zend-Avesta*, vol. ii. pp. 363–397, where the full list of favourites of the goddess is given. Her name Ardvî-Sûra Anâhita seems to signify *the lofty and immaculate power* (JUSTI, *Handbuch der Zendsprache*, p. 30; J. DARMESTETER, *op. cit.*, vol. ii. p. 363). For her nature, cf. SPIEGEL, *Erânische Alterthumskunde*, vol. ii. pp. 54–60, and J. DARMESTETER, *op. cit.*, vol. ii. pp. 363–366.

[3] This is the definition given by Eugène Burnouf (*Commentaire sur le Yaçna*, p. 270).

[4] Drawn by Faucher-Gudin, from LOFTUS, *Chaldæa and Susiana*, p. 379).

[5] The legend of the descent of the Fravashis to dwell among men is narrated in the Bundehesh; cf. SPIEGEL, *op. cit.*, vol. ii. p. 93; J. DARMESTETER, *op. cit.*, vol. ii. p. 502.

[6] Cf., for the interpretation of the name as " nourisher," *supra*, p. 573, note 3.

[7] Drawn by Faucher-Gudin, from a coin of King Huvishka, published by PERCY GARDNER, *The Coins of the Greek and Scythian Kings*, pl. xxviii. No. 10.

it?" And if they find a man to hearken to their request, they bless him: "May his house be blessed with herds of oxen and troops of men, a swift horse and a strongly built chariot, a man who knoweth how to pray to God, a chieftain in the council who may ever offer us sacrifices with a hand filled with food and raiment, with a prayer which bestows sanctity on him who offers it!"[1]

Ahura-mazdâ created the universe, not by the work of his hands, but by the magic of his word, and he desired to create it entirely free from defects. His creation, however, can only exist by the free play and equilibrium of opposing forces, to which he gives activity: the incompatibility of tendency displayed by these forces, and their alternations of growth and decay, inspired the Iranians with the idea that they were the result of two contradictory principles, the one beneficent and good, the other adverse to everything emanating from the former.[2] In opposition to the god of light, they necessarily formed the idea of a god of darkness, the god of the underworld, who presides over death, Angrô-mainyus.[3] The two opposing principles reigned at first, each in his own domain, as rivals, but not as irreconcilable adversaries: they were considered as in fixed opposition to each other, and as having coexisted for ages without coming into actual conflict, separated as they were by the intervening void. As long as the principle of good was content to remain shut up inactive in his barren glory, the principle of evil slumbered unconscious in a darkness that knew no beginning; but when at last "the spirit who giveth increase"—Spentô-mainyus—determined to manifest himself, the first throes of his vivifying activity roused from inertia the spirit of destruction and of pain, Angrô-mainyus.[4] The heaven was not yet in existence, nor the waters, nor the earth, nor ox, nor fire, nor man, nor demons, nor brute beasts, nor any living thing, when the evil spirit hurled himself upon the light to quench it for ever, but Ahura-mazdâ had already called forth the ministers of his will— Amêsha-spentas, Yazatas, Fravashis—and he recited the prayer of twenty-one words in which all the elements of morality are summed up, the Ahuna-vairya: "The will of the Lord is the rule of good. Let the gifts of Vohu-manô be

---

[1] *Yasht* 13, §§ 49–52, in J. DARMESTETER, *Le Zend-Avesta*, vol. ii. pp. 518, 519.

[2] Spiegel, who at first considered that the Iranian dualism was derived from polytheism, and was a preliminary stage in the development of monotheism, held afterwards that a rigid monotheism had preceded this dualism (*Erânische Alterthumskunde*, vol. ii. p. vi.). The classical writers, who knew Zoroastrianism at the height of its glory, never suggested that the two principles might be derived from a superior principle, nor that they were subject to such a principle, as is shown by the passages collected together by RAPP, *Die Religion und Sitte der Perser und übrigen Iranier*, in the *Z. d. D. Morgenl. Gesells.*, vol. xxx. pp. 83–89, which are the more significant as Rapp does not believe in the dualism. The Iranian books themselves nowhere definitely affirm that there existed a single principle distinct from the two opposing principles, and the existence of the dualism, as known from their testimony, is admitted for the Achæmenian and Median periods by J. Darmesteter (*Le Zend-Avesta*, vol. iii. pp. lxvi.-lxix.).

[3] HERODOTUS, VII. cxiv.: τῷ ὑπὸ γεὰν λεγομένῳ εἶναι θεῷ, to whom human sacrifices were offered.

[4] SPIEGEL, *Erânische Alterthumskunde*, vol. ii. p. 143, following the first chapter of the Bundehesh.

bestowed on the works accomplished, at this moment, for Mazda. He makes Ahura to reign, he who protects the poor."[1] The effect of this prayer was irresistible : "When Ahura had pronounced the first part of the formula, Zânak Mînoî, the spirit of destruction, bowed himself with terror ; at the second part he fell upon his knees ; and at the third and last he felt himself powerless to hurt the creatures of Ahura-mazdâ."[2] The strife, kindled at the beginning of time between the two gods, has gone on ever since with alternations of success and defeat; each in turn has the victory for a regular period of three thousand years; but when these periods are ended, at the expiration of twelve thousand years, evil will be finally and for ever defeated.[3] While awaiting this blessed fulness of time, as Spentô-mainyus shows himself in all that is good and beautiful, in light, virtue, and justice, so Angrô-mainyus is to be perceived in all that is hateful and ugly, in darkness, sin, and crime. Against the six Amesha-spentas he sets in array six spirits of equal power— Akem-manô, evil thought; Andra, the devouring fire, who introduces discontent and sin wherever he penetrates ; Sauru, the flaming arrow of death, who inspires bloodthirsty tyrants, who incites men to theft and murder ; Nâongaithya, arrogance and pride ; Tauru, thirst; and Zairi, hunger.[4] To the Yazatas he opposed the Daêvas, who never cease to torment mankind, and so through all the ranks of nature he set over against each good and useful creation a counter-creation of rival tendency.[5] " ' Like a fly he crept into ' and infected ' the whole universe.' He rendered the world as dark at full noonday as in the darkest night. He covered the soil with vermin, with his creatures of venomous bite and poisonous sting, with serpents, scorpions, and frogs, so that there was not a space as small as a needle's point but swarmed with his vermin. He smote vegetation, and of a sudden the plants withered. . . . He attacked the flames, and mingled them with smoke and dimness. The planets, with their thousands

[1] For this act of creation by the Ahuna-vairya, refer to the translation with commentary of *Hâ 19* of the *Yasna*, in J. DARMESTETER, *Le Zend-Avesta*, vol. i. pp. 161–171, which is entirely devoted to this episode.

[2] Theopompus (*Fragm.* 71, in MÜLLER-DIDOT, *Fragm. Hist. Græc.*, vol. i. p. 279) was already aware of this alternation of good and bad periods. According to the tradition enshrined in the first chapter of the Bundehesh, it was the result of a sort of compact agreed upon at the beginning by Ahura-mazdâ and Angrô-mainyus. Ahura-mazdâ, fearing to be overcome if he entered upon the struggle immediately, but sure of final victory if he could gain time, proposed to his adversary a truce of nine thousand years, at the expiration of which the battle should begin. As soon as the compact was made, Angrô-mainyus realised that he had been tricked into taking a false step, but it was not till after three thousand years that he decided to break the truce and open the conflict. Cf. DARMESTETER, *Ormuzd and Ahriman*, pp. 114–117.

[3] *Yasna* 30, §§ 3–8, in J. DARMESTETER, *Le Zend-Avesta*, vol. i. pp. 220–223 ; cf. *Yasna* 45, § 2, in ID., *ibid.*, p. 296.

[4] The last five of these spirits are enumerated in the *Vendidad*, 10, §§ 9, 10 (J. DARMESTETER, *Le Zend-Avesta*, vol. ii. pp. 175, 176), and the first, Akem-manô, is there replaced by Nasu, the chief spirit of evil.

[5] SPIEGEL, *Eránische Alterthumskunde*, vol. ii. pp. 125, 126, where it is remarked that the Daêvas appear to be above all things of the male sex. For the meaning of the word itself, cf. DARME-STETER, *Ormuzd and Ahriman*, pp. 265–272. The modern form is Dêv, Dîv.

of demons, dashed against the vault of heaven and waged war on the stars, and the universe became darkened like a space which the fire blackens with its smoke." And the conflict grew ever keener over the world and over man, of whom the evil one was jealous, and whom he sought to humiliate. The children of Angrô-mainyus disguised themselves under those monstrous forms in which the imagination of the Chaldæans had clothed the allies of Mummu-Tiamât, such as lions with bulls' heads, and the wings and claws of eagles, which

the Achæmenian king combats on behalf of his subjects, boldly thrusting them through with his short sword. Aêshma of the blood-stained lance, terrible in wrath, is the most trusted leader of these dread bands,[1] the chief of twenty other Daêvas of repulsive aspect — Astô-vîdhôtu, the demon of death, who would devote to destruc-

ONE OF THE BAD GENII, SUBJECT TO ANGRÔ-MAINYUS.[3]

tion the estimable Fravashis;[2] Apaosha, the enemy of Tishtrya, the wicked black horse, the bringer of drought, who interferes with the distribution of the fertilising waters;[4] and Bûiti, who essayed to kill Zoroaster at his birth.[5] The female demons, the Druges,[6] the Incubi (Yâtus), the Succubi (Pairîka), the Peris of our fairy tales, mingled familiarly with mankind before the time of the prophet, and contracted with them fruitful alliances, but Zoroaster broke up their ranks, and prohibited them from becoming incarnate in any form but that of beasts; their hatred, however, is still unquenched, and their power will only be effectually overthrown at the consummation of time.[7] It is a matter of uncertainty whether the Medes already admitted the possibility of a fresh revelation,

[1] SPIEGEL, *Erânische Alterthumskunde*, vol. ii. pp. 131–133; the name Aêshma means *anger*. He is the Asmodeus, Aêshmo-daevô, of Rabbinic legends.

[2] ID., *ibid.*, p. 133. The name of this demon signifies *He who separates the bones* (E. BURNOUF, *Commentaire sur le Yaçna*, p. 465).

[3] Drawn by Faucher-Gudin, from a photograph taken from the original bas-relief in glazed tiles in the Louvre; cf. MARCEL DIEULAFOY, *L'Acropole de Suse*, pl. xi.

[4] SPIEGEL, *op. cit.*, vol. ii. pp. 133, 134.

[5] Cf. *supra*, p. 573. The Greater Bundehesh connects the demon Bûiti with the Indian Buddha, and J. Darmesteter (*Le Zend-Avesta*, vol. ii. p. 259, note 4) seems inclined to accept this interpretation. In this case we must either admit that the demon Bûiti is of relatively late origin, or that he has, in the legend of Zoroaster, taken the place of a demon whose name resembled his own closely enough to admit of the assimilation.

[6] SPIEGEL, *Erânische Alterthumskunde*, vol. ii. pp. 136, 137.

[7] ID., *ibid.*, pp. 138–140, 146–148.

preparing the latest generations of mankind for the advent of the reign of good. The traditions enshrined in the sacred books of Iran announce the coming of three prophets, sons of Zoroaster—Ukhshyatereta, Ukhshyatnemô, and Saoshyañt[1]— who shall bring about universal salvation. Saoshyañt, assisted by fifteen men and fifteen pure women, who have already lived on earth, and are awaiting their final destiny in a magic slumber, shall offer the final sacrifice, the virtue of which shall bring about the resurrection of the dead. " The sovereign light shall accompany him and his friends, when he shall revivify the world and ransom it from old age and death, from corruption and decay, and shall render it eternally living, eternally growing, and master of itself." The fatal conflict shall be protracted, but the champions of Saoshyant shall at length obtain the victory. "Before them shall bow Aêshma of the blood-stained lance and of ominous renown, and Saoshyañt shall strike down the she-demon of the unholy light, the daughter of darkness. Akem-manô strikes, but Vohu-manô shall strike him in his turn ; the lying word shall strike, but the word of truth shall strike him in his turn ; Haurvatât and Ameretât shall strike down hunger and thirst ; Haurvatât and Ameretât shall strike down terrible hunger and terrible thirst." [2] Angrô-mainyus himself shall be paralysed with terror, and shall be forced to confess the supremacy of good : he shall withdraw into the depths of hell, whence he shall never again issue forth, and all the reanimated beings devoted to the Mazdean law shall live an eternity of peace and contentment.[3]

Man, therefore, incessantly distracted between the two principles, laid wait for by the Daêvas, defended by the Yazatas, must endeavour to act according to law and justice in the condition in which fate has placed him.[4] He has been raised up here on earth to contribute as far as in him lies to the increase of life and of good, and in proportion as he works for this end or against it, is he the *ashavan*, the pure, the faithful one on earth and the blessed one in heaven, or the *anashavan*, the lawless miscreant who counteracts purity.[5] The highest grade in the hierarchy of men belongs of right to the Mage or the *âthravan*, to the priest whose voice inspires the demons with fear, or the soldier whose club despatches the impious, but a place of honour at their side is assigned to the

---

[1] The legend ran that they had been conceived in the waters of the lake Kañsu (SPIEGEL, *Erânische Alterthumskunde*, vol. i. pp. 705, 706, vol. ii. pp. 161, 162 ; J. DARMESTETER, *Ormuzd and Ahriman*, pp. 224–238). The name Saoshyañt signifies *the useful one, the saviour ;* Ukshyatereta, *he who makes the good increase ;* Ukshyatnemô, *he who makes prayer increase.*

[2] *Yasht* 19, §§ 89–96 ; J. DARMESTETER, *Le Zend-Avesta*, vol. ii. pp. 636–638.

[3] For the classical texts which prove that the doctrine of the resurrection of the body existed in the time of the Achæmenids, cf. WINDISCHMANN, *Zoroastrische Studien*, p. 236 ; RAPP, *Die Religion und Sitte der Perser und übrigen Iranier*, in the *Z. d. D. Morgenl. Gesells.*, vol. xx. p. 57, et seq. ; SPIEGEL, *op. cit.*, pp. 158–160 ; J. DARMESTETER, *op. cit.*, vol. iii. pp. lxvi., lxvii.

[4] For the idea of destiny in the Iranian religion, cf. SPIEGEL, *op. cit.*, vol. ii. p. 11, and J. DARMESTETER, *Ormuzd and Ahriman*, p. 322.

[5] J. DARMESTETER, *Le Zend-Avesta*, vol. ii. pp. 21, 22, where the author has greatly simplified the over-subtle definition he had given of the *asha* in his *Ormuzd and Ahriman*, pp. 7–18.

peasant who reclaims from the power of Angrô-mainyus the dry and sterile fields. Among the places where the earth thrives most joyously is reckoned that " where a worshipper of Ahura-mazdâ builds a house, with a chaplain, with cattle, with a wife, with sons, with a fair flock ; where man grows the most corn, herbage, and fruit trees; where he spreads water on a soil without water, and drains off water where there is too much of it." He who sows corn, sows good, and promotes the Mazdean faith ; " he nourishes the Mazdean religion as fifty men would do rocking a child in the cradle, five hundred women giving it suck from their breasts.[1] When the corn was created the Daêvas leaped, when it sprouted the Daêvas lost courage, when the stem set the Daêvas wept, when the ear swelled the Daêvas fled. In the house where corn is mouldering the Daêvas lodge, but when the corn sprouts, one might say that a hot iron is being turned round in their mouths." And the reason of their horror is easily divined : " Whoso eats not, has no power either to accomplish a valiant work of religion, or to labour with valour, or yet to beget children valiantly ; it is by eating that the universe lives, and it dies from not eating." [2] The faithful follower of Zoroaster owes no obligation towards the impious man or towards a stranger,[3] but is ever bound to render

THE KING STRUGGLING AGAINST AN
EVIL GENIUS.[4]

help to his coreligionist. He will give a garment to the naked, and by so doing will wound Zemaka, the demon of winter.[5] He will never refuse food to the hungry labourer, under pain of eternal torments,[6] and his charity will

---

[1] The original text says in a more enigmatical fashion, " he nourishes the religion of Mazdâ as a hundred feet of men and a thousand breasts of women might do."

[2] *Vendidad*, 3, §§ 2–4, 30–33, in J. DARMESTETER, *Le Zend-Avesta*, vol. ii. pp. 34, 42–44.

[3] Charity is called in Parsee language, *ashô-dâd*, the *gift to a pious man*, or the *gift of piety* (J. DARMESTETER, *op. cit.*, vol. ii. pp. 44, 63), and the pious man, the *ashavan*, is by definition the worshipper of Ahura-mazdâ alone.

[4] Drawn by Boudier, from the photograph in MARCEL DIEULAFOY, *L'Art de la Perse Antique*, vol. iv. pl. xvii. ; cf. J. DIEULAFOY, *La Perse, la Chaldée et la Susiane*, p. 401.

[5] *Vendidad*, 4, § 49ª, in J. DARMESTETER, *op. cit.*, vol. ii. p. 62. The passage is translated thus : " He strives against the winter, clothing himself in the thinnest raiment ; " but it seems as if, later on, the translator reverted to the traditional rendering I have indicated in the text, for in the index of vol. iii. p. 235, he refers to this phrase for the name of the demon Zemaka. Allusion is made to the gift of raiment in the *Vendidad*, 18, § 34 ; cf. J. DARMESTETER, *op. cit.*, vol. ii. p. 248, note 44.

[6] *Vendidad*, 18, § 29, in J. DARMESTETER, *op. cit.*, vol. ii. p. 247 ; in *Vendidad*, 3, § 35 (J. DARMESTETER, *op. cit.*, vol. ii. pp. 44, 45), he " who has not given charity to the faithful cultivator of the soil " is threatened with hell.

extend even to the brute beasts, provided that they belong to the species created by Ahura-mazdâ : he has duties towards them, and their complaints, heard in heaven, shall be fatal to him later on if he has provoked them. Asha-vahista will condemn to hell the cruel man who has ill-treated the ox, or allowed his flocks to suffer ; [1] and the killing of a hedgehog is no less severely punished—for does not a hedgehog devour the ants who steal the grain ? [2]   The dog is in every case an especially sacred animal—the shepherd's dog, the watch-dog, the hunting-dog, even the prowling dog.   It is not lawful to give any dog a blow which renders him impotent, or to slit his ears, or to cut his foot, without incurring grave responsibilities in this world and in the next ; it is necessary to feed the dog well, and not to throw bones to him which are too hard, nor have his food served hot enough to burn his tongue or his throat.[3]   For the rest, the faithful Zoroastrian was bound to believe in his god, to offer to him the orthodox prayers and sacrifices, to be simple in heart, truthful, the slave of his pledged word, loyal in his very smallest acts.[4]   If he had once departed from the right way, he could only return to it by repentance and by purification, accompanied by pious deeds : to exterminate noxious animals, the creatures of Angrô-mainyus and the abode of his demons, such as the frog, the scorpion, the serpent or the ant, to clear the sterile tracts, to restore impoverished land, to construct bridges over running water, to distribute implements of husbandry to pious men, or to build them a house, to give a pure and healthy maiden in marriage to a just man,—these were so many means of expiation appointed by the prophet.[5]   Marriage was strictly obligatory,[6] and seemed more praise-worthy in proportion as the kinship existing between the married pair was the closer: not only was the sister united in marriage to her brother, as in

---

[1] *Yasna*, 29, § 3, in J. DARMESTETER, *Le Zend-Avesta*, vol. i. p. 215. The whole of chap. 29 is occupied with the lament of the bull, and the assurances given to him by Ahura-mazdâ that he shall be well treated as soon as Zoroaster has ensured the triumph of the law.

[2] *Vendidad*, 13, §§ 1–4, in J. DARMESTETER, *op. cit.*, vol. ii. pp. 193–195.

[3] For the condition of the dog, cf. the thirteenth Fargard of the Vendidad (J. DARMESTETER, *op. cit.*, vol. ii. pp. 192–209), which is entirely devoted to this subject; for pregnant bitches, cf. the fifteenth Fargard (ID., *ibid.*, vol. ii. pp. 221, 224–229).

[4] HERODOTUS, I. cxxxvi. : παιδεύουσι δὲ τοὺς παιδὰς . . . τρία μοῦνα, ἱππεύειν καὶ τοξεύειν καὶ ἀλη-θίζεσθαι.

[5] For this category of praiseworthy actions, cf., among others, *Vendidad*, 14, § 10–16 ; 18, §§ 73, 74, in J. DARMESTETER, *op. cit.*, vol. ii. pp. 216–218, 254, 255. There is even enumerated how many noisome beasts must be slain to accomplish one full work of expiation—" to kill 1000 serpents of those who drag themselves upon the belly, and 2000 of the other species, 1000 land frogs or 2000 water frogs, 1000 ants who steal the grain," and so on.

[6] *Vendidad*, 4, § 47 : " And I tell thee, O Spitama Zarathustra, the man who has a wife is above him who lives in continency " (J. DARMESTETER, *Le Zend-Avesta*, vol. ii. pp. 60, 61) ; and, as we have seen in the text, one of these forms of expiation consisted in " marrying to a worthy man a young girl who has never known a man " (*Vendidad*, 14, § 15). Herodotus of old remarked that one of the chief merits in an Iranian was to have many children : the King of Persia encouraged fecundity in his realm, and awarded a prize each year to that one of his subjects who could boast the most numerous progeny (HERODOTUS, I. cxxxvi.).

Egypt,[1] but the father to his daughter, and the mother to her son, at least among the Magi.[2] Polygamy was also encouraged and widely practised: the code imposed no limit on the number of wives and concubines, and custom was in favour of a man's having as many wives as his fortune permitted him to maintain.[3] On the occasion of a death, it was forbidden to burn the corpse, to bury it, or to cast it into a river, as it would have polluted the fire, the earth, or the water—an unpardonable offence.[4] The corpse could be disposed of in different ways. The Persians were accustomed to cover it with a thick layer of wax, and then to bury it in the ground: the wax coating obviated the pollution which direct contact would have brought upon the soil.[5] The Magi, and probably also strict devotees, following their example, exposed the corpse in the open air, abandoning it to the birds or beasts of prey.[6] It was considered a great misfortune if these respected the body, for it was an almost certain indication of the wrath of Ahura-mazdâ, and it was thought that the defunct had led an evil life.[7] When the bones had been sufficiently stripped of flesh, they were collected together, and deposited either in an earthenware urn or in a stone ossuary with a cover, or in a monumental tomb either hollowed out in the heart of the mountain or in the living rock, or raised up above the level of the ground.[8] Meanwhile the

[1] For the Egyptian marriages between brothers and sisters, especially in the royal family, cf. *Dawn of Civilization*, pp. 50, 51, 270.

[2] The information given by the classical authors on these various marriage connections has been brought together in RAPP, *Die Religion und Sitte der Perser und übrigen Iranier nach den Griechischen und Römischen Quellen*, in the *Z. d. D. Morgenl. Gesells.*, vol. xxx. pp. 112, 113; cf. SPIEGEL, *Erânische Alterthumskunde*, vol. ii. p. 300, note 1, vol. iii. pp. 678, 679, and more particularly J. DARMESTETER, *Le Zend-Avesta*, vol. i. pp. 126–134, where the evidence from Iranian sources is given as well as that from classical authors.

[3] HERODOTUS, I. cxxxv.: Γαμέουσι δὲ ἕκαστος αὐτῶν πολλὰς κουριδίας γυναῖκας, πολλῷ δ' ἔτι πλέονας παλλακὰς κτῶνται. For the passages from other classical writers confirming the statement of Herodotus, cf. RAPP, *op. cit.*, pp. 107, 108.

[4] Cf., for the legal prohibition to burn the corpse, HERODOTUS, III. xvi.; CTESIAS, *Fragm.* 29, § 57 (in MÜLLER-DIDOT, *Ctesiæ Cnidii Fragmenta*, p. 57); NICOLAS OF DAMASCUS, *Fragm.* 68 (in MÜLLER-DIDOT, *Fragm. Hist. Græc.*, vol. iii. p. 409); the penalty of death was inflicted on him who was guilty of perpetrating this crime (STRABO, XV. iii. § 14, p. 732). For the prohibition to pollute the water or throw into it anything dead, cf. HERODOTUS, I. cxxxviii., and STRABO, XV. iii. § 16, p. 733.

[5] HERODOTUS, I. cxl., where the author seems to imply that it was more especially the custom of the Persians: κατακηρώσαντες δὲ ὦν τὸν νέκυν Πέρσαι γέᾳκ ῥύπτουσι. Cf. CICERO, *Disp. Tusculan.*, i. 45, and STRABO, XV. iii. § 20, p. 735, who establishes, as Herodotus had done, a distinction of usage between the Persians and the Magi. The kings seem to have been buried in this fashion; cf. the legend of the death and burial of Astyages, in Ctesias (*Fragm.* 29, § 5, in MÜLLER-DIDOT, *Ctesiæ Cnidii Fragmenta*, pp. 46, 47).

[6] HERODOTUS, I. cxl., and, among the Bactrians, ONESICRITUS, *Fragm.* 6, in MÜLLER-DIDOT, *Scriptores rerum Alexandri Magni*, pp. 49, 50. The other classical authors agree in declaring that, at least in the Parthian epoch, the skeleton was buried as soon as the flesh had been destroyed, as results from the passages collected by RAPP, *op. cit.*, pp. 55, 56, and by SPIEGEL, *Erânische Alterthumskunde*, vol. iii. pp. 703–705.

[7] QUINTUS CURTIUS, VII. v. § 40, probably following Aristobulus. For this belief and its development in later times, see the modern evidences brought together in A. HOVELACQUE, *L'Avesta, Zoroastre et le Mazdéisme*, p. 470, et seq.

[8] Marcel Dieulafoy discovered funeral urns at Susa (*L'Acropole de Suse*, pp. 426–428), and Malcolm brought back from Bushire a stone ossuary, which, according to the testimony of

soul remained in the neighbourhood for three days, hovering near the head of the corpse, and by the recitation of prayers it experienced, according to its condition of purity or impurity, as much of joy or sadness as the whole world experiences. When the third night was past, the just soul set forth across luminous plains, refreshed by a perfumed breeze, and its good thoughts and words and deeds took shape before it "under the guise of a young maiden, radiant and strong, with well-developed bust, noble mien, and glorious face, about fifteen years of age, and as beautiful as the most beautiful;" the unrighteous soul, on the contrary, directed its course towards the north, through a tainted land, amid the squalls of a pestilential hurricane, and there encountered its past ill deeds, under the form of an ugly and wicked young woman, the ugliest and most wicked it had ever seen. The genius Rashnu Razishta, the essentially truthful, weighed its virtues or vices in an un-erring balance, and acquitted or condemned it on the impartial testimony of its past life. On issuing from the judgment-hall, the soul arrived at the approach to the bridge Cinvaut, which, thrown across the abyss of hell, led to paradise. The soul, if impious, was unable to cross this bridge, but was hurled down into the abyss, where it became the slave of Angrô-mainyus. If pure, it crossed the bridge without difficulty by the help of the angel Sraôsha, and was welcomed by Vohu-manô, who conducted it before the throne of Ahura-mazdâ, in the same way as he had led Zoroaster, and assigned to it the post which it should occupy until the day of the resurrection of the body.[1]

The religious observances enjoined on the members of the priestly caste were innumerable and minute. Ahura-mazdâ and his colleagues had not, as was the fashion among the Assyrians and Egyptians,[2] either temples or tabernacles, and though they were represented sometimes under human or animal forms, and even in some cases on bas-reliefs, yet no one ever ventured to set up in their sanctuaries those so-called animated or prophetic statues to which the majority of the nations had rendered or were rendering their

Mr. Jivanji Modi (*Quelques Observations sur les ossuaires rapportés de Perse par M. Dieulafoy et déposés au Musée du Louvre*, in the *Comptes rendus de l'Académie des Inscriptions et Belles-Lettres*, 1889, pp. 369-374), represents the *Astodân* described in the Vendidad (6, § 51, in J. DARMESTETER, *Le Zend-Avesta*, vol. ii. p. 93) as being constructed of stone, plaster, or clay. We shall find later on, in Chapter VII., some illustrations giving the tombs of the Achæmenid kings.

[1] All this picture of the fate of the soul is taken from the *Vendidad*, 19, §§ 28-34 (J. DARMESTETER, *Le Zend-Avesta*, vol. ii. pp. 269-271), where the fate of the just is described, and in the *Yasht*, 22 (ID., *ibid.*, vol. ii. pp. 651-658), where the condition of faithful and impious souls respectively is set forth on parallel lines. The classical authors teach us nothing on this subject, and the little they actually say only proves that the Persians believed in the immortality of the soul (RAPP, *Die Religion und Sitte der Perser*, in the *Z. d. D. Morgenl. Gesells.*, vol. xx. pp. 57-62). The main outlines of the picture here set forth go back to the times of the Achæmenids and the Medes, except the abstract conception of the goddess who leads the soul of the dead as an incarnation of his good or evil deeds.

[2] HERODOTUS, I. cxxxi.; XENOPHON, *Cyropædia*, VII. vii. § 3; DINON, *Fragm.* 9, in MÜLLER-DIDOT, *Fragm. Hist. Græc.*, vol. ii. p. 91; and the passages from other classical authors collected by RAPP, *op. cit.*, pp. 80, 81.

solicitous homage. Altars, however, were erected on the tops of hills,[1] in palaces, or in the centre of cities, on which fires were kindled in honour of the inferior deities or of the supreme god himself. Two altars were usually set up together, and they are thus found here and there among the ruins, as at Nakhsh-î-Rustem, the necropolis of Persepolis, where a pair of such altars exist; these are cut, each out of a single block, in a rocky mass which rises some thirteen feet above the level of the surrounding plain. They are of

THE TWO IRANIAN ALTARS AT NAKHSH-Î-RUSTEM.[2]

cubic form and squat appearance, looking like towers flanked at the four corners by supporting columns which are connected by circular arches; above a narrow moulding rises a crest of somewhat triangular projections; the hearth is hollowed out on the summit of each altar.[3] At Meshed-î-Murgâb, on the site of the ancient Pasargadæ, the altars have disappeared, but the basements on which they were erected are still visible, as also the flight of eight steps by which they were approached.[4] Those altars on which burned a perpetual fire were not left exposed to the open air: they would have run too great a risk of contracting

[1] See in GOBINEAU, *Histoire des Perses*, vol. i. pp. 31, 32, the description of an artificially formed platform on the top of a hill opposite Demavend, which must be one of these "high places" destined to sacrificial rites (PERROT and CHIPIEZ, *Histoire de l'Art*, vol. v. p. 640).

[2] Drawn by Boudier, from a heliogravure in MARCEL DIEULAFOY, *L'Art Antique de la Perse*, vol. iii. pl. v.

[3] According to Perrot and Chipiez (*L'Histoire de l'Art*, vol. v. p. 643), "it is not impossible that these altars were older than the great buildings of Persepolis, and that they were erected for the old Persian town which Darius raised to the position of capital."

[4] MARCEL DIEULAFOY, *L'Acropole de Suse*, p. 291, et seq.

impurities, such as dust borne by the wind, flights of birds, dew, rain, or snow. They were enclosed in slight structures, well protected by walls, and attaining in some cases considerable dimensions, or in pavilion-shaped edifices of stone adorned with columns.[1] The sacrificial rites were of long duration, and frequent, and were rendered very complex by interminable manual acts, ceremonial gestures, and incantations. In cases where the altar was not devoted to maintaining a perpetual fire, it was kindled when necessary with small twigs previously barked and purified,[2] and was subsequently fed with precious woods, preferably cypress or laurel;[3] care was taken not to quicken the flame

THE TWO IRANIAN ALTARS OF MURGÂB.[5]

by blowing, for the human breath would have desecrated the fire by merely passing over it; death was the punishment for any one who voluntarily committed such a heinous sacrilege.[4] The recognised offering consisted of flowers, bread, fruit, and perfumes, but these were often accompanied, as in all ancient religions, by a bloody sacrifice; the sacrifice of a horse was considered the most efficacious,[6] but an ox, a cow, a sheep, a camel, an ass, or a stag was frequently offered;[7] in certain circumstances, especially when it was desired to conciliate the favour of the god of the underworld, a human victim, probably as a survival of very ancient rites, was preferred.[8] The king, whose royal

[1] Such is the temple of Firoz-Abad, notes of which were taken by Flandin and Coste (*Perse Ancienne*, pp. 36–38, and pl. xxxvii.); cf. the restoration by Coste, published by Perrot and Chipiez (*Histoire de l'Art dans l'Antiquité*, vol. v. p. 647), who assign good reasons for placing the date of the monument in the age of the Achæmenids. For another temple belonging to the same period, which has been discovered at Susa, see MARCEL DIEULAFOY, *L'Acropole d'Suse*, pp. 391, 411–416.

[2] STRABO, XV. iii. § 15, p. 733.

[3] NICOLAS OF DAMASCUS, *Fragm.* 66, in MÜLLER-DIDOT, *Fragm. Hist. Græc.*, vol. iii. p. 405; Pausanias, who witnessed the cult as practised at Hierocæsaræa, remarked the curious colour of the ashes heaped upon the altar (V. xxvii. § 3).

[4] STRABO, XV. iii. § 14, p. 732: ὑφάπτουσιν, ἔλαιον καταχέοντες, οὐ φυσῶντες, ἀλλὰ ῥιπίζοντες· τοὺς δὲ φυσήσαντας ἢ νεκρὸν ἐπὶ πῦρ θέντας ἢ βόλβιτον θανατοῦσι.

[5] Drawn by Boudier, from FLANDIN and COSTE, *La Perse Ancienne*, pl. cciii.

[6] The sacrifice of a horse is mentioned in HERODOTUS, VII. cxiii.; XENOPHON, *Cyropædia*, VIII. iii. § 24; ARRIAN, *Anabasis*, VI. xix. § 7. For the sacrifice of horses in the ancient Iranian rites, cf. the *Aban Yasht*, where an enumeration is given of the heroes who sacrificed a hundred horses to Anâhita Ardvî-sôura after the revelation to Zoroaster (*Yasht* 5, §§ 107, 112, 116; cf. J. DARMESTETER, *Le Zend-Avesta*, vol. ii. pp. 392–394).

[7] For the offering of these animals in sacrifice, cf. HERODOTUS, VII. xliii.; HERACLIDES OF CUMÆ, *Fragm.* 8, in MÜLLER-DIDOT, *Fragm. Hist. Græc.*, vol. ii. p. 96; ARRIAN, *Anabasis*, VI. xxix. § 7. The sacrifice of bulls and sheep is mentioned in the same passages as that of the horse (*Yasht* 5, §§ 108, 112, 116; cf. J. DARMESTETER, *op. cit.*, vol. ii. pp. 392–394), and elsewhere (*Vendidad*, 18, § 70; ID., *ibid.*, p. 254) that of thousands of smaller animals.

[8] HERODOTUS, VII. cxiii., cxiv. Most modern writers deny the authenticity of Herodotus' account,

position made him the representative of Ahura-mazdâ on earth,[1] was, in fact, a high priest, and was himself able to officiate at the altar,[2] but no one else could dispense with the mediation of the Magi.[3] The worshippers proceeded in solemn procession to the spot where the ceremony was to take place, and there the priest, wearing the tiara on his head, recited an invocation in a slow and mysterious voice, and implored the blessings of heaven on the king and nation.[4] He then slaughtered the victim by a blow on the head,[5] and divided it into portions, which he gave back to the offerer without reserving any of them, for Ahura-mazdâ required nothing but the soul; in certain cases, the victim was entirely consumed by fire,[6] but more frequently nothing but a little of the fat and some of the entrails were taken to feed and maintain the flame, and sometimes even this was omitted.[7] Sacrifices were of frequent occurrence. Without mentioning the extraordinary occasions on which a king

THE SACRED FIRE BURNING ON THE ALTAR.[9]

would have a thousand bulls slain at one time,[8] the Achæmenian kings killed each day a thousand bullocks, asses, and stags: sacrifice under such circumstances was another name for butchery, the object of which was to

because a sacrifice of this kind is opposed to the spirit of the Magian religion (SPIEGEL, *Erânische Alterthumskunde*, vol. iii. p. 593), which is undoubtedly the case, as far as the latest form of the religion is concerned; but the testimony of Herodotus is so plain that the fact itself must be considered as indisputable. We may note that the passage refers to the foundation of a city; and if we remember how persistent was the custom of human sacrifice among ancient races at the foundation of buildings (cf., for Egypt, LEFEBURE, *Rites Égyptiens*, pp. 4–6, 19–24, 36–38), we shall be led to the conclusion that the ceremony described by the Greek historian was a survival of a very ancient usage, which had not yet fallen entirely into desuetude at the Achæmenian epoch.

[1] PHANIAS OF ERESOS, *Fragm.* 9, in MÜLLER-DIDOT, *Fragm. Hist. Græc.*, vol. ii. p. 296: τιμᾶν βασιλέα καὶ προσκυνεῖν εἰκόνα θεοῦ τοῦ πάντα σώζοντος.

[2] XENOPHON, *Cyrop.*, VIII. v. § 26, where the sacerdotal functions of the king are clearly indicated.

[3] HERODOTUS, I. cxxxii.: ἄνευ γὰρ δή μάγου οὔ σφι νόμος ἐστι θυσίας ποιέεσθαι. Cf. XENOPHON, *Cyropædia*, VIII. iii. § 9, where it is stated that in religious matters the Persians strictly obeyed their Magi.

[4] HERODOTUS, I. cxxxii.   [5] STRABO, XV. iii. §§ 13–15, pp. 732, 733.

[6] XENOPHON, *Cyropædia*, VIII. iii. § 24, the accuracy of which is suspected by most historians (SPIEGEL, *Erânische Alterthums.*, vol. iii. p. 592; RAPP, *Die Religion und Sitte der Perser*, in the *Z. d. D. Morgenl. Gesells.*, vol. xx. p. 83; G. RAWLINSON, *The Five Great Monarchies*, 2nd edit., vol. ii. p. 346, n. 11).

[7] HERODOTUS, I. cxxxii.; STRABO, XV. iii. § 13, p. 733, where mention is made of the part of the victim cast on the fire: τοῦ ἐπιπλόου τι μικρὸν τιθέασι, ὡς λέγουσί τινες, ἐπὶ τὸ πῦρ. A relic of this custom may be discerned in the expiatory sacrifice decreed in the *Vendidad*, 18, § 70: "he shall sacrifice a thousand head of small cattle, and he shall place their entrails devoutly on the fire, with libations" (J. DARMESTETER, *Le Zend-Avesta*, vol. ii. p. 254).

[8] HERODOTUS, VII. xliii. The number 1000 seems to have had some ritualistic significance, for it often recurs in the penances imposed on the faithful as expiation for their sins: thus it was enjoined to slay 1000 serpents, 1000 frogs, 1000 ants who steal the grain (cf. *supra*, p. 588, note 5), 1000 head of small cattle (*Vendidad*, 18, § 70), 1000 swift horses, 1000 camels, 1000 brown oxen (*Vendidad*, 22, §§ 3, 4; cf. J. DARMESTETER, *Le Zend-Avesta*, vol. ii. p. 298).

[9] Drawn by Faucher-Gudin, from the impression of a Persian intaglio.

2 Q

furnish the court with a sufficient supply of pure meat.[1] The ceremonial bore
resemblance in many ways to that still employed by the modern Zoroastrians
of Persia and India.   The officiating priest covered his mouth with the bands
which fell from his mitre, to prevent the god from being polluted by his
breath; he held in his hand the baresman, or sacred bunch of tamarisk,[2] and
prepared the mysterious liquor from the haoma plant.[3] He was accustomed
each morning to celebrate divine service before the sacred fire,[4] not to speak
of the periodic festivals in which he shared the offices with all the members of
his tribe, such as the feast of Mithra,[5] the feast of the Fravashis,[6] the feast
commemorating the rout of Angrô-mainyus,[7] the feast of the Sakæa, during
which the slaves were masters of the house.[8] All the Magi were not necessarily
devoted to the priesthood ; but those only became apt in the execution of their
functions who had been dedicated to them from infancy, and who, having received
the necessary instruction, were duly consecrated.[9] These adepts were divided into
several classes, of which three at least were never confounded in their functions
—the sorcerers, the interpreters of dreams, and the most venerated sages—
and from these three classes were chosen the ruling body of the order and its
supreme head.   Their rule of life was strict and austere, and was encumbered
with a thousand observances indispensable to the preservation of perfect purity
in their persons, their altars, their victims, and their sacrificial vessels and

[1] HERACLIDES OF CUMÆ, Fragm. 2, in MÜLLER-DIDOT, Fragm. Hist. Græc., vol. ii. p. 96 ; cf. RAPP,
Die Sitte und Religion der Perser und übrigen Iranier, in the Z. d. D. Morgenl. Gesells., vol. xx. p. 83.

[2] STRABO, XV. iii. §§ 14, 15, pp. 732, 733. Dinon (Fragm. 8, in MÜLLER-DIDOT, op. cit., vol. ii.
p. 91) had already pointed out the use of the baresman for divination.

[3] The drink mentioned by the author of the De Iside (§ 46, ed. PARTHEY, pp. 81, 82), which was
extracted from the plant Omômi (ποάν γάρ τινα κόπτοντες ὄμωμι καλουμένην), and which the Magi
offered to the god of the underworld, is certainly the haoma. The rite mentioned by the Greek author,
which appears to be an incantation against Ahriman, required, it seems, a potion in which the blood
of a wolf was a necessary ingredient: this questionable draught was then carried to a place where
the sun's rays never shone, and was there sprinkled on the ground as a libation. J. Darmesteter
himself admits that the cult and myths of the haoma were already in existence in the Achæmenian
period (Le Zend-Avesta, vol. iii. p. lxix.).

[4] STRABO, XV. iii. § 15, p. 733.

[5] CTESIAS, Fragm. 55, in MÜLLER-DIDOT, Ctesiæ Cnidii Fragm., p. 79 ; DURIS OF SAMOS, Fragm. 13,
in ID., Fragm. Hist. Græc., vol. ii. pp. 472, 473.

[6] MENANDER, Fragm. 15, in ID., ibid., vol. iv. p. 220, speaks of this festival as conducted in his
own times, and tells us that it was called Furdîgan ; modern authorities usually admit that it goes
back to the times of the Achæmenids or even beyond (RAPP, op. cit., p. 92 ; SPIEGEL, Erânische
Alterthumskunde, vol. ii. pp. 96, 97).

[7] AGATHIAS, ii. 24, where every worshipper of Ahura-mazdâ is enjoined to kill the greatest possible
number of animals created by Angrô-mainyus, and bring to the Magi the fruits of his hunting.
Herodotus (I. cxl.) had already spoken of this destruction of life as one of the duties incumbent on
every Persian, and this gives probability to the view of modern writers that the festival went back
to the Achæmenian epoch (RAPP, op. cit., p. 92).

[8] The festival of the Sakæa is mentioned by Ctesias (Frag. 16, in MÜLLER-DIDOT, Ctes. Cnid. Frag.,
pp. 33, 34). It was also a Babylonian festival, and most modern authorities conclude from this double
use of the name that the festival was borrowed from the Babylonians by the Persians (RAPP, op. cit.,
p. 92), but this point is not so certain as it is made out to be, and at any rate the borrowing must
have taken place very early, for the festival was already well established in the Achæmenian period.

[9] J. DARMESTETER, Le Zend-Avesta, vol. iii. pp. lxxi., lxxii.

implements. The Magi of highest rank abstained from every form of living thing as food, and the rest only partook of meat under certain restrictions.[1] Their dress was unpretentious, they wore no jewels,[2] and observed strict fidelity to the marriage vow; [3] and the virtues with which they were accredited obtained for them, from very early times, unbounded influence over the minds of the common people as well as over those of the nobles: the king himself boasted of being their pupil,[4] and took no serious step in state affairs without consulting Ahuramazdâ or the other gods by their mediation.[5] The classical writers maintain that the Magi often cloaked monstrous vices under their apparent strictness, and it is possible that this was the case in later days, but even then moral depravity was probably rather the exception than the rule among them: [6] the majority of the Magi faithfully observed the rules of honest living and ceremonial purity enjoined on them in the books handed down by their ancestors.

There is reason to believe that the Magi were all-powerful among the Medes, and that the reign of Astyages was virtually the reign of the priestly caste; [7] but all the Iranian states did not submit so patiently to their authority, and the Persians at last proved openly refractory. Their kings, lords of Susa as well as of Pasargadæ, wielded all the resources of Elam, and their military power must have equalled, if it did not already surpass, that of their suzerain lords. Their tribes, less devoted to the manner of living of the Assyrians and Chaldæans, had preserved a vigour and power of endurance which the Medes no longer possessed; and they needed but an ambitious and capable leader, to rise rapidly from the rank of subjects to that of rulers of Iran, and to become in a short time masters of Asia. Such a chief they found in Cyrus,[8] son

---

[1] For these classes of Magi, cf. the passages of classical authors brought together in RAPP, *Die Religion und Sitte der Perser*, in the *Z. d. D. Morgenl. Gesells.*, vol. xx. pp. 72–74. The clearest, that of Eubulus (in PORPHYRY, *De Abstinentiâ*, iv. p. 16), speaks of three grades one above the other.

[2] DIOGENES LAERTIUS, *Procœmium*, § 2.

[3] Clement of Alexandria assures us that they were strictly celibate (*Stromates*, iii. p. 446), but, besides the fact that married Magi are mentioned several times, celibacy is still considered by Zoroastrians an inferior state to that of marriage; cf. on this subject the passages collected by HOVELACQUE, *L'Avesta, Zoroastre et le Mazdéisme*, pp. 461–463.

[4] In the Greek period, a spurious epitaph of Darius, son of Hystaspes, was quoted, in which the king says of himself, "I was the pupil of the Magi" (PORPHYRY, *De Abstinentiâ*, iv. p. 16).

[5] Cf. RAPP, *op. cit.*, pp. 74, 75, for the passages of classical authors which speak of the influence exercised by the Magi over the nobles and the sovereigns.

[6] These accusations are nearly all directed against their incestuous marriages (cf., for these marriages, *supra*, pp. 588, 589): it seems that the classical writers took for a refinement of debauchery what really was before all things a religious practice.

[7] G. RAWLINSON, *The Five Great Monarchies*, 2nd edit., vol. ii. p. 416; NÖLDEKE, *Aufsätze zur Persischen Geschichte*, p. 12.

[8] The original form of the name is Kûru, Kûrush, with a long *û*, as is shown by the quantity of the Greek form Κῦρος (ÆSCHYLUS, *Persæ*, 768), which forces us to reject the proposed connection (BRÉAL, *De Persicis nominibis*, pp. 23, 24; SPIEGEL, *Erânische Alterthumskunde*, vol. ii. pp. 270, 271) with the name of the Indian hero Kuru, in which the *u* is short (NÖLDEKE, *Aufsätze zur Persischen Geschichte*, p. 14, note 2). Numerous etymologies of the name Cyrus have been proposed: lately, Sayce has derived it from the Elamite, and translated it *the Shepherd* (*The Ancient Empires of the East*, p. 69, note 3). The Persians themselves attributed to it the sense of *the Sun* (PLUTARCH,

of Cambyses; but although no more illustrious name than his occurs in the list of the founders of mighty empires, the history of no other has suffered more disfigurement from the imagination of his own subjects or from the rancour of the nations he had conquered.[1] The Medes, who could not forgive him for having made them subject to their ancient vassals, took delight in holding him up to scorn, and not being able to deny the fact of his triumph, explained it by the adoption of tortuous and despicable methods. They would not even allow that he was of royal birth, but asserted that he was of ignoble origin, the son of a female goatherd and a certain Atradates,[2] who, belonging to the savage clan of the Mardians, lived by brigandage. Cyrus himself, according to this account, spent his infancy and early youth in a condition not far short of slavery, employed at first in sweeping out the exterior portions of the palace, performing afterwards the same office in the private apartments, subsequently promoted to the charge of the lamps and torches, and finally admitted to the number of the royal cupbearers who filled the king's goblet at table. When he was at length enrolled in the body-guard,[3] he won distinction by his skill in all military exercises, and having risen

Artaxerxes, § 1; CTESIAS, *Fragm.* 29, § 9, in MÜLLER-DIDOT, *Ctesiæ Cnidii Fragm.*, pp. 55–69; HESYCHIUS, *s.v.* Κῦρος). This interpretation is upheld by Oppert (*Le Peuple et la Langue des Mèdes*, p. 111) and Justi (*Iranisches Namenbuch*, p. 168).

[1] We possess two entirely different versions of the history of the origin of Cyrus, but one, that of Herodotus (I. cvii.–cxxx.), has reached us intact, while that of Ctesias is only known to us in fragments from extracts made by Nicolas of Damascus (*Fragm.* 66, in MÜLLER-DIDOT, *Fragm. Hist. Græc.*, vol. iii. pp. 397–406) and by Photius (ID., *Ctesiæ Cnidii Fragm.*, pp. 45–47, 59–62). Spiegel (*Erânische Alterthumskunde*, vol. ii. pp. 278, 279) and Duncker (*Gesch. des Alterthums*, 4th edit., vol. iv. pp. 281) thought to recognise in the tradition followed by Ctesias one of the Persian accounts of the history of Cyrus, but Bauer (*Die Kyros-Sage und Verwandtes*, pp. 30, 32, 33) refuses to admit this hypothesis, and prefers to consider it as a romance put together by the author, according to the taste of his own times, from facts partly different from those utilised by Herodotus, and partly borrowed from Herodotus himself: but it should very probably be regarded as an account of Median origin, in which the founder of the Persian empire is portrayed in the most unfavourable light (NÖLDEKE, *Aufsätze zur Persischen Gesch.*, p. 14). Or perhaps it may be regarded as the form of the legend current among the Pharnaspids who established themselves as satraps of Dascylium in the time of the Achæmenids, and to whom the royal house of Cappadocia traced its origin (cf. MARQUART, *Die Assyriaka des Ktesias*, in the *Philologus, Supplement*, vol. v. pp. 596–599). It is almost certain that the account given by Herodotus represents a Median version of the legend (DUNCKER, *Gesch. des Alterthums*, vol. iv. p. 272), and, considering the important part played in it by Harpagus, probably that version which was current among the descendants of that nobleman (NÖLDEKE, *op. cit.*, pp. 13, 14; PRASHEK, *Medien und das Haus des Kyaxares*, pp. 16, 17). The historian Dinon, as far as we can judge from the extant fragments of his work (*Fragm.* 7, in MÜLLER-DIDOT, *Fragm. Hist. Græc.*, vol. ii. pp. 90, 91), and from the abridgment made by Trogus Pompeius (JUSTIN, I. iv.–vi.), adopted the narrative of Ctesias, mingling with it, however, some details taken from Herodotus and the romance of Xenophon, the Cyropædia. For an analysis of the elements composing the legend of Cyrus and the analogies to it discovered among the different nations of the East and the West, cf. the instances collected by BAUER, *Die Kyros-Sage und Verwandtes*, 1882.

[2] According to one of the historians consulted by Strabo (XV. iii. § 6, p. 729), perhaps Polyclitus of Larissa (J. MARQUART, *op. cit.*, pp. 560–562), Cyrus himself, and not his father, was called Atradates.

[3] The tradition reproduced by Dinon narrated that Cyrus had begun by serving among the Kavasses, the three hundred staff-bearers, ῥαβδοφόροι, who accompanied the sovereign when he appeared in public, and that he passed next into the royal body-guard (*Fragm.* 7, in MÜLLER-DIDOT, *Fragm. Hist. Græc.*, vol. ii. pp. 90, 91), and that once having attained this rank, he passed rapidly through all the superior grades of the military profession.

from rank to rank, received command of an expedition against the Cadusians. On the march he fell in with a Persian groom named Œbaras,[1] who had been cruelly scourged for some misdeed, and was occupied in the transportation of manure in a boat: in obedience to an oracle the two united their fortunes, and together devised a vast scheme for liberating their compatriots from the Median yoke. How Atradates secretly prepared the revolt of the Mardians; how Cyrus left his camp to return to the court at Ecbatana, and obtained from

A ROYAL HUNTING-PARTY IN IRAN.[2]

Astyages permission to repair to his native country under pretext of offering sacrifices, but in reality to place himself at the head of the conspirators; how, finally, the indiscretion of a woman revealed the whole plot to a eunuch of the harem, and how he warned Astyages in the middle of his evening banquet by means of a musician or singing-girl, was frequently narrated by the Median bards in their epic poems, and hence the story spread until it reached in later times even as far as the Greeks.[3] Astyages, roused to action by the danger, abandons the pleasures of the chase in which his activity had hitherto found vent, sets out on the track of the rebel, wins a preliminary victory on the Hyrba, and kills the father of Cyrus: some days after, he again overtakes the rebels, at the entrance to the defiles leading to Pasargadæ, and

---

[1] This Œbaras whom Ctesias makes the accomplice of Cyrus, seems to be an antedated forestallment of the Œbaras whom the tradition followed by Herodotus (III. lxxxv.) knows as master of the horse under Darius, and to whom that king owed his elevation to the throne (NÖLDEKE, *Aufsätze zur Persischen Gesch.*, p. 14, note 1; J. MARQUART, *Die Assyriaka des Ktesias*, in the *Philologus, Supplement*, vol. v. pp. 596–598). For the resemblances between the story of the origin of Cyrus and that of the founder of the Sassanid monarchy, Ardashîr-î-Pâpakân, cf. GUTSCHMID, *Kleine Schriften*, vol. iii. pp. 133, 134, and NÖLDEKE, *Das Iranische Nationalepos*, in the *Grundriss der Iranischen Philologie*, vol. ii. p. 132; popular imagination must have transferred the legend of the ancient hero to his successor of a later age (NÖLDEKE, *Aufsätze zur Persischen Gesch.*, pp. 91, 92).

[2] Drawn by Faucher-Gudin, from the silver vase in the Museum of the Hermitage, reproduced in *Comptes rendus de la Commission Archéologique*, 1866, pl. iv. 1.

[3] According to Ctesias (NICOLAS OF DAMASCUS, *Fragm.* 66, in MÜLLER-DIDOT, *Fragm. Hist. Græc.*, vol. iii. p. 403), it was a singing-girl who revealed the existence of the plot to Astyages; according to Dinon (*Fragm.* 7, in ID., *ibid.*, vol. ii. pp. 90, 91), it was the bard Angarês. Windischmann (*Zoroastrische Studien*, p. 277) has compared this name with that of the Vedic guild of singers, the Angira; cf. A. WEBER, *Episches im Vedischen Ritual*, in the *Sitzungsberichte* of Acad. of Berlin, 1891, p. 46, note.

for the second time fortune is on the point of declaring in his favour, when the Persian women, bringing back their husbands and sons to the conflict, urge them on to victory.[1] The fame of their triumph having spread abroad, the satraps and provinces successively declared for the conqueror; Hyrcania, first, followed by the Parthians, the Sakæ, and the Bactrians:[2] Astyages was left almost alone, save for a few faithful followers, in the palace at Ecbatana. His daughter Amytis and his son-in-law Spitamas concealed him so successfully on the top of the palace, that he escaped discovery up to the moment when Cyrus was on the point of torturing his grandchildren to force them to reveal his hiding-place: thereupon he gave himself up to his enemies, but was at length, after being subjected to harsh treatment for a time, set at liberty and entrusted with the government of a mountain tribe dwelling to the south-east of the Caspian Sea, that of the Barcanians.[3] Later on he perished through the treachery of Œbaras, and his corpse was left unburied in the desert, but by divine inter-position relays of lions were sent to guard it from the attacks of beasts of prey: Cyrus, acquainted with this miraculous circumstance, went in search of the body and gave it a magnificent burial.[4] Another legend asserted, on the contrary, that Cyrus was closely connected with the royal line of Cyaxares; this tradi-tion was originally circulated among the great Median families who attached themselves to the Achæmenian dynasty.[5] According to this legend Astyages had no male heirs, and the sceptre would have naturally descended from him to his daughter Mandanê and her sons. Astyages was much alarmed by a certain dream concerning his daughter: he dreamt that water gushed forth so copiously from her womb as to flood not only Ecbatana, but the whole of Asia, and the interpreters, as much terrified as himself, counselled him not to

[1] This anecdote is omitted by Dinon in Trogus Pompeius (JUSTIN, i. § vi.), and by Nicolas of Damascus in Polyænus (vii. 45, 2). For the criticism of this part of Ctesias' narrative, cf. MARQUART, *Die Assyriaka des Ktesias*, in the *Philologus, Suppl.*, vol. v. pp. 600, 601, who considers that it contains traces of the same epic legends which have been partially utilised in the more recent traditions relative to the taking of Balkh from Lohrasp, father of Gushtasp (SPIEGEL, *Erân. Alterthums.*, vol. i. pp. 714, 715).

[2] This is the end of the narrative of Ctesias as known to us through Nicolas of Damascus (*Fragm.* 66, in MÜLLER-DIDOT, *Fragm. Hist. Græc.*, vol. iii. pp. 397–406). Herodotus places the sub-mission of the tribes of Central Asia after the fall of Crœsus (I. clxxvii.).

[3] CTESIAS, *Fragm.* 29, § 5 (MÜLLER-DIDOT, *Ctesiæ Cnidii Fragmenta*, pp. 46, 60, 61), has *Barcanians* where Trogus Pompeius has *Hyrcanians* (JUSTIN, I. vi.), perhaps following Dinon, or else by an unauthorised substitution of a well-known name for one of rare occurrence. Ancient geographers distinguished between the two; thus STEPHEN OF BYZANTIUM, *s.v.* Βαρκάνιοι, ἔθνος τοῖς Ὑρκανίοις ὅμορον; cf. DIODORUS SICULUS, ii. 2, and QUINTUS CURTIUS, iii. 2, 5. Marquart proposes to identify their country with the modern Farghâna (*op. cit.*, pp. 613, 614). It is, however, possible that we have here two different transcriptions of the name Vehrkâna (cf. *supra*, p. 451, note 3).

[4] CTESIAS, *Fragm.* 29, §§ 2, 5, in MÜLLER-DIDOT, *Ctesiæ Cnidii Fragm.*, pp. 45–47. The passage in Herodotus (III. lxii.) leads Marquart to believe that the murder of Astyages formed part of the primitive legend, but was possibly attributed to Cambyses, son of Cyrus, rather than to Œbaras, the companion of the conqueror's early years.

[5] This is the legend as told to Herodotus in Asia Minor, probably by the members of the family of Harpagus (cf. *supra*, p. 596, note 1), which the Greek historian tried to render credible by interpreting the miraculous incidents in a rationalising manner (BAUER, *Die Kyros-Sage und Verwandtes*, pp. 9, 10).

give Mandanê in marriage to a Mede. He therefore bestowed her hand on a Persian noble of the race of the Achæmenids, named Cambyses; but a second dream soon troubled the security into which this union had lulled him: he saw issuing from his daughter's womb a vine whose branches overshadowed Asia, and the interpreters, being once more consulted, predicted that a grandson was about to be born to him whose ambition would cost him his crown.

He therefore bade a certain nobleman of his court, named Harpagus—he whose descendants preserved this version of the story of Cyrus—to seize the infant and put it to death as soon as its mother should give it birth; but the man, touched with pity, caused the child to be exposed in the woods by one of the

REMAINS OF THE PALACE OF ECBATANA.[1]

royal shepherds. A bitch gave suck to the tiny creature, who, however, would soon have succumbed to the inclemency of the weather, had not the shepherd's wife, being lately delivered of a still-born son, persuaded her husband to rescue the infant, whom she nursed with the same tenderness as if he had been her own child. The dog was, as we know, a sacred animal among the Iranians: the incident of the bitch seems, then, to have been regarded by them as an indication of divine intervention, but the Greeks were shocked by the idea, and invented an explanation consonant with their own customs. They supposed that the woman had borne the name of Spakô: Spakô signifying *bitch* in the language of Media.[2] Cyrus grew to boyhood, and being accepted by Mandanê as her son, returned to the court; his grandfather consented to spare his life, but, to avenge himself on Harpagus, he caused the limbs of the nobleman's own son to be served up to him at a feast. Thenceforth Harpagus had but one idea, to overthrow the tyrant and transfer the crown to the young prince: his project succeeded, and Cyrus, having overcome Astyages, was proclaimed king

---

[1] Drawn by Boudier, from COSTE and FLANDIN, *Voyage en Perse*, pl. xxv.

[2] Herodotus (I. cx.) asserts that the child's foster-mother was called in Greek *Kynô*, in Median *Spakô*, which comes to the same thing, for *spaka* means *bitch* in Median. Further on he asserts that the parents of the child heard of the name of his nurse with joy, as being of good augury; "and, in order that the Persians might think that Cyrus had been preserved alive by divine agency, *they spread abroad the report that Cyrus had been suckled by a bitch.* And thus arose the fable commonly accepted" (I. cxxii.). Trogus Pompeius received the original story probably through Dinon, and inserted it in his book (JUSTIN, I. v.): "Invenit juxta infantem canem feminam, parvulo ubera præbentem, et a feris alitibusque defendentem." For the sacred character of the dog among the Iranians, cf. what is stated *supra*, p. 588.

by the Medes as well as by the Persians. The real history of Cyrus, as far as we can ascertain it, was less romantic. We gather that Kurush, known to us as Cyrus, succeeded his father Cambyses as ruler of Anshân about 559 or 558 B.C.,[1] and that he revolted against Astyages in 553 or 552 B.C.,[2] and defeated him. The Median army thereupon seizing its own leader, delivered him into the hands of the conqueror: Ecbatana was taken[3] and sacked, and the empire fell at one blow, or, more properly speaking, underwent a transformation (550 B.C.).[4] The transformation was, in fact, an internal revolution in which the two peoples of the same race changed places. The name of the Medes lost nothing of the prestige which it enjoyed in foreign lands, but that of the Persians was henceforth united with it, and shared its renown: like Astyages and his predecessors, Cyrus and his successors reigned equally over the two leading branches of the ancient Iranian stock, but whereas the former had been kings of the Medes and Persians, the latter became henceforth kings of the Persians and Medes.[5]

The change effected was so natural that their nearest neighbours, the Chaldæans, showed no signs of uneasiness at the outset. They confined themselves to the bare registration of the fact in their annals at the appointed date, without comment, and Nabonidus in no way deviated from the pious routine which it had hitherto pleased him to follow. Under a sovereign so good-natured there was little likelihood of war, at all events with external

[1] The length of Cyrus' reign is fixed at thirty years by Ctesias (*Fragm.* 27, § 8, in MÜLLER-DIDOT, *Ctesiæ Cnidii Fragm.*, p. 47), followed by Dinon (*Fragm.* 10, in ID., *Fragm. Hist. Græc.*, vol. ii. p. 91) and Trogus Pompeius (JUSTIN, i. 8, 14), but at twenty-nine years by Herodotus (I. ccxiv.), whose computation I here follow. Hitherto the beginning of his reign has been made to coincide with the fall of Astyages, which was consequently placed in 569 or 568 B.C., but the discovery of the *Annals of Nabonidus* obliges us to place the taking of Ecbatana in the sixth year of the Babylonian king (SCHRADER, *Die Nabonid-Cyrus-Chronik*, in *Keil. Bibl.*, vol. iii., 2nd part, pp. 128–131), which corresponds to the year 550 B.C., and consequently to hold that Cyrus reckoned his twenty-nine years from the moment when he succeeded his father Cambyses.

[2] The inscription on the *Rassam Cylinder of Abu-Habba*, col. i. ll. 28–33, seems to make the fall of the Median king, who was suzerain of the Scythians of Harrân, coincide with the third year of Nabonidus, or the year 553–2 B.C. But it is only the date of the commencement of hostilities between Cyrus and Astyages which is here furnished, and this manner of interpreting the text agrees with the statement of the Median traditions handed down by the classical authors, that three combats took place between Astyages and Cyrus before the final victory of the Persians.

[3] *Annals of Nabonidus*, col. ii. ll. 1–4; cf. SCHRADER, *op. cit.*, pp. 128–131, and HAGEN, *Keilschrifturkunden zur Geschichte des Königs Cyrus*, in the *Beiträge zur Assyriologie*, vol. ii. pp. 218, 219, 236.

[4] *Rassam Cylinder of Abu-Habba*, col. i. ll. 16–27; cf. LATRILLE, *Der Nabonidcylinder V Rawl. 64 umschrieben, übersetzt und erklärt*, in the *Zeitschrift für Keilforschung*, vol. ii. pp. 242–245, and PEISER, *Inschriften Nabonids*, in SCHRADER, *Keil. Bibl.*, vol. iii., 2nd part, pp. 98, 99.

[5] This equality of the two peoples is indicated by the very terms employed by Darius, when he speaks of them, in the *Great Inscription of Behistun*. He says, for example, in connection with the revolt of the false Smerdis, that " the deception prevailed greatly in the land, in Persia and Media as well as in the other provinces " (col. i. ll. 34, 35); and further on, that " the whole people rose, and passed over from Cambyses to him, Persia and Media as well as the other countries" (col. i. ll. 40, 41; cf. ll. 46, 47). In the same way he mentions " the army of Persians and Medes which was with him " (col. ii. l. 18), and one sees that he considered Medes and Persians to be on exactly the same footing. The evidence of classical authors, confirming this information and showing the complete equality of the two peoples, has been collected in MAX BÜDINGER, *Der Ausgang des Medischen Reiches*, pp. 8–16.

foes, but insurrections were always breaking out in different parts of his territory, and we read of difficulties in Khumê in the first year of his reign,[1] in Hamath in his second year,[2] and troubles in Phœnicia in the third year, which afforded an opportunity for settling the Tyrian question. Tyre had led a far from peaceful existence ever since the day when, from sheer apathy, she had accepted the supremacy of Nebuchadrezzar.[3] Baal II. had peacefully reigned there for ten years (574–564), but after his death the people had overthrown the monarchy, and various *suffetes* had followed one another rapidly—Eknibaal ruled two months, Khelbes ten months, the high priest Abbar three months, the two brothers Mutton and Gerastratus six years,[4] all of them no doubt in the midst of endless disturbances; whereupon a certain Baalezor restored the royal dignity, but only to enjoy it for the space of one year. On his death, the inhabitants begged the Chaldæans to send them, as a successor to the crown, one of those princes whom, according to custom, Baal had not long previously given over as hostages for a guarantee of his loyalty, and Nergal-sharuzur for this purpose selected from their number Mahar-baal, who was probably a son of Ithobaal (558–557).[5] When, at the end of four years, the death of Mahar-baal left the throne vacant (554–553), the Tyrians petitioned for his brother Hirôm, and Nabonidus, who was then engaged in Syria, came south as far as Phœnicia and installed the prince.[6] This took place at the very moment when Cyrus was preparing his expedition against Astyages; and the Babylonian monarch took advantage of the agitation into which the Medes were thrown by this invasion, to carry into execution a project which he had been planning ever since his accession. Shortly after that event he had had a dream, in which Marduk, the great lord, and Sin, the light of heaven and earth, had appeared on either side

[1] *Annals of Nabonidus*, col. i. l. 7; cf. SCHRADER, *Die Nabonid-Cyrus-Chronik*, in the *Keilinschrift-liche Bibliothek*, vol. iii., 2nd part, pp. 128, 129, and HAGEN, *Keilschrifturkunden zur Geschichte des Königs Cyrus*, in the *Beiträge zur Assyriologie*, vol. ii. pp. 214–217.

[2] *Annals of Nabonidus*, col. i. l. 9; this affair is dated in the month Tebeth: cf. SCHRADER, *Die Nabonid-Cyrus-Chronik*, in the *Keil. Bibl.*, vol. iii., 2nd part, pp. 128, 129, and HAGEN, *Keilschriftur-kunden zur Geschichte des Königs Cyrus*, in the *Beiträge zur Assyriologie*, vol. ii. pp. 216, 217, 235.

[3] All these events are known through the excerpt from Menander preserved to us by Josephus in his treatise *Against Apion*, i. 21 (*Fragm.* 2, in MÜLLER-DIDOT, *Fragm. Hist. Græc.*, vol. iv. pp. 446, 447); on the value of this fragment, and on its ascription to Menander the historian, cf. GUTSCHMID, *Kleine Schriften*, vol. iv. pp. 545–555.

[4] MOVERS, *Das Phönizische Alterthum*, 2nd part, vol. i. pp. 463, 534, and GUTSCHMID, *Kleine Schriften*, vol. ii. p. 71, suppose that one of the two *suffetes* had in his jurisdiction that part of Tyre which was on the island, and the other the part on the mainland.

[5] The fragment of Menander does not give the Babylonian king's name, but a simple chronological calculation proves him to have been Nergal-sharuzur.

[6] *Annals of Nabonidus*, col. i. ll. 14–17, where mention is made of a certain Nabu-makhdan-uzur —but the reading of the name is uncertain—who seems to be in revolt against the Chaldæans; cf. *Keilinschriftliche Bibliothek*, vol. iii., 2nd part, pp. 128, 129. Floigl has very ingeniously harmonised the dates of the *Annals* with those obtained from the fragment of Menander (*Fragm.* 2, in MÜLLER-DIDOT, *Fragm. Hist. Græc.*, vol. iv. pp. 446, 447), and has thence concluded that the object of the expedition of the third year was the enthroning of Hirôm which is mentioned in the fragment, and during whose fourteenth year Cyrus became King of Babylon (FLOIGL, *Cyrus und Herodot*, p. 56, note).

of his couch, the former addressing him in the following words : "Nabonidus, King of Babylon, with the horses of thy chariot bring brick, rebuild Ê-khul-khul, the temple of Harrân, that Sin, the great lord, may take up his abode therein." Nabonidus had respectfully pointed out that the town was in the hands of the Scythians, who were subjects of the Medes,[1] but the god had replied: "The Scythian of whom thou speakest, he, his country and the kings his protectors, are no more." Cyrus was the instrument of the fulfilment of the prophecy. Nabonidus took possession of Harrân without difficulty, and immediately put the necessary work in hand.[2] This was, indeed, the sole benefit that he derived from the changes which were taking place, and it is probable that his inaction was the result of the enfeebled condition of the empire. The country over which he ruled, exhausted by the Assyrian conquest, and de-populated by the Scythian invasions, had not had time to recover its forces since it had passed into the hands of the Chaldæans; and the wars which Nebuchadrezzar had been obliged to undertake for the purpose of strengthening his own power, though few in number and not fraught with danger, had tended to prolong the state of weakness into which it had sunk. If the hero of the dynasty who had conquered Egypt had not ventured to measure his strength with the Median princes, and if he had courted the friendship not only of the warlike Cyaxares but of the effeminate Astyages,[3] it would not be prudent for Nabonidus to come into collision with the victorious new-comers from the heart of Iran. Chaldæa doubtless was right in avoiding hostilities, at all events so long as she had to bear the brunt of them alone, but other nations had not the same motives for exercising prudence, and Lydia was fully assured that the moment had come for her to again take up the ambitious designs which the treaty of 585 had forced her to renounce. Alyattes, relieved from anxiety with regard to the Medes, had confined his energies to establishing firmly his kingdom in the regions of Asia Minor extending westwards from the Halys and the Anti-Taurus. The acquisition of Colophon, the destruction of Smyrna, the alliance with the towns of the littoral,[4] had ensured him undisputed possession of the valleys of the Caicus and the Hermus, but the plains of the Mæander in the south, and the mountainous districts of Mysia in the north, were not yet fully brought under his sway. He completed the occupation of the Troad and Mysia about 584, and afterwards made of the entire province an appanage for Adramyttios, who was either his son or his brother.[5] He even carried his arms

[1] Cf. *supra*, pp. 516, note 2, 519, of the present volume.

[2] *Rassam Cylinder of Abu-Habba*, col. i. ll. 8–53, and col. ii. ll. 1–46; cf. PEISER, *Inschriften Nabonid's*, in SCHRADER, *Keilinschriftliche Bibliothek*, vol. iii., 2nd part, pp. 96–103.

[3] Cf. *supra*, pp. 518–520, 530, 560.

[4] For the wars of Alyattes against the coast towns, and for his relations with the Greeks, cf. above, pp. 523–525.

[5] The doings of Alyattes in Troas and in Mysia are vouched for by the anecdote related by

into Bithynia, where, to enforce his rule, he built several strongholds, one of which, called Alyatta, commanded the main road leading from the basin of the Rhyndacus to that of the Sangarius, skirting the spurs of Olympus.[1] He experienced some difficulty in reducing Caria, and did not finally succeed in his efforts till nearly the close of his reign in 566. Adramyttios was then dead, and his fief had devolved on his eldest surviving brother or nephew, Crœsus, whose mother was by birth a Carian. This prince had incurred his father's displeasure by his prodigality, and an influential party desired that he should be set aside in favour of his brother Pantaleon, the son of Alyattes by an Ionian. Crœsus, having sown his wild oats, was anxious to regain his father's favour, and his only chance of so doing was by distinguishing himself in the coming war, if only money could be found for paying his mercenaries. Sadyattes, the richest banker in Lydia, who had already had dealings with all the members of the royal family, refused to make him a loan, but Theokharides of Priênê advanced him a thousand gold staters, which enabled Crœsus to enroll his contingent at Ephesus, and to be the first to present himself at the rallying-place for the troops.[2] Caria was annexed to the kingdom, but the conditions under which the annexation took place are not known to us;[3] and Crœsus contributed so considerably to the success of the campaign, that he was reinstated in popular favour. Alyattes, however, was advancing in years, and was soon about to rejoin his adversaries Cyaxares and Nebuchadrezzar in Hades. Like the Pharaohs, the kings of Lydia were accustomed to construct during their lifetime the monuments in which they were to repose after death. Their necropolis was situated not far from Sardes, on the shores of the little lake Gygæa; it was here, close to the resting-place of his ancestors and their wives, that Alyattes chose the spot for his tomb,[4] and his subjects did not lose the

Plutarch (*Banquet of the Seven Sages*, § 10, in DÜBNER-DIDOT, *Moralia*, vol. i. p. 182) concerning this king's relations with Pittakos. The founding of Adramyttium is attributed to him by Stephen of Byzantium (*s.v.* ᾿Αδραμύττειον), after Aristotle, who made Adramyttios the brother of Crœsus (*Fragm.* 191, in MÜLLER-DIDOT, *Fragm. Hist. Græc.*, vol. ii. p. 163). Radet [gives good reasons for believing that Adramyttios was brother to Alyattes and uncle to Crœsus (*La Lydie et le Monde Grec au temps des Mermnades*, p. 200, note 1), and the same person as Adramys, the son of Sadyattes, according to Xanthus of Lydia (NICOLAS OF DAMASCUS, *Fragm.* 68, in MÜLLER-DIDOT, *Frag. Hist. Græc.*, vol. iii. p. 396). Radet (*op. cit.*, p. 199, note 1) gives the year 584 for the date of these events.

[1] STEPHEN OF BYZANTIUM, *s.v.* ᾿Αλύαττα. Radet places the operations in Bithynia before the Median war, towards 594 at the latest (*op. cit.*, p. 201, note 1). I think that they are more probably connected with those in Mysia, and that they form part of the various measures taken after the Median war to achieve the occupation of the regions west of the Halys.

[2] XANTHUS OF LYDIA, in NICOLAS OF DAMASCUS, *Fragm.* 65, in MÜLLER-DIDOT, *Fragm. Hist. Græc.*, vol. iii. p. 397. A mutilated extract, in Suidas, of the same passage, seems to carry these events back to the time of the war against Priênê, towards the beginning of the reign (cf. above, p. 253). The united evidence of the accompanying circumstances proves that they belong to the time of the old age of Alyattes, and makes it very likely that they occurred in 566, the date proposed by Radet for the Carian campaign (*La Lydie et le Monde Grec au temps des Mermnades*, p. 196, note 2).

[3] The fragment of Nicolas of Damascus does not speak of the result of the war, but it was certainly favourable, for Herodotus counts the Carians among Crœsus' subjects (I. xxviii.).

[4] HERODOTUS, I. xciii.; cf. STRABO, XIII. iv. § 7, p. 627. The only one of these monuments,

opportunity of proving to what extent he had gained their affections.   His

THE TUMULUS OF ALYATTES AND THE ENTRANCE TO THE
PASSAGE.[2]

predecessors had been obliged to finish their work at their own expense and by forced labour;[1] but in the case of Alyattes the three wealthiest classes of the population, the merchants, the craftsmen, and the courtesans, all united to erect for him an enormous tumulus, the remains of which still rise 220 feet above the plains of the Hermus.   The sub-structure consisted of a circular wall of great blocks of limestone resting on the solid rock, and it contained in the centre a vault of grey marble which was reached by a vaulted passage.   A huge mound of red clay and yellowish earth was raised above the chamber, surmounted by a small column representing a phallus, and by four stelæ covered with inscriptions, erected at the four cardinal points.[4]   It follows the traditional type of burial-places in use among the old Asianic

ONE OF THE LYDIAN ORNAMENTS IN THE LOUVRE.[3]

races, but it is constructed with greater regularity than most of them;

besides that of Alyattes, which is mentioned by the ancients, belonged to one of the favourites of Gyges, and was called *the Tomb of the Courtesan* (CLEARCHUS OF SOLI, *Fragm.* 31, in MÜLLER-DIDOT, *Fragm. Hist. Græc.*, vol. ii. p. 314).   Strabo, by a manifest error, has applied this name to the tomb of Alyattes (SCHUBERT, *Geschichte der Könige von Lydien*, pp. 56, 57).

    [1] This, at least, seems to be the import of the passage in Clearchus of Soli (*Fragm.* 34, in MÜLLER-DIDOT, *Fragm. Hist. Græc.*, vol. ii. p. 314), where that historian gives an account of the erection of the *Tomb of the Courtesan.*

    [2] Drawn by Boudier, from the sketch by Spiegelthal, in ÖLFERS, *Ueber die Lydischen Königsgräber*, pl. iv.

    [3] Drawn by Faucher-Gudin, from a photograph.   Cf. another specimen of Lydian ornaments, also preserved in the Louvre, which is reproduced as a tailpiece, *supra*, p. 568.

    [4] HERODOTUS, I. xciii., xciv.   The tomb of Alyattes was excavated for the first time in 1853–1854, by Spiegelthal, Prussian consul at Smyrna, and his observations have been published and arranged by ÖLFERS, *Ueber die Lydischen Königsgräber bei Sardes und den Grabhügel des Alyattes* (in the *Memoirs* of the Berlin Academy of Sciences, 1858, pp. 539–556); cf. PERROT and CHIPIEZ, *Histoire de l'Art dans l'Antiquité*, vol. v. pp. 265-274.   Ölfers thought that he could conclude from Herodotus' remarks

Alyattes was laid within it in 561, after a glorious reign of forty-nine years.[1]

It was wholly due to him that Lydia was for the moment raised to the level of the most powerful states which then existed on the eastern shores of the Mediterranean. He was by nature of a violent and uncontrolled temper, and during his earlier years he gave way to fits of anger, in which he would rend the clothes of those who came in his way

MOULD FOR JEWELLERY OF LYDIAN ORIGIN.[2]

or would spit in their faces, but with advancing years his character became more softened, and he finally earned the reputation of being a just and moderate sovereign.[3] The little that we know of his life reveals an energy and steadfastness of purpose quite unusual; he proceeded slowly but surely in his

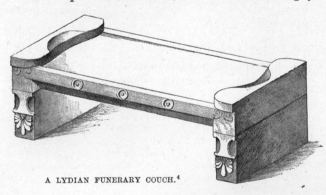

A LYDIAN FUNERARY COUCH.[4]

undertakings, and if he did not succeed in extending his domains as far as he had hoped at the beginning of his campaigns against the Medes, he at all events never lost any of the provinces he had acquired. Under his auspices

---

that the latter was speaking of the *tomb* from the observation of another person, but the comparison that Herodotus makes between it and the Egyptian pyramids and the Chaldæan ziggurâts (II. xciii.) proves that he had seen it during one of his journeys (SCHUBERT, *Geschichte der Könige von Lydien,* p. 56).

[1] HERODOTUS, I. xxv., gave fifty-seven years' length of reign to Alyattes, whilst the chronographers, who go back as far as Xanthus of Lydia, through Julius Africanus, attribute to him only forty-nine (EUSEBIUS, *Chronicon,* ed. SCHŒNE, vol. i. 69, 220); historians now prefer the latter figures, at least as representing the maximum length of reign (SCHUBERT, *Geschichte der Könige von Lydien,* pp. 14, 15; GUTSCHMID, *Kleine Schriften,* vol. ii. pp. 474, 475; RADET, *La Lydie et le Monde Grec au temps des Mermnades,* pp. 141–148, 191, 193, note 4).

[2] Drawn by Faucher-Gudin, from a photograph.

[3] NICOLAS OF DAMASCUS, *Fragm.* 64, in MÜLLER-DIDOT, *Fragm. Hist. Græc.,* vol. iii. pp. 396, 397.

[4] Drawn by Faucher-Gudin, from CHOISY, *Note sur les Tombeaux Lydiens de Sardes,* fig. 13.

agriculture flourished, and manufactures attained a degree of perfection hitherto unknown. None of the vases in gold, silver, or wrought-iron, which he dedi-

LYDIAN COIN BEARING A RUNNING FOX.[1]*

cated and placed among the treasures of the Greek temples, has come down to us, but at rare intervals ornaments of admirable workmanship are found in the Lydian tombs. Those now in the Louvre exhibit, in addition to human figures somewhat awkwardly treated, heads

LYDIAN COIN WITH A HARE.[2]

of rams, bulls, and griffins of a singular delicacy and faithfulness to nature. These examples

LYDIAN COIN WITH A LION.[4]

reveal a blending of Grecian types and methods of production with those of Egypt or Chaldæa, the Hellenic being predominant,[3] and the same combination of heterogeneous elements must have existed in the other domains of industrial art—in the dyed and embroidered stuffs,[5] the vases,[6] and the furniture.[7] Lydia, inheriting the traditions of Phrygia,[8] and like that state situated on the border of two worlds, allied moreover with Egypt as well as Babylon, and in regular communication

[1] Drawn by Faucher-Gudin, from a specimen in the *Cabinet des Médailles:* a stater of electrum weighing 14·19 grammes. I owe the cast of this coin to M. Babelon, who also has kindly undertaken the selection of the other coins reproduced below in the present work.

* [These illustrations are larger than the original pieces.—TR.]

[2] Drawn by Faucher-Gudin, from a coin in the *Cabinet des Médailles.* I am indebted to the courtesy of M. Babelon for a cast of this coin.

[3] For Lydian jewellery, see PERROT and CHIPIEZ, *Histoire de l'Art dans l'Antiquité,* vol. v. pp. 294–303, where Egyptian influence is rightly asserted. The ornaments, of which we have now no specimens, but only the original moulds cut in serpentine, such as the one reproduced above on p. 605, betray imitation of Assyria and Chaldæa (S. REINACH, *Deux Moules Asiatiques en serpentine,* in the *Revue Archéologique,* 1885, vol. vi. pp. 58–60).

[4] Drawn by Faucher-Gudin, from a coin in the *Cabinet des Médailles.* I am indebted to the courtesy of M. Babelon for a cast of this coin.

[5] On the transparent muslins called *sandykes,* from the name of the plant used to dye them a rosy flesh-colour, see the passage in JOHN OF LYDIA, *Roman Magistracies,* iii. 64. The custom of clothing themselves in dyed and embroidered stuffs was one of the effeminate habits with which the poet Xenophanes reproached the Ionians as having been learned from their Lydian neighbours.

[6] For the rare fragments of Lydian pottery which have come down to us, see PERROT and CHIPIEZ, *Histoire de l'Art dans l'Antiquité,* vol. v. pp. 292–294. M. Perrot points out that one of the vases discovered by G. Dennis at Bintépé is an evident imitation of the Egyptian and Phœnician chevroned glasses (*Histoire de l'Art dans l'Antiquité,* vol. v. p. 905). The shape of the vase is one of those found represented, with the same decoration, on Egyptian monuments subsequent to the Middle Empire, where the chevroned lines seem to be derived from the undulations of ribbon-alabaster.

[7] The stone funerary couches which have been discovered in Lydian tombs (CHOISY, *Note sur les Tombeaux Lydiens de Sardes,* in the *Revue Archéologique,* 1876, vol. xxxii. pp. 78–81; cf. the illustration, *supra,* p. 605) are evidently copied from pieces of wooden furniture similarly arranged and decorated (PERROT and CHIPIEZ, *Histoire de l'Art dans la Antiquité,* vol. v. pp. 303, 304).

[8] On the mixed character of Lydian art and civilisation, cf. PERROT and CHIPIEZ, *Histoire de l'Art dans l'Antiquité,* vol. v. pp. 305–308, and more especially RADET, *La Lydie et le Monde Grec au temps des Mermnades,* pp. 260–302.

with the Delta, borrowed from each that which fell in with her tastes or seemed likely to be most helpful to her in her commercial relations. As the country produced gold in considerable quantities, and received still more from extraneous sources, the precious metal came soon to be employed as a means of exchange under other conditions than those which had hitherto prevailed. Besides acting as commission agents and middle-men for the disposal of merchandise at Sardes, Ephesus, Miletus, Clazomenæ, and all the maritime cities, the Lydians performed at the same time the functions of pawnbrokers, money-changers, and bankers, and they were ready to make loans to private individuals as well as to kings. Obliged by the exigencies of their trade to cut up the large

COIN WITH LION'S HEAD.[1]

COIN BEARING HEAD OF MOUFLON GOAT.[2]

gold ingots into sections sufficiently small to represent the smallest values required in daily life, they did not at first impress upon these portions any stamp as a guarantee of the exact weight or of the purity of the metal: they were estimated, like the *tabonu* of the Egyptians,[3] by actual weighing on the occasion of each business transaction. The idea at length occurred to them to impress each of these pieces with a common stamp, serving, like the trade-marks employed by certain guilds of artisans, to testify at once to their genuineness and their exact weight: in a word, they were the inventors of money. The most ancient coinage of their mint was like a flattened sphere, more or less ovoid, in form: it consisted at first of electrum, and afterwards of smelted gold, upon which parallel striæ or shallow creases were made by a hammer. There were two kinds of coinage, differing considerably from each other; one consisted of the heavy stater, weighing about 14·20 grammes, perhaps of Phœnician origin, the other of the light stater, of some 10·80 grammes in weight, which doubtless served as money for the local needs of Lydia : both forms were subdivided into pieces representing respectively the third, the sixth, the twelfth, and the twenty-fourth of the value of the original.[4] The stamp which came to be impressed upon the money was in relief, and varied with the banker ;* when political communities began to follow the example of individuals, it also bore the name of the city where it was minted. The type of impression once selected, was little modified for fear of exciting mistrust among the people, but it was more finely executed and

[1] Drawn by Faucher-Gudin, from a coin in the *Cabinet des Médailles*, of which I am indebted for a cast to the courtesy of M. Babelon. Another specimen has been reproduced on p. 570.

[2] Drawn by Faucher-Gudin, from a coin in the *Cabinet des Médailles*. I am indebted to the courtesy of M. Babelon for a cast of it.

[3] On the *tabonu* of Egypt, cf. *Struggle of the Nations*, p. 490.

[4] BABELON, *Les Origines de la Monnaie considérées au point de vue historique et économique*, pp. 103–124, where this origin of coinage has been shown for the first time.

* [The best English numismatists do not agree with M. Babelon's "banker" theory. Cf. BARCLAY V. HEAD, *Historia Nummorum*, p. xxxiv.—TR.]

enlarged so as to cover one of the faces, that which we now call the *obverse.*
Several subjects entered into the composition of the design, each being impressed
by a special punch : thus in the central concavity we find the figure of a running
fox, emblem of Apollo Bassareus, and in two similar depressions, one above and
the other below the central, appear a horse's or stag's head, and a flower with
four petals. Later on the design was simplified, and contained only one, or at
most two figures—a hare squatting under a tortuous climbing plant, a roaring
lion crouching with its head turned to the left, the grinning muzzle of a lion,
the horned profile of an antelope or mouflon sheep : rosettes and flowers,

MONEY OF CRŒSUS.[1]

included within a square depression, were then used to replace the striæ and irregular lines of the reverse. These
first efforts were without inscriptions ; it was not long, however, before there came to be used, in addition to the figures,
legends, from which we sometimes learn the name of the
banker ; we read, for instance, "I am the mark of Phannes,"
on a stater of electrum struck at Ephesus, with a stag grazing on the right.[2]
We are ignorant as to which of the Lydian kings first made use of the new
invention, and so threw into circulation the gold and electrum which filled
his treasury to overflowing. The ancients say it was Gyges, but the Gygads
of their time cannot be ascribed to him ; they were, without any doubt,
simply ingots marked with the stamp of the banker of the time, and were
attributed to Gyges either out of pure imagination or by mistake.[3] The
same must be said of the pieces of money which have been assigned to
his successors, and, even when we find on them traces of writing, we cannot
be sure of their identification ; one legend which was considered to contain
the name of Sadyattes has been made out, without producing conviction, as
involving, instead, that of Clazomenæ.[4] There is no certainty until after the
time of Alyattes, that is, in the reign of Crœsus. It is, as a fact, to this prince
that we owe the fine gold and silver coins bearing on the obverse a demi-lion

---

[1] Drawn by Faucher-Gudin, from a coin in the *Cabinet des Médailles*, a cast of which I owe to the
courtesy of M. Babelon.

[2] BABELON, *Melanges de Numismatique,* vol. iii. p. 123. The coin is of electrum found at Halicarnassus, and is preserved in the British Museum : it weighs 14·06 grammes, and bears the inscription
Φαννος εμι σημα, written from left to right.

[3] The gold of Gyges, ὁ Γυγάδας χρυσὸς, is known to us through a passage in Pollux (*Onomasticon,*
iii. 87 ; cf. vii. 98). Fr. Lenormant attributed to Gyges (*Monnaies royales de la Lydie,* pp. 3, 4,
14, 15, 21 ; *La Monnaie dans l'Antiquité,* vol. i. pp. 128, 132, 133) the coins which Babelon restores to
the banks of Asia Minor (*Les Origines de la Monnaie,* pp. 222–226). Babelon sees in the Gygads only
" ingots of gold, struck *possibly* in the name of Gyges, capable of being used as coin, doubtless
representing a definitely fixed weight, but still lacking that ultimate perfection which characterises
the coinage of civilised peoples : from the standpoint of circulation in the market their shape was
defective and inconvenient ; their subdivision did not extend to such small fractions as to make all
payments easy ; they were too large and too dear for easy circulation through many hands."

[4] BABELON, *Mélanges Numismatiques,* vol. iii. p. 138.

couchant confronting a bull treated similarly.[1] The two creatures appear to threaten one another, and the introduction of the lion recalls a tradition regarding the city of Sardes; it may represent the actual animal which was alleged to have been begotten by King Meles of one of his concubines, and which he caused to be carried solemnly round the city walls to render them impregnable.[2]

Crœsus did not succeed to the throne of his father without trouble. His enemies had not laid down their arms after the Carian campaign, and they

VIEW OF THE SITE AND RUINS OF EPHESUS.[3]

endeavoured to rid themselves of him by all the means in use at Oriental courts. The Ionian mother of his rival furnished the slave who kneaded the bread with poison, telling her to mix it with the dough, but the woman revealed the intended crime to her master, who at once took the necessary measures to frustrate the plot; later on in life he dedicated in the temple at Delphi a statue of gold representing the faithful bread-maker.[4] The chief of the rival party seems to have been Sadyattes, the banker from whom Crœsus had endeavoured to borrow

---

[1] Lenormant ascribed an issue of coins without inscriptions to the kings Ardys, Sadyattes, and Alyattes (*Monnaies royales de Lydie*, pp. 4–7), but this has since been believed not to have been their work.

[2] On this tradition, cf. *supra*, p. 337.

[2] Drawn by Boudier, from a photograph.

[4] PLUTARCH, *De Pythiæ Oraculis*, § 16, in BÆHR-DIDOT, *Opera Moralia*, vol. i. p. 490, where the author simply says *the king's second wife;* he evidently designates thus the mother of Pantaleon (RADET, *La Lydie et le Monde Grec au temps des Mermnades*, p. 208). Herodotus mentions the statue of the bread-maker, giving no reason why Crœsus dedicated it. The author quoted by Plutarch would have it that in revenge he made his half-brothers eat the poisoned bread.

money at the beginning of his career,[1] but several of the Lydian nobles, whose exercise of feudal rights had been restricted by the growing authority of the Mermnadæ, either secretly or openly gave their adhesion to Pantaleon, among them being Glaucias of Sidênê; the Greek cities, always ready to chafe at authority, were naturally inclined to support a claimant born of a Greek mother, and Pindarus the tyrant of Ephesus, and grandson of the Melas who had married the daughter of Gyges, joined the conspirators. As soon as Alyattes was dead, Crœsus, who was kept informed by his spies of their plans, took action with a rapidity which disconcerted his adversaries. It is not known what became of Pantaleon, whether he was executed or fled the country, but his friends were tortured to death or had to purchase their pardon dearly. Sadyattes was stretched on a rack and torn with carding combs.[2] Glaucias, besieged in his fortress of Sidênê, opened its gates after a desperate resistance; the king demolished the walls, and pronounced a solemn curse on those who should thereafter rebuild them.[3] Pindarus, summoned to surrender, refused, but as he had not sufficient troops to defend the entire city, he evacuated the lower quarters, and concentrated all his forces on the defence of the citadel; he refused to open negotiations until after the fall of a tower at the moment when a practicable breach had been made, and succeeded in obtaining an honourable capitulation for himself and his people by a ruse. He dedicated the town to Artemis, and by means of a rope connected the city walls with the temple, which stood nearly a mile away in the suburbs, and then entreated for peace in the name of the goddess. Crœsus was amused at the artifice, and granted favourable conditions to the inhabitants, but insisted on the expulsion of the tyrant. The latter bowed before the decree, and confiding the care of his children and possessions to his friend Pasicles, left for the Peloponnesus with his retinue.[4] Ephesus up to this time had been a kind of allied principality, whose chiefs, united to the royal family of Lydia by marriages from generation to generation, recognised the nominal suzerainty of the reigning king rather than his effective authority. It was in fact a species of protectorate, which, while furthering the commercial interests of Lydia, satisfied at the same time the passion of the Greek cities for autonomy. Crœsus, encouraged by his first success, could not rest contented with such a compromise. He attacked,

---

[1] Cf. *supra*, p. 603.

[2] The history of Sadyattes and of his part in the conspiracy results from points of agreement which have been established between various passages in Herodotus (I. xcii.) and in Nicolas of Damascus (*Fragm.* 65, in MÜLLER-DIDOT, *Fragm. Hist. Græc.*, vol. iii. p. 397), where the person is sometimes named and sometimes not; cf. SCHUBERT, *Geschichte der Könige von Lydien*, p. 61, and RADET, *La Lydie et le Monde Grec au temps des Mermnades*, pp. 206–208.

[3] STRABO, XIII. i. § 42, p. 601, probably from Xanthus of Lydia, as the *Fragment* 24 of that author, in MÜLLER-DIDOT, *Fragm. Hist. Græc.*, vol. i. p. 43, seems to show.

[4] HERODOTUS, I. xxvi., where the outline of the story is given; the detailed account found in POLYÆNUS, *Stratagems*, vi. 50, and in ÆLIAN, *Hist. Var.*, iii. 26, is probably taken from Xanthus.

successively, Miletus and the various Ionian, Æolian, and Dorian communities of the littoral, and brought them all under his sway, promising on their capitulation that their local constitutions should be respected if they became direct dependencies of his empire.[1] He placed garrisons in such towns as were strategically important for him to occupy, but everywhere else he razed to the ground the fortresses and ramparts which might afford protection to his enemies in case of rebellion, compelling the inhabitants to take up their abode on the open plain where they could not readily defend themselves.[2] The administration of the affairs of each city was entrusted to either a wealthy citizen, or an hereditary tyrant, or an elected magistrate, who was held responsible for its loyalty; the administrator paid over the tribute to the sovereign's treasurers, levied the specified contingent and took command of it in time of war, settled any quarrels which might occur, and was empowered, when necessary, to exile turbulent and ambitious persons whose words or actions appeared to him to be suspicious.[3] Crœsus treated with generosity those republics which tendered him loyal obedience, and affected a special devotion to their gods. He gave a large number of ex-voto offerings to the much-revered sanctuary of Branchidæ, in the territory of Miletus;[4] he dedicated some golden heifers at the Artemision of Ephesus, and erected the greater number of the columns of that temple at his own expense.[5] At one time in his career he appears to have contemplated extending his dominion over the Greek islands, and planned, as was said, the equipment of a fleet, but he soon acknowledged the imprudence of such a project, and confined his efforts to strengthening his advantageous position on the littoral by contracting alliances with the island populations and with the nations of Greece proper.[6] Following the diplomacy of his ancestors, he began by devoting himself to the gods of the country, and took every pains to gain the good graces of Apollo of Delphi. He dispensed his gifts with such liberality that neither his contemporaries nor subsequent generations grew weary of admiring it. On one occasion he is said to have sacrificed three thousand animals, and burnt, moreover, on the pyre the costly contents of a palace—couches covered with silver and gold, coverlets and robes of purple,

---

[1] HERODOTUS, I. xxvi., xxviii. Mention of these capitulations, σύνθηκαι, is made with reference to Ephesus, in POLYÆNUS, *Stratagems*, vi. 50.

[2] He treated thus the Ephesians (STRABO, XIV. i. § 21, p. 640) and the Ilians (STRABO, XIII. i. § 25, p. 593).

[3] For the organisation of the dominion over Lydia under Crœsus, see the ingenious proof in RADET, *La Lydie et le Monde Grec au temps des Mermnades*, pp. 210–215.

[4] HERODOTUS, I. xcii., and V. xxxvi.

[5] HERODOTUS, I. xcii. The fragments of columns brought from this temple by Wood and preserved in the British Museum have on one of the bases the remains of an inscription confirming the testimony of Herodotus: Βα[σιλεὺς] Κ[ροῖσος] ἀνέ[θηκε]ν (MURRAY, *Remains of the Archaic Temple of Artemis at Ephesus*, in the *Journal of Hellenic Studies*, vol. x. pp. 1–10).

[6] HERODOTUS, I. xxvii.; DIODORUS SICULUS, ix. 25; POLYÆNUS, *Stratagems*, ii. 26. He seems to have been deterred from his project by a sarcastic remark made, as some say, by Pittakos the Mitylenian, or according to others, by Bias of Priênê.

and golden vials. His subjects were commanded to contribute to the offering, and he caused one hundred and seventeen hollow half-bricks to be cast of the gold which they brought him for this purpose. These bricks were placed in regular layers within the treasury at Delphi where the gifts of Lydia from the time of Alyattes were deposited, and the top of the pile was surmounted by a lion of fine gold of such a size that the pedestal and statue together were worth £1,200,000 of our present money. These, however, formed only a tithe of his gifts; many of the objects dedicated by him were dispersed half a century (548 B.C.) later when the temple was burnt, and found their way into the treasuries of the Greek states which enjoyed the favour of Apollo—among them being an enormous gold cup sent to Clazomenæ, and four barrels of silver and two bowls, one of silver and one of gold, sent to the Corinthians. The people at Delphi, as well as their god, participated in the royal largesse, and Crœsus distributed to them the sum of two staters per head. No doubt their gratitude led them by degrees to exaggerate the total of the benefits showered upon them, especially as time went on and their recollection of the king became fainter; but even when we reduce the number of the many gifts which they attributed to him, we are still obliged to acknowledge that they surpassed anything hitherto recorded, and that they produced throughout the whole of Greece the effect that Crœsus had desired. The oracle granted to him and to the Lydians the rights of citizenship in perpetuity, the privilege of priority in consulting it before all comers, precedence for his legates over other foreign embassies, and a place of honour at the games and at all religious ceremonies.[1] It was, in fact, the admission of Lydia into the Hellenic concert, and the offerings which Crœsus showered upon the sanctuaries of lesser fame—that of Zeus at Dodona,[2] of Amphiaraos at Oropos,[3] of Trophonios at Lebadæa,[4] on the oracle of Abæ in Phocis, and on the Ismenian Apollo at Thebes[5]—secured a general approval of the act. Political alliances contracted with the great families of Athens, the Alcmæonidæ and Eupatridæ,[6] with the Cypselidæ of Corinth,[7] and with the Heraclidæ of Sparta,[8] completed the policy of bribery which Crœsus

---

[1] HERODOTUS, I. l., li.; THEOPOMPUS, *Fragm.* 184, in MÜLLER-DIDOT, *Fragm. Hist. Græc.*, vol. i. pp. 309, 310; PHANIAS OF ERESOS, *Fragm.* 12, ID., vol. ii. p. 297.

[2] HERODOTUS, I. xlvi.

[3] HERODOTUS, I. xlvi., xlix., lii., xcii.; cf. the allusion to the consultation of the oracle in the scene at the funeral pile as described by NICOLAS OF DAMASCUS, *Fragm.* 68, in MÜLLER-DIDOT, *Fragm. Hist. Græc.*, vol. iii. p. 408.

[4] HERODOTUS, I. xlvi.

[5] HERODOTUS, I. xlvi., xcii.

[6] For Crœsus' relations with Alcmæon, cf. the traditions preserved by HERODOTUS, VI. cxxv.: The king compelled the inhabitants of Lampsacus, his vassals, to release the elder Miltiades, whom they had taken prisoner (HERODOTUS, VI. xxxvii.), and thus earned the gratitude of the Eupatridæ.

[7] Alyattes had been the ally of Periander, as is proved by an anecdote in HERODOTUS, III. xlviii. This friendship continued under Crœsus, for after the fall of the monarchy, when the special treasuries of Lydia were suppressed, the ex-voto offerings of the Lydian kings were deposited in the treasury of Corinth (HERODOTUS, I. l., li.; cf. PAUSANIAS, x. 13).

[8] HERODOTUS, I. lxix., lxx. According to Theopompus (*Fragm.* 219, in MÜLLER-DIDOT, *Fragm.*

had inaugurated in the sacerdotal republics, with the result that, towards 548, being in the position of uncontested patron of the Greeks of Asia, he could count upon the sympathetic neutrality of the majority of their compatriots in Europe, and on the effective support of a smaller number of them in the event of his being forced into hostilities with one or other of his Asiatic rivals.

This, however, constituted merely one side of his policy, and the negotiations which he carried on with his western neighbours were conducted simultaneously with his wars against those of the east. Alyattes had asserted his supremacy over the whole of the country on the western side of the Halys, but it was of a very vague kind, having no definite form, and devoid of practical results as far as several of the districts in the interior were concerned. Crœsus made it a reality, and in less than ten years all the peoples contained within it, the Lycians excepted—Mysians, Phrygians, Mariandynians, Paphlagonians, Thynians, Bithynians, and Pamphylians—had rendered him homage.[1] In its constitution his empire in no way differed from those which at that time shared the rule of Western Asia; the number of districts administered directly by the sovereign were inconsiderable, and most of the states comprised in it preserved their autonomy. Phrygia had its own princes, who were descendants of Midas,[2] and in the same way Caria and Mysia also retained theirs; but these vassal lords paid tribute and furnished contingents to their liege of Sardes, and garrisons lodged in their citadels as well as military stations or towns founded in strategic positions, such as Prusa[3] in Bithynia, Cibyra,[4] Hyda, Grimenothyræ, and Temenothyræ,[5] kept strict watch over them, securing the while free circulation for caravans or individual merchants throughout the whole country. Crœsus had achieved his conquest just as Media was tottering to its fall under the attacks of the Persians. Their victory placed the Lydian king in a position of great perplexity, since it annulled the treaties concluded after the eclipse of 585, and by releasing him from the obligations then contracted, afforded him an opportunity of extending the limits within which his father had confined himself. Now or never was the time for crossing the Halys in

---

Hist. Græc., vol. i. p. 314), the Lacedæmonians, wishing to gild the face of the statue of the Amyclæan Apollo, and finding no gold in Greece, consulted the Delphian prophetess: by her advice they sent to Lydia to buy the precious metal from Crœsus. Cf. Pausanias, III. x. § 10.

[1] Herodotus, I. xxviii.

[2] This is proved by the history of the Prince Adrastus in Herodotus, I. xxxv.–xlv.; cf. *supra*, p. 522.

[3] Strabo, XII. iv. § 8, p. 564, with the correction Κροίσου τοῦ πρὸς Κῦρον πολεμήσαντος. As Radet points out (*La Lydie et le Monde Grec au temps des Mermnades*, p. 222, note 2), Herodotus probably alluded to this colonisation by Crœsus, when he said that the Mysians of Olympus were descendants of Lydian colonists (VII. lxxiv.).

[4] Strabo, XIII. iv. § 17, p. 631, merely says that the Kibyrates were descended from the Lydians who dwelt in Cabalia: since Crœsus was, as far as we know, the only Lydian king who ever possessed this part of Asia, Radet, with good reason, concludes that Kibyra was colonised by him (*La Lydie et le Monde Grec au temps des Mermnades*, p. 222, note 3).

[5] Radet has given good reasons for believing that at least some of these towns were enlarged and fortified by Crœsus (*La Lydie et le Monde Grec au temps des Mermnades*, pp. 221–223).

order to seize those mineral districts with which his subjects had so long had commercial relations; on the other hand, the unexpected energy of which the Persians had just given proof, their bravery, their desire for conquest, and the valour of their leader, all tended to deter him from the project: should he be victorious, Cyrus would probably not rest contented with the annexation of a few unimportant districts or the imposition of a tribute, but would treat his adversary as he had Astyages, and having dethroned him, would divide Lydia into departments to be ruled by one or other of his partisans.   Warlike ideas, nevertheless, prevailed at the court of Sardes, and, taking all into consideration, we cannot deny that they had reason on their side.   The fall of Ecbatana had sealed the fate of Media proper, and its immediate dependencies had naturally shared the fortunes of the capital; but the more distant provinces still wavered, and they would probably attempt to take advantage of the change of rule to regain their liberty.   Cyrus, obliged to take up arms against them, would no longer have his entire forces at his disposal, and by attacking him at that juncture it might be possible to check his power before it became irresistible.[1] Having sketched out his plan of campaign, Crœsus prepared to execute it with all possible celerity.   Egypt and Chaldæa, like himself, doubtless felt themselves menaced; he experienced little difficulty in persuading them to act in concert with him in face of the common peril, and he obtained from both Amasis and Nabonidus promises of effective co-operation.[2]   At the same time he had recourse to the Greek oracles, and that of Delphi was instrumental in obtaining for him a treaty of alliance and friendship with Sparta.[3]   Negotiations had been carried on so rapidly, that by the end of 548 all was in readiness for a simultaneous movement; Sparta was equipping a fleet, and merely awaited the return of the favourable season to embark her contingent;[4] Egypt had already despatched hers, and her Cypriot vassals were on the point of starting, while bands of Thracian infantry were marching to reinforce the Lydian army.[5] These various elements represented so considerable a force of men, that, had they been ranged on a field of battle, Cyrus would have experienced considerable difficulty in overcoming them.   An unforeseen act of treachery obliged the Lydians to hasten their preparations and commence hostilities before the moment agreed on.   Eurybatos, an Ephesian, to whom the king had entrusted large sums of money for the purpose of raising mercenaries in the Peloponnesus,

---

[1] This is the motive ascribed to him by Herodotus: εἴ κως δύναιτο, πρὶν μεγάλους γένεσθαι τοὺς Πέρσας καταλαβεῖν αὐτῶν αὐξανομένην τὴν δύναμιν (I. xlvi.), to which elsewhere he adds that of avenging his brother-in-law Astyages (I. lxxiii.).

[2] HERODOTUS, I. lxxvii.

[3] HERODOTUS, I. xlvii.–lvi.; it was on this occasion that he gave to the Greek gods part of the presents described above, pp. 611, 612. For the treaty of alliance with Sparta, cf. HERODOTUS, I. lxix.

[4] HERODOTUS, I. lxx., lxxxiii.

[5] XENOPHON, *Cyropædia*, VII. ii. § 10, from some author now lost.

fled with his gold into Persia, and betrayed the secret of the coalition.[1] The Achæmenian sovereign did not hesitate to forestall the attack, and promptly assumed the offensive. The transport of an army from Ecbatana to the middle course of the Halys would have been a long and laborious undertaking, even had it kept within the territory of the empire; it would have necessitated crossing the mountain groups of Armenia at their greatest width, and that at a time when the snow was still lying deep upon the ground and the torrents were swollen and unfordable. The most direct route, which passed through Assyria and the part of Mesopotamia south of the Masios, lay for the most part in the hands of the Chaldæans, but their enfeebled condition justified Cyrus's choice of it, and he resolved, in the event of their resistance, to cut his way through sword in hand. He therefore bore down upon Arbela by the gorges of Rowandîz in the month Nisan, making as though he were bound for Karduniash; but before the Babylonians had time to recover from their alarm at this movement, he crossed the river not far from Nineveh and struck into Mesopotamia. He probably skirted the slopes of the Masios, overcoming and killing in the month Iyyâr some petty king, probably the ruler of Armenia,[2] and debouched into Cappadocia. This province was almost entirely in the power of the enemy;[3] Nabonidus had despatched couriers by the shortest route in order to warn his ally, and if necessary to claim his promised help. Crœsus, when he received them, had with him only the smaller portion of his army, the Lydian cavalry, the contingents of his Asiatic subjects, and a few Greek veterans, and it would probably have been wiser to defer the attack till after the disembarkation of the Lacedæmonians; but hesitation at so critical a moment might have discouraged his followers, and decided his fate before any action had taken place. He therefore collected his troops together, fell upon the right bank of the Halys,[4] devastated the country, occupied Pteria and the neighbour-

[1] DIODORUS SICULUS, ix. 32.

[2] *Annals of Nabonidus*, col. ii. ll. 15–18; cf. SCHRADER, *Die Nabonid-Cyrus-Chronik*, in the *Keilinschriftliche Bibliothek*, vol. iii., 2nd part, pp. 130, 131, and HAGEN, *Keilschrifturkunden zur Geschichte des Königs Cyrus*, in the *Beiträge zur Assyriologie*, vol. ii. pp. 218–221. Floigl (*Cyrus und Herodot*, pp. 125, 126)—the first to refer this passage in the *Annals* to the expedition against Crœsus—restored Is[parda] as the name of the country mentioned, and saw even the capture of Sardes in the events of the month Iyyâr, in direct contradiction to the Greek tradition. The connection between the campaign beyond the Tigris and the Lydian war seems to me incontestable, but the Babylonian chronicler has merely recorded the events which affected Babylonia. Cyrus' object was both to intimidate Nabonidus and also to secure possession of the most direct, and at the same time the easiest, route : by cutting across Mesopotamia he avoided the difficult marches in the mountainous districts of Armenia. A reminiscence of this invasion of Chaldæa is probably to be found in the brief notice of Justin (I. viii. § 3): "*Quum adversus Babylonios bellum gereret*, Babyloniis rex Lydorum Crœsus, cujus opes et divitiæ insignes eâ tempestate erant, in auxilium venit." Perhaps we should combine, with the information of the *Annals*, the passage of Xenophon (*Cyropædia*, II. iv. § 12), where it is said that the Armenians refused tribute and service to the King of Persia : Cyrus would have punished the rebels on his way, after crossing the Euphrates.

[3] DIODORUS SICULUS, ix. 31.

[4] On this point Herodotus (I. lxxv.) tells a current story of his time : Thales had a trench dug behind

ing towns, and exiled the inhabitants to a distance.[1] He had just completed the subjection of the White Syrians when he was met by an emissary from the Persians; Cyrus offered him his life, and confirmed his authority on condition of his pleading for mercy and taking the oath of vassalage.[2] Crœsus sent a proud refusal, which was followed by a brilliant victory, after which a truce of three months was concluded between the belligerents.[3] Cyrus employed the respite in attempting to win over the Greek cities of the littoral, which he pictured to himself as nursing a bitter hatred against the Mermnadæ; but it is to be doubted if his emissaries succeeded even in wresting a declaration of neutrality from the Milesians; the remainder, Ionians and Æolians, all continued faithful to their oaths.[4] On the resumption of hostilities, the tide of fortune turned, and the Lydians were crushed by the superior forces of the Persians and the Medes; Crœsus retired under cover of night, burning the country as he retreated, to prevent the enemy from following him, and crossed the Halys with the remains of his battalions. The season was already far advanced; he thought that the Persians, threatened in the rear by the Babylonian troops, would shrink from the prospect of a winter campaign, and he fell back upon Sardes without further lingering in Phrygia. But Nabonidus did not feel himself called upon to show the same devotion that his ally had evinced towards him, or perhaps the priests who governed in his name did not permit him to fulfil his engagements.[5] As soon as peace was

the army, which was probably encamped in one of the bends made by the Halys; he then diverted the stream into this new bed, with the result that the Lydians found themselves on the right bank of the river without having had the trouble of crossing it.

[1] HERODOTUS, I. lxxvi.

[2] DIODORUS SICULUS, ix. 31. Nicolas of Damascus records that Cyrus, after the capture of Sardes, for a short time contemplated making Crœsus a vassal king, or at least a satrap of Lydia (*Fragm.* 68, in MÜLLER-DIDOT, *Fragm. Hist. Græc.*, vol. iii. p. 409).

[3] We have two very different accounts of this campaign, viz. that of Herodotus (I. lxxvi., lxxvii.), and that of Polyænus (*Stratagems*, vii. 8). According to Herodotus, Crœsus gave battle only once in Pteria, with indecisive result, and on the next day quietly retired to his kingdom, thinking that Cyrus would not dare to pursue him. According to Polyænus, Crœsus, victorious in a first engagement owing to a more or less plausible military stratagem, consented to a truce, but on the day after was completely defeated, and obliged to return to his kingdom with a routed army. Herodotus' account of the fall of Crœsus and of Sardes, borrowed partly from a good written source, Xanthus or Charon of Lampsacus, partly from the tradition of the Harpagidæ, seems to have for its object the soothing of the vanity both of the Persians and of the Lydians, since, if the result of the war could not be contested, the issue of the battle was at least left uncertain. If he has given a faithful account, no one can understand why Crœsus should have retired and ceded White Syria to a rival who had never conquered him. The account given by Polyænus, in spite of the improbability of some of its details, comes from a well-informed author: the defeat of the Lydians in the second battle explains the retreat of Crœsus, who is without excuse in Herodotus' version of the affair. Pompeius Trogus adopted a version similar to that of Polyænus (JUSTIN, i. 7).

[4] HERODOTUS, I. lxxvi., where the attempted corruption of the Ionians is made to date from the beginning of the war, even before Cyrus took the field; cf. HERODOTUS, I. clxi., clxix.

[5] The author followed by Pompeius Trogus has alone preserved the record of this treaty. The fact is important as explaining Crœsus' behaviour after his defeat (JUSTIN, i. 7), but Schubert goes too far when he re-establishes on this ground an actual campaign of Cyrus against Babylon (*Geschichte der Könige von Lydien*, pp. 101, 102): Radet has come back to the right view in seeing only a treaty made with Nabonidus (*La Lydie et le Monde Grec*, p. 248).

proposed, he accepted terms, without once considering the danger to which the Lydians were exposed by his defection. The Persian king raised his camp as soon as all fear of an attack to rearward was removed, and, falling upon defence-less Phrygia, pushed forward to Sardes in spite of the inclemency of the season. No movement could have been better planned, or have produced such startling results. Crœsus had disbanded the greater part of his feudal contingents, and had kept only his body-guard about him, the remainder of his army   natives, mercenaries, and allies—having received orders not to reassemble till the following spring. The king hastily called together all his available troops, both Lydians and foreigners, and confronted his enemies for the second time. Even under these unfavourable conditions he hoped to gain the advantage, had his cavalry, the finest in the world, been able to take part in the engagement. But Cyrus had placed in front of his lines a detachment of camels, and the smell of these animals so frightened the Lydian horses that they snorted and refused to charge.[1] Crœsus was again worsted on the confines of the plain of the Hermus, and taking refuge in the citadel of Sardes, he despatched couriers to his allies in Greece and Egypt to beg for succour without delay.[2] The Lacedæmonians hurried on the mobilisation of their troops, and their vessels were on the point of weighing anchor, when the news arrived that Sardes had fallen in the early days of December, and that Crœsus himself was a prisoner.[3]

How the town came to be taken, the Greeks themselves never knew, and their chroniclers have given several different accounts of the event.[4]   The

---

[1] Herodotus' (I. lxxx.) mention of the use of camels is confirmed, with various readings, by Xenophon (*Cyropædia*, VII. i. § 48), by Polyænus (*Stratagems*, vii. 6), and by Ælian (*Hist. Animal.*, iii. 7); their employment does not necessarily belong to a legendary form of the story, especially if we suppose, with Radet (*La Lydie et le Monde Grec au temps des Mermnades*, p. 250, note 3), that the camel, unknown before in Asia Minor, was first introduced there by the Persian army. The site of the battle is not precisely known. According to Herodotus (I. lxxx.) the fight took place in the great plain before Sardes, which is crossed by several small tributaries of the Hermus, amongst others the Hyllus (*La Lydie et le Monde Grec au temps des Mermnades*, p. 249, note 4, 310). Radet recognises that the Hyllus of Herodotus is the whole or part of the stream now called the Kusu-tchaî, and he places the scene of action near the township of Adala, which would correspond with Xenophon's Thymbrara (*Cyropædia*, VI. ii. § 11). This continues to be the most likely hypothesis. After the battle Crœsus would have fled along the Hermus towards Sardes (Herodotus, I. lv.). Xenophon's story is a pure romance (*Cyrop.*, vii. 1), and Schubert in vain attempts to defend some of its details (*Geschichte der Könige von Lydien*, pp. 103, 104).

[2] Herodotus, I. lxxxi.

[3] Herodotus, I. lxxxiii. Radet (*La Lydie et le Monde Grec au temps des Mermnades*, p. 250, note 7) gives the date of the capture of Sardes as about November 15, 546; but the number and importance of the events occurring between the retreat of Crœsus and the decisive catastrophe—the negotiations with Babylon, the settling into winter quarters, the march of Cyrus across Phrygia—must have required a longer time than Radet allots to them in his hypothesis, and I make the date a month later.

[4] Ctesias (*Fragm.* 29, § 4, in Müller-Didot, *Ctesiæ Cnidii Fragmenta*, p. 46) and Xenophon *Cyrop.*, VII. ii.) seem to depend on Herodotus, the former with additional fabulous details concerning his Œbaras, Cyrus' counsellor (cf. what is said of this individual, *supra*, pp. 596, 597), which show the probable origin of his additions. Polyænus (*Stratagems*, vii. 6 and vii. 8) had at his disposal a different story, the same probably that he used for his account of the campaign in Cappadocia, for in

least improbable is that found in Herodotus. The blockade had lasted, so he tells us, fourteen days, when Cyrus announced that he would richly reward the first man to scale the walls. Many were tempted by his promises, but were unsuccessful in their efforts, and their failure had discouraged all further attempts, when a Mardian soldier, named Hyreades, on duty at the foot of the steep slopes overlooking the Tmolus, saw a Lydian descend from rock to rock in search of his helmet which he had lost, and regain the city by the same way without any great difficulty. He noted carefully the exact spot, and in company with a few comrades climbed up till he reached the ramparts; others followed, and taking the besieged unawares, they opened the gates to the main body of the army.[1] Crœsus could not bear to survive the downfall of his kingdom: he erected a funeral pyre in the courtyard of his palace, and took up his position on it, together with his wives, his daughters, and the noblest youths of his court, surrounded by his most precious possessions. He could cite the example of more than one vanquished monarch of the ancient Asiatic world in choosing such an end, and one of the fabulous ancestors of his race, Sandon-Herakles, had perished after this fashion in the midst of the flames.[2] Was the sacrifice carried out? Everything leads us to believe that it was, but popular feeling could not be resigned to the idea that a prince who had shown such liberality towards the gods in his prosperity should be abandoned by them in the time of his direst need. They came to believe that the Lydian monarch had expiated by his own defeat the crime by the help of which his ancestor Gyges had usurped the throne.[3] Apollo had endeavoured to delay the punishment till the next generation, that it might fall on the son of his votary, but he had succeeded in obtaining from fate a respite of three years only. Even then he had not despaired, and had warned Crœsus by the voice of the oracles. They had foretold him that, in crossing the Halys, the Lydians would destroy a great empire, and that their power would last till the day when a mule should sit upon the throne of Media. Crœsus, blinded by fate, could not see that Cyrus, who was of mixed race, Persian by his father and Median by his mother, was the predicted mule. He therefore crossed the Halys, and a great empire fell, but it was his own.[4] At all events, the god might have desired to show that

it can be recognised the wish to satisfy, within possible limits, the pride of the Lydians: here again the decisive success is preceded by a check given to Cyrus and a three months' truce. For the critical examination of these sources, see SCHUBERT, *Geschichte der Könige von Lydien*, pp. 106–108, and RADET, *La Lydie et le Monde Grec au temps des Mermnades*, pp. 251–253.

[1] HERODOTUS, I. lxxxiv. About three and a half centuries later Sardes was captured in the same way by one of the generals of Antiochus the Great (POLYBIUS, vii. 4–7).

[2] See what is said with regard to the death of Shamash-shumukîn, *supra*, pp. 422, 423. The first to recognise the true meaning of this final scene was RAOUL-ROCHETTE, *Sur l'Hercule Assyrien et Phénicien*, in the *Mémoires de l'Académie des Inscriptions et Belles-Lettres*, vol. xvii., 2nd part, p. 271, et seq., whose opinion, though long contested, is now generally adopted; see, nevertheless, the objections lately raised against it by SCHUBERT, *Gesch. der Könige von Lydien*, pp. 124–128.

[3] Cf. *supra*, pp. 389–391.   [4] HERODOTUS, I. xc., xci.

to honour his altars and adorn his temple was in itself, after all, the best of treasures. " When Sardes, suffering the vengeance of Zeus, was conquered by the army of the Persians, the god of the golden sword, Apollo, was the guardian of Crœsus. When the day of despair arrived, the king could not resign himself to tears and servitude; within the brazen-walled court he erected a funeral pyre, on which, together with his chaste spouse and his bitterly lamenting daughters of beautiful locks, he mounted; he raised his hands towards the depths of the ether and cried : ' Proud fate, where is the gratitude of the

gods, where is the prince, the child of Leto ? Where is now the house of Alyattes ? . . . The ancient citadel of Sardes has fallen, the Pactolus of golden waves runs red with blood ; ignominiously are the women driven from their well-decked chambers ! That which was once my hated foe is now my friend, and the sweetest thing is to die ! ' Thus he spoke, and ordered the softly moving eunuch [1] to set fire to the wooden structure. The maidens shrieked and threw their arms around their mother, for the death before them was

CRŒSUS ON HIS PYRE.[2]

that most hated by mortals. But just when the sparkling fury of the cruel fire had spread around, Zeus, calling up a black-flanked cloud, extinguished the yellow flame. Nothing is incredible of that which the will of the gods has decreed : Apollo of Delos, seizing the old man, bore him, together with his daughters of tender feet, into the Hyperborean land as a reward for his piety, for no mortal had sent richer offerings to the illustrious Pythô ! " [3] This miraculous ending delighted the poets and inspired many fine lines, but history could with difficulty accommodate itself to such a materialistic intervention of a divine being, and

[1] The word translated "softly moving eunuch " is here perhaps a proper name : the slave whose duty it was to kindle the pyre was called Abrobatas in the version of the story chosen by Bacchylides, while that adopted by the potter whose work is reproduced above on this page, calls him Euthymos.

[2] Drawn by Faucher-Gudin, from a photograph of the original in the Museum of the Louvre.

[3] BACCHYLIDES, *Ode III.*, 23–62.

sought a less fabulous solution. The legend which appeared most probable to the worthy Herodotus did not even admit that the Lydian king took his own life; it was Cyrus who condemned him, either with a view of devoting the first-fruits of his victory to the immortals, or to test whether the immortals would save the rival whose piety had been so frequently held up to his admiration. The edges of the pyre had already taken light, when the Lydian king sighed and thrice repeated the name of Solon. It was a tardy recollection of a conversation in which the Athenian sage had stated, without being believed, that none can be accounted truly happy while they still live. Cyrus, applying it to himself, was seized with remorse or pity, and commanded the bystanders to quench the fire, but their efforts were in vain. Thereupon Crœsus implored the pity of Apollo, and suddenly the sky, which up till then had been serene and clear, became overcast; thick clouds collected, and rain fell so heavily that the burning pile was at once extinguished.[1] Well treated by his conqueror, the Lydian king is said to have become his friend and most loyal counsellor; he accepted from him the fief of Barêné in Media, often accompanied him in his campaigns, and on more than one occasion was of great service to him by the wise advice which he gave.[2] We may well ask what would have taken place had he gained the decisive victory over Cyrus that he hoped. Chaldæa possessed merely the semblance of her former greatness and power, and if she still maintained her hold over Mesopotamia, Syria, Phœnicia, and parts of Arabia, it was because these provinces, impoverished by the Assyrian conquest, and entirely laid waste by the Scythians, had lost the most energetic elements of their populations, and felt themselves too much enfeebled to rise against their suzerain. Egypt, like Chaldæa, was in a state of decadence, and even though her Pharaohs attempted to compensate for the inferiority of their native troops by employing foreign mercenaries, their attempts at Asiatic rule always issued in defeat, and just as the Babylonian sovereigns were unable to reduce them to servitude, so they on their part were powerless to gain an advantage over the sovereigns of Babylon. Hence Lydia, in her youth and vigour, would have found little difficulty in gaining the ascendency over her two recent allies, but beyond that she could not hope to push her success;

[1] HERODOTUS, I. lxxxv.-lxxxvii., from Lydian traditions. The story told by Nicolas of Damascus (Fragm. 68, in MÜLLER-DIDOT, Fragm. Hist. Græc., vol. iii. pp. 406-409) comes down probably from Xanthus of Lydia, but with many additions borrowed directly from Herodotus (SCHUBERT, Geschichte der Könige von Lydien, pp. 120-124) and rhetorical developments by the author himself. Most other writers who tell the story depend for their information, either directly or indirectly, on Herodotus: in later times it was supposed that the Lydian king was preserved from the flames by the use of some talisman such as the Ephesian letters.

[2] HERODOTUS, I. lxxxvii.-xc., clv., clvi., ccvii., ccviii., ccxi., and later, in the reign of Cambyses, III. xxxiv.-xxxvi.; for his fief of Barêné, see CTESIAS, Fragm. 29, § 4, in MÜLLER-DIDOT, Ctesiæ Cnidii Fragmenta, p. 46, and the author followed by Pompeius Trogus (JUSTIN, i. 7).

her restricted territory, sparse population, and outlying position would always have debarred her from exercising any durable dominion over them, and though absolute mistress of Asia Minor, the countries beyond the Taurus were always destined to elude her grasp. If the Achæmenian, therefore, had confined himself, at all events for the time being, to the ancient limits of his kingdom, Egypt and Chaldæa would have continued to vegetate each within their respective area, and the triumph of Crœsus would, on the whole, have caused but little change in the actual balance of power in the East.

The downfall of Crœsus, on the contrary, marked a decisive era in the world's history. His army was the only one, from the point of numbers and organisation, which was a match for that of Cyrus, and from the day of its dispersion it was evident that neither Egypt nor Chaldæa had any chance of victory on the battle-field. The subjection of Babylon and Harrân, of Hamath, Damascus, Tyre and Sidon, of Memphis and Thebes, now became merely a question of time, and that not far distant; the whole of Asia, and that part of Africa which had been the oldest cradle of human civilisation, were now to pass into the hands of one man and form a single

A PERSIAN KING FIGHTING WITH GREEKS.[1]

empire, for the benefit of the new race which was issuing forth in irresistible strength from the recesses of the Iranian table-land. It was destined, from the very outset, to come into conflict with an older, but no less vigorous race than itself, that of the Greeks, whose colonists, after having swarmed along the coasts of the Mediterranean, were now beginning to quit the seaboard and penetrate wherever they could into the interior. They had been on friendly terms with that dynasty of the Mermnadæ who had shown reverence for the Hellenic gods; they had, as a whole, disdained to betray Crœsus, or to turn upon him when he was in difficulties beyond the Halys;[2] and now that he had succumbed to his fate, they considered that the ties which had bound them to Sardes were broken, and they were determined to preserve their independence at all costs. This spirit of insubordination would have to be promptly dealt with and tightly curbed, if perpetual troubles in the future were to be avoided. The Asianic peoples soon rallied round their new master —Phrygians, Mysians, the inhabitants on the shores of the Black Sea, and

---

[1] Drawn by Faucher-Gudin, from an intaglio reproduced in the *Antiquités du Bosphore cimmérien*, pl. xvi. Nos. 2, 3.

[2] On the subject of these unsuccessful negotiations of Cyrus with the Greek cities on the coast of Asia Minor, cf. *supra*, p. 616 of the present work.

those of the Pamphylian coast;[1] even Cilicia, which had held its own against Chaldæa, Media, and Lydia, was now brought under the rising power, and its kings were henceforward obedient to the Persian rule.[2] The two leagues of the Ionians and Æolians had at first offered to recognise Cyrus as their suzerain under the same conditions as those with which Crœsus had been satisfied; but he had consented to accept it only in the case of Miletus, and had demanded from the rest an unconditional surrender. This they had refused, and, uniting in a common cause perhaps for the first time in their existence, they had resolved to take up arms. As the Persians possessed no fleet, the Greeks had nothing to fear from the side of the Ægean, and the severity of the winter prevented any attack being made from the land side till the following spring. They meanwhile sought the aid of their mother-country, and despatched an embassy to the Spartans; the latter did not consider it prudent to lend them troops, as they would have done in the case of Crœsus, but they authorised Lakrines, one of their principal citizens, to demand of the great king that he should respect the Hellenic cities, under pain of incurring their enmity. Cyrus was fully occupied with the events then taking place in the eastern regions of Iran; Babylon had not ventured upon any move after having learned the news of the fall of Sardes, but the Bactrians and the Sakæ had been in open revolt during the whole of the year that he had been detained in the extreme west, and a still longer absence might risk the loss of his prestige in Media, and even in Persian itself.[3] The threat of the Lacedæmonians had little effect upon him; he inquired as to what Sparta and Greece were, and having been informed, he ironically begged the Lacedæmonian envoy to thank his compatriots for the good advice with which they had honoured him; "but," he added, "take care that I do not soon cause you to babble, not of the ills of the Ionians, but of your own."[4] He confided the government of Sardes to one of his officers, named Tabalos, and having entrusted Paktyas, one of the Lydians who had embraced his cause, with the removal of the treasures of Crœsus to Persia, he hastily set out for Ecbatana. He had scarcely accomplished half of his

[1] None of the documents actually say this, but the general tenor of Herodotus' account seems to show clearly that, with the exception of the Greek cities of the Carians and Lycians, all the peoples who had formed part of the Lydian dominion under Crœsus submitted, without any appreciable resistance, after the taking of Sardes.

[2] Xenophon, *Cyrop.*, VII. iv. § 2; Herodotus mentions a second Syennesis king of Cilicia forty years later at the time of the Ionian revolt (V. cxviii.).

[3] The tradition followed by Ctesias (cf. *supra*, p. 597) maintained that the submission of the eastern peoples was an accomplished fact when the Lydian war began. That adopted by Herodotus placed this event after the fall of Crœsus (I. clxxvii.); at any rate, it showed that fear of the Bactrians and the Sakæ, as well as of the Babylonians and Egyptians (I. cliii.), was the cause that hastened Cyrus' retreat.

[4] HERODOTUS, I. clii., cliii., and following him, but probably through Ephorus, DIODORUS SICULUS, ix. 36.

journey when a revolt broke out in his rear; Paktyas, instead of obeying his instructions, intrigued with the Ionians, and, with the mercenaries he had hired from them, besieged Tabalos in the citadel of Sardes. If the place capitulated, the entire conquest would have to be repeated; fortunately it held out, and its resistance gave Cyrus time to send its governor reinforcements, commanded by Mazares the Median. As soon as they approached the

THE PRESENT SITE OF MILETUS.[1]

city, Paktyas, conscious that he had lost the day, took refuge at Kymê. Its inhabitants, on being summoned to deliver him up, refused, but helped him to escape to Mytilene, where the inhabitants of the island attempted to sell him to the enemy for a large sum of money. The Kymæans saved him a second time, and conveyed him to the temple of Athene Poliarchos at Chios. The citizens, however, dragged him from his retreat, and delivered him over to the Median general in exchange for Atarneus, a district of Mysia, the possession of which they were disputing with the Lesbians.[2] Paktyas being a prisoner, the Lydians were soon recalled to order, and Mazares was able to devote his entire energies to the reduction of the Greek cities; but he had accomplished merely the sack of Priênê,[3] and the devastation of the suburbs of Magnesia on the

---

[1] Drawn by Boudier, from a photograph.

[2] A passage which has been preserved of Charon of Lampsacus (*Fragm.* 1, in MÜLLER-DIDOT, *Fragm. Hist. Græc.*, vol. i. p. 32) sums up in a few words the account given by Herodotus of the adventures of Paktyas (I. clvii.–clx.), but without mentioning the treachery of the islanders: he confines himself to saying Cyrus caught the fugitive after the latter had successively left Chios and Mytilene.

[3] HERODOTUS, I. clxi.; PAUSANIAS, VII. ii. § 10, attributes the taking of this city to the Persian Tabules, who is evidently the Tabalos of Herodotus.

Mæander, when he died from some illness. The Median Harpagus, to whom tradition assigns so curious a part as regards Astyages and the infant Cyrus, succeeded him as governor of the ancient Lydian kingdom, and completed the work which he had begun. The first two places to be besieged were Phocæa and Teos, but their inhabitants preferred exile to slavery; the Phocæans sailed away to found Marseilles in the western regions of the Mediterranean, and the people of Teos settled along the coast of Thracia, near to the gold-mines of the Pangæus, and there built Abdera on the site of an ancient Clazomenian colony. The other Greek towns were either taken by assault or voluntarily opened their gates, so that ere long both Ionians and Æolians were, with the exception of the Samians, under Persian rule. The very position of the latter rendered them safe from attack; without a fleet they could not be approached, and the only people who could have furnished Cyrus with vessels were the Phœnicians, who were not as yet under his power. The rebellion having been suppressed in this quarter, Harpagus made a descent into Caria; the natives hastened to place themselves under the Persian yoke, and the Dorian colonies scattered along the coast, Halicarnassus, Cnidos, and the islands of Cos and Rhodes, followed their examples, but Lycia refused to yield without a struggle. Its steep mountain chains, its sequestered valleys, its towns and fortresses perched on inaccessible rocks, all rendered it easy for the inhabitants to carry on a successful petty warfare against the enemy. The inhabitants of Xanthos, although very inferior in numbers, issued down into the plain and disputed the victory with the invaders for a considerable time; at length their defeat and the capitulation of their town induced the remainder of the Lycians to lay down arms, and brought about the final pacification of the peninsula.[1] It was parcelled out into several governorships, according to its ethnographical affinities; as, for instance, the governorship of Lydia, that of Ionia, that of Phrygia,[2] and others whose names are unknown to us. Harpagus appears to have resided at Sardes, and exercised vice-regal functions over the various districts, but he obtained from the king an extensive property in Lycia and in Caria, which subsequently caused these two provinces to be regarded as an appanage of his family.

While thus consolidating his first conquest, Cyrus penetrated into the unknown regions of the far East. Nothing would have been easier for him than to have fallen upon Babylon and overthrown, as it were by the way, the decadent rule of Nabonidus; but the formidable aspect which the empire still presented, in spite of its enfeebled condition, must have deceived him, and he

---

[1] HERODOTUS, I. clxi.–clxxvii.

[2] HERODOTUS, III. cxx., cxxvi., calls a certain Mitrobates satrap of Daskylion; he had perhaps been already given this office by Cyrus (KRUMBHOLZ, *De Asiæ Minoris Satrapis Persicis*, pp. 27, 28). Orœtes had been made governor of Ionia and Lydia by Cyrus (HERODOTUS, III. cxx., et seq.).

was unwilling to come into conflict with it until he had made a final reckoning with the restless and unsettled peoples between the Caspian and the slopes on the Indian side of the table-land of Iran. As far as we are able to judge, they were for the most part of Iranian extraction, and had the same religion, institutions, and customs as the Medes and Persians.[1] Tradition had already referred the origin of Zoroaster, and the scene of his preaching, to Bactriana, that land of heroes whose exploits formed the theme of Persian epic song.[2] It is not known, as we have already had occasion to remark, by what ties it was bound to the empire of Cyaxares, nor indeed if it ever had been actually attached to it. We do not possess, unfortunately, more than almost worthless

scraps of information on this part of the reign of Cyrus, perhaps the most important period of it, since then, for the first time, peoples who had been hitherto strangers to the Asiatic world were brought within its influence. If Ctesias is to be credited, Bactriana was one of the first districts to be conquered. Its inhabitants were regarded as being among the bravest of the East, and furnished the best soldiers. They

A LYCIAN CITY UPON ITS INACCESSIBLE ROCK.[3]

at first obtained some successes, but laid down arms on hearing that Cyrus had married a daughter of Astyages.[4] This tradition was prevalent at a time when the Achæmenians were putting forward the theory that they, and Cyrus before them, were the legitimate successors of the old Median sovereigns; they welcomed every legend which tended to justify their pretensions, and this particular one was certain to please them, since it attributed the submission of Bactriana not to a mere display of brute force, but to the recognition of an hereditary right. The annexation of this province entailed, as a matter of course, that of Margiana, of the Khoramnians,[5] and of Sogdiana. Cyrus

[1] For the Iranian origin of most of these peoples, see the testimony of ancient authors collected by RAPP, *Die Religion und Sitte der Perser und übrigen Iranier*, in the *Z. d. D. Morgenl. Gesells.*, vol. xix. pp. 11–21.

[2] Cf. *supra*, p. 572, et seq.

[3] The rock and tombs of Tlôs, drawn by Boudier, from the view in FELLOWS, *Lycia and Caria*, pl. vi.

[4] This is the campaign which Ctesias places before the Lydian war (*Fragm.* 29, § 2, in MÜLLER-DIDOT, *Ctesiæ Cnidii Fragmenta*, p. 46), but which Herodotus relegates to a date after the capture of Sardes (I. cliii., clxxvii.).

[5] Ctesias must have spoken of the submission of these peoples, for a few words of a description which he gave of the Khoramnians have been preserved to us (*Fragm.* 34, in MÜLLER-DIDOT, *Ctesiæ Cnidii Fragmenta*, p. 61).

2 s

constructed fortresses in all these districts, the most celebrated being that of Kyropolis, which commanded one of the principal fords of the Iaxartes.[1] The steppes of Siberia arrested his course on the north, but to the east, in the mountains of Chinese Turkestan, the Sakæ, who were renowned for their wealth and bravery, did not escape his ambitious designs. The account which has come down to us of his campaigns against them is a mere romance of love and adventure, in which real history plays a very small part. He is said to have attacked and defeated them at the first onset, taking their King Amorges prisoner; but this capture, which Cyrus considered a decisive advantage, was supposed to have turned the tide of fortune against him. Sparêthra, the wife of Amorges, rallied the fugitives round her, defeated the invaders in several engagements, and took so many of their men captive, that they were glad to restore her husband to her in exchange for the prisoners she had made. The struggle finally ended, however, in the subjection of the Sakæ; they engaged to pay tribute, and thenceforward constituted the advance-guard of the Iranians against the Nomads of the East.[2] Cyrus, before quitting their neighbourhood, again ascended the table-land, and reduced Ariana, Thatagus, Harauvati, Zaranka, and the country of Cabul;[3] and we may well ask if he found leisure to turn southwards beyond Lake Hamun and reach the shores of the Indian Ocean. One tradition, of little weight, relates that, like Alexander at a later date, he lost his army in the arid deserts of Gedrosia; the one fact that remains is that the conquest of Gedrosia was achieved, but the details of it are lost.[4] The period covered by his campaigns was from five to six years, from 545 to 539,[5] but Cyrus returned from these expeditions into the unknown only to plan fresh undertakings. There remained nothing now to hinder him from marching against the Chaldæans, and the discord prevailing at Babylon added to his chance of success. Nabonidus's passion for archæology had in no way lessened since the opening of his reign. The temple restorations prompted by it absorbed the bulk of his revenues. He made excavations in the sub-structures of the most ancient sanctuaries, such as Larsam, Uruk, Uru, Sippar, and Nipur; and when his digging was rewarded by the discovery of cylinders placed there by his predecessors, his delight knew no bounds. Such

---

[1] STRABO, XI. xi. § 4, p. 517, and ARRIAN, Anabasis, III. ii. § 1, iii. § 1–5 : there would have been altars dedicated by the conqueror in these cities (PLINY, Nat. Hist., vi. 49). Tomaschek identifies Kyra or Kyropolis with the present Ura-Tepe (Centralasiatische Studien, I., Sogdiana, pp. 57–59), but distinguishes it from the Kyreskhata of Ptolemy, to which he assigns a site near Usgent.

[2] CTESIAS, Fragm. 29, § 3, in MÜLLER-DIDOT, Ctesiæ Cnidii Fragmenta, p. 46.

[3] ARRIAN, Historia Indica, i. § 3, where all these peoples are confused under the general appellation of Indians on this side of the Indus.

[4] NEARCHUS, Fragm. 23, in MÜLLER-DIDOT, Scriptores Rerum Alexandri Magni, p. 65.

[5] Herodotus, I. clxxvii., sums up his conquests in few words : Τὰ δὲ ἄνω αὐτῆς [τῆς Ἀσίης] αὐτὸς Κῦρος [ἀνάστατα ἐποίεε], πᾶν ἔθνος καταστρεφόμενος καὶ οὐδὲν παριείς.

finds constituted the great events of his life, in comparison with which the political revolutions of Asia and Africa diminished in importance day by day.[1] It is difficult to tell whether this indifference to the weighty affairs of government was as complete as it appears to us at this distance of time. Certain facts recorded in the official chronicles of that date go to prove that, except in name and external pomp, the king was a nonentity. The real power lay in the hands of the nobles and generals, and Bel-sharuzur, the king's son, directed affairs for them in his father's name. Nabonidus meanwhile resided in a state of inactivity at his palace of Tima, and it is possible that his condition may have really been that of a prisoner, for he never left Tima to go to Babylon, even on the days of great festivals, and his absence prevented the celebration of the higher rites of the national religion, with the procession of Bel and its accompanying ceremonies, for several consecutive years.[2] The people suffered from these quarrels in high places; not only the native Babylonians or Kaldâ, who were thus deprived of their accustomed spectacles, and whose piety was scandalised by these dissensions, but also the foreign races dispersed over Mesopotamia, from the confluence of the Khabur to the mouths of the Euphrates. Too widely scattered or too weak to make an open declaration of their independence, their hopes and their apprehensions were alternately raised by the various reports of hostilities which reached their ears. The news of the first victories of the Persians aroused in the exiled Jews the idea of speedy deliverance, and Cyrus clearly appeared to them as the hero chosen by Jahveh to reinstate them in the country of their forefathers.

The number of the Jewish exiles, which perhaps at first had not exceeded 20,000,[3] had largely increased in the half-century of their captivity, and even if numerically they were of no great importance, their social condition entitled them to be considered as the *élite* of all Israel. There had at first been the two kings, Jehoiachin and Zedekiah, their families, the aristocracy of Judah, the priests and pontiff of the temple, the prophets, the most skilled of the artisan class and the soldiery.[4] Though distributed over Babylon and the

[1] The description of these works occupies most of the cylinder inscriptions of Nabonidus; cf. PEISER, *Inschriften Nabonid's*, in SCHRADER, *Keilinschriftliche Bibliothek*, vol. iii., 2nd part, pp. 81–119.

[2] *Annals of Nabonidus*, col. ii. ll. 5–25; cf. SCHRADER, *Die Nabonid-Cyrus-Chronik*, in the *Keilinschriftliche Bibliothek*, vol. iii., 2nd part, pp. 130–133, and HAGEN, *Keilschrifturkunden zur Geschichte des Königs Cyrus*, in the *Beiträge zur Assyriologie*, vol. ii. pp. 218–221.

[3] The body of exiles of 597 consisted of ten thousand persons, of whom seven thousand belonged to the wealthy, and one thousand to the artisan class, while the remainder consisted of people attached to the court (2 *Kings* xxiv. 14–16). In the body of 587 are reckoned three thousand and twenty-three inhabitants of Judah, and eight hundred and thirty-two dwellers in Jerusalem (cf. *supra*, p. 546). But the body of exiles of 581 numbers only seven hundred and forty-five persons (*Jer.* lii. 30; for this third deportation, see *supra*, p. 548, note 8). These numbers are sufficiently moderate to be possibly exact, but they are far from being certain.

[4] Cf. *supra*, p. 537.

neighbouring cities, we know from authentic sources of only one of their settlements, that of Tell-Abîb on the Chebar,[1] though many of the Jewish colonies which flourished thereabouts in Roman times could undoubtedly trace their origin to the days of the captivity; one legend found in the Talmud affirmed that the synagogue of Shafyâthîb, near Nehardaa, had been built by King Jehoiachin with stones brought from the ruins of the temple at Jerusalem.[2] These communities enjoyed a fairly complete antonomy, and were free to administer their own affairs as they pleased, provided that they paid their tribute or performed their appointed labours without complaint. The shêkhs, or elders of the family or tribe, who had played so important a part in their native land, still held their respective positions; the Chaldæans had permitted them to retain all the possessions which they had been able to bring with them into exile, and recognised them as the rulers of their people, who were responsible to their conquerors for the obedience of those under them, leaving them entire liberty to exercise their authority so long as they maintained order and tranquillity among their subordinates.[3] How the latter existed, and what industries they pursued in order to earn their daily bread, no writer of the time has left on record. The rich plain of the Euphrates differed so widely from the soil to which they had been accustomed in the land of Judah, with its bare or sparsely wooded hills, slopes cultivated in terraces, narrow and ill-watered wadys, and tortuous and parched valleys, that they must have felt themselves much out of their element in their Chaldæan surroundings. They had all of them, however, whether artisans, labourers, soldiers, gold-workers, or merchants, to earn their living, and they succeeded in doing so, following meanwhile the advice of Jeremiah, by taking every precaution that the seed of Israel should not be diminished.[4] The imagination of pious writers of a later date delighted to represent the exiled Jews as giving way to apathy and vain regrets: " By the rivers of Babylon, there we sat down, yea, we wept, when we remembered Zion. Upon the willows in the midst thereof we hanged up our harps. For there they that led us captive required of us songs, and they that wasted us required of us mirth, saying, Sing us one of the songs of Zion. How shall we sing the Lord's song in a strange land ? "[5] This was true of the priests and scribes only. A blank had been made in their existence from the moment when the conqueror had dragged them from the routine of daily rites

[1] *Ezek.* iii. 15. The Chebar or Kebar has been erroneously identified with the Khabur; cuneiform documents show that it was one of the canals near Nipur.

[2] NEUBAUER, *La Géographie du Talmud*, p. 322, note 4, pp. 350, 351.

[3] Cf. the assemblies of these chiefs at the house of Ezekiel and their action (viii. 1 ; xiv. 1 ; xx. 1).

[4] *Jer.* xxix. 1–7 ; cf. *supra*, p. 541.

[5] *Ps.* cxxxvii. 1–4.

which their duties in the temple service entailed upon them. The hours which had been formerly devoted to their offices were now expended in bewailing the misfortunes of their nation, in accusing themselves and others, and in demanding what crime had merited this punishment, and why Jahveh, who had so often shown clemency to their forefathers, had not extended His forgiveness to them. It was, however, by the long-suffering of God that His prophets, and particularly Ezekiel, were allowed to make known to them the true cause of their downfall. The more Ezekiel in his retreat meditated upon their lot, the more did the past appear to him as a lamentable conflict between divine justice and Jewish iniquity. At the time of their sojourn in Egypt, Jahveh had taken the house of Jacob under his protection, and in consideration of His help had merely demanded of them that they should be faithful to Him. " Cast ye away every man the abominations of his eyes, and defile not yourselves with the idols of Egypt ; I am the Lord your God." The children of Israel, however, had never observed this easy condition, and this was the root of their ills ; even before they were liberated from the yoke of Pharaoh, they had betrayed their Protector, and He had thought to punish them : " But I wrought for My name's sake, that it should not be profaned in the sight of the nations, among whom they were, in whose sight I made myself known unto them. . . . So I caused them to go forth out of the land of Egypt, and brought them into the wilderness. And I gave them My statutes, and showed them My judgments, which if a man do, he shall live in them. Moreover also I gave them My sabbaths, to be a sign between Me and them . . . but the house of Israel rebelled against Me." As they had acted in Egypt, so they acted at the foot of Sinai, and again Jahveh could not bring Himself to destroy them ; He confined Himself to decreeing that none of those who had offended Him should enter the Promised Land, and He extended His goodness to their children. But these again showed themselves no wiser than their fathers ; scarcely had they taken possession of the inheritance which had fallen to them, " a land flowing with milk and honey . . . the glory of all lands," than when they beheld " every high hill and every thick tree . . . they offered there their sacrifices, and there they presented the provocation of their offering, there also they made their sweet savour, and they poured out there their drink offerings." Not contented with profaning their altars by impious ceremonies and offerings, they further bowed the knee to idols, thinking in their hearts, " We will be as the nations, as the families of the countries, to serve wood and stone." " As I live, saith the Lord God, surely with a mighty hand and with a stretched out arm, and with fury poured out, will I be King over you." [1] However just the punishment, Ezekiel did not believe that it would last for ever. The

[1] *Ezek.* xx.

righteousness of God would not permit future generations to be held responsible for ever for the sins of generations past and present. " What mean ye, that ye use this proverb concerning the land of Israel, saying, The fathers have eaten sour grapes, and the children's teeth are set on edge ? As I live, saith the Lord God, ye shall not have occasion to use this proverb any more in Israel ! Behold, all souls are Mine ; as the soul of the father, so also the soul of the son is Mine ; the soul that sinneth it shall die. But if a man be just . . . he shall surely live, saith the Lord God." Israel, therefore, was master of his own destiny. If he persisted in erring from the right way, the hour of salvation was still further removed from him ; if he repented and observed the law, the Divine anger would be turned away. " Therefore . . . O house of Israel . . . cast away from you all your transgressions wherein ye have transgressed ; and make you a new heart and a new spirit ; for why will ye die, O house of Israel ? For I have no pleasure in the death of him that dieth . . . wherefore turn yourselves and live." [1] There were those who objected that it was too late to dream of regeneration and of hope in the future : " Our bones are dried up and our hope is lost; we are clean cut off." The prophet replied that the Lord had carried him in the spirit and set him down in the midst of a plain strewn with bones. " So I prophesied . . . and as I prophesied there was a noise . . . and the bones came together, bone to his bone. And I beheld, and lo, there were sinews upon them, and flesh came up and skin covered them above ; but there was no breath in them. Then said (the Lord) unto me, Prophesy unto the wind, prophesy, son of man, and say to the wind, Thus saith the Lord God : Come from the four winds, O breath, and breathe upon these slain, that they may live. So I prophesied as He commanded me, and the breath came into them and they lived, and stood up upon their feet, an exceeding great army. Then He said unto me . . . these bones are the whole house of Israel. . . . Behold, I will open your graves and cause you to come up out of your graves, O my people ; and I will bring you into the land of Israel. . . . And I will put My Spirit in you and ye shall live, and I will place you in your own land ; and ye shall know that I the Lord have spoken it and performed it, saith the Lord." [2]

A people raised from such depths would require a constitution, a new law to take the place of the old, from the day when the exile should cease. Ezekiel would willingly have dispensed with the monarchy, as it had been tried since the time of Samuel with scarcely any good results. For every Hezekiah or Josiah, how many kings of the type of Ahaz or Manasseh had there been ! The Jews were nevertheless still so sincerely attached to the house of

[1] *Ezek*. xviii.   [2] *Ezek*. xxxvii. 1–14.

David, that the prophet judged it inopportune to exclude it from his plan for their future government. He resolved to tolerate a king, but a king of greater piety and with less liberty than the compiler of the Book of Deuteronomy had pictured to himself,[1] a servant of the servants of God, whose principal function should be to provide the means of worship. Indeed, the Lord Himself was the only Sovereign whom the prophet fully accepted, though his concept of Him differed greatly from that of his predecessors: from that, for instance, of Amos— the Lord God who would do nothing without revealing "His secret unto His servants the prophets;"[2] or of Hosea—who desired "mercy, and not sacrifice; and the knowledge of God more than burnt offerings."[3] The Jahveh of Ezekiel no longer admitted any intercourse with the interpreters of His will. He held "the son of man" at a distance, and would consent to communicate with him only by means of angels who were His messengers. The love of His people was, indeed, acceptable to Him, but He preferred their reverence and fear, and the smell of the sacrifice offered according to the law was pleasing to His nostrils. The first care of the returning exiles, therefore, would be to build Him a house upon the holy mountain. Ezekiel called to mind the temple of Solomon, in which the far-off years of his youth were spent, and mentally re-built it on the same plan, but larger and more beautiful; first the outer court, then the inner court and its chambers, and lastly the sanctuary, the dimensions of which he calculates with scrupulous care: "And the breadth of the entrance was ten cubits; and the sides of the entrance were five cubits on the one side and five cubits on the other side: and he measured the length thereof, forty cubits; and the breadth, twenty cubits"—and so forth, with a wealth of technical details often difficult to be understood.[4] And as a building so well proportioned should be served by a priesthood worthy of it, the sons of Zadok only were to bear the sacerdotal office, for they alone had preserved their faith unshaken; the other Levites were to fill merely secondary posts, for not only had they shared in the sins of the nation, but they had shown a bad example in practising idolatry. The duties and prerogatives of each one, the tithes and offerings, the sacrifices, the solemn festivals, the preparation of the feasts,—all was foreseen and prearranged with scrupulous exactitude.[5] Ezekiel was, as we have seen, a priest; the smallest details were as dear to him as the noblest offices of his calling, and the minute ceremonial instructions as to the killing and cooking of the sacrificial animals appeared to him as necessary to the future prosperity

---

[1] See what is said of the king in Deuteronomy, *supra*, p. 509.

[2] *Amos* iii. 7.

[3] *Hos.* vi. 6.

[4] *Ezek.* xl. 5–xlvi. 24; for the explanation of these passages, cf. PERROT and CHIPIEZ, *Histoire de l'Art dans l'Antiquité*, vol. iv. pp. 243–271.

[5] *Ezek.* xliv. 1–xlvi. 24.

of his people as the moral law.　Towards the end, however, the imagination of the seer soared above the formalism of the sacrificing priest; he saw in a vision waters issuing out of the very threshold of the divine house, flowing towards the Dead Sea through a forest of fruit trees, "whose leaf shall not wither, neither shall the fruit thereof fail." The twelve tribes of Israel, alike those of whom a remnant still existed as well as those which at different times had become extinct, were to divide the regenerated land by lot among them—Dan in the extreme north, Reuben and Judah in the south; and they would unite to found once more, around Mount Sion, that new Jerusalem whose name henceforth was to be Jahveh-shammah, "The Lord is there." [1] The influence of Ezekiel does not seem to have extended beyond a restricted circle of admirers. Untouched by his preaching, many of the exiles still persisted in their worship of the heathen gods; most of these probably became merged in the bulk of the Chaldæan population, and were lost, as far as Israel was concerned, as completely as were the earlier exiles of Ephraim under Tiglath-pileser III. and Sargon. The greater number of the Jews, however, remained faithful to their hopes of future greatness, and applied themselves to discerning in passing events the premonitory signs of deliverance. "Like as a woman with child, that draweth near the time of her delivery, is in pain, and crieth out in her pangs; so have we been before Thee, O Lord. . . . Come, my people, enter thou into thy chambers, and shut thy doors about thee: hide thyself for a little moment, until the indignation be overpast.　For, behold, the Lord cometh forth out of His place to punish the inhabitants of the earth for their iniquity: the earth also shall disclose her blood, and shall no more cover her slain." [2] The condition of the people improved after the death of Nebuchadrezzar. Amilmarduk took Jehoiachin out of the prison in which he had languished for thirty years, and treated him with honour: [3] this was not as yet the restoration that had been promised, but it was the end of the persecution. A period of court intrigues followed, during which the sceptre of Nebuchadrezzar changed hands four times in less than seven years; then came the accession of the peaceful and devout Nabonidus, the fall of Astyages, and the first victories of Cyrus.　Nothing escaped the vigilant eye of the prophets, and they began to proclaim that the time was at hand, then to predict the fall of Babylon, and to depict the barbarians in revolt against her, and Israel released from the yoke by the all-powerful will of the Persians. "Thus saith the Lord to His anointed, to Cyrus, whose right hand I have holden to subdue nations before

[1] *Ezek.* xlvii., xlviii. The image of the river seems to be borrowed from the *vessel of water* of Chaldæan mythology.

[2] An anonymous prophet, about 570, in *Isa.* xxvi. 17, 20, 21.

[3] 2 *Kings* xxv. 27–30; cf. *Jer.* lii. 31–34.

him, and I will loose the loins of kings; to open the doors before him, and the gates shall not be shut; I will go before thee and make the rugged places plain: I will break in pieces the doors of brass, rend in sunder the bars of iron: and I will give thee the treasures of darkness, and hidden riches of secret places, that thou mayest know that I am the Lord which call thee by thy name, even the God of Israel. For Jacob My servant's sake, and Israel My chosen, I have called thee by thy name: I have surnamed thee, though thou hast not known Me." [1] Nothing can stand before the victorious prince whom Jahveh leads: "Bel boweth down, Nebo stoopeth; their idols are upon the beasts, and upon the cattle: the things that ye carried about are made a load, a burden to the weary beast. They stoop, they bow down together; they could not deliver the burden, but themselves are gone into captivity." [2] "O virgin daughter of Babylon, sit on the ground without a throne, O daughter of the Chaldæans: for thou shalt no more be called tender and delicate. Take the millstones and grind meal: remove thy veil, strip off the train, uncover the leg, pass through the rivers. Thy nakedness shall be uncovered, yea, thy shame shall be seen. . . . Sit thou silent, and get thee into darkness, O daughter of the Chaldæans: for thou shalt no more be called the lady of kingdoms." [3]

The task which Cyrus had undertaken was not so difficult as we might imagine. Not only was he hailed with delight by the strangers who thronged Babylonia, but the Babylonians themselves were weary of their king, and the majority of them were ready to welcome the Persian who would rid them of him, as in old days they hailed the Assyrian kings who delivered them from their Chaldæan lords. It is possible that towards the end of his reign Nabonidus partly resumed the supreme power; [4] but anxious for the future, and depending but little on human help, he had sought a more powerful aid at the hands of the gods. He had apparently revived some of the old forgotten cults, and had applied to their use revenues which impoverished the endowment of the prevalent worship of his own time. As he felt the growing danger approach, he remembered those towns of secondary grade—Uru, Uruk, Larsam, and Eridu—all of which, lying outside Nebuchadrezzar's scheme of defence, would be sacrificed in the case of an invasion: he had therefore brought away from them the most venerated statues, those in which the spirit of the divinity was more particularly pleased to dwell, and had shut them up in the capital,

---

[1] *Second Isaiah,* in *Isa.* xlv. 1–4.
[2] *Second Isaiah,* in *Isa.* xlvi. 1, 2.
[3] *Second Isaiah,* in *Isa.* xlvii. 1–5.
[4] This seems to follow from the part which he plays in the final crisis, as told in the *Cylinder of Cyrus* and in the *Annals;* cf. *infra,* pp. 634, 635.

within the security of its triple rampart.[1] This attempt to concentrate the divine powers, accentuating as it did the supremacy of Bel-Marduk over his compeers, was doubtless flattering to his pride and that of his priests, but was ill received by the rest of the sacerdotal class and by the populace. All these divine guests had not only to be lodged, but required to be watched over, decked, fed, and fêted, together with their respective temple retinues; and the prestige and honour of the local Bel, as well as his revenues, were likely to suffer in consequence. The clamour of the gods in the celestial heights soon re-echoed throughout the land; the divinities complained of their sojourn at Babylon as of a captivity in Ê-sagilla; they lamented over the suppression of their daily sacrifices, and Marduk at length took pity on them. He looked upon the countries of Sumir and Akkad, and saw their sanctuaries in ruins and their towns lifeless as corpses; " he cast his eyes over the surrounding regions; he searched them with his glance and sought out a prince, upright, after his own heart, who should take his hands. He proclaimed by name Cyrus, King of Anshân, and he called him by his name to universal sovereignty." [2] Alike for the people of Babylon and for the exiled Jew, and also doubtless for other stranger-colonies, Cyrus appeared as a deliverer chosen by the gods; his speedy approach was everywhere expected, if not with the same impatience, at least with an almost joyful resignation. His plans were carried into action in the early months of 538, and his habitual good fortune did not forsake him at this decisive moment of his career. The immense citadel raised by Nebuchadrezzar in the midst of his empire, in anticipation of an attack by the Medes, was as yet intact, and the walls rising one behind another, the moats, and the canals and marshes which protected it,[3] had been so well kept up or restored since his time, that their security was absolutely complete; a besieging army could do little harm—it needed a whole nation in revolt to compass its downfall. A whole nation also was required for its defence, but the Babylonians were not inclined to second the efforts of their sovereign. Nabonidus concentrated his troops at the point most threatened, in the angle comprised near Opis between the Medic wall and the bend of the Tigris, and waited in inaction the commencement of the attack. It is supposed that Cyrus put two bodies of troops in

---

[1] *Annals of Nabonidus*, col. iii. ll. 8–11; cf. SCHRADER, *Die Nabonid-Cyrus-Chronik*, in the *Keilinschriftliche Bibliothek*, vol. iii., 2nd part, pp. 132, 133, and HAGEN, *Keilschrifturkunden zur Geschichte des Königs Cyrus*, in the *Beiträge zur Assyriologie*, vol. ii. pp. 220–223. The chronicler adds that the gods of Sippar, Kutha, and Borsippa were not taken to Babylon; and, indeed, these cities being included within the lines of defence of the great city, their gods were as well defended from the enemy as if they had been in Babylon itself.

[2] *Cylinder of Cyrus*, ll. 1–12; cf. SCHRADER, *Inschrift auf dem Thoncylinder des Cyrus, Königs von Babylon-Persien*, in the *Keilinschriftliche Bibliothek*, vol. iii., 2nd part, pp. 120–123, and HAGEN, *Keilschrifturkunden zur Geschichte des Königs Cyrus*, in the *Beiträge zur Assyriologie*, vol. ii. pp. 208–211.

[3] Cf. what is said on this subject, *supra*, pp. 561–563.

motion : one leaving Susa under his own command, took the usual route of all Elamite invasions in the direction of the confluence of the Tigris and the Dìyala ; the other commanded by Gobryas, the satrap of Gutium, followed the course of the Adhem or the Dìyala, and brought the northern contingents to the rallying-place. From what we know of the facts as a whole, it would appear that the besieging force chose the neighbourhood of the present Bagdad to make a breach in the fortifications. Taking advantage of the months when the rivers were at their lowest, they drew off the water from the Dìyala and the Tigris till they so reduced the level that they were able to cross on foot ; they then cut their way through the ramparts on the left bank, and rapidly transported the bulk of their forces into the very centre of the enemy's position. The principal body of the Chaldæan troops were still at Opis, cut off from the capital ; Cyrus fell upon them, overcame them on the banks of the Zalzallat in the early days of Tammuz, urging forward Gobryas meanwhile upon Babylon itself.[1] On the 14th of Tammuz, Nabonidus evacuated Sippar, which at once fell into the hands of the Persian outposts ; on the 16th Gobryas entered Babylon without striking a blow, and Nabonidus surrendered himself a prisoner.[2] The victorious army had received orders to avoid all excesses which would offend the people ; they respected the property of the citizens and of the temples, placed a strong detachment around Ê-sagilla to protect it from plunder, and no armed soldier was allowed within the enclosure until the king had determined on the fate of the vanquished. Cyrus arrived after a fortnight had elapsed, on the 3rd of Marchesvân, and his first act was one of clemency. He prohibited all pillage, granted mercy to the inhabitants, and entrusted the government of the city to Gobryas. Bel-sharuzur, the son of Nabonidus, remained to be dealt with, and his energetic nature might have been the cause of serious difficulties had he been allowed an opportunity of rallying the last partisans of the dynasty around him. Gobryas set out to attack him, and on the 11th of Marchesvân succeeded in surprising and slaying him.[3] With him perished the last hope of the Chaldæans, and the nobles and

[1] For the strategic interpretation of the events of this campaign I have generally adopted the explanations of BILLERBECK, *Geographische Untersuchungen*, pp. 13–25. Herodotus' account (I. clxxxix.) with regard to the river Gyndes is probably a reminiscence of alterations made in the river-courses at the time of the attack in the direction of Bagdad.

[2] The *Cylinder of Cyrus*, l. 17, expressly says so : "Without combat or battle did Marduk make him enter Babylon." The *Annals of Nabonidus*, col. iii. ll. 15, 16, confirm this testimony of the official account.

[3] *Annals of Nabonidus*, col. iii. ll. 12–22 ; cf. SCHRADER, *Die Nabonid-Cyrus-Chronik*, in the *Keilinschriftliche Bibliothek*, vol. iii., 1st part, pp. 134, 135, and HAGEN, *Keilschrifturkunden zur Geschichte des Königs Cyrus*, in the *Beiträge zur Assyriologie*, vol. ii. pp. 222, 223. The passage dealing with the death of one of the king's sons is mutilated, and has been differently interpreted—by some as referring to the death of Nabonidus himself, by others as referring to that of Bel-sharuzur (TIELE, *Babylonisch-assyrische Geschichte*, pp. 475, 476 ; HOMMEL, *Geschichte Babyloniens und Assyriens*, p. 786).

towns, still hesitating on what course to pursue, now vied with each other in their haste to tender submission. The means of securing their good will, at all events for the moment, was clearly at hand, and it was used without any delay : their gods were at once restored to them. This exodus extended over nearly two months, during Marchesvân and Adar, and on its termination a proclamation of six days of mourning, up to the 3rd of Nisân, was made for the death of Belsharuzur, and as an atonement for the faults of Nabonidus, after which, on the 4th of Nisân, the notables of the city were called together in the temple of Nebo to join in the last expiatory ceremonies. Cyrus did not hesitate for a moment to act as Tiglath-pileser III. and most of the Sargonids had done ; he " took the hands of Bel," and proclaimed himself king of the country, but in order to secure the succession, he associated his son Cambyses with himself as King of Babylon.[1] Mesopotamia having been restored to order, the provinces in their turn transferred their allegiance to Persia ; " the kings enthroned in their palaces, from the Upper Sea to the Lower, those of Syria and those who dwell in tents, brought their weighty tribute to Babylon and kissed the feet of the suzerain." [2] Events had followed one another so quickly, and had entailed so little bloodshed, that popular imagination was quite disconcerted : it could not conceive that an empire of such an extent and of so formidable an appearance should have succumbed almost without a battle, and three generations had not elapsed before an entire cycle of legends had gathered round the catastrophe. They related how Cyrus, having set out to make war, with provisions of all kinds for his household, and especially with his usual stores of water from the river Choaspes, the only kind of which he deigned to drink, had reached the banks of the Gyndes. While seeking for a ford, one of the white horses consecrated to the sun sprang into the river, and being overturned by the current, was drowned before it could be rescued. Cyrus regarded this accident as a personal affront, and interrupted his expedition to avenge it. He employed his army during one entire summer in digging three hundred and sixty canals, and thus caused the principal arm of the stream to run dry, and he did not resume his march upon Babylon till the following spring, when the level of the water was low enough to permit of a woman crossing from one bank to the other

---

[1] Strassmaier has collected a certain number of contracts dated from the first year of this double reign. For the points of chronology which they settle, cf. PEISER, *Studien zur Altorientalischen Alterthumskunde*, pp. 2–8, where the dates are given one year earlier than throughout the present work. Krall (in the *Wiener Studien*, vol. ii. p. 48) has shown that the reign of eighteen years accorded to Cambyses by Ctesias (*Fragm.* 29, § 12, in MÜLLER-DIDOT, *Ctesiæ Cnidii Fragmenta*, p. 48) has been reckoned from the termination of the joint reign.

[2] *Cylinder of Cyrus*, ll. 25–36; cf. SCHRADER, *Inschrift auf dem Thoncylinder des Cyrus, Königs von Persien*, in the *Keilinschriftliche Bibliothek*, vol. iii., 2nd part, pp. 124–127, and HAGEN, *Keilschrifturkunden zur Geschichte des Königs Cyrus*, in the *Beiträge zur Assyriologie*, vol. ii. pp. 212, 213. The dates and the sequence of events after the entry of Cyrus into Babylon are furnished by the *Annals of Nabonidus*, col. iii. ll. 18–28.

without wetting her knees. The Babylonians at first attempted to prevent the blockade of the place, but being repulsed in their *sorties*, they retired within the walls, much to Cyrus's annoyance, for they were provisioned for several years. He therefore undertook to turn the course of the Euphrates into the Bahr-î-Nejîf, and having accomplished it, he crept into the centre of the city by the dry bed of the river. If the Babylonians had kept proper guard, the Persians would probably have been surrounded and caught like fish in a net, but on that particular day they were keeping one of their festivals, and continued their dancing and singing till they suddenly found the streets alive with the enemy.[1]

Babylon suffered in no way by her servitude, and far from its being a source of unhappiness to her, she actually rejoiced in it; she was rid of Nabonidus, whose sacrilegious innovations had scandalised her piety, and she possessed in Cyrus a legitimate sovereign since he had "taken the hands of Bel." It pleased her to believe that she had conquered her victor rather than been conquered by him, and she accommodated herself to her Persian dynasty after the same fashion that she had in turn accustomed herself to Cossæan or Elamite, Ninevite or Chaldæan dynasties in days gone by.[2] Nothing in or around the city was

[1] HERODOTUS, I. clxxxviii.–cxci. On the little that can be accepted as true in this story, cf. *supra*, p. 635, note 1.

[2] The table of the last kings of Babylon, according to the Canon of Ptolemy and the monuments, is given below—

747–733.	NABONAZIR [NABONASSAR]	Ναβονασσάρου.
733–731.	NABU-NADÎNZÎRU	} Ναδίου.
731.	NABU-SHUMUKÎN	
731–728.	UKÎNZÎR	} Χινζήρου καὶ Πώρου.
728–727.	PULU [TIGLATH-PILESER III.]	
727–721.	ULULAÎ [SHALMANESER V.]	Ἰλουλαίου.
721–709.	MARDUK-ABALIDDÎNA	Μαρδοκεμπάδου.
709–704.	SARGON	Ἀρκεάνου.
704–702.	[SENNACHERIB]	} Ἀβασίλευτα πρῶτα.
702.	MARDUK-ZAKÎRSHUMU	
702.	MARDUK-ABALIDDÎNA	
702–699.	BELIBNI	Βηλίβου.
699–693.	ASSUR-NADIN-SHUMU	Ἀπαραναδίου.
693–692.	NIRGAL-USHEZÎB	Ἡριγεβάλου.
692–689.	MUSHEZÎB-MARDUK	Μεσησιμορδάκου.
689–681.	[SENNACHERIB]	Ἀβασίλευτα δεύτερα.
681–667.	ESARHADDON	Ἀσαραδίνου.
667–647.	SHAMASH-SHUMUKÎN	Σαοσδουχίνου.
647–625.	KANDALANU [ASSUR-BANI-PAL]	Κινηλαδάνου.
625–604.	NABU-BALUZUR	Ναβοπολασσάρου.
604–561.	NEBUCHADREZZAR II.	Ναβοκολασσάρου.
561–559.	AMÎL-MARDUK	Ἰλλοραουδάμου.
559–555.	NERGAL-SHARUZUR	Νηριγασολασσόρου.
555.	LABASHI-MARDUK	
558–538.	NABONIDUS	Ναβοναδίου.

For the slightly different figures which can be deduced from the contracts, cf. the table of PEISER, *Studien zur Altorientalischen Alterthumskunde*, p. 7.

changed, and she remained what she had been since the fall of Assyria, the real capital of the regions situated between the Mediterranean and the Zagros. It seems that none of her subjects—whether Syrians, Tyrians, Arabs, or Idumæans —attempted to revolt against their new master, but passively accepted him, and the Persian dominion extended uncontested as far as the isthmus of Suez;[1] Cyprus even, and such of the Phœnicians as were still dependencies of Egypt, did homage to her without further hesitation. The Jews alone appeared only half satisfied, for the clemency shown by Cyrus to their oppressors disappointed their hopes and the predictions of their prophets. They had sung in anticipation of children killed before their fathers' eyes, of houses pillaged, of women violated, and Babylon, the glory of the empire and the beauty of Chaldæan pride, utterly destroyed like Sodom and Gomorrha when overthrown by Jahveh. "It shall never be inhabited, neither shall it be dwelt in from generation to generation: neither shall the Arabian pitch tent there; neither shall shepherds make their flocks to lie down there. But wild beasts of the desert shall lie there; and their houses shall be full of doleful creatures; and ostriches shall dwell there, and satyrs shall dance there. And wolves shall cry in their castles, and jackals in the pleasant palaces."[2] Cyrus, however, was seated on the throne, and the city of Nebuchadrezzar, unlike that of Sargon and Sennacherib, still continued to play her part in the world's history. The revenge of Jerusalem had not been as complete as that of Samaria, and her sons had to content themselves with obtaining the cessation of their exile. It is impossible to say whether they had contributed to the downfall of Nabonidus otherwise than by the fervency of their prayers, or if they had rendered Cyrus some service either in the course of his preparations or during his short campaign. They may have contemplated taking up arms in his cause, and have been unable to carry the project into execution owing to the rapidity with which events took place. However this may be, he desired to reward them for their good intentions, and in the same year as his victory, he promulgated a solemn edict, in which he granted them permission to return to Judah and to rebuild not only their city, but the temple of their God. The inhabitants of the places where they were living were charged to furnish them with silver, gold, materials, and cattle, which would be needed by those among them who should claim the benefits of the edict; they even had restored to them, by order of the king, what remained in the Babylonian treasury of the vessels of gold and silver which had belonged to the sanctuary of Jahveh. The heads of the community

[1] If the conjecture of Valois, who restores τὴν Περσῶν in a passage of Polybius (xvi. 40), is justified, Gaza held out for some time: we must in that case suppose that it very probably had the support of Egypt, and perhaps an Egyptian garrison.

[2] An anonymous prophet in *Isa.* xiii. 19–22.

received the favour granted to them from such high quarters, without any enthusiasm. Now that they were free to go, they discovered that they were well off at Babylon. They would have to give up their houses, their fields, their business, their habits of indifference to politics, and brave the dangers of a caravan journey of three or four months' duration, finally encamping in the midst of ruins in an impoverished country, surrounded by hostile and jealous neighbours ; such a prospect was not likely to find favour with many, and indeed it was only the priests, the Levites, and the more ardent of the lower classes who welcomed the idea of the return with a touching fervour. The first detachment organised their departure in 536, under the auspices of one of the princes of the royal house, named Shauash-baluzur (Sheshbazzar), a son of Jehoiachin.[1] It comprised only a small number of families, and contained doubtless a few of the captives of Nebuchadrezzar who in their childhood had seen the temple standing and had been present at its destruction. The returning exiles at first settled in the small towns of Judah and Benjamin, and it was not until seven months after their arrival that they summoned courage to clear the sacred area in order to erect in its midst an altar of sacrifice.[2] They formed there, in the land of their fathers, a little colony, almost lost among the heathen nations of former times—Philistines, Idumæans, Moabites, Ammonites, and the settlers implanted at various times in what had been the kingdom of Israel by the sovereigns of Assyria and Chaldæa. Grouped around the Persian governor, who alone was able to protect them from the hatred of their rivals, they had no hope of prospering, or even of maintaining their position, except by exhibiting an unshaken fidelity to their deliverers. It was on this very feeling that Cyrus mainly relied when he granted them permission to return to their native hills, and he was actuated as much by a far-seeing policy as from the promptings of instinctive generosity. It was with satisfaction that he saw in that distant province, lying on the frontier of the only enemy yet left to him in the old world, a small band, devoted perforce to his interests, and whose very existence

---

[1] The name which is written Sheshbazzar in the Hebrew text of the Book of Ezra (i. 9, 11; v. 14, 16) is rendered Σασαβαλάσσαρος in Lucian's recension of the LXX., and this latter form confirms the hypothesis of Hoonacker (*Zorobabel et le second Temple*, pp. 41–43), which is now universally accepted, that it corresponds to the Babylonian Shamash-abaluzur. It is known that Shamash becomes Shauash in Babylonian; thus Saosdukhînos comes from Shamash-shumukîn (cf. *supra*, p. 377, note 5): similarly Shamash-abaluzur has become Shauash-abaluzur. Imbert has recognised Sheshbazzar, Shauash-abaluzur in the Shenazzar mentioned in 1 *Chron.* iii. 18, as being one of the sons of Jeconiah (*Le Temple reconstruit par Zorobabel*, p. 60, note 1), and this identification has been accepted by several recent historians of Israel (RENAN, *Histoire du peuple d'Israel*, vol. iii. p. 519, note 2; ED. MEYER, *Entstehung des Judenthums*, p. 70, et seq.). It should be remembered that Shauash-abaluzur and Zerubbabel have long been confounded one with the other.

[2] The history of this first return from captivity is summarily set forth in *Ezra* i.; cf. v. 13–17; vi. 3–5, 14. Its authenticity has been denied : with regard to this point and the questions relating to Jewish history after the exile, the modifications which have been imposed on the original plan of this work have obliged me to suppress much detail in the text and the whole of the bibliography in the notes.

depended entirely on that of his empire.[1] He no doubt extended the same favour to the other exiles in Chaldæa who demanded it of him, but we do not know how many of them took advantage of the occasion to return to their native countries, and this exodus of the Jews still remains, so far as we know, a unique fact. The administration continued the same as it had been under the Chaldæans; Aramæan was still the official language in the provincial dependencies, and the only change effected was the placing of Persians at the head of public offices, as in Asia Minor, and allowing them a body of troops to support their authority.[2] One great state alone remained of all those who had played a prominent part in the history of the East. This was Egypt; and the policy which her rulers had pursued since the development of the Iranian power apparently rendered a struggle with it inevitable. Amasis had taken part in all the coalitions which had as their object the perpetuation of the balance of the powers in Western Asia; he had made a treaty with Crœsus, and it is possible that his contingents had fought in the battles before Sardes;[3] Lydia having fallen, he did all in his power to encourage Nabonidus in his resistance. As soon as he found himself face to face with Cyrus, he understood that a collision was imminent, and did his best in preparing to meet it. Even if Cyrus had forgotten the support which had been freely given to his rivals, the wealth of Egypt was in itself sufficient to attract the Persian hordes to her frontiers.

A century later, the Egyptians, looking back on the past with a melancholy retrospection, confessed that "never had the valley been more flourishing or happier than under Amasis; never had the river shown itself more beneficent to the soil, nor the soil more fertile for mankind, and the inhabited towns might be reckoned at 20,000 in number."[4] The widespread activity exhibited under Psammetichus II., and Apries, was redoubled under the usurper, and the quarries of Turah,[5] Silsileh,[6] Assuan,[7] and even those of Hammamât, were

[1] STADE, Geschichte des Volkes Israel, vol. ii. pp. 93, 94.

[2] The presence of Persian troops in Asia Minor is proved by the passage in Herodotus (III. cxxviii.) where he says that Orœtes had with him 1000 Persians as his body-guard.

[3] Cf. supra, p. 614.

[4] HERODOTUS, II. clxxvii.; cf. WIEDEMANN, Herodots Zweites Buch, pp. 604, 605, where will be found the passages in ancient authors referring to the number of Egyptian towns.

[5] HERODOTUS, II. clxxv.; cf. WIEDEMANN, Herodots Zweites Buch, p. 602. A stele of his forty-fourth year still exists in the quarries of the Mokattam (ROSELLINI, Monumenti Storici, vol. ii. p. 152, note 1).

[6] Inscriptions of Bigeh, in CHAMPOLLION, Monuments de l'Égypte et de la Nubie, vol. i. p. 163; LEPSIUS, Denkm., iii. p. 284 p; Inscriptions of Sehel, in J. DE MORGAN, De la Frontière de Nubie à Kom-Ombos, p. 84, No. 10; Inscriptions of Elephantinê, in PETRIE, A Season in Egypt, pl. xi. No. 302, and in J. DE MORGAN, De la Frontière de Nubie à Kom-Ombos, p. 115, No. 2. According to Herodotus (II. clxxv.), it was from the quarries of Elephantinê that Amasis caused to be brought the largest blocks which he used in the building of Sais.

[7] Inscriptions of the architects and engineers sent to the valley of Hammamât in the forty-fourth year of Amasis, to bring the stone for the king's monuments, in LEPSIUS, Denkm., iii. 275 a-d; cf.

worked as in the palmy days of the Theban dynasties. The island of Philæ, whose position just below the cataract attracted to it the attention of the military engineers, was carefully fortified and a temple built upon it, the materials of which were used later on in the masonry of the sanctuary of Ptolemaic times.[1] Thebes exhibited a certain outburst of vitality under the impulse given by Ankhnasnofiribri and by Shashonqu, the governor of her palace;[2] two small chapels, built in the centre of the town, still witness to the queen's devotion to Amon, of whom she was the priestess.[3] Wealthy private individuals did their best to emulate their sovereign's example, and made for themselves at Shêkh Abd-el-Gurnah and at Assassif those rock-hewn tombs which rival those of the best periods in their extent and the beauty of their bas-reliefs.[4] Most of the cities of the

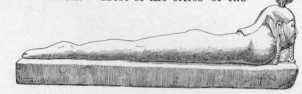

Saîd were in such a state of decadence that it was no longer possible to restore to them their former prosperity, but Abydos occupied too important a place

AN OSIRIS STRETCHED FULL LENGTH ON THE GROUND.[5]

in the beliefs connected with the future world, and attracted too many pilgrims, to permit of its being neglected. The whole of its ancient necropolis had been rifled by thieves during the preceding centuries, and the monuments were nearly as much buried by sand as in our own times. The dismantled fortress now known as the Shunêt ez-Zebîb served as the cemetery for the ibises of Thoth, and for the stillborn children of the sacred singing-women,[6] while the two Memnonia of

---

BRUGSCH, *Histoire d'Égypte*, pp. 258–261, and *Geschichte Ægyptens*, pp. 752–755; DÉVÉRIA, *Mémoires et Fragments*, vol. i. pp. 296–301.

[1] This fact, as far as I know previously unobserved, was noticed for the first time during an inspection made at Philæ in 1882.

[2] Concerning this queen, cf. *supra*, p. 558. Her tomb still exists at Deir el-Medineh, and the sarcophagus, taken from the tomb in 1833, is now in the British Museum (S. SHARPE, *Egyptian Antiquities in the British Museum*, pp. 104–185).

[3] Two of these temples are shown on Mariette's plan by the letters H and J, and some of their sculptures have been published partly by CHAMPOLLION, *Monuments de l'Égypte et de la Nubie*, pl. cclxxxii. Nos. 1–3; partly by ROSELLINI, *Monumenti Storici*, pl. xiii. Nos. 51–53; partly by LEPSIUS, *Denkm.*, iii. 274 *a–o*; and partly by MARIETTE, *Karnak*, pl. 56, and pp. 75–77; cf. BIRCH, *Lettre à M. Letronne sur la famille des Psammétichus de la XXVIe Dynastie*, in *Revue Arch.*, 1847, vol. iv. p. 622.

[4] The most important of these tombs is that of Petenit, the father of Shashonqu, who was associated with Ankhnasnofiribri in the government of Thebes; cf. CHAMPOLLION, *Monuments de l'Égypte et de la Nubie*, vol. i. pp. 552, 553.

[5] Drawn by Faucher-Gudin, after MARIETTE, *Monuments Divers*, pl. 25; cf. MASPERO, *Guide du Visiteur*, pp. 242, 243, No. 443. The monument is a statuette measuring only 15 centimetres in length; it has been reproduced to give an idea of the probable form of the statue seen by Herodotus. Wiedemann (*Herodots Zweites Buch*, pp. 603, 604) does not admit the probability of this resemblance.

[6] MARIETTE, *Catalogue général des Monuments d'Abydos*, pp. 440, 441, from which we see that, after the XXth dynasty, tombs of singing-women and of newborn children were constructed within the circuit of the walls. In the sloping mass of sand which has accumulated on the inside against the north

2 T

Seti and Ramses, now abandoned by their priests, had become mere objects of respectful curiosity, on which devout Egyptians or passing travellers— Phœnicians, Aramæans, Cypriots, Carians, and Greeks from Ionia and the isles —came to carve their names.[1] Amasis confided the work of general restoration to one of the principal personages of his court, Pefzââunît, Prince of Sais, who devoted his attention chiefly to two buildings—the great sanctuary of Osiris, which was put into good condition throughout, and the very ancient

AMASIS IN ADORATION BEFORE THE BULL APIS.[2]

necropolis of Omm-el-Gaâb, where lay hidden the *âlquhah*, one of the sepulchres of the god; he restored the naos, the table of offerings, the barques, and the temple furniture, and provided for the sacred patrimony by an endowment of fields, vineyards, palm groves, and revenues, so as to ensure to the sanctuary offerings in perpetuity. It was a complete architectural resurrection.[3] The

wall was buried, during the XXVIth dynasty, a considerable number of terra-cotta vases containing mummied ibises (MARIETTE, *Catalogue général des Monuments d'Abydos*, p. 579; cf. ROCHEMONTEIX, *Œuvres diverses*, p. 80).

[1] The position occupied by the graffiti on certain portions of the walls show that in these places in the temple of Seti there was already a layer of sand varying from one to three metres in depth. The Semitic and Phœnician or Aramæan graffiti have been published in the *Corpus Inscriptionum Semiticarum*. The Carian and part of the Greek graffiti have been collected by SAYCE, *The Karian Language and Inscriptions*, in the *Transactions* of the Bibl. Arch. Soc., 1887, vol. ix. pp. 126, 127, 147–153, and pls. i.–iii.; *Some Greek Graffiti from Abydos*, in the *Proceedings* of the same Society, 1888–1889, vol. xi. pp. 318, 319.

[2] Drawn by Faucher-Gudin, from a photograph taken in the Louvre; this is the stele of the bull that died in the twenty-third year of Amasis.

[3] *Statue A 93 of Pefzââunît in the Louvre*, published in PIERRET, *Recueil d'inscriptions inédites du Musée du Louvre*, vol. ii. pp. 39–41, and in BRUGSCH, *Thesaurus Inscriptionum Ægyptiacarum*, pp. 1252–1254, translated by PIEHL, *Saitica*, in the *Zeitschrift*, vol. xxxii. pp. 118–122; cf. CLARAC, *Musée de Sculpture*, vol. ii. pp. 243, 244. It seems that one of the buildings, the *âlquhah*, restored by

nomes of Middle Egypt, which had suffered considerably during the Ethiopian and Assyrian wars, had some chance of prosperity now that their lords were relieved from the necessity of constantly fighting for some fresh pretender. Horu, son of Psammetichus, Prince of the Oleander nome, rebuilt the ancient sanctuary of Har-shafaîtu at Hera-cleopolis, and en-dowed it with a munificence which rivalled that of Pefzââunît at Aby-dos.[1] The king himself devoted his resources chiefly to works at Memphis and in the Delta. He founded a temple of Isis at Memphis, which He-rodotus described as extending over an immense area and being well worth seeing ; un-fortunately nothing now remains of it, nor of the recum-bent colossus, sixty feet in length, which

THE NAOS OF AMASIS AT THMUIS.[2]

the king placed before the court of Phtah, nor of the two gigantic statues which he raised in front of the temple, one on each side of the door.[3] Besides these architectural works, Amasis invested the funerary ceremonies of the Apis-bulls with a magnificence rarely seen before his time, and the official stelæ which he carved to the memory of the animals who died in his reign exhibit a perfection of style quite unusual. His labours at Memphis, however, were eclipsed by the

Pefzââunît was the tomb of Osiris, discovered by Amélineau in 1897 (*Les Nouvelles Fouilles d'Abydos*, p. 38, et seq.).

[1] *Statue A 68 of the Louvre*, published in PIERRET, *Recueil d'Inscriptions inédites du Musée du Louvre*, vol. i. pp. 14–21.

[2] Drawn by Boudier, from the sketch of BURTON, *Excerpta Hieroglyphica*, pl. xli.

[3] HERODOTUS, II. clxxvi.: cf. WIEDEMANN, *Herodots Zweites Buch*, pp. 603, 604 ; MALLET, *Les Premiers Établissements des Grecs en Égypte*, p. 133.

admirable work which he accomplished at Sais. The propylæa which he added to the temple of Nît " surpassed most other buildings of the same kind, as much by their height and extent, as by the size and quality of the materials ; " he had, moreover, embellished them by a fine colonnade, and made an approach to them by an avenue of sphinxes. In other parts of the same building were to be seen two superb obelisks, a recumbent figure similar to that at Memphis, and a monolithic naos of rose granite brought from the quarries of Elephantinê. Amasis had a special predilection for this kind of monument. That which he erected at Thmuis is nearly twenty-three feet in height,[1] and the Louvre contains another example, which though smaller still excites the admiration of the modern visitor.[2] The naos of Sais, which amazed Herodotus, was much larger than either of the two already mentioned, or, indeed, than any known example. Tradition states that it took two thousand boatmen three years to convey it down from the first cataract. It measured nearly thirty feet high in the interior, twenty-four feet in depth, and twelve feet in breadth ;[3] even when hollowed out to contain the emblem of the god, it still weighed nearly 500,000 kilograms. It never reached its appointed place in the sanctuary. The story goes that " the architect, at the moment when the monument had been moved as far as a certain spot in the temple, heaved a sigh, oppressed with the thought of the time expended on its transport and weary of the arduous work. Amasis overheard the sigh, and taking it as an omen, he commanded that the block should be dragged no further. Others relate that one of the overseers in charge of the work was crushed to death by the monument, and for this reason it was left standing on the spot," where for centuries succeeding generations came to contemplate it.[4]

Amasis, in devoting his revenues to such magnificent works, fully shared the spirit of the older Pharaohs, and his labours were flattering to the national vanity, even though many lives were sacrificed in their accomplishment; but the glory which they reflected on Egypt did not have the effect of removing the unpopularity in which he was personally held. The revolution which

---

[1] *Description de l'Égypte, Antiquités*, vol. v. pl. 29, and *Texte*, vol. ix. pp. 370–373, and BURTON, *Excerpta Hieroglyphica*, pl. xli. The exact measurements as given in the *Description* are 23½ ft. in height, 12 ft. 9 ins. in width, and 10 ft. 6 ins. in depth. The naos of Saft el-Hinneh must have been smaller, but it is impossible to determine its exact dimensions.

[2] It measures 9 ft. 7 ins. in height, 3 ft. 1 in. in width, and 3 ft. 8 ins. in depth (E. DE RÒUGÉ, *Notice des Monuments*, 1849, pp. 88-90); the inscriptions have been published by PIERRET, *Recueil d'Inscr. inédites*, vol. i. pp. 74–80. It had been erected in the nome of Athribis, and afterwards taken to Alexandria about the Ptolemaic era; it was discovered under water in one of the ports of the town at the beginning of this century, and Drovetti, who recovered it, gave it to the Museum of the Louvre in 1825.

[3] According to Jomard's calculations, exactly 9 metres 70 by 3 m. 70 (*Description de l'Égypte*, vol. ix. p. 371, note 3).

[4] HERODOTUS, II. clxxv.; cf. WIEDEMANN, *Herodots Zweites Buch*, pp. 602, 603. The measurements given by Herodotus are so different from those of any naos as yet discovered, that I follow Kenrick (*The Egypt of Herodotus*, p. 219, and *Ancient Egypt*, vol. ii. p. 370) in thinking that Herodotus saw the monument of Amasis lying on its side, and that he took for the height what was really the width.

overthrew Apries had been provoked by the hatred of the native party towards the foreigners; he himself had been the instrument by which it had been accomplished, and it would have been only natural that, having achieved a triumph in spite of the Greeks and the mercenaries, he should have wished to be revenged on them, and have expelled them from his dominions.[1] But, as a fact, nothing of the kind took place, and Amasis, once crowned, forgot the wrongs he had suffered as an aspirant to the royal dignity; no sooner was he firmly seated on the throne, than he recalled the strangers, and showed that he had only friendly intentions with regard to them. His predecessors had received them into favour, he, in fact, showed a perfect infatuation for them, and became as complete a Greek as it was possible for an Egyptian to be.[2] His first care had been to make a treaty with the Dorians of Cyrene,[3] and he displayed so much tact in dealing with them, that they forgave him for the skirmish of Irasa, and invited him to act as arbitrator in their dissensions. A certain Arkesilas II. had recently succeeded the Battos who had defeated the Egyptian troops, but his suspicious temper had obliged his brothers to separate themselves from him, and they had founded further westwards the independent city of Barca. On his threatening to evict them, they sent a body of Libyans against him. Fighting ensued, and he was beaten close to the town of Leukon. He lost 7000 hoplites in the engagement, and the disaster aroused so much ill-feeling against him that Laarchos, another of his brothers, strangled him. Laarchos succeeded him amid the acclamations of the soldiery; but not long after, Eryxô and Polyarchos, the wife and brother-in-law of his victim, surprised and assassinated him in his turn. The partisans of Laarchos then had recourse to the Pharaoh, who showed himself disposed to send them help; but his preparations were suspended owing to the death of his mother. Polyarchos repaired to Egypt before the royal mourning was ended, and pleaded his cause with such urgency that he won over the king to his side; he obtained the royal investiture for his sister's child, who was still a minor, Battos III., the lame, and thus placed Cyrene in a sort of vassalage to the Egyptian crown.[4] The ties which connected the two courts were subsequently drawn

---

[1] See, on this revolution, above, pp. 555–558.

[2] HERODOTUS, II. clxxvii., distinctly says that he became a phil-Hellene, φιλέλλην δὲ γενόμενος ὁ Ἄμασις.

[3] For the events which occurred at Cyrene, see above, pp. 551–555.

[4] Herodotus narrates these events without mentioning Amasis (IV. clx., clxi.), and Nicolas of Damascus adopted Herodotus' account with certain modifications taken from other sources (*Fragm.* 52, in MÜLLER-DIDOT, *Fragm. Hist. Græc.*, vol. iii. p. 387). The intervention of Amasis is mentioned only by Plutarch (*De Mulier. virt.*, in the *Opera moralia*, DIDOT's ed., vol. ii. p. 260) and by Polyænus (*Stratagemata*, viii. 41); but the record of it had been handed down to them by some more ancient author—perhaps by Akesandros (cf. MÜLLER-DIDOT, *Fragm. Hist. Græc.*, vol. iv. pp. 285, 286); or perhaps, in the first instance, by Hellanicos of Lesbos, who gave a somewhat detailed account of certain points in Egyptian history. The passage of Herodotus is also found incorporated in accounts of Cyrenian origin: his informants were interested in recalling deeds which reflected glory on their

closer by marriage; partly from policy and partly from a whim, Amasis espoused a Cyrenian woman named Ladikê, the daughter, according to some, of Arkesilas or of Battos, according to others, of a wealthy private individual named Kritobulos.[1] The Greeks of Europe and Asia Minor fared no less to their own satisfaction at his hand than their compatriots in Africa; following the example of his ally Crœsus, he entered into relations with their oracles on several occasions, and sent them magnificent presents. The temple of Delphi having been burnt down in 548, the Athenian family of the Alcmæonides undertook to rebuild it from the ground for the sum of three hundred talents, of which one-fourth was to be furnished by the Delphians. When these, being too poor to pay the sum out of their own resources, made an appeal to the generosity of other friendly powers, Amasis graciously offered them a thousand talents of Egyptian alum, then esteemed the most precious of all others. Alum was employed in dyeing, and was an expensive commodity in the markets of Europe; the citizens of Delphi were all the more sensible of Pharaoh's generosity, since the united Greeks of the Nile valley contributed only twenty *minæ* of the same mineral as their quota.[2] Amasis erected at Cyrene a statue of his wife Ladikê, and another of the goddess Neît, gilded from head to foot, and to these he added his own portrait, probably painted on a wooden panel.[3] He gave to Athene of Lindos two stone statues and a corselet of linen of marvellous fineness;[4] and Hera of Samos received two wooden statues, which a century later Herodotus found still intact.[5] The Greeks flocked to Egypt from all quarters of the world in such considerable numbers that the laws relating to them had to be remodelled in order to avoid conflicts with the natives.

The townships founded a century earlier along the Pelusiac arm of the Nile had increased still further since the time of Necho, and to their activity was

country, like the defeat of Apries at Irasa (IV. clix.), but not in the memory of events so humiliating for them as the sovereign intervention of Pharaoh only a few years after this victory. And besides, the merely pacific success which Amasis achieved was not of a nature to leave a profound mark on the Egyptian mind. It is thus easy to explain how it was that Herodotus makes no allusion to the part played by Egypt in this affair.

[1] HERODOTUS, II. clxxxi. The very fact of the marriage is considered by Wiedemann (*Geschichte Ægyptens*, p. 184; *Ægyptische Geschichte*, p. 648; *Herodots Zweites Buch*, pp. 611, 612) as a pure legend, but there is nothing against its authenticity; the curious story of the relations of the woman with Amasis told by the Cyrenian commentators is the only part which need be rejected.

[2] HERODOTUS, II. clxxx.; cf. WIEDEMANN, *Herodots Zweites Buch*, pp. 609–611.

[3] HERODOTUS, II. clxxxi., clxxxii.; cf. WIEDEMANN, *Herodots Zweites Buch*, pp. 611–613. The text of Herodotus, καὶ εἰκόνα ἑωυτοῦ γραφῇ εἰκασμένην, can only mean a painted panel similar to those which have been found on the mummies of the Græco-Roman era in the Fayum.

[4] HERODOTUS, II. clxxxii.; cf. WIEDEMANN, *Herodots Zweites Buch*, pp. 613–615. It seems that one of these statues is that which, after being taken to Constantinople, was destroyed in a fire in 476 A.D. Fragments of the corselet still existed in the first century of our era (PLINY, *H. Nat.*, xix. 1), but inquisitive persons used to tear off pieces to see for themselves whether, as Herodotus assures us (III. xlvii.), each thread was composed of three hundred and sixty-five strands, every one visible with the naked eye.

[5] HERODOTUS, II. clxxxii.; cf. WIEDEMANN, *Herodots Zweites Buch*, p. 615.

attributable the remarkable prosperity of the surrounding region. But the position which they occupied on the most exposed side of Egypt was regarded as permanently endangering the security of the country; her liberty would be imperilled should they revolt during a war with the neighbouring empire, and hand over the line of defence which was garrisoned by them to the invader.[1] Amasis therefore dispossessed their inhabitants, and transferred them to Memphis and its environs. The change benefited him in two ways, for, while securing himself from possible treason, he gained a faithful guard for himself in the event of risings taking place in his turbulent capital.[2] While he thus

distributed these colonists of ancient standing to his best interests, he placed those of quite recent date in the part of the Delta furthest removed from Asia, where surveillance was most easy, in the triangle, namely, lying to the west of Sais, between the Canopic branch of the Nile, the mountains, and the sea-coast. The Milesians had established here some time previously, on a canal connected with the main arm of the river, the factory of Naucratis, which long remained in obscurity, but suddenly developed at the beginning of the XXVIth dynasty, when Sais became the favourite residence of the Pharaohs.[3] This town Amasis made over to the Greeks so that they might make it

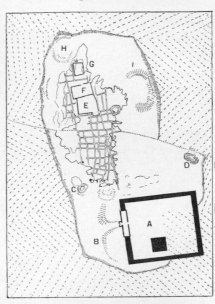

THE PRESENT SITE OF NAUCRATIS.[4]

the commercial and religious centre of their communities in Egypt. Temples already existed there, those of Apollo and Aphrodite,[5] together with all the political and religious institutions indispensable to the constitution of an Hellenic city; but the influx of immigrants was so large and rapid, that, after the lapse of a few years, the entire internal organism and external aspect of the city were metamorphosed. New buildings rose from the ground with incredible speed—the little temple of the Dioskuri, the protectors of the sailor,[6] the temple

---

[1] For these colonies, see above, pp. 496-498.

[2] HERODOTUS, II. cliv.: cf. WIEDEMANN, *Herodots Zweites Buch*, p. 563; MALLET, *Les Premiers Établissements des Grecs en Égypte*, pp. 128-131.

[3] For the origin of Naucratis, cf. *supra*, p. 497, note 2.

[4] Reduced by Faucher-Gudin from the plan published by PETRIE, *Naukratis*, vol. i. pl. xl., and vol. ii. pl. iv. The site of the Hellenion is marked A, the modern Arab village B, the temenos of Hera and Apollo E, that of the Dioskuri F, and that of Aphrodite G.

[5] For the temples in this earlier Naucratis, cf. PETRIE, *Naukratis*, vol. i. p. 11, et seq., and MALLET, *Les Premiers Établissements des Grecs en Égypte*, pp. 185-190.

[6] PETRIE and GARDNER, *Naukratis*, vol. i. pp. 16, 17; vol. ii. pp. 11, 30-32. Mallet (*Les Premiers*

of the Samian Hera, that of Zeus of Ægina,[1] and that of Athene;[2] ere long the great temenos, the Hellenion, was erected at the public expense by nine Æolian, Ionian, and Dorian towns of Asia Minor, to serve as a place of assembly for their countrymen, as a storehouse, as a sanctuary, and, if need be, even as a refuge and fortress, so great was its area and so thick its walls.[3] It was not possible for the constitution of Naucratis to be very homogeneous, when a score of different elements assisted in its composition. It appears to have been a compromise between the institutions of the Dorians and those of the Ionians. Its supreme magistrates were called timuchi, but their length of office and functions are alike unknown to us.[4] The inspectors of the emporia and markets could be elected only by the citizens of the nine towns,[5] and it is certain that the chief authority was not entirely in the hands either of the timuchi or the inspectors; perhaps each quarter of the town had its council taken from among the oldest residents.[6] A prytanæum was open to all comers where assemblies and banquets were held on feast-days; here were celebrated at the public expense the festivals of Dionysos and Apollo Komæos.[7] Amasis made the city a free port, accessible at all times to whoever should present themselves with peaceable intent, and the privileges which he granted naturally brought about the closing of all the other seaports of Egypt. When a Greek ship, pursued by pirates, buffeted by storms, or disabled by an accident at sea, ran ashore at some prohibited spot on the coast, the captain had to appear before the nearest magistrate, in order to swear that he had not violated the law wilfully, but from the force of circumstances. If his excuse appeared

---

Établissements des Grecs en Égypte, pp. 190, 191) thinks that the temple of which Petrie has discovered the remains was built about the time of Amasis, on the ruins of a previous temple, which also had been dedicated to the Dioskuri.

[1] PETRIE and GARDNER, *Naukratis*, vol. i. p. 16; vol. ii. pp. 49, 50; cf. MALLET, *Les Premiers Établissements des Grecs en Égypte*, pp. 191–193.

[2] The temple of Athene, the Nît of the Saite nome, is as yet known only by an inscription in PETRIE, *Naukratis*, vol. i. pl. xxx., and p. 17, and *Ten Years' Digging in Egypt*, p. 38; cf. MALLET, *Les Premiers Établissements des Grecs en Égypte*, p. 193.

[3] HERODOTUS, II. clxxviii.; cf. WIEDEMANN, *Herodots Zweites Buch*, pp. 607, 608. The site has been rediscovered by Petrie at the southern extremity of and almost outside the town (*Naukratis*, vol. i. pp. 23, 24); the walls were about 48 feet thick and 39 feet high, and the rectangular area enclosed by them could easily contain fifty thousand men. Cf. MALLET, *Les Premiers Établissements des Grecs en Égypte*, pp. 195–198.

[4] HERMIAS OF METHYMNOS, *Fragm.* 2, in MÜLLER-DIDOT, *Fragm. Hist. Græc.*, vol. ii. pp. 80, 81, where the timuchi are mentioned in connection with the festivals celebrated in the enclosure of the Hellenion. Hesychius' definition of a timuchos is: ἄρχων ἰσχυρότατος, μέγιστος. An inscription mentions a timuchos at Teos (*Corpus Inscriptionum Græcarum*, 3044), and this title may have been imported into Egypt by Tean colonists. The timuchi of Marseilles were not magistrates, but the six hundred life-members of the senate (STRABO, IV. i. § 5, p. 179).

[5] HERODOTUS, II. clxxviii.; cf. WIEDEMANN, *Herodots Zweites Buch*, p. 608.

[6] This, at least, is the opinion of CURTIUS, *Greek History* (translated by BOUCHÉ and LECLERQ, vol. i. p. 530), where the duties of the timuchi seem to be thus explained.

[7] For the civil and political organisation of the city of Naucratis, see the detailed account by MALLET, *Les Premiers Établissements des Grecs en Égypte*, pp. 357–360.

reasonable, he was permitted to make his way to the mouth of the Canopic branch of the Nile; but when the state of the wind or tide did not allow of his departure, his cargo was transferred to boats of the locality, and sent to the Hellenic settlement by the canals of the Delta.[1] This provision of the law brought prosperity to Naucratis; the whole of the commerce of Egypt with the Greek world passed through her docks, and in a few years she became one of the wealthiest emporia of the Mediterranean. The inhabitants soon overflowed the surrounding country, and covered it with villas and townships.[2] Such merchants as refused to submit to the rule of their own countrymen found a home in some other part of the valley which suited them, and even Upper Egypt and the Libyan desert were subject to their pacific inroads. The Milesians established depôts in the ancient city of Abydos;[3] the Cypriots and Lesbians, and the people of Ephesus, Chios, and Samos, were scattered over the islands formed by the network of canals and arms of the Nile, and delighted in giving them the names of their respective countries;[4] Greeks of diverse origin settled themselves at Neapolis, not far from Panopolis;[5] and the Samians belonging to the Æschrionian tribe penetrated as far as the Great Oasis;[6] in fact, there was scarcely a village where Hellenic traders were not found, like the *bakals* of to-day, selling wine, perfumes, oil, and salted provisions to the natives, practising usury in all its forms, and averse from no means of enriching themselves as rapidly as possible. Those who returned to their mother-country carried thither strange tales, which aroused the curiosity and cupidity of their fellow-citizens; and philosophers, merchants, and soldiers alike set out for the land of wonders in pursuit of knowledge, wealth, or adventures.[7] Amasis, ever alert upon his Asiatic frontier, and always anxious

---

[1] HERODOTUS, II. clxxix.; cf. WIEDEMANN, *Herodots Zweites Buch*, pp. 608, 609.

[2] On the prosperity and trade of Naucratis, cf. the work of MALLET, *Les Premiers Établissements des Grecs en Égypte*, pp. 199–364, where he has collected all the scanty information given by ancient authorities, and that which has resulted from the excavations of the *Egypt Exploration Fund* as set forth in PETRIE and GARDNER, *Naukratis*, i., ii.

[3] STEPHEN OF BYZANTIUM, *s.v.* Ἄβυδος, where the name of the town is said to be derived from that of the Milesian Abydos who founded it, probably on the testimony of Aristagoras (GUTSCHMID, *Kleine Schriften*, vol. i. p. 217). Letronne has seen that the historian meant a factory established by the Milesians probably in the reign of Amasis, at the terminus of the route leading to the Great Oasis (*Œuvres Choisies*, ed. FAGNAN, 1st series, vol. i. p. 166).

[4] HECATÆUS OF MILETUS, *Fragm.* 286, in MÜLLER-DIDOT, *Fragm. Hist. Græc.*, vol. i. p. 20, after STEPHEN OF BYZANTIUM, *s.v.* Ἔφεσος. The compiler confines himself to stating that there were in the Nile islands called Ephesus, Chios, Samos, Lesbos, Cyprus, and so on; the explanation I have given in the text accounts for this curious fact quite simply.

[5] HERODOTUS, II. xci.; cf. WIEDEMANN, *Herodots Zweites Buch*, p. 368, where Wiedemann, adopting Gutschmid's (*Kleine Schriften*, vol. i. p. 217) idea, shows that Neapolis is not, as has often been stated, the same as Kainêpolis, the Qeneh of the present day, but a large village near to Panopolis, or perhaps a Greek quarter within this last town.

[6] HERODOTUS, III. xxvi.; cf. MASPERO, *Études de Mythologie et d'Archéologie Égyptiennes*, vol. iii. pp. 422–426.

[7] In MALLET, *Les Premiers Établissements des Grecs en Égypte*, pp. 365–384, will be found a

to strengthen himself in that quarter against a Chaldæan or Persian invasion, welcomed them with open arms: those who remained in the country obtained employment about his person, while such as left it not to return, carried away with them the memory of his kindly treatment, and secured for him in Hellas alliances of which he might one day stand in need. The conduct of Amasis was politic, but it aroused the ill-feeling of his subjects against him. Like the Jews under Hezekiah, the Babylonians under Nabonidus, and all other decadent races threatened by ruin, they attributed their decline, not to their own vices, but to the machinations of an angry god, and they looked on favours granted to strangers as a sacrilege. Had not the Greeks brought their divinities with them? Did they not pervert the simple country-folk, so that they associated the Greek religion with that of their own country? Money was scarce; Amasis had been obliged to debit the rations and pay of his mercenaries to the accounts of the most venerated Egyptian temples—those of Sais, Heliopolis, Bubastis, and Memphis; and each of these institutions had to rebate so much per cent. on their annual revenues in favour of the barbarians, and hand over to them considerable quantities of corn, cattle, poultry, stuffs, woods, perfumes, and objects of all kinds. The priests were loud in their indignation, the echo of which still rang in the ears of the faithful some centuries later,[1] and the lower classes making common cause with their priests, a spirit of hatred was roused among the populace as bitter as that which had previously caused the downfall of Apries. As the fear of the army prevented this feeling from manifesting itself in a revolt, it found expression in the secret calumnies which were circulated against the king, and misrepresented the motives of all his actions. Scores of malicious stories were repeated vilifying his character. It was stated that before his accession he was much addicted to eating and drinking, but that, suffering from want of money, he had not hesitated in procuring what he wished for by all sorts of means, the most honest of which had been secret theft.[2] When made king, he had several times given way to intoxication to such an extent as to be incapable of attending to public business; his ministers were then obliged to relate moral tales to him to bring him to a state of reason.[3] Many persons having taunted

list of illustrious Greeks who according to tradition visited Egypt, or who really came thither in the Saite epoch—the poet Alcæus of Mitylene, the two Samian sculptors Theodorus and Telecles, Solon the Athenian, Thales of Miletus, and Pythagoras.

[1] Their expression of indignation has been preserved to us in one of the demotic papyri of the Bibliothèque Nationale translated by RÉVILLOUT, Le Roi Amasis et les Mercenaires, in the Revue Égyptologique, vol. i. pp. 11–13.

[2] HERODOTUS, II. clxxiv.; cf. WIEDEMANN, Herodots Zweites Buch, pp. 597, 598.

[3] This is the import of the story first published by RÉVILLOUT, Le Roi Amasis et les Mercenaires, in the Revue Égyptologique, vol. i. pp. 17–19; cf. MASPERO, Les Contes populaires de l'Égypte Ancienne, 2nd edit., pp. 297–308. The fondness of Amasis for wine and mirth is mentioned by HERODOTUS, II. clxxiii.

him with his low extraction, he had caused a statue of a divinity to be made out of a gold basin in which he was accustomed to wash his feet, and he had exposed it to the adoration of the faithful. When it had been worshipped by them for some time, he revealed the origin of the idol, and added "that it had been with himself as with the foot-pan. . . . If he were a private person formerly, yet now he had come to be their king, and so he bade them honour and reverence him." [1] Towards the middle and end of his reign he was as much detested as he had been beloved at the outset.

He had, notwithstanding, so effectively armed Egypt that the Persians had not ventured to risk a collision with her immediately after their conquest of Babylon. Cyrus had spent ten years in compassing the downfall of Nabonidus, and, calculating that that of Amasis would require no less a period of time, he set methodically to work on the organisation of his recently acquired territory; the cities of Phœnicia acknowledged him as their suzerain, and furnished him with what had hitherto been a coveted acquisition, a fleet. These preliminaries had apparently been already accomplished, when the movements of the barbarians suddenly made his presence in the far East imperative. He hurried thither, and was mysteriously lost to sight (529). Tradition accounts for his death in several ways. If Xenophon is to be credited, he died peaceably on his bed, surrounded by his children, and edifying those present by his wisdom and his almost superhuman resignation.[2] Berosus tells us that he was killed in a campaign against the Dahæ;[3] Ctesias states that, having been wounded in a skirmish with the Derbikes, one of the savage tribes of Bactriana, he succumbed to his injuries three days after the engagement.[4] According to the worthy Herodotus, he asked the hand of Tomyris, Queen of the Massagetæ, in marriage, and was refused with disdain. He declared war against her to avenge his wounded vanity, set out to fight with her beyond the Araxes, in the steppes of Turkestan, defeated the advance-guard of cavalry, and took prisoner the heir to the crown, Spargapises, who thereupon ran himself through with his sword. "Then Tomyris collected all the forces of her kingdom, and gave him (Cyrus) battle. Of all the combats in which barbarians have engaged among themselves, I reckon this to have been the fiercest. The following, as I understand, was the manner of it :—First, the

---

[1] HERODOTUS, II. clxxii.; cf. WIEDEMANN, *Herodots Zweites Buch*, pp. 594, 595.

[2] XENOPHON, *Cyropædia*, VIII. vii. §§ 3–38. A similar legend, but later in date, told how Cyrus, when a hundred years old, asked one day to see his friends. He was told that his son had had them all put to death : his grief at the cruelty of Cambyses caused his death in a few days (ONESICRITUS, *Fragm.* 32, in MÜLLER-DIDOT, *Scriptores rerum Alexandri Magni*, p. 57).

[3] If Eusebius (*Chronicon*, p. 29) can be trusted ; as Nöldeke has pointed out, Berosus might really have found the fact recorded in a Babylonian document similar to those from which we have learned the events that occurred at the beginning of Cyrus' reign (*Aufsätze zur Persischen Geschichte*, p. 24).

[4] CTESIAS, *Fragm.* 29, §§ 6, 7, in MÜLLER-DIDOT, *Ctesiæ Cnidii Fragmenta*, p. 47.

two armies stood apart and shot their arrows at each other; then, when their quivers were empty, they closed and fought hand to hand with lances and daggers; and thus they continued fighting for a length of time, neither choosing to give ground. At length the Massagetæ prevailed. The greater part of the army of the Persians was destroyed. Search was made among the slain by order of the queen for the body of Cyrus; and when it was found, she took a skin, and, filling it full of human blood, she dipped the head of Cyrus in the gore, saying, as she thus insulted the corse, ' I live and have conquered thee in fight, and yet by thee am I ruined, for thou tookest my son with guile; but thus I make good my threat, and give thee thy fill of blood.' " [1] The engagement was not as serious as the legend would have us believe, and the growth of the Persian power was in no way affected by it. It cost Cyrus his life, but his army experienced no serious disaster, and his men took the king's body and brought it to Pasargadæ. He had a palace there, the remains of which can still be seen on the plain of Murgâb.[2] The edifice was unpretentious, built upon a rectangular plan, with two porches of four columns on the longer sides, a lateral chamber at each of the four angles, and a hypostyle hall in the centre, divided lengthways by two

CYRUS THE ACHÆMENIAN.[3]

rows of columns which supported the roof. The walls were decorated with bas-reliefs, and wherever the inscriptions have not been destroyed, we can read in cuneiform characters in the three languages which thenceforward formed the official means of communication of the empire—Persian, Medic, and Chaldæan —the name, title, and family of the royal occupant. Cyrus himself is represented in a standing posture on the pilasters, wearing a costume in which Egyptian and Assyrian features are curiously combined. He is clothed from neck to ankle in the close-fitting fringed tunic of the Babylonian and Ninevite

[1] HERODOTUS, I. cciv.–ccxiv. (Rawlinson's trans.): cf. JUSTIN, i. 8; VALERIUS MAXIMUS, i. 10.

[2] For this palace of Cyrus, cf. PERROT and CHIPIEZ, *Histoire de l'Art dans l'Antiquité*, vol. v. pp. 665–670, and DIEULAFOY, *L'Art Antique de la Perse*, vol. i. p. 29, et seq.

[3] Drawn by Boudier, from the photograph by DIEULAFOY, *L'Acropole de Suse*, p. 49, No. 33.

sovereigns; his feet are covered with laced boots, while four great wings, emblems of the supreme power,[1] overshadow his shoulders and loins, two of them raised in the air, the others pointing to the earth; he wears on his head the Egyptian skull-cap, from which rises one of the most complicated head-dresses of the royal wardrobe of the Pharaohs.[2] The monarch raises his right hand

THE TOMB OF CYRUS.[3]

with the gesture of a man speaking to an assembled people,[4] and as if repeating the legend traced above his image: " I am Cyrus, the king, the Achæmenian." He was buried not far off, in the monumental tomb which he had probably built for himself in a square enclosure, having a portico on three of its sides; a small chamber, with a ridge roof, rises from a base composed of six receding steps, so arranged as to appear of unequal height. The doorway is narrow, and so low

---

[1] HERODOTUS, I. ccix.; cf. DIEULAFOY, *L'Art Antique de la Perse*, vol. i. p. 35.

[2] This is the diadem of the triple *hotesu*, No. xli. in the list of ROCHEMONTEIX, *Œuvres diverses*, pl. ii.

[3] Drawn by Faucher-Gudin, from the heliogravure of DIEULAFOY, *L'Art Antique de la Perse*, vol. i. pl. xix.

[4] Dieulafoy places in his closed hand " a statuette of which the double cap, very different from the *pshent*, is surmounted by the sacred uræus " (*L'Art Antique de la Perse*, vol. i. p. 35, and pl. xvii.): no other traveller has mentioned this emblem, and on closely examining the photographs of the monument, even that by Dieulafoy (*L'Acropole de Suse*, p. 49, No. 33), I can make out only a crack in the stone, beyond which can be easily seen the tips of the fingers, stretched out as in the illustration above on p. 652.

that a man of medium stature finds some difficulty in entering. It is surmounted by a hollow moulding, quite Egyptian in style, and was closed by a two-leaved stone door.[1] The golden coffin rested on a couch of the same metal, covered with precious stuffs; and a circular table, laden with drinking-vessels and ornaments enriched with precious stones, completed the furniture of the chamber. The body of the conqueror remained undisturbed on this spot for two centuries under the care of the priests; but while Alexander was waging war on the Indian frontier, the Greek officers, to whom he had entrusted the government of Persia proper, allowed themselves to be tempted by the enormous wealth which the funerary chapel was supposed to contain. They opened the coffin, broke the couch and the table, and finding them too heavy to carry away easily, they contented themselves with stealing the drinking-vessels and jewels.[2] Alexander on his return visited the place, and caused the entrance to be closed with a slight wall of masonry; he intended to restore the monument to its former splendour, but he himself perished shortly after, and what remained of the contents probably soon disappeared. After the death of Cyrus, popular imagination, drawing on the inexhaustible materials furnished by his adventurous career, seemed to delight in making him the ideal of all a monarch should be; they attributed to him every virtue—gentleness, bravery, moderation, justice, and wisdom. There is no reason to doubt that he possessed the qualities of a good general—activity, energy, and courage, together with the astuteness and the duplicity so necessary to success in Asiatic conquest—but he does not appear to have possessed in the same degree the gifts of a great administrator. He made no changes in the system of government which from the time of Tiglath-pileser III. onwards had obtained among all Oriental sovereigns; he placed satraps over the towns and countries of recent acquisition, at Sardes and Babylon, in Syria and Palestine, but without clearly defining their functions or subjecting them to a supervision sufficiently strict to ensure the faithful performance of their duties. He believed that he was destined to found a single empire in which all the ancient empires were to be merged, and he all but carried his task to a successful close: Egypt alone remained to be conquered when he passed away.

His wife Kassandanê, a daughter of Pharnaspes, and an Achæmenian like

[1] DIEULAFOY, *L'Art Antique de la Perse*, vol. i. p. 48.

[2] ARRIAN, *Anabasis*, VI. x. §§ 4–9, after ARISTOBULUS (*Fragm.* 37, in MÜLLER-DIDOT, *Scriptores rerum Alexandri Magni*, pp. 107, 108). Cf. PSEUDO-CALLISTHENES, II. xviii., where the author places the tomb of Cyrus and that of "Nabonasar, whom the Greeks call Nabukhodonosor," side by side. According to Oppert, the little building of Murghâb is not the tomb of Cyrus, but of his wife Kassandanê (*Journal Asiatique*, 1872, vol. xix. pp. 548, and *Le Peuple et la Langue des Mèdes*, pp. 110, 111). The description preserved by Arrian shows that it belongs to the conqueror, and not to one of his queens.

himself, had borne him five children ; two sons, Cambyses[1] and Smerdis,[2] and three daughters, Atossa, Roxana, and Artystonê.[3] Cambyses was probably born about 558, soon after his father's accession,[4] and he was his legitimate successor, according to the Persian custom which assigned the crown to the eldest of the sons born in the purple.[5] He had been associated, as we have seen, in the Babylonian regal power immediately after the victory over Nabonidus,[6] and on the eve of his departure for the fatal campaign against the Massagetæ his father, again in accordance with the Persian law, had appointed him regent.[7] A later tradition, preserved by Ctesias, relates that on this occasion the territory had been divided between the two sons : Smerdis, here called Tanyoxarkes, having received as his share Bactriana, the Khoramnians, the Parthians, and the Carmanians, under the suzerainty of his brother.[8] Cambyses,

[1] The Persian form of the name rendered Kambyses by the Greeks (HERODOTUS, II. i.) was Kābuzîyâ or Kambuzîya (JUSTI, *Iranisches Namenbuch*, pp. 153, 154). Herodotus calls him the son of Kassandanê (II. i., III. ii.), and the tradition which he has preserved is certainly authentic. Ctesias has erroneously stated that his mother was Amytis, the daughter of Astyages (*Fragm.* 37, in MÜLLER-DIDOT, *Ctesiæ Cnidii Fragmenta*, p. 63), and Dinon, also erroneously, the Egyptian woman Nitêtis (*Fragm.* 11, in MÜLLER-DIDOT, *Fragm. Hist. Græc.*, vol. ii. p. 91) ; Diodorus Siculus (i. 33) and Strabo make him the son of Meroê. For a good summary of information concerning Cambyses and the children of Cyrus, see PRASHEK, *Forschungen zur Geschichte des Alterthums*, vol. i. pp. 30–34.

[2] The original form was Bardîya or Barzîya, "the laudable" (JUSTI, *Iranisches Namenbuch*, p. 63), and the first Greek transcript known, in Æschylus (*Persæ*, 774), is Mardos, or, in the scholiasts on the passage, Merdias, which has been corrupted into Marphios by Hellanikos (*Fragm.* 164, in MÜLLER-DIDOT, *Fragm. Hist. Græc.*, vol. i. p. 68) and into Merges by Pompeius Trogus (JUSTIN, i. 9). The form Smerdis in Herodotus (III. xxx.), and in the historians who follow him (DIODORUS SICULUS, xix. 40), is the result of a mistaken assimilation of the Persian name with the purely Greek one of Smerdis or Smerdies (ARISTOTLE, *Politics*, Berlin ed., vol. ii. p. 1311) ; compare also the name of a son of Otanes rendered Smerdomenes for the same reason (HERODOTUS, VII. lxxxii., cxxi.).

[3] Herodotus says that Atossa was the daughter of Kassandanê (II. i., III. iii.), and the position which she held during three reigns shows that she must have been so ; Justi, however, calls her the daughter of Amytis (*Iranisches Namenbuch*, p. 398). A second daughter is mentioned by Herodotus (III. xxxi.), the one whom Cambyses killed in Egypt by a kick ; he gives her no name, but she is probably the same as (MARQUART, *Die Assyriaka des Ktesias*, in the *Philologus*, Suppl., vol. v. pp. 607, 608 ; PRASHEK, *Forschungen zur Geschichte des Alterthums*, vol. i. pp. 31, 32) the Roxana who according to Ctesias bore a headless child (*Fragm.* 29, § 12, in MÜLLER-DIDOT, *Ctesiæ Cnidii Fragmenta*, p. 48). The youngest, Artystonê, was the favourite wife of Darius (HERODOTUS, III. lxxxviii., VII. lxix., lxxii.). Josephus (*Ant. Jud.*, II. xi. § 2) speaks of a fourth daughter of Cyrus called Meroê, but without saying who was the mother of this princess.

[4] According to the very probable calculation of PRASHEK, *Forschungen zur Geschichte des Alterthums*, vol. i. pp. 34, 35.

[5] On this point, cf. HERODOTUS, VII. ii., iii., where tradition ascribes the establishment of this law to the Spartan Demaratos in the case of Xerxes I.

[6] On this first association, cf. *supra*, p. 636.

[7] HERODOTUS, I. ccviii., states the fact, Καμβύσῃ, τῷπερ τὴν βασιληΐην ἐδίδου; and elsewhere (VII. ii.) he formally says that the Persian law required the nomination of a successor in such a case.

[8] CTESIAS, *Fragm.* 29, § 8, in MÜLLER-DIDOT, *Ctesiæ Cnidii Fragmenta*, p. 47 ; Xenophon, who preserves the same legend, gives the name as Tanaoxares, and says that the Medes, the Armenians, and the Cadusians were his subjects (*Cyropædia*, VIII. vii. § 11). Duncker (*Geschichte des Alterthums*, 4th edit., vol. iv. p. 427) accepts the division of the empire between the two brothers, and the latest historian of Smerdis, Hutecker (*Der Falsche Smerdis*, p. 35), adopts the same view. Tanaoxares or Tanyoxarkes would then be only an epithet applied to Smerdis, Thanvarakhshathra, *the king of the bow* (DUNCKER, *Geschichte des Alterthums*, 4th edit., vol. iv. p. 437), Tanuvazraka, *the great of body* (OPPERT, *Mémoire sur les Inscriptions Akhéménides*, in the *J. As.*, 4th ser., 1851, vol. xvii. p. 262), Tanwakhshathaka, *established in a lesser kingdom* (KERN, *Specimen*

it is clear, inherited the whole empire, but intrigues gathered round Smerdis, and revolts broke out in the provinces, incited, so it was said, whether rightly or wrongly, by his partisans.[1] The new king was possessed of a violent, merciless temper, and the Persians subsequently emphasised the fact by saying that Cyrus had been a father to them, Cambyses a master.[2] The rebellions were repressed with a vigorous hand, and finally Smerdis disappeared by royal order, and the secret of his fate was so well kept, that it was believed, even by his mother and sisters, that he was merely imprisoned in some obscure Median fortress.[3] The ground being cleared of his rival, and affairs on the Scythian frontier reduced to order, Cambyses took up the projects against Egypt at the exact point at which his predecessor had left them. Amasis, who for ten years had been expecting an attack, had taken every precaution in his power against it, and had once more patiently begun to make overtures of alliance with the Hellenic cities; those on the European continent did not feel themselves so seriously menaced as to consider it to their interest to furnish him with any assistance, but the Greeks of the independent islands, with their chief, Polycrates, tyrant of Samos, received his advances with alacrity. Polycrates had at his disposal a considerable fleet, the finest hitherto seen in the waters of the Ægean, and this, combined with the Egyptian navy, was not any too large a force to protect the coasts of the Delta, now that the Persians had at their disposition not only the vessels of the Æolian and Ionian cities, but those

Historicum exhibens Scriptores Græcos de rebus Persicis Achæmenidarum Monumentis collatos, pp. 23, 24; Bréal, *De Persicis nominibus,* p. 27). Ctesias' story can be considered only as a purely imaginary one (Nöldeke, *Aufsätze zur Pers. Gesch.,* p. 26; Prashek, *Forsch. zur Gesch. des Alterth.,* vol. i. pp. 38, 39), probably modelled on what occurred, at the death of Darius II., between his two sons Artaxerxes II. and Cyrus the younger (Marquart, *Die Assyr. des Ktesias,* in the *Philologus,* Suppl., vol. v. pp. 619, 620).

[1] Herodotus, III. lxxxviii., speaks of peoples subdued by Cambyses in Asia, and this allusion can only refer to a revolt occurring after the death of Cyrus, before the Egyptian expedition; these troubles are explicitly recorded in Xenophon, *Cyropædia,* VIII. viii. § 2.

[2] Herodotus, III. lxxxix., where the term δεσπότης is explained as χαλεπός τε ἦν καὶ ὀλίγωρος.

[3] The inscription of Behistun (col. i. ll. 26–32) says distinctly that Cambyses had his brother Bardîya put to death before the Egyptian expedition (Weissbach and Bang, *Die Altpersischen Keilinschriften,* pp. 12–15); on the other hand, Herodotus makes the murder occur during the Egyptian expedition (III. xxx.) and Ctesias after this expedition (*Fragm.* 29, §§ 10, 11, in Müller-Didot, *Ctesiæ Cnidii Fragmenta,* pp. 47, 48). Ctesias' version of the affair adds that Cambyses, the better to dissimulate his crime, ordered the murderer Sphendadates to pass himself off as Tanyoxarkes, as there was a great resemblance between the two: Sphendadates—the historian goes on to say—was exiled to Bactriana, and it was not until five years afterwards that the mother of the two princes heard of the murder and of the substitution. These additions to the story are subsequent developments suggested by the traditional account of the Pseudo-Smerdis. In recent times several authorities, Beloch (*Griechische Geschichte,* vol. i. p. 345, note 1), Rost (*Untersuchungen zur Altorientalischen Geschichte,* pp. 107–109), and Winckler (in the *Orientalische Literatur-Zeitung,* 1898, pp. 39–45, and *Altorientalische Forschungen,* vol. ii. pp. 138–140), have expressed the opinion that all that is told us of the murder of Smerdis and about the Pseudo-Smerdis is merely a legend, invented by Darius or those about him in order to justify his usurpation in the eyes of the people: the Pseudo-Smerdis would be Smerdis himself, who revolted against Cambyses, and was then, after he had reigned a few months, assassinated by Darius. Winckler acknowledges "that certainty is impossible in such a case;" and, in reality, all ancient tradition is against his hypothesis, and it is best to accept Herodotus' account, with all its contradictions, until contemporaneous documents enable us to decide what to accept and what to reject in it.

of Phœnicia and Cyprus. A treaty was concluded, bringing about an exchange of presents and amenities between the two princes which lasted as long as peace prevailed, but was ruptured at the critical moment by the action of Polycrates, though not actually through his own fault. The aristocratic party, whose chiefs were always secretly plotting his overthrow, had given their adherence to the Persians, and their conduct became so threatening about the time of the death of Cyrus, that Polycrates had to break his engagements with Egypt in order to avert a catastrophe.[1] He made a treaty with the Persian king, and sent a squadron of forty galleys to join the fleet then being equipped in the Phœnician ports.[2] Amasis, therefore, when war at last broke out, found himself left to face the enemy alone. The struggle was inevitable, and all the inhabitants of the eastern coasts of the Mediterranean had long foreseen its coming. Without taking into consideration the danger to which the Persian empire and its Syrian provinces were exposed by the proximity of a strong and able power such as Egypt, the hardy and warlike character of Cambyses would naturally have prompted him to make an attempt to achieve what his predecessors, the warrior-kings of Nineveh and Babylon, had always failed to accomplish successfully. Policy ruled his line of action, and was sufficient to explain it, but popular imagination sought other than the very natural causes which had brought the most ancient and most recent of the great empires of the world into opposition; romantic reasons were therefore invented to account for the great drama which was being enacted, and the details supplied varied considerably, according as the tradition was current in Asia or Africa. It was said that a physician lent to Cyrus by Amasis, to treat him for an affection of the eyes, was the cause of all the evil. The unfortunate man, detained at Susa and chafing at his exile, was said to have advised Cambyses to ask for the daughter of Pharaoh in marriage, hoping either that Amasis would grant the request, and be dishonoured in the eyes of his subjects for having degraded the solar race by a union with a barbarian, or that he would boldly refuse, and thus arouse the hatred of the Persians against himself. Amasis, after a slight hesitation, substituted Nitêtis, a daughter of Apries, for his own child. It happened that one day in sport Cambyses addressed the princess by the name of her supposed father, whereupon she said, "I perceive, O king, that you have no suspicion of the way in which

---

[1] HERODOTUS, III. xxxix.-xliii., where the breach of the treaty is laid to the blame of the King of Egypt, and attributed to his fear of the constant good fortune of Polycrates. The latter's accession to power is fixed at about the year 540 by some (J. BELOCH, *Griechische Geschichte*, vol. i. p. 317), by others in the year 537 (DUNCKER, *Geschichte des Alterthums*, 5th edit., vol. v. p. 512), or in the year 533-2 (BUSOLT, *Griechische Geschichte*, vol. i. p. 602); his negotiations with Amasis must be placed somewhere during the last fifteen years of the Pharaoh.

[2] HEROD., III. xliv.-xlvi., where two opposing traditions are recorded: one that the Samians joined in the Egyptian campaign, the other that they went only as far as the neighbourhood of Karpathos.

you have been deceived by Amasis; he took me, and having dressed me up as his own daughter, sent me to you. In reality I am the daughter of Apries, who was his lord and master until the day that he revolted, and, in concert with the rest of the Egyptians, put his sovereign to death." The deceit which Cambyses thus discovered had been put upon him irritated him so greatly as to induce him to turn his arms against Egypt. So ran the Persian account of the tale,[1] but on the banks of the Nile matters were explained otherwise. Here it was said that it was to Cyrus himself that Nitêtis had been married, and that she had borne Cambyses to him; the conquest had thus been merely a revenge of the legitimate heirs of Psammetichus upon the usurper, and Cambyses had ascended the throne less as a conqueror than as a Pharaoh of the line of Apries.[2] It was by this childish fiction that the Egyptians in their decadence consoled themselves before the stranger for their loss of power. Always proud of their ancient prowess, but incapable of imitating the deeds of their forefathers, they none the less pretended that they could neither be vanquished nor ruled except by one of themselves, and the story of Nitêtis afforded complete satisfaction to their vanity. If Cambyses were born of a solar princess, Persia could not be said to have imposed a barbarian king upon Egypt, but, on the contrary, that Egypt had cleverly foisted her Pharaoh upon Persia, and through Persia upon half the universe.

One obstacle still separated the two foes—the desert and the marshes of the Delta. The distance between the outposts of Pelusium and the fortress of Ienysos [3] on the Syrian frontier was scarcely fifty-six miles, and could be crossed by an army in less than ten days.[4] Formerly the width of this strip of desert had been less, but the Assyrians, and after them the Chaldæans, had vied with each other in laying waste the country, and the absence of any settled population now rendered the transit difficult. Cambyses had his head-quarters at Gaza, at the extreme limit of his own dominions,[5] but he was at a loss how to face this solitary region without incurring the risk of seeing half his men buried beneath its sands, and his uncertainty was delaying his departure when a stroke of fortune relieved him from his difficulty. Phanes

---

[1] Herodotus, III. i.; Ctesias tells the same story, probably following Herodotus (*Fragm.* 37, in Müller-Didot, *Ctesiæ Cnidii Fragmenta*, p. 63).

[2] Herodotus, III. i.–iii. This account was borrowed from Herodotus by Dinon (*Fragm.* 11, in Müller-Didot, *Fragm. Hist. Græc.*, vol. ii. p. 91), and by Lycæas of Naucratis (*Fragm.* 2, in Müller-Didot, *Fragm. Hist. Græc.*, vol. iv. p. 441).

[3] The Ienysos of Herodotus (III. v.) is now Khân Yunes.

[4] In 1799, Napoleon's army left Kattiyeh on the 18th of Pluviose, and was at Gaza on the 7th of Ventose, after remaining from the 21st to the 30th of Pluviose before El-Arîsh besieging that place.

[5] This seems to follow from the tradition preserved by Servius, *Ad Æneidos*, i. 123, according to which Cambyses left his treasures at Gaza during the Egyptian campaign, and the town was thence called *Gaza*, " the treasury." The etymology is false, but the fact that suggested it is probably correct. considering the situation of Gaza and the part it must necessarily play in an invasion of Egypt.

of Halicarnassus, one of the mercenaries in the service of Egypt, a man of shrewd judgment and an able soldier, fell out with Amasis for some unknown reason, and left him to offer his services to his rival. This was a serious loss for Egypt, since Phanes possessed considerable authority over the mercenaries, and was better versed in Egyptian affairs than any other person. He was pursued and taken within sight of the Lycian coast, but he treated his captors to wine and escaped from them while they were intoxicated. He placed Cambyses in communication with the shêkh of the scattered tribes between Syria and the Delta. The Arab undertook to furnish the Persian king with guides, as one of his predecessors had done in years gone by for Esarhaddon, and to station relays of camels laden with water along the route that the invading army was to follow.[1] Having taken these precautions, Cambyses entrusted the cares of government and the regulation of his household to Oropastes,[2] one of the Persian magi, and gave the order to march forward. On arriving at Pelusium, he learned that his adversary no longer existed. Amasis had died after a short illness, and was succeeded by his son Psammetichus III. This change of command, at the most critical moment, was almost in itself a disaster. Amasis, with his consummate experience of men and things, his intimate knowledge of the resources of Egypt, his talents as a soldier and a general, his personal prestige, his Hellenic leanings, commanded the confidence of his own men and the respect of foreigners; but what could be

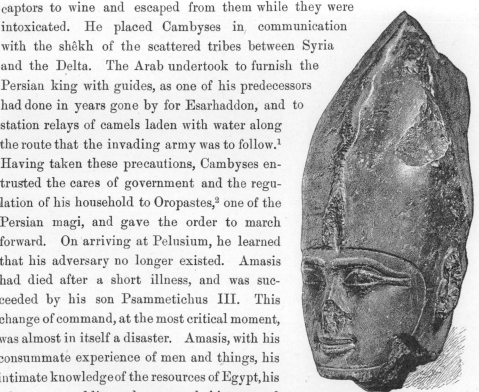

PSAMMETICHUS III.[3]

---

[1] HERODOTUS, III. iv.–x.; for the similar preparations of Esarhaddon, cf. *supra*, p. 371. In the account of Ctesias (*Fragm.* 29, § 9, in MÜLLER-DIDOT, *Ctesiæ Cnidii Fragmenta*, p. 47), Kombapheus, a eunuch, plays the same part as does Phanes in the tradition of Herodotus.

[2] Herodotus (III. lxi., lxiii.) calls this individual Patizeithes, and Dionysius of Miletus, who lived a little before Herodotus, gives Panzythes as a variant of this name: the variant passed into the Syncellus as Pauzythes, but the original form Patikhshâyathiya is a title signifying *viceroy, regent, or minister*, answering to the modern Persian *Padīshah*: Herodotus, or the author he quotes, has taken the name of the office for that of the individual. On the other hand, Pompeius Trogus, who drew his information from good sources, mentions, side by side with Cometes or Gaumata, his brother Oropastes (JUSTIN, i. 9), whose name Ahura-upashta is quite correct, and may mean, *Him whom Ahura helps* (BREAL, *De Persicis Nominibus*, p. 12). It is generally admitted that Pompeius Trogus, or rather Justin, has inverted the parts they played, and that his Cometes is the Pseudo-Smerdis, and not, as he says, Oropastes; it was, then, the latter who was the usurper's brother, and it is his name of Oropastes which should be substituted for that of the Patizeithes of Herodotus (JUSTI, *Geschichte des Alten Persiens*, p. 50; MARQUART, *Die Assyr. des Ktesias*, in the *Philologus*, Suppl., vol. vi. pp. 618, 619).

[3] Drawn by Boudier, from a photograph of the original in the Louvre; cf. G. BÉNÉDITE, *Une Tête*

expected of his unknown successor,[1] and who could say whether he were equal to the heavy task which fate had assigned to him ? The whole of the Nile valley was a prey to gloomy presentiment. Egypt was threatened not only, as in the previous century, by the nations of the Tigris and Euphrates, but all Asia, from the Indus to the Hellespont, was about to fall on her to crush her. She was destitute of all human help and allies, and the gods themselves appeared to have forsaken her. The fellahîn, inspired with vague alarm, recognised evil omens in all around them. Rain is rare in the Thebaid, and storms occur there only twice or three times in a century : but a few days after the accession of Psammetichus, a shower of fine rain fell at Thebes, an event, so it was stated with the exaggeration characteristic of the bearers of ill news, which had never before occurred.[2] Pharaoh hastened to meet the invader with all the men, chariots, and native bowmen at his disposal, together with his Libyan and Cyrenæan auxiliaries,[3] and the Ionians, Carians, and Greeks of the isles and mainland. The battle took place before Pelusium, and was fought on both sides with brave desperation, since defeat meant servitude for the Egyptians, and for the Persians, cut off by the desert from possible retreat, captivity or annihilation. Phanes had been obliged to leave his children behind him, and Pharaoh included them in his suite, to serve, if needful, as hostages. The Carians and Ionians, who felt themselves disgraced by the defection of their captain, called loudly for them just before the commencement of the action. They were killed immediately in front of the lines, their father being a powerless onlooker ; their blood was thrown into a cask half full of wine, and the horrible mixture was drunk by the soldiers, who then furiously charged the enemy's battalions. The issue of the struggle was for a long time doubtful, but the Egyptians were inferior in numbers ; towards evening their lines gave way and the flight

---

de statue royale, in the *Gazette des Beaux-Arts*, vol. xviii. pp. 35–42. This fragment, executed in very good style, has been given by Mme. André to the Egyptian Museum in the Louvre.

[1] Psammetichus III. has left us very few monuments (cf. WIEDEMANN, *Ægyptische Geschichte*, pp. 660, 661), which is accounted for by the extreme shortness of his reign. For the same reason doubtless several writers of classical times have ignored his existence, and have made the conquest of Egypt take place under Amasis (ARISTOTLE, *Rhetoric*, ii. 8 ; JOHN OF ANTIOCH, *Fragm.* 27, in MÜLLER-DIDOT, *Fragm. Hist. Græc.*, vol. iv. p. 552). Ctesias calls the Pharaoh Amyrtæus, and gives the same name to those who rebelled against the Persians in his own time, and he had an account of the history of the conquest entirely different from that of Herodotus (*Fragm.* 27, § 9, in MÜLLER-DIDOT, *Ctesiæ Cnidii Fragmenta*, p. 47).

[2] HERODOTUS, III. x. The inhabitants of the Saîd have, up to our own time, always considered rain in the valley as an ill-omened event. They used to say in the beginning of the nineteenth century, when speaking of Napoleon's expedition, "We knew that misfortune threatened us, because it rained at Luxor shortly before the French came." Wilkinson assures us that rain is not so rare at Thebes as Herodotus thought : he speaks of five or six showers a year, and of a great storm on an average every ten years (RAWLINSON, *Herodotus*, vol. ii. p. 338, note 4). But even he admits that it is confined to the mountain district, and does not reach the plain : I never heard of rain at Luxor during the six winters that I spent in Upper Egypt.

[3] DIODORUS SICULUS, x. 14.

began.[1] All was not, however, lost, if Psammetichus had but followed the example of Taharqa,[2] and defended the passage of the various canals and arms of the river, disputing the ground inch by inch with the Persians, and gaining time meanwhile to collect a fresh army. The king lost his presence of mind, and without attempting to rally what remained of his regiments, he hastened to take refuge within the White Wall. Cambyses halted a few days to reduce Pelusium,[3] and in the mean time sent a vessel of Mitylene to summon Memphis to capitulate : the infuriated populace, as soon as they got wind of the message, massacred the herald and the crew, and dragged their bleeding limbs through the streets. The city held out for a considerable time ; when at length she opened her gates, the remaining inhabitants of the Saîd who had hesitated up to then, hastened to make their submission, and the whole of Egypt as far as Philæ became at one stroke a Persian province. The Libyans did not wait to be summoned to bring their tribute ; Cyrene and Barca followed their example, but their offerings were so small that the conqueror's irritation was aroused, and deeming himself mocked, he gave way to his anger, and instead of accepting them, he threw them to his soldiers with his own hand (B.C. 525).[4] This sudden collapse of a power whose exalted position had defied all attacks for centuries, and the tragic fate of the king who had received his crown merely to lose it, filled contemporary beholders with astonishment and pity. It was said that, ten days after the capitulation of Memphis, the victorious king desired out of sport to test the endurance of his prisoner. Psammetichus beheld his daughter and the daughters of his nobles pass before him, half naked, with jars on their shoulders, and go down to the Nile to fetch water from the river like common slaves ; his son and two thousand young men of the same age, in chains and with ropes round their necks, also defiled before him on their way to die as a revenge for the murder of the Mitylenians ; yet he never for a moment lost his royal imperturbability. But when one of his former companions in pleasure chanced to pass, begging for alms and clothed in rags, Psammetichus suddenly broke out into weeping, and lacerated his face in despair. Cambyses, surprised at this excessive grief in a man who up till then had exhibited such fortitude, demanded the reason of his conduct. "Son of Cyrus," he replied, "the misfortunes of my house are too unparalleled to weep over, but not the

---

[1] HERODOTUS, III. xi., xii. ; eighty years later the battle-field used to be shown covered with bones and it was said that the Egyptians could be distinguished from the Persians by the relative hardness of their skulls.

[2] Cf. *supra*, pp. 372, 373.

[3] Polyænus (*Stratagems*, viii. 9) hands down a story that Cambyses, in order to paralyse the resistance of the besieged, caused cats, dogs, ibises, and other sacred animals to march at the head of his attacking columns : the Egyptians would not venture to use their arms for fear of wounding or killing some of their gods.

[4] HERODOTUS, III. xiii. The question as to the year in which Egypt was subdued by Cambyses has long divided historians : I still agree with those who place the conquest in the spring of 525.

affliction of my friend. When a man, on the verge of old age, falls from luxury and abundance into extreme poverty, one may well lament his fate." When the speech was reported to Cambyses, he fully recognised the truth of it. Crœsus, who was also present, shed tears, and the Persians round him were moved with pity. Cambyses, likewise touched, commanded that the son of the Pharaoh should be saved, but the remission of the sentence arrived too late. He at all events treated Pharaoh himself with consideration, and it is possible that he might have replaced him on the throne, under an oath of vassalage, had he not surprised him in a conspiracy against his own life. He thereupon obliged him to poison himself by drinking bulls' blood,[1] and he confided the government of the Nile valley to a Persian named Aryandes.[2]

No part of the ancient world now remained unconquered except the semi-fabulous kingdom of Ethiopia in the far-off south. Cities and monarchies, all the great actors of early times, had been laid in the dust one after another—Tyre, Damascus, Carchemish, Urartu, Elam, Assyria, Jerusalem, Media, the Lydians, Babylon, and finally Egypt; and the prey they had fought over so fiercely and for so many centuries, now belonged in its entirety to one master for the first time as far as memory could reach back into the past. Cambyses, following in the footsteps of Cyrus, had pursued his victorious way successfully, but it was another matter to consolidate his conquests and to succeed in governing within the limits of one empire so many incongruous elements—the people of the Caucasus and those of the Nile valley, the Greeks of the Ægean and the Iranians, the Scythians from beyond the Oxus and the Semites of the banks of the Euphrates or of the Mediterranean coast; and time alone would show whether this heritage would not fall to pieces as quickly as it had been built up. The Asiatic elements of the empire appeared, at all events for the moment, content with their lot, and Babylon showed herself more than usually resigned; but Egypt had never accepted the yoke of the stranger willingly, and the most fortunate of her Assyrian conquerors had never exercised more than a passing supremacy over her. Cambyses realised that he would never master her except by governing her himself for a period of several years, and by making himself as Egyptian as a Persian could be without offending his own subjects at home. He adopted the titles of the Pharaohs, their double cartouche, their royal costume, and their solar filiation;[3] as much to satisfy

[1] HERODOTUS, III. xiv., xv.; the Pharaoh, according to the account preserved by Ctesias, was left unharmed, and sent by Cambyses with six thousand of his people to Susa (*Fragm.* 29, § 9, in MÜLLER-DIDOT, *Ctesiæ Cnidii Fragmenta*, p. 47).

[2] HERODOTUS. IV. clxvi.; instead of Aryandes, Ctesias makes Kombarheus, whose treachery betrayed Egypt to Cambyses, the first satrap of Egypt (*Fragm.* 29, § 8, in MÜLLER-DIDOT, *op. cit.*, p. 47).

[3] The titles and cartouches of Cambyses, cut in relief on the inscriptions of Kosseir (BURTON, *Excerpta Hieroglyphica*, pl. vi. 1), and afterwards on the Naophoros statuette of the Vatican (VISCONTI, *Museo Pio-Clementino*, vol. vii. pl. 7 A), were first pointed out by Champollion and Rosellini (*Monumenti Storici*, vol. ii. pp. 153–155, 169).

his own personal animosity as to conciliate the Egyptian priests, he repaired
to Sais, violated the tomb of Amasis, and burnt the mummy after offering it
every insult.[1] He removed his troops from the temple of Nît, which they
had turned into a barrack to the horror of the faithful, and restored at
his own expense the damage they had done to the building.
He condescended so far as to receive instruction in the local
religion, and was initiated in the worship of the goddess by the
priest Uzaharrîsnîti.[2] This was, after all, a pursuance of the
policy employed by his father towards the Babylonians,[3]
and the projects which he had in view necessitated his
gaining the confidence of the people at all costs. Asia
having no more to offer him, two almost untried fields
lay open to his ambition—Africa and Europe—the
Greek world and what lay beyond it, the Carthaginian
world and Ethiopia. The necessity of making a final
reckoning with Egypt had at the outset summoned him
to Africa, and it was therefore in that continent that he
determined to carry on his conquests. Memphis was
necessarily the base of his operations, the only point
from which he could direct the march of his armies in
a westerly or southerly direction, and at the same time
keep in touch with the rest of his empire, and he
would indeed have been imprudent had he neglected anything which could make him acceptable to its inhabitants. As soon as he felt he had
gained their sympathies, he despatched two expe-
ditions, one to Carthage and one to Ethiopia. Cyrene had spontaneously

THE NAOPHOROS STATUETTE OF
THE VATICAN.[4]

---

[1] HERODOTUS, III. xvi., where a second account is given, which declares that Cambyses thus treated
the body, not of Amasis, but of some unknown person whom he took for Amasis. The truth of the
story is generally contested, for the deed would have been, as Herodotus himself remarks, contrary to
Persian ideas about the sanctity of fire. I think that by his cruel treatment of the mummy, Cambyses
wished to satisfy the hatred of the natives against the Greek-loving king, and so render himself more
acceptable to them. The destruction of the mummy entailing that of the soul, his act gave
the Saitic population a satisfaction similar to that experienced by the refined cruelty of those who,
a few centuries ago, killed their enemies when in a state of deadly sin, and so ensure not only
their dismissal from this world, but also their condemnation in the next.

[2] *Inscription of the Naophoros Stele*, ll. 10–22: cf. E. DE ROUGÉ, *Mémoire sur la Statuette Naophore*,
pp. 13–20; BRUGSCH, *Geschichte Ægyptens*, pp. 748–751; RÉVILLOUT, *Premier Extrait de la Chronique
Démotique de Paris*, in the *Revue Égyptologique*, vol. i. pp. 25–30; MARUCCHI, *Iscrizione Geroglifica
della Statuetta Naofora*, pp. 5–11. The priest's name is Uzaharrîsnîti, *the Eye of the Southern Horus*,
or rather, *the Eye of the Horus of the southern half of the temple*, a common name at the time, having as
its parallel Uzaharmihnîti, *the Eye of the Northern Horus*, or *the Eye of the Horus of the northern half
of the temple* (MASPERO, *Catalogue du Musée Égyptien de Marseille*, p. 67, No. 111).

[3] Cf. *supra*, pp. 635, 636.

[4] Drawn by Faucher-Gudin, from a photograph: the head and hands are a restoration of the last
century, in the most inappropriate Græco-Roman style.

offered him her homage; he now further secured it by sending thither with all honour Ladikê, the widow of Amasis,[1] and he apparently contemplated taking advantage of the good will of the Cyrenians to approach Carthage by sea. The combined fleets of Ionia and Phœnicia were without doubt numerically sufficient for this undertaking, but the Tyrians refused to serve against their own colonies, and he did not venture to employ the Greeks alone in waters which were unfamiliar to them.[2] Besides this, the information which he obtained from those about him convinced him that the overland route would enable him to reach his destination more surely if more slowly; it would lead him from the banks of the Nile to the Oases of the Theban desert, from there to the Ammonians, and thence by way of the Libyans bordering on the Syrtes and the Liby-phœnicians. He despatched an advance-guard of fifty thousand men from Thebes to occupy the Oasis of Ammon and to prepare the various halting-places for the bulk of the troops. The fate of these men has never been clearly ascertained. They crossed the Oasis of El-Khargeh and proceeded to the north-west in the direction of the oracle. The natives afterwards related that when they had arrived halfway, a sudden storm of wind fell upon them, and the entire force was buried under mounds of sand during a halt. Cambyses was forced to take their word; in spite of all his endeavours, no further news of his troops was forthcoming, except that they never reached the temple, and that none of the generals or soldiers ever again saw Egypt (524).[3] The expedition to Ethiopia was not more successful. Since the retreat of Tanuatamanu, the Pharaohs of Napata had severed all direct relations with Asia; but on being interfered with by Psammetichus I. and II., they had repulsed the invaders, and had maintained their frontier almost within sight of Philæ.[4] In Nubia proper they had merely a few outposts stationed in the ruins of the towns of the Theban period—at Derr, at Pnubsu, at Wady-Halfa, and at Semneh; the population again becoming dense and the valley fertile to the south of this spot. Kush, like Egypt, was divided into two regions—To-Qonusît, with its cities of Danguru,[5] Napata, Astamuras, and Barua; and Alo,[6] which extended along the White and

[1] HEROD., II. clxxxi.; cf. WIEDEMANN, *Herodots Zw. Buch*, pp. 611, 612, where the fact is doubted.

[2] HERODOTUS, III. xvii., xix.

[3] HERODOTUS, III. xvii., xxv., xxvi.; cf. DIODORUS SICULUS, x. 13; JUSTIN, i. 9, § 3, and compare the account of Alexander's march across the Libyan desert in ARRIAN, *Anabasis*, III. iii.

[4] On the Ethiopian wars of Psammetichus I. and II., cf. *supra*, pp. 504, 537, 538. The northern boundary of Ethiopia is given us approximately by the lists of temples in the inscriptions of Harsiatef and of Nastosenen: Pnubsu is mentioned several times as receiving gifts from the king (MASPERO, *Études de Myth. et d'Arch. Égyp.*, vol. iii. pp. 239, 243, 244), which carries the permanent dominion of the Ethiopian kings as far as the second cataract.

[5] Now Old Dongola; cf. MASPERO, *op. cit.*, vol. iii. pp. 256, 257.

[6] Berua is the Meroê of Strabo, Astaboras the modern Ed-Dameîr, and Alo the kingdom of Aloah of the mediæval Arab geographers (MASPERO, *op. cit.*, vol. iii. pp. 256–258).

the Blue Nile in the plain of Sennaar: the Asmakh, the descendants of the Mashauasha emigrants of the time of Psammetichus I., dwelt on the southern border of Alo.[1] A number of half-savage tribes, Madîti and Rohrehsa, were

settled to the right and to the left of the territory watered by the Nile, between Darfur, the mountains of Abyssinia, and the Red Sea; and the warlike disposition of the Ethiopian kings found in these tribes an inexhaustible field for obtaining easy victories and abundant spoil. Many of these sovereigns— Piônkhi, Alaru, Harsiatef, Nastosenen — whose respective positions in the royal line are still undetermined, specially distinguished themselves in these struggles, but the few monuments they have left, though bearing witness to their military enterprise and ability, betray their utter decadence in everything con-

ETHIOPIAN GROUP.[2]

nected with art, language, and religion.[3] The ancient Egyptian syllabary, adapted to the needs of a barbarous tongue, had ended by losing its elegance; architecture was degenerating, and sculpture slowly growing more and more

---

[1] On these Asmakh, cf. *supra*, pp. 498–500.

[2] Drawn by Boudier, from the photograph taken by BERGHOFF in 1881. M. Berghoff, who told me of the monument and sent me the photograph, was soon afterwards, in 1882, taken prisoner and beheaded by order of the Mahdi. Thanks to Gigler-Pasha, I was able to move the group to the Boulak Museum, and it is now at Gizeh; cf. MASPERO, *Guide du Visiteur*, p. 8, No. 6007, and *Archéologie Égyptienne*, p. 231, fig. 204.

[3] The monuments of these kings hitherto discovered have been translated and partly commented on by MASPERO, *Études de Mythologie et d'Archéologie Égyptiennes*, vol. iii. pp. 232–277; the stele of Nastosenen in the Berlin Museum (LEPSIUS, *Denkm.*, v. 16) has been translated into German by BRUGSCH, *Stele von Dongola*, in the *Zeitschrift*, 1877, pp. 23–27.

clumsy in appearance. Some of the work, however, is not wanting in a certain rude nobility—as, for instance, the god and goddess carved side by side in a block of grey granite. Ethiopian worship had become permeated with strange superstitions, and its creed was degraded, in spite of the strictness with which the priests supervised its application and kept watch against every attempt to introduce innovations. Towards the end of the seventh century some of the families attached to the temple of Amon at Napata had endeavoured to bring about a kind of religious reform; among other innovations they adopted the practice of substituting for the ordinary sacrifice, new rites, the chief feature of which was the offering of the flesh of the victim raw, instead of roasted with fire. This custom, which was doubtless borrowed from the negroes of the Upper Nile, was looked upon as a shameful heresy by the orthodox. The king repaired in state to the temple of Amon, seized the priests who professed these seditious beliefs, and burnt them alive. The use of raw meat, nevertheless, was not discontinued, and it gained such ground in the course of ages that even Christianity was unable to suppress it; up to the present time, the *brindê*, or piece of beef cut from the living animal and eaten raw, is considered a delicacy by the Abyssinians.[1]

The isolation of the Ethiopians had rather increased than lowered their reputation among other nations. Their transitory appearance on the battle-fields of Asia had left a deep impression on the memories of their opponents. The tenacity they had displayed during their conflict with Assyria had effaced the remembrance of their defeat. Popular fancy delighted to extol the wisdom of Sabaco,[2] and exalted Taharqa to the first rank among the conquerors of the old world;[3] now that Kush once more came within the range of vision, it was invested with a share of all these virtues, and the inquiries Cambyses made concerning it were calculated to make him believe that he was about to enter on a struggle with a nation of demigods rather than of men. He was informed that they were taller, more beautiful, and more vigorous[4] than all other mortals, that their age was prolonged to one hundred and twenty years and more, and that they possessed a marvellous fountain whose waters imparted perpetual

---

[1] *Stele of the Excommunication*, discovered and published by MARIETTE, *Monuments Divers*, pl. 10 (cf. *Quatre Pages des Archives officielles de l'Éthiopie*, in the *Revue Archéologique*, 1865, vol. ii. pp. 174, 175), translated with comments by MASPERO, *Études de Mythologie et d'Archéologie Égyptiennes*, vol. iii. pp. 71–79, 229–232. On the use of the *brindê* at the present time, see the curious information given by A. T. DE ROCHEBRUNE, *Toxicologie Africaine*, vol. i. pp. 703–710.

[2] On this subject, cf. *supra*, pp. 277, 278. The eulogy bestowed on him by Herodotus (II. cxxxvii., cxxxix.) shows the esteem in which he was held even in the Saite period (cf. DIODORUS SICULUS, i. 65); later on he seems to have become two persons, and so to have given birth to the good Ethiopian king Aktisanes (DIODORUS SICULUS, i. 60).

[3] STRABO, I. iii. § 21, p. 61, following authors of the flourishing Alexandrine period; cf. *supra*, pp. 362–364.

[4] HERODOTUS, III. xx. This exaggerated opinion was subsequently much modified, and Strabo (*e.g.*) says that the Ethiopians were small of stature.

youth to their bodies.[1]   There existed near their capital a meadow, perpetually furnishing an inexhaustible supply of food and drink ; whoever would might partake of this " Table of the Sun," and eat to his fill.[2]   Gold was so abundant that it was used for common purposes, even for the chains of their prisoners ; but, on the other hand, copper was rare and much prized.[3]   Cambyses despatched some spies chosen from among the Ichthyophagi of the Red Sea to explore this region,[4] and acting on the report they brought back, he left Memphis at the head of an army and a fleet.[5]   The expedition was partly a success and partly a failure.   It followed the Nile valley as far as Korosko, and then struck across the desert in the direction of Napata ; [6] but provisions ran short before a quarter of the march had been achieved, and famine obliged the invaders to retrace their steps after having endured terrible sufferings.[7]   Cambyses

[1] HERODOTUS, III. xxiii.

[2] HERODOTUS, III. xvii., xviii., xxiii. ; cf. POMPONIUS MELA, *De Situ Orbi*, iii. 15 ; SOLINUS, *Polyhist.*, xxx., who accept it as a fact, while Pausanias treats it as a traveller's tale.   Heeren thought that he saw in Herodotus' account a reference to intercourse by signs, so frequent in Africa.   The "Table of the Sun" would thus have been a kind of market, whither the natives would come for their provisions, using exchange to procure them.   I am inclined rather to believe the story to be a recollection, partly of the actual custom of placing meats, which the first comer might take, on the tombs in the necropolis, partly of the mythical "Meadow of Offerings" mentioned in the funerary texts, to which the souls of the dead and the gods alike had access.   This divine region would have transferred to our earth by some folk-tale, like the judgment of the dead, the entrance into the solar bark, and other similar beliefs.

[3] HERODOTUS, III. xxiii.

[4] HERODOTUS, III. xix.–xxv., where is set forth all the information traditionally said to have been acquired by the Ichthyophagi when on their expedition.

[5] Herodotus' text speaks of an army only (III. xxv.), but the accounts of the wars between Ethiopia and Egypt (cf., *e.g.*, the campaign of Piônkhi, *supra*, pp. 172–179) show that the army was always accompanied by the necessary fleet.

[6] It is usually thought that the expedition marched by the side of the Nile as far as Napata ; to support this theory the name of a place mentioned in PLINY (*H. Nat.*, vi. 29) is quoted, Cambusis or Καμβύσου ταμεῖα (PTOLEMY, iv. 7), " the stores of Cambyses," at the third cataract, which is supposed to contain the name of the conqueror (DUNCKER, *Geschichte des Alterthums*, 4th edit., vol. iv. pp. 411–415 ; KRALL, *Studien zur Geschichte des Alten Ægyptens, IV., Das Land Punt*, pp. 58–63 ; PRASHEK, *Forschungen zur Geschichte des Alterthums*, vol. i. pp. 67–70).   This town, which is sometimes mentioned by the classical geographers, is called Kambîusît in the Ethiopic texts (BRUGSCH, *Die Biblischen sieben Jahre der Hungersnoth*, p. 54), and the form of the name makes its connection with the history of Cambyses easy.   I think it follows from the text of Herodotus, οἱ δὲ στρατιῶται ἕως μέν τι εἶχον ἐκ τῆς γέας λαμβάνειν, ποιηφαγέοντες διέζωον, ἐπεὶ δὲ ἐς τὴν ψάμμον ἀπίκοντο, δεινὸν ἔργον αὐτῶν τινὲς ἐργάσαντο, that the Persians left the grassy land, the river-valley, at a given moment, to enter the sand, *i.e.* the desert.   Now this is done to-day at two points—near Korosko to rejoin the Nile at Abu-Hammed, and near Wady-Halfah to avoid the part of the Nile called the "Stony belly," Batn el-Hagar.   The Korosko route, being the only one suitable for the transit of a body of troops, and also the only route known to Herodotus (II. xxix.), seems, I think, likely to be the one which was followed in the present instance (RAWLINSON, *Herodotus*, vol. ii. p. 351, note 4 ; JUSTI, *Geschichte des Alten Persiens*, p. 49) : at all events, it fits in best with the fact that Cambyses was obliged to retrace his steps hurriedly, when he had accomplished hardly a fifth of the journey.

[7] HERODOTUS, III. xxv.   Many modern historians are inclined to assume that Cambyses' expedition was completely successful, and that its result was the overthrow of the ancient kingdom of Nepata and the foundation of that of Meroê (GUTSCHMID, *Neue Beiträge zur Geschichte des Alten Orient*, p. 68 ; DUNCKER, *Geschichte des Alterthums*, 4th edit., vol. iv. p. 413 ; ED. MEYER, *Geschichte des Alterthums*, vol. i. p. 611 ; JUSTI, *Geschichte des Alten Persiens*, p. 49 ; SAYCE, *The Ancient Empires of the East*, p. 241, note 1 ; KRALL, *Das Land Punt*, pp. 58–63 ; WIEDEMANN, *Ægyptische Geschichte*, pp. 670, 671 ; PRASHEK, *Forschungen zur Geschichte des Alterthums*, pp. 68–70) : Cambyses would have given the new town which he built there the name of his sister Meroê (DIODORUS SICULUS, i. 33 ; STRABO,

had to rest content with the acquisition of those portions of Nubia adjoining the first cataract—the same, in fact, that had been annexed to Egypt by Psammetichus I. and II. (523).[1] The failure of this expedition to the south, following so closely on the disaster which befell that of the west, had a deplorable effect on the mind of Cambyses. He had been subject, from childhood, to attacks of epilepsy, during which he became a maniac and had no control over his actions. These reverses of fortune aggravated the disease, and increased the frequency and length of the attacks.[2] The bull Apis had died shortly before the close of the Ethiopian campaign, and the Egyptians, after mourning for him during the prescribed number of weeks, were bringing his successor with rejoicings into the temple of Phtah, when the remains of the army re-entered Memphis. Cambyses, finding the city holiday-making, imagined that it was rejoicing over his misfortunes. He summoned the magistrates before him, and gave them over to the executioner without deigning to listen to their explanations. He next caused the priests to be brought to him, and when they had paraded the Apis before him, he plunged his dagger into its flank with derisive laughter : " Ah, evil people ! So you make for yourselves divinities of flesh and blood which fear the sword ! It is indeed a fine god that you Egyptians have here ; I will have you to know, however, that you shall not rejoice overmuch at having deceived me ! " The priests were beaten as impostors, and the bull languished from its wound and died in a few days ;[3] its priests buried it, and chose another in its place without the usual ceremonies, so as not to exasperate the anger of the tyrant,[4] but the horror evoked by this

XVII. i. § 5, p. 790 ; JOSEPHUS, *Ant. Jud.*, ii. 10, § 2, all three following Artemidorus of Ephesus). The traditions concerning Cambusis (cf. note 6 on the previous page) and Meroê belong to the Alexandrine era, and rest only on chance similarities of sound. With regard to the Ethiopian province of the Persian empire and to the Ethiopian neighbours of Egypt whom Cambyses subdued (HERODOTUS, III. xcvii.), the latter are not necessarily Ethiopians of Napata. Herodotus himself says that the Ethiopians dwelt in the country above Elephantinê, οἰκέουσι δὲ τὰ ἀπὸ 'Ελεφαντίνης ἄνω Αἰθίοπες ἤδη, and that half of what he calls the island of Takhompsô was inhabited by Ethiopians (II. xxix.) : the subjugated Ethiopians and their country plainly correspond with the Dodekaschênos of the Græco-Roman era.

[1] HERODOTUS, III. xcvii. ; on the reunion of this part of Nubia with Egypt effected by Psammetichus II., cf. *supra*, pp. 537, 538.

[2] HERODOTUS, III. xxxiii. Recent historians (HUTECKER, *Ueber den falschen Smerdis*, p. 16, et seq., 30, et seq. ; PRASHEK, *Forschungen zur Geschichte des Alterthums*, pp. 8–10) admit neither the reality of the illness of Cambyses nor the madness resulting from it, but consider them Egyptian fables, invented out of spite towards the king who had conquered and persecuted them.

[3] HERODOTUS, III. xxvii.–xxix. ; later historians improved upon the account of Herodotus, and it is said in the *De Iside*, § 44, that Cambyses killed the Apis and threw him to the dogs. Here there is probably a confusion between the conduct of Cambyses and that attributed to the eunuch Bagoas nearly two centuries later, at the time of the second conquest of Egypt by Ochus.

[4] Mariette discovered in the Serapæum and sent to the Louvre fragments of the epitaph of an Apis buried in Epiphi in the sixth year of Cambyses, which had therefore died a few months previously. This fact contradicts the inference from the epitaph of the Apis that died in the fourth year of Darius (§ 2274), which would have been born in the fifth year of Cambyses, if we allow that there could not have been two Apises in Egypt at once (WIEDEMANN, *Geschichte Ægyptens*, pp. 227–231). This was, indeed, the usual rule, but a comparison of the two dates shows that here it was not followed, and it is therefore simplest, until we have further evidence, to conclude that at all events in

double sacrilege raised passions against Cambyses which the ruin of the country had failed to excite. The manifestation of this antipathy irritated him to such an extent that he completely changed his policy, and set himself from that time forward to act counter to the customs and prejudices of the Egyptians. They consequently regarded his memory with a vindictive hatred. The people related that the gods had struck him with madness to avenge the murder of the Apis, and they attributed to him numberless traits of senseless cruelty,[1] in which we can scarcely distinguish truth from fiction. It was said that, having entered the temple of Phtah, he had ridiculed the grotesque figure under which the god was represented, and had commanded the statues to be burnt. On another occasion he had ordered the ancient sepulchres to be opened, that he might see what was the appearance of the mummies.[2] The most faithful members of his family and household, it was said, did not escape his fury. He killed his own sister Roxana, whom he had married, by a kick in the abdomen;[3] he slew the son of Prexaspes with an arrow;[4] he buried alive twelve influential Persians;[5] he condemned Crœsus to death, and then repented, but punished the officers who had failed to execute the sentence pronounced against the Lydian king.[6] He had no longer any reason for remaining in Egypt, since he had failed in his undertakings; yet he did not quit the country, and through repeated delays his departure was retarded a whole year. Meanwhile his long sojourn in Africa, the report of his failures, and perhaps whispers of his insanity, had sown the seeds of discontent in Asia; and as Darius said in after-years, when recounting these events, "untruth had spread all over the country, not only in Persia and Media, but in other provinces."[7] Cambyses himself felt that a longer absence would be injurious to his interests; he therefore crossed the isthmus in the spring of 521, and was making his way through Northern Syria, perhaps in the neighbourhood of Hamath,[8] when he learned that a revolution had broken out, and that its rapid progress threatened the safety of his throne and life. Tradition asserted that a herald

cases of violence, such as sacrilegious murder, there could have been two Apises at once, one discharging his functions, and the other unknown, living still in the midst of the herds.

[1] HERODOTUS, III. xxx.

[2] HERODOTUS, III. xxxvii. Pompeius Trogus added, on the evidence of some unknown historian, that he had the temple of Apis and those of other gods destroyed (JUSTIN, i. 9).

[3] HERODOTUS, III. xxxi., xxxii. On this woman's name, cf. *supra*, p. 655, note 3.

[4] HERODOTUS, III. xxxiv., xxxv. [5] HERODOTUS, III. xxxv.

[6] HERODOTUS, III. xxxvi. The whole of this story of Crœsus is entirely fabulous; on the real fate of that prince, cf. *supra*, pp. 617–620.

[7] *Inscription of Behistun*, col. i. ll. 32–35; cf. WEISSBACH and BANG, *Die Altpers. Keilins.*, pp. 14, 15.

[8] HERODOTUS, III. lxiv., calls the place where Cambyses died Agbatana (Ecbatana). Pliny says that the town of Carmel was thus named at first (*H. Nat.*, v. 19); but the place here mentioned cannot well have been in that direction. It has been identified with Batanæa in the country between the Orontes and the Euphrates (HYDE, *Religio Veterum Persarum*, p. 426), but the most likely theory is the one suggested by a passage in STEPHEN OF BYZANTIUM, *s.v.* Ἀμαθα, that the place in question is the large Syrian city of Hamath. Josephus (*Ant. Jud.*, xi. 2, § 2) makes him die at Damascus.

appeared before him and proclaimed aloud, in the hearing of the whole army, that Cambyses, son of Cyrus, had ceased to reign, and summoned whoever had till that day obeyed him to acknowledge henceforth Smerdis, son of Cyrus, as their lord. Cambyses at first believed that his brother had been spared by the assassins, and now, after years of concealment, had at length declared himself; but he soon received proofs that his orders had been faithfully accomplished, and it is said that he wept at the remembrance of the fruitless crime.[1] The usurper was Gaumâta, one of the Persian Magi, whose resemblance to Smerdis was so remarkable that even those who were cognisant of it invariably mistook the one for the other,[2] and he was brother to that Oropastes to whom Cambyses had entrusted the administration of his household before setting out for Egypt.[3] Both of them were aware of the fate of Smerdis; they also knew that the Persians were ignorant of it, and that every one at court, including the mother and sisters of the prince, believed that he was still alive.[4] Gaumâta headed a revolt in the little town of Pasyauvadâ on the 14th of Viyakhna, in the early days of March, 521, and he was hailed by the common people from the moment of his appearance. Persia, Media, and the Iranian provinces pronounced in his favour, and solemnly enthroned him three months later, on the 9th of Garma-pada;[5] Babylon next accepted him, followed by Elam and the regions of the Tigris.[6] Though astounded at first by such a widespread defection, Cambyses soon recovered his presence of mind, and was about to march forward at the head of the troops who were still loyal to him, when he mysteriously dis-appeared. Whether he was the victim of a plot set on foot by those about him,

[1] HERODOTUS, III. lxii., lxiii.

[2] Greek tradition is unanimous on this point, but the inscription of Behistun does not mention it; cf. HUTECKER, *Ueber den Falschen Smerdis*, pp. 40–42.

[3] Cf. on Oropastes, *supra*, p. 659, note 2. The inscription of Behistun informs us that the usurper's name was Gaumâta (col. i. l. 36; cf. WEISSBACH and BANG, *Die Altpersischen Keilinschriften*, pp. 14, 15); Pompeius Trogus alone, probably following some author who made use of Charon of Lampsacus (GUTSCHMID, *Kleine Schriften*, vol. v. p. 59), handed down this name in the form Cometes or Gometes, which his abbreviator Justin (i. 9) carelessly applied to the second brother. Ctesias gives the Mage the name Sphendadates (*Fragm.* 27, § 10, in MÜLLER-DIDOT, *Ctesiæ Cnidii Fragm.*, p. 47), which answers to the Old Persian Spentôdâta, "he who is given by the Holy One," *i.e.* by Ahura-mazdâ (JUSTI, *Iranisches Namenbuch*, pp. 308, 309). The supporters of the Mage gave him this name, as an heroic champion of the Mazdæan faith who had destroyed such sanctuaries as were illegal (cf. *infra*, p. 672), and identified him with Spentôdâta, son of Wistâspa (MARQUART, *Fundamente Israelitischer und Jüdischer Geschichte*, p. 48, note 3).

[4] HERODOTUS, III. lxi.

[5] *Inscription of Behistun*, col. i. ll. 35–43; cf. WEISSBACH and BANG, *Die Altpersischen Keilinschriften*, pp. 14, 15. On the identification of the Persian and Babylonian dates and those of the modern calender, see OPPERT, *Les Inscriptions du Pseudo-Smerdis et de l'usurpateur Nadintabel fixant le Calendrier perse*, in the *Acts of the Stockholm Congress*, vol. ii. pp. 254, 255.

[6] The tablets of the reign of Bardîya-Gaumâta, published by Fr. Strassmaier (*Inschriften von Nabopolassar und Smerdis*, in the *Zeitschrift für Assyriologie*, vol. iv. pp. 123–128), show that the usurper was recognised at Babylon from the month of Iyyâr onwards (OPPERT, *Les Inscriptions du l'seudo-Smerdis*, in the *Acts of the Stockholm Congress*, vol. ii. p. 257, and PRASHEK, *Forschungen zur Geschichte des Alterthums*, vol. i. pp. 22, 23; MARQUART, *Die Assyriaka des Ktesias*, in the *Philologus*, Suppl., vol. v. pp. 621, 622).

is not known.[1] The official version of the story given by Darius states that he died by his own hand, and it seems to insinuate that it was a voluntary act,[2] but another account affirms that he succumbed to an accident;[3] while mounting his horse, the point of his dagger pierced his thigh in the same spot in which he had stabbed the Apis of the Egyptians. Feeling himself seriously wounded, he suddenly asked the name of the place where he was lying, and was told it was "Agbatana" (Ecbatana). "Now, long before this, the oracle of Buto had predicted that he should end his days in Agbatana, and he, believing it to be the Agbatana in Media where were his treasures, understood that he should die there in his old age; whereas the oracle meant Agbatana in Syria. When he heard the name, he perceived his error. He understood what the god intended, and cried, ' It is here, then, that Cambyses, son of Cyrus, must perish !' " He expired about three weeks after, leaving no posterity and having appointed no successor.[4]

What took place in the ensuing months still remains an enigma to us. The episode of Gaumâta has often been looked on as a national movement, which momentarily restored to the Medes the supremacy of which Cyrus had robbed them; but it was nothing of the sort. Gaumâta was not a Mede by birth : he was a Persian, born in Persia, in the township of Pisyauvadâ, at the foot of Mount Arakadrish, and the Persians recognised and supported him as much as did the Medes. It has also been thought that he had attempted to foment a religious revolution,[5] and, as a matter of fact, he destroyed several

[1] That this was the case is believed by one of the latest of his historians (LINCKE, *Zur Lösung der Kambyses Frage*, pp. 5, 6, 14–24). He bases his opinion on two passages, one in Orosus (*Hist. adversus Paganos*, ii. 8, 2–4) and one in John of Antioch (*Fragm. 27*, in MÜLLER-DIDOT, *Fragm. Hist. Græc.*, vol. iv. p. 552), which he traces back to a Greek historian of the fifth century B.C., mediately through Apollodorus and Suetonius.

[2] *Inscription of Behistun*, col. i. l. 43; cf. WEISSBACH and BANG, *Die Altpersischen Keilinschriften*, pp. 14, 15. The passage is interpreted by Oppert as signifying a suicide (*Mémoire sur les Inscriptions Achéménides*, in the *Journal Asiatique*, 1851, vol. xvii. pp. 385, 386, and *Le Peuple et la Langue des Mèdes*, pp. 117, 165); also by BEZOLD, *Die Achämenideninschriften*, p. 5, and by SPIEGEL, *Die Altpersischen Keilinschriften*, p. 5; and in the same sense by most historians : DUNCKER, *Geschichte des Alterthums*, 4th edit., vol. iv. p. 442; JUSTI, *Geschichte des Alten Persiens*, p. 50; NÖLDEKE, *Aufsätze zur Persischen Geschichte*, p. 29; HUTECKER, *Ueber den falschen Smerdis*, pp. 49, 50; MARQUART, *Die Assyriaka des Ktesias*, in the *Philologus*, Supplement, vol. v. p. 622, note 422. Marquart thinks that the news of the revolt of the Babylonians was the cause of his suicide.

[3] HERODOTUS, III. lxiv. It has been pointed out, for the purpose of harmonising the testimony of the historian with that of the inscription of Behistun, that although the latter speaks of the death of Cambyses by his own hand, it does not say whether that death was voluntary or accidental (SPIEGEL, *Erânische Alterthumskunde*, vol. ii. p. 302, note 1; ED. MEYER, *Geschichte des Alterthums*, vol. i. p. 612; PRASHEK, *Forschungen zur Geschichte des Alterthums*, vol. i. pp. 78, 79).

[4] HERODOTUS, III. lxiv., whose account was reproduced in an abbreviated form by Pompeius Trogus (JUSTIN, i. 9). The story of a person whose death has been predicted to take place in some well-known place, and who has died in some obscure spot of the same name, occurs several times in different historians, *e.g.* in the account of the Emperor Julian (AMMIANUS MARCELLINUS, xxxv. 3), and in that of Henry III. of England, who had been told that he would die in Jerusalem, and whose death took place in the Jerusalem Chamber at Westminster. Ctesias has preserved an altogether different tradition—that Cambyses on his return from Babylon wounded himself while carving a piece of wood for his amusement, and died eleven days after the accident (*Fragm. 27*, § 11, in MÜLLER-DIDOT, *Ctesiæ Cnidii Fragmenta*, p. 48).

[5] Most of the ancient writers shared this opinion (HERODOTUS, III. lxi. lxxix.; PLATO, *Laws*, iii.,

temples in a few months.[1] Here, however, the reform touched less upon a question of belief than on one of fact. The unity of the empire presupposed the unity of the royal fire, and wherever that fire was burning another could not be lighted without sacrilege in the eyes of the faithful. The pyres that Gaumâta desired to extinguish were, no doubt, those which the feudal families had maintained for their separate use in defiance of the law, and the measure which abolished them had a political as well as a religious side.[2] The little we can glean of the line of action adopted by Smerdis does not warrant the attribution to him of the vast projects which some modern writers credit him with. He naturally sought to strengthen himself on the throne, which by a stroke of good fortune he had ascended, and whatever he did tended solely to this end. The name and the character that he had assumed secured him the respect and fidelity of the Iranians: "there was not one, either among the Medes or the Persians, nor among the members of the Achæmenian race, who dreamed of disputing his power" in the early days of his reign. The important thing in his eyes was, therefore, to maintain among his subjects as long as possible the error as to his identity. He put to death all, whether small or great, who had been in any way implicated in the affairs of the real Smerdis, or whom he suspected of any knowledge of the murder.[3] He withdrew from public life as far as practicable, and rarely allowed himself to be seen. Having inherited the harem of his predecessors, together with their crown, he even went so far as to condemn his wives to a complete seclusion.[4] He did not venture to hope, nor did those in his confidence, that the truth would not one day be known, but he hoped to gain, without loss of time, sufficient popularity to prevent the revelation of the imposture from damaging his prospects. The seven great houses which he had dispossessed would, in such a case, refuse to rally round him, and it was doubtless to lessen their prestige that he extinguished their pyres; but the people did not trouble themselves as to the origin of their sovereign, if he showed them his favour and took proper precautions to secure their good will. He therefore exempted the provinces from taxes and

---

ed. DIDOT, pp. 694, 695), and have been followed therein by many modern writers (NIEBUHR, *Vorträge*, vol. i. pp. 157, 399; GROTE, *History of Greece*, vol. iv. pp. 301, 302; SPIEGEL, *Erânische Alterthumskunde*, vol. ii. p. 310). Rawlinson was the first to show that Gaumâta's movement was not Median, and that he did not in the least alter the position of the Persians in the empire: but he allows the Magian usurpation to have been the prelude to a sort of religious reform (*On the Magian Revolution and the Reign of the Pseudo-Smerdis*, in the *Herodotus*, vol. iii. pp. 454–459).

[1] *Inscription of Behistun*, col. i. ll. 63, 64; cf. WEISSBACH and BANG, *Die Altpersischen Keilinschriften*, pp. 14, 15.

[2] The discovery of a similar event in the life of Ardashîr, the founder of the Sassanid dynasty (J. DARMESTETER, *Lettre de Tansar au roi de Tabaristân*, in the *Journal Asiatique*, 1894, vol. iii. pp. 530, 531), has enabled us to understand the passage of the Inscription of Behistun cited in the preceding note, and to explain it as I have done in the text (J. MARQUART, *Fundamente Israelitischer und Jüdischer Geschiche*, p. 48, note 3).

[3] *Inscription of Behistun*, col. i. ll. 43–53; WEISSBACH and BANG, *Die Altpers. Keilins.*, pp. 14, 15.

[4] HERODOTUS, III. lxviii.

military service for a period of three years.[1] He had not time to pursue this policy, and if we may believe tradition, the very precautions which he took to conceal his identity became the cause of his misfortunes. In the royal harem there were, together with the daughters of Cyrus, relatives of all the Persian nobility, and the order issued to stop all their communications with the outer world had excited suspicion : the avowals which had escaped Cambyses before the catastrophe were now called to mind, and it was not long before those in high places became convinced that they had been the dupes of an audacious imposture.[2]

A conspiracy broke out, under the leadership of the chiefs of the seven clans, among whom was numbered Darius, the son of Hystaspes, who was connected, according to a genealogy more or less authentic, with the family of the Achæmenides:[3] the conspirators surprised Gaumâta in his palace of Sikayauvatish, which was situated in the district of Nisaya, not far from Ecbatana, and assassinated him on the 10th of Bâgayâdîsh, 521 B.C.[4] The exact particulars of this scene were never known, but popular imagination soon supplied the defect, furnishing a full and complete account of all that took place. In the first place, Phædimê, daughter of Otanes, one of the seven, furnished an authentic

DARIUS, SON OF HYSTASPES.[5]

proof of the fraud which had been perpetrated. Her father had opportunely recalled the marvellous resemblance between Smerdis and the Magian, and remembered at the same time that the latter had been deprived of his ears in punishment for some misdeed : he therefore sent certain instructions to Phædimê, who, when she made the discovery, at the peril of her life, that her husband had no ears, communicated the information to the disaffected nobles. The conspirators thereupon resolved to act without delay ; but when they arrived at the palace, they were greeted with an extraordinary piece of intelligence. The Magi, disquieted by some vague rumours which were being circulated against them, had besought Prexaspes to proclaim to the people that the reigning monarch was indeed Smerdis himself. But Prexaspes, instead of making the desired

[1] HERODOTUS, III. lxvii., whose words Pompeius Trogus reproduced almost literally (JUSTIN, i. 9).

[2] HERODOTUS, III. lxviii., et seq., where Otanes plays the chief part.

[3] The passage in the Behistun inscription (col. i. ll. 1–11 ; cf. WEISSBACH and BANG, *Die Altpersischen Keilinschriften*, pp. 12, 13), in which Darius sets forth his own genealogy, has received various interpretations. That of Oppert seems still the most probable, that the text indicates two parallel branches of Achæmenides, which flourished side by side until Cambyses died and Darius ascended the throne. Such a genealogy, however, appears to be fictitious, invented solely for the purpose of connecting Darius with the ancient royal line, with which in reality he could claim no kinship, or only a very distant connection (WINCKLER, *Untersuchungen zur Altorient. Gesch.*, pp. 126–128).

[4] *Behistun Inscription*, col. i. ll. 53–61 ; cf. WEISSBACH and BANG, *op. cit.*, pp. 14, 15.

[5] Drawn by Faucher-Gudin, from M. DIEULAFOY, *L'Acropole de Suse*, p. 306, fig. 185.

declaration, informed the multitude that the son of Cyrus was indeed dead, for he himself had murdered him at the bidding of Cambyses, and, having made this confession, he put himself to death, in order to escape the vengeance of the Magi. This act of Prexaspes was an additional inducement to the conspirators to execute their purpose. The guard stationed at the gates of the palace dared not refuse admission to so noble a company, and when the throne-room was reached and the eunuchs forbade further advance, the seven boldly drew their swords and forced their way to the apartment occupied by the two Magi. The usurpers defended themselves with bravery, but succumbed at length to the superior number of their opponents, after having wounded two of the conspirators. Gobryas pinioned Gaumâta with his arms, and in such a way that Darius hesitated to make the fatal thrust for fear of wounding his comrade; but the latter bade him strike at all hazards, and by good fortune the sword did not even graze him. The crime accomplished, the seven conspirators agreed to choose as king that member of their company whose horse should first neigh after sunrise : a stratagem of his groom caused the election to fall on Darius. As soon as he was duly enthroned, he instituted a festival called the "magophonia," or "massacre of the Magi," in commemoration of the murder which had given him the crown.[1]

His first care was to recompense the nobles to whom he owed his position by restoring to them the privileges of which they had been deprived by the pseudo-Smerdis, namely, the right of free access to the king,[2] as well as the right of each individual to a funeral pyre;[3] but the usurper had won the affection of the people, and even the inhabitants of those countries which had been longest subject to the Persian sway did not receive the new sovereign favourably. Darius found himself, therefore, under the necessity of conquering his dominions one after the other.[4] The Persian empire, like those of the Chal-

---

[1] HERODOTUS, III. lxviii.–lxxxvii., whose account has been reproduced with some slight modifications by Pompeius Trogus (JUSTIN, i. 9,10; cf. GUTSCHMID, *Kleine Schriften*, vol. v. pp. 59–63). Ctesias gives a version (*Fragm.* 29, § 14, in MÜLLER-DIDOT, *Ctesiæ Cnidii Fragmenta*, pp. 48, 49) in which some of the names of the conspirators differ from those given by Herodotus. In at least three instances Ctesias gives the name of the son where Herodotus mentions the father (DUNCKER, *Geschichte des Alterthums*, 4th edit., vol. iv. p. 250, note 1), while the list of the Behistun inscription (col. iv. ll. 80–86) coincides with that of Herodotus, with one exception.

[2] HERODOTUS, III. cxviii.

[3] *Behistun Inscription*, col. i. ll. 61–71 ; cf.WEISSBACH and BANG, *Die Altpersischen Keilins.*,pp.14,15.

[4] The history of the early part of the reign of Darius is recorded in the great inscription which the king caused to be cut in three languages on the rocks of Behistun (cf. what is stated on this subject, *infra*, p. 682). This inscription was first edited and translated into English by H. RAWLINSON in the *J. R. As. Soc.*, vol. x. (cf. the latest English translation which he has published of this text under the title, *Inscription of Darius on the Rock at Behistun*, in the *Records of the Past*, 1st ser., vol. i. pp. 107–130); then into French by OPPERT, *Mémoire sur les Inscriptions achéménides conçues dans l'idiome des Anciens Perses*, in the *Journal Asiatique*, vol. xvii., 1851, pp. 256–296, 378–430, 524–567 ; vol. xviii. pp. 56–83, 322–366, 553–584 ; vol. xix., 1852, pp. 140–215 ; then into German by SPIEGEL, *Die Altpers. Keilins.*, and by WEISSBACH and BANG, *op. cit.*, pp. 12–33. The Babylonian version has been studied and translated separately by C. BEZOLD, *Die Akhemeniden-Inschriften,* and the third version by NORRIS, *Scythic Version of the Behistun Inscrip.* in *J. R. As. Soc.*, 1853, vol. xv., by OPPERT, *Le Peuple*

dæans and Medes, had consisted hitherto of nothing but a fortuitous collection of provinces under military rule, of vassal kingdoms, and of semi-independent cities and tribes; there was no fixed division of authority, and no regular system of government for the outlying provinces. The governors assigned by Cyrus and Cambyses to rule the various provinces acquired by conquest, were actual viceroys, possessing full control of an army, and in some cases of a fleet as well, having at their disposal considerable revenues both in money and in kind, and habituated, owing to their distance from the capital, to settle pressing questions on their own responsibility, subject only to the necessity of making a report to the sovereign when the affair was concluded, or when the local resources were insufficient to bring it to a successful issue. For such free administrators the temptation must have been irresistible to break the last slender ties which bound them to the empire, and to set themselves up as independent monarchs. The two successive revolutions which had taken place in less than a year, convinced such governors, and the nations over which they bore rule, that the stately edifice erected by Cyrus and Cambyses was crumbling to pieces, and that the moment was propitious for each of them to carve out of its ruins a kingdom for himself; the news of the murder, rapidly propagated, sowed the seeds of revolt in its course—in Susiana, at Babylon, in Media, in Parthia, in Margiana, among the Sattagydes, in Asia Minor, and even in Egypt itself[1]—which showed itself in some places in an open and undisguised form, while in others it was contemptuously veiled under the appearance of neutrality, or the pretence of waiting to see the issue of events. The first to break out into open rebellion were the neighbouring countries of Elam and Chaldæa: the death of Smerdis took place towards the end of September, and a fortnight later saw two rebel chiefs enthroned—a certain Athrîna at Susa, and a Nadinta-bel at Babylon.[2] Athrîna, the son of Umbadaranma, was a scion of the dynasty dispossessed by the successors of Sargon in the preceding century, but nevertheless he met with but lukewarm assistance from his own countrymen;[3] he was taken prisoner before a

et la Langue des Mèdes, pp. 112–214, and by WEISSBACH and BANG, *Die Achämenideninschriften zweiter Art.* The order of the events recorded in it is not always easy to determine. I have finally adopted, with some modifications, the arrangement of Marquart (*Die Assyr. des Ktesias*, in the *Philologus*, Suppl., vol. v. pp. 633–636), which seems to me to give the clearest "conspectus" of these confused wars.

[1] *Behistun Inscription*, col. ii. ll. 5–8; cf. WEISSBACH and BANG, *Die Altpers. Keilins.*, pp. 16, 17, where it is stated that insurrections broke out in all these countries while Darius was at Babylon; that is to say, while he was occupied in besieging that city, as is evident from the order of the events narrated.

[2] The latest known document of the pseudo-Smerdis is dated the 1st of Tisri at Babylon, and the first of Nebuchadrezzar III. are dated the 17th and 20th of the same month (BOSCAWEN, *Babylonian dated Tablets and the Canon of Ptolemy*, in the *Transactions* of the Bibl. Arch. Soc., vol. vi. pp. 31, 67, 68; OPPERT, *Les Inscriptions du Pseudo-Smerdis et de l'usurpateur Nadintabel*, in the *Actes du Congrès de Stockholm*, vol. ii. p. 255). The revolt of Babylon, then, must be placed between the 1st and 17th of Tisri; that is, either at the end of September or the beginning of October, 521 B.C.

[3] *Behistun Inscription*, col. i. ll. 72–77, 81–83; cf. WEISSBACH and BANG, *op. cit.*, pp. 14–17. The revolt cannot have lasted much more than six weeks, for on the 26th of Athriyâdiya following, that is

month had passed, and sent to Darius, who slew him with his own hand. Babylon was not so easily mastered. Her chosen sovereign claimed to be the son of Nabonidus, and had, on ascending the throne, assumed the illustrious name of Nebuchadrezzar; he was not supported, moreover, by only a few busybodies, but carried the whole population with him. The Babylonians, who had at first welcomed Cyrus so warmly, and had fondly imagined that they had made him one of themselves, as they had made so many of their conquerors for centuries past, soon realised their mistake. The differences of language, manners, spirit, and religion between themselves and the Persians were too fundamental to allow of the naturalisation of the new sovereign, and of the acceptance by the Achæmenides of that fiction of a double personality to which Tiglath-pileser III., Shalmaneser, and even Assur-bani-pal had submitted.[1] Popular fancy grew weary of Cyrus, as it had already grown weary in turn of all the foreigners it had at first acclaimed—whether Elamite, Kaldâ, or Assyrian— and by a national reaction the self-styled son of Nabonidus enjoyed the benefit of a devotion proportionately as great as the hatred which had been felt twenty years before for his pretended sire. The situation might become serious if he were given time to consolidate his power, for the loyalty of the ancient provinces of the Chaldæan empire was wavering, and there was no security that they would not feel inclined to follow the example of the capital as soon as they should receive news of the sedition. Darius, therefore, led the bulk of his forces to Babylon without a day's more delay than was absolutely necessary, and the event proved that he had good reason for such haste. Nebuchadrezzar III. had taken advantage of the few weeks which had elapsed since his accession, to garrison the same positions on the right bank of the Tigris, as Nabonidus had endeavoured to defend against Cyrus at the northern end of the fortifications erected by his ancestor. A well-equipped flotilla patrolled the river, and his lines presented so formidable a front that Darius could not venture on a direct attack. He arranged his troops in two divisions, which he mounted partly on horses, partly on camels, and eluding the vigilance of his adversary by attacking him simultaneously on many sides, succeeded in gaining the opposite bank of the river. The Chaldæans, striving in vain to drive him back into the stream, were at length defeated on the 27th of Athriyâdiya, and they retired in good order on Babylon. Six days later, on the 2nd of Anâmaka, they fought a second battle at Zazanu, on the bank of the Euphrates, and were again totally defeated. Nebuchadrezzar escaped with a handful of cavalry, and hastened to shut himself up in his city. Darius soon followed him, but if he cherished a hope that the Babylonians would open their gates to him without further resistance, as

to say, at the beginning of December, Darius had already joined issue with the Babylonians on the banks of the Tigris (col. i. ll. 89, 90).

[1] Cf. what is stated on this subject, *supra*, pp. 192, 193, 196–199, 209, 423, 424.

they had done to Cyrus, he met with a disappointment, for he was compelled to commence a regular siege and suspend all other operations, and that, too, at a moment when the provinces were breaking out into open insurrection on every hand.[1] The attempt of the Persian adventurer Martîya to stir up the Susians to revolt in his rear failed, thanks to the favourable disposition of the natives, who refused to recognise in him Ummanîsh, the heir of their national princes.[2] Media, however, yielded unfortunately to the solicitations of a

DARIUS PIERCING A REBEL WITH HIS LANCE BEFORE A GROUP OF FOUR PRISONERS.[3]

certain Fravartîsh, who had assumed the personality of Khshatrita[4] of the

---

[1] *Behistun Inscription*, col. i. ll. 83–96, col. ii. ll. 1–5; cf. WEISSBACH and BANG, *Die Altpers. Keilins.*, pp. 16, 17. The account given by Darius seems to imply that no interval of time elapsed between the second defeat of Nebuchadrezzar III. and the taking of Babylon, so that several modern historians have rejected the idea of an obstinate resistance (NÖLDEKE, *Aufsätze zur Persischen Geschichte*, pp. 31, 42, 43). Herodotus, however, speaks of the long siege the city sustained (III. clii.), and the discovery of tablets dated in the first and even the second year of Nebuchadrezzar III. (PINCHES, *The Egibi Tablets*, in the *Records of the Past*, 1st ser., vol. xi. p. 88) shows that the siege was prolonged into the second year of this usurper, at least until the month of Nisân (March–April), 520 B.C. No evidence can be drawn from the tablets dated in the reign of Darius, for the oldest yet discovered, which is dated in the month Sebat (Jan.–Feb.), in the year of his accession, and consequently prior to the second year of Nebuchadrezzar, comes from Abu-habba. On the other hand, the statement that all the revolts broke out while Darius was "at Babylon" (*Behistun Inscr.*, col. ii. ll. 5–8) does not allow of the supposition that all the events recorded before his departure for Media (col. ii. ll. 64, 65) could have been compressed into the space of three or four months. It seems, therefore, more probable that the siege lasted till 519 B.C., as it can well have done if credit be given to the mention of "twenty-one months at least" by Herodotus (III. clii., clv.); perhaps the siege was brought to an end in the May of that year, as calculated by Marquart (*Die Assyr. des Ktesias*, in the *Philologus*, Suppl., vol. v. p. 635).

[2] *Behistun Inscription*, col. ii. ll. 8–13; cf. WEISSBACH and BANG, *op. cit.*, pp. 16, 17.

[3] Drawn by Faucher-Gudin, from the impression of an intaglio at St. Petersburg; cf. MÉNANT, *Recherches sur la Glyptique Orientale*, vol. ii. pl. ix. No. 1, according to whom (*ibid.*, pp. 168–171) the prisoner whom the Achæmenian king is transfixing with his lance is none other than Gaumâta, the pseudo-Smerdis himself.

[4] *Behistun Inscription*, col. ii. ll. 13–17; cf. WEISSBACH and BANG, *op. cit.*, pp. 16, 17.

race of Cyaxares, and its revolt marked almost the beginning of a total break-up of the empire. The memory of Astyages and Cyaxares had not yet faded so completely as to cause the Median nobles to relinquish the hope of reasserting the supremacy of Media; the opportunity for accomplishing this aim now seemed all the more favourable, from the fact that Darius had been obliged to leave this province almost immediately after the assassination of the usurper, and to take from it all the troops that he could muster for the siege of Babylon. Several of the nomadic tribes still remained faithful to him, but all the settled inhabitants of Media ranged themselves under the banner of the pretender, and the spirit of insurrection spread thereupon into Armenia and Assyria. For one moment there was a fear lest it should extend to Asia Minor also, where Orœtes, accustomed, in the absence of Cambyses, to act as an autonomous sovereign, displayed little zeal in accommodating himself to the new order of things. There was so much uncertainty as to the leanings of the Persian guard of Orœtes, that Darius did not venture to degrade the satrap officially, but despatched Bagæus to Sardes with precise instructions, which enabled him to accomplish his mission by degrees, so as not to risk a Lydian revolt. His first act was to show the guard a rescript by which they were relieved from attendance on Orœtes, and " thereupon they immediately laid down their spears." Emboldened by their ready obedience, Bagæus presented to the secretary a second letter, which contained his instructions : " The great king commands those Persians who are in Sardes to kill Orœtes." "Whereupon," it is recorded, " they drew their swords and slew him."[1] A revolt in Asia Minor was thus averted, at a time when civil war continued to rage in the centre of Iran.

The situation, however, continued critical. Darius could not think of abandoning the siege of Babylon, and of thus both losing the fruits of his victories and seeing Nebuchadrezzar reappear in Assyria or Susiana. On the other hand, his army was a small one,[2] and he would incur great risks in detaching any of his military chiefs for a campaign against the Mede with an insufficient force. He decided, however, to adopt the latter course, and while he himself presided over the blockade, he simultaneously despatched two columns—one to Media, under the command of the Persian Vidarna, one of the seven ; the other to Armenia, under the Armenian Dâdarshîsh. Vidarna encountered Khshatrita near Marush, in the mountainous region of the old

---

[1] HERODOTUS, III. cxxvi.–cxxviii., where the context indicates that the events narrated took place shortly after the accession of Darius. Further on (III. cl.) Herodotus mentions, as contemporaneous with the siege of Babylon, events which took place after the death of Orœtes; it is probable, therefore, that the scene described by Herodotus occurred in 520 B.C. at the latest.

[2] " The army of Medes and Persians which was with me was small " (*Behistun Inscription*, col. ii. ll. 18, 19 ; cf. WEISSBACH and BANG, *Die Altpers. Keilins.*, pp. 16, 17).

Namri, on the 27th of Anâmaka, and gave him battle; but though he claimed the victory, the result was so indecisive that he halted in Kambadênê, at the entrance to the gorges of the Zagros mountains, and was there obliged to await reinforcements before advancing further. Dâdarshîsh, on his side, gained three victories over the Armenians—one near Zuzza on the 8th of Thuravâhara, another at Tigra ten days later, and the third on the 2nd of Thâigarshîsh, at a place not far from Uhyâma—but he also was compelled to suspend operations and remain inactive pending the arrival of fresh troops. Half the year was spent in inaction on either side, for the rebels had not suffered less than their opponents, and, while endeavouring to reorganise their forces, they opened negotiations with the provinces of the north-east with the view of prevailing on them to join their cause. Darius, still detained before Babylon, was unable to recommence hostilities until the end of 520 B.C. He sent Vaumisa to replace Dâdarshîsh as the head of the army in Armenia, and the new general distinguished himself at the outset by winning a decisive victory on the 15th of Anâmaka, near Izitush in Assyria; but the effect which he hoped to secure from this success was neutralised almost immediately by grievous defections.[1] Sagartia, in the first place, rose in rebellion at the call of a pretended descendant of Cyaxares, named Chitrañtakhma;[2] Hyrcania, the province governed by Hystaspes, the father of Darius, followed suit and took up the cause of Khshatrita,[3] and soon after Margiana broke out into revolt at the instigation of a certain Frâda.[4] Even Persia itself deserted Darius, and chose another king instead of a sovereign whom no one seemed willing to acknowledge. Many of the mountain tribes could not yet resign themselves to the belief that the male line of Cyrus had become extinct with the death of Cambyses. The usurpation of Gaumâta and the accession of Darius had not quenched their faith in the existence of Smerdis: if the Magian were an impostor, it did not necessarily follow that Smerdis had been assassinated, and when a certain Vahyazdâta rose up in the town of Târavâ in the district of Yautiyâ, and announced himself as the younger son of Cyrus, they received him with enthusiastic acclamations.[5] A preliminary success gained by Hystaspes at Vispauzatîsh, in Parthia, on the 22nd of Viyakhna, 519 B.C., prevented the guerilla bands of Hyrcania from joining forces with the Medes, and some days later the fall of Babylon at length set Darius free to utilise his resources to the utmost.[6] The long resistance of Nebuchadrezzar furnished a

---

[1] *Behistun Inscr.*, col. ii. ll. 18–57; cf. WEISSBACH and BANG, *Die Altpers. Keilins.*, pp. 16–19.

[2] *Behistun Inscr.*, col. ii. ll. 78–81; cf. ID., *ibid.*, pp. 20, 21.

[3] *Behistun Inscr.*, col. ii. ll. 92, 93; cf. ID., *ibid.*, pp. 20, 21.

[4] *Behistun Inscr.*, col. iii. ll. 10–12; cf. ID., *ibid.*, pp. 20, 21.

[5] *Behistun Inscr.*, col. iii. ll. 21–28; cf. ID., *ibid.*, pp. 22, 23.

[6] *Behistun Inscr.*, col. ii. ll. 94–98; cf. ID., *ibid.*, pp. 20, 21. For the confusion in the dates, and the actual order of events, cf. MARQUART, *Die Assyr. des Ktesias*, in the *Philologus*, Suppl., vol. v. pp. 634, 635.

fruitful theme for legend : a fanciful story was soon substituted for the true account of the memorable siege he had sustained. Half a century later, when his very name was forgotten, the heroism of his people continued to be extolled beyond measure. When Darius arrived before the ramparts he found the country a desert, the banks of the canals cut through, and the gardens and pleasure-houses destroyed. The crops had been gathered and the herds driven within the walls of the city, while the garrison had reduced by a massacre the number of non-combatants, the women having all been strangled, with the exception of those who were needed to bake the bread. At the end of twenty months the siege seemed no nearer to its close than at the outset, and the besiegers were on the point of losing heart, when at length Zopyrus, one of the seven, sacrificed himself for the success of the blockading army. Slitting his nose and ears, and lacerating his back with the lash of a whip, he made his way into the city as a deserter, and persuaded the garrison to assign him a post of danger under pretence of avenging the ill-treatment he had received from his former master. He directed some successful sallies on points previously agreed upon, and having thus lulled to rest any remaining feelings of distrust on the part of the garrison, he treacherously opened to the Persians the two gates of which he was in charge; three thousand Babylonians were impaled, the walls were razed to the ground, and the survivors of the struggle were exiled and replaced by strange colonists.[1] The only authentic fact about this story is the length of the siege. Nebuchadrezzar was put to death, and Darius, at length free to act, hastened to despatch one of his lieutenants, the Persian Artavardiya, against Vahyazdâta, while he himself marched upon the Medes with the main body of the royal army.[2] The rebels had hitherto been confronted by the local militia, brave but inexperienced troops, with whom they had been able to contend on a fairly equal footing: the entry into the field of the veteran regiments of Cyrus and Cambyses changed the aspect of affairs, and promptly brought the campaign to a successful issue. Darius entered Media by the defiles of Kerend, reinforced Vidarna in Kambadênê, and crushed the enemy near the town of Kundurush, on the 20th of Adukanîsh, 519 B.C. Khshatrita fled towards the north with some few horsemen, doubtless hoping to reach the recesses of Mount Elburz,

---

[1] HERODOTUS, III. cl.–clx. Ctesias (*Fragm.* 29, § 22, in MÜLLER-DIDOT, *Ctesiæ Cnidii Frag.*, p. 50) places the siege of Babylon forty years later, under Xerxes I.; according to him, it was Megabysus, son of Zopyrus, who betrayed the city. Polyænus asserts that the stratagem of Zopyrus was adopted in imitation of a Sakian who dwelt beyond the Oxus (*Stratagems*, viii. 11, § 8). Latin writers transferred the story to Italy, and localised it at Gabii (LIVY, i. 53, 54 ; OVID, *Fasti*, ii. 683–710), but the Roman hero, Sextus Tarquinius, did not carry his devotion to the point of mutilating himself.

[2] *Behistun Inscr.*, col. iii. ll. 28–33 : "Then I sent the army of the Persians and Medes which was with me. One named Artavardiya, a Persian, my servant, I made their general; the rest of the Persian army went to Media with me."

and to continue there the struggle; but he was captured at Ragâ and carried to Ecbatana. His horrible punishment was proportionate to the fear he had inspired: his nose, ears, and tongue were cut off, and his eyes gouged out, and in this mutilated condition he was placed in chains at the gate of the palace, to demonstrate to his former subjects how the Achæmenian king could punish an impostor. When the people had laid this lesson sufficiently to heart, Khshatrita was impaled; many of his principal adherents were ranged around him and suffered the same fate, while the rest were decapitated as an example.[1] Babylon and Media being thus successfully vanquished, the possession of the

REBELS BROUGHT TO DARIUS BY AHURA-MAZDÂ.[2]

empire was assured to Darius, whatever might happen in other parts of his territory, and henceforth the process of repressing disaffection went on unchecked. Immediately after the decisive battle of Kundurush, Vaumisa accomplished the pacification of Armenia by a victory won near Autiyâra,[3] and Artavardiya defeated Vahyazdâta for the first time at Rakhâ in Persia.[4] Vahyazdâta had committed the mistake of dividing his forces and sending a portion of them to Arachosia. Vivâna, the governor of this province, twice crushed the invaders,[5] and almost at the same time the Persian Dâdardîsh of Bactriana was triumphing over Frâda and winning Margiana back to allegiance.[6] For a moment it seemed

[1] *Behistun Inscr.*, col. i. ll. 64–68; cf. WEISSBACH and BANG, *Die Altpers. Keilins.*, pp. 18–21.
[2] This is the scene depicted on the rock of Behistun; cf. the illustration, *infra*, p. 683.
[3] *Behistun Inscr.*, col. ii. ll. 57–63; cf. WEISSBACH and BANG, *Die Altpers. Keilins.*, pp. 18, 19.
[4] *Behistun Inscr.*, col. iii. ll. 30–40; cf. ID., *ibid.*, pp. 22, 23.
[5] *Behistun Inscr.*, col. iii. ll. 52–75; cf. ID., *ibid.*, pp. 20–23.
[6] *Behistun Inscr.*, col. iii. ll. 12–21; cf. ID., *ibid.*, pp. 20–23.

as if the decisive issue of the struggle might be prolonged for months, since it was announced that the appearance of a new pseudo-Smerdis on the scene had been followed by the advent of a second pseudo-Nebuchadrezzar in Chaldæa. Darius left only a weak garrison at Babylon when he started to attack Khshatrita: a certain Arakha, an Armenian by birth, presenting himself to the Babylonian people as the son of Nabonidus, caused himself to be proclaimed king in December, 519 B.C.; but the city was still suffering so severely from the miseries of the long siege, that it was easy for the Mede Vindafrâ to reduce it promptly to submission after a month or six weeks of semi-independence.[1] This was the last attempt at revolt. Chitrañtakhma expiated his crimes by being impaled,[2] and Hystaspes routed the Hyrcanian battalions at Patigrabana in Parthia:[3] Artavardiya having defeated Vahyazdâta, near Mount Paraga, on the 6th of Garmapada, 618 B.C., besieged him in his fortress of Uvâdeshaya, and was not long in effecting his capture.[4] The civil war came thus to an end.

It had been severe, but it had brought into such prominence the qualities of the sovereign that no one henceforth dared to dispute his possession of the crown. A man of less energetic character and calm judgment would have lost his head at the beginning of the struggle, when almost every successive week brought him news of a fresh rebellion—in Susiana, Babylon, Media, Armenia, Assyria, Margiana, Hyrcania, and even Persia itself, not to speak of the intrigues in Asia Minor and Egypt: he would have scattered his forces to meet the dangers on all sides at once, and would assuredly have either succumbed in the struggle, or succeeded only by chance after his fate had trembled in the balance for years. Darius, however, from the very beginning knew how to single out the important points upon which to deal such vigorous blows as would ensure him the victory with the least possible delay. He saw that Babylon, with its numerous population, its immense wealth and prestige, and its memory of recent supremacy, was the real danger to his empire, and he never relaxed his hold on it until it was subdued, leaving his generals to deal with the other nations, the Medes included, and satisfied if each of them could but hold his adversary in check without gaining any decided advantage over him. The event justified his decision. When once Babylon had fallen, the remaining rebels were no longer a source of fear; to defeat Khshatrita was the work of a few weeks only, and the submission of the other provinces followed as a natural consequence on the ruin

[1] *Behistun Inscr.*, col. iii. ll. 75–91; cf. WEISSBACH and BANG, *Die Altpers. Keilins.*, pp. 24, 25.
[2] *Behistun Inscr.*, col. ii. ll. 82–91; cf. ID., *ibid.*, pp. 20, 21.
[3] *Behistun Inscr.*, col. iii. ll. 1–9; cf. ID., *ibid.*, pp. 20, 21.
[4] *Behistun Inscr.*, col. iii. ll. 40–19; cf. ID., *ibid.*, pp. 22, 23.

of Media.[1] After consummating his victories, Darius caused an inscription in commemoration of them to be carved on the rocks in the pass of Bagistana [Behistun], one of the most frequented routes leading from the basin of the Tigris to the table-land of Iran.   There his figure is still to be seen standing, with his foot resting on the prostrate body of an enemy, and his hand raised in the attitude of one addressing an audience, while nine figures march in file to meet him, their arms tied behind their backs, and cords round their necks, representing all the pretenders whom he had fought and put to death—Athrîna, Nadinta-bel, Khshatrita, Vahyazdâta, Arakha, and Chitrañtakhma; an inscription, written in the three official languages of the court, recounts at full length his mighty deeds. The drama did not, how-

THE ROCKS OF BEHISTUN.[2]

ever, come to a close with the punishment of Vahyazdâta, for though no tribe or chieftain remained now in open revolt, many of those who had taken no active share in the rebellion had, by their conduct during the crisis, laid themselves open to grave suspicions, and it seemed but prudent to place them under strict surveillance or to remove them from office altogether.   Orœtes had been summarily despatched, and his execution did not disturb the peace of Asia Minor; but

[1] Mention of some new wars is made towards the end of the inscription, but the text here is so mutilated that the sense can no longer be easily determined (*Behistun Inscr.*, col. v. ll. 1–31; cf. WEISSBACH and BANG, *Die Altpers. Keilins.*, pp. 28–31); we shall see in Chap. VII. that one of these wars was possibly directed against the Scythians.

[2] Drawn by Boudier, from FLANDIN and COSTE, *Perse Ancienne*, pl. xvi.; cf. J. DE MORGAN, *Mission en Perse*, vol. iv. pls. xxviii., xxix.

Aryandes, to whose rule Cambyses had entrusted the valley of the Nile, displayed no less marked symptoms of disaffection, and deserved the same fate. Though he had not ventured to usurp openly the title of king, he had arrogated to himself all the functions and rights of royalty, and had manifested as great an independence in his government as if he had been an actual Pharaoh. The inhabitants of Cyrene did not approve of the eagerness displayed by their tyrant Arkesilas III. to place himself under the Persian yoke: after first expelling and then recalling him, they drove him away a second time, and at length murdered him at Barca, whither he had fled for refuge. Pheretimê came to Egypt to seek the help of Aryandes, just as Laarchos had formerly implored the assistance of Amasis,[1] and represented to him that her son had fallen a victim to his devotion to his suzerain. It was a good opportunity to put to ransom one of the wealthiest countries of Africa; so the governor sent to the Cyrenaica all the men and vessels at his disposal.[2] Barca was the only city to offer any resistance, and the Persian troops were detained for nine months motionless before its walls, and the city then only succumbed through treachery.[3] Some detachments forced their way as far as the distant town of Euesperides,[4] and it is possible that Aryandes dreamt for a moment of realising the designs which Cambyses had formed against Carthage. Insufficiency of supplies stayed the advance of his generals; but the riches of their ally, Cyrene, offered them a strong temptation, and they were deliberating how they might make this wealth their own before returning to Memphis, and were, perhaps, on the point of risking the attempt, when they received orders to withdraw. The march across the desert proved almost fatal to them. The Libyans of Marmarica, attracted by the spoils with which the Persian troops were laden, harassed them incessantly, and inflicted on them serious losses;[5] they succeeded, however, in arriving safely with their prisoners, among whom were the survivors of the inhabitants of Barca. At this time the tide of fortune was setting strongly in favour of Darius: Aryandes, anxious to propitiate that monarch, despatched these wretched captives to Persia as a trophy of his success, and Darius sent them into Bactriana, where they founded a new Barca.[6] But this tardy homage availed him nothing. Darius himself visited Egypt and disembarrassed himself of his troublesome subject by his summary execution, inflicted, some said, because

---

[1] Cf. what is stated as to the relations between Amasis and Laarchus, *supra*, pp. 645, 646.

[2] HERODOTUS, IV. clxii.–clxviii.   [3] HERODOTUS, IV. cc., cci.

[4] HERODOTUS, IV. cciv.; this is the town which later on under the Lagidæ received the name of Berenice, and which is now called Benghazi.   [5] HERODOTUS, IV. cciii.

[6] HERODOTUS, IV. cciv. It is doubtless to these acts of personal authority on the part of Aryandes that Darius alludes in the Behistun Inscription, when he says, "While I was before Babylon, the following provinces revolted against me—Persia and Susiana, the Medes and Assyria, and the Egyptians . . ." (OPPERT, *Le Peuple et la Langue des Mèdes*, p. 125; the Persian text is mutilated in this passage, col. ii. l. 7; cf. WEISSBACH and BANG, *Die Altpers. Keilins.*, pp. 16, 17).

he had issued coins of a superior fineness to those of the royal mint,[1] while, according to others, it was because he had plundered Egypt and so ill-treated the Egyptians as to incite them to rebellion.[2] After the suppression of this rival, Darius set himself to win the affection of his Egyptian province, or, at least, to render its servitude bearable. With a country so devout and so impressed with its own superiority over all other nations, the best means of accomplishing his object was to show profound respect for its national gods and its past glory. Darius, therefore, proceeded to shower favours on the priests, who had been subject to persecution ever since the disastrous campaign in Ethiopia. Cambyses had sent into exile in Elam the chief priest of Sais—that Uzaharrîsnîti who had initiated him into the sacred rites; Darius gave permission to this important personage to return to his native land, and commissioned him to repair the damage inflicted by the madness of the son of Cyrus. Uzaharrîsnîti, escorted back with honour to his native city, re-established there the colleges of sacred scribes, and restored to the temple of Nît the lands and revenues which had been confiscated.[3] Greek tradition soon improved upon the national account of this episode, and asserted that Darius took an interest in the mysteries of Egyptian theology, and studied the sacred books,[4] and that on his arrrival at Memphis in 517 B.C., immediately after the death of an Apis, he took part publicly in the general mourning, and promised a reward of a hundred talents of gold to whosoever should discover the successor of the bull.[5] According to a popular story still current when Herodotus travelled in Egypt, the king visited the temple of Pthah before leaving Memphis, and ordered his statue to be erected there beside that of

---

[1] HERODOTUS, IV. clxvi. It is not certain that Aryandes did actually strike any coinage in his own name, and perhaps Herodotus has only repeated a popular story current in Egypt in his days (BABELON, *Mélanges numismatiques*, vol. ii. pp. 95, 96). If this money actually existed, its coinage was but a pretext employed by Darius; the true motive of the condemnation of Aryandes was certainly an armed revolt, or a serious presumption of revolutionary intentions (FR. LENORMANT, *Histoire de la Monnaie dans l'Antiquité*, vol. ii. p. 6).

[2] POLYÆNUS, *Stratagems*, vii. 11, § 7, where Aryandes is called Oryandros.

[3] *Inscription on the Statue of the Naophoros in the Vatican*, ll. 44–46: cf. E. DE ROUGÉ, *Mémoire sur la Statuette Naophore*, p. 23; E. RÉVILLOUT, *Premier Extrait de la Chronique Démotique de Paris*, in the *Revue Égyptologique*, vol. i. p. 29; MARUCCHI, *Iscrizione Geroglifica della Statuetta Naofora*, pp. 17–20. E. de Rougé (*Inscription de la Statuette Naophore*, p. 22) and Wiedemann read Aram instead of Elam (*Gesch. Ægyptens*, p. 239), and take Uzaharrîsnîti into exile only in Syria; I follow Brugsch (*Gesch. Ægyptens*, p. 750), however, in believing that Elam is intended, where Susa was one of the favourite residences of the great king.

[4] DIODORUS SICULUS, i. p. 96.

[5] POLYÆNUS, *Strat.*, vii. 11, § 7. This episode enabled Wiedemann to determine the date of Darius' visit to Egypt: the Apis referred to can only be the one which died in the fourth year of the king (S. 2274), or 517 B.C. (*Gesch. Ægyptens*, pp. 236, 237). The legend concerning the statue of Sesostris (HERODOTUS, II. cx.) at first led me to consider, with Ley (*Fata et Conditio Ægypti sub imperio Persarum*, pp. 11, 12) and Unger (*Manetho*, pp. 288, 289), that it was necessary to place this journey of Darius after the Scythian campaign (*Histoire Ancienne*, 4th edit., p. 522, note 7), but I now think that one is not justified in allowing the incidents in the tale of a dragoman (WIEDEMANN, *Herodots Zweites Buch*, p. 427) to outweigh those of a narrative based on a fact so precise as that of the mourning for an Apis.

Sesostris. The priests refused to obey this command, for, said they, "Darius has not equalled the deeds of Sesostris : he has not conquered the Scythians, whom Sesostris overcame." Darius replied that "he hoped to accomplish as much as Sesostris had done, if he lived as long as Sesostris," and so conciliated the patriotic pride of the priests.[1] The Egyptians, grateful for his moderation, numbered him among the legislators whose memory they revered, by the side of Menes, Asykhis, Bocchoris, and Sabaco.[2]

The whole empire was now obedient to the will of one man, but the ordeal from which it had recently escaped showed how loosely the elements of it were bound together, and with what facility they could be disintegrated. The system of government in force hitherto was that introduced into Assyria by Tiglath-pileser III., which had proved so eminently successful in the time of Sargon and his descendants;[3] Babylon and Ecbatana had inherited it from Nineveh, and Persepolis had in turn adopted it from Ecbatana and Babylon. It had always been open to objections, of which by no means the least was the great amount of power and independence accorded by it to the provincial governors; but this inconvenience had been little felt when the empire was of moderate dimensions, and when no province permanently annexed to the empire lay at any very great distance from the capital for the time being. But this was no longer the case, now that Persian rule extended over nearly the whole of Asia, from the Indus to the Thracian Bosphorus, and over a portion of Africa also. It must have seemed far from prudent to set governors invested with almost regal powers over countries so distant that a decree despatched from the palace might take several weeks to reach its destination. The heterogeneity of the elements in each province was a guarantee of peace in the eyes of the sovereign, and Darius carefully abstained from any attempt at unification : not only did he allow vassal republics, and tributary kingdoms and nations to subsist side by side, but he took care that each should preserve its own local dynasty, language, writing, customs, religion, and peculiar legislation, besides the right to coin money stamped with the name of its chief or its civic symbol. The Greek cities of the coast maintained their own peculiar constitutions which they had enjoyed under the Mermnadæ; Darius merely required that the chief authority among them should rest in the hands of the aristocratic party, or in those of an elective or hereditary tyrant whose personal interest secured his fidelity.[4] The

---

[1] HERODOTUS, II. cx.; DIODORUS SICULUS, i. 56 ; cf. WIEDEMANN, *Herodots Zweites Buch*, pp. 426, 427.
[2] DIODORUS SICULUS, i. 95.   [3] Cf. *supra*, p. 193, et seq.
[4] HERODOTUS, V. xxxvi.–xxxviii., where it is related how Aristagoras betrayed the great king, and how he seized the tyrants of the Greek cities in Asia in order to replace them by chiefs hostile to the Persians; cf. HERODOTUS, VI. xliii., where Mardonius, reversing the situation, put down the tyrants of these same cities to substitute for them the leaders of the democratic party.

Carians,[1] Lycians,[2] Pamphylians, and Cilicians[3] continued under the rule of their native princes, subject only to the usual obligations of the *corvée*, taxation, and military service as in past days; the majority of the barbarous tribes which inhabited the Taurus and the mountainous regions in the centre of Asia Minor were even exempted from all definite taxes, and were merely required to respect the couriers, caravans, and armies which passed through their territory. Native magistrates and kings still bore sway in Phœnicia[4] and Cyprus,[5] and

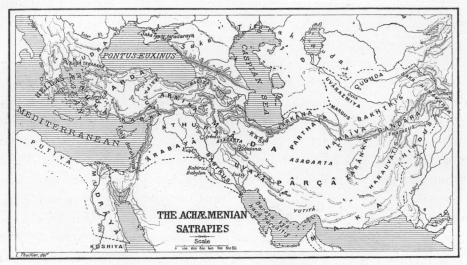

the shêkhs of the desert preserved their authority over the marauding and semi-nomadic tribes of Idumæa, Nabatæa, Moab, and Ammon, and the wandering Bedâwin on the Euphrates and the Khabur. Egypt, under Darius, remained what she had been under the Saitic and Ethiopian dynasties, a feudal state governed by a Pharaoh, who, though a foreigner, was yet reputed to be of the solar race; the land continued to be divided unequally into diverse principalities, Thebes still preserving its character as a theocracy under the guidance of the pallacide of Amon and her priestly counsellors,

---

[1] HERODOTUS, VII. xcviii., xcix., cites among the commanders of the Persian fleet three Carian dynasts, Histiæus, Pigres, and Damasithymus, besides the famous Artemisia of Halicarnassus.

[2] HERODOTUS, VII. xcviii., where a dynast named Kyberniskos, son of Sika, is mentioned among the commanders of the fleet. The received text of Herodotus needs correction, and we should read Kybernis, son of Kossika (SIX, *Monnaies Lyciennes*, pp. 13, 85), some of whose coins are still in existence (BABELON, *Les Perses Achéménides*, p. 64, Nos. 430, 431, and pl. xi. 2, 3). For the other Lycian dynasts of the same or a later period, cf. BABELON, *Les Perses Achéménides*, pp. xci.–cxiii.

[3] The Cilician contingent in the fleet of Xerxes at Salamis was commanded by Syennesis himself (HERODOTUS, VII. xcviii.; cf. ÆSCHYLUS, *Persians*, 324–326), and Cilicia never had a satrap until the time of Cyrus the younger (XENOPHON, *Cyropædia*, vii. 4, § 2).

[4] Three kings, viz. the kings of Sidon, Tyre, and Arvad, bore commands in the Phœnician fleet of Xerxes (HERODOTUS, VII. xcviii.).

[5] Cf. the Cypriot kings mentioned by Herodotus (VII. xcviii.) as commanding the vessels furnished by the island of Cyprus to the fleet of Xerxes; cf. in Book IV. civ., cix., cxii., in the account of the revolt against Darius, the reference to the chief Cypriot kings. For the coins of Cyprus and the names of the kings which they reveal during the sixth and fifth centuries B.C., cf. BABELON, *Les Perses Achéménides*, pp. cxiv.–cxx., cxxv.–cxxix., cxxxiv.–cxli., etc.

while the other districts subsisted under military chieftains. Our information concerning the organisation of the central and eastern provinces is incomplete, but it is certain that here also the same system prevailed. In the years of peace which succeeded the troubled opening of his reign, that is, from 519 to 515 B.C.,[1] Darius divided the whole empire into satrapies, whose number varied at different periods of his reign from twenty to twenty-three, and even twenty-eight.[2] Persia proper was not included among these, for she had been the cradle of the reigning house, and the instrument of conquest.[3] The Iranian table-land, and the parts of India or regions beyond the Oxus which bordered on it, formed twelve important vice-royalties—Media, Hyrcania, Parthia, Zaranka, Aria, Khorasmia, Bactriana, Sogdiana, Gandaria, and the country of the Sakæ—reaching from the plains of Tartary almost to the borders of China, the country of the Thatagus in the upper basin of the Elmend, Arachosia, and the land of Maka on the shores of the Indian Ocean. Ten satrapies were reckoned in the west—Uvayâ, Elam, in which lay Susa, one of the favourite residences of Darius; Babirus (Babylon) and Chaldæa; Athurâ, the ancient kingdom of Assyria; Arabayâ, stretching from the Khabur to the Litany, the Jordan, and the Orontes; Egypt, the peoples of the sea, among whom were reckoned the Phœnicians, Cilicians, and Cypriots, and the islanders of the Ægean; Yaunâ, which comprised Lycia, Caria, and the Greek colonies along the coast; Sparda, with Phrygia and Mysia; Armenia; and lastly, Katpatuka or Cappadocia, which lay on both sides of the Halys from the Taurus to the Black Sea. If each of these provinces had been governed, as formerly, by a single individual, who thus became king in all but name and descent, the empire would have run great risk of a speedy dissolution. Darius therefore avoided concentrating the civil and military powers in the same hands. In each province he installed three officials independent of each other, but each in direct communication with himself—a satrap,[4] a general, and a secretary of state. The satraps were chosen from any class

[1] Herodotus states that this dividing of the empire into provinces took place immediately after the accession of Darius (III. lxxxix.), and this mistake is explained by the fact that he ignores almost entirely the civil wars which filled the earliest years of the reign. His enumeration of twenty satrapies (III. xc.–xcv.) comprises India and omits Thrace, which enables us to refer the drawing up of his list to a period before the Scythian campaign, viz. before 514 B.C. (KRUMBHOLZ, De Asiæ Minoris Satrapis Persicis, pp. 12–15). Herodotus very probably copied it from the work of Hecatæus of Miletus (KLAUSEN, Hecatæi Fragmenta, p. 95; cf. p. 12), and consequently it reproduces a document contemporary with Darius himself.

[2] The number twenty is, as has been remarked, that given by Herodotus (III. xc.–xcv.), and probably by Hecatæus of Miletus. The great Behistun Inscription enumerates twenty-three countries (col. i. ll. 12–17; cf. WEISSBACH and BANG, Die Altpers. Keilins., pp. 12, 13; Inscription E of Persepolis, ll. 5–18; cf. ID., ibid., pp. 34, 35), and the Inscription of Nakhsh-î-Rustem gives twenty-eight (ll. 22–30; cf. ID., ibid., pp. 36, 37).

[3] In the great Behistun Inscription (col. i. l. 14) Darius mentions Persia first of all the countries in his possession. In the Inscription E of Persepolis he omits it entirely, and in that of Nakhsh-î-Rustem he does not include it in the general catalogue (ll. 17, 18).

[4] The Persian word khshatrapâ, khshathrapan, khshatrapâva, signifies the lord of the country.

in the nation, from among the poor as well as from among the wealthy, from foreigners as well as from Persians;[1] but the most important satrapies were bestowed only on persons allied by birth[2] or marriage with the Achæmenids,[3] and, by preference, on the legitimate descendants of the six noble houses. They were not appointed for any prescribed period, but continued in office during the king's pleasure. They exercised absolute authority in all civil matters, and maintained a court, a body-guard,[4] palaces and extensive parks, or *paradises*, where they indulged in the pleasures of the chase ; they controlled the incidence of taxation,[5] administered justice, and possessed the power of life and death. Attached to each satrap was a secretary of state, who ostensibly acted as his chancellor, but whose real function was to exercise a secret supervision over his conduct and report upon it to the imperial ministers.[6] The Persian troops, native militia and auxiliary forces quartered in the province, were placed under the orders, moreover, of a general, who was usually hostile to the satrap and the secretary.[7] These three officials counterbalanced each other, and held each other mutually in check, so that a revolt was rendered very difficult, if not impossible. All three were kept in constant communication with the court by relays of regular couriers, who carried their despatches on horseback or on camels, from one end of Asia to the other, in the space of a few weeks.[8] The most celebrated of the post-roads was that which ran from Sardes to Susa through Lydia and Phrygia, crossing the Halys, traversing Cappadocia and Cilicia, and passing through Armenia and across the Euphrates, until at length, after passing through Matiênê and the

[1] Herodotus mentions a satrap chosen from among the Lydians, Pactyas (I. cliii.), and another satrap of Greek extraction, Xenagoras of Halicarnassus (IX. cvii.).

[2] The most characteristic instance is that of Hystaspes, who was satrap of Persia under Cambyses (HEROD., III. lxx.), and of Parthia and Hyrcania under his own son (*Behistun Inscr.*, col. ii. ll. 93, 94 ; cf. WEISSBACH and BANG, *Die Altpers. Keilins.*, pp. 20, 21). One of the brothers of Darius, Artaphernes, was satrap of Sardes (HEROD., V. xxv.), and three of the king's sons, Achemenes, Ariabignes, and Masistes, were satraps of Egypt, Ionia, and Bactriana respectively (ID., VII. vii., xcvii., IX. cxiii.).

[3] To understand how well established was the custom of bestowing satrapies on those only who were allied by marriage to the royal house, it is sufficient to recall the fact that, later on, under Xerxes I., when Pausanias, King of Sparta, had thoughts of obtaining the position of satrap in Greece, he asked for the hand of an Achæmenian princess (THUCYDIDES, I. cxxviii.).

[4] We know, for example, that Orœtes, satrap of Sardes under Cyrus, Cambyses, and Darius (cf. what is said of him, *supra*, p. 678), had a body-guard of 1000 Persians (HERODOTUS, III. cxxvii.).

[5] Thus, Artaphernes, satrap of Sardes, had a cadastral survey made of the territory of the Ionians, and by the results of this survey he regulated the imposition of taxes, "which from that time up to the present day are exacted according to his ordinance" (HERODOTUS, VI. xlii.).

[6] The *rôle* played by the secretary is clearly indicated by the history of Orœtes, satrap of Sardes (HERODOTUS, III. cxxviii.); cf. the story related, *supra*, p. 678.

[7] While Darius appoints his brother Artaphernes satrap of Lydia, he entrusts the command of the army and the fleet to Otanes, son of Sisamnes (V. xxv., xxvi.). Similarly several generals are met with at the side of Artaphernes in the Ionic revolt (V. cxvi.).

[8] The Greeks translated by the word Ἄγγαροι or Ἀγγαρήϊοι (HEROD., VIII. xcviii.) the Persian term used to designate these couriers. Xenophon compares their speed in travelling to the flight of birds (*Cyropædia*, viii. 6, § 17). A good example of the use of the camel for the postal service is cited by Strabo (XV. ii. § 10, p. 724), on the occasion of the death of Philotas and the execution of Parmenion under Alexander.

country of the Cossæans, it reached Elam. This main route was divided into one hundred and eleven stages, which were performed by couriers on horseback and partly in ferry-boats, in eighty-four days.[1] Other routes, of which we have no particular information, led to Egypt, Media, Bactria, and India,[2] and by their means the imperial officials in the capital were kept fully informed of all that took place in the most distant parts of the empire. As an extra precaution, the king sent out annually certain officers, called his "eyes" or his "ears,"[3] who appeared on the scene when they were least expected, and investigated the financial or political situation, reformed abuses in the administration, and reprimanded or even suspended the government officials; they were accompanied by a body of troops to support their decisions, whose presence invested their counsels with the strongest sanction.[4] An unfavourable report, a slight irregularity, a mere suspicion, even, was sufficient to disqualify a satrap. Sometimes he was deposed, often secretly condemned to death without a trial, and the execution of the judgment was committed even to his own servants. A messenger would arrive unexpectedly, and remit to the guards an order charging them to put their chief to death—an order which was promptly executed at the mere sight of the royal decree.[5]

This reform in the method of government was displeasing to the Persian nobles, whose liberty of action it was designed to curtail, and they took their revenge in sneering at the obedience they could not refuse to render. Cyrus, they said, had been a father, Cambyses a master, but Darius was only a pedler greedy of gain.[6] The chief reason for this division of the empire into provinces was, indeed, fiscal rather than political : to arrange the incidence of taxation in his province, to collect the revenue in due time and forward the total amount to the imperial treasury, formed the fundamental duty of a satrap, to which all others had to yield.[7] Persia proper was exempt from the payment of any fixed sum, its inhabitants being merely required to offer presents to the king whenever he passed through their districts. These semi-

---

[1] HERODOTUS, V. li.–liii.; on the line and stages of this road in Asia Minor, cf. RAMSAY, *Historical Geography of Asia Minor*, pp. 27–35, and RADET, *La Lydie et le Monde Grec au temps des Mermnades*, p. 23, et seq., certain details of which have been corrected by the two authors themselves in several of their later works.

[2] Ctesias at the end of his work describes the routes leading from Ephesus to Bactriana and India (*Fragm.* 29, in MÜLLER-DIDOT, *Ctesiæ Cnidii Fragm.*, p. 58). It is probable that the route described by Isidorus of Charax in his *Stathma Parthica* (MÜLLER-DIDOT, *Geographi Græci Minores*, vol. i. pp. 244–254) already existed in the times of the Achæmenids, and was traversed by their postal couriers.

[3] Mention of the *Eye of the king* occurs in Herodotus (I. cxiv.), in Æschylus (*Persians*, 980), and in Plutarch (*Life of Artaxerxes*, § 12), of the *Ear* in Xenophon (*Cyropædia*, viii. 2, § 10) ; cf. the Persian proverb, according to which " The king has many eyes and many ears."

[4] Xenophon (*Cyropædia*, viii. 6, § 16) affirms that these inspections were still held in his day.

[5] Cf. the story of Orœtes in Herodotus (III. cxxviii.), related *supra*, p. 678.

[6] HERODOTUS, III. lxxxix. : Δαρεῖος μὲν κάπηλος, Καμβύσης δὲ δεσπότης, Κῦρος δὲ πατὴρ ὁ μὲν ὅτι ἐκαπήλευε πάντα τὰ πράγματα.

[7] HERODOTUS, III. lxxxix.

compulsory gifts were proportioned to the fortunes of the individual contributors; they might consist merely of an ox or a sheep, a little milk or cheese, some dates, a handful of flour, or some vegetables.[1] The other provinces, after being subjected to a careful survey, were assessed partly in money, partly in kind, according to their natural capacity or wealth. The smallest amount of revenue raised in any province amounted to 170 talents of silver—the sum, for instance, collected from Arachosia with its dependencies Gedrosia and Gandara;[2] while Egypt yielded a revenue of 700 talents,[3] and the amount furnished by Babylon, the wealthiest province of all, amounted to 1000 talents.[4] The total revenue of the empire reached the enormous sum of £3,311,997, estimated by weight of silver, which is equivalent to over £26,000,000 of modern English money, if the greater value of silver in antiquity is taken into consideration. In order to facilitate the collection of the revenue, Darius issued the gold and silver coins which are named after him. On the obverse side these darics are stamped with a figure of the sovereign, armed with the bow or javelin. They were

DARIC OF DARIUS, SON OF HYSTASPES.[5]

coined on the scale of 3000 gold darics to one talent, each daric weighing normally ·2788 oz. troy, and being worth exactly 20 silver drachmæ or Medic shekels; so that the relative value of the two metals was approximately 1 to 13½. The most ancient type of daric was thick and irregular in shape, and rudely stamped, but of remarkable fineness, the amount of alloy being never more than three per cent.[6] The use of this coinage was nowhere obligatory, and it only became general in the countries bordering on the Mediterranean, where it met the requirements of international traffic and political relations, and in the payment of the army and the navy. In the interior, the medium of exchange used in wholesale and retail commercial transactions continued to be metals estimated by weight, and the kings of Persia themselves preferred to store their revenues in the shape of bullion; as the metal was received at the royal treasury it was melted and poured into clay moulds, and was minted into money only gradually, according to the whim or necessity of the moment.[7] Taxes in kind were levied even more largely than

---

[1] ÆLIAN, *Var. Hist.*, i. 31.

[2] HERODOTUS, III. xci., where a list is given of the tribes comprised in this satrapy—Sattagydes (Thatagush), Gandarians, Dulikes, and Aparytes.

[3] HERODOTUS, III. xci.   [4] HERODOTUS, III. xcii.

[5] Drawn by Faucher-Gudin, from a specimen in the Bibliothèque Nationale, of which a cast has kindly been furnished me by M. Babelon.

[6] FR. LENORMANT, *La Monnaie dans l'Antiquité*, vol. i. p. 787; for the whole subject of darics, cf. BABELON, *Les Perses Achéménides, les Satrapes et les Dynastes tributaires de leur Empire*, pp. i.–xx.

[7] HERODOTUS, III. xcvi. Arrian relates that Alexander found 50,000 talents' weight of silver in the treasury at Susa (*Anabasis*, iii. 16); other hoards quite as rich were contained in the palaces of Persepolis and Pasargadæ (*Anabasis*, iii. 18).

in money, but the exact form they assumed in the different regions of the empire has not yet been ascertained. The whole empire was divided into districts, which were charged with the victualling of the army and the court, and Babylon alone bore a third of the charges under this head.[1] We learn elsewhere that Egypt was bound to furnish corn for the 120,000 men of the army of occupation, and that the fisheries of the Fayum yielded the king a yearly revenue of 240 talents.[2] The Medes furnished similarly 100,000 sheep, 4000 mules, and 3000 horses;[3] the Armenians, 30,000 foals; the Cilicians, 365 white horses, one for each day in the year;[4] the Babylonians, 500 youthful eunuchs;[5] and any city or town which produced or manufactured any valuable commodity was bound to furnish a regular supply to the sovereign. Thus, Chalybon provided wine; Libya and the Oases, salt;[6] India, dogs, with whose support four large villages in Babylonia were charged;[7] the Æolian Assos, cheese; and other places, in like manner, wool, wines, dyes, medicines, and chemicals. These imperial taxes, though they seem to us somewhat heavy, were not excessive, but taken by themselves they give us no idea of the burdens which each province had to resign itself to bear. The State provided no income for the satraps; their maintenance and that of their suite were charged on the province, and they made ample exactions on the natives. The province of Babylon was required to furnish its satrap daily with an *ardeb* of silver;[8] Egypt, India, Media, and Syria each provided a no less generous allowance for its governor, and the poorest provinces were not less heavily burdened. The satraps required almost as much to satisfy their requirements as did the king; but for the most part they fairly earned their income, and saved more to their subjects than they extorted from them. They repressed brigandage, piracy, competition between the various cities, and local wars; while quarrels, which formerly would have been settled by an appeal to arms, were now composed before their judgment-seats, and in case of need the rival factions were forcibly compelled to submit to their decisions. They kept up the roads, and afforded complete security to travellers by night and day; they protected industries and agriculture, and, in accordance with the precepts of their religious code, they accounted it an honourable task to break up waste land or replant deserted sites. Darius himself did not disdain to send congratulations to a satrap who had planted trees in Asia Minor, and laid out one

---

[1] HERODOTUS, I. cxcii.

[2] HERODOTUS, III. xci.; cf., for the fisheries of the Fayum, HERODOTUS, II. cxlix.; according to Diodorus Siculus, the daily revenue from these was assigned to the queen (i. 52).

[3] STRABO, XI. xiii. § 14, p. 525.   [4] XENOPHON, *Anabasis*, iv. 5, § 34, et seq.

[5] HERODOTUS, III. xcii.   [6] STRABO, XV. iii. §§ 21, 22, p. 735.

[7] HERODOTUS, I. cxcii.

[8] HERODOTUS, I. cxcii. This would be, by weight, about £104,000 a year.

of those wooded parks in which the king delighted to refresh himself after the fatigues of government, by the exercise of walking or in the pleasures of the chase.[1] In spite of its defects, the system of government inaugurated by Darius secured real prosperity to his subjects, and to himself a power far greater than that enjoyed by any of his predecessors. It rendered revolts on the part of the provincial governors extremely difficult, and enabled the court to draw up a regular budget and provide for its expenses without any undue pressure on its subjects; in one point only was it defective, but that point was a cardinal one, namely, in the military organisation. Darius himself maintained, for his personal protection, a bodyguard recruited from the Persians and the Medes. It was divided into three corps, consisting respectively of 2000 cavalry, 2000 infantry of noble birth, armed with lances whose shafts were ornamented below with apples of gold or silver—whence their name of *mêlophori* —and under them the 10,000 "immortals," in ten battalions, the first of which had its lances ornamented with golden pomegranates.[2] This guard formed the nucleus of the standing army, which could be reinforced by the first and second grades of Persian and Median feudal nobility at the first summons. Forces of varying strength garrisoned the most important fortresses of the empire, such as Sardes, Memphis,[3] Elephantinê, Daphnæ,[4] Babylon, and many others, to hold the restless natives in check. These were, indeed, the only regular troops on which the king could always rely. Whenever a war broke out which demanded no special effort, the satraps of the provinces directly involved summoned the military contingents of the cities and vassal states under their control, and by concerted action endeavoured to bring the affair to a successful issue without the necessity of an appeal to the central authority. If, on the contrary, troubles arose which threatened the welfare of the whole empire, and the sovereign felt called upon to conduct the campaign in person, he would mobilise his guard, and summon the reserves from several provinces or even from all of them. Veritable hordes of recruits then poured in, but these masses of troops, differing from each other in their equipment and methods of fighting, in disposition and in language, formed a herd of men rather than an army. They had no cohesion or confidence in themselves, and their leaders, unaccustomed to command such enormous numbers, suffered themselves to be led rather than exercise authority as guides. Any good qualities the troops may have possessed were neutralised by lack of unity in their methods of action,

---

[1] Cf. the letter of Darius to the satrap Gadatas, congratulating him on having planted some trees; it is published in the *Bulletin de Correspondance Hellénique*, 1889, p. 529, et seq.

[2] HERACLIDES OF CUMÆ, *Fragm.* 1, in MÜLLER-DIDOT, *Fragm. Hist. Græc.*, vol. ii. pp. 95, 96. Xenophon (*Cyropædia*, vii. 5, § 38) attributes the organisation of this force to Cyrus.

[3] HERODOTUS, III. xci., where it is stated that the army of Memphis included some Persian and auxiliary troops.

[4] HERODOTUS, II. xxx.; cf. WIEDEMANN, *Herodots Zweites Buch*, pp. 129, 130.

694 THE IRANIAN CONQUEST.

and their actual faults exaggerated this defect, so that, in spite of their splendid powers of endurance and their courage under every ordeal, they ran the risk of finding themselves in a state of hopeless inferiority when called upon to meet armies very much smaller, but composed of homogeneous elements, all animated with the same spirit and drilled in the same school.

By continual conquests, the Persians were now reduced to only two outlets for their energies, in two opposite directions—in the east towards India, in the west towards Greece. Everywhere else their advance was arrested by the sea or other obstacles almost as impassable to their heavily armed battalions: to the north the empire was bounded by the Black Sea, the Caucasus, the Caspian Sea, and the Siberian steppes; to the south, by the Indian Ocean, the sandy table-land of Arabia, and the African deserts. At one moment, about 512 B.C., it is possible that they pushed forward towards the east.[1] From the Iranian plateau they beheld from afar the immense plain of the Hapta Hindu (or the Punjab). Darius invaded this territory, and made himself master of extensive districts which he formed into a new satrapy, that of India, but subsequently, renouncing all idea of pushing eastward as far as the Ganges, he turned his steps towards the south-east. A fleet, constructed at Peukêla and placed under the command of a Greek admiral, Scylax of Caryanda, descended the Indus by order of the king;[2] subjugating the tribes who dwelt along the banks as he advanced, Scylax at length reached the ocean, on which he ventured forth, undismayed by the tides, and proceeded in a westerly direction, exploring, in less than thirty months, the shores of Gedrosia and Arabia. Once on the threshold of India, the Persians saw open before them a brilliant and lucrative career: the circumstances which prevented them from following up this preliminary success are unknown—perhaps the first developments of nascent Buddhism deterred them—but certain it is that they arrested their steps when they had touched merely the outskirts of the basin of the Indus, and retreated at once towards the west. The conquest of Lydia, and subsequently of the Greek cities and islands along the coast of the Ægean, had doubtless enriched the empire by the acquisition of active subject populations, whose extraordinary aptitude in the arts of peace as well as of war might offer incalculable resources to a sovereign who should know how to render them tractable and rule them wisely. Not only did they possess the elements of a

[1] India is not referred to in the Behistun Inscription, but is mentioned in one of the Inscriptions of Persepolis (E, ll. 17, 18; cf. WEISSBACH and BANG, *Die Altpersischen Keilins.*, pp. 34, 35), and in that of Nakhsh-î-Rustem (l. 25; cf. ID., *ibid.*, pp. 36, 37). The campaign in which it was subjugated must be placed about 512 B.C.

[2] HERODOTUS, IV. xliv. Scylax published an account of his voyage which was still extant in the time of Aristotle (*Politics*, viii. 13, § 1). Hugo Berger questions the authenticity of the circumnavigation of Arabia (*Gesch. der Wissenschaftlichen Erdkunde der Griechen*, vol. i. pp. 47-49), as that of the circumnavigation of Africa under Necho (cf. what is stated on this subject, *supra*, p. 533, note 1).

Two Soldiers of the Body guard of Darius

(FROM THE LOUVRE)

PRINTED BY FORTIER MAROTTE, IN PARIS. — FRANCE

navy as enterprising and efficacious as that of the Phœnicians, but the perfection of their equipment and their discipline on land rendered them always superior to any Asiatic army, in whatever circumstances, unless they were crushed by over-whelming numbers. Inquisitive, bold, and restless, greedy of gain, and inured to the fatigues and dangers of travel, the Greeks were to be encountered every-where—in Asia Minor, Egypt, Syria, Babylon, and even Persia itself; and it was a Greek, we must remember, whom the great king commissioned to navigate the course of the Indus and the waters of the Indian Ocean.[1] At the same time, the very ardour of their temperament, and their consequent pride, their impatience of all regular control, their habitual proneness to civic strife, and to sanguinary quarrels with the inhabitants of the neighbouring cities, rendered them the most dangerous subjects imaginable to govern, and their loyalty very uncertain. Moreover, their admission as vassals of the Persian empire had not altered their relations with European Greece, and commercial transactions between the opposite shores of the Ægean, inter-marriages, the travels of voyagers, movements of mercenaries, and political combinations, went on as freely and frequently under the satraps of Sardes as under the Mermnadæ. It was to Corinth, Sparta, and Athens that the families banished by Cyrus after his conquest fled for refuge, and every time a change of party raised a new tyrant to power in one of the Æolian, Ionian, or Doric communities, the adherents of the deposed ruler rushed in similar manner to seek shelter among their friends across the sea, sure to repay their hospitality should occasion ever require it. Plots and counterplots were formed between the two shores, without any one paying much heed to the imperial authority of Persia, and the constant support which the subject Greeks found among their free brethren was bound before long to rouse the anger of the court at Susa. When Polycrates, fore-seeing the fall of Amasis, placed himself under the suzerainty of Cambyses, the Corinthians and Spartans came to besiege him in Samos without manifest-ing any respect for the great king.[2] They failed in this particular enterprise,[3] but later on, after Orœtes had been seized and put to death, it was to the Spartans that the successor of Polycrates, Mæandrios, applied for help to assert his claim to the possession of the tyranny against Syloson, brother of Polycrates and a personal friend of Darius.[4] This constant intervention of the foreigner

[1] Cf. what is said of the expedition of Scylax, *supra*, p. 694.

[2] HERODOTUS, III. xxxix., xliv., lvi., with a mixture of romantic adventures.

[3] HERODOTUS, III. cxx., cxxv.; cf. STESIMBROTUS, *Fragm.* 12, in MÜLLER-DIDOT, *Fragm. Hist. Græc.*, vol. ii. pp. 56, 57. The date of the death of Polycrates must be placed between that of the conquest of Egypt and that of the revolt of Gaumâta, either in 524 or 523 B.C.

[4] HERODOTUS, III. cxxxix.–cxlix., and the simple fact, without the popular embellishments related by Herodotus in THUCYDIDES, I. xiii. The reinstatement of Syloson may be placed in 516 B.C., about the time when Darius was completing the reorganisation of the empire and preparing to attack Greece.

was in evident contradiction to the spirit which had inspired the reorganisation of the empire. Just when efforts were being made to strengthen the imperial power and ensure more effective obedience from the provincials by the institution of satrapies, it was impossible to put up with acts of unwarrantable interference, which would endanger the prestige of the sovereign and the authority of his officers. Conquest presented the one and only natural means of escape from the difficulties of the present situation and of preventing their recurrence; when satraps should rule over the European as well as over the Asiatic coasts of the Ægean, all these turbulent Greeks would be forced to live at peace with one another and in awe of the sovereign, as far as their fickle nature would allow. It was not then, as is still asserted, the mere caprice of a despot which brought upon the Greek world the scourge of the Persian wars, but the imperious necessity of security, which obliges well-organised empires to subjugate in turn all the tribes and cities which cause constant trouble on its frontiers. Darius, who was already ruler of a good third of the Hellenic world, from Trebizond to Barca, saw no other means of keeping what he already possessed, and of putting a stop to the incessant fomentation of rebellion in his own territories, than to conquer the mother-country as he had conquered the colonies, and to reduce to subjection the whole of European Hellas.

THE LAST DAYS OF THE OLD EASTERN WORLD.

THE MEDIAN WARS—THE LAST NATIVE DYNASTIES OF EGYPT—THE EASTERN WORLD ON THE EVE OF THE MACEDONIAN CONQUEST.

The Persians in 512 B.C.—European Greece and the dangers which its independence presented to the safety of the empire—The preliminaries of the Median wars: the Scythian expedition, the conquest of Thrace and Macedonia—The Ionic revolt, the intervention of Athens and the taking of Sardes; the battle of Ladê—Mardonius in Thrace and in Macedonia.

The Median wars—The expedition of Datis and Artaphernes: the taking of Eretria, the battle of Marathon (490)—The revolt of Egypt under Khabbisha; the death of Darius and the accession of Xerxes I.—The revolt of Babylon under Shamasherib—The invasion of Greece: Artemision, Thermopylæ, the taking of Athens, Salamis—Platæa and the final retreat of the Persians: Mycalê—The war carried on by the Athenians and the league of Delos: Inaros, the campaigns in Cyprus and Egypt, the peace of Callias—The death of Xerxes.

Artaxerxes I. (465–424): the revolt of Megabyzos—The palaces of Pasargadæ, Persepolis, and Susa; Persian architecture and sculpture; court life, the king and his harem—Revolutions in the palace—Xerxes II., Sekudianos, Darius II.—Intervention in Greek affairs and the convention of Miletus; the end of the peace of Callias—Artaxerxes II. (404–359) and Cyrus the Younger: the battle of Kunaxa and the retreat of the ten thousand (401).

Troubles in Asia Minor, Syria, and Egypt—Amyrtœus and the XXVIIIth Saite dynasty —The XXIXth Sebennytic dynasty—Nephorites I., Hakoris, Psammutis, their alliances with Evagoras and with the states of Continental Greece—The XXXth Mendesian dynasty— Nectanebo I., Tachôs and the invasion of Syria, the revolt of Nectanebo II.—The death of Artaxerxes II.—The accession of Ochus (359 B.C.), his unfortunate wars in the Delta, the conquest of Egypt (342) and the reconstitution of the empire.

The Eastern world: Elam, Urartu, the Syrian kingdoms, the ancient Semitic states decayed and decaying—Babylon in its decline—The Jewish state and its miseries—Nehemiah, Ezra—Egypt in the eyes of the Greeks: Sais, the Delta, the inhabitants of the marshes— Memphis, its monuments, its population—Travels in Upper Egypt: the Fayum, Khemmis, Thebes, Elephantinê—The apparent vigour and actual feebleness of Egypt.

Persia and its powerlessness to resist attack: the rise of Macedonia, Philippi—Arses (337) and Darius Codomannos (336)—Alexander the Great—The invasion of Asia—The battle of Granicus and the conquest of the Asianic peninsula—Issus, the siege of Tyre and of Gaza, the conquest of Egypt, the foundation of Alexandria—Arbela: the conquest of Babylon, Susa, and Ecbatana—The death of Darius and the last days of the old Eastern world.

A LION-HUNT, PERSIANS AND MACEDONIANS.[1]

CHAPTER VII.

THE LAST DAYS OF THE OLD EASTERN WORLD.

The Median wars—The last native dynasties of Egypt—The Eastern world on the eve of
the Macedonian conquest.

DARIUS appears to have formed this project of conquest immediately after his first victories, when his initial attempts to institute satrapies had taught him not only the condition and needs of Asia Minor, but of the various other regions subject to his laws. Two roads lay open before him by which to achieve his end. One by sea, from the Ionian to the Attic coast, straight through the Cyclades; the other by land, with the exception of the narrow straits of the Bosphorus or of the Hellespont, through Thrace and Macedonia. The first was by far the shorter, but the more perilous. It required the possession of an immense fleet, for such a bold undertaking could not be carried out without a considerable force of men,

---

[1] Drawn by Boudier, from one of the sarcophagi of Sidon, now in the Museum of St. Irene; cf. HAMDY-BEY and TH. REINACH, *La Nécropole de Sidon*, pls. xxxi., xxxiv. The initial letter, which is by Faucher-Gudin, represents the sitting cynocephalus of Nectanebo I., now in the Egyptian Museum at the Vatican.

and the largest vessels then built could transport only a small number of troops and horses in addition to their ordinary crew; it also incurred the risk of a naval engagement—an event always to be dreaded with vessels heavily laden with men and the material of war, when it was a question of encountering such experienced seamen as the Greeks of that period. Prudence, therefore, prompted its rejection, however great an economy of time and fatigue it promised, unless it were possible to avoid an encounter with the enemy's fleet, and on landing to be sure of meeting with partisans willing to throw open the gates of their towns, or at least facilitate the work of disembarkation. Attica was the point aimed at, for it was the key of the position, and the possession of it would have permitted Darius to adopt the sea-route without undue risk; but Athens was in the hands of the Pisistratidæ, and Hippias, although he was the vassal of Persia through holding the fief of Sigæum in the Troad, was not at all anxious to see Darius establish himself in the heart of Hellas. As long as Athens was hostile, the safest route, and, indeed, the only one practicable for the entire Persian army, was that bordering the north of the Ægean, debouching at the defiles of Thessaly. It was this road that the authorities at Susa finally selected, although its choice entailed a host of preliminary precautions which demanded time, men, and money; there were fresh Greek colonies to be subdued, and beyond them the warlike people of Thrace, while behind these lay the Scythian tribes. Even though a century had elapsed since the death of Madyes, the remembrance of the Scythians continued to alarm the whole of Asia; tales were still told among the Medes, in Lydia, in the sanctuary of Ascalon, on the frontier of Egypt, and in the sacred cities of Pteria,[1] of their wild raids over mountain and valley, their path marked by cities given to the flames or razed to the ground, populations carried away as slaves, violated temples, and always, as a sequel to these chapters of horrors, the vengeance which the offended gods wreaked upon them for these acts of sacrilege.[2] More recently the accounts given by the Greek colonists and the itinerant merchants of the northern shores of the Black Sea, without detracting from the report of their courage and ferocity, had added to it that of their wealth;[3] gold-mines were said to be scattered over the regions occupied by them, guarded by griffins, and worked for the good of the inhabitants by harmless ants as large as foxes. Besides this, Darius was constantly coming into conflict with

---

[1] Cf. *supra*, pp. 480, 481.

[2] The records of the Scythian invasion have been preserved by Herodotus, I. xv., ciii.–cvi.

[3] Herodotus, IV. xiii., xxvii., III. cxvi.; Ctesias, *Fragm.* 57, § 12, 70, in Müller-Didot, *Ctesiæ Cnidii Fragmenta*, pp. 82, 95–97; Strabo, XI. viii. § 4, p. 511. Most of these semi-fabulous traditions originated in Aristæus of Proconnesus and his Arimaspia (Hugo Berger, *Geschichte der wissenschaftlichen Erdkunde der Griechen*, vol. i. pp. 22, 23).

one or other of their hordes on his northern frontiers—on the Iaxartes, beyond Bactriana and Sogdiana, in the Caucasus, and latterly in Europe, on the Ister and the borders of Thrace. It is, therefore, not to be wondered at that, before attacking Greece, he desired to provide against all risks by teaching the Scythians such a lesson as would prevent them from bearing down upon his right flank during his march, or upon his rear while engaged in a crucial struggle in the Hellenic peninsula. On the other hand, the geo- graphical information possessed by the Persians with regard to the Danubian regions was of so vague a character, that Darius must have believed the Scythians to have been nearer to his line of operations, and their country less desolate than was really the case.[1] A flotilla, commanded by Ariaramnes, satrap of Cappadocia, ventured across the Black Sea in 515,[2] landed a few thousand men upon the opposite shore, and brought back prisoners who furnished those in command with the information they required.[3] Darius, having learned what he could from these poor wretches, crossed the Bosphorus in 514, with a body of troops which tradition computed at 800,000, conquered the eastern coast of Thrace, and won his way in a series of conflicts as far as the Ister. The Ionian sailors built for him a bridge of boats, which he entrusted to their care, and he then started forward into the steppes in search of the enemy. The Scythians refused a pitched battle, but they burnt the pastures before him on every side, filled up the wells, carried off the cattle, and then slowly retreated into the interior, leaving Darius to face the vast extent of the steppes and the terrors of famine. Later tradition stated that he wandered for two months in these solitudes between the Ister and the Tanais; he had constructed on the banks of this latter river a series of earthworks, the remains of which were shown in the time of Herodotus, and had at length returned to his point of departure with merely the loss of a few sick men. The barbarians stole a march upon him, and advised the Greeks to destroy the

---

[1] The motives imputed to Darius by the ancients for making this expedition are the desire of avenging the disasters of the Scythian invasion (HERODOTUS, IV. i., VII. xx.), or of performing an exploit which should render him as famous as his predecessors in the eyes of posterity (DIODORUS SICULUS, x. 5, certainly following Ephorus).

[2] The reconnaissance of Ariaramnes is intimately connected with the expedition itself in Ctesias (*Fragm.* 29, § 16, in MÜLLER-DIDOT, *Ctesiæ Cnidii Fragmenta*, p. 49), and could have preceded it by a few months only. If we take for the date of the latter the year 514–513, the date given in the Table of the Capitol (*Corpus Inscriptionum Græcarum*, No. 6355 *d*), that of the former cannot be earlier than 515. Ariaramnes was not satrap of Cappadocia, for Cappadocia belonged then to the satrapy of Daskylion (KRUMBHOLZ, *De Asiæ Minoris Satrapis*, p. 60).

[3] CTESIAS, *Fragm.* 29, § 16, in MÜLLER-DIDOT, *Ctesiæ Cnidii Fragmenta*, p. 49. The supplementary paragraphs of the Inscription of Behistun speak of an expedition of Darius against the Sakæ (col. v. ll. 21–31; cf. WEISSBACH and BANG, *Die Altpersischen Keilinschriften*, pp. 30, 31), which is supposed to have had as its objective either the sea of Aral or the Tigris. Would it not be possible to suppose that the sea mentioned is the Pontus Euxinus, and to take the mutilated text of Behistun to be a description either of the campaign beyond the Danube, or rather of the preliminary *reconnaissance* of Ariaramnes a year before the expedition itself?

bridge, retire within their cities, and abandon the Persians to their fate. The tyrant of the Chersonnesus, Miltiades the Athenian, was inclined to follow their advice; but Histiæus, the governor of Miletus, opposed it, and eventually carried his point. Darius reached the southern bank without difficulty, and returned to Asia.[1] The Greek towns of Thrace thought themselves rid of him, and rose in revolt; but he left 80,000 men in Europe who, at first under Megabyzos, and then under Otanes, reduced them to subjection one after another, and even obliged Amyntas I., the King of Macedonia, to become a tributary of the empire.[2] The expedition had not only failed to secure the submission of the Scythians, but apparently provoked reprisals on their part, and several of their bands penetrated ere long into the Chersonnesus.[3] It nevertheless was not without solid result, for it showed that Darius, even if he could not succeed in subjugating the savage Danubian tribes, had but little to fear from them; it also secured for him a fresh province, that of Thrace, and, by the possession of Macedonia, brought his frontier into contact with Northern Greece. The overland route, in any case the more satisfactory of the two, was now in the hands of the invader.[4]

Revolutions at Athens prevented him from setting out on his expedition as soon as he had anticipated. Hippias had been overthrown in 510, and having taken refuge at Sigæum, was seeking on all sides for some one to avenge him against his fellow-citizens. The satrap of Sardes, Artaphernes, declined at first to listen to him, for he hoped that the Athenians themselves would appeal to him, without his being obliged to have recourse to their former tyrant. As a matter of fact, they sent him an embassy, and begged his help against the Spartans. He promised it on condition that they would yield the traditional homage of earth and water, and their delegates complied with his demand, though on their return to Athens they were disowned

---

[1] HERODOTUS, IV. lxxxiii.–cxliii.: cf. CTESIAS, *Fragm.* 29, § 18, in MÜLLER-DIDOT, *Ctesiæ Cnidii Fragmenta*, p. 49, who limits the campaign beyond the Danube to a fifteen days' march; and STRABO, VII., iii. §§ 14, 15, p. 305, who places the crossing of the Danube near the mouth of that river, at the island of Peukê, and makes the expedition stop at the Dniester. Neither the line of direction of the Persian advance nor their farthest point reached is known. The eight forts which they were said to have built, the ruins of which were shown on the banks of the Oaros as late as the time of Herodotus (IV. cxxiv.), were probably tumuli similar to those now met with on the Russian steppes, the origin of which is ascribed by the people to persons celebrated in their history or traditions (KONDAKOFF and REINACH, *Antiquités de la Russie Méridionale*, pp. 157, 158).

[2] HERODOTUS, IV. cxlii.–cxliv., V. i., ii., xi.–xxvi., VII. cv.–cvii., with every sort of romantic detail borrowed from local, usually Macedonian, tradition.

[3] HERODOTUS, VI. xl., where the event is said to have taken place in the third year of Miltiades' government of the Chersonnesus.

[4] I had at first treated the whole subject of the Median wars at some length, and also given a general outline of the relations of that empire with the Greeks, but the necessity of keeping within the prescribed limits prevents me from giving more than a brief summary of events, and compels me to refer the reader to the latest histories of Greece. I have confined myself to the narration of facts which specially concern the ancient Eastern states of Egypt and Babylon, almost omitting the history—at least in the present edition—even of the Phœnicians and the Jews.

by the citizens (508).[1] Artaphernes, disappointed in this direction, now entered into communications with Hippias, and such close relations soon existed between the two that the Athenians showed signs of uneasiness. Two years later they again despatched fresh deputies to Sardes to beg the satrap not to espouse the cause of their former ruler. For a reply the satrap summoned them to recall the exiles, and, on their refusing (506),[2] their city became thenceforward the ostensible objective of the Persian army and fleet. The partisans of Hippias within the town were both numerous and active; it was expected that they would rise and hand over the city as soon as their chief should land on a point of territory with a force sufficient to intimidate the opposing faction. Athens in the hands of Hippias, would mean Athens in the hands of the Persians, and Greece accessible to the Persian hordes at all times by the shortest route. Darius therefore prepared to make the attempt, and in order to guard against any mishap, he caused all the countries that he was about to attack to be explored beforehand. Spies attached to his service were sent to scour the coasts of the Peloponnesus and take note of all its features, the state of its ports, the position of the islands and the fortresses; and they penetrated as far as Italy, if we may believe the story subsequently told to Herodotus.[3] While he thus studied the territory from a distance, he did not neglect precautions nearer to hand, but ordered the Milesians to occupy in his name the principal stations of the Ægean between Ionia and Attica. Histiæus, whose loyalty had stood Darius in such good stead at the bridge over the Danube, did not, however, appear to him equal to so delicate a task: the king summoned him to Susa on some slight pretext, loaded him with honours, and replaced him by his nephew Aristagoras. Aristagoras at once attempted to justify the confidence placed in him by taking possession of Naxos; but the surprise that he had prepared ended in failure, discontent crept in among his men, and after a fruitless siege of four months he was obliged to withdraw (499).[4] His failure changed the tide of affairs. He was afraid that the Persians would regard it as a crime, and this fear prompted him to risk everything to save his fortune and his life. He retired from his office as tyrant, exhorted the Milesians, who were henceforth free to do so, to make war on the barbarians, and seduced from their allegiance the crews of the vessels just returned from Naxos, and still lying in the mouths of the

---

[1] HERODOTUS, V. lxxiii.

[2] HERODOTUS, V. xcvi.; the date is fixed at the time when the Athenians first ostracised the principal partisans of the Pisistratids, and amongst others Hipparchus, son of Charmes, *i.e.* in 507–6.

[3] HERODOTUS, III. cxxix.–cxxxviii., where it is said that Darius sent spies with the physician Democedes of Crotona shortly before the Scythian expedition (III. cxxxiii.).

[4] HERODOTUS, V. xxx.–xxxiv., where an unlikely act of treachery is attributed to Megabates the Persian, who was commanding the Iranian contingent attached to the Ionian troops.

Mæander; the tyrants who commanded them were seized, some exiled, and some put to death. The Æolians soon made common cause with their neighbours the Ionians, and by the last days of autumn the whole of the Ægean littoral was under arms (499).[1] From the outset Aristagoras realised that they would be promptly overcome if Asiatic Hellas were not supported by Hellas in Europe. While the Lydian satrap was demanding reinforcements from his sovereign, Aristagoras therefore repaired to the Peloponnesus as a suppliant for help. Sparta, embroiled in one of her periodical quarrels with Argos, gave him an insolent refusal;[2] even Athens, where the revolution had for the moment relieved her from the fear of the Pisistratidæ and the terrors of a barbarian invasion, granted him merely twenty triremes—enough to draw down reprisals on her immediately after their defeat, without sensibly augmenting the rebels' chances of success; to the Athenian contingent Eretria added five vessels, and this comprised his whole force.[3] The leaders of the movement did not hesitate to assume the offensive with these slender resources. As early as the spring of 498, before Artaphernes had received reinforcements, they marched suddenly on Sardes. They burnt the lower town, but, as on many previous occasions, the citadel held out;[4] after having encamped for several days at the foot of its rock, they returned to Ephesus laden with the spoil.[5] This indeed was a check to their hostilities, and such an abortive attempt was calculated to convince them of their powerlessness against the foreign rule. None the less, however, when it was generally known that they had burnt the capital of Asia Minor, and had with impunity made the representative of the great king feel in his palace the smoke of the conflagration, the impression was such as actual victory could have produced. The cities which had hitherto hesitated to join them, now espoused their cause—the ports of the Troad and the Hellespont, Lycia, the Carians, and Cyprus—and their triumph would possibly have been secured had Greece beyond the Ægean followed the general movement and joined the coalition. Sparta, however, persisted in

---

[1] HERODOTUS, V. xxxv.–xxxviii. The Dorian cities took no part in the revolt—at least Herodotus never mentions them among the confederates. The three Ionian cities of Ephesus, Kolophon, and Lebedos also seem to have remained aloof, and we know that the Ephesians were not present at the battle of Ladê (HERODOTUS, VI. xvi.).

[2] HERODOTUS, V. xxxviii., xlix.–liv., from a Laconian tradition. Aristagoras had with him a map of the world engraved on a bronze plate (HERODOTUS, V. xlix.), which was probably a copy of the chart drawn up by Hecatæus of Miletus.

[3] HERODOTUS, V. xcvii., xcix.

[4] On the revolt of Paktyas, cf. *supra*, p. 623.

[5] HERODOTUS, V. xcix.–ci., where it is said that the Ionians on their return suffered a serious reverse near Ephesus. The author seems to have adopted some Lydian or Persian tradition hostile to the Ionians, for Charon of Lampsacus, who lived nearer to the time of these events, mentions only the retreat, and hints at no defeat (*Fragm.* 2, in MÜLLER-DIDOT, *Fragm. Hist. Græc.*, vol. i. p. 32). If the expedition had really ended in this disaster, it is not at all likely that the revolt would have attained the dimensions it did immediately afterwards.

her indifference, and Athens took the opportunity of withdrawing from the struggle.[1] The Asiatic Greeks made as good a defence as they could, but their resources fell far short of those of the enemy, and they could do no more than delay the catastrophe and save their honour by their bravery. Cyprus was the first to yield during the winter of 498–497. Its vessels, in conjunction with those of the Ionians, dispersed the fleet of the Phœnicians off Salamis, but the troops of their princes, still imbued with the old system of military tactics, could not sustain the charge of the Persian battalions; they gave way under the walls of Salamis, and their chief, Onesilus, was killed in a final charge of his chariotry.[2] His death effected the ruin of the Ionian cause in Cyprus, which on the continent suffered at the same time no less serious reverses. The towns of the Hellespont and of Æolia succumbed one after another; Kymê and Clazomenæ next opened their gates; the Carians were twice beaten, once near the White Columns, and again near Labranda, and their victory at Pedasos suspended merely for an instant the pro-

A CYPRIOT CHARIOT.[3]

gress of the Persian arms, so that towards the close of 497 the struggle was almost entirely concentrated round Miletus.[4] Aristagoras, seeing that his cause was now desperate, agreed with his partisans that they should expatriate themselves. He fell fighting against the Edonians of Thrace, attempting to force the important town of Enneahodoi, near the mouth of the Strymon (496);[5] but his defection had not discouraged any one, and Histiæus, who had been sent to Sardes by the great king to negotiate the submission of the rebels, failed in his errand.[6] Even when blockaded on the land side, Miletus could defy an attack so long as communication with the sea was not cut off.

---

[1] HERODOTUS, V. cii., ciii.; the Eretrians did not give up the contest. Later writers attributed to them an influence and achievements quite disproportionate to the smallness of their number (LYSANIAS OF MALLOS, in MÜLLER-DIDOT, *Fragm. Hist. Græc.*, vol. iv. p. 441).

[2] HERODOTUS, V. ciii., civ., cvii.–cxv. The movement in Cyprus must have begun in the winter of 499–498, for Onesilus was already in the field when Darius heard of the burning of Sardes (HERODOTUS, V. cv.); and as it lasted for a year (V. cxvi.), it must have been quelled in the winter of 498–497.

[3] Drawn by Faucher-Gudin, from the terra-cotta group in the New York Museum.

[4] HERODOTUS, V. cxv.–cxxii.

[5] HERODOTUS, V. cxxiv.–cxxvi., VI. i., where the town is not named, but a passage in Thucydides (iv. 102) shows that it was Enneahodoi, afterwards Amphipolis, and that the death of Aristagoras took place thirty-two years before the Athenian defeat at Drabeskos, *i.e.* probably in 496.

[6] See the account of the intrigues of Histiæus and of the adventurous close of his life, in Herodotus (V. cvi., cvii., VI. i.–xxv.–xxx.).

Darius therefore brought up the Phœnician fleet, reinforced it with the Cypriot contingents, and despatched the united squadrons to the Archipelago during the summer of 494. The confederates, even after the disasters of the preceding years, still possessed 353 vessels, most of them of 30 to 50 oars; they were, however, completely defeated near the small island of Ladê, in the latter part of the summer, and Miletus, from that moment cut off from the rest of the world, capitulated a few weeks later. A small proportion of its inhabitants continued to dwell in the ruined city, but the greater number were carried away to Ampê, at the mouth of the Tigris, in the marshes of the Nâr-Marratum.[1] Caria was reconquered during the winter of 494–493, and by the early part of 493, Chios, Lesbos, Tenedos, the cities of the Chersonnesus and of Propontis—in short, all which yet held out—were reduced to obedience. Artaphernes reorganised his vanquished states entirely in the interest of Persia. He did not interfere with the constitutions of the several republics, but he reinstated the tyrants. He regulated and augmented the various tributes, prohibited private wars, and gave to the satrap the right of disposing of all quarrels at his own tribunal. The measures which he adopted had long after his day the force of law among the Asiatic Greeks, and it was by them they regulated their relations with the representatives of the great king.[2]

If Darius had ever entertained doubts as to the necessity for occupying European Greece to ensure the preservation of peace in her Asiatic sister-country, the revolt of Ionia must have completely dissipated them. It was a question whether the cities which had so obstinately defied him for six long years, would ever resign themselves to servitude as long as they saw the peoples of their race maintaining their independence on the opposite shores of the Ægean, and while the misdeeds of which the contingents of Eretria and Athens had been guilty during the rebellion remained unpunished. A tradition, which sprang up soon after the event, related that on hearing of the burning of Sardes, Darius had bent his bow and let fly an arrow towards the sky, praying Zeus to avenge him on the Athenians; and at the same time he had commanded one of his slaves to repeat three times a day before him, at every meal, " Sire, remember the Athenians! "[3] As a matter of fact, the intermeddling of these strangers between the sovereign and his subjects was at once a serious insult to the Achæmenids and a cause of anxiety to the empire; to

[1] HERODOTUS, VI. vi.–xx. The year 497, *i.e.* three years before the capture of the town, appears to be an unlikely date for the battle of Lade (BUSOLT, *Griechische Geschichte*, vol. ii. pp. 39–42): Miletus must have fallen in the autumn or winter months following the defeat. Cf., on Ampê, the article of Andreas in PAULI-WISSOWA, *Real-Encyclopædie*, vol. i. pp. 1877–1880.

[2] HERODOTUS, VI. xxv.–xxxiii., xli.–xlii.

[3] HERODOTUS, V. cv.; the legend is clearly older than the time of Herodotus, for in the *Persæ* of Æschylus the shade of Darius, when coming out of his tomb, cries to the old men, " Remember Athens and Greece! "

leave it unpunished would have been an avowal of weakness or timidity, which would not fail to be quickly published in Syria, Egypt, Babylon, and on the Scythian frontiers, and would ere long give rise to similar acts of revolt and interference. Darius, therefore, resumed his projects, but with greater activity than before, and with a resolute purpose to make a final reckoning with the Greeks, whatever it might cost him. The influence of his nephew Mardonius at first inclined him to adopt the overland route, and he sent him into Thrace with a force of men and a fleet of galleys sufficient to overcome all obstacles. Mardonius marched against the Greek colonies and native tribes which had thrown off the yoke during the Ionian war, and reduced those who had still managed to preserve their independence. The Bryges opposed him with such

ALEXANDER I. OF MACEDON.[1]

determination, that summer was drawing to its close before he was able to continue his march. He succeeded, however, in laying hands on Macedonia, and obliged its king, Alexander, to submit to the conditions accepted by his father Amyntas; but at this juncture half of his fleet was destroyed by a tempest in the vicinity of Mount Athos, and the disaster, which took place just as winter was approaching, caused him to suspend his operations (492).[2] He was recalled on account of his failure, and the command was transferred to Datis the Mede and to the Persian Artaphernes. Darius, however, while tentatively using the land routes through Greece for his expeditions, had left no stone unturned to secure for himself that much-coveted sea-way which would carry him straight into the heart of the enemy's position, and he had

A PHŒNICIAN GALLEY.[3]

opened negotiations with the republics of Greece proper. Several of them had consented to tender him earth and water, among them being Ægina,[4] and besides this, the state of the various factions in Athens was such, that he had every reason to believe that he could count on the support of a large section of the population when the day came for him to disembark his force on the shores of Attica. He therefore decided to direct his next expedition against Athens itself, and he employed the year 491 in concentrating his troops and triremes in Cilicia, at a sufficient distance from the European coast to ensure

---

[1] Drawn by Faucher-Gudin, from a coin in the *Cabinet des Médailles*, a cast of which was courteously sent me by M. Babelon.

[2] HERODOTUS, VI. xliii.–xlv.

[3] Drawn by Faucher-Gudin, from a coin of Byblos in the *Cabinet des Médailles*, a cast of which was courteously sent me by M. Babelon.

[4] HERODOTUS, VI. xlviii., xlix., where it is said that *all* the island-dwelling Greeks, πάντες νησιῶται, submitted to the great king. But Herodotus himself says later on (VI. xcvi.) that the people of Naxos, at all events, proved refractory.

their safety from any sudden attack.　In the spring of 490 the army recruited from among the most warlike nations of the empire—the Persians, Medes, and Sakæ—went aboard the Phœnician fleet, while galleys built on a special model were used as transports for the cavalry.[1]　The entire convoy sailed safely out of the mouth of the Pyramos to the port of Samos, coasting the shores of Asia Minor, and then passing through the Cyclades, from Samos to Naxos, where they met with no opposition from the inhabitants, headed for Delos, where Datis offered a sacrifice to Apollo, whom he confounded with his god Mithra;

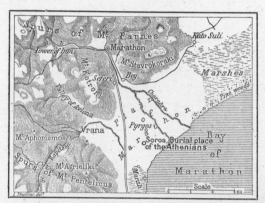

finally they reached Eubœa, where Eretria and Carystos vainly endeavoured to hold their own against them.　Eretria was reduced to ashes, as Sardes had been, and such of its citizens as had not fled into the mountains at the enemy's approach were sent into exile among the Kissians in the township of Arderikka.　Hippias meanwhile had joined the Persians and had been taken into their confidence.　While awaiting the result of the intrigues of his partisans in Athens, he had advised Datis to land on the eastern coast of Attica, in the neighbourhood of Marathon, at the very place from whence his father Pisistratus had set out forty years before to return to his country after his first exile.　The position was well chosen for the expected engagement.　The bay and the strand which bordered it afforded an excellent station for the fleet, and the plain, in spite of its marshes and brushwood, was one of those rare spots where cavalry might be called into play without serious drawbacks.　A few hours on foot would bring the bulk of the infantry up to the Acropolis by a fairly good road, while by the same time the fleet would be able to reach the roadstead of Phalerum.　All had been arranged beforehand for concerted action when the expected rising should take place; but it never did take place, and instead of the friends whom the Persians expected, an armed force presented itself, commanded by the polemarch Callimachus and the ten strategi, among whom figured the famous Miltiades.　At the first news of the disembarkation of the enemy, the republic had despatched the messenger Phidippides to Sparta to beg for immediate assistance, and in the mean time had sent forward

---

[1] The whole of this account, often somewhat legendary in character, is found in detail in HERODOTUS, VI. xciv.–cii.　The French reader may see a minute criticism of it in the remarkable work by AMÉDÉE HAUVETTE, *Hérodote historien des Guerres Médiques*, pp. 236–274, where the bibliography of the subject is given up to 1894.

all her able-bodied troops to meet the invaders. They comprised about 10,000 hoplites, accompanied, as was customary, by nearly as many more light infantry, who were shortly reinforced by 1000 Platæans. They encamped in the valley of Avlona, around a small temple of Heracles, in a position commanding the roads into the interior, and from whence they could watch the enemy without exposing themselves to an unexpected attack. The two armies

THE BATTLE-FIELD OF MARATHON.[1]

watched each other for a fortnight, Datis expecting a popular outbreak which would render an engagement unnecessary, Miltiades waiting patiently till the Lacedæmonians had come up, or till some false move on the part of his opponent gave him the opportunity of risking a decisive action. What took place at the end of this time is uncertain. Whether Datis grew tired of inaction, or whether he suddenly resolved to send part of his forces by sea, so as to land on the neighbouring shore of Athens, and Miltiades fell upon his rear when only half his men had got on board the fleet, is not known.[2] At any rate, Miltiades, with the Platæans on his left, set his battalions in movement without warning, and charged the enemy with a rush. The Persians and the Sakæ broke the centre of the line, but the two wings, after having dispersed the assailants on

[1] Drawn by Boudier, from a photograph by M. Amédée Hauvette.
[2] HERODOTUS, VI. ciii.–cxx. For the various hypotheses to which the account of the battle of Marathon has given rise, cf. A. HAUVETTE, *Hérodote historien des Guerres Médiques*, pp. 256-265.

their front, wheeled round upon them and overcame them : 6000 barbarians were left dead upon the field as against some 200 Athenians and Platæans, but by dint of their valiant efforts the remainder managed to save the fleet with a loss of only seven galleys. Datis anchored that evening off the island of Ægilia, and at the same moment the victorious army perceived a signal hoisted on the heights of Pentelicus apparently to attract his attention ; when he set sail the next morning and, instead of turning eastwards, proceeded to double Cape Sunion, Miltiades had no longer any doubt that treachery was at work, and returned to Athens by forced marches. Datis, on entering the roads of Phalerum, found the shore defended, and the army that he had left at Marathon encamped upon the Cynosargê. He cruised about for a few hours in sight of the shore, and finding no movement made to encourage him to land, he turned his vessels about and set sail for Ionia.

The material loss to the Persians was inconsiderable, for even the Cyclades remained under their authority ; Miltiades, who endeavoured to retake them, met with a reverse before Paros, and the Athenians, disappointed by his unsuccessful attempt, made no further efforts to regain them. The moral effect of the victory on Greece and the empire was extraordinary. Up till then the Median soldiers had been believed to be the only invincible troops in the world ; the sight of them alone excited dread in the bravest hearts, and their name was received everywhere with reverential awe.[1] But now a handful of hoplites from one of the towns of the continent, and that not the most renowned for its prowess, without cavalry or bowmen, had rushed upon and overthrown the most terrible of all Oriental battalions, the Persians and the Sakæ. Darius could not put up with such an affront without incurring the risk of losing his prestige with the people of Asia and Europe, who up till then had believed him all-powerful, and of thus exposing himself to the possibility of revolutions in recently subdued countries, such as Egypt, which had always retained the memory of her past greatness. In the interest of his own power, as well as to soothe his wounded pride, a renewed attack was imperative, and this time it must be launched with such dash and vigour that all resistance would be at once swept before it. Events had shown him that the influence of the Pisistratidæ had not been strong enough to secure for him the opening of the gates of Athens, and that the sea route did not permit of his concentrating an adequate force of cavalry and infantry on the field of battle ; he therefore reverted to the project of an expedition by the overland route, skirting the coasts of Thrace and Macedonia. During three years he collected arms, provisions, horses, men, and vessels, and was ready to commence hostilities in the spring of 487, when affairs in Egypt

[1] HERODOTUS, VI. cxii.

prevented him.[1] This country had undeniably prospered under his suzerainty. It formed, with Cyrene and the coast of Libya, the sixth of his satrapies, to which were attached the neighbouring Nubian tribes of the southern frontier.[2] The Persian satrap, installed at the White Wall in the ancient palace of the Pharaohs, was supported by an army of 120,000 men, who occupied the three entrenched camps of the Saites—Daphnæ and Marea on the confines of the Delta, and Elephantinê in the south.[3] Outside these military stations, where the authority of the great king was exercised in a direct manner, the ancient feudal organisation existed intact. The temples retained their possessions and their vassals, and the nobles within their principalities were as independent and as inclined to insurrection as in past times. The annual tribute, the heaviest paid by any province with the exception of Chaldæa and Assyria, amounted only to 700 talents of silver.[4] To this sum must be added the farming of the fishing in Lake Mœris, which, according to Herodotus,[5] brought in one talent a day during the six months

DARIUS ON THE STELE
OF THE ISTHMUS.[7]

of the high Nile, but, according to Diodorus,[6] during the whole year, as well as the 120,000 medimni of wheat required for the army of occupation,[8] and the obligation to furnish the court of Susa with Libyan nitre and Nile water;[9] the total of these impositions was far from constituting a burden disproportionate to the wealth of the Nile valley. Commerce brought in to it, in fact, at least as much money as the tribute took out of it. Incorporated with an empire which extended over three continents, Egypt had access to regions whither the products of her industry and her soil had never yet been carried. The produce of Ethiopia and the Sudan passed through her emporia on its way to attract customers in the markets of Tyre, Sidon, Babylon, and Susa, and the isthmus of Suez and Kosseir were the nearest ports through which Arabia and India could reach the Mediterranean. Darius therefore resumed the work

---

[1] HERODOTUS, VII. i.

[2] HERODOTUS, III. xcvii.; cf. VII. lxix. The Nubian tribes, who are called Ethiopians by the Greek historian and the cuneiform inscriptions (WEISSBACH and BANG, *Die Altpers. Keilins.*, pp. 36, 37), paid no regular tribute, but were obliged to send annually two *chœnikes* of pure gold, two hundred pieces of ebony, twenty elephants' tusks, and five young slaves, all under the name of a free gift.

[3] HERODOTUS, II. xxx., states that in his own time the Persians, like the Saite Pharaohs, still had garrisons at Daphnæ and at Elephantinê (cf. *supra*, p. 498). On the Persian garrison at Memphis, cf. HERODOTUS, III. xci.

[4] HERODOTUS, III. xci.; cf. *supra*, p. 691.

[5] HERODOTUS, II. cxlix., who says that the produce sank to the value of a third of a talent a day during the six other months.

[6] DIODORUS SICULUS, i. 52, who says that the revenue produced by the fisheries in the Lake had been handed over by Mœris to his wife for the expenses of her toilet.

[7] Drawn by Faucher-Gudin, from the *Description de l'Égypte, Antiquités*, vol. v. pl. 20.

[8] HERODOTUS, III. xci.

[9] DINO, *Fragm.* 15, 16, in MÜLLER-DIDOT, *Fragm. Hist. Græc.*, vol. ii. p. 92.

of Necho, and beginning simultaneously at both extremities, he cut afresh the canal between the Nile and the Gulf of Suez. Trilingual stelæ in Egyptian, Persian, and Medic were placed at intervals along its banks, and set forth to all comers the method of procedure by which the sovereign had brought his work to a successful end.[1] In a similar manner he utilised the Wadys which wind between Koptos and the Red Sea, and by their means placed the cities of the Saîd in communication with the "Ladders of Incense," * Punt and the Sabæans.[2] He extended his favour equally to the commerce which they

WALLS OF THE FORTRESS OF DUSH-EL-QALÂA.[3]

carried on with the interior of Africa; indeed, in order to ensure the safety of the caravans in the desert regions nearest to the Nile, he skilfully fortified the Great Oasis. He erected at Habît, Kushît, and other places, several of those rectangular citadels with massive walls of unburnt brick, which

[1] HERODOTUS, II. clviii., IV. xxxix.; cf. WIEDEMANN, Herodots Zweites Buch, pp. 560, 561. Several trilingual inscriptions discovered at different times in the Isthmus of Suez (Description de l'Égypte, Ant., vol. v. pl. 29, vol. v. pp. 150–153, and vol. viii. pp. 27–47; then MARIETTE, La Stèle bilingue de Chalouf, in the Revue Archéologique, 1866; MASPERO, Pièces relatives à la découverte du monument de Chalouf, in the Recueil de Travaux relatifs à la Philologie et à l'Archéologie Égyptiennes et Assyriennes, vol. vii. pp. 1–8; JAILLON and LEMASSON, Lettres à M. Golénischeff au sujet des Monuments Perses de l'Isthme, in the Recueil, vol. xiii. pp. 97–99), and translated or commented upon several times (OPPERT, Mémoire sur les rapports de l'Égypte et de l'Assyrie, pp. 123–127, and Le Peuple et la Langue des Mèdes, p. 214, et. seq.; J. MÉNANT, Les Achéménides, pp. 145–148, and La Stèle de Chalouf, in the Recueil de Travaux, vol. ix. pp. 331–357; DARESSY, Revision des textes de la Stèle de Chalouf, in the Recueil, vol. xi. pp. 160–171; GOLÉNISCHEFF, Stèle de Darius aux environs de Tell el-Maskhoutah, in the Recueil, vol. xiii. pp. 99–109; WEISSBACH and BANG, Die Altpersischen Keilinschriften, pp. 6, 7, 38, 39), confirm the classical tradition and furnish some curious information with regard to the work.

[* For the explanation of this term, cf. Struggle of the Nations, p. 245, note 3.—TR.]

[2] Several of the inscriptions engraved on the rocks of the Wady Hammamât show to what an extent the route was frequented at certain times during the reign. They bear the dates of the 26th, 27th, 28th, 30th, and 36th years of Darius (BURTON, Excerpta Hieroglyphica, pls. iii., iv., xiv.; ROSELLINI, Monumenti Storici, vol. ii. pl. 11 c, and p. 174; LEPSIUS, Denkm., iii. 283). The country of Saba (Sheba) is mentioned on one of the stelæ of the isthmus (GOLÉNISCHEFF, Stèle de Darius aux environs de Tell el-Maskhoutah, in the Recueil de Travaux, vol. xiii. p. 108).

[3] Drawn by Boudier, from the engraving by CAILLIAUD, Voyage à la Grande Oasis, pl. xii. Dush is the Kushît of the hieroglyphs, the Kysis of Græco-Roman times, and is situated on the southern border of the Great Oasis, about the latitude of Assuân.

resisted every effort of the nomad tribes to break through them ; and as the temple at Habît, raised in former times by the Theban Pharaohs, had become ruinous, he rebuilt it from its foundations.[1] He was generous in his gifts to the gods, and even towns as obscure as Edfu was then received from him grants of money and lands.[2] The Egyptians at first were full of gratitude for the favours shown them, but the news of the defeat at Marathon, and the taxes with which the Susian court burdened them in order to make provision for the new war with Greece, aroused a deep-seated

THE GREAT TEMPLE OF DARIUS AT HABÎT.[3]

discontent, at all events amongst those who, living in the Delta, had had their patriotism or their interests most affected by the downfall of the Saite dynasty. It would appear that the priests of Buto, whose oracles exercised an indisputable influence alike over Greeks and natives, had energetically incited the people to revolt. The storm broke in 486, and a certain Khabbîsha, who perhaps belonged to the family of Psammetichus, proclaimed himself king both at Sais and Memphis.[4] Darius did not believe

---

[1] For these buildings in the Oasis, cf. CAILLIAUD, *Voyage à l'Oasis de Thèbes*, p. 46, et seq. ; HOSKINS, *Visit to the Great Oasis*, p. 118 ; BRUGSCH, *Reise nach der grossen Oasen el-Khargeh*, p. 17, et seq.

[2] LEPSIUS, *Denkmäler*, iv. 43 *a*, l. 5, and *Eine Hieroglyphische Inschrift am Tempel von Edfu*, in the *Memoirs* of the Berlin Academy, 1855, p. 75 ; cf. DÜMICHEN, *Bauurkunde der Tempelanlagen von Edfu*, in the *Zeitschrift*, 1871, p. 96. The inscription shows us that the donation was made in the nineteenth year of Darius I.

[3] Drawn by Boudier, from the engraving by CAILLIAUD, *Voyage à l'Oasis de Thèbes*, pl. xviii.

[4] HERODOTUS, VII. i., who does not give the name of the leader of the rebellion, but says that it took place in the fourth year after Marathon. A demotic contract in the Turin Museum bears the date of the third month of the second season of the thirty-fifth year of Darius I. (RÉVILLOUT, *Notice des Papyrus démotiques archaïques*, pp. 435, 436): Khabbîsha's rebellion therefore broke out

the revolt to be of sufficient gravity to delay his plans for any length of time. He hastily assembled a second army, and was about to commence hostilities on the banks of the Nile simultaneously with those on the Hellespont, when he died in 485, in the thirty-sixth year of his reign.[1] He was one of the great sovereigns of the ancient world—the greatest without exception of those who had ruled over Persia. Cyrus and Cambyses had been formidable warriors, and the kingdoms of the East had fallen before their arms, but they were purely military sovereigns, and if their successor had not possessed other abilities than theirs, their empire would have shared the fate of that of the Medes and the Chaldæans; it would have sunk to its former level as rapidly as it had risen, and the splendour of its opening years would have soon faded from remembrance. Darius was no less a general by instinct and training than they, as is proved by the campaigns which procured him his crown; but, after having conquered, he knew how to organise and build up a solid fabric out of the materials which his predecessors had left in a state of chaos; if Persia maintained her rule over the East for two entire centuries, it was due to him and to him alone.

The question of the succession, with its almost inevitable popular outbreaks, had at once to be dealt with. Darius had had several wives, and among them, the daughter of Gobryas, who had borne him three children: Artabazanes, the eldest, had long been regarded as the heir-presumptive, and had probably filled the office of regent during the expedition in Scythia.[2] But Atossa, the daughter of Cyrus, who had already been queen under Cambyses and Gaumâta, was indignant at the thought of her sons bowing down before the child of a woman who was not of Achæmenian race, and at the moment when affairs in Egypt augured ill for the future, and when the old king, according to custom, had to appoint his successor,[3] she intreated him to choose Khshayarsha, the eldest of her children, who had been born to the purple, and in whose veins flowed the blood of Cyrus. Darius acceded to her request, and on his death, a few months after, Khshayarsha ascended the throne.[4] His brothers offered no opposition, and the Persian nobles did homage to their

---

between June and September, 486 (UNGER, *Manetho*, p. 289). Stern makes this prince to have been of Libyan origin (*Die XXII. Manethonische Dynastie*, in the *Zeitschrift*, 1882, p. 25). From the form of his name, Révillout has supposed that he was an Arab (*Chronique Égyptienne*, p. 5, note 2), and Birch was inclined to think that he was a Persian satrap who made a similar attempt to that of Aryandes (*On a Hieroglyphic Tablet of Alexander, son of Alexander the Great*, in the *Transactions* of the Bibl. Arch. Soc., vol. i. p. 24). But nothing is really known of him or of his family previous to his insurrection against Darius.

[1] HERODOTUS, VII. iv. According to Ctesias (*Fragm.* 29, § 19, in MÜLLER-DIDOT, *Ctesiæ Cnidii Fragmenta*, p. 49), he lived seventy-two, and reigned only thirty-one years.

[2] G. RAWLINSON, *The Five Great Monarchies*, 2nd edit., vol. iii. pp. 445, 446.

[3] Cf. *supra*, p. 655.

[4] HERODOTUS, VII. ii., iii.; Ctesias possibly tells a similar story, of which mention is made in Plutarch and in Justin (ii. 10).

new king. Khshayarsha, whom the Greeks called Xerxes, was at that time thirty-four years of age. He was tall, vigorous, of an imposing figure and noble countenance, and he had the reputation of being the handsomest man of his time, but neither his intelligence nor disposition corresponded to his outward appearance; he was at once violent and feeble, indolent, narrow-minded, and sensual, and was easily swayed by his courtiers and mistresses. The idea of a war had no attractions for him, and he was inclined to shirk it. His uncle Artabanus exhorted him to follow his inclination for peace, and he lent a favourable ear to this advice until his cousin Mardonius remonstrated with him, and begged him not to leave the disgrace of Mara-thon unpunished, or he would lower the respect attached to the name of Persia throughout the world.[1] He wished, at all events, to bring Egyptian affairs to an issue before involving himself in a serious European war. Khabbîsha had done his best to prepare a stormy reception for him. During a period of two years Khabbîsha had worked at the extension of the entrenchments

XERXES I.[2]

along the coast and at the mouths of the Nile, in order to repulse the attack that he foresaw would take place simultaneously with that on land, but his precautions proved fruitless when the decisive moment arrived, and he was completely crushed by the superior numbers of Xerxes. The nomes of the Delta which had taken a foremost part in the rising were ruthlessly raided, the priests heavily fined, and the oracle of Buto deprived of its possessions as a punishment for the encouragement freely given to the rebels. Khabbîsha disappeared, and his fate is unknown. Achæmenes, one of the king's brothers, was made satrap,[3] but, as on previous occasions, the constitution of the country underwent no modification. The temples retained their inherited domains, and the nomes continued in the hands of their hereditary princes, without a suspicion crossing the mind of Xerxes that his tolerance of the priestly institutions and the local dynasties was responsible for the maintenance of a body of chiefs ever in readiness for future insurrection (483).[4] Order was once more restored, but he was not yet entirely at liberty to pursue his own plan of action. Classical

---

[1] HERODOTUS, VII. ix.–xii.

[2] Drawn by Faucher-Gudin, from a daric in the *Cabinet des Médailles.* I owe a cast of the coin to the courtesy of M. Babelon.

[3] HERODOTUS, VII. vii.

[4] HERODOTUS, VII. vii.   The only detailed information on this revolt furnished by the Egyptian monuments is given in the Stele of Ptolemy, the son of Lagos, and published by MARIETTE, *Monuments Divers*, pl. 13, ll. 7–11 ; cf. BRUGSCH, *Ein Dekret Ptolemaios des Sohnes Lagi, des Satrapes*, in the *Zeitschrift*, 1871, pp. 4, 5, 10, 13 ; BIRCH, *On a Hieroglyphic Tablet of Alexander, son of Alexander the Great, recently discovered at Cairo*, in the *Transactions* of the Bibl. Arch. Soc., vol. i. pp. 22–25.   An Apis, whose sarcophagus still exists, was buried by Khabbîsha in the Serapæum in the second year of his reign (BRUGSCH, *Ein Dekret Ptolemaios*, in the *Zeitschrift*, 1871, p. 13), which proves that he was in possession of Memphis : the White Wall had perhaps been deprived of its garrison in order to reinforce the army prepared against Greece, and it was possibly thus that it fell into the hands of Khabbîsha.

tradition tells us, that on the occasion of his first visit to Babylon he had offended the religious prejudices of the Chaldæans by a sacrilegious curiosity. He had, in spite of the entreaties of the priests, forced an entrance into the ancient burial-place of Bel-Etana, and had beheld the body of the old hero preserved in oil in a glass sarcophagus, which, however, was not quite full of the liquid. A notice posted up beside it, threatened the king who should violate the secret of the tomb with a cruel fate, unless he filled the sarcophagus to the brim, and Xerxes had attempted to accomplish this mysterious injunction, but all his efforts had failed.[1] The example set by Egypt and the change of sovereign are sufficient to account for the behaviour of the Babylonians; they believed that the accession of a comparatively young monarch, and the difficulties of the campaign on the banks of the Nile, afforded them a favourable occasion for throwing off the yoke.[2] They elected as king a certain Shamasherib, whose antecedents are unknown; but their independence was of short duration,[3] for Megabyzos, son of Zopyrus, who governed the province by hereditary right, forced them to disarm after a siege of a few months.[4] It would appear that Xerxes treated them with the greatest severity: he pillaged the treasury and temple of Bel, appropriated the golden statue which decorated the great inner hall of the ziggurât, and carried away many of the people into captivity (581).[5] Babylon never recovered this final blow: the quarters of the town that had been pillaged remained uninhabited and fell into ruins; commerce dwindled and industry flagged. The counsellors of Xerxes had, no doubt, wished to give an object-lesson to the province by their treatment of Babylon, and thus prevent the possibility of a revolution taking place in Asia while its ruler was fully engaged in a struggle with the Greeks. Meanwhile all preparations were completed, and the contingents of the eastern and southern provinces concentrated at Kritalla, in

[1] CTESIAS, *Fragm.* 29, § 21, in MÜLLER-DIDOT, *Ctesiæ Cnidii Fragmenta*, p. 50. Ælian has preserved a more detailed account (*Various Stories*, xiv. 3). A similar legend was already current of the attempt that Darius made to open the tomb of Nitokris (HERODOTUS, I. clxxxvii.).

[2] CTESIAS, *Fragm.* 29, § 21, in MÜLLER-DIDOT, *Ctesiæ Cnidii Fragmenta*, p. 50, places this rebellion quite at the beginning of Xerxes' reign, before the Greek expedition (cf. J. MARQUART, *Die Assyriaka des Ktesias*, in the *Philologus*, Supplement, vol. v. pp. 514–526); others relegate it to a date after the return from Greece (ARRIAN, *Anabasis*, VII. xvii. § 3).

[3] This Shamasherib is mentioned only on a contract dated from his accession, which is preserved in the British Museum (Sp. ii. 19). Fr. Strassmaier, who discovered it, and was the first to publish it (*Arsaciden Inschriften*, in the *Zeitschrift für Assyriologie*, vol. iii. pp. 140, 141, 157, 158), pointed out that this prince belonged to the Achæmenian period; Oppert then showed that he must have been the leader of the rebellion in the time of Xerxes I. mentioned by Herodotus and by Ctesias (*Un Champion de l'indépendance chaldéenne*, in the *Journal Asiatique*, 1891, vol. xvii. pp. 543–545).

[4] CTESIAS, *Fragm.* 29, § 22, in MÜLLER-DIDOT, *Ctesiæ Cnidii Fragmenta*, p. 50, where the author attributes the act of devotion to Megabyzos which Herodotus (III. cl.; cf. JUSTIN, i. 10) tells of Zopyrus in the time of Darius (cf. *supra*, p. 680).

[5] STRABO, XVI. i. § 5, p. 738, says that Xerxes destroyed Bel's tomb; Arrian (*Anabasis*, III. xvi. § 4; cf. VII. xvii. § 2) more clearly states that he overthrew the temple of Bel and the other temples of the city.

Cappadocia, merely awaited the signal to set out. Xerxes gave the order to advance in the autumn of 481, crossed the Halys and took up his quarters at Sardes, while his fleet prepared to winter in the neighbouring ports of Phocæa and Kymê.[1] Gathered together in that little corner of the world, were forces such as no king had ever before united under his command; they comprised 1200 vessels of various build, and probably 120,000 combatants, besides the rabble of servants, hucksters, and women which followed all the armies of that period. The Greeks exaggerated the number of the force beyond all probability. They estimated it variously at 800,000, at 3,000,000, and at 5,283,220 men; 1,700,000 of whom were able-bodied foot-soldiers, and 80,000 of them horsemen.[2] The troops which they could bring up to oppose these

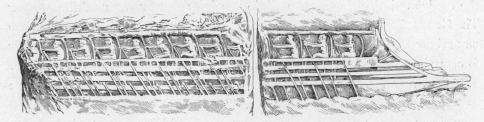

A TRIREME IN MOTION.[3]

hordes were, indeed, so slender in number, when reckoned severally, that all hope of success seemed impossible. Xerxes once more summoned the Greeks to submit,[4] and most of the republics appeared inclined to comply;[5] Athens and Sparta alone refused, but from different motives. Athens knew that, after the burning of Sardes and the victory of Marathon, they could hope for no pity, and she was well aware that Persia had decreed her complete destruction; the Athenians were familiar with the idea of a struggle in which their very existence was at stake, and they counted on the navy with which Themistocles had just provided them to enable them to emerge from the affair with honour. Sparta was not threatened with the same fate, but she was at that time the first military state in Greece, and the whole of the Peloponnesus acknowledged her sway; in the event of her recognising the suzerainty of the

[1] HERODOTUS, VII. xxvi.–xxxii.; Diodorus, who probably follows Ephorus, is the only writer who informs us of the place where the fleet was assembled (xi. 2).

[2] HERODOTUS, VII. clxxxiv.–clxxxvi.; elsewhere he records the epigram to the effect that 3,000,000 men attacked Thermopylæ (VII. ccxxviii.). Ctesias (*Fragm.* 29, § 23, in MÜLLER-DIDOT, *Ctesiæ Cnidii Fragmenta*, p. 50) and Ephorus adopt the same figures (DIODORUS SICULUS, xi. 3); Isocrates is contented with 700,000 combatants and 5,000,000 men in all (*Archidamus*, § 99, and *Panathenaic.*, § 49, ed. DIDOT, pp. 87, 156).

[3] Drawn by Faucher-Gudin: the left portion is a free reproduction of a photograph of the bas-relief of the Acropolis; the right, of the picture of Pozzo. The two partly overlap one another, and give both together the idea of a trireme going at full speed.

[4] HERODOTUS, VII. xxxii.

[5] For the feelings which animated the Greek cities at this crisis, cf. HERODOTUS, VII. cxxxviii.

barbarians, the latter would not fail to require of her the renunciation of her hegemony, and she would then be reduced to the same rank as her former rivals, Tegea and Argos. Athens and Sparta therefore united to repulse the common enemy, and the advantage that this alliance afforded them was so patent, that none of the other states ventured to declare openly for the great king. Argos and Crete, the boldest of them, announced that they would observe neutrality; the remainder, Thessalians, Bœotians, and people of Corcyra, gave their support to the national cause, but did so unwillingly.[1]

Xerxes crossed the Hellespont in the spring of 480, by two bridges of boats thrown across it between Abydos and Sestos; he then formed his force into three columns, and made his way slowly along the coast, protected on the left by the whole of his fleet from any possible attack by the squadrons of the enemy.[2] The Greeks had three lines of defence which they could hold against him, the natural strength of which nearly compensated them for the inferiority of their forces; these were Mount Olympus, Mount Œta, and the isthmus of Corinth. The first, however, was untenable, owing to the ill will of the Thessalians; as a precautionary measure 10,000 hoplites were encamped upon it, but they evacuated the position as soon as the enemy's advance-guard came into sight.[3] The natural barrier of Œta, less formidable than that of Olympus, was flanked by the Eubœan straits on the extreme right, but the range was of such extent that it did not require to be guarded with equal vigilance along its whole length. The Spartans did not at first occupy it, for they intended to accumulate all the Greek forces, both troops and vessels, around the isthmus. At that point the neck of land was so narrow, and the sea so shut in, that the numbers of the invading force proved a drawback to them, and the advantage almost of necessity lay with that of the two adversaries who should be best armed and best officered. This plan of the Spartans was a wise one, but Athens, which was thereby sacrificed to the general good, refused to adopt it, and as she alone furnished almost half the total number of vessels, her decision had to be deferred to. A body of about 10,000 hoplites was therefore posted in the pass of Thermopylæ under the command of Leonidas, while a squadron of 271 vessels disposed themselves near the promontory of Artemision, off the Euripus, and protected the right flank of the pass against a diversion from the fleet. Meanwhile Xerxes had been reinforced in the course of his march by the contingents from Macedonia, and had received the homage

---

[1] The behaviour of the Argives is shown by Herodotus in Books VII. cxlviii.–clii., VIII. lxxiii., that of the Corcyræans in Book VII. clxviii.; on the refusal of the Cretans, cf. HERODOTUS, VII. clxix.

[2] For the critical appreciation of Herodotus' account of the preliminaries of this expedition, I must refer the reader, as I did above, to the work of A. HAUVETTE, *Hérodote historien des Guerres Médiques*, pp. 290–340.

[3] HERODOTUS, VII. clxxii.–clxxiv.; cf. A. HAUVETTE, *ibid.*, pp. 340–350.

of the cities of Thessaly; having reached the defiles of the Œta and Eubœa, he began by attacking the Greeks directly in front, both fleets and armies facing one another. Leonidas succeeded in withstanding the assault on two successive days, and then the inevitable took place. A detachment of Persians, guided by the natives of the country, emerged by a path which had been left unguarded, and bore down upon the Greeks in the rear; a certain number managed to escape, but the bulk of the force, along with the 300 Spartans and their king, succumbed after a desperate resistance. As for the fleet, it had borne itself bravely, and had retained the ascendency throughout, in spite of the superiority of the enemy's numbers; on hearing the news of the glorious death of Leonidas, they believed their task ended for the time being, and retired with the Athenians in their wake, ready to sustain the attack should they come again to close quarters.[1] The victorious side had suffered considerable losses in men and vessels, but they had forced the passage, and Central Greece now lay at their mercy. Xerxes received the submission of the Thebans, the Phocæans, the Locrians, the Dorians, and of all who appealed to his clemency; then, having razed to the ground Platæa and Thespiæ, the only two towns which refused to come to terms with him, he penetrated into Attica by the gorges of the Cithæron.[2] The population had taken refuge in Salamis, Ægina, and Trœzen. The few fanatics who refused to desist in their defence of the Acropolis, soon perished behind their ramparts; Xerxes destroyed the temple of Pallas by fire to avenge the burning of Sardes, and then entrenched his troops on the approaches to the isthmus, stationing his squadrons in the ports of Munychia, Phalerum, and the Piræus, and suspended all hostilities while waiting to see what policy the Greeks would pursue.[3] It is possible that he hoped that a certain number of them would intreat for mercy, and others being encouraged by their example to submit, no further serious battle would have to be fought. When he found that no such request was proffered, he determined to take advantage of the superiority of his numbers, and, if possible, destroy at one blow the whole of the Greek naval reserve; he therefore gave orders to his admirals to assume the offensive. The Greek fleet lay at anchor across the bay of Salamis. The left squadron of the Persians, leaving Munychia in the middle of the night, made for the promontory of Cynosura, landing some troops as it passed on the island of Psyttalia, on which it was proposed to fall back in case of accident, while the right division, sailing close to the coast of Attica, closed the entrance to the straits in the

---

[1] HERODOTUS, VII. clxxv.–ccxxxix., VIII. i.–xxv.; cf. A. HAUVETTE, *Hérodote historien des Guerres Médiques*, pp. 350–379.

[2] HERODOTUS, VIII. xxvii.–xxxix., l.; cf. A. HAUVETTE, *Hérodote historien des Guerres Médiques*, pp. 380–389.

[3] HERODOTUS, VIII. l.–lv.

direction of Eleusis; this double movement was all but completed, when the Greeks were informed by fugitives of what was taking place, and the engagement was inevitable. They accepted it fearlessly. Xerxes, enthroned with his Immortals on the slopes of Ægialeos, could, from his exalted position, see the Athenians attack his left squadron: the rest of the allies followed them, and from afar these words were borne upon the breeze: "Go, sons of Greece, deliver your country, deliver your children, your wives, and the temples of the gods of your fathers and the tombs of your ancestors. A single battle will decide the fate of all you possess."

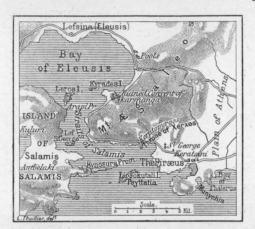

The Persians fought with their accustomed bravery, "but before long their numberless vessels, packed closely together in a restricted space, begin to hamper each other's movements, and their rams of brass collide; whole rows of oars are broken." The Greek vessels, lighter and easier to manœuvre than those of the Phœnicians, surround the latter and disable them in detail. "The surface of the sea is hidden with floating wreckage and corpses; the shore and the rocks are covered with the dead." At length, towards evening, the energy of the barbarians beginning to flag, they slowly fell back upon the Piræus, closely followed by their adversaries, while Aristides bore down upon Psyttalia with a handful of Athenians. "Like tunnies, like fish just caught in a net, with blows from broken oars, with fragments of spars, they fall upon the Persians, they tear them to pieces. The sea resounds from afar with groans and cries of lamentation. Night at length unveils her sombre face" and separates the combatants.[1] The advantage lay that day with the Greeks, but hostilities might be resumed on the morrow, and the resources of the Persians were so considerable that their chances of victory were not yet exhausted. Xerxes at first showed signs of wishing to continue the struggle; he repaired the injured vessels and ordered a dyke to be constructed, which, by uniting Salamis to the mainland, would enable him to oust the Athenians from their last retreat. But he had never exhibited much zest for the war; the inevitable fatigues and dangers of a campaign were irksome to his indolent nature, and winter was approaching, which he would be obliged to spend far from Susa, in the midst of a country

[1] ÆSCHYLUS, Persæ, 290-471, the only contemporaneous account of the battle, and the one which Herodotus and all the historians after him have paraphrased, while they also added to it oral traditions.

PART OF THE BATTLE-FIELD OF SALAMIS.

Drawn by Boudier, from a photograph by Monsieur Amédée Hauvette.

3 A

wasted and trampled underfoot by two great armies. Mardonius, guessing what was passing in his sovereign's mind, advised him to take advantage of the fine autumn weather to return to Sardes; he proposed to take over from Xerxes the command of the army in Greece, and to set to work to complete the conquest of the Peloponnesus. He was probably glad to be rid of a sovereign whose luxurious habits were a hindrance to his movements. Xerxes accepted his proposal with evident satisfaction, and summarily despatching his vessels to the Hellespont to guard the bridges, he set out on his return journey by the overland route.[1]

At the time of his departure the issue of the struggle was as yet unforeseen. Mardonius evacuated Attica, which was too poor and desolate a country to support so large an army, and occupied comfortable winter quarters in the rich plains of Thessaly, where he recruited his strength for a supreme effort in the spring. He had with him about 60,000 men, picked troops from all parts of Asia—Medes, Sakæ, Bactrians, and Indians, besides the regiment of the Immortals and the Egyptian veterans who had distinguished themselves by their bravery at Salamis; the heavy hoplites of Thebes and of the Bœotian towns, the Thessalian cavalry, and the battalions of Macedonia were also in readiness to join him as soon as called on.[2] The whole of these troops, relieved from the presence of the useless multitude which had impeded its movements under Xerxes, and commanded by a bold and active general, were anxious to distinguish themselves, and the probabilities of their final success were great. The confederates were aware of the fact, and although resolved to persevere to the end, their manœuvres betrayed an unfortunate indecision. Their fleet followed the Persian squadron bound for the Hellespont for several days, but on realising that the enemy were not planning a diversion against the Peloponnesus, they put about and returned to their various ports.[3] The winter was passed in preparations on both sides. Xerxes, on his return to Sardes, had got together a fleet of 200 triremes and an army of 60,000 men, and had stationed them at Cape Mycale, opposite Samos, to be ready in case of an Ionian revolt, or perhaps to bear down upon any given point in the Peloponnesus when Mardonius had gained some initial advantage. The Lacædemonians, on their part, seem to have endeavoured to assume the defensive both by land and sea; while their foot-soldiers were assembling in the neighbourhood of Corinth, their fleet sailed as far as Delos and there anchored, as reluctant to venture beyond as if it had been a question of proceeding to the Pillars of Hercules.[4] Athens, which ran the risk of falling into the enemy's hands for the second time through

---

[1] HERODOTUS, VIII. lvi.-cxx.; cf. HAUVETTE, Hérodote historien des Guerres Médiques, pp. 389-438.

[2] HERODOTUS, VIII. c., ci., cvii., cxiii., cxiv., where the number of troops remaining to Mardonius is estimated at 300,000 men.

[3] HERODOTUS, VIII. cviii.-cxii., cxxxi.   [4] HERODOTUS, VIII. cxxx.-cxxxii.

these hesitations, evinced such marked displeasure that Mardonius momentarily attempted to take advantage of it. He submitted to the citizens, through Alexander, King of Macedon, certain conditions, the leniency of which gave uneasiness to the Spartans; the latter at once promised Athens all she wanted, and on the strength of their oaths she at once broke off the negotiations with the Persians. Mardonius immediately resolved on action : he left his quarters in Thessaly in the early days of May, reached Attica by a few quick marches, and spread his troops over the country before the Peloponnesians were prepared to resist. The people again took refuge in Salamis; the Persians occupied Athens afresh, and once more had recourse to diplomacy. This time the Spartans were alarmed to good purpose; they set out to the help of their ally, and from that moment Mardonius showed no further consideration in his dealing with Athens. He devastated the surrounding country, razed the city walls to the ground, and demolished and burnt the remaining houses and temples; he then returned to Bœotia, the plains of which were more suited to the movements of his squadrons, and took up a position in an entrenched camp on the right bank of the Asopos. The Greek army, under the command of Pausanias, King of Sparta, subsequently followed him there, and at first stationed themselves on the lower slopes of Mount Cithæron. Their force was composed of about 25,000 hoplites, and about as many more light troops, and was scarcely inferior in numbers to the enemy, but it had no cavalry of any kind. Several days passed in skirmishing without definite results, Mardonius fearing to let his Asiatic troops attack the heights held by the heavy Greek infantry, and Pausanias alarmed lest his men should be crushed by the Thessalian and Persian horse if he ventured down into the plains. Want of water at length obliged the Greeks to move slightly westwards, their right wing descending as far as the spring of Gargaphia, and their left to the bank of the Asopos. But this position facing east, exposed them so seriously to the attacks of the light Asiatic horse, that after enduring it for ten days they raised their camp and fell back in the night on Platæa. Unaccustomed to manœuvre together, they were unable to preserve their distances; when day dawned, their lines, instead of presenting a continuous front, were distributed into three unequal bodies occupying various parts of the plain. Mardonius unhesitatingly seized his opportunity. He crossed the Asopos, ordered the Thebans to attack the Athenians, and with the bulk of his Asiatic troops charged the Spartan contingents. Here, as at Marathon, the superiority of equipment soon gave the Greeks the advantage : Mardonius was killed while leading the charge of the Persian guard, and, as is almost always the case among Orientals, his death decided the issue of the battle. The Immortals were cut to pieces round his dead body, while the rest took flight and sought refuge in their camp. Almost simultaneously the Athenians succeeded in routing the Bœotians. They took the entrenchments by assault, gained possession of an immense quantity of spoil, and massacred many of the defenders, but they could not prevent Artabazus from retiring in perfect order with 40,000 of his best troops protected by his cavalry. He retired successively from Thessaly, Macedonia, and Thrace, reached Asia after suffering severe losses, and European Greece was freed for

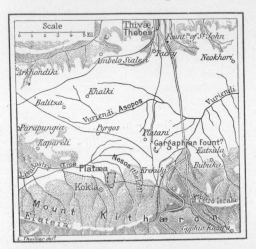

ever from the presence of the barbarians.[1] While her fate was being decided at Platæa, that of Asiatic Greece was being fought out on the coast of Ionia. The entreaties of the Samians had at length encouraged Leotychidas and Xanthippus to take the initiative. The Persian generals, who were not expecting this aggressive movement, had distributed the greater part of their vessels throughout the Ionian ports, and had merely a small squadron left at their disposal at Mycale. Surprised by the unexpected appearance of the enemy, they were compelled to land, were routed, and their vessels burnt (479).[2] This constituted the signal for a general revolt: Samos, Chios, and Lesbos affiliated themselves to the Hellenic confederation, and the cities of the littoral, which Sparta would have been powerless to protect for want of a fleet, concluded an alliance with Athens, whose naval superiority had been demonstrated by recent events. The towns of the Hellespont threw off the yoke as soon as the triremes of the confederates appeared within their waters, and Sestos, the only one of them prevented by its Persian garrison from yielding to the Athenians, succumbed, after a long siege, during the winter of 479–478.[3] The campaign of 478 completed the deliverance of the Greeks. A squadron commanded by Pausanias roused the islands of the Carian coast and Cyprus itself, without encountering any opposition, and then steering northwards drove the Persians from Byzantium.[4] The following winter the conduct of operations passed out of the hands of Sparta into those of Athens—from the greatest military to the greatest naval power in Greece; and the latter, on assuming command, at once

[1] HERODOTUS, VIII. cxxxvi.–cxliv., IX. i.–lxxxix.; A. HAUVETTE, *Hérodote historien des Guerres Médiques*, pp. 447–483.

[2] HERODOTUS, IX. xc.–cvii.; cf. A. HAUVETTE, *Hérodote historien des Guerres Médiques*, pp. 483–489.

[3] HERODOTUS, IX. cxv.–cxxii.; THUCYDIDES, I. lxxxix.

[4] THUCYDIDES, I. xciv.; DIODORUS SICULUS, xi. 44.

THE BATTLE-FIELD OF PLATÆA.

Drawn by Boudier, from photographs by Amédée Hauvette.

took steps to procure the means which would enable her to carry out her task thoroughly. She brought about the formation of a permanent league between the Asiatic Greeks and those of the islands. Each city joining it preserved a complete autonomy as far as its internal affairs were concerned, but pledged itself to abide by the advice of Athens in everything connected with the war against the Persian empire, and contributed a certain quota of vessels, men, and money, calculated according to its resources, for the furtherance of the national cause. The centre of the confederation was fixed at Delos; the treasure held in common was there deposited under the guardianship of the god, and the delegates from the confederate states met there every year at the solemn festivals, Athens to audit the accounts of her administration, and the allies to discuss the interests of the league and to decide on the measures to be taken against the common enemy.

Oriental empires maintain their existence only on condition of being always on the alert and always victorious. They can neither restrict themselves within definite limits nor remain upon the defensive, for from the day when they desist from extending their area their ruin becomes inevitable; they must maintain their career of conquest, or they must cease to exist. This very activity which saves them from downfall depends, like the control of affairs, entirely on the ruling sovereign; when he chances to be too indolent or too incapable of governing, he retards progress by his inertness or mis-directs it through his want of skill, and the fate of the people is made thus to depend entirely on the natural disposition of the prince, since none of his subjects possesses sufficient authority to correct the mistakes of his master. Having conquered Asia, the Persian race, finding itself hemmed in by insurmountable obstacles—the sea, the African and Arabian deserts, the mountains of Turkestan and the Caucasus, and the steppes of Siberia—had only two outlets for its energy, Greece and India. Darius had led his army against the Greeks, and, in spite of the resistance he had encountered from them, he had gained ground, and was on the point of striking a crucial blow, when death cut short his career. The impetus that he had given to the militant policy was so great that Xerxes was at first carried away by it; but he was naturally averse to war, without individual energy and destitute of military genius, so that he allowed himself to be beaten where, had he possessed anything of the instincts of a commander, he would have been able to crush his adversary with the sheer weight of his ships and battalions. Even after Salamis, even after Platæa and Mycale, the resources of Hellas, split up as it was into fifty different republics, could hardly bear comparison with those of all Asia concentrated in the hands of one man: Xerxes must have triumphed in the end had he persevered in his undertaking, and utilised the inexhaustible amount of fresh material with which his empire could have furnished him. But to do that he would have had to take a serious view of his duties as a sovereign, as Cyrus and Darius had done, whereas he appears to have made use of his power merely for the satisfaction of his luxurious tastes and his capricious affections. During the winter following his return, and while he was reposing at Sardes after the fatigues of his campaign in Greece, he fell in love with the wife of Masistes, one of his brothers, and as she refused to entertain his suit, he endeavoured to win her by marrying his son Darius to her daughter Artayntas. He was still amusing himself with this ignoble intrigue during the year which witnessed the disasters of Platæa and Mycale, when he was vaguely entertaining the idea of personally conducting a fresh army beyond the Ægean; but the marriage of his son having taken place, he returned to Susa in the autumn, accompanied by the entire court, and from thenceforward he remained shut up in the heart of his empire.[1] After his departure the war lost its general character, and deteriorated into a series of local skirmishes between the satraps in the vicinity of the Mediterranean and the members of the league of Delos. The Phœnician fleet played the principal part in the naval operations, but the central and eastern Asiatics—Bactrians, Indians, Parthians, Arians, Arachosians, Armenians, and the people from Susa and Babylon—scarcely took any part in the struggle. The Athenians at the outset assumed the offensive under the intelligent direction of Cimon. They expelled the Persian garrisons from Eion and Thrace in 476. They placed successively under their own hegemony all the Greek communities of the Asianic littoral. Towards 466, they destroyed a fleet anchored within the Gulf of Pamphylia, close to the mouth of the Eurymedon, and, as at Mycale, they landed and dispersed the force destined to act in concert with the squadron. Sailing from thence to Cyprus, they destroyed a second Phœnician fleet of eighty vessels, and returned to the Piræus laden with booty. Such exploits were not devoid of glory and profit for the time being, but they had no permanent results. All these naval expeditions were indeed successful, and the islands and towns of the Ægean, and even those of the Black Sea and the southern coasts of Asia Minor, succeeded without difficulty in freeing themselves from the Persian yoke under the protection of the Athenian triremes; but their influence did not penetrate further inland than a few miles from the shore, beyond which distance they ran the risk of being cut off from their vessels, and the barbarians of the interior—Lydians, Phrygians, Mysians, Pamphylians, and even most of the Lycians and Carians—remained subject to the rule of the satraps. The territory thus liberated formed but a narrow

---

[1] HERODOTUS, IX. cviii.

border along the coast of the peninsula; a border rent and interrupted at intervals, constantly in peril of seizure by the enemy, and demanding considerable efforts every year for its defence. Athens was in danger of exhausting her resources in the performance of this ungrateful task, unless she could succeed in fomenting some revolution in the vast possessions of her adversary which should endanger the existence of his empire, or which, at any rate, should occupy the Persian soldiery in constantly recurring hostilities against the rebellious provinces. If none of the countries in the centre of Asia Minor would respond to their call, and if the interests of their commercial rivals, the Phœnicians, were so far opposed to their own as to compel them to maintain the conflict to the very end, Egypt, at any rate, always proud of her past glory and impatient of servitude, was ever seeking to rid herself of the foreign yoke and recover her independent existence under the authority of her Pharaohs. It was not easy to come to terms with her and give her efficient help from Athens itself; but Cyprus, with its semi-Greek population hostile to the Achæmenids, could, if they were to take possession of it, form an admirable base of operations in that corner of the Mediterranean. The Athenians were aware of this from the outset, and, after their victory at the mouth of the Eurymedon, a year never elapsed without their despatching a more or less numerous fleet into Cypriot waters; by so doing they protected the Ægean from the piracy of the Phœnicians, and at the same time, in the event of any movement arising on the banks of the Nile, they were close enough to the Delta to be promptly informed of it, and to interfere to their own advantage before any repressive measures could be taken.

The field of hostilities having shifted, and Greece having now set herself to attempt the dismemberment of the Persian empire, we may well ask what had become of Xerxes. The little energy and intelligence he had possessed at the outset were absorbed by a life of luxury and debauchery. Weary of his hopeless pursuit of the wife of Masistes, he transferred his attentions to the Artayntas whom he had given in marriage to his son Darius, and succeeded in seducing her. The vanity of this unfortunate woman at length excited the jealousy of the queen. Amestris believed herself threatened by the ascendency of this mistress; she therefore sent for the girl's mother, whom she believed guilty of instigating the intrigue, and, having cut off her breasts, ears, nose, lips, and torn out her tongue, she sent her back, thus mutilated, to her family. Masistes, wishing to avenge her, set out for Bactriana, of which district he was satrap: he could easily have incited the province to rebel, for its losses in troops during the wars in Europe had been severe, and a secret discontent was widespread; but Xerxes, warned in time, despatched horsemen in pursuit, who overtook and killed him.[1] The incapacity of the king, and the slackness with which he held the reins of government, were soon so apparent as to produce intrigues at court : Artabanus, the chief captain of the guards, was emboldened by the state of affairs to attempt to substitute his own rule for that of the Achæmenids, and one night he assassinated Xerxes. His method of procedure was never exactly known, and several accounts of it were soon afterwards current. One of them related that he had as his accomplice the eunuch Aspamithres. Having committed the crime, both of them rushed to the chamber of Artaxerxes,[2] one of the sons of the sovereign, but still a child ; they accused Darius, the heir to the throne, of the murder, and having obtained an order to seize him, they dragged him before his brother and stabbed him, while he loudly protested his innocence. Other tales related that Artabanus had

ARTAXERXES I.[3]

taken advantage of the free access to the palace which his position allowed him, to conceal himself one night within it, in company with his seven sons. Having murdered Xerxes, he convinced Artaxerxes of the guilt of his brother, and conducting him to the latter's chamber, where he was found asleep, Artabanus stabbed him on the spot, on the pretence that he was only feigning slumber.[4] The murderer at first became the virtual sovereign, and he exercised his authority so openly that later chronographers inserted his name in the list of the Achæmenids, between that of his victim and his *protégé ;*[5] but at the end of six months, when he was planning the murder of the young prince, he was betrayed by Megabyzos and slain, together with his accomplices. His sons, fearing a similar fate, escaped into the country with some of the troops. They perished in a skirmish, sword in hand ;[6] but their prompt defeat, though it helped to establish the new king upon his throne, did not ensure peace, for the most turbulent provinces at the two extremes of the empire, Bactriana on the north-east and Egypt in the south-west, at once rose in arms. The Bactrians were led by Hystaspes, one of

[1] HERODOTUS, IX. cviii.–cxiii. ; cf. DIODORUS SICULUS, xi. 69.

[2] Artaxerxes is the form commonly adopted by the Greek historians and by the moderns who follow them, but Ctesias and others after him prefer Artoxerxes (*Fragm.* 29, § 29, in MÜLLER-DIDOT, *Ctesiæ Cnidii Fragmenta,* p. 51). The original form of the Persian name was Artakhshathra (*Inscription of Susa,* i. ll. 2, 4) ; cf. JUSTI, *Eranisches Namenbuch,* pp. 34–36.

[3] Drawn by Faucher-Gudin, from a daric in the *Cabinet des Médailles ;* I am indebted for a cast to the kindness of M. Babelon.

[4] Of the two principal accounts, the first is as old as Ctesias (*Fragm.* 29, § 29, in MÜLLER-DIDOT, *Ctesiæ Cnidii Fragmenta,* p. 51), who was followed in general outline by Ephorus, of whose account Diodorus Siculus preserves a summary compilation (xi. 69) ; the second was circulated by Dinon, and has come down to us through the abbreviation of Pompeius Trogus (JUSTIN, iii. 1). The remains of a third account are met with in ARISTOTLE, *Politics,* v. 10. Ælian (*Var. Hist.,* xiv. 3) knew a fourth in which the murder was ascribed to the son of Xerxes himself.

[5] The passages in these chronographers referring to the alleged reign of Artabanus are collected in UNGER, *Manetho,* p. 286.

[6] CTESIAS, *Fragm.* 29, § 30, in MÜLLER-DIDOT, *Ctesiæ Cnidii Fragmenta,* p. 51 ; DIODORUS SICULUS, xi. 69 ; JUSTIN, iii. 1.

the sons of Xerxes, who, being older than Artaxerxes, claimed the throne; his pretensions were not supported by the neighbouring provinces, and two bloody battles soon sealed his fate (462).[1] The chastisement of Egypt proved a harder task. Since the downfall of the Saites, the eastern nomes of the Delta had always constituted a single fief, which the Greeks called the kingdom of Libya. Lords of Marea and of the fertile districts extending between the Canopic arm of the Nile, the mountains, and the sea, its princes probably exercised suzerainty over several of the Libyan tribes of Marmarica. Inaros, son of Psammetichus,[2] who was then the ruling sovereign, defied the Persians openly. The inhabitants of the Delta, oppressed by the tax-gatherers of Achæmenes,[3] welcomed him with open arms, and he took possession of the country between the two branches of the Nile, probably aided by the Cyrenians;[4] the Nile valley itself and Memphis, closely guarded by the Persian garrisons, did not, however, range themselves on his side. Mean-while the satrap, fearing that the troops at his disposal were insufficient, had gone to beg assistance of his nephew. Artaxerxes had assembled an army and a fleet, and, in the first moment of enthusiasm, had intended to assume the command in person; but, by the advice of his counsellors, he was with little difficulty dissuaded from carrying this whim into effect, and he delegated the conduct of affairs to Achæmenes. The latter at first repulsed the Libyans (460), and would probably have soon driven them back into their deserts, had not the Athenians interfered in the fray. They gave orders to their fleet at Cyprus to support the insurgents by every means in their power, and their appearance on the scene about the autumn of 469 changed the course of affairs. Achæmenes was overcome at Papremis, and his army almost completely exterminated. Inaros struck him down with his own hand in the struggle; but the same evening he caused the body to be recovered, and sent it to the court of Susa, though whether out of bravado, or from respect to the Achæmenian race, it is impossible to say.[5] His good fortune

[1] CTESIAS, *Frag.* 29, § 31, in MÜLLER-DIDOT, *Ctes. Cnid. Frag.*, p. 52; DIOD. SICULUS, xi. 71. The date 462 is approximate, and is inferred from the fact that the war in Bactriana is mentioned in Ctesias between the war against the sons of Artabanus which must have occupied a part of 463, and the Egyptian rebellion which broke out about 462, as Diodorus Siculus (xi. 71) points out, doubtless following Ephorus.

[2] The name of the father of Inaros is given us by the contemporary testimony of Thucydides (i. 104).

[3] Achæmenes is the form given by Herodotus (III. xii., VII. vii.) and by Diodorus Siculus (xi. 74), who make him the son of Darius I., appointed governor of Egypt after the repression of the revolt of Khabbîsha (cf. *supra*, p. 715). Ctesias (*Fragm.* 29, § 32, in MÜLLER-DIDOT, *Ctesiæ Cnidii Fragmenta*, p. 52) calls him Achæmenides, and says that he was the son of Xerxes.

[4] The alliance of Cyrene and Inaros seems to be proved by the passage in PINDAR, 4th *Pythic Ode*, 53–56, and it goes back almost to the beginning of the rebellion, since Arkesilas carried off the prize in the third year of the LXXVIIIth Olympiad, *i.e.* in 461.

[5] CTESIAS, *Fragm.* 29, § 32, in MÜLLER-DIDOT, *Ctesiæ Cnidii Fragm.*, p. 50, and DIODORUS SICULUS, xi. 71, who says in so many words that the Athenians took part in the battle of Papremis; Thucydides (i. 104) and Herodotus (III. xii., VII. vii.) do not speak of their being there, and several modern historians take this silence as a proof that their squadron arrived after the battle had been fought.

did not yet forsake him. Some days afterwards, the Athenian squadron of Charitimides came up by chance with the Phœnician fleet, which was sailing to the help of the Persians, and had not yet received the news of the disaster which had befallen them at Papremis. The Greeks sunk thirty of the enemy's vessels and took twenty more,[1] and, after this success, the allies believed that they had merely to show themselves to bring about a general rising of the fellahîn, and effect the expulsion of the Persians from the whole of Egypt. They sailed up the river and forced Memphis after a few days' siege; but the garrison of the White Wall refused to surrender, and the allies were obliged to lay siege to it in the ordinary manner (459):[2] in the issue this proved their ruin. Artaxerxes raised a fresh force in Cilicia, and while completing his preparations, attempted to bring about a diversion in Greece. The strength of Pharaoh did not so much depend on his Libyan and Egyptian hordes, as on the little body of hoplites and the crews of the Athenian squadron; and if the withdrawal of the latter could be effected, the repulse of the others would be a certainty. Persian agents were therefore employed to beg the Spartans to invade Attica; but the remembrance of Salamis and Platæa was as yet too fresh to permit of the Lacedæmonians allying themselves with the common enemy, and their virtue on this occasion was proof against the darics of the Orientals.[3] The Egyptian army was placed in the field early in the year 456, under the leadership of Megabyzos, the satrap of Syria: it numbered, so it was said, some 300,000 men, and it was supported by 300 Phœnician vessels commanded by Artabazos.[4] The allies raised the blockade of the White Wall as soon as he entered the Delta, and hastened to attack him; but they had lost their opportunity. Defeated in a desperate encounter, in which Charitimides was killed and Inaros wounded in the thigh, they barricaded themselves within the large island of Prosopitis, about the first fortnight in January of the year 455, and there sustained a regular siege for the space of eighteen months. At the end of that time Megabyzos succeeded in turning an arm of the river,

---

[1] Ctesias (*Fragm.* 29, § 31, in Müller-Didot, *Ctesiæ Cnidii Fragmenta*, p. 52) is the only author who mentions this victory expressly, and he reduces the number of Athenian vessels to forty, but this number 40 = M has long been corrected to 200 = Σ, which was the number of vessels sent to Cyprus annually. It has also been proposed to alter the name Charitimides into Carmantides.

[2] The date of 459-8 for the arrival of the Athenians is concluded from the passage of Thucydides (i. 110), who gives an account of the end of the war after the cruise of Tolmides in 455, in the sixth year of its course.

[3] Thucydides, i. 109; cf. Diodorus Siculus, xi. 74. Megabyzos opened these negotiations, and his presence at Sparta during the winter of 457-6 is noticed.

[4] Ctesias (*Fragm.* 29, § 33, in Müller-Didot, *Ctesiæ Cnidii Fragmenta*, p. 52) here introduces the Persian admiral Horiscos, but Diodorus (xi. 74) places Artabazos and Megabyzos side by side, as was the case later on in the war in Cyprus, one at the head of the fleet, the other of the army (Diodorus, xii. 3); it is probable that the historian from whom Diodorus copied, viz. Ephorus, recognised the same division of leadership in the Egyptian campaign.

which left their fleet high and dry, and, rather than allow it to fall into his hands, they burned their vessels, whereupon he gave orders to make the final assault. The bulk of the Athenian auxiliaries perished in that day's attack, the remainder withdrew with Inaros into the fortified town of Byblos, where Megabyzos, unwilling to prolong a struggle with a desperate enemy, permitted them to capitulate on honourable terms. Some of them escaped and returned to Cyrene, from whence they took ship to their own country; but the main body, to the number of 6000, were carried away to Susa by Megabyzos in order to receive the confirmation of the treaty which he had concluded. As a crowning stroke of misfortune, a reinforcement of fifty Athenian triremes, which at this juncture entered the Mendesian mouth of the Nile, was surrounded by the Phœnician fleet, and more than half of them destroyed. The fall of Prosopitis brought the rebellion to an end.[1] The nomes of the Delta were restored to order, and, as was often customary in Oriental kingdoms, the vanquished petty princes or their children were reinvested in their hereditary fiefs; even Libya was not taken from the family of Inaros, but was given to his son Thannyras and a certain Psammetichus.[2] A few bands of fugitives, however, took refuge in the marshes of the littoral, in the place where the Saites in former times had sought a safe retreat, and they there proclaimed king a certain Amyrtæus, who was possibly connected with the line of Amasis, and successfully defied the repeated attempts of the Persians to dislodge them.[3]

The Greek league had risked the best of its forces in this rash undertaking, and had failed in its enterprise. It had cost the allies so dearly in men and galleys, that if the Persians had at once assumed the offensive, most of the Asiatic cities would have found themselves in a most critical situation; and Athens, then launched in a quarrel with the states of the Peloponnesus, would have experienced the greatest difficulty in succouring them. The feebleness of Artaxerxes, however, and possibly the intrigues at court and troubles in various other parts of the empire, prevented the satraps from pursuing their advantage, and when at length they meditated taking action, the opportunity

[1] The accounts of these events given by Ctesias (*Fragm.* 29, §§ 33, 34, in MÜLLER-DIDOT, *Ctesiæ Cnidii Fragmenta*, p. 52) and Thucydides (i. 109, 110) are complementary, and, in spite of their brevity, together form a whole which must be sufficiently near the truth. That of Ephorus, preserved in Diodorus (xi. 77), is derived from an author who shows partiality to the Athenians, and who passes by everything not to their honour, while he seeks to throw the blame for the final disaster on the cowardice of the Egyptians. The summary of Aristodemus (MÜLLER-DIDOT, *Fragm. Hist. Græc.*, vol. v. p. 14) comes directly from that of Thucydides.

[2] On this Psammetichus, cf. PHILOCHORUS, *Fragm.* 90, in MÜLLER-DIDOT, *Fragm. Hist. Græc.*, vol. i. pp. 398, 399; and on Thannyras, HERODOTUS, III. xv.

[3] On Amyrtæus, cf. THUCYDIDES, i. 110; according to HERODOTUS, II. cxl., the island where he took up his abode was Elbô—the same which had formerly furnished a retreat for the blind Anysis, and which was famous in the popular literature of this age.

had gone by. They nevertheless attempted to regain the ascendency over Cyprus; Artabazos with a Sidonian fleet cruised about the island, Megabyzos assembled troops in Cilicia, and the petty kings of Greek origin raised a cry of alarm. Athens, which had just concluded a truce with the Peloponnesians, at once sent two hundred vessels to their assistance under the command of Cimon (449). Cimon acted as though he were about to reopen the campaign in Egypt, and despatched sixty of his triremes to King Amyrtæus,[1] while he himself took Marion and blockaded Kition with the rest of his forces. The siege dragged on; he was perhaps about to abandon it, when he took to his bed and died. Those who succeeded him in the command were obliged to raise the blockade for want of provisions, but as they returned and were passing Salamis, they fell in with the Phœnician vessels which had just been landing the Cilician troops, and defeated them; they then disembarked, and, as at Mycale and Eurymedon, they gained a second victory in the open field, after which they joined the squadron which had been sent to Egypt, and sailed for Athens with the dead body of their chief. They had once more averted the danger of an attack on the Ægean, but that was all. The Athenian statesmen had for some time past realised that it was impossible for them to sustain a double conflict, and fight the battles of Greece against the common enemy, while half of the cities whose safety was secured by their heroic devotion were harassing them on the continent, but the influence of Cimon had up till now encouraged them to persist; on the death of Cimon, they gave up the attempt, and Callias, one of their leaders, repaired in state to Susa for the purpose of opening negotiations. The peace which was concluded on the occasion of this embassy might at first sight appear advantageous to their side. The Persian king, without actually admitting his reverses, accepted their immediate consequences. He recognised the independence of the Asiatic Greeks, of those at least who belonged to the league of Delos, and he promised that his armies on land should never advance further than three days' march from the Ægean littoral. On the seas, he forbade his squadrons to enter Hellenic waters from the Chelidonian to the Cyanæan rocks—that is, from the eastern point of Lycia to the opening of the Black Sea: this prohibition did not apply to the merchant vessels of the contracting parties, and they received permission to traffic freely in each other's waters —the Phœnicians in Greece, and the Greeks in Phœnicia, Cilicia, and Egypt. And yet, when we consider the matter, Athens and Hellas were, of the two, the greater losers by this convention, which appeared to imply their superiority. Not only did they acknowledge indirectly that they felt themselves unequal to the task of overthrowing the empire, but they laid down their arms before they had accomplished the comparatively restricted task which they had set

[1] THUCYDIDES, i. 112; PLUTARCH, *Life of Cimon*, § 18.

themselves to perform, that of freeing all the Greeks from the Iranian yoke: their Egyptian compatriots still remained Persian tributaries, in company with the cities of Cyrenaïca, Pamphylia, and Cilicia, and, above all, that island of Cyprus in which they had gained some of their most signal triumphs. The Persians, relieved from a war which for a quarter of a century had consumed their battalions and squadrons, drained their finances, and excited their subjects to revolt, were now free to regain their former wealth and perhaps their vigour, could they only find generals to command their troops and guide their politics. Artaxerxes was incapable of directing this revival, and his inveterate weakness exposed him perpetually to the plotting of his satraps or to the intrigues of the women of his harem. The example of Artabanus, followed by that of Hystaspes, had shown how easy it was for an ambitious man to get rid secretly of a monarch or a prince and seriously endanger the crown. The members of the families who had placed Darius on the throne, possessed by hereditary right, or something little short of it, the wealthiest and most populous provinces— Babylonia, Syria, Lydia, Phrygia, and the countries of the Halys—and they were practically kings in all but name, in spite of the *surveillance* which the general and the secretary were supposed to exercise over their actions. Besides this, the indifference and incapacity of the ruling sovereigns had already tended to destroy the order of the administrative system so ably devised by Darius : the satrap had, as a rule, absorbed the functions of a general within his own province, and the secretary was too insignificant a personage to retain authority and independence unless he received the constant support of the sovereign. The latter, a tool in the hands of women and eunuchs, usually felt himself powerless to deal with his great vassals. His toleration went to all lengths if he could thereby avoid a revolt ; when this was inevitable, and the rebels were vanquished, he still continued to conciliate them, and in most cases their fiefs and rights were preserved or restored to them, the monarch knowing that he could rid himself of them treacherously by poison or the dagger in the case of their proving themselves too troublesome. Megabyzos by his turbulence was a thorn in the side of Artaxerxes during the half of his reign. He had ended his campaign in Egypt by engaging to preserve the lives of Inaros and the 6000 Greeks who had capitulated at Byblos, and, in spite of the anger of the king, he succeeded in keeping his word for five years, but at the end of that time the demands of Amestris prevailed. She succeeded in obtaining from him some fifty Greeks whom she beheaded, besides Inaros himself, whom she impaled to avenge Achæmenes. Megabyzos, who had not recovered from the losses he had sustained in his last campaign against Cimon, at first concealed his anger, but he asked permission to visit his Syrian province, and no sooner did he reach it, than he resorted to hostilities. He defeated in succession Usiris and Menostates, the two generals despatched against him, and when force failed to overcome his obstinate resistance, the government condescended to treat with him, and swore to forget the past if he would consent to lay down arms. To this he agreed, and reappeared at court; but once there, his confidence nearly proved fatal to him. Having been invited to take part in a hunt, he pierced with his javelin a lion which threatened to attack the king: Artaxerxes called to mind an ancient law which

VIEW OF THE ACHÆMENIAN RUINS OF ISTAKHR.[1]

punished by death any intervention of that kind, and he ordered that the culprit should be beheaded. Megabyzos with difficulty escaped this punishment through the entreaties of Amestris and of his wife Amytis; but he was deprived of his fiefs, and sent to Kyrta, on the shores of the Persian Gulf. After five years this exile became unbearable; he therefore spread the report that he was attacked by leprosy, and he returned home without any one venturing to hinder him, from fear of defiling themselves by contact with his person. Amestris and Amytis brought about his reconciliation with his sovereign; and thenceforward he regulated his conduct so successfully that the past was completely forgotten, and when he died, at the age of seventy-six years, Artaxerxes deeply regretted his loss.[2]

Peace having been signed with Athens, and the revolt of Megabyzos being at an end, Artaxerxes was free to enjoy himself without further care for the future, and to pass his time between his various capitals and palaces. His

[1] Drawn by Boudier, from the engraving of FLANDIN and COSTE, *La Perse Antique*, pl. 58.

[2] These events are known to us only through Ctesias (*Fragm.* 29, §§ 34–41, in MÜLLER-DIDOT, *Ctesiæ Cnidii Fragmenta*, pp. 52, 53, 68). Their date is uncertain, but there is no doubt that they occurred after Cimon's campaign in Cyprus and the conclusion of the peace of Callias.

choice lay between Susa and Persepolis, between Ecbatana and Babylon, according as the heat of the summer or the cold of the winter induced him to pass from the plains to the mountains, or from the latter to the plains. During his visits to Babylon he occupied one of the old Chaldæan palaces, but at Ecbatana he possessed merely the ancient residence of the Median kings, and the seraglio built or restored by Xerxes in the fashion of the times: at Susa and in Persia proper, the royal buildings were entirely the work of the Achæmenids, mostly that of Darius and Xerxes. The memory of Cyrus and of the kings to whom primitive Persia owed her organisation in the obscure century preceding her career of conquest, was piously preserved in the rude buildings of Pasargadæ,[1] which was regarded as a sacred city, whither the sovereigns repaired for coronation as soon as their predecessors

THE TOMB OF DARIUS.[2]

had expired.[3] But its lonely position and simple appointments no longer suited their luxurious and effeminate habits, and Darius had in consequence fixed his residence a few miles to the south of it, near to the village, which after its development became the immense royal city of Persepolis.[4] He there erected buildings more suited to the splendour of his court, and found the place so much to his taste during his lifetime, that he was unwilling to leave it after death. He therefore caused his tomb to be cut in the steep limestone cliff

[1] On the buildings of Cyrus at Pasargardæ, his palace and his tomb, cf. *supra*, pp. 652, 653.

[2] Drawn by Faucher-Gudin, from the heliogravure by Marcel Dieulafoy, *L'Art antique de la Perse*, vol. ii. pl. x.; compare the tombs of the Achæmenids, in Flandin and Coste, *La Perse Ancienne*, pls. 173–176.

[3] Plutarch, *Artoxerxes*, § 3, where it seems very likely that the main part of the story has been borrowed from the historian Dinon, perhaps by an earlier writer than Plutarch, and then used by the latter.

[4] The history of Persepolis and the questions thereby raised have been briefly set forth by Nöldeke, *Aufsätze zur Persichen Geschichte*, pp. 135–146.

which borders the plain about half a mile to the north-west of the town. It is an opening in the form of a Greek cross, the upper part of which contains a bas-relief in which the king, standing in front of the altar, implores the help of Ahura-mazdâ poised with extended wings above him; the platform on which the king stands is supported by two rows of caryatides in low relief, whose features and dress are characteristic of Persian vassals, while other personages, in groups of three on either side, are shown in the attitude of

THE HILL OF THE ROYAL ACHÆMENIAN TOMBS AT NAKHSH-Î-RUSTEM.[1]

prayer. Below, in the transverse arms of the cross, is carved a flat portico with four columns, in the centre of which is the entrance to the funeral vault. Within the latter, in receptacles hollowed out of the rock, Darius and eight of his family were successively laid.[2] Xerxes caused a tomb in every way similar to be cut for himself near that of Darius, and in the course of years others were added close by.[3] Both the tombs and the palace are built in that eclectic style which characterises the Achæmenian period of Iranian art. The main features are borrowed from the architecture of those nations which were vassals or neighbours of the empire—Babylonia, Egypt, and Greece;[4]

[1] Drawn by Boudier, from the engraving of FLANDIN and COSTE, *La Perse Antique*, pl. 172.

[2] The description and technical criticism of these tombs are given at length in PERROT and CHIPIEZ, *Histoire de l'Art dans l'Antiquité*, vol. v. pp. 617-634.

[3] The tomb of Darius alone bears an inscription (WEISSBACH and BANG, *Die Altpers. Keilins.*, pp. 34-37). Darius III. was also buried there by command of Alexander; cf. ARRIAN, *Anabasis*, iii. 22, § 1, where the expression ἐς Πέρσας ἔπεμψε should be translated : "he sent the body to *Persepolis*."

[4] For the different elements borrowed from the art of vassals or neighbours, see the analysis of PERROT and CHIPIEZ, *Histoire de l'Art dans l'Antiquité*, vol. v. pp. 883-897.

3 B

but these various elements have been combined and modified in such a manner as to form a rich and harmonious whole. The core of the walls was of burnt bricks, similar to those employed in the Euphrates valley, but these were covered with a facing of enamelled tiles, disposed as a skirting or a frieze, on which figured those wonderful processions of archers, and the lions which now adorn the Louvre, while the pilasters at the angles, the

ONE OF THE CAPITALS FROM SUSA.[1]

columns, pillars, window-frames, and staircases were of fine white limestone or of hard bluish-grey marble. The doorways are high and narrow; the moulding which frames them is formed of three Ionic fillets, each projecting beyond the other, surmounted by a coved Egyptian lintel springing from a row of alternate eggs and disks. The framing of the doors is bare, but the embrasures are covered with bas-reliefs representing various scenes in which the king is portrayed fulfilling his royal functions—engaged in struggles with evil genii which have the form of lions or fabulous animals, occupied in hunting, granting audiences, or making an entrance in state, shaded by an umbrella which is borne by a eunuch behind him. The columns employed in this style of architecture constitute its most original feature. The base of them usually consists of two mouldings, resting either on a square pedestal or on a cylindrical drum, widening out below into a bell-like curve, and sometimes ornamented with several rows of inverted leaves. The shafts, which have forty-eight perpendicular ribs cut on their outer surface, are perhaps rather tall in proportion to their thickness. They terminate in a group of large

[1] Drawn by Boudier, from a photograph taken in the Louvre by Faucher-Gudin; this is one of the capitals brought back and set up by M. and Mme. Dieulafoy. Cf. DIEULAFOY, L'Acropole de Suse, p. 325, fig. 203.

GENERAL VIEW OF THE RUINS OF PERSEPOLIS.

Drawn by Boudier, from FLANDIN and COSTE, *La Perse Antique*, pl. 66.

leaves, an evident imitation of the Egyptian palm-leaf capital, from which spring a sort of rectangular fluted die or abacus, flanked on either side with four rows of volutes curved in opposite directions, generally two at the base and two at the summit.   The heads and shoulders of two bulls, placed back to back, project above the volutes, and take the place of the usual abacus of the capital.   The dimensions of these columns, their gracefulness, and the distance at which they were placed from one another, prove that they supported not a stone architrave, but enormous beams of wood, which were inserted between the napes of the bulls' necks, and upon which the joists of the roof were superimposed.[1]   The palace of Persepolis, built by Darius after he had crushed the revolts which took place at the outset of his reign, was situated at the foot of a chain of rugged mountains which skirt the plain on its eastern side, and was raised on an irregularly shaped platform or terrace, which was terminated by a wall of enormous polygonal blocks of masonry.   The terrace was reached by a double flight of steps, the lateral walls of which are covered

THE PROPYLÆA OF XERXES I. AT PERSEPOLIS.[2]

with bas-reliefs, representing processions of satellites, slaves, and tributaries, hunting scenes, fantastic episodes of battle, and lions fighting with and devouring bulls.   The area of the raised platform was not of uniform level, and was laid out in gardens, in the midst of which rose the pavilions that served as dwelling-places.   The reception-rooms were placed near the top of the flight

[1] For the detailed study of the elements of Persian architecture I refer the reader to PERROT and CHIPIEZ, Histoire de l'Art dans l'Antiquité, vol. v. pp. 447–588.

[2] Drawn by Boudier, from the heliogravure of MARCEL DIEULAFOY, L'Art antique de la Perse, vol. ii. pl. xii.; cf. PERROT and CHIPIEZ, Histoire de l'Art dans l'Antiquité, vol. v. pl. ii.

of steps, and the more important of them had been built under the two preceding kings. Those nearest to the edge of the platform were the propylæa of Xerxes—gigantic entrances whose gateways were guarded on either side by winged bulls of Assyrian type; beyond these was the *apadana,* or hall of honour, where the sovereign presided in state at the ordinary court ceremonies. To the east of the *apadana,* and almost in

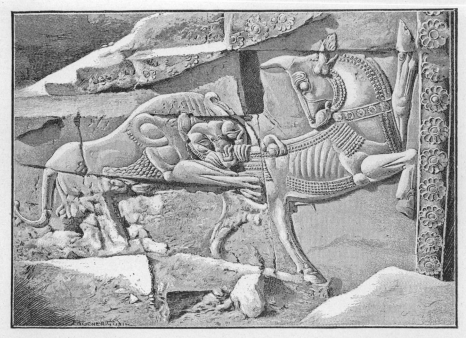

BAS-RELIEF ON THE STAIRCASE LEADING TO THE APADANA OF XERXES I.[1]

the centre of the raised terrace, rose the Hall of a Hundred Columns, erected by Darius, and used only on special occasions.[2] Artaxerxes I. seems to have had a particular affection for Susa. It had found favour with his predecessors, and they had so frequently resided there, even after the building of Persepolis, that it had continued to be regarded as the real capital of the empire by other nations, whereas the Persian sovereigns themselves had sought to make it rather an impregnable retreat than a luxurious residence. Artaxerxes built there an *apadana* on a vaster scale than any hitherto designed. It comprised three colonnades, which, taken together, formed a rectangle measuring 300 feet by 250 feet on the two sides, the area being approximately that of the courtyard of the

---

[1] Drawn by Faucher-Gudin, from MARCEL DIEULAFOY, *L'Art antique de la Perse,* vol. iii. pl. xviii.

[2] The monuments of Persepolis have been restored and described in the engravings and in the text of the great work of COSTE and FLANDIN, *Voyage en Perse,* 1st part, *Perse ancienne;* the analysis and the restoration will be found given in detail in PERROT and CHIPIEZ, *Histoire de l'Art dans l'Antiquité,* vol. v. pp. 675–750.

Louvre. The central colonnade, which was the largest of the three, was enclosed by walls on three sides, but was open to the south. Immense festoons of drapery hung from the wooden entablature, and curtains, suspended from rods between the first row of columns, afforded protection from the sun and from the curiosity of the vulgar. At the hour appointed for the ceremonies, the great king took his seat in solitary grandeur on the gilded throne of the Achæmenids; at the

THE KING ON HIS THRONE.[1]

extreme end of the colonnade his eunuchs, nobles, and guards ranged themselves in silence on either side, each in the place which etiquette assigned to him. Meanwhile the foreign ambassadors who had been honoured by an invitation to the audience —Greeks from Thebes, Sparta, or Athens; Sakæ from the regions of the north; Indians, Arabs, nomad chiefs from mysterious Ethiopia—ascended in procession the flights of steps which led from the town to the palace, bearing the presents destined for its royal master. Having reached the terrace, the curtains of the *apadana* were suddenly parted, and in the distance, through a vista of columns, they perceived a motionless figure, resplendent with gold and purple, before whom they fell prostrate with their faces to the earth. The heralds were the bearers of their greetings, and brought back to them a gracious or haughty reply, as the case might be. When they rose from the ground, the curtains had closed, the kingly vision was eclipsed, and the escort which had accompanied them into the palace conducted them back to the town, dazzled with the momentary glimpse of the spectacle vouchsafed to them.[2]

The Achæmenian monarchs were not regarded as gods or as sons of gods, like the Egyptian Pharaohs, and the Persian religion forbade their ever becoming so, but the person of the king was hedged round with such ceremonial respect as in other Oriental nations was paid only to the gods: this was but natural, for was he not a despot, who with a word or gesture could abase the noblest of his subjects, and determine the well-being or

---

[1] Drawn by Faucher-Gudin, from FLANDIN and COSTE, *La Perse Antique*, pl. 146; cf. similar scenes in the same work in pls. 155, 156.

[2] The palace of Susa, noticed by LOFTUS, *Travels and Researches in Chaldæa and Susiana*, pp. 343–355, 364–415, has been excavated by Dieulafoy, who has described it in *L'Acropole de Susa*, pp. 274–358.

misery of his people ?   His dress differed from that of his nobles [1] only by the purple dye of its material and the richness of the gold embroideries with which it was adorned,[2] but he was distinguished from all others by the peculiar felt cap, or *kidaris*, which he wore, and the blue-and-white band which encircled it like a crown ; [3] the king is never represented without his long sceptre with pommelled handle, whether he be sitting or standing, and wherever he went he was attended by his umbrella- and fan-bearers.   The prescriptions of court etiquette were such as to convince his subjects and persuade himself that he was sprung from a nobler race than that of any of his magnates, and that he

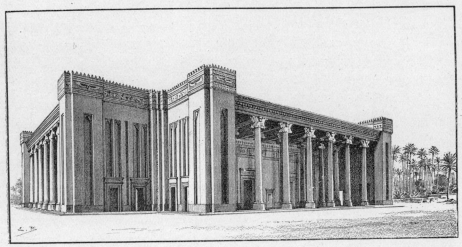

A VIEW OF THE APADANA OF SUSA, RESTORED.[4]

was outside the pale of ordinary humanity.   The greater part of his time was passed in privacy, where he was attended only by the eunuchs appointed to receive his orders ; [5] and these orders, once issued, were irrevocable, as was also the king's word, however much he might desire to recall a promise once made.[6] His meals were, as a rule, served to him alone ; [7] he might not walk on foot beyond the precincts of the palace, and he never showed himself in public

---

[1] It was the *Median robe*, called the *kandys*, whose adoption by the Persians dated, it was said, from the time of Cyrus (XENOPHON, *Cyropædia*, viii. 1, § 40).

[2] PLUTARCH, *Life of Artaxerxes*, § 24, asserts, probably following Dinon, that a royal costume of this description was estimated to be worth 12,000 talents, or nearly £2,750,000.

[3] The name is transliterated sometimes as *Kidaris* (ARRIAN, *Anabasis*, IV. vii. § 4), sometimes as *Kitaris* (PLUTARCH, *Life of Artaxerxes*, § 28).

[4] Drawn by Boudier, from the restoration by MARCEL DIEULAFOY, *L'Acropole de Suse*, pl. xv.

[5] JUSTIN, i. 9, where Pompeius Trogus relies probably on the testimony, direct or indirect, of Ctesias.

[6] For the impossibility of the king's retracting his word, even if he had pledged it imprudently, cf. the history of Xerxes and Amestris in HERODOTUS, IX. cix.

[7] HERACLIDES OF CUMÆ, *Fragm.* 2, in MÜLLER-DIDOT, *Fragm. Hist. Græc.*, vol. ii. pp. 96, 97, gives a very detailed description of the etiquette attending the royal meals, as well as all the other incidents in the life of the Achæmenian kings of Persia.

except on horseback or in his chariot, surrounded by his servants and his guards.[1] The male members of the royal family and those belonging to the six noble houses enjoyed the privilege of approaching the king at any hour of the day or night, provided he was not in the company of one of his wives.[2] These privileged persons formed his council,[3] which he convoked on important occasions, but all ordinary business was transacted by means of the scribes and inferior officials, on whom devolved the charge of the various departments of the government. A vigorous ruler, such as Darius had proved himself, certainly trusted no one but himself to read the reports sent in by the satraps, the secretaries, and the generals, or to dictate the answers required by each; but Xerxes and Artaxerxes delegated the heaviest part of such business to their ministers, and they themselves only fulfilled such state functions as it was impossible to shirk—the public administration of justice, receptions of ambassadors or victorious generals, distributions of awards, annual sacrifices, and state banquets: they were even obliged, in accordance with an ancient and inviolable tradition, once a year to set aside their usual sober habits and drink to excess on the day of the feast of Mithra.[4] Occasionally they would break through their normal routine of life to conduct in person some expedition of small importance, directed against one of the semi-independent tribes of Iran, such as the Cadusians, but their most glorious and frequent exploits were confined to the chase. They delighted to hunt the bull, the wild boar, the deer, the wild ass, and the hare, as the Pharaohs or Assyrian kings of old had done; and they would track the lion to his lair and engage him single-handed; in fact, they held a strict monopoly in such conflicts, a law which punished with death any huntsman who had the impertinence to interpose between the monarch and his prey being only abolished by Artaxerxes.[5] A crowd of menials, slaves, great nobles, and priests filled the palace; grooms, stool-bearers, umbrella- and fan-carriers, *kavasses*, "Immortals," bakers, perfumers, soldiers, and artisans formed a retinue so numerous as to require a thousand bullocks, asses, and stags to be butchered every day for its maintenance;[6] and when the king made a journey in full state, this enormous train looked like an army on the march. The women of the royal harem lived in seclusion in a separate wing of the palace, or in isolated buildings erected in the centre of the gardens. The legitimate wives of the sovereign were selected from the

---

[1] HERACLIDES OF CUMÆ, *Fragm.* 1, in MÜLLER-DIDOT, *Fragm. Hist. Græc.*, vol. ii. pp. 95, 96.

[2] HERODOTUS, III. lxxxiv.

[3] This is the council of the seven mentioned in the Book of *Ezra*, vii. 14.

[4] DURIS OF SAMOS, *Fragm.* 13, in MÜLLER-DIDOT, *Fragm. Hist. Græc.*, vol. ii. pp. 472, 473.

[5] Cf. what is stated on this subject, *supra*, p. 735.

[6] HERACLIDES OF CUMÆ, *Fragm.* 2, in MÜLLER-DIDOT, *Fragm. Hist. Græc.*, vol. ii. pp. 96, 97; cf. what is stated, *supra*, pp. 593, 594.

ladies of the royal house, the sisters or cousins of the king,[1] and from the six princely Persian families;[2] but their number was never very large, usually three or four at most.[3] The concubines, on the other hand, were chosen from all classes of society, and were counted by hundreds. They sang or played on musical instruments at the state banquets of the court, they accompanied their master to the battle-field or the chase, and probably performed the various inferior domestic duties in the interior of the harem, such as spinning, weaving, making perfumes, and attending to the confectionery and cooking.[4] Each of the king's wives had her own separate suite of apartments and special attendants, and occupied a much higher position than a mere concubine; but only one

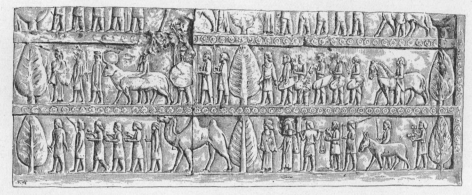

PROCESSIONAL DISPLAY OF TRIBUTE BROUGHT TO THE KING OF PERSIA.[5]

was actually queen and had the right to wear the crown, and this position belonged of right to a princess of Achæmenian race. Thus Atossa, daughter of Cyrus, was queen successively to Cambyses, Gaumâta, and Darius; Amestris to Xerxes; and Damaspia to Artaxerxes. Besides the influence naturally exerted by the queen over the mind of her husband, she often acquired boundless authority in the empire, in spite of her secluded life.[6] Her power was still further increased when she became a widow, if the new king happened to be one of her own sons. In such circumstances she retained the external attributes of royalty, sitting at the royal table whenever the king deigned to dine in the women's apartments, and everywhere taking precedence of the young queen; she was attended by her own body of eunuchs, of whom, as well as of her private

[1] For the consanguineous and incestuous marriages which were in vogue among the Iranians, and especially among the Magi, cf. *supra*, pp. 588, 589.

[2] HERODOTUS, III. lxxxiv.

[3] Cambyses had had three wives, including his two sisters Atossa and Roxana (cf. *supra*, p. 655, note 3, and p. 669). Darius had four wives—two daughters of Cyrus, Atossa and Artystônê, Parmys daughter of Smerdis, and a daughter of Otanes (HERODOTUS, III. lxxxviii.).

[4] DINON, *Fragm.* 17, in MÜLLER-DIDOT, *Fragm. Hist. Græc.*, vol. ii. p. 92; HERACLIDES OF CUMÆ, *Fragm.* 1, 2, in MÜLLER-DIDOT, *op. cit.*, vol. ii. pp. 93–95.

[5] Drawn by Faucher-Gudin, from plates in FLANDIN and COSTE, *La Perse Antique*, pl. 105, et seq.

[6] Thus Atossa induced Darius to designate Xerxes as his heir-apparent; cf. *supra*, pp. 714, 715.

revenues, she had absolute control. Those whom the queen-mother took under her protection escaped punishment, even though they richly deserved it, but the object of her hatred was doomed to perish in the end, either by poison treacherously administered, or by some horrible form of torture, being impaled, suffocated in ashes, tortured in the trough, or flayed alive.[1] Artaxerxes reigned for forty-two years, spending his time between the pleasures of the chase and the harem ; no serious trouble disturbed his repose after the suppression of the revolt under Megabyzos, but on his death in 424 B.C. there was a renewal of the intrigues and ambitious passions which had stained with bloodshed the opening years of his reign. The legitimate heir, Xerxes II., was assassinated, after a reign of forty-five days, by Secudianus (Sogdianus), one of his illegitimate brothers, and the *cortège* which was escorting the bodies of his parents conveyed his also to the royal burying-place at Persepolis. Meanwhile Secudianus became suspicious of another of his brothers, named Ochus, whom Artaxerxes had caused to marry Parysatis, one of the daughters of Xerxes, and whom he had set over the important province of Hyrcania. Ochus received repeated summonses to appear in his brother's presence to pay him homage, and at last obeyed the mandate, but arrived at the head of an army. The Persian nobility rose at his approach, and one by one the chief persons of the state declared themselves in his favour : first Arbarius, commander of the cavalry ; then Arxanes, the satrap of Egypt; and lastly, the eunuch Artoxares, the ruler of Armenia. These three all combined in urging Ochus to assume the *kidaris* publicly, which he, with feigned reluctance, consented to do, and proceeded, at the suggestion of Parysatis, to open negotiations with Secudianus, offering to divide the regal power with him. Secudianus accepted the offer, against the advice of his minister Menostanes, and gave himself up into the hands of the rebels. He was immediately seized and cast into the ashes, where he perished miserably, after a reign of six months and fifteen days.[2]

On ascending the throne, Ochus assumed the name of Darius. His confidential advisers were three eunuchs, who ruled the empire in his name— Artoxares, who had taken such a prominent part in the campaign which won him the crown, Artibarzanes, and Athôos; but the guiding spirit of his government was, in reality, his wife, the detestable Parysatis. She had already borne him two children before she became queen ; a daughter, Amestris, and a son, Arsaces,[3] who afterwards became king under the name of Artaxerxes.

---

[1] Cf. the history of Parysatis as narrated by Plutarch in his *Life of Artaxerxes*, §§ 4, 5, 14, 17, 19, etc.

[2] CTESIAS, *Fragm.* 29, §§ 43–48, in MÜLLER-DIDOT, *Ctesiæ Cnidii Fragm.*, pp. 54, 55 ; other authors mentioned by Diodorus Siculus (xii. 74) affirmed that the reign of Xerxes II. lasted a whole year.

[3] This is the spelling found in the extract from Photius (CTESIAS, *Fragm.* 29, § 49, in MÜLLER-DIDOT, *Ctesiæ Cnidii Fragm.*, p. 55), but Plutarch gives the form Arsikas (*Life of Artaxerxes*, § 1), which must be the original spelling; according to Dinon (*Fragm.* 22, in MÜLLER-DIDOT, *Fragm. Hist. Græc.*, vol. ii. p. 93), Artaxerxes was called Oartes before his accession.

Soon after the accession of her husband, she bore him a second son, whom she named Cyrus, in memory of the founder of the empire, and a daughter, Artostê; several other children were born subsequently, making thirteen in all, but these all died in childhood, except one named Oxendras.[1] Violent, false, jealous, and passionately fond of the exercise of power, Parysatis hesitated at no crime to rid herself of those who thwarted her schemes, even though they might be members of her own family; and, not content with putting them out of the way, she delighted in making them taste her hatred to the full, by subjecting them to the most skilfully graduated refinements of torture; she deservedly left behind her the reputation of being one of the most cruel of all the cruel queens, whose memory was a terror not only to the harems of Persia, but to the whole of the Eastern world. The numerous revolts which broke out soon after her husband's accession, furnished occasions for the revelation of her perfidious cleverness. All the malcontents of the reign of Artaxerxes, those who had been implicated in the murder of Xerxes II., or who had sided with Secudianus, had rallied round a younger brother of Darius, named Arsites, and one of them, Artyphios, son of

DARIUS II.[2]

Megabyzos, took the field in Asia Minor. Being supported by a large contingent of Greek mercenaries, he won two successive victories at the opening of the campaign, but was subsequently defeated, though his forces still remained formidable. But Persian gold accomplished what Persian bravery had failed to achieve, and prevailed over the mercenaries so successfully that all deserted him with the exception of three Milesians. Artyphios and Arsites, thus discouraged, committed the imprudence of capitulating on condition of receiving a promise that their lives should be spared, and that they should be well treated; but Parysatis persuaded her husband to break his plighted word, and they perished in the ashes.[3] Their miserable fate did not discourage the satrap of Lydia, Pissuthnes, who was of Achæmenian race: he entered the lists in 418 B.C., with the help of the Athenians.[4] The relations between the Persian empire and Greece had continued fairly satisfactory since the peace of 449 B.C., and the few outbreaks which had taken place had not led to any widespread

---

[1] Ctesias, *Fragm.* 29, § 49, in Müller-Didot, *Ctesiæ Cnidii Fragmenta*, p. 55. Since Ochus was not the son of Damaspia, the only legitimate wife of Artaxerxes I., the Greeks surnamed him Νόθος (Nothus), the bastard.

[2] Drawn by Faucher-Gudin, from one of the coins in the *Cabinet des Médailles*, of which a cast was kindly furnished me by M. Babelon.

[3] Ctesias, *Fragm.* 29, §§ 50, 51, in Müller-Didot, *Ctesiæ Cnidii Fragmenta*, p. 55. For the punishment of the ashes, cf. the statement of Valerius Maximus, ix. 2, 6: "Septum enim altis parietibus locum cinere complevit, superpositoque tigno prominente, benigne cibo et potione exceptos in eo collocabat, e quo somno sopiti, in illam insidiosam congeriem decidebant."

[4] Ctesias, *Fragm.* 29, § 52, in Müller-Didot, *Ctesiæ Cnidii Fragmenta*, pp. 55, 56.

disturbance. The Athenians, absorbed in their quarrel with Sparta, preferred to close their eyes to all side issues, lest the Persians should declare war against them, and the satraps of Asia Minor, fully alive to the situation, did not hesitate to take advantage of any pretext for recovering a part of the territory they coveted: it was thus that they had seized Colophon about 430 B.C.,[1] and so secured once more a port on the Ægean. Darius despatched to oppose Pissuthnes a man of noble birth, named Tissaphernes, giving him plenary power throughout the whole of the peninsula, and Tissaphernes endeavoured to obtain by treachery the success he would with difficulty have won on the field of battle: he corrupted by his darics Lycon, the commander of the Athenian contingent, and Pissuthnes, suddenly abandoned by his best auxiliaries, was forced to surrender at discretion. He also was suffocated in the ashes, and Darius bestowed his office on Tissaphernes. But the punishment of Pissuthnes did not put an end to the troubles: his son Amorges roused Caria to revolt, and with the title of king maintained his independence for some years longer. While these incidents were taking place, the news of the disasters in Sicily reached the East: as soon as it was known in Susa that Athens had lost at Syracuse the best part of her fleet and the choicest of her citizens, the moment was deemed favourable to violate the treaty and regain control of the whole of Asia Minor. Two noteworthy men were at that time set over the western satrapies, Tissaphernes ruling at Sardes, and Tiribazus over Hellespontine Phrygia. These satraps opened negotiations with Sparta at the beginning of 412 B.C., and concluded a treaty with her at Miletus itself, by the terms of which the Peloponnesians recognised the suzerainty of Darius over all the territory once held by his ancestors in Asia, including the cities since incorporated into the Athenian league. They hoped shortly to be strong enough to snatch from him what they now ceded, and to set free once more the Greeks whom they thus condemned to servitude after half a century of independence, but their expectations were frustrated. The towns along the coast fell one after another into the power of Tissaphernes, Amorges was taken prisoner in Iassos, and at the beginning of 411 B.C. there remained to the Athenians in Ionia and Caria merely the two ports of Halicarnassus and Notium, and the three islands of Cos, Samos, and Lesbos: from that time the power of the great king increased from year to year, and weighed heavily on the destinies of Greece. Meanwhile Darius II. was growing old, and intrigues with regard to the succession were set on foot. Two of his sons put forward claims to the throne: Arsaces had seniority in his favour, but had been born when his father was still a mere satrap; Cyrus, on the contrary, had been born in the purple, and his mother Parysatis was

---

[1] Thucydides, iii. 34.

passionately devoted to him.[1] Thanks to her manœuvres, he was practically created viceroy of Asia Minor in 407 B.C., with such abundant resources of men and money at his disposal, that he was virtually an independent sovereign. While he was consolidating his power in the west, his mother endeavoured to secure his accession to the throne by intriguing at the court of the aged king; if her plans failed, Cyrus was prepared to risk everything by an appeal to arms. He realised that the Greeks would prove powerful auxiliaries in such a contingency; and as soon as he had set up his court at Sardes, he planned how best to conciliate their favour, or at least to win over those whose support was likely to be most valuable.

CYRUS THE YOUNGER.[2]

Athens, as a maritime power, was not in a position to support him in an enterprise which especially required the co-operation of a considerable force of heavily armed infantry. He therefore deliberately espoused the cause of the Peloponnesians, and the support he gave them was not without its influence on the issue of the struggle: the terrible day of Ægos Potamos was a day of triumph for him as much as for the Lacedæmonians (405 B.C.).

His intimacy with Lysander, however, his constant enlistments of mercenary troops, and his secret dealings with the neighbouring provinces, had already aroused suspicion, and the satraps placed under his orders, especially Tissaphernes, accused him to the king of treason. Darius summoned him to Susa to explain his conduct (405 B.C.), and he arrived just in time to be present at his father's death (404), but too late

ARTAXERXES MNEMON.[3]

to obtain his designation as heir to the throne through the intervention of his mother, Parysatis; Arsaces inherited the crown, and assumed the name of Artaxerxes. Cyrus entered the temple of Pasargadæ surreptitiously during the coronation ceremony, with the intention of killing his brother at the foot of the altar; but Tissaphernes, warned by one of the priests, denounced him, and he would have been put to death on the spot, had not his mother thrown her arms around him and prevented the executioner from fulfilling his office.[4] Having with difficulty obtained pardon and been sent back to his province, he collected thirty thousand Greeks and a hundred thousand native troops, and, hastily leaving Sardes (401 B.C.), he crossed Asia Minor, Northern Syria,

[1] CTESIAS, *Fragm.* 29, § 49, in MÜLLER-DIDOT, *Ctesiæ Cnidii Fragmenta*, p. 55, and following him, PLUTARCH, *Life of Artaxerxes*, § 2. Cyrus was certainly not more than seventeen years old in 407 B.C., even admitting that he was born immediately after his father's accession in 424–3 B.C.

[2] Drawn by Faucher-Gudin, from one of the coins in the *Cabinet des Médailles*, of which the cast was kindly furnished me by M. Babelon.

[3] Drawn by Faucher-Gudin, from a coin in the *Cabinet des Médailles*, of which the cast was kindly furnished me by M. Babelon. This coin, which was struck at Mallos, in Cilicia, bears as a countermark the figure of a bull and the name of the city of Issus.

[4] CTESIAS, *Fragm.* 29, § 57, in MÜLLER-DIDOT, *Ctesiæ Cnidii Fragmenta*, pp. 56, 57, which was the source utilised by PLUTARCH, *Life of Artaxerxes*, §§ 2, 3; cf. JUSTIN, v. 11.

and Mesopotamia, encountered the royal army at Cunaxa, to the north of Babylon, and rashly met his end at the very moment of victory. He was a brave, active, and generous prince, endowed with all the virtues requisite to make a good Oriental monarch, and he had, moreover, learnt, through contact with the Greeks, to recognise the weak points of his own nation, and was fully determined to remedy them : his death, perhaps, was an irreparable misfortune for his country. Had he survived and supplanted the feeble Artaxerxes, it is quite possible that he might have confirmed and strengthened the power of Persia, or, at least, temporarily have arrested its decline. Having lost their leader, his Asiatic followers at once dispersed ; but the mercenaries did not lose heart, and, crossing Asia and Armenia, gained at length the shores of the Black Sea. Up to that time the Greeks had looked upon Persia as a compact state, which they were sufficiently powerful to conquer by sea and hold in check by land, but which they could not, without imprudence, venture to attack within its own frontiers. The experience of the Ten Thousand was a proof to them that a handful of men, deprived of their proper generals, without guides, money, or provisions, might successfully oppose the overwhelming forces of the great king, and escape from his clutches without any serious difficulty. National discords prevented them from at once utilising the experience they thus acquired, but the lesson was not lost upon the court of Susa. The success of Lysander had been ensured by Persian subsidies, and now Sparta hesitated to fulfil the conditions of the treaty of Miletus; the Lacedæmonians demanded liberty once more for the former allies of Athens, fostered the war in Asia in order to enforce their claims, and their king Agesilaus, penetrating to the very heart of Phrygia, would have pressed still further forward in the tracks of the Ten Thousand, had not an opportune diversion been created in his rear by the bribery of the Persians. Athens once more flew to arms : her fleet, in conjunction with the Phœnicians, took possession of Cythera; the Long Walls were rebuilt at the expense of the great king, and Sparta, recalled by these reverses to a realisation of her position, wisely abandoned her inclination for distant enterprises. Asia Minor was reconquered, and Persia passed from the position of a national enemy to that of the friend and arbiter of Greece; but she did so by force of circumstances only, and not from having merited in any way the supremacy she attained. Her military energy, indeed, was far from being exhausted; but poor Artaxerxes, bewildered by the rivalries between his mother and his wives,[1] did not know how to make the most of the immense resources still at his disposal, and he met with repeated checks as soon as he came face to face with a nation and leaders who refused to stoop to

---

[1] Cf., for the opening of the reign of Artaxerxes, the short notices given by CTESIAS, *Fragm.* 29, §§ 57, 59–61, in MÜLLER-DIDOT, *Ctesiæ Cnidii Fragmenta*, pp. 56–58.

treachery. He had no sooner recovered possession of the Ægean littoral than Egypt was snatched from his grasp by a new Pharaoh who had arisen in the Nile valley. The peace had not been seriously disturbed in Egypt during the forty years which had elapsed since the defeat of Inarus.[1] Satrap had peaceably succeeded satrap in the fortress of Memphis; the exhaustion of Libya had prevented any movement on the part of Thannyras; the aged Amyrtæus had passed from the scene, and his son, Pausiris, bent his neck submissively to the Persian yoke.[2] More than once, however, unexpected outbursts had shown that the fires of rebellion were still smouldering. A Psammetichus, who reigned about 445 B.C. in a corner of the Delta, had dared to send corn and presents to the Athenians, then at war with Artaxerxes I., and the second year of Darius II. had been troubled by a sanguinary sedition, which, however, was easily suppressed by the governor then in power;[3] finally, about 410 B.C., a king of Egypt had, not without some show of evidence, laid himself open to the charge of sending a piratical expedition into Phœnician waters, an Arab king having contributed to the enterprise.[4] It was easy to see, moreover, from periodical revolts—such as that of Megabyzos in Syria, those of Artyphios and Arsites, of Pissuthnes and Amorges in Asia Minor—with what impunity the wrath of the great king could be defied: it was not to be wondered at, therefore, that, about 405 B.C., an enemy should appear in the heart of the Delta in the person of a grandson and namesake of Amyrtæus.[5] He did not at first rouse the whole country to revolt, for Egyptian troops were still numbered in the army of Artaxerxes at the battle of Cunaxa in 401 B.C.;[6] but he succeeded in establishing a regular native government, and struggled so resolutely against the foreign domination that the historians of the sacred colleges inscribed his name on the list of the Pharaohs. He is there made to represent a whole dynasty, the XXVIIIth, which lasted six years, coincident with the six years of his reign. It was due to a Mendesian dynasty, however, whose founder was Nephorites, that Egypt obtained its entire freedom, and was raised once more to the rank of a nation.[7] This dynasty from the very outset

---

[1] Wiedemann thinks that Egypt was divided at that time into two satrapies: the first, that of Upper Egypt, being governed by a Persian; the second, by an Egyptian satrap such as Pausiris (*Geschichte Ægyptens*, pp. 252, 253).

[2] HERODOTUS, III. xv., who mentions him as ruling in Egypt in his own day.

[3] PHILOCHORUS, *Fragm.* 90, in MÜLLER-DIDOT, *Fragm. Hist. Græc.*, vol. i. pp. 398, 399.

[4] The revolt mentioned by CTESIAS, *Fragm.* 29, § 47, in MÜLLER-DIDOT, *Ctesiæ Cnidii Fragmenta*, p. 55, has nothing to do with the insurrection of the satrap of Egypt which is here referred to, the date of which is furnished by the Syncellus (p. 256, *d*).

[5] The name of this king has not been identified with any certainty on any of the contemporary hieroglyphic monuments. Neither Rudamanu nor Amen-iritrud (WIEDEMANN, *Gesch. Ægyptens*, p. 272; *Ægypt. Gesch.*, p. 694) seems to belong to the middle of the Persian epoch. In the *Demotic Rhapsody*, the reading of the name which seems to correspond to that of the Amyrtæus of the Greeks is not certain (RÉVILLOUT, *Une Chronique Égyptienne contemporaine de Manéthon*, pp. 2–5, and pl. iii. A, *Second Extrait de la Chronique Démotique de Paris* in the *Revue Égypt.*, vol. ii. pp. 53, 54).

[6] DIODORUS SICULUS, xii. 46.   [7] XENOPHON, *Anabasis*, i. 8, § 9.

adopted the policy which had proved so successful in the case of the Saites three centuries previously, and employed it with similar success. Egypt had always been in the position of a besieged fortress, which needed, for its complete security, that its first lines of defence should be well in advance of its citadel : she must either possess Syria or win her as an ally, if she desired to be protected against all chance of sudden invasion. Nephorites and his successors, therefore, formed alliances beyond the isthmus, and even on the other side of the Mediterranean, with Cyprus, Caria, and Greece, in one case to purchase support, and in another to re-establish the ancient supremacy exercised by the Theban Pharaohs.[1] Every revolt against the Persians, every quarrel among the satraps, helped forward their cause, since they compelled the great king to suspend his attacks against Egypt altogether or to prosecute them at wide intervals : the Egyptians therefore fomented such quarrels, or even, at need, provoked them, and played their game so well that for a long time they had to oppose only a fraction of the Persian forces. Like the Saite Pharaohs before them, they were aware how little reliance could be placed on native troops, and they recruited their armies at great expense from the European Greeks. This occurred at the time when mercenary forces were taking the place of native levies throughout Hellas, and war was developing into a lucrative trade for those who understood how to conduct it : adventurers, greedy for booty, flocked to the standards of the generals who enjoyed the best reputation for kindness or ability, and the generals themselves sold their services to the highest bidder. The Persian kings took large advantage of this arrangement to procure troops : the Pharaohs imitated their example, and in the years which followed, the most experienced captains, Iphicrates, Chabrias, and Timotheus, passed from one camp to another, as often against the will as with the consent of their fatherland. The power of Sparta was at her zenith when Nephorites ascended the throne, and she was just preparing for her expedition to Phrygia. The Pharaoh concluded an alliance with the Lacedæmonians, and in 396 B.C. sent to Agesilaus a fleet laden with arms, corn, and supplies, which, however, was intercepted by Conon, who was at that moment cruising in the direction of Rhodes in command of the Persian squadron.[2] This misadventure and the abrupt retreat of the Spartans from Asia Minor cooled the good will of the Egyptian king towards his allies. Thinking that they had abandoned him, and that he was threatened

---

[1] This is, at any rate, the idea given of him by Egyptian tradition in the time of the Ptolemies, as results from a passage in the *Demotic Rhapsody*, where his reign is mentioned (RÉVILLOUT, *Second Extrait de la Chronique Démotique de Paris*, in the *Revue Égyptologique*, vol. ii. p. 55.

[2] DIODORUS SICULUS, xiv. 79, where the name is written Nephereus. Pompeius Trogus (JUSTIN, vi. 2; cf. OROSIUS, iii. 1, § 8) had access to the works of an author who called the king Herkynium, who has been identified with Hakoris, but may well have been a pretender to the throne (JUDEICH, *Kleinasiatische Studien*, p. 153), or more likely one of those feudal lords of the Delta whom the Greeks treated as kings, as the Assyrians and Chaldæans had in old days treated their ancestors.

with an imminent attack on the shore of the Delta, he assembled, probably at Pelusium, the forces he had apparently intended for a distant enterprise.

Matters took longer to come to a crisis than he had expected. The retreat of Agesilaus had not pacified the Ægean satrapies; after the disturbance created by Cyrus the Younger, the greater number of the native tribes—Mysians, Pisidians, people of Pontus and Paphlagonia—had shaken off the Persian yoke, and it was a matter of no small difficulty to reduce them once more to subjection. Their incessant turbulence gave Egypt time to breathe and to organise new combinations. Cyprus entered readily into her designs. Since the subjugation of that island in 445 B.C., the Greek cities had suffered terrible oppression at the hands of the great king. Artaxerxes I., despairing of reducing them to obedience, depended exclusively for support on the Phœnician inhabitants of the island, who, through his favour, regained so much vigour that in the space of less than two generations they had recovered most of the ground lost during the preceding centuries: Semitic rulers replaced the Achæan tyrants at Salamis, and in most of the other cities, and Citium became what it had been before the rise of Salamis, the principal commercial centre in the island. Evagoras, a descendant of

HAKORIS.[1]

the ancient kings, endeavoured to retrieve the Grecian cause: after driving out of Salamis Abdemon, its Tyrian ruler, he took possession of all the other towns except Citium and Amathus. This is not the place to recount the brilliant part played by Evagoras, in conjunction with Conon, during the campaigns against the Spartans in the Peloponnesian war. The activity he then displayed and the ambitious designs he revealed soon drew upon him the dislike of the Persian governors and their sovereign; and from 391 B.C. he was at open war with Persia. He would have been unable, single-handed, to maintain the struggle for any length of time, but Egypt and Greece were at his back, ready to support him with money or arms. Hakoris had succeeded Nephorites I. in 393 B.C.,[2] and had repulsed an attack of Artaxerxes between 390 and 386.[3] He was not unduly exalted by his success, and had immediately taken wise precautions in view of a second invasion. After safe-guarding his western frontier by concluding a treaty

---

[1] Drawn by Faucher-Gudin, from LEPSIUS, *Denkmäler*, iii. 301, No. 80.

[2] The length of the reign of Nephorites I. is fixed at six years by the lists of Manetho (UNGER, *Chronologie des Manetho*, pp. 297, 298); the last-known date of his reign is that of his fourth year, on a mummy-bandage preserved in the Louvre (DEVÉRIA, *Catalogue des Manuscrits Égyptiens*, pp. 207, 208).

[3] This war is alluded to by several ancient authors (ISOCRATES, *Panegyric*, § 161; JUSTIN, vi. 6) in passages which have been brought together and explained by Judeich (*Kleinasiatische Studien*, pp. 158, 159); but unfortunately the detailed history of the events is not known.

with the Libyans of Barca,[1] he entered into an alliance with Evagoras and the Athenians. He sent lavish gifts of corn to the Cypriots, as well as munitions of war, ships, and money, while Athens sent them several thousand men under the command of Chabrias; not only did an expedition despatched against them under Autophradates fail miserably, but Evagoras seized successively Citium and Amathus, and, actually venturing across the sea, took Tyre by assault and devastated Phœnicia and Cilicia. The princes of Asia Minor were already preparing for revolt, and one of them, Hecatomnus of Caria, had openly joined the allies, when Sparta suddenly opened negotiations with Persia: Antalcidas presented himself at Susa to pay homage before the throne of the great king. The treaty of Miletus had brought the efforts of Athens to naught, and sold the Asiatic Greeks to their oppressors: the peace obtained by Antalcidas effaced the results of Salamis and Platæa, and laid European Greece prostrate at the feet of her previously vanquished foes. An order issuing from the centre of Persia commanded the cities of Greece to suspend hostilities and respect each other's liberties; the issuing of such an order was equivalent to treating them as vassels whose quarrels it is the function of the suzerain to repress, but they nevertheless complied with the command (387 B.C.). Arta-xerxes, relieved from anxiety for the moment, as to affairs on the Ægean, was now free to send his best generals into the rebel countries, and such was the course his ministers recommended. Evagoras was naturally the first to be attacked. Cyprus was, in fact, an outpost of Egypt; commanding as she did the approach by sea, she was in a position to cut the communications of any army, which, issuing from Palestine, should march upon the Delta. Arta-xerxes assembled three hundred thousand foot-soldiers and three hundred triremes under the command of Tiribazus, and directed the whole force against the island. At first the Cypriot cruisers intercepted the convoys which were bringing provisions for this large force, and by so doing reduced the invaders to such straits that sedition broke out in their camp; but Evagoras was defeated at sea off the promontory of Citium, and his squadron destroyed. He was not in any way discouraged by this misfortune, but leaving his son, Pnytagoras, to hold the barbarian forces in check, he hastened to implore the help of the Pharaoh (385 B.C.). But Hakoris was too much occupied with securing his own immediate safety to risk anything in so desperate an enter-prise.[1] Evagoras was able to bring back merely an insufficient subsidy; he shut himself up in Salamis, and there maintained the conflict for some years longer.[2] Meanwhile Hakoris, realising that the submission of Cyprus would oppose his flank to attack, tried to effect a diversion in Asia Minor, and by entering into alliance with the Pisidians, then in open insurrection, he procured for it a

[1] THEOPOMPUS, *Fragm.* 111, in MULLER-DIDOT, *Fragm. Hist. Græc.*, vol. i. p. 295.
[2] DIODORUS SICULUS, xv. 4–8.

respite, of which he himself took advantage to prepare for the decisive struggle.[1]
The peace effected by Antalcidas had left most of the mercenary soldiers of
Greece without employment. Hakoris hired twenty thousand of them, and
the Phœnician admirals, still occupied in blockading the ports of Cyprus, failed
to intercept the vessels which brought him these reinforcements.[2] It was
fortunate for Egypt that they did so, for the Pharaoh died in 381 B.C., and his
successors, Psamuthis II., Mutis, and Néphorites II., each occupied the throne
for a very short time, and the whole country was in confusion for rather more
than two years (381–379 B.C.) during the settlement of the succession.[3] The
turbulent disposition of the great feudatory nobles, which had so frequently
brought trouble upon previous Pharaohs during the Assyrian wars, was no less
dangerous in this last century of Egyptian independence; it caused the fall of the
Mendesian dynasty in the very face of the enemy, and the prince of Sebennytos,
Nakht-har-habît, Nectanebo I., was raised to the throne by the military faction.
According to a tradition current in Ptolemaic times, this sovereign was a son
of Nephorites I., who had been kept out of his heritage by the jealousy of the
gods;[4] whatever his origin, the people had no cause to repent of having accepted
him as their king. He began his reign by suppressing the slender subsidies
which Evagoras had continued to receive from his predecessors, and this
measure, if not generous, was at least politic.[5] For Cyprus was now virtually
in the power of the Persians, and the blockade of a few thousand men in
Salamis did not draught away a sufficiently large proportion of their effective
force to be of any service to Egypt: the money which had hitherto been devoted to the Cypriots was henceforth reserved for the direct defence of the Nile
valley. Evagoras obtained unexpectedly favourable conditions: Artaxerxes
conceded to him his title of king and the possession of his city (383 B.C.),

---

[1] THEOPOMPUS, *Fragm.* 111, in MÜLLER-DIDOT, *Fragm. Hist. Græc.*, vol. i. p. 296.

[2] DIODORUS SICULUS, xv. 29.

[3] Hakoris reigned thirteen years (MANETHO, in MÜLLER-DIDOT, *Fragm. Hist. Græc.*, vol. ii. p. 597),
from 393 to 381 B.C. The reigns of the three succeeding kings occupied only two years and four months
between them, from the end of 381 to the beginning of 378. Muthes or Mutis, who is not mentioned
in all the lists of Manetho, seems to have his counterpart in the *Demotic Rhapsody* (RÉVILLOUT,
Second Extrait de la Chronique Démotique, in the *Revue Égyptologique*, vol. ii. pp. 56, 57). Wiedemann
(*Geschichte Ægyptens*, p. 262, et seq.; *Ægyptische Geschichte*, pp. 696, 697) has inverted the order usually
adopted, and proposed the following series: Nephorites I., Muthes, Psamuthis, Hakoris, Nephorites II.
The discovery at Karnak of a small temple where Psamuthis mentions Hakoris as his predecessor
(MASPERO, *Découverte d'un petit temple à Karnak*, in the *Recueil de Travaux*, vol. ii. p. 20) shows that
on this point at least Manetho was well informed.

[4] Cf., for this tradition current in Ptolemaic times, the fairly full statement of the *Demotic
Rhapsody* which has been interpreted by RÉVILLOUT, *op. cit.*, p. 55.

[5] This is the interpretation which seems to me the best for the passage in the fragment of
Theopompus (*Fragm.* 111, in MÜLLER-DIDOT, *Fragm. Hist. Græc.*, vol. i. p. 296): καὶ ὡς Νεκτονέβοις
παρειληφότος τῆς Αἰγύπτου βασιλείας, πρὸς Λακεδαιμονίους ἀπέστειλεν Εὐαγόρας, τίνα τε τρόπον ὁ περὶ
Κῦπρον πόλεμος διελύθη. If the change of reign in Egypt had not been unfavourable to him at this
juncture, Evagoras would not have made the advances indicated to the Lacedæmonians, and would
not have capitulated shortly after.

and turned his whole attention to Nectanebo, the last of his enemies who still held out.

Nectanebo had spared no pains in preparing effectively to receive his foe. He chose as his coadjutor the Athenian Chabrias, whose capacity as a general had been manifested by recent events, and the latter accepted this office although he had received no instructions from his government to do so,[1] and had transformed the Delta into an entrenched camp. He had fortified the most vulnerable points along the coast, had built towers at each of the mouths of the river to guard the entrance, and had selected the sites for his garrison fortresses so judiciously that they were kept up long after his time to protect the country. Two of them are mentioned by name: one, situated below Pelusium, called the Castle of Chabrias; the other, not far from Lake Mareotis, which was known as his township.[2] The Persian generals endeavoured to make

PHARNABAZUS.[3]

their means of attack proportionate to the defences of the enemy. Acre was the only port in Southern Syria large enough to form the rendezvous for a fleet, where it might be secure from storms and surprises of the enemy. This was chosen as the Persian headquarters, and formed the base of their operations. During three years they there accumulated supplies of food and military stores, Phœnician and Greek vessels, and both foreign and native troops. The rivalries between the military commanders, Tithraustes, Datames, and Abrocomas, and the intrigues of the court, had on several occasions threatened the ruin of the enterprise, but Pharnabazus, who from the outset had held supreme command, succeeded in ridding himself of his rivals, and in the spring of 374 B.C. was at length ready for the advance. The expedition consisted of two hundred thousand Asiatic troops, and twenty thousand Greeks, three hundred triremes, two hundred galleys of thirty oars, and numerous transports.[4] Superiority of numbers was on the side of the Persians, and that just at the moment when Nectanebo lost his most experienced general. Artaxerxes had remonstrated with the Athenians for permitting one of their generals to serve in Egypt, in spite of their professed friendship for himself, and, besides insisting on his recall, had requested for himself the services of the celebrated Iphicrates. The Athenians complied with his demand, and while summoning Chabrias to return to Athens, despatched Iphicrates to Syria, where he was

---

[1] DIODORUS SICULUS, xv. 29; CORNELIUS NEPOS, Chabrias, § 2.

[2] Both are mentioned by Strabo: ὁ Χαβρίου λεγόμενος χάραξ (XVI. ii. § 33, p. 760) and ἡ Χαβρίου κώμη λεγομένη (XVII. i. § 22, p. 808); the exact sites of these two places are not yet identified. Diodorus Siculus, describing the defensive preparations of Egypt (xv. 42), does not state expressly that they were the work of Chabrias, but this fact seems to result from a general consideration of the context.

[3] Drawn by Faucher-Gudin, from a coin in the Cabinet des Médailles, of which a cast was kindly furnished me by M. Babelon; cf. BABELON, Les Perses Achéménides, pl. iv. No. 8.

[4] DIODORUS SICULUS, xv. 41.

placed in command of the mercenary troops.[1] Pharnabazus ordered a general advance in May, 374 B.C.,[2] but when he arrived before Pelusium, he perceived that he was not in a position to take the town by storm ; not only had the fortifications been doubled, but the banks of the canals had been cut and the approaches inundated. Iphicrates advised him not to persevere in attempting a regular siege : he contended that it would be more profitable to detach an expeditionary force towards some less well-protected point on the coast, and there to make a breach in the system of defence which protected the enemies' front. Three thousand men were despatched with all secrecy to the mouth of the Mendesian branch of the Nile, and there disembarked unexpectedly before the forts which guarded the entrance. The garrison, having imprudently made a sortie in face of the enemy, was put to rout, and pursued so hotly that victors and vanquished entered pell-mell within the walls. After this success victory was certain, if the Persians pursued their advantage promptly and pushed forward straight into the heart of the Delta; the moment was the more propitious for such a movement, since Nectanebo had drained Memphis of troops to protect his frontier. Iphicrates, having obtained this information from one of the prisoners, advised Pharnabazus to proceed up the Nile with the fleet, and take the capital by storm before the enemy should have time to garrison it afresh ; the Persian general, however, considered the plan too hazardous, and preferred to wait until the entire army should have joined him. Iphicrates offered to risk the adventure with his body of auxiliary troops only, but was suspected of harbouring some ambitious design, and was refused permission to advance. Meanwhile these delays had given the Egyptians time to recover from their first alarm ; they boldly took the offensive, surrounded the position held by Pharnabazus, and were victorious in several skirmishes. Summer advanced, the Nile rose more rapidly than usual, and soon the water encroached upon the land ; the invaders were obliged to beat a retreat before it, and fall back towards Syria. Iphicrates, disgusted at the ineptitude and suspicion of his Asiatic colleagues, returned secretly to Greece : the remains of the army were soon after disbanded, and Egypt once more breathed freely.[4] The check

ARTAXERXES II.[3]

---

[1] CORNELIUS NEPOS, *Chabrias,* § 3, and *Iphicrates,* § 2 ; DIODORUS SICULUS, xv. 29.

[2] As Kenrick (*Ancient Egypt under the Pharaohs,* vol. ii. p. 421) justly observes, "the Persian and Athenian generals committed the same mistake which led to the defeat of Saint Louis and the capture of his army in 1249 A.D., and which Bonaparte avoided in his campaign of 1798." Anyhow, it seems that the fault must be laid on Pharnabazus alone, and that Iphicrates was entirely blameless.

[3] Drawn by Faucher-Gudin, from a silver stater in the *Cabinet des Médailles,* of which I owe the cast to the kindness of M. Babelon.

[4] The story of this campaign is borrowed from Diodorus Siculus (xv. 41–43), but the details have been completed from information furnished by other authors, whose works have been brought together and carefully discussed by JUDEICH, *Kleinasiatische Studien,* pp. 159–163,

received by the Persian arms, however, was not sufficiently notorious to shake that species of supremacy which Artaxerxes had exercised in Greece since the peace of 387. Sparta, Thebes, and Athens vied with each other in obtaining an alliance with him as keenly as if he had been successful before Pelusium. Antalcidas reappeared at Susa in 372 B.C. to procure a fresh act of intervention; Pelopidas and Ismenias, in 367, begged for a rescript similar to that of Antalcidas; and finally Athens sent a solemn embassy to entreat for a subsidy. It seemed as if the great king had become a kind of supreme arbiter for Greece, and that all the states hitherto leagued against him now came in turn to submit their mutual differences for his decision. But this arbiter who thus imposed his will on states beyond the borders of his empire was never fully master within his own domains. Of gentle nature and pliant disposition, inclined to clemency rather than to severity, and, moreover, so lacking in judgment as a general that he had almost succumbed to an attack by the Cadusians on the only occasion that he had, in a whim of the moment, undertaken the command of an army in person,[1] Artaxerxes busied himself with greater zeal in religious reforms than in military projects. He introduced the rites of Mithra and Anâhita into the established religion of the state,[2] but he had not the energy necessary to curb the ambitions of his provincial governors. Asia Minor, whose revolts followed closely on those of Egypt, rose in rebellion against him immediately after the campaign on the Nile, Ariobarzanes heading the rebellion in Phrygia, Datames and Aspis that in Cilicia and Cappadocia, and both defying his power for several years. When at length they succumbed through treachery, the satraps of the Mediterranean district, from the Hellespont to the isthmus of Suez, formed a coalition and simultaneously took the field: the break-up of the empire would have been complete had not Persian darics been lavishly employed once more in the affair. Meanwhile Nectanebo had died in 361,[3] and had been succeeded by Tachôs.[4] The new Pharaoh deemed the occasion opportune to make a diversion against Persia and to further secure his own safety: he therefore offered his support to the satraps, who sent Rheomitres as a delegate to discuss the terms of an offensive and defensive alliance.

[1] PLUTARCH, *Life of Artaxerxes*, § 24; CORNELIUS NEPOS, *Datames*, § 1.

[2] Cf., in WEISSBACH and BANG, *Die Altpersischen Keilinschriften*, pp. 44–47, the passages from his inscriptions in which he invokes these two divinities.

[3] The lists of Manetho assign ten or eighteen years to his reign (MANETHO, in MÜLLER-DIDOT, *Fragm. Hist. Græc.*, vol. ii. p. 597). A sarcophagus in Vienna bears the date of his fifteenth year (BRUGSCH, *Recueil de Monuments*, vol. i. pl. vi. No. 1), and the great inscription of Edfu speaks of gifts he made to the temple in this town in the eighteenth year of his reign (LEPSIUS, *Denkmäler*, iv. 43; BRUGSCH, *Thesaurus Inscriptionum Ægyptiacarum*, p. 538, l. 3). The reading eighteen is therefore preferable to the reading ten in the lists of Manetho; if the very obscure text of the *Demotic Rhapsody* really applies the number nine or ten to the length of the reign (RÉVILLOUT, *Second Extrait de la Chronique Démotique*, in the *Revue Égyptologique*, vol. ii. pp. 57–59), this reckoning must be explained by some mystic calculations of the priests of the Ptolemaic epoch.

[4] The name of this king, written by the Greeks Teôs or Tachôs, in accordance with the pronunciation of different Egyptian dialects, has been discovered in hieroglyphic writing on the external wall of the temple of Khonsu at Karnak, by BOURIANT, *Notes de Voyage*, in *Recueil de Travaux*, vol. xi. pp. 153, 154.

Having inherited from Nectanebo a large fleet and a full treasury, Tachôs entrusted to the ambassador 500 talents of silver, and gave him fifty ships, with which he cruised along the coast of Asia Minor towards Leukê. His accomplices were awaiting him there, rejoicing at the success of his mission, but he himself had no confidence in the final issue of the struggle, and merely sought how he might enter once more into favour with the Persian court; he therefore secured his safety by betraying his associates. He handed over the subsidies and the Egyptian squadron to Orontes, the satrap of Daskylium, and then seizing the insurgent chiefs sent them in chains to Susa.[1] These acts of treachery changed the complexion of affairs; the league suddenly dissolved after the imprisonment of its leaders, and Artaxerxes re-established his authority over Asia Minor.

Egypt became once more the principal object of attack, and by the irony of fate Pharaoh had himself contributed to enrich the coffers and reinforce the fleet of his foes. In spite of this mischance, however, circumstances were so much in his favour that he ventured to consider whether it would not be more advantageous to forestall the foe by attacking him, rather than passively to await an onslaught behind his own lines. He had sought the friendship of Athens,[2] and though it had not been granted in explicit terms, the republic had, neverthe-

DATAMES III.[3]

less, permitted Chabrias to resume his former post at his side. Chabrias exhorted him to execute his project, and as he had not sufficient money to defray the expenses of a long campaign outside his own borders, the Athenian general instructed him how he might procure the necessary funds.[4] He suggested to him that, as the Egyptian priests were wealthy, the sums of money annually assigned to them for the sacrifices and maintenance of the temples would be better employed in the service of the state, and counselled him to reduce or even to suppress most of the sacerdotal colleges. The priests

[1] DIODORUS SICULUS, xv. 90, 92. The reason I have already had frequent occasion to allude to forces me to sacrifice the narration of the events which took place in Asia Minor and apply myself to giving forth the history of the Egyptian wars.

[2] The memory of this embassy has been preserved for us by a decree of the Athenian assembly, unfortunately much mutilated (*Corpus Inscriptionem Atticarum*, ii. No. 60), which has been assigned to various dates between 362 and 358 B.C. M. Paul Foucart has shown that the date of the decree must be referred to one of three archonships—the archonship of Callimedes, 360–59; that of Eucharistus, 359–8; or that of Cephisodotus, 358–7 (*Note sur deux inscriptions d'Athènes et de Priène*, in the *Revue de Philologie*, 1898, pp. 84–86). Without entering into a discussion of the other evidence on the subject, it seems to me probable that the embassy may be most conveniently assigned to the archonship of Callimedes, towards the end of 360 B.C., at the moment when Chabrias had just arrived in Egypt, and was certain to endeavour to secure the help of Athens for the king he served.

[3] Drawn by Faucher-Gudin, from a coin in the *Cabinet des Médailles*, a cast of which was kindly furnished me by M. Babelon; cf. BABELON, *Les Perses Achéménides*, pl. iv. No. 16.

[4] CORNELIUS NEPOS, *Chabrias*, § 2; cf. POLYÆNUS, *Stratagemata*, iii. 11, §§ 7, 12, where occurs the narration of several episodes relative to the preparations for this campaign. The conclusion from the discussion of the passages of Polyænus by Gutschmid (*Kleine Schriften*, vol. i. pp. 168, 169, 173–177) seems to be that they were borrowed from the work of Theopompus, in which the history of the wars between the king of Egypt and the great king was recounted at length.

secured their own safety by abandoning their personal property, and the king graciously deigned to accept their gifts, and then declared to them that in future, as long as the struggle against Persia continued, he should exact from them nine-tenths of their sacred revenues. This tax would have sufficed for all requirements if it had been possible to collect it in full, but there is no doubt that very soon the priests must have discovered means of avoiding part of the payment, for it was necessary to resort to other expedients. Chabrias advised that the poll and house taxes should be increased; that one obol should be exacted for each "ardeb" of corn sold, and a tithe levied on the produce of all ship-building yards, manufactories, and manual industries. Money now poured into the treasury, but a difficulty arose which demanded immediate solution. Egypt possessed very little specie, and the natives still employed barter in the ordinary transactions of life, while the foreign mercenaries refused to accept payment in kind or uncoined metal; they demanded good money as the price of their services. Orders were issued to the natives to hand over to the royal exchequer all the gold and silver in their possession, whether wrought or in ingots, the state guaranteeing gradual repayment through the nomarchs from the future product of the poll-tax, and the bullion so obtained was converted into specie for the payment of the auxiliary troops.[1] These measures, though winning some unpopularity for Tachôs, enabled him to raise eighty thousand native troops and ten thousand Greeks, to equip a fleet of two hundred vessels, and to engage the best generals of the period.[2] His eagerness to secure the latter, however, was injurious to his cause. Having already engaged Chabrias and obtained the good will of Athens, he desired also to gain the help of Agesilaus and the favourable opinion of the Lacedæmonians. Though now eighty years old, Agesilaus was still under the influence of cupidity and vanity; the promise of being placed in supreme command enticed him, and he set sail with one thousand hoplites. A disappointment awaited him at the moment of his disembarkation: Tachôs gave him command of the mercenary troops only, reserving for himself the general direction of operations, and placing the whole fleet under the orders of Chabrias. The aged hero, having vented his indignation by indulging a more than ordinary display of Spartan rudeness, allowed himself to be appeased by abundant presents, and assumed the post assigned to him. But soon after a more serious subject of disagreement arose between him and his ally; Agesilaus was disposed to think that Tachôs should remain quietly on the banks of the Nile, and leave to his generals the task of conducting the campaign.[3]

[1] Pseudo-Aristotle, *Economics*, ii. 25.

[2] Diodorus Siculus, xv. 92; for the devices resorted to by Chabrias in order to train the Egyptian rowers and to victual his fleet, cf. Polyænus, *Strategemata*, iii. 11, §§ 13, 14, and Pseudo-Aristotle, *Economics*, ii. 37.

[3] Diodorus Siculus, xv. 90–92; cf. [Xenophon], *Praise of Agesilaus*, ii. 28–30; Plutarch, *Agesilaus*, § 36; Theopompus, *Fragm.* 11, 23, in Müller-Didot, *Fragm. Hist. Græc.*, vol. i. pp. 279, 281.

The ease with which mercenary leaders passed from one camp to the other, according to the fancy of the moment, was not calculated to inspire the Egyptian Pharaoh with confidence: he refused to comply with the wishes of Agesilaus, and, entrusting the regency to one of his relatives, proceeded to invade Syria. He found the Persians unprepared: they shut themselves up in their strongholds, and the Pharaoh confided to his cousin Nectanebo, son of the regent, the task of dislodging them. The war dragged on for some time; discontent crept in among the native levies, and brought treachery in its train. The fiscal measures which had been adopted had exasperated the priests and the common people; complaints, at first only muttered in fear, found bold expression as soon as the expeditionary force had crossed the frontier. The regent secretly encouraged the malcontents, and wrote to his son warning him of what was going on, and advised him to seize the crown. Nectanebo could easily have won over the Egyptian troops to his cause, but their support would have proved useless as long as the Greeks did not pronounce in his favour, and Chabrias refused to break his oaths. Agesilaus, however, was not troubled by the same scruples. His vanity had been sorely wounded by the Pharaoh: after being denied the position which was, he fancied, his by right, his short

NECTANEBO I.[1]

stature, his ill-health, and native coarseness had exposed him to the unseemly mockery of the courtiers. Tachôs, considering his ability had been over-estimated, applied to him, it is said, the fable of the mountain bringing forth a mouse; to which he had replied, " When opportunity offers, I will prove to him that I am the lion." [2] When Tachôs requested him to bring the rebels to order, he answered ironically that he was there to help the Egyptians, not to attack them; and before giving his support to either of the rival claimants, he should consult the Ephors. The Ephors enjoined him to act in accordance with the welfare of his country, and he thereupon took the side of Nectanebo, despite the remonstrances of Chabrias. Tachôs, deserted by his veterans, fled to Sidon, and thence to Susa, where Artaxerxes received him hospitably and without reproaching him (359 B.C.); [3] but the news of his fall was not received on the banks of the Nile with as much rejoicing as he had anticipated. The people had no faith in any revolution in which the

---

[1] Drawn by Faucher-Gudin, from LEPSIUS, *Denkmäler*, iii. 301, No. 83.

[2] PLUTARCH, *Agesilaus*, § 36; cf. THEOPOMPUS, *Fragm.* 120, in MÜLLER-DIDOT, *Fragm. Hist. Græc.*, vol. i. pp. 297, 298, and LYCÆAS OF NAUCRATIS, in MÜLLER-DIDOT, *Fragm. Hist. Græc.*, vol. iv. p. 441.

[3] DIODORUS SICULUS, xv. 92; cf. [XENOPHON], *Praise of Agesilaus*, ii. 30. A somewhat foolish anecdote was current concerning the relations between Tachôs and Ochus (LYNCÆUS, or perhaps LYCÆAS OF NAUCRATIS, in MÜLLER-DIDOT, *Fragm. Hist. Græc.*, vol. ii. p. 466, note 1).

Greeks whom they detested took the chief part, and the feudal lords refused to acknowledge a sovereign whom they had not themselves chosen; they elected one of their number—the prince of Mendes—to oppose Nectanebo. The latter was obliged to abandon the possessions won by his predecessor, and return with his army to Egypt: he there encountered the forces of his enemy, which, though as yet undisciplined, were both numerous and courageous. Agesilaus counselled an immediate attack before these troops had time to become experienced in tactics, but he no longer stood well at court; the prince of Mendes had endeavoured to corrupt him, and, though he had shown unexpected loyalty, many, nevertheless, suspected his good faith. Nectanebo set up his headquarters at Tanis, where he was shortly blockaded by his adversary. It is well known how skilfully the Egyptians handled the pickaxe, and how rapidly they could construct walls of great strength; the circle of entrenchments was already near completion, and provisions were beginning to fail, when Agesilaus received permission to attempt a sortie. He broke through the besieging lines under cover of the night, and some days later won a decisive victory (359 B.C.). Nectanebo would now have gladly kept the Spartan general at his side, for he was expecting a Persian attack; but Agesilaus, who had had enough of Egypt and its intrigues, deserted his cause, and shortly afterwards died of exhaustion on the coast near Cyrene. The anticipated Persian invasion followed shortly after, but it was conducted without energy or decision. Artaxerxes had entrusted the conduct of the expedition to Tachôs, doubtless promising to reinstate him in his former power as satrap or vassal king of Egypt, but Tachôs died before he could even assume his post,[1] and the discords which rent the family of the Persian king prevented the generals who replaced him from taking any effective action. The aged Artaxerxes had had, it was reported, one hundred and fifteen sons by the different women in his harem, but only three of those by his queen Statira were now living—Darius, Ariaspes,[2] and Ochus. Darius, the eldest of the three, had been formally recognised as heir-apparent—perhaps at the time of the disastrous war against the Cadusians [3]—but the younger brother, Ochus, who secretly aspired to the throne, had managed to inspire him with anxiety with regard to the succession, and incited him to put the aged king out of the way. Contemporary historians, ill informed as to the intrigues in the palace, whose effects they noted without any attempt to explore their intricacies, invented several stories to account for the conduct of the young prince. Some

---

[1] Ælian (*Variæ Historiæ*, v. 1) narrates, probably following Dinon, that Tachôs died of dysentery due to over-indulgence at dinner.

[2] This is the form given by Plutarch (*Life of Artaxerxes*, § 30; Pompeius Trogus called this prince Ariarates (JUSTIN, x. 2), probably following Dinon.

[3] Cf., for this war, what is stated, *supra*, p. 758. Pompeius Trogus asserts that such co-regencies were contrary to Persian law (JUSTIN, x. 1); we have seen above (pp. 655, 716) that, on the contrary, they were obligatory when the sovereign was setting out on a campaign.

assigned as the reason of his conspiracy a romantic love-affair. They said that Cyrus the Younger had had an Ionian mistress named Aspasia, who, after the fatal battle of Cunaxa, had been taken into the harem of the conqueror, and had captivated him by her beauty. Darius conceived a violent passion for this damsel, and his father was at first inclined to give her up to him, but afterwards, repenting of his complaisance, consecrated her to the service of Mithra, a cult which imposed on her the obligation of perpetual chastity. Darius, exasperated by this treatment, began to contemplate measures of vengeance, but, being betrayed by his brother Ochus, was put to death with his whole family.[1] By the removal of this first obstacle the crafty prince found himself only one step nearer success, for his brother Ariaspes was acknowledged as heir-apparent: Ochus therefore persuaded him that their father, convinced of the complicity of Ariaspes in the plot imputed to Darius, intended to put him to an ignominious death, and so worked upon him that he committed suicide to escape the executioner. A bastard named Arsames, who might possibly have aspired to the crown, was assassinated by Ochus. This last blow was too much for Artaxerxes, and he died of grief after a reign of forty-six years (358 B.C.).[2]

Ochus, who immediately assumed the name of Artaxerxes, began his reign by the customary massacre: he put to death all the princes of the royal family,[3] and having thus rid himself of all the rival claimants to the supreme power, he hastened on preparations for the war with Egypt which had been interrupted by his father's death and his own accession. The necessity for restoring Persian dominion on the banks of the Nile was then more urgent than at any previous time. During the half-century which had elapsed since the recovery of her independence, Egypt had been a perpetual source of serious embarrassment to the great king. The contemporaries of Amyrtæus, whether Greeks or barbarians, had at first thought that his revolt was nothing more than a local rising, like many a previous one which had lasted but a short time and had been promptly suppressed. But when it was perceived that the native dynasties had taken a hold upon the country, and had carried on a successful contest with Persia, in spite of the immense disproportion in their respective resources;

[1] This is the version of the story given by Dinon and accepted by Pompeius Trogus (JUSTIN, x. 2). A chronological calculation easily demonstrates its unlikelihood. It follows from the evidence given by Justin himself (x. 2) that Artaxerxes died of grief soon after the execution of his son; but, on the other hand, that the battle of Cunaxa took place in 400 B.C.: Aspasia must then have been fifty or sixty years old when Darius fell in love with her.

[2] This is the length attributed by Plutarch to this reign (*Life of Artaxerxes*, § 30), and which is generally accepted. It was narrated in after-days that the king kept the fact of his father's death hidden for ten months (POLYÆNUS, *Stratagemata*, vii. 17), but it is impossible to tell how much truth there is in this statement, which was accepted by Dinon.

[3] According to the author followed by Pompeius Trogus (JUSTIN, x. 3), the princesses themselves were involved in this massacre. This is certainly an exaggeration, for we shall shortly see that Darius III., the last king of Persia, was accounted to be the grandson of Darius II.; the massacre can only have involved the direct heirs of Artaxerxes.

when not only the bravest soldiers of Asia, but the best generals of Greece, had miserably failed in their attacks on the frontier of the Delta, Phœnicia and Syria began to think whether what was possible in Africa might not also be possible in Asia. From that time forward, whenever a satrap or vassal prince meditated revolt, it was to Egypt that he turned as a natural ally, and from Egypt he sought the means to carry out his project; however needy the Pharaoh of that day might be, he was always able to procure for such a suitor sufficient money, munitions of war, ships, and men to enable him to make war against the empire. The attempt made by Ochus failed, as all previous attempts had done: the two adventurers who commanded the forces of Nectanebo, the Athenian Diophantes and Lamius of Sparta, inflicted a disastrous defeat on the imperial

EVAGORAS II.
OF SALAMIS.[2]

troops, and forced them to beat a hasty retreat.[1] This defeat was all the more serious in its consequences because of the magnitude of the efforts which had been made: the king himself was in command of the troops, and had been obliged to turn his back precipitately on the foe. The Syrian provinces, which had been in an unsettled condition ever since the invasion under Tachôs, flew to arms; nine petty kings of Cyprus, including Evagoras II., nephew of the famous prince of that name, refused to pay tribute, and Artabazus roused Asia Minor to rebellion. The Phœnicians still hesitated; but the insolence of their satrap, the rapacity of the generals who had been repulsed from Egypt, and the lack of discipline in the Persian army forced them to a decision. In a convention summoned at Tripoli, the representatives of the Phœnician cities conferred on Tennes, King of Sidon, the perilous honour of conducting the operations of the confederate army, and his first act was to destroy the royal villa in the Lebanon, and his next to burn the provisions which had been accumulated in various ports in view of the Egyptian war (351–350 B.C.). Ochus imagined at the outset that his generals would soon suppress these rebellions, and, in fact, Idrieus, tyrant of Caria, supported by eight thousand mercenaries under the Athenian Phocion, overcame the petty tyrants of Cyprus without much difficulty; but in Asia Minor, Artabazus, supported by Athens and Thebes, held at bay the generals sent to oppose him, and Tennes won a signal victory in Syria. He turned for support to Egypt, and Nectanebo, as might be expected, put Greek troops at his disposal to the number of four thousand,

---

[1] DIODORUS SICULUS, xvi. 48, who unfortunately has given us no detailed account of the course of events; perhaps he found none in Theopompus, who was the authority he followed for these Egyptian wars. To this expedition may be referred, with Wiedemann (*Gesch. Ægyptens*, pp. 294, 295), the stratagem of the Spartan Gastrôn, which, according to Polyænus (*Strat.*, ii. 16; cf. FRONTIN, *Stratagèmes*, ii. 3, § 13; GUTSCHMID, *Kleine Schriften*, vol. i. pp. 175, 176), secured the victory to the Egyptians.

[2] Drawn by Faucher-Gudin, from a coin in the *Cabinet des Médailles*, of which the cast was kindly furnished me by M. Babelon; cf. BABELON, *Les Perses Achéménides*, pl. xvii. No. 14.

commanded by one of his best generals, Mentor of Rhodes : Belesys, the satrap of Syria, and Mazæus, satrap of Cilicia, suffered a total defeat. Ochus, exasperated at their want of success, called out every available soldier, three hundred thousand Asiatics and ten thousand Greeks ; the Sidonians, on their side, dug a triple trench round their city, raised their ramparts and set fire to their ships, to demonstrate their intention of holding out to the end.[1] Unfortunately, their king, Tennes, was not a man of firm resolution. Hitherto he had lived a life of self-indulgence, surrounded by the women of his harem, whom he had purchased at great cost in Ionia and Greece, and had made it the chief object of his ambition to surpass in magnificence the most ostentatious princes of Cyprus, especially Nicocles of Salamis, son of Evagoras.[2] The approach of Ochus confused his scanty wits ; he endeavoured to wipe out his treachery towards his suzerain by the betrayal of his own subjects. He secretly despatched his confidential minister, a certain Thessalion, to the Persian camp, promising to betray Sidon to the Persian king, and to act as his guide into Egypt on condition of having his life preserved and his royal rank guaranteed to him. Ochus had already agreed to these conditions, when an impulse of vanity on his part nearly ruined the whole arrangement. Thessalion, not unreasonably doubting the king's good faith, had demanded that he should swear by his right hand to fulfil to the letter all the clauses of the treaty ; whereupon Ochus, whose dignity was offended by this insistence, gave orders for the execution of the ambassador. But as the latter was being dragged away, he cried out that the king could do as he liked, but that if he disdained the help of Tennes, he would fail in his attacks both upon Phœnicia and Egypt. These words produced a sudden reaction, and Thessalion obtained all that he demanded. When the Persians had arrived within a few days' march of Sidon, Tennes proclaimed that a general assembly of the Phœnician deputies was to be held, and under pretext of escorting the hundred leading men of his city to the appointed place of meeting, led them into the enemy's camp, where they were promptly despatched by the javelins of the soldiery. The Sidonians, deserted by their king, were determined to carry on the struggle, in the expectation of receiving succour from Egypt ; but the Persian darics had already found their way into the hands of the mercenary troops, and the general whom Nectanebo had lent them, declared that his men considered the position desperate, and that he should surrender the city at the first summons. The Sidonians thereupon found themselves reduced to the necessity of imploring the mercy of the conqueror, and five hundred of them set out to meet him as suppliants, carrying olive branches

---

[1] Diodorus Siculus, xvi. 44.

[2] Cf. the account of this king, under the name of Strato, given by the historian Theopompus, *Fragm.* 126, in Müller-Didot, *Fragmenta Historicorum Græcorum*, p. 299.

in their hands.　But Ochus was the most cruel monarch who had ever reigned in Persia —the only one, perhaps, who was really bloodthirsty by nature : he refused to listen to the entreaties of the suppliants, and, like the preceding hundred delegates, they were all slain.　The remaining citizens, perceiving that they could ńot hope for pardon, barricaded themselves in their houses, to which they set fire with their own hands ; forty thousand persons perished in the flames, and so great was the luxury in the appointments of the private houses, that large sums were paid for the right to dig for the gold and silver ornaments buried in the ruins.　The destruction of the city was almost as complete as in the days of Esarhaddon.[1]　When Sidon had thus met her fate, the Persians had no further reason for sparing its king, Tennes, and he was delivered to the executioner ; whereupon the other Phœnician kings, terrified by his fate, opened their gates without a struggle.[2]

Once more the treachery of a few traitors had disconcerted the plans of the Pharaoh, and delivered the outposts of Egypt into the hands of the enemy : but Ochus renewed his preparations with marvellous tenacity, and resolved to neglect nothing which might contribute to his final success.　His victories had confirmed the cities of the empire in their loyalty, and they vied with one another in endeavouring to win oblivion for their former hesitation by their present zeal : " What city, or what nation of Asia did not send embassies to the sovereign ? what wealth did they not lavish on him, whether the natural products of the soil, or the rare and precious productions of art ?　Did he not receive a quantity of tapestry and woven hangings, some of purple, some of diverse colours, others of pure white ? many gilded pavilions, completely furnished, and containing an abundant supply of linen and sumptuous beds ? chased silver, wrought gold, cups and bowls, enriched with precious stones, or valuable for the perfection and richness of their work ?　He also received untold supplies of barbarian and Grecian weapons, and still larger numbers of draught cattle and of sacrificial victims, bushels of preserved fruits, bales and sacks full of parchments or books, and all kinds of useful articles ?　So great was the quantity of salted meats which poured in from all sides, that from a distance the piles might readily be mistaken for rows of hillocks or high mounds." [3]　The land-force was divided into three corps, each under a barbarian and a Greek general.　It advanced along the sea coast, following the ancient route pursued by the armies of the Pharaohs, and as it skirted the marshes of Sirbonis, some detachments, having imprudently ventured over the treacherous soil, perished to a man.　When the main force arrived in safety

---

[1] For the destruction of Sidon by Esarhaddon, cf. *supra*, p. 352.
[2] The history of the Phœnician war is given at length by DIODORUS SICULUS, xvi. 41–45.
[3] THEOPOMPUS, *Fragm.* 125, in MÜLLER-DIDOT, *Fragm. Hist. Græc.*, vol. i. pp. 298, 299.

before Pelusium, it found Nectanebo awaiting it behind his ramparts and marshes. He had fewer men than his adversary, his force numbering only sixty thousand Egyptians, twenty thousand Libyans, and the same number of Greeks; but the remembrance of the successes won by himself and his predecessors with inferior numbers inspired him with confidence in the issue of the struggle. His fleet could not have ventured to meet in battle the combined squadrons of Cyprus and Phœnicia, but, on the other hand, he had a sufficient number of flat-bottomed boats to prevent any adversary from entering the mouths of the Nile. The weak points along his Mediterranean seaboard and eastern frontier were covered by strongholds, fortifications, and entrenched camps: in short, his plans were sufficiently well laid to ensure success in a defensive war, if the rash ardour of his Greek mercenaries had not defeated his plans. Five thousand of these troops were in occupation of Pelusium, under command of Philophrôn. Some companies of Thebans, who were serving under Lacrates in the Persian army, crossed a deep canal which separated them from the city, and provoked the garrison to risk an encounter in the open field. Philophrôn, instead of treating their challenge with indifference, accepted it, and engaged in a combat which lasted till nightfall. On the following day, Lacrates, having drawn off the waters of the canal and thrown a dyke across it, led his entire force up to the glacis of the fortifications, dug some trenches, and brought up a line of battering-rams. He would soon have effected a breach, but the Egyptians understood how to use the spade as well as the lance, and while the outer wall was crumbling, they improvised behind it a second wall, crowned with wooden turrets. Nectanebo, who had come up with thirty thousand native, five thousand Greek troops, and half the Libyan contingent, observed the vicissitudes of the siege from a short distance, and by his presence alone opposed the advance of the bulk of the Persian army. Weeks passed by, the time of the inundation was approaching, and it seemed as if this policy of delay would have its accustomed success, when an unforeseen incident decided in a moment the fate of Egypt. Among the officers of Ochus was a certain Nicostratus of Argos, who on account of his prodigious strength was often compared to Heracles, and who out of vanity dressed himself up in the traditional costume of that hero, the lion's skin and the club. Having imbibed, doubtless, the ideas formerly propounded by Iphicrates,[1] Nicostratus forced some peasants, whose wives and children he had seized as hostages, to act as his guides, and made his way up one of the canals which traverse the marshes of Menzaleh : there he disembarked his men in the rear of Nectanebo, and took up a very strong position on the border of the cultivated land. This enterprise, undertaken with a very insufficient force, was an extremely rash one ;

[1] Cf. what is stated on this subject, *supra*, p. 757.

if the Egyptian generals had contented themselves with harassing Nicostratus without venturing on engaging him in a pitched battle, they would speedily have forced him to re-embark or to lay down his arms. Unfortunately, however, five thousand mercenaries, who formed the garrison of one of the neighbouring towns, hastened to attack him under the command of Clinias of Cos, and suffered a severe defeat. As a result, the gates of the town were thrown open to the enemy, and if the Persians, encouraged by the success of this forlorn hope, had followed it up boldly, Nectanebo would have run the risk of being cut off from his troops which were around Pelusium, and of being subsequently crushed. He thought it wiser to retreat towards the apex of the Delta, but this very act of prudence exposed him to one of those accidental misfortunes which are wont to occur in armies formed of very diverse elements. While he was concentrating his reserves at Memphis, the troops of the first line thought that, by leaving them exposed to the assaults of the great king, he was deliberately sacrificing them. Pelusium capitulated to Lacrates; Mentor of Rhodes pushed forward and seized Bubastis, and the other cities in the eastern portion of the Delta, fearing to bring upon themselves the fate of Sidon, opened their gates to the Persians after a mere show of resistance. The forces which had collected at Memphis thereupon disbanded, and Nectanebo, ruined by these successive disasters, collected his treasures and fled to Ethiopia. The successful issue of the rash enterprise of Nicostratus had overthrown the empire of the Pharaohs, and re-established the Persian empire in its integrity (342 B.C.).[1]

[1] The complete history of this war is related by Diodorus Siculus (xvi. 46–51), who generally follows the narrative of Theopompus. The chronology is still sufficiently uncertain to leave some doubt as to the exact date of each event; I have followed that arrangement which seems to accord best with the general history of the period. The following table may be drawn up of the last Egyptian dynasties as far as they can be restored at present:—

XXVII. (Persian) Dynasty.

I. Masutrî Kanbuti	. . . .	Καμβύσης.
II. . . . [Gaumâta]	. . . .	[Σμέρδις].
III. Satôuturî Ntaraiuasha	. . . .	Δαρεῖος α'.
IV. Sanentonen-sotpuniphtah Khabbîsha	. . . .	
V. . . . . Khshayarsha	. . . .	Ξέρξης α'.
VI. . . . . Artakhshayarsha	. . . .	'Αρταξέρξης α'.
VII. . . . . Khshayarsha	. . . .	Ξέρξης β'.
VIII. . .	. . . .	Σεκυδίανος Σογδιανος.
IX. Miamunrî Ntaraiuasha	. . . .	Δαρεῖος β'.

XXVIII. (Saite) Dynasty.

I. . . .	. . . .	'Αμυρταῖος.

XXIX. (Mendesian) Dynasty.

I. Bînri-Mînutîru Nefôrîti I.	. . . .	Νεφερίτης α'.
II. Khnummarî-sotpunikhnumu Hakori	. . . .	Ἄκωρις.
III. Usiriphtahrî Psamutî	. . . .	Ψάμμουθις.
IV.	. . . .	Μύθης.
V. . . . . . . Nefôrîti II.	. . . .	Νεφερίτης β'.

XXX. (Sebennytic) Dynasty.

I. Snotmibrî-sotpunianhuri Nakhtharahbît-Mîanhuri-Siisît	Νεκτανέβης α'.
II. Irimaîtnirî Zadhu-Sotpunianhuri	. . . .	Τέως, Ταχώς.
III. Khopirkerî Nakhtunabuf	. . . .	Νεκτανέβης β', Νακτονάβοι

Egypt had prospered under the strong rule of its last native Pharaohs. Every one of them, from Amyrtæus down to Nectanebo, had done his best to efface all traces of the Persian invasions and restore to the country the appearance which it had presented before the days of its servitude ; even kings like Psamutis and Tachôs, whose reign had been of the briefest, had, like those who ruled for longer periods, constructed or beautified the monuments of the country.[1]

SMALL TEMPLE OF NECTANEBO, AT THE SOUTHERN EXTREMITY OF PHILÆ.[2]

The Thebaid was in this respect a special field of their labours. The island of Philæ, exposed to the ceaseless attacks of the Ethiopians, had been reduced to little more than a pile of ruins.[3] Nectanebo II. erected a magnificent gate there, afterwards incorporated into the first pylon of the temple built by the Ptolemies, and one at least of the buildings that still remain, the charming rectangular kiosk, the pillars of which, with their Hathor capitals, rise above the southern extremity of the island and mark the spot at which the Ethiopian

---

[1] *E.g.* the small temples built by Psamutis at Karnak (CHAMPOLLION, *Monuments de l'Égypte et de la Nubie*, pl. ccciii. 1, and ccix. 3; LEPSIUS, *Denkm.*, iii. 259, *a*, *b*; MASPERO, *Découverte d'un petit temple*, in the *Recueil de Travaux*, vol. vi. p. 20; WIEDEMANN, *On Two Temples of the 29th Dynasty at Karnak*, in the *Proceedings* of the Bibl. Arch. Soc., vol. vii., 1884–1885, pp. 108–112); also the works executed by Tachos in the quarries of Turah (BRUGSCH, *Histoire d'Égypte*, p. 282), and in the temple of Khonsu at Thebes (BOURIANT, *Notes de Voyage*, in the *Recueil de Travaux*, vol. xi. pp. 153, 154).

[2] Drawn by Boudier, from a photograph by Beato.

[3] As to the buildings of Amasis at Philæ, cf. p. 641, *supra*.

3 D

pilgrims first set foot on the sacred territory of the bountiful Isis.[1] Nectanebo I. restored the sanctuaries of Nekhabît at El-Kab,[2] and of Horus at Edfu, in which latter place he has left an admirable naos which delights the

NAOS OF NECTANEBO IN THE TEMPLE AT EDFU.[6]

modern traveller by its severe proportions and simplicity of ornament,[3] while Nectanebo II. repaired the ancient temple of Mînu at Coptos; [4] in short, without giving a detailed list of what was accomplished by each of these later Pharaohs, it may be said that there are few important sites in the valley of the Nile where some striking evidence of their activity may not still be discovered even after the lapse of so many centuries. It will be sufficient to mention Thebes,[5]

[1] CHAMPOLLION, *Monuments de l'Égypte et de la Nubie*, pls. lxxx., lxxxv., and pp. 201–206; ROSELLINI, *Monumenti Storici*, pl. 18; LEPSIUS, *Denkm.*, iii. 285, 286.

[2] Cf. the cartouches discovered in 1882 among the ruins of the great temple at El-Kab.

[3] DÜMICHEN, *Bauurkunde der Tempelanlagen von Edfu*, in the *Zeitschrift*, 1871, p. 95, et seq.

[4] MASPERO, *Notes*, § lxii., in the *Zeitschrift*, 1885, pp. 4, 5; PETRIE, *Koptos*, p. 17, and pl. xxvi. 2.

[5] *E.g.* the buildings of Nephorites I. at Karnak (CHAMPOLLION, *Monuments de l'Égypte et de la Nubie*, vol. ii. p. 290; LEPSIUS, *Denkm.*, iii. 284 *b, c*), of Hakoris at Karnak (CHAMPOLLION, *Monuments de l'Égypte et de la Nubie*, vol. ii. p. 264; ROSELLINI, *Monumenti Storici*, vol. ii. p. 213, and vol. iv. p. 218; LEPSIUS, *Denkm.*, iii. 284 *f, g*), and at Medinet-Habu (ROSELLINI, *Monumenti Storici*, vol. ii. pp. 211–213, and vol. iv. p. 218; LEPSIUS, *Denkm.*, iii. 284 *h, i*), of Psamutis at Karnak (CHAMPOLLION, *Monuments de l'Égypte et de la Nubie*, pl. ccciii. 1, cccix. 3; ROSELLINI, *Monumenti Storici*, pl. cliv. 4, vol. ii. pp. 214, 215, and vol. iv. pp. 219, 220; LEPSIUS, *Denkm.*, iii. 259 *a, b*; MASPERO, *Découverte d'un petit temple à Karnak*, in the *Recueil de Travaux*, vol. ii. p. 20), of Nectanebo I. at Karnak (CHAMPOLLION, *Monuments de l'Égypte et de la Nubie*, pl. cccviii. 2, and vol. ii. pp. 232, 238, 264, 273, et seq.; ROSELLINI, *Monumenti Storici*, vol. ii. p. 222; LEPSIUS, *Denkm.*, iii. 287 *b-h*), of Tachôs at Karnak (BOURIANT, *Notes de Voyage*, in the *Recueil de Travaux*, vol. xi. pp. 153, 154), of Nectanebo II. at Karnak (CHAMPOLLION, *Monuments de l'Égypte et de la Nubie*, pl. cccix. 2, and vol. ii. pp. 240, 256, 262, et seq.; LEPSIUS, *Denkm.*, iii. 284 *k*) and at Medinet-Habu (CHAMPOLLION, *Monuments de l'Égypte et de la Nubie*, pl. cxcvi.; ROSELLINI, *Monumenti Storici*, pl. cliv. 2, and vol. iv. pp. 222, 223; LEPSIUS, *Denkm.*, v. 1 *c*).

[6] Drawn by Boudier, from a photograph by Beato.

Memphis,[1] Sebennytos,[2] Bubastis,[3] Pahabît,[4] Patumu,[5] and Tanis.[6] Nor did the Theban oases, including that of Amon himself, escape their zeal, for the few Europeans who have visited them in modern times have observed their cartouches there. Moreover, in spite of the brief space of time within which they were carried out, the majority of these works betray no signs of haste or slipshod execution ; the craftsmen employed on them seem to have preserved in their full integrity all the artistic traditions of earlier times, and were capable of producing masterpieces which will bear comparison with those of the golden age. The

GREAT GATE OF NECTANEBO AT KARNAK.[7]

Eastern gate, erected at Karnak in the time of Nectanebo II., is in no way inferior either in purity of proportion or in the beauty of its carvings to what remains of the gates of Amenôthes III.[8] The sarcophagus of Nectanebo I. is

---

[1] Cf. the graffiti of the time of Hakoris and Tachôs in the quarries at Turah relating to the buildings carried out at Memphis (CHAMPOLLION, *Monuments de l'Égypte et de la Nubie*, vol. ii. p. 489 ; BRUGSCH, *Recueil de Monuments*, vol. i. pl. x. 10, 14–16, 20, 22, and *Histoire d'Égypte*, p. 282).

[2] NAVILLE, *The Mound of the Jews*, pp. 25, 26, and pl. vi. A ; cf. LEEMANS, *Papyri Græci*, vol. i. p. 122, where reference is made to the works carried out by Nectanebo II. in the temple at Sebennytos.

[3] NAVILLE, *Bubastis*, pp. 56–58, and pls. xliii.-xlviii., where the name of Hakoris is mentioned once (xliii. B) ; the greater part of the buildings dates from the time of Nectanebo I.

[4] NAVILLE, *The Mound of the Jews*, p. 26.

[5] NAVILLE, *Lettre à M. Lepsius*, in the *Zeitschrift*, 1883, p. 43 ; *The Store-City of Pithom*, p. 12, where we find the king responsible for the building was Nectanebo I. ; cf. PETRIE, *Tanis*, vol. i. p. 28, as to the statues of Nectanebo I. discovered at Tell el-Maskhutah.

[6] FLINDERS PETRIE, *Tanis*, vol. i. p. 21.

[7] Drawn by Boudier, from a photograph by Beato.

[8] CHAMPOLLION, *Monuments de l'Égypte et de la Nubie*, pl. cccix. 2, and vol. ii. p. 262, et seq. The gate and part of the wall adjoining it date from the time of Nectanebo II.

carved and decorated with a perfection of skill which has never been surpassed in any age, and elsewhere, on all the monuments which bear the name of this monarch, the hieroglyphics have been designed and carved with as much care as though each one of them had been a precious cameo.[1] The basalt torso of Nectanebo II., which attracts so much admiration in the Bibliothèque Nationale in Paris for accuracy of proportion and delicacy of modelling, deserves to rank with the finest statues of the ancient empire.[2] The men's heads are veritable portraits, in which such details as a peculiar conformation of the skull, promi-

FRAGMENT OF A NAOS OF THE TIME OF NECTANEBO II. IN THE BOLOGNA MUSEUM.[4]

nent cheek-bones, deep-set eyes, sunken cheeks, or the modelling of the chin, have all been observed and reproduced with a fidelity and keenness of observation which we fail to find in such works of the earlier artists as have come down to us. These later sculptors display the same regard for truth in their treatment of animals and their dog-headed divinities;[3] their dogs, lions, and sphinxes will safely bear comparison with the most lifelike presentments of these creatures to be found among the remains of the Memphite or Theban eras. Egypt was thus in the full tide of material prosperity when it again fell under the Persian yoke, and might have become a source of inexhaustible wealth to Ochus had he known how to secure acceptance of his rule, as Darius, son of Hystaspes, had done in the days of Amasis.[5] The violence of his temperament, however, impelled him to a course of pitiless oppression, and his favourite minister, the eunuch Bagoas, seems to have done his best to stimulate his master's natural cruelty. In the days when they felt themselves securely protected from his anger by their Libyan and Greek troops, the fellahîn had freely indulged in lampoons at the expense of their Persian suzerain ; they had compared him to Typhon on account of his barbarity,

[1] The sarcophagus was for a long time preserved near the mosque of Ibn-Tulun, and was credited with peculiar virtues by the superstitious inhabitants of Cairo ; cf. JOMARD, *Description des Antiquités de la Ville et de la Province du Kaire*, in the *Description de l'Égypte*, vol. ix. pp. 302–307, and *Antiquités*, vol. v. pl. xl.

[2] It has been reproduced in the *Description de l'Égypte, Antiquités*, vol. v. pl. lxix. 7, 8, and is now in the Bibliothèque Nationale in Paris.

[3] Cf. the cynocephalus of the Vatican, which is reproduced as an initial at the beginning of Chap. vii., on p. 699 of the present work.

[4] Drawn by Boudier, from a photograph by Flinders Petrie.

[5] As to the policy followed by Darius, son of Hystaspes, in dealing with the Egyptians, cf. pp. 684–686, *supra*.

and had nicknamed him "the Ass," this animal being in their eyes a type of everything that is vile. On his arrival at Memphis, Ochus gave orders that an ass should be installed in the temple of Phtah, and have divine honours paid to it; he next had the bull Apis slaughtered and served up at a set banquet which he gave to his friends on taking possession of the White Wall.[1] The sacred goat of Mendes suffered the same fate as the Apis,[2] and doubtless none of the other sacred animals were spared. Bagoas looted the temples in the most systematic way, despatched the sacred books to Persia, razed the walls of the cities to the ground, and put every avowed partisan of the native dynasty to the sword. After these punitive measures had been carried out, Ochus disbanded his

mercenaries and returned to Babylon, leaving Pherendates in charge of the reconquered province.[3] The downfall of Egypt struck terror into the rebellious satraps who were in arms elsewhere. Artabazus, who had kept Asia Minor in a ferment ever since the time of Artaxerxes

ONE OF THE LIONS IN THE VATICAN.[4]

II., gave up the struggle of his own accord and took refuge in Macedonia. The petty kings of the cities on the shores of the Hellespont and the Ægæan submitted themselves in order to regain favour, or if, like Hermias of Atarnæa, the friend of Aristotle, they still resisted, they were taken prisoners and condemned to death. The success of Ochus was a reality, but there was still much to be done before things were restored to the footing they had occupied before the crisis. We know enough of the course of events in the western provinces to realise the pitch of weakness to which the imbecility of Darius II. and his son Artaxerxes II. had reduced the empire of Darius and Xerxes, but it is quite certain that the disastrous effects of their misgovernment were not confined to the shores of the Mediterranean, but were felt no less acutely in the eastern and central regions of the empire. There, as on the Greek frontiers, the system built up at the cost of so much ingenuity by Darius was gradually being broken

[1] DINON, *Fragm.* 30, in MÜLLER-DIDOT, *Fragm. Hist. Græc.*, vol. ii. p. 95, from whom the details preserved in ÆLIAN, *Variæ Historiæ*, vi. 8, and x. 28, and in SUIDAS, *s.v.* ἄπιδες, κακοῖς ἐπισωρεύων κακά et Ὦχος have probably been borrowed.

[2] SUIDAS, *s.v.* ἄσατο, and ÆLIAN, *Fragm.* 256, which latter passage is probably taken from the same source as the statements in regard to the Apis.

[3] DIODORUS SICULUS, xvi. 51. It seems that a part of the atrocities committed by Ochus and Bagoas soon came to be referred to the time of the "Impure" (cf. *Struggle of the Nations*, p. 449, note 2) and to that of Cambyses (cf. p. 668, note 3, *supra*).

[4] Drawn by Faucher-Gudin, from a photograph by Flinders Petrie.

down with each year that passed, and the central government could no longer make its power felt at the extremities of the empire save at irregular intervals, when its mandates were not intercepted or nullified in transmission. The functions of the " Eyes " and " Ears " [1] of the king had degenerated into a mere meaningless formality, and were, more often than not, dispensed with altogether. The line of demarcation between the military and civil power had been obliterated : not only had the originally independent offices of satrap, general, and secretary ceased to exist in each separate province, but, in many instances, the satrap, after usurping the functions of his two colleagues, contrived to extend his jurisdiction till it included several provinces, thus establishing himself as a kind of viceroy. Absorbed in disputes among themselves, or in conspiracies against the Achæmenian dynasty, these officials had no time to look after the well-being of the districts under their control, and the various tribes and cities took advantage of this to break the ties of vassalage. To take Asia Minor alone, some of the petty kings of Bithynia, Paphlagonia, and certain districts of Cappadocia or the mountainous parts of Phrygia still paid their tribute intermittently, and only when compelled to do so; others, however, such as the Pisidians, Lycaonians, a part of the Lycians, and some races of Mount Taurus, no longer dreamed of doing so.[2] The three satrapies on the shores of the Caspian,[3] which a hundred years before had wedged themselves in between that sea and the Euxine, were now dissolved, all trace of them being lost in a confused medley of kingdoms and small states, some of which were ready enough to acknowledge the supremacy of Persia, while others, such as the Gordiæans, Taochi, Chalybes, Colchi, Mosynœki, and Tibarenians,[4] obeyed no rule but their own. All along the Caspian, the Cadusians and Amardians, on either side of the chain of mountains bordering the Iranian plateau, defied all the efforts made to subdue them.[5] India and the Sakæ had developed from the condition of subjects into that of friendly allies, and the savage hordes of Gedrosia and the Paropamisus refused to recognise any authority at all.[6] The whole empire needed to be reconquered and reorganised bit by bit

[1] As to these functionaries, cf. p. 690, *supra*.

[2] See the data supplied by XENOPHON, *Hellenica*, I. iv. § 3, III. ii. § 2, and *Anabasis*, I. i. § 11, ii. § 1, vi. § 7, ix. § 14, V. vi. § 8, etc.

[3] HERODOTUS, III. xciv.

[4] Cf. the descriptions of some of these countries given by XENOPHON, *Anabasis*, IV. i. § 8, VII. viii. § 25.

[5] They appear in the history of every epoch as the irreconcilable foes of the great king, enemies against whom even the most peacefully disposed sovereigns were compelled to take the field in person (CTESIAS, *Fragm.* 2, 25, in MÜLLER-DIDOT, *Ctesiæ Cnidii Fragmenta*, pp. 14, 42; DIODORUS SICULUS xv. 8, xvii. 6; CORNELIUS NEPOS, *Datames*, § 1; JUSTIN, x. 3; PLUTARCH, *Artaxerxes*, 24).

[6] The Sakæ fought at Arbela, but only as allies of the Persians (ARRIAN, *Anabasis*, III. viii.). The Indians who are mentioned with them came from the neighbourhood of Cabul; most of the races who had formerly figured in Darius' satrapy of India had become independent by the time Alexander penetrated into the basin of the Indus.

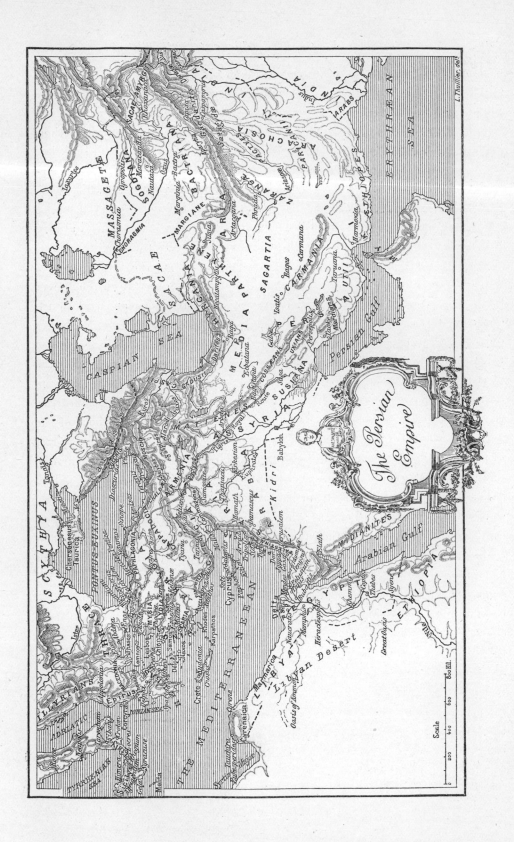

The Persian Empire

Scale

0   200   400   600   800 Kil.

L. Thuillier, del.

if it was to exercise that influence in the world to which its immense size entitled it, and the question arose whether the elements of which it consisted would lend themselves to any permanent reorganisation or readjustment.

The races of the ancient Eastern world, or, at any rate, that portion of them which helped to make its history, either existed no longer or had sunk into their dotage. They had worn each other out in the centuries of their prime, Chaldæans and Assyrians fighting against Cossæans or Elamites, Egyptians against Ethiopians and against Hittites, Urartians, Aramæans, the peoples of Lebanon and of Damascus, the Phœnicians, Canaanites and Jews, until at last, with impoverished blood and flagging energies, they were thrown into conflict with younger and more vigorous nations. The Medes had swept away all that still remained of Assyria and Urartu ; the Persians had overthrown the Medes, the Lydians, and the Chaldæans, till Egypt alone remained and was struck down by them in her turn. What had become of these conquered nations during the period of nearly two hundred years that the Achæmenians had ruled over them ? First, as regards Elam, one of the oldest and formerly the most powerful of them all. She had been rent into two halves, each of them destined to have a different fate. In the mountains, the Uxians, Mardians, Elymæans, and Cossæans—tribes who had formerly been the backbone of the nation—had relapsed into a semi-barbarous condition, or rather, while the rest of the world had progressed in civilisation and refinement, they had remained in a state of stagnation, adhering obstinately to the customs of their palmy days : just as they had harried the Chaldæans or Assyrians in the olden times, so now they harried the Persians ; then, taking refuge in their rocky fastnesses, they lived on the proceeds of their forays, successfully resisting all attempts made to dislodge them.[1] The people of the plains, on the other hand, kept in check from the outset by the presence of the court at Susa, not only promptly re-signed themselves to their fate, but even took pleasure in it, and came to look upon themselves as in some sort the masters of Asia. Was it not to their country, to the very spot occupied by the palace of their king, that, for nearly two hundred years, satraps, vassal kings, the legates of foreign races, ambassadors of Greek republics—in a word, all the great ones of this world—came every year to render homage, and had not the treasures which these visitors brought with them been expended, in part at any rate, on their country ? The memory of their former prosperity paled before the splendours of their new destiny, and the glory of their ancestors suffered eclipse. The names of the national kings, the story of their Chaldæan and Syrian conquests, the trophies of their vic-tories over the great generals of Nineveh, the horrors of their latest discords

[1] ARRIAN, *Anabasis*, III. xvii.

and of the final catastrophe were all forgotten; even the documents which
might have helped to recall them lay buried in the heart of the mound which
served as a foundation for the palace of the Achæmenides.[1] Beyond the vague
consciousness of a splendid past, the memory of the common people was a
blank, and when questioned by strangers they could tell them nothing save
legends of the gods or the exploits of mythical heroes; and from them the
Greeks borrowed their Memnon, that son of Tithonus and Eôs who rushed
to the aid of Priam with his band of Ethiopians, and whose prowess
had failed to retard by a single day the downfall of Troy. Further northwards, the Urartians and peoples of ancient Naîri, less favoured by fortune, lost ground with each successive generation, yielding to the steady
pressure of the Arme-
nians. In the time of
Herodotus they were
still in possession of
the upper basins of the
Euphrates and Araxus,
and, in conjunction

COINS OF THE SATRAPS WITH ARAMÆAN INSCRIPTIONS.[2]

with the Matieni and Saspires, formed a satrapy—the eighteenth—the boundaries of which coincided pretty closely with those of the kingdom ruled over
by the last kings of Van in the days of Assur-bani-pal; the Armenians, on
their side, constituted the thirteenth satrapy, between Mount Taurus and the
Lower Arsanias.[3] The whole face of their country had undergone a profound
change since that time: the Urartians, driven northwards, became intermingled
with the tribes on the slopes of the Caucasus,[4] while the Armenians, carried
along towards the east, as though by some resistless current, were now scaling the
mountainous bulwark of Ararat, and slowly but surely encroaching on the lower
plains of the Araxes. These political changes had been almost completed by
the time of Ochus, and Urartu had disappeared from the scene, but an Armenia
now flourished in the very region where Urartu had once ruled, and its princes,
who were related to the family of the Achæmenides, wielded an authority little
short of regal under the modest name of satraps.[5] Thanks to their influence,

---

[1] As to the trophies brought to Susa by the Elamite conquerors and discovered by M. de Morgan,
cf. pp. 227, 228, *supra.*

[2] Drawn by Faucher-Gudin, from coins in the *Cabinet des Médailles,* casts of which were very
kindly supplied to me by M. Babelon.

[3] HERODOTUS, III. xciii., xciv.; as to the kingdom of Urartu in the time of Assur-bani-pal,
cf. p. 394, *supra.*

[4] As to the ultimate fate of the Urartians, or, as they were afterwards called, the Alarodians, cf.
H. RAWLINSON, *On the Alarodians of Herodotus,* in G. RAWLINSON, *Herodotus,* vol. iv. pp. 203–206, and
FR. LENORMANT, *Les Origines de l'Histoire,* vol. ii. p. 299.

[5] As to these forward movements of the Armenians, cf. FR. LENORMANT, *Les Origines de l'Histoire,*
vol. ii. p. 370, et seq.

the religions and customs of Iran were introduced into the eastern borders of Asia Minor. They made their way into the valleys of the Iris and the Halys, into Cappadocia and the country round Mount Taurus, and thither they brought with them the official script of the empire, the Persian and Aramæan cuneiform which was employed in public documents, in inscriptions, and on coins. The centre of the peninsula remained very much the same as it had been in the period of the Phrygian supremacy, but further westward Hellenic influences gradually made themselves felt. The arts of Greece, its manners, religious ideals, and modes

A LYCIAN TOMB.[1]

STATUE OF MAUSOLUS.[3]

of thought, were slowly displacing civilisations of the Asianic type, and even in places like Lycia, where the language successfully withstood the Greek invasion, the life of the nations, and especially of their rulers, became so deeply impregnated with Hellenism as to differ but little from that in the cities on the Ionic, Æolian, or Doric seaboard. The Lycians still adhered to the ancient forms which characterised their funerary architecture, but it was to Greek sculptors, or pupils from the Grecian schools, that they entrusted the decoration of the sides of their sarcophagi and of their tombs.[2] Their kings minted coins many of which are reckoned among the masterpieces of antique engraving; and if we pass from Lycia to the petty states of Caria, we come upon one of the greatest triumphs of Greek art—that huge mausoleum in which the inconsolable

[1] Drawn by Faucher-Gudin, from a woodcut in BENNDORFF, *Reisen in Lykien und Karien*, vol. i. p. 33.

[2] Here again I have been obliged to omit all that I had written in regard to the infiltration of Hellenic ideas into Asia Minor. For details concerning Lycian art in particular, cf. PERROT and CHIPIEZ, *L'Histoire de l'Art dans l'Antiquité*, vol. v. pp. 361–399.

[3] Drawn by Faucher-Gudin, from a photograph of the original in the British Museum.

Artemisia enclosed the ashes and erected the statue of her husband. The Asia Minor of Egyptian times, with its old-world dynasties, its old-world names, and old-world races, had come to be nothing more than an historic memory; even that martial world, in which the Assyrian conquerors fought so many battles from the Euphrates to the Black Sea, was now no more, and its

neighbours and enemies of former days had, for the most part, disappeared from the land of the living. The Lotanu were gone, the Khâti were gone, and gone, too, were Carchemish, Arpad, and Qodshu, much of their domain having been swallowed up again by the desert for want of hands to water and till it; even Assyria itself seemed but a shadow half shrouded in the mists of oblivion. Sangara, Nisibis, Resaina, and Edessa still showed some signs of vigour, but on quitting the slopes of the Masios and proceeding southwards, piles of ruins alone marked the sites of those wealthy cities through which the Ninevite monarchs had passed in their journeyings towards Syria. Here wide tracts of arid and treeless country were now to be seen covered with aromatic herbage, where the Scenite Arabs were wont to pursue the lion, wild ass, ostrich, bustard, antelope, and gazelle; a few abandoned forts, such as Korsortê, Anatho, and Is (Hit) marked the halting-places of armies on the banks of the Euphrates.[3] In the region of the Tigris, the descendants of Assyrian captives who, like the Jews, had

LYCIAN SARCOPHAGUS DECORATED WITH GREEK CARVINGS.[2]

been set free by Cyrus, had rebuilt Assur, and had there grown wealthy by

[1] Drawn by Faucher-Gudin, from a silver stater in the *Cabinet des Médailles*, for a cast of which I am indebted to M. Babelon. The king in question was named Deneveles, and is only known by the coins bearing his superscription. He flourished about 395 B.C.

[2] Drawn by Faucher-Gudin, from a photogravure published by HAMDY-BEY and TH. REINACH, in *La Nécropole de Sidon*, pl. xiv. 1.

[3] XENOPHON, *Anabasis*, I. v. §§ 1–3.

husbandry and commerce,[1] but in the district of the Zab solitude reigned supreme.[2] Calah and Nineveh were alike deserted, and though their ruins still littered the sites where they had stood, their names were unknown in the neighbouring villages. Xenophon, relying on his guides, calls the former place Larissa, the second Mespila.[3] Already there were historians who took the ziggurât at Nineveh to be the burial-place of Sardanapalus. They declared that Cyrus had pulled it down in order to strengthen his camp during the siege of the town, and that formerly it had borne an epitaph afterwards put into verse by the poet Chœrilus of Iassus : " I reigned, and so long as I beheld the light of the sun, I ate, I drank, I loved, well knowing how brief is the life of man, and to how many vicissitudes it is liable." [4] Many writers, remembering the Assyrian monument at Anchialê in Cilicia, were inclined to place the king's tomb there. It was surmounted by the statue of a man—according to one account, with his hands crossed upon his breast, according to another, in the act of snapping his fingers —and bore the following inscription in Chaldaic letters : " I, Sardanapalus, son of Anakyndaraxes, founded Anchialê and Tarsus in one day, but now am dead." [5] Thus ten centuries of conquests and massacre had passed away like a vapour, leaving nothing but a meagre residue of old men's tales and moral axioms.

In one respect only does the civilisation of the Euphrates seem to have fairly held its own. Chaldæa, though it had lost its independence, had lost but little of its wealth ; its former rebellions had done it no great injury, and its ancient cities were still left standing, though shorn of their early splendour. Uru, it is true, numbered but few citizens round its tottering sanctuaries, but Uruk maintained a school of theologians and astronomers no less famous throughout the East than those of Borsippa. The swamps, however, which surrounded it possessed few attractions, and Greek travellers rarely ventured thither. They generally stopped at Babylon, or if they ventured off the beaten

[1] This seems to be indicated by a mutilated passage in the *Cylinder of Cyrus*, ll. 30–32 (cf. HAGEN, *Keilschrifturkunden zur Geschichte des Königs Cyrus*, in the *Beiträge zur Assyriologie*, vol. ii. pp. 212, 213), where Assur is mentioned in the list of towns and countries whose inhabitants were sent back to their homes by Cyrus after the capture of Babylon. Xenophon calls it Kænæ, this being, possibly, a translation of the name given to it by its inhabitants. Nothing could be more natural than for exiles to call the villages founded by them on their return " new." The town seems to have been a large and wealthy one (*Anabasis*, II. iv. § 28).

[2] Xenophon (*Anabasis*, II. iv. §§ 27, 28) calls this country Media, a desert region which the Ten Thousand took six days to cross.

[3] XENOPHON, *Anabasis*, III. iv. §§ 7-9. The name Larissa is, possibly, a corruption of some name similar to that of the city of Larsam in Chaldæa ; Mespila may be a generic term : cf. Mappela = *the ruins* (KIEPERT, *Handbuch der Alten Geographie*, p. 152, n. 2, 3). [Mespila is Muspula, " the low ground " at the foot of Kouyunjik ; Larissa probably Al Resen or Res-eni, between Kouyunjik and Nebi Yunus.—ED.]

[4] AMYNTAS, *Fragm.* 2, in MÜLLER-DIDOT, *Scriptores rerum Alexandri Magni*, p. 136. Cf. a variant of the same inscription, quoted as existing at Nineveh by CALLISTHENES, *Fragm.* 32, in MÜLLER-DIDOT, *op cit.*, pp. 21, 22, on the authority of Hellenicus of Lesbos or Dionysius of Miletus.

[5] ARRIAN, *Anabasis*, II. v. ; cf. the remarks of ED. MEYER (*Forschungen zur Alten Geschichte*, vol. i. pp. 203–209) in regard to these two gestures and their Assyrian prototypes.

track, it was only to visit the monuments of Nebuchadrezzar or the tombs of the early kings in its immediate neighbourhood.[1] Babylon was, indeed, one of the capitals of the empire—nay, for more than half a century, during the closing years of Artaxerxes I., in the reign of Darius II., and in the early days of Artaxerxes II., it had been the real capital; even under Ochus, the court spent the winter months there, and resorted thither in quest of those resources of industry and commerce which Susa lacked. The material benefits due to the presence of the sovereign seem to have reconciled the city to its subject condition; there had been no seditious movement there since the ill-starred rising of Shamasherîb, which Xerxes had quelled with ruthless severity.[2] The Greek mercenaries or traders who visited it, though prepared for its huge size by general report, could not repress a feeling of astonishment as they approached it. First of all there was the triple wall of Nebuchadrezzar, with its moats, its rows of towers, and its colossal gateways. Unlike the Greek cities, it had been laid out according to a regular plan, and formed a perfect square, inside which the streets crossed one another at right angles, some parallel to the Euphrates, others at right angles to it; every one of the latter terminated in a brazen gate opening through the masonry of the quay, and giving access to the river.[3] The passengers who crowded the streets included representatives of all the Asiatic races, the native Babylonians being recognisable by their graceful dress, consisting of a linen tunic falling to the feet, a fringed shawl, round cap, and heavy staff terminating in a knob.[4] From this ever-changing background stood out many novel features calculated to stimulate Greek curiosity, such as the sick persons exposed at street-corners in order that they might beg the passers-by to prescribe for them, the prostitution of her votaries within the courts of the goddess Mylitta, and the disposal of marriageable girls by auction: Herodotus, however, regretted that this latter custom had fallen into abeyance.[5] And yet to the attentive eye of a close observer even Babylon must have furnished many unmistakable symptoms of decay. The huge boundary wall enclosed too large an area for the population sheltered behind it; whole quarters were crumbling into heaps of ruins, and the flower and vegetable gardens were steadily encroaching on spaces formerly covered with houses.[6] Public buildings had suffered quite as much as private dwellings from the Persian wars. Xerxes had despoiled the temples, and no restoration had been attempted since his time.[1] The ziggurât of Bel lay half buried already beneath piles of rubbish; the golden statues which had once stood within its chambers had disappeared, and the priests no longer carried on their astronomical observations on its platform.[2] The palaces of the ancient kings were falling to pieces from lack of repairs, though the famous hanging gardens in the citadel were still shown to strangers. The guides, of course, gave them out to be a device of Semiramis, but the well-informed knew that they had been constructed by Nebuchadrezzar for one of his wives, the daughter of Cyaxares, who pined for the verdure of her native mountains. "They were square in shape, each side being four hundred feet long; one approached them by steps leading to terraces placed one above the other, the arrangement of the whole resembling that of an amphitheatre. Each terrace rested on pillars which, gradually increasing in size, supported the weight of the soil and its produce. The loftiest pillar attained a height of fifty feet; it reached to the upper part of the garden, its capital being on a level with the balustrades of the boundary wall. The terraces were covered with a layer of soil of sufficient depth for the roots of the largest trees; plants of all kinds that delight the eye by their shape or beauty were grown there. One of the columns was hollow from top to bottom; it contained hydraulic engines which pumped up quantities of water, no part of the mechanism being visible from the outside."[3] Many travellers were content to note down only such marvels as they considered likely to make their narratives more amusing, but others took pains to collect information of a more solid character, and before they had carried their researches very far, were at once astounded and delighted with the glimpses they obtained of Chaldæan genius. No doubt, they exaggerated when they went so far as to maintain that all their learning came to them originally from Babylon, and that the most famous scholars of Greece, Pherecydes of Scyros,[4] Democritus of Abdera,[5] and

---

[1] ARRIAN, *Anabasis,* VII. xvii. §§ 1, 2; cf. p. 716, *supra.*

[2] Herodotus (I. clxxxiii.) merely mentions that Xerxes had despoiled the temple; Strabo (XVI. i. § 5, p. 138) tells us that Alexander wished to restore it, but that it was in such a state of dilapidation that it would have taken ten thousand men two months merely to remove the rubbish.

[3] DIODORUS SICULUS, ii. 40; STRABO, XVI. i. § 5, p. 738, both of whom seem to have borrowed their main facts from Ctesias.

[4] PHILO OF BYBLOS, *Fragm.* 9, in MÜLLER-DIDOT, *Fragm. Hist. Græc.,* vol. iii. p. 572.

[5] MÜLLER-DIDOT, *Fragm. Hist. Græc.,* vol. ii. pp. 24–26. A legend of a later epoch affirms that he knew enough *Assyrian* to translate a book by the celebrated Achiacharus, who had been vizir to Sennacherib, and who is mentioned in the Jewish and Arab traditions (E. COSQUIN, *Le Livre de Tobie et l'Histoire du Sage Ahikar,* in the *Revue Biblique,* vol. viii. pp. 50–82). As to Democritus as alchemist, cf. BERTHELOT, *Les Origines de l'Alchimie,* p. 145, et seq., and in regard to the Egyptian origin of the traditions relating to him, cf. MASPERO, *Notes au jour le jour,* in the *Proceedings* of the Bibl. Arch. Soc., 1898, vol. xx. pp. 140–144.

Pythagoras,[1] owed the rudiments of philosophy, mathematics, physics, and astrology to the school of the *Magi*. Yet it is not surprising that they should have believed this to be the case, when increasing familiarity with the priestly seminaries revealed to them the existence of those libraries of clay tablets in which, side by side with theoretic treatises dating from two thousand years back and more, were to be found examples of applied mechanics, observations, reckonings, and novel solutions of problems, which generations of scribes had accumulated in the course of centuries.[2] The Greek astronomers took full advantage of these documents, but it was their astrologers and soothsayers who were specially indebted to them. The latter acknowledged their own inferiority the moment they came into contact with their Euphratean colleagues, and endeavoured to make good their deficiencies by taking lessons from the latter or persuading them to migrate to Greece. A hundred years later saw the Babylonian Berosus opening at Cos a public school of divination by the stars. From thenceforward "Chaldæan" came to be synonymous with "astrologer" or "sorcerer," and Chaldæan magic became supreme throughout the world at the very moment when Chaldæa itself was in its death-throes.

Nor was its unquestioned supremacy in the black art the sole legacy that Chaldæa bequeathed to the coming generations: its language survived, and reigned for centuries afterwards in the regions subjugated by its arms. The cultivated tongue employed by the scribes of Nineveh and Babylon in the palmy days of their race, had long become a sort of literary dialect, used in writings of a lofty character and understood by a select few, but unintelligible to the common people. The populace in town or country talked an Aramaic jargon, clumsier and more prolix than Assyrian, but easier to understand. We know how successfully the Aramæans had managed to push their way along the Euphrates and into Syria towards the close of the Hittite supremacy: their successive encroachments had been favoured, first by the Assyrian, later by the Chaldæan conquests, and now they had become sole possessors of the ancient Naharaîna, the plains of Cilicia, the basin of the Orontes, and the country round Damascus; but the true home of the Aramæans was in Syria rather than in the districts of the Lower Euphrates. Even in the time of the

---

[1] As to the supposed relations of Pythagoras with the Chaldæans or Assyrians, cf. NEANTHES OF CYZICUS, *Fragm.* 20, in MÜLLER-DIDOT, *Fragm. Hist. Græc.*, vol. iii. pp. 9, 10, and ALEXANDER POLYHISTOR, *Fragm.* 138, in MÜLLER-DIDOT, *Fragm. Hist. Græc.*, vol. iii. p. 239. The story which asserts that Pythagoras served under Nergilos, King of Assyria (ABYDENUS, *Fragm.* 7, in MÜLLER-DIDOT, *Fragm. Hist. Græc.*, vol. iii. p. 282), is probably based on some similarity of names: thus among the Greek kings of Cyprus, and in the time of Assur-bani-pal, we find one whose name would recall that of Pythagoras, if the accuracy of the reading were beyond question.

[2] In regard to the library of Assur-bani-pal at Nineveh, and the library in the temple of Bel-Marduk at Babylon which served as its prototype, cf. pp. 461-464, *supra*.

Sargonids their alphabet had made so much headway that at Nineveh itself and at Calah it had come into everyday use; when Chaldæan supremacy gave way to that of the Persians, its triumph—in the western provinces, at any rate—was complete, and it became the recognised vehicle of the royal decrees: we come upon it in every direction, on the coins issued by the satraps of Asia Minor, on the seals of local governors or dynasts, on inscriptions or stelæ in Egypt, in the letters of the scribes, and in the rescripts of the great king. From Nisib to Raphia, between the Tigris and the Mediterranean, it gradually supplanted most of the other dialects—Semitic or otherwise—which had hitherto prevailed. Phœnician held its ground in the seaports, but Hebrew gave way before it, and ended by being restricted to religious purposes, as a literary and liturgical language. It was in the neighbourhood of Babylon itself that the Judæan exiles had, during the Captivity, adopted the Aramaic language, and their return to Canaan failed to restore either the purity of their own language or the dignity and independence of their religious life. Their colony at Jerusalem possessed few resources; the wealthier Hebrews had, for the most part, remained in Chaldæa, leaving the privilege of repopulating the holy city to those of their brethren who were less plenteously endowed with this world's goods.[1] These latter soon learned to their cost that Zion was not the ideal city whose "gates shall be open continually; they shall not be shut day nor night; that men may bring unto thee the wealth of the nations;" far from "sucking the milk of nations and the breast of kings,"[2] their fields produced barely sufficient to satisfy the more pressing needs of daily life. "Ye have sown much, and bring in little," as Jahveh declared to them; "ye eat, but ye have not enough; ye drink, but ye are not filled with drink; ye clothe you, but there is none warm; and he that earneth wages earneth wages to put it into a bag with holes."[3] They quickly relinquished the work of restoration, finding themselves forgotten by all—their Babylonian brethren included—in the midst of the great events which were then agitating the world, the preparations for the conquest of Egypt, the usurpation of the pseudo-Smerdis, the accession of Darius, the Babylonian and Median insurrections. Possibly they believed that the Achæmenides had had their day, and that a new Chaldæan empire, with a second Nebuchadrezzar at its head, was about to regain the ascendency. It

[1] Cf. what is said on this subject on pp. 638, 639, *supra*. I should have liked to deal with the history of the Jewish community as fully as it deserves, but the necessity of condensing my work has rendered this impossible. I give here merely the necessary details, without quoting authorities; the reader will have no difficulty in identifying the works on which I have relied in dealing with the controversy which has arisen in regard to the chronology of the events mentioned in the books of Ezra and Nehemiah.

[2] An anonymous prophet in *Isa.* lx. 11–16.

[3] *Hagg.* i. 6.

would seem that the downfall of Nadintav-bel inspired them with new faith in the future and encouraged them to complete their task: in the second year of Darius, two prophets, Haggai and Zechariah, arose in their midst and lifted up their voices. Zerubbabel, a prince of the royal line, governed Judah in the Persian interest, and with him was associated the high priest Joshua, who looked after the spiritual interests of the community: the reproaches of the two prophets aroused the people from their inaction, and induced them to resume their interrupted building operations. Darius, duly informed of what was going on by the governor of Syria, gave orders that they were not to be interfered with, and four years later the building of the temple was completed.[1] For nearly a century after this the little Jewish republic remained quiescent. It had slowly developed until it had gradually won back a portion of the former territories of Benjamin and Judah, but its expansion southwards was checked by the Idumæans, to whom Nebuchadrezzar had years before handed

over Hebron and Acrabattenê (Akrabbim) as a reward for the services they had rendered. On the north its neighbours were the descendants of those Aramæan exiles whom Sargon, Sennacherib, and Esarhaddon, kings of Assyria, had, on various occasions, installed around Samaria in Mount Ephraim. At first these people paid no reverence to

CHALDÆAN SEAL WITH ARAMAIC
INSCRIPTION.[2]

the "God of the land," so that Jahveh, in order to punish them, sent lions, which spread carnage in their ranks. Then the King of Assyria allotted them an Israelitish priest from among his prisoners, who taught them "the law" of Jahveh, and appointed other priests chosen from the people, and showed them how to offer up sacrifices on the ancient high places.[3] Thus another Israel began to rise up again, and, at first, the new Judah seems to have been on tolerably friendly terms with it: the two communities traded and intermarried with one another, the Samaritans took part in the religious ceremonies, and certain of their leaders occupied a court in the temple at Jerusalem. The alliance, however, proved dangerous to the purity of the faith, for the proselytes, while they adopted Jahveh and gave Him that supreme

---

[1] *Ezra* iv.–vi.; the account given by JOSEPHUS, *Ant. Jud.*, x. 1, 2, of the two expeditions of Zerubbabel seems to have been borrowed partly from the canonical book, partly from the Apocryphal writing known as the *1st Book of Esdras*.

[2] Drawn by Faucher-Gudin, from a photogravure published in MÉNANT, *La Glyptique Orientale*, vol. ii. pl. ix. No. 4, and pp. 217, 218.

[3] *2 Kings* xvii. 24–40. There do not seem to have been the continual disputes between the inhabitants of Judæa and Samaria before the return of Nehemiah, which the compilers of the Books of Ezra and Nehemiah seem to have believed.

3 E

place in their devotions which was due to "the God of the land," had by no means entirely forsworn their national superstitions, and Adrammelek, Nergal, Tartak, Anammelek, and other deities still found worshippers among them. Judah, which in the days of its independence had so often turned aside after the gods of Canaan and Moab, was in danger of being led away by the idolatrous practices of its new neighbours ; intermarriage with the daughters of Moab and Ammon, of Philistia and Samaria, was producing a gradual degeneracy : the national language was giving way before the Aramæan ; unless some one could be found to stem the tide of decadence and help the people to remount the slope which they were descending, the fate of Judah was certain. A prophet—the last of those whose predictions have survived to our time—stood forth amid the general laxity and called the people to account for their transgressions, in the name of the Eternal, but his single voice, which seemed but a feeble echo of the great prophets of former ages, did not meet with a favourable hearing. Salvation came at length from the Jews outside Judah, the naturalised citizens of Babylon, a well-informed and wealthy body, occupying high places in the administration of the empire, and sometimes in the favour of the sovereign also, yet possessed by an ardent zeal for the religion of their fathers and a steadfast faith in the vitality of their race. One of these, a certain Nehemiah, was employed as cupbearer to Artaxerxes II. He was visited at Susa by some men of Judah whose business had brought them to that city and inquired of them how matters fared in Jerusalem. Hanani, one of his visitors, replied that "the remnant that are left of the captivity there in the province are in great affliction and reproach : the wall of Jerusalem also is broken down, and the gates thereof are burned with fire." Nehemiah took advantage of a moment when the king seemed in a jovial mood to describe the wretched state of his native land in moving terms : he obtained leave to quit Susa and authority to administer the city in which his fathers had dwelt.[1]

This took place in the twentieth year of Artaxerxes, about 385 B.C. Nehemiah at once made his way to Jerusalem with such escort as befitted his dignity, and the news of his mission, and, apparently, the sentiments of rigid orthodoxy professed by him from the beginning, provoked the resentment of the neighbouring potentates against him : Sanballat the Horonite, Tobiah the Ammonite, chief of the Samaritans, and Geshem the Bedâwin did their best to thwart him in the execution of his plans. He baffled their intrigues by his promptitude in rebuilding the walls, and when once he had rendered himself safe from any sudden attack, he proceeded with the reforms which he deemed

[1] *Nehemiah* i., ii.

urgent. His tenure of office lasted twelve years—from 384 to 373 B.C.—and during the whole of that time he refused to accept any of the dues to which he was entitled, and which his predecessors had received without scruple. Ever since their return from exile, the common people had been impoverished and paralysed by usury. The poor had been compelled to mortgage their fields and their vineyards in order to pay the king's taxes; then, when their land was gone, they had pledged their sons and their daughters; the moneyed classes of the new Israel thus absorbed the property of their poorer brethren, and reduced the latter to slavery. Nehemiah called the usurers before him and severely rebuking them for their covetousness, bade them surrender the interest and capital of existing debts, and restore the properties which had fallen into their hands owing to their shameful abuse of wealth, and release all those of their co-religionists whom they had enslaved in default of payment of their debts.[1] His high place in the royal favour doubtless had its effect on those whose cupidity suffered from his zeal, and prevented external enemies from too openly interfering in the affairs of the community : by the time he returned to the court, in 372 B.C., after an absence of twelve years,[2] Jerusalem and its environs had to some extent regained the material prosperity of former days. The part played by Nehemiah was, however, mainly political, and the religious problem remained in very much the same state as before. The high priests, who alone possessed the power of solving it, had fallen in with the current that was carrying away the people, and—latterly, at any rate —had become disqualified through intermarriage with aliens : what was wanted was a scribe deeply versed in sacred things to direct them in the right way, and such a man could be found only in Babylonia, the one country in which the study of the ancient traditions still flourished. A certain Ezra, son of Seraiah, presented himself in 369 B.C., and, as he was a man of some standing, Artaxerxes not only authorised him to go himself, but to take with him a whole company of priests and Levites and families formerly attached to the service of the temple. The books containing the Law of God and the history of His people had, since the beginning of the captivity, undergone alterations which had profoundly modified their text and changed their spirit. This work of revision, begun under the influence of Ezekiel, and perhaps by his own followers, had, since his time, been carried on without interruption, and by mingling the juridical texts with narratives of the early ages collected from different sources, a lengthy work had been produced, very similar in com-

[1] *Neh.* v.
[2] *Neh.* xiii. 6: "in the two and thirtieth year of Artaxerxes, King of Babylon, I went unto the king."

position and wording to the five Books of Moses and the Book of Joshua as we now possess them.[1]   It was this version of the Revelation of Jahveh that Ezra brought with him from Babylon in order to instruct the people of Judah, and the first impressions received by him at the end of his journey convinced him that his task would be no light one, for the number of mixed marriages had been so great as to demoralise not only the common people, but even the priests and leading nobles as well.   Nevertheless, at a general assembly[2] of the people he succeeded in persuading them to consent to the repudiation of alien wives.   But this preliminary success would have led to nothing unless he could secure formal recognition of the rigorous code of which he had constituted himself the champion, and protracted negotiations were necessary before he could claim a victory on this point as well as on the other.   At length, about 367 B.C., more than a year after his arrival, he gained his point, and the covenant between Jahveh and His people was sealed with ceremonies modelled on those which had attended the promulgation of Deuteronomy in the time of Josiah.[3]   On the first day of the seventh month, a little before the autumn festival, the people assembled at Jerusalem in " the broad place which was before the water gate."   Ezra mounted a wooden pulpit, and the chief among the priests sat beside him.   He " opened the book in the sight of all the people . . . and . . . all the people stood up: and Ezra blessed the Lord, the great God.   And all the people answered ' Amen, amen ! ' with the lifting up of their hands; and they bowed their heads and worshipped the Lord with their faces to the ground."   Then began the reading of the sacred text.   As each clause was read, the Levites stationed here and there among the people interpreted and explained its provisions in the vulgar tongue, so as to make their meaning clear to all.   The prolix enumeration of sins and their expiation, the threats expressed in certain chapters, produced among the crowd the same effect of nervous terror as had once before been called forth by the precepts and maledictions of Deuteronomy.   The people burst into tears, and so vehement were their manifestations of despair, that all the efforts of Ezra and his colleagues were needed to calm them.   Ezra took advantage of this state of fervour to demand the immediate application of the divine ordinances. And first of all, it was " found written in the law, how that the Lord had commanded by Moses that the children of Israel should dwell in booths."   For seven days Jerusalem was decked with leaves; tabernacles of olive, myrtle,

---

[1] This is the priestly revision presupposed by recent critics; here again, in order to keep within the prescribed limits of space, I have been compelled to omit much that I should have liked to add in regard to the nature of this work and the spirit in which it was carried out.

[2] *Ezra* vii.–xi., where the dates given do not form part of the work as written by Ezra, but have been introduced later by the editor of the book as it now stands.

[3] Cf. the account of these events on pp. 507–511, *supra*.

and palm branches rose up on all sides, on the roofs of houses, in courtyards, in the courts of the temple, at the gates of the city. Then, on the 27th day of the same month, the people put on mourning in order to confess their own sins and the sins of their fathers. Finally, to crown the whole, Ezra and his followers required the assembly to swear a solemn oath that they would respect "the law of Moses," and regulate their conduct by it.[1] After the first enthusiasm was passed, a reaction speedily set in. Many even among the priests thought that Ezra had gone too far in forbidding marriage with strangers, and that the increase of the tithes and sacrifices would lay too heavy a burden on the nation. The Gentile women reappeared, the Sabbath was no longer observed either by the Israelites or aliens; Eliashîb, son of the high priest Joiakim, did not even deprive Tobiah the Ammonite of the chamber in the temple which he had formerly prepared for him, and things were almost imperceptibly drifting back into the same state as before the reformation, when Nehemiah returned from Susa towards the close of the reign of Artaxerxes. He lost no time in re-establishing respect for the law, and from henceforward opposition, if it did not entirely die out, ceased to manifest itself in Jerusalem.[2] Elsewhere, however, among the Samaritans, Idumæans, and Philistines, it continued as keen as ever, and the Jews themselves were imprudent enough to take part in the political revolutions that were happening around them in their corner of the empire. Their traditions tell how they were mixed up in the rising of the Phœnician cities against Ochus, and suffered the penalty; when Sidon capitulated, they were punished with the other rebels, the more recalcitrant among them being deported into Hyrcania.[3]

Assyria was nothing more than a name, Babylon and Phœnicia were growing weaker every day; the Jews, absorbed in questions of religious ethics, were deficient in material power, and had not as yet attained sufficient moral authority to exercise an influence over the eastern world: the Egypt indestructible had alone escaped the general shipwreck, and seemed fated to survive her rivals for a long time. Of all these ancient nations it was she who appealed most strongly to the imagination of the Greeks: Greek traders, mercenaries, scholars, and even tourists wandered freely within her borders, and accounts of the strange and marvellous things to be found there were published far and wide in the writings of Hecatæus of Miletus, Herodotus of Halicarnassus, and Hellanicus of Lesbos.[4] As a rule, they entered the country from the west, as European

---

[1] *Neh.* viii., ix., with an interpolation in ver. 9 of chap. viii., inserted in order to identify Nehemiah with the representative of the Persian government.

[2] *Neh.* xiii.

[3] JOSEPHUS, *Ant. Jud.*, xi. 7, 1.; cf. NÖLDEKE, *Aufsätze zur Persischen Geschichte*, p. 78.

[4] As to the Greek historians who wrote about Egypt prior to the conquest of Alexander, cf. the

tourists and merchants still do ; but Rakôtis, the first port at which they touched, was a mere village,[1] and its rocky Pharos had no claim to distinction beyond the fact that it had been mentioned by Homer.[2]   From hence they followed the channel of the Canopic arm, and as they gradually ascended, they had pointed out to them Anthylla, Arkandrupolis, and Gynæcopolis, townships dependent on Naucratis,[3] lying along the banks, or situated some distance off on one of the minor canals ; then Naucratis itself, still a flourishing place, in spite of the rebellions in the Delta and the suppressive measures of the Persians.   All this region seemed to them to be merely an extension of Greece under the African sky : to their minds the real Egypt began at Sais, a few miles farther eastwards. Sais was full in memories of the XXVIth dynasty : there they had pointed out to them the tombs of the Pharaohs in the enclosure of Nît,[4] the audience hall in which Psammetichus II. received the deputation of the Eleians,[5] the prison where the unfortunate Apries had languished after his defeat.[6]   The gateways of the temple of Nît seemed colossal to eyes accustomed to the modest dimensions of most Greek sanctuaries ;[7] these were, moreover, the first great monuments that the strangers had seen since they landed, and the novelty of their appearance had a good deal to do with the keenness of the impression produced.   The goddess showed herself in hospitable guise to the visitors ; she welcomed them all, Greek or Persian, at her festivals, and initiated them into several of her minor rites, without demanding from them anything beyond tolerance on certain points of doctrine.[8]   Her dual attributes as wielder of the bow and shuttle had inspired the Greeks with the belief that she was identical with that one of their own goddesses who most nearly combined in her person this complex mingling of war and industry : in her they worshipped the prototype of their own Pallas.[9]   On the evening of the 17th day of Thoth, Herodotus saw the natives, rich and poor, placing on the fronts of their dwellings large flat lamps filled with a mixture of salt and oil which they kept alight all night in honour of Osiris and of

details collected by GUTSCHMID, *Kleine Schriften*, vol. i. pp. 35–149, 168–183, and by WIEDEMANN, *Ægyptische Geschichte*, pp. 103–117.

[1] BRUGSCH, *Dictionnaire Géographique*, pp. 66, 68, 451.

[2] ODYSSEY, iv. 354–359 ; cf. MALLET, *Les Premiers Établissements des Grecs en Égypte*, pp. 11, 12.

[3] HERODOTUS, II. xcvii., xcviii. ; WIEDEMANN, *Herodots Zweites Buch*, pp. 389–391.   None of the sites of these three places can now be fixed with certainty.

[4] HERODOTUS, II. clxix. ; cf. WIEDEMANN, *Herodots Zweites Buch*, pp. 580–583.

[5] Cf. what is said as to this embassy on p. 542, *supra*.

[6] HERODOTUS, II. clxix. ; cf. WIEDEMANN, *Herodots Zweites Buch*, pp. 580, 581.   As to these events, cf. pp. 557, 558, *supra*.

[7] HERODOTUS, II. clxxv. ; cf. WIEDEMANN, *Herodots Zweites Buch*, p. 598.

[8] HERODOTUS, II. clxxi. ; περὶ μέν νυν τούτων εἰδότι μοι ἐπὶ πλέον, ὡς ἕκαστα αὐτῶν ἔχει, εὔστομα κείσθω ; cf. WIEDEMANN, *Herodots Zweites Buch*, pp. 591, 592.

[9] Herodotus invariably calls Nît "Athenaiê ;" cf. II. lix. As to this assimilation, cf. MALLET, *Le Culte de Neith à Sais*, pp. 236–241.

the dead.[1] He made his way into the dwelling of the ineffable god, and there, unobserved among the crowd, he witnessed scenes from the divine life represented by the priests on the lake by the light of torches, episodes of his passion, mourning, and resurrection.[2] The priests did not disclose their subtler mysteries before barbarian eyes, nor did they teach the inner meaning of their dogmas, but the little they did allow him to discern filled the traveller with respect and wonder, recalling sometimes by their resemblance to them the mysteries in which he was accustomed to take part in his own country.[3] Then, as now, but little attention was paid to the towns in the centre and east of the Delta; travellers endeavoured to visit one or two of them as types, and collected as much information as they could about the remainder.

MODERN MOHAMMEDAN SHÊKHS' TOMBS.[4]

Herodotus and his rivals attached little importance to those

PART OF THE INUNDATION IN A PALM GROVE.[5]

details of landscape which possess so much attraction for the modern tourist. They bestowed no more than a careless glance on the chapels scattered up and down the country like the Mohammedan shrines at the present day, and the waters extending on all sides beneath the acacias and palm trees during the inundation, or the fellahîn trotting along on their little asses beside the pools, did not strike them as being of sufficient interest to deserve passing mention in an account of their travels. They

---

[1] HERODOTUS, II. lxii.; cf. WIEDEMANN, *Herodots Zweites Buch*, pp. 261, 262, where passages in classical authors referring to this festival are given. In my opinion, however, it is not the festivals of Athyr that are here referred to, but those of the month of Thoth, when, as the inscriptions show, it was the practice to *light the new fire*, according to the ritual, after first extinguishing the fire of the previous year, not only in the temple of the god, but in all the houses of the city.

[2] HERODOTUS, II. clxxi.; cf. WIEDEMANN, *Herodots Zweites Buch*, pp. 591–593.

[3] Cf., in regard to these points, P. FOUCART, *Recherches sur l'Origine et la Nature des mystères d'Eleusis*, 4to, 1895.

[4] Drawn by Boudier, from a photograph by Gautier.

[5] Drawn by Boudier, from a photograph by Gautier.

passed by the most picturesque villages with indifference, and it was only when they reached some great city, or came upon some exceptionally fine temple or eccentric deity, that their curiosity was aroused. Mendes worshipped its patron god in the form of a live ram,[1] and bestowed on all members of the same species some share of the veneration it lavished on the divine animal.[2] The inhabitants of Atarbêkhis,[3] on the island of Prosopitis, gave themselves up to the worship of the bull. When one of these animals died in the neighbourhood they buried it, leaving one horn above the earth in order to mark the spot, and once every year the boats of Atarbêkhis made a tour round the island to collect the skeletons or decaying bodies, in order that they might be interred in a common burying-place.[4] The people of Busiris patronised a savage type of religion. During the festival of Isis they gave themselves up to fierce conflicts, their fanatical fury even infecting strangers who chanced to be present. The Carians also had hit upon a means of outdoing the extravagance of the natives themselves: like the Shiite Mohammedans of the present day at the festival of the Hassanên, they slashed their faces with knives amidst shrieks and yells.[5] At Paprêmis a pitched battle formed part of the religious observances: it took place, however, under certain special conditions. On the evening of the festival of Anhuît, as the sun went down, a number of priests performed a hasty sacrifice in the temple, while the remainder of the local priesthood stationed themselves at the gate armed with heavy cudgels. When the ceremony was over, the celebrants placed the statue of the god on a four-wheeled car, as though about to take it away to some other locality, but their colleagues at the gate opposed its departure and barred the way. It was at this juncture that the faithful intervened; they burst in the door and set upon the priests with staves, the latter offering a stout resistance. The cudgels were heavy, the arms that wielded them lusty, and the fight lasted a long time, yet no one was ever killed in the fray—at least, so the priests averred—and I am at a loss to understand why Herodotus,

---

[1] Herodotus says that both the goat and the god were named Mendes in Egyptian (II. xlvi.), but he is here confusing ordinary goats with the special goat which was supposed to contain the soul of Osiris. It was the latter that the Egyptians named after the god himself, Baînibdîduît, i.e. *the soul of the master of the city of Diduît.* It was this form, popularly contracted into Bendidî, that was rendered by the Greeks Μένδης, Μένδητος.

[2] HERODOTUS, II. xlvi.; cf. WIEDEMANN, *Herodots Zweites Buch*, pp. 216–227.

[3] The old explanation of this name as the *City of Hathor* has been rightly rejected as inconsistent with one of the elementary rules of hieroglyphic grammar (WIEDEMANN, *Herodots Zweites Buch*, p. 195). The name, when properly divided into its three constituent parts, means literally *the Castle of Horus the Sparrow-hawk,* or *Hat-har-baki.*

[4] HERODOTUS, II. xli.; cf. WIEDEMANN, *Herodots Zweites Buch*, pp. 193–196.

[5] HERODOTUS, II. lix., lxi.; cf. WIEDEMANN, *Herodots Zweites Buch*, pp. 256–258.

who was not a native of Paprêmis, should have been so unkind as to doubt their testimony.[1]

It is nearly always in connection with some temple or religious festival that he refers to the towns of the Delta, and, indeed, in most of the minor cities of Egypt, just as in those of modern Italy there is little to interest visitors except the religious monuments or ceremonies. Herodotus went to Tanis or Mendes as we go to Orvieto or Loretto, to admire the buildings or pay our devotions at a famous shrine. More often than not the place was nothing in itself, consisting merely of a fortified enclosure, a few commonplace houses occupied by the wealthy inhabitants or by government officials, and on mounds of ancient *débris*, the accumulation of centuries, a number of ephemeral hovels built of clay or dried bricks, divided into irregular blocks by winding alleys. The whole local in-

terest was centred in the sanctuary and its inmates, human and divine. The traveller made his way in as best he could, went into ecstasies over the objects that were shown to him, and as soon as he had duly gone the rounds, set out for the next place on his list, deeming himself lucky if he happened to arrive during one of the annual fairs, such as that of Bubastis,

EPHEMERAL HOVELS OF CLAY OR DRIED BRICKS.[2]

for instance. Bands of pilgrims flocked in from all parts of Egypt; the river craft were overflowing with men and women, who converted the journey into one long carnival. Every time the vessel put in to land, the women rushed on shore, amid the din of castanets and flutes, and ran hither and thither challenging the women of the place with abuse to dance against them with uplifted garments. To the foreigners there was little to distinguish the festival of Bastît from many other Egyptian ceremonies of the kind; it consisted of a solemn procession, accompanied by the singing of hymns and playing of harps, dancing and sacrifices, but for weeks before and after it the town was transformed into one vast pleasure-ground. The people of Bubastis took a certain pride in declaring that more wine was drunk in it during

[1] HERODOTUS, II. lix., lxiii.; cf. WIEDEMANN, *Herodots Zweites Buch*, pp. 263–268. The god whom the Greeks identified with their Ares was Anhurît, as is proved by one of the Leyden Papyri (LEEMANNS, *Papyri Græci*, vol. i. pp. 123, 124, 128). So, too, in modern times at Cairo, it used to be affirmed that no Mohammedan who submitted to the *dôseh* was ever seriously injured by the hoofs of the horse which trampled over the bodies extended on the ground.

[2] Drawn by Boudier, from a photograph by Haussoullier.

a single day than during the rest of the whole year.[1] Butô enjoyed exceptional popularity among the Greeks in Egypt. Its patron goddess, the Isis who took refuge amid the pools in a moving thicket of reeds and lotus, in order that she might protect her son Horus from the jealousy of Typhon, reminded them of the story of Latona and the cycle of the Delian legends; they visited her in crowds, and her oracle became to most of them what that of Delos was to their brethren in Europe. At Butô they found a great temple, similar to all Egyptian temples, a shrine in which the statues of the goddess continued her mysterious existence, and, in the midst of the sacred lake, the little island of Khemmis, which was said to float hither and thither upon the waters.[2] Herodotus did not venture to deny this absolutely, but states that he had never seen it change its position or even stir:[3] perhaps his incredulity may have been quickened by the fact that this miracle had already been inquired into by Hecatæus of Miletus, an author who was his pet aversion. The priests of Butô declared that their prophets had foretold everything that had happened for a long time past, and for each event they had a version which redounded to the credit of their goddess: she had shown Pheron how he might recover his sight, had foretold how long the reign of Mykerinos would last, had informed Psammetichus that he would be saved by men of brass rising out of the sea, and had revealed to Cambyses that he should die in a town named Ecbatana.[4] Her priests had taken an active part in the revolt of Khabbîsha against Darius, and had lost a goodly portion of their treasure and endowments for their pains.[5] They still retained their prestige, however, in spite of the underhand rivalry of the oracle of Zeus Ammon. The votaries of the Libyan deity could bring forward miracles even more marvellous than those credited to the Egyptian Latona, and in the case of many of the revolutions which had taken place on the banks of the Nile, a version of the legend in his honour was circulated side by side with the legends of Butô.[6] The latter city lay on the very outskirts of one of those regions which excited the greatest curiosity among travellers, the almost inaccessible Bucolicum, where, it was said, no rebel ever failed

---

[1] HERODOTUS, II. lix., lx.; cf. WIEDEMANN, *Herodots Zweites Buch*, pp. 252–256.

[2] HECATÆUS OF MILETUS, *Fragm.* 284, in MÜLLER-DIDOT, *Fragmenta Historicorum Græcorum*, vol. i. p. 20.

[3] HERODOTUS, II. clv., clvi.; cf. WIEDEMANN, *Herodots Zweites Buch*, pp. 554–559.

[4] HERODOTUS, II. cxi., cxxxiii., clii., III. lxiv., lxv.

[5] Cf. what is said as to the part played by Butô under Khabbîsha on pp. 713–715, *supra*.

[6] This rivalry between the two oracles in the narrative of Herodotus had been noticed by GUTSCHMID, *Kleine Schriften*, vol. i. pp. 137, 138, 142, who believed the oracle in question to be that of the Theban Amon, and he might perhaps be right, were it possible to prove, what I believe to be the case, that the name Tementhes, in the legend of Psammetichus, is a corruption of Tandamanu. Nevertheless, I consider it more prudent for the present to admit, with MALLET, *Les Premiers Établissements des Grecs en Égypte*, pp. 45, 46, that it is the oracle of Zeus Ammon.

to find a safe refuge from his alien pursuers.[1] The Egyptians of the marshes were a very courageous race, but savage, poor, and ill fed.[2] They drank nothing but beer, and obtained their oil not from the olive, but from the castor-oil plant,[3] and having no corn, lived on the seeds or roots of the lotus, or even on the stalks of the papyrus, which they roasted or boiled.[4] Fish was their staple article of food, and this they obtained in considerable quantity from Lake Menzaleh, the lagoons along the coast, and the canals or pools left by the inundation.[5] But little was known of their villages or monuments, and probably they were not worth the trouble of a visit after those of the cities of the plain : endless stories were told of feats of brigandage and of the mysterious hiding-places which these localities offered to every outlaw, one of the most celebrated being the isle of Elbô, where the blind Anysis defied the power of Ethiopia for thirty years, and in which the first Amyrtæus found refuge.[6] With the exception of a few merchants or adventurers who visited them with an eye to gain, most travellers coming from or returning to Asia avoided their territory, and followed the military road along the Pelusiac arm of the Nile from Pelusium to Daphnæ or Zalu, and from Daphnæ or Zalu to Bubastis. A little below Kerkasoron, near the apex of the Delta, the pyramids stood out on the horizon, looking insignificant at first, but afterwards so lofty that, during the period of inundation, when the whole valley, from the mountains of Arabia to those of Libya, was nothing but one vast river, a vessel seemed to sail in their shadow for a long time before it reached their base.[7] The traveller passed Heliopolis on his left with its temple of the Sun, next the supposed sources of the Northern Nile, the quarries of the Red Mountain, and then entering at length the Nile itself, after a journey of some hours, came to anchor by the quays of Memphis.

To the Greeks of that time, Memphis was very much what Cairo is to us, viz. the typical Oriental city, the quintessence and chief representative of

[1] Cf. the description of the region about Bucolicum in *The Struggle of the Nations,* p. 89.

[2] This is the very description given of them by Herodotus, οἱ ἐν τοῖσι ἕλεσι κατοικημένοι (II. xcii.), or Αἰγυπτίων οἱ περὶ τὰ ἕλεα οἰκέοντες (II. xciv.), in the passages where he describes their customs.

[3] HERODOTUS, II. xciv. ; cf. WIEDEMANN, *Herodots Zweites Buch,* pp. 381–383. It seems, moreover, that this custom was not confined to the Delta ; Herodotus, in contrasting the custom of Bucolicum with that of the rest of Egypt, was evidently thinking of Sais, Memphis, and other great cities in which he had resided, where foreign olive oil obtained from Greece or Syria was generally used.

[4] HERODOTUS, II. xcii. ; cf. WIEDEMANN, *Herodots Zweites Buch,* pp. 373–379. As to food of this kind, cf. *Dawn of Civilization,* pp. 65, 66.

[5] HERODOTUS, II. xciii. ; cf. WIEDEMANN, *Herodots Zweites Buch,* p. 379.

[6] HERODOTUS, II. cxl. ; cf. WIEDEMANN, *Herodots Zweites Buch,* pp. 500, 501, and what is said on p. 732, *supra.*

[7] HERODOTUS, II. xv., xvii., xcvii. ; cf. WIEDEMANN, *Herodots Zweites Buch,* pp. 89, 90.

ancient Egypt.   In spite of the disasters which had overwhelmed it during the last few centuries, it was still a very beautiful city, ranking with Babylon as one of the largest in the world.   Its religious festivals, especially those in honour of Apis, attracted numberless pilgrims to it at certain seasons of the year, and hosts of foreigners, recruited from every imaginable race of the old continent, resorted to it for purposes of trade.   Most of the nationalities who frequented it had a special quarter, which was named after them; the Phœnicians occupied the *Tyrian Camp*,[1] the Greeks and Carians the *Hellenic Wall* and *Carian Wall*, and there were Caromemphites or Hellenomemphites side by side with the native inhabitants.[2]   A Persian garrison was stationed within the White Wall, ready to execute the satrap's orders in the event of rebellion, and could have held out for a long time even after the rest of the country had fallen into the hands of the insurgents.[3]   Animals which one would scarcely have expected to find in the streets of a capital, such as cows, sheep, and goats, wandered about unheeded in the most crowded thoroughfares; for the common people, instead of living apart from their beasts, as the Greeks did, stabled them in their own houses.[4]   Nor was this the only custom which must have seemed strange in the eyes of a newly arrived visitor, for the Egyptians might almost have been said to make a point of doing everything differently from other nations.   The baker, seen at the kneading-trough inside his shop, worked the dough with his foot; on the other hand, the mason used no trowel in applying his mortar, and the poorer classes scraped up handfuls of mud mixed with dung when they had occasion to repair the walls of their hovels.[5]   In Greece, even the very poorest retired to their houses and ate with closed doors; the Egyptians felt no repugnance at eating and drinking in the open air, declaring that unbecoming and improper acts should be performed in secret, but seemly acts in public.[6]   The first blind alley they came to, a recess between two hovels, the doorstep of a house or temple, any of these seemed to them a perfectly natural place to dine in.   Their bill of fare was not a

[1] HERODOTUS, II. cxii.; cf. WIEDEMANN, *Herodots Zweites Buch*, p. 432.   We find a *Quarter of the Hittites* in the environs of Memphis as early as the time of King Aî of the XVIIIth dynasty (DARESSY, *Notes et Remarques*, in the *Recueil de Travaux*, vol. xvi. p. 123).

[2] ARISTAGORAS OF MILETUS, *Fragm.* 5, in MÜLLER-DIDOT, *Fragm. Hist. Græc.*, vol. ii. p. 98: Ἑλληνικὸν καὶ Καρικὸν τόποι ἐν Μέμφιδι, ἀφ' ὧν Ἑλληνομεμφῖται καὶ Καρομεμφῖται, ὡς Ἀρισταγόρας, and Καρικόν, τόπος, ἰδιάζων ἐν Μέμφιδι, ἔνθα Κᾶρες οἰκήσαντες, ἐπιγαμίας πρὸς Μεμφίτας ποιησάμενοι, Καρομεμφῖται ἐκλήθησαν.   Cf. GUTSCHMID, *Kleine Schriften*, vol. i. pp. 135, 136, 141, 142.   Papyrus 50 in the British Museum contains a reference to one of these Hellenomemphites about the middle of the Ptolemaic epoch.

[3] HERODOTUS, III. xci., where he refers to the quantities of grain served out to the garrison of the White Wall.   Cf. the account of the revolt of Inaros on pp. 730, 731, *supra*.

[4] HERODOTUS, II. xxxvi.; cf. WIEDEMANN, *Herodots Zweites Buch*, pp. 157, 158.

[5] HERODOTUS, II. xxxvi.; cf. WIEDEMANN, *Herodots Zweites Buch*, pp. 159, 160.

[6] HERODOTUS, II. xxxv.; cf. WIEDEMANN, *Herodots Zweites Buch*, pp. 150, 151.

sumptuous one. A sort of flat pancake somewhat bitter in taste, and made —not of corn or barley—but of spelt,[1] a little oil, an onion or a leek, with an occasional scrap of meat or poultry, washed down by a jug of beer or wine; there was nothing here to tempt the foreigner, and, besides, it would not have been thought right for him to invite himself. A Greek who lived on the flesh of the cow was looked upon as unclean in the highest degree; no Egyptian would have thought of using the same pot or knife with him, or of kissing him on the mouth by way of greeting.[2] Moreover, Egyptian etiquette did not tolerate the same familiarities as the Greek: two friends on catching sight of one another paused before they met, bowed, then clasped one another round the knees or pretended to do so. Young people gave way to an old man, or, if seated, rose to let him pass. The traveller recalled the fact that the Spartans behaved in the same way, and approved this mark of deference;[3] but nothing in his home-life had prepared him for the sight of respectable women coming and going as they pleased, without escort and unveiled, carrying burdens on their shoulders (whereas the men carried them on their heads), going to market, keeping stalls or shops, while their husbands or fathers stayed comfortably at home, wove cloth, kneaded the potter's clay or turned the wheel, and worked at their trades;[4] no wonder that they were ready to believe that the man was the slave, and the wife the mistress of the family. Some historians traced the origin of these customs back to Osiris, others only as far as Sesostris: Sesostris was the last resource of Greek historians when they got into difficulties.[5] The city was crowded with monuments; there was the temple of the Phœnician Astarte, in which priests of Syrian descent had celebrated the mysteries of the great goddess ever since the days of the XVIIIth dynasty; then there was the temple of Râ, the temple of Amon, the temple of Tumu, the temple of Bastît, and the temple of Isis.[6] The temple of Phtah, as yet intact, provided the visitor with a spectacle scarcely less

---

[1] HERODOTUS, II. xxxvi.; it is this bread that he elsewhere calls κύλληστις (II. lxxvii.; cf. WIEDEMANN, *Herodots Zweites Buch*, pp. 326, 327); it was also known to Hecatæus of Miletus (*Fragm.* 290, in MÜLLER-DIDOT, *Fragm. Hist. Græc.*, vol. i. p. 20), and is identical with the *kurishtit* or *kulishtit* of Pharaonic times (LAUTH, *Drei Ægyptischen Namen des Brodes*, in the *Zeitschrift*, 1868, p. 91).

[2] HERODOTUS, II. xli.; cf. WIEDEMANN, *Herodots Zweites Buch*, pp. 187, 188.

[3] HERODOTUS, II. lxxx.; cf. WIEDEMANN, *Herodots Zweites Buch*, pp. 336-338.

[4] HERODOTUS, II. xxxv.; cf. WIEDEMANN, *Herodots Zweites Buch*, pp. 147-150.

[5] NYMPHODORUS OF SYRACUSE, *Fragm.* 21, in MÜLLER-DIDOT, *Fragm. Hist. Græc.*, vol. ii. pp. 380, 381, where a part of the thirty-fifth chapter of Herodotus is transcribed with additions of uncertain origin.

[6] This list is taken mainly from one of the mutilated letters found on the back of the *Sallier Papyrus*, iv. pl. i. l. 1, pl. ii. l. 11. The Phœnician Astarte, called a foreign Aphrodite by Herodotus, VI. cxii., was regarded by the Egyptians as a counterpart of Bastît, lady of Onkhtoui (BRUGSCH, *Die fremde Aphrodite in Memphis*, in the *Zeitschrift*, vol. i. p. 9).

admirable than that offered by the temple of the Theban Amon at Karnak. The kings had modified the original plan as each thought best, one adding obelisks or colossal statues, another a pylon, a third a pillared hall. Completed in this way by the labours of a score of dynasties, it formed, as it were, a microcosm of Egyptian history, in which each image, inscription and statue, aroused the attention of the curious. They naturally desired to learn who were the strangely dressed races shown struggling in a battle scene, the name of the king who had conquered them, and the reasons which had led him to construct this or that part of a monument, and there were plenty of busy-bodies ready to satisfy, as far as they could, the curiosity of visitors. Interpreters were at hand who bartered such information as they possessed, and the modern traveller who has had occasion to employ the services of a dragoman will have no difficulty in estimating the value of intelligence thus hawked about in ancient times. Priests of the lower class, doorkeepers and sacristans were trained to act as *ciceroni,* and knew the main ontlines of the history of the temple in which they lived.[1] Menes planned it,[2] Mœris added the northern propylæa,[3] Rhampsinitus those on the west,[4] Psammetichus the south,[5] Asychis those on the east, the most noteworthy of them all.[6] A native of Memphis, born at the foot of the pyramids, had been familiar with the names of Menes and Cheops from childhood; he was consequently apt to attribute to them everything of importance achieved by the Pharaohs of the old days. Menes had built the temple, Menes had founded the city, Menes had created the soil on which the city stood, and preserved it from floods by his dykes. The thoughtful traveller would assent, for had he not himself observed the action of the mud; a day's journey from the coast one could not let down a plummet without drawing it up covered with a blackish slime, a clear proof that the Nile continued to gain upon the sea.[7] Menes, at all events, had really existed; but as to Asychis, Mœris, Proteus, Pheron, and most of the characters glibly enumerated by Herodotus, it would be labour lost to search for their names among the inscriptions; they are mere puppets of popular romance, some of their names, such as Pirâui or Pruti, being nothing more than epithets employed by the story-tellers to indicate in general

---

[1] As to the persons meant by Herodotus when he speaks of "priests" and "Egyptians," cf. Maspero, *Études de Mythologie et d'Archéologie Égyptiennes,* vol. iii. pp. 343–345, and Wiedemann, *Ægyptische Geschichte,* pp. 113–115.

[2] Herodotus, II. xcix.; for the legend of Menes, cf. *Dawn of Civilization,* pp. 232–236.

[3] Herodotus, II. ci.; Wiedemann, *Herodots Zweites Buch,* pp. 401, 402.

[4] Herodotus, II. cxxi.; Wiedemann, *Herodots Zweites Buch,* pp. 445, 446.

[5] Herodotus, II. clii.; Wiedemann, *Herodots Zweites Buch,* p. 547.

[6] Herodotus, II. cxxxvi.; Wiedemann, *Herodots Zweites Buch,* pp. 490, 491.

[7] Herodotus, II. iv., v.; Wiedemann, *Herodots Zweites Buch,* pp. 58–61, 394–396. As to the observations made by the travellers and writers of the first Greek epoch in regard to these allusions, cf. Hugo Berger, *Geschichte der Wissenschaftlichen Geographie,* vol. i. pp. 120–126.

terms the heroes of their tales.[1]   We can understand how strangers, placed at the mercy of their dragoman, were misled by this, and tempted to transform each title into a man, taking Pruti and Piràui to be Pharaoh Proteus and Pharaoh Pheron, each of them celebrated for his fabulous exploits.   The guides told Herodotus, and Herodotus retails to us, as sober historical facts, the remedy employed by this unhistorical Pheron in order to recover his sight;[2]

THE STEP PYRAMID SEEN FROM THE GROVE OF PALM TREES TO THE NORTH OF SAQQARAH.[3]

the adventures of Paris and Helen at the court of Proteus,[4] and the droll tricks played by a thief at the expense of the simple Rhampsinitus.[5]   The excursions made by the Greek traveller in the environs of Memphis were very similar to those taken by modern visitors to Cairo : on the opposite bank of the Nile there was Heliopolis with its temple of Râ,[6] then there were the quarries of Turah, which had been worked from time immemorial, yet never exhausted, and from which the monuments he had been admiring, and the very

---

[1] As to these titles, cf. *Dawn of Civilization*, p. 263.   The equivalence of Pruti and Proteus was established by LAUTH, *Ægyptische Chronologie*, pp. 181, 182 ; that of Pharaoh and Pheron by MASPERO, *Études de Mythologie et d'Archéologie*, vol. iii. pp. 410–412.

[2] HERODOTUS, II. cxi. ; WIEDEMANN, *Herodots Zweites Buch*, pp. 427–430.

[3] Drawn by Boudier, from a photograph by Haussoullier.

[4] HERODOTUS, II. cxii.–cxx. ; WIEDEMANN, *Herodots Zweites Buch*, pp. 431–445.   Some dragomans identified the Helen of the Homeric legend with the " foreign Aphrodite " who had a temple in the Tyrian quarter at Memphis, and who was really a Semitic divinity (cf. p. 797, note 5, *supra*).

[5] HERODOTUS, II. cxxi. ; cf. MASPERO, *Les Contes populaires de l'Égypte ancienne*, 2nd edit., pp. xlvii.–li., 245–256 ; WIEDEMANN, *Herodots Zweites Buch*, pp. 445–452.

[6] HERODOTUS, II. iii. : ἐς Ἡλίου πόλιν αὐτῶν τούτων εἵνεκεν ἐτραπόμην.   Cf. WIEDEMANN, *Herodots Zweites Buch*, p. 50.

Pyramids themselves had been taken stone by stone.[1] The Sphinx probably lay hidden beneath the sand, and the nearest Pyramids, those at Saqqarah, were held in small esteem by visitors;[2] they were told as they passed by that the step Pyramid was the most ancient of all, having been erected by Uenephes, one of the kings of the first dynasty, and they asked no further questions.[3] Their whole curiosity was reserved for the three giants at Gizeh and their inmates, Cheops, Chephren, Mykerinos, and the fair Nitokris with the rosy cheeks.[4] Through all the country round, at Heliopolis, and even in the Fayum itself, they heard the same names that had been dinned into their ears

LONG STRINGS OF LADEN VESSELS.[6]

at Memphis; the whole of the monuments were made to fit into a single cycle of popular history, and what they learned at one place completed, or seemed to complete, what they had learned at another.[5]

I cannot tell whether many of them cared to stray much beyond Lake Mœris: the repressive measures of Ochus had, as it would appear, interrupted for a time the regular trade which, ever since the Saite kings of the XXVIth dynasty, had been carried on by the Greeks with the Oases, by way of Abydos.[7] A stranger who ventured as far as the Thebaid would have found himself in the same plight as a European of the last century who undertook to reach the first cataract.   Their point of departure—Memphis or Cairo—was very much the same; their destinations—Elephantinê and Assuan—differed but little.   They employed the same means of transport, for, excepting the cut of the sails, the modern dahabeah is an exact counterpart of the pleasure and passenger boats shown on the monuments.   Lastly, they set out at the same time of year, in November or December, after the floods had subsided.   The same length of time was required for the trip; it took a month to reach Assuan from Cairo if the wind were favourable, and if only such stoppages were made as were strictly

[1] These are "the quarries in the Arabian Mountain," τῶν λιθοτομιέων τῶν ἐν τῷ Ἀραβίῳ οὖρεϊ (HERODOTUS, II. cxxiv.), mentioned by Herodotus without indication of the local name; as to these quarries, cf. *Dawn of Civilization*, p. 383.

[2] Herodotus does not mention it, nor does any other writer of the Greek period. As to the covering of the Sphinx by the sand, cf. *Struggle of the Nations*, p. 294.

[3] MANETHO, in MÜLLER-DIDOT, *Fragm. Hist. Græc.*, vol. ii. pp. 539, 540.

[4] For the legends concerning the great pyramids and their founders, as well as Rhodopis, cf. *Dawn of Civilization*, pp. 377–382, 437–440.

[5] MASPERO, *Études de Mythologie et d'Archéologie Egyptiennes*, vol. iii. pp. 378–381, and *Les Contes populaires de l'Égypte Ancienne*, 2nd edit., pp. xxxiv.–xli.

[6] Drawn by Boudier, from a photograph by Gautier.

[7] Cf. what is said about the Samians who settled in the great Theban Oasis on p. 649, *supra*.

necessary for taking in fresh provisions. Pococke, having left Cairo on the 6th of December, 1737, about midday, was at Akhmîm by the 17th. He set sail again on the 18th, stayed at Thebes from the 13th of January, 1738, till the 17th, and finally moored at Assuan on the evening of January 20th, making in all forty-five days, fourteen of which were spent at various stopping-places. If the diary of a Greek excursionist or tourist had come down to us, we should probably find in it entries of a very similar kind.[1] The departure from Memphis would take place in November or December; ten or twelve days later the traveller would find himself at Panopolis;[2] from Panopolis to Elephantinê, stopping at Coptos and Thebes, would take about a month, allowing time for a stay at Thebes, and returning

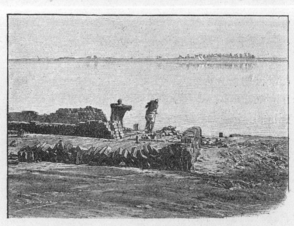

THE VAST SHEET OF WATER IN THE MIDDAY HEAT.[3]

to Memphis in February or March. The greater part of the time was employed in getting from one point to another, and the necessity of taking advantage of a favourable wind in going up the river, often obliged the travellers to neglect more than one interesting locality. The Greek was not so keenly alive to the picturesqueness of the scenes through which he passed as the modern visitor, and in the account of his travels he took no note of the long lines of laden boats going up or down stream, nor of the vast sheet of water glowing in the midday sun, nor of the mountains honeycombed with tombs and quarries, at the foot of which he would be sailing day after day. What interested him above all things was information with regard to the sources of the immense river itself, and the reasons for its periodic inundation, and, according to the

---

[1] Maspero, *Études de Mythologie et d'Archéologie Égyptiennes*, vol. iii. pp. 335–338. Herodotus (II. ix., clxxv.; cf. Wiedemann, *Herodots Zweites Buch*, pp. 68, 69, 602) fixes twenty days for the voyage from Sais to Elephantinê. This period of time must be probably correct, since at the present day dahabeahs constantly run from Cairo to the second cataract and back in two months, including stoppages of ten days to a fortnight for seeing the monuments. The twenty days of Herodotus represent the minimum duration of the voyage, without taking into account the stoppages and accidents which often delay sailing vessels on the Nile. Nine days, which Herodotus gives as the time for reaching Thebes (II. ix.), is not sufficient, if the voyage is undertaken in the usual way, stopping every evening for the night; but it would be possible if the navigation were uninterrupted day and night. This is now rarely done, but it might have been frequent in ancient times, especially in the service of the State.

[2] Herodotus, II. xci., from which it would seem clear that Herodotus stopped at Panopolis and had communications with the people of the town. [Panopolis or Khemmis is the present Ekhmîm.—Tr.]

[3] Drawn by Boudier, from a photograph by Gautier.

3 F

mental attitude impressed on him by his education, he accepted the mythological solution offered by the natives, or he sought for a more natural one in the physical lore of his own *savants*: thus he was told that the Nile took its rise at Elephantinê, between the two rocks called Krôphi and Môphi, and in showing them to him his informant would add that Psammetichus I. had attempted to sound the depth of the river at this point, but had failed to fathom it.[1] At the few places where the pilot of the barque put in to port, the population showed themselves unfriendly, and refused to hold any communication with the Greeks. The interpreters, who were almost all natives of the Delta, were not always familiar with the people and customs of the Saîd, and felt almost as completely foreign at Thebes as did their employers. Their office was confined to translating the information furnished by the inhabitants when the latter were sufficiently civilised to hold communication with the travellers. What most astonished Herodotus at Panopolis was the temple and the games held in honour, so he believed, of Perseus, the son of Danaë. These exercises terminated in an attempt to climb a regular "greasy pole" fixed in the ground, and strengthened right and left by three rows of stays attached to the mast at different heights;[2] as for Perseus, he was the ithyphallic god of the locality, Mînu himself, one of whose epithets—Pehresu, the runner—was confounded by the Greek ear with the name of the hero. The dragomans, enlarging on this mistaken identity, imagined that the town was the birthplace of Danaos and Lyncæus; that Perseus, returning from Libya with the head of Medusa, had gone out of his way to visit the cradle of his family, and that he had instituted the games in remembrance of his stay there.[3] Thebes had become the ghost of its former self; the Persian governors had neglected the city, and its princesses and their ministers were so impoverished that they were unable to keep up its temples and palaces. Herodotus scarcely mentions it, and we can hardly wonder at it: he had visited the still flourishing Memphis, where the temples were cared for and were filled with worshippers. What had Thebes to show him in the way of marvels which he had not already seen, and that, too, in a better state of preservation? His Theban ciceroni also told him the same stories that he had heard in Lower Egypt, and he states that their information agreed in the main with that which he had received at Memphis and Heliopolis, which made it unnecessary to repeat it at length.[4] Two or three things only appeared to him worthy of

---

[1] For the sources of the Nile at Elephantinê, cf. *Dawn of Civilization*, pp. 19, 38, 39. A *résumé* of the opinions held by the Greeks with regard to the sources of the Nile will be found in HUGO BERGER, *Geschichte der Wissenschaftlichen Erdkunde*, vol. i. pp. 104–120.

[2] See the illustration in MARIETTE, *Denderah*, vol. i. pl. 23.

[3] HERODOTUS, II. xci.; cf. WIEDEMANN, *Herodots Zweites Buch*, pp. 365–371.

[4] HERODOTUS, II. iii.; cf. *op. cit.*, pp. 46–51. He cites several facts and legends with regard to Amon (II. xlii., liv., lvi.–lviii., lxxxiii.), Heracles (II. xlii.), the Sacred Serpents (II. lxxix.), and about the infrequency of rain (III. x.).

mention. His admiration was first roused by the 360 statues of the high priests of Amon which had already excited the wonder of his rival Hecatæus; he noted that all these personages were, without exception, represented as mere men, each the son of another man, and he took the opportunity of ridiculing the vanity of his compatriots, who did not hesitate to inscribe the name of a god at the head of their genealogies, removed by some score of generations only from their own.[1] On the other hand, the temple servitors related to him how two Theban priestesses, carried off by the Phœnicians and sold, one in Libya and the other in Greece, had set up the first oracles known in those two countries: Herodotus thereupon re-

membered the story he had heard in Epirus of two black doves which had flown away from Thebes, one towards the Oasis of Ammon, the other in the direction of Dodona; the latter had alighted on an old beech tree, and in a human voice had requested that a temple consecrated to Zeus should be founded on the spot.[2] Herodotus is quite overcome with joy at the thought

THE MOUNTAINS HONEYCOMBED WITH TOMBS AND QUARRIES.[3]

that Greek divination could thus be directly traced to that of Egypt, for like most of his contemporaries, he felt that the Hellenic cult was ennobled by the fact of its being derived from the Egyptian.[4] The traveller on the Nile had to turn homewards on reaching Elephantinê, as that was the station of the last Persian garrison. Nubia lay immediately beyond the cataract, and the Ethiopians at times crossed the frontier and carried their raids as far as Thebes. Elephantinê, like Assuan at the present day, was the centre of a flourishing trade. Here might be seen Kushites from Napata or Meroë, negroes from the Upper Nile and the Bahr el-Ghazal, and Ammonians, from all of whom the curious visitor might glean information while frequenting the bazaars. The cataract was navigable all the year round, and the natives in its vicinity enjoyed the privilege of piloting freight boats through its difficult channel. It took four days to pass through it, instead of the three, or even two, which suffice at the present day. Above it, the Nile spread out and

---

[1] HERODOTUS, II. cxliii.; cf. WIEDEMANN, *Herodots Zweites Buch*, pp. 507–510.

[2] HERODOTUS, II. liv., lv.; cf. WIEDEMANN, *op. cit.*, pp. 242–246. I pointed out some time ago (BOUCHÉ and LECLERCQ, *Histoire de la Divination dans l'Antiquité*, vol. ii. p. 283, note 2) that this indicates a confusion in the minds of the Egyptian dragomans with the two brooding birds of Osiris, Isis and Nephthys, considered as *Zarait*, that is to say, as two birds of a different species, according to the different traditions either vultures, rooks, or doves.

[3] Drawn by Boudier, from a photograph by Gautier.

[4] HERODOTUS, II. liii., et seq.; cf. WIEDEMANN, *op. cit.*, p. 238, et seq.

resembled a lake dotted over with islands, several of which, such as Philæ and Biggeh, contained celebrated temples, which were as much frequented by the Ethiopians as by the Egyptians.[1]

Correctly speaking, it was not Egypt herself that the Greeks saw, but her external artistic aspect and the outward setting of Egyptian civilisation. The vastness of her monuments, the splendour of her tombs, the pomp of her ceremonies, the dignity and variety of her religious formulas, attracted their curiosity and commanded their respect : the wisdom of the Egyptians had passed into a proverb with them, as it had with the Hebrews. But if they had penetrated behind the scenes, they would have been obliged to acknowledge that beneath this attractive exterior there was hopeless decay. As with all creatures when

DARIUS III.[2]

they have passed their prime, Egypt had begun to grow old, and was daily losing her elasticity and energy. Her spirit had sunk into a torpor, she had become unresponsive to her environment, and could no longer adapt herself to the form she had so easily acquired in her youth : it was as much as she could do to occupy fully the narrower limits to which she had been reduced, and to maintain those limits unbroken. The instinct which made her shrink from the intrusion of foreign customs and ideas, or even mere contact with nations of recent growth, was not the mere outcome of vanity. She realised that she maintained her integrity only by relying on the residue of her former solidarity and on the force of custom. The slightest disturbance of the equilibrium established among her members, instead of strengthening her, would have robbed her of the vigour she still possessed, and brought about her dissolution. She owed whatever activity she possessed to impulses imparted to her by the play of her ancient mechanism—a mechanism so stable in its action, and so ingeniously constructed, that it had still a reserve of power within it sufficient to keep the whole in motion for centuries, provided there was no attempt to introduce new wheels among the old. She had never been singularly distinguished for her military qualities; not that she was cowardly, and shrank from facing death, but because she lacked energy and enthusiasm for warlike enterprise. The tactics and armaments by which she had won her victories up to her prime, had at length become fetters which she was no longer inclined to shake off, and even if she was still able to breed a military caste, she was no longer able to produce armies fit to win battles without the aid of mercenaries. In order to be successful in the field, she had to associate

[1] HERODOTUS, II. xxviii., xxix., where the context shows that the author went as far as Elephantinê ; cf. WIEDEMANN, *Herodots Zweites Buch*, pp. 113–127.

[2] Drawn by Faucher-Gudin, from a coin in the *Cabinet des Médailles*, of which I am indebted for a cast to the courtesy of M. Babelon ; cf. BABELON, *Les Perses Achéménides*, pl. ii. 19.

with her own troops recruits from other countries—Libyans, Asiatics, and Greeks, who served to turn the scale. The Egyptians themselves formed a compact body in this case, and bearing down upon the enemy already engaged by the mercenaries, broke through his ranks by their sheer weight, or, if they could not accomplish this, they stood their ground bravely, taking to flight only when the vacancies in their ranks showed them that further resistance was impossible. The machinery of government, like the organisation of their armies, had become antiquated and degenerate. The nobility were as turbulent as in former times, and the royal authority was as powerless now as of old to assert itself in the absence of external help, or when treason was afoot among the troops. Religion alone maintained its ascendency, and began to assume to itself the loyalty once given to the Pharaoh, and the devotion previously consecrated to the fatherland. The fellahîn had never fully realised the degradation involved in serving a stranger, and what they detested in the Persian

AN ELEPHANT ARMED FOR WAR.[1]

king was not exactly the fact that he was a Persian. Their national pride, indeed, always prompted them to devise some means of connecting the foreign monarch with their own solar line, and to transform an Achæmenian king into a legitimate Pharaoh. That which was especially odious to them in a Cambyses or an Ochus was the disdain which such sovereigns displayed for their religion, and the persecution to which they subjected the immortals. They accustomed themselves without serious repining to have no longer one of their own race upon the throne, and to behold their cities administered by Asiatics, but they could not understand why the foreigner preferred his own gods, and would not admit Amon, Phtah, Horus, and Râ to the rank of supreme deities. Ochus had, by his treatment of the Apis and the other divine animals,[2] put it out of his power ever to win their good will. His

---

[1] Drawn by Boudier, from a little terra-cotta group from Myrrhina now in the Louvre. This object dates from the time of the kings of Pergamos, and the soldier round whom the elephant winds his trunk in order to dash him to the ground is a Gaul of Asia Minor.

[2] Cf. for this subject, *supra*, p. 770.

brutality had made an irreconcilable enemy of that state which alone gave signs of vitality among the nations of the decaying East. This was all the more to be regretted, since the Persian empire, in spite of the accession of power which it had just manifested, was far from having regained the energy which had animated it, not perhaps in the time of Darius, but at all events under the first Xerxes. The army and the wealth of the country were doubtless still intact—an army and a revenue which, in spite of all losses, were still the largest in the world—but the valour of the troops was not proportionate to their number. The former prowess of the Persians, Medians, Bactrians, and other tribes of Iran showed no degeneracy : these nations still produced the same race of brave and hardy foot-soldiers, the same active and intrepid horsemen ; but for a century past there had not been the improvements either in the armament of the troops or in the tactics of the generals which were necessary to bring them up to the standard of excellence of the Greek army. The Persian king placed great faith in extraordinary military machines. He believed in the efficacy of chariots armed with scythes ; besides this, his relations with India had shown him what use his Oriental neighbours made of elephants, and having determined to employ these animals, he had collected a whole corps of them, from which he hoped great things. In spite of the addition of these novel recruits, it was not on the Asiatic contingents that he chiefly relied in the event of war, but on the mercenaries who were hired at great expense, and who formed the chief support of his power. From the time of Artaxerxes II. onwards, it was the Greek hoplites and peltasts who had always decided the issue of the Persian battles. The expeditions both by land and sea had been under the conduct of Athenian or Spartan generals—Conon, Chabrias, Iphicrates, Agesilas, Timotheus, and their pupils ; and again also it was to the Greeks—to the Rhodian Mentor and to Memnon—that Ochus had owed his successes. The older nations—Egypt, Syria, Chaldæa, and Elam—had all had their day of supremacy ; they had declined in the course of centuries, and Assyria had for a short time united them under her rule. On the downfall of Assyria, the Iranians had succeeded to her heritage, and they had built up a single empire comprising all the states which had preceded them in Western Asia ; but decadence had fallen upon them also, and when they had been masters for scarcely two short centuries, they were in their turn threatened with destruction. Their rule continued to be universal, not by reason of its inherent vigour, but on account of the weakness of their subjects and neighbours, and a determined attack on any of the frontiers of the empire would doubtless have resulted in its overthrow.

Greece herself was too demoralised to cause Darius any grave anxiety. Not only had she renounced all intention of attacking the great king in his own domain, as in the days of the Athenian hegemony, when she could impose her own conditions of peace, but her perpetual discords had yielded her an easy prey to Persia, and were likely to do so more and more. The Greek cities chose the great king as the arbiter in their quarrels; they vied with each other in obtaining his good will, his subsidies in men and vessels, and his darics; they armed or disarmed at his command, and the day seemed at hand when they would become a normal dependency of Persia, little short of a regular satrapy like Asiatic Hellas. One chance of escape from such a fate remained to them—if one or other of them, or some neighbouring state, could acquire such an ascendency as to make it possible to unite what forces remained to them under one rule. Macedonia in particular, having hitherto kept aloof from the general stream of politics, had at this juncture begun to shake off its lethargy, and had entered with energy into the Hellenic concert under the auspices of its king, Philip. Bagoas recognised the danger which threatened his people in the person of this ambitious sovereign, and did not hesitate to give substantial support to the adversaries of the Macedonian prince; Chersobleptes of Thrace and the town of Perinthus receiving from him such succour as enabled them to repulse Philip successfully (340). Unfortunately, while Bagoas was endeavouring to avert danger in this quarter, his rivals at court endeavoured to prejudice the mind of the king against him, and their intrigues were so successful that he found himself ere long condemned to the alternative of murdering his sovereign or perishing himself. He therefore poisoned Ochus, to avoid being assassinated or put to the torture, and placed on the throne Arses, the youngest of the king's sons, while he caused the remaining royal children to be put to death (336).[1] Egypt hailed this tragic end as a mark of the vengeance of the gods whom Ochus had outraged. A report was spread that the eunuch was an Egyptian, that he had taken part in the murder of the Apis under fear of death, but that when he was sure of his own safety he had avenged the sacrilege. As soon as the poison had taken effect, it was said he ate a portion of the dead body and threw the remainder to the cats: he then collected the bones and made them into whistles and knife-handles.[2] Ochus had astonished his contemporaries by the rapidity with which he had re-established the integrity of the empire; they were pleased to compare him with the heroes of his race, with Cyrus, Cambyses, and Darius. But to exalt him to such a level said little for their moral or intellectual perceptions, since in spite of his victories he was

---

[1] DIODORUS SICULUS, xvii. 5. Plutarch (*De Virt. Alexandri*, § 5) calls the successor of Ochus Oarses, which recalls the name which Dinon gives to Artaxerxes II. (cf. *supra*, p. 746, note 3). Diodorus says that Bagoas destroyed the whole family of Ochus, but he is mistaken. Arrian (*Anabasis*, III. xix. § 4) mentions a son of Ochus about 330, and several other members of the royal Achæmenian race are known to have been living in the time of Alexander.

[2] DIODORUS SICULUS, xvii. 5; ÆLIAN, *Variæ Hist.*, vi. 8. The body of the enemy thrown to the cats to be devoured is a detail added by the popular imagination, which crops up again in the Tale of Satni Khâmois; cf. MASPERO, *Les Contes populaires de l'Égypte ancienne*, 2nd edit., p. 200.

merely a despot of the ordinary type; his tenacity degenerated into brutal obstinacy, his severity into cruelty, and if he obtained successes, they were due rather to his generals and his ministers than to his own ability. His son Arses was at first content to be a docile instrument in the hands of Bagoas; but when the desire for independence came to him with the habitual exercise of power, and he began to chafe at his bonds, the eunuch sacrificed him to his own personal safety, and took his life as he had done that of his father in the preceding year (336).[1] So many murders following each other in rapid succession had considerably reduced the Achæmenian family, and Bagoas for a moment was puzzled where to find a king: he at length decided in favour of Codomannos,[2] who according to some was a great-grandson of Darius II.,[3] but according to others was not of the royal line, but had in his youth been employed as a courier.[4] He had distinguished himself in the hostilities against the Cadusians, and had been nominated satrap of Armenia by Ochus as a reward for his bravery.[5] He assumed at his accession the name of Darius; brave, generous, clement, and possessed with an ardent desire to do right, he was in every way the superior of his immediate predecessors, and he deserved to have reigned at a time when the empire was less threatened. Bagoas soon perceived that his new *protégé*, whose conduct he had reckoned on directing as he pleased, intended to govern for himself, and he therefore attempted to get rid of him; Bagoas was, however, betrayed by his accomplices, and compelled to drink the poison which he had prepared for Darius.[6] These revolutions had distracted the attention of the court of Susa from the events which were taking place on the shores of the Ægean, and Philip had taken advantage of them to carry into effect the designs against Persia which he had been long meditating. After having been victorious against the Greeks, he had despatched an army of ten thousand men into Asia under the command of Parmenion and Attalus (336). We may ask if it were not he who formed the project of universal conquest which was so soon to be associated with the name of his son Alexander. He was for the moment content to excite revolt among the cities of the Ægean littoral, and restore to them that liberty of which they had been deprived for nearly a century. He himself followed as soon as these lost children of Greece had established themselves firmly in Asia. The story of his assassination on the eve of his departure is well known (336), and of the difficulties which compelled

---

[1] DIODORUS SICULUS, xvii. 5; ARRIAN, *Anabasis*, II. xiv. 5, where it is stated that Codomannos had been Bagoas's accomplice in the murder of Arses. Cf. STRABO, XV. iii. § 24, p. 735.

[2] Pompeius Trogus gives him this name of Codomannos (JUSTIN, x. 3), probably following Dinon.

[3] DIODORUS SICULUS, xvii. 5, says that his grandfather was a certain Ostanes who would have been the brother of Artaxerxes II., probably the one whom Ctesias calls Oxandres (*Fragm.* 29, § 49, in MÜLLER-DIDOT, *Ctesiæ Cnidii Fragmenta*, p. 55).

[4] STRABO, XV. iii. § 24, p. 735; PLUTARCH, *Life of Alexander*, § 18.

[5] JUSTIN, x. 3, where Pompeius Trogus probably followed the account given by Dinon; cf. DIODORUS SICULUS, xvii. 6.

[6] DIODORUS SICULUS, xvii. 6.

Alexander to suspend the execution of the plans which his father had made. Darius attempted to make use of the respite thus afforded him by fortune; he adopted the usual policy of liberally bribing one part of Greece to take up arms against Macedonia—a method which was at first successful.   While Alexander was occupied in the destruction of Thebes, the Rhodian general Memnon, to whom had been entrusted the defence of Asia Minor, forced the invaders to entrench themselves in the Troad.   If the Persian fleet had made its appearance in

THE BATTLE-FIELD OF ISSUS.[1]

good time, and had kept an active watch over the straits, the advance-guard of the Macedonians would have succumbed to the enemy before the main body of the troops had succeeded in joining them in Asia, and it was easy to foretell what would have been the fate of an enterprise inaugurated by such a disaster. Persia, however, had not yet learnt to seize the crucial moment for action: her vessels were still arming when the enemy made their appearance on the European shore of the Hellespont, and Alexander had ample time to embark and disembark the whole of his army without having to draw his sword from the scabbard.   He was accompanied by about thirty thousand foot soldiers and four thousand five hundred horse; the finest troops commanded by the best generals of the time—Parmenion, his two sons Nikanor and Philotas, Crater, Clitos, Antigonus, and others whose names are familiar to us all; a larger force than Memnon and his subordinates were able to bring up to oppose him, at all

[1] Drawn by Boudier, from a photograph by Lortet; cf. LORTET, *La Syrie d'aujourd'hui*, p. 42.

events at the opening of the campaign, during the preliminary operations which determined the success of the enterprise.

The first years of the campaign seem like a review of the countries and nations which in bygone times had played the chief part in Oriental history. An engagement at the fords of the Granicus, only a few days after the crossing

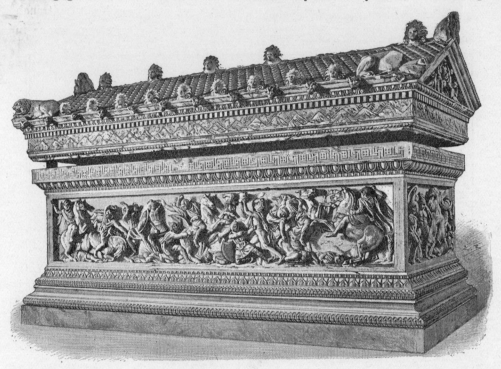

BAS-RELIEF ON A SIDONIAN SARCOPHAGUS REPRESENTING AN EPISODE IN THE BATTLE OF ISSUS.[1]

of the Hellespont, placed Asia Minor at the mercy of the invader (334). Mysia, Lydia, Caria, and Lycia tendered their submission, Miletus and Halicarnassus being the only towns to offer any resistance. In the spring of 333, Phrygia followed the general movement, in company with Cappadocia and Cilicia; these represented the Hittite and Asianic world, the last representatives of which thus escaped from the influences of the East and passed under the Hellenic supremacy. At the foot of the Amanus, Alexander came into conflict not only with the generals of Darius, but with the great king himself. The Amanus, and the part of the Taurus which borders on the Euphrates valley, had always constituted the line of demarcation between the domain of the races of the Asianic peninsula and that of the Semitic peoples. A second battle near the Issus, at the entrance to the Cilician gates, cleared the ground,

---

[1] Drawn by Boudier, from a photograph; cf. HAMDY-BEY and THÉODORE REINACH, *Les Sarcophages de Sidon*, pl. xxv.

and gave the conqueror time to receive the homage of the maritime provinces. Both Northern and Cœle-Syria submitted to him from Samosata to Damascus. The less important towns of Phœnicia, such as Arvad, Byblos, Sidon, and those of Cyprus, followed their example; but Tyre closed its gates, and trusted to its insular position for the preservation of its independence, as it had done of old in the time of Sennacherib and of Nebuchadrezzar. It was not so much a scrupu-

THE ISTHMUS OF TYRE AT THE PRESENT DAY.[1]

lous feeling of loyalty which emboldened her to take this step, as a keen realisation of what her conquest by the Macedonian would entail. It was entirely owing to Persia that she had not succumbed in all parts of the Eastern Mediterranean in that struggle with Greece which had now lasted for centuries: Persia had not only arrested the progress of Hellenic colonisation in Cyprus, but had given a fresh impulse to that of Tyre, and Phœnician influence had regained its ascendency over a considerable part of the island. The surrender of Tyre, therefore, would be equivalent to a Greek victory, and would bring about the decay of the city; hence its inhabitants preferred hostilities, and they were prolonged in desperation over a period of seven months. At the end of that time Alexander succeeded in reducing the place by constructing a dyke or causeway, by means of which he brought his machines of war up to the foot of the ramparts, and filled in the channel which separated the town from the mainland; the island thus became a peninsula, and Tyre henceforth was

---

[1] Drawn by Boudier, from a sketch by Lortet; cf. LORTET, *La Syrie d'aujourd'hui*, p. 133.

reduced to the rank of an ordinary town, still able to maintain her commercial activity, but having lost her power as an independent state (332). Phœnicia being thus brought into subjection, Judæa and Samaria yielded to the conqueror without striking a blow, though the fortress of Gaza followed the example set by Tyre, and for the space of two months blocked the way to the Delta. Egypt revolted at the approach of her liberator, and the rising was so unanimous as to dismay the satrap Mazakes, who capitulated at the first summons. Alexander passed the winter on the banks of the Nile. Finding that the ancient capitals of the country—Thebes, Sais, and even Memphis itself—occupied positions which were no longer suited to the exigencies of the times, he founded opposite to the island of Pharos, in the township of Rakotis, a city to which he gave his own name. The rapid growth of the prosperity of Alexandria showed how happy the founder had been in the choice of its site : in less than half a century from the date of its foundation, it had eclipsed all the other capitals of the Eastern Mediterranean, and had become the centre of African Hellenism. While its construction was in progress, Alexander, having had opportunities of studying the peculiarities and characteristics of the Egyptians, had decided to perform the one act which would conciliate the good feeling of the natives, and secure for him their fidelity during his wars in the East : he selected from among their gods the one who was also revered by the Greeks, Zeus-Ammon, and repaired to the Oasis that he might be adopted by the deity. As a son of the god, he became a legitimate Pharaoh, an Egyptian like themselves,[1] and on return- ing to Memphis he no longer hesitated to adopt the *pschent* crown with the accompanying ancient rites.[2] He returned to Asia early in the year 331, and crossed the Euphrates. Darius had attempted to wrest Asia Minor from his grasp, but Antigonus, the governor of Phrygia, had dispersed the troops despatched for this purpose in 332, and Alexander was able to push forward fearlessly into those regions beyond the Euphrates, where the Ten Thousand had pursued their victorious march before him. He crossed the Tigris about the 20th of September, and a week later fell in with his rival in the very heart of Assyria, not far from the village of Gaugamela, where he took up a position which had been previously studied, and was particularly suited for the evolutions of cavalry. At the Granicus and near Issus, the Greek element had played an important part among the forces which contested the field ; on this occasion, however, the great king was accompanied by merely two or three thousand mercenaries, while, on the other hand, the whole of Asia

[1] For the importance and significance of this act, cf. MASPERO, *Comment Alexandre devint Dieu en Égypte*, in *L'Annuaire de l'École des Hautes Études*, 1897, pp. 4–30.

[2] The fact is mentioned only in PSEUDO-CALLISTHENES, § xxxiv., ed. MÜLLER-DIDOT, p. 38. It is, however, so conformable with fact, that we may accept it as fully as if we had met with it in a trust- worthy historian : the author of the romance doubtless took it from some good source (MAHAFFY, *History of Egypt under the Ptolemaic Dynasty*, p. 4, note 2).

seemed to have roused herself for a last effort, and brought forward her most valiant troops to oppose the disciplined ranks of the Macedonians. Persians, Susians, Medes, Armenians, Iranians from Bactriana, Sakæ, and Indians were all in readiness to do their best, and were accompanied by every instrument of military warfare employed in Oriental tactics; chariots armed with scythes, the last descendants of the chariotry which had dominated all the battle-fields from the time of the XVIIIth Theban dynasty down to the latest Sargonids, and, employed side by side with these relics of a bygone day, were Indian elephants, now for the first time brought into use against European battalions. These picked troops sold their lives dearly, but the perfection of the Macedonian arms, and, above all, the superiority of the tactics employed by their generals,

THE BATTLE OF ARBELA, FROM THE MOSAIC OF HERCULANEUM.[1]

carried the day; the evening of the 30th of September found Darius in flight, and the Achæmenian empire crushed by the furious charges of Alexander's squadrons. Babylon fell into their hands a few days later, followed by Susa, and in the spring of 330, Ecbatana; and shortly after Darius met his end on the way to Media, assassinated by the last of his generals.

With his death, Persia sank back into the obscurity from which Cyrus had raised her rather more than two centuries previously. With the exception of the Medes, none of the nations which had exercised the hegemony of the East before her time, not even Assyria, had had at their disposal such a wealth of resources and had left behind them so few traces of their power. A dozen or so of palaces, as many tombs, a few scattered altars and stelæ, remains of epics preserved by the Greeks, fragments of religious books, often remodelled, and issuing in the Avesta—when we have reckoned up all that remains to us of

[1] Drawn by Boudier, from a photograph.

her, what do we find to compare in interest and in extent with the monuments and wealth of writings bequeathed to us by Egypt and Chaldæa? The Iranians received Oriental civilisation at a time when the latter was in its decline, and caught the spirit of decadence in their contact with it. In succeeding to the patrimony of the nations they conquered, they also inherited their weakness; in a few years they had lost all the vigour of their youth, and were barely able to maintain the integrity of the empire they had founded. Moreover, the great peoples to whom they succeeded, although lacking the vigour necessary for the continuance of their independent existence, had not yet sunk so low as to acquiesce in their own decay, and resign themselves to allowing their national life to be absorbed in that of another power: they believed that they would emerge from the crisis, as they had done from so many others, with fresh strength, and, as soon as an occasion presented itself, they renewed the war against their Iranian suzerain. From the first to the latest of the sovereigns bearing the name of Darius, the history of the Achæmenids is an almost uninterrupted series of internal wars and provincial revolts. The Greeks of Ionia, the Egyptians, Chaldæans, Syrians, and the tribes of Asia Minor, all rose one after another, sometimes alone, sometimes in concert; some carrying on hostilities for not more than two or three years; others, like Egypt, maintaining them for more than half a century. They were not discouraged by the reprisals which followed each of these rebellions; they again had recourse to arms as soon as there seemed the least chance of success, and they renewed the struggle till from sheer exhaustion the sword fell from their hand. Persia was worn out by this perpetual warfare, in which at the same time each of her rivals expended the last relics of their vitality, and when Macedonia entered on the scene, both lords and vassals were reduced to such a state of prostration, that it was easy to foretell their approaching end. The old Oriental world was in its death-throes; but before it passed away, the successful audacity of Alexander had summoned Greece to succeed to its inheritance.

INDEX.

THE END.

PRINTED BY WILLIAM CLOWES AND SONS, LIMITED, LONDON AND BECCLES.